Published by the Lockheed Employees Recreation Club
in cooperation with
the Lockheed Martin Skunk Works *Star*

Distributed by the LERC Employee Store
1011 Lockheed Way, Unit 12
Palmdale, CA 93599-3720

Lockheed's first publicist, Randall Irwin, resurrected an ancient Smith-Corona typewriter from the attic of a daughter's home in La Canada and typed out the first copy of the *Star* on his kitchen table in 1934. Lockheed employees have been reading the *Star* ever since. The editors at the helm during the Volume I years were Irwin, Hal Rosson, Bert Holloway, Paul Bailey, Kenneth Crist and Jack Prescott. Thanks, gentlemen, for a job well done.

Jerry Hall, 1996 *Star* editor

ISBN 0-9652837-0-4

Printed in Malaysia

THE LOCKHEED STAR

Published for the Employees of the Lockheed Aircraft Corporation

July 9, 1934 Vol. 1, No. 1

TEN LOCKHEEDS ENTERED IN LONDON-TO-MELBOURNE RACE

In pursuit of a $50,000 first prize, 64 contestants have entered the London-to-Melbourne MacRobertson international air races scheduled for next October. Of the 27 American airplanes entered in the race, 10 are single-motor Lockheeds, outnumbering even the most popular British make of airplanes. Of the 10 Lockheeds, six are entered from the United States, two from Australia, one from England and one from France.

Perhaps the best known American entry is our old friend, Wiley Post, who has equipped his Wasp-powered Vega, the Winnie Mae, for some real altitude work. With two superchargers building up pressure for the engine and for an air-tight flying suit, Wiley expects to go up on top, find a tail wind, and fly over some of the storms that are apt to impede the progress of pilots who are obliged to stay closer to the earth. In the upper regions, Wiley hopes to exceed 275 m.p.h. cruising speed. His supercharger equipment was recently installed here under the supervision of his personal mechanic. E. G. Mollenkopf, a former Lockheed employee.

As a champion defending his title, the amiable Sir Charles Kingsford-Smith will fly the race in an Altair which was built here and shipped to Australia late in June. Sir Charles established an England-to-Australia speed record of 10 1/2 days in 1930, and knows the route well. His co-pilot will be Capt. P. G. Taylor, MC, an able pilot in his own right and a first class navigator, according to Sir Charles. With a gasoline capacity of 500 gallons, Sir Charles' Altair will have a cruising range in excess of 3,000 miles. The Wasp is a new SE type, highly supercharged, with a 14 to 1 blower gear ratio. It has a rating of 500 horsepower at 11,500 feet. At 17,000 feet, Sir Charles cruised at 213 m.p.h. on a recent test flight over San Fernando valley.

In the factory now is an Orion which is being built to be flown in the race by Laura Ingalls, famous woman pilot who recently completed a 17,000-mile solo flight around South America in a Lockheed Air Express. Her Orion, entered in the race, will be powered with an S1D1 Wasp.

A local Lockheed entry is a Varney Speed Lines' Wasp-powered Orion, the "West Wind," which has been taken off the run of Lineas Aereas Occidentales, S.A., for entry in the race. Walter T. Varney and Franklin Rose plan to fly it.

Other American Lockheed entries on the list include Ruth Nichols, an Altair; Capt. Harry Lyon, an Altair, and the Lyon Flight Expedition Company, an Orion. Captain Lyon came into international prominence as the navigator of Sir Charles Kingsford-Smith on the Southern Cross flight from Oakland to Australia in 1928.

A French Lockheed entry is the noted military pilot, Michael Detroyat, who had an Orion built and shipped to France last winter. A Hispano-Suiza engine, believed to be of the French-built Wright Cyclone series, was installed after the plane arrived in France.

From Australia, a Vega has been entered by James Woods and Horace C. Miller, veteran Australian pilots. And English entry is Lieut. H. R. A. Kidston, R.N. The model of Lieutenant Kidston's Lockheed entry is not mentioned, but it is understood to be a Wasp-powered Vega in which his brother, Lieut-Comdr. Glen Kidston, R.N., made a fast flight from England to the Cape in 1931.

Other entries of California-built airplanes include a Douglas DC-2 Transport by K.L.M. airline of Holland, a Douglas by Harold Gatty (Post's navigator on his first round-the-world flight), a Keith Reider monoplane by Keith Reider, a Vance monoplane by Murray B. Dilley, and a Northrop Delta by Lieut. Marshall Lindholm of the Swedish airline, A.B. Aerotransport. Col. Roscoe Turner is listed with a Douglas, but reports here have it a Boeing bi-motor transport.

VEGA TO CUT W.P. FULLER'S TRAVEL TIME

Far into the mountains on the shore of Pillsbury Lake in Gravelly Valley, Lake County, W.P. Fuller, president of W.P. Fuller & Company, will commute this summer from the San Francisco municipal airport to his summer home some 150 miles to the north. He will fly in the new Wasp-powered Vega which was delivered last week to Mr. Fuller's personal pilot, Fred Hammer. The trip to Mr. Fuller's summer home, which requires eight tiring hours from San Francisco by ground transportation, will be made in the Vega in 45 to 50 minutes of scenic flight.

* * *

FIRST ELECTRA HARD AT WORK

The first Electra which was delivered to Northwest Airlines is carrying capacity loads on two round trips daily between Chicago and St. Paul, a distance of approximately 370 miles each way. Northwest officials were so fully satisfied with the operation of the Electra, they placed orders for four more. When additional Electras are delivered, they will be put into service between St. Paul and Seattle. This route is now being flown with single-motor Orions and tri-motor Fords.

* * *

TWENTY-TWO ELECTRAS ARE ON ORDER

Signed contracts are on hand for 22 Electras. First to come from the production line will be two for Northwest Airlines and six Wasp-powered models for Pan American Airways' Mexican affiliate, Aerovias Centrales, S.A.

Other orders include seven Electras for Nederlandsche Vliegtuigenfabriek, Anthony H.G. Fokker's international aircraft manufacturing organization in Amsterdam, Holland; two additional Electras for Northwest Airlines; one for Phillips Petroleum Company, Bartlesville, Okla.; one for Continental Oil Company, Ponca City, Okla.; one for Walker P. Inman of Sommerville, N.J.; one for Santa Maria Air Lines, Santa Maria, Calif.; and one for a foreign customer whose name is being withheld for the present, by request.

* * *

MORE ABOUT THE MacROBERTSON RACES

Because of the widespread interest in the event, information is given herewith on the prizes and route of the England-to-Australia air races. To encourage aviation and to mark the occasion of the Centenary of the State of Victoria, Australia, and its capital city, Melbourne, Sir MacPherson Robertson, a leading citizen of Melbourne, has donated the sum of L15,000 and a gold cup to be given as prizes in two races, which will be held concurrently. The races are known as the Speed Race and the Handicap Race, the commencing date of which will be on or about October 20.

Prices for the Speed Race are: First, L10,000 and a gold cup; second, L1,500, and third, L500. For the Handicap Race, prizes are: First, L2,000, and second, L1,000.

Competitors in the Speed Race will be required to land and check in at the following control points: Baghdad, Turkey; Allahabad, India; Singapore south of the Malay peninsula; and Darwin and Charleville, Australia. The first contestant to cross the finish line will be the winner of the Speed Race.

For the Handicap Race, checking points will be established at intervals of, roughly, 500 miles along the course. Winner of this race will be determined according to a handicap formula.

THE LOCKHEED STAR

Issued for the Employees of Lockheed Aircraft Corporation

July 27, 1934 Vol. 1, No. 2

FRANCHISE GRANTED DISTRIBUTOR FOR CHINA

Hosken Trading Company, Inc., New York City and Shanghai, has been granted the exclusive distributorship for Lockheed airplanes in all of China, including Manchoukuo. The arrangement includes an option to secure an exclusive license to manufacture the Electra, Orion, Altair and Vega in China.

The Hosken company's business is that of importing to China airplanes, locomotives and heavy machinery. In addition to Lockheeds, the company distributes Fairchild airplanes and aerial cameras.

* * *

PHILLIPS ORDERS ANOTHER LOCKHEED

Phillips Petroleum Company, Bartlesville, Okla., has placed an order for an Orion powered with a Wright Cyclone SR1820F33 engine, which is rated at 650 h.p. at 9500 ft. The cabin will provide seats for four passengers. Equipment will include General tires, a Sperry gyro horizon and a Westport radio.

Billy Parker, head of the company's aviation department, placed the order for the new Orion to replace an older Orion which Phillips sold to Aerovias Centrales, S.A., Pan American Airways' Mexican air line affiliate. The company also has an Electra on order.

* * *

LOCKHEED BALL TEAMS HAVE GOOD RECORDS

Employees of the Lockheed factory have two active ball teams which are putting up a good showing against other local clubs in competition. One team playing regulation baseball has won 7 out of 12 games, while the other team playing indoor ball has won 3 out of 5 games. Dusty Rhoads is manager of both teams, and Bob Mills is captain.

The Lockheed indoor team is a member of the Burbank Night League. It plays regular games on an average of once a week at the Burbank junior high school field.

Night league games are scheduled by the Lockheed team with the A.O.U.W. club at 7:30 p.m., Monday, July 30; with Bing Crosby's Groaners at 7:30 p.m., Friday, August 3, and with the Cleaners at 9:15 p.m., Friday, August 10.

The hardball team, which has played independently scheduled games since its formation in April, is entering the San Fernando Valley baseball league which is being organized. This will provide the Lockheed club with some fast competition.

The baseball team practices every Wednesday afternoon at 3:45 o'clock at Pioneer Park (Union Air Terminal). Rhoads states that new recruits are always welcome.

AUSTRALIANS WILL FLY LOCKHEEDS IN BIG RACE

Following the pleasant visit of Sir Charles Kingsford-Smith here to take delivery of a Wasp-powered Altair for entry in the London-to-Melbourne MacRobertson air race next October 20, another famous Australian pilot, James (Jimmy) Woods, visited the factory to confer with the engineering department in regard to fitting out a Vega for the 12,000-mile race.

Woods, who is western division manager of the MacRobertson-Miller Aviation Company of Australia, will fly a Vega owned by Horace C. Miller, managing director of the same company, a contract air mail carrier.

The Vega, with a Detroit-built metal fuselage, is the Lockheed in which the late Lieut-Comdr. Glen Kidston, R.N., made a fast flight from England to the Cape, South Africa, in 1931. It will be powered with a supercharged Wasp engine, and Woods is having a controllable pitch propeller installed.

Like Sir Charles, Woods has made several flights between London and Australia, so knows the route well. He left here, bound for London, where the plane is being conditioned for the long, gruelling flight.

* * *

PRELIMINARY REPORT ISSUED BY TREASURER

Orders on the books of the Lockheed Aircraft Corporation are now in excess of $900,000, as compared with $87,390.77 a year ago, according to a preliminary report contained in a letter to stockholders by Robert E. Gross, treasurer.

The letter which summarizes the effect of recent financing show that 48,959 additional shares of common stock were sold to stockholders at $2.00 a share through the offering of rights. Another block of 25,000 shares was sold to G. Brashears & Company at the same price. These two transactions made available to the company approximately $145,000 of new capital.

"This amount satisfactorily meets the requirements for which the financing was undertaken," the letter states.

The statement of Mr. Gross further points out that:

"Although it is expected the company will report a loss from operations for the first six months of 1934, favorable earnings are expected for the latter half of this year. During the first six months of this year, a concerted effort has been made to prepare for quantity production of the Electra regardless of its effect upon immediate earnings.

"Because of conditions affecting the entire industry, such as strikes and delayed delivery of materials, more time has been required to get into production on the Electra than was anticipated.

"It is expected that the second of the Electras will be completed within a few days.

"The manufacturing space occupied by the company has been increased from 75,000 feet to 150,000 feet, and the number of its employees has been increased from 160 to more than 500."

THE LOCKHEED STAR

Issued for the Employees of the Lockheed Aircraft Corporation

January 5, 1935 Vol. 2, No. 1

NEWS FLASHES

They are in the news spotlight again--these famous Lockheed pilots--Wiley Post, Laura Ingalls, Sir Charles Kingsford-Smith and Amelia Earhart Putnam.

STRATOSPHERE

Wiley Post flew in the other day to prepare his famous round-the-world Vega, the Winnie Mae, for a transcontinental non-stop speed flight at 30,000 to 35,000 feet altitude. Jimmy Gerschler, engineer, is working out the design of a landing skid under the fuselage. Yes, the reports are correct that Wiley plans to drop his landing gear right after his take-off. Elimination of the gear should give Wiley an additional 30 m.p.h. Meanwhile, the Wasp engine is being given a going-over by E.G. Mollenkopf, Wiley's personal mechanic and former Lockheed factory superintendent.

DISTANCE

Laura Ingall's new "black mystery" Orion is being prepared for Department of Commerce tests. Laura is quiet about her plans, but with the extra tankage and long-distant flight equipment in the Orion, it is assumed that she really plans to go places.

HOMEWARD

Sir Charles Kingsford-Smith, the gracious Australian "knight of the air," is returning to his own country by steamer, leaving his transpacific Altair in dead storage here. Because the "Lady Southern Cross" does not carry an N.C. license, the Australian government will not permit of its use, so as Sir Charles regretfully states, "I am forced to leave my other half behind."

TRANSPACIFIC

Amelia Earhart Putnam has her Wasp-powered Vega in Honolulu, where, according to persistent reports, she plans to take off for San Francisco. She is accompanied on her trip to Hawaii by her husband and Mr. and Mrs. Paul Mantz. Our sheet metal department built fuselage tanks for Amelia's Vega.

TRANSCONTINENT

F. C. Hall, Oklahoma oil man and backer of Wiley Post's first round-the-world flight, is preparing an Orion for a reported non-stop transcontinental speed flight. The Orion, purchased from John E. Mabee, is being overhauled at the Braniff shops in Dallas. Roy O. Hunt, famous Southwestern pilot, will fly the Orion.

RECOGNITION

In recognition of his six and a half years of service in the engineering department, James M. (Jimmy) Gerschler has been appointed assistant chief engineer by Hall Hibbard, vice president and chief engineer. "Jimmy" has contributed much toward the development of the Sirius, Orion, Altair and Electra.

BASEBALL

The Electras have games scheduled at Fernangeles for the next three Sundays in succession. Next Sunday, January 13, they play the Valley Cubs, and on January 20 Canoga Park.

THE LOCKHEED STAR

Issued for the Employees of Lockheed Aircraft Corporation

January 11, 1935 Vol. 2, No. 2

EMPLOYEES WILL HOLD DANCE

Employees of Lockheed will hold a dance at 9:30 p.m., Friday night, January 25, at the Whitley Country Club, formerly the Sunset Country Club, Burbank.

A committee of employees under Karl Roth, chairman, is handling arrangements and securing prizes. First prize of $10 cash has been donated by the Bankee Market in Burbank. The fee for the dance will be $1 per couple. Tickets must be purchased in advance.

NORTHWEST TO EXPAND SERVICE

Five Electras have been put in service and orders are in for eight additional Electras to be used to equip the northern transcontinental route completely with modern, high-speed transports. When radio and lighting installations are complete on the northern transcontinental airway, Northwest Airlines will double its air mail and passenger service between Chicago and Seattle, according to Fred A. Whittemore, vice president in charge of operations.

With three Electras in service, Northwest operated two of them a total of 16 hours and 50 minutes daily in the Twin Cities-Spokane service, and flew another Electra 10 hours and 10 minutes daily on two round trips between Chicago and Twin Cities. A third Chicago-Twin Cities schedule was flown with an Orion.

BALL "STARS" TO PERFORM

Three players of the Electras will represent the Lockheed team in an exhibition baseball game to be held Sunday, January 27, at 2 p.m., at the Circle Drive Park, Van Nuys. Major league scouts will view the game to uncover new material.

Representing the pick of the San Fernando Valley League, the players on the exhibition teams will include Randy Willis of the Lockheed production office, Morgan Keith, fuselage department, and Michael Draper, sheet metal.

"NEWS" ORION CREATES STIR

Considerable interest has been created throughout the East in the Detroit News Orion, which was recently flown to Detroit by James V. Piersol, pilot and aviation editor of The News. A flying newspaper office, the Orion has three camera installations which make it possible to take pictures from any angle.

Equipment of the plane includes three passenger seats, a desk for a flying reporter or radio operator, a radio transmitter for broadcasting outdoor events of public interest, a Sperry automatic pilot, and floats to replace the retractable wheels for seaplane operation.

Flying the Detroit News Vega, Piersol in the past has scored many world-wide news scoops on important stories. During four years of operation, the Vega was used on 350 assignments and made 1097 flights covering a distance of 121,511 miles without serious trouble.

THE LOCKHEED STAR

Issued for the Employees of the Lockheed Aircraft Corporation

March 12, 1937 Vol. 4, No. 9

SALES TAKE THE LEAD

It looks like a race between the sales and production departments, with sales in the lead at the moment. In the friendly race between the teams of R.A. Von Hake, superintendent, and Carl B. Squier, vice president and sales manager, the odds in favor of sales are expected to drop lower when the various shop departments get settled down and organized in their new quarters.

* * *

ORDERS MOUNT

Orders for "12's" just received include a 12A, equipped for photographic work, purchased by Standard Oil of New Jersey for use in Venezuela, a 12B by the Argentina Government for use by the chief of the Army Air Corps, and two 12A's by Varney Airlines for scheduled service between Denver and El Paso.

Expectations are being confirmed that the "14" will enjoy a ready market. Eighteen of the new planes have been sold to date.

DELIVERIES

Recent deliveries include No. 1084 to Sanford Airways, Sanford, Maine, and Nos. 1085 and 1086 to LOT Airlines, Poland.

Early deliveries will be made of No. 1215 to Byrd-Frost Airtransport, Dallas, Texas, and Nos. 1087 and 1088 to LOT. The Electras for Poland are flown to New York for shipment.

A.M.L. CALLS MEETING

A meeting, open to all employees, has been called for tonight at 8 o'clock in Jeffrie's Barn by the Aeronautical Mechanics Lodge of Burbank, of the International Association of Machinists, which has been recognized by this company as the sole collective bargaining representative for all employees.

Temporary officers of the organization are Max Stivers, president; Charles Tigar, vice president; James Guthrie, recording secretary; Ed Cruz, financial secretary, and Joe Lenz, treasurer. Permanent officers will be elected by the membership when the lodge receives its charter from Washington, D.C.

* * *

TICKETS FOR AIR SHOW

Special price tickets (25 cents) to the National Aircraft & Boat Show, March 13 to 21, are available in the Personnel Department for all employees. A large Lockheed attendance is expected "Lockheed Day," Wednesday, March 17.

Capt. G. Allan Hancock's special "12" will be Lockheed's exhibit, under the direction of James Griffin, publicity director. Harvey Christen was in charge of the difficult job of trucking the plane to the Pan-Pacific auditorium on Beverly Blvd. Jack Eaton's paint shop crew is busy shining it up.

* * *

CREDIT UNION ESTABLISHED

Lockheed Aircraft Employees Federal Credit Union has been officially launched; a charter received from the Federal Farm Bureau, and officers elected. Roger Lewis is president.

* * *

$858 PAID IN BENEFITS

Weekly benefits paid to Lockheed employees under the Group Accident and Sickness Policy totalled $858.31, during the months of January and February. The "flu" accounted for a large percentage of the 40 claims on which benefits were paid.

* * *

THE LOCKHEED STAR

Issued for the Employees of Lockheed Aircraft Corporation

April 5, 1937 Vol. 4, No. 10

ALL-TIME PEAK Lockheed reached an all-time peak in deliveries and personnel during March and enters this month with a schedule calling for the delivery of 10 planes and a slight increase in employment. Employees exceeded 1400 at the close of March, and nine planes were delivered during the month. Last summer, the company's payroll totalled 475 employees and in September, 1934, there were 75 employees.

FOREIGN SALES ARE HIGH Out of 19 Electras and "12's" delivered or scheduled for March and April, 13 were built for foreign customers. The domestic market accounted for only six planes, and four of those are to former Lockheed owners.

DELIVERIES IN MARCH March deliveries included four Electras to LOT Airline of Poland; two Electras to Industria Aeronautica Romana, a Roumanian airline; one Electra to Union Steamship Company for air transport use in New Zealand; one "12" to Las Vegas Gas Company of Nevada and a "12" to Byrd-Frost Air Transport Company of Dallas. LOT took delivery of its first four Electras late in 1935, whereas Byrd-Frost originally operated a single-engine Orion.

SCHEDULE FOR APRIL Delivery schedule for this month calls for two additional Electras for the Union Steamship Company; two Electras for the Roumanian air line; two Electras for Aeropout of Jugoslavia; one Electra for Hanford Airlines of Kansas City, and one "12" each to Phillips Petroleum Company of Bartlesville, Oklahoma, Superior Oil Company of Houston, Texas, and a Canadian customer. Hanford already operates two Electras; Phillips has operated both Orions and Vegas, and Superior Oil took delivery of an Electra in March, 1936.

EDUCATIONAL MEETING Educational group of the Lockheed Recreation Club will hold an open meeting at 7:30 p.m., Wednesday in the Burbank High School auditorium, according to H.C. Clark, chairman.

CREDIT UNION FUNCTIONS Lockheed Employees Federal Credit Union is now a going organization with 130 members and sufficient funds on deposit to make loans to members. Additional applications for membership will be approved by the officers the third Thursday of each month, according to Roger Lewis, president.

Loans are made for various purposes. For instance, it is pointed out, $5 deposited each payday between now and August will provide a member with a $50 fund for a vacation in that month.

DATE SET FOR DANCE Friday, April 16 has been set as the date for the LRC Spring Sport Dance, which will be held at the Burbank Elks Club. Norman Christopher is in charge, assisted by Louis Cummaro. Admission will be 50 cents per couple.

SHOP EMPLOYEES VACATION One hundred and eleven hourly wage employees will enjoy a one-week vacation with pay this year, as compared with 27 last year, according to a list prepared by the Personnel Department. Of the eligible employees, 18 are in the Sheet Metal Department, 14 in Final Assembly, 10 in Metal Fittings, 9 each in Jigs and Machine Shop, 8 in Fuselage and Center Section, 6 each in Inspection, Maintenance, and Wood Mill, and others in Stock, Precision Assembly, Wing, Trim, Paint, Electrical, Tool, Template and Experimental Departments.

All For Safety

THE Lockheed Star

Safety For All

PUBLISHED WEEKLY BY THE LOCKHEED AIRCRAFT CORPORATION FOR ITS EMPLOYEES

Vol. 7 BURBANK, CALIFORNIA, U.S.A. FEBRUARY 16, 1940 No. 7

The FACTORY ROUND TABLE

★ *Hibbard Looks Ahead.* In bold face type above every workbench and desk at Lockheed should be reproduced the prophesy recently expressed by Hall L. Hibbard, vice-president and chief engineer, before a meeting of department heads and foremen:

"As I look down the road, I see four things: First, a wise, careful, far-seeing management. Second, your unequalled and proven ability to produce. Third, your Engineering Department which I pledge will give you designs of which you will be justly proud. Fourth, a spirit with a determination to excel. Combine these four and you have Lockheed, which, in my opinion, is powerful, unbeatable and ever-lasting."

* * *

★ *Ambition—Virtue or Vice.* That good old American characteristic, ambition, can get a fellow into a peck of trouble if it is misdirected. Everyone knows the young man who has more ambition than common sense, and is so eager to get ahead he is always talking himself out of one job into another. Misdirected ambition has resulted in more failures than successes. True ambition is the earnest desire to excel in one's work—the desire for self-improvement. Example: The large enrollment in the trade extension classes. Upon such a foundation is based success.

* * *

★ *More for Our Efforts.* From "Southern California Business" we glean this cheerful note:

"American wage-earners outside agriculture average today over 70 cents per hour as against 10 cents per hour in 1840—a rise of 700 per cent. Meanwhile, the cost of living index has risen from 60 to 150, or 250 per cent. This means that the buying power of hourly

(Continued on page 2)

Vega Parking Space

L. O. Holter, Vega personnel supervisor, has called attention of Vega employees to the fact that adequate parking space has been provided on company property and urges that these facilities be used. He states:

"All employees are requested to use the company parking lots and not to park cars on the streets surrounding the plant, a practice which, if continued, will make restriction on parking time by city authorities inevitable. Such restrictions would impose inconveniences and hardships upon the many outside people who have business to transact with the company, but who are denied the use of the parking lots."

Job Vacancies Open For Senior Grade Mechanics

Several vacancies in the highly-skilled trades are announced by H. A. Beall, manager of the employment division of the Industrial Relations Department.

Applications will be received from employees or their friends at the interview window of the employment division. Applicants must be thoroughly experienced in the trades in which the vacancies exist. No additional "Learners" or "Juniors"

(Continued on page 2)

Basketball Team In Exhibition Games

A. A. U. Finals for Pacific Coast League February 29

The three strongest basketball teams in the Pacific Coast League of the A.A.U. will play four exhibition games with the national A.A.U. champions, Phillips 66 Oilers from Oklahoma, on February 21 and 22. Two games will be played each night with 20th Century-Fox and Lockheed starting competition Wednesday night at 7:15 at the Los Angeles City College, followed by Phillips 66 Oilers and Bank of America at 8:45. On Thursday night Bank of America and Lockheed will play at 7:15 and Phillips 66 and 20th Century-Fox at 8:45.

These four games promise some of the finest basketball to be witnessed locally as the Oilers have several times this year defeated the Denver Nuggets, last year's A.A.U. national champions, and the three local teams are about evenly divided for winners' honors in the Pacific Coast League, which winds up tournament play February 29.

The last game of the series will be played by Lockheed and Bank of America

(Continued on page 2)

"Silver Falcon" Dismantled for Conversion to Lodestar Model

Lockheed's Service Department, under the direction of J. R. Hargrove, is at present engaged in converting Major Max C. Fleischmann's Lockheed 14, the Silver Falcon, pictured above partially dismantled, into a Lodestar Model 18. This is the first of a series of similar conversion jobs planned by the Service Department and is expected to take four to six weeks to complete. Customers of Lockheed have in this department one of the most complete service organizations maintained by an aircraft factory. Here planes are serviced and kept in condition by the men who built them.

Dancing Classes Offered Employees' Children

Through efforts of L.E.R.C. officials, arrangements have been made for children of Lockheed employees to take dancing lessons at reduced rates from instructors of the well-known Ruth Ann Fowler Dancing School in Glendale.

Miss Fowler will offer a three-months' course beginning in March for instruction in tap, ballet and other types at twenty-five cents an hour, a considerable reduction from the regular dollar-an-hour rate. Ollie Arbelbide, L.E.R.C. program director, is making arrangements for the classes to be conducted in Burbank on Saturday mornings. The classes will be divided into groups of 15 students each, and are limited to children between the ages of 7 and 14 years. Upon completion of registration, which may be arranged by contacting Arbelbide at the canteen, as many classes as are necessary to absorb the number of students will be provided.

Arbelbide announces that ballroom dancing classes at special rates may be arranged at a later date for employees.

Choral Club Postpones Spaghetti Dinner

The Choral Club spaghetti dinner, previously set for February 17, has been postponed, according to Norman Hanson, president. Arrangements for this social function will be discussed further at the business meeting to be held Monday evening at 7:30 in the Pool Building in Griffith Park, and a new date announced later.

Semi-annual election of officers will take place at this meeting, and plans for the year's activities will be outlined to the members for approval and adoption.

Round Table

(Continued from page 1)

wages has risen since 1840 by almost 300 per cent." One of the greatest factors in making this advance possible is the development of labor-saving methods and machinery.

Job Vacancies Open

(Continued from page 1)

are needed in these occupations. Senior mechanics only are required.

The vacancies which exist in the senior grades are as follows:

Cutter Grinder, Sr.
Drop Hammer Operator, Sr.
Lathe Operator (tools), Sr.
Precision Bar Operators, Sr.
Process Inspector, Sr. (college chemistry required).
Template Inspectors, Sr.
Tool and Die Makers, Sr.

L.E.R.C. Calendar

Sunday, February 18—Baseball. Lockheed vs. Housel Trucking Company, Solon Park, Burbank, 2 p.m. Admission 15¢.

Monday, February 19—Basketball. Lockheed vs. Aero Industries Technical Institute, Glendale High School, 7:15. Admission free.

Monday, February 19—Choral Club. Semi-annual election meeting, Pool Building, Griffith Park, 7:30 p.m.

Tuesday, February 20—Bowling. Men's inter-departmental bowling league, Sunset Bowling Center, 8:30 p.m. Admission free.

Wednesday, February 21—Basketball. Exhibition game, Lockheed vs. 20th Century-Fox, Los Angeles City College, Monroe and Vermont, 7:15 p.m. Admission 40¢.

Thursday, February 22—Basketball. Exhibition game, Lockheed vs. Bank of America, Los Angeles City College, Monroe and Vermont, 7:15 p.m. Admission 40¢.

Thursday, February 22—Bowling. Mixed doubles bowling league, Sunset Bowling Center, 6:30 p.m. Admission free.

Friday, February 23—N.B.C. tour through Radio City, Sunset Boulevard and Vine Street, 7 p.m. Tickets 30¢ per person, available at the canteen.

Camera Club Meets To Plan Program

Operating under temporary by-laws and officials, the Lockheed Employees' Camera Club announces a regular meeting to be held at the home of Roland F. Holland, president, 608 West Ivy Street, in Glendale, on Thursday, February 22, at 7:30 p.m. At this meeting plans will be discussed concerning the club's first outing, a camera tour through railroad shops and yards.

"Outward Bound" Staged By Theater Workshop

Presentation of the famous New York stage play, "Outward Bound," on March 1, 2, 3 and 4, in the Footlight Theatre, 1455 North Laurel in Hollywood, by the Lockheed Theater Workshop will set a new standard in amateur dramatic presentations. Production of this play, which originally starred such stage and screen notables as Alfred Lunt, Leslie Howard, Beryl Mercer, Douglas Fairbanks, Jr., and Dudley Digges, is under the direction of Charles A. Bell. Among the Lockheed players featured are Art Schwerin, Bernard Benaway, Jean Mills, Juanita Vokrol, Bob McGaughey, Henry Sinderhauf, Charles A. Bell, Micki Schwerin and Earl J. Younker.

Tickets for the play are 35¢ each and will be available in the Publicity Department, the mail room, at the canteen and from members of the cast.

Bowling Tournament Awards Presented At Dinner

The Girls' Bowling Trophy was awarded to the Manufacturing Engineering team at the Bowling Dinner held Monday night. The trophy was held in 1938 by the Purchasing Department team, and in 1939 by Payroll Department. The five girls on this year's winning team rolled high score in the Girls' Bowling League, and will keep the trophy for the current year.

Teams receiving awards are:

First Place: Trophy and $25.00 to the Manufacturing Engineering Department team for the playing of Captain Doris Glastre, Harriet Waterbury, Ruth Simonson, Florence McGough and Betty Chambers.

A $10.00 award for second place went to the Personnel Department team consisting of Captain Leona Tyrell, Louise Davidson, Louise Reiner, Lorraine Rasmussen and Kay Dixon.

Basketball Team

(Continued from page 1)

on February 29. The winner of this game will be sent to Denver for the National A.A.U. championship games, unless 20th Century-Fox defeats Bank of America in the game scheduled to be played before that date, in which case a post-tournament play-off game between Lockheed and Fox will decide the league's winning team.

THE LOCKHEED STAR *is issued every Friday by the Lockheed Aircraft Corporation for its employees. Communications may be addressed to either the Industrial Relations Department or the Public Relations Department, Lockheed Aircraft Corporation, Burbank, California, U.S.A.*

Work Safely

THE Lockheed Star

Again Today

PUBLISHED WEEKLY BY THE LOCKHEED AIRCRAFT CORPORATION FOR ITS EMPLOYEES

Vol. 7 BURBANK, CALIFORNIA, U.S.A. APRIL 19, 1940 No. 16

★ *Employment Picks Up.* For the first time since the last of May of 1939, employment at Lockheed showed a decided up-turn last week, while the increase in Vega's employment continued at an accelerated rate. Most of the former Lockheed employees who were laid off due to shortage of materials at the beginning of this year have been called back. The employment division is conducting an active recruiting campaign to meet the need for experienced engineers and skilled craftsmen in certain lines. Employees of proven ability are being considered for promotion as new positions open up. Barring unforeseen circumstances, it looks like a good year ahead.

* * *

★ *What Makes a Good Supervisor?* At a time when employment is increasing, every one of us wonders how it will affect us. Not a few non-supervisory employees would like to know their chances of promotion to positions of supervision. Department heads and other executives, on the other hand, are trying to determine just who to select as the next supervisors. It is no easy task to decide. Many an excellent mechanic has failed when made a supervisor. It is a serious business to run the risk of making a second-rate supervisor out of a good mechanic. Assuming that he is dependable and conscientious, a mechanic is successful if he has technical knowledge and manipulative skill. As a supervisor, three-quarters of his job is "human relations" and one-quarter is technical knowledge. A supervisor may be "inflicted" on a group, but a real leader is made only by his being accepted by the employees whom he supervises. Lockheed and Vega want supervisors whom the other employees will cheerfully and enthusiastically follow.

NEW COMMERCIAL ORDERS SWELL BACKLOG

Parking Limited To Two Hours In Vega Area

An ordinance recently passed by the City of Burbank limits parking on San Fernando Road in the vicinity of the Vega factory to two hours. While this area has not yet been posted, the Burbank Police Department feels that sufficient warning has been given and traffic citations will be issued to violators of this ordinance.

Vega employees are requested to park in the company lot, which provides ample space for all cars. Entrance to the lot is on Cedar Street, one block south of San Fernando Road and one block west of Alameda.

Vacancies Listed For Skilled Workers

Vacancies have been announced by the employment division of the Industrial Relations Department for several types of experienced workers. Applications will be accepted at the employment window for any of the following:

Drop hammer operators.
Engineers: stress, layout, design, and senior draftsmen.
Form block makers.
Jig builders.
Precision bar operators.
Senior sheet metal workers
Tool designers.
Toolmakers.

Nine Lodestars, One Other Plane Contracted For In New Business Totalling More Than $1,000,000

New commercial orders amounting to more than $1,000,000 have been received by Lockheed, according to an announcement from Carl B. Squier, vice president and sales manager. This brings Lockheed's total current backlog to slightly in excess of $55,000,000.

Included in the new contracts are three Lodestars for Air France, doubling the order placed by this French company last February.

Regie Air Afrique, another French airline which has previously ordered planes of this model, has contracted for two additional Lodestars.

Continental Airlines have placed an order for three Lodestars for use on their schedules operating between Denver and El Paso.

One other executive Lodestar for an unnamed purchaser and one six-passenger personnel transport for the U. S. Navy complete the new business contracted for.

Thirty-six of the world's major airlines now either operate or have ordered Lockheed planes. To date more than 35 of the Lodestar model, introduced less than six months ago, have been ordered.

Sister Ship of the first Lodestar recently delivered to the Mid-Continent Airlines for use on their Great Plains Route. These planes are the first of the Lodestar model to be used in regular passenger transport service.

College-Level Accounting Course Offered

Thirty employees have already indicated intentions of entering a university-level course in Accounting offered at the John Muir Junior High School in Burbank starting next Monday, April 22, at 7 p.m.

This 45-hour course is to be completed before the summer vacation. A university fee of $18.00 will be charged and 3 units of university credit granted for successful completion of the course. No charge will be made for the first meeting, which will be primarily orientation and organization of the class.

Harry Simons, instructor in Business Administration at the University of California at Los Angeles, will direct the course.

Paul Sanderson Killed In Glider Accident

Paul A. Sanderson, 26, Lockheed stress analyst, died Sunday afternoon, April 14, as the result of a sailplane accident near Arvin, California, when his glider collided with another 500 feet in the air while flying in the third annual western championship glider tests.

Sanderson was employed in the Engineering Department, where he has worked since July, 1936, having previously been in the U.S. Naval Air Service. He was a graduate of the University of Michigan, holding degrees in aeronautical and mechanical engineering.

He is survived by his parents in Youngstown, Ohio, where funeral services and interment will be held.

Trade Classes Open

Attention of men working on the night shift is particularly directed to sheet metal layout, drafting, template layout and blueprint reading classes now being offered at the Frank Wiggins Trade School.

Due to the great number of placements of men in the aviation industry, vacancies in these classes have been announced. The classes are held daily from 10 a.m. to 2 p.m. in the aircraft division of the trade school, located at the corner of 11th and Flower streets in Los Angeles.

Softball Squad Formed

Employees who would like to play on the night softball squad now being formed are requested to call Ollie Arbelbide, L.E.R.C. program director, at the Canteen office, extension 556.

L.E.R.C. Calendar

Friday, April 19—Women's softball practice, Solon Park, Burbank, 4 p.m.

Saturday, April 20 — Children's dancing class, Ruth Ann Fowler Studio, 219½ North Brand Boulevard, Glendale, 9 a.m. to 12 noon.

Sunday, April 21—Baseball, Lockheed vs. Rosabelle Plumbers, Arroyo Seco Field, Pasadena, 2 p.m.

Monday, April 22—Softball. Inter-departmental game, Solon Park, Burbank, 4 p.m.

Monday, April 22—Band practice, John Muir Junior High School cafeteria, 7:30 p.m.

Monday, April 22—Choral Club. Rehearsal, Swimming Pool Building, Griffith Park, 7:30 p.m.

April 23, 24, 25—Softball. Inter-departmental games, Solon Park, Burbank, 4 p.m.

Aircraftsman Office Moved To Canteen

"Aircraftsman" headquarters have been moved from room 104, building 101, to an office in the canteen. This location will bring the staff of the employees' monthly publication closer to all members of the L.E.R.C. and facilitate the clearing of news items through the editor's office.

Protection Of Personal Property Advised

Employees are warned by the Police Department to take all possible precautions to protect their personal property from loss and possible theft by marking it for identification and keeping tool boxes locked when away from work.

Charles Phelps, chief of police, also points out the folly of leaving money or articles of value in coats or sweaters left hanging in unprotected places, and requests that any losses that occur at work be reported to the Police Department.

Regular inventories should be made of all personally owned tools to keep a proper check on them and report any missing items as quickly as possible. Accurate descriptions of lost tools and identification marks which they carry will materially assist in their recovery.

Burbank Educational Facilities Displayed

Burbank High School will hold open house twice next week when both the evening and day schools invite families and friends to inspect at first-hand the facilities offered in the two branches of education.

Wednesday, April 24, the trade extension classes of the evening school will be open to visitors and guides will be provided for escort through the building. Exhibits of the work being done in the various classes will be displayed.

Friday, April 26, an open house for the day school will be sponsored by the P.T.A. The annual affair will be under the direction of the president, Mrs. B. C. Boulton, wife of Lockheed's assistant chief project engineer. Dinner will be served in the school cafeteria at 6:30 p.m. for 35c per person. Following a tour through the school, guests will assemble in the auditorium at 8 p.m. when Svend Pedersen, Lockheed educational director, will speak on "Opportunities in Aviation."

Vega Employee Killed In Auto Accident

Melvin Jacobson, Vega Production-Dispatching Department, was killed Wednesday morning when the car in which he was en route to work collided with a truck at Castalar and North Figueroa in Los Angeles. Julian Nelson of Heat Treating, Austin Hanson of Wing and Tail and Sebastian Ramelli of Maintenance, all of Lockheed, were injured in the accident.

Course In Time Study Offered By U. S. C.

The University of Southern California will offer a 14 weeks' course in Time Study, to be conducted by Gerald C. Billman. The class will be held in room 302, Bridge Hall, on the university campus, every Tuesday. A fee of $14.50 will be charged for the course.

The class deals with the purposes of time study, the technique employed in timing, the determination of job elements, and the treatments of calculated results.

Blair Resumes Duties

R. A. Blair, auditor for Lockheed's British Reassembly Division, returned recently from England to resume his duties at the Burbank factory. Leigh Austin Newcomer left last week for the company's Liverpool reassembly plant.

THE LOCKHEED STAR *is issued every Friday by the Lockheed Aircraft Corporation for its employees. Communications may be addressed to either the Industrial Relations Department or the Public Relations Department, Lockheed Aircraft Corporation, Burbank, California, U.S.A.*

The Price of Liberty

THE Lockheed Star

Is Eternal Vigilance

PUBLISHED WEEKLY BY THE LOCKHEED AIRCRAFT CORPORATION FOR ITS EMPLOYEES

Vol. 7 BURBANK, CALIFORNIA, U.S.A., JULY 19, 1940 No. 29

Second Apprentice Group To Be Selected Soon

Lockheed and Vega Employees Eligible to Participate In Earn-as-You-Learn Program

For the second time in six months a group of apprentices will be selected from the Lockheed and Vega companies for training and actual work in the trades of machinist; tool, die and jig builder; wood pattern and jig builder; and sheet metal worker. This program is planned to offer qualified employees an opportunity to participate in the earn-as-you-learn program endorsed by the Federal Government.

The program is administered by a committee representing Lockheed Aircraft Corporation, the Aeronautical Mechanics of Burbank, Lodge 727 of the International Association of Machinists, and the Burbank Unified School System under standards established by the State and Federal governments.

The objective of the apprenticeship program is to develop broadly skilled craftsmen in their respective fields and covers a training period of four years

(Continued on page 3)

PERFORMANCE OF LOCKHEED HUDSON BOMBERS PRAISED IN WAR REPORTS

First Ten Months of War Prove Lockheed Planes Capable of Withstanding Strain in Action Far Greater Than Required by Specifications; Press and Radio Releases Praise Sturdy Construction

The excellence in design, workmanship and performance of Lockheed planes has been convincingly indicated in press releases and radio broadcasts emanating from the war zone. These reports provide an unofficial answer to the frequently repeated question, "How do Lockheed planes perform in actual war service?" On a recent radio program released over the Columbia Broadcasting System a British pilot officer stated in part, "The other day we were looking for targets on the Dutch Coast. Messerschmitts came up to us like a cloud of mosquitoes. We really tested our Lockheeds as they've never been tested before. We dived toward the sea at 400 miles an hour and that is faster than the manufacturers ever thought their planes would be likely to travel. We had to throttle through the gate for 35 minutes while the instructions allow us only three minutes at that maximum, but fifty feet above the sea, still trying to dodge the Messerschmitts, we rode and threw our machines about all over the place and they took it like birds.

"Last week-end a shell exploded inside the cabin of one of our aircraft. It blew dozens of holes in the fuselage, wrecked the radio, killed the gunner, and wounded the pilot and navigator. That aircraft looked like a sieve but they brought it back.

"Over Stavanger a few days ago, anti-aircraft fire knocked a hole in the wing

(Continued on page 4)

Visitors Registered On Lockheed Guest Book

Recent visitors to the Lockheed factory included a group of young Chinese army officers who were sent to this country by the Commission of Aeronautical Affairs of China. Included in this group, here for educational purposes, were Captains En-Wei Chen, Juo-Hong Chu, Herbert I. C. Yuan, Pao-Chun Shu, and Wen-Kwan Hwa.

(Continued on page 4)

Lockheed Hudson Bomber of type now being used for all types of warfare by Great Britain.

Procedure for Transfer Application Outlined

To avoid confusion and loss of time and effort through the improper "shopping" on the part of employees and supervisors for jobs and men, R. Randall Irwin, industrial relations manager, has issued a bulletin calling attention to the proper procedure to be followed by employees and supervisory personnel in applying for transfers.

Reviewing established rules, the bulletin states in part:

"No department head, foreman, or supervisor may discuss any aspect of a transfer with any employee without the con-

(Continued on page 4)

★ *A Reminder.* New employees continue to arrive at an all-time record rate. Do you remember how you felt when you first reported for work? Yes, that is the way 2,000 or more new Lockheed and Vega employees feel this month. Are you giving them that note of encouragement and helpful word of advice?

* * *

★ *Parking Problem.* Every new employee complicates the parking problem just a little more. More parking areas are being provided, but one of the best aids is to double up on transportation. If half the people who now drive their own cars would ride with someone else, it would cut the parking problem in half. A transportation exchange service is provided by the Employee Service Division of the Industrial Relations Department. Use it freely.

* * *

★ *A Tremendous Job.* It is variously predicted that it will require from 18 months to two years of strenuous work to produce the minimum amount of equipment needed to approximate the requirements of reasonable national defense. Some predict it will take longer. Even that will require the utmost cooperation between the government, industrial management and employees. The public, of which we all are a part, must learn self-sacrifice for the cause of defending the high principles and institutions of this country. Lack of unity and any widespread friction between various groups would bring defeat of the efforts to arm for defense. The government recognizes this important fact. A recent report from Washington suggested that, other things being equal, companies with the most harmonious internal conditions might secure preference in the allotment of orders. There is every reason for every individual and every group to try to work harmoniously with every other individual and group.

Gold Diggers' Ball Set for Next Week

Tickets for the Lockheed Girls' Gold Diggers' Ball, to be held at the Riverside Breakfast Club Saturday evening, July 27, are now on sale and may be secured from L.E.R.C. representatives.

The price is necessarily being increased to 40¢ per person as a result of tax regulations recently placed in effect and consequently will not be 35¢ as previously announced.

Dancing will be the order of the evening from 9 p.m. to 1 a.m. Sonny Crenshaw and his orchestra will furnish music for the event. Marjory Sargent, chairman of the Women's Committee, is planning special entertainment features for the evening. Dress will be informal.

Champion Archer In Exhibition July 26

Through special arrangements completed by Ollie Arbelbide, L.E.R.C. program director, Howard Hill, world champion archer, bow and arrow big game hunter and motion picture technical adviser, will give an exhibition in archery at Solon Park, Burbank, on Friday, July 26, at 4:15 p.m.

Hill will demonstrate his accuracy with the long bow in smashing skeet in full flight, cutting strings at twenty paces, and picking off small rolling targets from many positions.

★ *Defense or Defeat?* The complete story of just what happened in France may not be known for some time. But one thing is evident. The German army was well equipped, because the German industrial machine had been working efficiently for several years building war equipment. To accomplish this all individual liberties had been suppressed. In France, subversive elements had been allowed to run rampant and disrupt industry. The result was that the Army was poorly equipped — then defeated. When the French Army was defeated, democracy was killed, and France became a totalitarian state. Individual liberty became a thing of the past. If we are to preserve individual liberty, we must defend it by working together, not against each other. Voluntary, harmonious cooperation among groups and individuals never destroyed anyone's liberty. It is the essence of democracy and the modern American industrial system.

L.E.R.C. Calendar

Friday, July 19—L.E.R.C.-Foremen's Dinner, Hollywood Roosevelt Hotel, 7:30 p.m.

Saturday, July 20 — Riding Club meets at Roscoe Stables, 9989 Stonehurst, Roscoe, 9 a.m.

Monday, July 22—Softball playoff game, Timekeeping vs. Production and Planning, Solon Park, Burbank, 5 p.m.

Monday, July 22—Night softball, Lockheed vs. Corodi Music, John Muir Junior High School, Burbank, 8:30 p.m.

Tuesday, July 23—Band practice, John Muir Junior High School cafeteria, Burbank, 7:30 p.m.

Tuesday, July 23 — Hollywood Bowl Concert, Paul Robeson and David Broekman, tickets at Canteen, 50¢.

Wednesday, July 24 — Softball. Dispatching vs. Paint, Solon Park, Burbank, 5:30 p.m.

Thursday, July 25—Softball. Playoff game, Office League, Solon Park, Burbank, 5 p.m.

Thursday, July 25 — Hollywood Bowl Concert, Bartlett and Robertson, pianists; Albert Coates conducting. Tickets at Canteen, 50¢.

Friday, July 26—Archery exhibition, Howard Hill, world's champion, Solon Park, Burbank, 4:15 p.m. Admission free.

Friday, July 26—Hollywood Bowl Symphony, Bruno Walter conducting. Tickets at Canteen, 25¢.

Saturday, July 27—L.E.R.C. Girls' Gold Diggers' Ball, Riverside Drive Breakfast Club, 9 p.m. to 1 a.m., 40¢ per person.

Foremen Entertained By Recreation Club

The annual L.E.R.C. Foremen's dinner will be held this evening in the Florentine Room of the Hollywood Roosevelt Hotel at 7:30, according to Allen W. (Bill) Zinser, L.E.R.C. president.

Officers and foremen of the company will be guests of the L.E.R.C. council at this dinner. Committee chairmen of the recreation club's various activities will present reports covering the work accomplished and planned for this year.

THE LOCKHEED STAR *is issued every Friday by the Lockheed Aircraft Corporation for its employees. Communications may be addressed to either the Industrial Relations Department or the Public Relations Department, Lockheed Aircraft Corporation, Burbank, California, U.S.A.*

Human Relations Manual Circulated by Library

"Human Relations Manual for Executives" by Carl Heyel, manager of the Conference Planning Division of the American Management Association, is the title of one of the most recent additions to the library of the Lockheed education division. This book, covering reports from various companies on their dealings with employees also discusses problems of employee selection, training, and the general improvement of working conditions.

This book, especially recommended to executives, supervisors and personnel workers, may be borrowed from the library, though personal copies may be secured through the education division for $1.70 per copy.

Employees Invited to Join L.E.R.C. Band

All employees who play band instruments are invited by "Bob" Hanson, leader, to join the Lockheed Band. Rehearsals are held each Tuesday evening at 7:30 at the John Muir Junior High School in Burbank.

Courtlandt S. Gross, Thomas H. Corpe and S. W. Voorhes Take Over New Positions

Left: Courtlandt S. Gross. Center: Thomas H. Corpe. Below: S. W. Voorhes.

S. W. Voorhes has resigned his position as assistant general sales manager of Lockheed to take over the eastern sales organization which has its headquarters in New York City, according to a recent announcement from Carl B. Squier, vice-president and general sales manager.

Thomas H. Corpe is assuming the duties of assistant general sales manager, the announcement also disclosed. Corpe has been in charge of Lockheed's promotional activities and, until recently, also held the post of sales manager for the Vega Airplane Company.

Courtlandt S. Gross, formerly in charge of the New York office, was recently elected president of Vega and is at present active in this position.

J. G. Brown Appointed District Inspector

While he will continue to maintain his headquarters at Lockheed, J. G. Brown is at present taking over the work of Inspector In Charge, Western Aircraft Group, for the British Purchasing Commission.

E. H. Holman of the British Supply Board Inspectional Staff has been transferred to Lockheed as Resident Inspector for the board to take over the duties handled by Brown prior to his new appointment.

Second Apprentice Group

(Continued from page 1)

with a starting rate for apprentices without previous experience of 36¢ per hour, to be increased six cents each six months for the duration of the apprenticeship.

The apprentice is provided with a wide variety of work experiences supplemented by four hours of related technical instruction, at the same time receiving the regular apprenticeship rate of pay. Advanced credit up to a maximum of two years will be given to those applicants selected who can verify and demonstrate previous experience.

Application blanks are available from the telephone operator in the Lockheed employment division. These forms should be filled in completely, giving in detail courses taken in school, explanation of mechanical experience and special abilities or qualifications. They should be returned to the education division not later than August 3.

"Worth Your Salt"

By F. E. Poole, M.D.

The importance of salt in the diet has been recognized for thousands of years and it has been conjectured that some of the oldest trade routes were created for traffic in salt. So important was it considered both in the early history of the Roman army and in later times that an allowance of salt was made to officers and men, and from this ancient custom comes our expression—"Not worth his salt." In imperial times, however, an allowance of money was made for the salt, and our modern word "salary" is derived from the Latin "Salarium," meaning salt money.

It is doubtful whether the ancient Romans understood the scientific facts concerning the utilization of salt in the body, but experience probably was their best teacher in demonstrating that their soldiers had more endurance and less fatigue and heat stroke when provided with their salt allowance. This custom along with many others, however, was discontinued, and it now has the distinction of being probably the most recently revived of any of the "old Roman customs."

It has been only during the past 15 years that the direct relationship of loss of salt from the body to excessive fatigue with sweating, heat cramps, and heat stroke has been seriously studied and understood. The body normally needs at least two grams of salt daily under average conditions, and a person on a normal diet averages four or five times this amount. However, with hot weather and excess sweating an abnormal amount of salt is lost in the perspiration and it is essential to replace both the lost salt and water to keep the concentration in the blood stream at its normal level. So, if you are not inclined to be liberal with salt in your food during hot weather, take at least two salt tablets daily and drink plenty of water. There is no danger of taking too much salt, for the body uses only the amount it needs and excretes the rest.

During the summer eat your salt to make sure you are "worth your salt."

Lockheed Hudson Bombers at Union Air Terminal awaiting shipment to Great Britain to be put into service for the defense of that mighty empire.

Performance of Bombers Praised

(Continued from page 1)

big enough for two men to crawl through. For 400 miles the pilot could look down at the sea through that colossal hole between the fuselage and the engine, but he got it back home. We have done pretty well against the Dorniers and the twin-engine Heinkels. These Lockheeds have a terrific rate of climb even with a full load and if one motor goes out we still do well on the other one. I have flown these aircraft since before the war started, flown them blind in all weather and under all conditions the people who made them didn't exactly have in mind. They are good aircraft. Our squadron has been used for pretty well everything—bombing, reconnaissance, and photographic work. Occasionally we even have to do a bit of fighting. It is good to feel your aircraft isn't going to fall apart if it gets hit and that the wings will stay on when you pull it out of a power dive."

Commenting on one of the few comforts of warfare, he added, "And there is another thing which is very much appreciated by those of us who work in these aircraft. That is the heating system. It is really pleasant to be able to fly in your shirt sleeves even when there is ice on the wings."

North Sea Encounters

Fragments of news releases make frequent mention of the Lockheed Hudson in service. In one story a fight over the North Sea is described. Throughout the engagement both machines were within 20 feet of the water as "The British plane, a Hudson, was on patrol when the pilot saw a dark grey Dornier at sea level. The British pilot attacked from the beam, opening the fight with three short bursts from his front gun.

"The Dornier turned steeply to port, but the Hudson swung to starboard to bring his rear guns into action. Two bursts were fired as the enemy came into the fight. The German rear gunner replied with tracer bullets, but his shots went wide.

"The Hudson attacked again, and the German's rear gun was silenced. The British pilot made five more attacks from the tail, and there was still no reply from the German gun. The British pilot's ammunition ran out and he broke off the combat."

Close Call Recounted

Another account of a dive attack on a Dornier bomber over the North Sea an hour later tells of a successful engagement, but finishes, "The Hudson, however, was returning from a long patrol and the petrol began to run short. With a final burst from his gun the pilot broke off the combat and returned to his base. When he landed, he had only enough petrol in his tank for two minutes of flying time."

A recent Associated Press release by W. E. Yarbrough, in reference to the Lockheed Hudsons, makes the statement that "No German Messerschmitt has been able to shoot one down. Their job," this release quotes a Scottish flying officer as saying, "is to break the siege of Britain —getting ships safely into the harbors." This same officer told how three of the American planes had met 40 German machines, "Thirty flew on, leaving 10 to handle the American-made planes. When the shooting was over, five Germans were down and five had run away. All the British came home."

Procedure for Transfer

(Continued from page 1)

sent of the employee's present superior. This may be obtained by the employee or the department head, foreman or supervisor who is interested in the employee.

The Employment Division should be called upon to assist with arrangements that now take the time of operating supervision.

"An employee who desires a transfer to another job has two lines open to him. He may either obtain the permission of his superior to discuss a transfer with a specific department head, foreman, or supervisor, or he may go to the Employment Division to discuss his problem. The Employment Division will give all possible assistance including referral to the Education Division for any necessary guidance or other steps deemed advisable. The Employment Division, however, may not discuss a definite transfer with any employee without the permission of his present superior. If any of the parties involved feel that all care and fairness have not been exercised in arriving at a conclusion, the matter will be presented to the Industrial Relations Department for amicable adjustment."

Visitors Sign Guest Book

(Continued from page 1)

Other visitors included Brigadier General B. K. Yount, assistant chief of the Army Air Corps, who came here from Washington, D.C. Major C. C. Mosely, also of the Air Corps, was with him.

Airline representatives here for visits included B. H. Young who is stationed at Lima, Peru by Pan Air; R. L. Heinrich, George Page, and Don Woodward of United Air Lines; and Herman Pedersen of Continental Air Lines.

Wallace Carroll, a United Press staff correspondent, last week released a story commenting on the use of Lockheed Hudsons as a vital factor in preparations for the defense of the British Isles. His story, quoting a gray-haired squadron leader, said in part:

All-Purpose Planes

"At first we thought these planes would be all right for scouting and photography. Then the crews discovered they could do amazing things with them and that it took a lot of punishment to bring down a Lockheed. They were the first planes to drop bombs on Norway. When we abandoned a policy of not attacking land objectives in Germany, it was a Lockheed that dropped the first bombs and set fire to oil tanks at Bremen and Hamburg."

He said in conclusion that the planes had been in combat with every type of German aircraft and had always proved themselves the better.

Skilled Workers

THE Lockheed Star

Are Trained Workers

PUBLISHED WEEKLY BY THE LOCKHEED AIRCRAFT CORPORATION FOR ITS EMPLOYEES

Vol. 7 BURBANK, CALIFORNIA, U.S.A., SEPTEMBER 20, 1940 No. 38

4,000 Students Enroll In Trade Extension Classes

Extensive Education Program Organized to Help Overcome Shortage of Skilled Workers

Four thousand students employed by Lockheed and Vega started trade extension classes this week as part of the plant-wide program organized to overcome the current acute shortage of skilled workers. The students are enrolled in approximately 100 trade extension courses covering a period of 18 weeks, two evenings per week, and including virtually every phase of aircraft construction.

The courses, designed to train aircraft workers for positions in the aircraft factory which require experience or special training, are held in the three Burbank high schools, Hockaday Aircraft Corporation in Burbank, and at the Lockheed factory.

Most of the instructors of trade extension classes are employees of the Lockheed organization with long experience in aircraft construction, and a large portion of the equipment and supplies used will be furnished by Lockheed and Vega.

"Here, I believe, is the finest example of cooperation between employees and plant management to be found any place in the United States," said Svend Pedersen, director of education division of Lockheed. "A high degree of patriotism is being shown by the employees in this emergency. They are not only working extra hours to enable us to increase the

(Continued on page 4)

DRAFT MEASURE SIGNED BY PRESIDENT

REGISTRAR OF VOTERS AT LOCKHEED

In order to qualify for voting in the general election to be held Tuesday, November 5, all citizens must be properly registered. Thursday, September 26, is the deadline for such registration. A deputy registrar for voters has been stationed at Lockheed yesterday and today and will return to the plant Tuesday and Wednesday, September 24 and 25, of next week. The deputy will be at the Canteen from 11:30 a.m. to 12:00 m., at Gate 1 from 12:15 p.m. to 2 p.m., and at the Canteen again from 3 p.m. to 5 p.m.

Vega employees will have an opportunity to register Thursday, September 26, from 11 a.m. to 1 p.m. and from 4 p.m. on.

Registration to vote in the coming election is required of:

1. Anyone who has never registered;
2. Anyone who has moved since last registration;
3. Anyone who failed to vote either in the primary or general election of 1938.

Any citizen who will be 21 years of age by November 5 who has been a resident of the state for one year and of Los Angeles County for 90 days is eligible to register.

The first production model of the Lockheed P-38, world's fastest interceptor, underwent its preliminary test flights early this week with Marshall Headle at the controls.

October 16 Is Date Set For Registration of All Men Within Age Limits

President Roosevelt early this week placed his signature on the first peacetime draft in the nation's history, designated as the Selective Training and Service Act of 1940. This Act, which was enacted by Congress last Saturday, September 14, provides for conscription of the nation's man power and calls for industrial cooperation in the current rearmament drive.

Under the provisions of the bill the President proclaimed October 16 as national registration day, when, with few exceptions, all men from 21 to 35, inclusive, will be required to register for possible peace-time military training for the duration of one year.

Of the 16,500,000 men required to register 400,000 will be chosen by selection and lot for army training, scheduled to start late this fall. Thereafter it is expected that 900,000 men, the maximum number permitted by the bill, will be drafted each year for the next five years to be trained as a reservoir of man power for the nation's land and naval

(Continued on page 2)

War Department Places Order for Lockheed Planes

The War Department announced this week that an order totalling approximately $15,646,450 had been awarded to the Lockheed Aircraft Corporation for a number of pursuit planes. This new order brings the Lockheed backlog of unfllled business to more than $215,000,000.

The order was placed following an inspection of the P-38 interceptor two weeks ago by William S. Knudsen, production chairman of the National Defense Commission, and Major-General Henry H. Arnold, head of the Army Air Corps.

Early this week the first production model of the pursuit plane was flown in test flights from the Union Air Terminal by Marshall Headle, chief test pilot. Reports of the flight showed that it was "entirely normal."

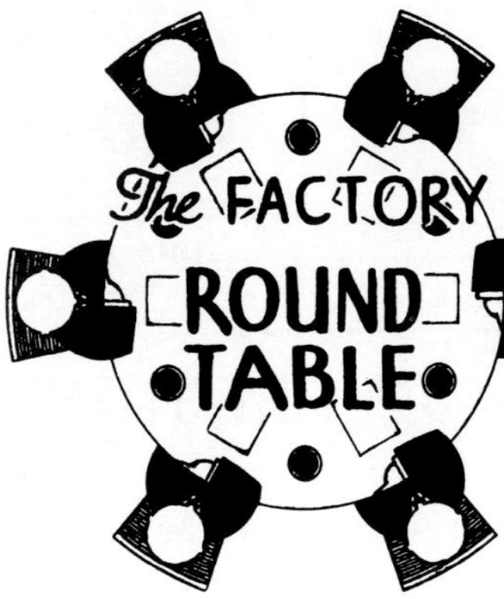

★ *Far Sighted.* In his annual report to stockholders, Vega President Courtlandt S. Gross said, "Events of the past year have served to strengthen the management's conviction as to the ultimate size and desirability of this market (small commercial and small private or family airplanes). However, these same events have additionally brought the conviction that enthusiastic and unselfish contribution of the company's energy and ingenuity to meeting the needs of national defense will remain during the period of emergency the principal concern . . . It is proposed wholeheartedly to direct this company's facilities to the country's needs, but it is intended concurrently to plan and design for the eagerly awaited peace time market."

* * *

★ *Military Leave.* Hardly had the ink dried on the Lockheed-Vega-Union contract when Congress passed and the President signed the so-called "National Guard Act" which contains provisions that persons called to military service shall be re-instated by their employers upon discharge from such service. The employee seeking reinstatement must (1) still be qualified to perform the duties of his position, and (2) make application for re-employment within 40 days after he is relieved from active military duty. The Union agreement likewise contains certain clauses protecting employees called to active military duty.

* * *

★ *Schools to Help.* Giving full support to the national defense program, Los Angeles Superintendent of Schools Vierling Kersey has given teachers instructions that should make the job of building defense easier. One is that high standards of instruction be maintained in the three R's. Arithmetic (and mathematics) are not to be neglected. Mr. Kersey has also instructed that tolerance toward subversive, Communistic or disloyal precepts be completely eliminated. Teachers of the Lockheed extension classes will be glad to hear that the Los Angeles schools are taking a stand against the so-called "progressive education" that neglects to require formal mathematics as a study. Too much time is wasted in the extension classes going back and giving mathematics that should have been taught in high school.

Draft Measure Signed

(Continued from page 1)

forces. Congress was asked by the President for an appropriation of $1,940,886,976, a large part of which is to be used to finance the proposed draft.

Declaring that it is imperative to increase and train the armed forces of the United States and that compulsory military training and service should be shared generally, measures of the provision require registration of all male citizens of the United States and all male aliens residing in this country between the ages of 21 and 36 (21 to 35, inclusive) on the registration date proclaimed by the President.

12 Month Training Periods

Training periods of 12 months are fixed by the bill except that they may be lengthened when Congress declares the national interest imperiled. Following the 12 months period of training, draftees will be placed on a reserve list for 10 years, or until they have reached the age of 45, for possible subsequent service in the Western Hemisphere or possessions of the United States. State draft quotas will be fixed on the basis of population with credits allowed for those men already in the military or naval service.

All Must Register

All men in the age group covered by the draft must register in accordance with rules and regulations, to be announced by the President, with the single exception of those now in active service. Under this ruling all aircraft workers are required to register regardless of the fact that they are employed in an industry that is considered essential to rearmament. While the President is permitted to defer training of persons employed in essential industries or agriculture and to issue regulations giving deferred status to married men, men with dependents or men who are suffering mental or physical disabilities, it is not anticipated that there will be any blanket exemption from service. Exemptions for draftees will be decided individually by draft boards to be established for that purpose.

Exempt from service, but not from registration, are men who have served three years in the Regular Army; National Guardsmen who have had active Federal duty and two additional years either in the Regular Army or National Guard in active duty or who are in active duty on the day proclaimed for registration and who have had six years national guard service; and reserve officers who will be on the eligible list for six years or more.

Re-employment Provisions

Provision is made for the re-employment of draftees when their year's service has been completed. Private employers are required to restore jobs unless their circumstances are so changed as to make it impossible or unreasonable. In any case of re-employment the draftee must still be qualified to fill the job and must apply for it within 40 days after his discharge from the Army or Navy. In cases of disagreement Federal District Attorneys are required to represent draftees in re-employment cases without fee and no court costs are to be assessed the draftee. The provision also expresses the policy of Congress that in no case shall a vacancy occurring in a business or industry as a result of the draft be filled by a member of the Communist party or the German-American Bund.

Industrial Conscription

To guard against the possibility of delay in procurement of materials, the bill empowers the President to conscript and operate plants, on a rental basis, which refuse to accept or give priority to defense contracts. Maximum penalties of three years' imprisonment and $50,000 fines are fixed for plant managers who

(Continued on page 4)

Expert Studies Traffic And Parking Problems

Lynn Harrison, expert at traffic and parking problems, is at present working with Chief of Police Charles Phelps and L. W. Wulfekuhler, assistant secretary, to work out the most satisfactory solution to the traffic and parking problem confronting the 12,000 Lockheed employees, a large number of whom drive their own cars to work each day.

Suggestions will be welcomed from employees for any methods for handling of the traffic problem or for the removal of as many inconveniences as possible. Any such suggestions may be forwarded to Harrison via the inter-office Mail Service.

Success of the entire program, according to Harrison, will be predicated on the assumption that each employee will be fully acquainted with the regulations established for his own benefit and will cooperate fully. One car out of line can cause a traffic tie-up.

THE LOCKHEED STAR *is issued every Friday by the Lockheed Aircraft Corporation for its employees. Communications may be addressed to either the Industrial Relations Office or the Public Relations Department, Lockheed Aircraft Corporation, Burbank, California, U.S.A.*

A Welcome To New Employees

Printed here are the names and department numbers of 308 new employees who started work during the week ending September 14, 1940.

The Lockheed and Vega managements and the officers of each company's recreation club sincerely wish that every employee shall feel at home and consider himself a vital part of his company. This means is being taken to extend a hearty welcome to new employees and appears as a regular weekly feature of the STAR.

In beginning a new job many problems and questions are bound to arise, and to meet this situation the employee service division of the Industrial Relations Department stands ready to give counsel and assistance whenever possible. Employees are welcome to call at the employee service division at any time during the business day.

Every employee is automatically a member of the Lockheed or Vega Employees' Recreation Club without cost and is invited to participate in any of the varied activities offered by these groups.

LOCKHEED

NAME	Dept.
ADAMS, Harold F.	1
AILMAN, Harry B.	48
ALDRICH, Harold	7
ALEXANDER, Lynn J.	12
ALMAN, Levi Ira	12
ARDIANA, Lewis M.	5
AVRIL, Edward V., Jr.	1
AXUP, Earl C.	42
BACHERTZ, Carl W., Jr.	14
BAIDA, Lafayette G.	1
BARNES, Thurman E.	7
BASSO, Marte B.	25
BEAN, Frances	25
BEERBROER, Milton J.	7
BENNETT, Charles D.	7
BENSON, Charles	7
BERRY, Millard D.	23
BEUTTLER, Otto L., Jr.	1
BICE, Harold K.	7
BLACKWELL, Craig R.	1
BOTZENHART, Chester A.	1
BOULRICE, Oliver	7
BOYER, Dwight S.	35
BRANUM, Carl D.	1
BRAUN, John	1
BREEDLOVE, Harry E.	14
BRICKMAN, Carl	1
BRIGGS, Dorian D.	1
BRIGHAM, Clare B.	7
BRILL, Robert Irving	12
BROWN, Andrew B.	1
BROWN, Don Bud	7
BURDICK, George A.	5
BURTON, Oliver	1
CAMPBELL, Dudley E.	53
CAREY, Paul W.	2
CARLESON, Robert E.	35
CARROLL, Robert H.	1
CHAMBERS, Robert W.	25
CHAPMAN, Donald A.	35
CLARK, Walter	7
CLODFELTER, Arthur B.	1
COBURN, Ward C.	22
COLLINS, Ernest H.	5
CONDON, John P.	1
COOK, Beverly B.	2
COURINGTON, Cranford G.	2
COWARDIN, Guy	5
COX, Hollis M.	40
COX, James E.	1
CRANDALL, Leonard C.	25
DAHL, Albert W.	5
DEXTER, Charles J.	42
DEXTER, Dennis D.	1
DOMENICI, Frank	12
DOYLE, Jeanne J.	25
DRUM, Velma Irene	96
EHRIG, Frank L.	7
EKSTROM, Orval F.	13
ELLIOTT, Marvin D.	7
EMMONS, John B.	7
ENOS, Harvey E.	14
ESLINGER, Clarence C.	1
ESPESETH, Clifford C.	12
FINLEY, Harold W.	7
FIRESTONE, John	7
FISH, Viron A.	1
FORCE, Albert C.	16
FORREST, Bernard A.	97
FOUTZ, Stuart R.	7
FOWLER, Myrl A.	1
FRANKEL, Melvin	5
FRICKE, William A.	32
FRIX, Elizabeth T.	25
GEANKOPLIS, Nicholas	34
GEILENFELDT, Edward	7
GOLDSTON, J. W.	7
GOUGH, Howard M.	7
GRANT, Kenneth R.	16
GRIMES, John K.	10
GROW, Earl W.	14
GUM, Ferrall D.	14
HABECKER, Clarence	24
HAGAR, Lee P.	14
HALL, Jack L.	2
HAMBY, Roy C.	7
HANSHUE, John	35
HARRISON, Charles M.	16
HARRISON, Lynn Hamilton	39
HARRISON, Ned. C.	12
HAZZARD, Frank F.	7
HERTEN, Robert	63
HIEBER, E. Ellsworth	25
HIGBEE, Adolph M.	12
HILLMAN, Walter P., Jr.	5
HOLECHEK, Russell H.	12
HOLMES, Frank R.	22
HOUSER, John Earl	32
HOVERSTEN, Jacob T.	1
HRYCENKO, Michael	22
HUBER, Clayton V.	24
JARRETT, Winifred H.	81

NAME	Dept.
JOHNSON, Alfred R.	35
JOHNSON, Claude A.	13
JOHNSON, Edward R.	7
JOHNSON, Mary Jane	95
JORGENSON, Israel M.	1
KAUTZ, Raymond	12
KELLEY, Richard E.	12
KEPPLER, Carl V.	14
KESSINGER, Earl R.	39
KINSEY, Mac Joseph	1
KITCHING, Elliott	22
KLAHS, Clifton D.	7
KRAMM, Hartzell M.	7
KRIEG, Allan D.	22
LACY, William G., Jr.	4
LANDER, Claude R.	35
LANTZY, Robert E.	7
LEE, William W.	42
LENTZ, Richard H.	5
LLOYD, Gaylord	7
LOUTZENHEISER, Virgil	5
LOVEJOY, George R.	16
LUHRING, Burdette	7
LUNDAHL, Albin T.	1
LUNKLEY, Charles	22
LYNXWILER, Burtis J.	14
LYON, Emmett J., Jr.	22
McCARTHY, John P.	32
McDOUGALL, George M.	22
MAILLET, Louis J.	1
MALLOY, Mary A.	25
MANKIEWICZ, Victor J.	6
MARTIN, Charles E.	5
MARTIN, Glenn E.	2
MARTIN, Rance N.	12
MAXEY, Theodore R.	1
MEADORS, Charles R.	16
MEREDITH, Robert L.	5
MEYER, Joseph J.	2
MEYERS, Floyd M.	12
MILAZZO, Gaetano	20
MILAZZO, Pasquale	22
MILLER, Warren C.	7
MIZE, William D.	12
MOCK, Edwin C.	1
MOISEVE, Mitchell	13
MOLLENHAUER, Raphael	7
MONG, Berl Eugene	7
MONROE, Benjamin F.	25
MONTGOMERY, James V.	52
MORGAN, John W.	7
MORROW, Dwight L.	7
MULLAN, Earle W.	95
MULLER, Jay C.	22
MURDAUGH, Norman D.	16
NAUMANN, Karl R.	97
NEIL, Vern L.	12
NEPTUNE, Robert J.	13
NEWELL, John D.	25
NICHOLS, Leonard	12
NORMAN, Robert W.	2

NAME	Dept.
OATES, Walter L.	40
OLINGER, Walter L.	24
OSBORNE, Robert W.	1
PAINE, Reith King	22
PEARSON, Curtis M.	12
PELTO, Edward	53
PETERSON, Gilbert	5
PHILLIPS, Burt Lee	95
PORTER, Mervyn H. Jr.	12
POSTEL, Edward	25
PRYOR, Herbert H.	5
PULIS, Mark	95
QUIGLEY, James J.	1
RAINS, Philip E.	20
RENZ, Edward	7
REPPE, Stanley H.	22
RICHARDS, Willard H.	5
RIDLEY, Grahame B.	38
ROBERTS, Joseph W.	1
ROUS, Jacques L.	16
ROWELL, Frederick S.	20
RUCKER, Nelson N.	13
RUTTINGER, Harold M.	7
RYAN, Roy J.	1
SCHAEFFER, Robert W.	52
SEDLACEK, Alfred G.	12
SEWELL, Rollin W.	7
SHAFFER, Paul E.	12
SHATTO, Theodore Carl	14
SHAW, Norman H.	14
SHEPARD, Harold	1
SHISLER, William O.	1
SHOWALTER, Henry C.	7
SICKLER, John M.	12
SIMMONS, Benjamin E. Jr.	12
SMITH, Fontaine E.	1
SMITH, John L.	1
SMITH, Phillip P.	22
SMYTHE, William H.	38
SOUTH, Veeder Jr.	23
STAHL, John Le Roy	1
STAMMER, Fred	7
STANLEY, Franklin Wm.	1
STEVENS, Le Roy Lester	7
STROWISS, Aaron	22
SWENNING, Irving M.	51
TARWATER, Jesse Wilson	48
THIEMAN, Arthur M.	20
THOMPSON, Marion Q.	14
TUONEN, Fred S.	12
VAJDA, Frank T.	5
VAUGHN, Josephine A.	32
VICKERY, Earl E. Jr.	35
WALIZER, Floyd	16
WARD, Bovell	14
WARREN, Walter	32
WATT, Walter W.	32
WELCH, Columbus Forrest	3
WELCH, Lawrence Calvin	16
WESTAPHER, Earl R.	1
WHATLEY, Glenn E.	12
WHEELER, Madeleine	72
WHEELING, Wm. K.	2
WILKE, Charles U.	35
WILLIAMS, Gertrude M.	68
WILSON, Eugene W.	52
WOOL, Justin M.	5
WREEDE, Forest Emerson	7
YOUNG, William T.	33
YOUNKERS, Gordon G.	1
ZELL, Lawrence	12

VEGA

NAME	Dept.
ALLEN, Edwin C.	31-2
AMELSBERG, George A. Jr.	39
BARRETT, Edward R.	55
BLAIR, Keyless Malone	60
BLAISDELL, Elaine	35-2
BLOMQUIST, Emil A.	29
BUTZ, Paul A.	7
CANADAY, John W.	35
CANNON, William A.	39
CARLSON, Harry L.	7
CHEPKE, Charles L.	7
CHRISTENSEN, Carl T.	29
CLARK, James P. Jr.	14
CLEWORTH, Alfred	28
COCHRAN, Louise R.	97
CORZATT, Peter S.	4
DARE, Edwin J.	26
DE BELLO, Frank A.	29
DODD, Richard	60
DORSETT, Blaine L.	4
DUNN, William O.	31-2
ELMORE, Austin E.	29
FAST, Ralph E.	25
FAUROT, G. Clement	10
FICKLING, William A.	35-2
FOERST, George A.	31
GARDNER, Jack	7
GREENLAW, Robert N. Jr.	27
GUILFORD, Lynden V.	39
HANAGAN, Hugh C.	4
HAYES, Robert B.	4
HILL, Ferris D.	28
HIRSCH, Maxon	7
HOLLENKAMP, William J.	94
HOOPER, John A. Jr.	39
HUGHES, Melvin N.	25
INGRAM, Howard L.	29
JOCHUM, William T.	65
KNEE, Seymour	95
LAMKIN, Everett C.	60
LANCE, Wilford L.	94
LEWIS, Herschel M.	4
LOCKWOOD, Howard C.	35
McCARTHY, Daniel L.	43
McDONALD, Otis W.	1
McGILVRAY, Walter S. Jr.	60
MAJOR, Charles N.	94
MALLOCK, Donald W.	65
MALLOY, Dorothy S.	94
MARELIUS, Robert W.	69
MARRIOTT, Henry A.	48
MATTSON, Dorothy	94
MILLER, Clarence J.	35
MILLER, Donald	39
MILLER, Gerald Arthur	60
MILLER, Haskell J.	29
MILLER, M. Maxine	90
MONTGOMERY, Nile V.	94
MUIR, William	1
NEWMAN, Marvin H.	35-2
OVER, Walter S.	29
PHELPS, Stowe Catlin	60
POWELL, Jack W.	60
RE, Carlo	60
ROUNDS, Howard J.	35-4
RYAN, William C.	60
SCHIRARD, Arthur W.	29
SCOTT, Herbert W.	39
SIEBERT, Theo. G.	13
SPIEKER, William F.	34
STATKIEWICZ, Stanislaus	29
TENNEY, John W. Sr.	6
WELLS, Thomas M.	26
WIDNER, Ray E.	28

Archery Club Elects Temporary Officers

Francis Stevenson was elected pro-tem chairman and Athena Smith was elected secretary of the Archery Club at a meeting held last Tuesday evening. Both officers will serve for a period of two months during which time permanent organization for the club will be established.

Plans are under way by the members of the group to provide a range for a Thanksgiving Turkey Shoot.

Camera Club Maps Program for Year

The Lockheed Employees' Camera Club extends to all employees seriously interested in photography an invitation to attend its meetings and join in the club's activities.

Meetings are held in the conference room of the Burbank Public Library the second and fourth Thursday of each month at 7:30 p.m. A number of educational meetings, field trips, contests and other events are being planned and will be announced in the near future as the plans are completed.

Red Cross Offers Classes in First Aid

The Glendale Evening High School is offering a series of First Aid classes at the American Red Cross headquarters, 117 North Maryland, Glendale, which were started this week. Anyone wishing to enroll in these classes may do so at the American Red Cross headquarters, or telephone CItrus 2-7529.

The following is a schedule of standard and advanced classes offered:

Advanced—Mon. 7:00 - 9:00 p.m.
Advanced—Tues. 7:00 - 9:00 p:m:
Standard—Tues. 9:30 - 11:30 a.m.
Standard—Wed. 7:00 - 9:00 p.m.
Standard—Thur. 7:00 - 9:00 p.m.

Draft Measure Signed

(Continued from page 2)

refuse to cooperate with the National Defense Act.

Pay Increased

The pay of Army privates is increased by the bill from $21 to $30 monthly, and of first class privates from $30 to $36 monthly.

Certain debt relief benefits of the 1918 Soldiers and Sailors Relief Act for draftees and reserves on active duty are provided for draftees, as are death and disability benefits accorded men in the Regular Army and Navy.

L.E.R.C. Calendar

Friday, September 20—Dramatics Club Meeting, Room 210 Personnel Building, 8 p.m.

Sunday, September 22—Meeting of Lockheed Rangers, Doc's Stables, Roscoe, 12:00 noon.

Monday, September 23—Choral Club Rehearsal, Swimming Pool Building, Griffith Park, 7:30 p.m.

Tuesday, September 24 — Band Rehearsal, John Muir Junior High School, Burbank, 7:30 p.m.

Tuesday, September 24—Archery meeting, Room 210, Personnel Building, 7:30 p.m.

Tuesday and Wednesday, September 24 & 25—Lockheed Men's Bowling League, Burbank Alleys, 7:00 p.m. and 9:00 p.m.

Wednesday, September 25—Dedication of Civic Center Park, Corner Glen Oaks and Amhurst Drive, Burbank. Exhibition tennis matches, 8:30 p.m.

Friday, September 27 — Opening night Lockheed Girls' Bowling League, Sunset Alleys, 6:15 p.m.

Registration of Night Crew Bowling Teams Requested

To assist plans which are underway for the organization of night-crew department bowling teams, it is requested that all such teams be registered with Mrs. Bucci in the L.E.R.C. office, extension 722, as soon as possible.

When a sufficient number of teams have been registered, arrangements will be announced for daytime bowling competition between these teams.

Aviation Dictionary On Sale at Special Rate

Baughman's Aviation Dictionary and Reference Guide, an Aero-Thesaurus, is on sale at the Employee's Tool Store at the special rate to aircraft employees of $3.50 per copy plus California sales tax.

This book, which sells regularly for $5.00, will be available to employees at the special rate until November 1, and is limited to one book per employee.

Employees Invited to Join Lockheed Band

Employees who are interested in band work are invited to attend rehearsals of the Lockheed Band held Tuesday evenings at 7:30 p.m. in the John Muir Junior High School, Burbank.

Employees Asked to Return Empty Bottles to Canteen

Employees are again requested by the Canteen management not to leave soft drink bottles on the parking areas. This practice causes considerable loss to the Canteen through lost bottles, and is a potential source of loss to employees through damage to tires.

Students Enroll in Classes

(Continued from page 1)

production of planes, but are putting in long hours of study to prepare themselves to fill positions in a few weeks that ordinarily would take five and six times as long.

"Our employees," he added, "show by their participation in the training program that they fully appreciate the fact that they are an important part of the nation's second line of defense."

Special Courses Given

A large number of the men enrolled in the present semester have just concluded courses in a special session held this summer. In addition to the men enrolled in the trade extension courses approximately 1500 men are receiving special training within the plant. This includes short, intensive courses for semi-skilled workers who are being trained on the job for special assignments for which they have shown aptitude.

Special courses are also being given to supervisors and foremen and to juniors being trained for such positions, and a number of lecture courses are being given in the plant after working hours for aeronautical engineers.

Engineers Receive Training

One hundred and twenty experienced engineers from other industries and engineering projects are completing a streamlined 16 weeks aeronautical course started at the California Institute of Technology last June. This special training program has been tried as an experiment to augment the supply of aeronautical engineers and, if it proves successful, it is expected to be repeated by Lockheed and elsewhere throughout the country.

During February of this year, Lockheed inaugurated an apprentice training program in conjunction with the International Association of Machinists in the Burbank schools. At that time 36 apprentices started on a full year training course and a second group was selected and assigned to apprentice training this summer.

The combined personnel of Lockheed and Vega is now in excess of 13,000. At the present rate of employment, this number, it is anticipated, will be almost doubled within the next six or eight months.

Skill To Do

THE Lockheed Star

Comes of Doing

PUBLISHED WEEKLY BY THE LOCKHEED AIRCRAFT CORPORATION FOR ITS EMPLOYEES

Vol. 7 BURBANK, CALIFORNIA, U.S.A., SEPTEMBER 27, 1940 No. 39

Regulations For Sick Leave Pay Reviewed

Rules Outline Procedure Under Union Agreement For Reporting Absences

In order to accomplish the "pay for sick leave" provisions of the Union Agreement adopted last month, the following procedure will apply for all employees:

1. **Each employee who is absent on account of illness must telephone, have someone telephone for him, or by other prompt means notify the Employee Relations Department during the first day's absence,** giving the reason for and probable length of disability. Any call which comes in to the department where the employee works must either be transferred to the Employee Relations Department or be reported immediately to that department.
2. **Each employee who is absent three days or more on account of illness must report to the Medical Division of the Employee Relations Department prior to returning to work.** It will not be necessary to report to the Medical Division of the Employee Relations Department if the absence is one or two days' duration.
3. **In order to receive pay for sick leave, an employee must file with the Employee Relations Department, not more than three days after returning to work, a written request on Form No. 1154, Request for Sick Leave Pay, designating which days and/or portions of days are involved.** (These

(Continued on page 2)

L.E.R.C. ASSISTS COMMUNITY FUND DRIVE

Voluntary Donations To Aid Burbank Youth Program

The Lockheed Employees' Recreation Club is cooperating with the City of Burbank in their drive for the 1940-41 Community and Red Cross fund. Money secured by voluntary donations from employees will be used to carry on work of the Burbank Boy Scouts and Girl Scouts of America, the Y.M.C.A., plus a substantial contribution to the Red Cross work.

During the last two weeks of October all employees will be given an opportunity of sign a confidential pledge card for donations to this important work. To facilitate collections the Company is cooperating by making payroll deductions wherever desired and authorized by the employee.

During the year from June 1, 1939 to June 1, 1940 several hundred boys and girls of the City of Burbank were provided with recreational activities through funds received during last year's drive. The goal for 1940-41 has been set at $12,500, which will provide for the maintenance of these character building activities. It is pointed out that while in no way are contributions to this fund compulsory, the Youth and Red Cross

(Continued on page 2)

Education Service Lists Six New Classes

Announcement is made by Education Service of the formation of six new trade extension classes. Included are:

PLASTER MOCK UP AND PATTERN MAKING CLASS
Tues. and Thurs. 6:30-9:30, Lockheed Aircraft Corp., Department 53.

STRESS ANALYSIS I (Force Applications)
Tues. and Thurs. 6:30-9:30, John Muir Jr. High, Room 111.

STRESS ANALYSIS II (Strength of Materials)
Tues. and Thurs. 6:30-9:30, Burbank High School, Room 260.

STRESS ANALYSIS III
Mon. and Wed. 6:30-9:30, John Muir Junior High, Room 105.

STRESS ANALYSIS IV
Mon. and Wed. 6:30-9:30, John Burroughs Junior High, Room 202.

STRESS ANALYSIS V
Mon. and Wed. 6:30-9:30, John Muir Jr. High, Room 111.

Anyone wishing further information regarding any of these courses is requested to contact the Education Service, room 205 in the Personnel Building. Employees of the Engineering Department may contact the Engineering Department personnel office for additional information regarding the Stress courses listed.

Pictured from left to right above with Lockheed's new fire truck are driver Elmer Schmutzler; J. M. O'Connor, fire chief; and firemen Dick Gottschalk, F. J. Aust, Bill Gates, and Ed Howell. This new equipment will be used by the company fire department in combatting fire hazards within the factory.

Otto P. Graff Receives Appointment To Vega Post

Appointment of Otto P. Graff as manager of the parts sales and customer service divisions of Vega Airplane Company was announced today by Thomas H. Corpe, general sales manager. Graff has been with the Lockheed Aircraft Corporation since 1936 and recently has been engaged in special assignments for the sales department.

Graff has been active in the aviation industry since 1929 as a sales executive and test pilot. In April, 1936, he was employed by the Lockheed corporation as a direct factory representative with offices in Chicago. In August, 1937, he was transferred to the home sales office and placed in charge of British Air Ministry contracts.

Princeton University

★ Your "columnist" this week is meeting with a group of industrial relations men gathered here from all sections of the country to discuss personnel and employment problems in rapidly expanding national defense industries.

Everyone is deeply impressed with the stupendous job ahead of us but each has full confidence that industry can and will do the job. Management-employees and workmen-employees, backed by the schools and every resource of the Government, are working together unselfishly and harmoniously for a common objective—equipping our military services with such superior airplanes and armaments that no foreign dictator power will dare attack us.

Of great concern to all is the shortage of skilled labor, but everyone here is confident that this lack will not stop the program of production. Employees of American industry are rising to the need by assuming greater responsibilities and putting forth greater efforts.

Regarding the supply of skilled labor, the conclusion is: if the supply is exhausted, industry can't hire them; the only alternative is more training. Happily, Lockheed-Vega and the Burbank schools already have developed the most extensive training program in the far-West, so are well equipped to meet this need.

From here at Princeton, the writer is going to Washington for a meeting of the Training Within Industry Committee of the National Defense Commission which will discuss proposals of a national program of training patterned closely after the Lockheed-Vega plan.

—Randall Irwin.

Lost and Found Service

Employees are requested to report all articles either lost or found to the Personnel office. This may be done in person by applying at the call-in desk or by phoning extension 753.

Lockheed Band Prepares For Public Appearances

The Lockheed Band will hold its regular rehearsal meeting at 7:30 Tuesday evening in the auditorium of the John Burroughs Junior High School in Burbank.

Rehearsals are under way at the present time for a number of regular appearances here at the factory and all employees or members of their families who play band instruments are invited to attend.

Sick Leave Pay Regulations

(Continued from page 1)

forms are available at all First Aid Units and at the Employee Relations Department.)

It will then be the responsibility of the Employee Relations Service to verify such requests and forward them to the Employment Department to determine the employee's eligibility to receive sick leave pay. Approved requests are sent to the timekeeping division. The following principles will apply in determining eligibility for receiving sick leave pay:

1. The provision for a total of five days per year means "during any twelve month period." This means that an employee's eligibility to receive pay for sick leave for any particular day is based upon whether or not he has received sick leave with pay for a total of five days during the twelve month period directly preceding his day or days of absence.
2. Payments for absence on account of illness apply only to each employee's five regular working days.
3. Exchanges of employment between Lockheed and Vega shall be counted as continuous employment.
4. **No pay will be allowed for non-occupational injuries.** Holders of group insurance receive compensation from the first day of the accident.
5. **Sick leave with pay will not be allowed for a lost time occupational injury.** However, a full day's pay will be allowed the day a lost time injury occurs and this allowed time will not be charged against the sick leave.
6. **Under no circumstances will more than five days per year or more than three days for any one illness be allowed.**

Community Fund Drive

(Continued from page 1)

work to be aided constitute one of the most deserving causes to which L.E.R.C. assistance can be given through its members.

Draft Instructions Are Issued By President

Everyone Within Age Limit Is Required To Register

Of interest to a majority of Lockheed employees are a number of provisions of the peace-time draft bill signed by President Roosevelt last week. While many details for operation of the draft have not yet been formulated, it is emphasized that ALL men between the ages of 21 and 36 must register on Wednesday, October 16, for possible draft.

No blanket exemptions have been, nor are likely to be prescribed, and all cases of deferred service will be decided upon by a draft board separately after any given individual has been drafted.

A 61 page book of detailed instructions covering initial stages for procedure for state organizations to carry out draft provisions was issued by the President early this week, stating that the purpose of the order is to obtain an "orderly, just and democratic method whereby the military man power of the United States may be made available for training and service in the land and naval forces of the United States, as provided by the Congress, with the least possible disruption of the social and economic life of the nation."

Fundamental regulations governing the selective service as outlined in the President's order require that under the general supervision of the governors of the 48 states registration will be handled by local election machineries or other designated agencies. Local draft boards with three or more members appointed by the President will classify registrants.

Men within the age limits set for the draft who are away from home on registration day are required to register at the designated station wherever they may be. Men who are too ill to register on the designated day may have a competent person register for them.

Lockheed Picnic Shown In Screen Snapshots

A premiere showing of pictures taken at the Lockheed picnic will be a feature of Columbia's Screen Snapshots to be shown at the El Portal theater, North Hollywood, Friday evening, September 27. The Screen Snapshot showing is scheduled to start at approximately 9:00 p.m.

THE LOCKHEED STAR *is issued every Friday by the Lockheed Aircraft Corporation for its employees. Communications may be addressed to either the Industrial Relations Office or the Public Relations Department, Lockheed Aircraft Corporation, Burbank, California, U.S.A.*

A Welcome To New Employees

Printed here are the names and department numbers of Lockheed and Vega employees who started work during the week ending September 21, 1940.

The Lockheed and Vega managements and the officers of each company's recreation club sincerely wish that every employee shall feel at home and consider himself a vital part of his company. This means is being taken to extend a hearty welcome to new employees and appears as a regular weekly feature of the STAR.

H. A. Beall

In beginning a new job many problems and questions are bound to arise, and to meet this situation the employee service division of the Industrial Relations Department stands ready to give counsel and assistance whenever possible.

H. A. Beall, employment director, is pictured above.

LOCKHEED

NAME	Dept.
ADAMS, Jack	10
ALLEN, Roy E.	52
ANDERSON, Fred	7
ASHWORTH, Glenn	12
ATHERTON, William	7
BALL, Robert F.	33
BARGER, Wilbur F.	38
BARTON, Herschel E.	10
BATCHELOR, Arthur	12
BELDEN, Frederick A.	32
BELIMAN, Leonard	32
BELLAS, Stanley A.	52
BENEFIEL, Eugene	34
BENGSTON, Clifford P.	16
BENSON, John	32
BERMAN, I. Leon	2
BESSOM, Leonard D., Jr.	14
BILLINGTON, Kennard L.	52
BISTAGNE, Tosia M.	52
BOMAR, Arsene T.	10
BONEY, Carvis W.	7
BOTELER, Lanham L.	80
BOTTOMS, Henry L.	52
BOYD, Robert	52
BOYER, Ralph W.	39
BREAULT, John L., Jr.	51
BROWN, Colin C.	2
BROWNING, Ralph	14
BURKETT, Alice L.	42
BURNES, Robert J.	7
BURTON, Carl W.	12
BUXTON, Thomas J.	7
BYRD, Frank P.	7
CAMPI, Richard	52
CANNON, Lowell F.	5
CANNON, William J.	2
CARNAHAN, Donald G.	12
CARSON, John J.	15 Pl. 3
CAVELL, Everett L.	7
CHAPMAN, Noland	1
CHRISTIE, Everett L.	5
CHRISTNER, George	52
CLARKE, John W. R.	14
COBB, Norman E.	52
COLE, Guy Winford	1
COLLING, Joseph D., Jr.	39
COLLINGHAM, Clinton	14
CONRAD, Frederick	7
COOPS, Richard W.	52
COPE, William L.	12
COTTRELL, Ross A.	20
COX, Walter G.	20
COWARD, James Burt	1
CROUCH, Robert E.	1
CRYER, Richard	1
CUKRAS, Arthur B.	95
DASNOIT, Walter E., Jr.	52
DAVIDSON, Carl R.	14
DEMMON, John Austin	35
DE MOTT, William H.	5
DERBES, Donald J.	10
DETTNER, Wilbur D.	52
DILKS, George L.	20
DIXON, Denny T.	10
DORN, Phillip Howard	52
DORSETT, Shirley V.	20
DOWD, Richard I., Jr.	39
DOWNS-PITTS, Donald L.	33
DOYLE, Grant H.	1
DUNCAN, Lester	12
DURELL, James R.	10
EARHART, Floyd M.	51
EDDINGTON, Lloyd H.	10
ELLIOTT, Charles F.	32
EMERY, Raymond L.	7
EPPERLY, Leslie E.	12
ERNEST, Robert	10
EVANS, Robert H., Jr.	20
EVERETT, Leon N.	56
FEINSTEIN, Harry	52
FORBES, F. Hallock	4
FOSKETT, Paul F.	46
FOTHERINGHAM, Albert O.	12
FREEMAN, Edwin C., Jr.	1
GALLAGHER, James J.	7
GAREY, Madeleine C.	42
GATES, James G.	7
GIDDINGS, Neil W.	10
GIVER, Harold W.	32
GLASS, Murvel O.	22
GODDARD, Harold K.	10
GOLLIN, Arthur	22
GRANATH, Leo R.	10
GRANELL, Jerald W.	10
GREENLEAF, Harvey	7
GRIFFITH, Kirby W.	1
GROENENSTEIN, Norbert J.	16
GROVE, C. Merle	52
GUEST, James W.	5
HAGENBURGER, Philip A.	10
HARDER, William J.	22
HARDIN, James C.	5
HARDING, William W.	39
HARTMAN, Rudolph R., Jr.	7
HARTNESS, Jim	5
HARVEY, Lawrence J.	14
HASTE, Albert E.	32
HAWKINS, Elwyn L.	7
HEADLEY, Bruce D.	14
HEALY, Roland E.	10
HEARD, Archie L.	7
HEARD, Charles L.	42
HEATH, Francis K.	14
HEBEIN, Frederick J.	10
HEDDEN, Hervey P.	14
HENSEL, Elgin C.	52
HERDRICH, Maynard M.	5
HERLICK, Stanford D.	10
HICKEY, Gerald E.	7
HINTON, M. Coleman	7
HOOD, Oscar H., Jr.	28
HORNER, Roy C.	7
HORNIG, Walter H., Jr.	2
HUGHES, William T.	28
HUNTSMAN, Rae M.	10
IRONS, Joseph	1
ISAACS, Jerome	31 Pl. 3
JAMIESON, Norman M.	12
JENKINS, Herbert W.	10
JOHNSON, Chester A.	10
JOHNSON, Clarence E.	20
JOHNSON, Jerome B.	95
JOHNSTON, Forest J., Jr.	12
JONES, Llewellyn J.	10
JORDAN, Daniel T.	10
KAISER, Oliver D.	10
KAUFMAN, Wallace L.	7
KEAS, William O., Jr.	52
KEEGAN, Donald C.	28
KELLEY, L. Felix	2
KELTON, Andrew J.	12
KENDLE, Robert E.	10
KENGLA, Kenneth O.	2
KILMER, Wesley L.	22
KILSTON, Ben B.	52
KIMBALL, Austin F.	7
KIMBALL, Leslie R.	7
KING, Charles	32
KLOPPER, Frederick H.	52
KNOX, Paul D.	22
KOPOCHUS, George M.	20
KORHONEN, Wilbert W.	10
KOZLOWSKI, Frank	20
KROM, John R.	10
KYZIVAT, Louis K.	95
LAMB, Elvis R.	7
LAMSON, Walter R.	10
LATHROP, John	7
LAWYER, Malvin E.	1
LEMKE, Elmer H.	22
LEVE, Ralph B.	12
LIERD, Richard	1
LOVITT, Ferdinand, Jr.	12
LUDWIG, Ernest N.	95
McCARROLL, Kenneth Wm.	28
McCORD, James B.	7
McDONALD, Agnes M.	44
McINTOSH, Stuart D.	20
McKENNA, Leonard C.	10
McVEY, Patrick R.	35
MacKENZIE, Donald J.	12
MAGUIRE, Thomas P.	14
MANGUS, J. Edward	5
MANUEL, E. George	52
MARINUCCI, William J.	7
MATHEWS, James M.	12
MATTEA, Ben W.	10
MEDLEY, Roy H.	12
MEEKS, Henry K.	5
MENNELL, Marc S.	10
MERRITT, Arthur H.	22
MEYER, Carl J.	1
MIELKE, Earl M.	10
MIKKELSON, Ward C.	28
MILHAM, Charles V. E.	23
MILLER, Howard R.	12
MILLER, Miles M.	14
MILLER, Robert A.	12
MILLS, James	28
MINNER, Walter, Jr.	10
MORGAN, Charles C.	3
MORIARTY, Kenneth L.	7
MORRIS, Coarson C.	28
MORRISON, Walter F.	40
MORSE, Jack B.	2
MULLEDA, Joseph J.	2
MULLENS, Frank A., Jr.	12
MULRENNAN, Margaret Mary	96
MURPHY, Frederick V.	1
MUSINSKI, Joseph J.	5
MYERS, Carl F.	1
MYERS, Edward E.	5
NELSON, Richard J.	52
NIBLEY, Merrill W.	32
NICHOLS, Orville	25
NICHOLS, Ruth Elizabeth	81
NOFREY, Clarence E.	1
NORTHUP, Kenneth D.	7
OEDING, Ruben W.	10
OLSEN, Glen A.	5
OLSON, Harold T.	5
OSTRANDER, Donald H.	34
OVITT, Edward L.	7
OXLEY, Wayne	12
PAGE, John W.	7
PARONELLI, Henry	16
PARTEE, Roy R.	14
PASCAL, Samuel	52
PATERSON, Carl J.	10
PETTIT, Howard E.	51
PHILLIPS, Jacob H.	51
PICKENS, Paul D.	10
POWER, William C.	7
PRESTON, Robert A.	12
PROCTOR, Clayton B., Jr.	28
RAMAY, Harry E.	56
REBBER, Robert W.	10
REEVES, Joseph W.	7
RENO, Joe T.	14
RICKETTS, W. Melville	5
RIDINGS, George T.	28
ROBERTS, Chester J.	37
ROGERS, Laurence	39
ROGERS, Robert N.	32
ROGERS, Robert V.	5
ROMPELL, Sherrill B.	5
ROSS, Harry F.	20
RYAN, Michael L.	25
RYDER, Arthur K.	35
SAATHOFF, Mervin A.	10
SAELMAN, Benjamin	52
SAINE, Charles C.	28
ST. CLAIR, Homer E.	7
SANDOVAL, Alfred	1
SANFORD, Kenneth C.	12
SAVORY, Robert E.	25
SCHICK, Donald K.	28
SHERWOOD, George B.	12 Pl. 3
SHORT, William C.	42
SIMMS, Allen Harris	52
SINCLAIR, Gerald	52
SKELTON, Richard L.	10
SMITH, Carl V.	1
SMITH, Clarence A.	16
SMITH, Clyde	12
SMITH, William F.	5
SOVERN, Vernon G.	7
SPRINGER, Edgar L.	16
SPRINGER, Frank B.	20
SPURGIN, Franklin	10
STANAGE, Tyler L.	5
STANFORD, J. T.	10
STEWARD, Lewis H.	3
STONE, Earl	22
STONE, George	56
STONE, Paul A.	10
SUGGETT, John W.	34
SUHOSKY, Edward J.	14
SUTER, Madison L.	20
SWANSON, Earl E.	20
SWEARINGEN, Richard Lee	39
SWETS, Boudewyn	1
TAYLOR, Glenn D.	10
TEBBE, James P.	28
THIELE, Carl L.	10
THIELMAN, Noral W.	5
THOMAS, Jack L.	14
THOMSEN, Thomas	10
TICHENOR, V. Clifford	14
TOMASSONI, Chester A.	22
VAN CLEEVE, Clarencey	10
VAN OSDELL, Lester L.	56
VAN RIPER, Dale H.	25
VIALL, Howard A.	1
VIETS, Vaughn C.	39
WAAS, Douglas E.	10
WACKER, Harry J.	7
WALKER, Joseph O.	12
WEBSTER, W. Allen	23
WEIR, Melvin R.	10
WEITHINGTON, Earl H.	12
WENTZ, Frederick R.	24
WENZEL, Robert F.	10
WESTEN, Albert	35
WHITLOCK, James B.	22
WIENER, Norton	52
WILBERGER, Howard E.	5
WILLIAMS, Richard F.	46
WILSON, Robert C.	5
WISE, George M.	10
WOLFE, Clifton P.	66
WOODS, Kenneth D.	7
WOODWARD, Herbert W., Jr.	14
ZAMPERINI, Louis S.	24 Pl. 1
ZIMMERMAN, Jack E.	1
ZUCKERMAN, Barbara L.	72

VEGA

NAME	Dept.
BALDWIN, William J.	43
BARBER, Jack E.	95
BARNES, Harvey C.	13
BAYLESS, Clifford C.	13
BECKER, Hubert	94-3
BELLAMY, Jesse A.	57
BELLMORE, Clifford J.	39
BROOKS, Manoka	94
BRUCE, Ralph J.	95
BULLARD, Chandler G.	39
CAMPBELL, Leroy Henry	60
CAVANAGH, Richard L.	27
CLOSE, Rodman E.	60
COBB, Donald E.	48
COLE, Clyde	13
CUNNINGHAM, Michael W.	29
CUNNINGHAM, Virginia M.	94
DE DONTNEY, Neil A.	27

(Continued on page 4)

The Traffic and Parking Problem

Announcement was made last week in the STAR of work and study being carried forward on the traffic and parking problems confronting some 12,000 Lockheed employees. For some time these problems have been recognized and corrective measures have been discussed and plans developed for relieving many of the unsatisfactory conditions existent.

Lynn Harrison, traffic expert, states that "Habit and practice observations and checks made on employees using areas provided for parking and driving on the streets indicate that a splendid opportunity exists for employees to contribute greatly to our program for improvement.

"These checks reveal that a serious loss of parking space exists within lane-marked areas as well as on unmarked but graded lots on which cars are parked. This is caused by the parking cars out of established lines, at other than indicated angles without regard to distance between cars and in driving lanes at entrances and exits, and in some cases even on sidewalks.

"It has been computed that because of this carelessness in parking a 12 per cent loss of space has been experienced in certain problem areas. This means that for approximately every seven cars parked one employee is cheated out of a space.

"The individual driver, by thoughtful and considerate acts and voluntary compliance with established systems and rules, will contribute more to desired improvement and safety in traffic matters than any other corrective measure that can be developed."

Comments or suggestions for facilitating the parking of cars will be appreciated and receive careful consideration if directed to Harrison via the inter-office mail service.

Heart Attack, Motorcycle Accident Cause Two Deaths

Funeral services were held last Wednesday afternoon for Dale A. Werle who passed away early last Sunday morning of a heart attack. Werle was employed in the Maintenance Department in June of this year, where he worked until the time of his death.

Jack Deal Ross, employed in the Metal Fittings Department for the past five years, died early Wednesday morning from injuries sustained in a motorcycle accident the previous day. Ross had worked for Lockheed since his graduation from Chaffey Junior College, Ontario, in 1935. Funeral arrangements have been announced on the company bulletin boards.

Rangers Hold Three Rides Each Saturday

All employees who are interested in riding with the Lockheed Rangers are urged to join that group in one of their rides each Saturday at Doc's Stables, Roscoe, at 6:00 a.m., 8:00 a.m., or 4:00 p.m.

Plans are now under way by this group to enter a drill team in the Saugus Rodeo to be held in October.

Night Crew Bowling Teams Requested To Register

The L.E.R.C. office requests that all bowling teams for daytime bowling call extension 722 and register with Mrs. Bucci.

If enough of these teams composed of night crew workers sign up it is expected that definite plans will be completed by next week for this new bowling league.

L.E.R.C. Calendar

Friday, September 27 — Theater Workshop Meeting. Room 210, Personnel Building, 8:00 p.m.

Saturday, September 28—Meeting of Lockheed Rangers at Doc's Stables, Roscoe, 6:00 a.m., 8:00 a.m. and 4:00 p.m.

Sunday, September 29 — Tennis matches. Lockheed vs. North American Aviation, Civic Center Park, Burbank, 9:00 a.m. to 1:00 p.m.

Sunday, September 29 — Golf match. Lockheed vs. El Segundo Division of Douglas Aircraft, Brookside Park, Pasadena, 9:15 a.m.

Monday, September 30 — Choral Club rehearsal. Swimming Pool Building, Griffith Park, 7:30 p.m.

Tuesday, October 1 — Band rehearsal. John Burroughs Jr. High School, Burbank, 7:30 p.m.

Tuesday and Wednesday, October 1 and 2—Men's Bowling League. Burbank Alleys, 7:00 p.m. and 9:00 p.m.

Thursday, October 3 — Theater Workshop. Barnsdall Park clubhouse, Vermont Avenue at Hollywood Boulevard, 7:30 p.m.

A Welcome To New Employees

(Continued from page 3)

NAME	Dept.
DOUGLAS, Emile C.	60-64
DOWLING, Donald E.	39
DUGAN, Walter N.	27
DUNN, Virginia M.	42
EDGERTON, John J.	27
ELLIOTT, Edwin	31
EVANS, Everett J.	35
FOULKES, Harry M., Jr.	95
GIBBONS, Donald B.	31-2
GLUSHYN, Wladimir	29
GOLDSWORTHY, Charles	35
GRAHAM, Zeb	53
GRAY, Millard E.	27
GREEN, Max	57
HALES, Arthur	39
HAMBLEY, Edwin Wm.	55
HAMLIN, Benson	60
HANSEN, Edward M.	1
HARGROVE, Rex S.	13
HARRINGTON, John W.	27
HARRIS, Lewis S.	16
HART, Frank L.	55
HOBRECKER, Sam H.	4
HOLZ, Arthur A.	27
HUBENET, Bernard J.	60
HUNT, William H.	39
JACKSON, George B.	27
JANSSE, Edward	84
JARVI, Albert O.	60
JOHNSON, Clell	39
KAESTNER, Walter G.	27
KELLER, Laurine B.	35-7
KELLOGG, Clarence S.	57
KOKOR, Eric	27
KRATZ, Donald	57
LACY, Elizabeth F.	36
LAKE, Henry S.	39
LARSH, Leander S.	39
LARSON, Harold K.	1
LAWHEAD, Robert	13
LEMM, Frederick L.	29
LEWIS, Ralph K.	35-4
LUDDERS, William C.	35-1
LUPPENS, Charles L.	27
McDANIEL, Darrel C.	31
McFEELY, Betty A.	35
MACK, Edward G.	39
MACKE, Arthur Ray	82
MARTIN, John W.	94
MATHES, Rothel B.	39
MEILI, Rudolph	25
MITCHELL, Leonard M.	55
MULLER, Gustav L.	27
NICHOLS, Charles	57
O'BRIEN, Clarence	39
PARNALL, Edgar	29
PAULSEN, Robert A.	60
PENNOCK, Robert M.	27
PERRA, Joseph D.	13
PERRY, Thomas J.	39
PERRY, Wilbur T.	60
PIERCE, Starr C.	44
PIRCH, Otto W.	95
PRICE, Jack W.	13
PRUITT, Elda J.	13
PUETZ, Ernest N.	91
RAITER, Chris	35-1
RICHTER, Hugo E. Jr.	27
ROBERTS, Ned L.	60
ROSS, Anthony L.	44
RUSSELL, Walbur R.	57
SCHMIDT, Walter C.	1
SHIPPEE, Elmer J.	35-7
SHORE, Ray E.	10-17
SIRYK, Nix Peter	13
SMITH, Earl N.	7
SMITH, Raymond P.	13
STOLTE, Conrad E.	94
STOREY, Hayes V.	39
STRAUSS, Max B.	60
SWACKENBERG, Vincent P.	10-4
TALLANTYRE, Renee	85
TAUSIG, Arthur E.	27
THATCHER, William C.	35
THOMPSON, Clyde H.	45
THOMSON, James U. Jr.	41
TODD, Harry	27
TYLER, Vern M.	7
VAN NOY, Henry	27
WALCOTT, Edvarda M.	94
WALLACE, Robert J.	27
WEIGOLD, Curtis B.	57
WELTY, George	10
WILLIAMS, John H.	27
WILLIAMS, Richard D.	27
WOLF, Russell M.	19
WYMAN, Winfield W.	13

Playing Safe

★ ★ ★ THE Lockheed Star ★ ★ ★

Wastes No Time

PUBLISHED WEEKLY BY THE LOCKHEED AIRCRAFT CORPORATION FOR ITS EMPLOYEES

Vol. 8 BURBANK, CALIFORNIA, U.S.A., FEBRUARY 28, 1941 No. 9

In "Final"

Scene in Lockheed's 325 by 600-foot Final Assembly Hangar.

Sympathy For Our "Grievous Loss"

The following two telegrams were received from Sir Henry Self, K.B.E., C.B., head of the British Air Commission, and Morris Wilson, special representative of Lord Beaverbrook in Canada and the United States, immediately following announcement of the death of Marino Guglielmetti and Robert McKee in a Hudson bomber crash during a delivery flight last week.

WB WASHINGTON DC 1215 P FEB 20 1941
ROBERT GROSS
LOCKHEED AIRCRAFT CORPN BURBANK CALIF
DEEPLY DISTRESSED TO LEARN OF YESTERDAYS UNHAPPY EVENT. PLEASE ACCEPT YOURSELF AND ALSO CONVEY TO THE RELATIVES OF THOSE CONCERNED OUR VERY PROFOUND SYMPATHY IN THEIR BEREAVEMENT. ENGLAND WILL NEVER FORGET THE SACRIFICES MADE ON HER BEHALF BY THE LOCKHEED CORPORATION AND ALL THOSE ASSOCIATED WITH IT.
HENRY SELF BRITISH AIR COMMISSION.

PXX WASHINGTON DC 1200P FEB 20 1941
ROBERT GROSS, LOCKHEED AIRCRAFT CORPN
BURBANK CALIF
LORD BEAVERBROOK SHARES MY GREAT DISTRESS AT THE GRIEVOUS LOSS YOU AND YOUR COLLEAGUES SUFFERED YESTERDAY. HE JOINS ME IN SENDING OUR HEARTFELT SYMPATHY TO THE RELATIVES OF THOSE WHO WERE LOST AND WHOSE QUIET COURAGE REMAINS AN INSPIRATION TO US ALL
MORRIS WILSON.

"NO PICTURES!" HANSON DEFINES RULES

Plant Protection Head Warns Employees To Observe Federal Regulations

Employees taking photographs at any point within the confines of the Lockheed and Vega factories are subject to possible heavy fines and imprisonment under federal laws, it was pointed out today by J. H. Hanson, Plant Protection director.

Under authority of a Congressional act of 1938 authorizing the president, in the interests of national defense, to "define certain vital military and naval installations or equipment as requiring protection against the general dissemination of information relative thereto," President Roosevelt has officially designated the vital military and naval installations coming under the restrictions.

Among those named is "any commercial establishment engaged in the development or manufacturer of military or naval arms, munitions, equipment, designs, ships or vessels for the United States Army or Navy." This unmistakably includes all property of the Lockheed and Vega companies.

The Act makes it "unlawful to make any photograph, sketch, picture, drawing, map or graphical representation of such vital military and naval installations or equipment" without first obtaining proper authority. Among many other restricted areas named in the President's proclamation were Army and Navy posts, naval harbors, military and naval equipment of all types designated as "secret," "confidential" or "restricted" and all official military or naval books, documents, designs, etc., which are in restricted classifications.

Employees are cautioned to strictly observe these federal regulations and should any question arise, to consult with the Plant Protection Department.

Income Tax Service

Federal income tax deputies will be on duty in Room 206 of the Burbank Post Office from 8:30 a.m. to 4 p.m. each day through March 15, the last day for filing federal income tax returns.

Deputies will also be on duty during the same hours in Glendale at 220 East Colorado boulevard.

★ *Wading In.* During the recent downpour, Lockheed's sandbag artists did themselves proud. Maintenance men, plant engineers, transportation men, and members of the Police Department moved in on the situation with a sandbag on each shoulder. Commendations are in order for performance well above the line of duty.

* * *

★ *Growing Up.* With the leasing of the Ford Plant, Lockheed-Vega has grown to five plants. Vega Plant 1 is the new plant at Union Air Terminal. Vega Plant 2 is located at San Fernando Blvd. and Alameda. Lockheed Plant 1 is at Victory and Empire. The recently leased Ford Building will be designated as Lockheed Plant 2. Lockheed Plant 3 is north of Lockheed Plant 1 just off San Fernando Road, which formerly was the 3-G distillery.

Another recent acquisition is the Union Air Terminal which is to be renamed Lockheed Air Terminal.

In addition, reassembly of airplanes is being carried on in England and branch offices are maintained in New York City and Chicago.

* * *

★ *Inspection.* Whenever you feel that Inspection is holding you up, remember that high standards in Inspection is one of the factors responsible for Lockheed's excellent reputation.

Basil de Guichard Joins Manufacturing Office

The appointment of Mr. Basil W. de Guichard to the staff of the Lockheed-Vega Manufacturing Office was announed recently by H. E. Ryker, Assistant in Charge of Manufacturing.

Mr. de Guichard, who will co-ordinate and be responsible for all outside production activities of the two companies, was for 21 years associated with the A. C. Spark Plug Company having started as a clerk and advanced to the presidency of the firm.

LOCKHEED WORKER GIVES LIFE IN RESCUE ATTEMPT

TRADE EXTENSION CLASSES

The education service division of the Industrial Relations Department announces the formation of the following trade extension classes, to be conducted in connection with the Burbank Adult Education program.

MACHINE SHOP — Monday, Wednesday and Friday, Burbank High School Shop, 10 p.m. to midnight.

TOOL AND DIE MAKING—Tuesday and Thursday, Jackman Building, 1809 Magnolia Avenue, 1 a.m. to 4 a.m.

WELDING — Wednesday and Friday, 68 North Orange Grove, 1 a.m. to 4 a.m.

Students may enroll in these classes by going directly to the classrooms at the first meeting of the class.

Richard Burr Phelps Dies Saving Woman Caught In Flood

In an heroic attempt to rescue Mrs. Bernice Coleman as she was being washed down Chevy Chase boulevard in flood waters, Richard Burr Phelps, aged 19, lost his life last week.

Phelps was originally employed by Lockheed on October 14 of last year as a riveter learner and at the time of his death was working as a skin fitter. He is survived by his parents, Mr. and Mrs. W. S. Phelps of Watsonville, California, and one married sister.

The management and employees of the Lockheed and Vega companies all join in a sincere expression of sympathy to members of Phelps' family at the tragic outcome of his courageous sacrifice.

Reading Habit Hints

B. C. Boulton, assistant chief project engineer, recently prepared the following article suggesting some excellent rules to apply to the development of the habit of reading. It is reproduced from the Engineers' Weekly Bulletin.

"There are two basic types of reading: one for short range purposes and one for long. This division extends both to general and technical reading. Each type has its place, but we can read more wisely if we understand the difference.

"Our minds should not be treated like attics in which we store odds and ends with the vague thought that some day they may be of use to us. Short range reading yields information of a specific type that may be applicable to some work that we may be doing, and hence is useful, but too often we conscientiously read article after article, filling our minds with fact and information that has no direct or immediate application. In a short time these ideas lose their clear-cut outlines and tend to become a jumbled mass.

"On the other hand, if in the course of our reading we are able to discover a new principle, then we should read it carefully, study it until it becomes part of ourselves, retaining its clarity and vitality. The application of a principle is not merely specific, but broad; and at the time it is hard to see how wide its usefulness may be.

"There is a great deal of difference in the way in which people read. Too many of us skim through the pages and read with our eyes but not with our minds. Too often in a few days there is little left but a hazy impression. It is better to read a little, wisely chosen, and to absorb, than to read much and be none the wiser.

"One should not assume that what one reads is necessarily true, but should be critical of it and test it against the touchstone of one's own previous knowledge and experience. If it rings true, then retain it. A great deal of the value of reading depends on this habit of weighing and comparing, and the act of doing this enables us to remember that which is worthwhile, making it an integral part of our mind.

"We can read for information and we can read for inspiration; of the two the latter is often much the more important. All of us need outside contacts to revitalize us. Otherwise, we tend to become ingrown and introspective. Wide horizons, new contacts, mean new life—they are the fountain of youth for our minds and spirits—the source of enthusiasm, of interest, and of creative work. There is something amiss in a man who, when in his reading stumbles across some new truth or principle, is not thrilled and inspired by it, and does not feel

"'. . . . like some watcher of the skies
When a new planet swims into his ken;
Or like stout Cortez, when with eagle eyes
He stared at the Pacific—and all his men
Look'd at each other with a wild surmise—
Silent, upon a peak in Darien.'"

THE LOCKHEED STAR *is issued every Friday by the Lockheed Aircraft Corporation for its employees. Communications may be addressed to either the Industrial Relations Department or the Public Relations Department, Lockheed Aircraft Corporation, Burbank, California, U.S.A.*

SINO-JAPANESE WAR FILM SHOWN FREE TO EMPLOYEES

Lockheed Bombers In A.A.U. Play-Offs

Fielding one of the finest teams in the history of basketball, Lockheed enters the play-off series for the Southern California AAU Championship tournament on Thursday, March 6, when the Lockheed quintet tangles with National Schools squad at the City College gym.

Winning teams in the play-off series are scheduled to journey to the National Basketball Tournament in Denver and Lockheed's five shows the type of play and material that 'champ' teams are made of.

"Don't think that our boys are going to have a walk-away," Leo Deason, veteran manager declares, "This National Squad is plenty hot and if you want to get behind your team next Thursday, you will see some top-notch basketball."

New Deadline For Aircraftsman

All material for the March issue of The Aircraftsman must be submitted to the office of The Aircraftsman by 5 p.m. Monday, March 3.

Contributors are requested to be certain that they obtain releases for photographic material and also that written news be limited to a page and one-half double-spaced typewriter copy.

Drama Club Meet On Sunday March 2

The regular monthly Party Meeting of the Lockheed Dramatic Club will be held Sunday evening March 2 at 1141 No. Gower Street, Hollywood, with business, a program, refreshments and dancing on the announced program.

All-Plant Dance Set For March 16

Honoring the venerable St. Patrick and all employees in the plant at the same event, the L.E.R.C. Entertainment Committee has completed details for a dinner dance to be held at Casa Manana Sunday night, March 16.

"This party marks the first all-plant dance the L.E.R.C. has ever attempted and from the way reservations are pouring into the L.E.R.C. office it looks like a sell out" a spokesman for the committee reports.

Reservations for the dinner dance may be made by phoning 1901 or 1902 between the hours of 8 p.m. and 5 p.m. Monday through Friday each week until March 14.

Boxers-Matmen Schedules Set

Loris Harrel, L.E.R.C. athletic chairman announces that once again Lockheed boxers and wrestlers may enjoy the facilities of Jeffrie's Barn on Victory Blvd.

"We can now offer this spot for the boys who want to keep in trim, from 3:30 p.m. to 5 p.m. daily except Thursdays and Sundays," Harrel declares.

"The recently acquired athletic equipment will soon be set up in a place of our own, but the Jeffrie Barn arrangement will keep us from getting stale and out of training," Harrel concludes.

Porter D. Dilley, Vega Executive To Offer Illustrated Talk Of 12,000 Mile Trek

"China at Bay" is the subject of a motion picture and commentary to be presented by Porter D. Dilley Friday evening, March 7, at 7:30 in the Burbank High School Auditorium, under the auspices of the L.E.R.C. Educational Committee.

Dilley spent two years travelling 12,000 miles to secure these pictures which graphically show why Japan, with all her mechanized forces, has not succeeded in conquering China.

Tickets, which will be required for admission to this program, may be secured free of charge from the V.E.R.C. or L.E.R.C. offices or from L.E.R.C. representatives. After the pictures have been shown the meeting will be devoted to an open forum discussion on the Japan-China situation.

Hygiene Talks Are Postponed

The scheduled hygiene talks have been postponed until those interested make definite reservations through the L.E.R.C. office.

The importance of these talks cannot be too strongly emphasized and employees are urged to notify the L.E.R.C. office if they wish to attend the sessions. If registration justifies re-scheduling the talks, they will be set for mid-March.

Ski Club In Trials

The second series of qualification races in the Giant Slalom is scheduled at McGee Creek Ski course Saturday and Sunday, March 1 and 2.

All interested are advised to notify Bob O'Hanlon, Station 1121. Directions and transportation can be arranged.

This series of races is being run off in anticipation of the scheduled meet at Yosemite on March 15 and 16 when it is hoped to have the top 30 skiers qualified in the A-B and C classes.

Employees Plan Flying Squadron

Arrangements have been completed to hold a meeting of all Lockheed flying enthusiasts Tuesday evening, March 4 at 7 p.m. in Room 215, Personnel Building.

It is expected that a good turn out will launch this group who are working on details for purchasing planes, offering training and flying time at very greatly reduced rates.

L.E.R.C. CALENDAR—MARCH 1 TO MARCH 7

Friday, February 28—Dramatics Club Meeting, Personnel Bldg., Room 215, 7:30 p.m.

Saturday, March 1 — Lockheed Rangers, Doc's Stables, Roscoe, 4:00 p.m.

Saturday and Sunday, March 1 and 2—Giant Slalom Qualifications Races, Ski Club, Call O'-Hanlon Ext. 1121 for details.

Sunday, March 2—Lockheed Baseball Team vs. Brotherhood of Railroad Clerks, Solon Park, Burbank, 2:00 p.m.

Lockheed Rangers, Doc's Stables, Roscoe, 8:00 a.m.

Monday, March 3—Choral Club, Swimming Pool Bldg., Griffith Park, 7:30 p.m. Band Rehearsal, John Burroughs Junior high, Burbank, 7:30 p.m.

Tuesday, March 4 — Dramatics Club Meeting, 1141 N. Gower, Hollywood, 8:00 p.m. Organization Discussion, Lockheed Flying Group, Room 215, Personnel Bldg., 7:15 p.m.

Thursday, March 6 — Lockheed Basketball Team vs. National Schools. AAU Championship play-off game, City College.

Tuesday and Wednesday, March 4 and 5 — Men's Bowling League, Burbank Alley, 7:00 p.m. and 9:00 p.m.

Tuesday, Thursday and Friday, March 4, 6 and 7 — Men's Bowling League (Night Crew) Burbank Alleys, 12:00 noon.

Monday, Tuesday, Wednesday and Friday, March 3, 4 and 5—Second Round, Inter-department Basketball Games, Burbank High School gym, 7:00 to 10:00 p.m.

L.E.R.C. ELECTION DETAILS NEED CLOSE COOPERATION

Incumbents Must File Intent If They Seek Reelection To Employee Council

The final arrangements for the L.E.R.C. Representative election will be announced within a few days according to Carl Sroufe, chairman of the election committee.

"One point that the election committee is very anxious to stress again is the fact that representatives now serving on the L.E.R.C. must send in an ANVO stating their desire to serve again next year," Sroufe emphasizes.

There are only seven incumbents who are serving two year terms and all other incumbents who intend to represent their departments must file their intentions to run with the election committee or their names will not appear on the ballot.

Incumbents are advised to send their notices to the L.E.R.C. office immediately so that the committee can set up the ballots for the election, determine the date for the balloting and set forth regulations on electioneering, campaign posters and other pertinent election regulations.

New Merchandise On Sale At The L.E.R.C. Canteen

Several new items are being offered employees at the L.E.R.C. Canteen, John Jordan, manager announces.

Included in the list of new offerings are new P-38 lapel pins, a new type of Lodestar ashtrays and a recently designed combination badge and pass case made of leatherette.

The ashtrays and badge cases will be available March 4, while the pins will go on sale March 8.

Jury Duty Exemptions May Be Arranged

Employees who are called for jury duty are reminded that arrangements have been made to grant exemption to aircraft employees or employees engaged in essential industries. Lockheed and Vega employees should contact the Employee Relations Department for arranging certification of exemption.

It is not necessary for anyone to appear personally before the Jury Commissioner to obtain such exemption if the matter is taken care of through the Employee Relations Department.

Dramatic Club Casting Play

Final casting for the Lockheed Dramatic Club production of "The Night of January 16th" will take place at two club meetings scheduled for next week.

On Tuesday evening, March 4, and on Friday evening, March 7, the club will meet at 1141 No. Gower, Hollywood, to determine final cast and production plans.

Dick Walsh, coach of the drama group urges all dramatic enthusiasts to come out to the meetings.

L.E.R.C. Movie Being Planned

Two meetings to consider the details of the production of the L.E.R.C. motion picture have been called by Dick Walsh, Dept. 25, dramatic club head. March 3 and March 6 at 1141 No. Gower at 8 o'clock in the evening. These meets will establish cast, production crews, and all other details of the picture which the Dramatics Club has planned to portray the importance of the L.E.R.C. to the new and old employees alike.

Debate Club Organizing

Plans are being pressed for the formation of a debate club under the auspices of the Education Committee of the L.E.R.C.

All those interested are requested to send or phone in their names to the L.E.R.C. office (Station 1901) as an organization meeting is scheduled for early next month.

Mechanical Guards And Mental Guards

Mechanical guards play an important part in making our plant safe. However, to complete the program, the assistance of each employee is also needed.

To accomplish the best results in our safety efforts, every employee in the factory must be in a state of mind that is receptive to and enthusiastic about things that will prevent accidents.

When everyone has the determination to perform his job the correct and safe way, then injuries will be eliminated.

Lockheed Epic Film Opens Glendale Run

Lockheed employees and their friends will have an opportunity to see the Lockheed sound motion picture, "Look to Lockheed for Leadership," when it appears at the Capitol Theatre in Glendale from March 5 to March 8 inclusive.

Following a preview of the new Lockheed sound motion picture by Fox West Coast Theater executives it was decided to show the picture in their largest Glendale theater because of the high public interest in aviation and the particular interest of the people of Glendale and vicinity in the Lockheed company.

The picture, which will be shown in addition to the regular Capitol Theatre program, will be publicized by a large banner across the front of the theater and an elaborate lobby display of photographs of Lockheed products and processes.

Marksmen Plan Election Meet

Lockheed Pistol and Rifle devotees are urged to attend the election meeting of the newly organized shooting club which is scheduled for Sunday afternoon, March 9, in Room 215 of the Industrial Relations Building, at 1 o'clock.

"It is very important that we have a big membership turn-out," Fred Good, Dept. 25, temporary chairman declares, "For this newly organized club hopes to be able to offer members their own shooting range, once organization details have been completed."

Call Issued For Softball Squads

All day and night departmental softball squads are advised to send in team rosters to the L.E.R.C. office immediately for the schedules on the Fifth Annual Softball tourney are to be drawn up during early March.

Ben Franklin, manager of the Lockheed Girls Softball squad has announced that he is now accepting ANVO's from girl softball players and requests that girls send their entries to him in care of Department 35. Turnouts are set for late March, weather permitting.

Entries Being Received For Model Airplane Contest

A model airplane contest is being sponsored Sunday, March 2, 1941, at the Los Angeles County Fairgrounds in Pomona, by the Jack Ford, Jr. Chapter 9 post of the Disabled American Veterans of the World War.

Contest rules and application blanks may be secured from the L.E.R.C. office, 2400 Empire Avenue.

A Welcome To New Employees

Printed here are the names and department numbers of Lockheed and Vega employees who started work during the week ending February 22, 1941

The Lockheed and Vega managements, together with the officers of each company's recreation club, sincerely wish that every employee shall feel at home and consider himself a vital part of his company. Since it is impossible to greet every new employee individually, this means is taken to extend a hearty welcome to each one.

LOCKHEED

Name	Dept.
AHRENS, K. W.	10
ALBERTSON, E. A.	12
ALLISON, H. H.	38
ANDERSON, W. A.	53
ANDREW, C. P.	1
APPLEBY, T. N.	10
ARMSTRONG, L. H.	7
ASHTON, J. W.	46
BAILEY, E. I.	10
BAINES, K. W.	7
BAKER, R. E.	10
BAKER, R. F.	12
BALLESTER, N. P.	2
BALES, S. C.	7
BARNES, L. S., Jr.	35
BARNETT, B. G.	6
BASSETT, H. A.	10
BAXTER, M. G.	16
BEAUCHAMP, E. H.	1
BEEGHLEY, E. G.	12
BENNETT, R. W.	38
BIDDLE, J. A.	12
BLACKSTONE, Guy N.	1
BLAKE, R. S.	2
BLANCHARD, L. A.	16
BODENHORN, G.	56
BOLLER, D. L.	36
BONE, M. L.	10
BONHAM, H. H.	12
BOWMAN, F. G.	16
BRASH, F. B.	13
BREITWIESER, R. J.	10
BREWER, F. K.	22
BREWSTER, W. D.	33
BRICKA, J. W.	34
BRIDGEMAN, W. F.	36
BRINKLEY, W. A.	12
BRINSMEAD, B.	12
BRUNE, A. D.	18
BRYAN, L. V.	10
BUCHENAU, W. S.	54
BUCK, A. G.	16
BUCKLAND, H. C.	34
BUCKLES, R. L.	20
BUNCH, T. O.	35
BURNS, W. C.	16
BURR, R. H.	22
BURROWS, W. F.	34
BURSEY, Fred W.	1
BUXKEMPER, C.	43
BYERS, L. R.	12
CARLTON, C. B.	7
CARR, J. S.	5
CARRICK, G.	10
CASSITY, J. J.	32
CHAGI, L.	34
CHAPMAN, H. J.	10
CHENEY, L. L.	54
CLARK, C. G.	34
CLARK, D. N.	32
CLARK, F. A.	12
CLARK, J. C.	1
CLAYBROOK, G. C.	6
CODY, P. T.	16
COLE, C. C.	39
COLLINS, V. H.	34
COMEY, E. L.	33
COOPER, B. B.	12
COOPER, D. L.	12
CORDER, R. W.	16
COX, W. E.	16
COX, W. T.	16
CRAGO, T. W.	16
CRISWELL, D. T.	5
CROOK, E. C.	3
CROT, A.	25
CULLIS, J. R.	16
CUNNINGHAM, Paul	2
DALE, V. W.	1
DAMBRUCH, L. E.	10
DANIELSON, D. W.	2
DAVERN, L. P.	10
DE BERE, H.	1
DE CORDOVA, R. L.	10
DELP, S. H.	10
DERBY, Donald W.	1
DICK, F. E.	22
DICKEY, W. A.	22
DICKSON, J. W., Jr.	90
DILLINGHAM, H. A.	16
DODGE, G. A.	6
DOLLMEYER, W. G.	90
DOSSEY, N. G.	13
DOUGHERTY, R. H.	34
DRAKE, A. G.	16
DRYDEN, R. R.	3
DUDDY, J. R.	7
DUITSMAN,, P. W.	10
DUKE, F. E.	1

Name	Dept.
DUPREE, F. L.	16
DURBIN, W. R.	4
DURGIN, J. R.	23
EGAN, A. J.	12
EHRLICH, P.	10
EIDE, P. M.	12
ELLIOTT, R. E.	10
EMERY, F. K.	7
EPLING, H. O.	33
ERICKSON, P. H.	7
ERLANDSON, A. O.	12
EVERETT, J. W.	16
FALLIS, W. S.	16
FENSTERMACHER, D. M., Jr.	22
FITZSIMMONS, F. D.	48
FLATTUM, R. L.	12
FORMAN, K. M.	95
FRASER, R. B.	10
FREEDE, W. J.	38
FREITES, T.	16
FULLER, B. W.	12
GABEL, P. E.	7
GALLAGHER, R. T.	2
GARDNER, C. B.	56
GARDNER, T. J.	42
GEBELE, L. E.	23
GERBER, J.	25
GERSON, J. G.	7
GIBBS, D. L.	95
GILLILAND, J. C.	16
GLAUS, C. G.	7
GODE, D. R.	10
GOLDEN, H.	10
GOLDEN, W. E.	12
GOLDMAN, G.	10
GOWER, E. T.	10
GREEN, S. L.	54
GREENWOOD, A. W.	7
GROGAN, C. A.	34
GUENTHER, H. E.	10
GUNTRUP, C. T.	22
HALBEISEN, L. E.	10
HALLOWELL, L. B.	16
HANCOCK, W.	7
HANSEN, R. J.	16
HANSON, L. L.	5
HARDING, J. A.	10
HARPER, M. E.	6
HARRIS, G. N.	37
HARRIS, R. D.	3
HARTSTROM, H. A.	12
HASKINS, T. C., Jr.	13
HAYES, G. W.	53
HAYNES, R. H.	39
HAYNES, W. H.	6
HEINZE, G. W.	34
HELZER, M. L.	10
HENDRY, M. S.	7
HENSLEY, C. F.	2
HERMANSON, R. W.	34
HICKEY, F. W., Jr.	10
HINEMEYER, H. M.	16
HOFFPAUIR, J. S.	10
HOGE, A. L.	35
HOLCOMB, F. E.	32
HOMER, G. W.	10
HOMEWOOD, Ivan D.	7
HOOP, H. H.	10
HOORNBEEK, P. S.	10
HRACHOVEC, J. J.	10

Name	Dept.
HUBLER, D. D.	10
HUMES, J. P.	2
HUMMER, H. W.	16
HUNGERFORD, B. R.	16
HUNTER, F. F.	6
HUNTER, W. T.	12
HUNZEKER, C. P.	11
HUSTON, J. V.	11
INGRAHAM, L. B.	12
INGRAM, K. A.	11
JACOBS, J. R.	1
JENNINGS, J. W.	16
JENSEN, L. H.	12
JENSEN P. A.	7
JOHNSON, C. D.	53
JOHNSON, L. R.	5
JOHNSON, O. S.	12
JOHNSON, W. H.	16
JORDAN, J. B.	28
JUHNKE, E. C.	1
KANE, T., Jr.	53
KARR, H. E.	16
KEELER, L. M.	26
KELLY, W. R.	23
KEMP, Frank W.	38
KERR, K. E.	12
KILLION, L. L.	12
KIMBALL, W. L.	14
KING, Amos W.	10
KING, E. R.	12
KLING, E.	10
KLOETZLI, Fred	34
KNIGHT, L. I.	10
KRAMER, B. A.	10
KREITZMAN, L.	16
KREUTER, W. G.	10
KUHL, M. L.	10
KUHNS, J. W.	1
LADEN, G. C.	35
LANDERS, B., Jr.	10
LANE, D. S.	6
LARSEN, J.	5
LARSON, N. A.	11
LAUGHLIN, L. E.	69
LAWSON, G. L.	12
LAWSON, W. G.	38
LAYFIELD, E. W.	11
LEHN, A. J.	13
LEIFHEIT, F. R.	7
LEIM, M. L.	32
LINDBERG, W. M.	1
LINDER, F.	12
LINK, R. J.	16
LINNAN, C. C.	34
LIVINGSTON, P.	16
LUCKENBILL, F. F.	16
LUTHER, C. E.	10
LYNCH, F. L.	16
MANIORD, D. L.	12
MARAK, V. L.	16
MARGOLIN, A.	16
MARKEY, M. A.	34
MARTIN, R. E.	5
MASCARA, A. V.	66
MASON, M. D., Jr.	12
MASTERS, H. C.	39
MAYNARD, D. C.	12

NAME	Dept.
McADAMS, J. W.	1
McCLELLAN, D. E.	54
McCORMICK, J. E.	56
McCREA, H. T.	6
McCREA, R. W.	39
McDONALD, D. B.	16
McINTYRE, D. S.	23
McINTYRE, H.	22
McKENNA, B. C.	7
McKINNEY, K. D.	12
MELVILLE, R. R.	10
MILLER, C. D.	22
MILLER, C. L.	7
MILLER, D. B.	10
MILLER, H. R.	35
MILLER, M. J.	50
MILLER, W. C.	10
MILNES, H.	6
MISKE, E. G.	10
MOE, M. V.	12
MORAN, C. F.	11
MORGAN, G. B.	10
MORRILL, T. A.	12
MORRIS, J. L.	56
MORROW, P. G.	9
MORTON, R. W.	1
MOYETTE, M. T.	22
MULLER, C. W.	10
MUNN, R. A.	10
MUNSELL, R. M.	97
MURRAY, E. L.	23
MYERS, E. A.	14
NEAL, W. M.	90
NELSON, J. A.	35
NICHELSON, H. L.	16
NOVAK, A. E.	12
NYGARD, M.	11
O'CONNOR, A. W.	23
O'LAUGHLIN, E. J.	22
OLSEN, O. M.	10
OLSEN, W. R.	12
OSKEY, K. J.	10
PACKER, H. J.	11
PARKKINEN, W. W.	35
PATTISON, W. G.	10
PATTON, C. M.	10
PEARMAN, R. D.	16
PEARSON, E. A.	16
PERRY, H. E.	54
PESEK, D. A.	93
PFAFF, C. W.	10
PIEPER, D. M.	12
POGUE, O. M.	1
PORTELA, L.	13
POWELL, D. V.	16
POWELL, W. J.	7
PYEATT, R. T.	10
QUIBELL, R. B.	3
RANUM, D. E.	10
RASK, H. G.	10
RASMUSSEN, C. N.	4
READ, H. C.	7
REED, D. F.	66
REESE, W. C.	96
REESER, C. T.	12
REINER, K.	54
REMER, G. B.	11
RESLOCK, P. G.	32
REYNOLDS, R. W.	28
RICHARDS, Burt T.	1
RIGGS, C. M.	66
RINK, V. N.	95
ROBERTS, G.	2
ROBERTS, L.	22
ROBERTS, S. E.	7
ROBINSON, C. R.	96
ROGERS, W. M.	16
ROSE, J. L.	10
ROTHSCHILD, W. F.	23
ROUNTREE, E. H.	10
ROWLEY, S. A.	90
RUSSELL, Janet C.	25
RUPERT, R. A.	33
SACKETT, G. C.	16
SCHMIDT, A. G.	23
SCHNEIDER, P. M.	11
SCHOLL, G.	1
SCHWARZ, A. P.	12
SCHWEIZER, W. W.	16
SCOTT, L. M.	54

(Continued on page 6)

Refunds Possible On Annual Pay Deductions

Refunds Available To Those Receiving More Than $3,000 From Two Or More Employers

Employees who have worked for two or more employers during the past year and have received more than $3,000 are reminded by D. E. Browne, chief accountant, that each employer has been required to withhold 1 percent tax and that a refund of the tax paid may now be secured if the salary received exceeded $3,000 in the single year provided that:

1. **Claim for refund on form 843 is filed within two years of the payment of such payroll taxes.**
2. **That it be accompanied by Form SS-9 "Employer's Statement." Three copies of this form for each employer should be obtained—the original for the Collector of Internal Revenue, the second for the employer in question and the third to be retained by the applicant.**
3. **If unable to secure an "Employer's Statement," an explanation of the applicant's inability to submit such statement.**

Copies of these forms may be obtained by calling extension 2186 in the Accounting Department or by calling the Employee Relations Department.

Tom Tull Elected Credit Union Head

Following a dinner meeting held in the Sky Room at Union Air Terminal last week the board of directors of the Lockheed Aircraft Employees' Federal Credit Union elected officers for the year 1941.

Officers elected are Tom W. Tull, Lockheed assistant coordinator, president; John Hartman, Engineering Department, vice president; D. E. Browne, chief accounting officer, treasurer; Harry E. Richardson, Credit Union cashier, assistant treasurer; William I. Hawkes, Assistant Secretary's Office, clerk.

Retiring president and vice president, L. D. Bonham, Engineering Department, and Vern Beckman, Tool Cribs, retain their membership in the board of directors.

RED CROSS ACKNOWLEDGMENT

A letter of formal acknowledgement and appreciation for contributions made by Lockheed and Vega employees to the American Red Cross has been received from David Rittenhouse, chairman of the Burbank branch of the American Red Cross.

In acknowledging the $3,653.11 contributed by company employees, Rittenhouse wrote, "We are deeply indebted to you, not only for the funds which you provided to alleviate some of the human suffering in this area, but also for the spirit in which your offering was made."

The American Red Cross Roll Call was conducted in the Lockheed and Vega plants in conjunction with the Burbank Community Fund Campaign. A total of more than $9,000 was contributed by Lockheed and Vega employees.

Special arrangements have been made through the L.E.R.C. for workers on the night shift to play golf on the Chevy Chase Golf Club course during the day.

A Welcome to New Employees

(Continued from page 5)

Name	Dept.
SCOTT, R. L.	95
SEABOLD, G. H.	10
SEBREN, H. V.	33
SHERMAN, E. I.	34
SHERMAN, R. F.	12
SHINNEFIELD, J. H.	16
SILVERMAN, A.	7
SLAYBAUGH, J. B.	35
SMITH, H. C.	16
SMITH, L. F.	11
SMITH, M. C.	10
SMITH, R. W.	7
SMITHSON, C. H.	22
SNELL, Carroll R.	25
SNYDER, J. C.	54
SOLOW, Henry A.	2
SPETH, P. J.	22
SPILMAN, B. F.	10
STEEN, Billie A.	2
STEERE, J. E.	16
STEVENS, L. V.	12
STEVENSON, T. I.	74
STEWART, R. T.	12
STINE, Vance D.	25
STOLTZ, K. J.	16
STORBECK, B. E.	16
STOUT, C. L.	10
STRAND, A. J.	2
SULLIVAN, D. L.	54
SUTTON, J. O.	22
SWANTZ, L. D.	12
TAYLOR, D. M.	10
TERRELL, C. O.	23
THOMAS, C. R.	10
THOMAS, H. K.	38
THOMAS, W. J.	16
THOMPSON, M. K.	22
THOMPSON, W. F.	12
TILLOTSON, D. S.	12
TOBIN, C. J.	16
TOBIN, Raymond L.	3
TONKIN, S. A.	16
TORRANCE, R. M.	12
TUCKER, C. A.	35
TURGEON, L. A.	10
VAN ORSDEL, M. L.	2
VASSAR, V. M.	12
WACHTER, M. J.	95
WALKER, W. C.	35
WALTERS, L. M.	2
WARDWELL, H. W.	16
WEBSTER, J. D.	2
WHITE, S. H.	90
WIENS, H. L.	10
WILLIAMS, D. D.	10
WILLIAMS, G. V.	12
WILLIAMS, J. L.	42
WILSON, H. J.	12
WINSOR, M. W.	10
YOUNG, J. D.	16
ZELLER, W. M.	12

VEGA

Name	Dept.
ADAMS, Jerry L.	27
AUNE, Edward S.	27
AUSTIN, James W., Jr.	57
AUSTIN, Maynard B.	35
BAILEY, Donald S.	57
BELL, William D.	96
BOARDMAN, Richard J.	31
BUCK, Harold J.	35
BUSH, William F.	57
BUSHNELL, T. Stewart	55
BYRNES, Ralph	1
CAFFREY, Edgar B.	57
CAMERON, Donald H.	67
CAMPBELL, Colin S.	95
CANADAY, Harold E.	29
CANNING, James T.	27
CASTLER, Thomas E.	16
CHAMBERS, Gilbert B.	35
CHARLES, Claude H., Jr.	27
CLODFELTER, Robert R.	35
COIT, Robert D.	35
COX, Leonard A.	34
DONAHUE, James A.	34
DONAHUE, Terence B.	46
DOUGHERTY, Frank M.	51
DOWNING, William J.	34
DOWNS, Lewis O.	55
EARLEY, Melvin C.	27
ECK, Knut E.	39
FARNELL, Jack W.	68
FIFE, Robert C.	27
FIKE, Thelma A.	68
FRY, James C.	45
GAMBLE, Thomas J., Jr.	94
GARDNER, Albert O.	29
GEIGER, William N.	34
GILBERT, Henry	7
GILLESPIE, Edward W.	31
GLASS, S. Odell	46
GORRIS, Margaret W.	67
GOTTSCHALK, Richard B.	55
GRAVES, Byron L.	46
GRIMES, Evelyn C.	63
HAGENBAUGH, James W.	35
HANSHAW, Ellsworth S.	34
HANSON, Carl	60
HASLAM, William E.	60
HAWKINS, John A.	29
HEALD, James R.	27
HILL, Robert W.	35
HILLMAN, Ruth M.	50
HITOON, Serge E.	35
HOBART, Ernest L.	64
HOWARD, James E.	27
HUDSON, Glen R.	51
HUGHES, William E.	60
IANNARONE, Eugene F.	94
ILG, Paul F.	46
JOHNSON, David C.	27
JONES, John R.	45
JONES, Russel V.	6
JUDSON, Hale D., Jr.	94
KAMIN, Herbert I.	31
KELLEY, Eugene W.	16
KENNEDY, Douglas L.	55
KENNEDY, Roi	28
KIEBEL, Roland K.	27
KING, Ruth A. Bell	50
KIRCHHOFF, Joseph G.	29
KIRST, James J.	27
KNUTSSON, Arthur V.	60
KOBERNE, George E.	62
KOYEN, James W.	94
KRUGER, Melvin E.	52
LAUS, Darold N.	46
LEES, Walter L.	57
LESNER, William M.	29
LINDSAY, W. Glen	34
LINDSTROM, Gene F.	27
LIST, Edgar G., Jr.	27
McCAULOU, Kenneth G.	94
McGINNESS, Howard A.	55
McKNIGHT, Douglas K.	95
MARTIN, Lanie W.	55
MECHAM, Paul W.	16
MEIER, Harold S.	27
MILLER, Charles B., Jr.	57
MILLER, Henry A.	31
MILLER, Herbert H.	57
MONROE, Lester G.	49
MOORE, George C.	59
MOORE, George W.	50
MOORE, Royda C.	94
MURRAY, Edward B.	94
NELSON, Alfred R.	55
NELSON, Forrest A.	29
NESEL, Charles J., Jr.	46
NOLAN, Albert H.	46
ORR, Robert A.	27
OSTMAN, Robert L.	35
OWEN, Robert G.	31
PALMER, William R.	40
PARKER, H. Putnam	34
PLUMMER, Charles R.	51
PLUNKETT, Walter A.	39
POSTE, Helen A.	67
PURVIS, Howard Jay	55
RAWAK, Bertram J.	27
RICHTER, August L. M.	28
ROBERTSON, Robert R.	57
RYAN, William M.	46
SCHERREI, William F.	62
SCOTT, George O.	31
SHIRLEY, Charles Earl	51
SIMRELL, E. Byrdgess	27
SMALLWOOD, Cyril T.	64
SMITH, Arthur Gale	16
SMITH, Harry C.	55
SMITH, Oliver Leslie	51
SMOOT, Harry H.	64
STANFORD, Grant L., Jr.	35
STARR, Donald E.	60
STEVENSON, Bernard Richard	96
SUTPHEN, Joseph W., Jr.	63
THOMPSON, Harold J.	39
TILLMAN, Edwin J.	28
TWEED, John S.	95
U'REN, Robert M.	27
WEATHERILL, Gordon P.	27
WERNER, George J.	94
WICE, Theodore	55
WILLIAMS, Russell	16
WILSON, Clarence P.	51
WINSLOW, John R.	34
WOODWARD, William E.	46
YOUNG, George O.	94
ZERMAN, Frederick A.	82
ZITLOW, Steven, Jr.	14

THE ★ ★ Lockheed-Vega Star ★ ★

Vol. 8 BURBANK, CALIFORNIA, U.S.A., MARCH 21, 1941 No. 12

Vega Report Shows Record Plant Expansion

Vote Results In L.E.R.C. Election

With a record total of nearly 17,000 votes cast, a vote practically as big as that of the average small city, employees of the Lockheed Aircraft Corporation have elected the following as their representatives on the Lockheed Employees Recreation Club Council for the term starting the third week in April, it is announced by Carl Sroufe, chairman of the election committee:

Women
- Eleanor V. Clark
- Harriet Slater
- Verna Mae Tinker

Plant Three-Day Shift
- George Margien
- Allan G. Morrison

Plant Three-Night Shift
- Casper J. Heilman

Depts. 1 & 41-Day Shift
- Carl Sroufe

Dept. 1 & 41-Night Shift
- Elmer Lamb

Depts. 2 & 50
- Oscar C. Bowman

Depts. 4 & 53
- Larry Billups

Dept. 5
- Chester Leigh

Dept. 6
- Charles Alexander

Dept. 7
- M. L. Caldwell
- Bill Reardon
- J. A. Whitehead

Dept. 7—Night Shift
- Louie Tarr

Dept. 10—Day Shift
- Wm. Briggs
- Dan Lamberth
- A. L. Rankin

Dept. 10—Night Shift
- Bob Metz
- John A. Steele

Dept. 12—Day Shift
- Jud Judson
- Frank Tuttle

Dept. 12—Night Shift
- Joe Kohler

Depts. 13 & 14
- R. K. Browning

Dept. 16—Day Shift
- E. J. Beall
- Bruce Frost
- Don R. Winegar

Dept. 16—Night Shift
- Maurice Kittredge
- E. E. Thompson

Depts. 18 & 20
- Jack Mohr

Dept. 23
- Frank Arrico

Depts. 24 & 28
- Curt Houck

Dept. 25
- James F. Mosher
- Bob O'Hanlon
- Bill Paxton
- Frank Zehrbaugh

Depts. 26, 31, 37, 38, 55, 56, 60, 61, 63, 64 to 71, 75 to 85, 90 to 94 & 97
- John Barnum

Depts. 29, 36, 72 & 74
- Buck Hadley

Depts. 33, 54, 96
- Bob Sihler

Dept. 34
- Donald T. McGregor

Dept. 35—Day Shift
- Norman MacTaggart

Dept. 35—Night Shift
- Fred Berliner

Dept. 39
- Day H. Dunning

Depts. 42, 43, 44, 45, 46, 48
- Roger Hope

Depts. 51 & 52
- Elmer L. Steiner

Depts. 95, 30, 40
- H. B. Jimmie Ramsey

In Appreciation

The motion picture unit of the L.E.R.C. Drama Club wishes to take this opportunity to thank each and every member present at the St. Patrick's Day dance last Sunday, at the Casa Manana, for their splendid cooperation and considerate patience while the pictures were being shot. The consideration and patience shown during the delay was truly the Lockheed spirit. Again may we say thank you!

President Reveals Huge Order Gain

Courtlandt S. Gross

LOCKHEED EXECS' TIME WELL FILLED

Pressure of the National Defense Program is keeping some of the key Lockheed executives on the hop to a degree that threatens to result in them becoming strangers in their own homes.

For instance, Svend Pedersen, director of training for the company and the U.S. Administration's latest dollar-a-year recruit in the capacity of training specialist on shipbuilding for the West Coast, was in Washington only a few days ago conferring with the heads of OPM.

After making a three-week survey of East Coast shipyards at the Government's request, he hopped back to Burbank and is now putting in hectic days and nights

(Continued on page 5)

512 Employees Become 4866 In 14 Months

At the close of a year marked by a record plant expansion, Vega Airplane Company has entered 1941 with an increase in unfilled orders on its books approximately 234 times larger than was the case at the end of 1939, according to the financial report of the company for 1940, released today.

The new peak backlog was reached March 1 of this year, when unfilled orders amounted to $74,407,192, up from the $318,000 total on the company's books as of December 31, 1939.

Nineteen-forty was primarily a year of preparation, of tooling up and plant expansion, for the tremendous increase in present activities, President Courtlandt S. Gross pointed out in his covering report. Because of this and the concurrently necessary training of personnel, net profits for the year to December 31, 1940, were lower than in 1939, although sales last year were much greater than in the previous period.

Earned net for the year totaled $71,654, on gross sales of $1,950,554, after provision for income and excess profits taxes, equivalent to approximately 16 cents a share on the 460,000 shares of $1.50 par value common stock outstanding. By comparison, the 1939 net was $86,311, on net sales of $592,168.

The three highlights of President Gross' report were the peak backlog, the increase in personnel to 3815 by comparison with 512 as of December 31, 1939, and the increase in factory floor area last year from 160,000 square feet to some 1,100,000 square feet, part of which is

(Continued on page 6)

Note

The annual report of President Robert E. Gross to Lockheed employees is now being prepared and will be issued soon.

LOCKHEED'S PAYROLL

★ *Average Annual Earnings.* The average annual earnings of all types of companies and industries have lately been publicized nationally. Earnings at Lockheed compare very favorably with those of automobile and steel companies. The annual average for weekly-salaried Lockheed employees during 1940 was about $1,800.

This is considerably higher than the $1,629.05 reported by a large automobile manufacturer in a recent nation-wide advertisement, or the $1,635 reported for all automobile manufacturers in 1939. Steel earnings in 1937—a big year—averaged $1,628.

* * *

★ *Payroll vs. Profits.* Lockheed made less profit per payroll dollar than a representative car manufacturer. The total payroll at Lockheed in 1940 was $30,983,492.47. The profit was $3,165,675—about 10 cents returned on each payroll dollar.

A large automobile manufacturer made a profit of 183 million dollars on a payroll of 386 million dollars—50 cents returned on every payroll dollar spent. This comparison illustrates that aircraft manufacturing is not so profitable as automobile companies.

* * *

★ *Amount of Money Spent on Payroll.* 35 cents of every dollar spent by Lockheed went to employees in the form of wages and salaries during the year. In 1939, 17 cents out of every dollar spent by automobile manufacturers went out in payroll.

* * *

★ *Regularity of Payroll.* Since *1934,* Lockheed has had no more than a 10 per cent layoff. Few manufacturers have such a consistent record.

Employees who have rides to offer, please contact the Employee Relations Department.

Lewis Harding Moore Dies At Sawtelle

It is with deep regret that we announce the death of Lewis Harding Moore, age 46, Thursday morning, March 13, at the Sawtelle Veterans' Hospital. Mr. Moore had been ill for some time and underwent a serious operation the previous week. He had been employed at Lockheed since July, 1938, starting as a cabinet maker and was later transferred to the Jig Department as a jig and fixture builder.

He leaves his widow, Adelaide Moore of 546 Rose Avenue, Venice, and his father, William Moore of Santa Cruz, California.

Funeral services were held in the Chapel at Sawtelle Hospital Monday morning, March 17, at 11:00 o'clock.

To his family we extend the sincere sympathy of his many friends at Lockheed.

Prizes Offered In Vega Amateur Talent Contest

An amateur talent contest is being sponsored by the Vega Employees Recreation Club. The contest is open to all Vega employees who are interested in displaying any talent they may have, such as dancing, singing or playing an instrument. Fifty dollars in prizes will be awarded to the winners. All applications are to be submitted to the V.E.R.C. office before Friday, April 11.

The contest is to be held at the Riverside Breakfast Club, Saturday evening, April 12. No admission will be charged. Dancing throughout the evening will also be free to employees and their friends. The contest will be augmented by the appearance of well-known theatrical agents and music composers who will act as judges for the contest.

Vega employees are asked to bring their identification passes.

HUDSONS HANG HIGH

All over the world Hudsons now grace the home walls of aviation's enthusiasts. Since the recent offer of "a colored picture of the Hudson suitable for framing"—at the bottom of the Lockheed advertisements in "Life," "Time," "Newsweek," "National Geographic" and "New Yorker" a veritable flood of requests have been pouring in. This proof of the popularity of Lockheed equipment has had the Advertising and Sales Promotion Departments thinking of the proverbial "Straw on the Camel's Back." Plant employees were afforded an opportunity to obtain the pictures through a coupon that recently appeared in the "Star." This method of distribution was adopted to avoid the loss of employee time caused by individuals calling at the Advertising office. New employees may obtain the pictures by addressing a post card to the Advertising Department using the key number appearing in any of the above advertisements. Employees are requested not to add to the pressure on the Advertising Department by attempting to secure the pictures by phone. The above picture gives a fair idea of the load the Advertising Department is carrying in filling the hundreds of requests received. Left to right are Don Wood, Cliff Butterfield, Angelica Donnelly and, seated, John Norman Reid.

THE LOCKHEED STAR *is issued every Friday by the Lockheed Aircraft Corporation for its employees. Communications may be addressed to either the Industrial Relations Department or the Public Relations Department, Lockheed Aircraft Corporation, Burbank, California, U.S.A.*

British Squadron Leader Lauds Hudson Bomber After Million Miles Flown

SAYS CRAFT FIRST CLASS AIR WEAPON

Further evidence of the fine materials, advanced engineering and skilled workmanship that goes into the building of Lockheed planes is indicated in a talk recently broadcast by the Commanding Officer of a Hudson squadron in Great Britain recounting the completion of one million miles flown in these planes by his squadron. He said in part:

"We clocked up our millionth mile quite quietly. It happened the other night when we had a number of aircraft out over the North Sea. After they came back we logged up the mileage, and found we were well over the million mark. Incidentally, we've used up enough petrol in those million miles to send a fleet of 400 family cars right around the world.

"Our work is general reconnaissance —known in the Service as 'G. R.'—and we are a unit of the Coastal Command of the Royal Air Force. A reconnaissance really means going somewhere to see what is there. But while that is the essence of our job, there is actually a great deal more to it than that. For instance, we do a lot of bombing, and, when we run into enemy aircraft, we have to be fighters as well.

All Weather Job

"I'm not going to try to shoot a line about hair-raising exploits in which our squadron has played a part—not because we haven't had plenty, but because that would be putting such incidents in a false perspective. Our work is not spectacular in the main. It is hard, plodding routine of patrols. Every day, in sunshine, rain or snow, we go out over the North Sea to find out what's happening on the other side. And the data have been invaluable.

"In the early part of the war the squadron did a good deal of U-boat hunting. There was scarcely a pilot who had not had a crack at one or more, and our total bag of enemy submarines is quite impressive.

"Even if a U-boat sees us coming and crash-dives as fast as it can, it may still be within reach of our bombs. They are timed to explode beneath the surface of the sea. Then a shuddering and a disturbance of the water, and masses of dark brown oil coming up. These tell what has happened in the sea below. Other U-boats, which we caught by surprise on the surface, proved easy prey. Some of my pilots have seen their heavy bombs burst right on the hulls. Now, of course, there aren't so many U-boats about.

Used As Fighters

"—We have to look out for such hazards as enemy fighters patrolling the coast and anti-aircraft fire which is of an accuracy not to be sneezed at. It is on such occasions that we use our Hudsons as fighters. To match an aircraft built for reconnaissance work against a modern fighter is rather like putting a retired boxing champion against the newest holder of the title. The fighters have an advantage over us in speed, but we carry pretty useful armament, and our big aircraft can take an enormous amount of punishment.

"There's no doubt about it, our Hudsons are first-class aircraft for the job of reconnaissance. They have far more room in them than the average Service machine; indeed, there's the same internal space as in the civil counterpart, the Lockheed 14 airliner, in which some of you have probably flown before the war. There is a row of windows in each side of the cabin, a folding bed, hot and cold air regulator—in fact, every modern convenience. The seats, of course, have been taken out, and there is a gun turret in the tail.

Exceptional Performance

"The operational performance, too, is exceptionally good. The fact that we use these landplanes so much for long re-

(Continued on page 5)

WINGED, BUT STILL IN THE FIGHT

It's hard to believe, but the Hudson Bomber shown above, badly shot about as it was by German anti-aircraft fire, got itself and its crew home safely after a flight of several hundred miles from German occupied territory. R.A.F. flyers report that such feats are not unusual for Hudsons.

L.E.R.C. Calendar

Friday, March 21—Drama Club rehearses the play, "The Night of January 16," 7:30 p.m., 1141 N. Gower St., Hollywood.
Tour for Lockheed employees through the Los Angeles Times, 1:00 and 8:00 p.m., 5th Floor of Times Bldg.

Saturday and Sunday, March 22 and 23 — Lockheed Rangers, Doc's Stables, Roscoe, 4:00 p.m. Patrol leaders go on hike to Camp Verdugo. Leave 3:00 p.m. Saturday.

Sunday, March 23 — Baseball game, Lockheed vs. Twentieth Century Fox at Soldiers Home, Sawtelle, 2:00 p.m.
Pistol and Rifle Club will meet in Room 215 of the Personnel Bldg., 1:30 p.m.
Lockheed Rangers, Doc's Stables Roscoe, 8:00 a.m.
Model Club meeting, Room 215, Personnel Bldg., 2:00 p.m.
Drama Club rehearses the play, "The Night of January 16," 7:30 p.m., 1141 N. Gower St., Hollywood.

Monday, March 24—Choral Club Swimming Pool Bldg., Griffith Park, 7:30 p.m. and rehearsal, John Burroughs Junior High, Burbank, 7:30 p.m.

Tuesday, March 25—Drama Club rehearses the play, "The Night of January 16," 7:30 p.m., 1141 N. Gower St., Hollywood.

Tuesday and Wednesday, March 25 and 26 — Men's Bowling League, Burbank Alley, 7:00 p. m. and 9:00 p.m.

Tuesday, Thursday and Friday, March 25, 27 and 28—Men's Bowling League (Night Crew) Burbank Alleys, 12:00 noon.

Monday, Tuesday, Wednesday and Friday, March 24, 25, 26 and 28—Second Round, Inter-department Basketball Games, Burbank High School Gym, 7:00 to 10:00 p.m.

Thursday, March 27—Ski Club Meeting, 7:30, 1141 N. Gower St., Hollywood.
Camera Club Meeting, Burbank Library, 7:30 p.m. Speaker, Dr. Doran. Subject, Chemistry of Photography.

Friday, March 28—Meeting of the new troop of Majoretts, Doc's Stables, 7:00 p.m.

OPPORTUNITIES WIDE OPEN FOR FREE TRAINING

Need for ever increasing numbers of workers in defense industries has led the Lockheed Aircraft Corporation and its affiliate, the Vega Airplane Company, to urge their employees to acquaint members of their families or friends with the fact that training for the development of required skills is available at no cost to the trainees.

With such training acquired, jobs are plentiful and will become even more so in the future, not only in the aircraft industry but in every other industry affected by the National Defense Program.

The training plan, known as National Defense Pre-employment Training, works as follows: at the request and direction of the Federal Government, school districts throughout California are cooperating with the State Department of Employment and the state's industrial organizations in a coordinated program of pre-employment training.

A procedure has been adopted whereby applicants for employment who have no skill, or those needing refresher courses, will register with the State Department of Employment and upon selection will be assigned to shops where training will be given by the public school districts. The Department maintains offices in Glendale, Pasadena, Van Nuys, Los Angeles and other communities.

The training period varies from three to ten weeks, depending upon the type of training given and the aptitude of the individual. There is absolutely no cost to the trainee. Tools, equipment and supplies are being furnished by the Federal Government, the schools supplying space and instruction. At the present time classes in riveting, sheet metal work, machine shop, pattern and wood jig building, elementary tool and die making and aircraft detail assembly are being given.

Industrial organizations are lending invaluable assistance to the State Department of Employment by supplying information as to equipment and tools, types of work to be trained for, and coordination in placement after training. Instructors are being selected from among skilled men in industry recommended for their ability.

A meeting for the purpose of organizing a flying club will be held in Room 212, Lockheed Personnel Building, at 2 p.m. Sunday, it is announced by Jack Enright. All company employees interested in flying are urged to attend.

Main purpose of the club will be to cut the cost of flying for beginners.

L.E.R.C. Sport Shorts

Here is a swell opportunity for all of the Lockheed girls that like to go horseback riding. Those who would be interested in joining a troop called "The Majoretts," please contact Miss Graham in the Personnel Building. Those desiring to make this formation, please come to the meeting to be held at Doc's Stables for this purpose, March 28, at 7:00 p.m.

★

A tennis tournament is under way and will start around the first of April.

Everyone concerned in the previous tennis tournament last year was so busy, we did not have very good turn-outs, but this year we would like to have EVERYBODY, that possibly can, be conscientious about it and get your matches played off as soon as possible in order that we may start with the tournaments the first of next month.

★

A very good showing in the form of a large attendance will be needed at the next meeting of the Pistol and Rifle club says T. K. Formes, secretary.

The meeting will be held in room 215 of the Personnel building at 1:30 o'clock Sunday afternoon, March 23.

All present members and others interested in the shooting sport are invited to show their interest by showing up for this meeting.

Mattson Assigned To New York Office

M. V. Mattson has been assigned to the New York Office as Eastern Industrial Relations Representative of Lockheed and Vega. He will continue to function as a member of department 44 and take charge of eastern employment activities on the return to Burbank of Robert C. Storment. Meanwhile Mulvey White is in charge of the Lockheed-Vega Central Employment Service Department during the absence of Mr. Storment.

Vega Reports

The report of President Courtlandt S. Gross to Vega employees was distributed to the employees last Tuesday, March 18.

Those of the company's employees who wish complete copies of the President's report to Vega stockholders, highlights of which are given in this issue of the Star, may secure them by applying at the office of L. W. Wulfekuhler, assistant secretary, Room 260 in the Vega Administration Building.

THE HUDSON CAN "TAKE" IT

This is what sometimes happens when a fighting plane gets in the way of German ground fire. Few makes of planes other than the Hudson can take this kind of punishment and still reach the home airdrome. British fighter pilots are often amazed at the plane's ability to absorb punishment and still function.

(Continued from page 3)

connaissance over the sea speaks for itself. Nobody ever worries about engine failure, which used to cause so much anxiety in the last war. A typical remark was made by one of my pilots as he taxied in the other day after a long trip. He turned to his navigator and said, 'You'd think these blinking engines would go on turning over for ever.' "

The successful under-fire operations of these squadrons of Hudson reconnaissance bombers are not due alone to the ships themselves, but to the important factor of expert handling and maintenance of these planes by Royal Air Force pilots and crews.

Safety in National Defense

These are the days in which all loyal Americans are concerned about the defense of our country.

With a world at war we suddenly realize that forces are at work which threaten seriously the security and freedom of our American way of life.

To withstand those forces we must have not only wise and energetic public officials, but each one of us must accept the responsibility for that part of this national problem which comes within the scope of his personal life.

National defense and national safety are closely coordinated. How closely related they are may be seen when we interpret them as personal defense and personal safety. To contribute our part toward the security of our country and its people, we must exert ourselves to carry out all the principles of safety as completely as we can.

We must conserve man power. Our country needs the utmost of productive work from every individual. It cannot spare a single mechanic or truck driver, engineer or teacher, business man or public official, farmer or home maker through accidental injury.

We must increase our productive capacity through intensive training. We must avoid wastage of raw materials. We must conserve all our material and human resources. We MUST play SAFE all along the line!

V.E.R.C. Calendar

Sunday, March 23—Plant 2 Leaders Breakfast. 9:00 a.m., Riverside Breakfast Club.

Sunday, March 23—Golf Match with Northrop. 9:00 a.m., Fox Hills Golf Course. — Baseball Game, Double - Header, Solon Park; Opener, Vega Blues vs. East Pasadena Merchants; 2:30, Vega Club vs. Walker's Roofing. Mixed Doubles Bowling, Hollywood Recreation, 7:00 p.m.

Monday, March 24 — Orchestra practice, Burbank High, 7:00-9:00 p.m. Vega Girls' Chorus, Social Hall, Burbank High, 7:00-9:00 p.m.

Tuesday, March 25—Male Chorus, Griffith Park Bldg., 7:00 to 9:30 p.m. Little Theatre, Barnsdall Park, Olive Hill, 7:30-9:00 p.m.

Tuesday, March 25—Vega Male Chorus dinner at the California Hotel, Glendale, 7:30 p.m.

Wednesday, March 26 — Night Men's Bowling League, Burbank Bowl, 12 noon. Men's Bowling, Hollywood Recreation, 7:00p.m.

Thursday, March 27—Little Theater Group, Barnsdall Park, Olive Hill, 7:30-9:00 p.m. Orchestra Practice, Burbank High, 7:00-9:00 p.m.

Friday, March 28—Girls' Bowling, Sunset Recreation, 7:00 p.m.

Lockheed Executives

(Continued from page 1)

catching up on company work. Then this week-end he will hop for San Francisco where, starting Monday, he will take part in the Fourth Annual Industrial Relations Conference at Stanford University, where he will speak on problems of training in a rapidly expanding industry and will deal with both shipbuilding and airplane manufacturing.

Another Lockheed executive who may have his hands full between his functions for the company and governmental calls on his time is R. Randall Irwin, director of industrial relations, who was called to Washington to spend two days conferring with OPM heads early this week and who will join Mr. Pedersen at the Stanford Conference next week.

Mr. Irwin is scheduled to speak on the subject that he has made his specialty and on which he is recognized as an authority.

Letters Tell Of Life In "Hell's Corner" Of Britain

A member of the editorial staff of the Star recently received two letters from two relatives at present in England, a brother and a cousin. Both are residing in the "Hell's Corner" area of the south of England, one in Haslemere, Surrey, not far from the great Bramshott military camp of World War 1, the other in Sussex.

In the belief that first hand reports from the hottest of the British battle zones will be of interest to Star readers, and also in the belief that such reports are well calculated to impress us all with the vital need to keep war away from American shores, a few observations from the letters follow in quotes.

Incidentally, both letters were opened by English "examiners" and resealed, but unlike previous communications from the same writers, they were not heavily censored.

Confirming the lack of need for any more man power in the islands, one writer said: "At the moment it is not man so much as machine power that we are in need of . . . and if we get it in sufficient quantity, there is a good chance that this war will never reach American shores. You'd better hope it doesn't, for this new type of Hitler warfare is something no one ever dreamed of in even the most terrible nightmare.

Last War "Easy"

"You and I went through the last "do" and we know *that* was pretty bad; but there is really no comparison between this war and the last one, certainly not as far as civilians are concerned.

"It's a grim business, but you would be surprised to see how really cheerfully people are taking it. It is genuinely astounding what the human frame and brain can stand up to.

"I cannot give you . . . detailed information about bomb damages, etc., as we are asked to be careful what we write . . . but I can tell you that perhaps most of the places you knew so well during the last war are flat. It is incredible the terrific amount of damage that can be done in one night. It makes the last war seem as if we had been playing with penny balloons.

"So far the wife and I are alright although we have had several (bombs) plenty close enough and we live under the same strain, of course. This last seven or eight days (during the last lull in the luftwaffe strafing. Ed.) has seemed quite unreal, not having the planes buzzing over every few minutes at night. I really believe it is getting on peoples' nerves more than the raids do. It has given us a few nights back in bed, though, which is very acceptable after sleeping downstairs on the floor with a table over our heads for a month or two."

With regard to German invasion of the isles, the writer gave it as his opinion that this danger is becoming more real every day.

"There still are a number of people who think he (Hitler) will not try it, but it is my opinion that the more successes we have against him in other parts of the war, the more sure we make invasion of these islands. He has got to keep on having successes, and the one thing that would solve all his troubles would be the successful invasion of this country. And I think he is a big enough gambler to risk it. Still, we're here if he comes, and he's going to have a toughish job on his hands."

No Hunger

In the matter of food stuffs, both writers were positive in their statements that there is apparently an adequate supply of basic commodities reaching Great Britain, in spite of the German submarine and aerial blockade, and the population generally is in good health.

"You must not believe any propaganda about us starving over here," said one. "True, there are many things we can't get at all, and others that are hard to come by, but we're a long way from starving. The biggest "grouse" we've got here is, where the price is not controlled by the government, the profiteers get busy and the prices of some things are out of all reason. However, the government has taken adequate steps to cure these conditions as they arise."

In the case of one of the writers, this "grouse" loomed much larger in her mind than the fact that two nights before she wrote the letter a bomb had blown out all the back end of her home.

Drama Club Star Sings With Garber

Jean Brown, Department 26, star of the L.E.R.C. Drama Club's new show, "Night of January 16," accepted Jan Garber's gracious invitation to sing as guest artist with his famous orchestra at the L.E.R.C. dance held at the Casa Manana last Sunday evening.

Taking full advantage of the unexpected opportunity, the motion picture unit made several excellent shots of Jean with Mr. Garber.

VEGA REPORTS RECORD PLANT EXPANSION

(Continued from page 1)

still under construction at the Lockheed Air Terminal.

The extent of the growth in personnel, indicating the vital part the aircraft industry is playing in the employment situation in Southern California, is revealed in the fact that 1051 new employees were added to the company's payroll between December 31 and March 1 of this year. Company employees on the latter date totaled 4866 and this number is steadily increasing as new production units swing into action.

Inventories alone increased from $328,161 to $4,975,127, during the twelve-month period, the report showed, and this figure, based on average cost, was below market value.

Included in the company's $74,407,-192 backlog is $72,792,703, representing sub-contracts from Lockheed Aircraft Corporation, its affiliate, covering the firm's new Vega-Ventura Model 37 twin-engined bomber, now under construction and destined for Great Britain. In connection with the work to be done on these sub-contracts, Lockheed has advanced the company $10,197,262, the report discloses.

This loan has been made in accordance with an agreement between Vega and Lockheed by which Lockheed agreed to advance Vega funds in amounts substantially equivalent to the advances Lockheed receives from the British Purchasing Commission. It will automatically liquidate itself as the sub-contracts are completed.

Drama Tickets On Sale April 1

Due to the exceedingly favorable interest and already heavy advance reservations, tickets for the L.E.R.C. Drama Club's new show, "Night of January 16" will go on sale April 1, Frank C. Trumble, publicity director of the club announces. Employees wishing choice seats are urged to place their reservations early and should contact Bernie Koch, Extension 571, for further details.

The club also is looking for some one to do some poster and art work. Anyone interested should call Dick Walsh, Extension 1983.

Crockett And Holland Camera Club Stars

Camera Club Quarterly Salon was held March 13 at the Burbank Library. Doug Crockett walked off with first and second prize, while Rolly Holland trailed along with third. The judging was done by Ralph W. Browne, well-known portrait photographer.

RECORD DELIVERY MONTH—PAGE 3

THE Lockheed-Vega Star ★ ★

Vol. 8 BURBANK, CALIFORNIA, U.S.A., MAY 9, 1941 No. 19

"LOCKHEED ON 'ALL OUT' FOOTING!" PRES. GROSS

NEWSREEL MEN 'SHOOT' P-38

Left: Lineup of Lockheed Hudson bombers at test hangar. Below: P-38 cuts figure 8's for newsreels.

PUBLIC TO HAVE OPPORTUNITY TO SEE PLANE IN ACTION

Lockheed and all its humming activity will take a bow from the movie screens of America as the result of an enterprise which recently brought the cameras of all leading newsreel companies into the plant.

Through the courtesy of Lieut. Col. Frank Allen, Jr., of the U.S. Army's Bureau of Public Relations, permission was received for the newsreels and leading photo syndicates to enter the plant and photograph Lockheed planes and production.

Working in conjunction with our public relations department, the cameramen of Universal, Hearst Metrotone, Paramount, Pathe and Fox Movietone spent three days "covering" Lockheed. Photo syndicates represented included Acme, Wide World, Associated Press, International News and Life Magazine.

Highlights of the filming are expected to start appearing on the movie screens of the country sometime next week. An effort is being made to get exact dates on which Lockheed employees, who may be interested, may see the newsreels in local theaters.

NEW BUS SERVICE FROM HOLLYWOOD

As the outcome of a conference held recently in the office of the City Manager of the City of Burbank between Lynn Harrison, Lockheed and Vega traffic coordinator, and representatives of the several transportation companies of Southern California, a new and additional bus service for Lockheed and Vega employees has now been placed in operation.

This service will add 12 schedules in each direction every week-day over the following routes:

Leaving Hollywood Bus Depot, 1627 Cahuenga Blvd.
Cahuenga Blvd., to Barham Blvd.
Barham Blvd. to Olive Avenue.
Olive Avenue to Hollywood Way.
Hollywood Way to San Fernando Rd. (serving Vega).
San Fernando Rd. to Empire Avenue (serving Lockheed).
Empire Avenue to Hollywood Way.
Hollywood Way to Olive Avenue.
Olive Avenue to Barham Blvd.
Barham Blvd. to Cahuenga Blvd.
Cahuenga Blvd. to Hollywood Bus Depot.

Also as a result of the conference, which was sponsored by Lockheed and Vega, a reduced round trip and commu-

(Continued on Page 6)

10,000 Men Work On Night Shifts; Total Near 29,000

Responding to President Roosevelt's call to American industry to immediately embark on a 24-hour, seven-day a week schedule on the National Defense effort, President Robert E. Gross promptly pledged that Lockheed, in cooperation with its affiliate, Vega Airplane Company, would continue this policy which it had inaugurated in its plants some time ago.

Ten thousand men working on two night shifts have already added their efforts to the work of 19,000 day shift employees to maintain the 24-hour, seven day a week schedule, President Gross revealed, and this number is constantly being increased.

Mr. Gross declared that of the 28,930 employees of the two affiliated companies, 10,722 are on night duty. The day shift at the two companies consists of 18,208 men, ten thousand more than were working on all shifts at both companies one year ago.

"We are training men, and hiring trained men, just as fast as we can," said Mr. Gross. "We have more than 8,000 employees attending trade extension classes in the city schools of Burbank and nearby communities, and are hiring at the rate of more than 2,500 a month. In fact, in the month of April we hired 3,540 men.

"Lockheed is on an 'all-out' footing.

(Continued on Page 8)

Medico Issues Warning On Hot Spell Treatment

There have been a number of "casualties" in the plants during the current hot spell due to the taking of too many salt tablets, Dr. Seymour Dudley, of the Medical Service, reports.

To prevent this, he asks the personnel to remember that the taking of salt is not for cooling purposes. It is to replace salt lost from the system by perspiration, thus preventing heat prostration and sunstroke.

For best results, Dr. Dudley says, one-half tablet per half day is plenty.

L.E.R.C. CALENDAR

Saturday, May 10 — Lockheed Rangers, Doc's Stables, Roscoe, 5:00 p.m. to 7:00 p.m.

Saturday & Sunday, May 10 & 11 —Lockheed All-Stars and Lockheed No. 850 Bowling Teams will compete in the State Bowling League, Oakland, Calif.

Sunday, May 11—Rifle & Pistol Club Shoot, Pasadena Police Range, 9:00 a.m. to 5:00 p.m.

Skeet Shooting, Roaring Gulch Skeet Club, 9:00 a.m.-5:00 p.m. Aircraft Mounted Review, Riviera Country Club, 2:00 p.m.

Motion Picture Unit Shooting Service Committee, 10:00 a.m.

Motion Picture Second Unit Shooting Rangers.

Aircraft Mounted Review, Riviera Country Club, 2:00 p.m.

Monday, May 12—Band & Choral Club joint rehearsal, John Burroughs Junior High School, 7:30 p.m. sharp.

Wednesday, May 14 — Lockheed Rangers, Doc's Stables, Roscoe, 7:00 p.m. to 9:00 p.m.

Thursday, May 15—Motion Picture Production Meeting, 1141 North Gower Street, Hollywood, 8:00 p.m.
Lockheed Rangers (Nite Crew) Doc's Stables, Roscoe, 10:00 a.m. to 12:00 noon.

Thursday, May 15—Rangerettes, Doc's Stables, Roscoe, 7:00 to 9:00 p.m.

LEONARD HUNTRESS BACK FROM TRIP TO THE EAST

Leonard Huntress, Lockheed employee relations manager, returned Monday from a trip to the East coast.

Due to R. Randall Irwin's absence, he read a paper entitled, "Safety in the Aircraft Manufacturing Industry," before the Greater New York Safety Convention in New York City.

Managers of defense industry plants are becoming more conscious of the increased need for keeping employees continually on the job and consequently are devoting more emphasis to perpetual safety, he reports.

While East, Mr. Huntress visited various manufacturing and aircraft plants and he says that easterners generally feel we are practically in the war and take the war situation much more seriously.

He found immediate and widespread interest in every activity connected with Lockheed and Vega.

MANY LOCKHEED, VEGA 'ESSENTIAL' WORKERS DEFERRED

That armaments manufacture, in the present national emergency, is of importance equal to military service, has been frequently stressed by the government and press of late. Much comment has appeared on the danger of depriving industries engaged in the National Defense Program of skilled men engaged in the production of airplanes and other vital defense weapons.

For this reason it is of interest to note that the Selective Service Division of the Lockheed and Vega organization had written, up to April 26, approximately 3000 letters to Selective Service Boards requesting occupational deferments for employees.

According to a report by J. Caden Jenkins, in charge of this division, the companies have so far been notified that about 1500 of these employees have been granted deferment by their local boards as a result.

"We assume that nearly all of the others have been similarly deferred, but have not yet reported their classifications to us," said Mr. Jenkins.

Whenever a Selective Service registrant is deferred, he is under orders to report his classification to his employer, but the Selective Service office reports that "a terrific amount of difficulty is being experienced in getting the men to do this." It is pointed out in Mr. Jenkins' report that failure to comply with the boards' order may make it difficult, or bring a refusal to grant a request to apply for an extension of deferment upon expiration of the first period.

Therefore, in order to keep the records straight and up to date, and for his own protection, a Lockheed or Vega employee is urgently requested to get in touch with the Selective Service Division in the Industrial Relations Building, Lockheed plant, as soon as his deferment has been granted.

Company requests for deferment are limited to those men filling the classification of "essential" employees.

WESTERN FLIERS WILL MEET NEXT SUNDAY

Western Fliers, flying club organized by Lockheed employees, will hold its next meeting Sunday, May 11, at 1 p.m., in Room 215, Industrial Relations building, according to Charles Duley, one of the directors.

On the agenda will be discussion of initial membership fees and dues, and the cost per hour for flying.

The club is now awaiting approval of its incorporation papers in Sacramento.

V.E.R.C. CALENDAR

Sunday, May 11 — Flying Club, Group Breakfast Flight to Norconian Club, breakfast to be followed by swimming.

Baseball Game, Vega vs. Northrop at Santa Monica Municipal Stadium, 2:00 p.m.

Monday, May 12—Girls' Chorus, Michiel Marsman's home, 700 E. Lomita, Glendale, 7:30 p.m.

Tuesday, May 13—Male Chorus, Griffith Park Building, 7:00-9:00 p.m.

Wednesday, May 14 — Night Men's Bowling League, Burbank Bowl, 12 noon.

Men's Bowling, Hollywood Recreation, 7:00 p.m.

Thursday, May 15—Little Theatre Group, Barnsdall Park, Olive Hill, 7:30-9:30 p.m.

Friday, May 16—Riding Club Instruction Classes, Ride-A-While Stables, 7:00 p.m.

AIRMAIL CAMPAIGN GIVEN ENDORSEMENT

The campaign to stimulate the transportation of all first class mail by air, launched by Lockheed at the suggestion of President Robert E. Gross, has received strong impetus during the past two weeks, according to J. Caden Jenkins, sales promotion manager.

As the result of letters written by his department, Mr. Jenkins reports, more than 50,000 sheets of the stamps, which appear in all Lockheed advertising and which read "All First Class Mail By Air," have been requisitioned by various business and civic organizations wholeheartedly supporting the idea. The stamp also contains a picture of a Lockheed Lodestar.

The letters offering a free supply of the stamps went out to 250 leading business concerns throughout the country.

In times of national emergency the question of rapid communication is one of paramount importance and for this reason the campaign appears to have struck at a psychological time, Mr. Jenkins commented. He added a request that employees do not ask for these stamps as they are designed solely for the use of industrial and business organizations in connection with their own mailings.

"You are judged by the record you make, Not by your ability to make a record."

NEW RECORDS ON EMPLOYEE TOTAL, DELIVERIES

FABULOUS LOST MINE RE-DISCOVERED

Part of the crowd of Vega employees who participated in the search shown at jumping-off point in the Clipper Mountains. All members of the party and the V.E.R.C. will share in the proceeds of the mine.

WHAT STARTED AS GAG ENDS UP IN REAL GOLD FIND

When Vega employees went out on the desert to search for the Lost Dutch Oven Gold Mine, there were no straining oxen or covered wagons; instead the trip was made in swiftly moving automobiles and in airplanes. Preparations, which would have taken months in 1849, were made in hours and minutes in 1941. And the most amazing thing about the whole venture is that a mine was actually found.

The lowdown on the search for gold is that the expedition was really only an outing for the employees of the Vega Airplane Company. As planned, the searchers left Los Angeles after work on Friday night, April 25, in buses, automobiles and airplanes. Other amateur, but enthusiastic prospectors followed as their week's work at the aircraft factory was completed. All returned, according to schedule, Sunday afternoon and evening.

The search took place in the Clipper Mountains north of Danby, California. As searchers arrived at a camp established in advance by the Vega Employees Recreation Club, they were assigned to parties which were to cover specific areas throughout the territory where the Lost Dutch Oven Mine was said to be located. All through Saturday and Sunday

(Continued on Page 6)

R. C. STUNKEL HEADS NEW ASSOCIATION

Recognizing the need for coordinating their efforts and eliminating mutual service problems, a group of service engineers and managers met in Hollywood recently and formed an association of aircraft service men. The new body was officially named the "Aircraft Manufacturers Service Association."

Represented at the meeting were Lockheed, Douglas, North American, Harlow, Hughes, Ryan, Vega, B. G. Corporation, Bendix, Vultee, Pacific Airmotive, Aircraft Accessories, Northrop, Menasco, Pratt & Whitney and Wright.

Officers elected were: Reagan C. Stunkel, Lockheed, president; Otto Graff, Vega, vice-president; James B. Thompson, Vultee, secretary; Thomas Bond, North American, treasurer. Don Sprague of Douglas, Eddie Cooper of Bendix and James Misner of Hughes Aircraft were elected committeemen-at-large.

In general, it will be the aim of this association to afford a means of interchange of service information and to organize research into service problems. It is expected that the transactions of the organization will constitute a source of excellent design information from the maintenance point of view, as well as creating a source through which aircraft manufacturers may accumulate the latest information regarding maintenance policies and procedures of the Army, Navy and airline operators.

3,540 New Men Hired In April; Lead Continues

Illustrative of accelerating defense production in Southern California's aircraft industry, the Lockheed Aircraft Corporation in Burbank not only set a new employment record in April but also exceeded by three million dollars its best previous month in the dollar value of airplanes delivered.

According to figures made available today, the company built and delivered $12,150,000 worth of planes, exceeding the previous record of $9,100,000 established in March. These figures brought the total for the first four months of 1941 to $32,998,000, as compared to $44,000,000 for the entire year of 1940.

The company hired 3,540 men during the month, bringing the total employees of Lockheed and its affiliate, Vega Airplane Company, to 28,930. Of these, 23,488 were employed at Lockheed and 5,442 at Vega.

This record hiring placed the Lockheed and Vega organization as the largest employer in America of manpower used exclusively in the production of airplanes.

Proportions of the defense speed-up were indicated by the fact that in one single day 802 applicants for jobs were interviewed at Lockheed, and during one four-day period beginning April 26, a total of 645 men were hired and "cleared in" for work, according to B. W. Messer, director of employment at this plant. Lockheed is producing the P-38 interceptor pursuit plane for the United States Army Air Corps, and Great Britain, and the famous Hudson bomber for the Royal Air Force. Vega is rushing to completion its new $7,000,000 plant in which among others a new bomber, the Vega Ventura, will be built for the British.

SPEEDING AT AIR TERMINAL, COMPLAINT

The Air Terminal has made several complaints that Vega employees are exceeding the speed limit in and around the Terminal area between the hours of midnight and 1:00 a.m.

The most serious accidents often occur at night when traffic rules are ignored. The cooperation of Vega employees in eliminating this hazard, by strict observance of the speed limits posted at the airport entrance, is therefore requested.

AIRCRAFT MOUNTED REVIEW SCHEDULED FOR MAY 11 SHOW

The Lockheed Rangers, in conjunction with the North American Flying Horsemen and the Vultee Mounted Vanguards will present, May 11, at the Riviera Country Club, the "Aircraft Mounted Revue."

The program will start at 2 p.m. and will include several professional acts as well as specialty drill exhibitions by the three mounted groups. Leading among the professional acts will be the "Taxi-meter Mule," a trained animal comedy act declared to be the funniest ever presented.

Another well-known exhibition will be Miss Carol Henry and her highly trained horse "Sweetheart." This horse presents some of the most difficult tricks a horse can perform and has been booked on the stage throughout the Middle Western states and in Hawaii, as well as the San Francisco Shriners indoor circus, the Rose Bowl, and other noteworthy events.

There will be many other exciting events, including a relay race which will see a team of Lockheed horsemen race against teams from North American and Vultee.

Tickets are now on sale at the Canteen and from the Rangers. Ticket sales will be divided between the three companies and it is hoped that a good many Lockheed employees will be on hand to root home the Lockheed team.

The program will be completed with an All Star polo game, participated in by many well-known polo stars.

OPPORTUNITIES IN AIRCRAFT AT PEAK

Are you prepared for advancement?

Never before in history has the opportunity been as great for trade preparation as it is today. The Burbank schools and the National Defense have purchased and installed the very latest of equipment for your use in trade extension classes, in all trades of the aircraft industry.

Classes are held day and night for your convenience. Information as to subjects, time and locations may be obtained at the Education Department, 203 Industrial Relations Building, or at any school office in Burbank.

LOCKHEED RANGERS TO RIDE

Here are the boys who will give the crowd a thrill at the Riviera Country Club May 11 when the Aircraft Mounted Review will be presented. Left to right: Lieut. Claude Rucker, Lieut. F. A. Chafee, Capt. E. E. Thompson, Lieut. Arthur Sledge, and Lieut. Vern Arthur.

SPORT SHORTS

SKEET SHOOTERS MEET. As a result of the splendid response to calls for Skeet Shooters, the Lockheed Pistol and Rifle Club announces that a shoot will be held this Sunday at the Roaring Gulch Skeet Range between the hours of 9 a.m. and 5 p.m.

★

THE TIME LIMIT FOR ALL TENNIS MATCHES will be one week (from Sunday to Sunday). Applications will still be accepted for mixed doubles, men's doubles and women's singles.

When opponents are arranging for a match, kindly contact one another before each match, giving them your home telephone number and address as well as your Extension here at Lockheed.

★

THE LOCKHEED ALL-STARS and the Lockheed No. 850 Bowling Teams will leave to play in the State Bowling Tournament to be held at Oakland, California. Members of the respective teams are as follows:

Lockheed All-Stars	Lockheed No. 850
Ned Shaefer	Joe E. Brown
Jim Hogan	Dudley Browne
John Cadrobbi	Gordon Brown
Don Gaskill	Dick Wayman
Carl Nylander	Don Denoyer

Team members will roll in the team events in the Singles and the Doubles.

VEGA LITTLE THEATRE GROUP EXTENDS BID TO THOSE 'OUTSIDE'

The Vega Little Theatre Group *has* something, and they want to share it with other Vega employees!

Those who have not yet joined the ranks—or even attended a meeting—of this "uppen-comin" organization have promoted a feeling of deep compassion from those who have sampled the fruits of the Little Theatre.

Thursday night—once the voo-doo of the week—has become the red letter evening, the focal point of the entire week (recreationally speaking). Those who are either vaguely or actively interested in theatrical work have found these meetings a real boon to their dramatic instincts.

The fun of casting and rehearsing plays is followed up at each meeting by entertainment. At present, casting for a three-act comedy, as well as for two one-act plays, is in progress.

Now is the time for interested persons to avail themselves of the opportunity before the dramas are actually launched. Your husband, wife or sweetheart is cordially invited, too.

AIRCRAFT BLUEPRINT READING IS MOST POPULAR COURSE

Aircraft Blueprint reading is the most popular class in the Burbank Trade Extension Program, both in number of classes and students enrolled.

Because of the industry's recent growth and rapid development and the frequent changes in design and methods of fabrication and assembly, blueprints are used to a much greater extent by the workman than in most industries. Without the ability to interpret the information to be found on the blueprint, a man is severely handicapped both in his ability to do his daily work and in justifying advancement to greater responsibility.

The ability to read a blueprint involves two principal phases: (1) to interpret the lines and figures and visualize the shape of the part or the assembly, (2) to interpret the dimensions, notes and information with respect to fabricating operations, material, heat treatment and finishes.

The complete ability to read a blueprint means that the workman can take a blueprint, secure the material, have the operations made, inspect for workmanship after each operation, and carry the project out to completion.

It is also extremely important for him to be able to make freehand sketches for the benefit of those who are unable to interpret the blueprint. The ability to read a blueprint to the extent outlined makes it very likely that less skilled workmen will be assigned to his direction.

A remark frequently heard is, "I don't have to read blueprints; I never see any, why should I learn how?" If the truth were known, his inability to read them is recognized and he is never called upon to do so.

Blueprint reading classes are being conducted in Burbank, Glendale, North Hollywood and Van Nuys, to mention only those in the vicinity, all of them being conducted by instructors from the industry. Employees are urged to visit the classes and take advantage of this opportunity.

Funeral Services Held For Earl W. Brink

Funeral services for Earl Warren Brink of the Vega Airplane Company were held at 11 a.m. Tuesday, May 6, at the Sawtelle Chapel in the Veteran's Home at Wilshire and Sepulveda, in Sawtelle.

The company expresses condolences to his relatives.

AMERICAN AIRPLANE PRODUCTION HIT ALL-TIME RECORD IN APRIL

According to a United Press report from Washington this week, American airplane production reached an all-time high mark of 1493 for the month of April, as against a previous record output of 1216 for March.

Of the April total, informed sources said, only 78 planes of commercial type were manufactured and delivered. All the rest went to the United States Army, the United States Navy, British and other governments. The number that went to each branch of the armed services was not revealed.

Of the March output of 1216 planes, only 75 were of the commercial type. Of the total, 879 went to the United States Army and Navy and the British.

Following are United States aircraft production figures since last December: December, 799; January, 1036; February, 972; March, 1216; April, 1493.

OPM Director General William S. Knudsen said recently that the March production figures would be doubled by August 31.

VEGA COST DIVISION THROWS SURPRISE PARTY FOR CHIEF R. A. PEARSON

The cost division of the Vega Accounting Department surprised their boss, R. A. Pearson, with a surprise birthday party Tuesday, May 6, at Eaton's Rancho on Ventura boulevard, North Hollywood.

The group of 163 employees consisted of the Cost Division, Accounting Tabulating, Timekeeping, and special guests James J. Norton, chief accountant at Vega; A. J. Vanderschoot, assistant chief accountant; Jack Boyle of Lockheed, and C. M. Ferguson, and their wives.

Mr. Pearson was presented with a large birthday card made by two of the employees, inscribed with the names of all those who participated, and a fine black onyx pen set.

The esteem in which Mr. Pearson is held was evidenced by the enthusiasm of those present.

The theme of the birthday card and place cards was the cartoon "Jiminy Cricket," drawn by Victor Popiel and lettered by Paul Lee, both of the cost division.

The ceremony was presided over by O. C. Metter, supervisor of the cost division.

The committee in charge of arrangements included the following: M. B. Bates, Adele Miller, Eleanor Peterson, George Davies, Betty Meek and Gordon Palmer.

SAFETY ENGINEER'S WORK HELD VITAL TO DEFENSE SPEED

He neither designs bombers nor builds pursuit planes. Yet, in the aircraft factories of the nation his efforts are as vital to the success of America's vast defense program as the aeronautical engineer or the men who drive the rivets in the wings of swift new combat craft.

He is the safety engineer. His task is a many-sided one. He must direct a campaign of education. He must make certain all possible hazards are eliminated from a factory where thousands of workers and hundreds of machines are busy day and night. He must analyze each accident and devise methods of preventing its recurrence.

The fruits of his efforts are two-fold —protection of the lives and well-being of thousands of wage earners and increased production of the American airplanes which are vital to the safety of the world's democracies.

How efficiently this nationwide accident prevention work is progressing is disclosed by a survey just completed by the Aviation News Committee of the Aeronautical Chamber of Commerce.

The rate of exposure to accidents has risen sharply in airplane and engine plants, due to the rapid hiring of thousands of new employes, many of them unskilled or only semi-skilled in aircraft work. Yet the survey showed that the frequency of accidents in the same plants, instead of taking a corresponding rise, has decreased sharply.

The result has been that men who might otherwise have been laid up have been on the job—a substantial contribution to the tremendous acceleration of national defense production.

Future articles of this series will discuss the methods and results achieved in various plants now engaged in producing planes, engines and accessories for the United States and Great Britain.

Aircraft Beach Club In 48-Hour Barbecue

Setting an all-time record for barbecues, the Aircraft Beach Club is offering its facilities in a 48-hour barbecue to all L.E.R.C. members.

This new beach club is being opened by Hal Mars, formerly of Department 3 at Lockheed, and in making his offer to the L.E.R.C., Mars declares that all the attractions of the club will be available under a very nominal blanket charge.

The affair is scheduled for Saturday and Sunday, May 17 and 18.

WHAT STARTED AS GAG ENDS UP IN REAL GOLD FIND

(Continued from Page 3)

morning, parties were dispatched to the hills until the hunt took on the appearance of a major military operation. At one time, during the progress of the hunt, it was impossible to point out a mountain peak or a valley in which searching parties could not be seen.

Because of the rugged character of the country, the total area covered by the larger searching parties was perhaps no greater than 30 square miles. The locating of the Lost Dutch Oven Mine was accomplished by two men who were working independently of the main searching parties. These men, Mr. Eckel and Mr. Rollow, had been transported to the foothills in the farther reaches of the Clipper Mountains by automobile and had stumbled on to the lost mine on their return trip to camp.

Upon the return of the expedition to Los Angeles, it had not been definitely determined that the location found by Eckel and Rollow was actually the Lost Dutch Oven Mine, nor was it known that the ore samples taken from the mine were of any value.

After checking all accounts of the Lost

(Continued on Page 7)

NEW BUS SERVICE FROM HOLLYWOOD

(Continued from Page 1)

tation rate for the service is announced by the Asbury Rapid Transit System. The new round trip rate is 35 cents as against the previous rate of 45 cents; and the new commutation book, containing 12 one-way trips, sells for $1.70 as against the previous price of $2.10.

Information concerning the timetable and other fares can be obtained by calling Extension 1774, or at Window No. 8, Lockheed Industrial Relations building.

NEW REGULATIONS FOR SELECTIVE SERVICE MEN

J. Caden Jenkins announced today that new regulations have been promulgated by Selective Service headquarters which will affect all men called for service.

Instead of the usual five day notice prior to actual induction into the service, the Local Boards will hereafter give 10 days' notice and MAY extend the time in which the Selectee will report for service up to 60 days if the registrant can demonstrate that such delay is necessary to prevent great personal hardship.

Mr. Jenkins has been advised unofficially that the Local Boards must now complete the classification of all remaining registrants as rapidly as possible. It is suggested that as soon as any Lockheed or Vega employee gets his questionnaire, he contact his Employee Relations Department WITHOUT DELAY, as any statement requesting deferment for occupational reasons must accompany the questionnaire.

Bowling Dinner Dance For All Lockheedians

All Lockheed personnel will have an opportunity to obtain tickets to the annual Bowling Dinner-Dance scheduled at Casa Manana, Sunday evening, June 1, according to word from the committee in charge of the celebration.

"Last year many bowlers were unable to obtain tickets to this annual party, so we made tickets available to bowlers first this year," J. E. Brown states. "Now that all bowlers have had first chance at the tickets, all Lockheedians will be given an opportunity to attend the dance."

Reservations will be taken care of in rotation with tickets available through the L.E.R.C. office and the ticket sales booth at Gate 11.

SAYS AIR INDUSTRY PROGRESS 'MIRACLE'

Progress made by the American aircraft industry is "nothing short of a miracle," in the opinion of Merrill C. Meigs, chief of the aircraft section of the Office of Production Management.

In California on an inspection tour of airplane factories, Mr. Meigs pointed out that it took 25 years to develop the American automobile industry.

"It is nothing short of a miracle," he said, "that the airplane industry has risen almost fully-winged in so short a time. We in America have raised aircraft production to above 1000 planes a month—more than Britain was able to do after months of war—and we're moving faster and faster along the assembly lines."

Mr. Meigs was equally enthusiastic about the quality of American warplanes, declaring:

"I wish to state with emphasis that the present American combat planes are not only equal, but better, than any European aircraft and that airplanes now in production—in the hands of trained American pilots—will outfly and outperform any aircraft that has ever been built in all the world."

In the matter of aircraft engines, Mr. Meigs pointed out that the major manufacturers had increased their output over January of last year by 29 per cent.

"American industry has not lagged," he continued. "It has not slumped and is not failing to meet the challenge. This conflict will be fought and won by airplanes; and the victor will be the nation which has the best, the swiftest and the strongest. If freedom is to survive in the world, we must be that nation."

LIBRARY LISTS NEW BOOKS FOR STUDENTS

New Technical Books in Library:

A.B.C. of Aviation $1.93
Aircraft and Engine Mechanics Manual 2.40
Aircraft Hydraulic System 2.53
Aircraft Inspection Methods .... .99
Aircraft Radio and Electrical Equipment 3.43

All of the above books are available for circulation or purchase. Purchase may be made by cash or by payroll deduction.

Book of the Week:

Airplane Blueprint Reading by Alex Robson .... $ .95

A basic textbook for the airplane sheet metal worker, machinist, tool and die-maker, patternmaker, loftsman, draftsman, engineer, and inspector.

"You are judged by the record you make, Not by your ability to make a record."

REGISTER YOUR BOAT NOW

Here's where Lockheed boatmen get the low-down on each other. The Lockheed "Aircraftsman" has offered to further their activities by publishing a list of Lockheed-owned boats in the June issue.

Now, of course, this Yacht Register won't be complete unless YOUR boat is listed too. So fill out this blank and give it to your departmental L.E.R.C. representative, or mail it direct to the L.E.R.C. office. Deadline for the "Aircraftsman" is near, so don't delay!

BOAT OWNER'S QUESTIONNAIRE

Name........................ Dept........................

Address........................ Home Telephone........................

Name of Boat........................ Type........................

Length................ Beam................ Draft................

Sail Area........................ Engine........................

Designer........................ Builder........................

Where do you do your boating?........................

FUTURE ENGINEERS GET POINTERS

Engineer Instructor G. W. Papen, 2nd, of Lockheed, previews an engineering course with a few of his students.

OVER 400 ENGINEERS ENROLL IN CLASSES

Going full-blast and nearing the home stretch are some fourteen University Extension Classes for engineers. These classes are being given under the Engineering Defense Training Program, financed by a federal appropriation.

Supervision is maintained by the Mechanical Engineering Department of the University of California through the University Extension Division. E. D. Kane of the university is here from Berkeley as coordinator.

Most of the instructors are top-notch men from our own Engineering Department. Ten of the classes are being held in classrooms in the Industrial Relations Building. Over 400 engineers from Lockheed and Vega are enrolled.

Such subjects as Fabrication and Assembly Methods, Materials and Processes, Power Plant Installation, Structures, Hydraulics, Electrical Design, and Design Sketching are offered.

Present classes will end in June. It is expected that new courses will begin some time in August.

WHAT STARTED AS GAG ENDS UP IN REAL GOLD FIND

(Continued from Page 6)

Dutch Oven Mine, leaders of the expedition became convinced that the Eckel-Rollow discovery was actually the fabled lost mine, and it was decided to have assays run on the ore. All of this was done without any excitement or any actual expectation that the ore would prove valuable. When the assayer's report was made public, the members of the expedition were completely dumbfounded and greatly elated.

When the trip was originally planned, every precaution was taken to see that all of those taking part in the search would receive an equal share in any find that was made. Each participant in the Lost Dutch Oven Mine venture will receive one share in the ownership of the mine. The total number of shares which were issued is equal to the total number of participants plus five shares. These five shares will go to the Vega Employees Recreation Club.

"Jack has given up smoking."
"How did he manage it?"
"Knocked out his pipe on a gasoline pump."

EX-EMPLOYEE TELLS PRIDE IN FORMER LOCKHEED ASSOCIATES

It is not often that an individual who has worked for an organization and who has severed his connection with it, voluntarily takes pen in hand to express to that organization his appreciation of the treatment he received.

For this reason the following letter from Richard P. O'Meara, former Lockheed employee now with Cal-Aero Academy, Oxnard, to Gil Causey of Lockheed, is worth quoting for the light it sheds on the harmony of Lockheed employer-employee relations and the pride former employees continue to take in the company and its achievements.

Dated Wednesday, April 30, 1941, O'Meara's letter says:

"I can't say how much I really appreciate the fine and gentlemanly way I was treated while an employee at Lockheed. Never before have I seen a group of men gathered from all parts of the country, from all walks of life, assemble under one roof and work with such cooperative spirit towards one objective —namely, to build the best in their line.

"Their workmanship is exemplified in the fine planes they build. All take a personal pride in Lockheed's leadership.

"We (the Academy) are preparing our Cadet Magazine for next month and the fellows would like a personal interest story about the progress and building of the P-38 in it. Could you give me a few highlights on the P-38 as to the trouble and time taken to make this plane? I'm sure some of the engineers slept in it while it was in the experimental stage.

"The men up here want to hear about them and are very anxious to give space in their new magazine for such news. I'll send you our first copy."

It is this kind of personal interest on the part of Lockheed and ex-Lockheed men that has helped spread the fame of the company and its products throughout the land.

WRIGHT AERONAUTICAL IN RECORD OUTPUT

Reflecting the production advances reported throughout the aeronautical industry, a record monthly high in the output of Cyclone and Whirlwind aircraft engines—a total of 1,430,000 horsepower during March—was announced recently by Guy W. Vaughan, president of Wright Aeronautical Corp.

The March production represents a 23 per cent increase over January, 1941, and a 500 per cent increase over September, 1939, when the European war began.

"You are judged by the record you make, Not by your ability to make a record."

THE Lockheed-Vega Star

The LOCKHEED-VEGA STAR is issued every Friday for the employees of the Lockheed Aircraft Corporation and the Vega Airplane Company. Communications may be addressed to either the Industrial Relations Office or the Public Relations Department, Lockheed Aircraft Corporation, Burbank, California. U.S.A.

H. L. (Hal) Rosson, Editor

Volume 8 Number 19

Service Assistance Asked

The following appeal is made to all Lockheed Foremen by C. R. R. "Buck" Hadley, chairman of the Service Committee:

To All Lockheed Foremen:

On behalf of the L.E.R.C. Service Committee may I ask for your wholehearted cooperation in the matter of reporting all cases of sickness and accident in your several departments in order that we of the Committee may be enabled to do our part in the alleviation of distress on the part of our unfortunate fellow employees.

Our employee enrollment is getting so large that a great deal of call is made upon us in aiding some cases who find themselves in poor financial state at time of illness or accident. Many times we of the Service Committee are not informed of cases until too late to be of any service. In case of deaths in the family it is our custom to send a wreath for the funeral. In a number of instances of late we have not had any knowledge of some of the funerals until after all was over. On occasion we have fellow employees at home ill for some time before we are aware of their condition. That means very often that these people are unable to have certain things needed for their betterment and their recovery is delayed. Again, they ofttimes are deeply worried while on the job and that worry is reflected in their work. You, as foremen, feel the loss of your employee in the matter of lost time and results obtained from their work.

I ask that you arrange some way in your department whereby someone, probably the personnel clerk, would advise the Service Committee of an absence or known illness or accident of any employee under your supervision. With this knowledge we of the Committee will be able to go ahead and find out if there is any need of our help. We find that in most cases a little loan of a few dollars at such a time is of great help. It is our province to provide such help. Without your aid and cooperation we are unable to function properly.

May I ask that you consider this matter seriously and direct all information to Buck Hadley, 2231-2, Frank Arrico, 1316, or to Head Nurse, Miss Davidson at 1185. Or Lew Large, 1234, Miss Eleanor Clark, 2112, Verna Mae Tinker, 364 or Dan Dunning, 1155.

Sincerely,

C. R. R. "Buck" Hadley,

Chairman, Service Committee.

"LOOK BEFORE YOU SIGN" SAYS BETTER BUSINESS BUREAU

Latest bulletin of the Better Business Bureal of Los Angeles to appear on company bulletin boards advises "Before You Sign, Examine Carefully!"

Pointing out that it's too late to change your mind after you have signed, the Bureau says that many people sign up for various purchases without realizing the seriousness of their act.

"They believe it is easy to have the contract cancelled or to discontinue payments and surrender the property, if they change their mind," the bulletin states. "It is not quite so simple.

Double Charge For Parking Forbidden

L. O. Holter, manager of employee relations for Vega, calls to the attention of Vega employees the fact that when they pay a parking fee on Vega employee lots, they are entitled to leave and return to the same lot as many times as they wish during the day, as long as they retain the check stub handed them as they pay their fee on first entering.

There have been complaints from employees who use their cars during the noon period that they have been required to pay two fees. This is contrary to the company arrangement and should not be tolerated.

10,000 MEN WORK ON NIGHT SHIFTS; TOTAL NEARS 29,000

(Continued from Page 1)

We are driving toward our objective of filling out our complement of personnel to three full shifts working 24 hours a day on military aircraft for the United States Army Air Corps and the British Royal Air Force."

AVIATION MEETING GETS WARNING ON SECURITY THREAT

WICHITA, Kans., — "So long as there is a single German or Italian transport plane, pilot, ground crewman or trace of German financial interest in any commercial or civil aviation activity in the Western Hemisphere, we face a threat to our security that is little less dangerous than the German air raiders over London!"

The Southwest Aviation Conference heard this warning from Irving H. Taylor, manager of the Trade Development Department of the Aeronautical Chamber of Commerce of America.

Mr. Taylor told how German and Italian airlines are, without economic justification, operating and maintaining ground establishments over almost 22,000 miles of strategically located routes in South America.

Calling that situation "the greatest threat to the Americas," Mr. Taylor proposed unstinted United States assistance to Latin American airline development, urging that:

(1) Our Government recognize the necessity of providing against further aviation aggression by the Axis; (2) U.S. airline operators cooperate freely in advancing aviation throughout the hemisphere; (3) Manufacturers be granted encouragement and authority by the Government to produce advanced types of transport planes which will assure commercial air supremacy; (4) There be ample production of light airplanes for air transport and pilot training needs.

New Insurance Schedule In Effect

Because of numerous requests for additional coverage, the Lockheed and Vega group insurance contract has been amended and the following schedule placed in effect as of today:

Class	Weekly Wage	Life	Acc. D. & D.	A. & S. Wkly. Ben.	Hosp. Surg. Med. Reimb.	Empl. Wkly. Cost
B	Less than $28	$1000	$1000	$15	Same	.74
C	$28 but less than $34	1500	1500	20	"	.90
D	$34 but less than $45	2000	2000	25	"	1.06
E	Over $45	3000	3000	30	"	1.29
F	Executives	5000	5000	30	"	1.48

From this schedule you will note that Class "A" insurance is no longer available. Employees now carrying this class may continue to do so, but no new insurance will be written under this classification.

The regular procedure for increasing insurance classification will be followed in putting this schedule into effect. All employees eligible for a higher classification will be notified and given the opportunity to sign a waiver of the increase if they wish to maintain their present coverage. If a waiver is not signed, the increase will be made automatically.

In accordance with our insurance contract, increases become effective on the first day of the calendar month, providing the employee is actively at work on that date; otherwise, they become effective on the day the employee returns to work.

Interpretation of the above schedule will be gladly given by the Insurance Division of the Employee Relations Department.

LORD HALIFAX 'HITS A HOMER'

Volume 8 BURBANK, CALIFORNIA, U.S.A., JULY 18, 1941 No. 30

THE *Lockheed-Vega Star* ★ ★

36,000 GIVE "THUMBS UP" TO ENVOY

Top view shows the assembly of Lockheed workers who welcomed Lord Halifax yesterday when he voiced the thanks of the British Empire for the magnificent aid given by Lockheed and Vega to her fighting forces. At right, scene in the Vega Final Assembly building as the British Ambassador greeted Vega Plant 1, Vega Plant 2, and Lockheed Plant 3 employees.

Cheers Of Vega, Lockheed Men Heard By World

The 1000th Hudson bomber, a favorite of the British Royal Air Force, roared up and away from the Lockheed Burbank plant yesterday with a Godspeed from Lord and Lady Halifax.

While over 20,000 aircraft workers cheered the take-off, the British Ambassador and his Lady waved good luck as the plane began winging its way on the long flight that will end with a hop across the north Atlantic. At the controls at the takeoff was Jimmie Mattern, famous round-the-world flier who has been for many years a Lockheed test pilot.

The event was a highlight of the first visit of the British Ambassador to the Pacific Coast, timed to receive the thousandth Hudson from the assembly line. Lord and Lady Halifax arrived in Cal-

(Continued on Page 7)

STABILIZATION OF WAGES PROGRESSES

The meeting of aircraft manufacturers to discuss wage stabilization was concluded last week in Washington, D.C. Representatives of all of the major aircraft plants in Southern California had met at the request of the OPM, along with the manufacturers from the East and Middle West, to determine some program of wage stabilization.

The aircraft manufacturers of Southern California in meeting with the OPM, Army and Navy, agreed that they would "Actively support a regional labor wage stabilization program calculated to issue maximum and uninterrupted aircraft production for national defense, if the government approves the program and makes it economically possible."

As a result of this meeting, the Southern California aircraft manufacturers have started local meetings to work out a program for the Southern California region.

Before the stabilization group convened in Washington, Robert E. Gross, president of Lockheed, and Courtlandt S. Gross, president of Vega, assured Aeronautical Lodge 727 that Lockheed and Vega employees would benefit with employees of other aircraft companies and promised that certain

(Continued on Page 8)

L.E.R.C. CALENDAR

Saturday, July 19 — Boy Scouts Camping until Thursday, Big Tujunga.

Sunday, July 20 — Golf Tournament, Woodland Hills, Ventura Blvd., near Girard.

Motion Picture Unit shooting Golf Tournament and Tennis sequence.

Lockheed All-Star Baseball team vs. 20th Century Fox, Soldiers' Home, Sawtelle, 2 p.m.

Lockheed Rangers Drill team, 7 a.m. to 9 a.m., Doc's Stables, Roscoe.

Monday, July 21—Band Rehearsal, John Burroughs Junior High, Burbank, 7:30 p.m.

Tuesday, July 22—Lockheed Girls' Softball practice, John Muir Junior High, 5 p.m.

Wednesday, July 23—Choral Club Rehearsal, Social Room, Burbank Senior High School, 7:30 p.m.

Lockheed Rangers, Doc's Stables, Roscoe, 7 p.m. to 9 p.m.

Lockheed All-Star Softball practice, 7:30 p.m., Burbank Civic Park.

Regular Boy Scout meeting, 1935 Brighton, Burbank, 7 p.m. to 9 p.m.

Thursday, July 24—Camera Club, Lecture and Shooting, James N. Doolittle Studio, 1045 South La Cienega, Los Angeles, 7:30 p.m. Bring your cameras.

Roller Skating Club, Shrine Roller Rink, 32nd & Figueroa, Los Angeles, 6:30 p.m.

Lockheed Rangers (Nite Crew) Doc's Stables, Roscoe, 10 a.m. to 12 noon.

Rangerettes, Doc's Stables, Roscoe, 7 to 9 p.m.

ALL-LOCKHEED GOLF TOURNEY NEXT SUNDAY

Don't forget the All-Lockheed Golf Tournament next Sunday morning at Woodland Hills Golf Club. A few starting times are still available, phone 1901.

A prize for everyone and a good time for all will be the theme of the day, according to I. J. Baldaseroni, golf chairman. Woodland Hills boasts a splendid swimming pool and ample 19th hole facilities.

All entries are reminded to pick up their tickets 15 minutes in advance of starting time. *Please be on time!*

TICKET TUSSLE

Joe Lenz, Dept. 10 foreman, and Ray Buckminster, Superintendent of Dept. 10, stage an informal tussle over the first of the ducats for the First Annual Picnic being staged for the 6000 members of the department at Pop's Willow Lake, Sunday, July 27. An extensive program of athletic events, a dance, a gigantic barbecue and motion pictures will highlight the day-long celebration.

V.E.R.C. GOLF TOURNEY TO BE HELD AUGUST 3

The V.E.R.C. Golf Tournament will be held Sunday, August 3, at the Woodland Hills Golf Club, Girard. This club may be reached by driving out Ventura boulevard to Canoga avenue (approximately three blocks this side of the city of Girard) and turning left. The club is about one and a half miles from Ventura boulevard.

Those wishing definite reserved starting times should report their reservations to the V.E.R.C. office not later than August 1. The tournament will be held on a blind hole handicap basis. Three holes in each nine will be selected by the "Pro" at the golf course and put in a sealed envelope, and each player's handicap will be figured from the score he turns in on these particular holes.

Prizes will be given for the following events:

1. Low Medal Score.
2. Runner-up for Low Medal Score.
3. Low Handicap Score.
4. Runner-up for Low Handicap Score.
5. Blind Bogey winner.

There will also be prizes awarded for accuracy in driving and approaching.

The V.E.R.C. will have reserved starting times starting at 7 a.m. and lasting until late afternoon. GREEN FEES WILL BE $1.00. It will be necessary that all participants register at the starting tee with the V.E.R.C. representative. Those who do not register will not be eligible for any prizes.

In addition to the golf tournament, all entrants are invited to bring their families. A swimming pool, picnic grounds and clubhouse facilities will also be available. Come and bring your family and make it an all-day outing.

V.E.R.C. CALENDAR

Sunday, July 20—Ice Skating Club, Special meeting for Election of Officers to be held Sunday morning at 9:30 a.m., Pan Pacific Ice Rink. Ice skating for all to follow meeting. All employees who are interested in ice skating are invited to join by attending this meeting.

Baseball Game—Vega vs. Kenedome Wildcats at Salon Park, Burbank, 2:30 p.m.

Monday, July 21—Girls' Chorus, Michiel Marsman's home, 700 E. Lomita, Glendale, 7:30 p.m. Riding Club Instruction Class, Ride-A-While Stables, 7-8:30 p.m.

Mixed Doubles Bowling League, Hollywood Recreation, 7 p.m.

Tuesday, July 22—Male Chorus, Griffith Park building, 7:30 to 9 p.m.

Rifle & Pistol Practice, Glendale Rifle & Revolver Range, 7:30 p.m.

Girls' Bowling League, Hollywood Recreation, 7 p.m.

Softball Game, Playground League, Vega Blues vs. Newsboys Local No. 75, Echo Park, 9 p.m.

Wednesday, July 23—Vega-Lockheed Night Men's Bowling, Burbank Bowl, 12:30 p.m.

Men's Bowling League, Hollywood Recreation, 2 sections: 1st section, 6:45 p.m.; 2nd section, 9 p.m.

Ice Skating Club, Weekly meeting, 8:30 p.m., Pan Pacific Ice Rink. Ice skating before and after meeting.

Thursday, July 24—Little Theatre Group, Barnsdall Park, Olive Hill, 7:30-9:30 p.m.

Friday, July 25 — Riding Club, Drill team practice, 7:30-9 p.m., Trail Ride, 7-9 p.m., for those who wish straight riding from Ride-A-While Stables, Burbank, with business meeting at 9 p.m.

L.E.R.C. Offers Cut Rate Golf Practice

Special arrangements concluded between the L.E.R.C. and Golfer's Paradise, driving range at Hollywood Way and Victory boulevard, Burbank, offer L.E.R.C. members special night rates on both instruction and driving practice, according to an announcement from the L.E.R.C. office.

KNUDSEN VOICES PRAISE OF AIRCRAFTSMEN

O. P. M. CHIEF SEES P-38 A-BUILDING

William S. Knudsen, chief of the Office of Production Management, is here shown watching man at work on the nascelle of a P-38 Lightning during his visit to the Lockheed and Vega plants last Tuesday. Left to right, facing the camera, are Thomas H. Corpe, assistant general sales manager, Lockheed; Richard A. Von Hake, vice-president in charge of manufacture, Lockheed; Major General George H. Brett; Mr. Knudsen.

FIRST SUPERVISORY CONFERENCES HELD

The first of a continuing series of Supervisory conferences was held last week for foremen at Vega Plant 1. This was followed by a conference for Lockheed foremen, while a third conference group for Plant 2 foremen of Vega met last Monday.

Added to these three initial groups will be others consisting of assistant foremen and supervisors. They will be organized just as soon as space can be arranged for the holding of the conferences.

While the subjects to be discussed as these conferences progress will cover many problems of supervision, the opening conferences are being devoted to the improvement of the apprenticeship program now in operation at Lockheed and Vega. One of the aims of these conferences is to prepare the foremen so that they can in turn conduct similar meetings with their assistants and sub-leaders.

AEROQUIZ

Q.—What part of an airplane is designated as the empennage?

A.—Empennage (French) is the collective name for the entire tail group, or tail assembly, of an airplane.

VEGA FAMILIES TO PICNIC AT CATALINA

An excursion to Catalina for all Vega employees will be held over the week-end of August 9-10.

Featured this "Vega" week-end will be the baseball games between Vega and the Catalina Cubs baseball team, the first Saturday afternoon and the second Sunday morning.

Round-trip transportation from Wilmington, through the medium of this excursion, special price $2.50. Accommodations can be had in the rear section of the Villa Park Beacon at the rate of $2.25 for one or two persons.

For further information please contact the V.E.R.C. office, Extensions 356 and 357.

LOCKHEED BALL TEAM BEATS NORTH AMERICAN

Tuesday night Lockheed beat North American by a score of 2 to 1. Bridgens pitched four-hit ball, and Red Ramsey drove in the winning run in the eighth inning.

The second State Tournament game will be played Sunday evening at Torrance, at 8 o'clock, against Kelman Electric.

Impressed By Speed, Efficiency At Lockheed, Vega

Whatever doubts William S. Knudsen, chief of the Office of Production Management, may have had regarding America's ability to arm herself effectively and in time for all-out National Defense, were largely dispelled Tuesday by what he saw on his inspection trip through the great Lockheed and Vega plants, where more than 20,000 men are at work on the day shift alone.

Escorted by Robert E. Gross and Courtlandt S. Gross, presidents respectively of Lockheed and Vega, and by Cyril Chappellet, secretary, Richard A. Von Hake, vice-president in charge of manufacture, Thomas S. Corpe, assistant sales manager of the two companies, and Ken Smith, of the Sales Department, Mr. Knudsen was deeply impressed by the activity and efficiency in production which he saw all about him.

He praised the record speed with which Lockheed had got into production on the famed Hudson bomber for Great Britain, the 1000th of which will be dispatched to that embattled island Thursday; and he whistled appreciatively as the P-38 Lightning, world's fastest airplane, shot overhead in a routine test flight, stood on its tail in a sensational climb and disappeared before the roar of its twin engines had died away.

But it was the long production line of the P-38, now being turned out in increasing numbers for the U.S. Army Air Corps and the British Royal Air Force, which caused him the greatest amazement. This plane was only in its cradle when the O.P.M. chief visited Los Angeles last year.

There was much talk of production quotas—2,000 planes a month by the end of the year throughout the country as a whole; 3,700 planes a month by September of 1942. But chiefly Knudsen talked of the men who build the planes.

"The greatest contribution the American aircraft worker can make to the national defense program is to give his job everything he's got," Knudsen declared. "I believe he is doing exactly that. With the workman doing his part, America can make more planes and better planes than any other nation on earth!

"The manner in which the aircraft

(Continued on page 6)

LIBRARY OFFERS BOOK SUGGESTIONS

New books recently received include the following titles:

How to Teach a Job	$1.35
Managerial Control	4.10
Machine Woodworking	2.49
Materials of Aircraft Construction	4.05
Graphic Routes to Greater Profits	2.05
Oxyacetylene and Arc Welding	4.55

There are still a few copies of the following specials available:

Winged Warfare	$2.45
Fortune—March issue	2.00
Roget's Thesaurus	.65
Lightplane Flying	1.98
Air Navigation	4.05
Die Design and Die Making Practice	4.85
The Engineers' Manual	2.25

Suggested library selections for toolmakers:

Die Design and Die Making Practice	$4.85
Tool Making, by Cole	2.45
Jigs and Fixtures	2.85
Jig and Fixture Design	2.45
Die Design Manual	2.35
Punches and Dies	3.25
Tool Engineering	2.45

Copies of the Library book-list may still be obtained by those who wish to have a complete, classified list of all the volumes.

A Word TO THE WISE—

TODAY'S REAL BATTLE

•

Conservation and Safety against Waste and Carelessness

Division of MATERIAL CONSERVATION

FIGURES REVEAL PAYROLL SPURT

The rapid growth of Lockheed and Vega personnel is revealed in figures released this week by officials of the Personnel Departments of both companies.

These show that Lockheed, as of January 2, 1941, had 16,588 on the payroll; on July 10, 30,080. Vega, January 2, had 3818; on July 10, 6796 giving a total payroll for the two affiliated companies as of July 10, 36,876, largest in America employed solely on aircraft production.

These figures show almost identical percentages of increase, and follow plant enlargements in both companies to take care of increasing demands for National Defense.

VIEW FROM SPEAKER'S STAND

Looking out from speaker's stand, Lord Halifax is shown as he voiced his message of appreciation to thousands of Lockheed workers at Plant 1, Thursday, for the vital aid Lockheed and Vega have given the R.A.F. in the Empire's battle for democracy.

SPORT SHORTS

NOTICE TO RANGERS & RANGERETTES. Regular riding time for the Rangers Drill team is 7 a.m. to 9 a.m. Sundays, Doc's Stables, Roscoe. For the Lockheed Rangers it is 7 p.m. to 9 p.m. on Wednesdays, and for the Rangerettes on Thursdays from 7 to 9 p.m.

* * *

THE MOTION PICTURE MEETING JULY 26. The regular July party meeting of the Dramatic group will be held July 26 at the Hollywood headquarters at 8 p.m. At that time full plans and schedules for the next production, "Room Service," will be announced. Charlie Bell, chairman of the advisory committee, is in charge for the casting of this production. All members of the Dramatic group who are planning to participate in the party meeting should send an ANVO to Dick Walsh this week, so that the program can be drawn up. Material may be in the form of scenes, pantomime or sketches.

* * *

ATTENTION! PAN PACIFIC SKATING FANS. Club Sessions will be held each week through the summer season with the same prices as were in effect last winter. Admission from *6 p.m. until 7 p.m., 45¢;* after 7 p.m. the regular evening rate of 55¢ will prevail; skates rental 25c, figure skates 35c. This admission entitles you to remain over for the evening session from 8 p.m. until 11 p.m. without further charge.

* * *

NOTICE TO WRESTLERS AND BOXERS on night shift! The gymnasium at Jeffries' Barn will be opened every day from 12:30 noon to 5:30 p.m., with the exception of Thursdays and Sundays. Shower facilities will be available.

"Hopped-Up" Cars Held Lawbreakers

It has been called to the attention of the Lockheed management by the office of the Chief of Police of Los Angeles, that "hopped-up" automobiles bearing out-of-state licenses and Lockheed emblems, are in many cases being driven recklessly and without regard to speed and traffic laws.

Besides being dangerous to both the drivers and the public, this constitutes an unfair reflection on the company.

In his letter of complaint, Deputy Chief of Police B. R. Caldwell asks for the cooperation of all Lockheed and Vega employees in observing local and state traffic rules.

LOCKHEED 6-MONTH OUTPUT TOPS ALL 1940

IMPRESSIVE SCENE AT VEGA

A section of the audience at Vega who greeted Lord and Lady Halifax on the occasion of their visit of inspection.

ATTENTION CALLED TO SECRECY PACT

A recent communication from Lieut. Colonel Chas. E. Branshaw, Air Corps Western District Supervisor, to the Vega Airplane Company, again calls attention to the need for strict compliance of all persons engaged in National Defense industries with the Secrecy Agreement covering government and War Department contracts.

In his letter, Colonel Branshaw said:

"Gentlemen:

"In view of a recent incident wherein several Air Corps contractors in the Western procurement District disclosed classified information to an individual without proper authorization, this office desires to again call your attention to the necessity for strict compliance with War Department directives, policies and procedures relating to the dissemination of classified information, and to particularly call your attention to the fact that real or presumed authority from one government department, permitting the release of classified information, does not constitute authority for release or disclosure of such information under the control of another government department.

"CHAS. E. BRANSHAW,
"Lt. Col., Air Corps,

LOCKHEED SHOOTERS TAKE 3-WAY MATCH

At the Pasadena Pistol Range, July 8, in a 3-way team match, Lockheed won its fourth consecutive match of the year.

Lockheed, 1382; Altadena Pistol and Revolver Club, 1379; Adel Precision Products Gun Club of North Hollywood, 1198.

Scores of the Lockheed high five were: Carl Hirdler (35) 289; J. B. Crawford (73) 284; Clyde Crowley (22) 280; Fred Good (25) 268; Jim French (25) 261. Mrs. Herbert McKown was high lady shooter of the evening. The high score of the Altadena team which fired second place was 293, fired by Wallace Good.

The Lockheed-Vega Pistol Match held a week earlier was won by Lockheed with a score of 1363. The Vega team had a score of 1221. Adel also shot in this match, totaling 1191 for their group. The high score on the Lockheed five-man team was J. B. Crawford, and Mrs. McKown took second place. High shooter on the Vega team was Mrs. J. W. Colbertson with a score of 263.

2 Companies Now Have High Backlog Of $420,169,513

Lockheed's stride in the march of the nation's aircraft industry toward its goal of complete National Defense, gave this company an all-time production record during the first six months of 1941, according to figures released this week by Robert E. Gross, president.

Its 29,290 men turning out warplanes on schedule, the Lockheed company built and delivered $56,900,000 worth of airplanes during the six-month period ending June 30. Hudson bombers for Great Britain, and P-38 "Lightning" Interceptors for the U.S. Army Air Corps and Great Britain, constituted the bulk of this output.

During the same six-month period of last year, from January through June, 1940, total sales of completed airplanes, spare parts and assemblies were $19,268,434, while sales for the same period in 1939 were only $12,565,117.

The high production mark achieved during the past six months at Lockheed surpassed the total for the entire year of 1940, when the company built and delivered $44,936,594 worth of airplanes.

Lockheed and its affiliate, the Vega Airplane Company, now have a backlog of $420,169,513, of which Lockheed has $304,863,930 and Vega $115,305,583. To complete this huge volume of business on schedule, the two companies are hiring men at a rate of between three and four thousand a month and will continue to do so indefinitely.

Personnel department figures reveal that 3,984 men hired in June bring the total of Lockheed and Vega employment to 35,902. Of these, 6,612 are on the Vega payroll as the company's new $7,000,000 factory moves toward production of Vega Ventura bombers for the British and "Flying Fortresses" for the U.S. Army Air Corps.

One year ago Lockheed had only 10,772 men, and Vega approximately 1,500. The companies at the time had a combined backlog of $169,845,414. Now the Vega backlog figures alone have passed the $115,000,000 mark.

AEROQUIZ

Q.—What is a Pitot tube?

A.—A thin tube projecting from the leading edge of an airplane wing, used to measure air speeds.

BOMBER MARKS MILESTONE

Prior to their appearance before the more than 20,000 Lockheed employees at Plant 1 yesterday, Lord and Lady Halifax, center, pose before the 1000th Hudson which took off en route for Great Britain at the conclusion of the ceremony. Flanking the Ambassador and his wife are, left, Hall Hibbard, chief engineer and vice-president, and right, Robert E. Gross, president of Lockheed.

NEW LOCKHEED OFFICE BUILDING ON EMPIRE

Russell Weil, manager of Lockheed Plant Engineering, announced this week that work had begun on the new Lockheed office building on Empire avenue, opposite the Service Hangar.

The building, when complete, will contain 40,000 square feet of space and will house Lockheed office departments now operating under crowded conditions. The first unit is expected to be ready for occupancy by September 10.

DRIVERS LICENSES

The Industrial Relations Office has been notified that the Division of Drivers Licenses of the Glendale office of the motor Vehicles Department will be closed until August 1.

It will be necessary to go into Los Angeles to obtain drivers licenses until that date. The Glendale Division of Registration, however, will remain open.

Tomorrow's forgotten man is the man who stopped learning today.

KNUDSEN PRAISES LOCKHEED-VEGA

(Continued from page 3)

industry has designed America's new warplanes, made the tools to manufacture them, built the plants to house the construction and trained the men to build the planes is an achievement unparalleled in the history of the world's industrial progress.

"As I look at these men of Lockheed and Vega performing their tasks today, my faith is restored in that native quality of the American to do the job assigned to him and get it done on time!"

Following his tour of the Lockheed and Vega plants, Mr. Knudsen made an inspection trip through the North American Aviation plant in Los Angeles, and the Douglas plants at El Segundo and Santa Monica. Accompanying Mr. Knudsen on the tours were Major General George H. Brett, Colonel K. B. Wolfe, Lieut. R. P. Wollenberg, Colonel A. M. Martenstein, Major T. A. Sims, Brigadier General George Kenney and Dean Jennings.

THOUSANDS APPLY FOR SUPERVISORY TRAINING

The Supervisory Development Division of the Education Department is entering its second week of intensive training for selected men in subjects pertaining to the problems of supervision.

When this program was announced several weeks ago, more than 3,000 men applied for admission to the classes, and 2,600 were approved for training after careful checking of personnel records. Because of space limitations, only about 800 are now attending classes. The remaining 1,800 will be put into classes as rapidly as space becomes available.

L.E.R.C. Pistol Team Beats Douglas Squad

Bringing home the kudos from their match with the nationally famous Douglas Aircraft pistol team, the L.E.R.C. small bore squad tallied a 1398 score for a one point victory Tuesday night at the Pasadena Police Pistol Range.

Aside from the fact that the Lockheed team has been in competition for but four months, the remarkable fact that Warren Orr of Department 83, borrowed a gun to score enough points for the win over Douglas is something of a record in itself.

Individual team score: Carl Hirdler, 25, 288; J. B. Crawford, 73, 281; Herbert McKown, 24, 281; Richard Mosher, 16, 276, and Warren Orr, 83, 272. Kenneth Irwin of Douglas tallied 284 to lead the Douglas marksmen.

CHEERS OF VEGA, LOCKHEED MEN HEARD BY WORLD

(Continued from Page 1)

ifornia this morning for a ten-day tour of the aircraft and shipbuilding industries of the state.

Following a press conference in one of the executive offices of the company, Lord and Lady Halifax were introduced to the thousands of Lockheed workers gathered beside the thousandth bomber just outside the main manufacturing building. Here, in a ceremony which was heard by radio throughout the nation and, over facilities of the British Broadcasting Corporation, in England and other parts of the British Empire, Lord Halifax addressed the aircraft workers.

"This occasion does not mark the achievement of a goal, not even a pause in our efforts," declared Robert E. Gross, president of Lockheed, in introducing the Ambassador. "Even now, down in the back of our factory, we are starting number 1266 in our production line. Rather, we are gathered here to pledge renewed efforts, more hundreds, more thousands of bombers and pursuits. That's the keynote, more and more in a never-ending stream, until the battle is won."

In a gesture of encouragement to the millions of British subjects listening in, the Lockheed employees welcomed Lord Halifax with a rousing "Thumbs Up!," after which the Ambassador thanked them for "the skill, craftsmanship, work and goodwill that you are putting into these fighting ships I see around me," and declared that he would take back to England with him "a great story of encouragement and of expanding production."

"All you give us will be used in the defense of freedom of speech, thought and religion, and personal liberties, which things the English-speaking people the world over value more highly than life itself," Lord Halifax declared. "You know, we know, and if the Nazis do not already know, they soon will, what you are doing."

Praising the planes and ships being turned out in this country for the cause of freedom, the Ambassador said: "In making these two vital parts of war equipment, California is doing a job second to none, and the men and women of Lockheed and Vega may well be proud of their part in it.

"This time last year our people were feeling very much alone. France had fallen—defeated in a few short weeks. Our own production of fighting machines of all kinds was just beginning to come in. You, at that time, were already contributing to the support of our air force, of which our Prime Minister, Winston Churchill, so truly said—'Never in the history of the world have so many owed so much to so few.'

"We were alone but unafraid, and unafraid to a great extent because we felt that this great industrial giant, the United States, was well forward on the road to give us the mechanical means of carrying on this new form of warfare. We knew our men, given enough of the right tools, could, man for man, beat the Nazis."

Lord Halifax declared that in visiting some of the industrial cities of the middle west he had begun to realize the enormous power of industrial production in the United States. In addition to the Lockheed Hudsons, the Ambassador expressed the high regard of his countrymen for the Curtiss Tomahawks, the Glenn Martin Marylands, the Martlets and the Buffaloes from the Grumman and Brewster plants, the Liberators and Catalinas from Consolidated, the Douglas Bostons and Havocs, the Boeing Flying Fortresses, the Harvard Trainers of North American and the Vultee Vanguards.

He spoke highly in praise of the Wright, and Pratt and Whitney engines, and of the Allison liquid-cooled motors such as he saw in scores of Lockheed P-38 "Lightning" Interceptors lined up down the production line and beside the landing field ready for delivery to the U.S. Army Air Corps and the R.A.F.

Speaking more specifically of the Hudsons, such as the one which Mattern took off today, Lord Halifax said that it has "the quality of sturdiness that has led many high officers of the Royal Air Force to use the words: 'The Hudson Lockheed Bomber is a household word in our coastal command.' Your planes are able to take a beating in battle and still fly home.

"With the planes we are producing at home, with your help and that of similar factories of the United States, we will surely keep our boys flying in the finest ships that skill can give them until we have driven the enemy from the skies."

Lord Halifax later addressed a gathering of several thousand workers of the Vega Airplane Company, an affiliate of Lockheed, to whom he was introduced by Courtlandt S. Gross, president. He inspected the new plant which soon will be in production of Vega Ventura bombers for the Royal Air Force.

While Lord Halifax was on a tour of the Lockheed factory, where in addition to rows of Hudsons he saw an 820-foot assembly line of the "Lightning," world's fastest airplane, Lady Halifax, famous for her activities in the field of social welfare abroad, made a tour of inspection of the Lockheed and Vega employee service departments, interviewing personnel executives.

Lord and Lady Halifax and members of their party lunched informally. They were to leave tonight for San Francisco via United Airlines, where they will spend three days, returning to Los Angeles next week to inspect aircraft and ship building plants here. They will be entertained by the motion picture industry and also will visit numerous British war relief agencies locally. The Ambassador and party will visit San Diego before returning to Washington.

On the speakers' platform during the address of Lord Halifax to employees of Lockheed were the following:

Lord Halifax, Lady Halifax, Eric Cleugh, Mrs. Cleugh, Miss Palmer Gross, Mrs. C. S. Gross, Robert E. Gross, Courtlandt Gross, Colonel A. McDonnell, C. Peake, Fred Sigrist, Group Captain Wincott, Wing Commander Addams, Col. John Whiteley, Col. Chas. Branshaw, Col. Benson, Cyril Chappellet, Charles Barker, Hall Hibbard, Max Short, Dale Reed, H. E. Ryker, Charles Tigar, E. H. Holman, R. A. Von Hake, John McCabe and James Mattern.

SEA OF FACES GREETS HALIFAX

Cut shows just one section of the enthusiastic crowd of Lockheed men and women who gathered to do honor to Lord and Lady Halifax at Lockheed Plant 1 Thursday. In far background is the 1000th Hudson bomber, which took off with Jimmy Mattern at the controls at conclusion of ceremony.

THE Lockheed-Vega Star ★ ★

The LOCKHEED-VEGA STAR is issued every Friday for the employees of the Lockheed Aircraft Corporation and the Vega Airplane Company. Communications may be addressed to either the Industrial Relations Office or the Public Relations Department, Lockheed Aircraft Corporation, Burbank, California, U.S.A.

H. L. (Hal) Rosson, Editor

Volume 8 No. 30

A New Man Speaks

Great is the prestige of the Lockheed name in the far places of the earth. So great, indeed, that not only do men come from those far places to buy the ships that have blazed the world's air trails, but also come to stay and help build them.

Latest, and one of the most colorful instances of this, is personified in Alvin W. Horton, of Department 95, Lockheed Plant 3. From far off Shanghai by way of the fabled ports of three continents he has come to Lockheed, and in a letter to the editor of the STAR he recounts what he learned about Lockheed planes abroad, and why he was so determined to join the company that he travelled halfway around the world to do so. But let him tell his own story:

"Dear Editor:

"I am one of the new men at Lockheed and my interest in the company came about in rather a peculiar way, which might be of interest to relate. For the past nine years I have been in business at Shanghai, China. Sick of four years of war I sold out to return to the United States.

"On my way home I visited Japan, Hongkong, Formosa, Borneo, Malaya, Ceylon, Africa from Mombasa and Zanzibar to Capetown, South America and the West Indies. At the port of Lourenco Marques, Portuguese East Africa, I rented a small plane for a flight over the jungle to see wild elephant herds. In the big hangar sat two Lockheed Lodestars. The Portuguese pilot fondly patted one and said, 'Here is the airplane for me.' It did look sleek.

"I have flown many times in the interior of China and am very airminded. When I left China I had aviation in mind vaguely, but no concrete plans to get into the industry had been laid. That Portuguese pilot's remark set me to thinking. A few days later at Capetown, South Africa, I came aboard ship preparatory to sailing at daybreak for Buenos Aires, Argentina. I had a new cabin mate who was already in bed asleep when I came aboard.

"It was my very pleasant surprise the next morning to meet Johnny Gormly of Lockheed, who had been in South Africa the past several months setting up some new Lockheeds for South African Airways. A more enthusiastic Lockheed booster I have yet to meet. Johnny and I talked aviation for two weeks until we reached South America. I liked the pictures he showed me of Lockheed ships, I liked the reputation of the company, I liked Johnny and before we docked at Buenos Aires I resolved to become identified with Lockheed Aircraft.

"Here I am. I commenced work on June 16 as timekeeper. But I like everything about Lockheed and I am resolved to become a permanent fixture here. It is a swell company and the people I work with are as fine as one could wish for and I intend to go to the top.

"Yours very truly,
(Signed) "Alvin W. Horton."

"P.S.

"I might mention that I have a little boy, Charlie, aged three and one-half years, who has crossed the Pacific three times, the equator twice and had his first airplane ride at the age of one and one-half years.

"Another coincidence that strengthened my desire to get into Lockheed was this. One of my closest friends is a former University mathematics instructor, Dr. Carroll V. Newsom, President of the American Society of Mathematicians and a member of the American Society for the Advancement of Science. Dr. Newsom studied mathematics with Hall Hibbard, chief engineer and vice-president of Lockheed. Dr. Newsom liked my idea and helped me to that end." A.W.H.

STABILIZATION OF WAGES PROGRESSES

(Continued from Page 1)

changes, if made, would be made retroactive to July 1, 1941.

According to R. Randall Irwin who was an invited observer on behalf of Lockheed at the Washington meeting, it is not known how entire process of wage stabilization is to be achieved, except that it is recognized that the plan will be one of constant study of the various jobs in aircraft factories and an agreement between the manufacturers on what the different jobs consist of, with ultimately the rate of pay for each job classification to be approximately the same in all factories.

In attendance at the Washington meetings, representing West coast aircraft manufacturers in addition to Lockheed representatives, were Richard Millar, Vultee; John Rogers, Douglas; R. H. Fleet, Consolidated; La Motte Cohu, Northrop; and A. T. Burton, North American.

Larry Becht, manager of the Industrial Relations Research Department, accompanied R. Randall Irwin as special assistant.

"A good accident record is a sign of good character."

Dept. 10 Free Of Accidents In First Half of July

By PROF. ACCIDENT

It is the aim of Lockheed Department 10 to make July an accident-free month. The first half of the month showed a perfect record.

It has been wisely said that "Eternal vigilance is the price of freedom." We can also say that "Eternal vigilance is the price of Safety." This is doubly true now, because every dollar spent for medical care and every man-hour lost due to injury is lost to National Defense.

Commenting on 10's fine record, Harvey Christen, chairman of the Safety Committee, told members:

"We are happy to note the cooperation and unity you have shown in this campaign, because it indicates that you are taking an interest in your work, your company, and your country. It is this spirit of unity and cooperation which will enable us to meet the demands placed upon our company by our government."

TIGHTEN RULE ON VACATION CHANGES

When the Lockheed and Vega vacation program was put into effect, it was the intention of the management to keep vacation changes and cancellations to an absolute minimum. The only reasons authorized for changes were illness of an employee prior to the scheduled vacation period, or "other *extreme* emergencies."

The Industrial Relations Department reports that these rules are not being observed and that as a result an increasing volume of extra and unnecessary paper work is falling upon the department. Consequently, all departments have been requested to carefully review requests for changes and cancellations and to recommend them only when considered absolutely necessary.

Also, in view of the increasing pressure of National Defense work, the departments have been asked to deny leaves in addition to vacations except in cases of *extreme personal emergency.*

Son: "Dad, I understand that some of the African men don't know their wives until after they are married."

Dad: "Why Africa, son?"

« « CONSERVATION OF MATERIAL IS A PATRIOTIC DUTY » »

IN THIS ISSUE - FULL FALL SEMESTER SCHEDULE

Volume 8 BURBANK, CALIFORNIA, U.S.A., SEPTEMBER 5, 1941 No. 38

THE *Lockheed-Vega Star* ★★

PERFECT RECORD ON ALASKA RUN

Above is shown an NC-47-M, one of the Alaska Coastal Airlines Lockheed-Vega seaplanes which has been flying up and down the Alaska coast for the past 12 years without an accident. It is shown taking off at Juneau where, on the mountainside in the background, can be seen the world's largest gold mine. These Vegas perform a shuttle service for Pan American Airway's Lockheeds to island communities. Photo was taken by Keith T. Petrich, PAA operations man stationed at Juneau and forwarded to V. A. Kemmerer, Lockheed advertising manager.

Vega Veteran In 12-Year Hitch

Pioneers in the flying of world-wide airlanes, Lockheed-Vega planes daily cover the toughest kind of assignments, but few on any continent are tougher, day in and day out, than those faced by the Alaska Division of Pan American Airways on which Lockheed equipment is used exclusively.

Keith T. Petrich, Pan-Am operations man at Juneau, who sent the above photograph of one of the Vega veterans of the line to V. A. Kemmerer, Lockheed advertising manager, had some interesting observations to make on his company's Alaskan operations.

"Lockheed equipment is the only type of aircraft we use," he said in a

(Continued on Page 6)

CREDIT UNION SELLS U. S. DEFENSE STAMPS

Personnel of Lockheed and Vega companies may buy Defense Savings Stamps at the Federal Credit Union offices.

This announcement is made in answer to numerous requests as to how U.S. Defense Savings Stamps and Bonds may be purchased with the greatest convenience.

Defense Savings Stamps are available in denominations of 25c, 50c and $1.

With your first purchase of a stamp in any denomination, you are given a stamp album in which to place stamps of the same denomination until the required amount necessary for the purchase of a Defense Bond is acquired.

This plan for the installment purchase of Defense Savings Stamps and Bonds is an easy way to put aside funds for future personal use and at the same time give valuable help toward national defense.

Program Includes Tuition In All Aircraft Skills

The complete schedule of the Education Department's Trade Extension Classes for the Fall Semester, of vital interest to every ambitious member of the Lockheed and Vega forces, appears on pages 4 and 5 of this issue.

These classes, providing unprecedented opportunities to learn new skills during the National Defense emergency, are made available through the cooperation of the companies and the Burbank, Glendale and Pasadena school districts. ALL OF THEM ARE FREE AND ARE TIMED TO SUIT THE CONVENIENCE OF MEN ON EVERY SHIFT.

All phases of aircraft design and construction are embraced in these classes. The instructors are "tops" in their specialized fields and, in addition, the most modern scientific and mechanical facilities are provided to give students the identical instruction they would receive in actual work on the job in the factories.

Enrollment in these classes should be made directly with the instructor of the course selected. THERE IS NO CHARGE.

ENGLAND TELLS EPIC STORY OF HUDSON'S BATTLE

The STAR received a clipping this week of a story which appeared in the Northampton Chronicle, Northampton, England, July 11, which, taken in conjunction with the thousands of other stories of the Hudson's prowess, gives the impression that the Germans are merely wasting their ammunition when they try to down one of these famous planes.

The story details the adventure of a Hudson which attacked a convoy of three German ships off Ushant (Netherlands coast) destroying the largest of them, a 1200-ton mine sweeper, and getting back to its drome although both motors concked under the impact of enemy fire.

"The ship," the report said, "was the largest of three sighted by the Hudson (of the R.A.F. Coastal Command) which closed to investigate.

"As soon as the aircraft came within range, the 1200-ton ship opened fire, fol-

(Continued on Page 3)

L.E.R.C. CALENDAR

Friday, September 5 — Drama Club Rehearsal for "Room Service," Hollywood headquarters, 7:30.

Sunday, September 7—Lockheed Basket Picnic, Santa Anita Race Track and Park, 6 a.m. to 6:30 p.m.

Motion Picture Unit shooting Picnic, Santa Anita, 11 a.m.

Rifle and Pistol Club shoot match with Los Angeles Club.

Drama Club Rehearsal, "Room Service," Hollywood Headquarters, 7:30 p.m.

Lockheed Rangers Drill Team, 7 a.m. to 9 a.m., Doc's Stables, Roscoe.

Monday, September 8—Band Rehearsal, John Burroughs Junior High, Burbank, 7:30 p.m.

Tuesday, September 9 — Drama Club Rehearsal "Room Service," Hollywood Headquarters, 7:30.

Lockheed Night, Golfer's Paradise; Victory Blvd. and Hollywood Way, Burbank, 8 p.m.

Lockheed Girl's Softball practice, John Muir Junior High, 5 p.m.

Wednesday, September 10—Regular Boy Scout Meeting, 1935 Brighton, Burbank, 7 p.m. to 9 p.m.

Lockheed Rangers, Doc's Stables, Roscoe, 7 p.m. to 9 p.m.

Lockheed All-Star softball practice, 7:30 p.m., Burbank Civic Park.

Choral Club Rehearsal, Social Room, Burbank Senior High School, 7:30.

Thursday, September 11—Roller Skating Club, Shrine Roller Rink, 32nd and Figueroa, Los Angeles, 6:30 p.m.

Lockheed Rangers (Nite Crew) Doc's Stables, Roscoe, 10 a.m. to 12 noon.

Rangerettes, Doc's Stables, Roscoe, 7 to 9 p.m.

Friday, September 12 — Drama Club Rehearsal, "Room Service," Hollywood Headquarters, 7:30.

Judge: What is the source of your income?

Rastus: Ah ain't got but two, yo' honor.

Judge: Well, what are they?

Rastus: Seben and 'leben.

LIBRARY IN RESALE OF SCHOOL BOOKS

The Lockheed-Vega Education Library still offers the following Ford Trade School publications for resale:

Physics Course	**.35**
Shop Trigonometry	**.25**
Mechanical Drawing	**.75**

Some of the War Department technical manuals which may be obtained at the Library include:

Airplane Sheet Metal Work	**.25**
Airplane Inspection Guide	**.20**
Airplane Induction, Fuel and Oil Systems	**.20**
Study Guide for Commercial Radio Operator's Examinations	**.15**
Airplane Hydraulic Systems	**.15**

These are available at either the Lockheed Library in Room 210 of the Industrial Relations Building, or at the Vega branch library in Room 113, Building 67, at Vega Plant 1.

During the last month several new books on industrial relations, engineering, machinery and general aviation were added to the library for circulation. These are loaned for two weeks each. New employees are invited to use the library.

BEACHCOMBERS FROLIC PROMISES GAY TIME

The frivolous Beachcomber's Frolic slated for Saturday, September 13, looms as a gay event. Art Whiting's Band has been signed to furnish the music for dancing until 1 a.m. Plans for the floor show entertainment are near completion.

Everyone is invited but tickets are limited and may be obtained from Camera Club Members or by phoning the L.E.R.C. Office. The regular meeting of the Camera Club at the Burbank Public Library, Thursday, September 11, will feature a showing of natural color slides taken by various members.

SALVAGE DEPARTMENTS ARE NOW CONSOLIDATED

Consolidation of Lockheed Salvage, Tool Salvage, Material Conservation and Material Reclamation departments into one unit, Salvage Department 19, is now in effect according to J. H. Sreenan, works manager.

The consolidation has been made to insure more efficient functioning of the departments. The present personnel of the three additional groups is being transferred to Department 19, where the reorganization is being conducted under the supervision of Walter White, who will continue as manager of the division.

V.E.R.C. CALENDAR

Saturday, September 6 — Pistol Practice, Burbank Police Range, 9 to 12 a.m.

Sunday, September 7—Ice Skating Club Meeting, 9:45 a.m., Tropical Ice Gardens, Westwood Village, Ice Skating for all will follow meeting.

Rifle Practice, Glendale Rifle and Revolver Range, 9:30 a.m.

Pistol Practice, Burbank Police Range, 9 a.m. to 2 p.m.

Baseball Game, Vega vs. San Fernando Merchants, Solon Park, 2:15 p.m.

Choral Club, 4:30 p.m., over KIEV, Glendale. Tune in for this program every Sunday.

Monday, September 8 — Girls' Chorus, Michiel Marsman's home, 700 E. Lomita, Glendale, 7:30 p.m.

Riding Club Instruction Class, Ride-A-While Stables, 7-8:30 p.m.

Mixed Doubles Bowling League Hollywood Recreation, 7 p.m.

Tuesday, September 9 — Male Chorus, Griffith Park Building, 7:30-9 p.m.

Rifle Practice, Glendale Rifle and Revolver Range, 7:30 p.m.

Girls' Bowling League, Hollywood Recreation, 7:30 p.m.

Wednesday, September 10—Vega Lockheed Night Men's Bowling, Burbank Bowl, 12:30 p.m.

Men's Bowling League, Hollywood Recreation, 2 sections, 1st section, 6:45 p.m.; 2nd section, 9 p.m.

Ice Skating Club Meeting, 7:30-8 p.m., Polar Palace, Melrose and Van Ness, Ice Skating before and after meeting.

Thursday, September 11 — Little Theatre Group, Barnsdall Park, Olive Hill, 7:30-9:30 p.m.

Friday, September 12 — Riding Club, Drill Team practice (7:30-9 p.m.) Trail Ride (7-9 p.m.) for those who wish straight riding from Ride-A-While Stables, Burbank, with business meeting at 9 p.m.

Dance Club, Wilshire Music Center, Corner of Wilshire and Western, 8 p.m.

A naval officer fell overboard. He was rescued by a deck hand. The officer asked what he could give in reward.

"The best way, sir, is to say nothing. If the other fellows knew I'd pulled you out, they'd chuck me in."

ENGLAND TELLS HUDSON'S BATTLE

(*Continued from Page 1*)

lowed by the other two. The ships had arranged themselves on three sides of a square, leaving the fourth side open for the aircraft's course, and they concentrated their fire on this passage.

"To attack the Hudson had to weave its way almost at sea level through an intense barrage. It was only 50 yards from the largest ship when the pilot let go his salvo of heavy bombs with a slight delay action on them to allow him to get clear before they exploded.

"Every bomb hit, and as the Hudson pulled away the crew saw the ship become a mass of flame. She ceased fire immediately, listed heavily to port, and appeared likely to sink at any moment.

"Then the Hudson's crew had to look to their own safety. The aircraft had been hit many times and came out of the attack with the port-engine on fire. The flames died down, but the other engine cut out, after the pilot had pulled the aircraft up to a thousand feet. The crew found that no fuel was reaching the engine, and it picked up again after petrol had been pumped from the tank by hand. Then they also managed to get the port engine going too and made a safe landing."

MYRON SUGARMAN, 25, DIES OF INJURIES

Seriously injured in an auto crash near Taft, California, September 3, Myron Sugarman, of Department 25, died later the same day in the Taft hospital.

Mr. Sugarman joined the Lockheed Company in May of 1940 and all members of Engineering sincerely regret his passing.

"ENGINEERING" SAYS GOODBYE TO E. R. HARMAN

The Engineering Personnel group said "goodbye" last week to a good friend and fellow worker, E. R. Harman.

Mr. Harman has been in charge of Personnel Research and Guidance for some time and is well known throughout the department. He leaves to take over the post of Director of Industrial Relations for another aircraft company where the scope of his service to the industry will be enlarged.

Marksmen Attention!

Since Sunday, September 7, is the date of the L.E.R.C. Picnic, the following Gun Club events falling on that date are to be canceled until further notice:

1. The Lockheed Rifle Team vs. Los Angeles Times Rifle team inter-club match.

2. Regular practice shoot at Pasadena Police Range.

BOB HOPE 'HOPEFUL'

Comedian Bob Hope takes time out during shooting of Paramount's "Louisiana Purchase" to chat with stars of L.E.R.C.'s "Room Service." Left to right: Charlie Bell, Burt Miller, Hope, and Lloyd Hansen.

Supervisory Examinations Classes Take Vacation

All Supervisory Development classes in both Course I, "Job Instruction Planning and Presentation," and Course II, "Orientation," will close for a two-week's vacation beginning Monday, September 8. All classes will be resumed on Monday, September 22.

TOOL PURCHASE PAYROLL DEDUCTION PLAN DESCRIBED

New employees who desire to purchase tools through the Lockheed and Vega Employees' Tool Store on the payroll deduction plan are advised by the Accounting Department of the procedure under which payment for such purchases may be made.

Purchases of $3 or less are on a cash basis. Tools to an amount of $25 may be purchased on the payroll deduction plan, payable in five weekly installments. If the amount terminates in odd cents, the odd cents together with one-fifth of the remaining amount will be deducted from the first check following date of purchase. No deduction will be made for less than $1.

If an employee makes additional purchases before completion of payments, the new amount will be payable on the same basis. As an example: If an employee is paying $2 per week for tools purchased, and buys another $10 worth, his payments will then be $4 per week until the original amount has been paid, at which time his payments revert back to $2 weekly.

BIRDS WINNERS IN TILT WITH PLANES

Two freak accidents in which two buzzards brought down two airline airplanes were reported last week from Managua, Nicaragua, in a U.P. dispatch which John Mihalic, of 840 East Magnolia boulevard, Burbank, was kind enough to clip and send to the STAR.

The U.P. story, under an August 15 dateline, reported as follows:

Two airplanes brought down by buzzards, underwent repairs at the airport here today.

A disaster was narrowly averted when a buzzard attacked a *Lockheed transport plane* of the Taca Airways enroute from here to San Jose, Costa Rica, with passengers. The pilot, Floyd Wright, had changed his course to avoid a flock of buzzards when one wheeled and swooped down on him, crashing through the metal nose of the plane at a 200-mile-an-hour clip. Wright brought the plane down and the dead bird was extricated with difficulty. A new nose for the plane was being flown here.

A United States Army Douglas DC-2 plane crashed with a buzzard earlier in the week and has been laid up for repairs since.

LOCKHEED VETERAN DIES AFTER LONG ILLNESS

William R. DeMuth, of Department 16 and one of the veterans of Lockheed, having joined the company on October 5, 1934, died Sunday, August 31, after a long illness. His passing came as a shock to his hundreds of friends throughout the organization.

Funeral services were held Thursday, September 4, at the Little Church of the Flowers, Forest Lawn Memorial Cemetery, Glendale.

LOCKHEED NIGHTS AT ICE FOLLIES

Sunday, September 14, and Monday, September 15, will be Lockheed Nights at the Ice Follies, Pan Pacific Auditorium, 7600 Beverly Blvd.

Through special arrangement, Lockheed employees may purchase regular $2.20 tickets for $1.70 and regular $1.65 tickets at $1.15. Tickets now on sale at L.E.R.C.

Brig. General Lachland To Speak At Picnic

Word has been received that Brigadier General Frank D. Lachland, commander of the First Bombardment Wing, U.S. Air Corps, has accepted the honor of being Air Corps representative at the L.E.R.C. Picnic.

General Lachland is a very forceful and impressive speaker and Lockheedians are honored in the fact that he will address them.

PRACTICAL JOKE VICTIMS FACE 100 PER CENT LOSS

Practical jokers who are inclined to practice their horseplay in the plants are given a jolt this week by Jack Hatton, Lockheed safety engineer, who reports that injuries incurred by employees due to this cause are not covered by the California Workmen's Compensation Act.

"In spite of many previous warnings against acts coming under the heading of 'horseplay,' we find some employees still are prone to play a prank on a fellow worker," says Mr. Hatton.

"They have been observed wadding paper up into a ball and throwing it. Rivets are sometimes blown through tubing, which can easily cause the loss of an eye. Stools and chairs have been pulled out from behind a person about to sit down. Air hoses have been used to dust off other fellows clothes, and if this practice continues it will sooner or later result in a fatality.

"To be sure, none of these acts is deliberately performed to cause bodily harm to a fellow workman. That is probably farthest from the prankster's mind, but the unfortunate part of the whole thing is, that they frequently result in a serious injury.

"The injured man does not have the benefits of compensation insurance to pay his medical and hospital bills. Neither does he receive the weekly compensation insurance check to help take care of his family until he recuperates. He must either stand these costs himself, or have other valid insurance.

" 'Horseplay' tactics are not at all necessary in this or any other factory. They always lead to painful injuries that might otherwise have easily been averted.

" 'Horseplay' is something we at Lockheed and Vega can and must get along without. Let's each of us act as a personal crusader against pranks of this sort and thereby eliminate, first, the painful injuries and, second, the recommending of disciplinary action against the offender."

ACCIDENT SLATE CLEAN OVER LONG HOLIDAY

Despite the heavy toll of traffic deaths and serious injuries recorded throughout California during the three-day Labor Day holiday, Lockheed and Vega came near having a perfect record. Several minor injury cases were reported but otherwise the accident slate was clean.

The personnel of both companies merit high praise for their splendid efforts in helping to reduce traffic accidents through careful driving.

STARTLING FIGURES ON DEFENSE NEEDS

An article appearing in the current issue of Factory Management & Maintenance presents some startling figures on America's production requirements in both defense and non-defense industry.

The article quotes $68,000,000,000 as being the value of all goods turned out by all of America's factories in our best peacetime year (1929). It further points out that $17,000,000,000 worth of defense products will be required for the year 1941. In other words, manufacturers will be called upon to show an increase in production of 25 per cent over the best industrial year in U.S. history.

In quoting national income in comparison to production, the article further states that during that peak peacetime year (1929), the national income was $83,000,000,000. With the estimated increase in production scheduled for the current year, income may reach an all-time high of $104,000,000,000.

L. C. Morrow, editor of Factory Management & Maintenance, pointed out the tremendous task faced by industry in doing this huge national defense job "right" while at the same time enabling Americans to continue to enjoy their present living standard.

"If America is to do this over-all job successfully," he said, "five principal procedures are necessary: (1) put all machines to work; (2) work machines all the time; (3) use the most efficient methods; (4) build an adequate working force; (5) keep this working force at work.

"This is a big job, so big that every unit of industry and labor must do its part and do it well.

"America cannot and will not bog down on the biggest job it has ever tackled," he concluded.

A total of 353,478 passengers traveled by air during June in the U.S., the largest number in the history of American aviation.

VEGA VETERAN IN 12-YEAR HITCH

(Continued from Page 1)

covering letter. "Seven are in use at present with others on order. You might be interested in knowing that Alaskans don't call our ships "Clippers," but Lodestars or Electras.

"We have three Lockheed Lodestar 18's in service now between Seattle, Prince George, Juneau, Whitehorse and Fairbanks. They leave Seattle at 10 a.m., (PST) and arrive at Fairbanks at 6 p.m. (PST) the same day, a journey which required eight days, less than two years ago! Four Lockheed Electras are in operation between Fairbanks and Nome, Fairbanks and Anchorage (a new run) and Fairbanks and Bethel."

Petrich stated that in June 4000 pounds of mail were carried, but in July these seven Lockheeds carried over 8500 pounds of mail.

"A drop in the bucket when compared to that carried in California," he commented, "but remember all this mail was directed to but 60,000 people. Every ship is full on every section and reservations must be made at least a month in advance."

TULLY M. STANSELL KILLED IN AUTO CRASH

Word has been received by the Employee Relations Department of the death of Tully M. Stansell, who was killed in an automobile accident at Alamogorda, N. M., August 28. He had been with Lockheed, Department 14, since June of this year.

According to information available Mr. Stansell, together with four other Lockheed employees, was traveling across country when the accident occurred. The report states the others escaped with minor injuries.

Mr. Stansell is survived by his widow, to whom the deepest sympathy of the company and his fellow workers is extended.

"ROOM SERVICE" tickets on sale Daily at Gate 8—11:30 to 12:30.

Motor Vehicle Offices Now Open Until 5 P.M.

The Department of Motor Vehicles has announced a change in office hours at all of its branches, effective September 2.

Driver licenses and automobile registrations may now be obtained from 9 a.m. to 5 p.m. (Saturdays, 9 a.m. to 12 noon).

The main office is located at 3500 South Hope street, Los Angeles; Glendale branch at 1246 South Brand boulevard; Hollywood branch at 6433 Homewood avenue; Pasadena branch at 1297 East Green street.

ATTENDANCE RECORD LOOMS AT SEPT. 7 PICNIC

MUSICAL STARS AT PICNIC

Marion MacCormack, vocalist with Lee Yanders' Band. Marion is well known, having appeared with this band and with Gilbert and Sullivan companies on the Pacific Coast.

Lee Yanders, leader of the Dance Band for the Picnic. Lee is in Department 23 and his band is considered to be one of the coming name bands in this territory.

SPLIT PARKING IS ARRANGED AT SANTA ANITA PARK

The Picnic Committee has completed arrangements to have parking facilities available for 30,000 cars at the Parking Area adjacent to the Santa Anita Race Track.

Suggested routes for travel to and from the Picnic have been drawn up for the convenience and safety of all Lockheedians *(see cut, Page 8)*.

The suggested routes are:

FROM BURBANK, GLENDALE—San Fernando to Colorado Boulevard—Colorado through Pasadena.

FROM LOS ANGELES — Huntington Drive direct to Park.

FROM HOLLYWOOD, (North of Sunset)—Los Feliz to Glendale Blvd., Glendale Blvd. to Colorado—Colorado through Pasadena to Park.

FROM HOLLYWOOD, (South of Sunset)—Sunset to North Main Street, L.A.—North Main to Mission—Mission to Huntington Drive — Huntington Drive to Park.

North Glendale, La Canada, Montrose, Sunland, Tujunga, etc.—FOOTHILL BOULEVARD to Double Drive Arcadia, turn right direct to Park.

Whittier, East Los Angeles Area—North on Atlantic to Huntington Drive, turn right direct to Park.

RADIO BROADCAST TOUR IS PLANNED

A free tour of the Columbia Broadcasting Radio and Television studio in Hollywood has been arranged for Sunday evening, September 14, at 7 o'clock, according to Bill Briggs, chairman of the L.E.R.C. Educational Committee.

"Lockheed employees will have an opportunity to make this popular tour at no charge," Briggs announced. "Following the tour, they will be able to attend an actual broadcast of the program 'I Was There,' if they obtain tickets through the L.E.R.C."

Tickets for the tour may be obtained at the new L.E.R.C. Office, west of Personnel, early next week. Due to the fact that the capacity of both the tour parties and the "I Was There" broadcast are limited, persons wishing to attend are asked to obtain their tickets promptly.

Hydraulics Examinations

Entrance examinations for Hydraulics and Plumbing II will be given at the Jackman Building, Burbank, on Monday, September 8 at 6:30 p.m., according to L. Stearns, instructor.

Over $2700 In Prizes Offered Contest Winners

With more than 200 merchandise prizes valued above $2,000, and with cash prizes in excess of $700, the Annual Lockheed Family Picnic promises to bring out one of the largest picnic crowds ever assembled.

"With requests for tickets totalling nearly 90,000, and with additional requests flooding the L.E.R.C. office each day, there is little doubt that the entire Lockheed family will be on hand September 7 to celebrate the seventh annual picnic in fitting style," Norman MacTaggart and Ollie Arbelbide, chairman and recreation director, declare.

Day Starts at 6 a.m.

The day's activities will commence at 6 a.m. when golfers registered in the tournament will tee off in two sections; one at the Santa Anita course and the other at Altadena.

At 8 o'clock the Midget Cars will be available for youngsters along Santa Anita Avenue.

Starting at 9 a.m. the several prize contests for adults and children will commence.

The children's events will be held in the grass area between the swimming pool and the baseball field, while the adult events are set for the baseball field proper.

Swimming-Tennis-Horseshoes

The entire facilities of the Santa Anita County Park will be available all day to Lockheed employees, their families and their friends.

The tennis courts, the swimming tank, putting greens, horseshoe courts are all to be open for our use.

Other free attractions include the Puppet Show, free Vita-C orange juice, free soft drinks, and free ice cream novelties for which tickets have been issued through the L.E.R.C.

At 10 a.m. the Lockheed Girls' Softball squad is scheduled to play an exhibition game.

Time Out for Lunch

All entertainment, prize contests and other events at the County Park will be suspended at 12 Noon so that everyone may enjoy their lunch without being left out of any of the scheduled events.

(Continued on Page 8)

THE Lockheed-Vega Star ★ ★

The LOCKHEED-VEGA STAR is issued every Friday for the employees of the Lockheed Aircraft Corporation and the Vega Airplane Company. Communications may be addressed to either the Industrial Relations Office or the Public Relations Department, Lockheed Aircraft Corporation, Burbank, California, U.S.A.

H. L. (Hal) Rosson, Editor

Volume 8 Number 38

Education Information Schedule

For the benefit of new employees, the following Education Information schedule is reprinted:

Day Shift—
11:30 a.m. to 12 noon—Booth at rear of Industrial Relations Bldg.
3:30 to 4 p.m.—Booth at rear of Industrial Relations Bldg.

Swing Shift—
3 to 4 p.m.—Booth at rear of Industrial Relations Bldg.
8 to 8:30 p.m.—Library, Room 210, Industrial Relations Bldg.

Graveyard Shift—
11 to 12 midnight—Library, Room 210, Industrial Relations Bldg.

ATTENDANCE RECORD LOOMS AT SEPTEMBER 7 PICNIC

(Continued from Page 7)

Promptly at 1:30 the Lockheed Band will start its concert in the special infield stand erected at Santa Anita Race Track.

For a half hour, this popular musical aggregation will entertain the crowd, which will be seated in the main grandstand.

Gate prize drawings are to be conducted at the Race Track, and starting at 2 p.m., the famous radio crew of Al Pierce and his Gang will stage a show to be broadcast through the Columbia Broadcasting System hook-up.

Ranger Show Planned

The Lockheed Rangers are to be on hand with a fine program of formation riding worked out to fit into the 20 minutes following Al Pierce.

"Promptly at 3 p.m. a two hour vaudeville show is planned," MacTaggart promises, "and this variety of acts is certain to delight everyone."

The final phase of the Seventh Annual Lockheed Family Picnic will be the two hour dancing on the mezzanine of the Race Track Grandstand, between 5 and 7.

Lee Yanders' Band

The committee has been fortunate in obtaining Lee Yanders' 12 piece name-band for the picnic.

Yanders is working in Lockheed Department 23. Rob Lee, Department 2, plays tenor sax, while Bob Bedford, formerly of Lockheed and now of Vega, is first trumpet.

This band has played at the opening of the Hilton Hotel in Long Beach, at the Del Mar Club, at the Deauville Club, the Beverly Hills Hotel and the Santa Barbara Biltmore.

Last summer, it appeared on the Stairway to Fame program with Gus Arnheim.

The feature attraction of the band is Marion MacCormack, Santa Barbara State co-ed, who "arrived" when she was selected to sing the lead in a Gilbert and Sullivan organization. At the same time has maintained her standing in the dance band vocalist field with her splendid singing, both with Yanders Band and with the Santa Barbara State College Swing Band.

FOLLOW THE ARROWS FOR FUN

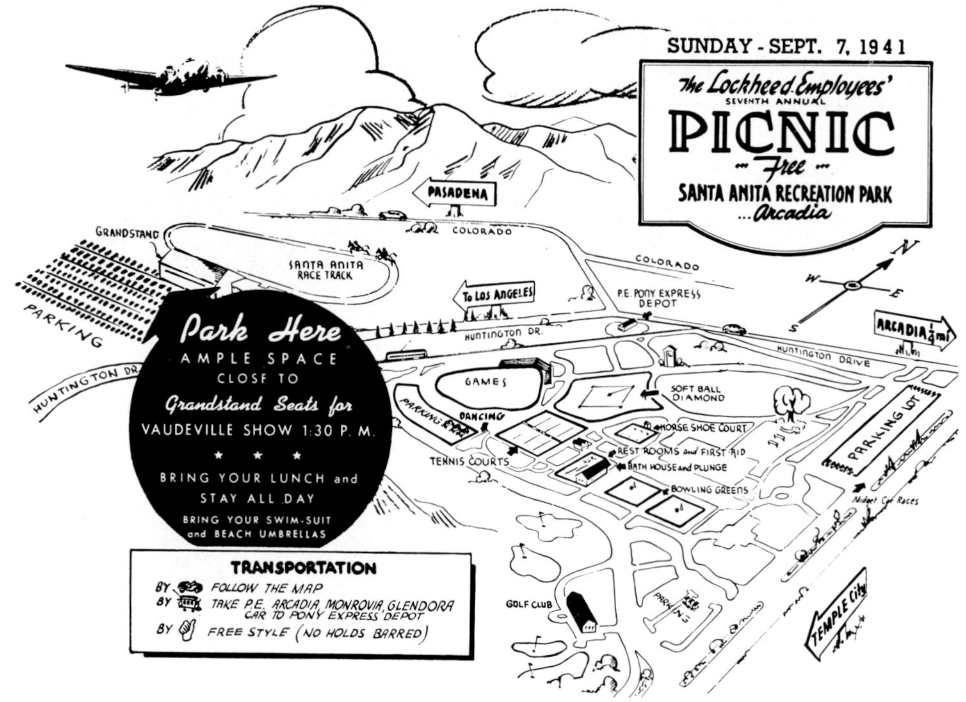

Revised Hourly Events Of The Day

6:00 a.m.—FIRST TEE-OFF SANTA ANITA GOLF COURSE
6:30 a.m.—FIRST TEE-OFF ALTADENA
8:00 a.m.—MIDGET CARS FOR YOUNGSTERS
9:00 a.m.—PRIZE CONTESTS
Children 50 yd. dash
Boys, 5-7.
9:05 a.m.—Girls, 5-7
9:10 a.m.—Boys, 8-10
9:15 a.m.—Girls, 8-10
75 YARD DASH
9:20 a.m.—Boys, 10-12
9:25 a.m.—Girls, 10-12
100 YARD DASH
9:30 a.m.—Boys, 12-15
9:35 a.m.—Girls, 12-15
SACK RACE
9:40 a.m.—Boys, 9-15
9:45 a.m.—Girls, 9-15
3-LEGGED RACE
9:50 a.m.—Boys, 9-12
9:55 a.m.—Girls, 9-12
10:00 a.m.—Boys, 12-15
10:05 a.m.—Girls, 12-15
10:15 a.m.—5-12, Pie Eating Contest
10:30 a.m.—MEN'S 100 Yard Dash
10:45 a.m.—WOMEN'S 100 Yard Dash
11:00 a.m.—R.A.F. PILOTS NURSING CONTEST
11:15 a.m.—WATER BALLOON RELAY
11:30 a.m.—WOMEN'S SHOE KICKING CONTEST
11:40 a.m.—ADULT 3-LEGGED RACE
11:50 a.m.—ADULT EGG-THROWING CONTEST
12 NOON—OFFICE-SHOP TUG-O-WAR
BASKET LUNCH
1:30 p.m.—LOCKHEED BAND CONCERT, Race Track Grandstand
2:00 p.m.—Al Pearce and His Gang RADIOCAST CBS, featuring Frances Langford and Jon Hall
2:30 p.m.—Ranger Review
2:50 p.m.—Drawings—$700 in cash
3:00 p.m.—Vaudeville
5:00 p.m.—Dancing, Lee Yanders' Band
7:00 p.m.—Good Night.

Throughout the day, midget cars 'til noon, free ice cream, Vita-C orange juice, soft drinks, the swimming pool and tennis courts and horseshoe pits will be available for all Lockheedians.

AIRCRAFT MOTOR OUTPUT SETS FAST PACE

Volume 8 BURBANK, CALIFORNIA, U.S.A., SEPTEMBER 26, 1941 No. 41

THE *Lockheed-Vega Star* ★ ★

U. A. C. CHIEF LOCKHEED GUEST

Eugene E. Wilson, left, president of United Aircraft Corporation, inspects a Hudson bomber during his recent visit to Lockheed and Vega. Two of the companies that his company controls, Pratt and Whitney and Hamilton Propellers, provide much of the equipment that goes into the building of Hudsons. Shown in the picture with Mr. Wilson are Leonard K. Schwartz, public relations director for Lockheed and Vega, center, and Lauren D. Lyman, who directs the same functions for United Aircraft.

CITY OFFICIAL LAUDS PLANT PERSONNEL AND MANAGEMENT FOR COOPERATION

The following letter, revealing the spirit of cordial cooperation on traffic problems which exists between officials of the City of Burbank and employees and management of Lockheed and Vega, was received this week by Assistant Secretary L. W. Wulfekuhler from H. I. Stites, city manager of Burbank.

Said Mr. Stites:

"I cannot overlook this opportunity to express appreciation on behalf of the City of Burbank for the fine spirit of cooperation shown by your employees in assisting the City to solve the traffic problems in the vicinity of your plants. Observation shows that, while in recent months the number of employees at your combined plants has grown from 20,000 to 45,000, the time of dispersal remains unchanged.

"The City of Burbank wishes to do all within its power to get these men to and from work as quickly as possible, and we appreciate that the measure of success which we have experienced is due in a large degree to the fine spirit of these employees.

"Your company is to be congratulated for having brought together such a high class of personnel.

"Sincerely,

"H. I. Stites, City Manager."

Executive Tells Of Ten-Fold Gain In Production

With a ten-fold increase in engine output since the National Defense program went into effect, the nation's aircraft motor manufacturers are keeping pace with the production tempo of the aircraft manufacturers of Southern California.

This was the statement of Eugene E. Wilson, president of United Aircraft Corporation, of East Hartford, Conn., during a visit to the Lockheed and Vega plants last week. United Aircraft controls Pratt & Whitney, one of the world's largest manufacturers of airplane motors; Vought-Sikorsky, aircraft makers, and Hamilton propellers.

Mr. Wilson said his firm, which has been supplying engines for commercial and military aircraft for many years, has increased its output ten-fold.

"We were 3100 engines ahead of our customers when I left Hartford," he said, "but after visiting the Los Angeles plants and watching their impressive round-the-clock activity, I feel I ought to hurry home and try to turn them out even faster."

The Eastern aviation executive paid high tribute to all Lockheed and Vega employees when he told President Robert E. Gross that he had the "most cheerfully energetic" group of workmen that he had ever seen. Mr. Wilson was accompanied on his tour by Lauren D. Lyman, public relations director for United Aircraft.

PAYCHECK LATE? HERE'S SUGGESTION

In response to complaints of employees who have failed, for various reasons, to receive their paychecks on Fridays, the Paymaster's Office requests that when this occurs, the employee concerned will immediately contact his Personnel Clerk and give him any information that might aid in locating it. Recent transfers, change of shift or extended absence can hold up delivery of the check.

If the check is not delivered by the end of the shift it is recommended that, when possible, the employee give the Department an additional day to locate it. In this connection, it is pointed out, an employee absent on Friday must obtain a Paycheck Release from Window No. 3 in the lobby of the Industrial Relations Building.

L.E.R.C. CALENDAR

Friday, Sept. 26—"Circle of Fire" Movie, Burbank High School, 7 p.m.

Final Clean-up Rehearsal for "Room Service," Hollywood headquarters, 7:30 p.m.

Sunday, Sept. 28—Sneak preview. Location withheld. Staff report, 11 a.m. Cast report, 2 p.m.

Rifle and Pistol Club SPECIAL day, Pasadena Police Range, 9 a.m. to 5 p.m.

Rangers Box Social and Barn Dance, Legion Hall, Sunland Blvd. (north of Roscoe), 7 p.m.

Lockheed Rangers Drill team, 7 a.m. to 9 a.m., Tex' Stonehurst Stables, Roscoe.

Monday, Sept. 29—Band Rehearsal, John Burroughs Junior High, Burbank, 7:30 p.m.

Tuesday, Sept. 30—Baseball practice, Solon Park, San Fernando Road, across from Plant 1, after work.

Drama Club cast, Final check-up rehearsal, Hollywood headquarters, 7:30 p.m.

Drama Club Staff, Hollywood Assistance League Playhouse. Set up entire production, 6 p.m.

Lockheed Night, Golfer's Paradise, Victory Blvd. & Hollywood Way, Burbank, 8 p.m.

Wednesday, Oct. 1 — Lockheed Rangers, Tex' Stonehurst Stables, Roscoe, 7 to 9 p.m.

Lockheed All-Star Softball practice, 7:30 p.m., Burbank Civic Park.

Regular Boy Scout meeting, 1935 Brighton, Burbank, 7 to 9 p.m.

Choral Club rehearsal, Burbank High School, 7:30 p.m.

Drama Club dress rehearsal, Assistance League Playhouse, 7 p.m.

Thursday, Oct. 2 — Lockheed Rangers (Nite Crew), Tex' Stonehurst Stables, Roscoe, 10 a.m. to 12 noon.

Rangerettes, Doc's Stables, Roscoe, 7 to 9 p.m.

Press Preview for Company Officials and L.E.R.C. Council. Curtain, 8:30 sharp. Company call, 7 p.m.

Baseball practice, Solon Park, San Fernando Road, across from Plant 1, after work.

Friday, Oct. 3, 4 and 5—Opening nights of "Room Service." Curtain 8:30 p.m. Company call, 7 p.m.

R. A. F. TRAINEES TO PLAY SOCCER MATCH

Soccer enthusiasts will have an opportunity Sunday, September 28, to not only see a good game between "the boys who make 'em" and "the boys who fly 'em," but also to give support to a worthy cause sponsored by their friends of the Canadian Legion.

The occasion is a soccer football match to be held that day at 3 p.m., between a team from the R.A.F. trainees at Lancaster and the Douglas Aircraft soccer team. Place is the Loyola Stadium, 1907 Venice Boulevard, Los Angeles, and all proceeds will go to the Canadian Legion Last Post Fund, which takes care of the burial of indigent veterans of the British Empire and maintains the British Veterans plot at Inglewood Park cemetery.

The game will be preceded by an hour-and-a-half of entertainment, starting at 1:30. Movie Star Alan Mowbray will be master of ceremonies and many stellar attractions will be on the bill.

MUSICIANS WANTED FOR NEW DANCE ORCHESTRA

A brand new, bang-up Lockheed-Vega dance orchestra should shortly be providing first-class entertainment for employee social affairs if Phil Grogan, of Department 5, Graveyard shift, can put his plan into effect.

Phil, who was formerly with the George Olsen, Orrin Tucker and Johnnie "Scat" Davis orchestras, is a member of Ascap, one of his songs, "Especially for You," having been a Lucky Striker. He is sending out a call to both Lockheed and Vega employees for musicians to form the orchestra.

To turn out a first rate dance band, he says, he will need four saxes, four brass, four rhythm, one girl singer and a copyist. He offers his services free as musical arranger and director, the group to operate on a purely non-profit basis.

After hours Phil can be contacted at WAlnut 2553, or replies can be sent care of this publication for forwarding.

CAMERA CLUB BIDS FOR NEW MEMBERS

The Lockheed Camera Club is bidding for new members to take part in the varied and interesting programs of the organization.

Regardless of the ability or experience of camera enthusiasts, they are welcome to join the Camera Club. No fees or dues are collected and the only responsibility entailed is regular attendance at the Club meetings.

V.E.R.C. CALENDAR

Saturday, Sept. 27 — Pistol practice, Burbank Police Range, 9 a.m.-12 noon.

Sunday, Sept. 28 — Ice Skating Club meeting, 9:45 a.m., Tropical Ice Gardens, Westwood Village. Ice skating for all will follow meeting.

Rifle practice, Glendale Rifle and Revolver Range, 9:30 a.m. Pistol practice, Burbank Police Range, 9 a.m.-2 p.m.

Baseball Game, Vega vs. Fullerton Firemen at Fullerton, 2:15 p.m.

Vega Choral Club Time, 4:30-4:45 p.m., Station KIEV, 870 on your dial.

Monday, Sept. 29 — Riding Club Instruction class, Ride-A-While Stables, 7 to 8:30 p.m.

Tuesday, Sept. 30 — Vega Mixed Chorus, Male Chorus, Girls' Chorus, Griffith Park Recreational Center, Los Feliz and Riverside Drive, 7:30-9:30 p.m.

Rifle practice, Glendale Rifle & Revolver Range, 7:30 p.m.

Vega Fencing Club, Falkner's Studio, 5610 Hollywood Blvd., 7:30 p.m. The club will meet on Tuesday until further notice.

Wednesday, Oct. 1—Men's Bowling League, Hollywood Recreation; 2 sections, first section, 6:45 p.m.; second section, 9 p.m. Sunset Bowling Center, one section, 6:15 p.m.

Mixed Chorus for Swing Shift and Graveyard will meet at Michiel Marsman's home, 700 E. Lomita, Glendale, at 1 p.m.

Ice Skating Club meeting, 7:30-8 p.m., Tropical Ice Gardens, Westwood, 7:30 p.m. Skating before and after meeting.

Thursday, Oct. 2—Little Theatre Group, Wilshire Music Center, 3771 Wilshire Blvd., 7:30 to 8 p.m.

Men's Bowling League, Sunset Bowling Center, 6:15 p.m.

Friday, Oct. 3—Swingphony Club (recordings and dance), Wilshire Music Center, corner Wilshire and Western, 7:30 p.m.

Riding Club, drill team practice, 7:30-9 p.m., Trail Ride, 7-9 p.m. for those who wish straight riding from Ride-A-While Stables, Burbank, with business meeting at 9 p.m.

Union Contract Questions Answered

The following questions and answers are of general interest on the Union Agreement, signed September 15, 1941. Any further questions should be taken up directly with Personnel Representatives.

Minimum Rates

Q. If a man is hired now at $24 weekly when does he receive $30 weekly?

A. At the completion of 12 full work weeks as follows: At the end of four full work weeks he shall receive 65c per hour ($26 weekly). At the end of eight full work weeks, he shall receive 70c per hour ($28 weekly) and upon completion of 12 full work weeks he shall receive 75c per hour ($30 weekly). FULL weeks shall form the basis for these reviews. Example: An employee starting to work on Saturday, Sunday or Monday shall be considered to have completed a full work week on the following Friday. If he starts work on Tuesday or later, the following Monday shall be the actual starting day of his first FULL working week.

Q. Will rate changes be made for employees who become eligible for new minimum rates during the 60-day freezing period?

A. Yes, when eligible.

Reviews and Rate Changes

Q. Will an employee's first regular review be scheduled six months after he is hired or six months after he receives the minimum rate of 75c?

A. All employees will be reviewed 24 weeks after hiring date.

Q. During the period of 60 days from date of signing agreement are there to be absolutely no rate changes?

A. Only changes in classification will be made with rates changed accordingly. No merit increases will be made during this period.

Q. When an employee is changed to a higher paid job, the intent is to pay him the scale for that job AT ONCE. What is the interpretation of AT ONCE?

A. In the new agreement all rate reviews are frozen for a period of 60 days from Sept. 15, 1941. In case of a classification change however, such change will become effective within a reasonable period after such classification change is made.

Overtime

Q. Will an employee, if he does not work on the first overtime day (Saturday) of a week, receive double-time if he works the second overtime day (Sunday)-?

A. Yes, under the new agreement he will receive two times the regular rate for all hours worked on Sunday or on his second overtime day should he be on an odd-work week.

Q. Do the double-time provisions affect regular working day?

A. No.

Q. Is double-time retroactive?

A. No. Double-time for second overtime day of week went into effect Sept. 15, 1941.

Rates

Q. Will rates continue to be handled in 3c increments?

A. No. All rates will now be computed to the nearest cent for straight-time and to the nearest half-cent for overtime. Example: If any employee formerly got $1.02 per hour for straight-time on graveyard shift it was because the rate figured at $1, but was put forward to the nearest 3c interval. If the rate now figures to be $1, the new rate will be applicable.

Q. What rate will apply in the case of a rehire to an employee who left the company between July 1 and the present date and who was eligible for the 75c minimum on July 1?

A. Upon termination of employment the employee loses his seniority rights and may be rehired as a new employee.

Q. Will the rate schedule be increased by 10c in each grade of each classification?

A. No. Anyone hired since July 1 at $30 a week or more, or going to a higher rated job since July 1, does not necessarily receive more than the minimum listed in the present wage schedule. It is possible the wage schedule may be increased from time to time.

Retroactive Checks

Q. Will employees who have terminated since July 1 have to pick up their retroactive checks, or will they be mailed?

A. They will be mailed.

Q. When will retroactive checks be distributed?

A. As soon as they have been completed and checked for accuracy.

MULVEY Z. WHITE IN NEW POSITION

Effective September 1, Mulvey Z. White relinquished his duties in Department 44, Lockheed-Vega Central Employment, to become assistant manager of Department 42, Employment, according to B. W. Messer, manager of the Employment Department.

Mulvey Z. White

Mr. White has been with the company since August, 1940, having started as a special interviewer. He is a graduate of U.S.C. and after his graduation served as assistant secretary to President R. B. von Kleinsmid, of U.S.C. He also served as assistant coordinator of the university and for four years was director of employment at that institute of learning.

Boarder: Ah, your steak is like the weather this evening, madam, rather raw.

Landlady: Indeed? By the way, your account is like the weather too—unsettled.

THIS REMINDER MAY SAVE AVOIDABLE LOSS

For the convenience of Lockheed and Vega employees who may have the misfortune to lose personal property, Lost and Found bureaus have been set up in Lockheed Plant 1 and Vega Plants 1 and 2.

In case of loss, Vega personnel should notify the clerk on Extensions 1142, 396 or 7333.

Lockheed Plant 1 personnel should call Extension 1774 and lost articles should be delivered to Window 8, Employee Relations Department.

Wanted! Service Mechanics

During the coming year, expansion of the Service Divisions of Lockheed and Vega will require a number of certificated "A" & "E" mechanics.

Men holding such certificates and desirous of entering this service work should send their names and qualifications, especially aircraft experience, to B. W. Messer, Department 42, for Lockheed employees; or to Ralph B. Smith, Department 67, for Vega employees.

R. RANDALL IRWIN NAMED ON COUNCIL

R. Randall Irwin, industrial relations director of Lockheed and Vega, has been appointed Aircraft Representative on the State Advisory Committee for the Council of State Administrators for National Defense Training.

This committee, which includes representatives of industry, labor and agriculture, serves as advisor to the State Departments of Education and Employment and the National Youth Administration in all national defense training activities within the state, under the federal training program.

Mr. Irwin is also a member of the National Advisory Committee on the Training Within Industry Section of O.P.M., and a member of the California State Apprenticeship Council.

Brakes now being made by industry for defense purposes are so powerful that they must stop 80-ton bombing planes rolling along the ground at 80 miles per hour in 10 seconds flat.

THE DIFFERENCE A FEW MONTHS MAKE

The two photographs above show the intersection of Empire avenue and Hollywood Way, adjacent to the Vega No. 1 Plant, as it was (top) just six short months ago, and (bottom) as it is today. It is because of these vital highway improvements in the Lockheed-Vega plant areas, brought about through the cooperation of the companies and the City of Burbank, that it takes no longer now for employees to disperse to their homes than it did six months ago when the working forces were less half what they are at present.

R. B. ROBERTSON HONORED BY STATE APPOINTMENT

R. B. Robertson, assistant director of Industrial Relations for the Lockheed and Vega companies, has been appointed a member of the Manufacturing Wage Board of the California Industrial Welfare Commission.

Mr. Robertson, who has been with Lockheed since 1938, will represent the aircraft industry on this important board.

Baldwin Kite On Radio

Those who heard Baldwin Kite, of Vega Department 57, sing over the radio last August 29, will have a chance to hear him again tomorrow night, Saturday, September 27.

Due to the letters and cards mailed in by Lockheed and Vega employees, he placed second in a popular contest, thereby earning a chance to try again. Listen in tomorrow night on "Tune Out Time," KFI at 9:00 p.m.

SPORT SHORTS

BASEBALL PLAYERS at Lockheed are requested again to attend the turn-outs on Tuesday and Thursday evenings immediately after work. Turn-outs are held at Solon Park, across San Fernando Road from Lockheed.

* * *

BASKETBALL ENTHUSIASTS are advised that inter-departmental play will commence shortly after November 1 and all teams must be made up from each department before that date. When teams have been signed up, send list to L.E.R.C. office promptly.

* * *

THE LOCKHEED PISTOL AND RIFLE Club is planning a five-point meeting this coming Sunday, September 28, at the Pasadena Police Range. A practice shoot, a rifle match, a business meeting, election of officers and ratification of the proposed by-laws are scheduled to fill the day-long event, and all club members are urged to attend.

* * *

FANTASIA TICKETS may be obtained by Lockheed-Vega employees at the Carthay Circle Theatre Box Office at half-price. Just show your Lockheed-Vega pass.

"YANK IN THE R.A.F." STARS HUDSON BOMBERS

Hailed as a great air picture, "A Yank In The R.A.F." had its gala world premiere last night, Thursday, at Grauman's Chinese Theater. Following the premiere, the production set a new precedent by playing three local first-run houses at once, opening today at the Four-Star, Loew's State and the Chinese.

The picture, starring Tyrone Power and Betty Grable, is of special interest to Lockheedians and Vegans because of the authentic aviation background filmed in England and the spectacular part played by Lockheed Hudson bombers. Several of the scenes were filmed at the Lockheed Air Terminal in Burbank.

Packed with thrilling excitement of air duels, bombings and the sensational evacuation of Dunkirk, the production is listed as a "must-see" by those who saw the previews.

Tickets At Half Price

Tickets to "Mamba's Daughters," now playing at the Biltmore Theatre, may be obtained at half-price by Lockheed-Vega employees who show their passes at the box office. The run of this New York hit will close on October 4.

WRONG TOOL IN RIGHT MOTOR CAN SLOW YOU DOWN

"Hey, this blankety-blank motor is no good!"

Such was the comment overheard by one of the Tool Service men out in the shop the other day. Stepping over to the source of the vociferous complaint, he inquired into the cause of the trouble.

"Well," said the operator, laying down the handful of rags with which he was holding the motor and gingerly juggling it over onto a bench, "the darn thing won't pull; it chatters and it gets hotter than a depot stove!"

T.S. man casts experienced eye over the situation; notes as follows:

1. 5000 R.P.M. electrical motor, with, of course, a 3/16" chuck.
2. 5/16" reamer, shank ground down to fit chuck.
3. Operation, ream bolt holes approximate 3/8" thickness of material.

The Tool Service man patiently explained, for perhaps the twenty-fifth time that day, that:

1. 5000 R.P.M. motors are to be used for 3/16" maximum drilling, hence the 3/16" chuck.
2. Satisfactory life of reamers depends on operation at slow speeds, otherwise chatter dulls or breaks flutes and produces rough work.
3. A combination of the two forms of abuse results also in excessive maintenance on motors, replacement of burned out armatures, ruined chucks, etc.

P.S. John J. Operator, who was so hot under the collar the other day, is now using a 500 R.P.M. motor for his reaming. He whistles while he works, but the reamer doesn't! Incidentally, it is saving the company money.

GLENN MARTIN VISITS VEGA

Shown at right, during the recent visit of Glenn L. Martin to the Vega and Lockheed plants are, left to right: W. G. Hoskinson, chief inspector, and M. A. Deeds, assistant chief inspector, Vega; Mr. Martin and B. F. Roehrig, receiving inspector of Department 45, Vega, who was the first man to give the noted aircraft builder his first ride in an airplane back in 1910. Mr. Martin was a guest of Robert E. Gross, president of Lockheed, during his visit to the plants.

NATIONAL MAGAZINES FEATURE LOCKHEED-VEGA IN NEWS, PICTURES

For the information of those who may desire to procure them, the following articles and pictures on Lockheed and Vega appeared in leading national and trade magazines during September:

AERO DIGEST—September
"Development of Aircraft Control Cables," by Carl Beed.
"Using Cameras as Aircraft Production Tools," by J. H. Washburn.
Article and picture of the Vega Ventura.
Article and picture of the N.E.I. Parachute Troop Lodestars.

AIR TRAILS—September
Picture of the P-38.
Picture of the Trans-Canada Airlines Lodestars.

AMERICAN AVIATION—September 15
"Vega Gets Funds to Expand Plant."

AVIATION—September
"Specification Engineering," by Peter A. Beck and Richard H. Robb.
Article on the Vega Production System, by H. A. Ryker.
Article on Vega's Fluorescent Lighting.
Article on Army Mechanics Learning to Service the P-38.

COMMERCIAL AVIATION—August
Article on the Yukon Lodestars.

MACHINERY—September
Article on Lockheed's Photo-Loft Template System, by R. A. Von Hake.

WAR ACES—September
Picture of Hudson Bombers.

WESTERN FLYING—September
Vega Test-Flies First Ventura.
Picture of P-38 Assembly Line.

WESTERN INDUSTRY—September
"The X-Ray Does Its Part Speeding Industry Toward Defense."

HOLDS REUNION WITH MAN WHO TAUGHT HIM TO FLY

A reunion unique in the history of aviation highlighted the recent visit of Glenn L. Martin, famed airplane builder, to the plants of the Lockheed and Vega companies, for among those in the Vega reception party for the noted guest was the man who gave him his first airplane ride way back in 1910 — B. F. Roehrig, now Receiving Inspector in Department 45, Vega.

Added interest was given the reunion by the fact that it brought together again, after many years, the two men who hold the first two flying licenses ever issued on the Pacific Coast. Mr. Roehrig holds the first, Mr. Martin the second.

It was back in 1909 that Mr. Roehrig built his first ship in San Diego and demonstrated to Mr. Martin, who was then in the auto business in the same city, that it would actually fly. First plane ever seen by the man who now heads one of the biggest aircraft companies in America, the ship was of the Farman type fitted with a 90 h.p. 6-cylinder "Featherweight" motor, but with it Mr. Roehrig made an altitude record in 1910 by soaring 500 feet into the air for 20 minutes of sustained flight, for which he was awarded the Knabenshue Cup.

Among other famous fliers whom he introduced to aviation was Lincoln Beechey. That picturesque pioneer took his first airplane ride with and was taught

(Continued on Page 7)

LOCKHEED TRAINS OWN 'HELLO' GIRLS

The first Lockheed training course for new Lockheed telephone operators was recently completed under the supervision of Miss Vera Doane, in charge of the Telephone Department, and Glenn Cole, of the Works Manager's office.

The seven girls who participated were trained PBX operators, but they were new to Lockheed and not acquainted with the complication of names, departments and locations which now make up this huge organization. In the past, operators have been trained on the main switchboard, training time being sandwiched in between calls and the regular day's business. This, naturally, was not satisfactory, so Miss Doane decided on the "school" idea, which quickly taught the new operators the "who's who"—the names and positions of executive and department heads and their secretaries—thus considerably speeding up service.

To complete the course, the girls were taken on a tour of the huge Lockheed 1 Plant so that they could see for themselves just where the various departments are located and could confirm Miss Doane's statement that "the Service Building is quite a distance from the Wind Tunnel."

All seven girls passed the course and tests with flying colors.

Mother: "After all, he's only a boy, and boys will sow their wild oats."

Father: "Yes, but I wouldn't mind if he didn't mix so much rye with it."

CLASS ANNOUNCEMENTS

Blueprint Reading II Class—
This class is for men who have had one semester of Blueprint Reading and who wish to continue studies along this line. The class is held Mondays and Wednesdays from 4 to 6:30 p.m. at the John Burroughs Evening High School, 1920 Clark, Burbank.

Lofting I—
Mr. Parmalee's Lofting class, which meets on Tuesday and Thursday from 6:30 to 9:30 p.m., will be held at the Luther Burbank school, Third and Magnolia, Burbank.

Spot Welding—
The Spot Welding class, which meets from 7 to 9 p.m. Tuesdays and Thursdays at the John Burroughs Evening High School, has room for additional students.

Hydraulics and Plumbing—
This class is to be held from 11 a.m. to 2 p.m. at the Frank Wiggins Trade School, Venice and Olive, Los Angeles, on Mondays and Wednesdays. It will begin Monday, September 29.

ARTISTS ARE SUCH FUNNY 'PIPPLE'

Coming to the forefront in "equestorial" circles is Lockheed's artist, George E. Nettleton, Jr. Having recently acquired Anthony (George calls him "Tony"), Nettleton has donned a MIXture of cowboy raiment and is now well on the way to being a rough rider. Picture at the right well illustrates the amazed impression his friends received of his exhibition, wi h perfect control, in last Saturday's Fiesta Parade in Glendale.

WARN AGAINST DEALING IN BACK PAYCHECKS

With issuance of thousands of checks for retroactive pay looming in the near future, a practice has sprung up among some employees of Lockheed and Vega, anxious to get cash immediately, of selling these prospective checks at a heavy discount, according to reports reaching the management.

These sales, it is reported, are being made between employees inside the plants as well as to outsiders. While there is nothing illegal in dealing in this form of "futures," nevertheless there is always someone on the losing end in each transaction and these losses tend to create ill-feeling when the day for settlement comes.

For this reason the management requests the cooperation of all employees in bringing about a discontinuance of the practice.

THE MULE

A mule can't pull while he's kickin'—
  The reverse is also true:
He can't kick while he's pullin';
  And neither can I or you.

The best way to move the wagon
  From out of the place where it's ditched
Is stand on your feet and quit kickin',
  At least until you're unhitched.

Mules bray and are called plain stubborn,
  Unable troubles to stem;
They kick at the least provocation—
  But who wants to be like them?

—Harrington Barrus

SUPERVISOR CLASSES TO START SEPT. 29

New classes in Supervisory Development will start Monday, September 29, and Tuesday, September 30.

Formal acceptance notices showing class number, time, days, and place have been issued by Supervisory Development to 2000 new students. Including the new students, the total enrollment of present and potential basic leaders attending these classes will be increased to 4000.

Arrangements to handle the increased enrollment have been made and new instructors have been added. The staff of instructors at present includes J. B. Calhoon, L. E. Eyre, H. Gabar, J. D. Keyes, F. L. Naylor, L. T. Peterson, J. Pettker and H. C. Rundle, of the Education Department.

The courses being offered by Supervisory Development are:

Course No.	Subject
1	Job Instruction Planning and Presentation
2	Orientation of New Employees
3	Setting Up and Conducting Departmental Training Programs
4	Basic Supervisory Techniques
5	(To be announced later)

Application for enrollment in Supervisory Development classes must be made to department heads.

The aircraft industry in this country increased its floor space 246 per cent and hired nearly 193,000 more employees in only 27 months' time between 1939 and 1941.

NEW L.E.R.C. PRESIDENT

John McCabe, retiring president of the L.E. R.C., hands the gavel of authority to the new incoming president, Harold E. Davis.

Following the resignation of John McCabe, members of the Lockheed Employees' Recreation Club Council elected Harold E. Davis, Department 34, to fill the presidential position.

The unanimous selection of Davis as head of the recreation club makes the second time Davis has been selected to head the organization.

Davis was president in 1938; served as vice-president for a part of the 1940 term and was reelected vice president for 1941.

The vacancy created in the vice presidential spot with Davis' election to president, was filled by James Mosher, of Department 25.

ENGINEERS PLAY LEAD ROLES IN 'ROOM SERVICE'

No less than five engineers and two ex-engineers are working on the L.E. R.C. Drama Club play, "Room Service," to be presented in October.

Charles Bell and Burt Miller, of Engineering, both of whom will be remembered for their fine job in the last play, have leading roles. Norman Ford and R. R. Steinberg are playing supporting parts, and Frank Lindsay is working on details. Susie McCallum, a former Group Clerk, is to be in the production, and Dick Walsh, formerly of Engineering, is directing.

VEGA VAQUEROS TAKE HONORS

★

The Vega Vaqueros shown strutting their stuff down Brand Boulevard during the Glendale Fiesta last Saturday. The troup is aiming for the Pasadena Tournament of Roses parade next New Year's Day.

★

GLENN L. MARTIN IN HISTORIC REUNION

(Continued from Page 5)

to fly by Mr. Roehrig, who continued his barnstorming trips throughout the country after Beechey was killed. A companion barnstormer in 1910 and 1911 was Didier Masson, who later became Air Minister of France.

Among Mr. Roehrig's souvenirs of those stirring times are his Number 1 license and yellowed clippings from the San Diego newspapers showing pictures of his original "crate," and stories depicting the pride of San Diego in his achievements.

GLENDALE CLASSES

Four lectures are being given by Miss Floy A. Taylor in the Glendale Evening High School on Wednesday evenings for feminine office employees.

These lectures deal mainly with office manners and personality. The first was given Wednesday, September 24. Three more will follow on consecutive Wednesdays.

The Blueprint Reading course at the Hoover High School, Glendale, on Monday and Wednesday evenings, from 7 to 10 p.m., is open for additional enrollment. Clyde Newman, of the Lockheed Engineering Department, is conducting the class in room 706.

Electrical assembly and installation classes are to be held from 7 to 10 p.m. in room 702 of the Glendale High School, 1440 East Broadway, on Tuesdays and Thursdays.

WIN SECOND PLACE IN FIESTA PARADE

Following their very successful gymkhana, entitled "Horse-Capades," the Vega Vaqueros again demonstrated fine horsemanship by winning for Vega second place in the Glendale Fiesta Parade.

This achievement is especially noteworthy because of the high quality of competition furnished by the many star riders in the event.

The Vega Vaqueros are newcomers to the field of equestrian team competition and is composed of men and women of Vega. In less than a year the group has turned out a strikingly uniformed team, able to compete with such noteworthy veteran organizations as the "Glendale Grayettes," "Lockheed Rangers" and the "North American Flying Horsemen."

This ambitious, fast-moving organization is heading for honors in the New Year's Day Tournament of Roses parade in Pasadena.

A Word TO THE WISE—

SEGREGATION —FOR SATISFACTORY SALVAGE

Division of MATERIAL CONSERVATION

THE *Lockheed-Vega Star* * *

The LOCKHEED-VEGA STAR is issued every Friday for the employees of the Lockheed Aircraft Corporation and the Vega Airplane Company. Communications may be addressed to either the Industrial Relations Office or the Public Relations Department, Lockheed Aircraft Corporation, Burbank, California, U.S.A.

H. L. (Hal) Rosson, Editor

Volume 8 Number 41

Dollars For Defense

The personnel of Lockheed and Vega know the urgent need for increased national defense. It is our job. The President has asked for speed and more speed—and we are giving it.

Our supplying of better and faster planes is one of the most important factors in national defense—however, it is not the full job. Hundreds of other types of armament are needed; munitions, supplies and trained man-power to use them are essential.

All this costs money, lots of money, and our government has called upon us to help pay the bill—to pay for it with dollars and cents, which is asking little when you consider that the people of other nations must pay with human lives.

Each employee of Lockheed and Vega can do his or her share by resolving right now to purchase at least one Defense Bond. This is your way of contributing your own individual share toward your country's defense. You can buy Defense Bonds "on time" by purchasing Defense Stamps each week until you have a sufficient number to equal the value of one Bond. Moreover, you can buy both Bonds and stamps very conveniently by stopping at your Credit Union window.

Each penny you put into Defense Stamps or Defense Bonds will pay you a profit—but that is not the important thing. What *is* important is that you are showing your faith in the future of your country—you are proving that you believe in democracy, freedom for human rights, and that you are willing to back up both your faith and your belief with *immediate action*.

OLD AND NEW IN BADGES

At far right is shown a sample of the new type of badge which is being distributed as the new system of personnel control goes into effect in all plants of the Lockheed and Vega companies.

THIS IS STRICTLY A PARTY STORY

Now here's a story you must believe, it concerns a party held at Plant 3—Fred Ward was the sponsor, Monday the day, they said refreshments would be given away, and those who came would have to stay . . . Oh, My.

The cause of it all came from a hunch, Fred Ward wanted his gang to meet Bill Rau's bunch, so the suite vacated by B.A.M. got a 958 job done by Hamm, and Plant Personnel moved in with a wham . . . Oh, My.

A handful of days went swiftly by, then a gleam appeared in this Ward's eye, the joint was dressed up fit to kill, and flowers appeared on each window sill, and the dive was as clean as a doctor's pill . . . Oh, My.

The invitations were black on white, and delivered in person, both day and night, Bill Rau and his Foremen, and Assistants, et al., came in a bunch for this fancy brawl, and when they saw what they saw, they started to crawl . . . Oh, My.

We figured a punchbowl with champagne or gin, and tid-bitty sandwiches for good measure thrown in, but our hopes were blasted like a toy balloon, and one by one we started to swoon, and we couldn't be saved with a Crosby tune . . . Oh, My.

Now take it easy as you read on through, 'cause I don't want the same shock to happen to you, but with do-nuts and cider they smiled, "How-dy-do" and instead of one you had to take two, and you had to eat them, they saw to that, too . . . Oh, My.

The Day Crew could take it and smile and smile, they knew they could leave in a little while, and head for a joint out Burbank way, and wash it down in a Wally Wells way, and mister that ain't eating hay . . . Oh, My.

But the poor old Night Crew had nothing to say, they had to take it and they had to stay, and the Personnel crowd very grand and nice, kept feeding 'em do-nuts not once but twice, and God help the man who didn't take thrice . . . Oh, My.

Well, the eight o'clock lunch was a sad ordeal, for hardly a man could eat a meal, but we learned our lesson and this we say, "if an apple will keep a doctor away, Plant 3 Personnel gets a barrel today" . . . Oh, My.

Well, Hal, there's the story, and with tongue in cheek, I've written it for the Star this week, but don't get me wrong we had a swell time, and Fred and his gang are really divine, but I'm bringing a sandwich and beer next time . . . Oh, My!

JERRY ISAACS, Plant 3.

NEW SYSTEM OF PERSONNEL CONTROL GOES INTO EFFECT

Huge and rapid increase in Lockheed and Vega personnel, plus the need to maintain effective control over the circulation of employeees and non-employees within company premises, has resulted in a decision by the management to install a uniform system of badges and passes for all plants of the Lockheed-Vega organization, according to a notification by L. W. Wulfekuhler, assistant secretary, to department managers.

Installation of the new system is now under way through the office of J. H. Hanson, plant protection director, who is charged with responsibility for carrying it into effect. Certain temporary records of department personnel will have to be kept until the system is in full operation, instructions concerning which, as well as details of the installation procedure, are being distributed to department heads by the Identification Bureau.

Company executives, officials, department and division heads will receive their new identification cards and badges through special arrangement with the Identification Bureau. The white administrative type badge will be retained until the new pass and badge system is complete.

Any questions concerning this matter should be referred to Mr. Hanson.

« « CONSERVATION OF MATERIAL IS A PATRIOTIC DUTY » »

THE *Lockheed-Vega Star* ★★

Hudsons Over England

(See Story Page 3)

COMMUNITY FUND DRIVE WEDNESDAY

Report Reveals Govt. Efforts To Prevent Inflation

The cost of consumer goods being of direct concern to everyone, the following review of what is being done to combat the tendency to inflation should be of interest to all Lockheed and Vega employees.

In its efforts to combat price inflation, the government is proceeding along two general lines. First, individual prices are being regulated through the establishment of price maximums and secondly, further pressure on prices is to be relieved through taxation and bond sales, or through further limiting of consumer credit.

As an initial step toward curbing consumer credit buying, certain regulations have already been put into effect through the Federal Reserve Board. They include higher down payments on the purchase of certain commodities and the shortening of maturity payments on time contracts. A further stiffening of consumer credit terms may be expected in future months. This has already been suggested by the Board of Governors of the Federal Reserve as a supplemental instrument to be used in conjunction with the broader, more basic fiscal policy of other governmental powers in combatting price inflation.

The Brookings Institution, in a report made public last week, takes exception to the government policy of attempting to halt inflation through price fixing without including control of farm prices and wages.

Chief factors in rising prices, said Brookings, are higher farm prices and higher wages.

The report further points out that Defense spending increased the national income from a rate of 70 billion dollars a year in the spring of 1940 to the present rate of 85 billions. Manufacturing got the most, its share of the national income being increased by 17 per cent, at least in 1940, beyond which no Department of Commerce figures are available. Agriculture got only 3.45 per cent more, Government 3.03 per cent, Finance 1.64 per cent. Of 1940's extra 5.3 billion dollars (over 1939), Manufacturing got more than half.

But Manufacturing is not just corpor-

(Continued on Page 7)

FEATURE MOVIES OFFERED GRATIS

The first all-talking, double feature motion picture offered free to Lockheedians through the Educational Committee of the L.E.R.C. will be shown tonight at 7 p.m. in the auditorium of Burbank High School.

Admission will be by your Lockheed pass. Two outstanding pictures will be shown: a travelogue, and a documentary film entitled "Ghost Town Saves Itself."

A second short subject, "Romance of Radium" has also been booked for this evening's program.

The hour: 7 p.m. The place: Burbank High Auditorium and the Admission, Free with your Lockheed pass.

Proposal Made For Kiddies Day Nursery

The L.E.R.C. is working with Louise Davidson, head of the Visiting Nurses Unit, on a proposal to establish a day nursery for employees' children of pre-school age.

Those employees interested are requested to send an ANVO to the L.E.R.C. office giving their name, the number of children of pre-school age and indicating "yes" or "no" on the question of paying a small daily fee per child.

The results of this survey will determine whether a day nursery shall be established. Therefore everyone interested is urged to "vote" at the earliest possible date.

Full-Out Aid Is Requested Of Lockheed - Vega

Along with the Burbank Community Fund, which devotes its efforts locally, the American Red Cross is in dire need of funds to carry on with its works of mercy, not only among the women and children of war-devastated Europe and Asia, but among the unfortunates of our own country who have been rendered homeless by recent floods, hurricanes and other major disasters.

With the all-out support of the companies, the L.E.R.C. and the V.E.R.C. and the Union, the Community Fund and Red Cross will hold on Wednesday and Thursday, October 15 and 16 in all plants, a joint drive for funds.

Lockheed and Vega personnel have earned a great reputation for generosity in the past and it is hoped that this year they will set an all-time record for contributions to these worthy causes. They need help more than ever before.

It is well known that there are many in Burbank and other parts of our nation who are actually in want and depend on the Community Fund and the Red Cross almost for their very existence.

For your convenience and to spread payments over a longer period so that it will be easier for you, your companies have agreed that you may authorize deductions from your pay checks.

Pledge cards will be distributed with time cards (those on monthly salary will receive cards in their pay envelopes). You will have a choice as to the pay days on which you wish deductions to be made. If more convenient, you may make cash donations to the Fund.

The Union has authorized its chairmen to collect the pledge cards and cash contributions.

Give whatever you can afford and help those who cannot help themselves.

SWING SHIFT JAMBOREE

Enjoy an evening of fun to the tune of Jimmy Grier and his band at the Florentine Gardens, 5955 Hollywood Blvd., Hollywood, California, Sunday, October 19. A seven course dinner plus three great floor shows. For tickets contact Chester Leigh at the L.E.R.C. office between 3:30 and 4 p.m.

WING BROKEN, HUDSON FIGHTS TO VICTORY

MAIMED BUT TRIUMPHANT

Although badly damaged by her wing tip striking the sea early in an attack on a German convoy, a Lockheed Hudson of the R.A.F. Coastal Command was still to out-fly, out-fight the German protecting air and naval forces and complete the bombing of a German naval convoy. Photograph above shows an R.A.F. aircraftsman kneeling on the wing, examining the damage a few minutes after the plane had landed at its own aerodrome. The picture was sent to Lockheed by the British Air Ministry.

UNION AGREEMENT IN BOOKLET FORM

Booklets containing the complete agreement recently signed between Lockheed and Vega and Aeronautical Lodge 727 of the International Association of Machinists, which became effective September 15 last, are being distributed to employees in all plants of both companies.

Aeronautical Lodge 727 has been sole representative of Lockheed and Vega employees on matters pertaining to wages, hours and conditions incident to their employment since March 12, 1937. In a covering letter issued over the signature of Cyril Chappellet, secretary of both companies, the management affirms that the joint relationship of the companies with the Union has been continuous and harmonious.

Any employee who has not yet received a copy of the agreement should ask his Plant Personnel representative for one.

TEMPLATE PROCESS EXHIBIT FEATURED

"Star" of the recent 54th Convention of the Photographers Association of America, held in Chicago, was the complete exhibit of the Lockheed template process prepared by the Lockheed Photo Department for Eastman Kodak Company and given the most prominent display in that company's booth.

The exhibit, according to Joe Washburn, chief photographer, who attended the convention as Lockheed and Vega representative, was studied with the greatest interest by technicians and photographers from such organizations as Studebaker, General Motors, General Electric, Western Electric, Boeing Aircraft, Teletype Corporation, the Electro-Motive Corporation, International Harvester and others.

Incidentally, Joe, who attended in the modest role of an observer, got "drafted" to conduct the first clinic on industrial photography ever sponsored by the PAA.

Flying Cross Award Reveals Epic Adventure

How Lockheed Hudsons can stand up to almost anything in the way of punishment and still fly is shown by the award of the Royal Air Force Distinguished Flying Cross to a British pilot whose Hudson reconnaissance bomber, attacking a German naval convoy protected by no less than five destroyers, hit the sea, broke off the entire tip of the port wing, and still recovered and completed its attack. The following account of the action was received direct from the British Air Ministry in London. The pilot's name was not revealed.

This particular Hudson was one of two which were on a daylight offensive patrol looking for enemy shipping off the Dutch coast. When they sighted the convoy they were not surprised by the unusual number of escorting warships, as the Royal Air Force has so whipped German convoys in those waters that the German Admiralty has been forced to increase drastically their convoy protecting vessels.

The weather was bad, which made the Hudson attack especially difficult. The moment they were sighted by the

(Continued on Page 6)

Britain Welcomes Sight Of Hudsons Overhead

One of the best pictures of Hudsons serving with the R.A.F. to come out of England is that which appears on Page 1 of the Star this week.

The picture, an official photograph released by the British Air Ministry, shows a squadron of Hudsons of the Coastal Command returning from convoy duty patrol over the Atlantic, in which vital task they have long played a leading role. Most outstanding example of the spectacular part they are playing was the recent capture of a German submarine by a single Hudson bomber — the only case of its kind in the history of aerial warfare.

Note the peaceful, checkered pattern of the English countryside below, reminiscent of some of the older parts of New England. Such a sight must be more than welcome to the intrepid air crews after their hazardous hours on patrol and bombing forays. But even more cheering is the knowledge that they are flying Hudsons, the plane which has earned fame for "always bringing them back."

R. A. F. MEN IN TRAINING HERE

★

Left to right: Sgt. R. R. Tilbury and Sgt. C. F. Cockle of the R.A. F., Sgt. G. L. Purvis, U.S. Army technician from Ladd Field, Alaska; Sgt. R. H. Anderson and V. Denham, technician, both of the R.A.F.

★

VEGA EMPLOYEES PLAN BIG DANCE

One of the biggest dances of the year will be staged by Vega employees Friday night, October 17, at the Riverside Breakfast Club. It will be an all-night affair, all-night meaning right through to breakfast time Saturday morning, thus giving day and night shift workers an opportunity to take part in the event.

Starting at 8 o'clock Friday evening, an hour of coaching in the tango, rhumba and la conga will be given by glamorous Marguerite Price, former Follies star and now a Hollywood dancing teacher. Admission tickets will include this course of instruction. Hal Lomen's popular dance orchestra will provide everything from sweet swing to jive.

Day workers who arrive at 8 or 9 Friday night can stay as long as they wish, right on through the program for the swing-shift workers who will arrive around 1 a.m., if they care to. A map showing the location of the club is on the back of every ticket. Tickets are on sale by Departmental Representatives and at the V.E.R.C. office.

Prices are: 75 cents for couples; 50 cents for stags, for those arriving before midnight. For swing-shift workers who arrive after midnight, the price will be 50 cents a couple and the same price for stags.

The Riverside Breakfast Club is located at 3213 Riverside Drive, just south of Los Feliz Boulevard, near Griffith Park and the Los Feliz plunge.

LEARN TO SERVICE VEGA VENTURA, P-38

Four British R.A.F. technical instructors this week arrived at Lockheed-Vega to take a six-weeks course in servicing the Vega Ventura bomber and the Lockheed Model 322, or "Lightning," the British version of the P-38.

The men, Sergeants R. R. Tilbury, C. F. Cockle and R. H. Anderson, and V. Denham, technician, will spend their first three weeks learning how to service the "Lightning," their last three on the Ventura.

The Lockheed-Vega Education Department instructors are teaching the R. A.F. men all about servicing the two airplanes. On their return to England, it will be the job of these four technicians to teach scores of other flight and service mechanics how to keep the Lightning and the Ventura flying.

CREDIT UNION WARNS ON MAIL REMITTANCES

Many Credit Union members are in the habit of transmitting cash deposits to the offices either by mail or by way of the "pony" service.

Occasionally, these remittances are delayed in the mails and for this reason Manager Harry E. Richardson points out that the Credit Union cannot assume responsibility for cash sent in this manner until it has actually been received by a duly authorized representative of the Credit Union.

In other words, such remittances are made at the sender's own risk.

AVERAGE INCOME TAX PAYABLE TOLD BY DEPT. CHIEF

Under the new income tax schedules the average employee at Lockheed and Vega who has been on a weekly salary since January 1, 1941, will earn for the year an amount that will require an income tax of $125.64, if he is single, and $50.64 if he is married or the head of a house, according to R. E. Baumgarten, head of the Reports and Statistics Division, Lockheed.

The full significance of the responsibility to be carried for the first time by persons of lower incomes has been realized by the Government through issuance of tax anticipation warrants. The banks are sponsoring savings for income tax purposes by the creation of special income tax savings accounts.

As a partial offset to this inevitable responsibility, the retroactive wage adjustments to be received by employees on the payrolls as of July 1 may be considered more than sufficient to cover the tax payment of the married individual, and a substantial portion of the tax to be paid by the single individual can be offset in this manner, Mr. Baumgarten pointed out. In other words, to many employees this retroactive adjustment will serve as an excellent opportunity to anticipate the income tax liability.

In the case of new employees who will not have been on the payrolls for the full year of 1941, the income tax liability will fall somewhere in the brackets which were indicated in the STAR of last week. In any event, the retroactive cash adjustment could be an excellent offset against the new income taxes.

DEATH TAKES CLIFFORD GUY DICKSON OF VEGA

The friends and co-workers of Clifford Guy Dickson, of Vega Employees' Tool Store, will grieve to learn of his death last Sunday.

Mr. Dickson entered the employ of Vega in August of this year. He is survived by a sister, to whom the company and employees extend their deepest sympathy.

L.E.R.C. Main Canteen Will Open Monday

The L.E.R.C. main Canteen will be open for business Monday, October 13, in the paved recreation area west of the Credit Union-L.E.R.C. building.

Sixteen windows offering service on all four sides will eliminate much of the service delay experienced at the Canteen when it was located near the main clock house.

L.E.R.C. CALENDAR

Drama Club

October 10 and 11, last two days of Drama Club Play "Room Service" at Hollywood Assistance League Playhouse, 1367 North St. Andrews Hollywood, 8:30 p.m.

Education

Double-Feature motion picture, Free with Lockheed Pass, 7 p.m., Friday, October 10, Auditorium of Burbank High School.

Camera Club

Sunday, October 12, Field Trip to take place at Noah Beery's Paradise Ranch.

Rangers

Lockheed Rangers Drill Team, 7 a.m. to 9 a.m., Tex' Stonehurst Stables, Roscoe, Sunday, October 12.

Lockheed Rangers, Tex' Stonehurst Stables, Roscoe, 7 p.m. to 9 p.m., Wednesday, October 15.

Lockheed Rangers (Nite Crew), Tex' Stonehurst Stables, Roscoe, 10 a.m. to 12 noon, Thursday, October 16.

Band

Band rehearsal, John Burroughs Junior High, Burbank, 7:30 p.m., Monday, October 13.

Pistol & Rifle

Small bore rifle meet, Sunday, October 12, Times Rifle Range.

Sunday, October 12, 9:00 a.m., I.C.S. B.R.L. match with L. A. Times R. & R. Club, at Times Range.

Baseball

Baseball Practice, Solon Park, San Fernando Road across from Plant 1 after work, Tuesday, October 14 and Thursday, October 16.

Boy Scouts

Regular Boy Scout Meeting, 1935 Brighton, Burbank, 7 p.m. to 9 p.m., Wednesday, October 15.

Choral Club

Choral Club Rehearsal, Burbank High School, 7:30 p.m., Wednesday, October 15.

Golf

Lockheed Night, Tuesday, October 14, Golfer's Paradise, Victory Blvd. and Hollywood Way, Burbank, 8 p.m.

Rangerettes

Doc's Stables, Roscoe, 7 to 9 p.m., Thursday, October 16.

Ski Club

Ski Club meeting, Tuesday, October 14, at 7:30 p.m., Burbank Women's Club, Burbank.

Ice Skating

All Lockheed employees will be admitted free at the Pan Pacific Ice Skating Rink, Thursday, October 16, between 6:30 and 7 p.m.

CHUCK KEYS MADE TO SAVE INJURIES, EXPERIENCE SHOWS

"Better use your chuck key, Joe."

Such was the advice of the Tool Service man the other day as he observed another case of the so-called "quick way"—slapping the chuck with the "heel" of the hand to loosen it.

"Aw, s'too slow," was the reply. "I always do it this way; never have any trouble."

The truth is that "Joe," like many another operator in the shop, was under the misguided impression that to use a chuck key was the mark of a tenderfoot. So he went on doing it his own way—for a couple of days.

What happened is old stuff. The First Aid stations could very nicely use a rubber stamp for writing up the report. The chuck somehow tightened more than usual. Joe banged it a couple of licks and it still stuck. Losing patience, he hauled off and took a real pass at it. You know the rest; nice, sharp little No. 40 drill, and somehow, Joe still doesn't know why that third finger didn't get out of the way.

Here's how Joe is saving the company money, now that he is using a chuck key when changing drills:

1. He's not galling drill shanks by insufficiently tightened chuck jaws.
2. He's actually saving time by not having to stop and take another "grab" at the chuck every few minutes.
3. He is getting reasonable service out of a set of chuck jaws.
4. He has more than cut in half the risk of serious damage to the motor by dropping.
5. Last, but by no means least, he is not running the risk of injury to the hands that earn him his daily bread.

Think it over. Use your *head and your hands—AND your chuck key!*

"Keep 'em Flying"

V.E.R.C. CALENDAR

V.E.R.C. Dance

Fall Dance—Friday, October 17, 9 p. m., Riverside Breakfast Club. Hal Lomen and his orchestra will furnish music. Dancing instructions from 8 to 9 p.m.

Bowling

Men's Bowling League, Wednesday, October 15, Hollywood Recreation, 2 sections; first section 6:45 p.m.; second section, 9 p.m. Sunset Bowling Center, one section, 6:15 p.m.

Men's Bowling League, Thursday, October 16, Sunset Bowling Center, 6:15 p.m.

Choral Clubs

Vega Choral Club Time, Sunday, October 12, 4:30 p.m., Station KIEV, 870 on your dial.

Vega Mixed Chorus, Male Chorus, Girls' Chorus, Tuesday, October 14, Griffith Park Recreational Center, Los Feliz and Riverside Drive, 7:30-9:30 p.m.

Mixed Chorus for Swing Shift and Graveyard, Wednesday, October 15, 700 E. Lomita, Glendale, 1 p.m.

Fencing Club

Meeting, Tuesday, October 14, Falkner's Studio, 5610 Hollywood Blvd., 7:30 p.m.

Ice Skating Club

Meetings, Sunday, October 12 at 9:45 a.m.; Wednesday, October 15 at 7:30-8 p.m., Tropical Ice Gardens, Westwood Village. Skating before and after meetings.

Little Theatre Group

Meeting, Thursday, Oct. 16, Barnsdall Park, Olive Hill, 7:30-9:30 p.m.

Riding Club

Instruction Class, Monday, Oct. 13, Ride-A-While Stables, 7-8:30 p.m.

Drill Team Practice, 7:30-9 p.m.; Trail Ride, 7-9 p.m., Friday, October 17, Ride-A-While Stables. Business Meeting at 9 p.m.

Rifle and Pistol Club

Pistol Practice, Sunday, Oct. 12, 9 a. m. to 2 p.m., Burbank Police Range.

Rifle Practice, Sunday, Oct. 12 at 9:30 a.m.; Tuesday, October 14 at 7:30 p.m., Glendale Rifle and Revolver Range.

Swingphony Club (Recordings and Dance)

Meeting, Friday, October 10, Wilshire Music Center, corner Wilshire and Western, 7:30 p.m.

Appointment Announced

Appointment of Robert J. McCullough, as Personnel Representative of Lockheed Plant 3, was announced today.

The appointment is effective immediately. He will replace Fred Ward, who has been transferred to Vega Plant 1 to assume other duties.

FIRST WOMEN IN SUPERVISORY CLASSES

These girls from the Electrical Precision Department, Vega Plant 1, are the first to avail themselves of the Lockheed-Vega training program for leaders in the airplane industry. Left to right: Fay Freeman, Elaine Piisponen, Mable Wilson, Murrle Davis, Laura Lane and Ruby Blond.

FREAK AIR HOSE ACCIDENT TOLD

A recent rather unusual injury demonstrates the need for special precautions when using compressed air.

The victim of this particular accident was a Lockheed Machine Shop employee who had stuck his right palm with a pencil. Later, he used an air hose to clean some tools held in the injured hand. When he opened the nozzle, the air under 100 pounds pressure struck and entered the tiny pencil wound, and before he realized what had happened, the back of his hand and wrist were blown up as big as an orange.

Besides being painful, the accident could have been very serious had the air forced its way into the blood stream.

This and similar accidents can be easily avoided by directing the air in such a way that its blast does not contact either the operator or a fellow worker. A hand brush can be substituted for an air blast in a good many cases, eliminating the risk of injury.

V.E.R.C. ORGANIZING ORCHESTRA, BRASS BAND

A dance orchestra and a brass band, to be made up entirely of Vega employees, is being organized by the V.E.R.C.

This is an opportunity for those who can play a saxaphone, bass drum, trombone, accordian, xylophone, clarinet, vibra-harp, French horn, violin, piccolo or flute, trumpet, piano, guitar, or bassoon to contribute to the enjoyment of their fellow workers. Just go to the V.E.R.C. office and fill out a questionnaire they have prepared.

The club is also anxious to hear from those who have had experience in leading dance orchestras or brass concert bands.

AIRCRAFT MANUAL SOLD AT LIBRARY

The new Sixth Edition of the Standard Aircraft Workers' Manual is for sale to all Lockheed-Vega employees through the Lockheed Library at the special price of one dollar.

Only four months old, the sixth edition is completely up-to-date and is recognized as being the most complete and accurate manual of its kind. It serves as a dependable and useful source of information on aircraft construction from the workers' point of view.

Replete with drawings and illustrations to show uses and characteristics of aircraft material, tools, drawings, blue prints, mathematics, A, AN and B standard parts, practices and a glossary of terms, the manual is considered authentic in every respect.

Of handy pocket size, the 4 inch by 7 inch lexide covered wire bound book is easily read and fits into any tool box.

LOCKHEED SHOOTERS BRING HOME MEDALS

Based on the record turn-out of October 4 and 5 small bore rifle shooters at Lockheed are destined to make a name for themselves and for Lockheed.

In the Southern California Small Bore Registered Meet held at the Glendale range, Lockheed riflemen made a splendid showing.

Taking sixth place in the matches, which brought together some of the outstanding teams of the country, the 19 Lockheed representatives felt that their score was highly creditable in a match with 18 other sharpshooters.

Frank Faye, 16; Harry McClure, 10; Ray Robison, 18, and Alden Foster, 22, brought home medals.

AWARD REVEALS EPIC ADVENTURE

(Continued from Page 3)

enemy, all five destroyers—as well as the various ships of the convoy itself—opened fire. The Hudson leader was shot down in flames almost immediately.

The defensive fire was so tremendous that the pilot of the surviving Hudson was compelled to throw his plane about in the sky like a snipe. With the intention of making a mast-high attack he dived to only a few feet above sea level. Still twisting and turning to avoid shell bursts, he and his crew felt a violent blow which shook the plane from propellors to tail. Realizing that he had struck the sea the pilot pulled the stick back and, to his relief, the Hudson responded so well that he was able to fly it up into cloud-cover.

Out of sight, they had a look to see the extent of the damage. Three feet six inches of the port wing had been torn clean away by the impact with the waves and the loose ends of the de-icing equipment were flapping about in the slip-stream.

This rather looked as if no attack could be made, but as the pilot found that the Hudson still flew and maneuvered splendidly he and his crew decided to carry on and bomb the convoy.

Putting her nose down he slipped quietly out of the clouds and dived towards the convoy. Again a most fierce fire was opened upon him. Still, the Hudson stood up to every strain the pilot put upon it, and the bombing attack was carried out.

With shells bursting all around him, the pilot turned for home. Immediately two German fighters attacked him. The convoy was very near to the German occupied coast-line and the destroyers had obviously wirelessed for help.

It was not a pleasant position for the Hudson crew. Their plane was badly damaged and things were critical. Everything depended, if adequate evasive action were to be taken, upon the remaining maneuverability of the plane. In spite of every aerobatic trick the German fighters brought into play, the Hudson responded so well that the British pilot succeeded in eluding them and in bringing his Hudson safely home—with himself and his crew unwounded.

Engineers Sponsor Red, White, Blue Jig

With the announcement that Lud Gluskin's popular band and Martha Tilton, captivating vocalist, are signed to play and sing for the Engineers' Red, White and Blue Dance on November 8 at the Los Angeles Breakfast Club, the committee anticipates a sell-out of the limited number of tickets available.

REPORT REVEALS INFLATION BARS

(Continued from Page 2)

ations, the report continues. Industrial wage earners benefited (as a class) still more. In the same year, through June 1941, in which profits rose 16 per cent, average weekly earnings in 90 manufacturing industries rose 26 per cent (from $25.25 to $31.84). In the first quarter of 1941, total wages of all Social Security registrants (approximately 31,300,000 names) were 16 per cent more than the year before.

The Brookings report concludes that since farm products and wages have risen faster and farther than the price of manufactures in the past two years, the price of manufactures will soon be under terrific pressure to catch up. Inflation will then be well under way. Retail price increases have not yet been great, but their turn is coming, and the Office of Price Administration is helpless since even the proposed laws on price control do not give control over wages or over farm products until 110 per cent of parity has been reached. Yet these two factors, the report states, are chiefly responsible for the 21 per cent rise in wholesale prices since 1939.

"ROOM SERVICE" CAST WINS IN LAUGH WAGER

Early in the second act of the Lockheed Drama Club's production of "Room Service," the laugh judges from the Vega dramatic group conceded a victory to the Lockheed players for the dinner wager on the relative laugh-getting ability of the "Room Service" cast versus the "Boy Meets Girl" cast, which recently appeared under the sponsorship of the V.E. R.C.

The two final nights of "Room Service" are set for this Friday and Saturday night at the Assistance League Playhouse in Hollywood. A few seats are still available at the box office.

NEW CLASSES

Final Assembly—Installer

The above class will be held Monday, Wednesday and Friday from 6:30 p.m. to 9:30 p.m. at the new High School shop, Glenoaks and Grinnell, Burbank.

Machine Maintenance—

Tuesday and Thursday from 4 p. m. to 7 p.m. at the Burbank High School, Third and Fairmount, Burbank.

Sheet Metal—

Wednesday and Friday from 1 a. m. to 4 a.m. at the Jackman Building, 1809 Magnolia St., Burbank.

EVERYTHING BUT THE HORSE AND BUGGY

Thanks to the magic of the photographer's art, the P-38 superimposed on the above picture completes a visualization of all modes of transportation, except the horse and buggy, which feature the vicinity of Lockheed Plant 1 during the 3:30 shift-changing time. Clearly apparent are the various problems that confront the company and the City of Burbank in solving the traffic problem in the vicinity of the plants. Except for the plane, the picture is an actual photograph taken at 3:30 on a week-day afternoon. In addition to trucks and autos, a freight train, a pedestrian and a cyclist can be seen. And when those cars start coming off the railroad right-of-way, some one is certainly going to be late getting home.

CASHIER'S OFFICE NOW IN EMPIRE ST. BUILDING

In order to facilitate the handling of business through the Cashier's Office, the main unit is now located in Room 212, Building 167, corner of Empire and Valpreda streets, according to G. F. Duvall, manager of the Credit and Finance Division.

Office hours are 8 a.m. to 5:30 p.m.; Saturdays, 8 a.m. to 4:40 p.m. A subcashier's branch is located in Room 295, Building 103, with office hours from 11 a.m. to 12 noon and 3 p.m. to 4 p.m.; Saturdays, 11 a.m. to 12 noon.

DEPARTMENT 5 ENLARGED

Department 5, precision assembly, has recently been forced to enlarge its floor space, due to increased production schedules and the fact that all "322" assemblies, previously handled at Lockheed Plant 3, are now being assembled at Plant 1.

The increase in floor space, together with other changes, have streamlined the department to meet the ever increasing demand for "all-out" production.

LOCKHEED GUN CLUB ELECTS NEW OFFICERS

The Lockheed Gun Club combined a business meeting and a special shoot recently at the Pasadena Police Range, which brought out an enthusiastic crowd of members. The following new officials were elected: Thomas Dudley, president; Fred Good, vice-president; N. S. Hopkins, secretary; and Esther Valentine, treasurer. Dick Keeney was reappointed publicity chairman and Carl Hirdler executive officer for the group.

The constitution and by-laws were approved, thereby enabling the club to affiliate with the National Rifle Assn.

SHORT STORY DEADLINE EXTENDED TO OCTOBER 13

Due to the heavy response to the Short Story Contest being sponsored by The Aircraftsman, deadline for entries has been extended to permit contestants time to brush up their prize stories.

Entries must be sent into the L.E.R.C. Office not later than Monday, October 13, 5 p.m., to be considered for this month's contest. Late entries will be judged for the November contest.

THE *Lockheed-Vega Star* ★★

The LOCKHEED-VEGA STAR is issued every Friday for the employees of the Lockheed Aircraft Corporation and the Vega Airplane Company. Communications may be addressed to either the Industrial Relations Office or the Public Relations Department, Lockheed Aircraft Corporation, Burbank, California, U.S.A.

H. L. (Hal) Rosson, Editor

Volume 8 No. 43

Look Before You Leap

In these days of huge defense employment and consequent plentiful paychecks, the temptation is strong on everybody with a steady pay envelope to splurge a bit, not only on necessities but on luxuries.

There are various reasons, all coupled with the national defense economy, why the Government is advocating that this urge be restrained, principal of which is the existing and potential shortages in the supply of vital defense materials.

Where, however, this advice is disregarded and free spending is indulged in, the consumer should get not only value for his dollars but protection against chisellers who always spring up like a poisonous growth in times of "easy money." To supply this protection the public pays for its police and other governmental agencies. Unfortunately, the efforts of these organizations must be confined to prosecuting crime and fraud after it has been committed.

On the principle of "Prevention is Better Than Cure," the Los Angeles Better Business Bureau was created. Supported by ethical business firms for the purpose of protecting the public against fraudulent and unfair schemes, its protective services are offered free.

"Before you invest, investigate," is its slogan. Any employee of Lockheed and Vega who is considering a purchase or an investment and who, for some reason, is hesitant about going through with the deal, may phone the Bureau at TRinity 6305 and have his doubts either confirmed or set aside.

Such consultation costs absolutely nothing.

ADDITIONAL ESMDT CLASSES ARRANGED

The courses in Industrial Organization and Scientific Management offered under the ESMDT program have been so enthusiastically received that an additional class with R. W. Burbridge, of Vega, as instructor, is being arranged.

This course covers the principles of Industrial Management and the various processes of organization; the economic, administrative, and operational aspect of industrial organization through the consideration of such functions as the technical and managerial organization of production; time and motion study; production control; plant layout; budget evaluation; planning of production operations; production design and standardization; and budgetary control.

Class meetings will be held on Mondays from 7 p.m. to 9 p.m. in Room 122, Royce Hall, U.C.L.A. The course will consist of nineteen meetings, the first of which will be held October 13.

Mountain Guide: "Be careful not to fall here, it's dangerous. But if you do fall remember to look to the left, you get a wonderful view."

DO YOU REMEMBER WHEN ?

Lockheedians who are well acquainted with Lockheed Plant 1 as it is today should find the above historic photograph, taken only as recently as 1932, of special interest. It shows how the plant looked that year, when all the buildings combined wouldn't have much more than filled the Final Assembly building of today. Across the upper left hand corner of the picture is Victory Place, with the then administration buildings fronting on it. In the lower foreground is Empire Avenue, with a handful of employees' cars parked either side. But small as the plant was in 1932, compared with what it is today, it was at that time one of the largest in the United States, which position it still retains nine years later.

AIRCRAFT ECONOMICS COURSE IS OFFERED

A new course in Economics of Aircraft Manufacturing under the ESM DT program, will begin October 13 at U.C.L.A. G.M. Giannini, of Vega, will be instructor.

The course will cover distribution of aircraft manufacturing costs and their control by proper engineering design and breakdown.

Also analyzed will be design trends in military, commercial, and private airplanes and their future influence on the economics of the industry. Classes will be held in Room 126, Royce Hall, on Mondays from 7 to 9 p.m.

BASKETBALL

Once again this year Lockheed expects to field one of the outstanding basketball teams in the Los Angeles area. A call has been issued to all experienced basketball players who would like to play on the team.

Below is a registration form for players in the plant. When filled out please send to the L.E.R.C. Office.

NAME______________ DEPT.__________ PLANT__________

Experience__________ Prep-School__________ College__________

No. of Years__________ Position__________ Last Year of Play__________

Fill Out and Send to L.E.R.C. Office Immediately

LOCKHEED JOINS IN U.S. NUTRITIONAL SURVEY

Volume 8 BURBANK, CALIFORNIA, U.S.A., NOVEMBER 21, 1941 No. 49

THE Lockheed-Vega Star ★ ★

VITAMIN FEEDING TO BE TRIED

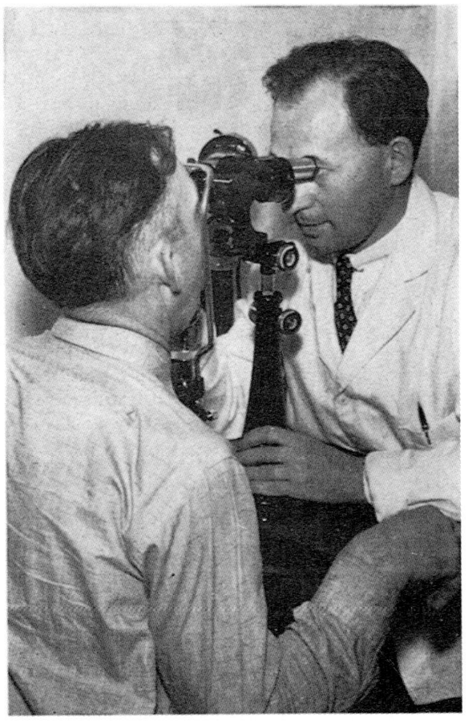

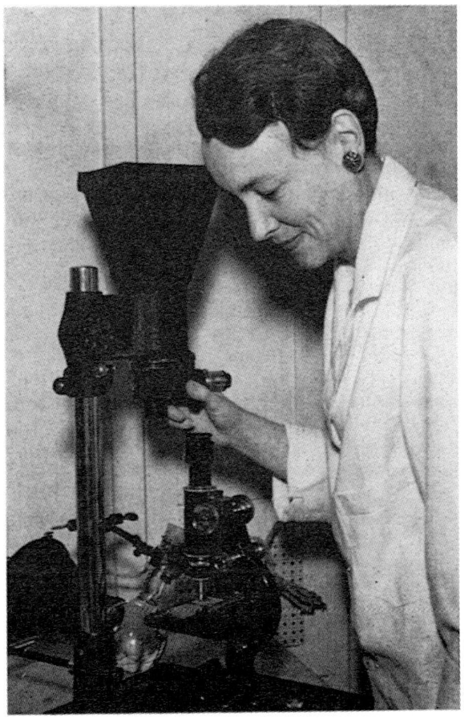

Step 1 (top picture) in the vitamin survey consists of establishing a nutritional history to ascertain the quality of present diet. Left to right: Richard L. Roland; Josephine Piazza and Mildred Way from the Los Angeles County Bureau of Medical Social Service, and Richard C. Swingler.

Lower left, Dr. H. Borsook of Caltech, examines patient with the aid of a Slit-lamp to measure the deficiency of Vitamin A and B_2. This instrument is one of only four at present in use in the United States.

Lower right, Beulah T. Waterbury, Bureau of Laboratories, Los Angeles County Health Department, shown making a microscopic examination to determine quality of blood.

When the six to nine months tests are completed, the United States Government Health Service believes it will have a far more complete guide to what is wrong with United States public health than it has ever had in the past.

Tests Designed To Improve The National Health

A man can have a full stomach seven days a week, 52 weeks in the year—and yet be half-starved!

This is not a matter of opinion but a provable fact based upon exhaustive scientific research by the National Research Council among industrial workers of the United States. The Council, which is the official advisory body to the United States Government on all scientific subjects, is at present conducting a survey among industrial workers throughout the country to determine their state of nutrition as a first step toward improving the national health through improvement of the national diet.

To this end, a number of organizations have contributed a $60,000 fund on the Pacific Coast alone, among them, besides the Council: Lockheed Aircraft Corporation, North American Aviation, Inc., the County of Los Angeles, the California Institute of Technology and the University of Southern California.

In the two aircraft factories, about 1300 employee selectees have been chosen to undergo feeding tests lasting

(Continued on Page 6)

LOCKHEED AND VEGA CONTRIBUTE $37,668 TO COMMUNITY FUND

A $37,000 tribute to the generosity of Lockheed and Vega employees and to the cooperation of more than 1000 Union chairmen in both companies plants, was recorded during the recent annual drive for funds for the Burbank Community Fund and the Red Cross.

As of Tuesday of this week, but before the books are finally closed, the actual amount subscribed by the personnel of the two companies amounted to $37,668, $9809 of which was donated by Vega men and women, $27,859, the balance, by Lockheed personnel in the three plants. Lockheed plants 1 and 3 subscribed $23,777; Lockheed plant 2, $4082, and both the Vega plants, $9809.

The campaign was jointly sponsored on behalf of the Community Fund and the Red Cross by the managements of both companies, the Union and the Recreation Clubs, to all of whom congratulations for the highly satisfactory results are due.

"OUT-OF-STATERS" GIVEN ADVICE ON CAR REGISTRATION

Non-residents of California who drive automobiles are urged by Howard Deems, registrar of the Department of Motor Vehicles, to go to the nearest office of the Department and determine what procedure they will be required to follow to register their vehicles in this state.

Deems said there are thousands of persons who have come here from other states within the last few months who will be required to register their vehicles when the annual renewal season begins January 2, if they desire to continue driving in California.

Inasmuch as registration requirements differ according to the state from which the non-resident comes, such persons can save themselves much delay and inconvenience by having their cars inspected and rated now instead of waiting until the renewal rush is on.

Registrar Deems said this applies particularly to the owners of Fords because the motors of this brand of car must have a serial number stamped on them before they may be registered under California regulations.

Application blanks and all necessary information will be given non-residents who call at branch offices of the Department at this time.

Deems' admonition was directed particularly at non-resident service men and workers in national defense factories.

Consistency certainly becomes a rare jewel when you see motorists with Safety First windshield stickers doing 75.

NEW CLASSES

Aircraft Rigging—
M-W-F, 6:30-9:30 p.m.
New High School Shop, Glenoaks and Grinnell, Burbank. Begins November 24.

Electrical Assembly and Installation—
T-Th, 12 noon-3 p.m.
Burbank High School, Third and Fairmont, Burbank. Begins November 25.

Detail Design and Drafting—
M-W, 6:30-9:30 p.m.
Drafting Room, John Burroughs School, 1920 Clark Street, Burbank. Begins November 24.

Aircraft Blueprint Reading—
T-Th, 6:30-9:30 p.m.
Senior High School, Room 214. Begins November 24.

Tool Design—
T-Fri, 12 noon-3 p.m.
Burbank High School, Third and Fairmont, Burbank. Begins November 25.

COLOR IS NO BAR TO EMPLOYMENT AT LOCKHEED AND VEGA

By Fleming R. Waller
Department 14, Lockheed

There are now approximately 125 Negroes employed by Lockheed and its affiliate, the Vega Airplane Company. I am one of them. And herein I am setting forth an accounting of my experiences and impressions gained at Lockheed for the past four weeks.

F. R. Waller

I was struck by the courtesy of my fellow-white employees and still marvel at the fact that of the thousands here, I have met with no insult, either open or veiled, and that I am given to feel that the Lockheed man is fair and is an ideal citizen.

I am in Department 14 where I gained my most favorable impressions of the Lockheed man. From Harold Gammill, the foreman, and his associates, Red Johnson and Harold Stiers, I gathered a broad view of the defense program at Lockheed. I found these supervisors to be a fine, intelligent trio and they are respected by every man in my department.

There is something unique in being given equal opportunity and the same chances of advancement alongside one's fellow-white American when one is a Negro. The psychological effect is stimulating and I am given to believe that industrial democracy is possible in America.

Now as regards the practical application of democracy. Lockheed is in the lead in Southern California among aircraft plants. I feel prepared to speak for the members of my group who are now employed at Lockheed. I have talked with a goodly number of them and without exception they all agree that Lockheed is an ideal place to work and that their experiences with their fellow-white workers are of the highest order. I also feel prepared to speak for the many young Negro men and women of Los Angeles who clamor at the gates, seeking entrance. They yearn to become an integral part of this vital force. I plead with Lockheed to let them in. Tap their youthful energies and enthusiasm. Guide them along vocational lines and lend a sympathetic ear to their problems. For these efforts, I can assure the company that no more capable and loyal group will be found in America.

The defense effort is not yet in high gear. The grand symphony of defense is not synchronized. There is lack of harmony. There is need of unison and keener cooperation between the black worker and the white worker. Just as the melody is made complete by the playing of both black and white keys, so must this defense symphony be unified by all black and white Americans, that the rising crescendo may boom into a thundering finale.

RIDES FOR PASADENA EMPLOYEES ARE NEEDED

There is a strange dearth of rides offered Lockheed and Vega employees residing in Pasadena, according to the Employee Service Department. Few are listed in the file at the Transportation Desk, yet many are needed.

Car owners phone Ext. 1774.

STATISTICIAN IS RED IN THE FACE

Nominated for first place in "Embarrassing Moments Department" is none other than John J. Macfadden of Accounting-Tabulating. "Mac" as he is familiarly known, is the man largely responsible for the efficient manner in which the huge task of getting out retroactive checks was accomplished.

Questionnaire No. 1, pertaining to an error in the amount of the retroactive check, came from a young lady in "Mac's" own office. She was a recent employee and had a check due her for $1.60. She received but 80c. Needless to say, the questionnaire followed.

Incidentally, in connection with the job of computing and making out these thousands upon thousands of checks, the amazing efficiency of the Accounting-Tabulating Department was evidenced by the fact that up to the early part of this week, less than a dozen complaints had been received that the checks were not correct. In most cases, it is reported, the checks totalled more than the recipients had computed.

'APRIL FOOL' PHONE CALLS BADLY TIMED

Suffering from a rather misguided sense of humor, certain individuals at Lockheed 1 are indulging in "April Fool" telephone calls which, while not serious in number, could be responsible for delays in important work.

It should be evident to these "humorists" that if the companies are to live up to their motto "First Things First," there is no time for this kind of foolishness.

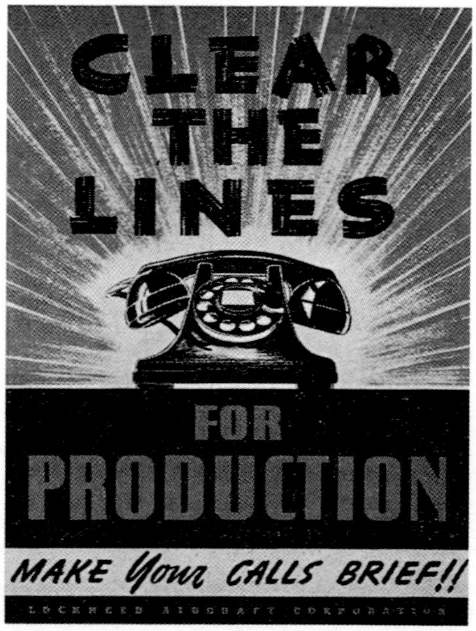

New Employees Continue To Sing Company Praises

A few weeks ago the STAR reprinted a few letters from present employees of Lockheed and Vega who had obtained employment with the companies through their State Employment Offices and who had gone to the trouble of writing back their appreciation of the service rendered them and of their employment here.

Much interest and considerable comment was evoked by the letters from the "Out-of-Staters." Several more have now been received, of which we have room in this issue to reprint the following (names deleted):

To The Fargo, N.D., Office:

"Just a few lines to let you know that I got here Monday. I started work at Lockheed and like it fine. I didn't get in the electric department as yet. They started me in the precision assembly. It is very interesting work and I like it fine. It sure is a nice factory to work in. I have a lovely place to live so am very well satisfied."

Signed..

To The Jamestown, N.D., Office:

"Got here on the 20th. and reported at Lockheed on the 21st. I went to work in Dept. 16, final assembly. A beginner starts at 60c per hour with 5c raises every four weeks until he is getting 75c. Graveyard and swing shift pays a 6c bonus. At present I am making 71c per hour. I work on the swing shift, 4 p.m. to 12:30 a.m. We work 8 hours overtime a week and get paid time and one-half for it. That is Saturdays."

Signed..

To the Bismarck, N.D., Office:

"I decided to work a month before writing you so as to give you more accurate information. Lockheed is now starting men at a minimum of 60c per hour and a 5c raise every four weeks. After six months we will be getting about 80c per hour. The work is not hard but requires a lot of care. I was placed on the detail assembly of the P-38 and the foremen all seem to be nice fellows. It is quite hard to find rooms for rent less than 2 miles from the plant, but we were lucky and found a place within ten minute walking distance."

Signed..

(Continued on Page 7)

ROGER B. SMITH ON LOCKHEED LEGAL STAFF

The Lockheed legal staff has been enlarged with the addition of Roger B. Smith who will act as assistant to Harold Tallmadge, Lockheed general counsel. Smith is a native Angeleno and attended schools in Claremont prior to his pre-legal course at Pomona.

A graduate of the Harvard Law School, Mr. Smith has practiced in Los Angeles for the past 10 years, the last three of which were with his own firm.

DOES 20 HOURS WORK IN 15 MINUTES

★

John E. Browne, Lockheed Department 1, Plant Engineering, left, confirming with John F. Fechtig, Department 3, the speed and accuracy with which his Electrical Tester invention checks all the electrical equipment in an airplane in a fraction of the time formerly required. The Tester now does in 15 minutes what it formerly took two men eight to ten hours each to do.

★

RESEARCH DEPT. IN AIR TRAVEL QUIZ

In a test mailing of its latest questionnaire, the Lockheed Market Research Division is realizing returns which are unusually great for any type of questionnaire. For example, the returns from the Los Angeles area total 40% of those mailed out. The questionnaire is designed to determine public reaction to two or four engine equipment, and to air travel in general.

"What About Flying" is its title. Twenty-five hundred are being sent to non-air travelers, 2500 to Travel Card holders, and 8000 to Cadillac owners.

Indicative of the artistic appeal of the questionnaire is the fact that in a great many instances the first page has been torn off and retained.

34 MORE LOCKHEEDIANS AWARDED FIVE-YEAR PINS

Lockheed congratulates the following members of the company personnel upon achieving their eligibility to receive the Five-Year diamond service pin this month:

NAME	DEPT.	NAME	DEPT.
Loren R. Hemphill	3	Wallace B. Pierce	25
Wilbur M. Ball	4	Robert G. Vencill	25
M. Larry Billups	4	Raymond L. Weaver	25
Sidney C. Grassie	4	Ralph A. Conover	27
Robert W. Barrow	5	Howard A. Werner	28
Alfred P. Hottum	5	James C. Borger	31
Joseph J. Schlarb	6	Lowell W. Besack	34
George D. Asdel	12	Frederick P. Fuller	34
Harold DuBois	13	Ellwood E. Flood	35
Harry B. Harmon	20	Joachim C. Hein	46
Alfred J. Poland	22	Don H. Thatcher	46
Kyle P. Hancock	24	William A. Shott (in England)	49
Jack K. Maloney	24		
Charles H. Munson	24	Clair E. Hacker	51
Willis R. Orcutt	24	Rowland F. Holland	56
Edward W. Schmuck	24	Oliver A. Schoening	59
John Frick Baht	25	William J. Hanlon, Jr.	73
Philip F. Nelson	25		

"You hit your husband with a chair? Pray tell me, why did you do it?"

"I did it," sighed the lady, "because I could not lift the table."

Lockheed Expert 'Ups' Output With New Wiring Tester

In their never-ending search for methods to cut production time on defense aircraft, the personnel of Lockheed and Vega have made some of the most notable contributions in the history of aviation.

Now comes the newest invention, developed by John E. Browne, Lockheed Department 1, Plant Engineering. It is an invention which cuts the time required to check and double-check the maze of electrical installations in our planes from an average of 16 to 20 hours to only 15 minutes.

While working as electrical inspector in Precision Assembly over a year ago, Mr. Browne designed and had built by Plant Engineering a universal electrical tester that gives continuity, checks for shorts and duplicates ship operation of all electrical sub-assemblies equipped with special plugs. Since then he has re-designed the original design to meet new assembly requirements and the new machine is the finished product of his efforts, which have been ably aided throughout by Plant Engineering.

Principle of Mr. Browne's invention is based on the fact that the main switch box is the heart of a plane's electrical circuit, the connecting link between all electrical equipment on the ship. Hundreds of wires pass through it, going from forward to aft, starboard to port. There are many plugs and receptacles with as many as 36 pins on one plug. But most important, there are about 100 loose wire ends which go out through various conduits to fuse panels and equipment.

(Continued on Page 7)

"BROWN BOMBER" SEES BOMBER BUILT

World Champion Joe Louis, the "Brown Bomber," sees a Lockheed Hudson Bomber in the making during his recent visit to the Lockheed plant. Among those who greeted him was Hamilton Payne, electrical conduit installation worker, one of the Negro employees of the aircraft firm. Left to right are Floyd Covington, director of the Los Angeles Urban League; Lt. Lawrence Oxley, Social Security Board, Washington, D.C.; Joe Louis, Hamilton Payne and Robert Brown, personnel assistant of the N.Y.A.

WATCHES HUDSONS BEING RUSHED FOR HITLER KNOCKOUT

Brown Bomber met Hudson Bomber here last week when World Champion Joe Louis visited Lockheed and saw thousands of workers, many of them Negroes, turning out brown Hudson bombers for the British, and P-38 "Lightning" Interceptors for the U.S. Army Air Corps and the R.A.F.

Accompanied by an official party that included Lt. L. A. Oxley of the Social Security Board, Washington, D.C.; Floyd Covington, director of the Los Angeles Urban League, and Robert Brown, personnel assistant of the N.Y.A., Louis chatted with Negro workers on the job.

During the noon lunch hour the champion answered questions fired at him by the workers over the public address system at the canteen. The workers were particularly interested in the champion's immediate plans, whether he will defend his title while in the army, who was his toughest opponent and whether he would like to fly the P-38.

"I'd like to fly the P-38, but I don't think I know how," he admitted. "I'll defend my title if the army will let me out long enough to train, and I have no intention of retiring." Louis said the best man he ever fought was Max Schmeling, but he had his toughest fight from Billy Conn.

Louis was shown through the plant by Harvey Christen, assistant works manager, and Svend Pedersen, director of education.

AERONAUTICAL LIBRARY ANNOUNCES NEW HOURS FOR NIGHT STUDENTS

Due to continued requests for evening hours from the workers in the West Coast aviation industry, the newly-founded Pacific Aeronautical Library in Hollywood announces today the following schedule started November 17:

Monday, 9 a.m. to 5 p.m.; other week-days, 9 a.m. to 9 p.m.; Saturdays, 9 until 12 noon.

This library, organized by the librarians of the local aircraft companies and already proved popular with aeronautical engineers and shop men, has been open to the public for reading privileges since October 1.

PLANE DELIVERIES TO GREAT BRITAIN HIT RECORD HIGH

Aid to Britain, in the form of delivery of warplanes and aeronautical equipment from American aircraft factories, reached a record high of $330,000,000 during the first eight months of 1941.

Reporting this development, the Aviation News Committee stressed that production of military aircraft for Great Britain and her far-flung outposts is still largely in its original phase, with a vast majority of United States manufacturers rushing work on contracts awarded prior to inception of the Lend-Lease law.

In other words, the output of airplanes, engines, propellers and other equipment for the British is proceeding at a pace of more than $40,000,000 monthly, though the Lend-Lease phase of aerial aid to Britain is just getting under way.

Story in Figures

Statistics and estimates show:

1—Original British orders placed with American aircraft manufacturers prior to Lend-Lease inception totaled approximately $2,000,000,000.

2—Total aeronautical deliveries to the British from Jan. 1 to Sept. 1 amounted to $330,000,000.

3—During the first six months' operation of the Lend-Lease law—March 1 to Sept. 1—approximately $1,300,000,000 worth of aircraft and equipment was contracted for under Lend-Lease authority.

4—Total aeronautical exports to the British under Lend-Lease authority (March 1 to Sept. 1) amounted to $6,016,045.

Thus, total 1941 deliveries to the British to September 1 were 50 times greater than Lend-Lease deliveries.

Under Prior Contracts

A survey among nine leading aircraft companies who jointly represent more than 60 per cent of the aircraft industry's backlog of unfilled orders disclosed that from 85 to 100 per cent of their 1941 British deliveries are under contracts preceding Lend-Lease.

This data, the Aviation News Committee pointed out, lends added emphasis to the fact that a record-breaking pace is being maintained on original British orders, to clear the way for even greater deliveries under the Lend-Lease law.

Traffic safety, says the Department of Motor Vehicles, is a good bit like what Mark Twain said about the weather—everybody talks about it but nobody ever does anything about it.

L. E. R. C. RECREATIONS FOR THE WEEK

TOWN THEATER FOR SWING SHIFTERS

Through special arrangements concluded with the L.E.R.C. Entertainment Committee, the Town Theatre, 5th and Hill streets will hold free Owl Shows for Swing Shift employees starting tonight at 2 a.m.

Featuring "Dive Bomber" and "The Next Time I Marry," the opening program will run for three nights. Employees merely bring this story and pay the 2 cent Federal Tax for admittance.

LOCKHEED RANGERS PLAN GYMKANA EXHIBITION SHOW

Members of the Lockheed Rangers are working out routines for their participation in the San Fernando Valley Horse Show and Gymkana scheduled at Strickland Arena, Riverside Drive, Burbank on this Sunday, November 23.

In the day-long show, a varied program of riding exhibitions and competitive drills will be featured and the Lockheed troop is expected to make a splendid showing.

LOCKHEED-VEGA BASEBALL SQUADS PLANNING EXHIBITION

Planned to show their followers that baseball at Lockheed and Vega are really on the way up . . . through joint efforts of the L.E.R.C. and V.E.R.C. an exhibition game will be played at Wrigley Field on Sunday, December 7th.

Tickets through both clubs.

BASEBALL
Lockheed vs. Pacific Clay Products
2 P.M., Sunday, November 23
SOLON PARK, BURBANK

FINAL SMALL-BORE SHOOT SET FOR 23rd

With the wind-up of the Small Bore Rifle League scheduled at the Times Range, Burbank, Sunday, November 23, the Lockheed Squad is all primed to bring home the trophies, according to a spokesman for the nimrods.

"Starting at 7:30 a.m., marksmen from the Inter-Club league will bang targets 'til 5 and Lockheed expects to tally team and individual scores which will rate us up among 'em," Carl Hirdler, range-master emphasizes.

"ALL-LOCKHEED" PLAY DRAMA CLUB NEXT BILL

With "Quote-Unquote," fast moving comedy written by Norman Ford, Department 25 as their next play, the Lockheed Drama Club is now holding readings prior to casting which will be made early next month.

"Readings are scheduled for each Tuesday, Friday and Sunday evening at 1141 North Gower street, Hollywood," Burt Mill, business manager states. "And any Lockheedian with dramatic talent is asked to turn out."

Girl Bowlers Invited

Girl bowlers, notify Harriet Slater or Eleanor Clark if you want to get a vacant spot on one of the girls' teams.

ALL-PLANT DANCE SET FOR PALLADIUM

Through special arrangements concluded between the management of the Hollywood Palladium and the L.E.R.C. Entertainment Committee, Lockheedians from all shifts will obtain special 41 cent admission rates on Sunday, November 30th.

"We of the L.E.R.C. Entertainment Committee feel extremely fortunate in being able to bring Lockheedians into the Palladium where Stan Kenton and his 14 piece band will furnish the rhythm," Curt Houck, committee chairman declares.

Under the plan worked out, each Lockheed employee may have five guests in his party for which the 41 cent rate is available. All tickets will be sold at the door to those carrying Lockheed identification passes.

"Kenton's band with Kay Gregory and Red Doris vocalists have been packing 'em in for some time at the Palladium and the Lockheed deal looks like a sell-out," Houck says.

SOUTH SEA FILM FREE TO LOCKHEEDIANS

Capt. Dwight Long's all color film, "Seven Seas on a Shoestring" will be shown free to Lockheedians Friday evening November 28th at John Muir Junior High School, 7 o'clock.

This film is obtained through the efforts of the L.E.R.C. Educational Committee headed by Bill Briggs.

SKI CLUB DIRECTORS SCHEDULE BUSINESS MEET

A business meeting of the Board of Directors of the Lockheed Ski Club has been called for Friday evening, November 28th, 7:30 at 608 Clybourne street, Burbank.

Tennis Finalists Announced

Tennis finalists: Jane Mayo—96, over Elsie Purcell—25; default. Hughes-Murray over Smith-Fisher, 6-1, 6-3; Hughes over Fisher, 6-0, 6-2.

CAMERA CLUB members! "Mechanics and Industrial" print night on November 27, Burbank Library.

BADMINTON PLAYERS register with L.E.R.C. office for special court rates.

BASKETBALL OFFICIALS are still needed. Register at L.E.R.C. office via ANVO.

L.E.R.C. CALENDAR
November 21-28

Choral Club
Choral Club Rehearsal, Burbank High School, 7:30 p.m., Wednesday, Nov. 26.

Band
Band Rehearsal, John Burroughs Junior High, Burbank, 7:30 p.m., Monday, Nov. 24.

Baseball
Lockheed All-Stars vs. Pacific Clay Products, Solon Park, Sunday, Nov. 23, 2 p.m.
Baseball practice, Solon Park, Tuesday and Thursday.

Basketball
All-Star practice, CYO Gym, Friday, Nov. 21 and 28.

Camera Club
Print night, Thursday Nov. 27, 7:30 p.m., Burbank Library Conference Room.

Rifle and Pistol Club
Interclub small bore league, L. A. Times Range, Sunday, Nov. 23, 9 a.m.
Regular meet, Pasadena Police Range, 9 a.m.-4 p.m.

Boy Scouts
Regular Meeting, Scout House, Wednesday, Nov. 26, 7:30 p.m.

Ice Skaters
Lockheed Night, Pan Pacific Auditorium, Thursday, Nov. 27, 7:30 p.m.

Drama Club
Readings, Sunday, Tuesday and Friday, Nov. 23, 25 and 27, 7:30 p.m., 1141 N. Gower St., Hollywood, on Play, "Quote-Unquote."

Rangers
Tex' Stonehurst Stables, Roscoe, Drill Team, Sunday, Nov. 23, and Wednesday, Nov. 26, 7-9 p.m.
Nite Crew, Thursday, Nov. 27, 10 a.m. to 12 noon.
Rangerettes, Doc's Stables, Thursday, Nov. 27, 7 to 9 p.m.

STAR PINCH-HITS FOR STAR

★

When Bob "Bazooka" Burns was unable to appear Monday noon at the L.E.R.C. Recreation Area because of sickness, Gail Patrick, movie lovely, stepped in and pinch-hit for him, with Bob wired in from his sickbed. Both stars will appear during the lunch period next Monday in the new Canteen area. Russ Weil, plant engineer, acted as M.C. at last Monday's show, introducing Gail Patrick, Louetta Ward's accordion band and talking to Bob Burns by phone.

★

LOCKHEED JOINS U.S. NUTRITIONAL SURVEY

(Continued from Page 1)

from six to nine months, upon which will be based findings as to what is lacking in the ordinary diet to promote robust health and the enjoyment of living. Definite, scientific answers to these and other questions, the Council believes, will make it possible to increase the national health many fold.

People are only just beginning to understand that a man with a full stomach is not necessarily a man well fed, say the doctors. Unless an amplitude of food includes the vitamins and minerals the body needs, then the body's hunger is not satisfied. A deficiency in the diet is a hidden hunger making itself known, not by a gnawing at the stomach, but by a gnawing at the heart, muscles, eyes and nervous system. The hidden hunger of vitamin and mineral deficiency, according to medical authorities, makes many people old before they are 50, old before their time. IN OTHER WORDS, A MAN SHORT ON FOOD BUT LONG ON VITAMINS IS ACTUALLY BETTER OFF THAN A MAN LONG ON FOOD AND SHORT ON VITAMINS.

The Lockheed volunteers for the test will each furnish information about his regular diet. They will not be asked to change their present eating habits.

(Continued on Page 8)

GEORGE WASHINGTON HIGH ANNOUNCES NEW CLASSES

To better serve the educational needs of Lockheed employees living in the Los Angeles area, the George Washington High School, 10860 South Denker street, announces the following classes:

I. Aircraft Drafting
M-T-W-T-F, 2:25 p.m.-3:15 p.m.

II. Aircraft Sheet Metal Fabrication
M-T-W-T-F, 3:15 p.m.-5:15 p.m.

III. Blueprint Reading and Shop Mathematics
M-T-W-T-F, 2:25 p.m.-3:15 p.m.

IV. Template Layout and Development
M-T-W-T-F, 4 p.m.-6 p.m.

V. Advanced Shorthand (Emphasizing Aircraft Terminology)
M-T-W-T-F, 2:25 p.m.-3:15 p.m.

VI. Advanced Mathematics
M-W-F, 1:30 p.m.-2:25 p.m.

Employees may enroll at any time, as the work is largely of an individual nature. The instructors of these courses all have had recent experience in shops and factories.

Plane Deliveries Doubled

"In this year's first seven months American manufacturers sent to England nearly twice as many combat planes as were lost defending the British Isles during the whole of 1940." Walter D. Fuller, president of the National Association of Manufacturers, recently announced.

TRAFFIC PROBLEM BROUGHT TO FORE BY EDITORIAL

Commenting upon the highly controversial issue of alleged reckless driving on the part of aircraft workers, the Aviation News recently carried the following: "Police departments and traffic officers in the vicinity of aircraft plants have been accused of conducting a campaign of persecution against aircraft workers who drive automobiles. Police, in turn, accuse aircrafters with driving on crowded traffic arteries with utter abandon for the lives and safety of other persons.

"The quarrel has developed beyond the point of where it is merely a subject for noon-hour talk of bent fenders and flat tires, for during the past week, two of the largest automobile insuring agencies in Southern California have announced they will not accept automobile insurance from persons employed in aircraft plants who have not carried previous policies, which we think is the most serious indictment we have heard against the men who work in building the planes for this nation's defense.

"The fact that insurance agencies who normally want all the business they can get, refuse to grant new insurance to aircraft employees, shows there is something wrong with highway safety near the aircraft plants."

The Lockheed-Vega organization is so concerned with the situation outlined above that it is now conducting a survey to determine the specific facts from which may evolve a solution to the problem fair to everyone concerned.

"We have only one life to live and it cannot be postponed."

NEW EMPLOYEES CONTINUE PRAISES

(Continued from Page 3)

From the Greeley, Colo., Office:

"I am at the Vega plant, have worked for a week and like it very much. Can't say too much about my work, I may let something out. I do a lot of filing and countersinking on aluminum. Made it out here on $9 counting eats and everything. The work here is not hard but has to be perfect and it never can be too perfect for them. I like it here very much. Room and board for $9 per week and only one block from the plant."

Signed..............................

From the Winona, Minn., Office:

"Just a line to acknowledge receipt of your letter sent to General Delivery at Burbank. I was put to work in Vega Plant 2 before receipt of your letter, but thanks for your efforts and cooperation. Working conditions are fine here and the Lockheed company intends to hire many more men, according to the company newspaper of today."

Signed..............................

From the Boise, Idaho, Office:

"It has taken me quite some time to write you in regard to the Lockheed Aircraft Corp. and how it is to work for and as to a person's future with them. They are a fine company to work for, I have had more than fair treatment in the two months I have been here. More than I had in the mines and smelters all the time I was there. Lockheed is at Burbank and with all the families living here, it has caused a shortage of houses, so I live in a place (Venice) about 20 miles from there. Wages are good and I make $30.55 a week for five days and most of the time we work six days a week so I make around $37. I am more than grateful to you for the help you gave me and am sorry that I did not write sooner."

Signed..............................

S. P. RAILROAD AGAIN WARNS ON TRACK SITTING

Several months ago L. O. Holter, manager of the Employee Service division at Vega, received complaints from the Southern Pacific Railroad Company regarding Vega employees sitting on the railroad tracks to eat lunch and thereby risking injury to themselves and a possible tie-up of railroad service.

For some time there was an improvement in the condition, but apparently new employees taken on since have not been made aware of the danger of this practice. Now comes another complaint from S. P., quoting the reports of several of its engineers. In one the statement is made that "as the train approaches, the men, either in a spirit of fun or because they don't know any better (?) wait until the engine is too close for comfort.

. . . "I am afraid that if we would get an engineer on the head end of one of these long trains who might be overcautious and feel the men didn't see or hear him coming, (he might) make an emergency application and tie up the railroad."

MORE PROMOTIONS AT VEGA-LOCKHEED

The Review Section of Vega Plant Personnel announces the following promotions to group leader, effective November 22:

	DEPT.		DEPT.
L. F. Eaker	21	J. V. Blair	25
D. J. Goldsmith	24	R. A. Canini	25
J. Llelyn Haggart	24	L. O. Dixon, Jr.	25
Ed. E. Mullaney	24	R. W. Kroneberger	25
J. D. Baer	25	Walter Frisby	28
Alva Baker	25	Nicholas Claiser	57
W. L. Bickel	25	Dillon M. Dyer	57

The following promotions to section leader are effective December 1:

	DEPT.		DEPT.
Irving W. Howe	31	Kirk Lee Page	33
Ira A. Smith, Jr.	31	L. L. Scott	61
Herbert R. Wilson	31		

Review Section of Lockheed Plant Personnel announces the following promotions to section leader, effective November 22:

	DEPT.		DEPT.
P. K. Berkland	50	H. B. Waller	50
E. F. Davis	50	R. A. Watson	50
R. G. Hamilton	50	H. G. Wilhelm	50
W. M. Robertson	3	E. R. Crotser (group leader)	22

PLANT ENGINEERING HOLDS MONTHLY DINNER

The regular monthly departmental dinner of Plant Engineering, Department No. 1, was held Wednesday, November 12, in the main dining room of the Walt Disney Studios.

Featured guests were E. J. Dolan, staff assistant to the Works Manager, and Ray Buckminster, superintendent of Assembly.

EXPERT 'UPS' OUTPUT WITH NEW TESTER

(Continued from Page 3)

It is these units which have presented a problem to Production and Inspection because it required many hours of work to check the continuity of the circuits. When so many wires were being checked and a man had to hunt for the other end, there were too many chances for mistakes if the job was hurried.

Consequently, these main switch boxes required considerable rework after they were installed in the ships, work which would have taken only a few minutes on the bench but required many hours after installation. Mr. Browne's idea was to literally transfer this bench testing to the installed apparatus.

His new Tester does just this, in minutes as against hours. It checks all wires for shorts to the frame of the box and indicates by a red light those that are shorted. It also checks all plug terminals for shorts to the shell and adjacent pins, indicating by lights which are shorted and where. All switches in the switch box operate on the Tester the same as in the ship, and each switch has a separate light on the test panel to indicate if it is properly wired.

The Tester shown in the picture is for the Model No. 322. Another of similar design is now being completed for the P-38E main switch box. Mr. Browne, before coming to Lockheed, designed and manufactured electrical testing equipment in Chicago.

SOFT HEART, HARD STEEL SPELLS LOSS OF EYE TO ONE MAN

If you have ever been tempted to criticize your leadman, group leader, or foreman because of his continually harping about wearing safety goggles, we suggest you read the following: It actually happened in another factory.

A machine shop foreman passed through the shop and observed Joe chipping a steel casting, with his goggles around his neck. The foreman said nothing for fear of offending a good friend and a good workman.

Twice more the foreman passed by and noticed Joe doing the same thing. After the third time a metal chip struck Joe in the eye and sent him to the hospital where the eye was removed.

Two days later the foreman visited Joe and received the bad news.

Joe said, "Boss, why in the name of God didn't you send me home for a week when you saw me the first time? I'd have lost a little time, but I'd still have my two eyes."

Draw your own conclusion.

THE *Lockheed-Vega Star* ★★

The LOCKHEED-VEGA STAR is issued every Friday for the employees of the Lockheed Aircraft Corporation and the Vega Airplane Company. Communications may be addressed to either the Industrial Relations Office or the Public Relations Department, Lockheed Aircraft Corporation, Burbank, California, U.S.A.

H. L. (Hal) Rosson, Editor

Volume 8 Number 49

Time Lost Problem

In this period of national emergency, one of the most serious problems industry has to face and try to overcome is the productive time lost by employees absenting themselves from work. In many cases, of course, sickness accounts for the absences, but investigation has revealed that in the majority of cases this is not the cause. All too many are accounted for by the fact that a certain type of individual, his pockets full of money, loses sight of the urgency of National Defense and decides to lay off for a day to "rest."

The extreme gravity of the problem was revealed this week in an analysis of absences at Lockheed. In one five day week, from November 3 to November 7, out of a total man-days of 192,450 for the period, 9731 man-days, or 77,848 man-hours of production were lost through employees staying away for various reasons. And this did not include short shifts or tardiness.

Absentees ranged from a percentage of 5.9 on Monday to 3.9 on Friday of the entire company payroll, or an average absentee percentage for the week of 5.1.

Employment statistics indicate that Lockheed is not alone in this experience.

The lesson is plain. National Defense comes first. Every American worthy of the name will put it ahead of self-indulgence.

LETTERS

Paymaster,
Lockheed Aircraft Corp.,
1705 Victory Pl.,
Burbank, Calif.

588 Ladera St.,
Pasadena, Calif.
Nov. 17, 1941.

This is to acknowledge the receipt of a check, persumably for "back pay," for which I am extremely grateful.

Having severed mv connections with your company prior to the settlement of your negotiations with the Union, I hardly expected this retroactive measure to apply to my case. However, this is just one of the policies of the Lockheed Aircraft Corp. which has elevated them to a very high place in my esteem. . . .

Wishing the highest success for "Lockheed," I am

Respectfully and appreciatively yours,

JOSEPH E. RUFFENACH.

Some machine tools used in making defense equipment weigh more than 50 tons and stand as high as a three-story house.

METAL PROCESSING LISTED BY LIBRARY

BOOK OF THE WEEK: *Metal Processing* by Orlan William Boston. First edition, 1941; 630 pages; $4.05. Research and practice results have been combined to produce this new volume. Written principally as a college text, the book is admirably adapted for collateral reading in extension courses and serves as a valuable reference for engineers, foremen and those interested in Machine Shop Practice. *Metal Processing* emphasizes the subject of machinability and the author has devoted much space to specific practical recommendations for speeding production in the shop. Worthy of note are the many up-to-date illustrations of machine tools, operation and practice. This book is available for purchase or loan at the library.

Below is a partial list of new books which have recently been added to the Library for free circulation among employees of Lockheed and Vega:

Aeronautical Dictionary and Reference Library, Hartley.
Aircraft Descriptive Geometry, Vaughn.
Making, Shaping and Treating of Steel, U.S. Steel Corp.
Gregg Shorthand, Gregg.
Aircraft Mechanic's Pocket Manual, Ashkouti.

LODESTAR USED IN RECORD PARACHUTE JUMP

America was thrilled recently by the world's record delayed parachute jump of 30,800 feet made by Arthur H. Starnes, of Calumet City, Ill., above Rubinkam airport, near Harvey, in that state.

One piece of news that few of the newspapers carried, but which is brought to our attention by Elmer J. Schmutzler, of Lockheed Department 39, is that the plane from which he made his daring jump, was a Lockheed Lodestar, one of the few commercial planes capable of climbing to that altitude. The plane is owned by the Phillips Petroleum Company.

Starnes plummetted down 29,800 feet before pulling the ripcord on his first parachute, a distance of about six miles in one minute and 56 seconds.

VEGA DEPT. 4 PRAISES SUPERVISORY CLASSES

Leadmen of Department 4, Vega, who have been attending Supervisory Development classes held at Vega plant 2, are high in their praise for the benefits received from this training.

D. McAdam, foreman of Department 4, reports that parts are now being fabricated through the methods taught at these classes.

LOCKHEED JOINS U.S. NUTRITIONAL SURVEY

(Continued from Page 6)

Each will receive a thorough physical examination, including a check-up on heart, lungs, eyes, mouth, tongue, skin, blood and nervous system. It is estimated that the medical fee for an examination as complete as this, if obtained privately, would cost about $100 per man.

Then, throughout the six to nine month period, each selectee will be given free a nutritional supplement to his ordinary diet of vitamins and minerals (the cost of which, at current retail prices, is about 50 cents per day per man).

At the end of the testing period, all of the volunteers will be given a second physical examination to determine the extent of improvement in their general health. All records will be kept in strictest confidence by the medical officials, closed even to company officials, and the information obtained will be used for statistical purposes only.

While the National Research Council will bear the heaviest share of the cost of this survey, that of the aircraft companies will not be light. Both Lockheed and North American will contribute, in addition to substantial cash sums, the services of medical staffs, the cost of keeping records and the cost of men's time while they are being examined and receiving their nutritional supplements.

At the end of the survey, all the selectees will be informed on how they can maintain a good nutritional status.

The survey is being conducted by Dr. H. Borsook, of Caltech, in charge of Vitamin and Nutritional Survey, in collaboration with Dr. Elmer Alpert, specialist in Nutritional Medicine, on loan from the National Research Council, Washington, and, for Lockheed, with Dr. F. E. Poole, medical director for the company.

TRIBUTE TO RALPH VIRDEN

'Tis done; the pilot folds his earthly wings,
No more his flashing plane is seen on high;
No more the whirling prop its message sings
As plane and pilot sweep across the sky.

No doubt he often glimpsed the pearly gate,
Or heard an echo from the bugle's call,
As winging on, he took his chance with fate,
Prepared to meet whatever might befall.

No fear, no apprehension filled his mind
He had a task to do, and did it well;
He served not only man, but humankind
By giving all he had before he fell.

No gallant patriot ever offered more
No hero ever met a nobler fate,
No athlete ever gained a greater score
No airplane ever winged a finer mate.

'Tis done and well indeed; the task is o'er,
The God of all has loosed the binding tie;
We'll meet again upon that Golden Shore,
Till then farewell, old friend, but not goodbye.

—M. L. QUINN.

« « 'SPIRIT'S' ANNIVERSARY -- PAGES 2-3 » »

THE Lockheed-Vega Star ★ ★

Volume 9 BURBANK, CALIFORNIA, U.S.A., DECEMBER 19, 1941 No. 1

BRAZILIAN AIR OFFICERS VISIT COMPANIES

LATIN FRIENDS GET COMFORTING CLOSE-UP

Brazilian air mission visits Lockheed and inspects executive type Lodestar being built for Brazilian Minister of Aeronautics. Left to right are, Capt. Mendes da Silva; Capt. Gomez da Silva; Capt. Oswaldo Balloussier; Ferris M. Smith, manager, Lockheed Export Sales Division; Col. Armando Ararigboia; Maj. Leigh Wade, U.S. Army, and Capt. Miguel Lampart.

See How Planes Are Produced At Lockheed-Vega

A group of ranking Brazilian Air Force officers, under the leadership of Col. Armando Ararigboia, Air Attache with the Brazilian Embassy in Washington, last week visited Lockheed and Vega and saw first-hand how one American aircraft company is meeting the demands of war-time emergency.

Col. Ararigboia, who visited Germany in 1939 and inspected a number of Nazi plane plants, declared he saw nothing in Germany to compare with Lockheed as to size and efficiency.

The party, which was accompanied by Major Leigh Wade, U.S. Army Air Force, and Ferris M. Smith, export sales manager for Lockheed and Vega, also inspected an executive type Lodestar now under construction for the Brazilian Minister of Aeronautics.

Other Brazilian officers in the party were: Capt. Miguel Lampart, Capt. Joaquin da Silva Gomes, Capt. Jose Mendes da Silva, and Capt. Oswaldo Balloussier.

Buy Defense Bonds

DEPT. 9, LOCKHEED WINS SAFETY TROPHY

Department 9, Miscellaneous Sub-Assembly at Lockheed Plant 3, is the proud recipient of the company's safety trophy for a no-accident record during November. Despite the fact that it has about 1331 employees, the department worked a total of 257,480 hours last month without a single lost time industrial injury, according to Safety Engineer Jack Hatton.

Sixteen other departments of Plants 1, 2, and 3 completed the month with perfect safety records as far as lost time injuries were concerned.

PARKING FOR EMPLOYEES PLANNED AT PLANT 4

Negotiations have been started by the company to lease property suitable for parking facilities immediately west of and adjoining Plant 4 at Maywood. This area when available will be placed at the employees' convenience on an unrestricted basis. On completion of these proposed plans, it is hoped that all employees will use care and consideration for each other in parking cars so that the most efficient use may be obtained from this area.

In addition, local transportation officials have been contacted in connection with providing service to Plant 4 from already existing facilities of Metropolitan Los Angeles.

Don't 'Join' If It Will Interfere With Production

For the guidance of employees in the present emergency, the management urgently requests that they DO NOT sign up with any outside defense organization if a call from such an organization would interfere with their work at the plants. This includes outside police duty, etc.

The civil and military authorities recognize that aircraft production must now go forward at ever increasing tempo, and that nothing must be allowed to interfere with this vital duty. "First Things First"—and the first thing is more Hudsons and P-38's off the assembly lines.

VEGA ENGINEERING DEVELOPMENT WILL AID CONSERVATION

The Vega Engineering Department cracks through this week with an idea that will SAVE—save material, save dollars, and, best of all, save time in the production of vitally needed aircraft.

The idea, operating through the medium of photography, results in the reduction of large engineering drawings to one-quarter the area of the original tracing through development of what are known as "Lithotee" prints. These reductions are a boon to the craftsman at his bench, the planner at his desk, the engineer at his drafting board, as they can be opened to full size without inconveniencing neighboring workers. The whole print, in a very small area, is even clearer than the original, as the "Lithotee" photographic process tends to sharpen the lines of a drawing, according to J. E. Boyce, assistant engineering manager for Vega.

In addition to these advantages, another of great importance is the saving in material and cost. It is estimated that by reducing the size of the large drawings, 50 per cent of the blueprint paper now used can be conserved. When it is remembered that Lockheed and Vega combined use about a million and a half square feet of the paper a month, it can be appreciated that in dollar savings alone the new idea will constitute an important aid in reduction of operational costs, as well as conservation of material.

Two other great advantages of the new system, Mr. Boyce points out, lie in the fact that it will expedite the services of the Blueprint Department by enabling it to turn out twice as many large prints in a given period of time; and will, through reduction in size of the working prints, save approximately 20 per cent in filing space.

VEGA MOURNS DEATHS OF TWO OF ITS MEMBERS

The Vega Airplane Company regrets to announce that death came December 13 to Lieut. Charles Frederick Warrell following a heart attack, and to Eley Nelson Gunn, who passed away suddenly on December 15.

Lieut. Warrell entered Vega's employ February 15 as a guard in the Plant Protection Department. Funeral services were held Tuesday, December 16, in the Little Church of the Flowers, Forest Lawn Cemetery.

Mr. Gunn joined Vega December 8 of this year, only a few days before his death. He was a member of the Operations Control Department. Funeral services were held last Tuesday.

British Air Ministry Report On 'Spirit' Comes On First Anniversary

Just a year ago, Lockheed and Vega employees, inspired by the gallantry of the last-ditch battle the people of Great Britain were putting up against the Nazi hordes of Hitler, made the British a gift in token of their admiration.

That gift was the "Spirit of Lockheed-Vega Employees," built on their own time with material contributed by the companies. The famed Hudson was flown to Canada and immediately entered into the Battle of the Atlantic. From time to time since, word has been received of her, and every mention has added to that great record of service which the Hudsons and all American aircraft have made in England.

This week, from the British Air Ministry, comes the most comprehensive report yet made on the great work the "Spirit" is doing, and with the report are pictures of a few of its activities (see opposite page). Far out over the convoy lanes of the North Atlantic the "Spirit" keeps vigil over the ships that must reach England. Its adventures, and those of its intrepid R.A.F. crew, would fill a book if they could be told. And some day they will be.

For instance, if it had not been for the fact that the "Spirit" was being flown by another crew than its own the day a Hudson made the first capture of a submarine in the history of war, the "Spirit" would have added that distinction to her laurels. She had been laid up a day for a tune-up and test. That day her own crew, composed of Squadron Leader J. H. Thompson, D.F.C.; Flying Officer J. Coleman, D.F.C.; Rear Gunner Sgt. F. J. Drake and Wireless Operator Sgt. D. W. Strode, manning another Hudson, brought to bay and forced the surrender of the German submarine somewhere off the coast of England. The same audacious crew, however, has been flying her since, according to the British Air Ministry report.

Perhaps nothing tells the story of this famous aircraft better (and in paying tribute to the "Spirit" the Ministry pays tribute to the entire American aircraft industry) than the words of the Ministry's report. Here are excerpts:

". . . The Spirit of Lockheed-Vega Employees"—the "Six Spirit" as she is known to the Squadron,—is not only a show-piece of which the Squadron is proud, but an operational aircraft, taking turn with all the others in the Battle of the Atlantic.

"The 'Spirit' has done the job well. She has flown thousands of miles now over the Atlantic, watching and guarding the convoys of ships bringing munitions and supplies from the United States to Britain. The Navy has seen her, circling ahead of the shipping lines, sweeping the path clear of U-boats. She has given cc fort to the merchantmen, steaming east in the bitterest Atlantic weather. Looking through glasses from the bridge, they

(Continued on Page 7)

NOTICE

Because Christmas Day comes on Thursday next week, the STAR will go to press Tuesday for distribution Wednesday afternoon. The issue will contain four pages instead of the usual eight. Deadline for important, spot news that must go has therefore been moved up to Monday noon. Please cooperate by observing this deadline.

Ed.

BOOK OF THE WEEK AT THE LIBRARY

BOOK OF THE WEEK: *Aircraft Instruments* by George Ellis Irvin. First edition, 1941. 506 pages. $4.05. This modern text was prepared for students, operators, manufacturers and those who install and repair all types of aircraft instruments. It is presented in the simplest language possible and contains excellent photographs, drawings, diagrams and tables furnished by leading instrument manufacturers.

Lockheedians Ask Soldiers To Dine December 24-25th

In response to many suggestions, Lockheedians wishing to have as Christmas Dinner guests soldiers from the units detailed to this area, are requested to list their names at the L.E.R.C. Office as follows:

Note: It is suggested that at least two boys be invited, for they will then have someone with them with whom they have something in common.

Name ....

Date of dinner, Dec. 24.......Dec. 25.......

Hour of dinner ....

Time you will pick up soldiers at

Victory Place and Victory Blvd..............

Number of soldiers invited..........................

Your home state..

'SPIRIT' PLAYS STAR ROLE IN NORTH ATLANTIC

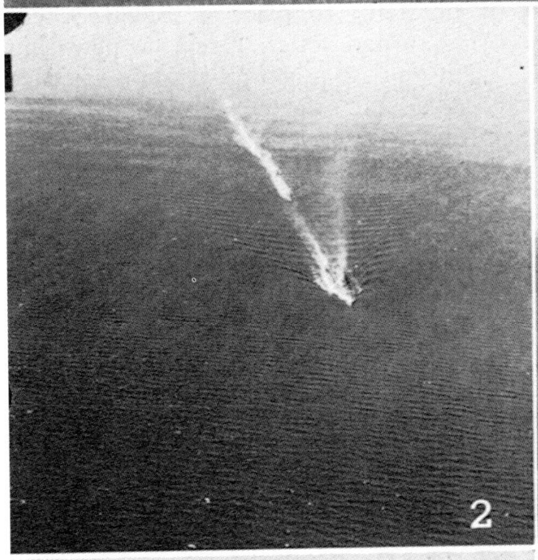

THE PHOTOGRAPHS ON THIS PAGE, FORWARDED BY THE BRITISH AIR MINISTRY IN LONDON TO BURBANK, ARE NOT ONLY OF HISTORIC INTEREST IN CONNECTION WITH THE BATTLE OF THE ATLANTIC, BUT ARE OF VERY SPECIAL INTEREST TO THE EMPLOYEES OF LOCKHEED AND VEGA WHO LAST YEAR TOUCHED THE HEARTS OF THE BRITISH BY PRESENTING THEM WITH A SURPRISE GIFT OF THE FAMED HUDSON "SPIRIT OF LOCKHEED AND VEGA EMPLOYEES." AS THESE PICTURES GRAPHICALLY REVEAL, THE "SPIRIT" HAS BEEN, AND STILL IS AT LAST REPORTS, CARRYING THE PROUD BANNER OF ALL MEMBERS OF LOCKHEED AND VEGA INTO THE THICK OF THE DECISIVE ATLANTIC CONFLICT. (SEE STORY, PAGE 2.) FIVE PICTURES ON THIS PAGE WERE SHOT FROM THE "SPIRIT."

1—The "Spirit of Lockheed-Vega Employees" with its crew who captured a submarine. (Names, left to right, in story, page 2.)

2—Naval forces that accompanied Mr. Winston Churchill to his meeting with President Roosevelt—H.M.S. Prince of Wales carrying the Prime Minister at the head of the line—photographed by the navigator of the "Spirit of Lockheed-Vega Employees."

-Convoys—line after line of merchantmen strung out across the waters. The "Spirit" on reconnaissance flight with the R.A.F. Coastal Command offers photographic proof that "the tools" the U.S. promised Great Britain are being delivered.

4—U.S. Naval patrols guarding approaches to their country are photographed from the "Spirit" on scouting assignment. This U.S. aircraft carrier was sighted steaming placidly with escort "somewhere in the Atlantic."

5—Strangest of all wartime assignments is probably the ice-pack patrol flown by the "Spirit." These icebergs off the coast of Greenland were photographed from the long range Hudson bomber now scouting Arctic regions.

6—Famous glacial mountain, Vatna Jokul, photographed from the "Spirit" making regular scouting flights over Arctic territory to discover enemy shipping, U-boats and meteorological information for the R.A.F.

CHRISTMAS RUSH ON L.E.R.C. CANTEEN ITEMS

GOLFERS CLOSE 1941 SEASON

One hundred and nine golfers rang down the curtain on Lockheed's 1941 Golf Season at Altadena last Sunday, December 14. Low Gross, Blind Bogey and Special Putting events were featured on the program.

Jim Tebbe won the All-Lockheed 1941 Championship by carding a 74, giving him an average of 72.3 strokes per tournament round for the season. Mr. Tebbe receives the special Lockheed trophy. In the Blind Bogey event, the numbers drawn were 78-77-76-79-74-72. Winners please call for prizes at L.E. R.C. office.

The results:

Low Gross—Winner: 1st, R. Jensen, 73; 2nd, J. Tebbe, 74; 3rd, W. Crooks, 75; 4th, J. Middleton, 75.

Blind Bogey—Flight One (70185): 1st, C. Markham; 2nd, W. MacCarty, 3rd, R. E. Rohne.

Blind Bogey—Flight One (70-85): 1st, 1st, C. Mundorf; 2nd, G. Brown; 3rd, R. E. Palm; 4th, L. Baggio; 5th, J. Jordan.

Blind Bogey—Flight Three (101-115): 1st, C. E. Sharpe; 2nd, L. Slupko; 3rd, L. J. Sayer.

Blind Bogey—Flight Four (116 and over): J. L. Mahony, J. Sellers.

Putting: G. Coffee, guest; J. Garagliano, employee.

Guests: 1st, R. Simpson; 2nd, A. Swoboda.

Special Seasonal Trophy: J. Tebbe—(average 72.3).

BOWLERS SUSPEND LEAGUE DURING CHRISTMAS WEEK

Bowlers now rolling in the Lockheed League are advised that all games in the league are suspended between Monday, December 22 and Friday, January 2.

League play will be resumed on regular schedules starting Monday, January 5, 1942.

L.E.R.C. CALENDAR

December 19-26

Band

Band Rehearsal, John Burroughs Junior High, Burbank, 7:30 p.m., Monday, Dec. 22.

Badminton

Friday, December 19, 7:30 p.m., Hollywood Sport Center, 1424 North Bronson, Hollywood.

Rangers & Rangerettes

Tex' Stonehurst Stables, Roscoe, Drill Team, Sunday, December 21, 7 to 9 p.m. Rangerettes, Night Crew, Tuesday, December 23, 10 a.m.

BASEBALL

LOCKHEED vs. BROTHERHOOD OF RAILROAD CLERKS
2 P.M. SUNDAY
SOLON PARK, BURBANK

SPECIAL GYMNASIUM FACILITIES READY

Through special arrangements made by the L.E.R.C. Athletic Committee with the Los Angeles Athletic Club, Lockheedians wishing to avail themselves of gymnasium facilities may do so at moderate rates.

Notify the L.E.R.C. office, Plant 1, Extension 1901, giving name and department number and shift.

L.E.R.C. BASKETBALL TOURNEY GOES INTO SECOND WEEK PLAY

The L.E.R.C. sponsored inter-departmental basketball tourney is starting on its second bracket.

Play will be held on the Tuesday schedule of both Christmas and New Year's week but, of course, as Christmas and New Year's both fall on Thursdays, there will be no league play.

Thursday night league will start again on Thursday, January 8, 1942.

LOCKHEED BADMINTON PLAYERS DEFEAT "B-O"

Lockheed employees are going strong for the badminton facilities which were arranged for by Chet Leigh, if attendance figures can be accepted.

"This is one recreational activity which cannot be affected by blackouts, because the courts are located in one of the old sound stages at the Sunset Blvd. Warner Studios," Mr. Leigh points out.

Lockheedians are playing on Friday evenings at 7:30 at the 1424 North Bronson courts. Beginners as well as experts are welcome.

SPECIAL RATES ARRANGED FOR ED HORTON PICTURE

Lockheedians wishing to attend the production, "Springtime for Henry," a stage feature starring Edward Everett Horton, are advised that special rates for Lockheed employees may be obtained by showing your Lockheed pass.

No tickets are on sale at the L.E.R.C. office.

This special offer is for four nights only, starting this Sunday, December 21, at the El Capitan theatre, Hollywood.

Candy, Ash-Trays Most Popular For Yule Remembrance

Stressing the point that additional help has been employed to handle the last minute Christmas shoppers at the Canteens, John Jordan, manager, advises all Lockheedians to come around early to have first choice.

"The popularity of the two pound Lockheed Special pack Christophers candy selling at $1.00 has already made it necessary to place a second order," Mr. Jordan states, "and the new shipment of P-38 ash trays is going rapidly."

The scale model ash trays in both chrome and bronze are selling at $3.95 and can only be compared to similar merchandise retailing elsewhere for $5 to $7.

FLASH: Your Canteen has just received a limited number of charm bracelets with eight airplane charms which are a special Christmas value at $4.45.

Sales of the magnificent Lockheed Christmas cards are already nearing the record set last year, for Lockheedians are enthusiastic over the handsome full-color cards depicting the Atlantic Ferry of Hudson Bombers.

"The last shipment of P-38 lapel pins and buttons selling for $1.00 are a "must" on any Christmas list," Mr. Jordan declares.

Additional Christmas merchandise now available at the Canteen Office includes Lockheed photos, rings and new orders of typical Lockheed gift merchandise.

"Under the anticipated strain upon the L.E.R.C. funds during the present crisis, it is gratifying to have Lockheedians buying at their Canteens for they realize that the profits are plowed back into service and recreation," Mr. Jordan concluded.

ENTERTAINMENT DRAWS LARGE CROWD TO HEAR NBC SINGING FEATURE

An enthusiastic Lockheed crowd enjoyed the excellent entertainment provided by Jimmie Cash-NBC-singing star from the Burns and Allen show.

Cash appeared in the recreation ar· on Empire through the efforts of the L. E.R.C. Entertainment Committee and is another star in a brilliant program being mapped out by that committee.

'DONATIONS FOR DOUGHBOYS' PLAN NOW IN OPERATION

In connection with the voluntary donations of comforts for the Anti-Aircraft Detail at Lockheed, Harold E. Davis, president of the L.E.R.C., has issued the following announcement:

To all L.E.R.C. Council Members and to All Employees:

The suggestions regarding cigarettes, candy and similar gifts to the Anti-Aircraft Detail located on Lockheed property are presently coming from individuals and groups throughout the entire plant.

That these suggestions are being made with the greatest of sincerity and with a spirit of generosity is unquestioned. However, the L.E.R.C. has concluded arrangements with the approval of representatives of the Lockheed Company to concentrate all these proposals into one simple and direct procedure.

At several places around Plants 1 and 3 large containers will be available into which anyone who so desires may place cigarettes or candy bars to be turned over to the officer in charge of the Lockheed Anti-Aircraft Detail for distribution.

It has also been decided that in the event of inclement weather, coffee and doughnuts will be provided to the Army boys without charge for the time being, at least.

This will be done from the L.E.R.C. general fund which, as you know, depends entirely upon your patronage of the L.E.R.C. Canteen system.

Your cooperation in connection with the above procedures will be greatly appreciated by all those concerned.

Very truly yours,

HAROLD E. DAVIS, President.
Lockheed Employees Recreation Club.

In view of the above, both L.E.R.C. and the company management take this opportunity to state that no solicitation of funds FOR ANY PURPOSE will be allowed among employees.

Buy Defense Bonds

Victory Place Tunnel Opened To Employees

The new pedestrian tunnel from the main administration building, Lockheed Plant 1, passing under Victory Place and the S.P. railroad tracks to San Fernando road, is now open and should be used at all times by those wishing to cross the tracks, announces L. W. Wulfekuhler, assistant secretary.

GIFTS FOR SOLDIERS POUR IN

Cut shows Harold E. Davis, president of L.E.R.C., (center) helping to distribute the generous gifts of cigarettes and candy that Lockheed and Vega employees are eagerly making to the members of the Anti-Aircraft Unit in this area.

FIVE YEAR SERVICE PIN RECIPIENTS

The following 61 employees of Lockheed will achieve the distinction of receiving the Five-Year diamond studded service pin this month:

NAME	DEPT.	NAME	DEPT.
Goforth, Frank D.	2	Adams, Dewey E.	24
Owens, George F.	2	Fromm, Frederick W.	24
Geiger, George W.	3	Cowles, Frederick B.	25
Leipelt, Carl J.	3	Crichton, Gaylord A.	25
McMillan, Damon L.	3	Cutshaw, Carl L.	25
Rosin, Bruno	4	Gasser, Thomas W.	25
Aleshire, Otis C.	6	Hargraves, Robert R.	25
Chauncey, Roy A.	6	Hawkins, Jack D.	25
Coutu, Clarence G.	7	Johnson, Merrit H.	25
Jackson, Louis B.	7	Kehoe, Walter C.	25
King, Elmore C.	7	Ross, David T.	25
Siebert, Ralph	7	Scott, John G.	25
Sorensen, Robert L.	9	Sipple, Howard B.	25
Cupp, Harvey M.	10	Gain, Cameron E.	27
Roth, David W.	13	Theis, Harry L.	29
Carter, Otis E.	14	Hodgins, James D.	34
Shaw, Harold S.	14	Marshall, Ernest J.	34
Shiells, Frank D.	14	Roberts, Malcolm W.	34
Shull, Allen B.	14	Barnes, Charles W.	35
Pagel, Howard H.	16	Farley, Sherwood N.	94-49
Redmond, John	16	(In England)	
Rivers, Claude W.	16	Slusser, Ralph T.	94-49
Sandifur, Cecil C.	16	(In England)	
Glasgow, William P.	17	Lukerman, Hyman D.	51
Wilkinson, John R.	19	Kampmann, Norvie J.	52
LaVerne, George	20	Jones, Leander C.	53
Croan, Kenneth F.	22	Huber, Norman R.	56
Croan, Robert J.	22	Dahle, William C.	61
Laudeman, Jesse O.	22	Shigley, Joseph W.	95-71
Minklein, Hubert C.	22	Hargrove, Joseph R.	95-75
Ross, Alexander H.	22	Cook, William J.	96-91
Roughcore, William L.	22		

Salesgirl: "Here's a lovely doll. You lay it down and it closes its eyes and goes to sleep like a real baby."

Customer (mother of seven): "Have you ever tried to put a real baby to sleep, girlie?"

Buy Defense Bonds

MAGAZINES CARRY MANY ARTICLES ON L & V ACTIVITIES

For the guidance of those who like to follow the activities of Lockheed and Vega in national and international monthly publications, the following articles (and the magazines they appeared in) appeared during November and in December to date:

AERO DIGEST—November
Picture of Hudson Bombers overseas.

AERO DIGEST—December
"Aspects of Practical Standardization," by B. C. Boulton, Lockheed Administrative Engineer.
"Certification of Army and Navy Welders," by W. R. Allen, Lockheed Senior Inspector, Outside Production Welding.
Lockheed's Nine Months' Production.
Lockheed-Vega Pay Retroactive Salaries.

AVIATION—December
"The War and Aircraft Maintenance," by Reagan Stunkel, Lockheed Customer Service Manager.

AIR FORCE REVIEW—November
Hudsons Overseas.
Vega Venturas.
N.E.I. Parachute Lodestars.

AUTOMOTIVE INDUSTRIES—Nov. 15
Onsrud Milling Machine.
Vega—History of Plant.

CANADIAN AVIATION—November
Hudsons Overseas.

(Continued on Page 6)

MAGAZINES CARRY MANY ARTICLES

(Continued from Page 5)

CANADIAN AVIATION—December
Onsrud Extrusion Miller Saves Time.

CANADIAN AIR CADET—November
Picture of P-38.

FLYING & POPULAR AVIATION—Dec.
Picture of P-38.
Picture of N.E.I. Parachute Lodestars.

FLYING & POPULAR AVIATION—Jan.
Pictures of Coast Guard Lodestars.

GO—November
"Trucks Keep 'Em Flying."

HOUSING—Book No. 4
"Defense Housing and the Aircraft Industry," by Maxwell Stiles, Lockheed-Vega News Bureau.

MACHINERY—December
"Modern Machines Produce Vega's Jigs & Fixtures."

POPULAR MECHANICS—December
Color Picture of P-38.

SOUTHERN FLIGHT—November
50,000th Employee.

REVISTA AEREA, Latin America Edition of Aero Digest—December
Picture of Lodestar.

SOUTHERN FLIGHT—December
Lockheed Nine Months' Production.

U.S. AIR SERVICES—November
Picture of Vega Ventura.

WESTERN FLYING—December
C. L. (Kelly) Johnson Awarded Wright Bros. Medal.
Group Picture of P-38's in Flight.
Lockheed Nine Months' Production.

WESTERN MACHINERY & STEEL WORLD—December
Onsrud Extrusion Miller.
50,000th Employee.

CANCELLATION

Due to present unsettled conditions, the Lockheed Drama Club has cancelled the scheduled production of "Quote-Un-Quote," the business manager, Burt Miller, says.

Judge: "You are sentenced to hang by the neck till dead."
Prisoner: "Judge, I believe you're stringing me."

MAYOR HINTON NAILS EVACUATION RUMORS

Rumors that families will be evacuated from the defense production areas adjacent to Lockheed and Vega are entirely without foundation, according to Mayor Walter Hinton of Burbank, chairman of the Burbank Defense Council.

"So far we have received no instructions from the Army to evacuate civilians," Mayor Hinton declared. "No such orders are anticipated, but if they do come they will originate with the Army and we shall be obliged to comply."

LETTERS REVEAL FIGHTING SPIRIT OF LOCKHEED-VEGA ORGANIZATION

Never has the fighting spirit of the entire Lockheed and Vega organization shone more brightly than now when America has been plunged into a war not of her choosing. And never has this spirit and determination been more adequately expressed than in the following exchange of letters between Harold E. Davis, president of the L.E.R.C., speaking for the Executive Committee, and Robert E. Gross, president of Lockheed.

Mr. Davis' letter:

Mr. Robert E. Gross, President
Lockheed Aircraft Corporation
Dear Mr. Gross:

In the face of the present national crisis, which by its very impact affects conditions at Lockheed, the Executive Committee of the Lockheed Employees' Recreation Club, speaking for the Employee Council and all Lockheed Employees, pledges its every resource and all of its collective strength to the Lockheed Management.

It is the fervent hope of the Lockheed Employees, for whom this Committee speaks, that Lockheed will call upon them whatever the demand may be.

It is the firm belief of this Executive Committee that all members of the Lockheed Employees' Recreation Club, which means every Lockheed Employee, will, by his diligence and an intelligent application to his work, provide the fighting aircraft to our Nation's forces in an ever increasing number.

The Executive Committee of the Lockheed Employees' Recreation Club, takes this opportunity to assure both employees and management that we are so organized as to provide to industry the production lines in unlimited quantities and to supplement this tremendous power with a surging spiritual energy that can be used to maintain that constant "Spirit of Lockheed."

Respectfully yours,
HAROLD E. DAVIS, President
for
EXECUTIVE COMMITTEE
Lockheed Employees Recreation Club

Mr. Harold E. Davis, President
Executive Committee
Lockheed Employees Recreation Club
Lockheed Aircraft Corporation
Burbank, California

Dear Harold:

Your letter of December 10, with its pledge of wholehearted cooperation of all of the people of Lockheed in the job at hand, is deeply appreciated.

The "Spirit of Lockheed" has never let us down before, and I am sure that it will not be found wanting in this crisis.

Please be assured that we take your offer to assist us deeply to heart, and will call on you whenever the need occurs.

The occurrences of the past few days have proven unquestionably, the importance of aircraft in modern warfare, and with the kind of spirit expressed in your letter, there is no question in my mind that the United States will speedily be supplied with the aircraft it so vitally needs.

Respectfully yours,

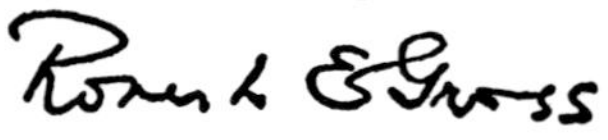

President.

GOVERNOR WARNS ON HOLIDAY TOLL

Motorists were asked today by Governor Culbert L. Olson to guard against pedestrian accidents during the coming holiday season.

In a special message received by the STAR Governor Olson said that for 14 consecutive years in California the season had been marked by an increase in traffic casualties.

Of the 3139 persons killed in traffic accidents during the first 11 months of this year, he said, more than one-third were pedestrians and many of these were young children or aged persons. He said December is always the worst month of the year for pedestrian mishaps because of Christmas weather and traffic.

CABLE FROM HAWAII VOICES CONFIDENCE IN VEGA AND LOCKHEED

Direct word from the Hawaiian battle front has been received by I. A. Crawford, of the Manufacturing Office at Vega, from his friend, William Soper, president of the Honolulu Paper Company.

The cable, received late this week, reads:

"Hawaii has met the test. Military forces have the situation fully controlled. Advise Vega and Lockheed we know they will quadruple efforts unloosening American tornado of force."

A tribute to the courage of Americans in Hawaii, to Lockheed and Vega, and the expression of a confidence in this organization's ability and determination that the future will prove was well placed.

Company Salutes Britons By Radio New Year's Eve

When Britain's millions of radio listeners tune into B.B.C. at midnight on New Year's Eve they will hear the voice of a Lockheed employee wishing them a victorious New Year. The voice will be that of Neal Thomas, one of Assistant Works Manager Harvey Christen's crew of expediters.

Neal Thomas

Columbia Broadcasting System, which recorded the program here for the B.B.C., selected Lockheed to represent the United States aircraft industry and Neal Thomas was chosen to send greetings in behalf of all aircraft workers. Neal's talk, during which he mentioned the Hudson bomber and Lockheed, lasted more than two minutes and was recorded on two disks. One of these was immediately dispatched to London aboard bomber and the other was retained in the New York office of BBC to be played back to London over trans-Atlantic telephone in case anything happens to the first one.

Neal's talk follows:

"Hello, England! This is Neal Thomas speaking and sending New Year's greetings to all of you from all of us in the aircraft factories here in Southern California.

"Perhaps you are acquainted with the Lockheed Hudson bomber. Well, I help build them; I am what is known as an expediter. I'm one of the gang that irons out all production problems and keeps the Hudsons rolling off the line so you can keep them flying.

"I have lived here in Southern California for 18 years and consequently know a number of the fellows in the other airplane factories. And right down the line, we feel that the best possible New Year's greetings we can send to you will be in the form of bombers and fighters . . . more and more of them . . . hundreds and thousands of the toughest, fightingest, most hard-hitting ships that we can possibly build.

"Over here, in judging the worth of man, we often ask, 'He can dish it out, but can he take it?' Well, we have seen how you British can take it. Now Hitler can learn how you dish it out.

"I think you in England and we in the United States understand each other

(Continued on Page 8)

PLAYTIME IN BLACKOUT TIME

It's going to take more than the little yellow man to break the morale of America's aircraft workers if the above picture is any criterion. It was taken in Lockheed Plant 1 during the first air raid alarm and shows Swing Shift and Tabulating employees playing a game of miniature dominoes with Guard William Steffen (center) as referee. Yes . . . and there was the usual line-up of kibitzers.

MINISTRY REPORTS ON FAMED 'SPIRIT'

(Continued from Page 2)

have sometimes been able to pick out the lettering on her fuselage — "Spirit of Lockheed-Vega Employees."

"GERMAN U-BOAT COMMANDERS HAVE SEEN HER, TOO. As they have been riding on the surface in dirty weather, trying to replenish their batteries for underwater attacks on the convoys, they have heard the 'achtung' from the lookouts and have crash-dived beneath the sea as the "Spirit" has dived on them through the air.

"THE VICTORIES OF THE BATTLE OF THE ATLANTIC MUST REMAIN A SECRET, THE DETAILS CANNOT BE GIVEN. BUT THIS CAN BE SAID—THAT THE "SPIRIT" IS A VALUED AIRCRAFT IN A SQUADRON WHICH HAS HAD SOME STRIKING SUCCESSES."

The presentation plaque which the "Spirit" carried when it was presented to the R.A.F. now hangs in the headquarters of the Royal Air Force squadron in England. Upon receiving the plane, Lord Beaverbrook, then Minister of Aircraft Production, thanking Lockheed and Vega employees, said in part, and under strong emotion:

"Long after this war is fought and won, when the aircraft and the battles are no more than heroic memories, the plaque will remain, recalling to future generations of our people the comradeship shown to us in the hour of peril by the men and women who work in the Lockheed-Vega factories."

The "Spirit" left Burbank last December 22, arrived in Montreal on Christmas Day, flew the Atlantic and landed in England less than a week from the time of the takeoff here.

U. OF C. ANNOUNCES NEW SERIES OF DEFENSE COURSES

The University of California, under the Engineering, Science, and Management Defense Training Program, has arranged new courses for the Burbank region to serve the men of the Lockheed and Vega companies. As these courses are of an engineering college level, they should be of particular benefit to the engineers at Lockheed and Vega.

A list of courses and their starting dates is as follows:

Week of January 5:

Monday—Aircraft Hydraulic Systems and Equipment, Aircraft Detail Design.

Tuesday—Production Design III, Aircraft Heating and Ventilating I, Airplane Dynamic Loads and Fatigue.

Wednesday — Aircraft Power Plant Installation, Aerodynamics for Designers, Statically Indeterminate Structures.

Thursday—Aircraft Mechanisms, Aircraft Structural Analysis, Technical Report Writing.

Week of January 12:

Monday—Aircraft Materials and Processes (non-ferrous), Production Design II, Thin-Sheet Analysis.

Tuesday—Aircraft Design Sketching, Production Design I.

Wednesday—Aircraft Structural Design, Aircraft Manufacturing Organiza-

(Continued on Page 8)

THE Lockheed-Vega Star ★ ★

The LOCKHEED-VEGA STAR is issued every Friday for the employees of the Lockheed Aircraft Corporation and the Vega Airplane Company. Communications may be addressed to either the Industrial Relations Office or the Public Relations Department, Lockheed Aircraft Corporation, Burbank, California, U.S.A.

H. L. (Hal) Rosson, Editor

Volume 9 Number 1

Enemy Has Many Ears

The Plant Protection Department, through Manager John Hanson, today issued the emphatic warning that during this period of national emergency it is vitally essential to the best interests of the United States that all persons, both military and civilian, engaged in the National Defense program, keep close guard on their talk as well as the work in which they are taking part.

Employees should not discuss outside the plant matters of business or production, i.e., number of planes being manufactured or any other confidential data. If they do so, Mr. Hanson points out, they might be adjudged guilty of violating the Espionage Act, of which all employees have been furnished copies.

COMPANY TO SALUTE BRITONS BY RADIO

(Continued from Page 7)

pretty well; but in your hour of adversity it probably was a little difficult to understand why we didn't do more over here. Well, we are six, seven and eight thousand miles away from the fighting front, so it took a little while for us to realize that this Hitler was a menace to us too. We know now! AND ON THIS FIRST DAY OF A NEW YEAR, LET ME ASSURE YOU THAT HERE IN THE UNITED STATES WE HAVE MADE UP OUR MIND THAT HITLERISM AND AGGRESSION AND NAZISM AND FASCISM MUST BE WIPED OFF THE EARTH. BRITAIN AND AMERICA TOGETHER CAN DO THE JOB. ON THAT SCORE WE SPEAK THE SAME LANGUAGE.

"Both of us were late getting started. Neither of us wanted war. We tried everything to prevent it . . . yes, we even tried appeasement. But that's all over now. As our President, Franklin D. Roosevelt said when he first took office, "We're on our way, and we're headed in a new direction."

"May 1942 see us both on the threshold of victory; may this New Year bring to every one of you in England, the assurance that your dark hours have not been suffered in vain . . . that this old world still rewards the stout heart and the iron will. I cannot and will not say, A Happy New Year to you. But I do say a Victorious New Year to you all."

CASUALTY PERCENTAGES DURING AIR RAIDS BASED ON SHELTER TYPES FOR COMPARISON

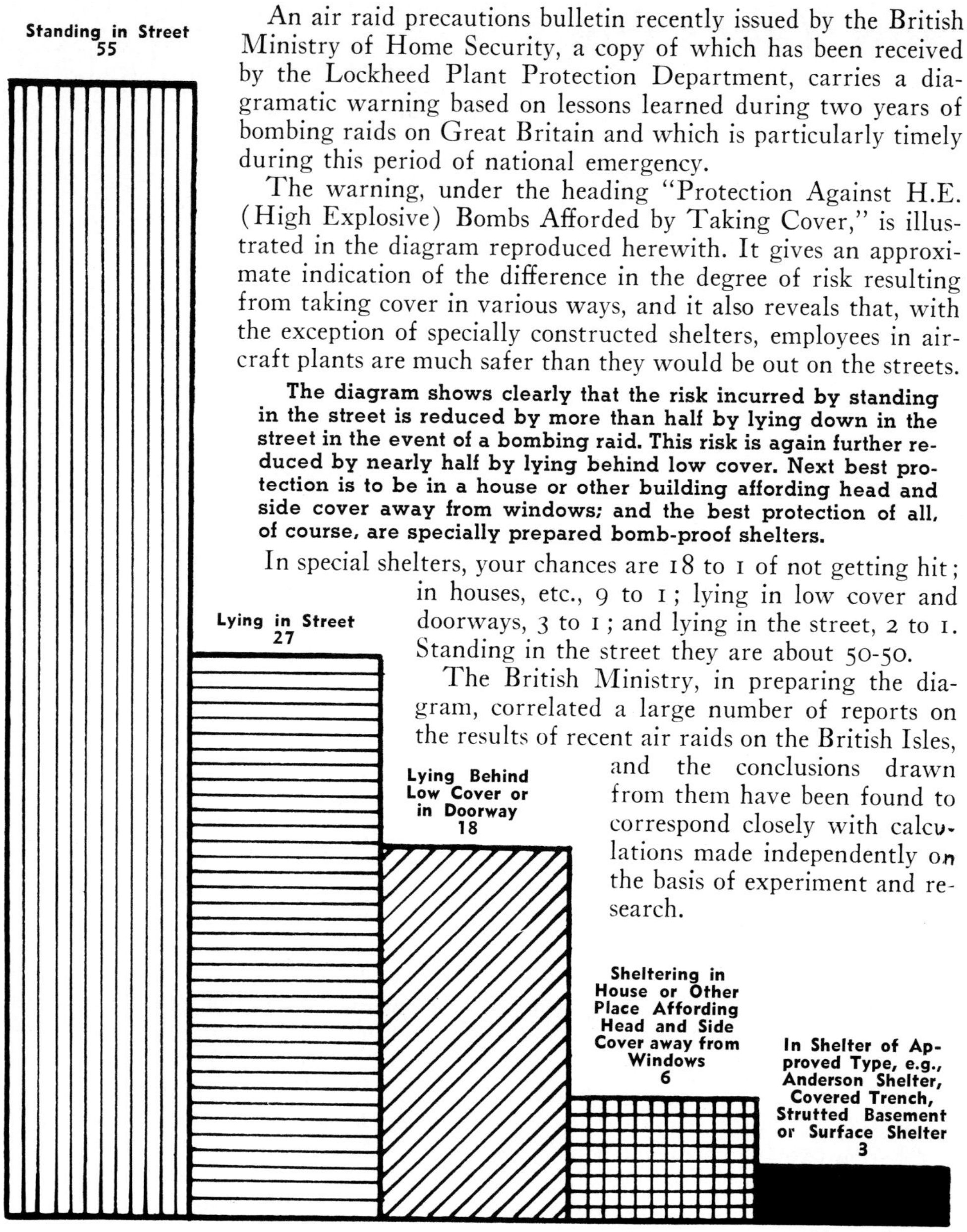

An air raid precautions bulletin recently issued by the British Ministry of Home Security, a copy of which has been received by the Lockheed Plant Protection Department, carries a diagramatic warning based on lessons learned during two years of bombing raids on Great Britain and which is particularly timely during this period of national emergency.

The warning, under the heading "Protection Against H.E. (High Explosive) Bombs Afforded by Taking Cover," is illustrated in the diagram reproduced herewith. It gives an approximate indication of the difference in the degree of risk resulting from taking cover in various ways, and it also reveals that, with the exception of specially constructed shelters, employees in aircraft plants are much safer than they would be out on the streets.

The diagram shows clearly that the risk incurred by standing in the street is reduced by more than half by lying down in the street in the event of a bombing raid. This risk is again further reduced by nearly half by lying behind low cover. Next best protection is to be in a house or other building affording head and side cover away from windows; and the best protection of all, of course, are specially prepared bomb-proof shelters.

In special shelters, your chances are 18 to 1 of not getting hit; in houses, etc., 9 to 1; lying in low cover and doorways, 3 to 1; and lying in the street, 2 to 1. Standing in the street they are about 50-50.

The British Ministry, in preparing the diagram, correlated a large number of reports on the results of recent air raids on the British Isles, and the conclusions drawn from them have been found to correspond closely with calculations made independently on the basis of experiment and research.

This diagram is based on a large number of reports of the results of recent air raids in England and is an approximate indication of the difference in the degree of risk resulting from taking cover in various ways.

U. OF C. ANNOUNCE DEFENSE COURSES

(Continued from Page 7)

tion, Advanced Aircraft Weight Control.

Thursday—Strength of Materials, Analytical Mechanics.

Week of January 19:

Wednesday—Engineering Physics.

Thursday—Engineering Mathematics.

Week of January 26:

Thursday — Elementary Engineering Mathematics.

All classes will meet at 5245 West San Fernando Road (Aero Industries Technical Institute near California Avenue).

Applications for enrollment and further detailed information are available at these offices:

Lockheed Engineering Department, Personnel Office, F. P. Gibbs.

Vega Engineering Department, Personnel Office, E. V. Gustavson.

Education Department, Room 150, Building 167, J. Kadushin.

All interested employees are requested to avail themselves of enrollment blank as soon as possible to assure a place in the desired course.

Buy Defense Bonds

THE *Lockheed-Vega Star* ★ ★

Vol. 9 BURBANK, CALIFORNIA, U.S.A., APRIL 24, 1942 Number 19

GLAMOUR QUEEN SPURS BOND SALES

Giving of her high-priced time freely and generously in behalf of the nation's all-out war effort, Dorothy Lamour was guest of honor last Monday night at Vega and Lockheed main plants. Left to right: Ralph Richert, president of V.E.R.C.; Miss Lamour and Fred Jones, business manager of the club.

SHARING CAR NOT TO HIT INSURANCE

Employees who are now driving their own cars to and from work are advised that they may, without jeopardizing the liability insurance on their automobiles, arrange with other employees to share the cost of transportation.

Eighty-two of the principal companies writing this type of insurance voluntarily modified their underwriting rules last August to cooperate with the defense program, according to H. Everett Charlton, chairman of the General Insurance Committee of the Los Angeles Chamber of Commerce. Since that time all policies written by these companies have permitted any policyholder to cooperate with

(Continued on Page 6)

BIKE RIDERS ASSURED LOW RATE INSURANCE

The Employees Transportation Committee reports bicycle insurance coverage may be obtainable at approximately $2.50 a year. Contact Employee Transportation offices of Lockheed or Vega.

Monthly Personnel Check-Up

For the duration of the war it is imperative that the Personnel Office have available at all times personal information on all Lockheed employees. To provide automatically for keeping a current file of basic data, Emergency Information cards are distributed ONCE EACH MONTH to all employees. As these cards are kept for one month only, it is essential that they be filled out and returned immediately, regardless of whether the information required has changed or not. The next cards will appear in time-card racks on May 1.

Dorothy Lamour Gives Campaign Eloquent Support

The Lockheed and Vega "War Bond" sales drive was given added momentum last Monday night when Cinema Star Dorothy Lamour contributed her services in a "Buy Bonds" message to the Swing Shifts of the two companies in their respective recreation areas.

With the same glamorous appearance that has brought her world fame, Miss Lamour delivered a powerful message on behalf of whole-hearted support of the War Bond purchase drive.

Accompanying the motion picture star was Ivan Staufer, representing the United States Treasury Department, and the L.E.R.C. Band provided a splendid musical program for the Lockheed appearance while the Vega Band furnished the musical background for Miss Lamour's appearance at Vega.

Arrangements were concluded by Curt Houck and Steve Leeds for both Lockheed and Vega. Harold Davis, president of L.E.R.C., introduced the guests at the Lockheed appearance, while Ralph Richert presented Miss Lamour and Mr. Staufer to the Vega Swing Shifters.

SELECTIVE SERVICE ACT DEFINITIONS

All men between the ages of 18 and 65 have been brought under the operation of the Selective Service Act and, sooner or later, will be placed in one of the classifications shown below, according to a statement issued by the Lockheed-Vega Selective Service Section. The explanation following each class has been abbreviated except in the case of Class II-B (occupational deferment) which is quoted in full from the Act:

CLASS I-A: Available for general military service when found acceptable to the land or naval forces.

CLASS I-A-O: Available for noncombatant general military service when found acceptable to the land or naval forces; conscientious objector.

CLASS I-B: Available for limited mil-

(Continued on Page 7)

West Los Angeles Bus Schedules Are Announced

Lockheed employees of Plants 1 and 3 and Vega employees of Plants 1 and 2 residing in Santa Monica, Ocean Park, Venice, Westwood, and West Los Angeles are advised by the Employee Transportation Committee that "all-shift bus transportation" will be made available for them starting Monday morning, April 27.

Ticket books are now on sale at all Lockheed and Vega Employee Transportation offices. Each book contains ten tickets and is priced at $3.00, affording employees the opportunity of riding to and from work at a cost far below that of driving their own automobiles, to say nothing of the savings on tires, etc.

Busses will leave Ocean Blvd. and Broadway, Santa Monica, on the following schedule:

For 7 a.m. shift	5:40 a.m.
For 8 a.m. shift	6:40 a.m.
For 4 p.m. shift	2:30 p.m.
For 12:30 a.m. shift	11:10 p.m.

Busses will leave railhead (Ocean Blvd. and Broadway, Santa Monica) over two routes with stops for passenger pick ups as follows: Route 1, Ocean Blvd. via Santa Monica. Stops at Santa Monica & Lincoln; Santa Monica & 14th; Santa Monica & Sawtelle Blvd.; Santa Monica & Westwood. Non-stop between here and plants.

Route 2: Stops at Wilshire & Lincoln; Wilshire & 14th; Wilshire & 26th; Wilshire & Centinella and Wilshire & Westwood Blvd. Non-stop between here and plants.

Busses will be routed for Lockheed Plant 1 and Vega Plant 2 with others going to Vega Plant 1 and Lockheed Plant 3.

At the present time no stops can be made in Beverly Hills and employees desiring service from there are advised to contact their Employee Transportation Offices immediately as additional railheads will be set up as rapidly as the demand justifies.

CLASSES

"Make-Up" classes in Supervisory Development courses, 1 and 4, are now under way for the benefit of those who missed one or more sessions earlier.

The meetings will be held at Lockheed, Plant 2; Vega, Plant 2, and Lyn's restaurant at Lockheed, Plant 1. Employees wishing to attend may call Vega, Plant 2, Extension 7211 for further information.

SHIFT IN PLANT PROTECTION HEADS

Commissioned last week a Major in the U.S. Army Air Forces, B. Mason Value, for the past year Army Plant Pro-

Major B. Mason Value

tection Chief at Lockheed with jurisdiction over the entire San Fernando Valley

(Continued on Page 6)

O.P.A. TELLS STAND ON TIRE RECAPS

The Office of Price Administration has no objection to issuance of purchase certificates for new tires of obsolete sizes to List B vehicle owners who have changed wheels and rims to permit use of those sizes instead of the recapped casings that otherwise would be the only kind available to them.

This stand is taken by O.P.A. in a letter to State rationing administrators.

"As long as the supply of 'obsolete' sizes meets the needs of present List A and List B eligibles, this office can see no reason to oppose such 'changeovers' or to refuse certificates," the O.P.A. letter says. "HOWEVER, ADMINISTRATORS OR BOARDS MAY WELL POINT OUT TO SUCH APPLICANTS THAT THERE IS CONSIDERABLE RISK INCURRED IN THESE CHANGEOVER EXPENDITURES, SINCE THE AVAILABLE TIRE SUPPLY IS LIMITED TO THOSE OBSOLETE SIZES NOW ON HAND."

NEW GLARE-PROOF GOGGLES INVENTED BY LOCKHEEDIAN

Solving a problem of many years, perfection of new welding goggles that will help speed up production of Hudson bombers and "Lightning" P-38 interceptors by entirely eliminating glare from aluminum welding operations is announced by Lockheed. These goggles will be made available to all airplane manufacturers. For years aluminum welders have been handicapped by the glare from the hydrogen torches. This glare is caused by the low temperature at which aluminum melts, the high temperature of the hydrogen torch and the large amount of flux required in this type of welding.

Dr. R. C. Burt

This glare problem was solved by Dr. R. C. Burt, a member of the Lockheed Plant Engineering Department, who, with the help of Corning Glass Works technicians, produced a pair of goggles with the optical properties that would filter out the glare.

First trial of the new goggles was by the foreman of Lockheed's welding section. He took them off almost immediately to see why his torch had gone out, but found it burning brightly. Finally, after once more taking the goggles off he remarked it was the first time in his life he had ever welded "without a flame."

As now used by Lockheed welders, the improved lenses allow a small cone of flame to be seen at the burner tip.

UNIVERSITY EXTENSION OPENS PILOTS GROUND COURSE

Open to new students upon consent of the instructors will be a new section of a current University of California Extension Division course in ground school work of pilot training. The new section opens on Tuesday evening, April 28, 7 o'clock at the Hill street building, 813 South Hill street in downtown Los Angeles.

WILBUR I. McCOY, OF VEGA, IS TAKEN BY DEATH

Funeral services were held last Saturday in the Wee Kirk o' the Heather, Forest Lawn Cemetery, Glendale, for Wilbur I. McCoy, of Vega, who was killed by a train April 14. At the time of his death, Mr. McCoy was a storekeeper in the Material Control Department.

Byrd's Companion, Now At Lockheed, Paid Signal Honor

In the winter of 1934-35, E. J. Demas, now a Lockheed structures research engineer, kept a tractor going through the barren wasteland of ice and snow a hundred miles from Little America to reach the isolated hut where Rear Admiral Richard E. Byrd was staying alone.

The small party, out for triangulations, had decided to push on 10 days beyond their normal operations just to pay their commander a visit. It was fortunate that they did, for they arrived just in time to save Admiral Byrd from asphyxiation by carbon monoxide gas.

The temperature on that occasion was 70 below zero, which was good training for Mr. Demas, who often works at that temperature in the pressurize chamber in the structures research laboratory at Lockheed. Yesterday, as he stepped out of this "cold room," Mr. Demas was handed a letter from Admiral Byrd. It read:

Dear Pete:

While trying to find the unknown coastline on our last expedition halfway between Little America and South America, we discovered a range of mountains. They will probably be on all charts of the Antarctic, even the small scale ones. In fact they are on the small scale government hydrographical chart now being printed.

I suggested to the Government that these mountains be named after you. This recommendation was approved.

It is not as much honor as I would like to show you, or as much as you deserve, but with it goes my admiration, gratitude and affection.

Faithfully yours,
Richard E. Byrd,
Rear Admiral, USN, Rtd.

Mr. Demas has never seen the range of mountains named after him. His duties on the last Antarctic expedition included supervision of all equipment, including tractors and airplanes.

Mr. Demas' connection with the Admiral began when he applied to go along on Byrd's North Pole trip. He was taken on as an assistant steward and engine mechanic.

On his return from the North Pole expedition, Mr. Demas worked for Wright Aeronautical. He was called by Byrd for the first Antarctic expedition, after which he was given a scholarship by Byrd at New York University, where he studied aeronautical engineering until he left in May, 1933, on the second Antarctic expedition.

Later the Admiral sent him back to New York University, from which he graduated in 1937 with a B.S. and a degree in Aeronautical Engineering. He joined Lockheed last June.

SUB-ARCTIC MOUNTAINS NAMED AFTER HIM

A distinction that comes to few men, especially during their lifetime, was conferred upon E. J. Demas, Lockheed structures research engineer last week when he received from Rear Admiral Richard E. Byrd, famed Arctic explorer, notification that the Admiral had named after him a range of mountains located between Little America and South America. Mr. Demas was with Admiral Byrd on three expeditions, one to the North Pole, two to the Antarctic. Shown (right) congratulating him is Hall Hibbard, Lockheed vice-president and chief engineer.

CHARLES T. McALEER, OF LOCKHEED, DIES IN CRASH

Traffic took toll of another Lockheed employee last Friday when Charles T. McAleer, Dept. 25, Day Shift, died in Georgia street Receiving Hospital as the result of an automobile accident.

Mr. McAleer joined Lockheed in May of '41. Funeral services were held at the Sawtelle Chapel, Sawtelle, last Tuesday morning. The deceased is survived by his widow, Mrs. Ruth C. McAleer, to whom the sincere sympathies of the company are extended.

REHEARSAL SCHEDULED

The regular monthly Program Meeting of the L.E.R.C. Drama Club featuring a one-act play, playreading sketches and musical varieties will be held at 7377 Santa Monica Blvd., Saturday evening, May 2.

ADVANCED COURSE SCHEDULED BY U OF C

An additional course in the Tool Design program of the ESMDT unit of the University of California starts April 27. The title of the course is "Advanced Die Design." Instructor is E. E. James, Department 34, Lockheed.

Prerequisites are high school graduation, experience in shop work and practice and knowledge of metal characteristics. Prospective students should have completed algebra, geometry, trigonometry and a year of mechanical drawing.

The course will be presented on Monday and Wednesday evenings from 6:30 to 9:30 p.m. for a period of 16 weeks, and will be held in Room 18, Aero Industries Technical Institute, 5245 San Fernando Blvd.

Complete information and application blanks may be obtained from Ivan Breetwor, Plant Personnel Unit, Lockheed Department 34.

"MARCH AHEAD, in production, EVERYBODY!"

TORPEDO VICTIM TO GIVE LECTURE

Lockheedians are to be offered a special treat when Second Officer Finn Burnby, hero of three Nazi attacks, speaks at John Muir Jr. High School, 220 North Grinnell Drive, Burbank, April 29 at 8 p.m.

Held under the auspices of the Norwegian Lecture Bureau, this thrilling talk will bring first-hand revelations of the trials of being torpedoed, being on a prison ship, being in a concentration camp and finally being rescued by the British. No charge is being made for the event.

DRAMA CLUB ROTATES REHEARSAL LOCATIONS

Adding their weight to the drive for tire conservation, members of the cast of the L.E.R.C. Drama Club are rotating rehearsal locations for their forthcoming production of "The Importance of Being Earnest" which will be presented in mid-May.

Produced under the direction of Russ Brinley, this fine play will feature the talents of Frances Bishop, Everett Vilander, Fred Murray and Harris Finklestein.

SCHEDULE TENNIS TOURNEY FOR APRIL 26

Weather permitting, the Lockheed inter-departmental tennis tournament will start Sunday, April 26, as previously announced.

Registrations for men's doubles can still be made through the L.E.R.C. office, or through Art Fiedler, Dept. 25, with a 50c court charge being collected from each pair of registrants. The L.E.R.C. provides the balls for this tournament.

L.E.R.C. GETS SPECIAL RATE FOR HOLLYWOOD MUSICAL

Through special arrangements concluded between the L.E.R.C. and the management of the Trouper's Theatre, Hollywood, special 50 percent discount rates for tickets to the latest musical show, "Music To My Ears" are available to Lockheedians who show their identification badges at the box office. Reservations may be made by phoning HIllside 9488.

Badminton Tourney Tonight

The third, fourth and fifth rounds in the L. E. R. C. All-Plant Badminton Tournament will be played tonight starting at 7 on the Hollywood Sports Center courts, 1424 North Bronson.

ICE CAPADE SPECIAL

Once again, the L.E.R.C. has made arrangements to handle tickets for the world famous "Ice Capades" for a two-day special Lockheed series on May 3 and 4.

Special rates will be available for the two performances with regular $2.25 seats at $1.70 and $1.65 seats at $1.15. Tickets go on sale at the L.E.R.C. office next Monday, April 27.

DEPARTMENT 34 WILL STAGE DANCE AT BARNEY'S

Department 34 has arranged an L.E.R.C. approved dance at Barney Oldfield's Country Club on Saturday, May 2, with tickets selling at 50 cents, including tax.

"This dance will feature the music of Art Whiting and dancing will start at 9, with 'Home, Sweet Home' scheduled for 1," Gordon Ford, L.E.R.C. Entertainment Committee, states.

Golf Tourney Scheduled For April 26

Lockheed's inter-departmental golf tournament will have its annual tee-off this Sunday, April 26, at both Montebello and Altadena golf courses. "This is the first plant-wide golf tournament," states athletic chairman Jack Mohr, "and with over 40 teams entered, the tourney should prove successful."

HOOPSTERS TO MEET VEGA CHAMPIONS

In a basketball game to top all games the Lockheed Champs will meet the Vega Champs at the C.Y.O. Gym., 1947 Venice Blvd. at 2 p.m., Sunday, April 26.

With Lockheed's Department 32 hoopsters set to pull a Lockheed victory away from an equally determined Vega quintet from Department 57, this match promises real basketball.

A special feature of the event will be the appearance of the Vega Band and a large crowd of rooters is expected to fill the stands for this free championship game.

SOFTBALL TOURNAMENT IS WELL UNDER WAY

First games in the plant-wide inter-departmental softball tourney started Monday, April 20, and will continue throughout the next few weeks, according to the L.E.R.C. office.

"High caliber play features the matches, which have thus far been closely contested, and a real tussle is in the wind for the Lockheed champ spot this year," Frank Davis, assistant program director declares.

L. E. R. C. CALENDAR—April 24 - May 1

Badminton Tournament
Hollywood Sports Tournament, Friday, May 1, 7 p.m.—Swing Shift, Monday, April 27, Defense Recreation Building, 11 a.m. to 1 p.m.

Department Dance
Dept. 34 Dance, Barney Oldfield's Country Club, Saturday, May 2, 9 p.m.

Basketball
Lockheed Champs vs. Vega Champs, CYO Gym, 1947 Venice Blvd., Sunday, April 26, 2 p.m.

Free Lecture
Norwegian lecture by Second Officer Finn Burnby, Wednesday, April 29, John Muir Jr. High School, 220 North Grinnell Drive, Burbank, 8 p.m.

Golf Tournament
Tournament play begins Sunday, April 26, at Altadena & Montebello courses.

Tennis Tournament
Tournament play begins Sunday, April 26, La Cienega Courts, one block east of Wilshire Blvd. on La Cienega Blvd.

Speaker's Club
Monday, April 27, Rafail's Cafe, Burbank and Victory Blvds., 5:30 p.m.

Band
Band Rehearsal, John Burroughs Junior High, Burbank, 7:30 p.m., Monday, April 27.

Rangerettes & Rangers
Tex' Stonehurst Stables, Roscoe, Drill Team, Sunday, April 26, 8 to 10 a.m. and Wednesday, April 29, 7 to 9 p.m.—Nite Crew, Thursday, April 30, 10 a.m. to noon.—Rangerettes, Tex' Stables, Thursday, April 30, 7 to 9 p.m., and Sunday, April 26, 10 a.m. to noon.—Nite Crew, Tuesday, April 28, 10 a.m.

Boy Scouts
Regular Meeting, George Washington School, Wednesday, April 29, 7 p.m.

Chess Games
Wednesday, April 29, 7:30 p.m., Burbank Recreation Center, 1111 West Olive, Burbank.

Drama Club
Friday, Tuesday and Thursday, April 24, 28 and 30, Rehearsal, "Importance of Being Earnest," Hollywood Headquarters, 1141 N. Gower, Hollywood, 7:30 p.m. — Tuesday and Thursday, April 28 and 30, May 2, Monthly Program Scene, rehearse at cast's home, 7:30 p.m.—Sunday, April 26, Rehearse "Importance of Being Earnest." 237C Fairmont, Burbank, 2:30 p.m. Wednesday, April 29, Rehearse "Importance of Being Earnest," Burbank Defense Recreation Center, 7:30 p.m.—Wednesday, April 29, May 2, Monthly Program ("Escape by Moonlight") rehearse at Hollywood Headquarters, 7:30 p.m.—Friday, May 1, DRESS REHEARSAL, May 2 Monthly Program, Hollywood Headquarters, 7:30 p.m.—Saturday, May 2, DRAMA CLUB MONTHLY PROGRAM, Plummer Park, 7377 Santa Monica Blvd., Hollywood, 8 p.m. Program of one-act play, playreading, sketches and musical varieties, followed by dancing and refreshment. EVERYBODY INVITED. 25c, tax included.

First, Last, All The Time, Hudsons Are On The Job

When the British Government called upon American aircraft manufacturers for bombers to meet the threat of impending war in 1938, Lockheed transformed its Model 14 transport into the Hudson and within a few months was delivering these planes in quantity to England. . . .

When Great Britain declared war on Germany in September, 1939, and sent its first reconnaissance squadron out over the English Channel, the Hudson was on the assignment. . . .

When the first bombs were dropped on German-held Norway, and on German shipping in the North Sea, the Hudson did the job. . . .

When England needed warplanes to help out in the evacuation of Dunkirk, the Hudson was there. . . .

When England fought for her very life in the Battle of Britain and turned back the Nazis, the Hudson was there. . .

When the German battleship Bismarck left Nazi waters and docked in a Norwegian port en route to the open sea, she was spotted by a Lockheed Hudson. . . .

When submarines threatened the lifelines of the Atlantic, when the fighting grew tense in Africa and the Near East, when the Japs struck at Singapore and the Dutch East Indies and Australia, the Hudson was there. . . .

And when American bombers last Saturday made their first raid on Tokyo and other Japanese cities—according to Japanese pilots—the Hudson, too, was THERE!

First intimation that Lockheed planes may have participated in the Tokyo bombings was contained in press dispatches out of the Japanese capital last Tuesday, when a Japanese pilot was quoted to the effect that he had sighted a Lockheed Hudson flying southward over Mito and that he had chased it to Chiba prefecture, the southernmost point of Japan. Although he says he scored hits on the Hudson, he had to confess that the Lockheed had "disappeared, still in the air."

SPEAKERS CLUB OPENS IN FIRST OF INTERESTING SERIES

The first of a series of speaker training classes sponsored by the L.E.R.C. Speaker's Club is set for Monday evening, April 27 at Rafail's Cafe, Burbank and Victory Blvds., starting at 5:30.

YEP! WAR BONDS ARE IN DEMAND

This is the way the men and women of Lockheed and Vega are responding this week to the "Buy War Bonds" drive. Left to right above are: Marty Donlan, foreman, Lockheed Dept. 16; Jean Rypinski, Lockheed Dept. 63; Vivian Mattson, Genevra Pond and Supervisor Art Bliss, all of Dept. 16.

FIVE-YEAR SERVICE EMBLEMS AWARDED

The following members of the Lockheed personnel were presented with their five-year diamond-studded service pins on April 15.

NAME	DEPT.
Joseph Earl Anders	22
Robert D. Ash	19
John H. Baukind (Father)	31
Robert H. Baukind (Son)	95-73
Benhard Leo Berg	10
William J. Bowns, Jr.	6
Henry W. Brummel	28
Milo G. Burcham	36
Reed C. Clarke	59
George A. Coombs	22
John T. Cooney	8
Guy B. Collins	4
Felix E. Conahan	1
Harold F. McIntosh	35
Gene Durand	22
Herbert W. Eggleston	25
Lawrence E. Ganahl	24
Alfred Gertsch	22
Leonard H. Gustafson	4
Robert H. Hafenfield	22
Robert E. Harris	7
Leonard V. Herauf	10
Vern Edwin Herrick	4
William Ray Holcomb	31
John P. Jacobs	22
Evan Wilson	4

NAME	DEPT.
Morris S. Kasperson	4
Robert M. Keiser	10
Adrian P. Ladish	7
Daniel Elton Lamberth	27
Howard A. Leatart	5
Dale Long	55
George William Means	16
Joseph E. Miner	19
Herbert M. Munson	1
Harold E. McDowell	10
John B. McFarlane	8
Ralph J. Osborn	26
Gerard George Paquet	8
Frederick C. Parsons	4
William S. Pickering	33
John W. Prosser	34
Claude L. Rucker	7
Louis E. Schock	7
Bob Sinclair	7
Elroy Smith	53
Rudolph Andrew Suk	20
Harold Martin Thorpe	7
William Waggett	22
Eric H. Wickman	35
William M. Young	7
Robert A. Blair	95-78
Victor V. Day	17
Matt Reisdorf	10
William F. Dawson	5

Other members of the personnel who have received their pins during the last two months (some of whom are now at Vega) are:

NAME	DEPT.
Dudley Brown	Comptroller of Lockheed
Wilton Darrell Collins	73
Virgil Zeigler	53

VEGA

NAME	DEPT.
John A. MacDonald	20
Robert Evenson	23
George Pentland	14
William S. Dunlop	43

SURVIVOR OF THREE ATTACKS TO BE FEATURED SPEAKER

Company officials, department heads and all members of Lockheed and Vega next Wednesday night will learn all about how it feels to be torpedoed and bombed at sea when they hear an address by Second Officer Finn Burnby, of the Norwegian Merchant Marine, at John Muir Junior High School in Burbank.

Officer Burnby has had two ships torpedoed and sunk under him, and a third one wrecked by bombs. Captured by Nazis and placed on a ship under a German prize crew, he discovered his own brother among prisoners aboard. When the ship was torpedoed by the British he and his brother were rescued, but 87 others were drowned.

He spent three months in a German concentration camp. Escaping on skis from Norway into Sweden, he crossed Sweden, Finland, Russia, Turkey and Syria to Suez and made his way aboard a British troop ship from Suez to South Africa and to New York. He will speak to the Lockheed group through the cooperation of the Norwegian Lecture Bureau.

ANALYSIS REVEALS HOW EARNINGS INCREASE DIVIDED

With the Government proposing drastic new taxes to pay for the war effort and curb inflation by mopping up the increased purchasing power resulting from the war program, it is interesting to know how this increase is at present divided among the various sections of the American public.

According to an annual review recently published in Current Business, the people of the United States received 17.2 billions more dollars in 1941 than in 1940.

A "breakdown" shows that of this increase: 70 percent, or 12.1 billion dollars, went to wages and salaries.

About 10 percent, or 1.8 billions, went to farmers.

Less than 2 percent, 0.3 billions, went as dividends to corporation stockholders. In addition, about 8 percent, or 1.3 billions, was earned by corporations but was put back in the hands of management to expand the work of these concerns or to strengthen them for future emergencies.

The following table showing these facts is from figures published by the United States Department of Commerce.

NATIONAL INCOME BY GROUPS
(Billions of Dollars)

	1940	1941	Increase
Total compensation of employees	52.6	64.7	12.1
Dividends to stockholders	4.3	4.6	0.3
Reinvested corporation earnings	1.3	2.6	1.3
Agriculture (net)	4.4	6.2	1.8
Unincorporated business	7.1	8.4	1.3
Interest (net)	5.2	5.3	0.1
Net rents and royalties	2.2	2.5	0.3
Totals	77.1	94.3	17.2

Prisoners Of War Bureaus Functioning

A Prisoners of War Information Bureau and an Alien Enemy Information Bureau have been established in the office of the Provost Marshal General at the War Department, Washington, D.C., according to information received from the Naval Department at Washington.

Purpose of these bureaus is to exchange information with enemy countries through the International Red Cross Committee at Geneva.

Requests for information and correspondence relative to our prisoners of war and civilian internees in the hands of the enemies should be addressed to:

Prisoners of War Information Bureau,
Office of the Provost Marshal General,
War Department,
Washington, D.C.

NEW BUS SERVICE EXTENSIONS NEAR

Further expansion of mass transportation bus services to the Vega and Lockheed plants in the Burbank area looms this week as the result of negotiations between the companies, city officials of Burbank and C. H. Eckles, head of the Burbank Bus Service.

Evidence and facts have been developed to substantiate the conclusion that the local bus system should be increased to more satisfactorily serve the Lockheed and Vega plant areas and these facts were presented Mr. Eckles by Traffic Manager Lynn Harrison and the Employee Transportation Committee. Conferences have also been held with Councilman Paul Brown, chairman of the Burbank City Transportation Committee, and City Manager Howard Stites.

Following these conferences, Mr. Eckles stated he would file an application with the Burbank City Council immediately for an operative franchise to inaugurate at least three additional routes of service to the Lockheed and Vega plant areas of the city. It has been proposed that a new cross-town route run along Buena Vista, interconnecting with the now existing routes on Victory, Burbank and Verdugo, as well as serving Alameda avenue territory. Such a route would provide direct and fast service by looping Lockheed 1 and 3 and Vega 1, L.A.T. districts.

It is further proposed that more direct service be provided for employees by inauguration of lines, possibly along Kenneth Road and Glenoaks Boulevard, avoiding the congested conditions along San Fernando Road. Owing to the urgent need of more adequate and direct bus service for local employees to plants, immediate action is anticipated.

'BUCK-OF-MONTH' CLUB TO GIVE THE RED CROSS $35,000

The first fruits of the Lockheed and Vega employees' "Buck-of-the-Month Club" will be given the American Red Cross next Friday when approximately $35,000 in checks will be distributed among 15 Red Cross chapters and a Burbank branch in which Lockheed-Vega workers live.

The checks will be presented by L.E.R.C. and V.E.R.C. members of the "Buck-of-the-Month Committee" to representatives of the various chapters at a ceremony to be held during the noon lunch hour at the main Lockheed Recreation Area. The Vega band will play.

A feature of the ceremony will be a demonstration of a Red Cross emergency field unit showing the efficiency of the Red Cross personnel and equipment.

The donation to the Red Cross is but the first of a series of monthly presentations to be made to various deserving charities or war relief agencies. The money comes from the employees, a majority of whom have authorized paycheck deductions for the duration of the war as a generous and continuous mass attack on the problem of wartime charities.

No other solicitations for charity are made of club members, either at work or at home, their contributions to the "Buck-of-the-Month" organization constituting their full obligation for the duration of the war. Under this plan, several hundred thousand dollars will be donated to accredited wartime charities by Lockheed and Vega employees this year.

SHIFT IN PLANT PROTECTION HEADS

(Continued from Page 2)

area, is now San Diego Area Plant Protection Officer.

Major Value left this week for San Diego to set up offices in the Consolidated Aircraft plant.

SHARING CAR NOT TO HIT INSURANCE

(Continued from Page 1)

others by forming groups and all riding together to and from work.

No special endorsement is required to make this effective, Mr. Charlton states. This means, in effect, that even though an assured may have an old form policy, his insurance is still good if he is transporting fellow workers and charging them for it.

SELECTIVE SERVICE ACT DEFINITIONS

(Continued from Page 1)

itary service when found acceptable to the land or naval forces.

CLASS I-B-O: Available for noncombatant limited military service when found acceptable to the land or naval forces; conscientious objector.

CLASS I-C: Member of land or naval forces of United States.

CLASS I-H: Man deferred by reason of age. At the present time there is no deferment by reason of age; however, military service is limited to men between the ages of 20 and 45.

CLASS II-A: Man necessary in his civilian activity.

CLASS II-B: Man necessary to the war production program. (a) In Class II-B shall be placed any registrant found to be a "necessary man" in any industry, business, employment, agricultural pursuit, governmental service, or in any other service or endeavor, or in training or preparation therefor, the maintenance of which is necessary to the war production program. (b) Class II-B deferments shall be for a period of 6 months or less. If there is a change in the registrant's status during tne period of deferment in Class II-B, his classification shall be reopened and considered anew. At the expiration of the period of the registrant's deferment in Class II-B, his classification shall be reopened, and he shall be classified anew. In again classifying the registrant, care should be taken not to impede the war production program. The registrant should be again classified in Class II-B for a period of 6 months or less if such classification is warranted and if the registrant's employer has made a reasonable but unsuccessful effort to secure or train a replacement for the registrant during the period of deferment. The same rule shall be applied when again classifying such a registrant at the end of each successive period for which he has been classified in Class II-B.

CLASS III-A: Man deferred by reason of dependency.

CLASS IV-A: Man who has completed service. (In time of war, no registrant shall be placed in this class and all registrants previously placed in this class shall be reclassified.)

CLASS IV-B: Official deferred by law.

CLASS IV-C: Neutral aliens requesting relief from liability, and unacceptable alien enemies.

CLASS IV-D: Minister of religion or divinity student.

CLASS IV-E: Available for general service in civilian work of national importance; conscientious objector.

CLASS IV-E-LS: Available for limited service in civilian work of national importance; conscientious objector.

CLASS IV-F: Physically, mentally, or morally unfit.

Further information concerning Selective Service matters is available to Lockheed employees through the Selective Service Section of their Employee Service Division located in the Lockheed Industrial Relations Building. Vega employees may obtain draft information from the Military Desk in their Employee Service Division, Vega Personnel Building.

THIRTEEN YEARS IN ARCTIC SERVICE

Above is shown a 13-year-old Lockheed "Vega" plane, the CF-AAL, maker's number 30, which was delivered in April, 1929. It has been in continuous service ever since under the most exacting climatic and flying conditions and is still giving first-class service. It is now being operated by the Canadian Pacific Railway in Canada's Far North.

VEGA SPEEDS UP 'FORTRESS' OUTPUT

The story of how production of "Flying Fortresses" under the Boeing, Vega, Douglas pooled facilities program has been advanced six months, through the use of an electrolytic transfer process by which the master pattern, or work template, can be reproduced in five minutes, was told this week by Mac Short, vice-president in charge of engineering for Vega.

The template is the same thing to aircraft manufacture as the tailor's pattern is to the making of a suit of clothes, and no work can be done on a given part in the shop until the corresponding template has been drawn, made and cut out to within a few thousandths of an inch tolerance.

"There was in existence only one complete set of these templates for the B-17 Flying Fortress," Mr. Short explained. "This set was at the Boeing Aircraft Company plant in Seattle. Duplicate sets were needed at both Vega and Douglas to enable those two companies to start work. The electrolytic

(Continued on Page 8)

VETERAN CRAFT PROVES LOCKHEED'S LEADERSHIP SLOGAN

In the way of aviation history, here's something for the book. We are indebted for it to J. H. Campbell, press representative of the Canadian Pacific Railway, Winnipeg, Manitoba, Canada.

In a letter to the STAR accompanying the photograph reproduced herewith, Mr. Campbell says:

"As you are no doubt aware, the Canadian Pacific Railway has recently taken over a number of the northern flying companies, including Yukon Southern, Wings, Starrett and Canadian Airways.

"The equipment taken over includes a Lockheed "Vega" CF-AAL, which I understand was first acquired by Commercial Airways in Edmonton in 1929 and taken over by Canadian Airways in 1931. The original certificate of the craft was issued April 18, 1929, and the maker's number is 30.

This aircraft, which is still in fine serviceable condition, operates in the sub-Arctic regions and has figured in some hair-raising operations in the bush and lake country in northern Canada."

Thirteen years of the most exacting service under the most punishing climatic conditions in the world—and still going strong! No wonder the worthy descendants of this worthy craft—the Hudson Bomber and the "Lightning"—have won world-wide acclaim.

THE *Lockheed-Vega Star* ★★

The LOCKHEED-VEGA STAR is issued every Friday for the employees of the Lockheed Aircraft Corporation and the Vega Aircraft Corp. Communications may be addressed to either the Industrial Relations Office or the Public Relations Department, Lockheed Aircraft Corporation, Burbank, Calif., U.S.A.
BERT W. HOLLOWAY, Editor-in-Chief
H. L. (Hal) ROSSON, Managing Editor

Volume 9 Number 19

Joined for Victory

America's leading aircraft companies have joined forces against aggression.

Under a cooperative plan and a wholesale exchange of blueprints, the big manufacturing companies are pooling resources on tested and proven models of warplanes

Employing complete tooling lists and detail drawings of the jigs and tools used by Boeing, Douglas and Vega Aircraft companies are turning out mighty Flying Fortresses so identical that their individual parts are interchangeable.

The joint Flying Fortress program is an outstanding example of the aircraft industry's devotion to the national defense program. Despite the fact that both Douglas and Vega have prominent designs of their own in the bomber field, the companies promptly and unselfishly turned over part of their facilities to help meet the Army's demand

VEGA SPEEDS UP 'FORTRESS' OUTPUT

(Continued from Page 7)

transfer process, a Lockheed invention and patent, was utilized as a means of eliminating the tedious, time-consuming hand reproduction of these duplicate working patterns, effecting a substantial savings of both time and money.

"Twenty-seven men from the Vega template group spent four months in Seattle reproducing 28,000 templates by hand from the master boards of the Boeing company. Each of these 28,000 patterns was sent to Burbank where reproductions were made of each template by the new electrolytic process which required only five minutes for each reproduction.

"Complete sets of templates were turned out for Douglas, others were retained by Vega and duplicate sets were sent Boeing to back up the master set from which the Vega men had made the drawings by hand. This saved each company about 50,000 man hours, or a total of some 150,000 work hours that would have to be completed before any manufacturing of parts, tooling or jig building could even have started."

The total cost of template layout copying by this new method, including labor and materials, has been found to be less than ten cents per square foot of layout area, as contrasted with $1 per square foot by hand.

WHEEL ALIGNMENT IS BIG TIRE SAVER

The third of the series on tire conservation issued by the Lockheed-Vega Employee Transportation Committee deals with the problem of wheel alignment.

Improper front wheel alignment will wear out tires faster than any other factor connected with tire wear. *A front wheel out of alignment one-half inch (toe-in or toe-out) will cause the tire to be dragged sideways 87 feet for every mile driven—literally grinding off the tire tread.*

Front wheel alignment should be checked every six or twelve months. Tires should be inspected at more frequent intervals to see if there are telltale signs of improper wheel alignment such as feather edges on the tread, excess wear on one side of tread and waves in the tread surface. Front wheels must be toed in at the front (toe-in) and slanting outward slightly at the top (camber) to be in proper alignment. The front wheels should also have "caster," which is defined as the amount (in degrees) that the top of the front axle is tilted toward the rear of the car. This produces the trailing effect of a common furniture caster, makes the front wheels straighten out as a car comes out of a turn, and tends to prevent shimmy and wandering from one side of the road to the other when the car is driven straight ahead.

TOE-IN OR TOE-OUT MISALIGNMENT WEAR

If any of these conditions are not within the limits of the car manufacturer's specifications, excessive and expensive tire wear will be the result, in addition to certain steering faults. It is especially important that alignment be checked after a minor collision involving the wheels, or hitting an obstacle, curb, or large chuck hole in the road. The tire casing should also be examined carefully in a case such as this. Most reputable dealers have adequate equipment and make reasonable charges or no charge at all for checking front wheel alignment.

Even if the tires are unevenly worn now due to improper alignment, the tread will smooth out if the fault is corrected and the tires are run a few hundred miles.

DONALD M. NELSON ANSWERS QUERIES ON VACATIONS

Question as to the Government's policy in regard to vacations for defense workers was answered this week by Donald M. Nelson, chairman of the War Production Board, who stated that employees of American industry should be allowed rest periods to restore their energy.

The Lockheed and Vega managements suggest that employees in those departments in which work is relatively slow at this time take their vacations as soon as they can be arranged with their supervisors. The full text of Mr. Nelson's statement follows:

"Experience here and abroad is indicating that the worker, even when stimulated by the urgency of the Allied war situation, cannot work long hours and maintain peak output indefinitely. We know that he benefits in peacetime from an annual vacation. After the extensive overtime and the added emotional strain of the war effort, we can be sure some rest period this year is going to prove doubly effective in the restoration of his energy and determination.

"In planning the vacation program in 1942, it is particularly necessary in each plant that American industry show its ingenuity in securing the vacation benefits without paying a counterbalancing cost in productive hours lost. This can be accomplished by doing work ahead in the departments affected, by further overtime of the workers not on vacation, by a special program of training substitutes for those workers scheduled to go on vacation, by the spreading of the vacations over the whole year in those sections where this is possible and spreading them evenly over the full May-through-September period in those sections where the greatest vacation benefits are secured in summer.

"I am depending upon American Industry to embrace the vacation opportunity, and solve its accompanying problem, in a way that will not let our current output suffer and yet will fortify our working force for the still greater accomplishments the President's program demands. *Under no circumstances can the desire or need for vacations be permitted to excuse any shut-down of any department of any war production plant."*

The regular vacation period started on March 1 and an employee's eligibility date is based on the completion of one full year of service from date of hiring.

Dept. 48 clerks will furnish Lockheed factory employees with any information desired relative to vacations, eligibility and proper application procedure. Office employees desiring such information may obtain same from the department clerk assigned to handle vacations in their departments.

Vega personnel should contact Attendance Desk for information.

THE Lockheed-Vega Star ★ ★

Official publication of the Lockheed and Vega Aircraft Corporations

Vol. 9 BURBANK, CALIFORNIA, U.S.A., MAY 29, 1942 Number 24

CHAMPION MEETS CHAMPION

Lockheed's mighty "Lightning" P-38 meets Britain's famous "Spitfire" at Lockheed Air Terminal. This historic "handshaking" of the two champion defenders of the Democracies took place this week after Col. Ben Kelsey of the U.S. Army Air Forces flew in from Wright Field. The "Spitfire" is generally credited with having saved England during the Battle of Britain in 1940, while the "Lightning" P-38 is now recognized as the World's fastest airplane.

PASADENA BUS RUN TO LOCKHEED-VEGA PLANTS STARTS JUNE 1

The Pasadena run as a part of the Employee Transportation Bus set-up to Lockheed Plants 1 and 3 and Vega Plants 1 and 2 will start service Monday morning, June 1.

The railhead on this line will be Sierra Madre Ave. and Colorado Street. Fare will be 15c each way and ticket books are now on sale at all Employee Transportation Offices.

Time schedule and passenger pick-up stops are as follows:

STARTING POINT—Sierra Madre and Colorado Streets.

Schedule

Colorado St. at Sierra Madre St.—
6 a.m., 7 a.m., 2:30 p.m., 11:30 p.m.
Colorado St. at Oak St.—
6:01 a.m., 7:01 a.m., 2:31 p.m., 11:31 p.m.
Colorado St. at Allen St.—
6:02 a.m., 7:02 a.m., 2:32 p.m., 11:32 p.m.
Colorado St. at Hill St.—
6:04 a.m., 7:04 a.m., 2:34 p.m., 11:34 p.m.
Colorado St. at Marvista St.—
6:05 a.m., 7:05 a.m. 2:35 p.m., 11:35 p.m.

(Continued on Page 7)

BUCK-OF-THE-MONTH DONATES $5000 TO CHINA RELIEF FUND

Buck - of - the - Month Club and the United China Relief Association joined hands for the relief of suffering in China when the Club today presented the association with a check for $5000 on behalf of all Lockheed and Vega employees.

The presentation was made during the lunch hour in the north Recreation Area at Vega Plant 1 and the stellar attraction at the event was the appearance of famed cinema star Anna May Wong to receive the gift on behalf of her countrymen. Miss Wong, who was given an enthusiastic welcome, eloquently expressed the gratitude of the association, in which she is playing a leading role, for the generosity of the gift. The Vega band provided background music.

The check was handed Miss Wong by Hal Davis, president of the Club, in the presence of T. K. Chang, Chinese Consul in Los Angeles, who also expressed thanks on behalf of his country.

Analysis Reveals What Happens To Company Income

Did you ever get to the end of the month and ask yourself, Where did all the money go? If you actually try to figure out exactly what happened to each penny, you may get a surprise. It's two to one you didn't realize how much you were spending on some little thing like cigarettes or candy—unless you're one of those mythical characters who have a budget and stick to it.

An industry has to ask itself the same question. Moreover, if the company is to succeed, the answer must be exact and reflect a wise, carefully planned distribution of the company's money. For example, the Accounting Department at Lockheed has made a report on how each dollar of the company's money is spent. You may be interested in the results.

During the past four years, each Lockheed dollar was spent in the following manner:

	1938	1939	1940	1941	Aver.
For wages & salaries:	.33	.27	.27	.27	.2725
For parts, materials, etc:	.61	.60	.62	.58	.5917
For taxes:	.03	.03	.0475	.11	.0817
For dividends:	.00	.02	.0175	.0066	.0133
For surplus to meet future needs, etc.	.03	.08	.04	.0333	.0408
Total	$1.00	1.00	1.00	1.00	1.00

The distribution is a little easier to see if we cut up an average dollar and show the relative size of the pieces:

On the average, the stockholders received only a little over 1 per cent. Parts and materials (including wages paid by vendors and sub-contractors to their em-

(Continued on Page 8)

ASK GOVERNMENT PARTICIPATION IN WAGE ADJUSTMENT

In the interests of all concerned, the Company and the Union have mutually agreed to ask the aid of the U. S. Conciliation Service in interpreting and making application of the findings of the joint Union-Management job evaluation study which has recently been completed.

DESIGN CLASS PROJECT REPORTED READY FOR LOFTING

Progress of the Mira No. 11, the low-wing bimotor transport plane being designed by the Aircraft Design & Layout Drafting classes at the Burbank Evening High School, has been such that the project is now scheduled for lofting by the Contour Design classes to commence with the summer semester, July 1.

The Mira is a modern all-metal design having fully-retractable tricycle landing gear, and using two 12-cylinder "V" engines. The wind-tunnel model of the ship is being completed and tests are planned in the near future.

The Design & Layout Drafting classes, conducted by Franklin Naylor, are organized along lines used by a modern Aircraft Engineering Department with design group leaders in charge of each phase of the project.

These principles will be followed in the Contour Design class conducted by Tom McClain. In this class, the airplane will be drawn full size on the loft table, and lines of the fuselage, wing and nacelles "faired." The contours so designed will be then transmitted to the Layout class for final drawing of the fuselage bulkheads, wing ribs and other structure.

Registration in the class should be made on Monday and Wednesday evenings from 6:30 to 9:30 in Room 407, Burbank Evening High School, starting next week.

IDENTIFYING BUS TICKETS MAY SAVE YOU CASH LOSSES

The Employee Transportation Office at Lockheed Plant 1 reports the recovery of several lost bus ticket books.

As these represent an actual monetary investment, the suggestion has been made that when an employee purchases one of these ticket books, he write his name, department number and clock number on the cover.

This simple identification will aid in returning lost books to their rightful owners.

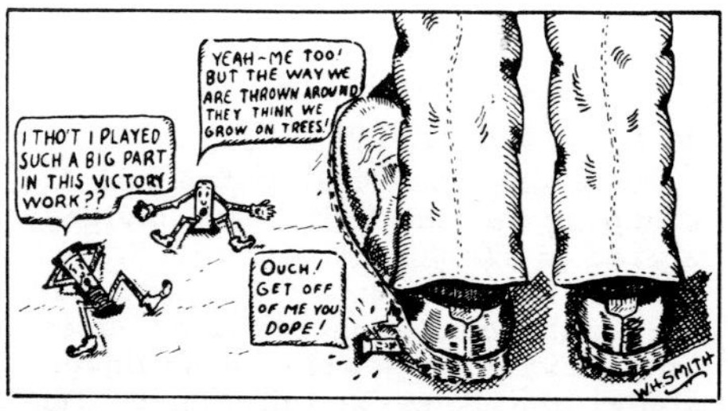

Waste Rivets—Waste War Effort

MacARTHUR'S KIN WORKING AT VEGA

Douglas MacArthur is now building airplanes.

Right here in Southern California.

He was discovered last week at Vega Plant 1 where he works on the day shift.

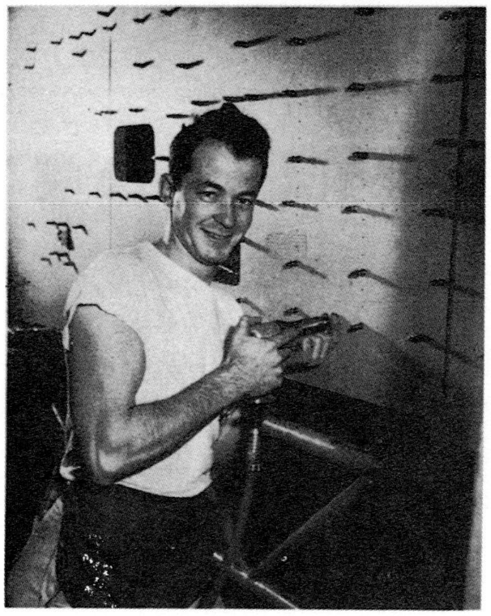

Douglas MacArthur

His only weapon is a hand drill which he uses in fuselage assembly work on the Vega Ventura bomber.

Douglas MacArthur is only 20 years old, he has been at Vega seven months and is trying to get into the Air Forces. He came to Southern California three years ago from Roundup, Montana.

Yes, they DO call him "General" and he is IS related to THE General Douglas MacArthur. His great-grandfather and General MacArthur's grandfather were brothers.

Conserve—Or You May Have To Use Solid Gold Bathtubs!

On May 5, 1942, thousands of manufacturing plants were ordered by the War Production Board to stop using iron and steel in the manufacture of more than 400 common civilian products. Included in the list were bathtubs, pie plates, cigarette lighters, mail boxes and fountain pens.

The ironic twist, however, is that while iron and steel are banned, any of the above may be made from what were formerly considered the more precious metals, gold and silver. That should remove even a war worker from the bathtub market!

Heretofore, conservation of the lighter metals, magnesium and aluminum, was considered to be most essential to the war effort, but now iron and steel join the list of strategic materials.

LETTER REFLECTS APPRECIATION OF TRANSPORT SYSTEM

The following letter of appreciation, received by the Lockheed-Vega Transportation Committee, is published herewith as a reflection of many similar letters which have been received by the STAR:

"Gentlemen:

"I wish to take this occasion to express my appreciation of the efforts of your committee in working out the transportation problems for the employees of Lockheed and Vega. It was and is a big job and I wish on behalf of myself, and I think I can speak for many of my fellow workers, to commend you for the results that you have accomplished to date.

"It sure is a pleasure to get aboard a bus and relax without the strain of driving, to say nothing of the economy involved and I wonder how many of the employees who live adjacent to this bus transportation and who persist in driving their cars realize that when their present tires are worn out, and even though they are defense workers, they will undoubtedly be denied replacements. Would it not be well to stress this point in a forthcoming issue of the Lockheed-Vega STAR?

"Again let me thank you for the good work that you have accomplished.

Yours sincerely,
N. E. CANFIELD
Dept. 96-95, Lockheed."

DANGER STRESSED IN USE OF WRONG EQUIPMENT

Jack Hatton, Lockheed Safety Engineer, points out that several injuries have occurred to employees who attempted to "short cut" the job by using makeshift equipment.

The latest injury involved an employee who decided to make up a mandrel for honing with emery cloth. A piece of dural scrap tubing was used and, it being too weak for the job, twisted, locked, and broke, cutting the worker's fingers quite badly.

This is another instance where failure to think things out boomeranged and resulted in delaying production rather than increasing it.

Let's use our heads and save our bodies.

HEAT WARNING!

DON'T TAKE TOO MANY SALT TABLETS!!

One tablet in four hours is plenty. If more than this is taken one is liable to become nauseated and have severe cramps.

Salt does not cool the system, but replaces the salt lost from the system by sweating, thus preventing heat prostration and sun stroke.

EAT LIGHT FOODS—DRINK PLENTY OF WATER—USE PLENTY OF SALT ON FOODS—DO NOT DRINK LIQUOR.

Keep heads covered when working in the sun.

Meetings Held To Stimulate Airplane Output

Exchanging ideas in an effort to help one another step up warplane production for the fighting fronts, representatives of eight Southern California aircraft companies, comprising the advisory council on production of Aircraft War Production Council, Inc., toured the Lockheed and Vega plants last week.

The men were taken on a tour of the Vega plant by H. E. Ryker, and of Lockheed by R. A. Von Hake, vice-presidents in charge of manufacturing of Vega and Lockheed, respectively.

At the Vega plant the group showed much interest in the white B-17 innerwing jigs, which are three stories high; in the method of assembling fuselages on the Ventura, using two working surfaces, and subsequent mating operations.

At the Lockheed plant most members were interested in the system of parts spray-painting and drying and in the P-38 fuselage assembly line.

The electrolytic method of reproducing template layouts also aroused their interest.

The following representatives were present:

Herbert Bowling and J. L. Kelley of Consolidated, J. E. Young of Douglas, H. Virgil Gaudette and R. A. Von Hake of Lockheed, R. E. Dawe and Harold Raynor of North American, Paul Buckner of Northrop, S. E. Barton and Lawrence C. Martin of Ryan, Harris McIntosh and H. E. Ryker of Vega, J. E. I'Anson and R. A. Lawson of Vultee.

BUY WAR BONDS!

PRODUCTION 'BRAINS' TOUR LOCKHEED-VEGA

Above is shown a group of leading production executives of the Southern California aircraft industry as they visited the Lockheed and Vega plants this week: Left to right: Paul Buckner, Northrup; Herbert Bowling, Consolidated; J. E. I'Anson, Vultee; F. Penn Holter, Lockheed (standing); R. A. Lawson, Vultee; H. Virgil Gaudette, Lockheed; J. H. Sreenan, Lockheed; J. L. Kelley, Consolidated; R. A. Von Hake, Lockheed, (standing); Lawrence C. Martin, Ryan; S. E. Barton, Ryan (standing); Harold Raynor, North American; R. E. Dawe, North American (standing); J. E. Young, Douglas, (standing); and Harvey Christen, Lockheed.

NEW BUS TICKET OFFICES ARE OPENED

As a further convenience to personnel who ride the big yellow busses to and from work, bus ticket books may now be purchased at the following conveniently located ticket offices:

LOCKHEED PLANT 1—West end of Industrial Relations Bldg.; Receptionist in the Purchasing Department Lobby; Mr. Morrison's Desk in Dept. 34, and Receptionist in the Finance Bldg. Lobby (Bldg. 167).

LOCKHEED PLANT 3—Plant Personnel Unit.

VEGA PLANT 1—Employee Transportation Office, just east of Bldg. 61; Employee Service Lobby (Graveyard Shift only).

VEGA PLANT 2 — Plant Personnel Unit.

Inter-Plant Golf Tourney Starts Sunday, June 7

In the first inter-plant golf tourney of the year, engineering golfers from Lockheed and Vega are scheduled to tee off on Sunday, June 7, at the Altadena Golf Club.

Starting times may be obtained by sending an ANVO to Gordon Brown, Lockheed Dept. 25, and the committee which has worked out the tourney announces that a fine list of prizes have been posted for winning golfers.

U.C.L.A. ANNOUNCES NEW CLASSES IN TOOL ENGINEERING

Twelve more evening classes and one afternoon class in Tool Engineering are scheduled to start on the U.C.L.A. campus the week of June 1, according to an announcement from the University of California War Training office.

This new group of tuition-free courses is in addition to the nine classes started on the U.C.L.A. campus last week, plus an Advanced Tool Planning class that opened in Van Nuys.

All of the Tool Engineering courses, with one exception, are evening classes and meet one evening a week, from 7 to 10, for 16 weeks. One course, Aircraft Materials and Processes, is a two-hour course, starting at 7:30 p.m.

The one exception to the evening class is a course in Body Plan Interpretation for Template Layout which meets Thursday afternoon, from noon to 3 o'clock, to be available for night shift men. A parallel class opens Thursday evening from 7-10 p.m.

Other Tool Engineering courses, and their starting days, include: Tuesday,

(Continued on Page 6)

'AH WILDERNESS' PREMIERE TO BE GALA EVENT

EMPLOYEES IN KFWB BROADCAST JUNE 7

Free studio tickets will soon be available to Lockheed-Vega employees for the "Meet Another American" broadcast slated for June 7, over K.F.W.B.

Representatives of the L.E.R.C. and V.E.R.C. will participate in this program of which Joe Crail is master of ceremonies.

The popularity of this "Meet Another American" broadcast has gained wide listening audience, and the Lockheed-Vega program promises to be an outstanding link in a long chain of interesting and entertaining Sunday evening K.F.W.B. performances.

JUNE 3 IS DEADLINE FOR ANNIVERSARY EDITION

Deadline notice for the Anniversary issue of the "Aircraftsman" is set for Wednesday, June 3, according to information received from the employee publication office this week.

Special emphasis should be given to senior employees and events relating to the past, emphasizing the tenth anniversary edition of the employee magazine, representatives of the publication point out.

EMPLOYEE BICYCLE CLUB WILL BE INAUGURATED

Arrangements for the inauguration of an employee bicycle club are nearing completion, according to an L.E.R.C. representative. The club will be formed for Lockheedians who ride the two wheelers to the plant. Conservation of indispensables will be the principle object of the organization. Employees interested should send an ANVO to the L.E.R.C. office.

EXECUTIVE POSTS FILLED IN L.E.R.C.

As a result of elections held at the L.E.R.C. council meeting last week, Bob O'Hanlon was elected secretary-treasurer, and Bill Mealer was voted into the vice-president seat.

O'Hanlon, long a member of the L.E.R.C. council, is employed in Department 25, while Mealer was formerly Plant 3 representative. Vacancies in the executive posts were opened when Allan Morison and Lyle Dewey, secretary-treasurer, and vice-president respectively, terminated at Lockheed.

NEW PROBLEMS AS BIKE RIDING GAINS

Since bicycles have become an increasingly popular means of transportation, new problems have arisen at the Lockheed and Vega parking lots for the guards on duty at the times shifts change.

Several complaints have been made to the companies Plant Protection departments that pedestrians on the sidewalks outside the plants have been injured by cyclists dashing hell-bent-for-election out of the gates. The departments point out that this is not only bad for the pedestrian but also bad for the cyclist, who lays himself open to a suit for damages.

And it also gives the guards a lot of headaches, for which reason they ask the cooperation of all employees who ride bikes in observing safety and traffic rules. The same rules that apply to the driving of automobiles apply in almost every instance to the riding of bicycles. Boiled down to the simplest term, these rules require that you "Ride Safely—the Pedestrian has the Right-of-Way."

L.E.R.C. Drama Club Suggests Theater 'Parties' Organize

Various departments and groups throughout Lockheed this week began organizing theater parties to attend en masse the major drama club production, "Ah Wilderness."

Stressing full department recreation, as well and tire and gasoline conservation, theater parties are encouraged among employees. A worthy successor to last year's "Room Service," the 5-day run of Eugene O'Neill's famous drama will be produced and directed by Dick Walsh who is remembered for his previous successes.

Tickets are on sale for 50 cents and may be secured from drama club members, L.E.R.C. representatives, and the L.E.R.C. Office. First curtain call is scheduled for Wednesday, June 24.

'YOUTH HOSTELING' FILM FREE TO LOCKHEEDIANS

Lockheedians may still see the motion picture, "Youth Hosteling in Southern California," according to Education Committee Chairman Bruce Frost, who adds that admission is free to Lockheed employees.

Only showing of the film is at the Burbank High School auditorium. The performance will begin at 8 tonight.

PREVENTION GETS ATTENTION

L.E.R.C. CALENDAR—MAY 29 - JUNE 5

Drama Club

Rehearsals at 1141 N. Gower St., Hollywood, 7:30, Friday, May 29, Sunday, May 31, Tuesday, June 2, Friday, June 5. Production meeting, 7:30 p.m., Wednesday, June 3.

Band

Band rehearsal, John Burroughs Junior High, Burbank, 7:30 p.m., Monday, June 1.

Badminton

Day Shift every Friday night, 7:30 p.m., Hollywood Sport Center, 1424 North Bronson, Hollywood, Group play. Swing shift every Monday morning, 11:00 a.m., Defense Area Building, 1111 W. Olive Ave., Burbank.

Rangers and Rangerettes

Day shift Rangers and Rangerettes ride together Wednesday nights, 7 p.m. 'till 9 p.m.

Night Shift Rangers and Rangerettes ride together Mondays from 10 a.m. til 12 m. Sunday morning all shifts ride together from 8 until 10.

Boy Scouts

Regular meeting, George Washington School, Wednesday, June 3, 7 p.m.

Educational Film

"Youth Hosteling in Southern California—The Thrill of New Trails," Burbank High School Auditorium, Friday, May 28, 8 p.m.

MORE SAMPLES OF DISNEY INSIGNIA ON VENTURAS

Above are three more reproductions of the Disney characters appearing on the sides of the Ventura bombers as they roll off the lines at Vega. The characters are used, free, by permission of Walt Disney but the slogan ideas are Randy McGraw's own, Randy being one of Vega's best in the Paint Department. The Nip will have no difficulty recognizing where these planes are from if he gets a closeup of the sides of the fuselages. And if he does it will be too bad—for him.

LONG LIST OF PROMOTIONS AT VEGA ANNOUNCED

The following list of personnel promotions at Vega has been announced by R. E. Winter, Vega Review Section. They are effective on dates shown:

DEPT.	NAME	OCCUPATION
	Effective May 2, 1942	
24	Russell G. Hanson	Group Leader, B
	Effective May 16, 1942	
1	Harold Larson	Asst. Foreman
1	William Muir	Asst. Foreman
7	Lewis W. Standage	Supervisor
9	Charles Alfred Swirsky	Supervisor
14	Simon P. Severson	Supervisor
15	Ralph L. Marinari	Supervisor
15	H. Edward Perkins	Supervisor
16	Lionel H. Chamness	Supervisor
19	Walter F. Winseman	Asst. Foreman
22	Robert E. Gunckel	Supervisor
26	Paul P. Pierson	Asst. Foreman
32	Melvern L. Wilson	Supervisor
33	Albert Mathey	Section Leader
35	Preston Y. Bowman	Div. Supervisor
36	Marshall Prothero	Div. Supervisor
36	Jean A. Waller	Div. Supervisor
39	George W. Rose	Supervisor
39	Walter W. Safford	Section Leader
42	Roland Douglas	Supervisor
45	William Chester Bunch	Section Leader
45	Damon L. McMillan	Div. Supervisor
55	Arthur B. Wink	Captain-Guard
66	Wardwell D. Evans	Section Leader
66	R. A. Hurley	Safety Engineer
96	David G. Beauchaine	Section Leader
96	Leland J. Brown	Section Leader
96	Robert V. Fredeen	Section Leader
96	Wm. F. Glass	Section Leader
96	Walter J. Lantz	Section Leader
96	Norman B. Riesch	Section Leader
4-2	Albert Henry Coulombe	Group Leader, A
11	Thorman Lehmann	Group Leader, B
11	Stanley Severson	Group Leader, B
15	Todd R. Lewis	Group Leader, B
16	Carl R. Ast	Group Leader, A
16	Frederic M. Gillet	Group Leader, A
21	Llewellyn J. Jones	Group Leader, B
22	James C. Hedges	Group Leader, B
22	Merton A. Oliver	Group Leader, B
25	Thomas T. Grady	Group Leader, B
25	W. C. Heselton	Group Leader, B
25	Roy E. Peterson	Group Leader, B
	Effective May 23, 1942	
12	Gerald B. Royalty	Group Leader, B
13	John A. Brown	Group Leader, B
13	Benjamin F. Habeger	Group Leader, B
13	Thomas L. Ward	Group Leader, B
13	Dudley E. Young, Jr.	Group Leader, B
13	Steven J. Zitlow, Jr.	Group Leader, A
15	Irving I. Blonder	Group Leader, B
26	Louis M. Kingsley	Group Leader, A
26	Everette D. Masters	Group Leader, B

RULES MEMORIAL DAY NOT A HOLIDAY

The following telegram has been received from Brig. Gen. Charles E. Branshaw, Western District Supervisor, AAF., for the attention of all Lockheed and Vega employees:

"The Secretary of War has ruled that Memorial Day is not a holiday and that production must continue in all plants without interruption."

MONTEBELLO RED CROSS EXPRESSES AID THANKS

A gift of $128.80 to the Montebello Branch of the American Red Cross has recently been made by the Lockheed-Vega Buck-of-the-Month Club on behalf of all the employees.

In acknowledging the check, Margaret H. Malone, Montebello Branch Chairman of the Red Cross, said:

"This donation is particularly gratifying because the small branches seldom get big donations, and this very fair and just way of handling this fund is outstanding and unusual.

"The employees who were so generous, and the companies who aided the plan, are to be congratulated and thanked for their generosity and fairness in distribution to these small branches, who will be able to do untold good work with this unexpected assistance."

MEMORIAL SERVICE HELD FOR LOCKHEED-VEGA WAR DEAD

A Memorial Service for former members of the Lockheed-Vega organization who have died in the service of their country was held last Sunday by the Lockheed-Vega American Legion Post No. 581 in Masonic Hall, Burbank.

Courtlandt S. Gross, president of Vega, had been scheduled to make the address of eulogy, but was unavoidably detained in Washington. In his absence, the eulogy was delivered by L. P. Brewer, staff assistant of Vega Dept. 35, whose son John, formerly of Vega Dept. 24, is now in the U.S. Army Military Intelligence Service.

Former employees honored at the service, all of whom have paid the supreme price in the service of the United States are: Warren C. Dunaway, Ivan P. Ellis, Richard Long and Hubert March. They were all members of Lockheed and lost their lives in line of duty.

In addition, honor was paid to Raymond Eckle, reported missing and believed dead, who formerly worked in Vega Production Control; and Raymond E. Miller, Jr., formerly of Vega Dept. 4, Plant 2, who was recently killed while on a training flight at Perrin Field, Texas.

BUY WAR BONDS!

LEARNS ABOUT UNKNOWN RESERVE

★

Cut shows Willis J. Bradbury, of Lockheed Dept. 7, who has been seriously ill since January 13 of this year, as he received the welcome news in hospital from Arthur F. Dignum, of the Lockheed-Vega Group Insurance Section, that he still had approximately $375 hospital benefits available, plus surgical fees if necessary, under his Lockheed-Vega Group Insurance policy, in spite of the fact that his lost time benefits under the policy expired April 23.

★

CLARENCE F. ROEDER, LOCKHEED DEPT. 11, DIES

Funeral services were held last Monday at St. Mary's Catholic Church, Whittier, for Clarence Frederick Roeder, formerly of Dept. 11, Lockheed, who died May 20 as the result of an auto-train crash in Whittier. Rosary was held in the White & Emerson Chapel Sunday night, with interment following on Monday at the Rose Hill Mausoleum.

Mr. Roeder is survived by his mother, Mrs. Marie Hurley, of 129 North Pickering, Whittier, to whom deepest sympathy is extended.

ARMY MAN SURPRISED AS RETROACTIVE CHECKS ARRIVE

L. O. Holter, of the Personnel Division at Vega, has received the following expression of appreciation from Lt. William A. Fickling, former Vegan now stationed at Hickam Field, T.H. The letter, delayed in transit, acknowledged receipt of retroactive paychecks. The letter said, in part:

"Receipt (of retroactive paychecks) is indeed a great surprise, and could not be more pleasant to help relieve the tensity since our 'party' of December 7th. With genuine sincerity I thank you for the checks and wish the very best for Ventura. Let's keep 'em flying!"

U.C.L.A. ANNOUNCES NEW CLASSES IN TOOL ENGINEERING

(Continued from Page 3)

Tool Design, Machine Jig and Fixtures; Machine Jig and Fixtures Laboratory; Wednesday, Aircraft Drafting Standards; Aircraft Materials and Processes; Tool Planning; Lofting Lines; and Die Design Laboratory; Friday, Tool Design, Die Design; Tool Design, Assembly Jig and Fixtures; Aircraft Descriptive Geometry; and Tool Design, Machine Jig and Fixtures Laboratory.

In addition to the tooling program, there is an industrial management class, Production Management, which opens an 18-weeks course starting Tuesday in room 100, Education building, on the campus, and two courses in Production Control starting on the campus on Tuesday and Wednesday.

NEW CLASSES

Blueprint Reading—
M-W, 6:30-9:30 p.m., Room 104, John Burroughs.

Welding Classes—
Interested employees should contact Charles Fisher, Friday nights between 6 p.m. and 12 midnight at the Burbank school on Magnolia Blvd. at Jackson.

INSURANCE EXPIRES BUT HE DISCOVERS COVERAGE IN FORCE

Few of us have to go through the pain and mental turmoil that Willis J. Bradbury, of Dept. 7, Lockheed, has suffered in order to learn the value of insurance coverage at time of illness or accident. But any of us may be forced to undergo the experience at any time, and if we do it may bring to us as it did to Mr. Bradbury a realization of the additional advantages to be derived from a self-administered Group Insurance Program such as is in force at Lockheed and Vega.

Here, briefly, is Mr. Bradbury's experience:

He has been disabled and off duty since January 13 of this year. Payment of $260 for 13 weeks of lost time benefits was completed April 23. Not being able to return to work, he was notified that his Group Insurance coverages would be cancelled until such time as he did return, when all would be reinstated.

Some time after he had been notified of cancellation, with, however, the privilege of converting his policy to an individual life insurance policy, it was found necessary to place him in a hospital. Study of his Group Insurance certificate then revealed that although his hospital coverage had been cancelled, he was entitled to additional hospital benefits of which he was unaware.

The result was that Arthur F. Dignum, of the Group Insurance Section, called on Mr. Bradbury and broke the good news to him that up to $375 in hospital benefits was available to him, and that should surgery be found necessary, an additional allowance could be made for surgical fees.

The Group Insurance Section points out that administration of the Lockheed-Vega Plan is handled entirely by Lockheed-Vega employees whose primary desire and duty is to see that sick and injured members of the companies' personnel receive the maximum insurance benefits to which they are entitled. Settlement of claims is authorized and completed in the Insurance Section and employees presenting claims are dealing with fellow employees rather than with an insurance claim adjuster interested in keeping settlements at a minimum.

Appointment

Announcement of the appointment of Merrill J. Cate as Supervisor of the Vega Plant Personnel Division was made this week by Ralph B. Smith, personnel manager. Mr. Cate will relieve D. H. Cameron, who is to devote his full time to labor relations at Vega.

VEGA ARTIST SPURS WAR BOND SALES

★

The drawing shown here, submitted by Harry A. Schafer of Vega Department 6, Processing and Heat Treating, is a fine example of the spirit shown by Lockheed and Vega personnel in the purchase of War Bonds.

★

Hudsons Not Only Bomb Hun But Take Home Part Of Ship

In the following recent B.B.C. broadcast a 20-year-old Scottish pilot of R.A.F. Coastal Command tells what happened one night when he made a low-level attack in a Lockheed Hudson on a ship off the Norwegian coast:

"When we got over the Norwegian coast the moon was shining brightly—just like daylight. It was a lovely night—and a grand night for spotting Hun ships crawling along near the shore. I'd been patrolling for about half an hour when I saw a convoy of medium-sized ships. They seemed to take little notice of us. Maybe they hoped we hadn't seen them and didn't want to stir anything up by firing at us.

"I selected one of them as my target and dipped the nose of the Hudson. Well, I got down to sea level and made straight at the ship. I held on to the last second before releasing my bombs. Then I pulled back on the stick to climb. But the ship was an old-fashioned sort of a tub with two very tall radio masts.

"The Hudson made a gallant effort to get over, but didn't quite make it. There was a crash, and a scraping, tearing kind of noise, and a sudden violent wind. I

(Continued on Page 8)

UNUSABLE TIRES VALUABLE AID IN RUBBER SHORTAGE

Tires worn to the point where they are no longer usuable can help relieve the rubber shortage situation if they are turned in immediately to a scrap or junk dealer or a local collecting charity, Leon Henderson, administrator of the OPA, said recently.

Mr. Henderson emphasized that it is a mistake to believe that casings worn or damaged beyond repair are acceptable as "basic carcasses" for retreading or recapping. The tires sought as scrap are those that are completely worn out or have suffered damage which makes them unfit for recapping.

"There is a pressing demand for scrap rubber to augment the nation's restricted crude rubber supply," the OPA administrator said. "Old tires are the main source of scrap rubber supply."

PASADENA BUS RUN TO L. & V. PLANTS STARTS JUNE 1

(Continued from Page 1)

Colorado St. at Lake St.—
6:07 a.m., 7:07 a.m., 2:37 p.m., 11:37 p.m.
Colorado St. at Los Robles St.—
6:09 a.m., 7:09 a.m., 2:39 p.m., 11:39 p.m.
Colorado St. at Marengo St.—
6:10 a.m., 7:10 a.m., 2:40 p.m., 11:40 p.m.
Colorado St. at Fair Oaks St.—
6:12 a.m., 7:12 a.m., 2:42 p.m., 11:42 p.m.
Route from Pasadena is: In:—
Colorado St. and San Fernando Road to Alameda St. Vega Plant No. 2 and Victory Blvd. to Lockheed Plant No. 1, Empire St. to Hollywood Way Vega Plant No. 1 and Hollywood Way to Lockheed Plant No. 3.

BOND SALES KEEP PACE WITH 'ALL-OUT' WAR PRODUCTION

"All out for War Production—and all out for War Financing" are the two primary principles which govern the conduct of the Vega and Lockheed personnel, judging from a report on War Bonds purchases in the two companies up to May 14.

As of that date, Lockheed-Vega employees had bought, through the Lockheed-Vega Federal Credit Union AND FOR CASH, $505,648 worth of War Bonds, of which amount $113,156 has been purchased since December 7. In addition to this total, $3402 worth of War Stamps has also been sold.

Maturity value of this cash investment in the U.S. and the War Effort is approximately $678,000.

In addition to these cash purchases, Lockheed, under the payroll deduction plan, was buying $131,712 worth of bonds a month, and Vega $84,782. Both companies are showing a steady increase each month.

In connection with the payroll deduction plan for bond purchases, it should be noted that only the amounts indicated on the authorization cards can be deducted for this purpose because of the enormous task involved in tabulating these deductions. Since the cards were distributed, filled in and returned, many requests have come to Accounting-Tabulating regarding the possibility of pledging 10 per cent of one's earnings. Unless this percentage was stated in the original card, employees are advised to make their additional purchases through the Federal Credit Union, as being the simplest and quickest way to acquire their quota.

NEW BOOKS IN LIBRARY

The following new titles are now on sale at the Lockheed Library in Room 210, Industrial Relations Bldg.:

Mathematics Dictionary—James......$2.60
Blueprint Reading Made Easy—Walsh 3.30
Aircraft Propellers—Hashacher........ 2.38

VEGA, DEPARTMENT 12, RINGS THE BELL ON BONDS

Again showing that good old American Drive spirit, which the men of Department 12 demonstrated in being the first department to beat the schedule, the Inner Wing Assembly Department claims the distinction of being the first Vega department to sign up 100% for the purchase of war bonds.

Now the campaign is on to make those bond dollars produce the greatest possible number of units. The boys say, "If I have to pinch MY pocketbook to buy bonds to pay MY wages, then I'm going to see to it that I get my money's worth."

THE Lockheed-Vega Star * *

The Lockheed-Vega Star is issued every Friday for the employees of the Lockheed Aircraft Corporation and the Vega Aircraft Corporation and is the official publication of both companies. Communications may be addressed to either the Industrial Relations Office or the Public Relations Department, Lockheed Aircraft Corporation, Burbank, California, U.S.A. Although news and cartoon contributions are welcome, circumstances make it impossible to give any promise that they will be returned to sender when not used, nor can individual acknowledgment be made.

BERT W. HOLLOWAY, Editor-in-Chief

H. L. (HAL) ROSSON, Managing Editor

Volume 9 Number 24

'Brighten The Corner'

Month after month the "Brighten the Corner" list appears in the *Aircraftsman*. This is not just a list of men who are not working, but a list of your fellow employees confined to hospitals or their homes because of severe illness. Each of these men wishes that he were back on the job doing his part in the "Victory Drive."

To employees who are fortunate enough to be well and working, may we suggest that you think of these fellow workers a little more often. A card, a letter, or a visit, is a small thing; but to those so anxious to keep up with the activities of their plant, it means a great deal.

There is yet another way that you might help to cheer up these boys. There are two Lockheed employees in the Olive View Sanitarium in San Fernando who refuse to remain idle. In the workshop they are cutting out and hand-painting very clever wooden lapel pins. We hope that these will soon be on sale in the canteens, but for the present orders for them will be taken in the Nurses' office.

Things are moving fast these days and every minute counts, but surely somewhere along the line each of us can spare a moment for the fellow who used to work next to us.

Modern cars are Winterproofed but not fool-proofed. Drive Carefully!

SECOND INSTALLMENT ON INCOME TAX DUE JUNE 15

Don Hicks, of Lockheed Dept. 23-G, comes through with a timely suggestion. Says he:

"It might perhaps save a number of employees embarrassment if the STAR carries a reminder that the second payment on Income Tax comes due June 15."

Well, here's the reminder. And if the STAR hadn't given it, your Uncle Samuel would have. Better be sure that installment is in the mail so that it reaches the Collector of Internal Revenue NOT LATER than June 15 in a certified check or money order. Penalties for nonpayment on time are pretty stiff!

LOCKHEED PROMOTIONS

The following personnel promotions, effective on the dates shown, have been reported by Lockheed Review Section:

	Effective May 16, 1942	
7	Marvin C. Larsen	Group Leader
10	Jack A. Felling	Group Leader
15	George Holznagel	Group Leader
	Effective May 23, 1942	
7	Arthur J. Forrester	Group Leader
7	Earl R. Garn	Group Leader
7	James G. Wyatt	Group Leader
12	Wilfred H. Stabenow	Group Leader
12	Edward B. Soltwedel	Group Leader
15	A. M. Rice	Group Leader
12	Lloyd C. Payne	Group Leader
10	Edward W. Parshall	Group Leader
15	Theron L. Mason	Group Leader
15	Robert B. Crevier	Group Leader

ANALYSIS REVEALS WHAT HAPPENS TO COMPANY INCOME

(Continued from Page 1)

ployees) took over 59 per cent. Lockheed employees received more than 27 per cent. Taxes took over 8 per cent, and slightly more than 4 per cent was set aside to meet the company's future problems.

Thus, of the individuals who profit from the company's earnings, employees (including also the employees of companies which furnish parts and materials to Lockheed) receive a large share. Stockholders' wages (dividends) have been consistently low, and at times actually non-existent. The money which the company makes is to a large extent being turned back to the men and women who are turning out the planes.

HUDSONS SCORE ON NAZI CRAFT

(Continued from Page 7)

knew I'd hit the ship or the masts, but we were still flying. Just then there were bright flashes as the bombs went off on the ship. We'd got her all right.

"Then I had a look round to see what damage had been done to the Hudson. First of all I found the perspex nose had been bashed in. A bitterly cold wind was sweeping in at hurricane force and nearly knocking me off the seat. The starboard main plane had been damaged and the wing lights knocked off, and the de-icing system had also been put out of action. I decided to get home on the shortest possible course.

"We also found that the radio had packed up and we couldn't get any help from it in finding our way home. With that hurricane howling through the hole in the nose of the aircraft it was next to impossible to hold a chart by which to navigate. I thought I'd call in the rear gunner to help; but I couldn't get a reply from him. The navigator went back to the turret to see what was wrong and found that the gunner had smacked his head against the turret when I pulled up over the ship; he was dazed, but he soon recovered, and I think he had the most comfortable place in the Hudson.

"The navigator, the wireless operator and I were half frozen up in front. We stamped our feet to try and keep warm; but it wasn't much use.

"When we finally circled our base our hands were numb; our feet were like lead; and our faces were blue with cold.

"We were a bit apprehensive about the landing, for we didn't know if the Hudson had been much damaged underneath. But everything went off all right.

"Riggers got to work at once on the damaged aircraft and they found that we had brought back the aerial from the Jerry ship. It had wound itself round our starboard airscrew and engine cowling. The wing tip had had quite a bashing too. But two days later the Hudson was ready for action again, which says a lot for the Hudson and R.A.F. ground crews who do a marvelous job of work.

"Well, it was a grand trip that—except for the cold—and we are certain that one enemy ship at least won't sail again. When we last saw it, it was burning merrily."

How Company Dollar Is Divided

"KEEP'EM FLYING!"

VEGA BREAKS OUTPUT RECORD

THE Lockheed-Vega Star ★ ★

Official publication of the Lockheed and Vega Aircraft Corporations

Volume 9 BURBANK, CALIFORNIA, U.S.A., JUNE 5, 1942 Number 25

'FLYING FORTRESS' PRODUCTION MONTHS AHEAD

Months ahead of schedule, Vega is now in full mass production of B-17 "Flying Fortresses" for the U.S. Army Air Forces. Vega was the first to make deliveries of these heavy bombers under a pooled facilities agreement with two other aircraft manufacturers, and is now pushing production ahead on a 24-hour schedule. Photo shows Vega employees looking on proudly and enthusiastically while one of the four-engine sky giants moves off the line during the noon lunch period.

ACHIEVEMENTS ARE HAILED BY ARMY CHIEFS

Six months ahead of schedule, massive "Flying Fortresses" now are rolling off the assembly lines at Vega to increase the hitting power of the U.S. Army Air Forces.

This latest bad news for the Axis came in an announcement by Courtlandt S. Gross, president, simultaneously with a telegram from Lt. Gen. Henry H. Arnold, Commander of the U.S. Army Air Forces, to the employees of Vega. The telegram—

"Congratulations on your splendid record of being six months ahead of schedule. This accomplishment is the result of your untiring efforts in following through on an outstanding case of long range planning. Upon you depends how soon victory will be ours."

Mr. Gross announced that Vega, newest of the large Southern California aircraft factories, was fully launched into an accelerated production schedule on the B-17 "Fortresses," and stated the plant's record of speed had been achieved without slowing down its output of Vega Ventura twin-engine bombers for the British.

"In fact, the men are well ahead of schedule on the Ventura bombers," President Gross said.

The young Vega organization, whose initial tooling was begun less than a year ago, was the first aircraft manufacturer to make deliveries under the pooled facilities arrangement which was hailed as an outstanding industrial plan by the U.S. Army Air Forces to extend production of hard hitting big bombers.

Under the production pooling, Vega and Douglas are manufacturing Boeing's B-17 along with Boeing.

One hundred Vega engineers, under Chief Engineer Mac Short, Vega vice-president, spent several weeks at Boeing last fall obtaining engineering data on the B-17. Now the "Fortresses" are being manufactured completely by the Vega organization and its component parts subcontractor, with the exception of such

(Continued on Page 5)

QUIP PRIZE TEST TO STIR INTEREST IN 'AH WILDERNESS'

With the slogan "you too can win five dollars," the L.E.R.C. Drama Club is staging a contest to get the best quip line with a pay-off for their forthcoming production, "Ah Wilderness," which opens June 24 at the Hollywood Assistance League Playhouse.

Such a line as:—As Doolittle said, looking back at Tokyo—"Ah Wilderness," or perhaps, "As the leadman said when they transferred him to Plant 4—"Ah Wilderness."

Anyway, it's simple and no soap wrappers are needed and you stand a chance to win five dollars or tickets to the Drama Club laugh riot . . . "Ah Wilderness."

SPECIAL RATES ARRANGED FOR 'LIFE WITH FATHER'

Through special arrangements concluded between the L.E.R.C. and the management of the Music Box Theatre, Hollywood, Lockheedians may enjoy reduced rates for the stage hit "Life With Father."

In order to obtain these rates, Lockheedians are to show their Lockheed passes. These special rates are available only on Mondays, Tuesdays and Thursdays.

PROMOTERS WARNED ON SCHEDULING DATES

All groups and departments are cautioned once again to clear dates with the L.E.R.C. office to avoid conflict and to eliminate embarrassment and confusion.

"This simple procedure will not only give each event full support of the L.E.R.C. but will have the tendency to help make each event more successful because of elimination of competition," states Ollie Arbelbide, program director.

TICKETS FOR SALE TO 'AH WILDERNESS'

Tickets for the L.E.R.C. Drama Club production of "Ah Wilderness," which opens a five-day run June 24, may be obtained through Drama Club members, L.E.R.C. representatives or the L.E.R.C. office at 50 cents each.

Production of Eugene O'Neill's remarkable drama, "Ah Wilderness," marks a new high for the L.E.R.C. Drama Club and present indications point to plant-wide support of the play.

BUY WAR BONDS!

L.E.R.C.-V.E.R.C. CLUBS COMBINE BASEBALL TEAMS THIS YEAR

Merging in the interest of a stronger baseball team, the L.E.R.C. and the V.E.R.C. have consolidated into one organization for this season.

Dropping the opener to the Fullerton Firemen with an 8 to 7 score, the new Lockheed-Vega squad expects to stage a comeback this Sunday, 2 p.m., when they meet the Arcadia Merchants at Arcadia Park.

"All ball players are urged to come to turn-outs," Coach Mike Gazzella, former Yankee diamond star states, "For the teams we field on Sundays are made up from men who turn out at the North Hollywood field on Tuesday and Thursday afternoons at 4."

L.E.R.C. CALENDAR
June 5 - 12

Badminton

Swing Shift every Monday morning, 11 a.m., Defense Area Building, 1111 W. Olive Ave., Burbank.

Boy Scouts

Regular meeting, George Washington School, Wednesday, June 10, 7 p.m.

Camera Club

Meeting, Thursday, June 11, 7:30 p.m. Conference Room, Burbank Public Library.

Band

Band Rehearsal, John Burroughs Junior High, Burbank, 7:30 p.m., Monday, June 8.

Rangers and Rangerettes

Day shift Rangers and Rangerettes ride together Wednesday nights, 7 p.m. till 9. Night Shift Rangers and Rangerettes ride together Mondays from 10 a.m. till 12 m. Sunday morning all shifts ride together from 8 until 10.

Drama Club

"AH WILDERNESS" Schedule

Rehearsals, Friday, Wednesday, Thursday and Friday, June 5, 10, 11 and 12, at 7:30 p.m. Sunday, June 7, Rehearsal, 1:30 p.m. First run through 7:30 p.m. Tuesday, June 9, Rehearse Act I, 7:30 p.m.

Inter-Plant Golf Tournament

Engineering golfers, Sunday, June 7, Altadena Golf Club.

Employees' Broadcast

"Meet Another American" Sunday, June 7, K.F.W.B.,—L.E.R.C. and V.E.R.C. representatives will participate.

Ski Club

June 6 and 7, Ski Club Outing at Ski Area. Hiking and Picnic. Bring your lunch or stay overnight.

L.E.R.C. Picks New Program Director: Arbelbide Resigns

The L.E.R.C. will have a new Program Director effective Monday, June 8 as result of the resignation of Ollie Arbelbide, who leaves the post which he pioneered to enter the Industrial Relations field with another concern.

Ollie's successor is to be Harry Pierson, former athletic manager of the Pasadena Athletic Club, swimming coach of Olympic teams and recently recreation director for the Officer's Club at Coronado. He brings to the L.E.R.C. many years of successful athletic and recreational experience.

FREE RADIO TICKETS TO L.E.R.C.-V.E.R.C. SHOW

Interest in the Lockheed-Vega Recreation Club participation in Joe Crail's "Meet Another American" radio show Sunday evening, 6:30 to 7 over Station K.F.W.B., has found the limited number of studio tickets almost exhausted by the V.E.R.C. and L.E.R.C. members who wish to attend.

Included on the program will be the Lockheed Band, officers of both the V.E.R.C. and L.E.R.C. . . . a fine quartet, solo numbers by Jean Machin and Bob McCrae and a humorous skit presented by the Drama Club.

PISTOL SECTION NEWS

The pistol section of the Lockheed Employees Rifle and Revolver Club lost its second match of the year to the Altadena Pistol Club Tuesday, May 26, by a score of 1389 to 1410. Those on the Lockheed team were: Carl Hirdler, Mrs. Florence Hopkins, Mrs. Mirian McKown, Evan Nelson, and Ward Robinson. Another match is scheduled in about a month.

Rifle Section Coming Events

There is a rifle match scheduled between Lockheed and the Los Angeles Times for Sunday, June 7. This match, which is to be fired on the range of the L.A. Times, about two miles north of Plant 1 on Glenoaks avenue, will begin at 8:30 a.m. Medals are to be given in both individual and team events.

One steel company gives cigars and cigarettes to departments establishing production records. Workers decided to pool their winnings and send them to buddies in the services. Last month's production record means 10,000 packages of cigarettes for fighting ex-steel workers.

Tribute Paid To Men Now In U.S. Armed Services

Brief Memorial Day services were held in the Lockheed Plant 1 Recreation Area on Friday, May 29, during the noon lunch period.

Bill Mealer, vice-president of L.E.R.C., acted as Master of Ceremonies and introduced Jean Machin, Lockheed Department 28, Experimental Production Planning, who sang "My Buddy."

Harvey Christen, Lockheed assistant works manager, spoke briefly, paying a tribute to the employees who are now serving in the armed forces and who are represented by blue stars on the Lockheed-Vega Service Boards. Also to those who have already given their lives and are now represented by Gold Stars.

He pointed out that the way we of the production forces can best pay tribute to these men is to see that they are adequately furnished with the finest fighting material available, that we at home might survive and that those who have made the supreme sacrifice shall not have died in vain.

"Taps," by a member of the L.E.R.C. Band, was sounded at the conclusion of Mr. Cristen's address.

As of this week, there are more than 3100 stars on the Lockheed-Vega Service Boards.

FORMER LOCKHEED MAN WINS AIR FORCE WINGS

Aviation Cadet John C. Fehrs, Azusa, California, has received his commission as a Second Lieutenant, U.S. Air Forces and wings of an Aerial Bombardier from the Air Corps Advanced Flying School at Albuquerque, New Mexico.

Lieutenant Fehrs, son of Mr. and Mrs. J. C. Fehrs, is a former student of Citrus Junior College and former employee of Lockheed Aircraft Corp.

Prior to his advanced training at Albuquerque, Lt. Fehrs was stationed at Ellington Field, Texas.

As a lieutenant in the Air Corps, ready for active duty, his destination is not disclosed.

NEW BUS SCHEDULE

Effective Monday, June 8, busses on the Pomona run will stop for passengers at the corner of Garfield Avenue and Foothill Blvd. in Alhambra. The fare from this point to Lockheed Plants 1 and 3 and Vega Plants 1 and 2 will be 20c each way. Leaving time from this new stop will be 6 a.m., 2:42 p.m. and 11:20 p.m.

MORE THAN 3100 STARS ON HONOR ROLL

Honor was paid to former Lockheed and Vega employees now in the armed services of their country at a brief ceremony held at Lockheed Plant 1 last Friday to commemorate Memorial Day. Picture shows the Honor Roll Board as it appears today with more than 3100 stars upon it. Harvey Christen, Lockheed assistant works manager, foreground, spoke briefly; Jean Machin, of Lockheed Dept. 28, sang "My Buddy," and Bill Mealer, vice-president of L.E.R.C., acted as master of ceremonies.

ANNOUNCE REVISION ON 'SHORT TIME' LEAVES

A revision of the present procedure relating to weekly employees leaving Lockheed plants on "short time" on personal business has been issued by the Industrial Relations Department.

Three-tenths of an hour has been established as the minimum deduction for weekly salaried employees granted permission to leave the plants on personal business and return during working hours.

This covers the loss in production time necessary for an employee to obtain permission to leave, obtain a Traffic Card or notation on Time Card, proceed to the gate nearest the employee's business, complete the personal business, report back and return to work.

Any time which is clocked absent more than the minimum three-tenths of an hour is deducted at the rate of one-tenth for each tenth of an hour or fraction thereof that the employee is absent.

SKI CLUB LIBRARY

Two copies of the National Ski Association's "Manual of Ski Mountaineering" are now available. Write to Bob O'Hanlon, Dept. 25.

MEDICAL SECTIONS HARD HIT BY WAR

Two of the departments most heavily hit by terminations for Army and Navy service are the Medical Sections of the Health & Safety Divisions of Vega and Lockheed.

Proud of its contribution to the Armed Forces, and wondering whether any other department can boast such a high percentage, the Lockheed Medical Section reports that it has lost 13 members of its personnel. They are:

Vaughn Wright	USN	John T. Davis	USN
Melvin P. Fowler	USN	John G. Davis	USN
H. M. Mangold	USN	Charles Leininger	USN
Sam Isaacs	USN	Ed Davies	USN
W. E. Downing	USN	Roy Hudson	USN
Don Lyttle	USA	Willard Beckman	USA
Leonard Kroloff	USN		

From Vega's Medical Section have gone five members of the staff, all of them to the Navy. They are:

R. O. Kercheval	USN	E. H. Harrington	USN
R. J. Lyons	USN	"Pop" Arnison	USN
Zeb Graham	USN		

Take care of your job and your job will take care of you.

GIANTS WILL CARRY DOOM TO JAPS

Vega-built "Flying Fortress" taking off from a West Coast airport

Center section finished 2 weeks ahead of schedule

"Jig-Time" Vegans in action

"Launching" one of the sky giants

A "Flying Fortress" near completion

UNIFIED EFFORT SPEEDS 'FLYING FORTRESS' OUTPUT

One of the Vega-built sky giants in flight over Southern California

Looking up to a big job

They roar night and day—engine testing

Vega's B-17 mechanics service the sky giant

(Continued from Page 1)

purchased parts as engines, instruments, propellers and tires.

Congratulatory messages to Vega employees also came from Brig. Gen. A. W. Vanaman, Commanding General of the Army Air Forces Material Center at Wright Field, and from T. P. Wright, Assistant Chief of the Aircraft Branch, War Production Board. Sales Manager F. B. Dollins of the Boeing Airplane Company, Seattle, wired—"It's a slap for the Japs so keep 'em rolling."

Vega occupied its present quarters little more than a year ago, and the company has been consistently ahead of schedule in every phase of its program, from construction of buildings and installation of equipment to the hiring and training of personnel by the thousands, from tooling and jig building to the production of Vega Venturas and now the building of four-engine bombers for the U.S. Army Air Forces.

The Venturas and "Flying Fortresses" now are rolling down adjacent assembly lines 24 hours a day, six days a week to augment the steadily mounting air power of America and the United States.

Much credit for the advanced production of these four-engine giants must go to Mac Short, vice-president in charge of Engineering, and all his crew; H. E. Ryker, vice-president in charge of Manufacturing; Mort Bach, works manager, and his assistant, George Pruden; Harry Allen, superintendent of assembly, and his capable staff of both day and night shifts.

But chiefly it was team work from the newest employee on the line to top management, each and all giving out just a little, more each minute of each hour to step up the B-17 production program to its present stage.

Analysis Shows Southland Wage Earner Lucky

Eddie Cantor once boasted he owned a dog worth $50,000. He was asked: "How do you know your dog is worth $50,000?"

He replied: "Why, I swapped him for two $25,000 cats."

Everybody knows that the true value of a dollar is its purchasing power—what it will buy. The European workman who gets paid 20,000 rubles or kronen or marks every week may find himself able to buy only a single pair of shoes with them. Therefore, we say that his "real wage" is the equal of a pair of shoes, or $5 in cold American cash.

Likewise, with American wages. Living costs vary in different parts of the country. In one section of America, a $30 pay envelope provides just enough for "vittles" and carfare. In another region a $30 pay envelope enables a man to live the proverbial "Life of Riley," and to buy a War Bond, too.

Los Angeles has nearly the lowest cost of living found in 10 key cities of America (see cut). According to the Bureau of Labor Statistics charts shown here—as of September 15, 1941—a worker in Washington, D.C., Detroit, and other cities would have to receive *more* money to maintain the *same* standard as does the worker in Los Angeles. Since that time, with all the changes in cost of living, Los Angeles still ranks lower than most key cities. It takes $1.11 for a Chicago worker to buy as much as you buy here with your $1.00.

The real worth of your pay envelope then rests on a comparison of the living costs of your community and your dollar wages.

The following chart shows the rise of weekly wages enjoyed by Lockheed-Vega workers in Southern California—compared with the rise of the local cost of living. The cost figures were compiled by the Bureau of Labor Statistics and are based upon the 1935-1939 level. This is defined as average and is represented by an index of 100. Lockheed-Vega's average weekly earnings have been charted in respect to this starting point.

From January, 1940, to April, 1942, the cost of living in Los Angeles increased 17%. During the same period, the rise in earnings of weekly salaried Lockheed-Vega employees amounted to 29%. "Real earnings," which are found by dividing money wages by the cost of living index, have risen 11% during this period. In other words, the Lockheed-Vega employee who has maintained his same way of life during the last two years has been able not only to "beat the rising cost of living" but to retain 11% of his wages for other uses.

L. A. SECOND LOWEST IN LIVING COST

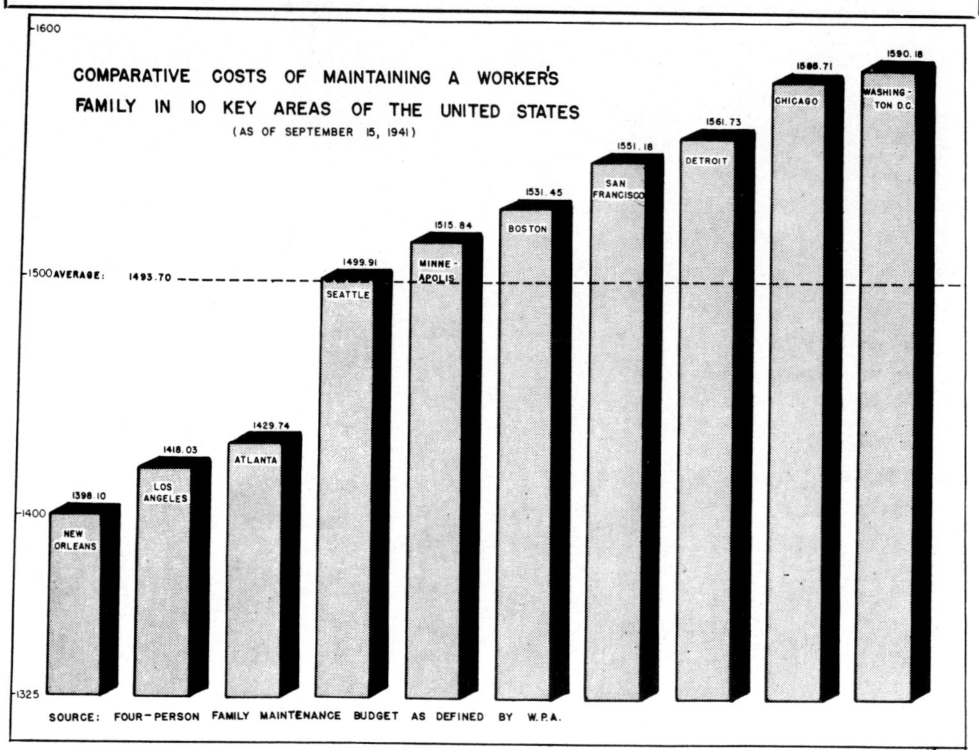

COMPARATIVE INCOME-OUTGO REVEALED

INDEX TREND OF WEEKLY SALARIED EMPLOYEES FOR LOCKHEED-VEGA, COMPARED WITH COST OF LIVING

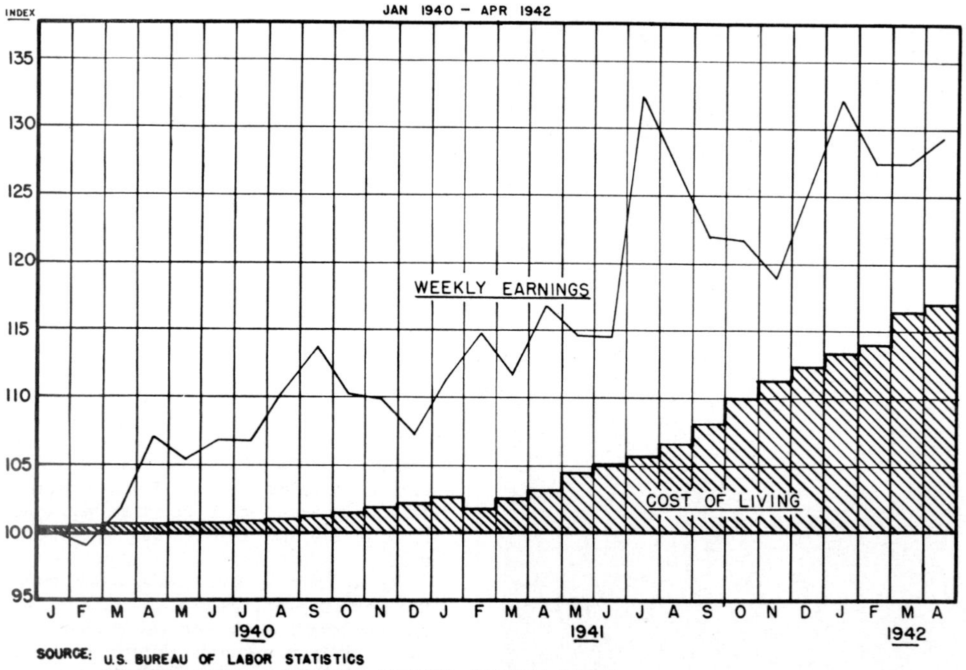

SOURCE: U.S. BUREAU OF LABOR STATISTICS
LOCKHEED-VEGA – INDUSTRIAL RELATIONS RESEARCH RECORDS

Rabid Dog Warning

All Lockheed and Vega employees residing in the Burbank area, and who own dogs, are advised by Dr. P. H. Ransom of the Burbank Health Department to keep their animals under close observation for the next week or so, because the fox terrier dog which went mad and bit twelve persons in Glendale is known to have been in Burbank over the past week-end.

Dr. Ransom also advises anyone who has been bitten by any dog in the past few days to report immediately to the Public Health Officer in Burbank, or to his or her own physician.

Clean-up Week For Material Saving Planned

Mark a red ring on your calendars around the dates "June 22 to June 27," for in that week "something new will have been added" to the Material Conservation program in all Lockheed and Vega plants and departments.

The week has been designated by Secretary L. W. Wulfekuhler as "Housecleaning Week" and all Department Managers and Supervisors have been so notified through an Inter-Departmental Communication issued earlier this week. The "week" has nothing to do, except indirectly, with cleaning up work benches and keeping floors clear of safety hazards.

It is directed particularly at the "hidden treasures" in desk drawers and tool boxes as well as in miscellaneous storage cabinets other than the recognized authorized storerooms or sources of supply. Practically all these "treasures" are small parts held out of circulation and use by loyal and patriotic employees whose only thought is that, if a temporary shortage occurs in any certain part needed on their job, they'll have some on hand with which to carry on their Fight for Victory task.

The motive is worthy, but the effects are a headache to Salvage Survey Department 19, which recently conducted a cross section survey of this hoarding. F. C. Weber, division supervisor of the department, reports that in one man's desk, picked at random, $9.60 worth of valuable small parts. Alclad sheet metal pieces, moulded extrusion and solid brass were found. Multiply this by the thousands of desks, benches and tool boxes in the Lockheed and Vega plants and the total rises to astronomical figures—figures which represent not only a heavy financial cost but may occasion a slowing-up in vital plane production.

The "Housecleaning Week" is primarily the outgrowth of scores of suggestions made to the Management by employees who have noticed the tendency to hoard on the part of some of the personnel and who have felt strongly enough about it to send in Anvos suggesting cures. The clean-up will include not only nuts, bolts, rivets, small extrusions, bearings and small purchased parts requisitioned from stockrooms and never used, but also such articles as miscellaneous sheet metal parts made into ash trays, paper weights, pen and pencil receptacles, etc.

So, in the spirit of cooperation and leadership for which our companies are noted, let's make the week of June 22 to June 27 a real clean-up week and get every department, desk drawer, closet, tool box and the like to give up its hoarded treasure wherewith to build more planes for Uncle Sam.

CHINESE BEAUTIES GRACE GALA OCCASION

Believed to be the first feminine member of her race to be employed in an American aircraft plant, Miss Marian Shu Ying Loo, left, above, had the honor last week of presenting to Anna May Wong, famous Chinese movie star, the check for $5000 donated by Buck-of-the-Month Club to United China Relief. With Miss Loo, in the picture, left to right, are: Ralph Richert, past president of the V.E.R.C.; Don Simmons, president of V.E.R.C.; Miss Wong; Fred Jones, business manager of V.E.R.C.; and T. K. Chang, Chinese Consul in Los Angeles.

LETTERS

The following letter, which speaks for itself, has been received by Svend Pedersen, director of the Education Department for Lockheed-Vega:

Dear Mr. Pedersen:

Before leaving for the Lockheed Overseas Corp., I want to express my appreciation for all that you and your staff have done for me in the two years time I have been with the Lockheed Aircraft Corp.

You have not only made it possible for me to attend classes in all branches of aircraft work but also have been ready and willing to help whenever I needed advice. I believe that everyone has a grand opportunity at sometime during his life, but everyone working at Lockheed has a grand opportunity all of the time if they get acquainted with the Education Department.

Two years ago I started at the minimum rate of fifty-one cents per hour, now I have a senior rating and am getting top wages. This would not have been possible without the help of the Education Department.

Sincerely yours,
(Signed) JAMES O'SHEA.

MARIAN SHU YING LOO, VEGA, HANDS MISS WONG CHECK

From the hands of Marian Shu Ying Loo, Chinese-American file clerk in the Engineering Department at Vega, Anna May Wong last Friday received in behalf of the United China Relief a check of $5000 from the Lockheed-Vega Employees Buck-of-the-Month Club.

The ceremony was held during the noon lunch hour at the Vega recreation area. Present also was T. K. Chang, Chinese Consul in Los Angeles; Courtlandt S. Gross, president of Vega, and various V.E.R.C. and Buck-of-the-Month Club officials.

Miss Wong, well-known motion picture star, expressed to the Vega employees her appreciation and that of her people for the donation which, she said, would feed and clothe hundreds of Chinese families hard hit by the misfortunes of war.

Miss Loo, who joined Vega two weeks ago, was born 24 years ago in

(Continued on Page 8)

THE *Lockheed-Vega Star* * *

The Lockheed-Vega Star is issued every Friday for the employees of the Lockheed Aircraft Corporation and the Vega Aircraft Corporation and is the official publication of both companies. Communications may be addressed to either the Industrial Relations Office or the Public Relations Department, Lockheed Aircraft Corporation, Burbank, California, U.S.A. Although news and cartoon contributions are welcome, circumstances make it impossible to give any promise that they will be returned to sender when not used, nor can individual acknowledgment be made.

BERT W. HOLLOWAY, Editor-in-Chief

H. L. (HAL) ROSSON, Managing Editor

Volume 9 No. 25

BUCK-OF-THE-MONTH FINANCIAL REPORT REVEALS BIG GIFTS

An outstanding record of individual and collective generosity in support of a coordinated charitable effort was revealed this week in the financial report of the Buck-of-the-Month Club to May 31, as submitted by Chairman Hal Davis.

The report shows that since inception of the Club early this year, Lockheed and Vega employees have contributed $89,308 of their wages as an over all contribution to cover gifts to worthy causes, and to eliminate separate and frequent solicitations that in the past resulted in much overlapping of effort and consequent higher cost of collection and distribution.

Under the Club plan, all donations to any cause of whatever nature are covered by an employee's authorized deduction from his paycheck. He is not subject to further solicitation if he shows his Buck-Of-The-Month Club button.

Mr. Davis' report follows in detail:

Financial Report — Buck-of-the-Month Club as of May 31, 1942

Contributions		
Lockheed Employees	$59,801.25	
Vega Employees	28,571.75	
Triplett & Barton	192.00	
L.E.R.C. Employees	26.00	
V.E.R.C. Employees	17.00	
Publication Employees	2.00	
Miscellaneous	652.00	
British Reassembly Division	46.00	
TOTAL		$89,308.00
Disbursements		
Refunds	$ 40.25	
Bonding	360.00	
Red Cross (already donated)	20,117.95	
(Due L.A. Chapter $14,233.05)		
(Total Red Cross—$34,351.00)		
Infantile Paralysis	3,435.00	
Iron Lung	500.00	
United China Relief	5,000.00	
Poppy Day	1,000.00	
Junior Chamber of Commerce	50.00	
TOTAL		$30,503.20
BALANCE		$58,804.80

LOCKHEED PLANT 4 NOW IN BUS SYSTEM

Extension of the bus transportation service to include employees working at Lockheed Plant 4 has been announced by the Employee Transportation Committee.

Effective Monday, June 8, the first line will serve those living in the Pasadena, South Pasadena and Alhambra districts. The railhead has been established at Foothill Blvd. and Fair Oaks where busses will leave at 5:45 a.m., 2:15 p.m. and 11:15 p.m. The following passenger pick-up stops, together with leaving times will be in effect:

Foothill & Fair Oaks	5:45	2:15	11:15
Montana & Fair Oaks	5:48	2:18	11:18
Wash'ton & Fair Oaks	5:50	2:20	11:20
Wash'ton & Los Robles	5:52	2:22	11:22
Mountain & Los Robles	5:54	2:24	11:24
Orange Grv. & Los Rob.	5:55	2:25	11:25
Walnut & Los Robles	5:57	2:27	11:27
Colo. & Los Robles	6:00	2:30	11:30
Calif. & Los Robles	6:03	2:33	11:33
Glenarm & Los Robles	6:05	2:35	11:35
Miss. St. & Los Rob.	6:08	2:38	11:38
Hunt. & Los Robles	6:12	2:42	11:42
Alham. Rd. & Atlantic	6:15	2:45	11:45
Main St. & Atlantic	6:18	2:48	11:48
Valley Blvd. & Atlan.	6:25	2:55	11:55
Hellman & Atlantic	6:28	2:58	11:58
Garvey Blvd. & Atlan.	6:31	3:01	12:01 a.m.

Ticket books for this run are now on sale at the Employee Transportation Office in the Plant Personnel Unit of Lockheed Plant 4.

MARIAN SHU YING LOO, VEGA, HANDS MISS WONG CHECK

(Continued from Page 7)

Shanghai. Her father was born in Honolulu. Both her father and mother are now in China. She has one brother who is an engineer on the Burma Road, another who is a student at University of Missouri, and a third who is with the U.S. Engineering Department in Honolulu. A sister is a student in San Francisco.

She was graduated from the Peiping American school in 1936, was in Shanghai when the Japanese war started in 1937, was present when the Chinese people presented General Chaing Kai Shek with 50 warplanes on his 50th birthday and left Peiping two years ago. She knows General Stilwell.

Miss Loo worked for awhile in the Hollywood medical offices of Dr. Berto Olson as a nurses' assistant. At Vega she wears conventional Chinese costumes while working and is believed to be the first Chinese girl to be employed in any American aircraft factory.

Aerial photographs are being used to reveal defects in the fire drill precautions in shipyards, aircraft factories, and other war plants on the West Coast.

SUGGESTION GIVEN: 'DON'T CANCEL YOUR GROUP INSURANCE'

Occasionally, employees call at the Group Insurance Section requesting cancellation of their insurance coverages, giving as their reasons that the premium rates are too high or that they are able to secure similar coverages elsewhere at lower rates. Usually, employees making such requests do so because they do not have a clear understanding of the extent of their coverages, nor of the individual rates charged for each coverage which, added together, make up the weekly or semi-monthly deduction for Group Insurance.

The Lockheed-Vega Group Insurance program offers more complete protection than that which is available to most other groups of comparable size. On the other hand, the rates charged for each portion of the plan will compare favorably with those charged under any other plan for similar coverage. In order that all may understand just what rates we are paying, we will use Class "C" insurance as an illustration:

	WKLY. PREM. RATE	SEMI-MTHLY. PREM. RATE
Life Insurance	.173	.375
Acc. Death & Dis.	.035	.075
Acc. & Sick Wk. Ben.	.369	.80
Hospitalization	.162	.35
Surgical Benefits	.069	.15
Medical Benefits	.092	.20
	90c	$1.95

Class "C" insurance provides $1500 life insurance, $1500 accidental death and dismemberment, $20 weekly benefits for lost time, hospitalization at the rate of $5 per day for a period of 70 days, with special benefits up to $25; surgical benefits ranging from $5 to $150, and medical benefits up to $75. The hospital, surgical and medical benefits are the same for each class of insurance and, of course, the rates remain the same. The benefits payable under life, accidental death and dismemberment, and the accident and sickness lost time coverages, vary with the class of insurance, and the rates are decreased or increased proportionately.

In setting up the Group Program, the Management has attempted to secure insurance coverages which will benefit the greatest number of employees at the lowest possible rates.

Golf Club Privilege Cards

Special privilege cards which will allow the holder to obtain a $5 membership in the Chevy Chase Golf Club, Glendale, for a total price of $4 may be obtained at the V.E.R.C. office. Vega employees and their families may purchase these cards.

SPARE PARTS PRODUCTION DRIVE LAUNCHED

Volume 9 BURBANK, CALIFORNIA, U.S.A., JULY 10, 1942 Number 30

THE *Lockheed-Vega Star* ★ ★

'FIREWORKS' ON PRODUCTION LINE

It's all "Thumbs Up!" among these Zone Two and Zone Five workers in Vega Department 23 (Sub-assembly) at the completion of their eight-hour shift on the Fourth of July, which they celebrated by far exceeding their normal production quotas.

Former Vega Man Lost In Raid Over Holland

It is July 7, 1941. A young man is hired as a learner plumber at Vega. He proves to be a good worker and is well liked by everyone.

"He's just a baby," say these friends two months later when young Marshall Draper is called to begin training as a bombardier in the U.S. Army Air Forces.

One year goes by. Maxwell Field, Ala. Next an advance flying school in Albuquerque. Then overseas.

It is now July 4, 1942.

A group of American airmen are visiting an R.A.F. base in England. "How would some of you boys like to go along and celebrate the Fourth?" asks one of the R.A.F. officers.

One of those who cries, "Fine!" is

(Continued on Page 5)

VEGA GROUPS HIT BALL (AND AXIS) CELEBRATING '4th'

Once again the Spirit of Lockheed-Vega rises to new heights. This time through the sensible and practical method of celebrating the Fourth of July.

The spirit expressed by all Lockheed and Vega employees is best exemplified by the production efforts of the personnel in Department 23, fuselage sub-assembly at Vega, last Saturday.

The employees of Zones two and five decided the best way to celebrate the Fourth would be to produce the absolute maximum number of their respective units possible. At the close of the day shift, the scoreboard read: Zone two, one hundred and twenty-five per cent of scheduled daily quota; Zone five, one hundred seventy-five per cent of quota.

This clearly emphasizes the determination of Lockheed-Vega employees to do more than their bit in helping to defeat the Axis.

Christen Stresses Importance Of 'Extras' For P-38

Closely following the Lockheed "Lightning" P-38's debut under a baptism of fire in the Aleutian Islands recently, the company has launched a concerted manufacturing drive to produce spare parts concurrently with deliveries of airplanes to the fighting fronts.

Characterizing spare parts manufacture as one of the most urgent production efforts Lockheed has been called upon to make, Harvey Christen, Assistant Works Manager and recently appointed coordinator of spare parts production, had this to say:

"The Army now requires this type of delivery as a necessary move to keep our fighting planes in the field ready for instant action at all times. It is a condition of our Lockheed airplane contracts, and one that must and will be met. What it actually means to our production is that spare parts must be produced ahead of the airplane for which they are intended because of the increase in spares requirements per plane. In view of increased production spare parts for Lockheed ships are now required in a greater proportion than ever before. If we want to hear more successful reports of Lockheed ships in action, we must furnish the spare parts for those ships or they will not be allowed in the air."

50 Per Cent Efficiency

Referring to a recent report on the exploits of General Claire Chennault's "Flying Tigers" in Burma, Christen recalled that Gen. Chennault was able to get 100 P-40's, but because of spare parts requirements he could keep only 50 of these in the air. Therefore, his fighting forces were only 50 percent effective. Adequate supplies would have doubled his striking power and made possible a

(Continued on Page 5)

TIRES !

Employees in need of tire service, who have properly authorized applications on file with their local tire rationing boards, which the boards have been unable to fill to date, are advised that through the efforts of the Transportation Committee of the Aircraft War Production Council additional new quotas have been made available. They are advised to contact their rationing boards immediately to bring their applications up to date, and that if they fail to secure rubber requisitions authorizing recaps or recap service, they should report the matter at once to the office of Robert Storment, Chairman, Lockheed-Vega transportation committee. Telephone 1188.

NEW EDUCATION DEPT. QUARTERS

★

Photo shows interior of one of the offices in the new Education Department building at 2817 Empire Boulevard. Standing at extreme left in photo is Svend Pedersen, Director of Education for Lockheed and Vega.

★

HOT AND STUFFY? SO ARE THE BOYS!

With the arrival of summer hot weather and less comfort on the job, employees in some departments of our various plants may find temperature and ventilation conditions not the most desirable. This condition, to a great extent, is due to, or aggravated by, necessary plant protection measures prescribed by the government for black out against air attack.

Although the government recognizes the special problems of comfort and efficiency occasioned by passive defense installations and proposed plans for camouflaging the factories, it is also faced with the more important problem of immediately protecting our facilities against the danger from air attacks.

The question of whether vital material should be used for the purpose of ventilation when it could be used for a more direct contribution to the war effort, is a serious one, and is presently under consideration by the United States Engineers, who are making a study of our situation prior to submitting recommendations to the government as to what action should be taken. They, of course, have many similar situations to handle in other defense plants.

This fact, plus unavoidable priority delays and growing scarcity of ventilation and other equipment, make early relief unlikely. However, when one considers the dangers and physical hardships common to our fighting services at home and abroad, it goes without saying that those of us on the home front can "take it" too.

If the average family of four saves its tin cans for two weeks it will have 18, or enough to supply tin for a portable flame thrower; for four weeks, enough to make the bushings for three .30 caliber machine guns.

BUCK-OF-MONTH CLUB FINANCIAL REPORT

The following financial report of the Buck-of-the-Month Club as of June 30, 1942 has been issued by Chairman Hal Davis.

CONTRIBUTIONS	
Lockheed Employees	$ 74,362.25
Vega Employees	39,257.00
Triplett & Barton	334.50
L.E.R.C. Employees	71.00
V.E.R.C. Employees	45.00
Publication Employees	7.00
Miscellaneous	664.00
British Reassembly Division	92.00
TOTAL	$114,832.75
DISBURSEMENTS	
Refunds	$ 42.50
Bonding	360.00
Infantile Paralysis	3,435.00
Iron Lung	500.00
United China Relief	5,000.00
Poppy Day	1,000.00
Red Cross (already donated,	20,117.95
Due L.A. Chapter $14,233.05	
Total Red Cross ......$34,351.00)	
*Junior Chamber of Commerce (Burbank)	100.00
United Service Organization	34,351.00
Veterans of Foreign Wars (Burbank Post)	150.00
Canteen Service	200.00
**Asbury Rapid Transit System (Bus tickets for Soldiers)	190.00
Navy Aid Auxiliary	500.00
TOTAL	$65,946.45
BALANCE	$48,886.30

*A sum of $50 per month for a period of six months has been pledged to this fund. This money is being used for the sole purpose of buying coffee and doughnuts for the soldiers stationed in the Valley.

**This sum was used for the purchase of bus tickets for the soldiers guarding Lockheed and Vega plants who had no other means of transportation to and from Los Angeles and Hollywood on the limited time they had off from guard duty. This is on a one month trial basis.

SERVICE FOR BOTH COMPANIES AGAIN UNDER ONE ROOF

Serving employees of both Lockheed and Vega, the Education Department (45) has once more gathered under one roof most of its divisions and activities which, for the last few months, have been scattered in various locations in the Lockheed and Vega plants. It is now housed in its new building at 2817 Empire Boulevard, about half way between Lockheed Plant 1 and Vega Plant 1.

The Lockheed Library, located on the second floor of the Industrial Relations Building, and the Vega Library, in Room 107 of the new addition to the Administration Building at Vega Plant 1, will continue to operate in their present locations. The only other division of the Education Department which is not housed in the new building is the Maintenance and Operations Training Section which, because of the nature of its work, continues to have its office and classrooms in Hangar 4 at Hollywood Way and Winona Avenue.

The new building on Empire Boulevard provides office space for all the rest of the department, including the mimeographing unit, which busily turns out much of the training and educational material used in classes both in the plants and in the schools of Burbank, Glendale, Pasadena and other places. Most of the Supervisory Development classes which, up to a week ago, had been held in Vega Plant 2, at Lyn's Restaurant and in other nearby locations, have been moved into the four large classrooms which are included in the new building. These classrooms, each with a seating capacity of about 60, provide quiet and pleasant facilities which will add much to the comfort of those attending classes.

First occupied on Monday of Lockheed's tenth anniversary week, the "Education Building" marks another milestone in the development of Lockheed and Vega. Ten years ago Lockheed had no Education Department and little attention was given to the problems and techniques of training newcomers. Seven years ago the Education Department got its start when a series of lectures given by Svend Pedersen, then in charge of tooling, awakened a number of Lockheed employees to the benefits to be obtained from outside study. Today, Mr. Pedersen is the head of the Education Department, employing 94 people and giving almost every kind of educational service to all Lockheed and Vega employees. Also, as a direct result of the expansion of the Army Air Forces, it is helping to train more than 500 enlisted mechanics a month.

Albert T. Helbing, assistant director of the Education Department, joined Lockheed in that capacity in February of 1941.

Premiere Of 'Wings For The Eagle' July 15

Ann Sheridan in Warner Bros. Feature Filmed Within Gates of Lockheed

Premiere showing of "Wings for the Eagle," filmed by Warner Bros. within the gates of the Lockheed plant, will be held for Swing Shift employees of Lockheed and Vega at 1:30 a.m. Wednesday, July 15 (after the regular Tuesday night shift), at Warner Bros. Hollywood Theater.

This is the first Swing Shift premiere in Hollywood motion picture history.

The picture, which stars Ann Sheridan, Dennis Morgan, Jack Carson and George Tobias under the direction of Lloyd Bacon, opens to the general public at 11 a.m. Wednesday, July 15, at Warner Bros. Downtown Theater, and 12:30 p.m. the same day at Warner's Hollywood.

Written and filmed as Warner Bros.' tribute to the men and women in the aircraft industry, "Wings for the Eagle" marks the first time that a motion picture company has been permitted to bring its cameras inside a big airplane factory for other than stock shots. The huge Lockheed plant opened its doors —doubly guarded in war time—to permit Warner Bros. to tell the story of the men and women who are behind the men behind the guns.

The story is that of men and women who work in the aircraft industry and many thousands of Lockheed employees at work are seen in the film. The picture presents the manufacture of P-38 "Lightning" interceptors and Hudson bombers, shows close-ups of work on the assembly lines and in other parts of the factory and winds up with Ann Sheridan working in the Personnel Department.

Every important member of the cast plays the part of a Lockheed employee.

The film has been approved by Lockheed and military officials as an important contribution to the record of wartime effort.

The plot touches several timely problems of the aircraft industry—the "essential defense work" angle, the exclusion of aliens with sons in Uncle Sam's service, and the vital drive for production. It ends when the right man enlists, the "indispensable man" stays in the factory to turn them out, and the "2000th bomber" roars from the assembly line ahead of schedule.

"Corky" Jones (Dennis Morgan), a very cocky young fellow, gets a job at Lockheed working for Jake Hanso (George Tobias) and with Jake's son, Pete (Russell Arms). "Corky" gets his start in a tool crib.

Fellow employees are "Brad" Maple (Jack Carson) and his wife Roma (Ann Sheridan), over whom a rivalry develops after Roma, because of domestic troubles with "Brad," leaves home.

When Roma refuses to have anything further to do with "Brad," "Corky" settles down to serious work at Lockheed and soon starts climbing right up the ladder in Final Assembly.

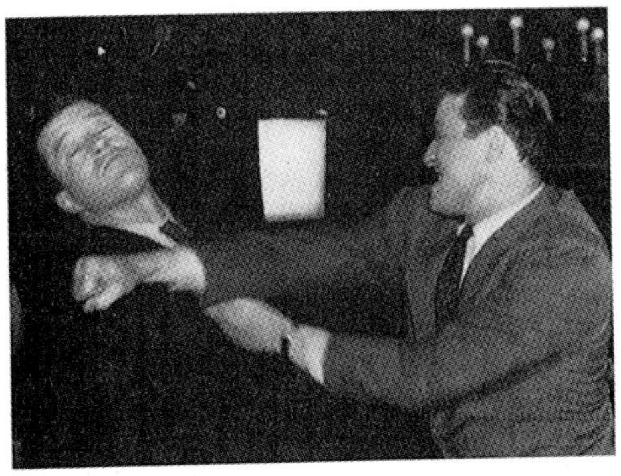

The feud between "Corky" and "Brad" for Roma's affections culminates in a wild night club brawl. Police haul both away and Roma, indignant and denying she knows either, is stuck with the check.

The Jones-Hanso production team at Lockheed is broken up when Jake is forced to leave his important post because he doesn't have his final citizenship papers, and Pete joins the Army Air Forces.

Comes Pearl Harbor, and "Corky" follows Jake's son into the Air Corps. He says good-bye to "Brad" and Roma, who have made up and who, he realizes, are still very much in love with each other.

After securing his final papers and taking the oath of allegiance to the United States, Jake gets his old job back and urges the workers to double their efforts as the 2,000th bomber comes off the line.

"Corky" vows to carry on for Jake's son, who has been killed in action, as Lockheed employees, gathered for a ceremony just outside the assembly hangar, watch the 2,000th bomber take off in a glorious roar.

LOCKHEED GIRLS VIE FOR QUEEN IN AQUACADE

Deadline is drawing near for the selection of the Lockheed Miss who will reign as queen of the Aquacade in Pasadena on July 19th.

On this page you will find a ballot for your vote. Fill in the name of the girl you would like to see as Lockheed queen. Send it to the L.E.R.C. office today. Contest closes Monday.

The L.E.R.C. Aquacade, which promises to be the coolest event of the season, will be held at the Vista del Arroyo Swimming Pool in Pasadena. World's greatest swimmers and divers will perform, including: Sammy Lee, Bill Lewin, and Marjorie Gestring.

Tickets for this cool splash may be obtained for 50 cents from the L.E.R.C. office. Vista del Arroyo pool seating capacity is limited and the event is a one-day treat, according to Aquacade committeeman Bob Boyles, who urges employees to purchase tickets today.

Employees Asked To Vote Only Once For Lockheedienne Queen

Aquacade Queen Ballot

I vote for Miss..

of department..................., Plant............... for Queen of the L.E.R.C. Aquacade.

My name is..

My clock number is..

Fill out and send to L.E.R.C. Office today. Contest deadline, July 13.

DRAMA CLUB CAST OF "AH WILDERNESS" GETS WILL ROGERS, JR., PRAISE

Cast and Staff of the recent drama club production, "Ah Wilderness" were highly praised last week when they received a letter of congratulation from Will Rogers Jr., son of the late, great stage, screen and radio star.

Rogers was highly commendable in his comment of the play, saying: "Since 'Ah Wilderness' was one of the better shows acted by my father, I have always been interested in the play. When I saw that the Lockheed employees were staging the production, I made quick arrangements to purchase tickets."

L.E.R.C. CALENDAR
July 10 - 17

Band

Band rehearsal Monday nights, 7 p.m. Swing Shift Concert, 8 to 8:30 p.m., L.E.R.C. Recreation area. Swing Shift Concerts, Fridays, 8 to 8:30 p.m., L.E.R.C. Recreation area.

Drama Club

Tuesday and Friday, July 14 and 17, casting for "The Front Page," 1141 North Gower, Hollywood, 7:30 p.m.

Chess Enthusiasts

Chess games Wednesday nights, 7:30 p.m., Burbank Recreation Center, Olive St., Burbank.

Badminton

Swing Shift every Monday morning, 11 a.m., Defense Area Bldg., 1111 W. Olive Ave., Burbank.

Boy Scouts

Regular meeting, George Washington School, Wednesdays, 7 p.m.

Baseball Practice

Lockheed-Vega team practice, Tuesday and Thursday, N. Hollywood playground, 4 p.m.

Rangers and Rangerettes

Day Shift Rangers and Rangerettes ride together Wednesday nights, 7 p.m. till 9. Night Shift Rangers and Rangerettes ride together Mondays from 10 a.m. till 12m. Sunday morning all shifts ride together from 8 until 10.

L.E.R.C. Double-Feature Movies

"Look to the L.E.R.C. for Fun" and "Look to Lockheed for Leadership," July 10, 11 and 12, Hollywood Assistance League Playhouse, 7 p.m., Sunday showing, 2 p.m. Special Swing Shift showings, Friday and Saturday, 11 a.m.

Bicycle Enthusiasts

Bicycle Club starts rolling, Sunday, July 12, 9:30 a.m., Burbank Recreation Center, Olive and Victory Blvds.

BICYCLE CLUB TO MEET SUNDAY

The newly organized L.E.R.C. bicycle club starts rolling Sunday, July 12th, at 9:30 a.m. Bike lovers who would like to join the club are asked to meet at the Burbank Recreation Center, on Olive and Victory Blvds., says chairman Milt Entwistle, adding that many activities are planned for club members and their friends.

SPECIAL RATES AFFORDED EMPLOYEES AT GOLF CLUB

Special tickets may be obtained by Lockheed employees for monthly rates at the Chevy Chase Golf Club, according to L.E.R.C. Athletic Director, Frank Davis.

Regular $5.00 tickets will be sold to Lockheedians for $4.00, and holders will have the privilege of the club on week days, Sundays, and Holidays.

Lockheed Films To Start 3-Day Run Tonight In Hollywood

Both new and old employees will be interested to learn the L.E.R.C. Film Committee is re-showing the two films, "Look to Lockheed for Leadership," and "Look to the L.E.R.C. for Fun," at the Hollywood Assistance League Playhouse for a three-day run starting tonight.

The two films are an example of the smooth functioning between management and employee in the industrial field, declares committeeman Bruce Frost, who cordially invites all Lockheedians and friends. Night performance begins at 7 p.m., while swing shifters may view the films at 11 a.m., July 10 and 11, and 2 p.m. on Sunday, July 12th.

"MIRACLE" ESCAPE IN HUDSON BOMBER

From the London Daily Express of Sunday, May 17, there comes the following thrilling account of escape from death in a Lockheed Hudson:

"Out of control after a heavy A.A. shell had burst under its starboard wing, off the Norwegian coast at dusk, a Coastal Command Hudson turned over and spun towards the sea.

Its crew "shuttlecocked" from roof to floor and side to side as the plane plunged down at 320 miles an hour to what seemed certain destruction—so certain that the German gunners stopped firing.

But the Hudson cheated them at the last moment.

On his back only 200 ft. above the waves, the captain, a pilot officer, from Manchester, got his foot on the rudder, flattened the aircraft out and, before the Germans knew what had happened, it had disappeared into the clouds.

The crew was unhurt and their plane undamaged. They had been searching for enemy shipping off Norway."

SWING SHIFT POLO FOUR WHIPS DAY TEAM, 3-2

Polo enthusiasts at Lockheed played their first organized game last Sunday at the Riviera Country Club. Featuring the day shift team against the night shift marauders, the fracas offered high excitement for onlookers.

Dick Collins, captain of the day shifters, reports a 2-2 tie at the end of the third quarter, an extra point made by the swing shift squad in the last quarter, making them winners, 3-2.

MANUFACTURE OF EXTRA PARTS FOR P-38 PUSHED UP

(Continued from Page 1)

great many more attacks than he was able to complete successfully.

"Spare parts usually require special handling," Christen declared. "This is necessary because the same parts, when in production, receive inspection and finishing as they are assembled on the airplane. Because these spare parts are not to be available to mating with parts at Lockheed, the inspection must be doubly strict in order to discover even the slightest error.

"Spare parts must be available in usable condition at an air base before the effectiveness of that base and the ships allocated to it can be felt. Therefore, spare parts should be completed and in transit before the ship on which the parts are to be used is in final inspection."

Parts Arrive Last

Because of the necessity of transporting spare parts by comparatively slow methods such as water, rail or truck, the airplanes for which the spares are built are usually at their destination long before the parts necessary to keep the ship in active service. As a consequence, airplanes have had to be dismantled after arrival at the point of service, and parts of them used as spares. This cuts down the striking power of the squadron at that air base.

"The quantities of spare parts required to insure having a supply at all necessary bases and depots has increased three-fold during the past year, due to the ever-widening battlefronts of this war," Christen continued. "If we are to maintain our forces on these fronts with the striking power necessary, every ship must be complete and 100 per cent effective. That is possible only through an ever-increasing flow of spare parts.

"A ship grounded for want of a single spare might as well be back at the factory for repairs. In fact, it would be better so, for it would not then be vulnerable to attack and after repair would be able to reach the point of service in much less time than the spare part required.

Our First Problem

"Intelligent planning is needed in order to provide spares so that they will not interfere with production of planes. In the past, this problem has not been of the same magnitude as at present, consequently it would receive only the attention it deserved. However, since Lockheed ships are increasingly in action with our armed forces, spares requirements have become uppermost as a production problem and the help of every person at Lockheed is needed to maintain the unceasing flow of parts that is demanded to keep abreast of Lockheed's increasing spares delivery schedules."

The number of people directly working for the various Lockheed spare parts departments has been greatly increased in the last two months, Christen said.

BROTHER, CAN YOU SPARE . . . ?

IT'S REALLY ZERO WHEN JAP "ZERO" SUFFERS DAMAGE

With Lockheed production chiefs now launched upon an intensified spare parts production effort, it is of interest to note how much the presence of these spares at our A.A.F. air bases overseas will add to the superiority of the P-38 "Lightning" over the Japanese Zero fighter plane.

It is pointed out by the Aeronautical Chamber of Commerce that inspection of Zero fighters shot down shows that the Zero's wings and fuselage are made in one piece. This means that damaged wings cannot be changed—the whole job must be replaced. A badly damaged Zero is a zero Zero in the box-score of the war, while the P-38 can go back into service using such spare parts as wing tips, wing panels, wing flaps, landing gear, booms, inter-coolers, etc.

Former Vega Man Missing In Raid Over Holland

(Continued from Page 1)

Second Lieut. Marshall Draper of Beverly Hills, California. Twenty-four boys go over—the first U.S. Army Air Forces men to cross the Channel and drop bombs on German-held Holland in this war. Eight do not come back.

Among those "missing in action"—Second Lieut. Marshall Draper, Vega's first war hero.

Services Held For Two Lockheed-Vega Men

Funeral services for one Lockheed and one Vega employee were held during the past week.

James Edwin Colter was buried at Lamar, Colorado, after being killed in an automobile-motorcycle collision in Burbank on Tuesday morning, June 30. Colter, 20, Department 10, Lockheed swing shift, is survived by his mother, Mrs. Vera O. Whitney of Burbank.

Clifford C. Miller, 64, Vega Department 36, Plant 2, died July 3 at the Glendale Sanitarium. He is survived by his daughter, Mrs. M. Irene Henzel of Los Angeles. Services were held July 7 at the Little Church of the Flowers in Forest Lawn.

BUY WAR BONDS!

AGAIN 'OLD BOOMERANG' BRINGS 'EM BACK

SHOT TO BITS OVER NORWAY, HUDSON MAKES HOME BASE

A Hudson of the R.A.F. Coastal Command has added one more to the long list of adventurous escapes for which these remarkable planes are famous in British operational records.

Says the latest report from the British Ministry of Aircraft Production:

Flying on the offensive is seldom comfortable and never safe, and you can't expect to dodge all of the flak all of the time—but the way Hudsons can take anything and get away with it—not only away, but safe home again, is a very striking proof of the soundness of their construction.

This Hudson went to attack a radio station in Norway. It was met by a storm of heavy anti-aircraft fire. The radio station was effectively disposed of, but the Hudson had had a gruelling time in the process—and it's a long, long way home from Norway.

Part of the starboard rudder was shot away. The tail-plane was badly hit, and both wings were pierced by cannon-shells. However, it appears that if there's anything left of a Hudson to fly with, it'll stay up in the air; and this one, true to the established Hudson tradition, made its way back, apparently not much hampered by its somewhat unbalanced condition.

Nobody but the pilot himself can guess at the hazards of such a journey with controls and trim knocked out of true. The sum of his and the Hudson's struggle and success is contained in the final phrase of the flight's official record.

It ends with the laconic but heartening words:

"Despite this damage, the pilot landed his aircraft safely at his base."

PERIODIC REVIEW PLAN EXPLAINED

For the benefit of the newer employees, the Industrial Relations Office offers the following explanation of the present procedure for periodic reviews given each employee every six months:

Whenever a new employee, or a re-hired employee, attains the rate of $30.00 per forty hour week, a permanent review group number is assigned to insure that the review will be automatically scheduled for the correct date.

The review group to which an employee is assigned is determined by the hiring date; those hired on Tuesday through Monday are effective on the Saturday of that week. Thus if an employee is hired on Tuesday, he is assigned to the review group which becomes effective six months from the following Saturday, and every six months (twenty-six weeks) thereafter. Likewise, if an employee is hired on Monday, he is assigned to the review group which becomes effective six months from the preceding Saturday and every six months thereafter.

The review dates for employees hired prior to July 1, 1941 may not agree precisely with the present procedure. However, in accordance with the Union agreement, Article V, Section 1, "The rate and record of each employee shall be reviewed every six months," hereafter the effective date of each employee's periodic review will be six months (twenty-six weeks) from the effective date of his last regular review which is always on Saturday.

Electrical Classes

The Education Department announces that the following classes will start July 13 at Glendale High School: Electrical Assembly and Installation, M-W-F, 7 to 10 p.m.; T-Th., 7 to 10 p.m.

Seat Pads, Auto Floor Mats Offered In Rubber Drive

Lockheed and Vega employees apparently are growing dissatisfied with their own contributions to the rubber drive.

An increasing number of them are calling or writing in to the office of L. W. Wulfekuhler, Lockheed secretary, and suggesting that rubber doormats, chair pads and floor mats are not pulling their weight in the war effort.

They have created a new classification: "In daily use but non-essential," and some of them urge that the contribution of such articles be made compulsory.

The company prefers to leave it to the individual employees to prove their interest in this national emergency. The "Leave Scrap Here" boxes used in the Housecleaning Week campaign are being distributed again. They yawn for non-essential rubber—anything that can be spared.

"If the White House can be stripped of rubber, so can Lockheed and Vega," say these all-out employees. So can every home and garage in the country, with every filling station building up its salvage pile from its immediate neighborhood.

There are many 'hidden' rubber items, such as automobile floor and trunk mats—a large and valuable source of rubber.

Let's take this last chance to put tires on Army trucks.

NEW PRODUCTION METHODS COURSES

An airplane being 90 per cent sheet metal in some form or another, a complete understanding of the fabricating and assembling processes involved will prove invaluable, in whatever capacity one may be employed.

Production Methods Courses No. 1 and No. 2 offered at the Burbank High School is available to help all those who are interested to gain that knowledge for use in their daily work; particularly those who would like to get into tool planning, Tool and Production Engineering.

Production Methods I—Analyze plants organization: The functions of the non-productive departments, Engineering Research Laboratories; and a general discussion on machines and equipment.

Production Methods II—Discusses the functions of the Tool shops, and Production departments. A thorough study of sheet metal tooling and fabricating machines, and an analysis on Tool Planning and Production Engineering.

Magazines Print Many Articles On Company Doings

Iron Age, one of the oldest and most highly respected metal trades magazines in the country, reports that it has received an enthusiastic response from readers to a series of four articles on various aspects of sheet metal forming, written by members of the Lockheed Engineering Department. These articles were published in the issues of May 28, June 4, June 11 and June 18.

Their titles and authors follow:

IRON AGE—May 28
"Drawing Dies for Airframe Stampings," by G. A. Brewer.
IRON AGE—June 4
"Stretch - Forming Contoured Sheet Metal Aircraft Parts," by T. H. Hazlett and M. M. Rockwell.
IRON AGE—June 11
"Forming Convex Flanges and Joggles," by William Schroeder and R. Glassco.
IRON AGE—June 18
"Hydro-press Forming With Rubber Platens," by T. H. Hazlett and William Schroeder.

Other recently published articles:

LOOK—June 30
"Industrial Worker, War Model." Vega.
WESTERN MACHINERY & STEEL WORLD—June
Transports, Pursuit Ships, Bombers.
Women in Industry. Vega electrical assembly workers.
Antarctic Range Named After Lockheed Engineer E. J. Demas.
AMERICAN ROLLING MILL CO. BULLETIN
Lockheed's Photo Template Process.
DIXIE AIR NEWS—May
Merry-Go-Round Hydro-Press.
Vega Women at Work.
Lockheed Diary.
MACHINERY—June
"Manufacturing Rivets for Airplanes," Part 2, by M. W. Seavey.
AERO DIGEST—June
Cover Picture, Formation Flight of P-38's.
Electrolytic Process of Template Reproduction.
Dr. R. C. Burt's Anti-Glare Welding Goggles.
"Practical Rivet Standardization," by L. J. Fila.
AVIATION—June
"Women in Slacks," by Don Wharton. Vega.
"Perspective Drawings Speed Plane Assembly."
WESTERN FLYING—June
Mountains Named for Engineer E. J. Demas.
Dr. Burt's Anti-Glare Welding Goggles.
CANADIAN AVIATION—June
Dr. Burt's Anti-Glare Welding Goggles.
COLLIER'S—June 13
"Twin Booms," fiction by Douglas Ruth
MODERN INDUSTRIAL PRESS—June
Plastics in Aircraft Tooling. Vega.
Dr. Burt's Welding Goggles.
MONETARY TIMES (Canada) — June 27
Machine Tools from Walnuts. Vega.
CHARM—July
Part 2 of "Swing Shift Girl," by Alyce Canfield. Vega.
KODAK—May
Triplett & Barton X-Ray Laboratory.
AUTOMOTIVE & AVIATION INDUSTRIES—June 15
"Scrap Salvage," by Raymond Kay.
"WINGS"—June
Slant Top Table for Electric Drill Operator. Vega.
AMERICAN HAIRDRESSER & FINESSE
"Women Who Make Planes," by S. A. Lewis. Vega.

During recent large-scale air attacks on the continent, the English have lost approximately 3 out of every 100 planes used in each raid. In other words, the best efforts of German fighter planes and anti-aircraft guns have caused the destruction of about 3 per cent of Allied planes taking part in raids.

Lockheed-Vega's employees who do not report for work are causing twice that amount of damage to the Allied cause.

Workers who are absent from their jobs are reducing our total working force by about 6 per cent every day. That is, 3½ minutes out of every hour, half an hour out of every 8-hour day, almost 2/3 of a month every year, are lost because of absences.

In many cases, of course, sickness accounts for the absences. However, a large amount of time is lost because of easily preventable accidents. What is worse, many absences admittedly have no legitimate reason.

The conclusion to be drawn is obvious. Absenteeism among our workers is losing the Allies more planes than are being destroyed by our declared enemies.

Have you been absent unnecessarily this month?

Buy Bike Now Or It's Bye-Bye Bike

Because of certain restrictions being placed on the manufacture of bicycles, employees desiring to obtain a bicycle under the liberal purchase plan through the Employee Transportation Committee are advised to contact the Employee Transportation Office immediately. A limited number of bicycles are now available and any further shipments will depend upon the number of applications received.

FIRST-AID TRAINING PROVES BIG ATTRACTION

The enthusiasm shown by Lockheed personnel for the Red Cross First-Aid training, made available by the Education Department, has been most gratifying, according to Jack Fowle, of the Health and Safety Division.

Many employees who enrolled in the First-Aid classes have already completed their training, 41 having been fully certified as Red Cross instructors.

Because of transfers to other departments, it has been found necessary to reorganize the emergency first aid squads throughout the various plants and this work of bringing squads up to their regular complement will be completed this week, Mr. Fowle stated.

Emergency first-aid equipment, consisting of adequately equipped cabinets, army litters, Stokes stretchers and war casualty boxes, have been placed at strategic points throughout the plants.

Five new classes are to be started, which will place in training approximately 200 more men with additional instructors and classroom space available.

The steel, copper wire and brass used to make an average piano would be enough to produce a dozen bayonets, a signal corps radio set and 66 .30 caliber cartridges.

THE Lockheed-Vega Star * *

The Lockheed-Vega Star is issued every Friday for the employees of the Lockheed Aircraft Corporation and the Vega Aircraft Corporation and is the official publication of both companies. Communications may be addressed to either the Industrial Relations Office or the Public Relations Department, Lockheed Aircraft Corporation, Burbank, California, U.S.A. Although news and cartoon contributions are welcome, circumstances make it impossible to give any promise that they will be returned to sender when not used, nor can individual acknowledgment be made.

BERT W. HOLLOWAY, Editor-in-Chief
H. L. (HAL) ROSSON, Managing Editor

Volume 9 Number 30

Freedom

So little truly great literature has come out of the present war, so few great songs and such a poverty of poetry worthy to be ranked with "In Flanders Fields," "I Have a Rendezvous With Death" and "The Soldier" of the last war, that when some really fine writing does come along, we feel it worth reprinting. Particularly when it carries so poignant a message as these lines written by Hazel Parker in the Louisville Courier-Journal:

From the archives of broken peace we are bringing out old words and dusting them off for use again as shining lanterns to lead us through the darkness of another war.

Words like freedom, justice and truth—all of them hard to define, none of them used more frequently than freedom.

You cannot say what freedom is, perhaps, in a single sentence. It is not necessary to define it. It is enough to point to it.

Freedom is a man lifting a gate latch at dusk and sitting for awhile on the porch, smoking his pipe before he goes to bed.

It is the violence of an argument outside an election poll; it is the righteous anger of the pulpits.

It is the warm laughter of a girl on a park bench.

It is the rush of a train over the continent and the unafraid faces of people looking out of the window.

It is all the howdys in the world and all the hellos.

It is Westbrook Pegler telling Roosevelt how to raise his children; it is Roosevelt letting them raise themselves.

It is Lindbergh's appeasing voice raised above a thousand hisses.

It is Dorothy Thompson asking for war; it is General Hugh S. Johnson asking her to keep quiet.

It is the sea breaking on the wide sands somewhere and the shoulders of a mountain supporting the sky.

It is the air you fill your lungs with and the dirt that is your garden.

It is a man cursing all cops.

It is the absence of apprehension at the sound of approaching footsteps outside your closed door.

It is your resentment of intrigue, the tilt of your chin and the tightening of your lips sometimes.

It is all the things you do and want to keep on doing.

It is all the things you feel and cannot help feeling.

Freedom—it is you.

You Can Help Save Watersheds

The Forest Service of the U.S. Department of Agriculture has created a civilian group called the Forest Fire Watchers Corps. This organization is composed of civilians volunteering to act as "watch dogs" over the national forests, especially during the summer months.

Many uninformed persons do not fully realize the important part Southern California water sheds play in our every day life. Southern California is a semi-arid land which has very little rainfall from May to October. Under these conditions the hills, mountains, and national forests are turned into dry hot tinder boxes where the smallest spark or flame may start a fire that can burn many thousands of acres. These fires destroy nature's means of storing reservoirs of water through retention of excessive rainfall by the trees, bushes, and other foliage. When these protective agencies are destroyed, ground hardens and the rain runs off, causing floods and land erosion.

It is true war workers have been discouraged from participating in defense activities outside of their jobs because of possible loss of time from work. However, membership in the Forest Fire Watchers Corps is one job that everyone can do in spare time spent in the hills and national forests.

Briefly, a Forest Fire Watcher in visiting a National Forest should find the ranger at the guard station giving the location where he can be found in case of emergency. At the same time he should obtain from the forest officer in charge the telephone number that he should use in reporting fires.

Thereafter, the Forest Fire Watcher should maintain constant alertness for outbreak of fire. If any fire is observed, it should be reported at once to the forest officer in the district. Should the F.F.W. observe acts of carelessness of fire, matches, or cigarettes on the part of other visitors, the member should inform the violator courtesously as to the danger of his conduct and instruct him in the fire and smoking rules.

Application for membership in this Corps appears below.

Labor Code Sets Procedure For Injury Cases

The following article appeared in the Star on April 3 and is being republished to serve as a reminder that the California State Labor Code establishes very definite procedures for the treatment of industrial accidents.

"Definite procedures for the treatment of industrial accidents sustained while an employee is on the job are established under the California State Labor Code," states Ronald P. King, assistant treasurer of the company, in charge of insurance, in commenting on cases where an employee has obtained medical service outside the company without having first secured consent from either the company or the insurance carrier.

The companies maintain approved medical units under the supervision of licensed and approved doctors where medical service is available on a 24-hour basis. Employees are advised that in the event of injury, no matter how slight, they should report to the nearest First Aid unit at once.

In order to eliminate any misunderstanding relative to medical treatment of industrial accidents, the following is given as an authoritative interpretation of the law:

The employer is not liable for the cost of medical treatment where given no opportunity to furnish same. There is a duty upon the employee to give his employer prompt notice, both of his injury and his need for treatment. This eliminates free choice of doctor and hospital by the individual injured. If the injured person prefers to select his own doctor and treatment he may do so, but it will be at his own expense unless the employer or insurance carrier consents and agrees to pay for such service.

The Medical Division is responsible for the treatment of all injuries and illness resulting from or during working hours. Company rules require that injury or illness be reported to the nearest First Aid unit immediately. It should also be remembered that self-treatment should never be undertaken.

Lockheed Employees Recreation Club
Attention: Harold E. Davis, President

Please forward my application for membership in the Forest Fire Watchers Corps to the Forest Defense Coordinator of the U. S. Forest Service. I am over 18 years of age, and it is my understanding that my primary function is to report to the proper authorities the discovery of any fire in the National Forests. Would you please send my membership card and instructions to—

NOTE: If you intend to visit National Forests this summer, please give approximate date.

____
Name

____
Street Address

____
City and State

THE *Lockheed-Vega Star* ★ ★

Official publication of the Lockheed and Vega Aircraft Corporations

Volume 9 | BURBANK, CALIFORNIA, U.S.A., OCTOBER 30, 1942 | Number 46

Companies Add New Bus Service From Glendale

Further expansion of the Employee Transportation bus system was announced today by Robert C. Storment, manager of the Employee Transportation Department, through the addition of two lines in the Glendale area.

This new service, resulting from negotiations between the companies and the Glendale City Lines, Inc., operators of bus service in that city, makes available a fleet of 30-passenger coaches for service between various points in Glendale and Lockheed Plants 1 and 3 and Vega Plants 1 and 2.

Service on these lines will become effective Monday, November 2 and will be maintained for all shifts with transfer privileges offered on all Glendale City Line busses without additional fares.

In commenting on this newest addition to the vast network of busses now being operated as a transportation service to employees, Mr. Storment pointed out that every effort is being made to assure adequate transportation for all employees and that regardless of "mileage rationing" in connection with gasoline and tires, bus transportation will be available from practically every residential district throughout the area.

"As it is the aim of all of us to do the best kind of a job in conserving our vital rubber supply, the use of these busses for transportation to and from work cannot be too highly emphasized," concluded Mr. Storment.

Following are the time schedules and passenger pick-up stops on the Glendale lines, effective Monday, November 2.

PACIFIC AND GLEN OAKS LINE
Fare from these points is 12½c

	A.M.	A.M.	P.M.	A.M.
Glen. Blvd. & San Fernan.	6:15	7:15	3:00	12:00
Glen. Blvd. & Brunswick	6:16	7:17	3:01	12:01
Appleton & Brunswick	6:17	7:17	3:02	12:02
Los Feliz & Brunswick	6:18	7:18	3:03	12:03
Los Feliz & San Fernan.	6:19	7:19	3:04	12:04
Chevy Chase & San Fernan.	6:20	7:20	3:05	12:05
Pacific & Colorado	6:22	7:22	3:07	12:07
Pacific & Broadway	6:23	7:23	3:08	12:08
Pacific & Lexington	6:24	7:24	3:09	12:09
Pacific & Glen Oaks	6:25	7:25	3:10	12:10
Concord & Glen Oaks	6:26	7:26	3:11	12:11
Norton & Glen Oaks	6:27	7:27	3:12	12:12
Grand View & Glen Oaks	6:28	7:28	3:13	12:13
Sonora & Glen Oaks	6:29	7:29	3:14	12:14
Western & Glen Oaks	6:30	7:30	3:15	12:15
FARE FROM THIS POINT IS 5c				
Alameda & Glen Oaks	6:31	7:31	3:16	12:16

(Continued on Page 2)

Orson Welles Will Produce New Weekly Lockheed-Vega Radio Show Starting Nov. 9

The aviation industry makes its debut in the field of radio on November 9 when Lockheed and Vega launch the first of a series of Monday evening programs over the coast-to-coast Columbia Broadcasting System.

Orson Welles

Heard locally over station KNX at 8:15 p.m. each Monday evening, the program will feature Orson Welles as narrator.

Planned to inform the American people as to the part that American aviation is playing today and will play in the future, the program will deal with the personalities, planes and dramatic events of the industry. The 15-minute dramatizations will be written and directed by Welles. An orchestra of 16 men will supply the musical background for the episodes. The size of the cast will vary according to the dramatizations.

It is felt by the company that radio provides the most effective means of

(Continued on Page 2)

New Selective Service Set-up Announced

Because of the increased demand for services rendered in connection with selective service, the Lockheed Selective Service Section, formerly a part of Employee Service Division, 43, has been expanded and will hereafter be known as Selective Service Division, 42. This newly created division will be under the supervision of Edmund Davies, who in turn will report directly to J. Caden Jenkins, personnel manager. The office is prepared to advise and assist employees in problems arising from selective service.

War Bond Deliveries Cut To 17 Days

Employees are requested to allow 30 to 40 days for receipt of bonds paid for subsequent to the bond drive and up to the present. The Lockheed Accounting Department reports that the tremendous amount of work involved in setting up deduction and bond purchase records on 20,000 new subscriptions resulting from the recent bond drive put them behind schedule.

The handicap has been overcome, however, and in the future the schedule from the ending date of the payroll period in which the last deduction was collected to issuance of the bond by the California Bank will approximate 17 days.

Lockheed At "Newsreel"

Five minutes of closeup glimpses of Lockheed will be on the screen at the Newsreel Theatre, 744 S. Broadway, starting at 6 p.m. today when Tex McCrary's feature, "Your Ringside Seat At World War II," presents "Eagle's Nest." This is an exclusive showing.

WAR DEPARTMENT APPROVES

Orson Welles, left, seen at lunch in Washington with Major General Alexander Surles, Chief of Public Relations for the War Department and the U.S. Army. The War Department, through General Surles, has expressed its aproval of the new radio program sponsored by Lockheed and Vega, in which Welles will tell the dramatic story of the aviation industry and what America's armed forces are doing with planes turned out by the nation's aircraft manufacturers.

LOCKHEED-VEGA RADIO PROGRAM

(Continued from Page 1)

presenting the dramatic story of aviation, particularly the many years of progress crowded by the industry into the last two, in serving the nation in its war effort.

The program will dramatize the accomplishments of our armed forces, justifying the public confidence in the products of the aircraft industry, and thereby building up a future that will help provide jobs for workers in days to come.

Material for the programs will be documented by research. Harold R. Isaacs, who has been borrowed from his research activities on the CBS program, "Report to the Nation," will head a research office in Washington; a second man will be detailed to the west coast to gather material on the airplane industry, and a third source of information will be the special services of the United Press.

In addition to a 57-station release in this country, the full CBS short-wave facilities will be used to send the program to America's armed forces abroad.

ART EXHIBIT OPEN TO ALL AIRCRAFT WORKERS

Lockheed and Vega artists are invited to enter any worthy works in an art exhibit which opens November 22 at Raymond & Raymond, Inc., 8652 Sunset Boulevard. Contributions may be of any size in any medium including sculpture, but must be ready for hanging, framed or mounted. The exhibit is intended to show the work of war workers in this medium of expression.

The L.E.R.C. office will receive entries from both Lockheed and Vega artists. The gallery will be prepared to receive all exhibits November 9 and 10 from 10 a.m. to 7:30 p.m.

NEW GLENDALE BUS SERVICE

(Continued from Page 1)

CHEVY CHASE & SAN FERNANDO LINE
Fare from these points is 12½c

	A.M.	A.M.	P.M.	A.M.
Verdugo & Chevy Chase	6:15	7:15	3:00	12:00
Broadway & Chevy Chase	6:16	7:16	3:01	12:01
Colorado & Chevy Chase	6:17	7:17	3:02	12:02
Adams & Chevy Chase	6:19	7:19	3:04	12:04
Glendale & Chevy Chase	6:20	7:20	3:05	12:05
Brand & Chevy Chase	6:21	7:21	3:06	12:06
Central & Chevy Chase	6:22	7:22	3:07	12:07
San Fernan. & Chevy Chase	6:23	7:23	3:08	12:08
San Fernan. & Windsor	6:24	7:24	3:09	12:09
San Fernan. & Colorado	6:25	7:25	3:10	12:10
San Fernan. & Broadway	6:26	7:26	3:11	12:11
San Fernan. & Doran	6:27	7:27	3:12	12:12
San Fernan. & Grand View	6:28	7:28	3:13	12:13
FARE FROM THIS POINT IS 5c				
San Fernan. & Alameda	6:31	7:31	3:16	12:16

Transfer points have been established at three intersections in Glendale and 12½c tickets are good for transfers at the following points (Glendale City Lines ONLY):

To the East Broadway-Atwater Line at Chevy Chase and San Fernando.
To the Victory-East Colorado Line at Colorado and Chevy Chase.
To the Burbank-Glen Oaks Line and the Rossmoyne-Mountain Lines at Glen Oaks and Pacific.

WATCH THOSE RIVETS!

The appeal for material conservation contained in the following quotation taken from a letter just received from L. E. Smith, former leadman of Department 11 at Lockheed Plant 2, who is now located "somewhere in Africa," needs no comment.

To Inspectors, Dept. 03:

P.S. Give this to the Dept. 11 office, and take heed you guys.

I've often thought of those boxes of mixed rivets, nuts, bolts, screws, etc. If we had the waste for one week, it would keep us supplied for at least six months. So when you fellows drop those rivets, bolts, etc., think of the fellows over here that are trying to repair aircraft with hand made rivets and drills.

Smitty—Overseas Service

ARMY AIR FORCES AID IN EMPLOYEE TRANSPORTATION

Further cooperation between Washington and local aircraft companies in solving the employee transportation problem was indicated here this week with the visit of Capt. Arthur E. Neelley, in charge of employee transportation, Division of Traffic and Transportation Base Services, the Army Air Forces.

Capt. Arthur E. Neelley

Working closely with the Highway Division of the Services of Supply of the War Department, Capt. Neelley's position is coordinating and setting up employee transportation facilities with civilian firms which are contractors to the Army Air Forces, which includes Lockheed and Vega.

During his visit to Lockheed and Vega, Capt. Neelley coordinated with Robert C. Storment, the companies' employee transportation manager, in seeking ways and means of getting workers to their jobs after gasoline rationing becomes effective.

NEW V.E.R.C. BOOTHS

Fred L. Jones, Business Manager of the V.E.R.C., announces that the sale of pins and novelties has been taken out of the office proper of the V.E.R.C. These articles may now be purchased at the Recreation Club booths located at Gate No. 8 on Hollywood Way and at Gate No. 3 on the West side of the factory.

Club members should acquaint themselves with the services available at these booths, as an excellent line of Christmas gifts and novelties is planned to be placed on sale there during the months of November and December.

Eugene M. Daoust

Eugene Michel Daoust, Dept. 20, died of a heart attack on October 21. The body was shipped to Worcester, Mass., for burial. The deceased, who was 52 years of age, is survived by his sister, Mrs. Corona Vigeant.

YOUR BUS SCHEDULE

Employees living in the vicinity of SANTA MONICA BLVD. and WESTERN AVENUE or who have easy access to this point, should be interested in the following bus schedule:

	A.M.	A.M.	P.M.	P.M.
Sta. Mon. & West.	6:05	7:10	2:50	11:35
Sunset & Western	6:06	7:11	2:51	11:36
Sunset & Vine	6:07	7:12	2:52	11:37

INSURANCE DEPT. TELLS LESSON IN GROUP COVERAGE

In the past two weeks five deaths have occurred within the Lockheed and Vega personnel. Four of these employees were covered under the Group Insurance Plan, according to P. V. Myers in charge of group insurance, and benefits totalling in excess of $8000 are payable. Unfortunately, the fifth employee was not a subscriber to the Group Insurance Plan and consequently no benefits were payable to his survivors.

While this employee may have had outside coverage, the benefits payable under his participation in the Group Insurance Plan would have to some extent eased the burden which always follows a death.

Within five hours after notification of death had been received, the Insurance Section had delivered drafts in payment of life benefits to the beneficiaries of three of the deceased employees. In the case of the fourth employee, he had named his estate as beneficiary and settlement must be held in abeyance until an administrator has been appointed.

While it is never a pleasant duty to call on a bereaved family immediately following the death of a member to discuss insurance matters, the Insurance Section does feel that its prompt settlement of death claims often aids in a financial way, to assist the family during its greatest hour of need.

TRANSPORTATION DEPT. TO MOVE

New and larger quarters is the order of the day for Department 75, Lockheed-Vega Employee Transportation, effective Wednesday, November 4.

Because of the rapid expansion in services rendered by this department in connection with forthcoming gasoline rationing, tire service, bus tickets, etc., more space was required to serve efficiently the thousands of employees who now ride the busses and contact this department in all other matters pertaining to transportation to and from work.

Wednesday morning will find the department located in the East section of the building formerly occupied by Lyn's Restaurant on Empire, directly opposite Lockheed Plant 1 Recreation Area.

This move affects the transportation office at Lockheed Plant 1 ONLY, all other Employee Transportation Offices remaining in their present locations.

A CLOCK WITH WASTED TIME ON ITS HANDS

The picture printed above is an actual photograph of sabotage at Lockheed and Vega.

It may only be a card rack and time clock to you, but it is good news to the Axis. It means that for each of those cards in the rack, we have lost one man-day from our production.

For many months now, Allied propaganda has been short-waved to occupied countries in Europe telling workers that they can achieve the most effective sabotage by being absent unnecessarily or by taking time off for a minute here or two minutes there.

But such attempts are amateurish compared to our performance here. The daily loss caused by absenteeism at Lockheed and Vega right now, in the midst of a drive for all-out production, is equal to the amount of time which would be lost if *every single employee stopped work for a full half-hour each day.*

Some of this loss may be attributed to accidents or sickness; but an alarming amount of absenteeism is completely unnecessary. Even the "legitimate" absenteeism, caused by accidents or ill health, could be reduced drastically if we all realized our duty to protect ourselves against sickness and to work and play safely.

The fact that you were absent because of a strained back doesn't excuse your foolishness in trying to show off before the kids in a back-lot football game.

If your card is in that rack through any fault of your own, you are helping the Axis to win this war. You are A.W.O.L. from the production army. How about getting all the way into the fight?

Robert Snider

Following a short illness, Robert Snider, 19, Lockheed Dept. 7-D, died on October 21. Services were held October 23 at the Glasband Mortuary in Los Angeles. Snider is survived by his parents, Mr. and Mrs. Sam Snider.

L. E. R. C. Golf Tourney Times Are Still Open

A few early starting times are still available for the Fall Golf Tourney scheduled at Altadena Golf Club Sunday, November 8, according to Bob Mercer who is helping to coordinate the event for the L.E.R.C.

The Blind Bogey handicap tournament will be run off in foursomes and a fine list of awards has been obtained for Lockheedians who enter the contest. Times may be obtained through the L.E.R.C. office, Extension 1901.

'PROF. ACCIDENT' IS TOUGH TEACHER

As has been said before, if Old Man Accident is worth the powder to blow him up, it is only because he teaches a sound, intelligent safety lesson every time he traps somebody.

It goes without saying that enrolling in Professor Accident's Safety School is really learning your safety the hard way. The tuition is a broken arm, bandages around your head, or some other evidence you have been the victim of an accident.

Professor Accident belongs to an even older school of teaching discipline than the spinster school ma'am who used to rap your knuckles with a ruler when you did something wrong. The Old Professor takes one of your legs or knocks your teeth out when you don't do things according to Hoyle.

His method of teaching safe working habits is effective, but very painful. For instance, one member of his class last month learned that you shouldn't attempt to cut sheet metal with a pair of tin snips unless goggles are worn. This individual almost lost an eye—he was trimming a small piece off the sheet and as he completed the cut, the piece flew, burying itself deeply in his eyeball. Other Lockheed employees have learned to their sorrow that this is poor business.

The Professor teaches his safety lessons very well, all right. His pupils don't forget, but he certainly charges a high price for his instruction.

Phil James Alldritt

Funeral services for Phil James Alldritt, 50, Dept. 16 Swing, were held October 19 at Bresee Brothers and Gillette Mortuary in Los Angeles. Alldritt died October 15 of a heart attack. Alldritt is survived by his wife, Mildred Alldritt.

MARJORIE BRENTANO
Lockheed Dept. 72, Day

BADMINTON SEASON OPEN TO EMPLOYEES

Day Shift Badminton players are now meeting each Wednesday night at the Burbank Recreation Center, 1111 W. Olive between 7 and 10:30 it is announced by Howard Daub, a top player from last season who is coordinating the activity for the L.E.R.C. this year.

"Swing Shifters wishing to play badminton can enjoy the Recreation Center facilities Monday mornings starting at 11 and running for two hours," Bob Stryker, Department 2, who has taken over the badminton program for Swing players.

Four 'Miss Victory' Candidates Named; Contest Still On

As a result of the popular vote of their fellow workers, two Lockheed and two Vega girls were selected as "Miss Victory" candidates during the intermission at the all-Lockheed-Vega dance held last Sunday night at the Palladium.

Marjorie Brentano, Dept. 72 Lockheed; Lillian Pryor, Dept. 23 Vega; Vivienne Worl, Dept. 50 Lockheed, and Mildred Williams, Dept. 45 Vega received the top honors after being interviewed before the microphone by a representative of the Hearst papers who acted as judge.

Based largely on their contribution to the current war effort, entrants were registered in the $1000 War Bond contest and latest word from the contest officials is that any Lockheed or Vega girl may yet enter the final regional contest by directing an ANVO either to the L.E.R.C. or V.E.R.C. before November 23.

Drama Club Offers Instruction

Lockheedians interested in dramatic instruction are cordially invited to attend classes in dramatics being offered by the L.E.R.C. Drama Club on Fridays and Tuesdays.

Classes are held at 1141 North Gower, Hollywood with Dick Walsh in charge of instruction.

VIVIENNE WORL
Lockheed Dept. 50, Swing

SWING CAMERA CLUB HOLDS FIRST MEET

Judging from the turn-out at last night's meeting of the Swing Shift Camera Club, this new activity promises to afford pleasure and recreation to a large group of Lockheedians.

"The meeting place in the Burbank Recreation Center has been established as regular headquarters and subsequent meeting dates will be announced when organization details have been completed," one of the group states.

Details are available through the L.E. R.C. office.

Every motor vehicle accident is the result of somebody doing something the wrong way at the wrong time.

L.E.R.C. CALENDAR October 30 to November 6

Choral Club
Rehearsal Monday, November 2, 7:30 p.m., Burbank High School Auditorium.

Bridge Club
Thursday evenings, 7:30 p.m., Burbank Recreation Center, 1111 W. Olive.

Hallowe'en Jamboree
Depts. 7, 40 and 58, Riverside Drive Breakfast Club, Saturday, October 31.

Dept. 5 Hallowe'en Dance
Oakmont Country Club, Saturday, October 31.

Drama Club
Advanced Class in Acting, Friday, October 30. Beginning Class in Acting, Tuesday, November 3. Advanced Class in Acting, Friday, November 6. All classes at 1141 North Gower, Hollywood, 7:30 p.m.

Ski Club
Work trek to Buckhorn leaves Angeles Crest and Foothill Blvd., 8:50 Sunday, November 1. Watch next week's Star for first Ski Club Meeting.

Ice Skating
Pan-Pacific Ice Arena, Thursday evenings, Day Shifters. Pasadena Winter Gardens, 171 S. Arroyo Parkway, Pasadena, 1 a.m. to 3:15 a.m., Swing Shifters.

Rhumba Classes
Every Monday night, Burbank Recreation Center, 1111 W. Olive, 7:30 p.m.

Boy Scouts
Regular meeting, George Washington School, Wednesdays, 7 p.m.

Polo
Regular practice at Riviera Country Club, Day Shift, Thursday, November 5, 3:30 p.m., and Swing Shift, Wednesday, November 4, 11:30 a.m.

Band
Friday, October 30, Concert, Main recreation area. Rehearsal, Monday, November 2, 7:30 p.m., Burbank Civic Auditorium at San Fernando and Scott Road, Burbank, Friday, November 6, 11:30 a.m., Concert, Main Recreation Area.

Badminton
Swing Shift every Monday morning, 11 a.m. to 1 p.m., Defense Area Bldg., 1111 W. Olive, Burbank. Day Shift players are now meeting each Wednesday night at 1111 W. Olive between 7 and 10:30 p.m.

Drill Team (Men and Women)
Burbank Civic Park, softball diamond, Wednesday, November 4, 1 p.m. N.E. of Turkey Crossing at San Fernando Rd.

Penguin Club
Meeting at Los Angeles Breakfast Club Monday, November 2, 7 p.m. (day shift). Swing Shift, Friday, November 6, 12:15.

Rangers and Rangerettes
Night Shift Rangers and Rangerettes, Thursday mornings, 7 to 9 a.m. Day shift Rangers and Rangerettes, Wednesday nights, 7 to 9 p.m. All shifts, all members, Sunday mornings, 7 to 9 a.m.

Industrial Relations Dance
Midwick Country Club, Saturday, October 31.

Rifle and Pistol
Annual Meeting to be held November 1 at the Burbank Recreation Center, 1111 West Olive in Burbank at 2 p.m. Election to be held in conjunction with meeting.

TRANSCRIPTION FOR SOLDIERS OVERSEAS MADE AT LOCKHEED

Swing shifters at Lockheed Plant 1 were mystified Monday evening when they came into the Empire Recreation Area for lunch and found a radio program in full swing on the bandstand, unannounced.

It was a recording made by the Overseas Division of the Office of War Information, for shortwave broadcast by transcription to troops in Australia and the Southwest Pacific and later to all English-speaking peoples of the United Nations. This "Voice of Lockheed-Vega" program will be played from the records some 20 times, assuring the allies that planes are being built fast and well.

The Lockheed band was the musical backbone of the half-hour program, backed up by brief interviews with Jimmy Mattern and Jim Allison, test pilots; Harvey Christen, Assistant Works Manager, and Henrietta Sumner Plume, group leader in final assembly inspection at Vega. The OWI has promised records of the program, which will be played during lunch periods at the various plants.

SWING GIRLS BOWLING SETS UP TWO LEAGUES

Reports filtering in on the Girls Swing Shift Bowling indicate that both the league rolling at the Burbank bowl after work and the before work teams rolling at Sunset are proving popular with Swing Girls.

"Not only are these girls finding that they get fine exercise but they are finding that these once-a-week get togethers are really pleasant social gatherings as well," Eleanor Clark, Swing Bowling coordinator emphasizes.

Due to change of work schedules, there are a few vacancies on teams in both groups and girls who are not yet affiliated with any bowling team are asked to join as soon as possible so no team will get too far behind the balance of the league. Details may be obtained from Eleanor Clark or from the L.E.R.C. office.

BRIDGE CLUB SPONSORED

Details on the newly sponsored L.E.R.C. Bridge Club may be obtained from Glenn Wilkie, Department 2, who states that the Club is open to tournament stars and beginners alike and play is held every Thursday evening starting at 7:30 in the Burbank Recreation Center, 1111 West Olive.

Once a pretty girl
With a Veronica curl
Showed safety rule scorn.
Now she is shorn.

VEGA CHORAL CLUB GIVES CONCERT AT PLANT TWO

The "Swing Shift Premier" of "Ballad for Americans" was presented by the Vega Choral club during the lunch hour at Vega, Plant Two this week and was well received by an enthusiastic audience.

This performance marked the first appearance in many months of the popular Vega choristers at their own plant, although they have been giving recitals and concerts at many places all over the Southland.

"Ballad for Americans" is easily the outstanding number in the repertoire of the Club, receiving much favorable comment wherever it was presented. Stowe Phelps, Dept. 59, Vega One, took the part of narrator and baritone soloist. Plans are under way for similar performances at Plant One and Lockheed, according to Orville Sims, Dept. 28, President of the club. Mr. Sims also announces that casting for the solo parts of "H.M.S. Pinafore" will begin at the next regular rehearsal, Tuesday, November 3, at 7:30 p.m. held at the Hollywood Roosevelt Hotel.

FIRST AID TRAINING

Red Cross First Aid training in the vicinity of your own home! This is being planned by the Education Department for employees of Lockheed and Vega.

Those interested in attending these Red Cross classes are asked to send an ANVO to H. F. Blackmore, Lockheed Department 45, giving home address and time they could attend. Instructors will be furnished by the Education Department.

SURVEY REVEALS 39,000 WOMEN IN AIRCRAFT INDUSTRY

A survey by the Aeronautical Chamber of Commerce of America shows that more than 39,000 women are now employed in productive capacities in the aircraft manufacturing industry as compared with only 1,900 one year ago.

The number of women actually building warplanes in the industry, the Chamber says, has increased 1,952 per cent since October, 1941. Employment of women in the industry started on a small and in many cases an experimental basis. Now, women having proved they can handle almost any job in an aircraft plant as well as men, their employment is being expanded as manpower wanes.

In addition to those in strictly production work, thousands of other women hold clerical positions in the industry. About 1,900 women were in productive jobs in October, 1941, and by November there were 2,500. This figure had more than doubled by January, 1942, to 6,900. Two months later the industry again more than doubled its number of feminine employees, having 16,000. Then further increasing production raised the total to above 39,000 by July.

Thus, what was once looked upon as a dubious although necessary expedient to meet war demands, now is an accomplished fact. All aircraft companies give preference to wives and widows of men in the armed forces.

The Chamber's survey shows they represent an average cross-section of the feminine populace. There are ex-shop girls and former school teachers. There are housewives, stenographers, waitresses, farm girls, textile and garment workers, youngsters not long out of school or college, and some grandmothers.

Services For Frank Bird At East Walpole, Mass.

Funeral services for Frank Bird, Lockheed engineer who was killed in the spectacular crash of an airline transport at Palm Springs last Friday, were held last Tuesday at East Walpole, Mass. Bird, 24, had been with Lockheed since his graduation from Harvard University in 1941. He was a section head in cataloging for the Army.

At the time of his death Bird was en route east on vacation and personal business, and to visit his mother at East Walpole. He is also survived by two sisters.

Uncensored Weather Report

"Looks like rain, doesn't it?"
"Yeah, and it's supposed to be coffee."

PLANT 'THREE MUSKETEERS'

★

In an "all for one and one for all" gesture the boys of Department 17, Lockheed this week purchased a flag and flagpole which were presented to all employees of Plant 3 in an impressive ceremony which featured a talk by Capt. A.L. Schluttig of the Air Forces. A short greeting from the Lockheed management was delivered by Chief Counsel H. C. Tallmadge, and the ceremony was climaxed with the raising of the American and Treasury Dept. Bull's-Eye flags. U. S. Army color bearers participated.

★

NEW EMPLOYMENT SET-UP ANNOUNCED BY ROBERTSON

Department 44, previously known as Personnel Procurement Department, is now the Lockheed-Vega Employment Department, according to a communication issued by R. B. Robertson, assistant industrial relations director.

All functions and personnel related to the employment processes of Lockheed Division 42 and Vega Division 67 have been transferred to the reorganized Department 44 under M. V. Mattson, manager. All communications relating to employment should hereafter be addressed to Mr. Mattson.

To facilitate applicant interviewing and hiring without transportation inconvenience to prospective employees, four new employment offices have been opened. These offices located at 5820 Hollywood Boulevard in Hollywood, 2100 South Figueroa Street in Los Angeles, 713 East Green Street in Pasadena and 131 East Magnolia in Burbank will be operated and staffed by members of Department 44.

Applicants may now be interviewed, hired and assigned to the various plants directly from any one of the above offices, eliminating the necessity of first having to clear through employment offices at Plant 1.

NO 'OPEN SEASON' ON CYCLISTS

Abraham Lincoln once said, "It is the duty of every man to protect himself and those associated with him from accidents which may cause injury or death."

The great emancipator was not thinking of our present day motorists when he uttered these words, but they are just as timely today, and in this connection the hundreds of bicyclists who travel to and from work daily ask their fellow workers who still drive automobiles, to exercise a little more caution when driving on our crowded highways.

They point out that while the two-wheel method of transportation is their contribution to the conservation of vital rubber, it is extremely hazardous, particularly when one wonders if motorists think there is an "open season" on bicycle riders.

With the days getting shorter and darkness coming on earlier than usual, all automobile drivers are earnestly requested to DRIVE CAREFULLY and show a little more consideration for their fellow worker who rides a bicycle.

$2 Dividend Declared By Lockheed Directors

The directors of Lockheed Aircraft Corporation this week declared a dividend of $2.00 payable November 14, 1942, to stockholders of record as of November 5, 1942.

HARRISON TELLS HOW TO FIGURE 'GAS' MILEAGE

Many employees will want to know as nearly accurate as possible just what can be expected from their own cars in travel distance from each gallon of gasoline rationed to them. Up to now we have all, more or less, been satisfied with "about this or that number of miles per gallon," however, because of varied gear ratios in different cars, quality of gasoline used, condition of car and actual conditions under which the car is driven, the wise individual should make some simple checks and determine facts pertinent to his or her own travel.

Lynn H. Harrison, Traffic Engineer, suggests the following procedure because it can be done without gauges or checking instruments of any kind:

To determine what 'miles per gallon' you have been getting, (1) simply have your gasoline tank filled up to a definite point in the filler neck, or throat of the gas tank. (Do not fill until it overflows.) (2) Take note of the speedometer reading. (3) Drive for a day or two as you normally would, back and forth to work, shopping, etc. (4) Have tank filled again to the same level of gasoline. (5) Check the mileage. (6) Divide the number of gallons of gasoline used by the number of miles registered as traveled, and you have your actual miles per gallon, under your normal habits of travel.

VAQUEROS TO FROLIC ON HALLOWE'EN

The Vega riding club, The Vaqueros, are to hold their second annual Hallowe'en party, Saturday, October 31, at 8 p.m. A special invitation is extended to all members and to any one else who has ever ridden with the club. To complete a really "rugged" week end, the Vaqueros will attend the Lockheed Rangers Field Day at Tex's Stables in Roscoe on Sunday, November 1.

Shareholders To Vote On Retirement Income Plan

A special meeting of the shareholders of Lockheed Aircraft Corporation has been called for December 3, 1942, to afford them an opportunity to vote on a proposed employees' retirement income plan.

The plan, if approved by the shareholders, will be open to participation by all full-time employees of Lockheed Aircraft Corporation and its subsidiaries, Vega Aircraft Corporation and Lockheed Air Terminal, Inc., who have been with the companies more than one year and whose salaries or wages are in excess of $250 per month. The proposed plan is similar to those now in effect in numerous leading corporations.

L.E.R.C. CHORAL CLUB APPEALS TO CROWD

The outlook for a most successful Choral Club season was seen in the response and attendance at the first 1942 meeting of the group held the past Monday night.

"We expect even a larger turn-out on each succeeding Monday night when the group attends the regular rehearsals in the Burbank High School Auditorium," a spokesman for the Choral Club states.

Any Lockheedian or any member of a Lockheedian's immediate family may take part in this L.E.R.C. sponsored activity and rehearsals start promptly at 7:30 with Victor Boggis serving as director.

THREE HALLOWE'EN DANCES SCHEDULED

Three Departmental Hallowe'en Dances are on the calendar for October 31st according to the L.E.R.C. office.

Departments 7-40 and 58—Department 5 and the Industrial Relations groups are planning parties at The Riverside Drive Breakfast Club—The Oakmont Country Club and the Southern California Country Club respectively.

Tickets for Industrial Relations dance may be obtained from Betty Dixon of the Nurses Office, and Harold Blackmore of Education while the Department 5 tickets are available through Chet Leigh and deputy L.E.R.C. representatives.

Jerry Sickler, L.E.R.C. representative for 7-40-58 states his party will be a near sell-out at $1.50 a couple and $1.00 for singles.

FIELD DAY PROGRAM SET FOR NOVEMBER 1

Final details of the Ranger and Rangerette three-event celebration scheduled for November 1st are shaping up rapidly according to word from the committee planning the show at Tex Stonehurst stables.

"The Horse Show portion of the program which starts at one in the afternoon will find riders from both Lockheed and Vega and other Valley organizations putting on a free field day to top all previous shows," a Committee spokesman states, "and the barbecue and barn dance which are set to fill the balance of the day and evening, will wind up the affair as one of the best events ever sponsored by the Lockheed Rangers and Rangerettes."

Lockheed Tool Store Hours

The Lockheed Employees' tool store hours are 6 a.m. to 8:30 p.m., Monday through Friday, and 8 a.m. to 4:45 p.m. Saturdays.

SAVES SCRAP

An interesting saving of important material was created in the Vega Machine Shop by the simple process of welding together scrap butt ends of Cast Manganese Bronze Cored Bar Stock used in the making of Landing Gear Shims, resulting in an almost 100 per cent saving of scrap. Mr. Orville Wait is pointing to the weld which makes possible the machining of hundreds of additional shims and the saving of this critical material. Your ingenuity, too, can be of great service. Your suggestions are needed.

MORE BOWLERS NEEDED

The "825 Scratch" league, Bowling at Magnolia Bowling Center in Burbank, is in need of additional bowlers. This is Vega's fastest league, made up of the top-notch bowlers of the plant. Book averages of 150 and up are enough to qualify you to enter in this league.

Bowlers, LIVING IN THIS AREA are urged to turn out next Tuesday evening at 6:45 to fill vacancies created in the league by terminations, military service, etc.

You may call the V.E.R.C. office, Ext. 1735, if you care to fill in on one of these teams.

Espeseth Honor Man

Herbert Randall Espeseth, 28, former employee of Lockheed and Vega, has been graduated from recruit training as honor man of his company at the Great Lakes Naval Training Station. He has been selected to attend one of the Navy's service schools.

Osmond Wins Honors

David John Osmund, former Lockheed employee, has just rung the gong at Great Lakes Naval Training Station. Osmond, 24, was graduated recently as honor man of his company and will attend one of the Navy's service schools.

NEW CLASSES SET FOR EMPLOYEES

Following is a list of classes just announced by the Lockheed-Vega Education Department:

Blueprint Reading, T-Th, 6:30-9:30 p.m., North Hollywood H.S.
Blueprint Reading, M-W, 6:30-9:30 p.m., Van Nuys H.S.
Blueprint Reading, M-W, 7:00-10:00 p.m., Los Angeles H.S.
Blueprint Reading, T-Th, 7:00-10:00 p.m., Los Angeles H.S.
Blueprint Reading, M-W, 6:30-9:30 p.m., Beverly Hills H.S.
Portuguese, Th-F, 6:00-8:00 p.m., JMES
Electrical Assembly and Install., M-W-F, 6:30-9:30 p.m., BES
Mach. Shop (The.) T-W, 7:00-9:00 p.m., JMES.
Time & Mot. Study, T-Th, 6:30-9:30 p.m., JMES.
Mater. & Processes, T, 6:30-9:30 p.m., JMES.
Machine Shop, T-Th, 4:00-7:00 p.m., BES.
Mach. Shop, Maint., F-S, 4:00-7:00 p.m., BES.
Tool & Die Making, W-S, 6:00-9:00 p.m., BES.
Tool Planning, Sat., 11:30-3:30 p.m., BES.
Machine Shop, M-W-F, 4:00-7:00 p.m., BES.
Blueprint Reading—Sheet Metal, M-W, 6:30-9:30 p.m., JBES.
Los Angeles High School, 4600 W. Olympic
Beverly Hills High School, 241 Moreno Drive.
Van Nuys High School, 6535 Cedros Ave.
John Muir Evening School (JMES), 220 E. Grinnell Drive, Burbank.
Burbank Evening School (BES), 901 N. Third Street, Burbank.
John Burroughs Evening School, 1920 Clark Street, Burbank.
North Hollywood High School, Magnolia Blvd. at Colfax.

Blueprint Reading for aircraft workers in all departments will be featured in a number of courses to be given by the Burbank City Schools through their War Training Program.

Many of the classes will be pointed to the needs of women who have recently entered the aircraft industry and who must know what they are doing as well as how to do the aircraft production job to which they are assigned. Trainees will be instructed in the reading of all types and kinds of drawing.

Classes which will be given at the Burbank Evening High School, 901 North Third, are:

Blueprint Reading (Beginning), M-W, 6:30-9:30 p.m., Room 208.
Blueprint Reading (Beginning), M-W, 6:30-9:30 p.m., Room 374.
Blueprint Reading (Beginning), T-Th, 6:30-9:30 p.m., Room 208.
Blueprint Reading (Advanced), M-W, 6:30-9:30 p.m., Room 271.

Classes scheduled at the John Muir Evening School, 320 East Grinnell Drive, are:

Blueprint Reading (Introductory), M-W, 6:30-9:30 p.m., Room 110.
Blueprint Reading (Introductory), M-W, 1:00-3:00 p.m., Room 3.
Blueprint Reading (Beginning), M-W, 6:30-9:30 p.m., Room 105.
Blueprint Reading (Beginning), T-Th, 1:00-3:00 p.m., Room 105.
Blueprint Reading (Advanced), M-W, 1:00-3:00 p.m., Room 105.
Blueprint Reading (Advanced), M-W, 6:30-9:30 p.m., Room 111.
Blueprint Reading for Machinists, T-Th, 1:00-3:00 p.m., Room 3.

Classes scheduled at the John Burroughs Evening School, 1920 Clark Avenue, are:

Blueprint Reading (Introductory), M-W, 6:30-9:30 p.m., Room 204.
Blueprint Reading (Introductory), M-W, 4:00-6:30 p.m., Room 204.
Blueprint Reading (Introductory), T-Th, 6:30-9:30 p.m., Room 104.

YOUR JOB

By

R. RANDALL IRWIN

Everyone—or nearly everyone—wants to do more than he is now doing to help win the war. All that he wants is a bigger opportunity.

En route to Washington. On the plane, a master sergeant, meteorologist from the Air Corps base at Victorville (Calif.), flying east for unknown assignment, eager for foreign service. A civilian flying instructor from an Army contract school, heading East to try for a commission so he will be eligible for duty overseas. A famous motion picture director reporting for active duty as a lieutenant colonel.

The only passenger content with her lot is an elderly woman whose two sons are in the service. She has contributed greatly, but give her a few more months and she will want to take an active part in the war effort.

Danger of this "urge to do more" is that it creates an unwise, disorderly moving around from job to job. The result is that many war industries are experiencing a 100 per cent annual turnover in employees. Departmental establishments of the Federal Government are approaching a civilian employee "quit rate" of 100 per cent a year. You cannot successfully produce airplanes, ships and munitions—and run an efficient wartime Government—with this kind of turnover of employees.

In Washington. Everyone is talking about National War Service legislation. How will it affect you and me and our jobs? Does it mean "freezing us" to our present work?

The chances are that it will not directly affect us at all. The powers under a National Service Act will only be used where necessary to the war effort. The Government will depend on you and me to be willing to accept and stay on the job where our highest skill will be fully utilized in the prosecution of the war. The authority of the Government will be exercised only if we start jumping around from job to job without any sound reason —or if we decide to go fishing or to accept a non-essential job when we are needed in some war industry. Then of course, we will be told to "get to work— or else."

Actually, it is doubtful if we will have immediate enactment of a National Service Act. Organized labor is opposed to it unless all other methods to accomplish the purpose have been tried and proved inadequate.

A subcommittee of the War Manpower Commission's Policy Committee has been working on a draft of a National War Service Act—at the request of the President. However, all labor and management members of the committee agree that the leadership and the full present authority of the President and the War Manpower Commission should be exercised to solve the manpower problem before additional legislation is passed.

Through cooperative efforts of government, labor and management, it is hoped that most of the nation's manpower problems will be solved.

DON'T SEAL YOUR AIR MAIL MATTER, EXCEPT LETTERS

Don't seal your air mail matter, except letters in their ordinary and usual form!

This is the new rule which applies both to company and personal air mail correspondence or packages as a result of new orders issued this week by the Postmaster General, an excerpt from which reads:

"No mail matter, either sealed or unsealed, intended for AIR MAIL except letters in their ordinary and usual form and official matter, shall be accepted for transmission by air mail until they have been thoroughly examined and endorsed by two postal employees."

In order to comply with the above instructions, all company air mail bigger than ordinary letter size envelopes must be delivered to the Lockheed or Vega mail room unsealed. Company mailroom clerks will submit such matter to postal employees and seal same in the presence of these official inspectors.

Employees having personal air mail of this type must take their mail in person, and unsealed, to their Post Office for inspection. The company cannot handle personal air mail in this manner because of the volume of company air mail that must be taken to the Post Office for inspection. Do it yourself—and DON'T SEAL IT except in the presence of the postal employees!

THE *Lockheed-Vega Star* ★★

The Lockheed-Vega Star is issued every Friday for the employees of the Lockheed Aircraft Corporation and the Vega Aircraft Corporation and is the official publication of both companies. Communications may be addressed to either the Industrial Relations Office or the Public Relations Department, Lockheed Aircraft Corporation, Burbank, California, U.S.A. Although news and cartoon contributions are welcome, circumstances make it impossible to give any promise that they will be returned to sender when not used, nor can individual acknowledgment be made.

BERT W. HOLLOWAY, Editor-in-Chief
H. L. (HAL) ROSSON, Managing Editor

Volume 9 Number 46

WHAT'S WRONG WITH THIS PICTURE?

What's wrong with this picture? You're wrong—he HAS his badge. That was two weeks ago when he didn't have it. Last week he had an empty cart, which was worse. Today's the worst yet. He has his cart loaded so badly that everything's about to fall off, risking damage to precious parts. Keep on trying, Buddy, you may get it right yet!

They're Not Kidding; Keep It Under 35

City, county and state police officers received praise for their cooperation in citing speed offenders from rationing chief Paul Barksdale d'Orr. Speaking before a meeting of the Los Angeles Peace Officers' Traffic Council, d'Orr said:

"If you loyal and patriotic officers continue doing what you have been doing voluntarily, everything will be accomplished that is desired."

Pointing out that thousands of copies of citations given to motorists for exceeding the 35-mile-per-hour speed limit have already been sent to his office, the administrator said these would soon be turned over to the appropriate government agency. Mr. d'Orr also reported to the group the receipt of a bulletin from Washington, outlining a proposed plan which would give the Office of Defense Transportation the legal power to make operation of an automobile over the 35-mile-per-hour maximum, cause for impounding the vehicle.

War time inventors with all their ingenuity have yet to produce a combination more dangerous than a driver with a fast car, a bottle of hooch and an open road.

THE *Lockheed-Vega Star* ★ ★

Official publication of the Lockheed and Vega Aircraft Corporations

Volume 9 | BURBANK, CALIFORNIA, U.S.A., DECEMBER 11, 1942 | Number 52

VEGA VENTURAS HAMMER HUNS IN EUROPE

Swarms of Vega Ventura bombers such as those seen above struck their first reported blow of the war at Axis held territory on Sunday, December 6, when R.A.F. pilots swept them in waves over Eindhoven, Holland. Dispatches from London stated that the Venturas, built at the Vega Aircraft plant in Burbank, California, formed part of the second wave of attacking bombers engaged in the biggest daylight raid of the war against the Nazis. Flying at roof-top height with great speed, the Venturas scored direct hits on their targets. The effect of the raid was described as "devastating."

Lightnings Even Score With Best German Planes

Dispatches from the war fronts in Tunisia, where air superiority in the Mediterranean area may be determined, continue to bring heartening news of the increasingly important role being played by the Lightning in that theatre of operations.

In Washington this week Lieut. General Henry H. Arnold, Commanding General of the Army Air Forces, said American planes and personnel are going up against first-class air power for the first time in this war.

"The new American Lockheed P-38 pursuit ship now is engaging the best planes the Germans possess — the Focke-Wulfe 190 and Messerschmitt

(Continued on Page 7)

News Reports From Britain Reveal 'Vega's Own' Playing Important Role In Smashing Vital Enemy Targets

Strictly "hush-hush," as far as the newsfronts of the world are concerned, has been the Vega Ventura Bomber. And up until last Monday the same censorship shrouded its performance on the battlefronts of the world.

But now, as with the P-38 three weeks ago, the news has broken and the men and women of Vega, who have given of themselves in unstinted measure to produce this grand fighting plane for the Allies, know at last that it is helping to carry Allied wrath and might to the enemy—and so do the Nazis!

Associated Press dispatches last Monday from London gave the story full play. They told how, in the R.A.F.'s sweep over Nazi-occupied Holland the day before, the Venturas participated in a hedge-hopping raid that blasted some of the most important munitions works in German held territory, among them the Philips Radio Tube Works at Eindhoven, largest of its kind in all Europe.

(Continued on Page 6)

TAKE A TIP—LISTEN TO THE 'ARMY HOUR' SUNDAY

A program of greatest interest to all Lockheed and Vega employees will be broadcast on the NBC "Army Hour" at 12:30 p.m. this Sunday, December 13th. The Army Hour goes to an estimated 40,000,000 listeners internationally. Listen in on Station KFI, at 12:30 Sunday noon.

VEGA ENGINEERS HOSTS AT DINNER

★

Guests at the Vega Engineering Supervisors' dinner last Friday evening heard a stirring commentary on the war today by John B. Hughes, popular Mutual network analyst and commentator. Mr. Hughes also paid tribute to Vega engineers in his 9:30 news program over KHJ. Among those present were, left to right, at table: Bert Holloway, John B. Hughes, Richard Gearing (behind Mr. Hughes), E. M. Wales, Lt. Harak of the WAAC, Joe Washburn and Paul Riggs.

★

'UNSUNG HEROES' IN PLANTS AS WELL AS ON BATTLEFRONTS

Unsung heroes of the fighting forces, whose efforts and personal contributions often go unrecognized, have their counterparts at Vega in the employees who put their efforts for national defense above their personal comfort.

Such a one is Lillian W. Jolson of Department 7 who stumbled over a basket and broke her knee one day several weeks ago, went to the hospital and had it set, and reported back to work with only one day of lost time.

Then there is Robert H. Love of Department 13, Plant 2, who received a one and one-half inch laceration of the forearm which cut into the biceps muscle. He reported to the hospital, had the wound sutured and returned to work with no lost time.

Within the last two months, many employees with painful hand and foot injuries have lost no time from their jobs. Pat S. Runnion of Department 23 had a comminuted finger fracture — which means a painfully smashed finger—but took no time off from her work. Francis H. Williams of Department 13, Plant 2, had a fracture and contusion of the right hand; Annie Mannix of Department 15 had a chip fracture and sprain of the left hand; Thomas J. King of Department 13 received a fracture and laceration of the finger; and several men in the Material Control department have had puncture wounds in their feet—all continued on their jobs with no lost time.

This is what we mean when we say "they have what it takes."

Gal: "My goodness, that boy friend of mine is trying at times."

Pal: "That's nothing, mine is trying at all times."—*Trade Winds.*

WAR WORKERS AGAIN ASSURED OF ENOUGH NECESSARY GASOLINE

A previous statement that Lockheed and Vega employees are assured all the gasoline they need for essential driving was reaffirmed today by Robert C. Storment, manager of the Employee Transportation Department.

With the issuance of supplemental ration books almost completed (except for cases where the employee delayed sending in his application or where it was improperly made out), the Employee Transportation Department has asked those who have received supplemental books but who feel these do not cover their necessary requirements, to please contact the department immediately. Adjustments, if in order, will be made.

A number of supplemental books are still unclaimed at the Transportation office and employees who have not yet been notified to pick up their books are asked to contact the department. You must do this in person *and bring your white or blue registration slip with you.*

TOOL PLANNING AND MANUFACTURE ENGINEERING

The University of California War Training Program is offering a course in Advanced Tool Planning and Manufacturing Engineering to begin on January 5. Classes will be held at the U.C.L.A. War Training Center, 3700 Magnolia Boulevard, Burbank. The course will be instructed by Dan White, assisted by Sherman Martin. Prospective students may contact the University War Training Office or Sherman Martin, Lockheed extension 3174.

The University has requested that prospective students bring their forms for requests for Supplemental Gas Rations.

John B. Hughes, Radio Star, Is Guest Of Honor

The monthly Vega Engineering Supervisors' dinner was held last Friday evening, December 4, at Eaton's Rancho Cafe in North Hollywood. One hundred and fifteen engineers and guests were present. This was the first meeting attended by both men and women supervisors of Vega.

With Richard Gearing, Vega Engineering photographic correlator acting as Master of Ceremonies, the program featured John B. Hughes, popular Mutual network news analyst and commentator. In his talk Mr. Hughes gave a comprehensive picture of the war today, predictions as to the next theatre of war operations, and prognostications of the world peace to come.

He also paid tribute to Vega engineers in his 9:30 news program which was broadcast by remote hook-up and released through KHJ.

Following the radio broadcast, short talks were made by Lieut. Horak of the WAAC's, Lieut. Shoup of the WAVE's, and Joe Washburn, chief photographer of Lockheed and Vega.

Other guests included Paul Briggs, manager Lockheed-Vega Customer Service; J. B. Wassall, Vega chief engineer; E. M. Wales, Vega executive engineer; J. W. Anderson, Vega assistant executive engineer; and Shavenau Monsen, group head, Vega Photographic Department.

A surprise feature of the evening was the presentation of an award to John W. Borquist, Vega production engineer, for his article appearing in the November issue of Product Engineering on "Standardization of Surface Roughness." Albert A. Peterson, Vega staff engineer, presented the check.

The showing of colored motion pictures of all models of Vega aircraft in flight concluded the program.

Design and Drafting Class

The class in aircraft and aircraft accessory designing and drafting at Burbank Technical Institute is still open for enrollments. This class has as its objective the upgrading of students from all departments of the industry when the making and interpreting of drawings is so all important. Class meets Monday, Wednesday and Friday evenings from 6:30 to 9:30 p.m in Room 5 (second floor front, Main Building) 1809 W. Magnolia Blvd., Burbank.

If Bonds Haven't Arrived, Be Patient; Here Are Reasons For Delay

Improvement in the delivery of War Bonds to Lockheed and Vega employees who are purchasing bonds regularly through the payroll deduction plan, was announced this week by the Accounting and Finance departments.

Decision by the Treasury Department to permit bonds to be mailed under a new system which eliminates the registered envelopes that were a source of innumerable delays, will greatly facilitate transmission.

Also many hours of labor incident to registration for delivery of the bonds now can be devoted to other phases of the tremendous task.

The departments who have been working on the task, as well as the bank which is registering and issuing all bonds purchased by Lockheed and Vega employees, believe the new step will speed delivery time by several days.

It was explained that the initial task of setting up machinery for payroll deductions and bond purchases proved a tremendous job for the accounting departments, which had to devise a complex and foolproof system to assure exact registration of all bonds. An entirely separate bookkeeping system also had to be established to record all bond transactions in the account of each employee.

Work of the Finance Departments on the project was impeded by errors on the part of employees in filling out their original authorization cards. Many thousands of these cards had to be corrected.

The bank to which the departments turned for help in registration and issuance of bonds, has encountered numerous difficulties, first obtaining additional trained personnel for the job and secondly in getting special office machinery now on high priority. Exacting requirements of the Treasury Department, closely observed by the issuing bank, complicated the problem of setting up an organization to handle several thousand weekly orders for bonds.

The Finance and Accounting Departments made the following points clear:

1. The companies acting as trustees for funds deducted from paychecks for war bond purchases, assume full responsibility for these funds until the bonds are registered.

2. War Bonds can be negotiated only by the registered owner and therefore Lockheed and Vega employees who are experiencing temporary delays in delivery need not be alarmed if the bonds do not reach their homes when expected.

3. Money deducted from paychecks is placed in a separate "trustee" bank account which earns no interest. Within a few days after the final deduction, the funds are forwarded to the Government and put to work for the Government.

Every effort is being made by the companies and the bank to eliminate delays in deliveries, and the steady improvement in the complex organization for the task is expected to bring satisfactory delivery in the near future.

2 MORE GOLD STARS ON HONOR ROLLS

Two more Gold Stars have been added to the Lockheed-Vega Honor Rolls in memory of former employees who have given their lives while serving with our armed forces.

Lieut. George H. Cummings, formerly employed in Lockheed Department 46, was killed in action at Guadalcanal while serving with the U.S. Infantry.

Lieut. Forrest J. Johnston, Jr., a former employee of Lockheed Department 10, was killed while serving with the U.S. Air Corps this year. He is survived by his mother, Mrs. Roselyn Johnston, now at Vega; and a brother and sister.

LIBRARY

The Lockheed and Vega Libraries and Book Stores have received many new titles as well as some older books which are in demand. Employees at Plant 4 may obtain books and magazines through the Branch Library located there.

The following are some of the titles in stock at present:

Mathematics Refresher—A. Hooper, R.A.F.
Blueprint Reading Made Easy.
Handbook of Chemistry and Physics.
Aircraft Yearbook, 1942.
Engineering Drawing, French.
Hydraulics—Aircraft Specialties.
Hydraulics As Applied to Machines—Ford Apprentice School.

PUTTING THE 'PROD' TO PRODUCTION

VEGA WOMAN TEAM BREAKS PRODUCTION RECORD IN DEPT. 15

"Putting the prod to production" is the logical caption for this picture. Shown are Vega Swing Shiftresses, Wilhelmina Morris and Margie Guyott, who together have formed a team typical of the efforts of Department 15 to speed up production of its thousands and one sub-assemblies.

Recently these two combined their zeal in the record breaking feat of completing 435 Oxygen Valve Support assemblies in eight hours time. The operations consisted of installing the part in the jig, drilling, dismantling, burring, and assembling the parts with clecos. Note the caps, goggles, regulation wearing apparel, and lack of jewelry; all indicative of the fact that Dept. 15 is one hundred per cent in accord with the safety rules and regulations as prescribed by the Company and the State.

NOTICE !
Change In Bus Schedules

Effective Monday morning, December 14, the schedule of busses from Pasadena on FACTORY SHIFTS ONLY, will be advanced five minutes.

Busses on the Orange Grove line will leave the railhead at Colorado and Sierra Madre at 5:45 a.m., 2:15 p.m. and 11:15 p.m. Those on the Colorado Street line will leave the same railhead at 5:50 a.m., 2:20 p.m. and 11:20 p.m. Time of arrival and departure at all passenger pick-up stops will be advanced accordingly.

HOLD 'PHILADELPHIA STORY' REHEARSALS

Rehearsals are being held regularly every Tuesday, Friday and Sunday evening for the forthcoming L.E.R.C. Drama Club production of "Philadelphia Story," which will be presented to Lockheedians starting January 29.

Rehearsals start promptly at 7:30 and share-the-ride arrangements are working out satisfactorily, Dick Walsh, director, reports. "When we open at the Hollywood Assistance League Playhouse on January 29, we expect to have a comprehensive share-the-ride plan worked out."

L.E.R.C. SWING CAMERA CLUB GAINS IN NEW MEMBERSHIP CAMPAIGN

Widespread interest in the L.E.R.C. Swing Shift Camera Club is reported by officials of the organization.

Any Lockheedian, or member of a Lockheed family, may join this club, which holds its meetings at the Burbank Recreation Center, 1111 West Olive, Burbank.

SKIERS SCHEDULE MEET TO PLAN HOLIDAY TREK

Plans are completed for the Yosemite Dinner, sponsored by the L.E.R.C. Ski Club, to be held tonight at the Hofbrau Gardens, 6361 Sunset Boulevard starting at 6:45, according to Bob O'-Hanlon of Department 25, who has made all arrangements for the affair.

O'Hanlon may be reached at Extension 1780 by those who have not made reservations.

PLANT 2 SWING GOLF PLAYERS MEET WEEKLY

The recently organized Plant 2 L.E.R.C. Swing Shift Golf Club is meeting Monday mornings at the Griffith Park course, according to Jim Arbogast, Plant 2, athletic committeeman coordinating the activity for the L.E.R.C.

Any Plant 2 Swing Shifter interested in playing with this group is urged to show up at Griffith Park. Share-the-rides are available and details may be worked out with Arbogast by contacting him at the plant.

"... IN THIS CORNER"

Empire Recreation Area, Tuesday, December 15, WRESTLING, 11:30 Lunch Period. Iron Mike Works vs. Herb Scherb.

Empire Recreation Area, Tuesday evening, December 15, WRESTLING, Swing Lunch Period, Maintenance Madman vs. Herb Scherb.

L.E.R.C. CALENDAR
December 11-18

Choral Club
Rehearsal Monday, December 14, 7:30 p.m., Burbank High School.

Bridge Club
Thursday evenings, 7:30 p.m., Burbank Recreation Center, 1111 West Olive, Burbank.

Rhumba Classes
Every Monday night, Townsend Hall, Burbank at 7:30 p.m.

Boy Scouts
Regular meeting, George Washington School, Wednesday, 7:00 p.m.

Band
Friday, December 11, Concert Main Recreation Area. Rehearsal Monday, December 14 at 7:30 p.m., John Burroughs Junior High School, Burbank. Friday, December 18, Concert in Main Recreation Area.

Ice Skating
Pan-Pacific Ice Arena every Thursday, Day Shift. Pasadena Winter Garden, 6-7 Thursday evenings, special rates for skating and skates.

Badminton
Day Shift every Friday evening between 7 and 10, Hollywood Recreation Center, Hollywood.

Rangers and Rangerettes
Night shift Rangers and Rangerettes Thursday mornings, 7 to 9 a.m. Day Shift Rangers and Rangerettes, Wednesday nights 7 to 9 p.m. All shifts, all members Sunday mornings, 7 to 9 a.m.

Wrestling
Tuesday, December 15, noon lunch period. Tuesday, December 15, swing lunch period.

Drama Club
Advanced class in acting every Monday at 7:30, 1141 N. Gower, Hollywood. Rehearsal for "Philadelphia Story" Tuesday, Friday and Sunday at 7:30 p.m., Hollywood Headquarters.

Plant 2 Golf Club
Swing Shift golf club meeting each Monday morning at the Griffith Park Course at 8 a.m.

Basketball
Mondays, plant 3 girls meet at 4:15, Burbank Recreation Center, Tuesdays at 5:15.

Ski Club Sun Valley Dinner
December 11, Hofbrau Gardens, 6361 Sunset Blvd., starting at 6:45. Call 1780 for reservations.

Camera Club (Swing Shift)
Meeting scheduled for Thursday, December 17, at the Burbank Recreation Center, 1111 West Olive. Meeting will feature "Table Talk" prints and is scheduled for 1:00 p.m.

Penguin Meeting (Day Shift)
Los Angeles Breakfast Club, December 17.

Swing Camera Club Meet

The next meeting of the L.E.R.C. Swing Shift Camera Club will feature "Table Talk" prints. Prizes will be awarded during the meeting which is scheduled for 1 p.m. Thursday, December 17, at the Burbank Recreation Center, 1111 W. Olive.

CHRISTMAS SALES AT L.E.R.C. CANTEEN SMASHING RECORDS

Stressing the fact that there are but 13 days until Christmas, Walter Crooks, of the L.E.R.C. Canteen System, urges Lockheedians to "shop" the various gift items offered at L.E.R.C. Canteens.

"The demand for the special Christmas cards has surpassed the demands of past seasons—the purchase of novelty items has created certain definite shortages, and all those who have not made selections from the L.E.R.C. Christmas line should do so promptly to avoid disappointment," Crooks declares.

Among the items still available are five choices in Christmas cards, ash trays, some novelty jewelry items, the special Pyrex candied fruit packet and a special Lockheed 2-pound package of candy packed by Watkins.

L.E.R.C. INTERDEPARTMENT CASABA TOURNAMENT IN DRIVE FOR ATTENDANCE

The 1942 inter-departmental L.E.R.C. Basketball tourney is rapidly nearing the half-way point, according to Frank Davis of the L.E.R.C., who points out that most of the teams are making their schedules with a minimum of interference.

"All the games are open to the public, free, and the splendid quality of ball being played makes these games well worth attending," according to Mr. Davis. "Check the L.E.R.C. office for the game being played nearest your home, the next night you are looking for some real fun."

During the two holiday weeks, starting with the Christmas holiday, no games will be played but schedules will resume during the first week of January.

WOMEN'S BASKETBALL PRACTICE WEEKLY EVENT

Two sessions of basketball for Lockheed women are to be held at the Burbank Recreation Center, according to word from the L.E.R.C. office.

On Mondays the Plant 3 girls meet at 4:15; on Tuesdays the sessions start promptly at 5:15.

Penguin Clubs Meeting

The Swing Shift Penguins have adjourned for this year but will take up again with a meeting scheduled for January 8, according to John McCabe, entertainment chairman for the group. The Day Shift Penguins have one more meeting before the new year, December 17, at the Los Angeles Breakfast Club.

BUCK-OF-THE-MONTH CLUB'S FINANCIAL REPORT HEALTHY

Lockheed-Vega members of the Buck-of-the-Month Club who are planning to enter the second letter contest now being sponsored by the club, have until Monday evening, December 14, to send in their entries.

A pair of tickets to the very popular "Blackouts of 1942" is being given each week to the member who tells briefly and sincerely "Why I am a Member of the Buck-of-the-Month Club."

Send entries to Buck-of-the-Month Club office.

As membership in the Buck of the Month Club increases at both Lockheed and Vega, the ninth monthly statement of the income and allocation of funds from this Lockheed-Vega employees voluntary charity organization is herewith submitted.

FINANCIAL REPORT
Buck of the Month Club as of
November 30, 1942

CONTRIBUTIONS		
Lockheed Employees	$186,931.00	
Vega Employees	95,101.25	
Triplett & Barton	608.50	
L.E.R.C. Employees	155.00	
V.E.R.C. Employees	140.00	
Publications Employees	13.00	
Miscellaneous	943.51	
Brit. Reassem. Div.	269.00	
		$284,161.26
DISBURSEMENTS		
Refunds	46.75	
Bonding	360.00	
Miscellaneous (Check Book)	1.00	
Infantile Paralysis	3,435.00	
Iron Lung	500.00	
United China Relief	5,000.00	
Poppy Day	1,000.00	
Red Cross	29,606.65	
Canteen Service to Soldiers in Burbank	300.00	
United Service Orgs.	34,351.00	
Veterans of Foreign Wars	150.00	
Canteen Service	1,200.00	
Asbury Rapid Transit Sys.	760.00	
Naval Aid Auxiliary	3,000.00	
Navy Relief Society	10,000.00	
All Serv. Rec. Center	600.00	
Gideon Testament Ministry	500.00	
Queen Wilhelmina Fund	2,000.00	
Travelers Aid Society	800.00	
Army (Canteen Credit)	2,000.00	
Navy (Canteen Credit)	2,000.00	
Army Emergency Relief	15,000.00	
British War Relief	5,000.00	
Marine Corps (Cant. Cred.)	2,000.00	
Russian War Relief	5,000.00	
Serv. Men Rec. Fund	200.00	
Community Chest (L.A. and 15 other branches)	60,001.00	
Am. Soc. Hyg. Asso.	500.00	
Christmas Cigarettes, Former Emp. in Serv. (part pay.)	500.00	
Salvation Army	10,000.00	
Am. Wom. Vol. Serv., Inc.	1,150.00	
TOTAL		$196,961.40
Nov 30. *** BALANCE		87,199.86

CHRISTMAS DAY TO BE OBSERVED AS HOLIDAY

In compliance with the wish expressed by Donald Nelson for a one-day holiday out of the year for war workers, all plants of Lockheed and Vega will close down Christmas Day. Only the necessary skeleton maintenance and plant protection personnel will be on duty.

RICKENBACKER RESCUE RECALLS EARLY DAYS

Recent news of the rescue of Col. Eddie Rickenbacker was especially welcome to one member of the Lockheed-Vega organization, his long-time friend of early dirt track racing and pioneer aviation days, L. M. Bach, Vega Works Manager. This photo was taken in 1929 at the Metropolitan Airport, Van Nuys, which was then one of the city's largest. Rickenbacker visited the Bach Aircraft Company to look over the "Airyacht," radical in design for its time, but prototype of the modern luxury airliner as later developments proved. Captain Eddie often visited "Mort," as he is familiarly known, to watch the progress of Bach's planes, which held many speed, altitude and endurance records for early passenger ships.

LOCKHEED-VEGA MEN WIN MODEL CONTEST

Lockheed and Vega cleaned up in the model airplane meet sponsored by the Southern California Gas Model Association last weekend.

Robert L. Holland, of Dept. 25, Lockheed Plant 1, had a field day. He won (using the same plane each time) the Class A event, the Northrop Trophy for longest single flight of the day; the Academy of Model Aeronautics trophy for the longest flight of an A.M.A. member; the Adel Trophy for the winning two-flight total in Class A; a $25 check from the Gas Model Association for first in Class A; and, last but not least, a $25 War Bond from Lockheed.

Fred Gillett, of Vega, was winner of second place in the Class A. event, and Ray Acord, of Lockheed Dept. 45, took third place.

Bridge Club Grows

Interest in the L.E.R.C. Bridge Club is growing, according to Glenn Wilkie, Department 2, who is coordinating the Thursday evening sessions held in the Burbank Recreation Center.

'OUT-OF-STATERS' ADVISED ON 1943 LICENSE RENEWALS

The Department of Motor Vehicles has called attention to the fact that many employees of defense plants have renewed their automobile licenses in the states in which they previously lived, and while the California Motor Vehicle Code allows a certain amount of reciprocity, this should only be interpreted to mean the time in the current year in which they made their entry into California.

Lockheed and Vega employees who are driving cars with out-of-state plates are herewith advised that upon the expiration date of their plates, they must secure California licenses if they are employed and living in this state.

Following are office hours and addresses of Motor Vehicle branch offices within this area:

LOS ANGELES—Weekdays, 9 a.m. to 5 p.m.; Saturdays, 9 a.m. to 12 noon. 3500 South Hope Street.

EAST LOS ANGELES—Hours same as L.A. Office, 5210 East Olympic Blvd.

(Continued on Page 7)

$50 REWARD FOR ONE IDEA

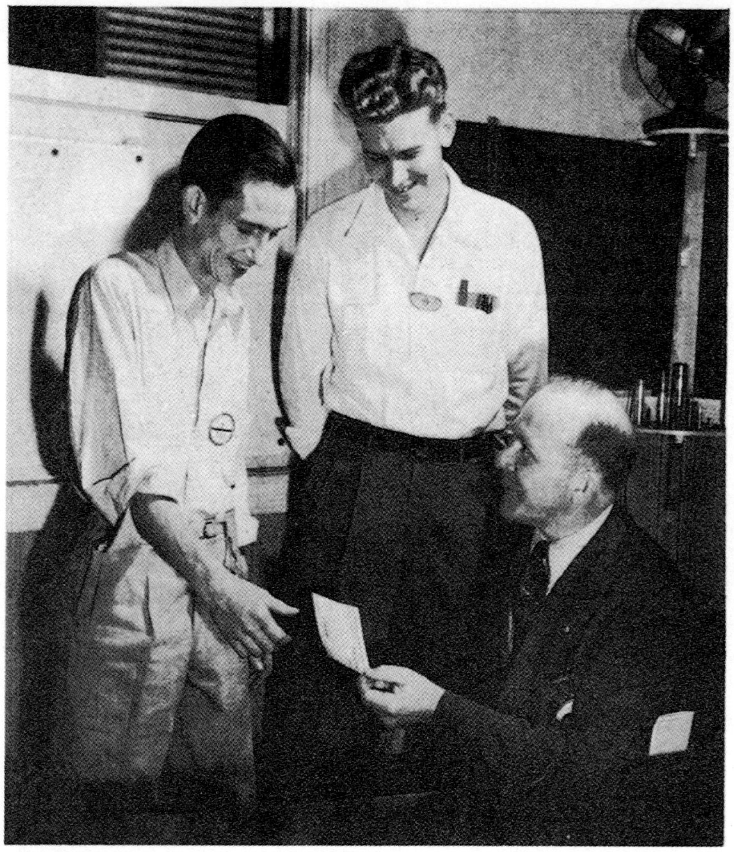

George McCreary, Department 9, Lockheed Plant 3 receives a check for $50 from L. B. Darby, Foreman of Department 9 for his suggestion and idea on the installation of a mono-rail. Steve Sinclair, supervisor of the same department (center) looks on approvingly. This is one of the many awards made through the Work Simplification Offices.

LOCKHEED 3 MAN WINS $50 CHECK

George McCreary of Lockheed Plant 3 was presented with a check for $50 recently as a reward for suggesting the installation of a mono-rail on the aft boom drill jig. This addition to the jig permits handling the assembly in and out of the jig more easily and saves valuable time, in addition to making the job safer.

The outlying Lockheed plants are doing a fine job in putting into practice the principles of Work Simplification and several awards have been made to their employees who have submitted ideas.

NOTICE TO EMPLOYEES PARTICIPATING IN THE GROUP INSURANCE PLAN

Many employees have had wage increases since September 1, 1942, which place them in a higher Group Insurance coverage bracket. This will necessitate an automatic increase in the payroll deduction amount effective December 1, 1942.

This plan was explained in the August 14 issue of the Lockheed-Vega Star. A short review of the procedure should serve to explain the increased payroll deduction many employees found on their first payroll checks in December.

The schedule of benefits and deductions is as follows:

	Classification by Basic Weekly Wage	Life Ins.	Accidental Death & Dismem. Ins.	Wkly. Acci. & Sick Bene.	Daily Hosp. Bene.	Special Hosp. Bene.	Max. Surg. Bene.	Med. Exp. Non-Surg.	Employee's Contribution Wkly.	Employee's Contribution Semi. Mthly.
B	Less than $28.00	$1000	$1000	$15.00	$5.00	$25.00	$150	$75.00	$ .74	$1.60
C	$28 but less than $34	1500	1500	20.00	5.00	25.00	150	75.00	.90	1.95
D	$34 but less than $45	2000	2000	25.00	5.00	25.00	150	75.00	1.06	2.30
E	$45 but less than $70	3000	3000	30.00	5.00	25.00	150	75.00	1.29	2.80
F	$70 but less than $95	4000	4000	30.00	5.00	25.00	150	75.00	1.43	3.10
G	$95.00 and over	5000	5000	30.00	5.00	25.00	150	75.00	1.56	3.40

The contributions shown above are the employees' costs; the company pays the balance of premium.

AUTOMATIC CHANGE IN CLASSIFICATION. When an employee's wage entitles him to a change in insurance coverage, that change will automatically become effective on the first day of March, June, September or December next following his increase in wage, provided he is actively at work on that date; otherwise on the first day of the next increase period following his return to work, provided he is actively at work on that day.

ALL INSURED EMPLOYEES WILL BE AUTOMATICALLY PLACED IN THEIR PROPER CLASSIFICATION ON THE FIRST DAY OF THE NEW QUARTER IF ACTIVELY AT WORK ON THAT DAY; OTHERWISE AS STATED ABOVE.

LOCKHEED SERVICE STAR WOMEN NAME CLUB OFFICIALS

Service Star Women of Lockheed gathered for their first regular meeting Sunday, December 6 at Sardi's in Hollywood.

Approximately one hundred women with near relatives in the armed forces of the allied nations attended. Officers elected include Eleanor Sewall (Department 43) president; Monona Campbell (Department 94-65) fist vice president in charge of membership; Gladys Egan (Department 35) second vice president in charge of service; Maurine Parnell (Department 42) third vice president in charge of entertainment; and Betty French (Department 88) secretary-treasurer. Members at large, who with the officers will comprise the Executive Committee, include Ella Blair (Department 48, Plant 2); Esther Johnston (Department 1, Plant 3) and Libby Benson (Department 8, Plant 4).

Any woman of Lockheed who has a brother, son, father or husband in the armed forces is eligible for membership.

VEGA-VENTURAS HAMMER HUNS OVER EUROPE

(Continued from Page 1)

To quote from the A.P. report:

"The Venturas were part of the second wave of the Eindhoven attack on the tube works when the German defenses were in full action and several of them were brought down, the news service said.

"But the squadrons swept in to their target at rooftop height and dropped their loads of high explosive and incendiary bombs right on the target," it added. "A very experienced pilot said he never had seen a more concentrated and effective bombing."

Specifications and performance data of the Vega Ventura are still restricted. About all that has been officially released is that it is a military version of the Lodestar, from which the rows of windows on each side of the cabin have been removed and which is designed as a medium attack bomber.

It is bigger, faster, more heavily armed and carries a bigger bomb load than the Hudson, which it resembles. Both the Ventura and the "Flying Fortress" (known at Vega as the B-17) are now rolling off the company's assembly lines and, as in the case of the P-38 and the B-17, there is no question in the minds of military aviation experts, that this latest entry in the Allies sky armada will give fully as important service as all the other famed planes which have fought and are fighting, the Axis.

LIGHTNINGS EVEN SCORE WITH REST OF GERMAN PLANES

(Continued from Page 1)

109G—and in their initial trials the score is about even," the General stated.

In the struggle to determine which side shall be supreme in the air over the Mediterranean and Europe, the Germans in North Africa "are feverishly endeavoring to build up a superiority before we can gather our strength," General Arnold continued.

"At present," he said, "it is touch and go as to who is the stronger. In some sections we are; in others they are."

He also revealed that P-38's have been in England since August, but that, "for some unaccountable reason the Germans refused to close in and fight with them. We didn't know how good the P-38 was. We knew it had been operating in the Aleutians, where it gave a good account of itself against both Zeros and other Japanese types. But in Australia we never were able to get the enemy into combat with the P-38's."

And a United Press War Department report from Washington early this week disclosed that "U.S. Army P-38 Lockheed Lightning fighters continued sweeping operations over Southern Tunisia . . . and destroyed two enemy planes. One American plane was missing."

If American planes can continue to meet the German fighters on equal terms (and he seems confident they can); General Arnold said the outcome is only a question of time, according to an A.P. dispatch Monday. Germany, he said, because of its smaller productive capacity, will have to destroy two Allied planes for every German plane lost in order to retain equality in the air.

"Our strength in the air is growing; theirs is decreasing," he said. "There is every indication we are now shooting down Japanese aircraft faster than they are building them. Mr. Churchill told you recently that we are combining with the British to do the same thing to the Germans. The Germans have a wasting air power."

Aircraft Engine Mechanics

Several new engine classes are opening at Burbank, December 14. These classes are planned to prepare the student for an "E" license, C.A.A. tests. They are:

ENGINES 1—M-W-F, 7 to 10 p.m.
ENGINES 2—M through F, 4-7 p.m.
ENGINES 1—M-W-F, 10 a.m.-1 p.m.
ENGINES 1 & 2—M through F, 8:30 a.m.-2:30 p.m.

All classes will meet in Room 525, John Burroughs Evening School, Shop Building at Grinnel Ave. and Glenoaks Blvd. in Burbank. The last class mentioned above is open to all qualified students, employed or unemployed.

SIMPLIFICATION PROPOSAL EARNS $81

A proposal submitted through Vega Work Simplification office for simplifying the wiring of the main instrument panel of the B-17 earned a reward of $81 for Jean Glazer, of Department 7. Shown in the picture as Miss Glazer received her check from M. Hoopes, sub-foreman, Department 7, are, left to right: Harry Allen, superintendent of Assembly; Mr. Hoopes, Al Jennings, general foreman of Department 10; Miss Glazer and Al Winters, group leader, Electrical Detail Assembly.

GASOLINE IS ALLOTTED TO CAR, NOT TO OWNER, COMMITTEE EXPLAINS

Gasoline, under rationing regulations of OPA, is alloted to the vehicle and not to the individual owner.

Certain specific regulations pertaining to change of residence address, change of occupational address or sale of the automobile have been made a part of the rationing program and should be complied with to avoid penalties which are included in the rationing set up.

The following instructions should be carefully noted:

Surrender of "A," "B" or "C" ration books must be made within five days from the date of sale of the automobile to which any of these books have been issued.

Change of residence or occupational address make it necessary for the holder of a "B" or "C" book to surrender them within five days.

Such books should be surrendered to the Employee Transportation Department when a new application covering the current status will be issued.

Industry now has in use the first 1,000,000-volt industrial X-ray machines for boiler-drum and pressure-vessel inspection, capable of penetrating eight inches of steel in good commercial time. The unit operates at 2½ times the maximum voltage previously available in industrial equipment and weighs only 1,500 pounds.

'OUT-OF-STATERS' ADVISED ON 1943 LICENSE RENEWALS

(Continued from Page 5)

GLENDALE—Hours same as L.A. Office, 1246 South Brand Blvd.

SANTA MONICA — Tuesdays and Wednesdays ONLY; 10 a.m. to 5:30 p.m. Board of Education Bldg., 1333 Sixth Street.

HOLLYWOOD—Hours same as L.A. Office, 6433 Homewood Ave.

Limited service at branches in Compton, Orange, Hawthorne and San Pedro.

To record a change of address on driver's license and on the automobile registration slip, employees may obtain necessary forms at the Employee Service Divisions of either Lockheed or Vega. This pertains to change of address only and the employee should bring his driver's license and white or blue registration slip with him.

FREE FIREWOOD

All Lockheed and Vega employees are urged to take advantage of the free firewood that may be had at the Lumber Salvage Yard on Empire St. just east of the new building now under construction. Just drive in and help yourself to what you need.

THE Lockheed-Vega Star **

The Lockheed-Vega Star is issued every Friday for the employees of the Lockheed Aircraft Corporation and the Vega Aircraft Corporation and is the official publication of both companies. Communications may be addressed to either the Industrial Relations Office or the Public Relations Department, Lockheed Aircraft Corporation, Burbank, California, U.S.A. Although news and cartoon contributions are welcome, circumstances make it impossible to give any promise that they will be returned to sender when not used, nor can individual acknowledgment be made.

BERT W. HOLLOWAY, Editor-in-Chief
H. L. (HAL) ROSSON, Managing Editor

Volume 9 Number 52

"Beginning the End"

Allied troops are driving the Nazis and Italians out of North Africa. The Marines are pushing the Japs out of New Guinea. American tanks and planes are helping the Russians shove back the Germans from Stalingrad.

The news has been good, but this is no time to grow over-confident. Now, when our enemies are on the defensive all over the world, is more than ever a time to remember what Britain's Prime Minister Churchill said about Allied successes:

"This is not the beginning of the end. It is the end of the beginning."

The beginning, which meant victories for the enemy and Dunkerques and Pearl Harbors for ourselves, is over.

Now with the beginning over, we can look ahead to bringing about the enemy's end. That means making a greater effort than ever, because the enemy is more desperate than ever.

This is the time to dig in for the long pull. The time to boost our production of war stuff to new levels. The time to roll out more guns, more planes, more tanks. Faster and faster.

This is no time to coast. No time for unnecessary days off. No time for showing up late. No time for "monkey-business" of any kind. No time to gripe about rationing.

The Yanks are in action now. They're burning up machines by the hundreds and tossing tons of metal at the enemy. They need everything we can send them and they need it NOW. Not tomorrow, but TODAY and EVERY DAY.

WAR RESTRICTS MAILING

Why do we send Christmas cards? Simply because it has been man's method of expressing his friendship to others during the Yuletide Season. In normal times we accept this printed message, via the mails, as a foregone conclusion. But these are not normal times; and the Postoffice Department has also felt the effects of the manpower shortage. Let's save the MAILS for the fighting MALES and express our Christmas greetings through the PERSONAL CONTACT we have with our friends throughout the year.

★ Your JOB ★

By . . . .
R. RANDALL IRWIN

New Manpower Authority Established

President Roosevelt's executive order creating a new War Manpower Commission gives to Chairman Paul V. McNutt sweeping powers "to promote the most effective mobilization and utilization of the national manpower."

How effectively Mr. McNutt will discharge his new responsibilities will depend, not only upon his ability to develop a sound operating organization, but upon the caliber of his leadership and his ability to secure the wholehearted, active participation of management and labor.

The nation's manpower problems cannot be solved in Washington. Only broad policies can be established there. The real job must be performed in Los Angeles, San Diego, San Francisco and in the several hundred other industrial and agricultural areas in the United States.

An Answer To "Shall I Enlist?"

The President's order does not answer all of the questions that are in your minds and mine. They cannot be answered all at once. However, the President has given a definite answer to the thousands of young men who have been asking, "Should I enlist now, or wait to be drafted."

The answer clearly is "No male person who has attained the eighteenth anniversary and has not attained the thirty-eighth anniversary of the day of his birth shall be inducted into the enlisted personnel of the armed forces," except through selective service.

This means that everyone must wait until he is called. Then he will have an equal opportunity with all other inductees to be considered for the branch of the service of his choice. Thus ends the bitter competition between the various branches of the armed services for the cream of America's young manhood.

Meanwhile, the young man in an essential war production activity can rest assured that Uncle Sam wants him to stay right where he is until or unless he is called.

A Big Job Ahead

There will continue to be some confusion in the manpower picture until a sound field organization is established and until the operation of the War Manpower Commission and the Selective Service System are integrated. For the time being at least, selective service will operate as a separate bureau under the War Manpower Commission, but as time goes on, the functions of the two organizations will be brought closer together.

The local Selective Service Boards, the members of which are public spirited citizens serving without pay, will continue to determine what men are to be called to the armed services, and when.

Buy Christmas Seals

Joan Wadsworth and Jean M. Parrish, Lockheed, are shown selling Christmas seals.

BUCK O' MONTH CLUB PURCHASES CHRISTMAS SEALS FOR MEMBERS

As a result of special arrangements concluded with the Combined Christmas Seal Fund, members of the Lockheed-Vega Buck-of-the-Month Club may obtain an allotment of seals at canteens at both Lockheed and Vega and at the V.E.R.C. and L.E.R.C. offices.

"We have arranged to purchase $10,000 worth of these seals in behalf of Buck of the Month Club members," Don Simmons, chairman, reports. "We feel confident that this $10,000 will serve a very worthy purpose in aiding the control of tuberculosis in the Los Angeles area."

The quartermaster sergeant was equipping a new recruit with battle dress. The trousers fitted perfectly, the tunic might have been made for him in Saville Row, the cap was just right.

"Lor' love a duck," exclaimed the sergeant, "you must be deformed."—*Trade Winds.*

THE Lockheed-Vega Star ★★

Official Publication of the Lockheed and Vega Aircraft Corporations

BURBANK, CALIFORNIA, U.S.A.

First major event on 1943's aviation calendar was the take-off of Lockheed's big, fast Constellation transport, the four-engined culmination of Lockheed's engineering research to combine high speed with long range and great cargo capacity in one airplane. Faster than a Japanese Zero fighter or any four-engined bomber now in active service, the giant new Lockheed will cross the continent non-stop in less than nine hours, fly to Honolulu in twelve. Wearing a wartime garb of Army camouflage, the Constellation, designed originally by Lockheed engineers for TWA, is the largest, fastest and most powerful land- based cargo or transport plane. It can carry 55 passengers and a crew of nine nonstop from Los Angeles to New York in record time. Powered by four 2000-horsepower Wright engines, the Constellation at cruising speed at half power is approximately 100 miles an hour faster than standard air-cargo or airline ships of today.

THREE VITAL SERVICES REPRESENTED

Pictured at the presentation of the coveted Army-Navy "E" award for efficiency at Vega Aircraft last Wednesday are, left to right: Brig. General Edwin M. Morris, representing the U.S.Army; Mrs. Naomi Dewey, representing the V.E.R.C. and all Vega employees; and Rear Admiral Joseph R. Defrees, representing the U.S. Navy.

High Officers Present 'E' Flag Award To Vega

Men and women of the Vega Aircraft Corporation took a bow Wednesday.

They paused for a brief moment during their noon lunch hour to witness a ceremony at which they and the Vega management were awarded the coveted Army-Navy "E" for efficiency, then returned briskly to the war work for which they were so honored—the work of building B-17 and PV-1 bombers.

After Rear Admiral Joseph R. Defrees had explained the significance of the "E" pennant, originated by the Navy in 1906, Brig. Gen. Edwin M. Morris, representing the Army, presented the "E" award on behalf of Robert P. Patterson, Under Secretary of War, and James V. Forrestal, Under Secretary of the Navy. Courtlandt S. Gross, President of the Company, accepted on behalf of the men and women of Vega.

(Continued on Page 3)

'CONNIE' GOES UP

Lockheed's revolutionary new transport, the "Constellation," shown as she took off from the airport on her initial test flight. It was a tense moment for observers, all of whom breathed a sigh of relief as the giant plane headed north and east for Muroc Dry Lake, flying as though she were a veteran of the airways instead of an advanced-design ship which may revolutionize air travel in the future.

Lockheed's 'Plane Of Tomorrow' Passes Initial Tests Successfully; New Sky Giant Has Amazing Qualities

TOMORROW'S TRANSPORTATION, HERE AND READY TO MEET TODAY'S MILITARY EMERGENCY BY FLYING GREAT CIRCLE COURSES ABOVE THE WEATHER IN A DIFFERENT WORLD, TO THE BATTLE FRONTS OF A GLOBAL WAR. . . .

THE HEAVIEST LOAD, FLOWN OVER THE LONGEST DISTANCE IN THE SHORTEST TIME, WITH THE GREATEST SAFETY AND AT THE LEAST COST. . . .

THE LARGEST, FASTEST AND MOST POWERFUL LAND-BASED CARGO OR TRANSPORT PLANE, IN A WARTIME GARB OF ARMY CAMOUFLAGE. . . .

This is the condensed story of the big but practical Lockheed "Constellation," newest aircraft in Lockheed's long list of record-breakers with star names which made its first successful test flight last week.

As a military cargo plane, the Constellation modernizes the time-honored recipe for winning battles: "Get there firstest with the mostest." At a top speed comparable with the cruising speed of fighter planes, it will fly a light tank and its complement of troops across an ocean. As a task-force transport it will move many men and their armament, and get there first.

Faster than the tiny Japanese Zero fighter or any four-engined bomber now in active service, the Constellation will cross the continent in less than nine hours or fly to Honolulu in twelve.

In a future peacetime role as a high-performance luxury liner of the air oceans it could carry 55 passengers and a crew of nine nonstop from Los Angeles to New York in record time—or, under today's airline procedure with frequent fueling stops, it could fly 60 passengers across the country for less than railroad rates.

Its four 2,000-horsepower Wright en-

(Continued on Page 4)

THESE MEN TOOK CONSTELLATION UP ON FIRST FLIGHT

There were five men aboard the Lockheed Constellation when it took off on its first flight:

EDDIE ALLEN, pilot. Allen was appointed by the Army because he has probably had more experience with four-engined aircraft than any pilot available. Allen was first to fly Lockheed's first twin-engined transport—the Electra. He flies for numerous companies and has been testing four-engine B-17's for Boeing.

MILO BURCHAM, co-pilot. Burcham is the Lockheed test pilot who did most of the pioneer sub-stratosphere testing of the Lockheed Lightning P-38. He has had considerable experience with four-engine aircraft and will do most of the engineering test flying of the Constellation.

C. L. (KELLY) JOHNSON, Lockheed's Chief Research Engineer—an aerodynamics expert of international standing.

RUDY THOREN, Johnson's assistant in the solving of the many aerodynamics and other engineering problems that arise during the engineering test flights of all Lockheed aircraft.

DICK STANTON, chief mechanic. Stanton, sub-foreman of the experimental flight shop section, knows every working part and control of the big ship—and how to fix it if necessary.

'CONSTELLATION' POWERED BY FOUR 2000 H.P. ENGINES

The Constellation is powered by four cyclone 18s, the world's most powerful aircraft engines in service. These air cooled radial engines, manufactured by the Wright Aeronautical Corporation of Patterson, New Jersey, are of the 2,000 horsepower series. These are 18 cylinder engines built in two banks of 9 cylinders each. They are advanced models of the 2,000 horsepower Cyclones now powering the world's largest airplanes. All models of this engine have a displacement of 3350 cubic inches. Like the Wright Cyclone 14, the Cyclone 18 has the low-weight ratio of 1.1 pounds per horsepower. This weight ratio plus low fuel consumption and high horsepower takeoff with heavy load is a factor in the long range of the Constellation.

BUY WAR BONDS AND STAMPS !

THOUSANDS WITNESS CEREMONY

Long shot of the huge crowd which witnessed presentation of the "E" award to Vega last Wednesday. Lower left: Flag-draped platform on which ceremony was performed at Vega Plant 1.

Smoking Periods Established By Lockheed-Vega

In keeping with its established policy of always maintaining ideal working conditions for its employees, the management of Lockheed and Vega has approved the inauguration of smoking and rest periods in all Lockheed and Vega plants.

Effective, Monday, January 18, two 10-minute rest periods will be given factory employees of both Day and Swing shifts. Day shift rest periods will be from 9 to 9:10 a.m. and 1:45 to 1:55 p.m. Swing shift employees will have their rest periods from 6 to 6:10 p.m. and from 10:30 to 10:40 p.m.

These rest periods will not apply to employees on Graveyard shift, but such employees will be allowed to smoke within the designated SMOKING AREAS during their regular lunch periods. Neither will the rest and smoking periods apply to departments where smoking is now permitted during regular working hours.

Clearly defined SMOKING AREAS will be established throughout all plants and under no circumstances should employees smoke elsewhere within the factory areas. These SMOKING AREAS will be plainly indicated and arrangements have been made to insure their availability in the immediate vicinity of the employee's work, making it unnecessary to race to distant areas during the

(Continued on Page 4)

THREE LOCKHEEDIANS TAKEN BY DEATH

Lockheed lost three valuable members recently when death took Robert Y. Zachary, Dept. 96-97, James F. Armstrong, Dept. 24, days, and Charles R. Chambers, Dept. 27-5.

Mr. Zachary, 50, a general accountant, died December 29, of a heart attack. He is survived by his widow, Mrs. Suzanne Zachary. Services were held at Forest Lawn Memorial Park, Glendale.

Mr. Armstrong, 63, died December 26 from natural causes. He is survived by his widow, Mrs. Johanna Mary Armstrong. Funeral services were held December 28.

Mr. Chambers, 43, died December 29 and funeral services were held January 2 at Pierce Bros. Mortuary, Hollywood. He is survived by his widow, Mrs. Mildred Chambers, and four children.

High Officers Present 'E' Flag Award To Vega

(Continued from Page 1)

Because transportation limitations made it impossible to bring men and women of Vega Plant 2 to the ceremony, the program was broadcast over Radio Station KMPC and released over the Plant 2 public address system. The broadcast also brought the program into the homes of Swing and Graveyard workers who were unable to be present.

In part, Admiral Defrees said:

"The Navy is indebted to Vega for a new, improved type of land-based sea raider of great striking power, adequate range, and defensive armament locally known as the PV-1, a Navy modification of the company's well-known Ventura, the design and production of which has been one of the highlights of American aircraft industry's record of war-time achievement.

"This plane is faster, larger, more heavily armed, carries deadlier explosive charges and possesses qualities which constitute a far greater menace to enemy submarines, warships and transports than any land-based aircraft of similar type previously built in this country. I am informed that its production is considerably ahead of schedule.

"In the United States Navy, "E" stands for Excellence. For 35 years the Navy "E" has been the goal hard-fought for by Navy men who have vied with one another for the privilege of bearing the "E" on the bridge, conning tower, funnel or turret of their ships and for the coveted honor of achieving an "E" to wear on the sleeve of their uniforms. It is the Navy's reward for work well-done and is the highest of all Naval honors. It is largely responsible for the Fleet's readiness for battle today.

General Morris was then presented and said: "Men and women of Vega: I am before you as a representative of the Under Secretary of War, the Honorable Robert P. Patterson and the Under Secretary of the Navy, the Honorable James V. Forrestal, to tell you—each and every one of you—that your country is grateful for your accomplishments here in this war plant, and each of you has every right to be proud of your production record.

"You will be called upon to make greater sacrifices (in 1943). But no matter how hard or how long you have to work, or what sacrifices in money, time

(Continued on Page 5)

THESE FOUR CONTRIBUTED GREATLY

At left are four experts in the Lockheed organization who worked ceaselessly in the production and perfecting of the great Constellation. Left to right they are: Kelly Johnson, Chief Research Engineer; Mel Maurer, Assistant Works Manager in charge of Experimental and New Developments and Coordinator of the Constellation Project; Milo Burcham, Chief Engineering Test Pilot; and M. C. Haddon, Chief Project Engineer.

THORNTON AVE. PARKING RESTRICTED

In order to make possible the movement of airplanes from Lockheed to the Air Terminal, it has been necessary for the city of Burbank to establish parking restrictions on Thornton avenue, from Hollywood Way to Buena Vista avenue.

Effective immediately therefore, all parking will be prohibited on Thornton avenue, between 6 p.m. and 6 a.m. In addition, requirements of the Vega Company and certain problems of the Army units located in this area make it necessary that parking restrictions be effective on Hollywood Way, from Empire avenue to San Fernando Road.

In view of this, Vega has requested the city of Burbank to enforce NO PARKING along Hollywood Way at all times. The company therefore asks employees to comply with these no parking requirements. Employees are warned that if cars are parked in violation of the above restrictions, the city has authority to have them towed off the streets and impose such towing charge and fines the court may impose.

Full cooperation of employees is requested, as parked cars on these streets have caused serious and costly delays.

SMOKING PERIODS FOR BOTH COMPANIES SET

(Continued from Page 3)

short rest periods for the purpose of smoking.

As in any such plan, cooperation is the keynote of success. Therefore a few simple rules pertaining to the smoking privilege within factory areas should serve to answer all questions. They are:

1. **A warning signal will be sounded at the beginning and end of each rest period.**
2. **Do not at any time smoke anywhere within the factory area unless the area is clearly defined as a SMOKING AREA.**
3. **Smoke only during the rest periods as designated above.**
4. **Use the SMOKING AREA nearest your work station.**
5. **Throw cigarette stubs in the containers placed in the SMOKING AREAS for this purpose. Do not throw them on floors.**
6. **If there is any doubt about a SMOKING AREA, ask your immediate supervisor BEFORE you smoke.**
7. **Employees must not leave factory areas during these rest periods.**

Remember that fire hazard is always increased by smoking, therefore exercise extreme caution and help prevent fires.

These smoking and rest periods are on a trial basis and their continuance depends upon the cooperation of every employee.

Lockheed's 'Plane Of Tomorrow' In Successful Tests

(Continued from Page 2)

gines, mounted in an airframe of new aerodynamic efficiency, will lift a heavy load. At cruising speed at about half power the Constellation is approximately 100 miles an hour faster than standard air-cargo or airline ships of today, while eliminating most of the time lost in fuel stops.

This unique performance is possible, with new comfort to passengers in transport duty, because the Constellation is able to cruise through thin air at 20,000 feet-above 90 per cent of all rough-air weather disturbances, and with ample reserve fuel to fly around most of the others. The pressurized cabin, heated or cooled according to climate and always air-conditioned, will maintain the air density of the 8,000-foot level, and in case of need the Constellation can rise comfortably to 35,000 feet.

Partial engine failure would have little effect upon the Constellation, for the ship will maintain a 25,000-foot altitude on three of its engines, and will fly at 16,500 feet on only two. This reliability, together with its exceptionally long range nonstop flight, will enable the Constellation to blaze new travel routes.

It will fly the Great Circle courses which bring Chicago closer to parts of Europe than is New York, or trace a shorter route from San Francisco to Singapore, or wheel across the North Pole to bridge the world more compactly than by the Equator. Its speed and range will link the three Americas into a sleeper jump; its 8,000-horsepower eagerness to carry a useful load will draw new maps of military logistics and intercontinental commerce.

Its economy is a long stride forward in airplane operation, for the Constellation is a "practical" ship. There are bigger planes, and planes which will carry more cargo, but none will "get there firstest with the mostest," especially at the Constellation's economical operating cost. Lockheed's super-transport will fly its full load, using one gallon of gasoline per mile, hour upon hour. No transport of today approaches its combination of speed, range, and useful load capacity.

"I believe this airplane is the greatest contribution to air transit yet made by Lockheed," said President Robert E. Gross. "It is designed and built to do a necessary job as well as it can be done today, happily timed for the war cargo emergency which confronts us, and for the reconstruction to follow the victory we must first win."

THE Lockheed-Vega Star ★★

Official publication of the Lockheed and Vega Aircraft Corporations

Volume 10 BURBANK, CALIFORNIA, U.S.A., FEBRUARY 19, 1943 Number 10

ON THE TRAIL OF THE WOLF-PACK—Here is the Navy's mighty new land-based patrol plane, the Vega PV-1, a nautical version of the Vega Ventura Bomber. Now in production at Vega, the PV-1 is hailed as the new scourge of the submarine and may prove to be America's answer to the No. 1 war problem of 1943—the problem of licking the enemy's wolf-pack submarine. The PV-1 carries "ash can" depth charges or torpedoes and is the first sub-buster in production to fill the Navy's needs for twin-engined, land-based aircraft with adequate range plus both defensive and offensive armament. The Ventura is bigger, faster, more heavily armed and able to pack a deadlier explosive wallop than the famous Lockheed Hudson which it closely resembles. Yet it retains all the sturdy qualities of the Hudson, known to the R.A.F. as "Old Boomerang" because of its ability to return to its base. Carrying more radio equipment than any plane Vega or Lockheed have ever built, as well as droppable gas tanks that give it a tremendous range, the PV-1 constitutes a far greater menace to enemy submarines, warships and transports than any land-based aircraft yet built in this country. It is powered by two 2000 horsepower Pratt & Whitney engines.

VEGA EARNINGS STATEMENTS TO BE DISTRIBUTED FEB. 26

Earnings statements for 1942 will be distributed to all Vega employees on February 26. The statements will be released with the paychecks from the Paymaster's office.

If the statement is not received on February 26, it may be obtained at the Paymaster's office upon identification by the employee.

Earnings for last year are computed as follows: Weekly Salary: From December 27, 1941 to and including December 25, 1942. Monthly Salary: January 1, 1942 to and including December 31, 1942.

Terminated employees may obtain statements by writing to the Paymaster. Clock number should be given to facilitate distribution.

PV-1, Mighty New Allied Air Weapon, Now 'Rolling' At Vega

SCOURGE OF THE SUBMARINE, A NEW LAND-BASED SEA RAIDER OF GREAT STRIKING POWER IS NOW IN PRODUCTION AT VEGA FOR USE BY THE UNITED STATES NAVY AGAINST ENEMY SHIPPING OF ALL KINDS, IT WAS ANNOUNCED THIS WEEK BY COURTLANDT S. GROSS, PRESIDENT.

Equipped to destroy anything flying hostile colors within its long range, particularly to strike terror among enemy submarines, Vega's first Navy warplane is a nautical version of the Ventura bomber which the company has been delivering to the Army and the British in quantity for many months. Its Navy designation is PV-1, but to the thousands of men and women who are building it and the men who fly it the plane is known as the Vega Ventura.

Unlike the British Ventura, however, the Navy ship is not primarily a bomber. Carrying either "ash can" depth charges or a standard torpedo, this seabird that nests on land can pounce upon an enemy submarine or surface craft like a gigantic albatross swooping down upon its prey.

(Continued on Page 2)

Near-Deadline Advice Given On U.S. Tax Returns

As you doubtless know, millions of Americans will, for the first time, file Federal income tax returns and pay income tax on their 1942 income this year. The tremendous cost of the war hits every pocketbook. As stated in last week's STAR, arrangements have been made to make income tax return forms available to employees who need them.

Who Must Pay

If you are single and made $500 in 1942, or if you are married and made $1200 or more last year, you must file an income tax return. Even though your credits and deductions are enough so that you have no tax to pay, this is necessary for information.

Pay-As-You-Go

Congress is considering legislation which will require employers to withhold from salary and wages most of your income tax on a current pay-as-you-go basis. The committees of Congress have said, however that this action will not affect the requirement of filing a return for 1942 income on or before March 15, 1943. You will, in all probability, then have to pay one-quarter of the tax, even though the "pay-as-you-go" plan is adopted for use thereafter.

Obtaining Proper Forms

If you have never before paid income tax, you must obtain the proper forms for your tax return. The companies have arranged for a supply of the return forms which will be available commencing Friday, February 19 at the following locations:

LOCKHEED

Plant 1, Entrance Old Service Hangar (Bldg. 146)
Cotton Shed—Distribution through Supervisory Channel
Engineer's Exit on Empire
Gate 8
Gate 7
Canteen—Between Gates 4 and 5
Gate 35
L.E.R.C.—Office counter (8 a.m. to 8:45 p.m.)
Canteen—Office counter (7 a.m. to 4:45 p.m.)
Employee Service Office
Plant 2, Employee Service Office
Plant 3, Gates 1 and 4
Plant 4, Employee Service Office
Plant 5, Gate 18
Plant 6, L.A.T.—both gates
Plant 7, Timeclock

VEGA

Plant 1, Plant Personnel Units
V.E.R.C. Booths
Gates 3 and 8
Employees Service Division
Plant 2, Personnel Office

For the assistance of employees, the companies have prepared a brief statement outlining important points with respect to Federal income tax, which will be available, together with the proper forms, at the above locations. You may also obtain the blanks by writing the Collector of Internal Revenue, Los Angeles, California, or telephoning Michigan 8111. If you made an income tax return last year, the Government mails forms to you at your known address.

Types of Forms

The Government has two types of income tax return forms for use by individuals. If your total income did not exceed $3,000 in 1942, you may use a special form, No. 1040-A. This form, known as the "optional method," has a simple table on which you can find the amount of your tax without filling in all the entries and making all the calculations necessary in the regular form. This form makes allowance for a reasonable amount of deductions and credits, but you should not use this form if you have more than an ordinary amount of deductions and credits. The regular form, No. 1040, *may* be used by *any* taxpayer, but *must* be used if your total income was more than $3,000, or if the total income of you and your wife was more than $6,000. You must also use the regular form if you received income other than wages, salary or dividends and annuity, such as income from rental property.

Preparing Your Return

The first step is to make up an accur-

(Continued on Page 7)

Survivor Of Pacific Ocean Epic To Speak Here

Lieut. James C. Whittaker, above, co-pilot of the Eddie Rickenbacker plane which met disaster in the Pacific, will be guest speaker next Monday, 11 to 11:30 a.m., in the main L.E.R.C. Recreation area at Lockheed Plant 1. Lieut. Whittaker will give some hitherto unrevealed details of the epic adventure of him and his companions, including Capt. Rickenbacker, during their 21 days adrift in life rafts on the vast expanses of the South Pacific. His talk will be broadcast throughout Plant 1 over the P.A. system. Listen for it.

PV-1, MIGHTY NEW ALLIED AIR WEAPON, 'ROLLING' AT VEGA

(Continued from Page 1)

"The Navy is expecting great things of the Ventura, as this sub-buster is the first airplane in production to fulfill their needs for twin-engined, land-based patrol aircraft with adequate range, plus both defensive and offensive armament," Mr. Gross said. "We hope that it will be the answer to America's No. 1 war problem of 1943—the problem of the wolf-pack submarine."

Bigger, faster, more heavily armed and able to pack a deadlier explosive wallop than the famous Lockheed Hudson, which it closely resembles, the Navy's new Ventura possesses qualities which constitute a far greater menace to enemy submarines, warships and transports than any land-based aircraft yet built in this country. Yet it retains all the sturdy qualities of the Hudson, known to the R.A.F. as "Old Boomerang" because of its ability to return to its base through flak and flame.

The Ventura was under military wraps for months, though it had seen action against the enemy on many fronts. Many of its features still are cloaked in wartime secrecy. About all that has been revealed even of the original British model is that it is "fiercer, farther and faster" than the Hudson.

Exact performance may not be given, but the gun-studded Ventura will fly farther than the Hudson with a heavier useful load, with a cruising speed approximating the top speed of the Hudson, and has an enlarged "bomb bay" for accommodating the depth charges and torpedoes which make it so deadly a weapon to employ against enemy ships.

In addition it carries more radio equipment than any plane Vega or Lockheed have ever built.

The Navy's Ventura is powered by two 2000 horsepower Pratt & Whitney engines and attains a remarkably high service ceiling. Droppable gas tanks, to-

(Continued on Page 6)

If You Need Supplemental Gasoline Ration, Read This

Employees whose supplemental gasoline ration books expire in March and who have not already received a renewal application blank, or did not fill out one of the questionnaire cards recently distributed, are requested to contact their Employee Transportation Office in person as soon as possible.

The Employee Transportation Department MUST have your questionnaire card on file before a renewal application for supplemental gas rationing can be sent to you; therefore, if you have not received a renewal application, contact the above office in person.

Victory Committee Elects New Officers

The regular Monday meeting of the Lockheed-Vega Employee Victory Committee was highlighted this week with election of two officers. Al Pimsner, of Vega Department 29, who is also a trustee and delegate of Lodge I. D. L. 727, I.A.M. was elected chairman, and Ray Baur, staff assistant in Vega Department 67, was re-elected secretary. Pimsner succeeds Don Simmons, president of V.E.R.C., who for the past six months has held the chairmanship.

Al Pimsner

Representatives of Lockheed, Vega, L.E.R.C., V.E.R.C., Lodge 727, I.A.M., the Vega Blue Star Service Women and the Lockheed Service Star Women's Club make up the membership of this committee and its functions consist primarily of aiding fellow employees in all phases of the war effort by following through on programs to emphasize the importance of material conservation, health and safety, morale, etc.

Under the committee's sponsorship and coordination, the employees of Lockheed and Vega were among the first to be awarded the Minute Man and Bulls-Eye Flag of the U. S. Treasury Department for their participation in the purchase of War Bonds. High praise from officials of the American Red Cross for their generous donations of blood during the Committee-sponsored Blood Donor Drives has also been earned by employees of both companies.

Ray Baur

The Employee Victory Committee has no delegated authority but acts purely as a representative body of all employees in matters pertaining to conservation, health and safety, morale, etc. through the use of posters, publicity and its recommendations to management.

Tell L.E.R.C. Of Transfer

Service Star members who have transferred since joining the group are requested to notify the L.E.R.C. office of their new location so that bulletins and other information will reach them promptly.

'On, To Victory!'

Kaye Spencer, of Lockheed Dept. 7-44, symbolizes the "Will To Win" of America.

PLEA MADE TO 'KEEP THE FLAGS FLYING'

Yes, the Minute Man Bullseye Flag you see flying underneath "Old Glory" belongs to Lockheed and Vega. We won the right to fly it last September, by our Second Front War Bond Drive, when 97 per cent of our employees pledged 10.6 per cent of their gross payroll towards the purchase of War Bonds under the Lockheed-Vega War Bond Payroll Deduction Savings Plan. We feel justly proud that Lockheed-Vega employees were the first of any major aircraft manufacturer on the Pacific Coast to win this honor and to merit Government recognition.

We may feel, because of the approach of income taxes or because of the 5 per cent Victory Tax, that we cannot afford to continue our bond payroll deductions, but can the boys fighting the Japs and the Nazis afford to stop fighting because they are tired or haven't received an increase in pay? If we cancel, aren't we breaking our faith with those who are giving more than we at home could ever possibly sacrifice? Before stopping our bond purchases, let us all take a walk and look at our Honor Roll Boards. In particular, let us pause and grasp the significance of the Gold Stars.

TEN LOCKHEED TEAMS IN HEREX TOURNEY

NEW L.E.R.C. DANCE BAND SCHEDULED FOR MARCH 6 MEET

In the first all-shift dance sponsored by the Lockheed Tooling Division, the recently established L.E.R.C. Dance Band will make its initial appearance.

"Made up of former musical stars from well known name bands, these Lockheedians have organized a top-flight musical organization," Dave Praeger, chairman of the Tooling Dance, declares, "We feel fortunate in having them make their first appearance at our party."

Included in the band membership are "Red" Farrington and "Ken" Baker, and between the hours of 9 p.m. and 5 a.m., this troupe promises to give real dancing melody for those who get in on the special 75 cent per person deal.

March 6 has been selected for the party. With the all-night feature a large turn-out from all shifts is expected.

FINAL DEADLINE FOR BAND AUDITIONS

Final deadline for auditions for those seeking feature spots with the L.E.R.C. Dance Band is Friday evening, February 26, at 4 p.m. Burbank Recreation Center, 1111 W. Olive.

Lockheedians with special talents are urged to come to the February 26th turn-out, bringing music or other properties needed for the audition.

DEPARTMENT 02 TO GIVE DANCE

Tickets for the Department 02 Dance at the Riverside Drive Breakfast Club February 28 are moving well, according to Joe Quint, who is coordinating the affair for the L.E.R.C. Art Whiting and his orchestra have been engaged and tickets may be obtained through the L.E. R.C. or from Quint and his deputies in Department 02.

CLUB SYMPHONY FEB. 21

Due to the response made in a survey on a proposed Symphony Orchestra to be sponsored by the L.E.R.C., it has been decided to launch this organization with Oliver Alberti as director.

The first meeting of the newly sponsored activity will be held Sunday, February 21. Full details of the time and place may be obtained from the L.E. R.C. office.

L.E.R.C. CALENDAR
February 19-26

Friday, February 19
Band Concert Main Recreation Area, noon.

Sunday, February 21
First meeting of Symphony Orchestra Group. Details may be obtained at L.E.R.C. Office.
Herald-Express War Industry Basketball Tourney at CYO Gym. First game scheduled for 8 a.m. with Lockheed appearances scheduled hourly.
Opening of Swing Shift Drama production "Return Engagement." Assistance League Playhouse. Curtain 2 a.m. After Saturday work.
Ranger and Rangerette Ride 8-10 a.m.

Monday, February 22
Choral Club rehearsal at 7:30 p.m., Burbank High School.
Badminton at Burbank Recreation Center, 7-10 p.m.
Band rehearsal, 7:30 p.m., John Burroughs Junior High.

Tuesday, February 23
Rifle and Pistol 7-10 p.m. Glendale High School range.

Wednesday, February 24
Boy Scouts to meet at John Muir School, Third and Cypress in Burbank at 7 p.m.

Thursday, February 25
Bridge Club meeting at Burbank Recreation Center at 7:30 p.m.
Ice-Skating at Pasadena Winter Gardens, 6-7 p.m.
Ice-Skating at Pan-Pacific regular time.
Day and Swing Shift Camera Club members to meet. Day Shift 7:30 p.m. Burbank Recreation Center and Swing Shift 1 p.m.
9-11 Swing Rangers, Rangerettes.

Friday, February 26
Band concert main recreation area. Noon.
Auditions for feature spots with L.E. R.C. Dance Band being held at 4 p.m. Burbank Recreation Center, 1111 W. Olive.

L.E.R.C. CHORAL CLUB ELECTS OFFICERS

Moving rapidly ahead in their program for the 1943 season, the L.E.R.C. Choral Club held an election of officers at the last meeting and charged these new leaders with coordinating a well rounded season of public appearances.

Those elected include Barbara O' Hanlon, president; John Harbottle, vice-president; Mary Lou Burr, secretary; and Mary May, librarian.

Meetings of the group are held Monday evenings in the Burbank High School at 7:30, and any Lockheedian or member of a Lockheed family may join the group.

Departmental Champs To Meet Squads From Other War Plants

With 10 top ranking basketball squads set for play in the Herald-Express War Industry tournament, Lockheed is given a better than average chance to cop one of the top awards in the seven-day-and-night event which opens this Sunday. The first game is scheduled for 8 a.m.

The first Lockheed game will find Department 15, Plant 4, tangling with North American at 9 a.m. and subsequent Lockheed appearances will continue almost hourly throughout the preliminary phases of the tourney.

"Tickets for the entire series, with proceeds going to relief, may be obtained through L.E.R.C. offices and representatives at outlying plants," Frank Davis, L.E.R.C. recreation director, reports.

SCHEDULE OF LOCKHEED GAMES

Sunday A.M.
9 a.m. No. 15 Plant 4 vs. No. American
10 a.m. No. 22 vs. Douglas Long Beach

SUNDAY P.M. (SWING)
2 p.m. Lockheed Plant 2 vs. Douglas El Segundo
3 p.m. Lockheed (Wednesday) vs. No. Americans R.U.
4 p.m. Lockheed Runner-up vs. North American Champs
5 p.m. Dept. No. 35 vs. Interstate Envoys

SUNDAY NIGHT
7 p.m. Dept. No. 25 vs. Douglas Santa Monica B's
8 p.m. Plant 2 (Thursday Machiners) vs. Vultee

MONDAY NIGHT
7 p.m. Plant 2 Wingbuilders Dept. 12 vs. North American

CAMERA CLUBS SET PRINT NIGHT 25TH

Both the Swing and Day Shift Camera Clubs have set a special print event for February 25 with a specialty subject . . . "Song Titles" as the assignment.

Swing members will meet at the Burbank Recreation Center at 1 p.m., and Day members will meet at the Burbank Public Library at 7:30.

This is the last salon in which prints may be entered to be eligible for judging in the Annual Salon March 28.

VEGA PLANT 1 BUS SERVICE FACILITATED

To eliminate traffic congestion and facilitate bus service from Vega Plant 1, the Employee Transportation Department has arranged special bus loading zones to become effective Monday, February 22, with the 7 a.m. outgoing busses.

Busses will no longer circle the plant before leaving for their respective rail-heads but will leave DIRECTLY from loading zones at regularly scheduled departure time.

The diagram shown here clearly designates the entire loading zone and employees using busses are requested to study it, familiarize themselves with the location of their respective bus and use exit gates accordingly.

A shuttle service will be placed in operation between the Old Bendix Building and Hollywood Way to accommodate persons working in that area when going off shift.

There will be no change in the in-coming service. Busses will continue to circle the plant as in the past.

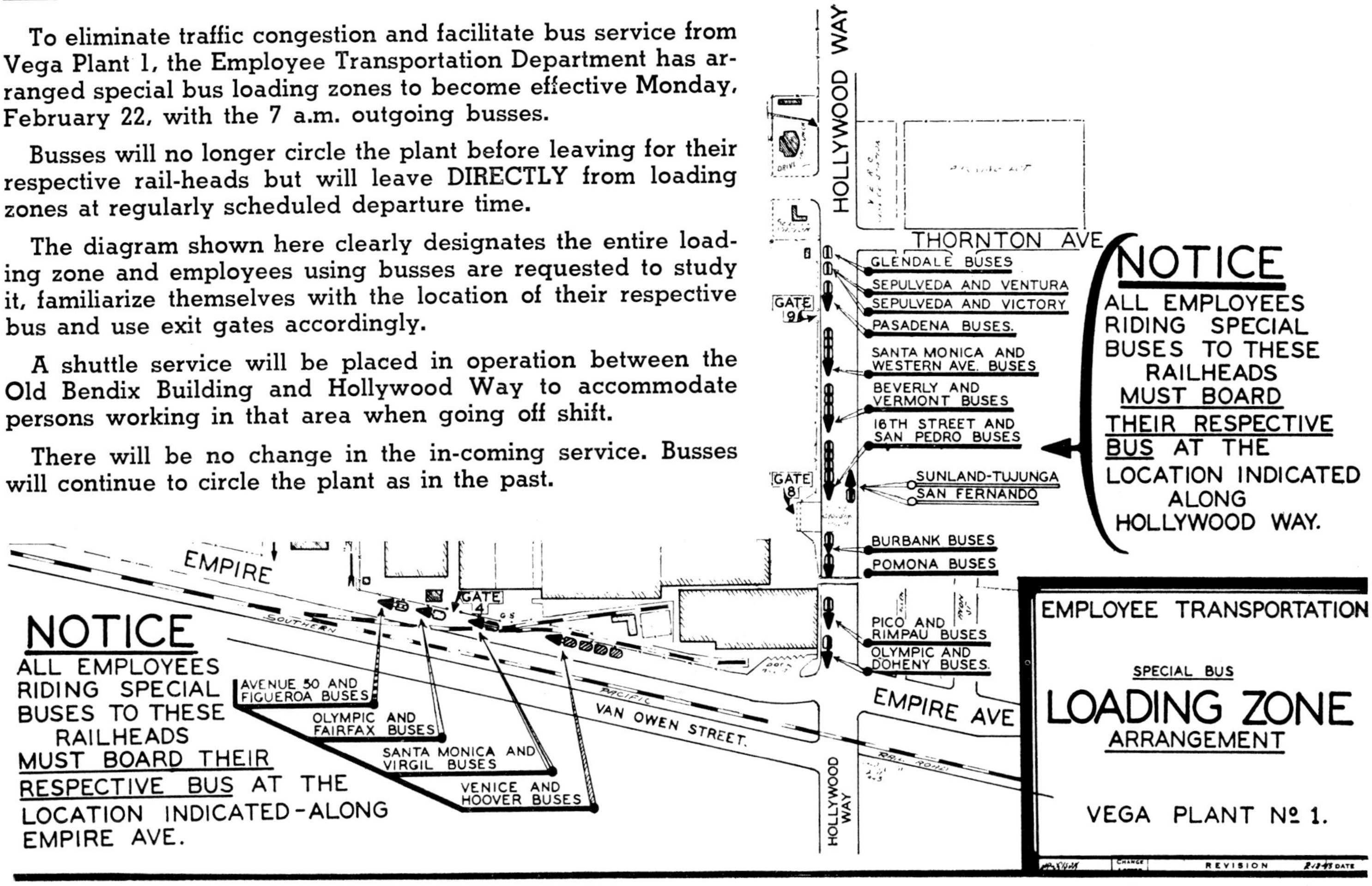

ARRANGEMENTS MADE TO REPLACE DRAFTEES' LOST DRAFT CARDS

To assist men in the 18 to 45 draft age group who may have lost or mislaid, had destroyed or stolen either or both their Classification Card (Form 57) or Registration Certificate (Form 2), Vega Plant 1 announces that duplicates may now be arranged for through its Selective Service Dept., ground floor Bldg. 62.

As previously announced, all men, except those in the 45 to 65 age group at time of registration, must now carry on their person at all times both their Classification Card and their Registration Certificate.

In order to replace lost, mislaid, destroyed or stolen draft cards, registrants must file an official affidavit. Proper forms, covering both types of draft cards, are now available and may be filled out and notarized at the Selective Service Department instead of at the draft board.

In addition, the Department will forward all affidavits to the registrants' draft boards in order that no work hours need be lost in the transaction. In turn, duplicate cards will then be mailed direct to all registrants by the draft boards.

Story Of Lockheed-Vega's Dallas Modification Base Told For First Time

Biggest of Uncle Sam's modification bases in the United States, and the first to get into operation, is the Lockheed-Vega modification center in Dallas, Texas, officials of the allied companies announced today. Modification—another word for modernization-up-to-the-minute—is one of the tricks that keep American fighting planes superior to the aircraft of all the world. "Basic" airplanes are turned out with all the speed of mass production, then put through modification to meet specific requirements of climate and combat, always on special order.

Lockheed "Lightning" P-38 fighters, the twin-tailed speed demons of world flying, are "winterized" or "summerized" for arctic or tropic regions by special treatment of oil and fuel lines. New navigational instruments are installed as they are developed or acquired. Many ships are re-camouflaged at Dallas, when an emergency change of orders sends them to a desert instead of a jungle region, or to over-the-water flying.

Vega "Ventura" bombers are fitted for several missions suggested by their great power and range. Some will operate on off-shore patrol against submarines. Others will tow the gliders which have been developed by the Army Air Forces.

Lockheed "Hudson" bombers, the "Old Boomerang," which has earned its reputation for coming home in British service even when shot half to pieces, is joining the AAF at Dallas, too. American guns are replacing British armament, new standard instruments are installed, and general modernization of older models diverted from British delivery is under way.

"Production methods would require planning and tooling for 18 months to two years, to build perhaps 300 ships for a special purpose," says Reagan C. Stunkel, general service manager for Lockheed and Vega. "We can modify the same number of basic airframes in

(Continued on Page 6)

WINS PERMANENT SAFETY TROPHY

By winning the Lockheed Safety Trophy the greatest number of times during 1942, Department 1-23, Tool Cribs, Lockheed, has gained permanent possession of this coveted symbol of outstanding safety performance. Mel Stirling, department manager, is shown accepting the trophy from Harvey Christen, assistant works manager and chairman of the Lockheed General Safety Committee, as Ed Stackhouse, assistant works manager, beams his approval of the accomplishment. Ten other Lockheed departments—Metal Fittings, Jig, Sheet Metal, Precision Assembly, Customer Service, General Stores, Misc. Sub-Assembly Plant 3, Spot Welding Assembly, Final Assembly Plant 3, and Detail Assembly Plant 2—have been awarded the trophy for one month during 1942 which signified that during that period, they had accumulated the largest number of accident-free manhours of any department in the Lockheed organization. All of these departments are to be congratulated for their part in preventing needless injuries during the past year and it should be remembered that now is the time to start winning permanent possession of the 1943 Lockheed Safety Trophy.

STORY OF LOCKHEED AND VEGA DALLAS MODIFICATION BASE

(Continued from Page 5)

a fraction of that time. It's a short-cut to modify, specialize, and modernize the ships individually."

The Dallas center was authorized about a year ago, and five days later it was operating—with men and materials flown to Texas from Burbank. Now the modification plant comprises four huge hangars at famed Love Field, an extensive shop area, and other new buildings. The Lockheed-Vega Education department has used as many as 40 classrooms in Dallas public schools for the training of unskilled labor, and about 60 per cent of the personnel now being hired are women.

Except that the Army Air Forces is practically the sole "customer," the Dallas base is essentially a link in Lockheed-Vega's worldwide Service Division, under general direction of Carl B. Squier, vice-president of both companies, which maintains and services the companies' ships in the four corners of the earth.

Don Marshall is base manager of the Dallas operation, assisted by Mark Crawford as assistant base manager; Evan Harrington, plant engineer; Pete Cavender, chief pilot; Ted Weed, factory manager; Dave Osborne, financial manager; Herb Putman, chief inspector, and Floyd Hargiss, industrial relations manager.

TIRE INSPECTION WARNING!

February 28 is the deadline for tire inspection for all motorists who hold "B" or "C" supplemental ration books. You must have your tires inspected by a duly authorized O.P.A. tire inspector before you can obtain a renewal "B" or "C" gasoline book. The tire inspection form must accompany your renewal application when it is returned to the Employee Transportation Department.

PV-1, MIGHTY NEW ALLIED AIR WEAPON, 'ROLLING' AT VEGA

(Continued from Page 2)

gether with tanks within the fuselage that are regarded as standard equipment, give the Ventura a cruising range and ability to stay in the air in search of submarines and other enemy shipping far in excess of any high-speed planes until now possessed by the Navy.

The Ventura normally carries a crew of four. It has a wing span of 65 feet 6 inches. It is heavily armed by machine guns protecting all vital points, as well as in the nose for strafing or attack purposes.

The plane will land under 80 miles an hour, a safety feature which adds greatly to its prestige among the men who fly it, and which enables it to operate off small islands in remote places where long runways are not feasible.

Under the leadership of Courtlandt S. Gross, president, and vice-presidents Mac Short and H. E. Ryker, in charge of engineering and manufacturing respectively, production on the Ventura has been one of the highlights of the American aircraft industry's record of wartime achievement. Despite the complexities of participation in the Vega-Boeing-Douglas B-17 pool, the five-year-old Vega company finished the initial British contract ahead of schedule and is now building the Ventura for the Navy and still another version of the Ventura for the Army at a pace four times what company and Army expectations had been a year ago.

This was made possible by many ingenious production shortcuts and by the smoothly flowing methods of material handling in a modern new plant that is the show window of the aircraft industry in Southern California.

COMPANIES ARRANGE FOR VOTERS REGISTRATION

The Lockheed and Vega Employee Service Divisions have made arrangements for a deputy registrar of voters to register employees living in Burbank. Registration will start on Monday, February 22, and end on Thursday, February 25, between the hours of 11 a.m. and 6 p.m. These deputy registrars will be located as follows:

Lockheed Plant 1—
Gate 8 on Victory Place
Gate 11 on Empire Boulevard
Vega Plant 1—Gate 8, North Lunch Area
Vega Plant 2—Location and time will be announced at that plant later.

Registration of Burbank residents at this time will permit voting in the April 6, 1943, general election which provides for the election of a police court judge and two city councilmen.

NEAR DEADLINE ON U.S. TAX RETURNS

(Continued from Page 2)

ate record of your 1942 income. Within a few days after this article appears, all employees will have received from the companies their copies of Form 1099, which shows the amount of wages or salary paid you by the companies in 1942. This information is required to be given by the companies to the Government and will be checked against your return. When you have determined your total 1942 income, unless you are using the "optional method," you must determine your deductions and credits and enter them on the return. This year, for the first time, no oath is required on the return, so you will not need a notary; the return is completed merely by signing it. The form may be made in duplicate so that you may keep a copy for your record.

Community Returns

In community property states, such as California, a community return *may* be made separately by husband and wife. The return should show all income received and deductions allowable by either spouse, but should report one-half of the resulting net income on the return of each spouse.

Filing And Paying

You must file your Federal income tax return with the Collector of Internal Revenue not later than March 15. You may do this by mail, or in person at one of the Collector's offices located in various cities. The law provides that you may pay all at once, in two equal installments, or in four equal installments. If a "pay-as-you-go" plan is enacted by Congress, the requirements for installments after March 15 may be changed.

The Bureau of Internal Revenue has arranged to send Deputy Collectors to our various plants primarily for the convenience of the day shifts on the following dates and locations, between 9 a.m. and 5:30 p.m.:

LOCKHEED

Plant 1, Monday through Sunday, February 22 to February 27, incl., Employees Service Office

Plant 2, Tuesday, February 23, Employees Service Office

Plant 4, Wednesday, February 24, Employees Service Office

Plant 3, Thursday, February 25, Room next to Plant Personnel Office

Plant 6, (L.A.T.) Friday, February 26, Pilot House Gate

VEGA

Plant 1, Monday through Saturday, February 22 to February 27, incl., Employees Service Office

Plant 2, Monday, February 22, Plant Personnel Office

If, after you have obtained your return and read the statement outlining important points furnished by the companies, you still have questions, please consult the Deputy Collectors at the times mentioned.

Star-Spangled Show

Marlene Dietrich

Are you listening? More particularly, are you listening to the new, more glamorous, star-studded, drama-potent "Ceiling Unlimited" broadcasts each Monday night over KNX, Los Angeles, and associated CBS stations from coast to coast?

If you aren't you've been missing something good, a very big program, a show whose excellence even radio producers are enviously discussing. The time is 8:15 p.m., Pacific war time, each Monday.

Just how good the new Lockheed and Vega radio dramas are is aptly illustrated by the fare of the past two. February 8, Ronald Colman in person was the guest star of the episode entitled "Dive Bomber." February 15, Marlene Dietrich dazzled the CBS studios when she appeared as guest star in "Bombs over Germany."

Next Monday, Washington's birthday, Lockheed and Vega have secured the services of Private Alan Ladd, U.S. Army Air Force, celebrated, before joining the army, for his spontaneous rise to stardom through the Paramount picture, "This Gun for Hire." By special arrangement, the army has given Private Ladd permission to appear on the "Ceiling Unlimited" series in "Arctic Rescue."

New Course On Planes And Parts Opens Monday

A new course in The Airplane and its Components will open on Monday, February 22, from 6:30 to 9:30 p.m. This class is of six weeks duration, meeting twice weekly in Room 102 of the John Burroughs Evening School, 1920 Clark Avenue, Burbank. Of special interest to all new aircrafters, the course is replete with slides, movies, and many other visual aids.

NEW ENGINEERING COURSES, SPONSORED BY UCLA, TO START

Engineering courses, sponsored by the War Training Division of U.C.L.A., have been scheduled as follows:

MECHANICAL PERSPECTIVE—Feb. 22, Mon. & Wed., 6:30-9:30 p.m., 15 weeks, 3700 Magnolia Blvd., Burbank.

METALS IN AIRCRAFT DESIGN—Feb. 22, Mondays, 7-9 p.m., 16 weeks, Room 101, John Muir Evening School, Burbank.

APPLIED AERODYNAMICS — Feb. 23, Tuesdays, 7-9 p.m., 18 weeks, Room 103, John Muir Evening School, Burbank.

AIRCRAFT STRUCTURAL ANALYSIS—Feb. 23, Tuesdays, 7-9 p.m., 16 weeks, Room 204, John Muir Evening School, Burbank.

DESCRIPTIVE GEOMETRY — Feb. 23, Tuesdays, 6:30-9:30 p.m., 20 weeks, 3700 Magnolia Blvd., Burbank.

THIN SHEET ANALYSIS—Feb. 23, Tuesdays, 7-9 p.m., 16 weeks, Room 102, John Muir Evening School, Burbank.

STRENTH OF MATERIALS — Feb. 24, Wednesdays, 7-9 p.m., 16 weeks, Room 101, John Muir Evening School, Burbank.

PLASTICS IN AIRCRAFT DESIGN—Feb. 24, Wednesdays, 7-9 p.m., 16 weeks, Room 102, John Muir Evening School, Burbank.

PLASTIC FORMING OF METALS FOR DESIGNERS—Feb. 24, Wednesdays, 7-9 p.m., 16 weeks, Room 204, John Muir Evening School, Burbank.

AIRCRAFT DESIGN SKETCHING—Feb. 25, Thursdays, 7-9 p.m., 16 weeks, 3700 Magnolia Blvd., Burbank.

ANALYTICAL MECHANICS — Feb. 25, Thursdays, 6:30-8:30 p.m., 16 weeks, Room 102, John Muir Evening School, Burbank.

STRESS ANALYSIS FOR DESIGNERS—Feb. 25, Thursdays, 7-9 p.m., 16 weeks, Van Nuys.

FERROUS METALLURGY FOR AIRCRAFT DESIGNERS—Mar. 1, Mondays, 6:30-8:30 p.m., 16 weeks, Room 102, John Muir Evening School, Burbank.

DESIGN FOR SERVICE AND MAINTENANCE—Mar. 2, Tuesdays, 6:30-8:30 p.m., 16 weeks, Room 202, John Muir Evening School, Burbank.

FABRICATION AND DESIGN OF MACHINED PARTS—Mar. 4, Thursdays, 7-9 p.m., 16 weeks, Room 204, John Muir Evening School, Burbank.

PRODUCTION DESIGN—Mar. 9, Tuesdays, 7-9 p.m., 16 weeks, Room 203, Room 201, John Muir Evening School, Burbank.

Call Lockheed, Ext. 3338 or Vega Ext. 1716 for further information.

Further Cooperation In Vitamin Research Requested

Employees who have been participating in the Nutritional Study conducted by Cal-Tech under the supervision of Dr. H. Borsook, and who have been notified to appear for re-examination, are asked to extend their cooperation in this work by keeping their appointments.

If appointments for the re-examinations are not kept it may be necessary to discontinue issuance of vitamins to such persons, according to a statement issued by officials of the Nutritional Study.

THE *Lockheed-Vega Star* ★★

The Lockheed-Vega Star is issued every Friday for the employees of the Lockheed Aircraft Corporation and the Vega Aircraft Corporation and is the official publication of both companies. Communications may be addressed to either the Industrial Relations Office or the Public Relations Department, Lockheed Aircraft Corporation, Burbank, California, U.S.A. Although news and cartoon contributions are welcome, circumstances make it impossible to give any promise that they will be returned to sender when not used, nor can individual acknowledgment be made.

BERT W. HOLLOWAY, Editor-in-Chief
H. L. (HAL) ROSSON, Managing Editor

Volume 10 Number 10

'Clock 96660 Speaks'

(The following tribute to our fighting men anonymous except for the Clock number "96660," was received this week by the STAR. It is printed just as it was received and needs no comment or editing.)

Well, there was Adams, a rather small man with curly black hair who loved a good scrap, played good basketball, lived to enjoy life. He was a good friend of mine. He was shot down over France. Maybe he had the wrong attitude.

Then there was Freddie, rather a long awkward kid with reddish hair and plenty of freckles. His grin spread all over his homely mug whenever he played a good joke on some one, which was frequent. Just a country boy who believed in God and his fellow men. He was a good friend of mine. He's at the bottom of the Atlantic. Didn't come back from a patrol flight. Maybe he had the wrong attitude.

Parks was a big fellow, easy going, a guy everybody liked. Father and mother on the shady side of life. Their only child. He was a good friend of mine. He won't be back from the Solomons. Maybe he had the wrong attitude.

Carl Blomgren, one of the Vega boys, a good-humored kid just past 21, entered the service and died before he could get a crack at the Axis. He was a good friend of mine. Maybe he had the wrong attitude.

There are many more, your friends and mine, all over the world sticking out their necks to save ours. Maybe they had the wrong attitude.

I'm just a punk dispatcher who is fool enough to holler my head off to anybody and everybody when I'm pushing hot parts. Every minute I save may mean the life of a friend of ours. I'll go out of my way to cooperate with anyone. I like to think that the 20 or 30 minutes extra I put in each day will help to bring back one of those fellows with whom I like to hunt and fish.

If I have the wrong attitude, thank God, I was born that way.

#96660

★ Your JOB ★

By . . . .
R. RANDALL IRWIN

NOTES FROM THE NATION'S CAPITAL

LID ON PRICES AND WAGES

Economic Stabilization Director Byrnes, so-called "Assistant President," is bearing down on the War Labor Board and the Office of Price Administration to keep a tight lid on wages and prices to halt the inflationary spiral.

AIRCRAFT WAGE CASE NEXT

Now that the WLB has the "Big Four" meat packing cases out of the way, it is directing most of its attention to Pacific Coast aircraft wage stabilization. A directive order is expected soon.

In the Packers' decision, WLB refused to grant a general wage increase. In its directive order, WLB pointed out, "The primary and controlling purpose of this stabilization is to protect the incomes of all, and particularly wage earners, against the destructive effects of uncontrolled inflation. It has become increasingly evident that the stabilization of our domestic economy, as conceived by Congress and by the President, can only be achieved by a determination to maintain present levels. This applies to both wages and prices."

IS RICKENBACKER RIGHT?

Eddie Rickenbacker's speeches have stirred up heated controversy throughout the nation. He has said, for instance, "If our soldiers knew all the facts, they would be madder than they are." On another occasion he said that if the soldiers were brought back and put in the factories, production would increase 30 to 40 per cent. Is he right?

My guess is that Rickenbacker is only partly right, and here is why. The great majority of American employees and employers in war industries are devoting themselves wholeheartedly to their jobs. The "slackers" constitute a small minority.

In the words of a Washington Post columnist, Samuel Grafton, "I think we can cure absenteeism by drawing a line between workers who are absentees and workers who are not. What does one cure by drawing a line between workers and soldiers?

And here is the answer of a Lockheed-Vega employee who wrote—

"While it is physically impossible to really do as much, we can well make the following our objective. **At least try to do as much for the boys over there as they are doing for us over here.** May I add that I really feel we are working for **them** under Lockheed supervision."

PRIZES FOR SAFETY RECORDS SECURED

Both Lockheed and Vega have again secured handsome new trophies to be awarded this year to the factory departments with the best safety records.

The trophy will be awarded monthly on the basis of employee hours worked in relation to the NUMBER OF LOST TIME INJURIES sustained in a department. So that the smaller departments can also participate in the awards, it has been decided to accumulate all consecutive, accident free, departmental employee hours worked each month in computing the winner. All departments will start from scratch on January 1 and July 1.

The trophy will become the permanent possession of the department which wins it most times during the year.

The famous White Elephant awards will be displayed each month by the factory department with the poorest safety record. This award will be based not only upon the number of lost time injuries but upon their severity as well.

The companies wish to point out that to achieve possession of the safety trophy is a distinct honor and the STAR will take pleasure in announcing each month the department to which it will be awarded.

BUCK 'O MONTH OFFERS BADGES

Lockheed and Vega members of the Buck of the Month Club may obtain March of Dimes lapel insignia to denote that they have contributed, because the Buck of the Month Club has given $7300 to this fund.

Insignia may be obtained at L.E.R.C. offices and representatives at all plants according to Voltaire Perkins, executive secretary.

Hero Of Bataan Battle Will Be Guest Speaker

Col. Henry G. Thorne, Jr., of the U.S. Army Air Forces, 4th Fighter Command, and the last man to fly a plane out of Bataan before our forces retired to Corregidor, will be a guest of the Employee Victory Committee at Lockheed Plant 1 on Wednesday, February 24 and at Vega Plant 1 on Thursday, February 25.

Col. Thorne will speak in the Recreation Areas during the lunch periods at 11 a.m. and at 11:30 a.m. His visit to the plants was arranged by the Employee Victory Committee through the courtesy of L.E.R.C. and V.E.R.C.

THE *Lockheed-Vega Star* ★ ★

Official publication of the Lockheed and Vega Aircraft Corporations

Volume 10 BURBANK, CALIFORNIA, U.S.A., MARCH 19, 1943 Number 14

1000th VENTURA COMPLETED AHEAD OF SCHEDULE

President Courtlandt S. Gross, left, receives congratulations from Capt. R. E. Farnsworth, Inspector of Naval Aircraft for the Burbank District, upon completion in record time of the 1000th Vega Ventura bomber. Mr. Gross responded on behalf of all Vega employees, every one of whom gave his fullest effort to making the record possible. Also shown above are Major Howard W. Angus, AAF Plant Representative at Vega; and Group Capt. J. A. T. Ryde, Western Headquarters Chief for the British Air Commission.

IMPORTANT NOTICE

For information on payment of the retroactive bonus, please turn to Page 2, Column 2, of this issue of the STAR.

Climaxes Production Record Which Brought Vega The Army-Navy 'E' Award

With wartime speed and secrecy, and without ceremony, the 1000th twin-engined bomber rolled from the new Vega Aircraft Corporation factory at Burbank recently and took off to fight.

Representatives of the three air services which have absorbed the thousand ships were there to see it go, and to congratulate President Courtlandt S. Gross upon a production record which recently won Vega an Army-Navy "E" award, but workers remained at their jobs and delivery of the ship was not delayed.

(Continued on Page 7)

Job Classification Order Will Be Retroactive

On March 3, 1943, the National War Labor Board, after nearly nine months of deliberation, issued a wage stabilization order for the West Coast airframe industry.

Among its several provisions this directive order contained the mandate that the manufacturers covered by the order "shall promptly" make job classifications, as provided elsewhere in the order, applicable to all employees, and, further, that employees so classified "shall immediately receive at least the minimum hourly wage rate attached to the labor grade in which the jobs are classified."

In conformance with this directive order, the company immediately undertook the task of applying those portions of the order which did not require any additional interpretation and about which there were no questions. After considering all factors, it was decided that the pay period beginning March 20 was the earliest date on which these changes could be made effective.

On March 17, 1943, we received a telegram signed by William H. Davis, Chairman of the War Labor Board, requesting us to "withhold application of the West Coast Airframe Directive until subsequent order of aircraft committee chairman." In conformance with this request we immediately stopped all preparation toward application of job classification and rate provisions of the order.

When the situation is clarified, the company will apply the job classifications and wage structure retroactively to such date as may be permitted by the Board.

DON'T SEND ORIGINALS TO STAR—COPIES ONLY

Many contributions of a widely varied nature come to the STAR each week—letters from sons overseas, family portraits, poems, clipping from home town newspapers, etc. — all of which are warmly welcomed and which would appear in the STAR if only sufficient space were available. As much of it as possible is used, but necessarily much of it is "held over" and soon loses its news value.

Wartime restricted facilities make it impossible for this publication to undertake to return any editorial contributions and it is therefore urgently requested that *originals* of the items *be not* submitted—*only copies*—so that in the event they are not used there will be no personal loss to the contributors.

War Labor Board Directive Details Adjustment Rules

The War Labor Board Directive calls for a retroactive adjustment for all employees on the payroll (whose wages come under the jurisdiction of the W.L.B.) as of July 6, 1942 and March 3, 1943. Employees eligible for the full bonus of $64.75 will be given a card along with their regular time card of March 23, 1943, on which they are to indicate the manner in which payment of this adjustment is to be made. Payment in cash or in a combination of war bonds and cash is optional, as indicated on the card. These cards must be returned to your timekeeper or deposited in your time card box not later than March 26.

Eligible employees on the payroll as of March 3, 1943, but who have a seniority date later than July 6, 1942, will be paid a bonus of $1.85 a week for each week worked through March 3, 1943. Employees whose employment began either before or after July 6, 1942, and whose entry into the Armed Forces of the United States was the immediate cause of termination, will be paid a bonus of $2.50 a week for weeks worked after July 6, 1942 through March 3, 1943.

It has not yet been clarified as to how retroactive adjustments will be made regarding employees who were transferred either from monthly to weekly salary or from weekly to monthly salary during the period from July 6, 1942 to March 3, 1943. An announcement regarding such employees will be made later.

VENTURAS SPEARHEAD FRENCH COASTAL ATTACK

Almost coincident with the launching of the 1000th Vega Ventura bomber came word from London over the weekend that Venturas in the service of the R.A.F. had spearheaded another blazing attack on the German-occupied French coast. This time the target was St. Brieuc, in Brittany, an important sector in the German coastal defenses and site of an enemy airfield. Only one of the Venturas, which were escorted by a strong cover of British Spitfires, was lost. The raid followed strong attacks on enemy shipping off the Dutch coast by RAF Typhoons.

THREE ELECTIONS IN TOP MANAGEMENT ARE ANNOUNCED

Creating a better balanced organization to meet the increased responsibilities brought on by vastly increased output, the Board of Directors of the Vega Aircraft Corporation last week announced three elections in top management.

Carl B. Squier

Carl B. Squier, Lockheed Vice-President in charge of sales and service, was elected to a Vega vice-presidency and given responsibility for the same departments. He will have charge of the worldwide "service empire" which trains mechanics and maintains Lockheed and Vega ships on duty.

Cyril Chappellet

Cyril Chappellet, also a Lockheed Vice-President, was elected a vice-president of Vega in charge of general administration, industrial relations and plant protection. At the same time he resigned his Vega office as Secretary, and Louis Wulfekuhler was elected to the vacancy.

Mr. Wulfekuhler, who holds the secretary's post at Lockheed, previously had been serving as Vega's assistant secretary under Mr. Chappellet. As Secretary of both companies, he will head the office management organizations in addition to discharging the usual duties of a corporate secretary.

Louis Wulfekuhler

All three men have been associated with the aircraft industry for many years, and are widely known throughout the world of aviation.

Second Half Of Kegler Match Set

The second half of the total pin winner-take-all V.E.R.C. match will be rolled this Sunday at the Magnolia Bowling Center in Burbank. Both matches will start at 6 p.m.

P-38's In Action Portrayed In Full-Color Page

The Lockheed P-38 is featured in the April issue of ESQUIRE in a full-page full-color painting by Alexander Leydenfrost, a black and white reproduction of which appears herewith. Each fighter pilot brings an enemy plane into his gunsight and pumps a thick stream of lead into the doomed target which falls, a mass of flaming debris, says the explanatory note accompanying the picture.

No airplane, our Army declares, can withstand the full fire-power of the Lightning. Designed as a high-altitude interceptor, to dive upon enemy bombers at their greatest heights and destroy them before they can reach their objectives, the P-38 has proved versatile beyond all expectations in the actual test of battles and has won for itself the all-around designation of "fighter."

Official communiques placed the first battle-testing area of the P-38 in the Aleutians, where they made many fighter sweeps and escorted squadrons of bombers over Kiska. On one of these escort trips, two Lightnings brought down two four-engined Japanese flying boats, according to Lt. Gen. H. H. Arnold, AAF Chief. And Lt. Col. K. H. Gibson, in command of bomber operations in Alaska, reported that a single flight of P-38's downed five Zeros and one four-engined flying boat in a single dive. Still another Army account relates that in one "plastering" of Kiska, four Zeros were shot down and an estimated 500 Japanese soldiers were killed or wounded.

News dispatches from Tunisia and from other African theaters of war mention the brilliant action of the P-38's, where they have proved their fire-power greater than the nearest German equivalent (the Me-110).

DANCES GET SPOTLIGHT FOR COMING WEEK-ENDS

Ticket sales for four Lockheed dances set for the next four weeks, indicate that attendance will be far above average, according to the L.E.R.C. office.

The Department 7 dance featuring the California Rhythm Rascals and scheduled for Saturday night, March 27, is a near sell-out. The Department 4 party, set for next Saturday night at the Blossom Room of the Hollywood-Roosevelt with Art Whiting's orchestra, is enjoying a strong ticket sale, and the Lockheed-Vega Service dance set for April 10 in the Terrace Room to the music of Matty Harmon's band is already getting department-wide endorsement.

'ESQUIRE' STARS THE LIGHTNING

Above is a black and white reproduction of the striking full color painting of the P-38 which appears, with a story in the April issue of "Esquire," now on the newsstands.

BATTLE TESTS MAKE P-38 EVEN DEADLIER

The fiery furnaces of aerial combat have forged new temper into every American fighting plane, as lessons learned on the battle fronts were applied to production lines. Every fighter in the world has been improved since Pearl Harbor, and through this swift evolution the Lockheed "Lightning" P-38 with its unique design, "like a sword mounted on two bullets," has remained the fastest, highest flying, hardest hitting and best protected of all fighters. Also it has become the most versatile.

In mass production for many months with increasing volume, the "Lightning" is now striking the Axis in North Africa, over Europe and in the Pacific as only lightning can strike. New tactics

(Continued on Page 6)

L.E.R.C. TO ELECT NEW REPRESENTATIVES

All Shift Ballots In Time Racks On Monday, March 29

Starting with the Graveyard shift March 29, the annual L.E.R.C. departmental representative election will be held for all shifts, all departments and all plants, according to Jerry Sickler, chairman of the L.E.R.C. election committee.

Twenty-three representative vacancies are to be filled and ballots for departments affected will be distributed with time cards on March 29.

Speaking on the subject of the election, Sickler cautions all voters to consider candidates in the light of the following responsibilities which representatives must assume:

Can the candidate devote sufficient time to his duties as a representative? Is the candidate able to assist in conducting the many-sided business problems which the L.E.R.C. presents? Does the candidate appreciate his responsibilities and will the candidate conscientiously serve the best interests of those he represents?

In studying the following list of candidates, weigh them against the above factors.

OFFICIAL BALLOT

Instructions to Voters: Mark candidates preferred with an "X". Vote only for candidates in your department and shift. Vote for number of candidates indicated on the card. If you wish to vote for a candidate not on the ballot write in the same. Ballots not in by the end of the swing shift will be invalid.

Dept. 101 Swing — Vote for 1
Byard Taylor (inc)....[ ]
Richard Cryer............[ ]
Jeff Williams ....[ ]
..............................[ ]

Dept. 102 All Shifts — Vote for 1
Joe Quint (inc)........[ ]
Dorothy Blake ....[ ]
..............................[ ]

Depts. 131-137-138-726-765-867-768-769-770-771-781-795-796 All Shifts — Vote for 1
Eleanor Clark ....[ ]
Kathryn Boehm........[ ]
..............................[ ]

Depts.. 107-140-158—Swing — Vote for 1
J.W. (Rocky) Williams[ ]
Juanita Smith............[ ]
..............................[ ]

Depts. 107-140-158—Graveyard — Vote for 1
Arnold Davis ....[ ]
Tommy Willemsen....[ ]
..............................[ ]

Depts. 218-220-234—All Shifts — Vote for 1
Jack Mohr (inc)......[ ]
Bill Lindenberg ....[ ]
..............................[ ]

Dept. 124—Swing Graveyard — Vote for 1
Ben Cogan................[ ]
Al Malavsky..............[ ]
..............................[ ]

Dept. 135—Swing Graveyard — Vote for 1
Larry Lappi................[ ]
Bill Moran ....[ ]
Evan Worley..............[ ]
..............................[ ]

Dept. 135 Days — Vote for 1
Bordie Deane ....[ ]
Evelyn Kinsey............[ ]
..............................[ ]

Dept. 110 Days — Vote for 1
Otto Bobo ....[ ]
Hazel King................[ ]
..............................[ ]

Dept. 110—Swing & Graveyard — Vote for 1
Edward Kisner............[ ]
Edith Yates................[ ]
Fay Brauch................[ ]
..............................[ ]

Dept. 325 All Shifts — Vote for 2
Wally Bison (inc)......[ ]
Bob O'Hanlon............[ ]
Joe McDonald............[ ]
..............................[ ]
..............................[ ]

Dept. 116 Days — Vote for 1
Howard Clark (inc)....[ ]
Harry Mannell..........[ ]
..............................[ ]

Dept. 116 Swing — Vote for 1
Fred Garrison............[ ]
..............................[ ]

L. E. R. C. CALENDAR

FRIDAY, MARCH 19—Class in Acting, 1141 North Gower, Hollywood, 7:30 p.m. —Band Rehearsal, 10 a.m. in Main Recreation Area. Concert following.
SUNDAY, MARCH 21—Rangerettes and Rangers ride, 8-10 a.m.—Symphony rehearsal, 2:30 p.m. at Renoff & Renova Studio, 6151 Wilshire Blvd.—Department 4 Dance, Blossom Room, Hotel Roosevelt, Hollywood. Dancing 8-12.
MONDAY, MARCH 22—Penguin Meeting, 7 p.m., Los Angeles Breakfast Club.—Choral Club rehearsal, 7:30 p. m., Burbank High School.
TUESDAY, MARCH 23—Class in Acting, 1141 North Gower, Hollywood, 7:30 p. m.—Badminton, 7-9:30 p.m., John Burroughs Junior High School, Parrish and Clark Sts.
WEDNESDAY, MARCH 24 — L. E. R. C. Model Club to meet at 7 p.m., Burbank Recreation Center.—Regular Boy Scout Meeting at John Muir School, Third and Cypress, 7 p.m.—Rangers & Rangerettes ride, 7-9 p.m.
THURSDAY, MARCH 25—Ice Skating, Pan-Pacific Auditorium, before 7 p.m., special rate.
FRIDAY, MARCH 26—Band rehearsal, 10 a.m., Main Recreation Area. Concert following.

CAMERA CLUBS IN ANNUAL MEETING

A last call for dinner reservations for the Annual L.E.R.C. Camera Club Dinner Salon at Gastons, March 28, has been issued by the committee.

This annual affair will this year find entries from both Day and Swing Camera Club members and judging will be done by Joe Washburn and Jimmie Doolittle, with a third judge yet to be named.

Giesler To Address Penguins

Featured speaker for the Monday, March 22, meeting of the Day Penguins will be Attorney Jerry Giesler who will address the group at their evening meeting at the Los Angeles Breakfast Club at 7 p.m.

Dept. 750 All Shifts — Vote for 1
Albin Lundahl (inc)..[ ]
Frank Benedict..........[ ]
..............................[ ]

Depts. 743-744-745-746-747-748-749—All Shifts — Vote for 1
Phyllis Bubser............[ ]
Susan Laughlin..........[ ]
Charlotte Beeson......[ ]
Delia Bria ....[ ]
..............................[ ]
..............................[ ]

Plant 2 Graveyard — Vote for 1
Gob Arnold (inc)......[ ]
Kenny Jones..............[ ]
..............................[ ]
..............................[ ]

Plant 3—Swing & Graveyard — Vote for 1
John Lauerman ....[ ]
Mary Swanson............[ ]
..............................[ ]
..............................[ ]

Plant 5 All Shifts — Vote for 1
Al Silverman (inc)....[ ]
Howard Doub............[ ]
Amber McCoy ....[ ]
..............................[ ]
..............................[ ]

Plant 6 Days — Vote for 1
Don Hayes (inc)........[ ]
Lester L. Rainwater..[ ]
..............................[ ]
..............................[ ]

Plant 6—Swing & Graveyard — Vote for 1
Bruce Frost (inc)......[ ]
Charles Kreuger........[ ]
..............................[ ]
..............................[ ]

SIX SHOOTERS RATE IN PISTOL MATCHES

In the two-night .22 caliber pistol shoots held last week at the Glendale High School range, six Lockheedians were rated awards under the N.R.A. Gallery regulations.

Hopkins rated "Expert"; Gold and Dudley, "Sharpshooter" and Jacobson, F. Hopkins and Edwards qualified as "Marksman." Scores are being sent to N.R.A. headquarters and awards will be sent winners soon.

In the rifle division of the club, Swing Shift riflemen shoot every Friday at the Burbank American Legion range and anyone interested in joining this group is advised to contact T. L. Johanson, Plant 3, for full details. Many newcomers were noted at the shoots and club officials are hoping that more will continue to turn out.

TEAMS SIGN UP FOR SOFTBALL TOURNEY

Following the first announcement of the opening of interdepartmental softball play, the L.E.R.C. office has already received a number of team line-ups.

"From present indications, it should be possible to open the interdepartmental tourney on April 15 as planned," Frank Davis, recreation director, declares. "Kay Swindler is also lining up a number of women's teams which may require a separate tourney."

All departments planning to enter teams are advised to get line-ups into the L.E.R.C. offices of their respective plants immediately.

DEPARTMENT 35 FIVE WINS TOURNEY

Going down to defeat in the final minutes of play, the Department 27, Plant 3 basketball team lost a heart-breaker to a strong Department 35 quintet in the 1942-43 L.E.R.C. Championship hoop play.

With but five men and no reserves, this Plant 3 gang really earned their way to the finals, but the sharp eyes of Morgie Morganthaler and Chet Freeze's airtight defense spelled victory for the 35 squad as they tallied their 19th straight victory.

COMPANIES REPORT RESULTS OF FIRST TEST SATISFACTORY

Completion of their first week's work in Lockheed Department 2-20, Tool Shop, found six boys from Pasadena Junior College, now working under the "four and four" plan recently inaugurated by Lockheed and Vega, taking inventory of their accomplishments.

Approximately 10 sets of form blocks had been turned out by these youngsters and according to Axel Sorensen, foreman of the department, and E. McMurray, instructor, the boys may well be proud of their work.

These lads are just six of the more than 400 who have become half-time aircraft builders. The boys attend school for four weeks, then build airplanes for four weeks. In this way, they not only help the war effort but earn regular wages for their war production work and at the same time complete their scholastic grades, it being the intention that every boy working under this "four and four" plan will receive his high school diploma.

This group of junior aircraft builders consists of Carl Berglund, Everett Herrick, Peter Nightingale, Jackie O'Gara, Elmer Pedersen and William Richards.

SERVICE DEPT. WINS FEB. SAFETY TROPHY

To Department 473, Lockheed-Vega Service (Jack Hill, factory foreman and A. N. Smith, assistant foreman at night) goes the honor of winning the Lockheed Safety Trophy and banner for the month of February. This department, with a working force of about 365 employees, built up during the months of January and February a total of more than 167,000 accident-free manhours.

Fifteen other factory departments have accumulated thousands of accident-free manhours during the same period. They are: Guards, Final Assembly at Plant 3, Tool Shop, Template, Lockheed-Vega Training, Metal Fittings, Paint and Finish, Salvage Survey, Intra-Factory Transportation, Wood Shop, Pattern, Plaster and Foundry, Fire Prevention, Heat Treat and Process, Model 49 Fuselage and Trim Shop.

The proverbial White Elephant has journeyed down Maywood way and taken up his residence, at least temporarily, in Fabrication and Assembly at Plant 4.

Cross switch your tires now and then and help the boys double-cross Hitler!

SCHOOLBOYS COMPLETE FIRST WEEK

E. McMurray, left, instructor in Lockheed Department 2-20, congratulates young Carl Berglund, Pasadena Junior College student working part time in the plant, on his aptitude in acquiring expert mechanical knowledge on finishing plane parts. Hundreds of other students from Pasadena, Burbank, North Hollywood and Verdugo Hills are working on the Lockheed-Vega "four-four" plan.

Collection of household waste fats throughout the country for the month of December, 1942, exceeded five million pounds—a new record but only about a third of the goal set in the waste fats campaign.

Parking Restrictions Again Put Into Effect

During recent weeks, while certain necessary work was being done on parking lots adjacent to Lockheed Plant 1 and Vega Plant 1, Burbank city officials cooperatively suspended street parking restrictions to permit Lockheed and Vega employees to park in the streets in the vicinity of the plants.

However, effective Monday, March 22, these restrictions will again become operative as work on the lots has now been completed and the areas are again open for use. So, to avoid parking tags, remember to put your car back in your former parking stall starting next Monday.

DRAMA CLUB PICKS A NEW DIRECTOR

Selecting Robert Lewis, former professor of Drama at Yale University as director, the L.E.R.C. Drama Club will launch a five-week class series starting Friday, March 19, and continuing Tuesday and Friday evenings until the five week series has been completed.

Mr. Lewis is currently affiliated with Fox Studios where he is an actor-director and his professional touch is expected to result in some fine productions.

Turn-outs start promptly at 7:30. Interested Lockheedians are cordially invited to take part. These sessions are held at 1141 North Gower, Hollywood.

Lessons Learned In Battle Incorporated In Lockheed P-38's

(Continued from Page 3)

and missions have been developed to match the peerless performance of the ship; deliveries to worldwide fronts have been solved by increasing its range until it can be ferried anywhere and even then the turbo-supercharged P-38 was long reserved as a new development to be hurled against the enemy in crushing force when all was ready, and not before.

This twin-engined, twin-boomed fury of the sky is rated as the most versatile of fighters partly because it is the greatest weight-carrier of all. This is due to the 2300 horsepower of its two Allison liquid-cooled engines, to its highly efficient wing, and to its amazingly clean aerodynamic lines.

On the score of versatility the Lockheed P-38 will carry bombs over medium fighting ranges. Without these loads it will climb to more than 40,000 feet and fly "well over 400 miles per hour," yet it lands at 80 miles an hour and maneuvers effectively against fighters with half the P-38's unusually heavy wing-loading. These advantages are not gained by sacrificing sturdiness, for the ship is vastly more rugged than most, and the pilot is better armored.

The value of the twin-engined fighter has been proved in action by these Lockheeds, which on one engine alone can fly with ease. This tremendous safety margin has saved many pilots, and will save more. In the Aleutians a Lightning pilot flew 150 miles back to his base with one engine shot away.

Another hidden virtue in the twin engines, rotating in opposite directions on the Lightning, is equal maneuverability to left or right with no torque effect to be overcome. Many Nazi ships have been shot down since it was learned that they could come out of a dive *only* toward the right, because of torque reaction at high speed. The Lightning has no torque reaction and will turn readily in either direction at any speed.

Fire power is another quality in which the P-38 excels. Its four big machine guns and cannon are concentrated in the nose where they can fire all-out, without being slowed down to synchronize with the propeller, and they are aimed with rifle accuracy by the pilot. Thus, the P-38 pumps a deadly column of lead, effective at any range and able to chop the wing off a Messerschmitt or saw a Zero in two.

Bombs are released with the same deadly accuracy as cannon shells, and with the same sights, for the speed of the Lightning hurls the bomb straight into its target from low altitudes—then whips the ship away from the blast. The P-38 was not designed for bombing originally, but its willingness to lift thousands of pounds with slight loss of speed has pressed it into service on this unexpected assignment.

CHAS. BOYER STARS 'CEILING UNLIMITED'

"Ceiling Unlimited," the Lockheed and Vega weekly radio program over CBS stations from coast to coast, soars to a new high next Monday, March 22,

CHARLES BOYER

when Charles Boyer, Filmdom's "big moment," appears as guest star.

Long a favorite among women with his quiet yet forceful interpretations of French-American roles, Boyer plays the part of Brazil's great aviator and aviation pioneer, Alberto Santos-Dumont.

That all American flying accomplishments are not traceable direct to the United States will be proved in next Monday's drama. Santos-Dumont, a daredevil but scientific type of flyer, is regarded in his native Brazil in the light of national hero.

Ideally cast for the part, with his friendly foreign accent, Boyer doubtless will create a rush to loud speakers when the program opens with Announcer Patrick McGeehan calling:

"Ceiling———Unlimited!"

The program is heard locally over KNX at 8:15 p.m.

A new sterling silver P-38 brooch at $2.35 is now available at the L.E.R.C. Canteens and a limited number of the popular P-38 lapel pins at $1.25.

STATE OFFERS AID IN FILING INCOME TAX RETURNS FOR '42

Similar to the Federal law, the California Personal Income Tax Act requires returns if—as a married person or head of a family—you have received income of $2,500 or more—or, as a single person or married, but not living with husband or wife—you have received income of $1,000 or more.

During the week of March 22 to 27, inclusive, representatives of the Franchise Tax Commissioner's office will be stationed at the following locations, on the days and hours indicated, for the purpose of assisting Lockheed-Vega employees in the preparation and filing of returns. In addition, appropriate explanation forms, prepared by the Lockheed-Vega Tax Division, will be made available.

LOCKHEED

Plant 1—Monday through Saturday, March 22-27 8:30 a.m.-5 p.m., Employee Service Office
Plant 2—Friday and Saturday, March 26-27 8:30 a.m.-5 p.m., Employee Service Office
Plant 3—Wednesday and Thursday, March 24-25 8:30 a.m.-5 p.m., Room next to Plant Personnel Office
Plant 4—Friday and Saturday, March 26-27 8:30 a.m.-5 p.m., Employee Service Office
Plant 6—Monday and Tuesday, March 22-23 8:30 a.m.-5 p.m., Pilot House Gate

VEGA

Plant 1—Monday through Saturday, March 22-27 8:30 a.m.-5 p.m., Employee Service Office
Plant 2—Monday and Tuesday, March 22-23 8:30 a.m.-5 p.m., Plant Personnel Office

These returns will be due not later than April 15, 1943.

State Form 540-B, similar to the yellow short form (Federal) will be provided, which can be used in reporting earnings up to $5,000 for each individual, and will be found not only easy to prepare but also a means of saving tax, if your allowable deductions do not exceed 6% of gross income. A supply of these forms, in addition to Forms 540 and 540-A, will be available Monday, March 22, at the following locations:

LOCKHEED

Plant 1—Entrance Old Service Hangar (Bldg. 146)
Cotton Shed—Distribution through Supervisory Channel
Engineer's Exit on Empire
Gate 8
Gate 7
Canteen—Between Gates 4 and 5
Gate 35
L.E.R.C.—Office counter, 8 a.m.-8:45 p.m
Canteen—Office counter, 7 a.m.-4:45 p.m.
Employee Service Office
Plant 2—Employee Service Office
Plant 3—Gates 1 and 4
Plant 4—Employee Service Office
Plant 5—Gate 18
Plant 6—L.A.T.—both gates
Plant 7—Timeclock

VEGA

Plant 1—Plant Personnel Units
V.E.R.C. Booths
Gates 3 and 8
Employees Service Division
Plant 2—Personnel Office

Special Skating Rates

Through arrangements concluded between the L.E.R.C. and the management of the Pan-Pacific Auditorium, special ice skating rates are available.

FORMER LOCKHEED DEPT. 23 MAN TELLS OF SEA ADVENTURES

Revealing the type of adventure that many former Lockheed and Vega men are now experiencing in the armed services throughout the world, and also containing an interesting eye-witness account of just one such adventure in which a Hudson played a leading part, comes the following letter from Bob Harmon, formerly of Lockheed Dept. 23, Plant 3.

Addressed to his friends in the department and the companies, Harmon says:

"After 10 months of service and some 35,000 miles in combat zones outside the United States, I'm inclined to think back to my days at Lockheed as the 'good old days.' It takes days like these to bring back days like those.

"I'm on a Coast Guard manned, Navy Operated P.C. boat and we're salty deep water sailors—and how. We've seen a fair share of death and destruction at point blank range (as the newspapers put it). We haven't seen any subs, but we've certainly tried our best to make those which came our way difficult for anyone else to see—ever again.

"Not long ago we helped polish off a Schickelgruber sub some 300 miles off the mouth of the .... river, when lo! and behold! a Lockheed Hudson bomber hove into view. It barely cleared our crows nest and in passing dropped a message streamer. The message directed us to a boatload of survivors some 40 miles south by west—and as always Lockheed led the way. We made it—and in time.

"Regards to all the folks I knew. (Wish some of them would write.) We all need the Lockheeds, keep 'em flying, and we'll keep the subs sinking. Yours,

"BOB HARMON
(Ex-Lockheed Dept. 23, Plant 3)
Gunners Mate, USS PC 469
c/o Fleet Postmaster, New York."

1000th VENTURA COMPLETED AHEAD OF SCHEDULE

(Continued from Page 1)

These big, fast Vega Ventura bombers are fighting for the Royal Air Force and the Army Air Forces of the United States over many fronts, and another version of the same basic airplane is in mass production for the U.S. Navy as the PV-1.

Representing the three fighting services were Group Captain J. A. T. Ryde, Western Headquarters Chief for the British Air Commission; Captain R. E. Farnsworth, Inspector of Naval Aircraft for the Burbank district; and Major Howard W. Angus, AAF Plant Representative at Vega.

In addition to producing the Ventura at a record-breaking pace, Vega remains well ahead of its schedule in building B-17 bombers under the Boeing-Vega-Douglas pool.

WRIGHT EXPERTS INSPECT HANDIWORK

Officials of the Wright Aeronautical Corp., visited Lockheed and Vega last week on a tour of inspection of their installations. Here the visitors are examining one of their famous Wright radial engines, which have made aviation history. Left to right: Paul Briggs, Manager of Lockheed-Vega Customer Service Division; W. D. Kennedy, Wright Aeronautical Corp. Vice-President in Charge of Sales and Service, of Paterson, N.J.; R. E. Johnson, Chief Field Engineer for Wright; and T. F. Bergman, West Coast Representative of the Paterson, N.J., corporation.

BURBANK DRAFT BOARD VEGA GUESTS

In order to learn at first hand the problems encountered in the mass production of warplanes, Selective Service Board No. 180, Burbank, believed to be California's largest draft board, was the guest of Vega Plant 1 last week.

Members of the Board who visited Vega included Frank C. Mattison, chairman; Lew Fink, Roby Green; Mrs. Ann Creel, chief clerk; Miss Martha W. Shaw, assistant; and Miss Land from Capt. H. A. Raider's office, coordinator for the district. They were taken on their first tour of the Vega plant by H. A. Andrews, supervisor of Vega Selective Service—Dept. 53.

After the tour, which took in all phases of manufacture, from engineering through B-17 final assembly, the entire board enjoyed a luncheon in the Terminal Sky Room, arranged for them by Ralph B. Smith, Vega personnel director.

Mr. Mattison expressed the feelings of his group when he stated that the trip through the plant had been not only a wonderful experience but one that had proved extremely instructive and educational as well.

BUY WAR STAMPS AND BONDS!

Seek Softball Umpires

In order to provide suitable officials for the forthcoming softball tourney, Frank Davis of the L.E.R.C. has issued a call for experienced officials from all shifts. Register at L.E.R.C. giving name, department, shift, extension number and home phone.

ALL OF NAVY MAN'S FAMILY WORKING AT VEGA PLANT ONE

Luman E. Haynes, F2/c of the United States Naval Reserve, has a family all of whom are working at Vega Plant 1. His father is in Dept. 8, Hydro Swing; his mother is in Dept. 1, Swing; his wife is in Dept. 13, Day Shift; and his sister is in Dept. 19, Days.

Recently, in a letter received by his parents, he gave a typical service man's description (in verse) of what he may write under Army and Navy regulations. Because it applies to every man in the armed services, it is reproduced herewith:

Hello everybody
Can't write a thing,
The censor's to blame,
Just to say I am well,
And sign my name.
Can't tell where we leave from
Can't mention the date
Can't even mention the meals that we ate
Can't say where I am going
Don't know where I'll land
Couldn't inform you
If I was met by a band,
Can't mention the weather
Can't tell if there's rain,
All military secrets
Must secret remain,
Can't have a flashlight
To guide me at night
Can't smoke a cigaret
Unless out of sight
For such is sin,
Can't keep the envelopes
Your letters come in
Can't say for sure
Just what I can write,
So I'll close this letter
And close with good night.

THE Lockheed-Vega Star

The Lockheed-Vega Star is issued every Friday for the employees of the Lockheed Aircraft Corporation and the Vega Aircraft Corporation and is the official publication of both companies. Communications may be addressed to either the Industrial Relations Office or the Public Relations Department, Lockheed Aircraft Corporation, Burbank, California, U.S.A. Although news and cartoon contributions are welcome, circumstances make it impossible to give any promise that they will be returned to sender when not used, nor can individual acknowledgment be made.

BERT W. HOLLOWAY, Editor-in-Chief
H. L. (HAL) ROSSON, Managing Editor

Volume 10 Number 14

Navy Day On Maui

Recently a letter from a sailor to his Mom revealing the spirit actuating the people of Hawaii, those closest to the Jap peril, came to the attention of the Treasury Department. Because it so clearly illustrates the spirit which must animate us all, we reprint it. Here it is:

"Dear Mom, Dad, Al and Kay:

"Day before yesterday was Navy Day. Fortunately I had a chance to take part in it, and believe me it was one of the most impressive things I have ever seen. It wasn't the displays that made the show but instead a few thousand people buying bonds. I only wish they could have taken moving pictures of the show and then could have sent it back to the States, so the people back there could really see true Americans in action. Folks, could you imagine about half the people in Marin County (Calif.) getting together and buying $160,000 worth of bonds in one day? Well, that's the way they celebrated Navy Day on Maui. Everybody dug way down into their socks and pulled every last cent to buy as many bonds as they could. They hadn't saved up especially for this one day. It was all spontaneous and above their regular buying. Many of them apologized for not being able to buy more

"You should have heard the comment though, yesterday and today. They all say 'It's too bad it couldn't have gone another day to take care of all the buyers.' Frankly, I don't see how there could have been anybody left to buy. If everybody in the States was like the people out here, we could really cut a lot of time out of this war. Out here they work until they are about ready to drop, and instead of complaining they turn right around and make a showing as they did on Navy Day. Maybe that explains some of my true feelings toward this Island. You have to forget race and color when you see such things as above.

"I was planning to send you a paper telling all about it, but they didn't print half the story. Guess they are too busy to spend any time bragging about their accomplishments.

"Loads of love. (Sgd.) STEVE"

NOTED INVENTOR HONORED GUEST

Dr. Moss (center), General Electric scientist and "father" of the Turbo-Supercharger, shown inspecting the latest development of his invention. With him, left to right, are: R. G. Standerwick, chief engineer, Supercharger Division, G.E., Lynn, Mass.; R. E. Johnson, chief engineer, Aviation Division, G.E., Los Angeles; E. S. Thompson, manager, Aviation Division, G.E., Los Angeles; Dr. Sanford A. Moss; Lon Storey, Jr., Lockheed Engineering; and H. Wayne Allen, G.E. district manager. Dr. Moss of General Electric Corp., was a visitor to the Lockheed and Vega plants last weekend.

★ Your JOB ★

By . . . .
R. RANDALL IRWIN

WHAT? ABSENTEEISM AGAIN!

I am sure you are tired of reading about absenteeism. I am. But as long as criticisms continue to bombard war production employees, we had better face the problem squarely and do something about it.

The first step toward solving the problem is to get the facts. The second is to see that the facts are made known to the public and to Government officials.

This week I had an opportunity to help put the record straight with two Government groups.

On Monday I conferred with the Aircraft Production Board, consisting of Generals Knudson and Echols of the Army, Admiral Davison of the Navy, and Charles E. Wilson and T. P. Wright of the War Production Board.

On Tuesday I appeared before the House Labor Committee, of which Congresswoman Mary J. Norton is chairman. They all showed a keen and sympathetic interest in the problems faced by aircraft employees in their efforts to maintain good attendance records.

Why Workers Are Absent

The facts, boiled down, are these:

To date, materials and equipment shortages, not absenteeism, have been the most important factors retarding production. However, if allowed to grow, it is true that absenteeism WILL seriously retard production.

The great majority of aircraft employees have excellent attendance records. A minority contributes most of the absenteeism.

Criticism of war workers and legislation aimed to penalize them will not answer the problem. Efforts should be concentrated on correcting the primary causes. The principal causes are:

1. Personal illness (including fatigue).
2. Illness or death in the family.
3. Necessary personal business and domestic responsibilities, including shopping, child care.
4. Inadequate transportation and housing, or failure of transportation facilities.
5. Temporary lack of work (such as due to material shortages).
6. Lack of full appreciation of importance of each individual's job to the over-all war effort.

These conditions can only be improved by a coordinated program, in which management, labor, the community and the Government all work together in a united effort. Disunity and criticism will only complicate the problem.

STATEMENT BARES HUGE PRODUCTION GAIN

Volume 10 BURBANK, CALIFORNIA, U.S.A., APRIL 2, 1943 Number 16

THE Lockheed-Vega Star ★ ★

Official publication of the Lockheed and Vega Aircraft Corporations

CEREMONY MARKS BUCK-O-MONTH GIFT

The Lockheed-Vega Employees' Buck of the Month Club celebrated its first anniversary this week with a gift of $60,000 to the American Red Cross. The ceremony marking the event, held at Lockheed Plant 1, was highlighted by the presence of Bob Hope, celebrated radio and screen star who volunteered his services, a Marine Corps and a Naval hero and company and Red Cross executives. Left to right above are: R. Randall Irwin, director of Industrial Relations, Lockheed and Vega; Cyril Chappellet, vice-president, Lockheed and Vega; Paul K. Yost, chairman of the Los Angeles County Red Cross drive; Nurse Doris Hornbecker; Bob Hope; Sergeant Joseph Royal, U.S. Marine Corps, who took part in three Commando raids in the Marshall Islands; Chief Aviation Machinists Mate E. N. Silver, who was aboard the U.S. Aircraft Carrier Hornet when she was sunk; and Nurse Betty Barker.

APRIL FOR ATTENDANCE

There are no plants in the world which produce more critical war material than Lockheed and Vega. Reports from the front depict, more vividly every day, the vital parts played by our P-38s, B-17s, PV-1s, A-29s, and transports.

We have willingly shouldered a tremendous responsibility. The Army and Navy want more and more of our ships. We have promised to provide them, and we WILL provide them. It will be a tough job, and personal sacrifices will be necessary. This has become a personal war for all of us.

The men and women of Lockheed and Vega have been doing their part—and doing it well. Thirty per cent of us ARE NEVER ABSENT. A larger percentage are only rarely reported "missing from the production front."

All of us are here because the companies believe that each one of us can—and WILL—carry our shares of the war. We all have difficulties, and disappointments. We have had interruptions due to manufacturing changes, material shortages, and other obstacles. We will have more of them. Superior ships are the result of constant design changes.

But every one of us is needed every day, subject to the normal absentee rate of about 3 per cent, for illnesses or other compelling reasons. Our rate is a little higher than that—not dangerously high, but higher than needful.

So April is for Attendance. Let's bring that rate down. Watch your departmental bulletin board, and see how you compare with other departments. Attendance is everybody's problem. Answer it for yourself, and it's answered for your country. Please—April is for Attendance!

Pres. Robt. E. Gross Issues Eleventh Annual Report

Robert E. Gross, president of Lockheed Aircraft Corporation, this week rendered his eleventh Annual Report to the stockholders on the operations of the Corporation and its wholly owned subsidiaries, Vega Aircraft Corporation, Lockheed Air Terminal, Inc., and Lockheed Overseas Corporation, Inc., for the year 1942.

The report revealed that the total production of $491,160,470 REPRESENTED A THREE-FOLD INCREASE OVER 1941 AND WAS APPROXIMATELY ELEVEN TIMES THAT OF 1940.

In pointing out that such a record could not have been made without the whole-hearted cooperation of all Lockheed and Vega people, Mr. Gross added: "In expressing grateful appreciation to employees, to stockholders, and to the public for the loyalty and understanding that they have received from all, your companies continue their pledge to do all that they can to perform faithfully and well the tasks assigned to them."

The report to stockholders explained that certain Congressional legislation of the last year provided that certain Government contracts must be renegotiated and that since this renegotiation had not been completed the figures on net earnings could not be regarded as final.

It was further pointed out that the company had offered to reduce prices by approximately $31,000,000 on work done in 1942 in the renegotiating proceedings and had made provision for paying this amount back to the Government in their financial statement, but that this offer had not been accepted as yet by the Government.

After reflecting this offer and after providing for reserves for contingencies and post-war adjustments, the net earnings of the company and its subsidiaries for the year 1942 amounted to $8,163,721. This represented $7.59 per share on the outstanding stock of the company compared to net earnings of $7,416,536 after reserves, or $6.89 per share for the previous year 1941.

It was pointed out that 1942 dividends paid to stockholders amounted to $2 per share, the balance of the net earnings of the company having been retained in surplus for future needs.

The net income earned was at the rate of 1.66 per cent on sales for 1942 compared to 4.65 per cent for 1941.

Total taxes paid or accrued during the year were $60,159,428, compared with $25,007,089 in the previous year.

(Continued on Page 6)

BUCK O' MONTH IN FIRST ANNIVERSARY GIFT TO RED CROSS

Marking its first anniversary with a two appearance double-header ceremony, at which $60,000 was presented to the Red Cross, the Lockheed-Vega Employees' Buck-of-the-Month Club closed the year with $421,000 voluntarily contributed to this giant employee charity organization.

Of this amount $373,000 has been voted to 53 worthy charities.

A complete break-down of monies collected and voted to charities follows:

BUCK OF THE MONTH CLUB
As of March 31, 1943

Contributions		
Lockheed Employees	$283,656	
Vega Employees	134,811	
Triplett & Barton	812	
L.E.R.C. Employees	224	
V.E.R.C. Employees	250	
Publication Employees	217	
Miscellaneous	1,411	
British Reassembly Division	359	$421,742
Disbursements		
Refunds	66	
Bonding	720	
Miscellaneous (Check Book)	2	
Infantile Paralysis	10,759	
Iron Lung	500	
United China Relief	5,000	
Poppy Day	1,000	
Red Cross	81,787	
Canteen Service to Soldiers in Burbank	300	
United Service Organizations	34,351	
Veterans of Foreign Wars	150	
Canteen Service	1,200	
Bus Tickets for Soldiers	950	
Naval Aid Auxiliary	4,000	
Navy Relief Society	10,000	
All Service Recreation Center	1,200	
Gideon Testament Ministry	1,500	
Queen Wilhemina Fund	2,000	
Travelers Aid Society	1,600	
Army (Canteen Credit)	6,000	
Navy (Canteen Credit)	6,000	
Army Emergency Relief	15,000	
British War Relief	5,000	
Marine Corps (Canteen Credit)	6,000	
Russian War Relief	5,000	
Service Men Recreation Fund	550	
Community Chest (L.A. and 15 other branches)	60,001	
American Social Hygiene Asso.	500	
Christmas Cigarettes—former Employees in Service	6,783	
Salvation Army	10,100	
American Women's Vol. Serv., Inc.	1,150	
L.A. County Tuberculosis Asso.	10,000	
Christmas Week Theater Tickets to Soldiers	350	
Valley Civilian Defense	1,000	
American Soc. for Control of Cancer	1,000	
Air Raid Ground Observer Vols.	500	
Disabled American Veterans	1,500	
Citizens Com. Army & Navy	1,000	
Hazel Hurst Foundation for Blind	5,000	
Children's Hospital Society	10,000	
Nursery School for Blind Children	2,500	
Crescenta Val. Wel. & War Fund	250	
Inter. War Prisoners Aid Com.	5,000	
Vega Blue Star Service Women	150	
Children's Home Society	5,000	
United Nations War Relief	35,000	
Service Star Women of Lockheed	386	
L.A. Orthopaedic Foundation	10,000	
Conval. Home for Crippled Children	1,000	
Children's Hearing & Speech Clinic	200	
L.A. Tuberculosis Sanitorium	550	
John Tracy Clinic	300	
Braille Institute for Blind	1,000	
Florence Crittenton Home	1,000	
San Fernando Valley Y.M.C.A.	1,000	
Native Sons & Daughters Homeless Children	1,000	
TOTAL		$373,558
March 31	*Balance	48,183

*A balance of $40,000 to be maintained at all times by the Club as an emergency fund to be used in case of a civilian war disaster.

PRESTON FOSTER ON "CEILING UNLIMITED"

PRESTON FOSTER

When Preston Foster takes over the starring role in Lockheed and Vega's "Ceiling Unlimited" broadcast April 5, coast-to-coast listeners over CBS networks will hear a timely presentation, "Tribute to Test Pilots."

Account will be made for the heroism of "testers" such as Ed Allen, who lost his life not so long ago when his ship dived into a packing plant at Seattle; Jimmie Mattern, of Lockheed and Vega, and many others who have distinguished themselves for daring and bravery. The story should help increase the already established respect and admiration for men who are not serving for fame and their names in headlines, but for freedom.

Foster's personal enthusiasm for the test pilots promises to add zest to what is expected to be an exciting performance over "Ceiling Unlimited" this week.

The program emanates from KNX at 8:15 p.m. (PWT), Monday evenings.

SUGGESTION OFFERED ON TRANSPORT SERVICE

To expedite the service rendered by the Employee Transportation Department in connection with rationing transactions, employees are advised to take their application forms to the department in person. Do not send them in the mail.

In this way, considerable time will be saved, as the application can be checked while you are at the office and thus eliminate the necessity of having to make a second trip.

SITE FOR NEW UNIT GIFT OF LOCKHEED

Sisters of Charity of the House of Providence, on the Centenary Anniversary of their foundation, this week laid the cornerstone of their new St. Joseph Hospital in Burbank. The Most Reverend John J. Cantwell, Archbishop of Los Angeles, delivered the blessings.

St. Joseph, now under construction at 501 South Buena Vista street, Burbank, will accommodate 100 patients. It is the newest of 47 hospitals, 89 schools and orphanages, and 34 homes and asylums established by the House of Providence since it was established in Montreal, Canada, March 25, 1843.

The Federal Works Agency allocated $230,000 toward the cost of the building, on property donated by the Lockheed Aircraft Corporation.

Other speakers at the ceremony included Mayor Walter R. Hinton of Burbank, and the Hon. Joseph Scott, K.C.S.G. A. L. Whitten, who is a staff assistant in Dept. 10, has been appointed chairman of the hospital board. Mr. Whitten has spent much time on this project.

INSTRUCTIONS FOR REPORTING ABSENCES

Starting Monday, April 5, employees who find it necessary to be absent from work should so inform THEIR DEPARTMENT directly by telephone at the earliest possible moment. The central call-in desks are being eliminated at both companies and the extension number to call when reporting your absence will be posted on the bulletin board in your department. Here are the principal questions you will be asked when you call your department:

1. **What is your name, clock number and shift?**
2. **What is your address and telephone number?**
3. **What is the reason for absence?**
4. **How long have you been absent?**
5. **If hospitalized, what hospital, and name of attending physician?**
6. **When do you expect to return to work?**

PLEASE REMEMBER TO ASK FOR YOUR OWN DEPARTMENT WHEN CALLING IN—NOT THE CALL-IN OR ABSENTEE DESK.

If at any time you know in advance that you must be absent from work, please notify your immediate superior prior to the expected absence.

When you return following an absence and before you actually resume work, report to your immediate supervisor. This will serve as his notice that you are back on the job. You will then be requested to fill out an absence interview form which in turn will be sent to the Attendance Division.

Adjustments In Wage Rates Being Made Rapidly

On March 27, 1943, the weekly payroll factory occupations were changed over to the new War Labor Board occupations, and each employee was automatically brought up to the minimum basic hourly rate of his new occupational grade, unless he was already at or above this amount. Errors which inevitably occurred from improper classification or other reasons are being adjusted as quickly as possible.

Attention is called to the fact that adjustments above the minimum rate to place each factory employee in his proper position in the new rate range (in-grade adjustments) still remain to be made. IT IS INEVITABLE THAT MALADJUSTMENTS OR INEQUALITIES IN INDIVIDUAL RATES WILL BE APPARENT UNTIL THESE ADJUSTMENTS HAVE BEEN COMPLETED. However, application of this portion of the WLB directive has been withheld at Lockheed and Vega at the request of the West Coast Aircraft Committee. The Lockheed-Vega companies and Lodge 727 are attempting to dispose of this question as expeditiously as possible. At a Senior Labor Relations Committee meeting held Friday, March 26, the companies and the Union agreed on a method of making these in-grade adjustments, and this proposal has been submitted to the West Coast Aircraft Committee for approval. An announcement of the means of making these adjustments will be made as soon as an agreement is reached by all interested parties.

All weekly payroll technical and office occupations (non-productive) which come under the jurisdiction of the War Labor Board were changed over to the new job codings on March 27. However, in accordance with the WLB directive of March 3, 1943, the titles and rates for the technical and office occupations will remain the same as the current Lockheed-Vega titles and rates for these occupations until further changes are negotiated. The directive provides that any rate adjustments which may result from the negotiations shall be made upon the same principle as those adjustments made for factory employees.

The county ration board has allotted Houston, Texas, firemen an extra pound of coffee per man because of the special requirements of fire-fighting.

'RESULTS SPEAK FOR THEMSELVES'

WAR DEPARTMENT
COMMANDING GENERAL, ARMY AIR FORCES
WASHINGTON

March 23, 1943

Mr. Robert E. Gross
Lockheed Aircraft Corporation
Burbank, California

Dear Bob:

Thanks very much for your congratulations on the honor recently bestowed upon me by the President. We are all extremely gratified at this signal honor not only to me personally but to the Army Air Forces as a whole. We realize that we have gone a long way in a short time and too much can not be said for the splendid job done by you fellows who are getting out the airplanes for us. Your efforts have been untiring and the results speak for themselves.

I wish you would extend my personal greetings to all of your personnel who are doing so much to help and, of course, my very best to you.

Sincerely,

H. H. ARNOLD,
General, U. S. Army.

From the Chief of the U.S. Army Air Forces himself, the only four-star General ever to command the U.S. A.A.F., comes the above tribute to the wonderful work being done by the men and women of the Lockheed and Vega companies. General H. H. ("Hap") Arnold, only American airman ever to wear the four stars of a full General and one of only a half-a-dozen Generals in the history of the U.S. Armed Forces, was promoted to that highest Army rank by President Roosevelt a few days ago in recognition of his outstanding services to the Allied cause. General Arnold expressed his gratitude for the outstanding job being done by Lockheed and Vega plants in the above personal letter to his long-time friend, Lockheed's President Robert E. Gross.

'PRODUCTION DESIGN' COURSE STARTS APRIL 9

A course in Production Design, sponsored by the University of California, begins April 9 at the John Muir School in Burbank, and will meet on Friday evenings from 7 to 9 p.m.

Prerequisites for the course include graduation from an engineering college or equivalent in experience, and employment in an aircraft industry as an engineer, senior layout man or engineering trainee.

NEW DIVISIONS TO DEAL WITH ABSENTEEISM

An attendance program to reduce avoidable absenteeism has been inaugurated by the Personnel Departments of both Lockheed and Vega. These divisions, under the supervision of Ray Baur of Vega Department 67 and Karl Kunze, Lockheed Department 7-48, have established the necessary facilities to bring the problem of absenteeism to the attention of all concerned.

These newly organized divisions report employees showing a keen interest.

PLAN 'MID-SPRING' FROLIC DANCE

James Burruss, left, of Lockheed Dept. 19 and chairman of the committee which will stage the "Mid-Spring Frolic," checks with Frank Davis, L.E.R.C. Program Director, the April 17 date on which the dance will be held.

HOBBYISTS MOVE TO NEW QUARTERS

The Hobby and Model Club will henceforth meet at the Burbank High School in order to take advantage of better facilities available.

"The popularity and widespread interest in this newly formed organization indicates that the Burbank High School will provide the needed additional space," President "Scotty" Barker says. "Those who belong or those who are interested in joining are advised to watch the STAR for meeting dates."

L.E.R.C. DANCE BAND TO PLAY APRIL 10

Plans for the Department 02 dance call for dancing from 9 p.m. to 1 a.m., according to Joe Quint who is handling details of the affair. The date, April 10, at the Los Angeles Breakfast Club.

The new L.E.R.C. dance band, Red Ferrington conducting, will provide the rhythm for this party.

MIXED BOWLING STARTS TONIGHT

Play in the Lockheed Mixed Bowling League will start tonight (Friday), according to Frank Davis, recreation director, who requests those interested to register immediately as only team-play will be allowed in this tourney. Team entries may be made through the L.E. R.C. office regardless of the plant in which players work.

SWING DRAMA GROUP PLANS PLAY READING APRIL 8

Members of the "Lightning Players," made up of Swing Shift employees, are urged to attend a reading of "You Can't Take It With You" this coming Tuesday afternoon at 1 o'clock at the Burbank Recreation Center.

This session is designed to uncover additional talent for the next Lightning production but it has not yet been decided what play will be given.

L. E. R. C. CALENDAR

FRIDAY, APRIL 2—Class in Acting 1141 North Gower, Hollywood, 7:30 p.m.—Band Rehearsal, 10 a.m., in Main Recreation Area. Concert following.—Barn Dance at Los Angeles Breakfast Club.

SUNDAY, APRIL 4—Modern Symphonic Orchestra, 2:30 p.m. Edith James School of the Dance, 5601 Hollywood Blvd.—Rangers & Rangerettes Ride, 8 to 10 p.m.—Ski Club, White Stag Trophy Race and Carnival, 11 a.m., Lockheed Ski Area. Group rides leave Foothill and Angeles Crest Highway, 8:30 a.m.

MONDAY, APRIL 5—Choral Club Rehearsal, 7:30 p.m., Burbank High School.

TUESDAY, APRIL 6—Lightning Players to meet at Burbank Recreation Center at 1 p.m. for reading of "You Can't Take It With You."—Badminton, 7-9:30 p.m., John Burroughs Jr. High School, Parrish and Clark streets.—Class in Acting, 1141 North Gower, Hollywood, 7:30 p.m.

WEDNESDAY, APRIL 7—Model & Hobby Club, 7:30 p.m., Burbank High School. —Regular Boy Scout Meeting at John Muir School, 3rd and Cypress, 7 p.m.—Rangers & Rangerettes Ride, 7-9 p.m.

THURSDAY, APRIL 8—Rhumba Class, 7:30 at Ballard's Studio, 1753 North Highland, Hollywood.—Ice Skating, Pan Pacific Auditorium; before 7 p.m. special rates.

FRIDAY, APRIL 9—11:30 Luncheon for Swing Shift Penguins, Los Angeles Breakfast Club.—Band Concert, Main Recreation Area.

RHUMBA CLASSES WILL START SOON

As a result of the keen interest in last year's Rhumba sessions, a new series of classes will be started Thursday evening, April 8, with Paul Ballard, well-known dancing instructor directing the 12-class session.

Both beginning and advanced instruction will be offered. Both divisions will meet Thursday evenings at 7:30 at Ballard's Studio, 1753 North Highland, Hollywood.

'EBONY COLLEGIANS' TO PLAY FOR PARTY

Tickets for the Mid-Spring Frolic and dance will go on sale next week, according to James Burruss, chairman of the committee planning the affair, which is set for April 17 at the Polish Auditorium, 4204 Avalon Boulevard.

George Brown and his Ebony Collegians have been engaged for the party and a number of guest artists have been invited to attend.

The 75-cent admission to this party practically assures a sell-out for the event.

'HOT' BARN DANCE FOR ALL TONIGHT

Interest in the Barn Dance to be held at the Los Angeles Breakfast Club tonight indicates that this party will be one of the big social events of the spring season. Sim Steinberger's "Skyridin' Ranger" orchestra will furnish music for the party. Dancing will be between the hours of 8 and 12 and tickets may be obtained through the L.E.R.C.

NO TICKETS AT DOOR FOR ENGINEERS' DANCE

With all plans completed for the Engineer's Sports Informal April 24, at the Los Angeles Breakfast Club, the committee reports that no tickets will be on sale at the door and that those planning to attend this $1.50 party with Rudy Friml, Jr., and his band, had better get their tickets promptly.

Swing Penguin Meeting

The regular luncheon meeting of the Swing Shift Penguin Club will be held Friday, April 9, at 11:30, in the Los Angeles Breakfast Club.

BUY WAR STAMPS AND BONDS!

COMPANIES' MEDICAL SERVICES HONORED

Dr. Seymour Dudley, left, supervisor of Lockheed Medical Department, and Dr. F. E. Poole, director of Lockheed and Vega Medical Division, admire the American College of Surgeons certificate awarded the companies in recognition of their high standards of medical service.

A.M.A. Certificate Evidence Of Units High Standing

Further recognition of the high standards in medical service maintained at Lockheed and Vega was recently received when a certificate of merit authorized by the American College of Surgeons was awarded both companies.

During a visit to the West Coast, Dr. Paul Ferguson, Hospital Inspector for the American College of Surgeons, was asked to survey the medical facilities of both companies and make recommendations with a view toward improving the facilities and services in the field of Industrial Medicine rendered by the Lockheed-Vega Medical Division. Following this survey, official findings were requested of the College and the result was the award of the certificate.

In conforming to minimum standards, a corporation must show that its medical staff is made up of graduates of Medical Colleges rated Class "A" by the American Medical Association and have received post-graduate instruction in emergency surgery and the field of Industrial Medicine.

In addition, the special consultants in the various surgical and medical specialties must be certified by the various specialty boards as having completed

(Continued on Page 6)

NEW FIRST AID OFFICE

The Emergency First Aid Office, under the supervision of Ray Pedregon, assisted by Dwight J. Wieman, Days, Kenneth Gillum, Nights, and Benham Nymeyer, Graveyard, is now located at 1903 Empire street, Lockheed Plant 1. All communications from detachment leaders and team members should be sent to the new address. The phone extension is 2781.

British Aircraft Designer Lauds L. & V. Sky Fighters

There's no hearsay or guesswork about what Lockheed and Vega planes are doing in this war. Apart from news dispatches from the fighting fronts which tell their own vivid stories of Lightnings, Venturas and Hudsons in action, there comes occasionally to the companies' offices first person tributes from the men who design and build some of the world's other great air fighters—the Hurricanes, Spitfires, Typhoons and the great British bombers which are currently blasting the heart out of Naziland.

Such a tribute was received last week from John W. R. Taylor of the Design Department of Hawker Aircraft, Ltd., which builds the R.A.F.'s famous Hurricane and Typhoon fighters and Hurribombers. Acknowledging receipt of a group of photographs of Vega and Lockheed planes, Mr. Taylor said, in part:

"Lockheed-built aeroplanes have certainly been making history in these last few months. I was recently privileged to visit a station in England from which the U.S. A.A.F. is operating against Germany with Fortress bombers. They are certainly grand machines, and although they do not carry as great a bomb load as our heavy bombers, they can certainly look after themselves in a fight with the best German fighter planes. With Fortresses and Liberators pounding them by day and the R.A.F. carrying on the good work at night, the lot of the Germans cannot be a very happy one now.

"We in England were very delighted to hear about the daylight raids on Germany. Raids on the occupied countries are quite commonplace, but it is the German people who must be made to feel the might of the United Nations.

"The Lockheed Venturas have also

(Continued on Page 6)

Playgrounds Open For Working Mothers' Kiddies

As an aid to working mothers with children who find Saturdays a problem day because of school holidays, arrangements have been made whereby a school playground in this area will be open from 6 a.m. to 6 p.m.

The playgrounds at the Fernangeles School, 8851 Laurel Canyon Blvd., Roscoe, will be open and under the supervision of a playground director on Saturday, starting April 3. Children will be expected to bring their own packed lunches and should they desire to do handicraft work, a charge of five to ten cents will be made for materials used. Children from six to twelve years of age are eligible.

Annual Statement Bares Tremendous Production Gain

(Continued from Page 1)

The average weekly paycheck in December, 1942, was $50.07, compared to $41.48 in December of 1941.

Total payroll for Lockheed and Vega in 1942 was $142,415,013, compared to $81,233,662 in 1941.

In explaining the offer which the company had made to reduce prices under renegotiation, Mr. Gross pointed out that the Government had suggested a basis of price adjustment which was unacceptable to the company, but which would further reduce company reserves for contingencies and post-war needs by $1,500,000 and net income after reserves by $3,900,000.

The report showed that in accordance with Congressional provisions in the Revenue Act of 1942 for a refund of 10% of excess profits taxes of corporations to assist the taxpayers in meeting problems of post-war adjustments, an actual reduction of taxes resulted to the corporations, by reason of liquidation of indebtedness, as provided by the Act, in the amount of $5,651,517. The company has purchased United States Treasury Notes totaling $5,000,000 and set them aside as a fund against this and other contingency reserves of the corporation.

"Taken as a whole, most of the 1942 business of the corporation and its subsidiaries was done under fixed price contracts," Mr. Gross stated, "which basis, as opposed to cost-plus-a-fixed-fee, your management fundamentally prefers."

Total bank indebtedness, to finance large inventories, reached a maximum of $42,500,000 during 1942, but as of December 31, 1942, all bank indebtedness had been liquidated.

Since that date, a "V" loan credit of $90,000,000 to the corporation and its subsidiary, Vega Aircraft Corporation, has been arranged with a group of banks, it was explained, and a substantial amount has been borrowed against the credit. This type of loan has been provided for by the Government to substitute for large advance payments from the Government on war contracts.

Mr. Gross pointed out that numerous problems were encountered in achieving increasing production quotas, most important of which was the procurement of necessary materials and the recruiting of an adequate personnel. It was emphasized that in trying to solve these problems the management was confronted by many factors which it itself did not control.

The report also described the warplane

(Continued on Page 8)

BRITISH DESIGNER LAUDS L & V PLANES

(Continued from Page 5)

won their spurs over the Continent of Europe in several hard battles. The bombing of the radio factory at Eindhoven in Holland must surely have been one of the most damaging blows yet struck at the Nazi war machine. The fact that Venturas were chosen for the job on their first big operation proves that the pilots who flew them must have great confidence in their machines.

"I have not yet had a chance to have a good look at a Lightning fighter, but have seen them in the air and was chiefly impressed by their rocket-like climb.

"Yes, Lockheeds are certainly playing their part in the victory of the United Nations. With our Typhoon and the latest Spitfires as short-range fighters and the Lightning for long-range work we have a record-breaking team that will prove too much for the Germans.

"I have recently had a number of my articles published in 'The Aeroplane' and if I can be of any service to you by doing a write-up on any Lockheed machines please do not hesitate to let me know.

"Thank you once more for the excellent photos. Best wishes to Lockheeds.

"Yours faithfully,
"John W. R. Taylor
"Design Department,
"Hawker Aircraft, Ltd."

A.M.A. HONORS BOTH COMPANIES MEDICOS

(Continued from Page 5)

the minimum number of years of post-graduate study in hospitals approved by the American Medical Association.

F. E. Poole, M.D., is medical director of the Lockheed-Vega Medical Division. The Lockheed and Vega Medical Departments are under the supervision of Seymour Dudley, M.D., and T. A. Le Valley, M.D., respectively. Albert Chaney, Ph.D., occupies the position of Industrial Hygienist and Toxicologist. Special consultants are Charles Gilfillan, M.D., Orthopaedics; Cyril Francis, M.D., Internal Medicine; and Stanley O. Chambers, M.D., Dermatology.

Vega Plant I Opens New Transportation Office

Opening of the new Employee Transportation Office at Vega Plant 1 has just been announced. This new office, fully staffed and equipped to handle all transportation matters for the thousands of Vega employees who ride the big yellow busses or participate in the Share-Your-Car Plan of rider-driver transportation, is conveniently located opposite the south entrance of Building 62.

The office is open on a 24-hour basis to handle sales of bus tickets, rationing applications, information on automobiles for sale by Vega employees, etc.

A.E.R. OFFERS HELP TO DEPENDENTS OF MEN IN SERVICE

Just being away from home is not the soldier's or the sailor's only grief and worry. They expect that in the Services. Another, and generally the toughest of all, is wondering about the family left behind—whether it's making out all right and if it will be taken care of if an emergency arises.

It is to do away with this worry, to ease the minds of our fighting men, that the Army Emergency Relief has been organized, a branch of which is located on the ground floor of the Chamber of Commerce Building, Los Angeles. Administered by the Army Air Forces, aided by the Red Cross, the services of the organization are available to dependents of service men regardless of which branch of the service they may be in.

Relief may take the form of a loan or an outright grant of money to dependents, according to the circumstances involved. The AER does not solicit funds, nor are contributions asked for; it was a grant of a million and a half dollars from the American Red Cross that got it started and it is now carrying on with money donated through benefits and the like.

The officers in charge of the L.A. office therefore urge service men's dependents who may have legitimate money problems to get in touch with the AER at once. The phone number is PRospect 8647. Lt. Col. William H. Dayton and Lt. Col. Wilson are the officers in charge.

NUTRITION COURSES OPEN TO WOMEN WAR WORKERS

Courses in nutrition are now being offered women war workers by the Los Angeles County Committee on Nutrition in Industry, of which Dr. H. Borsook of Caltech is chairman.

The course consists of four lectures and demonstrations in cooking with actual food. Preparation of food to save nutrition value, menu planning, preparation of inexpensive foods and economical buying under the point rationing system are a few of the subjects to be discussed.

These courses can be given to groups of women at a time convenient to all and in most every community in the county. Simply send your name and address and the hours and day most convenient for you to the Woman Counselor of your department. Arrangements will then be made to start a class for your convenience.

TWO NEW CLASSES IN STRESS ANALYSIS TO OPEN APRIL 5

Lockheed and Vega are building bigger and better airplanes and it takes highly qualified and well informed craftsmen to construct the jigs and fixtures and to carry on the extensive construction of large assembly jigs, etc.

It is now necessary to stress-analyze all the major jigs and fixtures, and consequently it is reasonable to suppose that jig builders and tool makers will be interested in having some knowledge of simple stress analysis and strength of materials in order to more thoroughly appreciate the designs and construction methods.

Two new classes of the supplementary type under the War Production Training program will be inaugurated on April 5. The objective of these classes is to accommodate mechanics in the shop who wish to gain an appreciation of applied stress analysis and strength of materials.

Classes to be held at John Muir Evening School, 3rd and Grinnel streets, Burbank.

Introductory Stress Analysis I (Applied Analytical Mechanics). Prerequisites: Past acquaintance with the simpler portions of Algebra, Geometry and Physics; Trigonometry desirable; Calculus not necessary. Mon.-Wed., 6:30 to 9:30 p.m., April 5-7, Room 110 for 13 weeks.

Introductory Stress Analysis II (Applied Strength of Materials). Prerequisites: Course I or its equivalent. Tu.-Th., 6:30 to 9:30 p.m., April 6-8, Room 101 for 13 weeks.

The instructor in both courses will be C. E. Noerenberg of Dept. 1-01, Lockheed. Applications for supplemental gasoline rationing will be endorsed for those who need it.

TWENTY-FIVE LOCKHEEDIANS ELIGIBLE FOR FIVE-YEAR PINS

The following Lockheed employees became eligible for Five-year Diamond Service Pins during the month of March:

NAME	DEPT.	NAME	DEPT.
Ernest W. Ahlberg	1-24	Iola Morrow	1-98
Lee E. Allen	1-03	Vernon R. Morse	7-51
Hughcollen Babcock	1-16	John K. McGraw	1-24
Dale E. Baker	1-05	Gerald F. McMindes	1-58
Shipman S. Biegler	8-95	Frank Omodt	1-03
Norman C. Boardman	7-72	Jack K. Painter	3-25
James H. Brimson	1-09	Charles W. Peale	1-89
Donald O. Carmichael	1-13	Carl A. Pederson	7-51
Raymond R. Carter	1-12	Fred F. Penny	1-16
Margaret C. Cox	7-33	Arnold V. Pesek	2-22
Wayne O. Curtis	4-73	Howard C. Pittenger	1-12
Charles A. Ferguson	1-24	Alden E. Pruett	1-11
Kenneth G. Fletcher	1-27	Iven H. Rankin	1-35
Samuel M. Galer	1-38	James H. Rassat	1-10
Robert H. George	2-51	Manuel Sandoval	1-03
Edna L. Udall	8-68	Wayne M. Scott	2-22
Eugene B. Gumm	1-10	William A. Sing	1-35
Raymond F. Hentschel	1-31	Floyd E. Smith	1-17
Raymond C. Hill	1-09	Oliver J. Smith	7-61
Raymond T. Hobbs	1-16	Clark A. Sneve	1-02
Harold H. Hopkins	Dallas	John B. Trenor	B.R.D.
Clarence A. Irvine	1-24	Spiro M. Vuscovich	1-48
Merle E. Jones	1-24	Rex M. Wilson	1-24
Clark H. Kirkham	1-12	Robert M. Woodside	1-03
Wendell J. Mercer	Dallas	Miller R. Yoder	4-73

NOW--BOND BUYING MADE EASY

★

With War Bond purchases now available on the payroll deduction plan at all departmental offices, Marion Roberts, Lockheed Department 48, accepts an authorization card from Robert Harwick of Department 16. Through this convenient method of buying War Bonds, the army of 10-per-centers is rapidly growing at Lockheed and Vega.

★

'TRANSPORTATION' ADDS A NEW SERVICE

A new service has been added by the Employee Transportation Department. If you have an automobile for sale or desire to buy a used car, this department can help you.

A list of cars offered for sale by Lockheed and Vega employees will be posted on departmental bulletin boards at frequent intervals.

If you are in the market for an auto, contact your Employee Transportation office, give the file number shown on the listing and full information on the particular car you are interested in will be furnished you. Such requests must be made in person as no information can be given over the telephone.

DAY SHIFT EMPLOYEES GET BREAK ON LICENSES

The Lockheed and Vega Employee Service Divisions have been notified by the Glendale branch office of the Division of Registration, Department of Motor Vehicles, that day shift employees are being given an opportunity to secure their driver's and chauffeur's licenses on Wednesday nights from 5:30 to 7 p.m.

This service starts on Wednesday, April 7. Since it is being provided solely for day shift employees, appointments must be made through the Employee Service Divisions by calling Lockheed Extension 1238 or Vega Extension 1142. Appointments will not be accepted later than noon of each Wednesday.

DEPARTMENT PLAN BOOSTS BOND SALES

Since it became generally known by employees that they could now authorize payroll deductions for the purchase of War Bonds at their respective departmental offices, the Industrial Relations Office has been swamped with requests for additional authorization cards.

Apparently not satisfied with their efforts to build P-38s, Hudsons, Venturas and Flying Fortresses better, faster and ahead of schedule, Lockheed and Vega employees, despite income taxes, rationing, etc., are determined to set a new record in War Bond purchases.

Needless to say, such reports regarding War Bond activity at the Lockheed and Vega plants are received with a great deal of interest by Treasury Department officials, who, ever since the Second Front Campaign of last September, have looked to our companies to set the pace in War Bond sales through payroll deduction.

It is self-evident that War Bonds and Income Taxes are both necessary, but, if Congress should pass a 20 per cent withholding tax, employees will be devoting no more money to the war effort than at present.

The difference will be that when income tax time rolls around next year, there will be no worry and scramble for money with which to pay these taxes. It will largely have been paid in advance *and in some cases, there may even be a refund.*

BUY WAR STAMPS AND BONDS!

THE *Lockheed-Vega Star* * *

The Lockheed-Vega Star is issued every Friday for the employees of the Lockheed Aircraft Corporation and the Vega Aircraft Corporation and is the official publication of both companies. Communications may be addressed to either the Industrial Relations Office or the Public Relations Department, Lockheed Aircraft Corporation, Burbank, California, U.S.A. Although news and cartoon contributions are welcome, circumstances make it impossible to give any promise that they will be returned to sender when not used, nor can individual acknowledgment be made.

BERT W. HOLLOWAY, Editor-in-Chief
H. L. (HAL) ROSSON, Managing Editor

Volume 10 Number 16

Admiral Salutes Buck-O-Month

For those (if there are any) who doubt that the good works of the Buck-of-the-Month Club are not recognized and appreciated by the highest as well as the lowest ranks in our Armed Services, as well as in civilian organizations, the following exchange of correspondence between Admiral C. W. Nimitz, Commander in Chief of the United States Pacific Fleet, and President Robert E. Gross, of Lockheed, should set their minds at rest.

Early last month Admiral Nimitz addressed the following letter to Mr. Gross:

The Chief of Naval Personnel has informed me that through the generosity of the employees of your company, $1,000 is available to provide free cigarettes, candy and other items contributing to the morale of enlisted Naval personnel in the Pacific Ocean areas. I have sent this gift to the Commander, South Pacific Force, for distribution among the enlisted personnel of his command in outlying areas.

I wish to take this occasion to thank you and your employees for their generosity to the men of the Navy now in the Pacific. This gift will contribute in a substantial degree to the morale of all hands.

With kindest personal regards,
Sincerely,
C. W. NIMITZ,
Admiral, U.S. Navy,
Commander in Chief
United States Pacific Fleet.

Acknowledging the Admiral's courtesy on behalf of the Buck-of-the-Month Club and all Lockheed and Vega employees, Mr. Gross replied:

Dear Admiral Nimitz:

Having just returned from a business trip East, I find your kind letter of March 1 and hasten to personally acknowledge it.

It was very good of you to take the trouble to write as you did and I assure you it is most appreciated by myself and my fellow employees. We are glad it was possible for us to make the contribution we did.

With best wishes, I am
Sincerely yours,
ROBERT E. GROSS
President.

★ Your JOB ★

By . . . . R. RANDALL IRWIN

Your Job is not only important to you. Your letters to this column show that most of you realize that Your Job actually is one of the most important things in the world today.

As Randolph Branner of Lockheed Tool Cribs, Department 1-23, says, "Show me how my activity at bench, lathe, or jig is translated into a hurtling Zero, or a Messerschmidt descending to destruction, or a block-buster in the streets of Stuttgart, and you make my otherwise humdrum job breathe fire and resound with resolve."

Of course it is often difficult to understand just how important one's own job is in a large organization. Martin H. Boisen of Lockheed Experimental Department 1-24 found the answer through taking a course in Industrial Management. He says, "Many of the conditions I used to consider as 'bone-headed red-tape' have been clarified as necessary functions. Through a study of the company organization, I believe it is possible to gain a new understanding of the relativity of our jobs to the organization as a whole."

Not from a classroom but from a personal experience, Philip W. Oberg of Lockheed Dispatching Department 1-35, found the same answer. In a letter to Hall L. Hibbard, vice-president and chief engineer, Oberg told of a recent critical shortage in Department 1-10. Everyone went to work and cleared the necessary paper-work, tools and materials through Departments 1-02, 1-07, 1-10, 2-18, 1-23, 1-35, 2-51, 2-52, 1-58, and 7-61, and completed the job within one shift. "What I felt elated about," says Oberg, "was the spirit that seemed to animate every man connected with the job. Each one was anxious to play his role and play it right. Talk about teamwork, cooperation, oneness of purpose and that high voltage something called enthusiasm—here it was personified in a dozen or more men. Believe me, I was proud to be a member of the team that night."

Or perhaps all we need to remember is this idea from Kenneth Lloyd of Lockheed Plant Personnel Division 7-63, "The simple thought that a job well done saves the life of a fighting friend should give each of us a feeling of individual responsibility. Why should not each of us 'adopt' a fighting man?"

CREDIT UNION MOVES ONE OFFICE

Lockheed men and women wishing to use the facilities of the Credit Union may do so at the same Lockheed Plant 1 location. Last week's "house moving" only affects the bookkeeping division of the Credit Union.

"The bookkeeping division is located across Empire avenue from Gate 10, but employees do not have to contact this office directly for status information," says W. R. Livingston, assistant treasurer.

Members seeking loan or share-balance information should go to the main Credit Union office where they will fill out an information request which will be completed by the Credit Union and sent back to the employee.

FINANCIAL STATEMENT

(Continued from Page 6)

types produced by Lockheed and Vega, featuring the Lockheed "Lightning" P-38 fighter and the B-17 bomber, manufactured by Vega by arrangement with the Boeing Airplane Company, and it was reported that all types were believed to be performing satisfactorily on the fighting fronts.

LIBRARY

Some new arrivals at the Lockheed and Vega book stores:

- AMERICAN AIR ALMANAC $1.00
- AMERICAN PRACTICAL NAVIGATOR—Bowditch, U.S. Navy Dept. Hydrographic Office 2.70
- CIVIL AERONAUTICS MANUAL 04 AIRPLANE AIRWORTHINESS .... .50
- ENGINE LATHE OPERATIONS—Whipple & Baudek 1.39
- METHODS OF MEASUREMENTS—Cornetet 1.39
- RADIO AMATEURS HANDBOOK .... .75

Hours: 7 a.m.-12:30 p.m. daily except Saturdays when the libraries and book stores close at 4:45 p.m.

The Lockheed Library and book store is located in the Personnel Building on the second floor, Room 210. At Vega, it is located in Building 62.

Employees may check library books out for two weeks by showing their pass. Books may be purchased for cash, or, if the purchase amounts to $3 or more, it may be on payroll deduction.

SYMPHONIC MEETINGS

The L.E.R.C. Modern Symphonic Orchestra is growing so rapidly that it has become necessary for it to make its headquarters in Edith James School of the Dance, 5601 Hollywood Blvd., where it meets every Sunday afternoon at 2:30.

SEE PAGE 3 FOR WAGE RULINGS

THE *Lockheed-Vega Star* ★ ★

Official publication of the Lockheed and Vega Aircraft Corporations

Volume 10 | BURBANK, CALIFORNIA, U.S.A., APRIL 16, 1943 | Number 18

Nation's Aircraft Chiefs Visit Lockheed Plants

Presidents of Eastern aircraft companies, assembled for a series of meetings with western presidents, inspected the Lockheed and Vega factories as a preliminary to their conferences. Left to right: Lieut. J. O. Christian, acting Inspector of Naval Aircraft at Vega; Courtlandt S. Gross, President, Vega Aircraft Corporation; P. G. Johnson, President, Boeing Aircraft Co.; J. Carlton Ward, Jr., President, Fairchild Engine and Aircraft Corp.; L. C. Goad, General Manager, Eastern Aircraft Division, General Motors Corp.; Lieut. David E. Irwin, representing the General Inspector of Naval Aircraft; Glenn L. Martin, President, The Glenn L. Martin Co.; L. D. Bell, President, Bell Aircraft Corp.; Major Howard W. Angus, AAF Resident Representative at Vega; Guy W. Vaughan, President, Curtiss-Wright Corp.; Frank F. Russell, President, National Aviation Corp.; Robert E. Gross, President, Lockheed Aircraft Corp.; Dr. A. E. Lombard, Aircraft Resources Control Office, War Production Board; H. E. Ryker, Vega Vice-President in Charge of Manufacturing, and L. M. Bach, Vega Works Manager.

NATIONAL COUNCIL OF MANUFACTURERS FORMED AT MEETING

Launching a series of teamwork conferences among the manufacturers of 90 per cent of American air power, Vega and Lockheed played host on Monday to the chief executives of practically all the najor Eastern aircraft companies.

The occasion which brought together, for the first time in aviation history, this total concentration of the industry, was the blending of the Aircraft War Production Council, Inc. (West Coast), with the Aircraft War Production Council, East Coast. The two groups jointly organized the National Aircraft War Production Council further to speed the output of war planes through nationwide interchange of technical information, materials, and facilities.

Frank F. Russell, president of Nation Aviation Corp. and a director of Lockheed and also of Bell Aircraft Corporation on the East Coast, was selected as General Manager of the national council. With offices in Washington, he will coordinate the eastern and western organizations and fit them into the requirements of governmental war agencies.

The national council epitomizes the spirit of unity and teamwork which it takes to win a World War. Robert E.

(Continued on Page 7)

Mementos Of Solomons Battles Bare Jap Weakness

A shell-riddled fragment of a vertical stabilizer from a Jap Zero plane shot down in flames on the beach near Henderson Field. A bullet-pierced penny and a dented nickel taken off the body of a dead Jap. A marker bomb, a flare bomb and the wooden nose plug from a Jap 500-pound bomb. Some Japanese and New Caledonia folding money.

These are the souvenirs of war in the Solomons, brought home to Los Angeles recently by Walter W. Parris, a Chief Commissary Officer of the Merchant Marine, as gifts to his half-brother, Randall Updyke, a Lockheed Aircraft hydropress operator on the Graveyard shift.

Updyke, who lives at 7705 Whitsett street, Los Angeles, brought the articles to Lockheed one day last week where the construction details of the Zero's vertical fin proved to be of particular interest to heads of the fabrication and assembly departments that are turning out one of the Zero's chief foes, the Lockheed Lightning P-38.

The Zero's stabilizer was found to be light, fragile and "tinny" in comparison with the sturdy alclad stabilizer of the Lightning. Most of the rivets on the Zero were corroded with rust, indicating poor anodization, and all were turned so badly that not one would have passed inspection in the Lockheed plant, it was said.

Attached to the Army Transport Command, Parris landed at Guadalcanal last January and remained four days.

"We steamed past the Hardly-Ables and made a safe run for it," Parris recalls. "The Hardly-Ables were a Japanese coast artillery battery on the southeast tip of Guadalcanal. They were so named because they were hardly able to hit anything.

"I went ashore every day, and was escorted by a Marine sergeant up to the front lines. On the way up we passed by heaps of Jap dead which the Marines were burning. They just poured gasoline over the bodies and set the whole mess ablaze. Everything in sight was riddled by gunfire, and several times Jap snipers fired at us from the tops of trees.

"This Marine sergeant gave me two coins, which he had taken from the body of a Jap he'd killed a few days before. Evidently the Jap had taken them off the body of a Marine, and then had found them insufficient armor to protect his own hide. Both the penny and the

(Continued on Page 6)

ZERO 'SOUVENIR' SHOWS INFERIOR WORK

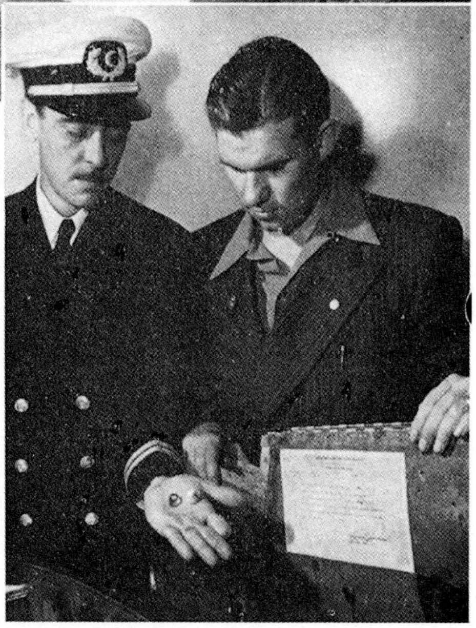

Walter Parris, left, shown with his half-brother, Randall Updyke, Lockheed Graveyard shift hydropress operator, and trophies of war in the Solomons brought home by Parris, a Chief Commissary Officer aboard a merchant marine ship that stopped at Guadalcanal last January. In top photo Updyke inspects vertical stabilizer of a Jap Zero fighter shot down at Guadalcanal. Parris inspects corresponding part of a Lockheed P-38. In lower photo Parris shows his brother a bullet-riddled American penny and a nicked nickel taken from the body of a dead Jap sniper.

LAUREL CANYON BUS LINE ADDED

A new bus line to serve employees of Lockheed Plants 1 and 3 and Vega Plants 1 and 2 living in the Laurel Canyon area will commence operation next Monday morning, starting with the 7 a.m. shift. The Employee Transportation Department has announced the following schedule of time and passenger pick-up stops from the railhead at Wicks and Laurel Canyon. Fare on this line will be 10c. One coach will serve all plants.

Wicks & Laurel Canyon	6:10	2:55	11:40
Neenach & Laurel Canyon	6:11	2:56	11:41
Saticoy & Laurel Canyon	6:12	2:57	11:42
Sherman Way & Laurel Canyon	6:13	2:58	11:43
Van Owen & Laurel Canyon	6:14	2:59	11:44
Victory & Laurel Canyon	6:15	3:00	11:45
Victory & Radford	6:17	3:02	11:47
Victory & Lankershim	6:18	3:03	11:48
Victory & Tujunga	6:20	3:05	11:50
Victory & Cahuenga	6:22	3:07	11:52

ENGINEER COURSE OFFERED BY U.C.L.A.

Graduate engineers, or those with equivalent experience in design, testing or research of fluid flow equipment, may enroll in a new tuition-free War Training class—Fluid Mechanics for Aircraft Design—at the University of California in Los Angeles.

Beginning next Monday (April 19) at 7 p.m., the 14 meetings of the class will be held in Room 127, Chemistry Building, on the U.C.L.A. campus. Lecture topics will include a brief review of thermodynamics of gases, general laws of hydrostatics and hydrodynamics, including metering, friction and turbulence of compressible fluids, and introduction to airfoil theory.

SUMMARY OF ACTION ON W.L.B. DIRECTIVE

TO KEEP EMPLOYEES FULLY INFORMED REGARDING THE STATUS OF ALL WAGE AND SALARY MATTERS, MANAGEMENT PRESENTS THE FOLLOWING REVIEW OF ACTION TAKEN, OR TO BE TAKEN, IN THE APPLICATION OF THE WAR LABOR BOARD DIRECTIVE, AND REQUESTS THE CO-OPERATION OF ALL EMPLOYEES DURING THE PERIOD LOCKHEED AND VEGA ARE FACED WITH THE TASK OF CHANGE-OVER IN APPLYING THIS DIRECTIVE.

WEEKLY PAYROLL FACTORY EMPLOYEES

Retroactive Bonus:

On April 14th all weekly payroll factory employees who were on the payroll during the period from July 6, 1942 to March 3, 1943, received a retroactive wage adjustment, less the required Federal and State deductions, of $64.75 in cash, or three $25.00 war bonds, plus $10.00 in cash. On this same date all weekly factory payroll employees whose employment with Lockheed-Vega companies began subsequent to July 6, 1942, and who remained on the payroll to March 3, 1943, received a retroactive wage adjustment of $1.85 per week for such time worked between these dates.

Conversion to New War Labor Board Occupations and Minimum Rates:

On March 27, 1943, all weekly factory payroll occupations were changed over to the new W.L.B. occupations and each employee was automatically brought up to the minimum basic hourly rate of his new occupational grade unless he was already at, or above, this amount. All such adjustments will be retroactive to March 6, 1943. Errors which occurred from improper classifications, or other reasons, are being adjusted as quickly as possible.

In-Grade Adjustments:

Up to the present time adjustments above the minimum rate to place each factory employee in his proper position in the new rate range (in-grade adjustments) have been withheld at Lockheed and Vega at the request of the War Labor Board's West Coast Aircraft Committee. However, an agreement on the procedure for making these in-grade adjustments has now been reached by the company and the Union, and approved by the West Coast Aircraft Committee, and the companies may now apply this portion of the Directive. In order to do this, it will be necessary to review all eligible factory employees and the departments are now reviewing these employees to consider their correct classification and proper position in the new rate range. The magnitude of this task makes it necessary to declare a moratorium on all regular and special reviews for factory employees. It is inevitable that maladjustments or inequalities in individual rates will be apparent until these in-grade adjustments have been completed. The above in-grade adjustments will be completed and placed into effect May 8, 1943, and will be retroactive to March 6th.

Joint Company-Union Committee to Review Conversion of Old Lockheed-Vega Factory Occupations and Rates to New W.L.B. Factory Occupations and Rates.

A joint Company-Union committee was established and has reviewed and analyzed the conversion of the old Lockheed-Vega factory occupations, grades and rates to the new W.L.B. occupations, grades and rates. This committee has recommended changes deemed necessary. However, in accordance with the W.L.B. Directive, it will be necessary that such proposed changes be taken to the West Coast Aircraft Committee for final decision.

WEEKLY PAYROLL TECHNICAL AND OFFICE (NON-PRODUCTIVE) EMPLOYEES

Retroactive Bonus:

On April 14th all weekly payroll technical and office employees who were on the payroll during the period from July 6, 1942 to March 3, 1943, received a retroactive wage adjustment, less the required Federal and State deductions, of $64.75 in cash, or three $25.00 war bonds, plus $10.00 in cash. On this same date all weekly technical and office payroll employees whose employment with Lockheed-Vega companies began subsequent to July 6, 1942 and who remained on the payroll to March 3, 1943, received a retroactive wage adjustment of $1.85 per week for such time worked between these dates.

Negotiations on Non-Productive Job Classifications and Wage Rates:

All weekly payroll technical and office occupations (non-productive) were changed over to the new job codings on March 27, 1943. However, in accordance with the W.L.B. Directive the titles and rates for these occupations will not be changed until negotiations have been completed on a uniform job classification and wage rate schedule and such schedule has received approval of the West Coast Aircraft Committee. It is anticipated that the Company and the Union will start these negotiations within the next week and an attempt will be made to dispose of this question as expeditiously as possible. The Directive provides that any rate adjustments which may result from the approved schedule shall be made upon the same principle as those adjustments made for factory employees. Until such time as an agreement is reached on the new occupation and rate schedule by all interested parties, and the new schedule is applied, special and regular reviews on technical and office occupations will continue to be made as long as they are within the present wage ranges.

WEEKLY-MONTHLY EMPLOYEES

Retroactive Bonus:

The portion of the W.L.B. Directive regarding retroactive bonus adjustments for Lockheed and Vega employees who were transferred either from weekly to monthly, or monthly to weekly salary during the period from July 6, 1942 to March 3, 1943, has been interpreted by the West Coast Aircraft Committee, as follows: Eligible employees on the payroll as of March 3, 1943, and who have a seniority date of July 6, 1942, or later, will participate in the retroactive bonus on the basis of $1.85 per week for such time between these dates that they were on the weekly payroll only.

Delay in the clarification of this portion of the Directive made it impossible to issue checks to this group on April 14th. However, checks will be issued at the earliest possible date.

MONTHLY SALARIED EMPLOYEES

The War Labor Board Directive calling for retroactive bonus applies only to employees over whom the Board has jurisdiction, namely, those on an hourly basis.

Lockheed and Vega monthly salaried employees rates come under the jurisdiction of the Treasury Department at the present time and not under the W.L.B. and therefore, are not covered by the recent Board Directive.

In the past the companies were free to, and did, make regular adjustments of monthly salaries in recognition of increased responsibility and promotions. Recent rulings, however, have made it necessary to secure Treasury Department approval of such salary adjustments which are initiated by the companies. Such adjustments for the monthly salaried group, where justified will continue to be put into effect as the necessary Treasury Department approval can be secured.

(Continued on Page 8)

'BUCKSHOT' BLANKS AT L.E.R.C. OFFICES

Applications for the "Buckshots" may be obtained through the L.E.R.C. office, according to Kay Swindler, who is co-ordinating this Service Star Women's activity along with Margaret Olson, Dept. 35, and Patsy Jenkins, Dept. 5, Graveyard.

Any child between 6 and 16 whose parents are employed at Lockheed may join this organization. It is planned to have programs run at the same time that Service Star Women meet so that children may enjoy proper supervision while their mothers are attending the Service Star Women affairs.

Applications may be obtained at the L.E.R.C. office and through the Counselors at outlying plants.

Mid-Spring 'Frolic' Sell-Out

The Mid-Spring Frolic slated at the Polish Auditorium tomorrow night promises to be a sell-out, according to Jimmie Burruss and his committee who have planned the affair.

"For those who do not know where the Polish Auditorium is, please note that it is located at 4202 Avalon Blvd.," says Burruss. "When George Brown and his Ebony Collegians strike up the band, we expect a full crowd for the 75-cent event."

L. E. R. C. CALENDAR

FRIDAY, APRIL 16—Class in Acting, 7:30 p.m., 1141 North Gower. — Band Rehearsal, 10 a.m., Main Recreation Area. Concert following.

SATURDAY, APRIL 17 — Mid-Spring Frolic, Polish Auditorium, 4202 Avalon Blvd.

SUNDAY, APRIL 18—Meeting of Modern Symphonic Orchestra, 2:30 p.m., 5610 Hollywood Blvd. — Rangers & Rangerettes Ride, 8-10.

MONDAY, APRIL 19—Choral Club Rehearsal, 7:30 p.m., Burbank High School. —Class in Acting, 7:30 p.m., 1141 North Gower.

TUESDAY, APRIL 20—Badminton, 7-9:30 p.m., John Burroughs Jr. High School.

WEDNESDAY, APRIL 21 — Model and Hobby Club, 7:30 p.m., Burbank High School. — Boy Scout Meeting, John Muir School, 7 p.m. — Rangers & Rangerettes Ride, 7-9 p.m. — Drama Class, 7:30 p.m., 1141 North Gower.

THURSDAY, APRIL 22 — Rhumba Class, 7:30 p.m., Ballard's Studio, 1753 North Highland, Hollywood. — Ice Skating, Pan-Pacific, before 7 p.m., special rates. —Bridge Club Meeting, Burbank Recreation Center, 7:30 p.m. — Lightning Players Casting for "You Can't Take It With You," 1 a.m., Burbank Little Theater, San Fernando and Amherst.— Stagecraft Class, 7:30, 1141 N. Gower.

FRIDAY, APRIL 23—Band Concert, Main Recreation Area. — Drama Class, 7:30 p.m., 1141 N. Gower.

DEPARTMENT 4 KEGLERS NAMED BOWLING CHAMPS

Battling their way through a tough preliminary game against the Butchers, 2851 to 2722, the Department 4 Keglers won the 1942-43 Lockheed League Championship by downing the Modelers by a score of 2893-2440 to bring the annual Lockheed Bowling League to a close.

Highlighted by McCutchins 607 series the Keglers rolled into first place, cinching this year's top spot.

GOLF TOURNAMENT SLATED FOR MAY 16

The first all-plant, all shift golf tournament sponsored by the L.E.R.C. this year will be held May 16 at the Flintridge course between Montrose and Altadena.

"This is the first L.E.R.C. tournament to be held at this course and from reports made by some of the top golfers, this first L.E.R.C. tournament should enjoy a tremendous response from golfers from all plants," Bob Mercer, L.E.R.C. athletic chairman, reports.

SOFTBALL PLAY STARTS APRIL 19

Play in the softball league will start on Monday, April 19, according to Frank Davis, recreation director for the L.E.R.C. Rules and schedules have been sent to teams.

Additional information may be obtained from the L.E.R.C. office or from Jim Arbogast, L.E.R.C. recreation director for Plants 2 and 4.

STAGECRAFT CLASSES

Classes in stagecraft are now being planned by the L.E.R.C. Drama Club and Andy Calderwood, whose sets for "Philadelphia Story" were one of the high points of the production, has agreed to conduct the sessions.

Classes are scheduled on the second and fourth Thursday evenings each month starting April 22 at 7:30 at 1141 North Gower. Work covered will include every phase of behind-the-scenes activity.

Plants 3 And 4 Party

Promising to set a new high for social events, the Plant 3 and 4 party May 2 at the Palm Room of the Royal Palms Hotel will feature the L.E.R.C. Dance Band under the direction of Red Ferrington. Tickets from L.E.R.C. representatives at $1.10 per couple and 65 cents for single admissions.

TENNIS TOURNAMENT ENTRIES PILING IN

Hoping to close the registration for the coming L.E.R.C. Tennis Tournament so that play may start shortly, the committee in charge of this activity urges all tennis players to register at the L.E.R.C. office, or at Plants 2 and 4 through Jim Arbogast, who will be available to collect fee and ball deposit on Tuesdays, Wednesdays and Thursdays, Plant 2, and Mondays and Fridays at Plant 4.

Players at Plants 1 and 3 may register through the main L.E.R.C. daily from 8 a.m. to 8:45 p.m.

SPECIAL ICE-CAPADES TICKETS AT L.E.R.C.

Special rates for L.E.R.C. members who wish to attend the Ice-Capades have been obtained through the L.E.R.C. office. Three Lockheed performances, May 2, 3 and 9 have been arranged and regular $2.20 tickets will be available at the L.E.R.C. office for $1.70, and $1.65 seats go for $1.15, under this plan.

A special preview performance April 27 will make it possible for those purchasing War Bonds to obtain ticke free. Purchases must be made at the rink or through regular ticket outlets.

Engineers Planning Dance

Warning that no tickets will be sold at the door, the committee in charge of the Engineers Sports Informal at the Los Angeles Breakfast Club on April 24 urges everyone planning to attend this party to get their tickets promptly, as only a limited number will be sold. Rudolph Friml Jr.'s band, so popular at the last engineers' party, has again been engaged for the event which starts promptly at 9 p.m., with "Home Sweet Home" scheduled at 1 a.m.

Additional representatives elected in the recent L.E.R.C. election include Joe MacDonald, Department 25, and Arnold Davis, Departments 7-40 and 58, Graveyard.

SWING DRAMA GROUP TO CAST PLAY APRIL 22

Casting for the next Lightning Players production, "You Can't Take It With You," is scheduled for the night of April 22, according to Jack Wright, president of the L.E.R.C. sponsored group.

There are nineteen parts in this play and all Swing employees interested in dramatics are invited to turn out on April 22 at 1 a.m. at the Burbank Little Theater, San Fernando and Amherst.

COMPANIES JOIN TO AID SELECTIVE DRAFT REGISTRANTS

In order that all registrants of draft boards may be kept fully informed regarding changes in official classification procedure, Selective Service Divisions of both Lockheed (7-42) and Vega (53) have collaborated to bring to the attention of all employees the following information which became effective April 12:

All Class 3-B's have now been eliminated, nationally.

Class 3-A has been reorganized, and it, together with the continuation of Class 2-B, will contain most of our employees. Whether a former 3-A or 3-B will now be classified 3-A depends entirely upon his marital status, i.e., in order to be eligible for a 3-A, a man must have been married prior to December 8, 1941, and a child born as a result of this marriage on or before September 14, 1942.

In addition, this father must have continuously maintained a bona fide relationship with his family during this time—his wife and child living with him.

No new 3-A can be drafted for military service until that class is made available by the National Director of Selective Service, or a change occurs in his marital status.

Those employees, aged 18 to 37, inclusive, not eligible for the new 3-A classification will be reclassified by their local boards. Classification 2-B includes all single men without dependents, single men with collateral dependents, married men without children, or married men whose marriage occurred after December 7, 1941, or whose child was born after September 14, 1942, or both.

Many former 3-A's and 3-B's will become 2-B's. Due to the enormous amount of work which this new processing order throws upon all local draft boards, new classifications, it is expected, may be a few weeks in arriving.

As we go to press we have just learned that Selective Service regulations have been amended to include step-children as recognized dependents for the new 3-A classification, provided they were acquired prior to December 8, 1941, and have lived continuously with the family since that time.

V.E.R.C. Service Station

Under the management of George Bunning, the V.E.R.C. Service station, on Hollywood Way directly across from the Air Terminal entrance, is undergoing an extensive "cleanup" and rearrangment.

'PIGGY-BACK' RIDE BROADCAST

★

Test Pilot Jimmy Mattern and Lieut. Ralph A. Likins, Army trainee pilot, ready to take off for their Army Hour broadcast. On the wing is Lt. Col. Warren E. Carey, District Safety Officer, who opened the program by describing the value of "piggy-back" instruction.

★

FOUR NEW CLASSES OPEN IN BURBANK

New classes in the Burbank School District still open for registration include the following:

Aircraft Components—Mon.-Wed., 6:30-9:30 p.m., John Burroughs Evening School.

Aircraft Drafting I & II—Tues.-Thurs., 6:30-9:30 p.m., John Burroughs Evening School.

Production Methods—Mon.-Wed., 6:45-9:15 p.m., Burbank Evening School.

Materials and Processes—Mon.-Wed., 7-9 p.m., John Muir Evening School.

Aircraft Drafting, Mr. Yapp, instructor, includes the mathematics and trigonometry needed by the average detailer. Simple arithmetic is the only prerequisite.

The course in Airplane Components includes slides, movies, and many other visual aids.

Due to the lack of instructors one class is being formed under the A and E Program to teach Civil Air Regulations, propellers, fabric and dope and paint, rigging and inspection methods. This class will meet on Monday, Wednesday, and Friday from 11:30 to 2:30 p.m., Burbank Evening School.

Many other classes are still open. Call CHarleston 6-1057 or CHarleston 6-4101 for further information.

The L.E.R.C. Band is seeking a competent tuba player who has his or her own tuba. Contact Ben Porter, Dept. 1-86, Ext. 1727, or L.E.R.C. office, Ext. 1901.

WORLD-GIRDLING AIRMAN THRILLS RADIO MILLIONS

Jimmy Mattern, Lockheed-Vega test pilot, probably spent seven of the busiest minutes in flying history last Sunday, when he flew a "Lightning" P-38 for 40,000,000 listeners in an NBC Army Hour demonstration of "piggy-back" instruction.

Flying with Mattern in the tiny streamlined enclosure was Lieut. Ralph A. Likins, a trainee P-38 pilot with peacetime experience as a radio announcer. The pair took off from a nearby Army air base with split second precision, just as the program was "handed" to them by New York Army Hour control.

Lieutenant Likins rode with both arms around Mattern's neck. In his right hand he held the microphone, passing it between Mattern and himself to pick up their conversation. In his left hand was the radio script, and as they read to the end of each page, Mattern would take one hand from the controls to rip off the page and drop it on the floor of the cockpit.

Reading constantly from the script, Mattern instructed the trainee in take-off procedure, banking, rolling, an Immelmann turn, and single-engine operation for seven minutes. At the close of the program he dived from 2500 feet, turned, and roared past a microphone on the field in a matter of seconds, to record the whistling thunder of the P-38 just as the program went off the air.

You can save with your Credit Union.

MEMENTOS OF SOLOMONS BATTLES

(Continued from Page 2)

Jap had been plugged right through the middle clean as a whistle.

"The first thing the sergeant told me was not to pick up anything myself—because I didn't know much about the Jap booby traps. The tales he and other Marines told me of Jap trickery and dirty tactics would make your hair stand on end. One favorite trick of theirs was to have three Japs walk out with hands raised, begging for mercy. They would walk toward a group of Marines with one of their number in the center and slightly ahead of the other two. Suddenly the leader would fall flat on his face with a yell and the other two would fall on top of him and kill the Marines with a machine gun that has been concealed on the back of the leader.

"Other times the raised Nip hands would suddenly begin heaving hand grenades. It was because of tactics like these on the part of the Japs that the Marines started using retaliatory methods of their own until it came so that no Jap would ever surrender to a Marine. Those boys were plenty sore at the little brown devils and they paid them back with interest some of their own style of medicine."

Parris said he found the marker bomb on Gavutu Island, about where a terrific battle had been fought August 8. "There are about 30 acres in all to Gavutu," Parris said. "And in all that area the tops of only three palm trees survived the terrific artillery and machine gun duels of August 8. All others had been shot away.

"Yes, I saw many amazing sights out there, but the most beautiful sight of all was to stand off at sea in our boat and watch the Lockheed Lightning P-38's take off from Henderson Field. Where other planes would come lumbering up and barely clear the treetops, the P-38's would shoot up as if they had been lifted by steel springs."

Doctor bills? Try a Credit Union Loan.

COMPANIES SIMPLIFY INDUCTION TRANSFERS

To assist men who receive induction orders from out-of-town or out-of-state draft boards, Lockheed Plants 1, 2 and 4 and Vega Plant 1 announce that transfers for delivery to the main Transfer Station, located at 333 West Second street, Los Angeles, may now be arranged through the Selective Service Divisions.

If you receive an Order to Report for Induction and prefer to be inducted in Los Angeles, please bring your order in person to: Selective Service Divisions, Lockheed Plant 1; Mr. Coffinberry, Plant 2; Mr. Hart, Plant 4; or the Selective Service Division at Vega Plant 1. Here complete arrangements may be made for the transfer of your induction from your draft board to Los Angeles.

WILLIAM POWELL ON 'CEILING UNLIMITED'

William Powell, master sophisticate of the screen and portrayor of the well-known character of Nick Charles in "The Thin Man" series, contributes his acting merits as star of "Ceiling Unlimited" Monday, April 19, the Lockheed and Vega program broadcast over CBS stations and KNX each week at 8:15 p.m., P. W. T. The story is entitled "God's Corporals" and enables Powell to achieve a departure from his usual debonair role.

William Powell

The narration will portray a battlefield where the injured are afforded emergency treatment and then transferred to bases behind the lines. The "sky-ambulances" are the vital factor in the recovery and ability of men to once again return to their fighting posts.

Powell's "smooth-tongued" voice will undergo an interesting transition when it describes the courage of our soldiers at the front.

FORMER LOCKHEED MAN DECORATED

Word was received this week that another ex-Lockheed man has won distinction on the battlefronts.

This time it is Lieutenant William E. Smith, A.C., formerly of Dept. 7, who has been awarded the Air Service Medal for "meritorious achievement while participating in an air flight December 23 (1942) against the enemy in the Solomon Islands."

William E. Smith

The Army citation continues: "Lieut. Smith, though low on fuel, pressed home a dive bombing and strafing attack on enemy shipping with relentless determination and aided greatly in the sinking of two enemy cargo vessels."

Lieut. Smith is the son of Mr. and Mrs. Albert T. Smith of 1328 Western avenue, Glendale. Mr. Smith, Sr., has been with Lockheed for 10 years and is now employed in Dept. 20.

Insurance Dept. Announces Plan To Speed Payments

In an effort to speed up settlement of claims and as a matter of convenience to Lockheed and Vega employees, provision has now been made for payment of hospital, medical and surgical benefits direct to hospitals, physicians and surgeons. This has been accomplished by incorporating an "Order to pay Hospital, Medical and Surgical Benefits" in the claim forms which are completed by the employee and his attending physician. Where an employee wishes drafts issued payable direct to a hospital or physician, he simply signs this portion of the form.

Under the old procedure, drafts in payment of hospital, medical and surgical benefits were made payable to the employees. In order to secure credit without payment in advance for services covered by the insurance, the Lockheed-Vega companies established the policy of securing the employee's endorsement on all such drafts in every case, unless the employee presented a receipted bill showing payment of the account. The drafts were then mailed direct to the hospital or doctor.

Quite often, settlement could not be completed until the employee returned to work after an extended illness, and it was then necessary for him to make several trips to the Insurance Division to endorse drafts. Most of these trips were made during lunch periods or before and after shift, but certainly were inconvenient. At the same time, hospitals and doctors were inquiring as to the reason no settlement had been made.

The new procedure represents a needed service to employees. Where accounts have already been paid, the drafts will be issued direct to the employee as in the past. On all other claims, it is optional with the employee as to whether the drafts shall be issued payable to the hospitals and doctors, or to himself.

VEGA IS SAFETY WINNER

In recognition of the accumulation of more than 122,000 man-hours without a lost-time accident, Precision Assembly at Vega, Department 20, has been awarded the Safety Trophy for March. Runners-up for the trophy were PV-1 Fuselage Sub-Assembly, Department 23, and Production Control, Department 35.

For the poorest safety record of the month, Welding and Metal Fitting, Department 4, became the recipient of the White Elephant.

Lightnings Prove 'Forked Terrors' In African Skies

Again becoming the fork-tailed terrors of the North African skies after a slight lull in their operations, Lockheed Lightning P-38 fighters knocked down 80 enemy planes in 36 hours over the Sicilian Straits and Tunisia last weekend, according to news dispatches.

On April 10 Virgil Pinkley, United Press manager in North Africa, wired from Allied headquarters:

"United States Lightning fighter plane pilots scored one of their greatest triumphs of the war today when they shot down 27 Italian and German aircraft, including 18 Junkers transports, in a 15-minute battle over the Sicilian narrows between Sicily and Tunis.

"The Yanks, flying speedy twin-motored Lightnings, sailed into an enemy formation of 30 to 50 planes between 7:45 a.m. and every American shot down or damaged an enemy ship. No American planes were lost.

"It was the second time this week the Americans had tangled with such a huge force of enemy transport planes. On Monday, in the same area, the Lightnings also bagged 18 big Junkers transports, most of which were believed carrying fuel for Rommel's tanks, and shot down 13 of their escort planes."

On April 11, the next day, the Associated Press reported:

"American Lightning fighters today knocked down 27 more enemy planes to run their 36-hour string to 80 Axis aircraft. (Note: actual count, 54 in the first two fights plus these 27 would equal 85 victims of the P-38's.) The Lightnings ranging out over the Sicilian Straits twice today ran into opposition, scoring heavily. Of the 27 enemy planes knocked down, 21 were transports."

In another Associated Press report on April 11, Daniel De Luce wired: "American Lightning fighters in two sweeps over the Sicilian Straits shot down 30 of these lumbering aircraft (Junkers 52 transports) and 11 fighters. Only one Lightning was lost in these battles. It clipped the tail of a Messerschmitt only a few feet above the water and both plunged into the sea."

Reporting on the same battle of the 11th, the United Press, presumably Pinkley, said: "Lightning pilots wiped out one entire formation of 20 Junkers, several of the big enemy planes being deliberately crashlanded at sea without being hit as their crews realized the futility of the fight.

"Six other enemy planes were shot down in the action, including two Messerschmitts which fell to the guns of 2nd Lieut. Don F. Sharp of Lewiston, Mont.

"'I was chasing a Messerschmitt 109 when I saw bullets whizzing past my side,' Sharp said. 'I realized a Messerschmitt 110 was on my tail. I throttled down as he went buzzing past me I let him have it. Then I got the other one.'"

RECORD LINEUP OF WAR BLOOD DONORS

That old familiar slogan, "Look to Lockheed for Leadership" again holds the spotlight, this time with the name Vega added. In this case it applies to the generous response accorded the Employee Victory Committee's call for blood donors at the American Red Cross Burbank headquarters.

Two hundred and forty Lockheed and Vega employees made blood donations at the local station on Monday of this week, when the mobile unit of the Blood Donor Service made the first visit to Burbank on a regular weekly schedule.

Next Monday will find members of the Swing and Graveyard shifts participating in this worthy cause. Employees are urged to make their appointments early. Lockheed Plant 1 employees should contact the Main Medical office, Clockhouse building, Extension 1541. Plant 3 personnel may make their appointments by contacting the First Aid Unit, Extension 20. Vega employees of Plant 1, please contact Employee Service Division, Extension 1142 and those of Vega Plant 2 call Extension 333.

Remember, this coming Monday is a Swing and Graveyard shift affair, 10 a.m. to 2 p.m., and if previous attendance is any criterion, it will "go over the top" as usual.

COL. KELSEY BAILS OUT AT SPEED OF SOUND; SPRAINS ANKLE

One of the most amazing escapes from death in the annals of aviation was written last week by Col. Ben Kelsey, veteran Army test pilot and the first man to fly a Lockheed Lightning in a record-breaking cross-country flight four years ago.

Entrusted with the risky task of testing an experimental control device, Col. Kelsey pointed the nose of his Lightning earthward, "gunned" it into a screaming terminal velocity dive at a speed approaching that of sound—then tested the gadget—*It failed!*

Only seconds intervened between him and death. Slapping the emergency canopy release with one hand and unbuckling his safety belt with the other, Col. Kelsey forced himself up into the powerful blast of the slip stream and was automatically thrown clear of the ship. As his 'chute opened and he floated down to earth he saw the plane crash beneath him near Calabasas.

Famed Lodestar Doing Splendid Training Job

Another "civilian" has been drafted for the Army by South Plains Army Flying School and is doing a job faithfully at this Lubbock, West Texas, advanced glider training school.

The C 60, converted into a cargo ship from the Lockheed Lodestar airliner of civilian days, has taken over the job of towing the huge troop and cargo carrying gliders to replace the C 47's which had been used previously.

The tough job of pulling the gliders is being handled faultlessly by the fleet of 60's which arrived only recently from the Lockheed-Vega factories. The training schedule calls for the ships to fly an average of 18 to 20 hours daily, making continuous landings and takeoffs.

The Lockheed twin-engine ship, when converted for Army use, was intended as a troop-carrying plane. But it has stepped into the harder job of towing and has proved its ability to "take it."

The planes have earned the nickname "workhorse" from the long schedule the program requires them to fly. The only time they fail to fly, day or night, is when weather conditions make flying a nightmare and landing almost impossible.

The routine for the 60's is to pull a glider several thousand feet into the air and tow it around to give fledgling pilots experience behind the plane. The glider is then cut loose to make its own landing and the plane returns to the ground to pick up another glider.

The job of towing these huge gliders is one of the toughest assignments and requires an exceptionally strong plane to stand up to the strain. That is where the C-60's are making a reputation for themselves.

NATIONAL COUNCIL OF MANUFACTURERS FORMED

(Continued from Page 3)

Gross, President of Lockheed and of the Aircraft War Production Council (West Coast), said: "This new organization completes the management team for close cooperation with the armed services, the War Production Board, and other government agencies.

"It is this kind of teamwork—management and workers, industry and government, fighting forces and civilians—which is the American way of fighting and winning a war."

A check-up on the whereabouts of 1602 rural young men in an Ohio county showed that about 40 per cent were in the armed services and 32 per cent had moved to nearby industrial centers.

THE Lockheed-Vega Star

The Lockheed-Vega Star is issued every Friday for the employees of the Lockheed Aircraft Corporation and the Vega Aircraft Corporation and is the official publication of both companies. Communications may be addressed to either the Industrial Relations Office or the Public Relations Department, Lockheed Aircraft Corporation, Burbank, California, U.S.A. Although news and cartoon contributions are welcome, circumstances make it impossible to give any promise that they will be returned to sender when not used, nor can individual acknowledgment be made.

BERT W. HOLLOWAY, Editor-in-Chief
H. L. (HAL) ROSSON, Managing Editor

Volume 10 Number 18

Why Buy War Bonds

Why buy United States War Bonds? Simply because they are the world's biggest bargain.

Here's what you do with every War Bond you purchase under the payroll allotment plan:

1. **You save your money at a high rate of interest.**
2. **You keep taxes down.**
3. **You build up post-war purchasing power for yourself.**
4. **You help to prevent disastrous inflation.**
5. **You get refunds against your Victory Tax.**
6. **You save time and tires by buying your bonds this easy way, instead of making trips to a bank or postoffice.**
7. **You build up a nest egg for any possible emergency.**
8. **You lend your money to Uncle Sam at the rate of $3 and get back $4.**
9. **You fulfill your duty as a real American.**
10. **You put your dollars to work for Victory.**

You may now authorize purchase of War Bonds on the payroll allotment plan at your departmental office. If you are not already a member of the Lockheed-Vega army of "10 Per Centers," join today. Remember, the slogan, "THEY GIVE their lives, you LEND your money."

Open House For Service Men

The Vega Blue Star Service Women are holding an open house for the service men in this locality Monday evening, April 19, at the Burbank Recreation Center, 1111 W. Olive street, Burbank.

ATTENTION—SWING AND GRAVEYARD SHIFTS

Frank Wiggins Trade School announces a tuition free class in Plexiglass Fabrication, meeting Monday, Wednesday and Friday and Tuesday and Thursday. Classes are now in session from 12 noon to 3 p.m. and enrollment may be made at the school at 644 West 17th street, Los Angeles. Content of the class includes the fundamentals of all plastics, use and working of plastic bonded plywood, both platen pressed and "cooked" process; and developing skill in all phases of fabricating plexiglass and lucite used in aviation work.

★ Your JOB ★

By . . . .
R. RANDALL IRWIN

In a "last ditch stand" against inflation, the President on April 8 issued an executive order further limiting wage, salary and price increases. In a statement accompanying the order, the President said in part:

"Some groups have been urging increased prices for farmers on the ground that wage earners have unduly profited. Other groups have been urging increased wages on the ground that farmers have unduly profited. Any continuance of this conflict will not only cause inflation but will breed disunity at a time when unity is essential.

"To hold the line we cannot tolerate further increases in prices affecting the cost of living or further increases in general wage or salary rates except where clearly necessary to correct sub-standard living conditions. The only way to hold the line is to stop trying to find justifications for not holding it here or not holding it there.

"The order also makes clear the authority of the Chairman of the War Manpower Commission to forbid the employment by an employer of any new employee except in accordance with regulations of the chairman, the purpose being to prevent such employment at a higher wage or salary than that received by the employee in his last employment unless the change of employment will aid in the prosecution of the war."

The burden of applying the wage provisions of this order falls upon the War Labor Board, and the salary provisions upon the Treasury Department, both subject to certain controls by Economic Stabilization Director Byrnes. Control over changes in employment is a responsibility of the Chairman of the War Manpower Commission, likewise subject to the approval of the Economic Stabilization Director.

If the Executive Order prohibited absolutely all wage and salary increases and all changes in employment, it would be rather simple to administer, but obviously no such rigid regulations will be forthcoming. Such a "freeze" would develop injustices and pressures that would be explosive.

On the other hand, it is an extremely complex problem to administer the economic stabilization (anti-inflation) program in such a way as to be fair and just to everyone concerned. The attempt to give all parties and factors full and fair consideration is one reason for many of the delays in correcting maladjustments.

SUMMARY OF ACTION ON WAR LABOR BOARD DIRECTIVE

(Continued from Page 3)

It is the intent of the companies to fully abide by the Executive Orders issued by the President or Directives issued by the War Labor Board and in so doing place every employee in his proper work classification for which he will receive the proper wage rate.

There have been some delays in the application of certain portions of the recent Directive issued by the W.L.B. as these required interpretation and clarification by the W.L.B. West Coast Aircraft Committee, which is composed of representatives of management, labor, and the public.

Employees are assured that as rapidly as any such points are cleared, full information will be released and the clarified portions of any such Directives placed in operation as quickly as possible.

CONSTELLATION DANCE DUCATS READY NEXT WEEK

Tickets for the Constellation dance, sponsored for departments that worked on the Constellation, are to go on sale next week, according to the ticket sale committee.

Featuring the music of Maury Paul and his Californians, with Maxine Conrad as soloist, this party will be held at the Burbank's Elk Lodge, 145 East Palm on Saturday evening, April 24.

LOCKHEED DEPT. 1-24 WINS SAFETY TROPHY

More than 300,000 accident-free man-hours during March is the proud record of Experimental Department 1-24, Lockheed Plant 1. By virtue of this fine performance the department is displaying the Lockheed Safety Trophy and banner for the month. B. J. Basolo, J. J. McCabe and F. W. Fromm, in charge of Day shift, Night shift and Graveyard, respectively, extend congratulations to their personnel on this accomplishment.

Eighteen other Lockheed factory departments were also on the list of accident-free departments for the same month. They were: Lockheed-Vega Training, Precision Assembly, Lockheed-Vega Service, Guards, Metal Fittings, Paint and Finish, Template, Pattern-Plaster and Foundry, Intra-Factory Transportation, Wood Shop, Machine Shop, Fire Prevention, Fighter Aft Booms, Traffic and Transportation, Heat Treat and Process, Model 49 Fuselage and Trim Shop.

Plant 4 proved an ungracious host to the infamous White Elephant who packed his trunk (no pun) and is now living in Assembly Department 1-27, at Plant 3.

Work absences in a Cleveland, Ohio, plant were reduced by a labor-management drive from 22,000 hours to 8,500 hours in a four-month period, in spite of increased employment.

SPECIAL TAX EDITION MONDAY. WATCH FOR IT!

Volume 10 BURBANK, CALIFORNIA, U.S.A., JUNE 18, 1943 Number 27

THE *Lockheed-Vega Star* ★ ★

Official publication of the Lockheed and Vega Aircraft Corporations

To Mr., Mrs., and Miss Lockheed and Vega:

Ever have someone who **isn't** in war work say, "Nice racket you war workers and your companies have! The companies hire all the people they can find at higher salaries than non-war industries can pay—then teach them how to stall on the job, to run up the costs of war goods. The employees draw fat checks for easy work—and spread the job out—and the company—on those "COST PLUS" contracts—cleans up because the higher the COST, the higher the PROFIT! Nice racket on the taxpayers' money!"

Dare say you've heard such talk!

CAN YOU DE-BUNK THEM?

A few weeks ago we sent Lockheed people a special message which gave some pertinent facts on constantly accelerating production schedules and planning problems (applied principally to the P-38) and cleared up those questions about "stalling on the job."

But **WHAT ABOUT** "COST PLUS" CONTRACTS?

What are **they?**

In the **last** war there were "cost plus a **percentage**" contracts—which meant that the contractor's **profit** was a **percentage** of the **actual** cost of the goods. The profit was determined **AFTER** the contract was completed and all the actual costs were added up.

Thus the higher the **cost**, the higher the **profit**.

There are no such contracts for aircraft in THIS war.

There is a form of contract which is called "COST PLUS A **FIXED** FEE."

It is **quite different** from the old "cost plus a **percentage**" type.

First—The **fee** is determined on the basis of the **estimated** cost of the goods, **before they are manufactured.** It is a **fixed dollars** and **cents** amount.

Second—The cost is estimated on the basis of calculations, not only by the contractor, but also by the government's production experts.

Third—(and this is **most** important). **No matter how much greater** the **actual cost** is than the **estimated cost**, the contractor does **not** receive **any more** than the **fixed amount** determined **before the work was done!**

Fourth—The government agrees in such contracts to pay only **what the government** considers are **actual production costs!**

This means that many of the normal overhead costs of doing business are **disallowed** by the government, and the **company must pay** them, thus materially reducing the fee..

Fifth—Such disallowed costs include taxes, advertising, etc., so that although the **fee** may be based on 4% or 5% of the **estimated costs,** this does not mean that the company's **profit** is anything like that amount.

In certain contracts, the **disallowed costs** have actually absorbed practically all the fee.

Thus you can see that it is ABSURD for anyone to say that a company which has "cost-plus-a-fixed fee contracts" is purposely increasing costs in order to make larger profits!

You should therefore be able to **de-bunk** any such misfounded rumors!

Sincerely,

YOUR MANAGEMENT

Certificate Of Exemption In Time Card Racks Tuesday

The Current Tax Payment Act of 1943, commonly known as "Pay as you go" income tax plan, is now a law and the Government will start collecting the tax next month — at Lockheed and Vega, and everywhere throughout the nation.

Collection will be made through wage deduction, and the law requires the companies to withhold income tax installments from paychecks.

On next Monday, June 21, a special edition of the Lockheed-Vega STAR will be distributed to all employees, giving detailed explanation of the Exemption Certificate and describing the procedure of collection.

It is vitally important to every employee that he receive a copy of this special edition, and that he retain the copy for reference on the following day when Exemption Certificates will be distributed.

These Exemption Certificates will be in the time card racks Tuesday morning, or distributed by department heads to monthly employees. They must be completed and returned by Friday, June 25.

The amount of tax to be withheld will be 20 per cent of the excess of each payment of wages or salaries over the Family Status Withholding Exemption allowable.

Hence the importance of filling out the Exemption Certificates correctly and promptly.

ONE THING MORE!

The tax will be 20 per cent of the excess OVER the exemption. Not 20 per cent of the total wage. A lot of people who have been talking—not figuring—about the tax plan, are going to be pleasantly surprised that the nick in the paycheck won't be as deep as they thought.

So-o-o, don't cancel your agreement to invest in War Bonds just because you mistakenly believe you can't pay your income tax and buy bonds too. Probably you won't be hurt as badly as you expect to be.

Remember, this is NOT a 20 per cent increase in income taxes; it's a new method of collecting income taxes.

And you'll still need the savings represented by those bonds.

CAMERA CLUB FIELD TRIP

★

In their first field trip of the spring and summer season, both the Day and Swing shift L.E.R.C. Camera Clubs spent an interesting day in Griffith Park. Note that both men and women belong and equipment is secondary for, like all L.E.R.C. sponsored activities, the camera clubs are for everyone without dues or fees for membership.

★

L.E.R.C. GUN CLUB OFFERS COURSE FOR INDUCTEES

In an effort to provide the Armed Services with men familiar with the use of firearms, the L.E.R.C. Rifle and Pistol Club has been authorized by the National Rifle Association to sponsor a small arms firing school as a part of the Army-approved program being launched all over the country.

The Hoover High School indoor range will be used and those interested are advised to notify the L.E.R.C. so that instruction sessions can be scheduled. A $4.75 fee is charged, but this includes cost of targets, ammunition and other equipment as well as fully sponsored instruction.

These courses will begin as soon as classes are signed up. Those who expect to be inducted should register.

Applicants are asked to fill out the following form:

Name.. **Age**.......

Home Address..

Home Phone...................... **Draft Class**..............

Department.................... **Extension**..................

L.E.R.C. DANCE CLUB MEETS ON TUESDAY

Success of the newly sponsored L.E.R.C. Dance Club seems assured with the announcement that more than 50 attended the first meeting of the organization. Meetings are every Tuesday evening at the Hollywood Roosevelt Hotel, starting promptly at 7:30.

Assembling in the Studio Lounge, the group has one hour of instruction followed by social dancing for the balance of the evening. Any Lockheedian is welcome to attend.

DANCES - PICNICS FILL L.E.R.C. SLATE

Dances and picnics will fill the social calendar for the L.E.R.C. during the coming weeks, according to word from the L.E.R.C. office.

On Saturday, June 19, Plant 4 Day shifters will swing to the tunes of Joe Gist at the Royal Palms Hotel and tickets are still available at $1.10 and 65 cents.

Three picnics feature the events for June 27, with 1-86 holding its 75-cent a family get-together in Pepper Tree Lane, Griffith Park; Department 1-24-18 gathering in the council circle area of Griffith Park for their 50 cents a family gathering; and Department 1-02 staging their picnic at Roscoe Park with tickets selling at 50 cents.

In the evening, on June 27, Plant 4 Swing shifters will dance at the Royal Palms. Tickets are $1.10 and 65 cents.

JAYHAWKERS TO BE FETED ON JUNE 23

Continuing the popular State Lunch Pail picnics during the lunch periods at the several Lockheed plants, the Jayhawkers of Kansas will meet on Wednesday, June 23, at Plants 1, 3 and 4.

Plant 2 will honor North and South Dakota and Montana on Thursday, June 24, and Lunch Pail Picnics for Graveyard shifts are to be held during the lunch period the morning of June 24.

This newly sponsored L.E.R.C. event has been especially helpful in bringing old friends and acquaintances together and it is planned to continue holding the picnics until all forty-eight states have been honored.

DRAMA CLUB PLAY IN HOLDOVER RUN

Due to the tremendous popularity of the L.E.R.C. Drama Club production of "Eve of St. Mark," which reached sell-outs on several occasions, the run for this play has been extended for three more performances starting tonight and closing on Sunday evening.

Accorded one of the most enthusiastic receptions from Los Angeles and Hollywood audiences (including many theatrical agents and motion picture executives) this L.E.R.C. production has enjoyed splendid support from Lockheedians as well.

Many who have been unable to secure tickets for the regular run may now get seats either at 75 cents or 50 cents. This week-end will definitely find the show closing, so immediate ticket purchases are advised.

L. E. R. C. CALENDAR

FRIDAY, JUNE 18—Nutrition Class, 1-3 p.m., 907 Cordova St., Burbank.—Band Concert, Main Recreation Area, Rehearsal, 10 a.m.—"Eve of St. Mark," 1367 N. St. Andrews Place, Assistance League Playhouse, 8:30 Curtain.

SATURDAY, JUNE 19—Plant 4 Dance, Palm Room, Royal Palms Hotel, 8-12 p.m.—"Eve of St. Mark," 1367 N. St. Andrews Place, Assistance League Playhouse, 8:30 Curtain.

SUNDAY, JUNE 20—Department 1-86 Picnic, Pepper Tree Lane, Griffith Park.—"Eve of St. Mark," 1367 N. St. Andrews Place, Assistance League Playhouse, 8:30 Curtain.—Rangerette & Rangers Ride, Tex Stonehurst Stables, 8-10 a.m.

MONDAY, JUNE 21—Choral Club Rehearsal, 7:30 p.m., Burbank High School.

TUESDAY, JUNE 22—Dance Club Meeting, 7:30 p.m., Hollywood Roosevelt Hotel.—Leatherspankers, English Riding Club, 4:30-5:30 p.m., Du Brock's Stables, Riverside and Los Feliz.—Badminton, 7-9:30 p.m., John Burroughs Junior High School.

WEDNESDAY, JUNE 23—Boy Scout Meeting, John Muir School, 7 p.m.—Ranger & Rangerette Ride, 7-9 p.m., Tex Stonehurst Stables.—Service Star Women, Plant 1, Bandage Rolling Meeting, 907 Cordova Ave., Burbank, 3:30-6:30 p.m.—Plant 4 Horseback Riding, 8 p.m., Flying Horse Stables.—Kansas Lunch Pail Picnic, all lunch periods, Plants 1, 3 and 4.

THURSDAY, JUNE 24—Ranger & Rangerette Ride, Tex Stonehurst Stables, 9-11 a.m.—Rhumba Class, 7:30 p.m., Ballard's Studio, 1753 North Highland.—Bridge Club Meeting, Burbank Recreation Center, 7:30 p.m.—Plant 4 Swing Shift Moonlight Ride, Flying Horse Stables, 1 a.m.—North and South Dakota and Montana Lunch Pail Picnic, Graveyard Shift, Plant 2.

FRIDAY, JUNE 25—Nutrition Classes for Swing Shift and Wives of Lockheed Employees, 1-3 p.m., Activity House, 907 Cordova, Burbank.—Band Concert, Main Recreation Area.

LAST HUDSON STANDS IN SOLITARY SPLENDOR

AS SEEN THROUGH FUSELAGE OF RIVAL

The above striking photo of the last Hudson to roll off the Lockheed assembly line was taken through a center fuselage section of a "Constellation." The Hudson was the first U.S. plane to fight in World War II. At right, above, taking farewell of the ship which he helped so much to create, is Richard A. Von Hake, Lockheed Vice-President in Charge of Manufacturing.

SUNSET FOR THE '414'

" " " But to we, who saw her evolve from the commercial ship of peaceful industry to the sturdy, faithful ship of war, the sun will never set on the place she holds in our hearts.

" " " With every Hudson that flies, proudly flies a little of the people who built her " " " who were confident that she would write a glowing page in the history of aviation.

" " " And though her successors, which we will build with the same confidence and pride, will equal and surpass her splendid record, we will always point with pride to the 414. " " " —KEN RAYZOR

Veteran Combat Plane Gives Way To 'Constellation'

The last Hudson flew off to the wars yesterday.

One of the great airplanes of World War II, the famous Lockheed Hudson bomber yielded to pressure for larger, faster aircraft and gave up its place on the production line at Lockheed to the great new Constellation.

The Hudson had been in constant production for more than five years, but now it could be discontinued because Vega has brought its hard-hitting Vega Ventura, big brother to the Hudson, into quantity production.

The Hudson was the first airplane ever to capture a submarine. Curiously, as the last Hudson left the line, there came an announcement from the Navy Department that the Vega Ventura had joined the anti-submarine warfare in the Atlantic and that one of the Venturas had fought a sub, and sunk it.

First American war plane to fight in this war, the Hudson has piled up an impressive history in manufacturing as well as in combat. It was accepted by the British after Lockheed technicians had performed a normal three-months' job in 10 days, building a complete mock-up of a bomber version of the Lockheed Model 14 commercial transport in time for inspection by a British commission. This was the Hudson which joined combat against the Axis on September 3, 1939. Highlights from its unique record follow:

The Hudson remained in production from January, 1939, to June, 1943, or four and one-half years, and during the period several thousand of these sturdy ships were delivered to the United Nations.

Until the ferrying of Lockheed "Lightning" fighters became standard practice, more Hudsons had flown the Atlantic than all other aircraft combined.

Hudsons are now operated on all six continents of the world by American, British, Canadian, Australian, Chinese, Dutch, and other air forces of the United Nations.

Although designed chiefly for reconnaissance and patrol duty, the Hudson has been used also as a dive bomber, medium-range bomber, mast-high raider, a skip-raider, sub-buster and escort fighter.

To gain the affectionate nick-name "Old Boomerang," Hudsons have strug-

(Continued on Page 6)

(See Pages 4 and 5 for Picture Spread)

Every Theatre Of World War II Has Thrilled To The

Another epic chapter in the history of the Hudson was written when our own "Spirit of Lockheed-Vega" crash-landed while on Icelandic patrol in 1941. At first believed to be a total loss, the ship was salvaged by herculean efforts, repaired and still in service with R.A.F.

Above is a picture of the "Spirit of Lockheed-Vega" and her crew in Iceland after she had been rebuilt and returned to active duty. Since that time she has participated in many a successful submarine hunt off the Atlantic coast of Canada.

High honor and distinction were accord
the Hudson when "Old Boomerang" wa
vorite aerial transport. Recent reports a
Prime Minister Winston Churchill's favo
above stepping out of his private plane
his current visit to American and British

★

At right is Artist W. Krogman's conception of the first and only time in the history of warfare that a submarine surrendered to an airplane. The action occurred in 1941 "somewhere" off the coast of England. The aircraft, a Hudson of the R. A. F. Coastal Command, located the German sub, bombed it to the surface and then held it under the threat of its bombs and guns until British surface vessels put out to sea and herded it back to port.

At upper left a Hudson bomber is shown flying protection over the English Channel during the historic evacuation of Dunkirk.

Lower left, another official R.A.F. photograph, shows what a Hudson can take and still keep going. The craft got this hit while bombing a German convoy off the Dutch coast, but flew back to England and made a perfect landing.

★

Gallantry Of 'Old Boomerang' And Its Fighting Pilots

d the Lockheed-Vega organization and selected by King George VI as his fa-
e to the effect that the Hudson is also
ite. It is believed that the King, shown
flew to North Africa in his Hudson on
troops in that area.

In the Battle of North Africa converted Hudsons and Lockheed Lodestars played a stellar role as hospital ships in flying American wounded back to base hospitals. Above is a Hudson delivering its load of casualties to an ambulance for their ride to a hospital.

Protecting vital convoys over the English Channel and through the submarine-infested waters near the coast of the British Isles is another service in which the Hudson has made an outstanding record. Above, "Old Boomerang" hovers over a Channel fleet.

★

Men who have worked on the Hudson fabrication and assembly lines for months at Lockheed gather during their lunch hour period to view with affection the last representative of this famous fighter as she prepares to take off for parts unknown. Perhaps never, in the history of the U. S. aircraft industry, has a plane of any type evoked such universal admiration for toughness, stability and fighting qualities, from friend and foe alike, as "Old Boomerang."

Top right are three Hudsons flying somewhere over Australia, and at lower right, by way of contrast and versatility, are three others silhouetted against the eternal snows of Mt. McKinley, Alaska, highest peak on the North American continent.

★

Robert Young Stars On "Ceiling Unlimited"

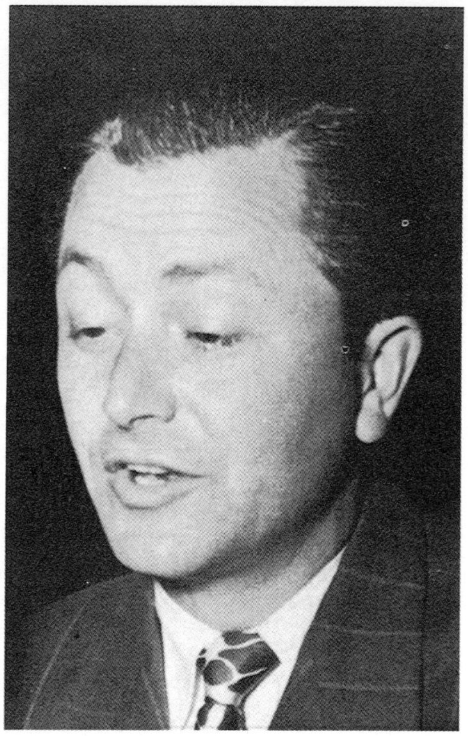

Robert Young salutes the men and women of Lockheed and Vega when he stars on their weekly CBS broadcast, "Ceiling Unlimited," Monday, June 21.

The story for this program tells of the North Atlantic air routes.

"Ceiling Unlimited" is heard over CBS stations at 7:15 p.m. (EWT) and at 8:15 p.m. (PWT) over KNX for local listeners.

A fast method of zinc plating, using AC or DC current, speeds production 100% to 200% in war plants and requires no new machinery.

LAST OF HUDSONS ROLL OFF LINE; MAKE ROOM FOR NEW CONSTELLATION

(Continued from Page 3)

gled back to base with half of a wing or tail shot away, the nose or an engine blown off, or the belly ripped open by collisions while strafing at sea level.

A Hudson once disabled a Nazi submarine by bombing; strafed it until the crew surrendered; and held it, with the help of another aircraft when the Hudson's fuel ran low, until surface vessels arrived to capture the U-boat intact. This was the only capture of a submarine, and all its crew, by an airplane in history.

Other Hudsons dive-bombed the Germans at Dunkirk; flashed word that the Nazi battleship Bismarck had left German waters on the foray which ended in its destruction; discovered the prison ship Altmark skulking in a Norwegian fjord with British prisoners aboard; served as the private plane of King George VI; carried on difficult Ice-Pack Patrol against submarines in the North Atlantic; protected most of the shores of the United Nations from the submarine menace; slaughtered 15,000 Jap troops attempting to land on the Malayan coast the same day the Japs attacked Pearl Harbor; performed shuttle duty carrying water, ammunition, fuel and other supplies to General Montgomery's British Eighth Army in pursuit of Rommel from El Alamein to Tripoli; and carried the fight into every quarter of the globe.

Shortly after the United States entered the war, delivery of Hudsons was diverted from the British to the United States Army Air Forces, and it was the AAF which accepted the last Hudson last week after test flights by Lockheed pilots. Conversion of facilities at the Lockheed factories has been under way for several weeks, as the Hudson assembly line gradually emptied.

VEGA GIRL CHOSEN FOR RADIO HONOR

Selected as an outstanding girl to represent the women who have made good in the Engineering Departments of aircraft industries, 19-year-old Mary Frances Sloan, Junior Detail Draftsman of

Mary Frances Sloan

Vega, was interviewed on the Blue network transcontinental radio program, "What Is Your War Job," June 16.

Mary Frances came to Vega in 1942 upon completion of the ESMWT Aircraft Drafting course at U.C.L.A. She is a graduate of Beverly Hills High School with majors in art and mathematics.

WARNING GIVEN PARKING AREA TO CLOSE MONDAY

Effective Monday, June 21, Lockheed company parking lot No. 2, between Wilson and Maria, south of San Fernando road, will be closed as a parking area for employees owing to commencement of construction of the new L.E. R.C. Cafeteria.

Ventura Wins Spurs In Combat

Another potent aerial weapon has been added to the imposing list of Southern California warcraft which already includes the "Lightning" P-38 fighter, the B-17 Fortress bomber which is built by two local plants, the Mitchell medium bomber and others.

The medium "Ventura" bomber, built by Vega in Burbank as the PV-1 for the Navy and the B-34 for the Army Air Forces, has won its spurs in combat. Rear Admiral John S. McCain, chief of the Naval Bureau of Aeronautics, yesterday wired the Vega workers as follows:

"TO THE MEN AND WOMEN OF VEGA AIRCRAFT CORPORATION:

"ALTHOUGH YOUR NEW 'VENTURA' PV-1s HAVE ONLY RECENTLY GONE ON ACTIVE DUTY WITH THE NAVY THEY ARE ALREADY PROVING THEMSELVES BY THEIR OUTSTANDING PERFORMANCE. THE EXCEPTIONAL FIGHTING QUALITIES OF THESE PLANES WERE DEMONSTRATED WHEN ONE OF THE FIRST PV-1s BATTLED AND SANK A NAZI SUB WHILE PROTECTING AN ATLANTIC CONVOY. DISPLAYING THE SPEED TO CATCH AND DESTROY U-BOATS BEFORE THEY CAN DIVE AWAY FROM DANGER THE 'VENTURA' ROARED DOWN ON THE SUB FROM SEVERAL MILES DISTANCE AND BLASTED IT TO THE BOTTOM WITH DEPTH CHARGES. THE BUREAU OF AERONAUTICS CONGRATULATES YOU ON THIS POWERFUL NEW ADDITION TO OUR ANTI-SUBMARINE FORCES. WE NEED MANY MORE OF THESE FINE 'VENTURAS' NOW!

JOHN S. McCAIN, Rear Admiral, U.S.N.
Chief of the Bureau of Aeronautics."

NAVAL AID TO SHOW GERMAN FIGHTER

The Buck-of-the-Month Club has been informed that the Naval Aid Society will have a Messerschmitt fighter on display this Friday, Saturday and Sunday on the grounds of the Edison School, Burbank.

Proceeds from this showing will go to the Naval Aid Society, which has already received the endorsement of the Buck-of-the-Month Club through donations made by that organization.

HONOR FALLS TO FERRY PILOT NOW WITH LOCKHEED

Credited with one of the top records in number of Hudsons ferried to England, Edward Browder, Jr., is the latest addition to Lockheed's famed group of test pilots.

Ed Browder's record reads like an aerial Cook's tour of all the oceans of the world. After learning to fly at Austin, Texas, while attending the University of Texas in 1936, he did considerable private flying until 1940 when he went to Canada and was commissioned in the R.C.A.F.

From 1940 to 1942 he served as a Flying Officer in the R.C.A.F. attached to the R.A.F. Ferry Command at Montreal. His real job then began—that of ferrying Hudsons across the Atlantic to England, at which nerve-racking task he spent approximately 500 hours. Later he was on coastal reconnaissance anti-sub patrol off both the Canadian and English coasts.

Since returning to the U.S. from service with the R.A.F., Browder, among other things, has worked with Pan-American Airways ferrying aircraft from Miami, Florida, to the British airforce in Africa and the Middle East; and later flew cargo and personnel from San Francisco to Australia for United Air Lines.

He joined Lockheed in March of this year and is currently engaged in test flying the "last Hudson" which rolled off the lines this week.

Speaking of Tools

Joe picks up a milling cutter from his bench and lightly tosses it to another spot. Joe has just rung up a fancy repair bill on a carbide tipped tool. While such tools are used to cut steel, the special cutting tips will break as easily as glass if they are handled improperly. Such things as dropping a cutter, laying it down roughly on a hard surface, or hitting the cutting tips in any way can put these tools out of commission.

Carbide tipped cutters are priority items, and they are expensive to buy and to recondition. Our shops depend on them to do most of their metal cutting.

Here are a few suggestions on handling a carbide tipped tool the right way:

1. When not in use keep the cutter in the special container supplied for the express purpose of protecting the tool.
2. Don't put cutters anywhere except in their own special containers.
3. When placing a cutter on a machine, be careful not to hit the cutting tips with your wrench or other equipment.
4. Don't let a cutter lay around, put it in its container IMMEDIATELY.

OCEAN FLYER TESTS LAST HUDSON

Edward Browder, Jr., holder of one of the top records on the Atlantic Hudson Ferry Service for the R.A.F., is now with Lockheed and Vega as a member of the companies' famed group of test pilots. Here he is shown standing under the nose of the "Last Hudson," which he is test flying this week. Wording on the ship was a sentimental tribute to "Old Boomerang" by the companies' pilots.

AUTO USE STAMPS ON SALE AT PLANTS

Through the cooperation of the U.S. Postoffice Department, it will be possible for employees of Lockheed and Vega to purchase their Federal Automobile Use Tax Stamps at Employee Transportation offices. These stamps must be purchased and placed on all automobiles not later than July 1. The tax is $5 and covers the full fiscal year, July 1, 1943 to July 1, 1944.

A representative of the Postoffice Department will be at Lockheed Plant 1 on June 21, 22 and 28. At Vega Plant 1 on June 23, 24 and 29. At Lockheed Plant 3 on June 25 and at Vega Plant 2 on June 26.

Stamps may be purchased at the above offices between the hours of 11 a.m. and 12:30 p.m. and 3 to 5:15 p.m.

Employees of Lockheed Plants 2, 4 and 7 may purchase their tax stamps at their Employee Transportation offices starting on June 21 and daily until July 1.

VICTORY GARDENS
"Weed 'em and Reap!"

L.&V. BLOOD DONOR DAY POSTPONED

Lockheed-Vega Blood Donor Day, scheduled for next Monday between the hours of 3:40 and 7:40 p.m. has been cancelled to permit the Red Cross Blood Donor Service unit to go to Warner Bros. Studio, where the all-soldier cast of the picture "This Is The Army" will make their contribution to the blood plasma bank before returning to their respective posts and camps.

A request from Warner Bros. to the Employee Victory Committee for the use of the mobile unit on this day brought instant approval. Norman Manning, public relations manager for the studio, in expressing appreciation for this cooperation stated, "It is only through the kindness and cooperation of your employees in giving up one of their regular dates for this fine cause that we are able to see this thing through. I would like to take this opportunity of expressing our thanks to Lockheed-Vega employees."

The next blood donor day for Lockheed Plants 1 and 3 and Vega Plants 1 and 2 will be Monday, June 28 between the hours of 3:40 and 7:40 p.m. Please make appointments early.

THE *Lockheed-Vega Star* ★ ★

The Lockheed-Vega Star is issued every Friday for the employees of the Lockheed Aircraft Corporation and the Vega Aircraft Corporation and is the official publication of both companies. Communications may be addressed to either the Industrial Relations Office or the Public Relations Department, Lockheed Aircraft Corporation, Burbank, California, U.S.A. Although news and cartoon contributions are welcome, circumstances make it impossible to give any promise that they will be returned to sender when not used, nor can individual acknowledgment be made.

BERT W. HOLLOWAY, Editor-in-Chief
H. L. (HAL) ROSSON, Managing Editor

Volume 10 Number 27

U.S.S. Los Angeles

Plans for the construction of a cruiser to be named the "U.S.S. LOS ANGELES" with funds raised through the purchase of War Bonds by citizens of Los Angeles County were announced early this week.

Representatives of the local War Savings committee said that all negotiations for the building of the cruiser have been completed by Secretary of the Navy Frank Knox and the Treasury Department.

Sale of $40,000,000 of bonds to finance the cruiser will be carried on during the entire month of July. Every community in the county will participate in the special cruiser campaign.

This will be the first time in naval history that a first-line ship has borne the name "LOS ANGELES."

Local War Savings committee workers said that a specific quota is being assigned to this community and that plans for the sale of War Bonds here during July in order to make the building of the cruiser possible are being made on a scale that will equal or surpass the recent second war loan drive.

More than 100 local committee chairmen from all sections of the county met last week in Los Angeles and heard plans for the drive outlined by Albert S. Scott, county War Savings chairman.

The spectacular "build the cruiser campaign" will be launched officially on June 30 under the personal auspices of Secretary of the Navy Knox. The secretary will make two formal "kickoff" speeches that day in Los Angeles—at a noon luncheon in the Biltmore Hotel and on the same evening in the Hollywood Bowl.

Tickets to the Hollywood Bowl meeting will be available here through the local War Savings committee.

Attention, All Vega Employees!

The V.E.R.C. office has been moved to a new location just outside the plant area. Located at 2425 Avon street, the office is one block east of Hollywood Way and the first house north of the ramp. Office hours remain from 7 a.m. to 12:30 a.m., and the telephone extension, 1735, is the same. All Mutual ticket agency contacts are to be made at this office, BUT NOT BY TELEPHONE.

WAR PRODUCTION BOARD CLARIFIES HOLIDAY POLICY

The following teletype from the Aircraft Production Board, Washington, has been received by the management:

Washington, D.C., June 11, 1943
Lockheed and Vega Aircraft Corporations
Burbank, Calif.

The Aircraft Production Board has established a policy by which it will insist that work proceed on the basis of normal operations through Sundays immediately preceding or following holidays, and on a full production basis on holidays at all companies in the aircraft industry that cannot meet their scheduled production for the months involved. Using your established schedules as a basis, you are requested to govern your operations through July 4, Labor Day, and subsequent holidays accordingly. You will be notified of any deviation from the above established policy.

C. E. Wilson, Chairman
Aircraft Production Board

L.E.R.C. NEEDS MORE PLANT TOUR HELP

Despite the enthusiastic response to a call for L.E.R.C. Plant Tour guides, the L.E.R.C. Educational Committee is still anxious to have more persons register for this activity.

Those willing to do this are asked to send in name, department number, shift and day or days they will serve as guides.

JOB CLASSIFICATION DEADLINE EXTENDED

In conformance with Order No. 30 of the West Coast Aircraft Committee, approved by the Tenth Regional War Labor Board, the Industrial Relations Office calls attention to the following notice issued by the committee:

NOTICE, NON-FACTORY EMPLOYEES

Because of the vast amount of detail work and study required, it has been found impossible for this Committee to order into effect a uniform job classification plan and wage rate schedule for non-factory workers by June 3, 1943, as provided in the National War Labor Board's Directive Order of March 3, 1943. The West Coast Aircraft Committee has, therefore, extended the time for concluding these schedules to July 3, 1943, and has ordered that all wage increases that may be provided in such schedule shall be retroactive to the payroll date nearest March 3, 1943.

Keglers In Wind-Up Plays

Concluding games in the Vega all-plant bowling tournament will be played Saturday and Sunday, June 19 and 20, at the Magnolia Bowling Center, announces Tom Barbour, bowling committee chairman. All Vegans are invited.

★ *Your* JOB ★

By . . . .
R. RANDALL IRWIN

From Burbank To Pantelleria

The fall of Pantelleria seemed far-off from the California plants and Dallas base of Lockheed and Vega. But every aircraft worker has reason to take pride and satisfaction in knowing that the planes he personally has helped to build have demonstrated beyond doubt that air power will be the one outstanding factor in winning the war.

In the words of Maj. Gen. James H. Doolittle, "The capitulation (of Pantelleria) proved conclusively that no agency can stand up under the prolonged, concentrated bombardment of properly selected objectives."

Congress Passes Anti-Strike Law

At this writing the Connally-Smith anti-strike bill has passed both houses of Congress and is on the President's desk for signature or veto. He is faced with a tremendously difficult decision.

The President's record as a friend of organized labor is clear. Seldom has he taken an action at variance with the wishes or demands of the leaders of organized labor. If he signs the Connally-Smith bill, he may lose their political support.

Adoption of anti-strike legislation was halted several months ago when organized labor gave the President a solemn pledge there would be no strikes for the duration. Most labor leaders have earnestly attempted to keep that pledge, but damaging strikes and work stoppages continue. Most of them have been "unauthorized" by labor leaders.

The result is that an overwhelming majority of the public favors anti-strike legislation. Congress is merely reflecting the mood of the public.

During the last 10 years there has been too much government in business. It looks as if organized labor is going to have a taste of the same experience.

It is hoped that some day a self-disciplined labor movement and industrial management will regain the public's confidence so that they can work together to throw off some of the shackles that will handicap the future development of American business and industry.

If we all want free enterprise in this country—and we do—now is the time for labor and agriculture and management to work together to preserve it. If we do, we will,—if we don't, we won't.

THE *Lockheed-Vega Star* ★ ★

Official publication of the Lockheed and Vega Aircraft Corporations

Volume 10 | BURBANK, CALIFORNIA, U.S.A., AUGUST 6, 1943 | Number 34

This Group Of USAAF Officers Made 'Lightning' History

The four officers of the U.S. Army Air Forces shown above have not only made aviation history by being the first to fly P-38's across the North Atlantic from America to England, but one of them, Lieut. Col. Cass S. Hough (second from the left) has established what, to date, appears to be the highest speed ever attained by any human being on earth. An official report, released this week, reveals that Col. Hough, test diving a Lightning over England, hit 780 miles an hour. In the picture above he is shown with Col. Ben S. Kelsey (extreme left), first man ever to fly a P-38; Col. James E. Briggs, and Col. John K. Gerheart.—Photo was taken at time of their epic transatlantic hop.

DRAFTING AIRCRAFT WORKERS DEFERRED FOR TWO MONTHS

Pursuant to a directive issued by the National Director of Selective Service, inductions into the Armed Forces of men engaged in the production of military aircraft will be stayed during the months of August and September.

Therefore, if you receive an order from your draft board to report for induction you should promptly notify the Selective Service Department at Lock-

(Continued on Page 6)

World Record P-38 Dive Told For First Time

"HE TOLD ME HE WENT STRAIGHT DOWN—VERTICAL—IN A FULL POWER DIVE, EVERYTHING WIDE OPEN, AND THAT HE HOLLERED LIKE A BANSHEE ALL THE WAY DOWN FROM 43,000 TO 18,000. THEN HE LEVELED OFF IN A WIDE ARC AND WAS IN LEVEL FLIGHT AGAIN AT ABOUT 8,000 FEET."

In these dramatic words Hall L. Hibbard, vice-president and chief engineer of Lockheed, this week described second-hand the longest vertical dive in history—nearly five miles—made at 780 miles an hour in a Lockheed Lightning P-38 by Lieut. Col. Cass Hough of Plymouth, Mich., last September.

(Continued on Page 6)

24 L. & V. 'VETS' RECEIVE 10-YEAR PINS

Twenty-four Lockheed and Vega veterans who completed a decade of service with the companies between January and August this year received their Ten-Year Service pins and certificates at a brief conference in the office of Lockheed President Robert E. Gross last Friday afternoon. Left to right, front row: Norman F. Loop, 124; Wayne Strong, Vega 57; Eldon W. Paine, 756; Theodore D. Boyd, 325; Carl Beed; 325; Second row: Harold Y. Read, 234; Robert W. Pearson, Vega 7; John C. Neill, 131; Robert E. Gross, President; Harold L. Gammill, 131; Albert T. Smith, 220; Henry M. Baker, 325. Third row: Frank Hontz, Vega 57; David U. Cartwright, 137; Jim K. Reynolds, 132; Jack L. Nichols, 325. Top row: Ivan H. Stearman, 119; Harry Sirsch, 104; John H. Sreenan, 137; Irvin Clifford, 115; John J. Gerber, 325; James E. Lewis, 131; Abraham J. Grafman, 49 Project; Washington I. Sweet, Vega 31. Not in the picture, although awarded 10-year pins recently, are William L. McFee, Vega 63; William Bernhard, 104; Vera L. Doane, 768; and La Verne K. Arthur and Belmont W. Messer, LOC.

IF YOU WANT YOUR VACATION CHECK, CHECK THESE RULES

The heavy volume of vacation paper work makes it necessary that the present procedure covering deadlines for vacation checks be strictly adhered to, D. H. Cameron, personnel manager of Lockheed, reports. He continues:

"Therefore, in order to issue vacation checks by the Friday before the employee goes on his vacation, it will be necessary that the approved VACATION REQUEST CARD (or Vacation Change Card) be submitted to the Personnel Records Department by 9 a.m. of the third Thursday prior to the actual vacation week.

"Beginning Saturday, August 7, all Vacation Request Cards submitted to the Personnel Records Department will be honored *only* according to this schedule. Consequently, employees expecting vacation checks by Friday, August 20, for vacations to begin Monday, August 23, must have their cards filed with their departments in time to reach Personnel Records by 9 a.m., Saturday, August 7. All subsequent requests shall be handled on the same time schedule, and no vacation checks will be issued prior to the vacation period, unless the above schedule is met."

TOO MANY STICKERS VIOLATE OPA RULING

A recent communication from the OPA points out that many automobile owners are violating rationing regulations by displaying more than one ration sticker on the windshield of their automobiles.

The regulations clearly provide that ONLY one gasoline ration sticker be so displayed and that this one be the "B" or "C" sticker if such a ration book has been issued. The OPA communication also points out the fact that it is a violation of the law to display an "A" sticker on the car if it is being operated under supplemental gasoline allowances, and subjects the owner to a penalty.

All gasoline coupons must be clearly marked on the front side with the name of the state in which they were issued and the license number of the car. Failure to so mark coupons makes the car owner liable to certain penalties.

Here Are Answers To What Material Conservation Means

Material conservation and waste prevention have long been recognized as two of the most important "musts" in the winning of this war.

While Lockheed and Vega personnel have made great strides in the field of conservation, many employees apparently do not believe they can play a part in this vital program for the simple reason that they appear to misunderstand the true meaning of the word "conservation."

To clarify this point and to show the importance of 100 per cent cooperation, the Material Conservation Departments have compiled a list of questions and answers which should materially aid in removing doubt from the minds of skeptical employees. The questions and answers follow:

Q. I am a riveter in a sub-assembly department. How can I conserve material?

A. You can see that small parts are not wasted and that rivets are not mixed or dropped.

Q. I am a Parts Lister. I don't handle any material. Does conservation concern me?

A. Yes, as on your accuracy depends the accurate procurement and disbursement of parts which in turn contribute to a saving of time.

Q. I am a truck driver and don't manufacture anything, therefore how would I waste anything?

A. Your job is most important. Improper handling of material and assemblies can be a severe handicap to production. Always be sure that your truck is properly loaded and handled so that material will not be damaged.

Q. I am a stenographer and my work is rather removed from material, isn't it?

A. No. Accuracy of your transcription and typing can contribute to economical uses of stationery, and correct interpretation of the letters and instructions you type for the guidance of persons using manufacturing material is a big contribution.

Q. I run a turret lathe in the machine shop. How can I help?

A. Have the first part checked before you complete the run. Save scrap but

(Continued on Page 8)

No Holding Mamma These Days

Russ Weil, Lockheed Plant Engineer, reports seeing on a trip to Pomona Plant 8 last week a sign on the highway saying: "Cease worrying—Mother does the cooking!"

About a hundred yards nearer the Lockheed plant was a second sign which read: "Closed for the duration—Mamma's working at Lockheed."

Signs of the times?

Joseph Cotten Now Maestro Of 'Ceiling Unlimited'

"Ceiling Unlimited" takes on a new meaning next Sunday, August 8, when the Lockheed and Vega radio program, "America—Ceiling Unlimited," appears for the first time under its revised formula over the Columbia network, coast to coast, at 11 a.m., Pacific War Time.

Occupying the spotlight will be Joseph Cotten as master of ceremonies, supported by comely Nan Wynn as vocal soloist, Wilbur Hatch and his orchestra of 24 pieces, a vocal chorus and Pat McGeehan as announcer.

The new "America—Ceiling Unlimited," supplanting James Hilton, has been extended to thirty minutes instead of the quarter-hour which has been the Monday procedure of the past.

As master of ceremonies, Cotten, currently appearing with Deanna Durbin in the film, "Hers to Hold," partly filmed at Vega, will have every opportunity to display the versatility for which he is noted, for he will repeat humorous stories Americans are telling, appear in the drama representing highlights of life in America and cite the books Americans are reading.

Designed to be up-to-the-minute in entertainment, "America—Ceiling Unlimited" provides for listeners a cross-section of what Americans are thinking, saying, reading and singing from week to week.

Miss Wynn, who came here recently from New York to appear in pictures, has drawn the assignment of singing each Sunday the song which is most timely in America. Her number for the opening program is the currently popular "You'll Never Know."

DRILL BREAKAGE IS BIGGEST DAMAGE BILL

Broken drills are responsible for half the cost of all damaged tools. The correct use of drills is of utmost importance in reducing the enormous cost of such breakage. Following are a few suggestions to keep in mind when drilling:

1. **When drilling always hold the drill at 90° to the surface of the work.**
2. **Always support an extension drill.**
3. **Select the proper drill for the proper motor. Make sure the motor and drill are correctly matched.**
4. **Use the correct speed motor for the drill size. Too high speed breaks drills.**
5. **Always center the drill in the bushing. Avoid angular approaches.**
6. **Tighten the drill in the chuck properly. Use a chuck key where possible.**
7. **Drill directly ahead; avoid side pressure.**
8. **Use a lubricant on the drill. The tool cribs will provide the correct lubricant.**

FEATURED ON NEW RADIO PROGRAM

Principals of new Lockheed and Vega radio program, "America—Ceiling Unlimited," are, left to right: Wilbur Hatch, musical director; Nan Wynn, vocalist, and Joseph Cotten, master of ceremonies. The program makes its debut next Sunday, August 8, over the Columbia network at 11 a.m., PWT, with KNX the local outlet. "America—Ceiling Unlimited" has been extended to thirty minutes for the new series.

New Classes To Open

New classes sponsored by the Burbank School System, University of California, and the California Institute of Technology will soon be open for enrollment.

The University of California is offering several new classes among which are:

Die Design, taught by Eugene E. James of Lockheed. The course will cover 16 weeks of lecture and laboratory work necessary as a foundation for the design of drawing dies. Class will begin August 9 and will meet every Monday and Wednesday nights from 6:30 to 9:30 p.m. at 3570 Magnolia boulevard, Room "A."

Tool Planning & Manufacturing Engineering, Part III, will be offered with Dan C. White of Lockheed as instructor, starting August 9. Class will meet on Mondays from 6:30 to 9:30 p.m. for a period of 16 weeks at 3820½ Magnolia boulevard, Burbank.

Free instruction in Machine Shop, including engine and turret lathe, surface grinder, milling machine, shaper, and jig borer, is available at the Burbank Technical Institute, 1809 West Magnolia on either Tuesday or Thursday from 6 to 12 midnight.

Radio Engineering, Part II, will start Thursday, August 12, at the U.C.L.A. Campus. Class will meet Thursdays in Room 126 of the Chemistry Bldg., from 7:30 to 9:30 p.m.

The California Institute of Technology is offering three courses in Plastics for which advance registration should be made. Apply at Lockheed-Vega Education Department.

ESTIMATED TAX DECLARATIONS DUE SEPTEMBER 15

The current Tax Payment Act of 1943, effective July 1, requires all persons who receive taxable income in excess of $2700 per year if single, or $3500 if married, from salaries, wages or commissions, to file on or before September 15, 1943, a Declaration of Estimated Tax for the year 1943. The Collector of Internal Revenue will shortly have available the forms to be used in the filing of such estimates, and a supply of these forms will be made available for Lockheed and Vega employees.

In the preparation of the Declaration of Estimated Tax employees will need information as to the probable amount of income that will be paid them in 1943 from Lockheed and Vega.

Early this year the company gave each employee a payroll accounting slip showing the earnings received during the year 1942 for assistance in preparation of employees' 1943 income tax

(Continued on Page 8)

DEANNA DURBIN NOW A VEGA 'BLUE STAR'

Honorary membership in the Vega Blue Star Service Women's organization was awarded to Deanna Durbin recently when 15 Blue Star members whose husbands are in the Air Corps were guests at Universal studios for dinner and a private showing of "Hers to Hold," new Deanna Durbin picture featuring Vega. Opal Lynch, whose husband is an aerial gunner, is shown above presenting the pin to Miss Durbin, while Frances Gladish, whose husband is a pilot in the Ferry Command, looks on. Deanna's husband, Vaughn Paul, is a Navy ensign.

Plant 2 Stages Wrestling Bout

Vega Plant 2 had its first wrestling match on the new stage in the lunch area recently when Mike Wark and the "Maintenance Mad Man," both of Lockheed, gave an exhibition performance for Plant 2 workers, according to Ellis Craig, V.E.R.C. entertainment director.

Vega All-Stars Beat Douglas

Vega All-Stars chalked up another victory last week when they won over the Douglas Long Beach softball team by a score of 15-0 in a match held in Long Beach.

Attention All Vega Employees!

Coffee cups, soft drink bottles, silverware, and china should not be taken from the luncheon areas.

The V.E.R.C. commissary is sustaining a loss of more than $200 each day for missing coffee cups. In addition to the monetary loss, because of priorities, it is not certain that the cups can be replaced. Since the commissary is not able to purchase paper cups, there is no alternative but to use china.

Your cooperation is requested. Please do not remove cups, bottles, and silverware from the canteen areas.

BUY WAR STAMPS AND BONDS!

V. E. R. C. ACTIVITIES—August 8 to 14

PLANT 2 RIDING CLUB—Every Friday evening at 7 p.m., at Ride-A-While Stables. $1.60 covers ride, dance and hot meal. Make reservations by Wednesday of the week in which you ride.

FENCING CLUB—Meeting Faulkner School of Fencing, 5610 Hollywood Blvd., Tuesday, 7:30 p.m. Swing shift meets 1 p.m., same place.

VEGA VAQUEROS—Every Friday, Pico Stables, 420 Riverside Drive, Burbank, 7 p.m. For reservations call CH. 6-5272.

BLUE STAR SERVICE WOMEN—Plan to attend the Open House for service men held at the Burbank Recreation Center, 1111 West Olive, Burbank, every Monday evening from 7 to 11 p.m. For further information, contact the V.E.R.C. office. The monthly "brunch" will be held Sunday, August 15, at 11 a.m. at the Hollywood Roosevelt Hotel. Tickets are on sale now at $1.10.

PLANT 2 SWIMMING CLUB—Pickwick Swim Park, Friday, from 4 to 6.

PENGUIN AND PENGUINETTE DANCE—"Get-Together" Dance to be held at the Oakmont Country Club, Glendale, on Saturday, August 21, from 9 p.m. until 1 a.m. Tickets are now on sale at $1.10 per person.

GOLF—Tournament on Sunday, August 22, at Inglewood Country Club. Open to all Vega golfers. Entry blanks at V.E.R.C. office.

NEELEY PLUMB'S BAND TO PLAY FOR COMBINED SOCIAL CLUBS AUG. 21

Neeley Plumb and his orchestra have been secured for the combined Penguin and Penguinette dance scheduled for Saturday evening, August 21, at the Oakmont Country club in Glendale, according to Frances Gotwalt, Day shift Penguinette president. Dancing will begin at 9 and continue until 1 a.m.

With the dance planned as a "get together" affair, the executive boards of the two organizations hope it will build a closer unity between the two clubs.

Tickets are now on sale at the V.E.R.C. office and booths and may also be secured from members of the two organizations. Deadline for ticket purchases is Wednesday, August 18.

VEGA BLUES TOPS IN 'TRIPLE A' LEAGUE

First place in the "Triple A" Municipal Sunday morning softball league is the honor won by the Vega Blues, a softball team composed of Graveyard, Swing and Day shift men. With only one game lost in league play, the Blues have won an enviable record, according to John Heinzman, assistant V.E.R.C. recreation director.

Playing at Rancho Park, San Vicente, and Culver City, the Vega team meets such opponents as the Bret Harte Dodgers, the Los Angeles Examiner, and M. G.M. Studios softball teams.

DONALD DUCK TO STAR AT WOMEN'S 'BRUNCH' MEET

Donald Duck in person will entertain members of the Vega Blue Star Service Women's club when they meet for their monthly "brunch" at the Hollywood Roosevelt Hotel on Sunday morning, August 15.

In addition to the "voice" of Donald Duck, Milton Neil, who draws the fighting duck for Walt Disney, will give a story board talk with cartoons. Also scheduled on the program for Blue Star entertainment is Johnnie Clark, tenor, in a repeat performance.

Tuesday, August 10, is the deadline for tickets, warns Betty Walker, social committee chairman for the Day shift.

Golf Tourney Entries Climb

More than 30 entries are already in for the all-plant golf tournament scheduled for Sunday, August 22, at the Inglewood Country club, reports Willie Barber, golf chairman.

Share Your Car For Victory!

BUCK OF THE MONTH BUILDS UP BIG FUND

In a regular report to the members, the Lockheed-Vega Employees' Buck of the Month Club statement shows that more than a half million dollars has been voluntarily given to the Buck of the Month Club since its inception and that almost $500,000 has been allocated to worthy charities in the same period of time.

"Anticipating certain large donations early in the fall, your Buck of the Month Club executive committee has a balance of $71,000 over and above the $40,000 Lockheed-Vega employee emergency fund to be available for county-wide war chest solicitations," Chairman Dale O. Reed emphasizes.

The complete financial report follows:

Financial Report

BUCK OF THE MONTH CLUB

July 31, 1943

Contributions		
Lockheed Employees	$379,655	
Vega Employees	217,388	
Triplett & Barton	1,004	
L.E.R.C. Employees	360	
V.E.R.C. Employees	802	
Publication Employees	32	
Miscellaneous	1,847	
British Reassembly Division	462	
		$601,552
Total amount donated for period March 31, 1942 to March 31, 1943, as previously reported in the STAR		$372,867
Disbursements (since March 31, 1943)		
Refunds	$ 73	
Bonding	720	
Miscellaneous (Check Book)	2	
Annual Audit	75	
Service Men's Recreation Fund	400	
Visiting Nurse Association	232	
Naval Aid Auxiliary	2,500	
Milton Berry Found'n (Paralytics)	1,000	
Service Men's Bible Committee	500	
Boys' Club of Hollywood	1,500	
Assistance League of So. Calif.	500	
Foothill Preventorium for Girls	200	
Pasadena Preventorium	200	
Crippled Children's Society	500	
Vets of Foreign Wars (Poppy Day)	1,250	
Amer. Legion Auxil. (Poppy Day)	750	
Army Canteen	4,000	
Navy Canteen	4,000	
Marine Corps Canteen	5,000	
Travelers Aid Society	900	
American Red Cross	25,663	
Battery F	40	
Battery F (Lockheed C. A.)	578	
Vega Blue Star Service Women	250	
Salvation Army	6,240	
Colored Boys' Home	300	
Service Men's Center	25	
Wounded Sailors at Norco Hospital	92	
Disabled American Vets, 9th Dist.	1,000	
Christian Service Organization	750	
Service Star Women of Lockheed	450	
Calif. Babies & Children's Hospital	1,000	
174th & 74th Chem. Unit—Army	48	
United Hospital Fund of L.A.	30,000	
Ruth Home	500	
St. Joseph's Hospital, Burbank	25,000	
Reynolds Tob. Co. (Xmas Gifts to Service Men)	3	
Citizens Committee—Army & Navy	125	
Nursery School	150	
Junipero Serra Boys' Home	250	
		$116,798
		$489,666
BALANCE*		$111,885

*Of this balance $40,000 is to be maintained at all times by the Club as an Emergency Fund to be used in case of a civilian war disaster.

ATTENDANCE RECORDS CLIMB

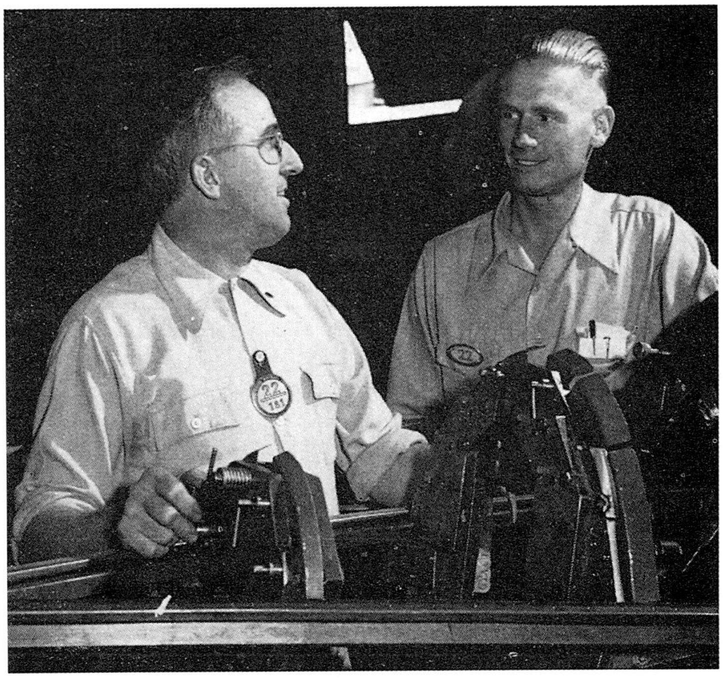

Allen O. Johnson, Dept. 2-22, Supervisor of Major Jigs, and John Jacobs, Dept. 2-22, discuss old times and compare their attendance records. Allen has been at Lockheed since January 14, 1935, and has been absent only six days. Allen introduced John Jacobs, left, to his job in 1937 on the Model 14 flap track assembly jigs. At that time Allen must have stressed attendance, because Jacobs has not been absent or tardy since.

LOCKHEED DEPT. 1-01 SETS BOND RECORD

Power of the printed word aided and abetted by the impetus of competitive war bond buying hit a new high in Lockheed Department 1-01 (Plant Engineering and Maintenance) last week-end.

In last Friday's issue of the STAR, page 2, appeared a picture and caption announcing the purchase by the department of $12,500 worth of bonds toward engineering and maintenance of the U. S. Cruiser Los Angeles. Plant Engineer J. Russell Weil vowed the total would climb to $15,000 by the end of the month.

Well, here's what actually happened—and if any other department can beat it, let's hear from them.

By Saturday evening, day after the story appeared, ANOTHER $9,000 WORTH OF BONDS WERE BOUGHT, bringing the total not to $15,000, BUT TO $25,014!

And incidentally, Plant 3, one of the smaller plants in the Lockheed organization, was way out in front, both in number of bonds bought and total of dollars invested. But that does not detract from the magnificent showing made by 1-01 in all units and, as stated above, if any other department can beat this record, the STAR would like to hear about it.

Dig deeper and send more dollars into the fight. Increase your payroll savings for War Bonds.

NO TIME LOST IN OVER FIVE YEARS

Since the first "STAR" article on employees with good attendance records appeared, many cases have been brought to light of Lockheed employees having noteworthy records.

John Jacobs, of Dept. 2-22, is one of them. He has been with Lockheed five and one-half years, says that the principal requirement for good attendance is a normal, healthy life, including plenty of sleep. Jake, as he is called by his associates, is a dyed-in-the-wool machinist and jig maker. In addition to his machinist's experience acquired before Lockheed, he has in his possession five certificates for technical courses related to his work.

Jake has not been absent or tardy since April 30, 1937, when he joined Lockheed and its 985 employees. He works in Dept. 2-22, Plant 2, and is building lower and upper rudder jigs for the P-38. Plant 2 is certainly proud of his record.

Despite his good attendance record, Jake takes a back seat to his father, who at 84, still packs eight hours into every day's work.

New L.E.R.C. Secretary

Eleanor Clark, Dept. 7-96 Swing shift, was elected to fill the position of secretary of the L.E.R.C., left vacant by the resignation of Betty Dixon Foust.

Miss Clark has served on the Executive committee as a departmental representative and has been especially active in women's bowling.

R. Randall Irwin Loaned To War Manpower Board

Appointment of R. Randall Irwin, for ten years Industrial Relations Director of Lockheed and Vega, to an important

R. Randall Irwin

executive post in the War Manpower Commission in Washington, was announced this week.

Administrative Vice-President Cyril Chappellet announced that Irwin had been loaned to the Commission at the urgent request of the government agency and of the aircraft industry, in view of the magnitude of the manpower problem and of Mr. Irwin's broad experience in the field of industrial relations.

He will be Executive Assistant to the management members of the War Manpower Commission's policy committee, having served as a member of this committee since its inception, dividing his time between Washington and Burbank.

At the same time it was revealed that Mr. Irwin had been appointed to a new position in the companies, that of Assistant to the Administrative Vice-President, in which he will advise the managements of Lockheed and Vega on industrial relations policies, trends and problems, nationally and locally. He will give full time to the government work however, as long as his services are needed in Washington, Chappellet stated.

William W. Aulepp was named Industrial Relations Director for Lockheed and Vega, with R. B. Robertson continuing as assistant director.

Mr. Aulepp previously was Assistant Industrial Relations Director in charge of personnel administration. He came to Lockheed and Vega a year ago from a manufacturing executive position in General Foods Corporation, to head up the work simplification program of these companies.

Mr. Irwin's promotion this month rounds out ten years of work with Lockheed, and 15 years in the aviation indus-

William W. Aulepp

try. He was editor of Western Flying Magazine for five years before coming to Lockheed. He established Lockheed personnel department and has been responsible for the company's selection, hiring and training of personnel since the days when Lockheed had fewer than 100 employees.

DRAFTING AIRCRAFT WORKERS DEFERRED FOR TWO MONTHS

(Continued from Page 1)

heed 1511 or 3111 or Vega 1715. If time permits you may do this by ANVO.

In order to expedite the handling of such cases the Selective Service Department will require the following information: name of employee, Clock number, job classification, Selective Service Board number and address, Selective Service Order number, and date employee is ordered to report for induction.

BUY WAR STAMPS AND BONDS!

LIGHTNING'S 780 MILE PER HOUR DIVE REVEALED

(Continued from Page 1)

Kept secret until now, first official report of Hough's feat was flashed out of London yesterday when United States Army Headquarters in England announced that Hough, who is Technical Director of the 8th Fighter Command, had been awarded the Distinguished Flying Cross for "flights which took him knowingly into unexplored fields."

"Col. Hough returned to the factory shortly after his dive, to give us a complete report on his findings," Hibbard revealed. "The dive was made in England in one of the first P-38's to fly across the Atlantic. Hough said one of the reasons why he did it was that he wanted to convince the British that the P-38 could do certain things they said it couldn't do.

"He made his dive on a very clear day in a standard P-38 that was in no way fitted out especially for a feat of this kind. Of course, he had plenty of oxygen, which he used throughout the high altitude phases of the flight and until he had pulled out of his dive.

"Hough told us that when he reached 43,000 feet he turned over on his back and slipped into the dive. He opened the throttle wide, gave the plane everything her two Allison engines had and kept her vertical until he hit 18,000 feet. Then he eased out. The noise, he said, was deafening as the wind struck the plane at such a high velocity. In fact, the two most definite impressions of the dive that he had afterwards were the noise of the wind and the crazy way in which the altimeter and rate of climb indicator dials kept spinning.

"He told us that he'd suffered no ill effects from the dive other than ears that were stopped up for a couple of days. The plane, he said, had taken it in stride and had felt very solid all the way down. There was no buffeting and the entire procedure including the pull-out was as easy as the flow of oil."

Hough was one of four Air Forces colonels who flew Lockheed Lightnings across the Atlantic a year ago in the first trans-oceanic flight by fighter aircraft. The officers were accompanied by scores of other P-38's and convoying bombers flying in mass formation.

Vega's Dunham Golf Wiz

After defeating Johnny Dawson, one of the world's leading amateur golfers, one up in match play Saturday, July 31, Bill Dunham of the Vega Department 12 Graveyard shift proceeded to follow this stunning victory Sunday by winning the pro-amateur tournament at Lakeside with Marian Stahl as his partner. Their score of 63 beat out the well-known John Montague and his partner by one stroke.

COUNSELING FOR EMPLOYEES PROVES VALUABLE SERVICE

Today, more than ever, due to wartime conditions, employees find themselves frequently in need of advice on personal problems. One of the most valuable services now being rendered Lockheed and Vega people through Employee Service is that of counseling. This service is available without cost and is conveniently located within the plant areas.

Advice and counseling on the following subjects are offered as a part of the service: Federal and State Income Tax, Withholding Tax, Real and Personal Property Taxes, Domestic Relations, Government Allotments for dependents of men serving with the Armed Forces, Personal problems, Financial problems, Traffic citations, Wills, Power of Attorney, Housing and many others.

Realizing the importance of familiarizing company personnel with their rights under the Social Security Act and the State Pension Act when they reach the eligible age, the personnel managers of Lockheed and Vega have each appointed a representative in the Employee Service section to handle matters of this nature.

Jack Fowle, Lockheed Department 763, whose Extension number is 3043; and Earl Lindley (days) or H. M. Weir (nights) in Vega Department 68, Extension 1717, have complete information regarding Social Security and State Pensions and their services are available to employees interested in such matters.

'LEARN TO SWIM' PROGRAM LAUNCHED

Glendale Park and Recreation Department, in cooperation with the American Red Cross, will hold a LEARN TO SWIM program at the Verdugo Swim Stadium, August 16 to 28, for the purpose of teaching swimmers and non-swimmers, junior and senior life savers, and water safety instructors.

These courses will be given with volunteer personnel. Instruction is free—pool fee only.

If you hold an active senior life saving or water safety instructor's certificate and can give some time to this campaign, please communicate with H. F. Blackmore, Lockheed-Vega Education Department.

Manager Russ Coggan of the Vega All-Stars softball team will lead his team into battle Sunday, August 15, against the powerful service team from Hammer Field, California. The game, to be played at North Hollywood playground, promises to be a thriller. Time, 2 p.m.

OVERSEAS ROMANCE IN L.O.C.

Here pictured is the happy ending to one of those "Yank Finds Rose in Ireland" stories, as Robert Louis Stevenson, civilian technical employee of the Lockheed Overseas Corporation, and his bride, the former Miss Isobel Steel Bannatyne, of Belfast, sign their wedding documents in the offices of the Rev. Dr. D. Frazer-Hurs, Presbyterian minister of the Northern Ireland capital. At left are Joan Thomas Bannatyne and Anne MacKenzie Bannatyne, two of the bride's five sisters; in center background are John Beach, usher and Don Blush, best man, fellow Lockheed associates of the groom. Stevenson, who is a Chicago-born third cousin of the famous writer, went to Northern Ireland from Burbank early last summer as a member of a civilian specialist group now working with America's 8th Air Force.

APPEAL MADE FOR MORE BLOOD PLASMA

At the beginning of this war the American Red Cross asked Americans to donate blood to the plasma bank for the purpose of helping save lives of our fighting men.

The response has been great but not great enough. The need for plasma is growing every day. Quotas have been set for every community in the country. Many have over-subscribed these quotas each month, but Southern California as a whole has fallen behind.

The Los Angeles area has a quota of 7000 pints of blood per month and the contributions made by Lockheed and Vega employees through the Employee Victory Committee-sponsored Blood Donor Days (each Monday) are credited first to the Burbank Chapter of the Red Cross and then toward the general total of the Los Angeles area.

Next Monday, August 9, is scheduled for Day shift employees (3:40 to 7:40 p.m.). Please make your appointments NOW. At Lockheed Plant 1 in the Main Medical office; Plant 3 at the First Aid Unit, and Vega Plants 1 and 2 employees should contact the Employee Service Sections.

Aid In Accident Prevention Brings Safety Emblems

Recognition of their outstanding work and assistance in contributing to factory safety practices has been accorded thirteen additional members of the Lockheed Safety Committees. The following have been awarded Lockheed safety lapel buttons, the emblem of outstanding service in connection with accident prevention:

Ralph Swedell
Ray Hill
Norman Davies
Norman Weaver
Edith Deatherage
Amber McCoy
Robert Gardner
Lieut. J. W. Kincannon
Richard C. Weisberg
Sirok Nazaretian
Clement Fletcher
Norman Williams
Douglas Rose

Each award was accompanied by a letter of appreciation and congratulations from R. Randall Irwin, director of Lockheed-Vega Industrial Relations Office, on the important work being done by the recipients in keeping industrial accidents at a minimum.

Camouflage colors are being standardized with an electronic device that distinguishes 2,000,000 different colors.

THE *Lockheed-Vega Star* ★★

The Lockheed-Vega Star is issued every Friday for the employees of the Lockheed Aircraft Corporation and the Vega Aircraft Corporation and is the official publication of both companies. Communications may be addressed to either the Industrial Relations Office or the Public Relations Department, Lockheed Aircraft Corporation, Burbank, California, U.S.A. Although news and cartoon contributions are welcome, circumstances make it impossible to give any promise that they will be returned to sender when not used, nor can individual acknowledgment be made.

BERT W. HOLLOWAY, Editor-in-Chief
H. L. (HAL) ROSSON, Managing Editor

Volume 10 Number 34

'This Is The Army'

The United States Army recognizes the fact that its fighting men must be unhampered by worries at home. A soldier cannot do his job well if he is concerned about the financial problems of his wife, mother or children.

That is why our military leaders formed Army Emergency Relief. It is through this agency that relatives of soldiers can find aid and comfort in time of need.

The Los Angeles office of Army Emergency Relief at Twelfth and Hill Streets, under the direction of Major William Woodlief, is daily taking care of the problems of many Southern California soldiers' families. In order to continue this important work Army Emergency Relief is constantly in need of funds.

Soon Los Angeles is going to have an opportunity to see a great movie and aid Army Emergency Relief by attending the three-theatre premieres of Warner Bros. technicolor production of Irving Berlin's great soldier show "This Is The Army." All of the proceeds from the premieres which will be held on August 17 at Warners Hollywood, Downtown and Wiltern theatres will go to Army Emergency Relief.

Advance reports indicate that the 350 soldiers of Uncle Sam's Army in the cast of the film, plus the movie stars also featured, combine to make "This Is The Army" outstanding entertainment.

What Material Conservation Means

(Continued from Page 2)

don't make it. Segregate your scrap properly and it will come back to you as new material.

Q. I am a Forms Control Clerk. How do I fit into the Conservation picture?

A. By insisting on the use of old stock wherever possible before new forms become effective. Design forms with fewer copies and standard sizes. Consolidate forms to make a few do the work of several.

Q. I am a clerk in a Foreman's office. As I am a non-productive employee, I don't have to worry about conservation, do I?

A. Yes, you do. Many things you use contain vital war materials. Paper clips, tape, paper, etc., have all gone to war. Conserve them and they will last, waste them and we may have to do without.

General Arnold Lauds 'White Collar' Workers

White collar workers in the aircraft industry came in for some high praise for their part in the war effort last week when General H. H. Arnold, Commanding General of the U.S. Army Air Forces, addressed a telegram to scores of Lockheed tool engineers attending their annual banquet at the Los Angeles Athletic Club.

The following telegram from Gen. Arnold was read by Austin H. Montgomery, Procedures Analyst for Lockheed:

Tool Engineers, Lockheed Aircraft Corporation
(c/o Los Angeles Athletic Club) Washington, D.C., July 29, 1943

We pay tribute to your work as engineers and designers whose knowledge, skill and industry make possible mass output and the high production rate of Lockheed Aircraft. Combat and transport planes for which you design the production tools have carried the battle to the enemy, and conclusive victory depends on your ability to keep pace with our needs. Now that we have the enemy on the run, if every man does his job and we continue to get maximum production, the result is assured. The Army Air Forces is confident it can rely on you.

ARNOLD

Principal speakers at the banquet were J. H. Sreenan, works manager of Lockheed; E. Stackhouse, assistant works manager in charge of tooling; George Betts, assistant superintendent of tooling, and A. Bittrick, manager of tool engineering. F. W. Johnson was toastmaster.

ACTIVITY HOUSES NOW OPEN FOR WAR WORK

As a "help the war" gesture, Activity Houses are now open in principal communities throughout the Southland. These houses are open to all groups engaged in war work. For instance, the Service Star Women of Lockheed use the Burbank Activity House at 907 Cordova avenue, for their weekly meetings. The group rolls bandages for the Office of Civilian Defense and to send out their monthly Buddy letters to former Lockheed employees in the Armed Forces.

One of the most interesting activities at these houses is the formation by various clubs of summer programs for children. To quote from the Activity House News, a paper published by Barker Bros., sponsor of these houses, "The increase of free time among all school-age children, coupled with the absence of one or both parents from homes because of war plant employment places a grave responsibility upon members of the community who are able to devote time and energy to this most important phase of our war effort."

Community groups who are desirous of using any one of these Activity Houses for this important war work should contact Mary Counselor at Barker Bros.

Tax Declarations Due Sept. 15

(Continued from Page 3)

return. Since the 1943 earnings of employees are approximately the same as in 1942, employees could very well use the amount of income as shown in the 1942 information advice as being the estimated annual income from Lockheed and Vega for 1943 in preparing their Declaration of Estimated Tax.

In the event employees need further assistance in the preparation of their Declaration of Estimated Tax, Employee Service will render every aid possible.

Bus Schedules

Attention of employees living in the Pasadena and Altadena areas who work at Lockheed Plants 1 and 3 and Vega Plants 1 and 2 is called to the following bus schedules.

Ticket books may be obtained from your Employee Transportation office or at the Lamanda Park Service Station, 2371 East Colorado street, Pasadena, railhead for the Colorado and Orange Grove lines.

(VIA COLORADO BLVD.)

	A.M.	A.M.	P.M.	P.M.
Colorado & Sierra Madre	5:45	6:55	2:25	11:25
Colorado & Oak	5:46	6:56	2:26	11:26
Colorado & Allen	5:47	6:57	2:27	11:27
Colorado & Hill	5:49	6:59	2:29	11:29
Colorado & Mar Vista	5:50	7:00	2:30	11:30
Colorado & Lake	5:52	7:02	2:32	11:32
Colorado & Oak Knoll	5:53	7:03	2:33	11:33
Colorado & Los Robles	5:54	7:04	2:34	11:34
Colorado & Marengo	5:55	7:05	2:35	11:35
Colorado & Fair Oaks	5:57	7:07	2:37	11:37
Colorado & Figueroa	6:01	7:11	2:41	11:41

(VIA ORANGE GROVE BLVD.)

Sierra Madre & Colorado	5:40	......	2:20	11:20
Orange Grove & Foothill	5:43	......	2:23	11:23
Orange Grove & Craig	5:45	......	2:25	11:25
Orange Grove & Allen	5:46	......	2:26	11:26
Orange Grove & Hill	5:47	......	2:27	11:27
Orange Grove & Lake	5:49	......	2:29	11:29
Orange Grove & El Molino	5:50	......	2:30	11:30
Orange Grove & Los Robles	5:51	......	2:31	11:31
Orange Grove & Marengo	5:52	......	2:32	11:32
Orange Grove & Fair Oaks	5:54	......	2:34	11:34
Orange Grove & Lincoln	5:55	......	2:35	11:35
Orange Grove & Rosemont	5:57	......	2:37	11:37

(VIA ALTADENA)

Foothill & Fair Oaks	5:45	......	2:30	11:15
Montana & Fair Oaks	5:48	......	2:33	11:18
Washington & Fair Oaks	5:50	......	2:35	11:20
Washington & Los Robles	5:52	......	2:37	11:22
Mountain & Los Robles	5:54	......	2:39	11:24
Orange Grove & Los Robles	5:55	......	2:40	11:25
Walnut & Los Robles	5:57	......	2:42	11:27
Colorado & Los Robles	6:00	......	2:45	11:30

NOTE: Busses on all three of the above line meet at the Flag Pole, Orange Grove avenue and Colorado street, to balance loads before proceeding to the plants.

Buy War Bonds and write your own ticket for the future.

THE *Lockheed-Vega Star* ★ ★

Official publication of the Lockheed and Vega Aircraft Corporations

Volume 10 BURBANK, CALIFORNIA, U.S.A., SEPTEMBER 3, 1943 Number 38

Central American Newsmen Pay Visit

Promoting inter-continental friendship and understanding, nine prominent newspapermen from Honduras, Panama and Guatemala toured the Lockheed and Vega plants this week. Above they are shown inspecting the belly gun turret of a B-17 at Vega.

EXTRA EFFORT PLEDGED FOR LABOR DAY

Statement by Dale O. Reed, President, Aeronautical Lodge 727, A.F.L.

Next Monday, September 6, is Labor Day—a day set aside for special recognition of the dignity and high estate of American Labor and its important contribution to the development of the American nation.

Normally, Labor Day, is observed throughout the nation as a holiday, but we are at war — and war recognizes no holiday. Last year we put in a full day's work at Lockheed and Vega, but this year we intend to do even more.

Lodge 727 is calling on all aircraft workers on the Day and Swing shifts to work their two rest periods on Labor Day; and for those on the Graveyard shift, who have no rest period, to work the first 10 minutes of their luncheon period.

The Commanding Officers of our Army and Navy are expecting a full day's production of airplanes to be delivered by us on Labor Day, and thousands of lives depend upon the weapons which only we can provide. A single employee who does not report for work on Labor Day will offset the extra time given by 24 loyal workers who are on the job.

The company will derive no benefits from this contributed time under the terms of their cost-plus-a-fixed fee contracts. The extra time we give will be evidence of our full support of the Armed Forces.

Statement by Cyril Chappellet, Vice-President of Lockheed and Vega

The Lockheed and Vega management is extremely pleased with the determination of the men and women of the two companies to keep faith with our Armed Forces, as demonstrated not only by their resolution to be on the job on Labor Day, but to voluntarily give an extra measure of effort by continuing work through the rest period.

We commend the Union and all of our employees for the fine spirit which has been demonstrated, and we are glad to cooperate in this voluntary movement to increase the production of warplanes on Labor Day.

Star Reporters From South View Production Here

Continuing the "Good-Neighbor" policy of providing the Latin-American republics with the latest information on the progress and developments of the U.S. aircraft industry, nine of the foremost journalists of Honduras, Panama and Guatemala were honored guests at Lockheed and Vega last Monday during a tour of the main plants. The newspaper men are touring the United States as guests of the Office of the Coordinator of Inter-American affairs, visiting important war industries in the States from coast to coast.

The visitors included three writers from Guatemala, three from Panama and three from Honduras, and escorts from the office of the Coordinator of Inter-American Affairs. The party was taken through Lockheed Plant 1 from the Research department, where designs are conceived and tested, down the mechanized assembly line where the famous Lockheed "Lightnings" are built, to the newest Lockheed assembly line, that of the Constellation, the Army's largest land-based transport.

From Lockheed the tour extended to Vega to see the work that is being done there in building B-17s for the Army and Vega Ventura PV-1s, or sub-busters, for the Navy.

Included in the party were: Ramon Blanco, Guatemala, representing *El Imparcial;* Ovidio Rodas Corzo, Guatemala, representing *El Imparcial;* Pedro Julio Garcia, Guatemala, representing *Nuestro Diario;* Carlos Sole Bosch, Panama, representing *Estrella de Panama;* Dr. Eduardo Morgan, Panama, representing *Renovacion;* Enrique Ruiz Vernacci, Panama, representing *Panama-America:* Vidal Mejia, Honduras, representing *El Norte;* Antonio Ochoa-Alcantara, Honduras, representing various newspapers of Buenos Aires, Havana, Lima, Madrid and Caracas; and Vicente Machado Valle, Honduras, representing *La Epoca.*

Those accompanying the group included: Richard Dyer, tour director; Thomas T. Driver, representative of the Office of Coordinator of Inter-American Affairs; James J. Baker, American Express Courier; and Joseph Rustan, of Acme Newspictures, Inc.

Major S. F. Robertson Named Lockheed Contract Officer

Lockheed welcomes to its resident Army staff Major Stafford F. Robertson, who has assumed the post with this company that he has occupied from February

MAJOR ROBERTSON

to July of this year with Vega—U.S. A.A.F. Contracting Officer.

Major Robertson, who was promoted from Captain to Major upon his transfer to Lockheed, is an old-time airman who joined the Army three days before the Jap attack on Pearl Harbor. Educated in engineering and the law, he graduated from the University of Utah Law School in 1926 and from then until the outbreak of war, was associated with the legal profession.

However, he had also been active in the mining industry throughout the Inter-Mountain states and was closely associated with aviation from 1926 to 1939, during part of which time he held a transport license (aircraft operation). Since Pearl Harbor he has been Contracting Officer at a number of aircraft plants, including Vega and now Lockheed.

Major Robertson is married, has three children and lives in Santa Monica. During his stay with Vega he became one of the most popular military men in residence.

Back the Attack—With War Bonds.

BUCK O' MONTH TOPS HALF MILLION GIFTS

Swinging into the spirit of the Buck of the Month Club, the Pomona Plant 8 sub-committee allocated $100 of their Buck of the Month Club monies to the Army Relief production of "This Is the Army" to purchase tickets for soldiers stationed in the Pomona area.

The regular monthly report of the Lockheed-Vega Employees Buck of the Month Club reveals that to date, this voluntary contribution organization has donated $501,000 to more than 70 worthy charitable organizations engaged in relieving war born difficulties.

The complete statement follows:

Financial Report

BUCK OF THE MONTH CLUB
August 31, 1943

Contributions		
Lockheed Employees	$405,883	
Vega Employees	240,054	
Triplett & Barton	1,039	
L.E.R.C. Employees	383	
V.E.R.C. Employees	842	
Publication Employees	34	
Miscellaneous	1,943	
British Reassembly Division	462	
		$650,641
Total amount donated for period March 31, 1942 to March 31, 1943, as previously reported in the STAR		$372,867
Disbursements (since March 31, 1943)		
Refunds	$ 73	
Bonding	720	
Miscellaneous (Check Book)	2	
Annual Audit	75	
Service Men's Recreation Fund	400	
Visiting Nurse Association	295	
Naval Aid Auxiliary	2,500	
Milton Berry Found'n (Paralytics)	1,000	
Service Men's Bible Committee	1,000	
Boys' Club of Hollywood	1,500	
Assistance League of So. California	500	
Foothill Preventorium for Girls	200	
Pasadena Preventorium	200	
Crippled Children's Society	500	
Vet. of Foreign Wars (Poppy Day)	1,250	
Amer. Legion Auxil. (Poppy Day)	750	
Army Canteen	5,000	
Navy Canteen	5,000	
Marine Corps Canteen	6,000	
Travelers Aid Society	1,200	
American Red Cross	30,663	
Battery E	40	
Battery F (Lockheed Coast Artillery)	578	
Vega Blue Star Service Women	500	
Salvation Army	6,240	
Colored Boys' Home	300	
Service Men's Center	25	
Wounded Sailors at Norco Hospital	342	
Disabled Amer. Vets., 9th Dist.	1,000	
Christian Service Organization	750	
Service Star Women of Lockheed	714	
Calif. Babies and Children's Hosp.	1,000	
174th and 74th Chem. Unit—Army	48	
United Hospital Fund of L. A.	30,000	
Ruth Home	500	
St. Joseph's Hospital, Burbank	25,000	
Reynolds Tobacco Co. (Xmas Gifts to Service Men)	3	
Citizens Committee—Army & Navy	125	
Nursery School	250	
Junipero Serra Boys' Home	250	
Hillside House (paralytics)	500	
All Pacific Recreation Fund	500	
Army Emergency (Pomona Buck of Month)	100	
Union Rescue Mission	200	
Los Angeles Officers Club	500	
Lockheed-Vega Service School	50	
Camp Cooke Day Rooms	500	
		$128,875
		$501,743
BALANCE*		$148,898

*Of this balance $40,000 is to be maintained at all times by the Club as an Emergency Fund to be used in case of a civilian war disaster.

NAN WYNN TO BE ON RADIO PROGRAM

"America—Ceiling Unlimited," Lockheed and Vega's weekly broadcast over CBS, enters upon its fifth week on Sunday, September 5, with Joseph Cotten as

NAN WYNN

master of ceremonies and Nan Wynn as featured vocalist for the variety half-hour program.

Cotten, stage and screen actor, takes over the dramatic portion of the program in a radio adaptation of Joseph Marshall's Saturday Evening Post story, "The Pop of Djebel-Saa'b." The theme recounts the adventures of two men in Tunisia, North Africa.

Nan Wynn, whose song fashions are prompting praise and increased popularity, will sing as song-of-the-week, "Sunday, Monday, or Always," and "Put Your Arms Around Me Honey."

"America — Ceiling Unlimited" may now be heard by a studio audience, and is heard locally over KNX at 11 a.m. and over other CBS stations at 2 p.m., Eastern War Time.

INCOME INFORMATION TO BE DISTRIBUTED

Information as to earnings for the year 1943 for *Lockheed and Vega weekly employees* will be distributed through the usual payroll channels on Wednesday, September 8.

Lockheed monthly employees will also receive this information on the same date.

Owing to technical difficulties, information as to the earnings of *Vega monthly employees* will not be distributed, as it is believed that they will have no difficulty in computing their estimated earnings for this period.

LIGHTNING COMBAT PILOT WRITES WAR EPIC

National 'Fire Prevention Week' October 3 To 9

The week of October 3 to 9 has been set aside this year as "National Fire Prevention Week" throughout the nation, a week which has particular significance to everyone employed in war production plants, especially aircraft factories.

Commenting upon the special importance of the annual event this year, Lockheed Fire Chief Jack O'Conner expresses the hope that the significance of fire prevention in aircraft plants is recognized by every American.

"One disastrous fire would destroy vital materials that might have won a major battle," he points out. "Also, let us not forget, in such case, the all important man-hours which have been irretrievably lost, even though a plant has been rebuilt and operations resumed.

"We cannot afford loss by fire," he concluded. "Consequently, we dare not relax our vigilance on the home front. Carelessness on our part now, causing a break in the flow of vital war weapons to the battlefronts, may cost the lives of our own soldiers."

So, make EVERY week Fire Prevention week, recommends Chief O'Conner, simply because the fate of *your* country, the lives of *your* buddies and *your own* job depends upon uninterrupted output of the war weapons we are forging.

L. A. COST OF LIVING RATED LOW BY BUREAU OF LABOR STATISTICS

According to a tabulation of living costs recently compiled by the Bureau of Labor Statistics, workers living in the Los Angeles area are in a much more favorable position than those living in many other large cities of the nation.

Actual living expenses for the average worker's family of four in Los Angeles are well below those of many large cities in a list of 33 shown in the report.

New York City occupies the top spot of the nation with an average of $1800 per year while the figures for Los Angeles show $1617 on a breakdown as follows: Food, $627; clothing, $213; housing, $250; fuel and light, $71; furnishings and household equipment, $41, and miscellaneous, $413.

The report shows San Francisco and Washington running a close second and third as the most expensive cities in the United States.

End Of Another Successful Mission

Capt. Newell O. Roberts, U.S.A.A.F., climbs out of the cockpit of his Lightning

True Story Of What Aerial Fighting Really Means Told In Collier's Magazine

The September 4 issue of Collier's carried one of the most exciting true stories of aerial combat in the Mediterranean theatre of war that has so far come out of World War II. Captioned "Three Seconds To Fight," Capt. Newell O. Roberts, 94th United States Pursuit Squadron, a Lightning pilot, tells how his combat group worked their P-38s against all-comers, from the ground up to 35,000 feet. For those members of the Lockheed and Vega families who did not obtain a copy of the issue, Collier's has generously granted the STAR *permission to reproduce it. The following is the first installment of the story, which will run serially in the following issues of the* STAR.

THREE SECONDS TO FIGHT

By CAPTAIN NEWELL O. ROBERTS
94th United States Pursuit Squadron

(Reprinted by permission of COLLIER'S *Magazine)*

I learned one thing from the first Jerry I shot down. In a fight with a Messerschmitt, three seconds is all the time you have to live or to die. The same goes for Jerry, too. People back home have the idea that fighter pilots zoom and dive and twist like a swarm of bees, spitting bullets right and left. It isn't like that at all. You take off in your twin-engined P-38 Lightning for a three-hour flight, patrolling, strafing, and escorting bombers. Altogether, you have about three minutes shooting in your guns, which pack the most concentrated firepower of any fighter plane. You hold your fire until you are a hundred yards from your enemy and let her go in three-second bursts. In three seconds you can squirt 300 shells. You get him, or he gets you.

My first Jerry was one of two Me.-110s cruising over Gabés at the southern end of Tunisia. I was the leader of my flight. We were patrolling that part of the Mediterranean to keep the U-boats under water. We also had orders to strafe German field concentrations around Gabés from thirty feet above the ground. We call that buzzing.

I saw two Jerries above us going the same direction as we were. We had the speed to overhaul them. There wasn't any time to maneuver. I gave my engine the blossom, pulled my nose up, got one Jerry in my sights,

(Continued on Page 6)

CORRECTION

The August 27 issue of the STAR incorrectly named Walter G. Rising as Manager of Lockheed Dept. 768. Mr. Rising is the Lockheed-Vega Technical Communications Advisor, Dept. 869. Miss Vera Doane is Dept. Manager of 768.

A hug is just energy gone to waist.

Graveyard Gaieties Ticket Sales Climb

Advance ticket sales to the Graveyard Gaieties Saturday night, September 11, at the Los Angeles Breakfast Club indicate that this revue and dance will establish a new high for attendance, according to word from the L.E.R.C. office.

Tickets are available at the L.E.R.C. office, Plant 1, daily between 8 a.m. and through all shifts until 1 a.m. Employees of other plants can obtain tickets from representatives at the respective plants.

Latest addition to the cast of Graveyard Gaieties is Ken Smith, of 1-03, who takes the place of Dale Newton, who recently terminated. Ken is "tops," according to Producer Les Capen, who is enthusiastic over the talent of the singing inspector.

DANCES AND PICNIC PLANNED FOR WEEKEND

The social events calendar for the first weekend in September finds Department 1-24-4-349 holding an opening dinner dance at the Oakmont Country Club on Saturday, September 4.

Also on Saturday night, Plant 4 Day and Graveyard Lockheedians will dance at the Royal Palms Hotel. Joe Gist and the L.E.R.C. Dance Band will provide the music.

On Sunday, September 5, Plant 8 Lockheedians are holding an all-shift, all-plant barbecue at Ganesha Park, Pomona.

Help put the skids under Hitler—Buy all the War Bonds you can and now.

SERVICE STAR WOMEN END JEWELRY DRIVE

Members of the Service Star Women of Lockheed are winding up their successful jewelry drive to provide members of the Armed Forces with a wide variety of "barter" currency for use in the South Pacific.

Plans are also being made by the Service Star Women to launch another game drive within the near future. Details will be announced shortly.

Canteen Needs Part-Time Help

The L.E.R.C. Canteen has several openings for part-time help on all shifts at all plants. Those interested are advised that wages are on the same basis as Lockheed wages. Applicants may contact Canteen managers at all plants.

LOCKHEED GIRLS VISIT CAMP COOKE

Soldiers at Camp Cooke, near Santa Barbara, were hosts to 39 Lockheed girls last weekend at this isolated station where the 559th Ordnance Company is located.

Accompanied by Merle Sproull, women's counselor, and Anne Smith of the L.E.R.C., the girls traveled in a chartered bus and enjoyed a pleasant weekend of dancing and beach parties.

Native Sons and Daughters of California will honor the Golden State at the next Lunch Pail Picnic Wednesday, September 8, during all lunch periods at both Plant 1 and Plant 3. This is for native Californians only.

L.E.R.C. HANDICAP BOWLING LEAGUE ENTRY BLANK

Team Name .... Approx. Team Av. ....

Captain ....

Captain's Dept. .... Plant .... Shift .... Ext. ....

Team Roster	Dept.	Average
1.		
2.		
3.		
4.		
5.		
Sub.		
Sub.		

Give name of houses you prefer and days. Give as wide a choice as possible to assist the committee in forming leagues.

Name of House	Day	Time
		6:45 P.M. ☐
1.	1.	9:00 P.M. ☐
2.	2.	1:30 A.M. ☐
3.	3.	11:45 A.M. ☐

BOWLING LEAGUE STILL REGISTERING

Lockheed bowlers who have not yet filled in the entry form which appeared in last week's STAR will find the form repeated again this week.

Two important factors must be remembered this year, Bob Mercer, L.E.R.C. athletic chairman and member of the Bowling Committee, points out. "First, this is a handicap league, and second, women's teams will have but four members to a team."

All bowlers are urged to register early so that teams may be scheduled on alleys of their choice. This plan is designed to tie in with the transportation conservation plan.

L. E. R. C. CALENDAR

FRIDAY, SEPT. 3—Drama Club Rehearsal, 734 Beacon St., Los Angeles, Beaux Arts Theater, 7 p.m.—Band Concert, Main Recreation Area, 10 a.m., Rehearsal.—Nutrition Class, 1-3 p.m., 907 Cordova, Burbank.

SATURDAY, SEPT. 4—Depts. 1-24-4-3-49 Dinner Dance, Oakmont Country Club. —Plant 4 Day and Graveyard Dance, Royal Palms Hotel.

SUNDAY, SEPT. 5—Plant 8 Barbecue, Ganesha Park, Pomona.—Drama Club Rehearsal, 734 Beacon St., Los Angeles, Beaux Arts Theater, 7 p.m.—Ranger & Rangerettes Ride, 8-10 a.m., Tex Stonehurst Stables.

MONDAY, SEPT. 6—Choral Club Rehearsal, 7:30 p.m., Burbank High School. —Drama Club Rehearsal, 734 Beacon St., Los Angeles, Beaux Arts Theater, 7 p.m.

TUESDAY, SEPT. 7—Ice Skating after work, 12:30 a.m., Pasadena Winter Gardens. — Leatherspankers, Du Brock's Riding Academy, 4:30-5:30 p.m.—Dance Club, Hollywood Woman's Club, 7:30-11 p.m.—Nutrition Class, 4:30-6:30 p.m., 907 Cordova, Burbank.—Drama Club Rehearsal, 734 Beacon St., Los Angeles, Beaux Arts Theater, 7 p.m.

WEDNESDAY, SEPT. 8—Opera Group, 7:30 p.m., Le Conte Jr. High School Auditorium, 1313 Bronson, Hollywood.—California Lunch Pail Picnic, Plants 1 and 3, all lunch periods.—Drama Club Rehearsal, 734 Beacon St., Los Angeles, Beaux Arts Theater, 7 p.m.—Boy Scout Meeting, 7 p.m., John Muir School.—Ranger & Rangerette Ride, 7-9 p.m., Tex Stonehurst Stables.

THURSDAY, SEPT. 9—Plant 4 Moonlight Ride, Decker's Riding Academy, Garfield Ave., Clearwater, 12:30 a.m.—Ranger & Rangerette Ride, Tex Stonehurst Stables, 9-11 a.m.—Bridge Club, 7:30 p.m., Burbank Recreation Center. —Rhumba Class, Ballard's Studio, 1753 North Highland.—Drama Club Rehearsal, 734 Beacon St., Los Angeles, Beaux Arts Theater, 7 p.m.

FRIDAY, SEPT. 10—Drama Club Rehearsal, 734 Beacon St., Los Angeles, Beaux Arts Theater, 7 p.m. — Band Concert, Main Recreation area.—Nutrition Class, 907 Cordova, Burbank.

John Law Puts Snatch On Two Tool Snatchers

In spite of the fact that the Plant Protection Departments of Lockheed and Vega have proven over and over again that it can't be done, there still appears to be a few of the companies' employees—a very few, fortunately—who believe that they can pilfer tools and small parts and get away with it.

The photograph, right, of vital small tools and parts taken from a former Vega employee, as reported by Vega Plant Protection Division Manager H. A. Smith, furnishes further proof that they can't. The man who appropriated these made the usual excuse that he put them in his pockets during the course of his work, found them when he arrived home and merely neglected to return them. He is now "ex-Vega."

To show how well-nigh impossible it is to get away with such thefts, a recent case reported by the Lockheed Plant Protection Department is interesting as showing the "Sherlock Holmes" methods employed by the departments to track down petty malefactors. The "subject" of this case is now doing 60 days in the Burbank City jail.

Among other tools that he had "borrowed" was a small electric drill motor from which he had filed the Lockheed control number, figuring that this would make identification impossible. But he forgot one all-important clue — a clue that must remain a secret. A department investigator, aided by an expert toolman, found the motor in the suspect's garage, along with a number of other tools and small parts which he had taken.

In a few minutes the tool expert had uncovered the clue which led through several company departments, the manufacturers and distributors organizations and right down to the actual tool crib from which the drill motor had been taken.

It was a clear trail, at the end of which the culprit confessed and the Burbank police put him in the pokey. Much credit for the successful solving of this and other similar cases is given by the Department to factory personnel, who have no more use for this type of wartime saboteur than have the police.

Notice—Gasoline Ration Holders

"A" book holders must have their tires inspected by September 30, "B" book holders by October 31, and "C" book holders by August 31.

If you have not had your last inspection, you should do so as soon as possible.

He Just Forgot To Return 'Em!

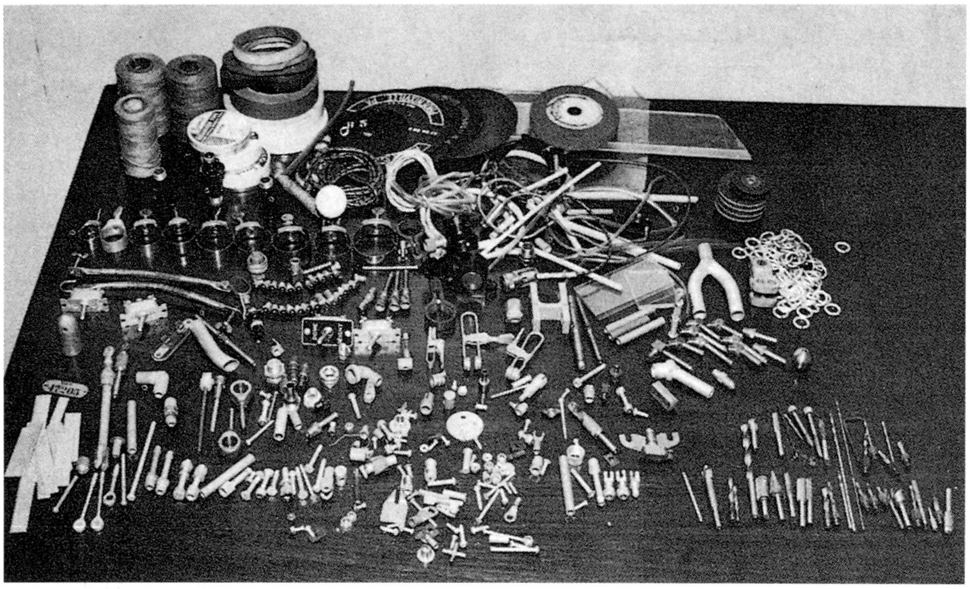

Above photo shows the collection of valuable small tools and parts which a former Vega employee "forgot to return" until the Plant Protection Department caught up with him.

U.S.C.'s FALL SCHEDULE FOR WARTIME EDUCATION TO START OCTOBER 11

The University of Southern California announces that their fall program will start the week of October 11. Are you interested in government-financed college training planned to increase your efficiency as a war worker? Would wartime education, with carry-over peacetime value, increase your contribution to the war effort? The War Training Office of the University of Southern California (Room 351, 3551 University avenue, Los Angeles 7) will send you, upon request, its fall program of more than 150 tuition-free, part-time courses in the fields of engineering, science, and management. The fall program includes such classes as:

Aeronautical, Chemical, Civil, Electrical, Mechanical and Radio Engineering. These include aerodynamics, aircraft design, fabrication methods, inspection, instruments, mathematics, materials and processes, applied mechanics, electronics, plastics, elementary electricity, radar, etc.

Management classes such as foremanship training, industrial management, industrial psychology, labor legislation, labor relations, etc.

Safety classes in safety engineering, and accident prevention.

Students are furnished signed certificates which may be used to support applications for additional gasoline. Preliminary application for classes should be made prior to their starting date. Application blanks may be secured from the University of Southern California, the Lockheed-Vega Education offices, or Education libraries.

EMPLOYEES APPEAL FOR AID IN FINDING HOUSES, APARTMENTS

Do you know of a house or apartment vacancy within commuting distance of Lockheed or Vega? If so, you are in a position to serve your fellow employees and the war effort. Here's how:

The Lockheed and Vega Employee Service Divisions have inaugurated a Housing Service. Current information on present and future vacancies is to be pooled and made available to employees in need of places in which to live.

Because of their own plans to move, or through leads from others, many Lockheed and Vega people possess information about living quarters that will become available in the near future.

If you know of such an actual or pending vacancy, contact your department clerk, women's counselor or the Plant Personnel Office and ask to fill out one of the simple forms. Your tip will then be sent immediately to Employee Service.

TIP FOR TAXPAYERS

Taxpayers having substantial deductions from income, or substantial income from sources other than wages, may find it desirable to use the alternative method of computing tax to be paid when submitting Declaration Form 1040-ES, due on or before September 15.

The "work sheet" furnished by the Government may be used or, if considerable detail is involved, a set of work sheets adapted for the purpose may be purchased at the Lockheed-Vega book store.

'THREE SECONDS TO FIGHT' TRUE STORY OF LIGHTNING PILOT

(Continued from Page 3)

gave him a squirt and he burst into flames. The job took about as long as it takes to tell it. A buddy of mine got the other one.

Air warfare is a percentage game. You fight in teams or you're dead. They'll shoot you down any time you go into acrobatic maneuvers. It takes a few seconds to go into a roll or a spin and the other fellow gets you the first second.

There isn't any room for grudge fighting. Almost all the pilots we lost were fellows who let themselves be sucked out of formation. The Jerries used to send one of their planes out in front and down low as a decoy. If one of our men dived on the decoy a whole team of Me.'s invariably dived on him. If our whole team took the bait, the Me. team usually stayed out of it. We could outfly and outshoot them.

Carrying on for Rick

Our squadron was a Pursuit. We still used the Hat-in-the-Ring insignia that Eddie Rickenbacker and his men used in the same squadron in the first World War. Ours was one of the first fighter groups to reach Algeria. We took off from England, flew nine hours and fifteen minutes with a Martin B-26 as a mother ship to guide us. Sitting that long strapped to the seat of a P-38 is bad enough. But in this flight an even worse strain was not knowing whether we would have to shoot our way into the airfield at Oran where we were to land.

Fortunately, the field had surrendered to our troops, but that didn't make it much better because Junkers 88s had just bombed the field and we had to dodge the holes that pocked the runway. The colonel's ship hit one and smashed up as flat as a pancake. He crawled out unhurt.

Winging that far overseas set a record for fighter planes, but it was duck soup for us after flying the North Atlantic in mid-winter. Ours was the first squadron of fighters to wing across the ocean. After Pearl Harbor we had been rushed out to San Diego and Long Beach to guard the Southern California coast. Everybody thought Tojo would be sending a carrier over to blast our aircraft factories. Our task was to head the Japs off at sea if they came. This was a break, because the P-38s were so new that nobody knew how to fly them. We had to work out an entirely new system of battle tactics.

Looking back, I would say this was the most dangerous flying I have done. Once in a formation so tight that our wing tips were only three feet apart, another pilot jammed his wing into my rudder. It was my first collision in the air. We got down all right—Roberts' luck. Another time I saw two P-38s below me fold together, back to back, and plunge into the ocean. Once, in another fog, a pilot came up under me, knocking both my engines out. He bailed out, but I like to stick with a ship. I pancaked in a small field without a scratch—more Roberts' luck.

One day they gave us new P-38s equipped with belly tanks, and the rumor spread that we were going overseas. By that time we knew what the P-38s would do—or thought we did. Our squadron flew from Southern California to Maine, and day after day we practiced long flights through the soup over the Atlantic. Next we flew to a base in Labrador. It was lost in the overcast. Every day the Flying Fortress carrying the navigator who was to get us to Greenland flew out and looked over the situation. The best weatherman in the world couldn't predict what we would find out there.

After several false starts, we took off again, hovering around the Fortress. Our flight made a tiny runway in Greenland. There were mountains all around the icebergs in the water. Our flight got down all right. But another, which started the same day, heading for another Greenland runway, landed on the icecaps and stayed there a long time before being rescued. We pushed on to Reykjavik, Iceland.

The next flight still gives me dreams more terrible than any fight I have been in. We took off in thick, soupy weather for Scotland with a Fortress for each four Lightnings. As the soup became thicker and thicker, we jammed ourselves closer under the wings of the Fortress. We were flying so tight that our wing tips almost touched. We flew like that for five hours. It seemed like fifty.

(TO BE CONTINUED NEXT WEEK)

Star Donates Blood At Lockheed 2

★

Culminating the Blood Bank drive at Lockheed Plant 2 on September 2, Olivia de Haviland, noted stage and screen star, not only spoke but also gave a pint of blood. Left to right are Superintendent Allan Hess, Miss de Haviland, Mrs. John T. Cooper of the Red Cross, and Jim Arbogast, representing the L.E.R.C. at Plant 2.

★

EMPLOYEE PLANT TOURS SERVING VALUABLE PURPOSE

The Employee Plant Tours currently being conducted by the Education Committee of L.E.R.C. are serving a valuable purpose.

Employees of Lockheed and Vega who have not yet had the experience of seeing Lockheed planes roll off the final assembly lines at Plant 1, are urged to take immediate advantage of these tours.

Arrangements may be made by visiting the L.E.R.C. office, or by contacting the L.E.R.C. chairmen in all outlying plants. Notice of desire to make the tour should be given well in advance so that necessary authorization may be secured from Plant Protection.

Schedules and further information may be obtained from bulletins posted on official company and departmental bulletin boards.

'SHARE YOUR HOME' CAMPAIGN STARTED

More than one million war workers who in the next year will take jobs away from their home towns must be housed in existing structures, the National Housing Agency announces as it maps a "Share Your Home" campaign in 160 key war industry centers. The long-term drive will open in various areas in September and October, centering around War Housing Week, October 3 to 9, and will continue until war housing needs in different areas are met.

An intensive advertising and promotional campaign on the theme "War Production Depends on War Housing" is to be conducted in the key areas where housing shortages are most acute. Prepared under the sponsorship of the War Advertising Council in cooperation with the National Housing Agency and the Office of War Information, the campaign is enlisting strong support of industry and business.

The campaign will stress a three-point program:

1. To encourage property owners and tenants to open their homes to war workers and to list with the local War Housing Center all vacant or soon-to-be vacant space available—houses, flats, apartments, rooms—which can be utilized without any expenditure of critical materials.

2. To encourage other owners, whose properties are not now suitable for use, to convert them into additional living accommodations for war workers—using either their own funds or conversion loans secured from private financial institutions.

3. To encourage property owners who are unable to convert their properties on their own responsibility, to lease their houses and buildings to the government and let the government do the job.

U. OF C. ANNOUNCES NEW WAR TRAINING CLASSES PROGRAM

War Training courses designed to prepare men and women for essential war jobs in a sub-professional, technical or supervisory capacity, will start soon under the University of California program of Engineering, Science and Management War Training.

The tuition-free classes will be held evenings at several convenient locations. High school graduation is required for this college-level training, and some courses require additional background.

A phone call to the University's War Training centers listed below will bring further information about these and other classes to start soon. Applications for supplemental gas rations needed to attend class will be endorsed at the first class meeting. The schedule:

Los Angeles, 714 S. Hill St., Phone VA 5142

Sept. 13—PRODUCTION PLANNING AND CONTROL, 7 to 9 p.m., Mondays, Rm. 410.

Sept. 16—PUMPING MACHINERY, *Its Application to Industrial Problems,* 7 to 9 p.m., Thursdays, Rm. 410.

Sept. 17—INDUSTRIAL ACCOUNTING, 7 to 9 p.m., Fridays, Rm. 410.

Sept. 17—INCENTIVES AND STANDARDS DEPARTMENT ADMINISTRATION, 7 to 9 p.m., Fridays, Rm. 410.

U.C.L.A. Campus, Phone BR 2-2171

Sept. 14—PRODUCTION CONTROL, 7:30 to 9:30 p.m., Tuesdays, Chemistry Bldg., Rm. 19.

Sept. 15—PERSONNEL AND EMPLOYMENT PSYCHOLOGY, 7 to 9 p.m., Wednesdays, Life Science Bldg., Rm. 105.

Sept. 15—INDUSTRIAL ORGANIZATION AND OPERATION, 7:30 to 9:30 p.m., Wednesdays, Royce Hall, Rm. 154.

Sept. 15—GRAPHICAL METHODS ON STATISTICAL WORK, 7 to 9 p.m., Wednesdays, Chemistry Bldg., Rm. 146.

Burbank, Phone CH 6-8355

Sept. 13—PRODUCTION PLANNING AND CONTROL, 7 to 9 p.m., Mondays, Burbank High School, Rm. 258.

Warning Whistle For Smoking Periods Installed

Lockheed employees now have no excuse for being late returning to their jobs at the end of the smoking periods on Day and Swing shifts.

Up until recently most members of the shifts waited until the whistle blew before starting back to their work. Much time was lost between the whistle blast and resumption of the work, according to E. A. Williams, staff assistant to the Assistant Works Manager in Charge of Experimental and New Development.

Therefore a warning whistle was suggested and has now been installed. It blows two minutes before the smoking periods are up and thus gives everybody a chance to be back on the job on time.

Tunisia Veteran Lauds The Lightning

Santa Ana—Lt. Benton E. Miller (right), fighter pilot from Los Angeles, uses P-38 model to illustrate battle maneuver to Warner Baxter and Jane Wyman, screen stars who entertained Santa Ana Army Air Base cadets here recently.

AWARDS TO BE GIVEN SAFE DRIVERS OF COMPANY VEHICLES

Motor vehicle accidents are *caused* . . . they don't "just happen."

That observation is made in a booklet now being distributed which describes the new Lockheed-Vega Transportation Safety Program. Its aim is to acquaint each employee of Lockheed, Vega and the Lockheed Air Terminal who may drive company-owned equipment, or any car on company business, with the full details of the plan. All such drivers are required to read the booklet and to acknowledge its receipt.

The purpose of the program is to reduce the number of motor vehicle accidents which cause lost time, costly repairs, higher insurance rates, and most important, loss of production.

Safe driving awards will be given drivers who maintain an accident-free record, while those charged by a Safety Committee with preventable accidents, will have demerits chalked against them. Twenty-two causes of unnecessary accidents are listed, most of which can be traced to carelessness.

Hereafter, all drivers on company business will be required to fill out "Accident Information Cards," at the scene of an accident and turn them in when they return to the plant to make their formal reports. All company-owned vehicles will be equipped with these cards.

'WORKHORSE' OF AIR FORCES, HE SAYS

Calling it the "workhorse of the Army Air Forces," Lt. Benton E. Miller, 21-year-old fighter pilot from Los Angeles, paid tribute to the Lockheed Lightning in an address before future flyers at the Santa Ana Army Air Base recently.

A member of the famed "Hat in Ring" squadron, Lt. Miller said the plane was equally useful at bomber escort, fighting, reconnaissance, dive-bombing, strafing or skip-bombing.

"And what's more," he said, "the Lightning is aerodynamically safe. This talk about the danger of bailing out of a P-38 is ridiculous. I can speak from experience."

During a wild dogfight over Tunisia, he recalled, his plane was set afire by German incendiary bullets. He tried to beat out the flames but it was no use. He had to bail out.

"I nosed her into a shallow dive. When I reached a speed of 275 m.p.h., I released the escape hatch and my safety belt simultaneously. A roaring wind scooped me out of the cockpit and sent me flying 1000 feet above the ship. All I did was sit there. The wind did the rest. The P-38 is just built that way."

Lt. Miller has three confirmed victories over Messerschmitt 109s. He wears the Purple Heart, Distinguished Flying Cross, the Air Medal and Croix de Guerre.

THE Lockheed-Vega Star ★★

The Lockheed-Vega Star is issued every Friday for the employees of the Lockheed Aircraft Corporation and the Vega Aircraft Corporation and is the official publication of both companies. Communications may be addressed to either the Industrial Relations Office or the Public Relations Department, Lockheed Aircraft Corporation, Burbank, California, U.S.A. Although news and cartoon contributions are welcome, circumstances make it impossible to give any promise that they will be returned to sender when not used, nor can individual acknowledgment be made.

H. L. (HAL) ROSSON, Editor

Volume 10 Number 38

You Can--If You Think You Can!

By Duke Branner, Lockheed

Have you ever watched someone do a job others thought difficult, and come away feeling that you could do it? Perhaps you even went home and tried it, failed three or four times and then—presto! You did it!

Every achievement begins with thinking—but it doesn't end with thinking! It takes courageous thinking to gain confidence, but even courageous and confident thinking aren't enough. It takes action, not merely assertion, to make achievement real.

Most of us, however, never even get to the point of thinking courageously. The result is, we don't get started. When we contemplate the thing to be done, it is so easy to conjure up reasons why we can't or shouldn't make the attempt, and so we don't get started.

Never mind the negatives! You can—if you think you can! Think of why you can and should, and then proceed to act on the reason why you can and should. You might fail? Certainly. What worthwhile success was ever attained without plowing through failures and licking them? Bell and Edison knew how true that is! So do Ford and MacArthur and Eisenhower!

Next time you're faced with the choice of doing or not doing something worthwhile, just remember: You can—if you think you can!

Next Monday morning you may face that question. Uncle Sam wants planes and wants them badly. Should you lie in the sun on this side of the ocean while our boys lie in the mud on the other side of the ocean? Or should you put aside play for the one day and come to your job prepared to give it "both barrels"?

You can—if you think you can!

SEPT. 19 DATE FOR BLUE STAR BREAKFAST

Blue Star members are reminded to reserve Sunday morning, September 19, for the September breakfast. An interesting program has been planned.

Carelessness The Great Destroyer

Picture at right shows what can happen during a moment of thoughtlessness. In this case the driver of the factory lift almost sheared off the tail of a P-38. Fortunately he swerved in time, otherwise there would have been one less Lightning to blast the Axis.

LIST PROMOTIONS IN HIGHER BRACKETS

Supervisory promotions recently announced by Lockheed included those of Paul F. Berger to Division Manager, 880; Paul Briggs, Division Manager, 473; Herbert G. Kimball, Division Manager, 880; Arthur M. Viereck, Superintendent, 325; Ellis W. Wright, Division Manager, 472; Paul K. Yost, Jr., Division Manager, 979, and Donald H. Cameron, Division Manager, 743.

Included in the list of Vega promotions were those of Leland B. Butt to Division Manager, 45; Frank N. Herzig, Division Manager, 45; William L. Robinson, Division Manager, 45; Mark Holmes, Division Manager, 46; O. P. Graff, Division Manager, 73; Gale M. Deam, Division Manager, 85; Lester G. Monroe, Division Manager, 58; Harold W. Baker, Assistant to Works Manager, 40; and John H. Gibbs, Division Manager, 48.

Swing Shift Penguin Meeting

The Executive Committee of the Vega Swing Penguins have announced their next meeting will be held Friday, September 10, at the Los Angeles Breakfast Club at 12 noon.

HANDLING OF PARTS CALLS FOR CAUTION

The need for careful handling of parts and material cannot be overestimated. It is one of the most important items in the all-out war effort. Finished assemblies particularly represent many thousands of manhours and one mistake can relegate an entire part or assembly to the scrap pile. While there is some slight value to the scrap material, the long arduous hours of labor and effort cannot be recovered.

Employees trusted with so vital a job as driving a truck, a factory lift, a tug or an electric crane or hoist, must be always aware of the tremendous responsibility of their job. Careful loading of material and parts is most important. It should be kept in mind that aluminum is not an easy material to handle. It is soft and scratches easily. Too much weight will crush it and *a dropped part is a spoiled part.*

An employee may do a fine job of fabrication and then spoil it by carelessly throwing the part into a box.

If you are one of the many employees trusted with material handling, remember the efforts of your fellow employees will accomplish nothing without your wholehearted support.

THE *Lockheed-Vega Star* ★ ★

Official publication of the Lockheed and Vega Aircraft Corporations

Volume 10 BURBANK, CALIFORNIA, U.S.A., OCTOBER 1, 1943 Number 42

Salvaged Zero Reveals Jap Secrets

Captured Jap Zero, salvaged by our boys in the South Pacific and reconstructed for exhibition by Lockheed Customer Service Division, drew huge crowds of curious sightseers in the recreation areas of Lockheed and Vega last week.

Need For Blood Typing Volunteers Voiced

An urgent appeal is made to Lockheed personnel to offer themselves for blood typing during the week beginning October 4. Employees who are typed will serve as a reserve source of blood for transfusions to their fellow workers in event of an emergency.

Blood typing, an action of potential protection to all Lockheed people, should not be confused with the current Red Cross drive for blood donations. Employees submitting to blood typing are not asked to furnish blood unless an emergency arises necessitating their particular type of blood. Blood typing itself is painless and consists of drawing one drop of blood from the finger under supervision of skilled Lockheed registered nurses, and takes but a few minutes.

PLANT 1—Wednesday, October 6

Employees working at Plant 1 are requested to visit the First Aid Station, Unit B, Building 128. This is the First Aid Station located just inside Gate 35 near the Personnel Building.

Day Shift October 6
between hours of 8 and 10 a.m.
Swing Shift October 6
between hours of 6 and 8 p.m.

PLANT 4—Tuesday, October 5

Personnel working at Plant 4 are requested to visit their Plant hospital.

Day Shift October 5
between hours of 9 and 11 a.m.
Swing Shift October 5
between hours of 6 and 8 p.m.
Graveyard Shift October 6
between hours of 1:30 and 3 a.m.

PLANTS 2 AND 7—Thursday, October 7

Those at Plant 2 are requested to visit their Plant hospital.

Day Shift October 7
between hours of 9 and 11 a.m.
Swing Shift October 7
between hours of 6 and 8 p.m.
Graveyard Shift October 8
between hours of 2 and 4 a.m.

Employees working at Plant 7 are requested to visit their Plant hospital.

Day Shift October 7
between hours of 1 and 3 p.m.
Swing Shift October 7
between hours of 8 and 10 p.m.

Plan now to have your blood typed for this worthy cause, which may save the life of a fellow Lockheed worker. Please contact your supervisor before going to the First Aid unit.

Failure To Match U.S., British Planes Clearly Shown

Shot down over Guadalcanal, salvaged by the Navy and rebuilt by the Lockheed Service Division, the first Japanese Zero fighter airplane to be placed on exhibition in this country was unveiled for the first time last week in the recreation areas of Customer Service, Lockheed Plant 1 and Vega Plant 1.

Rebuilt at the request of the Naval Aid Auxiliary, the plane will soon be taken on a nation-wide tour and exhibited for a small admission charge. Proceeds will go to the welfare group to continue their work for men in the Navy, Marines and Coast Guard, and their families.

The Zero, first seen by Lockheed and Vega employees, will be on exhibition at Pershing Square Park next week. Current plans call for a national tour covering about 125 cities.

The Zero was salvaged from a salt water resting place on a Guadalcanal beach. Turned over by the Navy to Naval Aid, it was delivered to Lockheed Customer Service in a badly damaged, corroded condition. It was necessary to do resurfacing of the wings and fuselage, and a general reconstruction job was completed by a special group of Customer Service workers in order to ready the plane for its exhibition tour.

A special steel dolly was built and placed directly under the fuselage for the specific purpose of carrying the plane during its tour. The ship is moved from one city to another by a specially built ten-ton truck and trailer, the inside of which has been specially constructed to house the Zero.

According to the best information available, most of the better points of the Zero were copied from American and British ships. The NAKAJIMI NK 1—14 cylinder twin row radial air cooled motor, developing approximately 900

(Continued on Page 6)

NOTICE!

Effective October 1, 1943, it will be necessary for all employees to show their identification card at the Medical Units when requesting treatment. This is necessitated by the institution of a tabulating system for medical records which require absolute accuracy of clock numbers.

F. E. POOLE, M.D.
Medical Director

'Fighting Fool' To Tell Epic Story

Sgt. Gary E. Gorsline is shown giving his experiences in the different theatres of the war to Capt. Carl J. Long, Public Relations Officer, United States Army Air Forces, at Vega.

BODILY INJURIES LEAD ALL OTHERS SURVEY REVEALS

According to Jack F. Hatton, chief safety engineer, the second quarter of this year's accumulated industrial injury experience still shows that more Lockheed and Vega employees are losing time from work because of injuries to the bodily trunk than to any other part of the body. These injuries are still manifesting themselves in the form of strains and sprains to the abdomen and back.

"If these injuries are to be kept at a minimum," Hatton reports, "employees will have to exercise greater care when lifting or attempting to move heavy objects. Employees should thoroughly familiarize themselves with the rules on lifting contained in the Lockheed and Vega safety rule books and follow them."

Illustrated below is a graphic presentation showing the percentage of lost-time industrial injuries incurred during this period by Lockheed and Vega workers.

Next in line comes injuries to the fingers, followed rather closely by injuries to the eyes and legs, which tied for third place.

SWING SHIFTERS NOW OFFERED DANCE CLUB

The first meeting of the newly organized Lockheed Swing Shift Dance Club will be held Tuesday afternoon, October 12, at 1 o'clock.

Mignon Callish, whose instruction for the Day Dance Club has proven so popular, will have charge of the Swing sessions which run from 1 until 2:30. There will be no charge for the first meeting.

CHILD CARE SERVICE ANNOUNCES NEW PROGRAM

Another feature of child care service has just been announced by the Los Angeles Department of Playgrounds and Recreation.

This time it is week-end outings for girls nine years of age and older in beautiful Griffith Park. Designed to aid working mothers with their child care problems, these "camping" trips afford an opportunity to live in and enjoy the great outdoors from Friday afternoon to Sunday afternoon for the small charge of $3, including six meals and lodging in comfortable cabins.

Swimming lessons, hiking, camp games, nature lore, handicraft and outdoor sports are all a part of the program under the supervision of trained women counselors. The camp is close to town, yet as hidden and remote as if in the heart of the High Sierras.

Enrollment may be made at your nearest Los Angeles Municipal Playground.

JIG PINS SMALL BUT VITAL TO PRODUCTION

Frequently seemingly little things assume large proportions if they are treated lightly. One of the major causes for jig damage and lost time where jigs are used is the misuse of jig pins. These little pins are most important. Valuable hours are lost trying to remove a broken pin or a "frozen" pin from a jig.

The chief cause for such damage is from forcing the pins into position by using a hammer. Pins are bent and broken and the jig is further damaged by enlarged alignment holes. The result is to tie up the jig for needed repairs, and production is delayed.

The primary rule is "Never use force." If a pin won't fit easily, use a lubricant. If this does not remedy the condition, call your Tool Contact man. But whatever is done, don't hammer the pin home. Use your weapons wisely. Be a good soldier.

Veteran Of Many Battles To Addres Penguin Day Shift

Battle experiences in the South Pacific area will be the subject of Flying Sgt. Gary L. Gorsline when he addresses the Vega Day Shift Penguin Club on October 7, at the Oakmont Country Club in Glendale.

Sgt. Gorsline, a veteran of every major mission in the South Pacific area, is in Southern California briefly on part of a nation-wide tour sponsored by the War Department.

As a Line Chief and Aerial Gunner in the USAAF, Sgt. Gorsline chalked up one of the greatest combat records to come out of this war. He participated in the Battle of the Bismarck Sea, the fall of Java, the Coral Sea battle, the beginning and the end of the Buna campaign and the Philippine campaign. Altogether, he spent 204 combat hours in 26 plane missions and among his decorations are the Distinguished Flying Cross, the Air Medal, Silver Star, Order of the Purple Heart and a citation from Wilhelmina, queen of the Netherlands.

He was shot down twice in combat, once over Jap-held Bali where he was rescued by friendly Dutch settlers; and the second time in the Buna campaign when it took him, wounded and with his pilot out of his mind, five days to traverse the 10 miles back to base through swamp and jungle. Prior to that, the day after the fall of Bataan, he flew non-stop from Australia to take part in the two-day bombing and strafing of the Japs in the Philippines. Sgt. Gorsline, a Los Angeles man, is at present assisting in forming a Lockheed-Vega Mobile Training Unit for use in the training of AAF personnel.

Sharing the speaking honors will be George L. Strehlke, district traffic manager of Pan American World Airways, who will tell of the important part the airlines are playing in winning the war.

Guests for the meeting will be Captain Carl J. Long, U.S. Army Representative at Vega; and Captain Mohnan, U.S. Army Representative at Lockheed, both former Penguin speakers. The celebrated technicolor training movie, "Flight Characteristics of the P-38," will also be shown. The meeting starts promptly at 7 p.m.

Lunch Pail Picnic October 6

Lockheed employees from Arizona and New Mexico are planning to attend the next Lunch Pail picnics for all shifts at Plants 1 and 3 on October 6, in the L.E.R.C. recreation areas.

LOCKHEED'S SECOND OLDEST EMPLOYEE STILL GOING STRONG

Second oldest employee of the company and one of its "indispensables," Henry Stolper, 78, Supervisor of Maintenance Carpentering, took a bow as guest of honor last week at a testimonial dinner tendered him by his associates in Department 1-01 in honor of his completion of 10 years service with Lockheed, and of receipt of his 10-Year Pin and a special "badge."

The ceremony, honoring a man whose name has become practically a legend in Works Engineering, was held at the Y.W.C.A., Glendale, with Russ Weil and Harvey Christen, Plant Engineer and Assistant Works Manager, respectively, playing a double-header as co-M.C.'s. Only man older in the company's service than Mr. Stolper is Guard Bill Steirs, who was similarly honored some months ago.

The 10-Year Pin was presented on behalf of Lockheed by Harvey Christen before a gathering of 117 members of the company from group leaders up, and the speaker of the evening was Bruce Coleman, Staff Assistant to the Works Man-‑er, who recounted a few of the legends, .morous and otherwise, that have grown up around Mr. Stolper's name and personality.

NEW FIRST AID CLASSES IN EVENING, DAY SCHOOLS

New first aid classes are now enrolling at the following public schools: Hollywood Evening High School, Monday and Wednesday evenings; Manual Arts Evening High School, Tuesday and Friday evenings; University Evening High School, Thursday evenings; Woodcrest Day School, 109th street and Normandie, Friday mornings; and 52nd Street Day School, 52nd street and Hoover, on Friday afternoons.

These classes are sponsored by the American Red Cross and the Board of Education under the instruction of Dr. Vance J. Hoyt, an authority on the subject. The courses cover all the phases of first aid with special stress upon the practical side of the subject, and are especially arranged so as to accommodate air-raid wardens, auxiliary police, nurses' aides and others who are interested in national defense work, as well as the general public.

An American Red Cross first aid certificate will be issued to those who complete the course and successfully pass the examinations.

'Grand Old Man' Of Dept. 1 Honored

Ray Longton, center, Maintenance Superintendent, Lockheed Dept. 1, pins the special "badge" on Henry Stolper to commemorate his tenth anniversary with the company and for "10 years endurance" with his department. Harvey Christen right, presented Mr. Stolper with his diamond-studded 10-year Service Pin at the testimonial dinner.

PROMOTIONS LISTED BY LOCKHEED, VEGA

Supervisory promotions at Lockheed and Vega just released for publication by the Industrial Relations Office include the following:

LOCKHEED

DEPT.	NAME	TO
720	William A. Baglin	Staff Assistant
741	Charles J. Dexter	Staff Assistant
843	Roger P. Johnson	Dept. Manager
186	Jack A. Malone	Dept. Manager
486	John L. Ross	Dept. Manager
896	Cleon C. Sparks	Asst. Div. Manager
186	Vaughn E. Thompson	Dept. Manager
198	Jack Tonkin	Staff Assistant
472	Ellis W. Wright	Staff Assistant
325	Walter W. West	Staff Assistant

VEGA

DEPT.	NAME	TO
91	Malcolm C. Williams	Staff Assistant
91	A. Carl Kotchian	Staff Assistant
10	Patrick M. Varraveto	Asst. Superintendent
22	Elwood L. Frame	Asst. Foreman, Night
31	Linus R. Collar	Dept. Manager
40	John F. Dunlap	Staff Assistant
60	Robert Kinkaid	Asst. Foreman
67	Robert J. Stevens	Asst. Personnel Manager
7	Frederic Powers	Staff Assistant
10	Sidney J. Akridge	Asst. Superintendent
10	Wayne E. Harness	Staff Assistant
10	Verner D. Vale	Asst. Superintendent
14	Joseph J. Pfeifer	Staff Assistant
21	Walter M. Hopkins	Staff Assistant
25	John Roach	Staff Assistant
25	Glen Smith	Staff Assistant
34	Herbert P. Van Streain	Dept. Manager
71	Thomas A. McDougall	Dept. Manager

LAMENT

I stand out by de tool creeb door,
I reeng de bell one hour or more
Nobodys answer when I reeng
I teenk I brake the G—D—theeng.

OCD OFFERS NEW 'SECURITY AWARD'

Establishment of a "National Security Award" as public recognition of outstanding achievement in protecting the safety of employees, plant facilities and production schedules was announced by the Office of Civilian Defense on September 26.

Almost unknown to the general public, American industry with the cooperation of the War and Navy Departments, the Office of Civilian Defense, management and labor, has achieved an unprecedented nation-wide program of plant protection to guard against interruptions or delay to the production of war supplies and essential civilian materials.

The National Security Award will honor plants for providing the safeguards to production without which the steady stream of material to our fighting forces and the necessary civilian supplies almost certainly could not be maintained."

The award will consist of a Certificate of Merit signed by the Director of Civilian Defense and a distinctive insigne bearing the words National Security Award.

Conservation Gals Show Top Form

They're off! Down the stretch come the women speedsters of the Material Conservation Department during the ladies' three-legged race at the all-shift departmental picnic last Sunday at Mineral Springs, Griffith Park

VAST INDUSTRIAL SAFETY TRAINING COURSES SCHEDULED

In-plant training courses for nearly two-thirds of a million foremen to improve safety conditions in war production are being inaugurated this month, the Department of Labor has announced. The courses will be directed by many of the 40,000 war plant supervisors who have completed safety training courses conducted in 116 engineering colleges.

The War Department also is adding emphasis to the accident-prevention programs of war plants by inviting representatives of private and governmental agencies to the meetings of the Safety Council of the Office of the Provost Marshal General. The meetings are held monthly.

The War Department's Safety Council was organized December 30, 1942, to encourage coordination of the safety effort in war industries, and assists the Office of the Provost Marshal General which has been charged by Lieutenant General Brehon Somervell, Commanding General of Army Service Forces, with responsibility for conduct of the War Department internal security program. The program includes accident and fire prevention, the guarding of plants, protection of vital information and all elements necessary to the safeguarding of war plant operation.

Then there was the moron who fell through a screen door and strained himself.

BOB MOHR WILL PLAY FOR SWING SHIFT DANCE

Bob Mohr and his Fitch Band Wagon orchestra will furnish the music at the Swing Shift Penguin-Penguinette Get-Together dance this Sunday, October 3, at the Los Angeles Breakfast Club, 3201 Los Feliz Blvd. In addition to the dance, a fine floor show has been booked for the occasion. Semi-formal dancing will be held from 9 p.m. to 1 a.m.

Here lie the bones of Kelly,
They buried him here today,
He lived the life of Reilly
While Reilly was away.

BUY WAR STAMPS AND BONDS!

VEGA CHORAL CLUB IN RADIO PROGRAM

With a radio program scheduled for next month, the Vega Choral Club is getting under way toward a highly successful season.

Mike Marsman, director, announces definite plans will be outlined by the Choral Club committees for recitals, socials and radio programs at the next meeting Monday, October 4, at the Hollywood Roosevelt Hotel. There is still room for a few more singers.

Vegans interested in joining this vocal group are asked to be on hand at the meeting which will convene at 7:30 p.m.

MILLION MORE WOMEN NEEDED BY WAR PLANTS

At least one million more women will be needed in munitions industries between now and January, 1944, and an additional 400,000 must enter similar work before July of next year, the War Manpower Commission has said in a report surveying the womanpower needs of industry and business.

At the same time vast numbers of women are urgently required in trade and service occupations. Part-time workers as well as many women who hav never been a part of the labor force will be relied upon to fill the labor gaps caused by the drafting of men and the transfer of both men and women to other jobs.

Latest WMC statistics show that 2.3 million women are employed in munitions, and 12.5 million are engaged in other occupations.

A Buffalo woman, confined to a wheel chair for 11 years, works in her own home as subcontractor for a large aircraft plant, sorting and inspecting rivets for a factory she has never seen.

V. E. R. C. ACTIVITIES

VEGA VAQUEROS—Every Friday, Pico Stables, 420 Riverside Drive, Burbank, 7 p.m. For reservations call CH. 6-5272.

BLUE STAR SERVICE WOMEN—Open house for service men every Monday at Burbank Recreation Center, 1111 West Olive, Burbank. Games, dancing, refreshments.

PLANT 2 RIDING CLUB—Every Friday evening at 7 p.m. at Ride-A-While stables. $1.60 covers ride, dance and hot meal. Make reservations by Wednesday of the week in which you ride.

FENCING CLUB—Meeting Faulkner School of Fencing, 5826 Hollywood Blvd., Tuesday, 7:30 p.m. Swing shift meets 1 p.m., same place.

BOWLING—Vega Majors, Magnolia Bowling Alleys, 6:45 p.m. every Thursday.

DEPT. 16 DAY SHIFT DANCE—Oakmont Country Club, Glendale, Saturday night, October 2, 9 p.m. to 1 a.m. Don Ricardo band.

SWING SHIFT PENGUIN--PENGUINETTE DANCE—Los Angeles Breakfast Club, 3201 Los Feliz Blvd., Sunday, October 3, 9 p.m. to 1 a.m. Bob Mohr band.

DEPT. 4 SWING SHIFT PICNIC—North Hollywood Park, Sunday, October 3, 11 a.m. to 7 p.m.

DEPT. 7 ALL-SHIFT PICNIC—Mountain Oaks Park, Verdugo City, Sunday, October 3, 11 a.m. to 7 p.m.

DAY PENGUIN DINNER—Oakmont Country Club, Glendale, Thursday, October 7, 7 p.m.

SWING SHIFT BLUE STAR WOMEN—Open house for service men, Burbank Recreation Center, 1111 West Olive. Every Friday, 12 noon until 3 p.m., starting Friday, October 8. Games, dancing, refreshments.

Difference Between Life And Death-- Three Seconds!

By CAPT. NEWELL O. ROBERTS
94th United States Pursuit Squadron

Fifth installment, reprinted by permission of COLLIER'S

As the Jerry tried to get set to dive on the bombers, we stayed in position to dive on them. As long as they let the bombers alone, we left them alone. They would send a couple of Messerschmitts down to make passes without shooting. We stayed in our places unless they actually attacked the bombers. That's how businesslike the deal was.

It took plenty of nerve for the Jerries to close in. The bombers were in formation so that no matter from which angle the Messerschmitts attacked, at least nine Fortresses' guns were on the attacker. In addition, our Lightnings were hitting them with all we had. Instead of dogfights that the movies picture as air battles, we dived, got in our burst, zoomed up for position, then dived again. We had the speed and power above 30,000 to do that.

About the only time we broke formation was when a Fortress was hit by ack-ack or fire from a Jerry, and fell behind or below the flight. The Jerries were always waiting like buzzards for this to happen. Then it was our task to hover over the injured bomber and fight off attackers while it limped home.

I was over Cagliari in Sardinia one day protecting a bomber after a battle. He was limping along at 150 miles an hour. Two Me.-109s came in above me. I climbed, trying to get up with them. They stayed on my tail. The other members of our squadron were spread out all over the sky after the battle.

The Jerries and I went around in a circle at 15,000 feet. I couldn't gain on them; they couldn't gain on me. I called in on my phone, "I've got two Me.-109s that need some help." Lieutenant Murdock heard me and swooped in. One Jerry got wise and went home. Murdock got the other in his sights and gave him a squirt. The Jerry went down in a long streamer of black smoke.

Over Tunis and Bizerte, these bombing missions were low-level operations. We could carry bombs under the wings and still have enough gas to fight and get home. In one, I was flight leader of twelve Lightnings protecting two dozen Fortresses.

We had reached our objective, bombed railroad yards, and were headed back. I had almost twisted my neck off looking around and up for Jerries. They're always trying to sneak in from the rear.

Just as the bombers warned us by radio, I saw a bunch of Me.-109s behind us. I called my planes on the radio, then made a fifteen-degree bank. I could see the pilot in the Lightning to my right eating a cholocate bar. You get as hungry as a horse on these long flights. I guess he didn't hear me, because the next time I looked, he wasn't there. The Jerry shot him down. Then they must have thought he was such easy meat that they could take on the rest of us.

We fought for seventy-five miles, going round and round in a circle about fifty feet off the ground—eleven P-38s and fifteen Me.-109s.

The Fortresses were there at the start, but they soon disappeared while we battled. It was one of the toughest fights I have been in.

(To Be Continued)

The Absentees Paid The Bill!

Lockheed Cribs 1-5A, B and C of Dept. 1-23 Swing, have proved in a novel way that absenteeism doesn't pay. The cribs held a contest to discover which of the three had the best work attendance record. No report on the winning crib or cribs has reached the STAR, but the losers anyway were stuck for dinner for all three at the Rancho in Burbank. The contest was declared such a success both in cutting down absenteeism and as a social event that the three cribs are holding another one this month.

Engineer Broadcasts

"In our plants we freeze nothing permanently—there are constant changes to improve performance and meet new tactical requirements," said Mac Short, Vega engineering vice-president and president of the Society of Automotive Engineers, on a transcontinental broadcast this week. Mr. Short headlined an Army Air Forces show with John A. C. Warner, SAE general manager; La Verne Browne, Douglas engineering test pilot, and Lt. Tony Lumpkin, over the Mutual coast-to-coast network. Shown are Lt. Lumpkin at the mike and Mr. Short.

APPEAL MADE TO HELP FIND HOMES

Lockheed and Vega Employee Service Divisions are urgently appealing to company personnel for their assistance in helping to alleviate the present housing difficulties of the two companies.

Many employees possess valuable information of vacancies, prospective vacancies and other housing data that could be used to assist other employees in securing houses, apartments and rooms.

Those knowing of actual or pending vacancies, are asked to contact their department clerks, women's counselors or Plant Personnel Offices to fill out The Housing Form. This information will be immediately sent to Employee Service where it will be made available to employees in need of a place to live. Be sure and include the telephone number of the prospective vacancy in the information you give.

CHORAL CLUB INVITES LOCKHEEDIANS TO JOIN

The enthusiastic response from Lockheed employees and members of their families to the newly sponsored Choral Club indicates that this group will become one of the outstanding L.E.R.C. organizations.

Turn-outs are held each Friday evening at the North Hollywood High School auditorium.

L.E.R.C. Troup To Stage Return Show

No wonder the boys at the Victorville Army Air Base are yelling for a return engagement of the L.E.R.C. Graveyard Gaieties. Shown returning last week from the first tour are, top, left to right, Bettie Stober, Jane Fisher, Flora Degen. Bottom row, Edith De Sylva, Sylvia Wosik, Lieutenant Jack J. Lyons, Beverly Roberts, Martha Oftendahl, Dorothea Clarke, Ruth Lee, Bettie Leavitt, and Dorothy Grotz.

GRAVEYARD GAIETIES PLAY FOR AIR CORPS TRAINEES ON DESERT

Following their highly successful appearance at the Victorville air base last week-end, the cast of the Graveyard Gaieties has gone into intensive rehearsals for the "popular demand" return engagement for their show, booked for the Elks Club, 607 South Parkview, Los Angeles, Saturday evening, October 16.

Once again, the Gaieties will be combined with a dance for which the L.E.R.C. Dance Band has been engaged, according to Les Capen, writer-director of the Graveyard Gaieties.

Tickets for the return engagement will be $1.10 and will go on sale this week-end. This production is a "must" for Lockheedians and marks a new high in L.E.R.C. sponsored entertainment features.

Jig and Fixture Classes

A class in Beginning and Advanced Jig and Fixture Design will start October 5 in Room 110, John Muir Evening School, 220 North Grinnell drive, Burbank. Meetings on Tuesday and Thursday evenings from 6:30 to 9:30. Lester W. Ferris, instructor.

Get "in the groove" and buy extra War Bonds now.

SPANISH LANGUAGE CLASSES OFFERED

Spanish language classes for local aircraft workers will be offered free at John Burroughs Junior High School, 1920 Clark street, Burbank, beginning October 4. The following schedule for Swing, Day and Graveyard shifts is announced:

Swing Shift—1 to 3 p.m.
Day Factory—4:15 to 6:15 p.m.
Day Office and Graveyard—7 to 9 p.m.

Monday-Wednesday....Beginning Spanish
Tuesday-Thursday..Intermediate Spanish
Friday ....Advanced Spanish

Those desiring to take the courses should enroll at the school.

COTTON SHED DANCE SET FOR OCTOBER 16

All details are completed for the long awaited Cotton Shed Dance on Saturday evening, October 16, at the Oakmont Country Club, according to Al Bevers, coordinator for the affair which is being given under L.E.R.C. sponsorship.

"This marks the first time that the guys and gals who have been putting the finishing touches on the P-38s have had a sponsored dance, and under the present seven-day production blitz the Cotton Shed gang have been stampeding the ticket representatives," reports Bevers.

FAILURE TO MATCH U.S., BRITISH PLANES CLEARLY SHOWN

(Continued from Page 1)

horsepower, is an imitation of the air cooled British Armstrong Siddeley Tiger 7. Many of the instruments which are calibrated in Arabic and western letters, are good copies of American type bank indicators, altimeters, pressure and oil gauges.

Outstanding, is the wing and fuselage construction of the Zero, which is built in one piece. This is absolutely contrary to the American method of building the wing and fuselage separately.

The ship on tour is a carrier based type Zero, as evidenced by its folding wing tips and deck hook, suspended below the tail. The ship's wing span is 39 feet 5 inches, and from nose to tail, measures 29 feet 6 inches.

The first reaction Naval experts had after examining the plane was its lightness. When fully loaded it weighs only 5207 pounds. This condition was traced to the absence of self-sealing gas tanks, parachutes and armor and the use of thin gauge metal throughout. Its basic protection is speed and maneuverability and the secret of its rapid climb is due to its light weight.

The Zero's armament consists of two 7.7 mm machine guns set in the nose of the ship and two 20 mm Oerlikan cannon projecting from the edge of each wing. All guns are controlled by a two-way switch, mounted on the throttle control lever.

The Zero's best performance is at approximately 200 miles per hour. At 230 miles per hour, the controls begin to stiffen (due to large control surfaces) and it is no longer capable of fast rolls and quick climbing turns. Flutter develops in vertical dives which warns of light construction.

In a straight level flight with full throttle, the Zero is capable of 345 miles per hour at about 11,500 foot ceiling. The service ceiling is 35,500 feet.

The fuel capacity is 145 United States gallons without the belly tank and 241 United States gallons with the belly tank. The maximum flying range is approximately 1400 miles with the extra tank fuel.

Patterson Gives High Praise To U.S. Air Engineers

When Undersecretary of War Robert P. Patterson returned recently to the United States from a 30,000-mile tour of Pacific posts, he said he had landed on Munda airfield in a medium U.S. bomber two or three weeks after it had been captured from the Japs.

Behind the repair and reconditioning of seized enemy airfields lies the speed, skill, and ingenuity of Army aviation engineers and Navy Seabees, highly praised by the Undersecretary of War, and backed by the comparable skill and speed of U.S. workers producing the war goods for the fighting engineers. Increasingly the flight engineers, the Office of War Information points out, will play an important part not only in providing maximum use of airfields as they are taken over from the enemy all over the globe, but in constructing new advance airdromes for United States heavy long-range bombers carrying the war straight to the heart of the Axis.

'DO'S AND DON'TS' FOR SIMPLIFICATION PROPOSALS

The Lockheed and Vega Work Simplification offices emphasizes the following "Do's and Don'ts" for employees submitting Proposals for Improvement. They are simple suggestions and will go a long way in expediting investigations.

"DO"

1. **Make your suggestion specific and complete.**
2. **Include all pertinent information concerning form or part numbers and names, tool numbers and names, job location by department and section or building and room number.**
3. **Be sure you have offered a solution, not merely recognized a problem.**
4. **Wherever possible confine your suggestions to ideas which can be put into effect through a better utilization of present equipment and facilities.**

"DON'T"

1. **Do not turn in a suggestion which will require large expenditures of money for more tools, machinery or equipment.**
2. **Do not suggest surveys, appointments of committees or other similarly vague means of accomplishing your improvement.**
3. **Do not leave the solution up to someone else.**
4. **Do not use the Proposal for Improvement Plan as a means of protest. Use it intelligently and constructively.**

The Work Simplification offices want to investigate thoroughly and accept all the ideas they possibly can and as quickly as possible.

Education Commissioner Visitor

★

Charged with the study of housing conditions in Southern California's war industry areas, and at the same time a check-up on the benefits accruing from the part-time employment of "boy-power" in war plants, Dr. John W. Studebaker, U.S. Commissioner of Education, was a recent distinguished visitor to Lockheed and Vega. Here he is seen, right, with Emery Olson, of the Lockheed Industrial Relations Department, inspecting a P-38 on the assembly line during a personally conducted tour of Lockheed Plant 1.

★

INCREASED DANGER OF SABOTAGE CITED

Increased dangers of sabotage activity in the United States may result from the reverses the Axis is meeting in the field and from the curb of the submarine menace, government agencies have warned in cautioning Americans against a "false sense of security."

The need to step up vigilance has been cited by the Federal Bureau of Investigation, and Army and Naval Intelligence, who have called upon the Office of War Information to conduct an informational program designed to prevent sabotage.

Four reasons for stepping up vigilance, say the Government agencies, are:

1. A sense of false security may result from the past good record of a minimum of sabotage.

2. The enemy himself has given strong indication of renewed zeal in sabotage efforts. It is an established fact that the Germans are turning out well-trained graduates of a saboteur school, and that some of the graduates may be sent to this country.

3. The enemy has been meeting enough reverses in the field so that desperation moves are very likely, and one of his favorites is sabotage.

4. Heretofore, enemy submarines have managed to destroy some war materials as they were being shipped to war zones. Now, however, we are beginning to conquer the submarine menace and it is logical to assume that, if the enemy can't destroy the material in transit, he will endeavor to destroy it at the source.

In cautioning the country against the possibility of sabotage, the Government agencies concerned stressed that it is important to remember that so far no major loss because of sabotage has been suffered. People should not get the erroneous idea, it was further insisted, that the country is filled with spies or that one is working in every plant, for this simply is not true.

THE Lockheed-Vega Star ★★

The Lockheed-Vega Star is issued every Friday for the employees of the Lockheed Aircraft Corporation and the Vega Aircraft Corporation and is the official publication of both companies. Communications may be addressed to either the Industrial Relations Office or the Public Relations Department, Lockheed Aircraft Corporation, Burbank, California, U.S.A. Although news and cartoon contributions are welcome, circumstances make it impossible to give any promise that they will be returned to sender when not used, nor can individual acknowledgment be made.

H. L. (HAL) ROSSON, Editor

Volume 10 Number 42

Every Shoulder To The Wheel

Swinging into its final week, the Third War Loan drive, which ends at midnight Saturday, October 2, must have the all-out support of every income-earner if Southern California's $422,000,000 quota is to be attained.

This was the word received today from Robert H. Moulton, chairman of the Treasury War Finance Committee for this area, who reported individual sales lagging.

All citizens who have not yet bought extra bonds and others who have bought but, by digging deep, are able to buy more were urged to turn every possible dollar of idle cash into War Bonds this week.

"The money to complete our part of this big job is here," Moulton said. "It is in the form of accumulated savings and surplus cash from current earnings.

"The government needs this money now to buy vital equipment and ammunition for our attacking soldiers, sailors and marines overseas. If we should lose the war because of lack of needed financing by the home front, these idle dollars will be of no value to their owners. But, invested in bonds, they will help win the war, make future security certain, ward off inflation and, at the same time, will return a good rate of interest. What better deal could any individual ask?

"Southern California has never failed and cannot on this loan."

LIBRARY

Here is a list of some of the recent arrivals in the bookstore of the Lockheed-Vega Education Library. You are cordially invited to come in and browse.

LOCKHEED PLANT I

Personnel Bldg., Room 210

Universal Machinist's Handbook, Shields $1.40
Mathematics Refresher, Hooper 1.95
Airplane Maintenance, Lesley 2.40
Aircraft Lofting & Template Layout, Thrasher 2.30
Aviation Mechanics Simplified, Williams 2.57

VEGA, PLANT I

"The Shacks," East of Bldg. 61

Practical Mathematics, 4 vols. ....ea. $1.00
Safety in Flight, Jordanoff 2.45

'Clothes For Work' Show At Plant 7

Plant 7 "Models" line up on stage in recreation area Thursday of last week to display what the well dressed feminine war worker will—and should—wear for comfort and safety.

'CEILING UNLIMITED' TO FEATURE FOREIGN BROADCAST SUNDAY

Hot off the German griddle, fliers of the R.A.F. and the American Eighth Army Air Forces will be heard from somewhere in England by American listeners when the pilots are introduced Sunday, October 3, by Major Ben Lyon on "America—Ceiling Unlimited."

As a salute to the combined military efforts of the British and Americans, Major Lyon, once prominent on the American stage and screen, will interview members of units who have been engaged in recent aerial activities on the continent.

Dramatic personal accounts of combat with enemy craft and contrasts of individual reactions to battle conditions will be offered by these airmen with a new technique in air-sea rescue work highlighting the flight story of the week.

Joseph Cotten, sinister-sophisticate and popular romantic leading man of films and the stage, presides as master of ceremonies and will enact a radio adaptation of the American Magazine story by Loring Dowst titled "Stranger in the Night." The selection is a mystery theme with the war as background.

Personable movie actress Nan Wynn occupies the vocal spotlight. She will sing for the second time this season, and by special request, "All Or Nothing At All."

EVENT VOTED BIG SOCIAL SUCCESS

Lockheed Plant 7 staged its feminine "Clothes for Work" fashion show Thursday of last week, a show which was not only notable for music, action and cameras, but also constituted the first real get-together of the plant personnel since the unit was opened last spring.

Distinguished for its sparkling color, six-piece orchestra, comic take-offs, models, and commentators, the affair was staged under the sponsorship of Employees Service at Plant 1, Mrs. Merle Sproull in charge.

The wide collection of slack suits, jumpers, blouses and caps shown are now available at cost through the Victory Shop in the Tool Store at Plant 1.

Frances Gifford, beautiful young star of M-G-M, acted as commentator and added a glamorous note to the performances. Maestro Casey Kuczborski, with his new Plant 7 orchestra, was a sensation. Frances Anderson and Olive St. John, women counselors, and all their able assistants share the credit for a "bang up" show.

Signs Of The Times

Recent classified ad from the L.A. Times:

MAN wanted, screwball inventor with spark of sanity. Box E-251, Times.

BAKERSFIELD AND TAFT EDITION

'E' DAY IS NEAR FOR FACTORY B

Volume 11 BURBANK, CALIFORNIA, U.S.A., MAY 12, 1944 Number 22

The LOCKHEED Star

OFFICIAL PUBLICATION OF THE LOCKHEED AIRCRAFT CORPORATION

Arctic Camouflage

Against a background of snow-swept mountain terrain, the Lockheed Ventura PV-1 is shown in snow-white battle array as she appears garbed for service in the Arctic regions. The U.S. Navy's sub-buster and patrol bomber, the Ventura also is flying under six other United Nation's flags, patrolling the shores of three continents. Spearhead of the Navy attack on the Kurile Islands, outpost of the Japanese empire, the Ventura also is a front-runner on Navy assaults on the Marshalls, Carolines, and the Marianas.

Follow These Directions To Flag Ceremony At Factory B-1 Next Wednesday

Here's how to get to the "E" award ceremonies.

The program will take place in the area just west of the end of the P-38 final assembly line, immediately south of Building 146.

To get to the area, proceed from your building to the rear of the plant and the old flying field and then due west toward Buena Vista street. In other words, employees who work in Department 18-04 or in administrative departments located adjacent to Gate 8 will follow the street in from Gate 8 to the flying field at the rear of the plant, turn west and proceed directly to the area adjacent to the cotton shed where the program will take place.

Employees who work outside of the plant on the north side of Empire avenue will follow Empire west to the end of the bomb shelters and enter the plant through Gate 17, opposite Lincoln street. Employees of B-1 and its branch plants will be excused from 9 a.m. to 9:40 a.m. to attend the ceremonies.

Plants To Receive 'E' Award May 17

Next Wednesday is "E" Day for Lockheed Factory B employees.

The hour is 9:05 a.m.

"For high achievement in the production of weapons of war," Factory B and its branch plants will be awarded the Army-Navy "E" for Excellence in ceremonies taking place just west of the end of the P-38 final assembly line, immediately south of Building 146.

When the whistle blows at 9 o'clock next Wednesday for the regular morning smoking period, employees will proceed directly to the program area.

Ceremonies will start promptly at 9:05 a.m. They will be broadcast over Radio Station KMPC for the benefit of Swing and Graveyard shift employees and their families and the families of Day shifters.

The entire program also will be carried to all Factory B branch plants where "E" pennants will also be raised simultaneously with the hoisting of the flag at the main ceremonies at B-1.

Temporary stands are being erected for the speakers, and plans are being made for a capacity audience to include all B-I employees. The L.E.R.C. band will furnish the music for the program.

THE PROGRAM—

1. Color guard raises the American flag.
2. Medley of martial airs by L.E.R.C. band.
3. Master of Ceremonies Major Howard Adams, Western District Public Relations Officer, gives background for "E" award.
4. Brig. Gen. Donald F. Stace, supervisor of the Western Procurement District, AAF Materiel Command, speaks for the Army Air Forces.
5. Lt. Colonel Howard Angus, Lockheed AAF Resident Representative, presents "E" pennant to color guard.
6. "E" pennant raised.
7. Robert E. Gross, president of Lockheed, accepts "E" award for Lockheed employees.
8. Captain D. L. Webb, Bureau of Aeronautics General Representative, speaks for the Navy.
9. Lieut. Commander Carlton D. Palmer, Lockheed Bureau of Aeronautics Representative, presents "E" pins to representative Lockheed employees.
10. Velma Biby, Dept. 18-16, Swing, accepts "E" pin for L.E.R.C.
11. C. O. McEfee, Dept. 36-01 Days, accepts "E" pin for Aeronautical Lodge 727, International Association of Machinists.
12. L.E.R.C. band plays "Star Spangled Banner."

U.S. Acts In Thefts

Carr Announces Drastic Drive To End Pilfering

Thefts of tools, gauges, small electrical equipment, copper materials, fittings and other "transportable" materiel have become so widespread in Southern California war plants that U.S. Attorney General Charles H. Carr has announced his intention of rigorously prosecuting all such cases which are brought to his attention, according to Plant Protection Manager John H. Hanson.

First action by Carr to halt these thefts, which can and do impair war production, was taken last Friday with the filing of criminal informations against five discharged employees of a local shipbuilding corporation. Charges against the quintet involved only $200, Carr said, but total losses in war plants in the Los Angeles area from employee thefts reach "a staggering figure," he added.

Army and Navy officials are cooperating in the drive launched by Carr, and criminal informations filed in such cases are in accordance with, and carry the penalties of, the statutes covering thefts from Government property in war time.

Famous Go-togethers — Petting on park benches—wedding bells; petting behind the wheels—tolling bells.

Families Will Hear 'E' Award Ceremony

All Lockheed Factory B employees and their families will be afforded an opportunity to hear at 9:05 a.m. next Wednesday morning the ceremonies at which the Army-Navy "E" for Excellence is awarded to Factory B and its coordinating units in outlying sectors.

The entire program will be broadcast over Radio Station KMPC from 9:05 a.m. to 9:35 a.m. for Swing and Graveyard shift workers and for the families of Day shifters.

At the same time, the program will be brought to all Factory B branch plants, either through a direct hook-up with the ceremonies at Factory B-1 or through a broadcast over the plant loud speaker systems of the KMPC broadcast.

Bunko Warning

Employees who are solicited to sign up for correspondence school training, or for any trade schools where fees are charged, should bear in mind that the company does not endorse any such schools and that under no circumstances is information pertaining to an employee given to such establishments.

Reports that salesmen for certain training courses are telling Lockheed personnel that the company has recommended them have recently been brought to light. Such statements are without foundation and any employee who is solicited in this manner should report it to the Employee Service Department immediately.

Mobile Blood Donor Unit

Change Visiting Days To Accommodate All

Because of more convenient working hours, Day shift employees who have registered as volunteer blood donors through the Lockheed program, outnumber their Swing shift co-workers by more than four to one; so, in order to permit all donors to visit the Blood Donor Station as early as possible, it is necessary that visits of the mobile unit of the American Red Cross Blood Donor service be revised.

Starting next Monday, May 15, the unit will come to Lockheed on the following schedule: Monday, May 15, Days; Monday, May 22, Days; Monday, May 29, Swing; Monday, June 5, Days; Monday, June 12, Days; Monday, June 19, Swing and Monday, June 26, Days.

Appointment cards will be sent to Department Clerks for distribution to volunteer donors several days prior to their appointment time. As a rigid schedule must be maintained, employees are requested to arrive at the Blood Donor Station *promptly at time shown on their appointment card.*

If for any reason the appointment cannot be kept, please so inform the Department Clerk so that card may be returned to the Blood Donor Station.

Spare Parts Program Behind Schedule

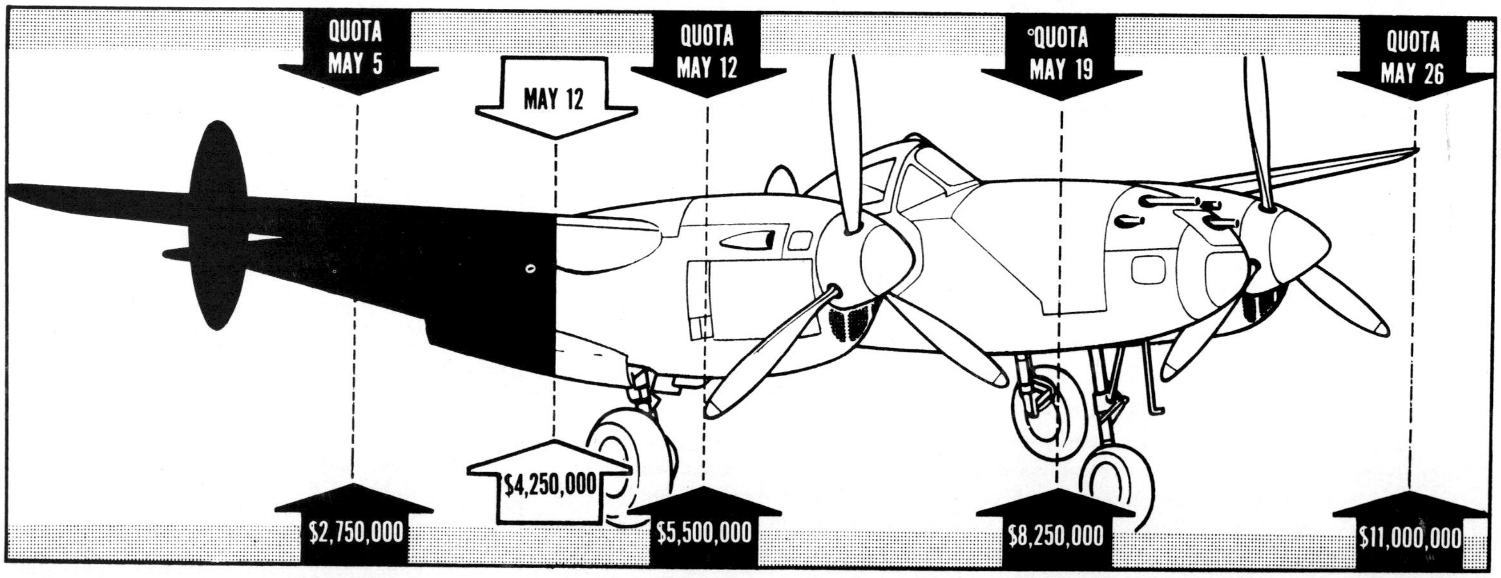

At the end of the second week in May, the Lockheed spare parts program was running considerably behind the schedule set up by the Army Air Forces, according to figures released today. While production figures for the month of April showed that Lockheed approximated the production quota set up as imperative, currently the production of spares is at only 77.3 per cent of schedule. The second week in May should have shown a spares production level of $5,500,000. Current figures list our spares production at $4,250,000—22.7 per cent behind quota. If the full quota for May is to be met, there will have to be a rapid improvement.

All So. Pacific Hails Bong And Plane

Thanks to Edmond Nasif, who, in a letter recently received, describes himself as "a G.I. photographer . . . in New Guinea," the two pictures at the top of this page and the one at the bottom have been made available to the STAR. The two photos above show, right, the victory flags on the nose of the Major's veteran Lightning, and left, a view of another P-38 at a New Guinea airdrome.

←Closeup of Major Bong and the trophies on his ship (left) taken at the time his score had reached 25 to tie Major Joe Foss and to fall only one short of Eddie Rickenbacker's record in World War I. (Acme photo.)

Army Photographer Edmond Nasif got this shot of the famous ace's Lightning after the Major had chalked up his 27th victory in the air over the Nips.

Pride In Ace's Feat Recounted

A lusty chorus from the South Pacific is joining with the nation's acclaim for Major Richard I. Bong, No. 1 American air ace. G.I. pride for the noted flyer's record of 27 Jap planes shot down is coupled with praise for the Lockheed product which is making such records possible. In such vein is the recent letter from Edmond Nasif, who calls himself "a G.I. photographer from somewhere in New Guinea—the garden spot of the world—of savages."

"You don't know me from Adam," he tells Lockheed, "but I would like *you* to know some of the results of *your* work.

"I happened to be on a job down on the line today, and saw Major 'Dick' Bong's ship sitting in its 'hod stand.' Those Nip flags looked good (on a P-38) so I decided to take a few spare 'public relations' shots. And tonight, upon viewing results, I decided to go a step farther and send Lockheed a couple of shots of a P-38 in her 'battle dress.'

"I'm not in a P-38 outfit, but I did spend six months in one back in '42. I learned to love that plane, and still cannot resist photographing her. Am enclos-

(Continued on Page 7)

NEWS OF BAKERSFIELD AND TAFT

Taft Reporter—
ALICE PARNELL

A Team In Work & Music

Close teamwork is the theme song of Nell McCamy and Perna Rankin, general assemblers in Department 19-54. The two girls started working together over a year ago putting hooks on the bomb rail assemblies. During rest periods and at lunch time you will usually find Nell and Perna entertaining fellow employees with cowboy songs and popular music of all kinds. They supply their own musical accompaniment. Nell with the guitar and Perna the accordion. Both girls contributed music and songs to the "Lockheed Morales of 1944" show presented by the L.E.R.C. recently.

Personality Corner

Plant 54

SKAGG'S HAGS bowling team, after striving to hold a place in the league, finally dropped to the basement position. . . . ADELEE BACON was welcomed back last Monday after a two weeks' vacation in San Francisco. . . . Farewells were said this week to LOUISE LESSLEY who has left Lockheed for a much needed rest. . . . While DORIS JONES paints her house, ARNOLD POPP goes fishing—they are both on vacation, being missed by the stockroom group. . . . Finance and Accounting Personnel Departments of Plant 54 held a picnic for members of the respective departments and other guests at the Kern County Park last Sunday. Softball was played during the day with a windup of fried chicken and refreshments.

BESSIE BUNDY is in Texas to see her son in the Air Force. . . . Did you know that BRUCE VOGLE played for five years with the Los Angeles Symphony Orchestra as clarinet soloist?

* * *

Plant 56

BETTY HUDSON is vacationing this week on her parent's ranch in Cuyama Valley. . . . MIKE ELLIS is supervising Bulkheads Nos. 7, 8 and 9, while COY SNIDER is away on his vacation. . . . NEMA THORNBRUGH'S husband has just returned home after ten months in the Aleutians. He hadn't seen his baby daughter since she was six days old.

AMOS CRAIG is wondering if he can make it to Alabama and back for a week's vacation—he has just received his 1-A.

Welcome to two newcomers—DOROTHY GRAHAM, formerly at Lockheed 54, and NORA LONG, formerly at Douglas Aircraft in Oklahoma City. . . . MARY BELTZ has just left on her vacation to visit her sister and brother who is home on furlough.

Bulkhead No. 6 is playing host to Bulkheads Nos. 10 and 11 with a pot-luck dinner during the regular lunch period on Thursday.

Wedding bells will ring May 6 for RUTH ROWELL and Lt. Roger Boon. They plan to tie the knot at Gardner Field. . . . Plant 56 really hated to see EARL MONSON leave last week. He will be missed by many. . . . ROBERT KIRKPATRICK, guard at 56, has just become the proud father of a little girl, born at the Taft Community Hospital. Both mother and baby are reported to be doing very nicely.

We haven't heard EILEEN KRUGER'S melodious voice lately. What's the matter, Eileen? . . . BETTY LLOYD is on vacation in Ohio. . . . Congratulations to BARBARA BRODIE and REGINA FOY for their efforts in making Bulkhead No. 11 the first to reach the (censored) ship serial mark at Plant 56.

ROBERT MUNS and JAMES MUNS, both of the Production Department at Plant 55, received "Greeting" from Uncle Sam this week. . . . BENTLEY TRODGEN of Plant 55 spent his vacation "swimming" in Missouri. Reason—with the exception of one day, it rained continuously

Bowling

Reds And Blues Enter Competition

Lockheed is now sponsoring two teams in the Merchant's League at Franks Bowling Alley on Monday nights. The two teams were picked from our regular bowling league as the 12 men having top bowling scores.

One team, the "Reds," is captained by Jim Mull. Members are: Wally Warren, Al Deifel, Zeke Romero, Kenny Duncanson, Jack Monan and Jim Mull.

During the first week of play this group established a nice high single team game of 980. On the second night of play they ran into a little difficulty and were able to win only one point, but are looking forward to a recovery next week. Kenny Duncanson, who rolled a high series the first game, was unable to play on the second night.

The other team, known as the "Blues" is captained by Ase Ebbutt. Members are: Eddie Ferrell, Sparky Carrico, Arnold Popp, Al Schulhof, Ira Smith, and Ase Ebbutt.

The "Blues" have been successful in their first two excursions, having won 3 points each time partially due to the outstanding efforts of Sparky Carrico, who has a 236 game for high and an average of 189 at present. He is assisted by Al Schulhof, who has maintained an average of more than 180.

'Hiding Behind Skirts'

Trailing edge assemblies shipped from Bakersfield Plant 54 to Plant A-I are "skirted" to prevent damage in shipping. A canvas skirt 22 feet long and 12 inches wide is attached to the bottom of the assembly to prevent scratching.

German flight captain reported to St. Peter.
Captain: "Flight Group 711 reporting."
St. Peter: "How many?"
Captain: "Seven officers, 33 men."
St. Peter: "Sorry! We have accommodations for only four. There aren't quarters here for the rest."
Captain: "Why?"
St. Peter: "That's all Goebbels reported shot down."

Credit P-38

South Pacific Flyers Praise Safety Margin

Captain Martin Foster and Captain Robert H. Eubank this week cashed in the rain checks they accepted months ago from Lockheed's field service representative Ed Packard, who invited the two P-38 fighter pilots to visit the factory when they returned to the United States from the Mediterranean theater.

Both officers flew P-38's exclusively overseas; and like all P-38 pilots, are "sold" on the ship.

"Several times I think I wouldn't have made it back if I hadn't been in a P-38," says Capt. Eubank, who holds the DFC and the Air Medal with three Oak Leaf clusters. During a dog fight only 40 feet from the ground, Eubank flew his P-38 right through an Me 109 as it exploded in mid-air from the P-38's concentrated firepower.

Captain Foster tells of returning 120 miles to base on a badly damaged right engine after the "blinkin' headlights" of an Me 109 destroyed most of the left side of his ship. In addition to the second engine, Foster praises the P-38's stability and absence of torque. "It makes high speed maneuvering close to the ground safer," he explains. Foster holds the Air Medal with nine clusters.

Citizenship Papers

Employees desiring to obtain their proof of citizenship papers from company files may do so by calling Extension 1242 at Factory B, or sending a memorandum to the Citizenship Desk, Dept. 90-62, B-I, giving clock number, department and plant number (A or B).

The papers will then be mailed to the employee through inter-office mail unless he desire to call for them in person at the Citizenship Desk, Industrial Relations building.

Do not call for citizenship documents without first notifying the Citizenship Desk at least 24 hours in advance of the time wanted.

The Family Car-

"How about gas?" was the query of many foot-weary when the meat rationing eased off. "Not so good," replied the OPA. "Washington recognizes the unique transportation problem arising from the unusually broad areas of Southern California. But increasing war needs will probably bring tighter restrictions on civilian supplies before more gasoline can be freed for use in the family car."

Lightning Fighters 'Sold'

★

Home from the Mediterranean fighting fronts for a well deserved rest, Capt. Martin Foster and Capt. Robert H. Eubank were visitors to Lockheed last week at the invitation of Lockheed's Field Service Representative Ed Packard. Both Capt. Foster (in cockpit) and Capt. Eubank flew Lightnings exclusively in combat and both credit the ship with having saved their lives by getting them back to base after being badly damaged.

★

Engineers Elected

Three Lockheed engineers were elected to responsible positions at the head of the Engineers and Architects Association of Southern California during the Fiftieth Anniversary dinner and installation of officers recently.

The three elected were:

New President—Dr. Robert C. Burt, Electrical Engineering group supervisor, Plant Engineering, Dept. 36-05.

New Vice-President—John G. Becker, Senior engineering checker, Design Engineering, Dept. 72-25.

Member of the Board of Directors—Harold R. Beck, Senior design engineer, Dept. 72-25, formerly a Senior electrical engineer in Plant Engineering.

The Engineers and Architects Association is the oldest engineering society in the southwest and was founded by the pioneers who engineered the Los Angeles harbor, aqueduct, civic center and much of our highway, railway and power systems.

Yield To Military Vehicles

As an immediate aid to our war effort, the Southern Securities District of the Ninth Service Command, U.S. Army, requests all citizens to yield the right-of-way to military convoys. With an increased tempo in the Pacific theater of war, our military vehicles must be aided in their movements to the greatest possible extent, says the Traffic Education Unit of the Los Angeles Police Department.

S-G Golf Opens

First Of Two May Meets Monday

Lockheed's Swing-Graveyard division of the L.E.R.C. Golf Club will hold the first of their two May meets on Monday morning, May 15, at Brookside Golf course in Pasadena and at the Griffith Park course, both events to start between 8:30 and 9:30 a.m.

Non-members of the two shifts who are interested in joining the divoteers must present four score cards signed by the prospective member and attested by another player. From these cards the club will decide his or her handicap. Players who have established handicaps will not have to present the four cards. Club membership is 50c with an additional charge of 50c for each tournament entered. The latter fee will be used to buy prizes for the winners of the events.

Uniform Gate Time

Effective Monday, May 15, gates at all Lockheed plants will be opened to incoming shifts on a uniform time basis. Starting next Monday they will open to incoming Day, Swing and Graveyard shifts 15 minutes prior to the starting time of each shift.

'Connie' Greets 15,000

One of the distinguished groups of Washingtonians which greeted the Constellation upon its arrival in the nation's capital is shown above. It includes Senators Alben W. Barkley of Ky., Harry S. Truman of Mo., Arthur H. Vandenberg of Mich., Ralph O. Brewster of Me., Allen J. Ellender of La., Ernest W. McFarland of Ariz., Homer Ferguson of Mich., Burnet H. Maybank of So. Car., and Theodore Francis Green of R.I. Also Wilson Wyatt, Mayor of Louisville, Ky., and L. L. Biffle, Secretarv to the Senate Majority. At left, Secretary of War Henry L. Stimson, with aide, and Howard Hughes, are shown leaving the giant ship after an interested inspection of her interior.

A little thought, with a little care, prevents accidents.

Constellation 'Wonderful' Orville Wright Verdict

Highlight to date in the career of Lockheed's giant new 57-passenger Constellation occurred when the mammoth plane arrived at Dayton's Wright Field. There, Orville Wright, surviving brother of the world-famous pair who invented and flew the first heavier-than-air machine to fly, and from whose baling wire and canvas original all modern aeroplanes are descended, sat at "Connie's" controls for five minutes during a one-hour flight.

Asked what he thought about the great ship, the 72-year old pioneer could say only one word: "Wonderful!"

Ex-Service Men Wear This Button

Whenever a serviceman is honorably discharged from duty in the armed forces, he is awarded this button by the War and Navy Departments to be worn in his lapel. The button is presented to him when he is given his discharge papers, or he may secure one upon presentation of his papers at any military or naval establishment. The button is made of plastic and plated with gold. Watch for it around the plants.

Like A Queen

Leaders Of The Land Pay Her Homage

April 17 to 26 was probably the busiest, most hectic period that the always bustling Washington National Airport had ever experienced in all its long operational history. For during those nine days an estimated 15,000 persons viewed the interior of the Constellation following its arrival after its record-breaking flight of 6 hours and 58 minutes from Lockheed Air Terminal, Burbank, to the capital's main airfield.

Ranking members of the Armed Forces, statesmen, and key figures in aviation circles boarded "Connie" for short flights and were piloted by Howard Hughes or Jack Frye, president of T.W.A. The roster of those who took these flights and those who contented themselves with inspecting the interior of the famous plane reads like a "who's who" of inner Administration circles, Congress and the Army and Navy Departments.

Prominent among those who were taken aloft were Chief of Air Staff Maj. Gen. B. M. Giles; Maj. Gen. Harold L. George, Commanding General of the Air Transport Command; Secretary of Commerce Jesse Jones; Robert P. Patterson, Under-Secretary of War; Donald Nelson, head of the War Production Board; Charles I. Stanton, Civil Aeronautics Administrator; L. Welch Pogue, Chairman of the CAB; Rear Admiral Emory S. Land, Chairman of the Maritime Commission; Rear Admiral Howard Vickery, also of the Maritime Commission; and William A. M. Burden, Assistant Secretary of Commerce.

Among those who inspected the plane's interior were Secretary of War Henry L. Stimson, and General H. H. Arnold, Commanding General of the USAAF. Both were shown through the plane by Howard Hughes.

Old Clothes Needed

The Russian War Relief, Inc. has notified the Buck-of-the-Month Club that a county-wide drive for old clothes for the Russian people in reoccupied areas will be put on from May 17 to May 28. They are not asking for money since the Buck - of - the - Month Club has already made a contribution to the United War Chest.

If you have any discarded clothes, the Russian people who have been under the heel of the Nazis need them badly. They should be delivered to 5512 Hollywood Blvd., near Western Ave., Los Angeles.

Shift Schedules

Newcomers Posted On Working Time Limits

Definite work shift schedules have long been established at Lockheed and all employees are presumed to be thoroughly familiar with them. For those who are not, the following information is issued by the Industrial Relations Department:

The time limits of work are the start and end of each shift, with designated rest periods for factory employees and designated lunch periods for all employees. A warning whistle is blown at the end of factory shifts, and an equivalent period is permitted on other shifts when necessary, for the specific purpose of enabling employees working away from their work stations, or who require preparation to complete a job, to *finish working time at their work station when the final quitting signal is given.*

A few employees have formed the habit of "rushing the clock"—standing in line inside plant gates at lunch time or near clock stations just before closing time, thereby gaining an advantage of fellow employees who do abide by company rules. They not only receive pay for time not worked but take unfair advantage over others during meal periods and in traffic.

"Clock rushing is one of the things we can well do without," says the department, "and effective Monday, May 15, any employee who loiters inside a plant gate just before lunch time, or near a clock station just prior to the end of a shift, will be given a warning through supervision which will be recorded in his or her permanent file. Further violations will be cause for suspension or dismissal."

Brainy Beauty Wins $437

★

Brainy, blonde and beautiful Naomi Riley, of Receiving Dept. 51-50, Factory B-1, is now $437 richer as the result of a Simplification idea which she submitted to simplify the work at the plant's Receiving Dock. Her proposal calls for a "Dock Record" which embodies a method of numbering designed to improve the recording and controlling of all incoming shipments saving much valuable time for the department. Here she is being handed her check by J. P. Elliot, Supervisor of Dept. 51-50.

★

Bits Breakage Costly

Cause Traced To Hand Made Tools

An operations report from Dept. 42-33 reveals that every week at Factory B over 2000 Phillips screwdriver bits are broken. At 20 cents each, this means a weekly breakage bill of more than $400, or approximately $20,800 per year.

A high percentage of this breakage is traced to the use of non-standard and poorly designed screwdrivers made in the shop.

As a means of reducing the number of broken bits, a supply of self-aligning screwdrivers and adaptors properly designed for Phillips bits has been placed on sale in the Lockheed Tool Stores at a nominal price. These drivers are to be used in conjunction with the standard Lockheed-furnished Phillips bits available at every tool crib.

The No. 1450 Apex Hand Driver is recommended for use with:

		Phillips Bits
No. 830-1	Lockheed Code	#5801022-221
830-2	" "	#5801022-210
830-3	" "	#5801022-223
830-4	" "	#5801022-214

The No. 1400 Apex Hand Driver is recommended for use with:

		Phillips Bits
No. 820-1	Lockheed Code	#5801022-214
820-2	" "	#5801022-213
820-3	" "	#5801022-219

Every employee requiring this type of tool in his work is urged to add one of these efficient screwdrivers to his personal collection of tools.

Recounts Bong's Feat

(Continued from Page 3)

ing a couple of other shots one of our fellows took recently.

"A plane is no better than the people who sweat blood building them. Keep it up—and we'll give you the South Pacific for Christmas."

Buck-A-Month Letter

A recent letter from the chairman of the Los Angeles Area War Chest reveals that 2500 boys are prisoners of war and that the War Chest gifts have helped to purchase for them books, musical instruments, games and other "luxuries" so much needed to keep up their morale. Members of the Lockheed Employees Buck-of-the-Month Club are proud of having a share in this fine work by reason of their donation of $250,000 last fall to the War Chest.

The LOCKHEED Star
OFFICIAL PUBLICATION OF THE LOCKHEED AIRCRAFT CORPORATION

The Lockheed Star is issued every Friday for the employees of the Lockheed Aircraft Corporation and is the official publication of the company. Communications may be addressed to either the Industrial Relations Office or the Public Relations Department, Lockheed Aircraft Corporation, Burbank, California, U.S.A. Although news and cartoon contributions are welcome, circumstances make it impossible to give any promise that they will be returned to sender when not used, nor can individual acknowledgment be made.

H. L. ROSSON, Editor

Volume 11 Number 22

Vaccination

Free Protection For Other Plants Starts

Vaccination of employees at Plants A-1 and A-2, and B-1, 3, 4, 5, and 6 against smallpox will begin next week, Dr. F. E. Poole, Medical Director, has announced.

Vaccination of employees at Plants B-2 and B-7 began May 1 following a warning by the Public Health Departments of Los Angeles City and County that there has been a recent increase in the incidence of smallpox in the State of California.

All employees are urged to contact their private physician, public health clinic, or to take advantage of this opportunity which is offered free of cost by the Medical Division for protection against this potentially serious disease.

Arrangements for vaccinations may be made by filling out the authorization card which will be distributed with time cards on Thursday, May 18.

These cards (illustrated below) should be placed in time card boxes with your time card without delay. When received by the Medical Department you will be notified when and where to report for vaccination.

Immunization against tetanus (lockjaw) is also available at the same time the vaccination is given. This immunization makes it unnecessary to give tetanus antitoxin serum in case of injury.

Both Health Departments advise all residents of the county who have not been vaccinated within the past five years to take advantage of this protection.

The Latin Touch Wins

In setting his recent record output of P-38 nose inter-cooler duct assemblies, John Igual De Montijo, center, general inspector in Dept. 18-58, was ably assisted by Virgil Kyle, left, and Jake Kupp, right.

Judge Jingle Sez . . .

A bomb run over Tokyo—
How our boys would like to try it!
Let's help them gain their hearts' desire . . .
Save for a Bond, then buy it!
If you drive as carefully as you can . . .
Don't better Oldfield's time, nor tie it,
You'll give the boys the bombs they need
To put a crimp in Tojo's Diet.

Mexican Inspector Proves Power House

That extra ounce of effort in war production was given a distinctly Latin flavor at Lockheed Factory B last week when John Igual De Montijo, general inspector in Dept. 18-58, was given a special commendation from H. A. Symonds, department head of 58-03 Inspection, for a job well done.

Under the driving force of energy exerted by this Mexican-born Spaniard, a naturalized American citizen since 1934, the Spot Weld Assembly department completed and sent through Inspection in one day 112 nose inter-cooler duct assemblies for the Lightning P-38. This was described by Symonds in his commendation as "a record for amount of assemblies passed through this department in one day."

IF YOU DESIRE TO TAKE ADVANTAGE OF THE COMPANY'S OFFER TO GIVE YOU, FREE OF COST TO YOURSELF, VACCINATION AGAINST SMALLPOX AND/OR IMMUNIZATION AGAINST TETANUS (LOCKJAW), FILL IN, DATE AND SIGN THIS CARD. DROP IT IN YOUR TIME CARD BOX AT END OF YOUR SHIFT, OR LEAVE IT AT ANY PLANT HOSPITAL OR FIRST AID STATION. YOU WILL RECEIVE NOTICE WHERE AND WHEN TO APPEAR. DO NOT CALL HOSPITAL FOR APPOINTMENT.

LOCKHEED AIRCRAFT CORPORATION

MEDICAL SERVICE AUTHORIZATION CARD

DESIRE TO HAVE MYSELF VACCINATED AGAINST SMALLPOX ☐ AND/OR

TO BE GIVEN IMMUNIZATION AGAINST TETANUS (LOCKJAW) ☐

EITHER OR BOTH TO BE GIVEN BY THE MEDICAL DIVISION OF THE LOCKHEED AIRCRAFT CORPORATION FREE OF COST TO ME.

DATE ____________ 1944 SIGNED ____________

DO NOT WRITE BELOW; FOR USE OF MEDICAL DIVISION ONLY

GIVEN		CHECKED	BY - PLANT PHYSICIAN
SMALLPOX	______ 1944	______ 1944 BY ______	______ M.D.
TETANUS	______ 1944 (FIRST)		______ M.D.
	______ 1944 (SECOND)		______ M.D.

DO NOT FOLD NOR TEAR THIS CARD

The LOCKHEED Star
OFFICIAL PUBLICATION OF THE LOCKHEED AIRCRAFT CORPORATION
Volume 11 BURBANK, CALIFORNIA, U.S.A., MARCH 31, 1944 Number 16

Take-off In The North

(Official U.S. Navy Photo)
Low-scudding clouds and the spray of snow thrown up by its propellers lend a wintry aspect to this picture of a Lockheed Ventura's take-off from an Aleutian air field.

Paramushiro, Round Trip

PV-1 Hailed As 'One Of Greatest Combat Planes' By Alaska's Navy Fliers

"One of the greatest combat planes in the fight!"

That's what the Navy fliers based in the Aleutians are saying about the Lockheed Ventura PV-I, according to Chester G. Petersen and Paul Von Essen, Lockheed Factory A service engineers who just returned from a visit to our northern bases.

The PV-Is are making the "Empire Express" run to Paramushiro with alarming regularity, bombing and strafing the installations of the Kurile Island outpost, northernmost bastion of the Japanese homeland. *The Lockheed planes are the first planes to be employed consistently on raids on the Nipponese home fortifications.*

There's very little that the Venturas won't do when put to the test, Navy pilots told Petersen and Von Essen on their visit to the Aleutians. They claim

(Continued on Page 2)

Blood Donor Restrictions Eased

In the past, donors to the Red Cross blood bank have been requested not to eat food of any kind during the four hours prior to making their donation. Now, according to word received from the Red Cross today, this restriction has been lifted. From now on, donors may eat what they like and as much as they like right up to the time of giving blood. So go ahead and eat your T-bone—and then toddle down to the company blood donor station before its effects wear off.

So Solly--No Like P-38

Nip Pilots Prefer To Dodge Lightning

What do Jap fliers think of the P-38? And how does the Jap stack up as an all-round aerial fighter?

These are two questions that thousands of the home folks ask, especially those with boys in the Central and South Pacific, and those here at Lockheed striving night and day to turn out more and more Lightnings. Perhaps an Associated Press dispatch from the 14th Air Force Base in Southeast China, under date of March 15, supplies some of the answers. Says A.P.:

American fliers using P-38 Lightning fighters have found that the average Japanese fighter pilot in China is anything but eager.

The suicidal psychology of Japanese tactics reported elsewhere is nonexistent in this area.

This may be accounted for by the sort of planes now used against them and their own fighters' lack of armor, or it may be, as some American commanders believe, that thus far the Japanese air force in China has consisted mainly of newly-winged fliers cautiously preening for action in the Southwest Pacific.

With the Lightnings especially, the Japanese show little inclination to tangle. A favorite tactic is to wheel around over their own anti-aircraft positions, hoping to draw the Americans into position where they can be brought under fire both from aloft and below.

The Japanese pilot generally plays a tight little game of aerial warfare. He is a good airman, but he doesn't like to fight unless the odds are in his favor. Even then he is unpredictable and may break off a fight and high-tail for home without visible cause.

He is wary of making offensive moves, preferring the defensive role, leaving the offensive stroke to his bombers.

The Japanese airman here has yet to demonstrate gallantry in battle. By gallantry I mean the deliberate act at great risk to save a comrade. In this sense, the Japanese airman is never brave. He may on rare occasions subject himself to grave danger, but even here there is no evidence that he thinks of anyone but himself.

Burma Bridge Bows Out

Top — The Mu River Bridge, west of Mandalay, offers a clean target to a raiding party of B-25's and P-38 escorts, which approached the target at 1000 feet or so, and wheeled into position for the bomb run.

Middle — Skimming the tree tops for better accuracy, a medium bomber sends a thousand-pound missile splashing into the river near the main supporting pier of the bridge. The full force of the explosion is not yet apparent.

Bottom — A closeup after the raid shows the complete destruction of the structure and the damage to the approaches. This will take a long time to repair.

Bombers, Escorted By Lightnings, Rip Jap Communications

Early this year, six B-25's of the Eastern Air Command, escorted by 16 P-38's, attacked and destroyed the Mu River bridge, a vital link in the Japanese supply system in Central Burma. The bridge which crosses the Mu River at Nyaungbinwun, west of Mandalay, controls traffic over a 250-mile stretch of the Burma railroad between Mandalay and Ye-U.

After pelting the target with thousand-pound bombs, crews reported that two spans had been knocked into the river and the others thrown out of alignment. Sections of track were torn up on both sides of the bridge and about 30 railroad cars in the vicinity were riddled by the P-38's and left in flames.

The pictures of the raid show a bomb being dropped from a B-25 which skimmed over the structure at about fifty feet. The pilot of this plane came straight for the bridge, but was forced to swerve to the right to avoid clipping a tree on the river bank. The bomb was delayed a fraction of a second to allow the plane to clear the target before the tremendous concussion took place.

These pictures illustrate *one* of the activities of U.S. airmen over Burma, and one of their most important assignments; for the reconquest of Burma depends largely on the disruption of Jap lines of communication and supply. The destruction of bridge after bridge in recent weeks is the handwriting on the wall for the Japanese.

Paramushiro And Back

(Continued from Page 1)

it is the fastest plane in the Navy—at least the fastest bomber—and it is as maneuverable as most fighter planes.

Navy pilots described to Petersen and Von Essen their raids on Paramushiro. (Details were eliminated for security reasons.)

Up to the time Petersen and Von Essen left the Aleutians, the Japs had never succeeded in bringing down a PV-I of the "Empire Express."

JAP SHIP ON DISPLAY

The Japanese Zero which was reconditioned by Lockheed's Service Division for display throughout the country will make its last Southern California appearance, according to Naval Aid Auxiliary officials, in Glendale today, tomorrow and Sunday. The ship will be spotted on Brand boulevard between Broadway and Wilson.

'Inspection' Takes Bow

Navy Commends 57-01 For Thorough Job

Factory A's Department 57-01 (Inspection) and its chief, Walter G. Hoskinson, are throwing their weight around this week. And with good cause. For the U.S. Navy is pleased with their work on the PV-1 and has officially expressed its pleasure in black and white in a communication to the corporation.

The commendation, over the signature of Resident Naval Representative Lt. Comdr. C. D. Palmer, U.S.N., and forwarded following the recent visit of Commander E. R. Sanders, U.S.N., to a Plant Engineering Conference at Factory A, said, in part:

"This letter is forwarded with the belief that you and your department will be interested in hearing some comments which were made by Commander E. R. Sanders during his recent meeting with the Navy inspection force in the Plant Engineering Conference. You will recall that Commander Sanders spoke to the company at their luncheon meetings indicating his appreciation to the people at Lockheed for their efforts in producing a good aircraft for the Navy. He was formerly Commanding Officer of VB137 which included the 101st PV-1 displayed on March 16, 1944. This squadron has been very successful in their operations against the Japs in the Mid-Pacific.

"In addressing the Navy inspectors, Commander Sanders stated, 'The ships that we have had out on advanced bases showed every evidence of good, thorough inspection. The inspectors have done a job which is an important one as far as the operations of the aircraft are concerned.'"

In conclusion, Lt. Comdr. Palmer stated:

"Your local Navy Representative takes considerable pleasure in forwarding this information and believes that these comments will be of value to you as a note of appreciation to your inspection force by those people who are using these particular Lockheed aircraft so successfully in combat."

P-38 CLOSEUP

A closeup of the P-38 to employees of Factory B-1 will be given next week for three days beginning Tuesday. The ship will be located adjacent to buildings 146 and 175 and a catwalk will be erected so that a close inspection may be made. Employees only may view the plane and then only during their lunch hour or before or after their regular shift. Entrance to the plane during off-shift hours will be through Gate 17.

'Blister' That Spits Death

Five top members of the Los Angeles County Citizens Manpower Commission, inspect a B-17 ball turret during a visit to Lockheed last week. They are left to right: Morris B. Pendleton, Paul Armstrong, Harold Wright, LeRoy Edwards, chairman, and Jack Smalley.

Old Dog Teaches New Tricks

Veteran Lightning Still Proving Fritz Has A Few Things To Learn

"Dear John," the Lightning fighter which carried Major Edward S. Newbury from Burbank to Tunisia and then safely through 300 hours of combat, is still teaching the Germans new tricks after more than two years of Army life.

Describing the veteran plane as "probably the oldest P-38 in combat," an article in *Stars and Stripes*, Army weekly, credits it with 92 missions over the enemy lines.

"Lockheed builds the toughest fighter plane in the world," said Capt. Richard A. Peterson of Chicago, engineering officer of the AAF Black Falcon squadron ever since Dear John joined up. "That airplane still is more than a match for the German Luftwaffe. It still draws its regular combat assignments."

When Major Newbury completed his operational tour and returned to the United States, Dear John was converted into a piggy-back for instructional use for a time. Later it was converted again, and Lt. James S. Alford took it back into combat.

Jumped by four Focke-Wulfs on a mission to Cae Fano in Italy, Lieutenant Alford slugged it out with them until forced to land with an aileron, boom, propeller and engine cowling riddled by their fire. Again Dear John was repaired and put back in service.

Major Newbury, now based on the West Coast, recently addressed the Day shift luncheon crowds at Factory B-1. He hopes to return to combat with the extra punch of the P-38J.

BUY WAR STAMPS AND BONDS!

NEWS OF BAKERSFIELD AND TAFT

By IRVING MILLER
Taft Reporter—ALICE PARNELL

Popular Spot At 55

The serene smile on Emma Hamilton's face above is not entirely for the benefit of the photographer who snapped this picture of the canteen at Plant 55. She's quite happy about the food that she has just purchased.

Since its opening, the canteen has increased in popularity by serving coffee and doughnuts before shifts, coffee at rest periods and hot lunches at noon. Soft drinks, candies and cigarettes are also sold.

Cities Split Twin Bill Bowling Clash

Lockheed's top men's and women's kegling teams from Taft and Bakersfield met at Frank's Bowling Academy Tuesday evening, for a return match.

Bakersfield men won from the Taft men by 97 pins. To even the score a bit, the Taft women took the honors from the Bakersfield women by 289 pins.

The star of the evening's play was Bertha Gordy of Taft, who bowled one 231 game and tallied another at 206.

Taft Men's Team	Bakersfield Men's Team
Pete Pankonin	Bob Yager
Al Turner	Al Schulhoff
Kenny Russell	Harold Cochran
Pete Bergman	Kenny Duncanson
Mike Ellis	Zeke Romero

Taft Women's Team	Bakersfield Women's Team
Jane Frank	Anita Miller
Ione de Amicis	Leo Adams
Eileen Kruger	Marjorie Owens
Fran Dickinson	Virginia Owens
Bertha Gordy	Evelyn Ferguson

'TWO GUN' WHITLOCK GETS 92 PER CENT—SHOOTING LEFT-HANDED

Performing pistol feats is an old-time sport for gunmen of the plains and many have awed audiences by their firearm fancy work, but getting down to hometown performers, A. D. Whitlock would be a mighty dangerous sharpshooter to start any gun play with.

Whitlock, a guard at Plant 54, recently set a shooting record in Bakersfield by pluggin' the bullseye 92 out of a possible 100 shots. But read on—this was only left-handed! Normally Whitlock is a right-handed shooter, but now his pistol prowess is well established with both hands. Yes sir, Mister Whitlock, here's my badge and pass!

All guards must shoot a score of 60, with hand other than one normally used, to qualify.

Pvt.: "Gosh, it's dark in this parlor. I can hardly see my hand in front of me."
She: "That's all right, don't worry I know where it is."

Noses and 'Seats' Changed

But No One's Hurt And All's Calm Again

Aladdin has rubbed his magic lamp again, playing tricks on some of the workers at Plant 54. Upon reporting to their customary working area they found:

Bombracks had suddenly turned to Pilot Seats and Noses had disappeared. After a bit of interrogation, everyone found what they were looking for and the world settled back down into its proper channels.

Pilot seats are now located where the Bombracks were, Bombracks moved into the previous Nose Section, and the Noses took over the original Pilot Seat location.

This assembly moving, which took place March 3, has resulted in a better coordination in the flow of work.

New Bowling League

The new bowling league of Bakersfield Lockheed Plants 54 and 55, sponsored by L.E.R.C., got under way Thursday, March 16. The new league is comprised of 12 teams, as follows, with their standing after the first night of play.

	GAMES PLAYED	POINTS WON	POINTS LOST
Timber Wolves	3	4	0
Knot Heads	3	4	0
Pinbusters	3	3	1
Pin Kings	3	2	2
Jiggers	3	2	2
Rolling Bombers	3	2	2
Floyd's Flirts	3	2	2
Skagg's Hags	3	2	2
Whiz Kids	3	2	2
Paper Dolls	3	1	3
Buck Passers	3	0	4
Rejectors	3	0	4

High game average for the men is held by Ase Ebbutt with 190; Odette Chudzinski of the women leads with 157.

What Can You Do?

Do you sing, dance or act? The "Lockheed Morals of 1944" cast is now being selected and the originators are looking for talent of all kinds. All employees interested are urged to contact Carl Boon in the personnel office at Plant 54. This may be your big chance to develop your talent and help the L.E.R.C. put on a big show.

Little boy (reading the newspaper): "What does it mean by seasoned troops, Dad?"
Dad: "Mustered by the officers and peppered by the enemy."

Paycheck Change Reminder

New System To Be Effective April 24

Employees now on monthly salary basis are reminded of the change in salary payment procedure which will become effective Monday, April 24, when the first bi-weekly pay checks will be issued.

In order to make the bi-weekly periods balance during the year, a one-week's salary will be paid on Monday, April 10, covering the period April 1-7. This check for one week will be issued in the gross amount, minus deductions for taxes, but not including deductions for bonds, group insurance, etc. The first bi-weekly check of April 24 will carry a three-week deduction for such premiums.

In the future all rates, increases or decreases quoted or recorded for salaried employees will be on a weekly instead of a monthly basis as heretofore. Monthly-to-weekly rate conversion charts have been distributed to all supervision for posting on departmental bulletin boards.

Noble Guy

GI Joe Is Hero On Sunday Radio Fare

A soldier finds it embarrassing being in love with two girls at the same time in Will F. Jenkins' story, "George Is A Noble Guy," to be heard next Sunday, April 2, over Lockheed's "America—Ceiling Unlimited."

Joseph Cotten, star of the weekly variety program, portrays the soldier whose marriage plans must be cancelled due to his sudden departure for another camp. Further complications arise when the fellow falls in love with a girl whose correspondence with his former sweetheart reveals some startling and hitherto unknown facts about himself.

Vocal fare is provided by Constance Moore who will sing the ballad favorite, "Suddenly It's Spring," and the new novelty, "It's Love, Love, Love," with orchestral accompaniment under the direction of Wilbur Hatch.

The broadcast is heard Sundays over KNX at 11 a.m. (PWT).

Hitler to Tojo (on phone): "Heil, Tojo, thought you would be in America in three weeks?"
Tojo: "So solly, Adolph! You phoning from Moscow?"

'Riveting With Rhythm'

★

Champion women riveters at Factory A are, left to right, Elizabeth Vernando and Cleo Glover who, setting a record pace of 104 rivets in 120 seconds, challenge any women riveters in Lockheed to equal them.

★

Rivet Gun Or Machine Gun, Makes No Difference, Rhythm's What Counts

One hundred and four rivets in 120 seconds!

All women riveters at Lockheed are challenged to beat this score by Elizabeth Vernando and Cleo Glover, the riveting team that set the record, attested by Joseph M. Alvey, group supervisor, who last week conducted a special time test. Elizabeth and Cleo work in Dept. 24, Factory A, on bomb bay doors for the PV-1.

One hundred and four 1/8 inch B.H. rivets were placed in the drilled holes and 120 seconds later were completely riveted by this team.

Elizabeth and Cleo started work at Lockheed one year ago, building PV-1 bomb doors. They came as green help but today are considered to be two of the fastest women riveters in the plant.

The pace set by Production Control at Factory A is a fast one. Components are delivered to the factory with rhythmic speed. Teamwork such as that of Miss Vernando and Miss Glover make it possible for the pace to be maintained.

When asked how they attained such a high degree of efficiency, Miss Vernando said, "You can become efficient doing anything if you have rhythm in your work."

Miss Glover said, "Whether you're using a machine gun or a rivet gun, you have to have rhythm."

And they prove it. For with rhythm of motion and the rhythmic rat-tat-tat of their rivet gun, they have established a record that has yet to be beaten under a stop watch at Lockheed.

Tragedy Strikes

Supreme Sacrifice Made By Lockheedian

Tragedy struck at Mr. and Mrs. T. J. Fluty, both of Factory A, this week when they received word that their son, 1st Lt. Joseph M. Fluty had been killed in action with the Eighth American Air Force while on a mission over Europe. Mr. Fluty is a guard at A and Mrs. Fluty works in Dept. 15-57.

Lt. Fluty, also a former employee of Lockheed, had the distinction of being the holder of two Distinguished Flying Crosses, two Air Medals and four Oak Leaf Clusters. The Guard Division at Factory A are planting a tree in his memory at the family home in Glendale.

The deepest sympathy of all, mingled with pride in his heroic accomplishments, goes out to his bereaved parents.

The LOCKHEED Star
OFFICIAL PUBLICATION OF THE LOCKHEED AIRCRAFT CORPORATION

The Lockheed Star is issued every Friday for the employees of the Lockheed Aircraft Corporation and is the official publication of the company. Communications may be addressed to either the Industrial Relations Office or the Public Relations Department, Lockheed Aircraft Corporation, Burbank, California, U.S.A. Although news and cartoon contributions are welcome, circumstances make it impossible to give any promise that they will be returned to sender when not used, nor can individual acknowledgment be made.

H. L. ROSSON, Editor

Volume 11 Number 16

Hop, Skip, Jump!

'Parts' Does Its Part To Speed Victory

Speed, and still more speed, not only in production of battle planes for the battle fronts but in keeping them flying once they are there, is one of the most important requirements demanded of Lockheed by our Air Forces overseas. How such demands are met, on time and mostly ahead of time, is revealed in the following incident.

A few days ago a code telegram from (censored) was received by the Parts Office of Lockheed Production Control. It told about one of our planes being grounded because of a damaged landing gear, holding up plane, crew and a vital mission.

"Hold the press" is a common phrase in the newspaper business, but "Hold the Hydro," as used by Lockheed's dispatchers, can mean putting a grounded plane and its crew back into the air in an unbelievably short time. The new landing gear for this particular plane was packed, boxed and followed through by our dispatchers for air transportation to the overseas freight terminal, placed aboard an air transport, arrived at its destination and was installed on the damaged ship *only 48 hours after receipt of the wire.*

Many such urgent requests from the Army and Navy air forces are received by Lockheed every day. The moment they arrive, dispatchers *hop* to their business, *skip* all red tape, and put the required parts on a plane for the big *jump* without a moment's delay. And moments can save lives, even save battles, in this war.

Said He: Say, that old gal sure gave you a mean look.
Said She: Who do you mean?
Said He (breaking into a run): Mother Nature.

FOOD FINDS

THIS TAKES THE PRIZE:

The Lockheed Medical Division announces the winner of the Contest for Fish Loaf. Five dollars goes to—

Leola Ann D. Guida, Clock No. 28538, Lockheed Plant B-4, Dept. 1-15

for her prize-winning recipe:

FISH LOAF SUPREME

Ingredients:

- 1 lb. cooked flaked fish (fresh or canned)
- 2 cups cooked drained rice
- 2/3 cup white sauce
- 1 tbsp. grated onions
- 1½ tsp. Worcestershire sauce
- 1 small bottle olives
- 1 sliced lemon (parsley)
- ¼ tsp. salt
- ⅛ tsp. pepper
- 1 cup dry bread crumbs

Method: First make a white sauce by combining over fire 1 tbsp. melted shortening and 2 tbsp. (level) flour. Add slowly 2/3 cup milk. Stir until smooth. Season. Set aside.

Now mix fish, rice, white sauce, onion, Worcestershire sauce, seasonings, and half of bread crumbs. Line a greased mold with half of remaining bread crumbs and fill with mixture. Put remaining crumbs on top. Bake in hot oven 450° F. 25 minutes. Unmold, garnish with the sliced lemon, sliced olives, and parsley. Serves 4.

Winner's Comment: This can be served with tomato sauce or mustard sauce. It is also delicious with white sauce.

Judges' Comment: Here's a tasty dish that takes little time if you use canned fish (be sure to drain off the oil first), and if you've planned to have the 2 cups of rice left over from an earlier cooking. Bread sticks—peas, carrots, or asparagus—and stewed tomatoes are good to have with this fish dish.

NEXT WEEK'S PRIZE: Contest No. 7 is designed to improve the lunch box. The subject of the contest is A LUNCH BOX MENU AND A SANDWICH FILLING. Five dollars will go to the contestant who submits a double header including: the best recipe for a sandwich filling, and the best combination of lunch-box foods to go with it. Fillings must be tasty, nutritious, and quick to prepare. Menus likewise.

Rules: Each recipe must be accompanied by full instructions. Each contestant may submit one recipe only. All entries must be in the hands of the judges by Friday noon, April 7. Mail your entries to This Takes the Prize, c/o Miss Josephine Williams, 1201 East California St., Pasadena 4, Calif. Be sure to include, besides your name and home address, your department, plant, and clock number.

At Last They Did It

It has finally happened! After skirting around the top many times, Production Control Division, Factory A, has won the Safety Trophy for the February period—and in a big way! The division accumulated over 570,000 accident-free man hours and not one hour has been lost during the year 1944 to date from occupational accidents.

Norm Stratton, manager, believes that the department will duplicate the performance for March if its personnel remain safety conscious. This is the first time in the history of the company that Production Control has won the Safety Trophy.

VETERANS PROPERTY TAX EXEMPTION

Arrangements have been made for ex-service men now employed at Lockheed to file their annual claim for tax exemption without losing time during working hours.

Veterans who are entitled to the $1000 property exemption may contact the County Assessor's Office on Sunday, April 16, 23 and 30, from 9 a.m. to 1 p.m. This office is located on the 4th floor, Hall of Justice, corner of Temple and Broadway, Los Angeles.

No claim for a veterans' exemption will be received by the County Assessor's Office after the last Monday in June.

TODAY IS DEADLINE ON BUS RIDE BOOST

Today is the deadline! From now on 12½ cent coupons in Lockheed-chartered bus books will not be accepted for rides on buses operating over the nine routes listed below.

This warning was issued today by Dale Cosgray, Manager of Employee Transportation, who said that starting tomorrow all who ride chartered buses must present the new tickets, which cost 15 cents each and which may be purchased in 16-ride books for $2.40.

Tickets outstanding in the old books may be turned in at any of the regular Employee Transportation units selling bus tickets. Exchanges will be made by paying the difference in cash. *Remember—it must be done before boarding the bus tomorrow!*

The following railheads are affected: **Santa Monica and Western, Beverly and Vermont, Ave. 39 and Figueroa, Olympic and Fairfax, Pico and Rimpau, Santa Monica and Virgil, Olympic and Doheny, Venice and Hoover, and 16th and San Pedro.**

A beginners' class in Radio Theory, preparing students for an F.C.C. Radio Telephone License, will begin Monday, April 3, at the John Burroughs Evening School, 1920 Clark street, Burbank. Classes will continue on Mondays and Thursdays from 6 to 9 p.m.

THE LOCKHEED
Star
OFFICIAL PUBLICATION OF THE LOCKHEED AIRCRAFT CORPORATION
Vol. I
BURBANK, CALIFORNIA, U.S.A., JUNE 2, 1944
No. 2
CONNIE GETS IN LINE
—Page Three

STAR GAZING from the proximity of a Lockheed homeward-bound bus, somewhere around last Friday afternoon.

Rudy Vallee

Lockheed Serenade By Famous Band

Lt. Rudy Vallee and his Coast Guard Band are coming to Lockheed to help launch the local campaign of the nation's Fifth War Loan Drive, June 9 to 24, inclusive.

The famous university graduate who became one of the nation's top-flight dance band leaders, is scheduled to entertain workers of Factory B-1 on Wednesday, June 7, during five lunch periods—three on the day shift and two on swing. On the following day, the program calls for his appearance at Factory A-1 for similar lunch periods.

To meet Lockheed's quota, employees will be urged to make their bond purchases total $100 each for this drive. Special booths and other convenient spots will be set up in every one of the company's plants.

Members of the Employees' Victory Committee in charge of the drive at Lockheed hope to increase participation in the payroll savings plan so that 90 per cent of the employees will be subscribing at least 10 per cent of their earnings

TURNING ON HEAT for their trumpet section are these seven zaneys in the Coast Guard Band of Lt. Rudy Vallee. The entire band is scheduled to appear during lunch periods at Factories A-1 and B-1, June 7 and 8.

Good Mixers

Lockheed's research chemical laboratory has put to the lie an old adage —that oil and water will not mix.

With test tubes and retorts they've not only proven it, *will* mix, but in accomplishing the seeming miracle they neatly sidestepped a threatened bottleneck in airplane production and licked a problem of corrosion which darkly loomed when paint solvents grew scarce.

For the first time in the history of the paint industry these Lockheed chemists, following research conducted by Glenn B. Weible, Factory B process engineer, and Robert J. Burns, research analyst, have perfected a method of mixing oily paint with water so that it won't flake off from weather-exposed metal surfaces.

Shortly after war's advent, the paint department was using about 400 gallons of paint thinner each day. This consisted of a liquid derived from petroleum. Gasoline also is made from petroleum and that's why the pinch began to be felt.

As the chemists explain it, there have been a number of water paints on the market for some time, but none of them could be applied directly to metal and stick there through all kinds of weather.

Now, give them a can of thick, oily paint and they'll thin it with water, using their patented process so that it can be applied directly to a metal surface as though it were lacquer. The water-thinned paint has been put to exacting tests and found to more than meet specifications.

Go West, Young Man

In five months' time the A.A.F. extended the American airplane bases 1,300 miles westward toward Tokyo.

Appointments

Supplementing the organizational change reported in *The Star* last week under which the Plant Engineering Departments of Factories A and B have been consolidated, Plant Engineer G. S. Rigdon announces the following personnel appointments:

Dept. 39-01 (Maintenance)—W. S. Taylor, Supt., Factories A and B; Charles Reynolds and H. D. Hamm, Gen. Foreman and Asst. Gen. Foreman, Factory B.

Dept. 39-36 (Buildings and Grounds)—J. G. Middleton and E. H. Erhard, Manager and Asst. Manager, Factories A and B.

Dept. 39-35 (Machine Design and Procurement)—R. J. Swonk and Carl R. Bowen, Manager and Asst. Manager, Factories A and B.

Dept. 39-37 (Control)—A. A. Silveri and A. H. Heinrich, Manager and Asst. Manager, Factories A and B.

Dept. 39-38 (Small Tool Repair) —G. V. Palmer and H. C. Greenman, Foreman and Asst. Foreman, Factories A and B.

K. C. Worden and T. O. Maxwell are confirmed in their positions of General Foreman and Asst. Gen. Foreman, Dept. 39-01, Factory A.

The consolidation combines design functions and plant engineering for all factories.

Honor Man

A former Lockheed experimental mechanic, Murray William Kershaw, was named honor man of the recently graduated Basic Engineers Class, U.S. Naval Training Center, San Diego. He led the class of 49 members with a mark of 96.25 per cent.

Coupons Invalid

B2 and C2 gasoline ration coupons, the old type without serial numbers, will be invalid on and after June 1, the OPA announced today.

Lockheed employees who are holders of unused B2 and C2 coupons may take them to the Employee Transportation Unit servicing their plant for exchange and the board will reissue the serially numbered strip-type B3 or C3 coupons.

However, no coupons will be accepted unless they are endorsed and accompanied by the cover of the book.

New Courses

CALIFORNIA INSTITUTE OF TECHNOLOGY

Techniques of Training Personnel—June 5—Mon. & Wed., 7:30 to 9:30 p.m. Hollywood High, Hollywood (13 weeks). Instructor: Oscar Schuster, Lockheed Aircraft Corp. (A basic course for superintendents, department heads, and foremen.)

Labor Relations—June 6—Tues. & Thurs., 7:30 to 9:30 p.m. Hollywood High (13 weeks).

Production Control—June 6—Tues. & Thurs., 7:30 to 9:30 p.m. Cal. Tech., Pasadena. Instructor: Trevor Gardner (13 weeks).

Motion and Time Study — June 5 — Two evenings per week, 7:30 to 9:30 p.m. Cal. Tech., Pasadena. Instructor: Edwin P. Hollywood and Wm. G. Barks, Jr. (13 weeks).

UNIVERSITY OF CALIFORNIA

Manufacturing Statistics and Surveys—June 13—Tues., 7:00 to 9:30 p.m. (15 weeks). 3570 Magnolia Blvd., Burbank. Room 3. Instructor: D. E. Hayes.

Mathematics for Electricians and Radiomen—June 1—Thurs., 7 to 9:30 p.m. (16 weeks). 3702 Magnolia Blvd., Burbank, Room 2. Instructor: R. L. Browning.

Differential Calculus—June 6, Tues, 7 to 9:15 p.m. (16 weeks). U.C.L.A. Campus, L. A., Room 126, Chemistry Bldg. Instructor: Paul H. Daus.

Fundamentals of Radio, Part I—June 12 —Mon. & Thurs., 7 to 9:30 p.m. U.C.L.A. Campus, Room 319, Physics Bldg. (16 weeks). Instructor: Chas. P. Hedges.

Fundamentals of Applied Aerodynamics —June 7—Wed., 7 to 9 p.m. 3570 Magnolia Blvd., Burbank. Instructor: George Toumanoff, Lockheed.

UNIVERSITY OF SO. CALIFORNIA

Basic Engineering Drawing—June 8—Thurs. & Fri., 7 to 10 p.m. 115B Harris Hall, U.S.C. Campus. Instructor: Henry A. Stafford.

Basic Engineering Mathematics—June 5 —Mon., 7 to 10 p.m. Room 333 Old College, U.S.C. Campus. Instructor: Earl Rex.

Basic Engineering Mechanics—June 6—Tues., 7 to 10 p.m. Room 333 Old College, U.S.C. Campus. Instructor: Fred Marer.

Basic Engineering Strength of Materials —June 7—7 to 10 p.m., Wed. Room 272, Science Hall. Instructor: George Gallagher.

Fundamentals of Radio II—June 6—Tues. & Thurs., 7 to 9 p.m. Room 167, Science Bldg., U.S.C. Campus (15 weeks). Instructor: R. H. Dishington.

OCCIDENTAL COLLEGE

Basic Engineering Drafting—June 6—Tues. & Thurs., 7 to 10 p.m. Room 3, Fowler Hall, Occidental College (16 weeks.) Instructor: I. E. Newlan.

Technical Illustration—May 29—Mon. & Fri., 7 to 10 p.m. Room 40, Fowler Hall, Occidental College (14 weeks). Instructor: C. K. Fiedler.

Basic Engineering Mathematics—June 5 —Mon., 7 to 10 p.m. (16 weeks). Room 34, Fowler Hall, Occidental College. Instructor: Dr. Henry Dieckmann.

Basic Engineering Physics—June 7—Wed., 7 to 10 p.m. (16 weeks). Room 28, Fowler Hall, Occidental College. Instructor: Gilbert Bell.

Basic Engineering Strength of Materials —June 9—Fri., 7 to 10 p.m. (16 weeks). Room 28, Fowler Hall, Occidental College. Instructor: Knute Nipedal.

For further information, call Joe Enarson, Extension 3371; University of California, ARizona 3-0970 or BRadshaw 2-2176; University of Southern California, RIchmond 4111 or PRospect 9877; Occidental College, ALbany 1151; Cal Tech, Ryan 17171 or Sycamore 6-7121.

ART OF WARFARE is holding the attention of Sgt. Sherman C. Loudermilk, who formerly was in the Lockheed spray paint department. Now serving with the Marines, Sgt. Loudermilk is shown here doing a war scene in the South Pacific. He has painted battle scenes at Vella LaVella, Bougainville, and Emirau Islands.

(U.S. Marine Corps Photo)

Exploring ★ ★ ★ ★

There is much talk about air routes of the future, and the part that diplomats will play in mapping them.

The scientist will play his part, too, and when all the diplomacy is done it may well be that the aircraft scientist will have determined aviation's network in the international skies.

Because Lockheed's scientists, leaders in aviation advances for many years, have given the world its first truly global airplane in the Constellation, it may be interesting to Lockheed's people if the editors of *The Star* explore the idea for a moment . . .

Air routes, as General George of the Air Transport Command has pointed out, primarily are systems of air fields and bases. As larger, rangier transports like the Constellation are developed, carrying more fuel, fewer landings will be required solely for refuelling purposes. Witness Connie's record-breaking transcontinental trip to Washington recently. But in today's war, air bases determine air routes.

And commercial routes of the immediate postwar period will be laid out along a system of U.S. bases, or international airports.

We acquired a string of military bases in New Foundland, Bermuda, British Guiana, Jamaica, Antigua, St. Lucia and Trinidad by the 1940 destroyers-for-bases deal with Great Britain. The question now is: Will our commercial planes be allowed to use them? Congressmen say yes, Englishmen say no, and another deal—to trade American transport planes for commercial rights to these bases—is on its way. If we get commercial rights to these bases, the U.S. will be well on its way to establishing an Atlantic network of air routes. If we do not, American international air transportation will be sorely handicapped.

In the Pacific our trouble is not bases. The available islands: Hawaii, Midway, Wake, Guam and the Philippines (within 800 miles of the Asiatic mainland), for the middle route, and Alaska and the Aleutians for the northern route, were American territory. But the middle route spanned the Pacific at one of its widest parts, adding tedious hours to the time required for the intercontinental flight. Weather difficulties cancel the advantages of the shorter North Pacific route. The apparent answer is the development of airplanes capable of flying the stratosphere, thus getting above the northern route's storms and fog.

The most-talked-of air routes—the routes to Asia over the top of the world —have waited for intensive development until planes of longer range and capable of flying above the weather of the Arctic, came along. But while total route mileages over the Arctic are shorter than more traditional routes, individual hops are long, the fuel load consequently large. Also, the Far North is without traffic-producing intermediate points, which can form the difference between profit and loss for airlines.

Add it all up, and what do you have? Just this—the air routes of the future may depend more on the kind of ship developed in the laboratories of Lockheed and other companies than on the devices of the diplomats.

—S. B. M.

Escape Over Amiens

In the lap of the co-pilot landed the pilot, left eye gone, arm broken and shell fragments in his chest, but the B-17 upon which an enemy shell caused this damage, got back to its base, with a former Lockheed worker navigating it.

The navigator was Capt. Charles Spare, former Hollywood High and City College student who worked in Department 5, Factory B-1, during 1941. Winner of several medals, he is now gunnery officer with the Eighth Air Force in England. The pilot recovered and the plane came back from a bombing mission over Amiens despite the fact her nose and turret guns had been knocked out by enemy fighters.

Pay Load

Perfectly packed, properly stowed, and carefully handled—a million dollars worth of airplane engines are transported efficiently and safely in a single box car.

THE COVER

The editors of *The Lockheed Star* have been permitted by military authorities to publish the first pictures of the Constellation's assembly line at Factory B-6. This unusual photo is the work of Erik Miller, Lockheed staff photographer, and shows four of the great sky birds in varied stages of construction.

THE LOCKHEED STAR

The Lockheed Star is issued every Friday for the employees of Lockheed Aircraft Corporation, and is the official publication of the company. Communications should be addressed to the Editor, Lockheed Star, Publicity Department, Lockheed Aircraft Corporation, Burbank, California, U.S.A. The editor assumes no responsibility for acknowledgment or return of contributions.

PAUL BAILEY, Editor.
Associates:
H. L. ROSSON, J. H. PRESCOTT.

Connie in Production

With P-38 production ahead of schedule as recognized by the recent award of the Army-Navy "E," the Army has authorized Lockheed to enter into "limited production" of the record-breaking C-69 Constellation supertransport.

For months Lockheed's entire effort has been concentrated on the versatile Lightning, described as America's Number One Fighter, but the photograph on the cover of *The Star* indicates that the Army now demands the best in transports as well.

The Constellation's production rate remains undisclosed, and every C-69 will go into Army service when completed. Transcontinental & Western Air, Inc., and Pan American World Airways System, both of which had ordered Constellations in quantity, have waived their rights in favor of the Government for the duration.

Unexpected Versatility

"Our test flying has brought out an unexpected versatility in this airplane," said President Robert E. Gross, announcing the C-69 to be in production. "It proves equally adapted to economical short-haul duty, and to long-range ocean and continental crossings. The Constellation will establish a new and higher standard in world transportation, with lower costs than today's."

At the same time a relaxation of War Department restrictions permits new information to be disclosed. Here are facts which you have never met concerning Connie:

Maximum take-off gross weight has been increased to 86,250 pounds (43 tons), of which more than 17 tons is "useful load" over and above the empty weight of the airplane.

One Gallon Per Mile

Top speed with this new and greater payload is 340 miles an hour. Connie will cruise with 65 per cent power at more than 300 miles an hour, and at her "economy cruising speed" of 275 miles (which is 100 mph faster than ordinary air liners), she burns only ONE GALLON OF GAS PER MILE. Long-range cruising at somewhat lower speeds requires even less gas consumption.

With a service ceiling of over 25,000 feet fully loaded, Connie will fly and climb at 20,000 feet on three engines, and at more than 6,700 feet on any two of her four engines. This safety factor is not approached in any other transport.

Ordinary Airports with Safety

Connie can use ordinary airports with complete safety, requiring less than 1,600 feet of actual runway when fully loaded. She can clear a 50-foot obstacle within less than 2,800 feet of her starting point on take-off, and in landing she can clear such an obstacle and stop within less than 2,500 feet.

Six interior versions are now projected, as follows:

The military personnel transport (now in production) seats 60; or sleeps 22 plus a relief crew of four.

A paratrooper version would carry 100 soldiers with full packs and rifles, in addition to crew.

Outstanding among the postwar "luxury liners" is an air coach seating 64 passengers with crew of six and cargo.

A convertible sleeper plane will carry 34 passengers in berths or 48 seated, with crew of six and cargo.

A "club cruiser" will carry 48 passengers in seats with de luxe accommodations, including a lounge and bar, with crew of six and cargo.

An Empire Cruiser, largely for ocean or nonstop transcontinental crossings, will seat 30 passengers in luxurious reclining chairs, plus crew of six, cargo, and a game room.

Connie's Measurements

Wing Span..............................123 feet
Overall Length...............95 ft. 1 3/16 in.
Fuselage Height.............18 ft. 8 3/16 in.
Vertical Tail Height......23 ft. 7 7/8 in.
Wing Area.......................1,650 sq. ft.
Mail-Baggage
Space...........450 cu. ft. (or more)

Fuselage assembly is now moving from Factory B-1 to permanent quarters in Factory A-1. The final assembly line will remain at Production Service, where the tempo will be rapidly stepped up until Connie is rolling out at the authorized rate.

Fighting 96th Wants Girl Friend

In Italy today a top Army Air Forces P-38 fighter squadron waits to know who will be their "Lightning Lady."

Veterans of 19 months' overseas action, twice recipients of the Presidential Citation, and top fighter squadron in the Italian theater for number of enemy planes downed, the enlisted men of the Fighting 96th want a girl friend—a special girl friend selected from the women at Lockheed who are building "the plane on which we pin our private hopes for final victory."

Who will be their "Lightning Lady?"

In answer to their request, LERC today announces the Belle Ballot, to discover her among women employed at all Lockheed plants working on the P-38.

To the girl the Fighting 96th elects as their "Lightning Lady," to represent their squadron, they promise "a spot of honor and dignity in our day room and our hearts. . . . Her name will be painted on one of our P-38's—possibly that of our squadron commander."

Through T/Sgt. John Fucciolo, spokesman for the squadron, the men write:

"We, the enlisted men of the Fighting 96th 'Slugging Jackrabbit' squadron, have decided after 19 months of actual combat operations, that we want a special, favorite girl-friend for our own. . . . Having worked with the P-38 for nearly three years now, and sincerely considering it the finest fighting plane in the air today, we want to choose our official girl from among the feminine workers in your plant who are helping to build the plane on which we pin our private hopes for final victory."

Belle Ballot Rules

1. Who is eligible?

The Fighting 96th say, "Would you—could you—have the girls who work on the P-38's send us their photographs? . . . We want to choose our official 'Lightning Lady.' So, every girl in all Lockheed plants concerned with production of the P-38 may enter the Belle Ballot.

2. What is the prize?

A very special place in the hearts of the Fighting 96th. "We will hold a long and solemn judgment to select the one girl who will officially receive the title "Lightning Lady" and will have her name painted on one of our P-38's — possibly that of our Squadron Commander."

3. You have 38 chances to win.

The Fighting 96th is eager to select its own "Lightning Lady." So, to save time, they have entrusted preliminary judging to the Army Air Forces test pilots resident at Lockheed, who will select 38 finalists. Pictures of *all* these 38 prettiest girls who build the P-38 will go to the boys in Italy. Each of the 38 finalists is a winner; her picture, too, will adorn the walls of the "sadly bare" squadron clubroom.

4. Your portrait will be taken.

It is not necessary to submit a studio portrait in the Belle Ballot—a snapshot will do. The 38 winners will be photographed by LERC, the portraits to be sent to the Fighting 96th for selection of the "Lightning Lady."

5. LERC is headquarters.

Mail or deliver your picture to Belle Ballot, LERC, Factory B-1, c/o Vic Stein. Write on the reverse side of your picture, or attach securely to it, the following information: name, clock number, department, job, shift, plant, and telephone extension. All photos will be returned, upon request, at LERC office at close of the contest.

6. Belle Ballot begins today.

CONTRIBUTION

"Our efforts—no matter how small our individual contributions may be—may shorten the war by hours or minutes," said Courtlandt S. Gross at the Memorial Day ceremonies. "By so doing we may be saving precious lives—the lives of our loved ones, of former Lockheed men. We may see our men return—instead of placing a gold star on our honor roll."

Overseas

Georgia Mott, formerly employed at Lockheed as general clerk, Factory B, has arrived in England to serve the armed forces as an American Red Cross staff assistant.

Previous to her coming to Lockheed Miss Mott was employed by the Watertown Recreation Association, Watertown, S. D., the Watertown Board of Education, and Leota School for Girls, Evansville, Wis. She is a graduate of State Teachers College, LaCrosse, Wis.

NOSE-GLOW Jennie Couch, swing shift worker on the Constellation assembly line at Factory B-6, makes final adjustments of signal lamp in nose of one of Connie's big sisters.

Hail and Farewell

In the Universal motion picture, "Hers to Hold," sequences of which were filmed at Lockheed, Deanna Durbin enacted the role of a lady aircraft worker. As background for one of the shots, two B-17's were lined up—Nos. 845 and 846, respectively. A few days ago, Deanna received a letter from Capt. Melvin R. Hecker, AAF pilot in England. He had flown these planes in combat.

"Whaletail, No. 845, was a good ship from the start," he disclosed. "It completed many missions against the Germans, and ended its life in the English Channel. It allowed all of its crew to escape safely, though.

"Tinker-Toy, No. 846, was a bad ship. It had the reputation of always getting home, but not without injury to its crew. Tinker-Toy met her end, also, in the English Channel.

"I thought you might find it interesting that these two ships, born at almost the same hour, met the same ending."

Payoff

In one month the RAF dumped as many bombs on Berlin—10,000 tons—as the Luftwaffe did on London in the blitz year of 1940-41.

Three-Way Victory

A two-year series of victories on three fronts — production quantity, production efficiency and costs—was reported today by Production Expediting Committee of the West Coast aircraft industry.

Keyed to a sober reminder that the war still remains to be won, the report, made by the Aircraft War Production Council at a meeting of its Production Expediting Committee, revealed that Pacific Coast aircraft manufacturers, in all their plants, including their Midwestern and Southern factories, produced 64,551 warplanes in 1942 and 1943, the first two years the United States was at war.

That was the equivalent of 1,075 bomber groups of 30 planes each, accompanied by an umbrella of an equal number of fighter planes, enough to launch 32 simultaneous 1,000-bomber raids on enemy territory.

The same manufacturers — Lockheed, Boeing, Consolidated Vultee, Douglas, North American, Northrop and Ryan, the seven companies constituting the Aircraft War Production Council—had built these planes with sharply reduced numbers of workers.

LOCKHEED HONORS ITS WAR DEAD

In ceremonies held Tuesday noon, Memorial Day, at Factory B, the 100th gold star—in honor of the 100th Lockheed man to give his life in the service of his country—was placed on the Lockheed Honor Roll.

The man who was honored thus was Robert Fenn Cole, who was employed as a riveter in the Lockheed Factory B Experimental Department from Nov., 1940, to Dec., 1941.

Cole enlisted in the Army Air Forces and was killed in action in China while serving as a pilot under Maj. Gen. Claire Chennault.

On the platform for the ceremonies were Mr. and Mrs. Oliver Fenn Cole, parents of the former Lockheed employee and both war workers themselves. Flanking them was a military guard of honor.

An Army bugler blew taps while Everett Eberhardt, who worked with young Cole, placed the gold star on the honor board which now contains the names of 17,230 former employees who left Lockheed to join the armed forces.

A floral wreath was placed at the foot of the honor roll by Miss Clara Hoback, woman's group chairman for Aeronautical Industrial District Lodge 727 of the International Association of Machinists.

Courtlandt S. Gross, vice-president and general manager of Lockheed, reminded those present that, while honoring the dead, the living—on the home front as well as those fighting on foreign soil—still have an enormous job to do.

Following the ceremonies, the 100th Fighting Memorial, a Lightning P-38, was dedicated in honor of Robert Fenn Cole.

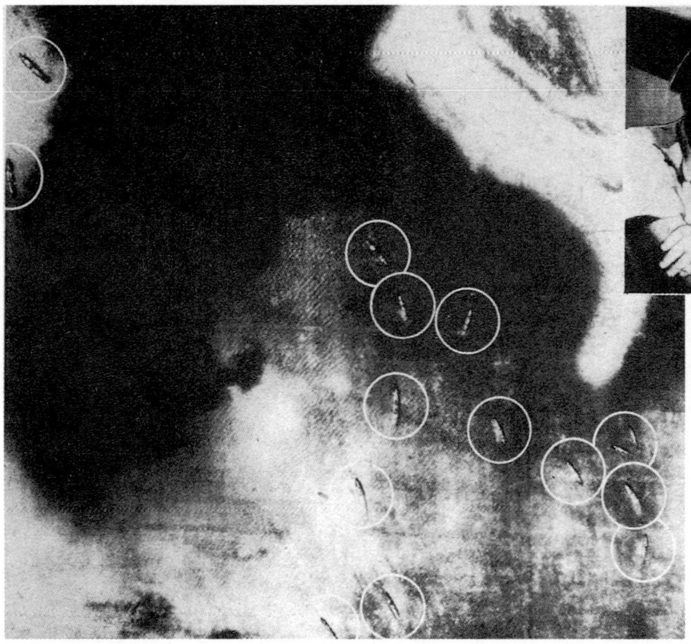

TRUK, the mighty Japanese sea and air base, was photographed by an Australian-manned Hudson two years before U.S. Navy airplanes began working it over with bombs. Flight Lt. R. Yeowart, who led the flight, and the only man of the crew now alive, is shown above.

—*Photos courtesy Australian News Bureau.*

Mikado Special

A Lockheed Hudson, one of the two "sweetest looking planes" their Marine pilots had ever seen, paved the way in 1942 for the Navy's historic attack on Truk that sank 19 Jap ships last February.

Nicknamed "Titwillow" in a flight that became known as "The Mikado Special," the plane brought back the all-important reconnaissance photos from which the successful attack two years later was planned.

Describing his experience in the May issue of the magazine *Flying,* Flight Lt. R. Yeowart says final details of the mission were planned after two newly arrived Hudsons had been assembled at their South Pacific base.

"These were the babies we had been waiting for and we didn't have any trouble getting crewmen. The whole squadron volunteered," he says.

Over Truk

One of the planes developed carburetor trouble, but the "Titwillow," in charge of Lieutenant Yeowart, took off from Kavieng on the morning of January 9. After a few hours he let the plane down from 13,000 feet, through a heavy squall and came out over the famous harbor the Japs thought was impregnable.

"Nice and peaceful all right," he continues. "There were many warships and, on one of the island's airstrips, heavy bombers were packed wing to wing.

Nips Wake Up

"We pulled up again and made a photographic run. We were halfway through before the Nips started to wake up and pour the ack-ack at us. Getting his gun ready, Sgt. Frank Marriner reported fighters taking off below.

"But we still had work to do and decided to make another run just to make sure of the pictures.

"We made the second run as low as possible and things were really popping. They had a lot of planes in the air and we were thankful for the squally weather. Enemy fighters were closing in on two sides and Marriner, his guns chattering, was singing 'You'll Come A-Waltzing, Matilda, with Me.'

Something Hit Our Tail

"We felt something hit our tail and the controls went sloppy for a moment. Then all right again. We climbed to 10,000 feet, evading three Jap float planes too close for comfort. What lovely things clouds can be.

"We dived through, leveling off at 500 feet in the midst of one of the prettiest and most welcome electrical storms I've ever seen. Then we high-tailed it for Kavieng where we found our only damage was a missing tail-plane tip the Japs shot away."

Other members of the Hudson's crew on this important flight were Flying Officer R. R. McDonald, co-pilot, and Sgt. Bill Ellis, radio man. The pictures were good—just how good, the Navy proved a few weeks later by its successful attack on the Jap bastion.

PRE-POSTWAR PLANNING

By PROFESSOR YIPPEE

(Burbank's Foremost World Traveler and Commentator)

Once a week and sometimes twice on Sunday the *Empire Avenue Bugle* or the *Fifth Avenue Evening Post* calls up and tells Lockheed what our postwar plan is going to be. Perish forbid that Lockheed should build airplanes yet; the bookmakers will bet you a doughnut against the hole in it that we're going into mass production with:

1—Prefabricated aluminum houses with a 400-mile cruising range and rubber sewer connections.

2—Three-wheeled automobiles with the engine in the glove compartment and a sewing machine attachment.

3—Trimotor spatulas, and if you don't know what a spatula is, ask your wife. If you haven't a wife, get married.

4—*Parfum,* as the French say, which will make MEN irresistible. It is high time somebody did this, as Prof. Yippee can prove by his batting average of .0000000001/4.

5—Heligyros, autocopters, aerosubmarines, tail-firsters, anything in the world but honest airplanes. One of our best little numbers is said to be a circular wing with eight engines which can fly rapidly away in all directions.

6—P-38's for the Salvation Army Air Forces.

7—Wings and a tail for New York City so it can come to California for the winter.

Your Uncle Lockheed is just sitting this one out, this flurry of postwar-planning-in-public, on the theory that nobody ever wrote a postscript to a letter before he wrote the letter. Your Uncle Lockheed is still writing his letter, filling the sky full of Lightnings, figuring to do plenty of fighting before he tools up for the postwar perfume business.

But.

Come to think of it, that "Constellation" is the solidest piece of postwar planning that's been done yet. While others are talking about Tomorrow's Airplane, your Uncle Lockheed is flying it places. Nobody knows even yet how good that airplane is. It will do to the rest of the industry just about what the steamboat did to the windjammer, or Professor Yippee is a washerwoman.

And.

More important than Connie are the brains that dreamed her out. She was dreamed out in principle five years ago. What have those brains been dreaming out since? Spatulas? A fat chance! Military secrets, that's what. Stick around, bretheren and cistern, and gradually these dreams will do a strip-tease.

So.

Anything those brains are dreaming on today is a postwar plan, if the war is short enough. If it's a longer war, they'll still be dreaming next year, and the year after.

Postwar planning is all right in its place, but it's much more than mere shouting about 4,000-passenger airplanes with built-in golf links; or flying subway systems; or skyhooks; or heligyros to land on your chimney; or *parfum.*

Postwar planning is hard work, brother, so Professor Yippee doesn't know a damn thing about it, but there are people here who do.

And they can't talk.

Clips Wings

Shearing off the wing tip of an enemy plane is not what a P-38 was built for, but that's what an unarmed, unescorted Lightning did on a photographic mission that brought its pilot the Distinguished Flying Cross.

"Under attack by enemy interceptors, he completed his photographic mission," read the citation presented with the medal to the pilot, Maj. Arthur L. Post of the Fifth Air Force.

"After he had evaded the attacking planes with great skill and had sheared off the wing tip of one of them, both of his engines were finally shot out."

After jumping, Maj. Post pulled his parachute's rip cord at only 500 feet, lived 100 days in the jungle and returned to his post.

Gavel from Cruiser

Part of an uncompleted warship—the *U.S.S. Los Angeles*—was presented last week to the Open Forum Breakfast Club by its executive vice-president, Charles E. Rachal of Department 90-58, Plant Personnel, of Factory B-1.

It was in the form of a gavel made from woodwork of the vessel now under construction in the Philadelphia Navy Yard. Authority to do it came from the late Secretary of the Navy, Frank Knox, personal friend of Rachal's.

Zero Vanishes

"Just like in the movies, the Zero sort of vanished when eight P-38's on its tail all fired at about the same time" in a raid described in a letter this week by Capt. George E. Brown, formerly with the Lockheed Medical Department.

Wrote Capt. Brown to Dr. Seymour Dudley here, "I can't tell you how much of a thrill it is to see those P-38's that I feel I have an interest in, flying around here. I am more than proud when the boys tell me they are tops and can't be touched by anything else."

Tabs Japs

Frank L. Acosta, Jr., aviation radioman first class, home in Burbank after South Pacific combat duty, told this week how his bomb-less Ventura kept tabs on a Jap task force until heavy American bombers arrived to take over.

"We were returning from a low-altitude bombing mission, when we spotted four Jap cruisers and six destroyers whose identity we weren't sure of until the ack-ack came up," he said.

Acosta radioed the location of the force to his base and the Ventura played "hide-and-seek" in the clouds because all its bombs had been dropped on the mission it was returning from. When heavy Army and Navy bombers arrived, the Ventura returned to its base.

Scores Again

Navy Ventura search planes flying more than 2,000 miles round trip, started several fires at Shimushu airfield in the Kuriles last week, Pacific fleet headquarters announced today.

It was the eleventh time in a month that bombers of either the Eleventh Army Air Force or Fleet Air Wing Four in the Aleutians have struck at the Kuriles, and the thirty-fifth attack of the war on Shimushu.

Affectionately nicknamed "The Empire Express" by the boys who fly them, the fast PV-1's are hanging up a fine record of successful operation for the Navy.

(Above) The broken plane, shown in pictures below, repaired under Lockheed supervision and ready to take off again.

(Right) A once battle-damaged P-38, repaired by Lockheed Field Service, rises again to meet the enemy.

(Center) Jay R. Whitmer, Lockheed Field Service representative, back from 17 months in Australia, New Guinea and New Caledonia, with headquarters at Brisbane. Fifty-five Jap bombings taught Jay the fine art of getting from tent to slit trench with speed and finesse.

Down Under WITH LOCKHEED

Lockheed Model 10 Electra after forced landing in clearing of scrub gum trees. Note eucalyptus logs in foreground.

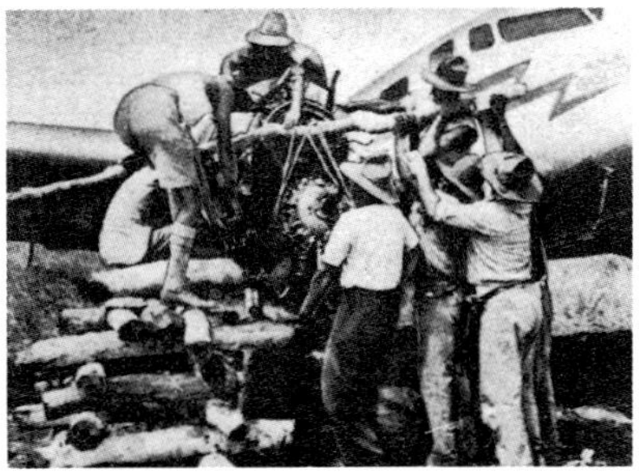

Plane has been jacked up on crossed logs and gear put down. Aussie mechanics (some civilian) labor to remove right engine.

Sudden and heavy rains complicate matters. Donkeys endeavor to drag plane from the sticky bog.

Jay Whitmer, Returned from Pacific War Zone, Tells How Lockheed Field Service Keeps 'Em Fighting and Flying

"The first thing to do after putting up a tent is to dig yourself a good slit trench—and then practice getting into it." So states Jay R. Whitmer, Lockheed Field Service representative, back from 17 months in Australia, New Guinea and New Caledonia.

After surviving 55 Jap bombing raids, Jay speaks with considerable authority. "At our New Guinea base," Jay discloses, "every moonlight night was good for from one to five bomb runs by the enemy. And a slit trench is valuable, not so much to hide yourself from Jap Betties, as to shield one's precious carcass from the Allied flack that descends from the sky like rain."

As a Lockheed Field Service representative Jay's first berth, after flying to the Pacific war zone from the U. S., was at New Caledonia, where he directed the assembly of the P-38's which later were used with such telling effect at Guadalcanal. From there he proceeded to Brisbane, from which base he supervised P-38 off-boat assembly and overhaul, maintenance and repair in the Australian and New Guinea air combat zones.

At that time the heat was on New Guinea, and Jay made eight separate trips to Allied advance bases, and spent considerable time in organizing repair facilities behind the lines. It was in New Guinea he perfected his slit-trench technique which was so instrumental in bringing him back to Burbank in one piece.

One of Jay Whitmer's New Guinea trips was made part way in General Kenney's own B-17—the "Sally"—with Generals Kenney and MacArthur both for company. However, the "Sally" was held over at Townsville, Australia, for brake repairs, and Jay's distinguished fellow travelers were whisked to the front in another plane. Jay followed them a day or so later.

"I suffered no shooting brushes with Japs during my New Guinea air jaunts," Jay confesses. "Once we came in on an alert, with a Jap recco tailing us, but we landed safely. We did, however, repair many an Allied airplane that hadn't come through so easily.

"While stationed at an airdrome near Port Moresby, a Lieutenant Auger (I'm not sure just how he spelled the name), landed a P-38 Lightning so full of holes it looked like a Swiss cheese. The pilot climbed out, unhurt, with a .30 caliber slug sticking from the sole of his shoe. We counted 100 small caliber bullet holes and 22 20mm cannon holes in the crippled Lightning. He'd gone through a formation of 18 Jap bombers, and had been caught in their crossfire. After they'd shot out his right engine he'd feathered his props, and when he pulled out of his dive at 550 mph, one engine was still windmilling. But he'd done some shooting, too, His credit was two definites and one possible. His P-38 had to be scrapped.

"Between mosquitoes, 'Gooba' storms and bombings, life in New Guinea never gets dull. And to haul crippled airplanes out of the Australian bush keeps mechanical ingenuity at top trim. In the air and on the ground, one sees many deeds of heroism."

The 25 pounds Jay lost in weight while "down under," he attributes to (a) heat, (b) bombs, and (c) Australian food. But for the efficiency and thoroughness of Lockheed's Field Service he has only the highest praise. By repair service, and mechanic and pilot instruction on the far-flung battle fronts of the world, Lockheed planes are more than doing the jobs for which they were designed.

A "down under" camp area after one of those sudden and frequent Australian showers.

Three of Lockheed's Australian mechanics pause long enough to dine at their eucalyptus log table.

A wounded P-38 after landing. Men are siphoning out the gas. Skillful repair will make it serviceable.

Plane finally removed to firm ground by 27-mule team. The donkeys were borrowed from ranchers.

Metal-and-wood service repair hangar somewhere in New Guinea. They are called "igloos" by the men who work under them.

Jay Whitmer stands beside wing of a P-38 shot up in combat over New Guinea. This has been replaced by new wing.

Pomona Nine Strong

Captain Clifford Sortland and Manager Willard Atteberry are whipping into shape a strong softball team which will compete in the Pomona civic league this summer.

The outfit, comprised of remnants of three teams which played a year ago, has shown potentialities in several practice games.

Vying for Lockheed honors is a women's team, captained by Frances Murphy, and managed by R. M. Chillcott. In several contests they have shown fine form.

Possibilities of teams recruited from men and women swing workers are being explored. Interested parties are asked to see Milt Brunk, Mel Deyo or Bill Knodel.

Hiring Program

Earle T. Cleveland, personnel assistant, is now on a split shift which covers both day and swing hours, to assist with the hiring program at Pomona, which should extend into July.

Employees who came into Plant 8 last week include Beatrice Rohrer of Ontario, Mabel and Guy Stapp of San Dimas, Clifford Base of Pomona, Effie Goodwin, Gwen Burleson, Doris Beck, John Clark and June Alton of Pomona, and Helen Chance of Ontario.

Starlights

Leaving Lockheed's Plant 8 for military service last week were HERB TROSIN, WILLIS LAWRENCE, LAURENCE ROBINSON, L. BERT MARTIN and Nurse HARRIETT STEFFENSEN, the latter joining the Army Nurses' Corps. . . . Master Sgt. HARRY L. DALTON, of Ontario, left the Army Tuesday after 35 years' continuous service and is now one of us at Plant 8. . . . TOM LAMBERT of Attendance was startled Thursday of last week when for the first time in six months no 14-28ers on days were tardy. When Friday repeated he nearly passed out.

MARY STAFFORD of Purchase Parts went to Arizona to vacation. . . . DONNA MASKER, stock clerk, tripped to Arizona to see her brother get his wings. . . . JIM SCHIZLER is better after an appendectomy. . . . ED SEBOURN had one, too, and is back. . . . ALICE WHITE saw the S. F. sights. . . . IRENE EITEL vacationed in Kansas, on the farm. . . . TOM CANTWELL was stumped for names for his twin sons, but he's proud. . . . VIRGINIA JOHNSON switched to days temporarily. . . . So did JOHNNIE LAWSON. . . . Many friends welcomed ETHEL EKLOFF back.

Roy L. Songer, seven years with Lockheed, and at Plant B-2 for the last three years, is a new section supervisor at Pomona, replacing John Anderson, who entered military service last month. He lives in Glendora.

Ira Lane, interim section supervisor, won high commendation from Assistant Superintendent Robert Sinclair for his excellent work. He is now group supervisor in left boom mating.

Group Supervisor Lloyd Payne returns to his regular post Monday, after holding down Section Supervisor Milt Kerner's post for two weeks while Kerner and his bride visited her parents in Nevada.

Well again, Jack Kingman is back in his framing section, Roy Gillett moving upstairs to Lynn Krogh's spot, Krogh having joined the armed forces. Dave Mason also is looking Navy-ward. He recently received his Lockheed 5-year pin.

All or Nothing

Soldier: "Let's get married or something."

WAC: "We'll get married or nothing."

SANTA BARBARA

Picnic Features Puppet Show

The "Family Day" picnic at Oak Park for all Santa Barbara Lockheedians and their guests, June 11, promises to be a day packed full of fun and excitement. Lloyd Monk, in charge of arrangements, has announced a puppet show at 1:30 p.m. The city recreation department will furnish music for both modern and old-time dancing. Also on the program are games and races for the youngsters, horseshoes, tennis, baseball, ping pong and volley ball.

Soft drinks and coffee will be furnished by the LERC. Employees who have been affected by the temporary layoff at Plants 59 and 60 and not actively employed at the present by the company are cordially invited to attend.

Channel City Chatter

The "I've Been with Lockheed Five Years Club" has a new member. DICK HOAG, supervisor of Dept. 19-19, just received his bright and shiny five-year pin last week. . . . MILDRED ROBBINS, 19-19, has just returned from her vacation spent in Burbank. . . . THOMAS GOODWIN, guard at 60, has recovered from an illness of several weeks and is now back on the job. . . . Hospitalized for an appendectomy is JEANETTE SPROAL, 19-59. . . . MARGARET CANNON, 19-20, was ill at home several days. . . . BEVERLY MILLER, 19-60, "pin-up" girl, terminated Saturday. She will attend school at the University of Washington. . . .

ALBERT PALM, guard at 59, vacationing this week. . . . GRACE HUBBARD, 83-40, spent last week end visiting her family in Long Beach. . . . BLANCHE OSBORN, 19-20, crammed a lot of excitement and fun in her four days' leave. Visiting first in Los Angeles, then by plane to San Francisco and back to work Thursday. . . . CHARLES SHIPLEY, supervisor 19-20, goes into the Navy on June 10 and has turned the helm of Blueprint Control over to JAMES LEE. . . . SAM POULLOS, 19-19, chief bidder in all the War Bond drives, terminated Saturday. . . . COLLEEN DE SCHAINE, 11-44, returned from a two weeks' vacation in Hollywood. . . . Superintendent William Barnett paid a visit to the Lockheed plants at Fresno, Bakersfield and Taft. . . . AURORA KAAL, Navy inspector, left Friday for a vacation in Michigan with her family.

Can't Get Rid of Him

A nip-and-tuck race at Pomona for the dubious honor of having custody of the White Elephant in the Swing Safety Contest last week ended with Group Supervisor Russell Rinard's right boom mating ahead 7 to 6 over Clemen Reiswig's preassembly section. This keeps the unpopular banner in the same location for the third straight week, despite shifts in supervision during that time.

BAKERSFIELD

Bowlers Top Two Tilts

The Reds again took three points from their opponents, Carroll's Liquor Store, and the Blues took their three from the Pepsi-Cola team at last week's Bakersfield bowling session. Jim Mull is leading the entire city league with an average of 188. Ase Ebbutt and Arnold Popp kept things in the clear for the Blues with high averages—Arnold bowled 192.

Personality Corner

PLANT 54—P/c Robert L. Subriar, son of Mr. and Mrs. Frank Subriar, has been graduated from the Army Air Forces Flexible Gunnery School. Along with his diploma he received a pair of aerial gunner's silver wings.

Enjoying vacations this week are: Madaline Fontes, Iola Wade and Francis Houk. Rose and Nadina Miranda also are taking this week on theirs. Alice Delanty has journeyed to the southland for her vacation—hadn't anyone noticed how quiet and peaceful the T. E. section is?

Plant 54 welcomes Ted Martins, who is stationed here temporarily, working with Harold Cochran.

PLANT 55—Two more casualties have been announced from the ball park—Erma Hopper's black eye and Ira Smith's sprained ankle. Leroy Lee announces the arrival of a bouncing baby boy recently.

Lillian Barnes, one of Lockheed's first employees here, is making her future home at Trona, California.

"Jim" Huzzard of Fresno was delighted to receive a token of appreciation from the girls in Detail Assembly, whom he has helped to become familiar with the new assemblies. The girls said the pleasure was all theirs.

Welcome to Cora McGilberry—recent transfer from Fresno. Also Juanita Jordan and Betty Bogue, the two new girls in Detail Assembly.

Otis Meece has joined the ranks of those having operations, while Margaret Landers rests nicely after hers.

Boys Beat Girls

Boys meet girls and boys beat girls.

It happened when a total score of 2078 to 1885 spelled victory for the LERC men's bowling team of 60 in a match game with the LERC-sponsored women's team of Plant 60 last Friday.

Chuck Buer led the men with an average of 158 in the three games rolled, followed closely by Joe Silva, Rollin Melvin, Chester Sampson and Kenneth Scheutz.

Hattie Edinger and Irene Albert, with their usual fine bowling, caused the boys a few moments of anxiety, as each chalked up a high game of 168. Willa Ross, Evelyn Hendry and Agnes Hildebrand completed the girls' team.

Mileage

Revenue passenger-miles exceeded 465 million for the first three months of 1944.

Lightnings Cop Softball Debut

The Lockheed Lightnings got off to a fast start in the Fresno City Softball League last week at Einstein Playground by winning their initial tilt with Vendorlator Aircraft, 7 to 3, in a lively 7-inning contest.

Chukker Warren Ludlow pitched scoreless ball until the first of the seventh, when Vendorlator stickers punched in two runs before Bob Logan relieved him on the mound. Logan allowed two hits and one run before retiring the side and icing the game at the 7-3 count.

Angelo Delecce, at third base, and player-manager Jimmy "The Gentleman" Corbett, at shortstop, sparkled for Lockheed in the infield, while Steini Thorsteinson starred at right field. First Baseman Joe Enos sparked the Lightning attack by collecting two singles and a double for four times at the plate.

The Lockheed Lightnings are entered in the International League of the city softball tournament leagues and will play Wednesday and Friday evenings at 8 o'clock. Schedule of games will appear in *Fresno Bee.*

Just for Fun

A group of girls formed a "Fun Club" in the Detail Department at Bakersfield Plant 55. As a matter of procedure, Ella Bryan elected herself president—just for "fun."

Associate members step out at least once a week in merrymaking time. Recently they visited a carnival after roller skating and bowling. They even had their fortunes told.

They all had a grand time and they keep the rest of us wondering what sort of highjinks will creep into their fun-loving heads next.

Golf Tournament

The tall tales are "who is the best golfer of Plants 59 and 60" will be replaced by facts next Sunday, June 4, when the LERC-sponsored handicap tournament is held at the Montecito Country Club. Time: 8:30 a.m. Prizes to be presented by the Santa Barbara LERC.

Jack Robbins, inspection supervisor and "uncrowned champion" at 60, has arranged all the details, and it appears that Jack is going to have some pretty tough competition from the fellows who have already signed up for the tournament.

Summertime

Once again vacation time for Bakersfield high school boys is here. But they, like our soldiers, find that now is not the time to play, but to work. Work to help build the planes their older brothers across the waters are calling for.

Last year these same boys gave us their hearts and hands, doing a fine job. Now they are back on the job. Ah, the good old summertime!

Taft Talk

A surprise to Plant 56 was the wedding of Joseph P. Markey and the former Norma Layton. The couple tied the knot in Bakersfield May 22.

Helen Risk, Betty Hudson and Janice Hayslett all celebrated wedding anniversaries last week. Congratulations, girls.

It has been rumored that there is an increase in the sale of liniment at the Taft drug counters. Can it be because of the baseball workouts the Lockheed boys have been getting?

We couldn't believe our eyes when we saw two girls on Bulkhead No. 6 giving their all with two rivet guns and two bucking bars at the same time. The riveter, Virginia Porcho, had both guns blaring, and the bucker, Louise Baisden, had both bars. Who can top this one?

Run Show

Here are ten of the fifteen newly elected LERC officers and committee, who will keep things moving entertainment-wise at Plant 56. Seated, foreground, are (left to right) Alice Parnell, secretary, and Jane Frank, president; in second row are Bertha Gordy, treasurer (left); Evelynne Nicholson, Inez Erlewine and Blanche Strang. Back row are Mildred Skinner, Betty Hofeling, Agnes Thomas and Jean Nash. Missing from photo are Louise Harris, vice-president; Sam Duvall, Joe Markey and C. A. Campbell.

FRESNO

What to Do With Junior

The burden of "What to do with junior this summer" has been lifted from the shoulders of Lockheed mothers in Fresno by the announcement that six Extended Day Care Centers and three additional Nursery Schools are to be opened Monday, June 12. These schools, recommended and supervised by the Federal Government and sponsored by Fresno City School Board, will care for the children from 6:30 a.m. until 5:30 p.m. every day except Saturdays.

Children of Plant 57 employees will attend the Webster School, which offers both nursery school and extended day care. The nursery school at Columbia and the extended day care facilities at Lincoln will accommodate the children of Plant 58 employees.

Further details concerning these schools may be obtained from the employees' counselors, Mrs. C. B. Pattison at Plant 57, and Mrs. Lillian Nilsson at Plant 58.

Plant 57, winner of the permanent Safety Trophy for 1943, was awarded the 1944 award last week for the first time, having accumulated a total of 428,530 consecutive man-hours without lost time injury for the period starting January 1. With a million man-hours as the goal, Plant 57 has accumulated to date 918,550 consecutive man-hours without lost time injury since October 1, 1943, according to Mr. Chamness.

A special order for 30 additional dorsal fins is being rushed through at Plant 58 in addition to the regular production schedule, Foreman Dick Becker has announced. The dorsal fin sections, already working at top speed under Group Supervisors Don Turner and Max Sloan to complete a cushion for outside production, will work two hours overtime for four days a week until the schedule is met, June 6, Becker added.

F. P. Berkenkamp has assumed the duties of assistant superintendent of Fresno Plants 57 and 58, according to an announcement by C. U. Wells, superintendent. Mr. Berkenkamp comes to Fresno well qualified for his position, having been with Lockheed for the past eight years, more recently as assistant superintendent of the graveyard shift at Plant 2.

The Fresno USO has declared Friday nights will be War Workers' Night, at which time employees of all Fresno war industries will be welcome to use the facilities of the club. Entertainment starts at 7:30 p.m., with a full-length motion picture lasting until 9 p.m. Dancing and other entertainment will follow until 11 o'clock. All Lockheed employees are especially invited.

Assembly Lines

Proud father of a 10-pound, 12-ounce baby boy is AUBREY BYARS, group supervisor at Plant 57 and pitcher for the Lockheed Interceptors. With an eye to the big leagues, Aubrey reports the baby has one of the finest pitching arms ever seen in the San Joaquin Valley. . . .

Another Plant 58 marriage has united MARY MARSHALL, 19-58, and LLOYD S. WARD of the U.S. Army, recently returned from Alaska. . . . MAVIS MILLS, 83-40, left Plant 58 last week to transfer to Los Angeles. . . . Joining the trek to Southern California is AUDREY HENRY LEHMAN, who is transferring from Plant A57 to B7. . . .

STILL more faces that will be missed:

ANSEL "WHITEY" CLAUS, ex-graveyard and swing shift group supervisor at Plant 58, who terminated last week; GERTRUDE DULING, 19-57, and ALTA RUMMEL, 57-24, who left last week for their home in Tennessee; ARSWELD McCREE, 19-57, who will take a short vacation at his home in Quitman, Mississippi, before joining the Army. . . . PAULINE NELSON, 19-57, who has turned in her Lockheed slacks for a maternity dress.

BRANCH PLANT STAFF

BAKERSFIELD, Personnel Dept.
FRESNO . Tom Geoghegan, Jr.
Dorothy Hornaday
POMONA . . . Milton Brunk
SANTA BARBARA . . .
Rosemary Martin
TAFT . . . . Alice Parnell

HISTORY REPEATS. This scene, taken February 27, during the first annual all-plant, all-shift golf tourney, will be repeated July 2, at Baldwin Hills and Inglewood courses in this year's second big golfing event.

All-Plant Tee Tourney Announced

Lockheed golfers will tee off in the second big all-plant, all-shift golfing event of the year at two favorite Los Angeles courses, Baldwin Hills and Inglewood, one month from today—Sunday, July 2.

The golf committee, headed by Chuck Markham, reveals the tourney will be a regular blind bogey four flight playoff with six blind holes. Extra features will include a driving contest, putting contest and golf ball awards to those hitting a circle on the 16th hole.

With the exception of the golf balls, all prizes and awards will be in War Bonds and Stamps in keeping with the patriotic Independence Day spirit. Players will be allowed to choose which of the two par 71 courses they wish to play with choice limited only to keep an even balance of players between the two courses. Starting June 17, reservations for the event will be taken at all LERC offices.

Double Feature

For the 16 golfers turning in the lowest gross scores, the July 2 event will be the qualifying round for a thirty-six-hole event to be run off the following Sunday, July 9, to determine Lockheed's low gross golfing champion. Champion and runner-up will receive trophies. Third place winner will receive a medal. The course for this second event has not been announced by the golf committee.

Picnic Playoff

A unique softball contest will be the feature of Factory A's Precision Assembly department picnic set for Sunday, June 11, in the Pepper Tree Lane section of Griffith Park.

Bob Gilliland, day chairman of the all-shift event, explains the game will be a triple feature attraction, with day girls *vs.* swing girls in the first round, day men *vs.* swing men in the second round and day supervision *vs.* swing supervision in the third game. The combined scores will determine which of the two shifts will be the winner of the trophy award.

Over 400 department employees, their families and friends, will be on hand for the day's outing to take part in the games, contests and picnic fun. A twenty-five dollar War Bond will be given as an attendance prize.

Mixed Doubles

Entries in the summer mixed doubles bowling leagues are coming in at both Factory A and B LERC offices. Lockheed's lady and gent bowlers interested in mixed doubles play are asked to apply at their LERC office, giving name of team, players' names, addresses, shift and preferred alleys.

League schedules will be mailed by the LERC office to all team captains, giving date and time of play.

Champs Clash

Lockheed's Lightnings, winners of the 1942 and '43 Los Angeles city and county softball crowns, have been selected to represent the Southern California aircraft industry in an aircraft-shipyard "World Series" against the Calship Mariners on Sunday afternoon, June 11, at Lakewood Stadium in Long Beach.

Sponsored by the *Aircraft and Shipyard Times*, the entire net proceeds will be donated to Service Sports, Inc., to provide athletic equipment for the men in the armed services. Both teams will enter the fray complete with movie star "mascots."

The event will be in the nature of a double-header with the second contest slated as another aircraft-shipyard battle. The clash came about as a result of a challenge issued by Russ Coggan, manager of the LERC-sponsored Lightnings, several weeks ago that was immediately taken up by Calship's recreation club who offered to meet the aircrafters "any time, any where." Odds are about even, with the Lightning's enviable record matched by the Mariners who took the Southern California softball championship last season.

Those who attend the classic will see two of Southern California's top squads in a contest spurred by old aircraft-shipyard rivalry and will have the satisfaction of knowing that the money they spend will be used to purchase additional sports equipment for our fighting men.

B-4 Bowling

The Cromate Lungers with an enviable record of 16 wins and 5 losses are heading up the Plant B-4 Scratch League, now in its eighth week. In addition the quintet holds the high team series for the league with 2540.

High team game for the season is held by the fourth place Sharks with 923 pins. I. Kennedy of the Millwrights sports a 590 to hold the high individual series for the league to date. Lunger Al Mertz rolled a 242 for high individual game.

The eight-team league meets every Tuesday at the Maywood Bowling Center.

Tops

Heading a recently graduated class of Aviation Machinist Mates at the Naval Air Technical Training Center, Norman, Oklahoma, was Charles M. Harrison of Santa Ana, California, former Lockheed metalsmith. He was presented with honor certificates and a Navy ring by the executive officer of the station.

SOFTBALL

Tallies and Standings Fourth Week

Interdepartmental softball competition with leagues well into their fifth week of play is beginning to show who is doing what to whom on the diamonds. Special interest in the game is being shown by the swing shifters. A new crop of swing shift teams will start a new league on Wednesday mornings at Griffith Park. The Thursday swing league, desiring to do double duty, has now added Tuesday mornings to their schedule, making two sessions each week for all teams . . . and just for the kicks!

Following are scores for the fourth week with relative standings for all teams:

DAY SHIFT—Monday, May 22

Team	Score	vs.	Team	Score
18-08	11		18-18	1
28-10	10		51-50	5
15-24	4		26-37	2

DAY SHIFT—Tuesday, May 23

Team	Score	vs.	Team	Score
58-03	10		50-30	2
28-10	5		43-28	3
18-20	7		15-08	0
44-22	10		55-21	6

DAY SHIFT—Wednesday, May 24

Team	Score	vs.	Team	Score
83-43	9		18-26	0
55-30	23		41-34	3
51-10	8		26-03	7
71-60	6		67-75	4

DAY SHIFT—Thursday, May 25

Team	Score	vs.	Team	Score
51-10	8		58-03	4
72-25	6		28-20	4
72-25	17		38-04	10

SWING SHIFT—Thursday, May 25

Team	Score	vs.	Team	Score
62-73	6		44-52	2
28-26	7		17-29	5
18-04	8		17-04	1

DAY SHIFT—Monday League

Name	Dept.	Plant	Won	Lost
Dept. 15-24	15-24	A-1	3	1
Knockabouts	18-08	B-1	3	1
Wolves	26-37	B-1	3	1
The Squirts	18-28	B-6	2	1
Templers	43-27	A-1	1	0
Tooling	28-10	B-1	1	2
Receivers	51-50	A-1	0	3
Finalist	18-18	B-1	0	4

Tuesday League

Name	Dept.	Plant	Won	Lost
Q.C.'s	58-03	B-1	4	0
P-38's	18-20	B-1	3	1
Dark Horse	28-10	B-1	3	1
B-1 Transp.	55-30	B-1	2	2
Block Busters	44-22	B-1	2	2
Wood Shop	43-28	A-1	2	2
The "8" Balls	15-08	A-1	0	4
Rebels	55-21	A-1	0	4

Wednesday League

Name	Dept.	Plant	Won	Lost
Office Gang	83-43	B-1	3	0
Transports	55-30	A-1	3	0
P-38 Preflight	18-26	B-1	3	1
Engineers	71-60	A-1	3	1
Material Control	51-10	A-1	2	2
Mechs	41-34	A-1	1	3
Mfg. Eng.	26-03	B-1	0	4
Spare Parts	67-75	B-1	0	4

Thursday League

Name	Dept.	Plant	Won	Lost
Ebees	72-25	B-1	4	0
Flying Tigers	51-10	B-1	3	1
Processers	38-04	B-1	2	2
Inspection	58-03	B-1	2	2
The Undecided's	72-25	B-1	1	3
Lards	28-20	B-1	0	4

STANDINGS: SWING SHIFT

Tuesday and Thursday League

Name	Dept.	Plant	Won	Lost
Wolves	18-04	B-1	4	0
Blue Jay's	28-26	B-1	3	1
Bumper's	17-13	A-2	3	1
Fiver's	62-73	B-5	2	2
Question Marks	44-52	B-1	1	3
Toolers	17-29	A-2	1	4
Welders	17-04	A-2	1	4

Checkers

Twenty-five swing shifters at Plant B-6 are currently pondering their way through a plantwide checker tournament in anticipation of crowning a B-6 swing shift champion who, in turn, will be pitted against other plant and shift champs in future tourneys.

The LERC office reveals a request from swing shifters at Plant B-3 for an additional dozen sets to satisfy their love for the game.

All this leads to the conclusion that the game is gaining momentum among Lockheed employees as a favorite lunchtime diversion. In view of this fact the LERC reminds checker players that sets may be obtained by contacting their LERC representative or LERC office. Many of the lunch areas are now supplied with numerous sets. Those that aren't will be furnished sets at employee request.

Barnyard Golf

The good old horse and buggy days never knew a crop of more enthusiastic barnyard golfers than those sporting Lockheed badges in this age of rockets and radar. The LERC, with thirty-six horseshoe courts dotting the lunch areas of almost all of Lockheed's several plants, are constantly on the lookout for new space, shoes and pegs to cope with the growing demand for this type of lunch hour and between shift recreation.

Many of the courts are equipped with proper lighting for night meets, many more will be so equipped when the material becomes available.

Home Again

More than a million discharged veterans have returned to civilian jobs since Pearl Harbor.

Fems at Bat

Those of the fair sex who have a yen for softball can get into the game individually or collectively.

Just write or phone your LERC office, giving name, department, shift, plant, extension and the position you like to play . . . or line up a team among your friends and co-workers. The LERC will form, schedule and equip teams for league play.

Swing shift girls at Plant B-2 "broke the ice" for the 1944 women's softball season and are now playing at Echo Park every Wednesday morning at 11 a.m.

Floating Airports

Trans-Atlantic airline routes may be spotted with floating airports after the war.

PEG HUDDLERS Three of Plant B-6 lunch-time horseshoe pitchers hug the pin for a little close calculation.

PEE WEE PEEVEY PEEVES

Lt. L. H. (Pee Wee) Peevey, Navy flyer on active duty, pilots a Lockheed PV-1. He likes his Ventura and its name—and his own name—but he wishes—

Well, here's a typical example of what frequently happens, according to Kenneth Duncan, Lockheed Field Service representative in the South Pacific, who overheard the ship-to-ground conversation in an advanced operations shack:

Lt. Peevey: 1200.

Operations Orderly: Plane?

Lt. Peevey: PV-113.

Operations Orderly: Pilot?

Lt. Peevey: Peevey.

Operations Orderly: Not the plane, sir; the pilot?

Lt. Peevey: Peevey! Peevey!

Operations Orderly: Yes, sir, I know the plane is a PV, but what is the pilot's name?

Lt. Peevey (beginning to get red): Look, son! I'M the pilot! I fly a PV, but my name is still Peevey. Lt. L. H. Peevey; P-E-E-V-E-Y!!

Operations Orderly: You don't understand, sir. Which PV are you talking about?

Lt. Peevey: I'm Pee Wee Peevey, and I'm in a PV. Which Peevey are *you* talking about?

This Is Rank

Quaint legend was used last week to explain what is symbolized by the bars, oak leaves and other rank insignia which indicates who salutes whom in the Army.

Said Capt. Carl J. Long, AAF public relations officer at Lockheed:

"A lieutenant, or subaltern as they were once called, may assume an elevated position in the field to watch the operations of his command. So he climbs on the first bar of a fence and can see his company from that vantage point. The captain, having more men to oversee, must stand on the top rail—two bars up.

"As I recall it, the legend goes on from there, placing the major in an oak tree, the lieutenant colonel in a silver spruce and the colonel way up among the eagles.

"General officers command so many men that they must obtain an exceptionally high point of view such as would be afforded by the stars."

Crutches will support a cripple, but not a family. Drive carefully!

Blonde Unpreferred

"Plane Talk," Consolidated Vultee publication, contained the following paragraph in an article, "Bombing Is Our Business," written by the pilot of a Liberator.

"Sometimes we have an escort of P-38's, and that is the most precious thing in the world. Every bomber pilot would rather have a P-38 alongside him than to have a beautiful blonde."

She's Proud of Her Union Card

Trudy Short, who teams with Polly Patterson in "The Care and Feeding of a Husband" on KHJ-Don Lee, is the proud possessor of a card in the machinist's union. Trudy got the card when she worked for fifteen and a half months at Lockheed as a dispatcher. She was senior union chairman of her department, which handled parts for Lockheed's B-17—sometimes as many as 5,000 in one order.

Sky Lanes

The best air routes between North America and Europe-Asia all traverse Canada.

LAST PV-1

Production Stops On Navy Ship

The last of the PV-1's rolled off the end of the Final Assembly Line at Factory A last week to make way for a newer Navy model, on the construction of which all employees who formerly worked on the PV-1 now have been absorbed.

The PV, or Ventura, has earned a lot of credit in a short time. Striking testimony to this effect was recently received by Lt. Com. C. D. Palmer, Bureau of Aeronautics representative at Lockheed, in a letter from a Navy squadron commander in the Central Pacific. Said this officer:

"In my opinion the PV-1 is the best in its class of any twin-engine airplane ever built and will remain the best until they put wings on Varga girls!"

Commander Palmer himself expressed the Navy's high regard for the plane in a congratulatory message to the men and women who have devoted all their time and talents to its production.

"I would like to congratulate all of you for the splendid production record you have established on the PV-1," he said. "It is your creation and the fighting record it has set in the combat areas of the world is, I know, a matter of justifiable pride for every PV-1 worker. This airplane outperforms any two-engine airplane the Japs have produced, and all their pilots have shown a healthy respect for it."

Similar praise was voiced by George Pruden, Works Manager of Factory A, who said:

"I want to take this opportunity to express my appreciation, and the company's, to all PV-1 craftsmen for their fine work in consistently meeting production schedules and maintaining, at the same time, the high quality standards for which Lockheed products are famed."

Man's fastest flight—a 780-m.p.h. power dive—was made in a P-38.

Science Space

With brick and concrete, men worked this week to provide extra space in the Research Building at Factory B-1 whose walls bulge with new machines and new ideas.

To this new structure will be moved some of the smaller laboratories where exacting tests can be better completed in greater isolation. Delicately balanced precision apparatus will also be located here.

For example, a magnifying camera that can make an almost invisible speck of dust look big as a rock will be moved further away from a guillotine-like device which makes the ground tremble when it tests the impact strength of materials.

On the first floor will be added several new machines capable of applying a force equal to the weight of as much as 300,000 pounds. These will handle work formerly done in outside laboratories.

Is it Here?

That refrigerator, alarm clock, bicycle, washing machine, iron, or car that you are not using may be just what the fellow working next to you needs to keep him doing a good job. This Classified Ad section, compiled and edited by Employee Service, is a medium through which articles that are scarce, due to existing priorities and lack of materials, can be put in the hands of employees who really need them.

Because we feel this service will be popular with employees, special forms have been printed for you to use in submitting your ads. They are available in Employee Service and Employee Transportation departments at all plants. They are also in stock at Stationery Stores. Ask for form No. 4929. Due to limited space, ads for essential articles and those made up in accordance with instructions on form No. 4929 will be favored.

A permanent file is maintained on cars for sale at Employee Transportation offices. This file includes additional information and prices. No telephone inquiries, please. Use file number in making inquiries. *Indicates owner is going in the service.

FOR SALE

HOUSEHOLD FURNISHINGS:

RUG, 9x12 and pad. Dishes and pans 10705 Riverside Dr., N. Hollywood.

BED, double, complete with spring and mattress. SUnset 18806.

CHEST of drawers, walnut; Frigidaire, 10 yrs. old. 600 Luton Dr., Glendale.

HOUSE furnishings and tools. Owner going east. 11337 Covello, Roscoe.

RECORD player and radio, bleached wood table model. WYoming 0459.

COMB. console radio, record player and recorder. 5515 Simpson, N.H.

PIANO, baby grand, like new. FItzroy 2181.

DINING room set, gas range, heaters, Frigidaire. WHitney 3536, 6 to 8 p.m.

DESK, limb lawn furniture, lawn swing. ANgeles 14990.

DINING set, round table, buffet, sideboard. ARizona 35986, nights.

SOFA and chair; rug; occasional chair; brkfst. set. 1923 Parkside, Burbank.

SOFA, brown friezette; table lamps. 1726 Beverly Blvd., Apt. 1, L. A.

MAYTAG gasoline washing machine. Good condition. CHurchill 91828.

WOODEN bunk beds with springs and pads. PLeasant 10534.

NEW radio tubes. 743-A Fairmont, Glendale.

4 RMS. furniture, complete. Includes washing mach. 7501 Lankershim, N.H.

REAL ESTATE:

5-RM. house, 3 yrs. old, landscaped. 14645 Vose St., Van Nuys.

5-RM. furnished house. Take trailer as part payment. 6506 Beeman Ave., N.H.

2 BDRM. house, corner lot, 3 yrs. old. SUnset 11718.

DUPLEX and 6-rm. house in rear. Good condition. NOrmandy 19762.

4-RM. furnished home, large lot. Units can be added. OLympia 4961.

4-RM. house, almost completed. Acre of land. NOrmandy 24404.

MISCELLANEOUS:

TENNIS racket; records: Nutcracker Suite. HIllside 0415.

COLLAPSIBLE baby buggy, like new. Ethelyn Colligan, 954 S. Normandie.

GASOLINE motor, 1-cylinder, suitable for bicycle. 6232 Atoll St., Van Nuys.

SUEDE pumps; blue-and-white spectators. 6½ AAA. 434 S. Ogden Drive, L. A.

NEW Webster's Unabr. Dict.; baby scales; infra-red lamp. SUnland 1396.

BOOK, "Organization & Management of Production," by Mitchell. HO. 6092.

WHITNEY collapsible baby carriage. SUnset 18947.

PREWAR metal baby buggy, springs, pad; auto bed and pad. AX. 27751.

DENNY Shute golf clubs; shotgun and shells. 7820 Claybeck, Roscoe.

TWO micrometers; 25-qt. pressure cooker; baby buggy. 12133 Hatteras, N.H.

3-HP. outboard motor. D. Fedderly, CItrus 24963.

CROWN Point spray gun, hose spray and cord. CItrus 35809.

LADY'S diamond ring, 5 diamonds, 3 rubies; 16-gauge shotgun. CL. 72524.

ALARM clock; trumpet; bathinett; tricycle; camera equip. NO. 25826.

SUIT, lady's size 14, beautifully tailored. Mrs. Jones, CL. 63633.

JERSEY cow, gentle; 10-weeks-old Guernsey calf. 3960 Vantage, L. A.

ONE set, new prewar ballon tires and tubes. SUnset 13060.

ENGLISH pointer puppies, pure bred. Liver-and-white. STate 52990.

DIAMOND engagement ring, dinner ring, watch, cameo pin. CI. 25001 after 2 p.m.

HENS, 6 Austra-white, laying; battery for 8 hens. 10742 Camarillo St., N.H.

WANTED

PORTABLE battery radio, any make. NOrmandy 8913 after 5 p.m.

STEEL fresh-water casting rod. 314 N. Chevy Chase Dr., Glendale.

BED spotlight. W. E. Stoddard, 1376 N. Ridgewood Pl., Hollywood.

METRONOME; gas stove; medium-sized refrigerator. CItrus 15373.

SHETLAND pony. 3960 Vantage, Los Angeles.

50 LBS. adjustable dumb-bells. W. McGaughey, 140 N. Jackson, Apt. 201, G.

SEWING machine, portable or treadle type. G. Ferguson, CH. 82871.

BOX couch and bamboo furniture. NOrmandy 16428 after 2 p.m.

ELECTRIC iron and cord. SUnset 18423.

SMALL radio. Ethel B. Raison, DRexel 1983.

TENNIS shoes, men's size 7; girls' size 5 or 7. CItrus 32580.

TO buy or rent, stucco brush. M. Greenberg, NOrmandy 6929 before 6 p.m.

LOST AND FOUND

Lost and found is an interesting place, especially to those who have lost articles. At Factory B, Room 200, Personnel Bldg., there is a lower dental plate that someone must be missing badly since rationing has eased a bit. There are gloves, scarfs, compacts and glasses, but suppose the ones who lost their glasses won't see this. Tell them about it, won't you? There are bracelets and lockets that must have more sentimental value to someone than they do to the custodians of Lost and Found,

LOST AND FOUND (Cont.)

though some of them have been around so long we have grown quite attached to them.

Factory A Lost and Found has a gold wedding band and a gold medal for service in the United States Navy during the Spanish campaign.

The Lost and Found departments are located in Employee Service at Factories B-1, A-1 and A-2.

LOST:

JACKET, man's tan windbreaker with zipper. Reward. 1138 Laguna Ave., L.A.

EXCHANGE

44-CAL. Smith & Wess. pistol and 70 rds. ammun., for typewr. CHurchill 91362.

VEHICLES FOR SALE

BICYCLES:

'44 Schwin electric, comp. with charger, 20 to 25 mph. No. 91.

LADY'S, front-wheel brake, prewar, like new. No. 92.

28", prewar, good shape. No. 93

MAN'S 28", lightweight, good condition. No. 139.

BUICK:

'37 sedan, will sell for best offer. 32,000 miles, new tires. No. 118.

*'39 special 4-door sedan, A-1 condition, new paint. No. 141.

CHEVROLET:

'39 coupe, good condition. No. 131.

'38 in good condition. No. 133.

'35 coach, 2 new grade I tires. New paint job. No. 142.

'41 club coupe, 28,000 miles, A-1 mechanically, radio. No. 110.

CHRYSLER:

'29 coupe, runs good, good tires, good transportation. No. 87.

DE SOTO:

'41 de luxe, 4-door sedan, radio, heater. Has to be sold. No. 111.

'38 sedan, mechanically A-1. Good tires, radio. No. 117.

DODGE:

'28 coupe, 5 good prewar tires, good motor, cheap trans. No. 137.

FORD:

'41 de luxe sedan, very clean, good motor and tires. Radio. No. 128.

'38 business coupe, in storage 2 years. Rebuilt motor, good tires. No. 134.

'35 V8, will trade for '40 or '41 Chev. or Olds., pay difference. No. 135.

'29 Model A, overhauled motor, good transportation. No. 136.

'38 sedan, radio, heater, overdrive. No. 115.

'38 coupe, fair tires, built-in radio, $15 battery. No. 116.

'35 sedan, tailored seat covers, clean, good running car. No. 121.

'35 tudor, new battery, motor overhauled. Cash only. No. 122.

'35 V8 tudor, new motor, new brakes, good rubber and upholstery. No. 123.

LINCOLN ZEPHYR:

'37 coupe, excellent radio, Lorraine spotlight. No. 119.

MERCURY:

'41 4-door sedan, radio, new paint, heater, 2 new grade I tires. No. 109.

MOTORCYCLES:

'42 Harley Davidson, model 61, low mileage, new tires. No. 89.

'41 Harley Davidson, model 74, new tires, low mileage. No. 90.

LATE model Harley Davidson, master de luxe, low mileage. No. 125.

'29 Harley Davidson, fair condition. No. 138.

'34 Indian, rebuilt, good tires. No. 126.

MOTOR SCOOTER:

LAWSON engine, side car, battery ignition, good tires. No. 127.

PLYMOUTH:

'40 de luxe sedan, clean, in good condition. 35,000 miles. No. 112.

'38 sedan, 2 new grade I tires; comp. overhauled. No. 114.

'36 coupe, must see to appreciate. No. 120.

'33 coupe, excel. mechanical cond.; good tires, generator. No. 124.

PONTIAC:

*'40 tudor sedan, excellent finish, overhauled engine. No. 130.

'40 4-door sedan, 5 recapped tires, radio, good condition. No. 140.

'39 sedan, excel. condition; 5 good tires, radio. No. 132.

STUDEBAKER:

'39 Commander club sedan, overdrive, good tires, hill holder. No. 113.

'40 custom coupe, 3 new recaps, good paint and upholstery. No. 129.

'29 sedan, excel. 6-ply, prewar tires and tubes. A-1 condition. No. 88.

'38 sedan, motor just overhauled. Must sell. No. 62.

TRAILERS:

'41 Schult, 18½', electric brakes, well-equipped. No. 94.

'40 Palace, 22', sleeps 4, refrigerator, A-1 condition. No. 95.

THE LOCKHEED Star
OFFICIAL PUBLICATION OF THE LOCKHEED AIRCRAFT CORPORATION
Volume I BURBANK, CALIFORNIA, U.S.A., JULY 7, 1944 No. 7

'Bad Penny' and the Japs ★ ★ ★

(Courtesy Chicago Times)

Betio Island, Tarawa Atoll, Gilbert Islands (delayed). The Japs at Wotje are living a tough life. They're cut off, deserted and hopeless, and all they can do is sit there and soak up our bombs.

"Sometimes I'm almost ashamed of myself," lanky Cal Morgan remarked, as we waited. "Every time I get to pitying them, though, I take a look at that and quit," he added, pointing to ranked white crosses hard by the runway.

Under the crosses lay the marines who died last November getting this airfield for Cal and his kind.

Ventura Loads Up

We were standing in the white, hot glare of Betio's coral runway while a gas truck dumped high octane fuel into the copious tanks of "Bad Penny," a Navy Ventura bomber with wings the size of a red bandana handkerchief and 4,000 horsepower to hurl her through the sky.

"Bad Penny's" thick belly was full of bombs for Wotje and we were waiting to take her up there across 500 miles of equatorial Pacific to deliver them.

We were getting a late start, at the last minute Cal's regular plane was reported ailing, and we switched to "Bad Penny," which is the regular chariot of Lt. (jg) Harold A. Tiegen, 6964 Oriole, Chicago. Tiegen was away bombing Naru that day with somebody's plane and so we took his.

Other planes, including one carrying Jack Bishop of the *Saturday Evening Post,* had gone ahead, leaving us to bring up the rear.

"She's okay," the crew chief said finally. We piled in, donned Mae Wests and stowed away a day's chow, a box containing a five-pound loaf of Spam, a hunk of whole wheat bread and a gallon can of sliced pineapple.

Pilot from Pomona

Cal, who is 24, comes from Pomona, Calif., and once flew Venturas in the Aleutians, taxied to the end of the runway, swung around and literally hurled "Bad Penny" into the air.

The meters registered—manifold pressure as her mighty engines opened their throats wide to gulp gas by the gallons, with a shot like a thunderbolt, the Ventura's tiny wings grabbed the air and clawed into the sky with a bellowing rush.

"Boy, oh, boy, we're a whole strike by ourselves," said Lt. (jg) John Friedeborn, of Queen's Village, Calif., the co-pilot. "I wonder what they're going to think when they see us coming in all alone a half hour after the other bunch leaves."

"I don't care what they think. I just care how good they shoot," answered Aviation Ordnanceman Albion F. Bpermeland, 30, of Los Angeles, navigator.

Like a leisurely bolt of Lightning, the swift Ventura circled Betio's scarred surface and squared away for the north. We bored along through bright sunlight over cobalt sea, which looked dangerous to only one of the plane's occupants—me.

"Bad Penny's" engines sang such a deep and confident song, however, that fears vanished, and I went to sleep lying on the belly gunner's cushion on the tail. I did not awake until young Aviation Ordnanceman Bill Curry, of New Stanton, Pa., prodded me to see the Jap base of Mille, gliding by beneath. I expected to see trouble coming up, but none came.

Sight Maloelap

After awhile an irregular gleaming white ring appeared far off on the surface.

Two writers described their rides in separate PV-1 Venturas which bombed Jap-held Wotje Island. Here's the story by one of them—Keith Wheeler of the Chicago Times. The other was John Bishop whose story is in the June 24 issue of the Saturday Evening Post.

"That's Maloelap. One plane got its turret shot off there yesterday," Bill said cheerfully.

I remembered the last time I'd seen Maloelap more than two years previously, when a cruiser shelled the place and got thoroughly bombed for its pains. It was funny now to see Maloelap so impotent and remembered back when I'd never expected to leave it alive. Hi, there, Maloelap. Remember me?

Suddenly Bill frowned, then handed me his earphones. Through the roar of the engines came the voice of William Mulvaney, 23, of Amenia, N. D., "Bad Penny's" radioman.

"The other planes have bombed," he said. "The plane your friend is on got hit by ack-ack. They got it bad. The rudder controls are gone."

I felt sick, but I didn't have much time for it. Bill suddenly wrenched out of the escape hatch so I could see alongside and below and then he flopped down and charged his twintail guns.

"We're going in, get set," he said.

There was a whining overhead as Aviation Mechanic Jack Harvey, of Binghamton, N. Y., swung the twin guns in the upper turret.

Huddles Beside Hatch

I huddled alongside the open hatch through which the wind blasted in a chilly hurricane. We'd know about this pretty soon now. Seconds, minutes at most.

All at once, "Bad Penny's" peacefully roaring motors were squawling with power and the plane quivered as 4,000 unleashed horses hurtled us through the sky. We were twisting from side to side. Below us lay fleecy clouds across which our shadow raced madly, always circled by a many-colored rainbow that had the look of a halo.

Suddenly we were out over the edge of the clouds and below us sprawled Wotje Island.

With 7,000 feet of thin air between us and the Japs, Cal roared alongside the island, reaching position for an attack. Down there were bomb-pocked, criss-crossing runways, many buildings, tattered palms, two dead ships on the reef—and

(Continued on Page 8)

PLANT BOND DRIVE ON THROUGH JULY

Although the bond booths have closed, the Fifth War Loan drive will continue at Lockheed through the month of July.

At Factory B-1, bond purchases may be made at the Federal Credit Union offices, Unit 54, 1829 Empire Avenue, daily except Saturdays from 10:50 a.m. to 1 p.m., from 3 to 4:30 p.m. and from 11:30 p.m. to 1 a.m.

At Factory A-1, bonds may be purchased at the Federal Credit Union offices, Building 77 (old Commissary Building), daily except Saturdays from 11 a.m. to 12:45 p.m. and from 3 to 4:30 p.m. A-1 Graveyard employees may make their purchases at the Employee Service Department, Building 62.

Employees in outlying plants can buy bonds through the Employee Service Department or the Paymaster's office of their plant.

All bond purchases by employees during July are applicable to the Lockheed quota. Those who buy bonds outside of Lockheed can apply their purchases to the Lockheed quota by calling the Bond Drive office, Factory B, 1742.

—Your Invasion—Buy War Bonds—

Yvonne Raises Ante

Bond purchases shot up 20 per cent among personnel of the Lockheed Air Terminal last week after Yvonne Davis, in a red, white and blue uniform of her own design, conducted a whirlwind campaign. The record shows 85 per cent of the department have bought bonds.

—Help Fight Inflation—

Wins Cluster

Staff Sgt. Clyde U. Bullock, former Lockheed worker, of 71 East Tujunga, Burbank, has had a second Oak Leaf Cluster added to his Air Medal.

CONSERVATION DOES IT!

These girls of the Conservation Department (11-38) clubbed together and bought war bonds to the tune of $600 at Factory A-1. Here they are signing the honor roll. At the left is Clarice Easler. Next in order are Lisette Cook, Anne Diamond, Mimi Edwards, Helen McCayne, Mildred Hartley.

THE COVER

This week's cover shows a bomb-scarred South Pacific landing strip similar to the one used by "Bad Penny" as described in the story accompanying the picture. The big bombs in the foreground are ready to be placed in a Navy Ventura about to take off on a mission of blasting Jap installations on another atoll. Palm trees on the island have been shredded by bombs and bullets.

TWO MESSAGES FROM 'BELLE BALLOT' BOYS

This week brought two messages from the Fighting 96th—originators of the Belle Ballot from their AAF base in Italy.

Ed Canada, Lockheed field service man just returned from the Mediterranean theatre, dropped in on Belle Ballot headquarters at the request of the squadron to see how things are coming along.

"The boys are really up in the air about this search," says Canada, who was with the enlisted men of the Fighting 96th when they wrote to Lockheed suggesting a contest among girls who help build their favorite plane—the P-38. Canada worked with the squadron in North Africa, moved into Italy with them early in October—one of the first groups to invade that country.

The second message from the Fighting 96th comes from the squadron's contest chairman, T/Sgt. John A. Fucciolo, who apologizes for not writing sooner, "but we've been pretty busy lately—especially the major."

The major is Major Clayton M. Isaacson, squadron commander, whose plane will carry the name of their "Lightning Lady," selected from the Belle Ballot.

"To a man, the squadron is looking forward to receiving the pictures of the Lockheed beauties with eager anticipation," he writes.

Replying to Belle Ballot inquiries for more information about the squadron, Sgt. Fucciolo explains that their two presidential citations were received for (1) leading a mass Lightning P-38 low-level attack on German air bases in the Foggia area, and (2) downing 24 Nazi planes out of 70 encountered on a bomber escort mission over Naples.

It is this crack P-38 fighter group that awaits pictures of Lockheed girls—the Belle Ballot was planned for them.

Rules are simple, and the Belle Ballot is still open. Closing date is midnight, July 15, when entries must be received at contest headquarters. All girls in all Factory B plants, and Factory A in Fresno, where P-38's are built are eligible. Send pictures to Belle Ballot, LERC, B-1, c/o Vic Stein.

Willie Barber Leads Golf

Willie Barber, who shot a 67 for the lowest gross score in last Sunday's all-shift, all-plant tourney at Inglewood and Baldwin Hills, will lead twenty of Lockheed's best in a 36-hole battle for the title of Lockheed's low-gross champion this Sunday at Baldwin and Fox Hills courses.

Barber, well known in Lockheed and Southern California golfing circles, took a 35 on the first nine and 32 on the back stretch at Inglewood for his 4 under par tally. Only other contender to turn in an under par score was Bob Barnard who shot 34 out and 35 in for a 69, also at Inglewood.

Of the near 300 starters in last Sunday's event, the twenty to tee off for the title this weekend all qualified with scores of 77 or under. As originally planned• by the LERC Golf Committee, the titlists were to be limited to the low sixteen, but with five turning in a 77 score, it has been necessary to raise the quota of starters to twenty. An attractive, two-foot, engraved trophy, donated by the LERC, will be awarded the new champion with other second and third place awards.

The medalist play will begin at 8:30 at Baldwin Hills Sunday morning for the first 18 holes. At 2:30 the second round will begin at Fox Hills.

Following is the list of the twenty titlists with their scores in last Sunday's qualifying round:

	OUT	IN	LOW GROSS
Willie Barber	35	32	67
Bob Barnard	34	35	69
Nick Petropolo	35	37	72
Tom Rasmussen	36	37	73
George Demko	38	35	73
Pat Lambert	36	37	73
Jack Gaines	36	38	74
Jim Sterling	35	39	74
Aubrey Devine	40	35	75
Warren Drew	36	39	75
Jack Segerdahl	37	38	75
Mike Gazella	36	39	75
Henry Hill	36	40	76
Charles Currier	39	37	76
Don Nak	40	36	76
Charles Hill	37	40	77
Clint Rubison	38	39	77
Ben Clinton	40	37	77
Nick Boukidis	37	40	77
Burt Barkelew	39	38	77

Winners of the putting contest were Joe Stein who turned in a 33 for the Baldwin Hills 18 followed by Imel Gryder who shot a 35. On the Inglewood 9-hole putting green, Warren Drew shot a 14 for first place, with R. A. Eddy and Jack Gaines tied for second with 15 strokes each.

Blind bogey winners in the July 2 event were Sid Miller, Kirk Venable, Gordon Brown, Irwin Ayres, F. Pratt, Tom Rasmussen, Garagliano, Glen Lee, Burr Cramer and Ray Galt. Blind bogey number was 70.

All prizes will be in the form of War Bonds and Stamps donated by the LERC, sponsors of both the July 2 and championship events. The ten winners in each of the three flights of last week's playoff will be notified by the LERC office as soon as computed by the Golf Committee.

Last week's tournament was handled by Jim Arbogast, Johnny Heinzman, Jack Phillips and Wilkie Byram with the assistance of Helen Worley

—Your Invasion—Buy War Bonds—

SHOOTS 67. Here's Willie Barber, last year's Lockheed golf champion, who got off to a good start in defense of his title by leading all comers in qualifying trials last Sunday.

New Library Location

Factory A-1's library is newly located in Room 20A, ground floor of Building 62. All the latest books, technical papers and trade publications pertaining to the aircraft industry will be found on its shelves. Hours remain the same as when it was in its former location.

Shoop on Air Sunday

Lt. Col. C. A. Shoop, who has been assistant A.A.F. resident representative at Lockheed and who recently returned to the U.S. from detached duty in the European war theatre, will be interviewed regarding his overseas experiences on the "I Was There" radio program over KNX, Columbia Pacific network, next Sunday from 9 to 9:30 p.m.

Col. Shoop will speak with first-hand knowledge of the invasion of Normandy, for on D-day at H-hour he flew a P-38 camera plane up and down the beachhead, taking reconnaissance pictures with which he was the first to return to England. Don't miss his interview—Sunday night, 9 to 9:30 p.m., over KNX.

Buck o' Month Aids Vets

Influx of disabled veterans into the Los Angeles area for hospitalization, brings increasing need of civilian aid in their rehabilitation. For this purpose Lockheed's Buck o' the Month Club reports a new donation of $600 to the Disabled American Veterans Association for use at the San Fernando and Sawtelle hospitals. Another donation of considerable importance, as revealed by the club's latest financial statement, was for $1000 to the Children's Home Society which has placed many homeless children for adoption in this area. The June statement follows:

BUCK OF THE MONTH CLUB—JUNE 30, 1944

CONTRIBUTIONS		
Lockheed Employees	$1,063,419	
Triplett & Barton	1,372	
L.E.R.C. Employees	3,263	
Miscellaneous	7,100	
British Reassembly Division	889	
		$1,075,045
Total amount donated for period March 31, 1942, to March 31, 1944, as previously reported in the *Star*.		880,660
DISBURSEMENTS (since March 31, 1944)		
Refund—V. H. Hagoes	1	
Audit—Buck of Month Books	100	
Premium on Bond for Executive Committee	360	
Marine Corps League	50	
Service Star Women of Lockheed—Buddy Letter, etc.	1,121	
Blue Star Service Club	375	
Beds for Servicemen, Hollywood High	1,360	
Salvation Army	205	
Knights of Columbus—Beds for Servicemen	75	
Birmingham Hospital	1,000	
Los Angeles War Chest, Final Payment	23,124	
Hollywood Guild & Canteen	300	
Travelers' Aid Society	900	
Marine Corps Canteen	3,000	
Navy Canteen	3,000	
Milton Berry School (paralytics)	1,000	
Visiting Nurses for Employees	55	
American Red Cross	51,000	
Poppy Day Donations	950	
Harlan Shoemaker Fund for Paralytics	1,300	
Clarke School for Paralytics	500	
Dawn Society (Blind Aid)	50	
Prisoners' Aid	50	
Air Corps Cadets' Club	500	
A.A.A. Battery (Lockheed)	15	
Veterans Rehabilitation Directory	135	
Servicemen (Aleutian Island) Radio	35	
Child Care—Nursery School	400	
Disabled American Veterans—Rehabilitation	600	
Children's Home Society	1,000	
Aircraft Women's Club—Hospital Robes	200	
		92,765
		$ 973,426
BALANCE ON HAND		$ 101,618

Step Up Drive On Thieves

A Lockheed general foreman is under indictment by a Federal Grand Jury on charges of theft of an altimeter and a bank-and-turn indicator which officials say he confessed stealing for his own airplane.

This tops a list of thefts uncovered by Plant Protection in a drive against tool pilfering in Southern California war plants directed by U.S. Attorney Charles H. Carr with the co-operation of Army and Navy officials.

Most of the thefts, it appears, are relatively petty, but an alarming increase in the number of them brought intensified efforts to stamp them out.

People think the loss of one drill won't break the company or the government and this may be true, explained John Hanson, plant protection manager, but one drill taken by each of a thousand people runs into an alarming total.

Theft of tools from a fellow-employee is an even more contemptible practice and one which often causes more trouble through production time lost by the worker who tries to get his tools back himself.

Often a piece of equipment as big as a drill motor is taken out through the gate after a worker has dissasembled it and put the parts in his pocket.

Sometimes a guilty conscience results in the return of stolen goods. Recently a worker brought back a whole bag of drills, wrenches and small tools which he handed to a gate guard with profuse apologies and the statement that he hadn't realized he was taking things.

—Invade with War Bonds—

Silly . . . Isn't It?

Sure, but it's just as silly to run through the factory area. However, since some people insist on doing just that, the *Star* photographer decided to show how it really should be done—in one easy lesson, with experts as teachers.

First of all, you should be a champion athlete—preferably a hurdler, broad jumper and pole vaulter. Model of the perfect champion athlete is Al Lawrence, star U.S.C. freshman who is one of the nation's best in the high and low hurdles, and who also scores points in the broad jump and pole vault. Al is the son of Scotty Lawrence, manager of Dept. 57-41 (Tool Inspection) at B-1.

It is also important to get off to a fair as well as an official start. So the photog called in Hal Powell, jig builder in Dept. 28-10, to fire the starting gun. Hal has been an A.A.U. official for 22 years, and has started such world-famous sprinters as Charley Paddock, Frank Wykoff and Jesse Owens. Be sure he is on hand with his gun (loaded with buckshot).

Directions and equipment are important, too. Safety Engineer Jack Hatton's counterpart of the Automobile Club put up the road signs reading "Walk, Don't Run—to Main Hospital." Al Lawrence is set and ready to "follow the red stripe" but he insists not only on being well and appropriately dressed for the occasion—in his Trojan track suit—but he also refused point-blank to take off on the hazardous journey unless he had a crutch.

"If the wind is in my favor," says Al, "I'll probably not need the crutch until I've run all of five feet."

Maybe it isn't so silly, at that!

Referral Honor Roll Listed

Honor roll of employees who have referred prospective new workers to the Employment and Placement Division, using the white Employee Referral forms, is listed below. The list represents the number of referrals received at Central Employment headquarters through June 30.

The following people referred two:

William A. Akler, Albert R. Ball, John G. Brown, Emil Eyer, S. H. Henderson, Mary Lee Jackson, Fay Lehman, K. P. Lloyd, Charles Loiselle, Lenora T. Markham, John T. Perry, Margaret Urdahl, Mattie Wilson.

The following people referred one:

Charles L. Allen, George E. Annand, Frances Auslander, Kathleen Baker, Eleanor M. Balch, Bertha C. Baldwin, Roscoe H. Beck, Elsie B. Belnap, Rufus Bias, Della O'Connor Bishop, Zenana Black, Homer Blair, Alice H. Bowler, Isaac E. Bowman, Brazilian Bradford, Frances G. Brown, James D. Browning, Arlo L. Brownley, Nina S. Bryant, Gloria L. Bumgardner, Thomas Burdine, Myrna C. Burke, Jr., George W. Byer, Preston A. Campbell.

Samuel C. Carbee, Zenobia S. Carney, Tom J. Carter, Thomas B. Castello, Mary Ceci, Madeleine M. Chanz, Florence F. Chapman, Glade M. Cherry, James B. Cherry, Belle Chmelik, William R. Chunn, Elizabeth Church, Daniel B. Cluck, Ralph W. Collins, Madge F. Compton, Felix E. Conahan, Robert Conrad, Marion Cowser, Alberta L. Crawford, Milton Cross, Catherine B. Cutler, Jesse E. Cutler, Gerald J. Denman, William DeRevere.

Ruth E. DeVall, Florence C. Deyo, Mary U. Diaz, Wallace E. Duncan, Duskin E. Earnest, Evelyn Ellis, L. J. Fitzpatrick, Earl A. Flanders, Ella L. Foster, Dwight T. Fox, Genevieve M. Frank, Jeannette Frenn, Lucy C. Geis, Alfred C. Gillman, A. T. Gilman, Dean E. Goldsmith, Orlandt Gottardi, Dorothy B. Gray, Joe B. Gross, Robert W. Gussom.

Frank W. Hackett, Charles R. Hamilton, John Hamilton, Wm. W. Hamlett, Sarah V. Hanlin, James V. Hanson, Jr., Willa S. Hardie, Helen H. Heard, Raymond P. Hentgers, John T. Hill, Lutetia R. Hines, Rosa E. Hollins, Lois B. Holly, Merle E. Hough, Brycie Houston, Marie R. Hubert, Merrill Huntoon, Ray E. Irwin.

Miguel M. Jackson, Fred E. Jeffress, Fred E. Jennings, Betty M. K. Johnson, Crobey Johnson, James R. Johnson, Rand Johnson, Deola W. Jones, Daniel Kempel, Lucretia Kent, Anton Kociemba, Eva L. Kunze.

W. Laymon Lee, John W. Lewis, Minnie Lewis, Niels G. Lindahl, George R. Little, Joe D. Lopez, John B. Lozano, Donald R. MacLean, Jannie B. McAllister, Wm. V. McAtee, Mary McClure, B. D. McConnell, Howard C. McDaniel, Harold McDonald, Jeanette McCown, Eddie Mae McGee, Audrey McMurry, Cora G. McMurry, E. McMurray, Clyde C. Mershon, Pauline Messing, Harry J. Mochel, Margaret B. Modell, Betty W. Morgan, Stanley A. Morris, Fred Motz, Bessie E. Munns, Matilda Munoz, Noah O. Narveson, Adam D. Nicodemo.

William J. O'Brien, Josephine M. Orozco, Pricilla Ortiz, John N. Padama, Jack K. Painter, Helen E. Parfitt, Ross I. Pierce, Jack R. Pike, Paul Piltz, Jay N. Patocka, William P. Rankin, Viola H. Raphael, Chas. C. Ray, Malissie A. Ray, Emma Renaas, Joseph F. Reso, Dolly K. Riken, Hannah L. Riley, Arland Roberto, Ray R. Robinson, Avery D. Roten, Lucille J. Roth.

Look at Lockheed...

With the Random Cameraman

MARTIN TURRET FOR VENTURA . . .
Frank Alten, Armorer, Factory A.

COLD METAL SPRAYER . . .
W. E. Murphy, Factory B.

PRINTING . . .
Renee Usab scans the sheets.

BLUEPRINTS . . .
Arline Burton, Junior Detail Draftsman, Factory B.

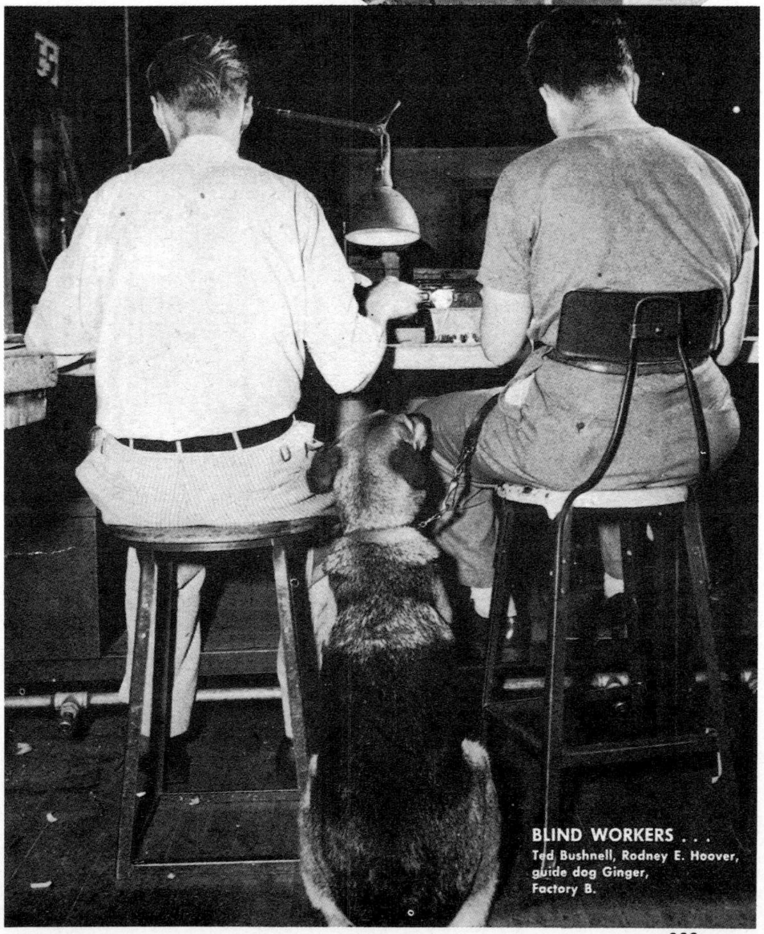

BLIND WORKERS . . .
Ted Bushnell, Rodney E. Hoover, guide dog Ginger, Factory B.

COMMISSARY . . .
John Knuesli, cook.

Last Ventura and Her Production Service Mechanics

JUST BEFORE **the Navy took delivery on this last Lockheed PV-1 Ventura, shown above. A new Navy model, details of which are restricted, is now the gang at Factory A Production Service was gathered for the group photo going into production.**

My Friend's Son

A Lockheed Father's Blood Bank Debt

(EDITOR'S NOTE—The Marine hero of the following story is the son of a Lockheed employee. Both father and son prefer to remain anonymous.)

I hadn't seen the boy since he had come back from New Guinea. Though delicate in health, I found him still fine looking, with strong features that indicated a good mind and a virile body. He had earned the silver bar, in action—a first lieutenant of the United States Marine Corps.

I remember when he left for Officers' Training camp—his eagerness, and the keen appreciation of what he was letting himself in for. As training weeks passed, his father had read me letters from the boy; letters which told of long, arduous hours of training, of difficult hikes, of amphibious rehearsals under actual battle conditions. Not once did the boy complain.

A Proud Moment

Then came the wire. He had made it! He had won his gold bar, as an officer in the Marine Corps. While proud of the achievement, he was not cocky. The only difference he suggested was that coffee cups now had handles, and he could walk into the officers' club.

One day came a call for volunteers, and he was one of three selected. I was almost as proud as was his father. One cold, foggy morning, the "slow boat" caught up with him and for three weeks there was no word.

Soon his letters began to arrive and we guessed wildly as to where he could be. He told of rain, more rain, and still more rain; of drilling in the mud, of the price of Scotch, and what fun they had with a case of beer. He told what fine men were in the Marines; of his colonel, "a real guy;" of his captain, "a born leader;" of his "he men" sergeants and corporals. The next letter told of his wearing the silver bar—a first lieutenant—and I shared the joy with my friend.

My friend's son went into action in New Guinea shortly after that. His training, plus inherent intelligence, stood him in good stead. My friend and I opened a bottle of twenty-year Scotch, toasted this son of his, and silently prayed to Almighty God that the boy be spared.

Both Arms Hit

Early one morning the phone rang and my friend read me a letter. His boy was in a base hospital; both arms had been hit. Of course "it was nothing serious"—the care he received "was perfect," and he "didn't suffer much."

Then came letters from those who had served with my friend's son. "He will be hard to replace," said his colonel, "for he is a fine officer, respected by his fellow officers and men alike." His buddy wrote that "he practically took one Jap machine gun nest alone," and that they were dropping hand grenades on a second nest when "the Japs got him in both elbows as he was about to let go with his grenades." "We covered him," said his buddy, "and pushed on and made the b——— pay for what they had done to him."

His men carried my friend's son back a short distance and gave him a plasma transfusion, for he was slipping fast. Then, on a stretcher made of rifles and raincoats, he was carried still farther back to a field hospital. Here a second and third plasma transfusion was given him, and a few hours later he was flown to the base hospital far from the front lines.

I visited my friend's son the other day. He appeared thinner. In his eyes was a hurt look, a terribly hurt look, that comes from excruciating pain over a long period, and from bewilderment of which I was to learn more later. He has been taken from the body cast in which he lay for four months. His arms are in steel and leather jackets. The fingers of one hand he can move a little; the other hand doesn't work yet.

Life-Saving Fluid

He asks no sympathy. All my friend's son wants is to get back the use of his arms, and rejoin his buddies. He doesn't particularly want to go through the suffering and horrors of war again, but he feels there is a job that must be done; that it is partly his job. His sense of duty, his belief in his country, leaves him no alternative.

We sat and talked, this friend's son who has grown into a man overnight—and I learned much. There is no selfishness on the fighting front. Men willingly give their lives that others may live.

My friend's son told me of the feeling of vitality, of the flow of life through his veins, when the blood plasmas were given him. "It saved my life," he said simply. "It has saved thousands of others from death."

He talked about our country, and his eyes shone. He loves this country, its past, and he and his buddies on the front intend to have something to say about this country's future when they return.

As steel is purified by white heat, maybe war purifies mankind. What I saw and learned this day gives me faith in the future of my country. And I am proud of my friend's son.

—Brayton Witherell.

—Your Invasion—Buy War Bonds—

Ideas for Dallas

From Dallas, Texas, last week came three men to busy Lockheed Air Terminal seeking ideas for remodeling their own Municipal Airport. They were Hart Bowman, aviation supervisor; Thomas Broad, architect, and V. R. Smithan, city manager. During their inspection of facilities here their host was L.A.T. Manager Dudley M. Steele.

A Shrinking World

As political campaigns gather momentum we hear more and more frequently the expression, "The world has shrunk, the airplane has made it into a small world." Juan Terry Trippe, president of Pan American Airways, challenges this current platitude in his recent speech at UCLA. "Only distances have shrunk," said the PanAm president.

Before the war, Mr. Trippe's airline system was the greatest in the world—the only United States international airline. He kept constantly in touch with events everywhere on earth. To most Americans before the war, the world was mainly the forty-eight states and a fringe of more or less civilized people in Europe, South America and Asia, but to the officers of Pan American Airways a local famine or a change in government in China or Brazil might mean life or death for an integral section of their system.

To mathematicians and travel agencies, perhaps the world seems smaller. But to the pilots and trouble shooters of our expanded international airlines, the world has grown suddenly to include all of its two billion inhabitants instead of just the 140,000,000 Americans in the United States. Great vistas have opened to all of us to travel in foreign countries, to become acquainted with people of a strange culture, to see the towns, the "sacred spots," the buildings and mountains and rivers that are only a dim story to us now.

The airplane brings the possibility of adventure to all of us. Opportunities only open to those of leisure and great wealth in the Sea Age will be open to the great majority of us in the Air Age. Victory will not immediately bring this greatly enlarged opportunity to us, of course, but it is a promise that the Air Age will eventually fulfill.

In the matter of time, distance, space, the world may have grown smaller. But in the vastly more important terms of the people living in it, it has, become huge.

People who live in strange places are now strangers to us and to other "foreigners" who live only a few hundred miles away. Only a relatively few people travel because it takes too long in most parts of the globe, and few countries can afford to build expensive railroads and highways. But travel by air may soon become the cheapest form of travel. Someday it may be possible for each of the two billion people who live on earth to have friends in "foreign" lands.

S.B.M.

"IF I HEAR THAT OUTA GAS GAG—JUST ONCE MORE . . ."

HORSESHOE QUEENS of Santa Barbara Plant 60 are Colleen De Schaine and (pitching) Eloise Mathews. Spectators left to right are Iris Jessup, Grace Hubbard, Rosalie Osborne, Dorothy Stevens, Lorraine Wooten and Sue Jacobus.

Pomona Pin-Up Winners

The Pomona pin-up girl contest came to a successful completion this week. On the day shift, Margaret Hendricks, 14-31 and Caroline Valincia, Dept. 14-28 were the winners.

The swing shift winners were Darlene Jertberg, Dept. 14-28 and Elanor Morwood, Dept. 14-28.

—5th War Loan—

Drops to Third Place

Leading the Pomona Civic Softball League for three weeks, the Lockheed club lost two tough contests the past week, falling into third place. But the boys remain very much in the running.

Lockheed lost a heartbreaker to Pomona Pumps 15 to 11. Manager Atteberry started his second-string pitcher for this contest, as he was saving Leonard Powers for a tougher game the following evening. But though Powers on that occasion hurled a fine game, he was beaten by Vortox, 5-0.

—Back the Attack—

Checker Tourney

A dynamic checker tournament started from a field of twenty players, is well on its way nearing the final play-offs at Pomona.

Walter Griffin, Paul Newhouse, Clayton Stevens, B. Dillon, and R. Chillcott are still in the running. Walter Griffin, the winner of the last tournament, is again in the finals.

—Invade with War Bonds—

Buck-of-the-Month

Pomona Buck-of-the-Month Club has released the following financial statement as of June 30:

Balance		$ 571.50
Receipts:		
Check No. 36800	$153.25	
Check No. 37163	104.25	
Check No. 37557	122.75	
Check No. 37893	109.75	
Check No. 37889	131.00	
	$621.00	$621.00
Disbursements	000.00	000.00
New Balance		$1192.50

—Back Our Boys—

BAKERSFIELD

Barn Dance

Queen Gingham and King Jean ruled when employees of Plants 54 and 55 gathered for an old-time barn dance and regular hoe-down recently at the Barn on Stine Road. All employees and their partners were admitted on their Lockheed passes for old-time music and modern, too, and the theme of the evening was grand right and left, and doce-do, choose your partners, kids, and let's go!

SANTA BARBARA

Channel City Chatter

Merton Oliver is in Texas on business. . . . Okey Wheeler has gone on his second honeymoon, from there reporting for induction at Los Angeles the 24th of July. Lots of luck! Okey! . . . Surprised to see Mrs. Ehrenborg's son in the cafeteria—fine looking chap, doing his part in the fire suppression crew of U. S. Forestry. . . . Ethel Trumbull is now in first aid at Plant 60, and Mildred Burrell is taking over the duties of visiting nurse in place of Marie Bockting. . . . Colleen De Schaine is whipping in and out of the parking lot in a new car. . . . A dinner meeting for section supervisors and department heads was held at the Montecito Country Club Wednesday at 7 p.m.

—Let's Go—For the Knockout Blow!—

POMONA

Starlights

WILBERT BOLLINGER of tool inspection changed from days to swing. ROY GILLETT of supervision, on leave, wired that he had received his induction papers, and terminated. DORIS WALKER, day timekeeper, fractured a couple of fingers playing soft ball.

Latest hires are: DON BRINDERSON, jigbuilder; GLEN PECK, EDYTHE PAGEL, EDITH BROWNELL, tool crib attendant; JUANITA SIEVERT, ditto; ERNEST McCABE, GWEN PIERCE, rehire; GENOA POWELL and NATIVIDAD REGALADO. Departures: ORA SMITH, JOSEPHINE ARROYO, ISABEL TAPIA, ELEANOR GARNIDA, EATHEL ALLEN, MYRTLE FINDLAY, ALICE WHITE, EDWARD SPEARS and CHARLES VANDERWERT.

Counselor MARGARET STEVENS' cryptic comment: "Life gets more interestinger and interestinger." Ex-day Nurse HARRIETT STEFFENSEN, army lieutenant, is stationed at Camp White, Ore. DON KENNARD is vacationing at Big Bear. JOE BROWN's bruised face is only evidence of his motorcycle accident. OLLIE and RAY LEWALLEN are in Oklahoma. BILLIE PARIS is on sick leave.

Sweet prayer uttered by a girl in finals every time she crawls into a boom: "I hope this boom brings somebody home safe." It's a thought worth passing along.

CHARLES HUBBELL, 69, janitor, is seriously ill. His son, CARL, is in supervision at Plant 1. TERESA McCRYNDLE has returned after a 2½ months' illness. MERILYN HIGLEE of Fontana has left Loma Linda and is recuperating at home. HELEN EDMONDSON will be out about two weeks, due to minor surgery at Pomona Valley hospital. WM. RUHL also underwent surgery and is now home. MILDRED FISCHER of Ontario, ill a month, hopes to return. MARY PACKARD has been ill several weeks. JOSEPHINE FORBES is at Pomona Valley Hospital convalescing after surgery.

MARLENE WALSTON, sweet little Okie of stock, is proudly flashing an engagement ring she received recently (by mail) from CHARLES BULLOCK, U.S.N., her schoolday sweetheart now at a destroyer school in Virginia. He's been in the Navy 2½ years, and gave up hope of placing it on her finger personally. LLOYD GEHRE, in mating, was with Lockheed in Ireland for nine months.

Charles Hadsell, Mrs. Millard Kirkman, Joe Gaglino, have all entertained the Lockheed swing shifters from the canteen platform during the past few days.

VACATIONISTS: Estelle Hines is expected back next Wednesday from a two-week vacation at Balboa Beach and points east. The following are now on vacation: Oliver Colburn, Ollie Bess, E. Asbury, Guy Lloyd, Sylvia Ness, Nellie O'Dell, Walter Teater, C. Heggs, L. Miller, Helen Abbott, John Borba, Charles Bertholdi, Wardwell Bottsford, Andrew Esslemont, Helen Ferguson, Loween Hall, Norman Palmer, Wanda Rhinehart, Ronald Rhinehart, Beatrice Smith, Lorena Stormer, Eldon Sutton, William Walston, Stanley Ruddell, Reber Walston and Mae Bauer.

Bakersfield Bowlers

The Rejectors were catching up in the Bakersfield bowling league but after last Thursday's games they still end up in second place with the Timber Wolves retaining a high lead. Standings at present are as follows:

	POINTS WON	POINTS LOST
Timber Wolves	49	15
Rejectors	42	22
Jiggers	36	28
Pinbusters	35	29
Whiz Kids	33	31
Knotheads	32	32
Buck Passers	32	32
Rolling Bombers	28	36
Pin Kings	29	35
Paper Dolls	23	41
Skaggs Hags	23	41
Floyd's Flirts	22	42

—Invade with War Bonds—

Personality Corner

Plant A-56 employees spent the three-day holiday in a variety of ways. Lucy Marsna, Bill Ellis, Faye Bartlett, Herman Tippitt, Bob Wilson, Lucille Taylor and their families spent the holiday at Pismo Beach. Sam Ramey and friends went picnicing. Julie Miller and family went motor boating. Helen Bostian visited friends in Los Angeles, and Cecille Van Epps entertained friends with a barbecue.

Katheryn Cooper was pleasantly surprised last week by a visit from her son, who is stationed in Redlands, taking naval training.

Edna Laevers' mother and father are visiting here from Arkansas. For the first time in 16 years the whole family is together for a reunion. Cause for a real celebration, don't you think?

Pete Pankonin, group supervisor, is pinch-hitting for Roy Lindstrom, foreman, while Roy is on vacation. 'Tis said Roy can be found up around Bishop wrestling with a fishing pole.

Bulkhead 7, 8 and 9 had a potluck Friday, June 30, in honor of Amos Craig, who is moving to Firebaugh, California, where he plans on taking the ministry of the Southern Baptist Church. He was presented with an engraved Bible by the employees in his group.

The Lockheed Bombers, softball team, won their first game of the season with a 4 to 0 victory over the Emporium. Congratulations to Woody Kreigbaum, pitcher, for pitching the first no-hit game in the league. Highlight of the game was a home run made by Roy Lindstrum with all bases loaded.

The Erlewines, Inez and Ed, entertained a group of friends with a chicken barbecue at their home in Taft Heights recently.

Dept. 19-16 employees honored Fern Caton and Cleta Rodman with a potluck luncheon at the plant last Friday. Cleta is leaving very shortly and Fern was celebrating her birthday.

Welcome to Hilda Fowler, newcomer at Plant 56.

Vacationeers this week include Jane Frank and Louise Harris.

Dorothy Blair, Section 4, has a new grandson, born at the Taft Community Hospital. Proud parents are Mr. and Mrs. Eugene Gregory.

Welcome to Ruth Bisig. Ruth is a recent transfer from Plant B1 and is now located in the Timekeeping Department at Plant 54.

We really hope Sparky Carrico enjoys his vacation this week. Sparky has an absolutely perfect record since date of hire at Plant 54—by absolutely perfect we mean—no tardies, no absences and no time off of any nature.

Both the Shipping Department and Production Records Department showed that they wanted a holiday on the Fourth of July in maintaining a perfect attendance record Sunday, June 26. The Stockrooms also had a 100 per cent attendance.

Mildred Winters is looking forward to a week end visit in Santa Ana with her son, who is in cadet training.

Notice Gene Williams' big broad smile since he became the proud papa of a baby boy.

Fresno Keglers Get Trophies

Lockheed men and women bowlers from both Fresno plants were rewarded for their fine showing, both in City League and plant competition, during the bowling season which ended recently, when they were awarded trophies and medals donated by the LERC at ceremonies held last week in the lunch areas at both plants.

The men's team, entered as the Vega All-Stars, placed fourth in the City League, which was made up of teams from other war industries, power companies and business firms.

The awards, presented at A57 by Superintendent C. U. Wells and at Plant 58 by Assistant Superintendent F. P. Berkenkamp, were given to the following bowlers:

Dick Foreman—High Season Average—170.

Edith Cavell Shield—High 3-Game Average—155.

Bob Becker—High 3-Game Series—577.

Edith Cavell Shield—High 3-Game Series—509.

Elmo Ballard—High Score—229.

Edith Allred—High Score—209.

First place in league competition with 31 wins and 17 losses went to the Bottlenecks, team members being Dave Harder, James Maggie, Ethel Longcor, Paul Bowman and Bill Brandon. The Lockettes, who took first place in feminine competition, were composed of Sharron Marshall, Ethel Longcor, Jean Mooney, Mary Baronian and Doris Hagopian. Taking high 3-game series honors with a total of 2495 pins were the Pirates, who included Dick Foreman, Walt Nilmeier, Lynn Coppedge, Wade Pfaffle and Hal Reese.

—Put Your Savings in Bonds—

Vet Praises P-38's

"That P-38 is the best ship in the air in the South Pacific," asserted P/M 2/C Loren Robison last week upon his return to his Fresno home after 18 months of active duty in the South Pacific battle area. Robison, brother-in-law of Jim Edwards, Dept. 57-24 employee, said no words of praise could be too high for the Lockheed ship, stating that it outclassed any other Allied or Axis plane encountered in that area.

—Build a Postwar Fund—

Children Benefit

The Fresno Buck-of-the-Month Club made its most recent contribution to charity last week when a check for $500 was presented to representatives of the Fresno Society for Crippled Children.

FRESNO

Combat Crews To Get Bonds

Not satisfied with merely putting forth their best efforts on a full-time job of building planes for America's vast air armada, Fresno workers have enthusiastically agreed to back the men who fly those planes on their first combat mission to the extent of a $25 War Bond for each member of the crew.

Scrolls carrying the best wishes of the Fresno employees as well as details of the unique offer will be placed inside one B-17 assembly at Plant 57, and ten P-38 assemblies at Plant 58. The message, addressed to the officer in command of the plane on its first combat mission, will specify that upon receipt of a list of the names of every member of the crew of that plane, a $25 bond will be mailed from the Fresno plants to each airman participating in the mission.

Money for the purchase of the bonds will be obtained by popular donation from the employees of the two subassemblies.

—Back the Attack—

10 Percenters Rate

Recognizing the value of the 10 per cent investor, the Fresno War Finance Committee Employees Division has planned a series of shows honoring the group whose purchases total six per cent of all bonds purchased since Pearl Harbor.

—Your Invasion—Buy War Bonds—

Assembly Lines

TOM HARRIS, staff assistant of Dept. 11-44, is relieving the monotony of wearing a cast with a series of tricky slings. TOMMY broke his left wrist in the second of the three game Softy Softball Series. . . . MARGIE COLEMAN, guardette at Plants 57 and 58, has transferred to production at Plant 57. . . .

The walls of the Personnel office at Plant 57 have been hung with maps of the various war fronts so that girls in that department may keep up with their husbands, one of whom is in England, one in Scotland, one in New Guinea, while a fourth is slugging it out in the foxholes of Fresno. . . .

AL NILMEIER, popular foreman at Plant 57, celebrated his birthday "Double-time Sunday" and left the next day for a well-earned two-weeks' vacation which he plans to spend at Huntington Lake. . . . Welcomed back in Nilmeier's office this week was his petite secretary, MARGI WALKER, who has been enjoying a few days leave with her husband, here on furlough from his camp in Texas. . . .

"Becker's Day" and "Reynolds' Day, universally observed at Plant 58 last week, proved so successful that DICK BECKER, foreman of the plant, and HERB REYNOLDS, department manager of Planning and Control, will again launch their own War Bond drives throughout the plant. BECKER exceeded the quota he had set for himself with several large sales, while REYNOLDS topped BECKER on individual sales of small denomination bonds.

ROD STEVENSON, ace hurler for Plant 58's Swivel Chair Artists, has noticed a decided jump in his fan mail since his pitching copped the Little World Series between Plants 57 and 58. . . . The West Fresno plant boasts some of the most ardent supporters of the Lockheed baseball team, including JACK ENGLERT, LES AKERS, HERB REYNOLDS and DICK BECKER—who can be seen, and heard, every game night rooting for the Interceptors from their own boxes at the Fresno State College ball park. . . .

After three and a half long and weary months, MRS. CORALYNN PATTISON, Employees' Counselor at Plant 57, has enthusiastically discarded the 30-pound plaster cast in which her left arm has been encased since an automobile accident in early March. What would seem an insurmountable obstacle to anyone else has only seemed to increase the activity of "PAT," who has been back at her desk for the past month and a half . . .

EMILY BAXTER, popular Dept. 19-18 employee, has transferred from Fresno A58 to Dept. 51-10, B-1. . . . One of Plant 58's most ardent endorsees of the "Share-the-Ride" plan is JACK McKEAN of Dept. 19-18, whose cooperative attitude should serve as an example for the rest of the employees. . . .

Employees of the Personnel Department at Plant 57 are anxiously scrutinizing each other for any signs of measles, since they were exposed to the childhood disease by Personnel Representative BERT SCHWARZ, who is languishing mournfully at his home counting red spots. . . .

Two Army inspectors bade a sad farewell this week to Plant 58, in particular to the girls of the Personnel Department there, before leaving for new assignments; BOB SCHROEBEL, chief of the Army inspectors, is off for the Pacific Northwest, where he will inspect B-29's being built at Seattle's Boeing plant. . . . while BARBARA KEENEY is transferring to the Standard Oil refinery at Richmond, California. . . .

BRANCH PLANT STAFF
BAKERSFIELD . Helen Newbury
FRESNO . Tom Geoghegan, Jr. Dorothy Hornaday
POMONA . . . Milton Brunk
SANTA BARBARA . . . Rosemary Martin
TAFT . . . . . . Alice Parnell

MALICAY FIRST NETTER IN QUARTER FINALS

Claude Malicay, 36-year-old tennis ace, has come from behind in a series of upsets to be the first to reach the quarter finals in the men's singles events of the current Lockheed tennis playoffs.

Playing out of Dept. 18-58, B-1, Malicay tromped Tom Forrester in the first round 6-2, 6-4 to meet Joe Quint in the second. Quint bowed out to Malicay after two sets of 6-2, 6-1. In the third round Malicay defeated seeded Paul Landwehr in two 6-1 sets to meet the winner of the Jim McDaniel-Joe Gallegos match in the quarter finals.

Malicay began his tennis career in 1936, later to take the doubles championship in the Filipino Southern California Tennis club in 1940 and '41 and to go to the semi-finals in the same loop singles the same years. Last year he reached the semi-finals in the Lockheed singles to be beaten by Leigh Newcomer after three fast sets.

Other netters in the quarter finals in the men's singles as announced by the LERC office are Leigh Newcomer and Don Phillips.

Men's doubles are now beginning the second round of play with the first round results listed as follows:

B. Richards and O. Effertz defeated G. Dishman and F. Gaiser 6-3, 6-4.

Bob Villaluz and Claude Malicay def. B. Manson and C. Armstrong 6-4, 6-4.

R. Shatz and MacHelzel def. Wm. Barker and Fred Dodge 6-2, 6-4.

Wm. Bradley and L. Snow won from O. Ayres and H. Kosieracki—default.

Phil Moore and Heron Riddle def. Roy Beesler and Chas. Locks 6-2, 6-2.

Don Phillips and F. Foster def. Bob Villaluz and C. Malicay 9-7, 8-6.

Kent Wilcox and Robert Browning def. Chas. Sharpe and Stan Gardner 6-2, 6-1.

E. Leppert and Art Bonney def. G. Vold and G. Anderson 6-3, 4-6, 6-1.

H. Bowen and J. Everington def. C. Kotchian and C. Inman 6-3, 6-2.

—Bonds — Good as Gold—

Activities

TOASTMASTERS CLUB—Tuesday, July 11, 1 p.m., Room 4, Commissary Bldg., B-1.

MODEL & HOBBY CLUB — Meeting every other Wednesday, 7 p.m., second floor of Swimming Pool Bldg., at Griffith Park.

PLANT TOURS—11 a.m., 1 p.m. and 7 p.m., every Monday, Tuesday and Wednesday. Apply at B-1 LERC office.

BOY SCOUTS—Troop No. 13 each Wednesday evening, 7 p.m., in Boy Scout Cabin at John Muir Jr. High School, Burbank. Troop No. 17 each Wednesday evening, 7 p.m., at Washington Street School, Burbank.

VICTORY SINGERS — Monday and Wednesday, 7 p.m., L. A. High School, Olympic and Rimpau, Room 423.

CHESS CLUB — Wednesday, 7 p.m., Rooms 1 and 2, Burbank Recreation Center, 1111 W. Olive.

BRIDGE CLUB—Thursday, 7:30 p.m., Burbank Recreation Center, 1111 W. Olive.

DANCES—Swing shift dances after work every Friday at the Burbank Recreation Center, 1111 W. Olive, 1 a.m. Bob Mohr's orchestra.

CONCERTS — Military Band, rehearsal Friday, 9:15 a.m., concerts begin 10:50 a.m., main recreation area, all day shift lunch periods.

SPEAKERS' CLUB — First and third Tuesdays of the month. Next meeting July 18.

BADMINTON—Tuesday and Thursday, 7 p.m., John Burroughs Jr. High gym, Burbank.

BLUE STAR WOMEN—Open House, Blvd. USO, 6551 Hollywood Blvd., Wednesday, 7:30 p.m.

DAY PENGUINETTES-A — Hostesses Hollywood USO, Cahuenga and Selma, every Tuesday, 7 p.m.

PISTOL AND RIFLE CLUB—Training course, Hoover High School, Glendale, Wednesday, 7 p.m.

RHUMBA CLASS—Thursday, 8 p.m., Perry Theatrical Studio, 1735 N. Highland.

GIRLS' SWIMMING—Tuesday, 7 p.m., Hollywood Y.M.C.A., 1553 N. Hudson, Hollywood. Swing shift: Tuesday, 10:30 a.m., same place.

RIDING CLUB — Lockheed Rangers, every Friday, 7 p.m., Pico Stables, 420 Riverside Drive, Burbank. Swing shift: After work Thursday, 1:30 a.m., Pico Stables, 420 Riverside Drive. Call LERC for reservations.

SERVICE STAR WOMEN—Plant B-1, first and third Wednesdays after work. Call LERC for meeting place. Swing shift: Friday, 3:15 p.m., July 7, in Room 3 of Cafeteria Factory B-1.

DAY PENGUINETTES-B — Cabaret Night hostesses, Blvd. USO, every Thursday evening.

—They Bring You Interest—

Keglers

A full season of bowling for Lockheed women was planned at last week's meeting of the Women's Bowling Committee of the LERC. Notable among the coming fall events will be the regular women's handicap leagues and a new 700 scratch league for women, sponsored by the LERC and sanctioned by the Women's International Bowling Congress. Both leagues will begin early in September. Entry blanks are available at either the A or B LERC offices.

—Build a Postwar Fund—

Enter L. A. Net Play

The eight quarter finalists in both the men's singles and doubles brackets of the Lockheed tennis tournament will be automatically entered in the forthcoming 16th Annual Los Angeles Industrial Tennis Tournament starting Sunday, July 23, according to LERC tennis co-ordinator, Art Fiedler.

The Los Angeles Recreation department, sponsors of the event, promise gold trophies for winners and runners up in each event.

This tournament will be open to all Lockheed netters. Applications are available now at either the A or B LERC offices.

—Bonds — A Good Buy—

New Quarters

The Lockheed Badminton club, just ending a successful winter and spring season, will move to the Burbank Recreation Center, 1111 West Olive, this week to begin a new series of meets. The club will meet one night a week with shower and dressing room facilities. There will be no charge for courts. Badminton players may contact Howard Doub, badminton co-ordinator or LERC offices for further particulars.

—Let's Go "Over the Top"—

Table Tourney

Twenty-two men and eighteen women from Unit 58 will begin a two-out-of-three elimination table tennis tourney in their recreation area this week according to Gene Long, LERC representative for the unit.

CONTENDERS. Eleanor Logan, Kathleen Turner and Barbara Challman, three of the seeded contenders for the Lockheed women's tennis crown, represent twenty-nine years of net play. Eleanor's nine years include Glendale and Lockheed tournaments. Kathleen's ten-year tennis career includes Los Angeles Municipal and Southern California mixed doubles play. Barbara began her ten years of tennis in LaGrange, Illinois, school tourneys, rose to quarter finals in Lockheed's '43 singles.

WOLVES NUDGE BUMPERS 1-0 FOR TWELFTH STRAIGHT WIN

The Wolves, undefeated leaders in the Tuesday-Thursday swing shift softball loop, came close to disaster last Tuesday morning at the hands of the Bumpers, who came through with their best game of the season to hold the league leaders to a 1 to 0 victory.

The only score of the day was made in the first inning when the Bumper's pitcher, Tommy Owen, walked Kautz, first man at bat for the Wolves. Catcher Sam Polis followed Kautz with a two-base hit into left field that allowed Kautz to score.

The Wolves, in shutting out the Bumpers, chalked up their 12th straight victory to be undisputed winners of the 1st and 2nd rounds of their league.

The speed play of the Thursday day shift league happened last week in the game between the Flying Tigers and Inspection. The Inspectors had a man on 1st and 2nd with no outs. Third man up hit a line drive to the Tiger's centerfielder, Bill Herrick, who tossed the ball to the 2nd baseman, Bob Mercer, who relayed to Norm Reis at 3rd. Reis tagged the runner for the second out. Reis fired the ball back to Bob Mercer at 2nd for the third out

Scores and standings in all leagues follow:

DAY SHIFT—Monday, June 26

Team	Score	vs.	Team	Score
38-04	7		18-08	5
28-10	7		43-27	5
18-30	7		51-50	0
15-24	9		60-86	2
Tuesday, June 27				
37-82	4		43-20	1
58-03	16		15-08	0
28-10	8		44-22	6
Wednesday, June 28				
55-30	10		71-60	8
18-26	7		51-10	0
83-43	9		26-03	3
67-75	15		41-34	5
Thursday, June 29 (Burbank Recreation)				
51-10	5		38-03	2
72-25	8		28-20	2
38-04	8		72-25	7
Thursday, June 29 (North Hollywood)				
35-37	11		27-31	5
57	7		35-38	5
60-86	22		81-22	6
SWING SHIFT				
Tuesday and Thursday—June 27 and 29				
18-04	1		17-13	0
28-26	7		44-52	0
17-29	7		62-73	0
Wednesday, June 28				
14-59	9		38-04	3
35-38	9		14-16	2
17-29	7		14-12	0
DAY SHIFT—Plant B-4				
81-24	4		14-21	3
44-29	8		81-24	4

STANDINGS:

Team	Dept.	Plant	Won	Lost
Monday League (Second Round)				
Dept. 15-24	15-24	A-1	2	0
The Squirts	18-28	B-6	2	0
Wolves	38-04	B-1	1	0
Templers	43-27	A-1	1	1
Tooling	28-10	B-1	1	1
Wilson's Okies	60-86	B-1	0	1
Receivers	51-50	A-1	0	2
Knockabouts	18-08	B-1	0	2
Tuesday League (Second Round)				
B-1 Transp.	55-30	B-1	2	0
Q.C.'s	58-03	B-1	2	0
Rebels	57-82	A-1	2	0
"P-38"	18-20	B-1	1	1
Dark Horse	28-10	B-1	1	1
The Eight Balls	15-08	A-1	0	2
Blockbusters	44-22	B-1	0	2
Wood Shop	43-28	B-1	0	2
Wednesday League (Second Round)				
Spare Parts	67-75	B-1	2	0
P-38 Preflight	18-26	B-1	1	0
Office Gang	83-43	B-1	1	0
Transports	55-30	A-1	1	0
Engineers	71-60	A-1	1	1
Mfg. Engrs.	26-03	B-1	0	1
Material Control	51-10	A-1	0	2
Mechs	41-34	A-1	0	2
Thursday League (Bur. Rec.) Second Round				
Flying Tigers	51-10	B-1	4	0
Processers	38-04	B-1	3	1
Inspection	38-03	B-1	2	2
Ebees	72-25	B-1	2	2
The Undecideds	72-25	B-1	1	3
Lards	28-20	B-1	0	4
Thursday League (North Hollywood)				
Shop Leaders	35-37	A-1	3	0
Rabble Rousers	60-86	A-1	2	1
Constellations	57	A-2	1	1
Sub-Majors	35-38	A-1	1	2
Yardbirds	27-31/13-20	A-1	0	1
Costers	81-22	B-1	0	2
SWING SHIFT STANDINGS:				
Tuesday & Thursday League (2nd Round)				
Wolves	18-04	B-1	6	0
Blue Jays	28-26	B-1	5	1
Bumpers	17-13	A-2	4	2
Toolers	17-29	A-2	3	3
Fivers	62-73	B-5	2	4
Welders	17-04	A-2	1	5
Wednesday League				
Sun Dodgers	14-59	B-2	4	0
The Outlaws	35-38	A-1	4	0
Vagabonds	17-29	A-2	2	2
Plant 7	14-16	B-7	1	3
Midnight Ramblers	14-12	B-2	1	3
Moonshiners	38-06	B-1	0	4
STANDINGS, DAY SHIFT, B-4:				
First Round				
Bums	44-29	B-4	1	0
Peppers	81-24	B-4	1	1
Wildcats	14-21	B-4	0	1
Spooks	14-21	B-4	0	0

LECTURER. "Runs begin and end here," Captain Nick Puglizevich, emphasizes as he dusts off home plate for all his teammates to see. The teammates are the crack swing shift Wolves who have weathered two rounds of the Tuesday-Thursday swing shift league undefeated. Last week's 1 to 0 battle with the Bumpers was their toughest.

His Gift—3 Lightnings

Idea Champion Hits with 110

Three Lockheed Lightning P-38 fighters a year—completely assembled and ready to fly away to the fighting fronts.

That is the personal, one-man gift to the Army Air Forces made by Jack Peslin, champion idea man of the Lockheed Work Simplification Employee Proposal for Improvement program. Peslin, 36-year-old former creamery company limerick contest manager and now an experimental mechanic at Lockheed Factory B-1, has submitted 322 proposals for improvement. Of these, 110 have been accepted and installed with an aggregate payoff to Peslin of $2423.50.

The 24,000 man-hours saved in one year by all of Peslin's accepted proposals are the equivalent of man-hours required to build and assemble three complete P-38 fighters. A few other Lockheed workers have saved even more man-hours but not one comes even close to Peslin in the number of ideas submitted or proposals accepted.

A majority of Peslin's proposals are for improvements in detail assembly at Factories B-2 and B-7 where he worked until recently. They range from reworking jigs to changes in operations and eliminations or revisions in area set-ups. His biggest single check was for $263, he has averaged $22.03 per check and he is known to his shop pals as "Jack Pot" Peslin because he often hits it with as many as half a dozen checks at one time.

Peslin's recipe for success in the Proposal for Improvement program is a right approach to the subject—that is, to confine his ideas in general to his own bench and that of others in his work section. He doesn't "go prospecting" with numerous theoretical improvements in departments other than his own.

—Your Invasion—Buy War Bonds—

Lockheed At War

AN EIGHTH AAF FIGHTER STATION, ENGLAND—1st Lt. Merle E. Blanchard, 24-year-old Lightning fighter pilot, and former worker in the experimental department at Lockheed, has been awarded the Distinguished Flying Cross. The award was for extraordinary achievement in shooting down a Messerschmitt 109 in an air battle with the Luftwaffe on the Dutch-German border, and for participating in 40 combat missions over occupied Europe.

PATTERSON FIELD, O.—Pvt. Ruth Pflueger, former Lockheed material control clerk, has now finished her WAC basic training and has been assigned to the Supply Division of Air Service Command headquarters here.

NEW HAVEN, CONN.—Leonard Bellman, formerly employed in Lockheed's Dept. 32 as parts investigator, has entered the Army Air Forces Training Command at Yale University as an aviation cadet in communications.

AN EIGHTH AAF FIGHTER STATION, ENGLAND — S/Sgt. Elmo K. Moen, former Lockheed stock clerk, has been awarded the Army's Good Conduct Medal. He is one of the ground personnel commended by headquarters when flyers from their station shot down 25 German planes in one afternoon.

AN EIGHTH AAF BOMBER STATION, ENGLAND—2nd Lt. Charles M. Hepworth, 24-year-old navigator on a B-17, has been presented an Oak Leaf Cluster to the Air Medal for meritorious achievement during heavy bombing raids on vital Nazi targets in Europe. He formerly served as general mechanic in Dept. 16.

NEW HAVEN, CONN.—Julian J. Schmidt, former Lockheed service mechanic, has entered the AAF Training Command School at Yale University as an aviation cadet in communications.

New Phone Numbers at A-1

Telephone numbers at Factory A-1 will be changed next Wednesday, July 12, making it necessary for all telephone users to consult new directories, which will be in their hands at that time.

Remember! Don't trust your memory in making a phone call to Factory A-1 next Wednesday and thereafter!

Consult your new directory before dialing any number there. Old ones will be obsolete. Look up the new ones and save confusion.

Not all Factory A-1 numbers will be changed, but to play safe, look them up in the new book before dialing.

Only numbers in the 300, 400, 500, and 600 groups will be changed as follows:

300 group will become 2600
400 group will become 2400
500 group will become 2500
600 group will become 1000

This change in numbers will affect the first two digits only. For example, if your number is 312, it will become 2612; if it is 412, it will become 2412; if it is 512, it will become 2512; if it is 612, it will become 1012. At the time of this number change the new directories will be in the hands of every employee.

'Bad Penny' and the Japs ★ ★ ★

(Continued from Page 1)

live Japs. You couldn't see them, but you knew they were there all right.

Then "Bad Penny" dipped her left wing, then her shark nose, and we went down in a wild dive. A screaming dive that seemed it would never end.

Down on my knees beside Bill, staring through the plexiglass floor windows, I saw first the breakers, then the shallow water of the reef, then the bomb-splattered shore line ripping into view so close, it seemed we could nearly touch it. Then "Bad Penny" was lurching up from the dive, pressing us so hard against the floor, it seemed we'd go through it.

"Bombs away," Bill yelled in my ear.

Then down there under our feet blossomed a great black and yellow geyser of earth and debris, then another and another, as our bombs stomped along the runway with giant strides.

There was no time to look for anti-aircraft. No time to be scared. Only time for swift exulting as the bombs chewed a furious way across that Jap airfield.

Grinning from ear to ear, Bill slowly sat up from the guns and raised and clasped hands in a prize-fighter's salute. Then with vast deliberation, he ran one grimy forefinger across his brow, squeezing about a quart of sweat.

"Whew," he said.

A few hours later we slipped down to Betio's runway and jeeped to the operations shack. A few minutes ahead of us landed the other plane with her rudder control shot away, a six-inch shattered hole in the tail and another hole as big as a man's head through the wing within a foot of the engine.

Bishop was standing thoughtfully in the middle of the room.

"You want to see a brand-new Christian?" he said.

THE LOCKHEED STAR

The Lockheed Star is issued every Friday for the employees of Lockheed Aircraft Corporation, and is the official publication of the company. Communications should be addressed to the Editor, *Lockheed Star*, Publicity Department, Lockheed Aircraft Corporation, Burbank, California, U.S.A. The editor assumes no responsibility for acknowledgment or return of contributions.

PAUL BAILEY, Editor.

Associates:
H. L. ROSSON, J. H. PRESCOTT.

Is it Here?

Ads "For Sale" and "Wanted" are to be written up on Form 4929 and sent to the Employee Service Dept. at either Factory A or B.

The procedure for selling cars is a little different. Car ads are sent to the Employee Transportation Dept. where a permanent file is made up on the cars listed. More information can be kept on file in Transportation than can be squeezed in two lines in the Classified Section. (That is the limit, two lines.) For this additional information on "Cars for Sale" ask the clerk in the Transportation Department, giving her the file number. The Transportation Dept. doesn't like telephone calls, they want to keep the cars in the Lockheed family.

FOR SALE

ANIMALS:

KITTENS, (4) 2 mos. old. Will give awa 1 or as many as wanted. CL 6-6768.
LAYING battery, doz. hens, roosts, nests, feed and water pans. 1721 N. Avon St.
PUPPIES, Great Dane, fawn and brindle. ST 5-1895, mornings or Sundays.
PUPPIES, English Pointer, purebred, liver and white. ST 5-2990 after 6:30.
LAYING battery and hens. AL 9371.

FURNITURE:

BED divan, club chair, rug, mattress, spring, stove, other furniture. CH 6-3268.
BEDROOM set, twin beds, chest, dresser, night stand and chair. WA 9412.
DINING set, walnut, large round table, 6 chairs. CH 6-1646.
FIREPLACE set, beautiful, highly polished, andirons, screen, etc. AL 1897.
FURNITURE, 4 rooms, linens, drapes, silverware, kitchenware. WA 6282.
FURNITURE. AL 9371.
ICE box, all metal, 100 lb. 2129 Pepper St., Burbank before 3:00 p.m.
LIVING room set, Monterey davenport, day bed, arm chairs. CH 8-8219 after 5:00 p.m.
RADIO, Stromberg Carlson, console. NO 2-1293.
SEWING machine, treadle. ST 5-4765.
STOVE, Detroit vapor, table top, 4 burners, good cond. NO 2-3858.
STOVE, table top, must sell quickly. RU 6-1724.
YOUTH bed, maple, like new, pre-war spring, innerspring mattress. AN 2-2224.
ROASTER, Everhot elec. Excel. cond. NO 21695, 5 to 6 p.m.
SCOOTER for child, like new. HI 4716 after 5 p.m.
TAYLOR TOT, excel. cond., prewar model. SU 18489.
BABY BUGGY, prewar. CL 66772.

HOUSES:

6 rm., with 3 bdrms. 1119 Leland Way, Burbank.
5 rm., stucco, newly redecorated, corner lot 95x130. Vacant. AT 2-1802.
5 rm. 14504 So. Brand Blvd., San Fernando. Call S. F. 3428.

MUSICAL INSTRUMENTS:

BANJO, tenor, Gibson, leather case. Good cond. AL 3076.
SAXOPHONE, E flat alto. Fred Reinecke, ST 4-4646.
SAXOPHONE, tenor, Buescher, overhauled, like new. Reasonable. CH 8-9505.
TRUMPET, Wurlitzer, with case. 3648 10th Ave., Los Angeles.

SPORTING GOODS:

BOAT, 20' commercial fishing, and equip. WE 3-1970.
CAMERA, Robot automatic sequence, F 2.8 Tessar lens. 7051 Coldwater Canyon, N. H.
GUN, Smith and Wesson Magnum 357, new F.B.I. model. Shells. SU 2-6320.
OCEAN fishing outfit, record changer. 3449 Mayfield Ave. La C.
REVOLVER, 32 Colt in A-1 cond. AX 2-6194.
SLOOP, small cabin, 2 bunks, sink and stove. Fast and roomy. CH 8-2419.
TENNIS racquet, men's "Keds," riding boots, size 11. 918 Beacon Ave., Apt. 408, L. A.

MISCELLANEOUS:

BABY buggy, good cond. AX 1-4150.
EARPHONE, new Zenith. H. Rogers, 517 S. Kenneth Rd., Burbank. CH 6-3342.
OXFORDS, lady's soft kid, leather soles, 8½B; silk housecoat. CI 1-5459.
PLAY pen, hardwood, on casters. Baby auto bed, A-1 cond. 1802 W. Winona, Burbank.
RADIO, '41 Chev., 8 tube, push button Motorola. Price reasonable. NO 2-2935.
TYPEWRITER, L. C. Smith standard. Good cond. NO 2-4514.
WATCH, Elgin railroad, 17 jewel, gold, small size, excel. cond. CI 1-4747.
CANNING jars, 3 doz. Kerr, quart size; 2 mattress covers. SU 2-0821.

WANTED

APRICOTS, for canning, will pick if near Burbank. CH 6-8835.
AUTO tire, 6:50x19. NO 2-1695, after 5.
BABY buggy, any style, cond. or age, to buy, rent or lease. WE 8768.
CAMERA, good candid, capable of taking fast pictures. RO 1842.
CHEVROLET, 1933-36 model. GR 9808.
LAMP, physio therapy, with stand. P. O. Box 406, Glendale.
REFRIGERATOR, elec., medium size, any make. 631 Hollywood Way, Burbank.
SPANISH language record set. CH 8-8401.
WASHING machine, in working cond. H. Klett, 6836 Cedros Ave., V. N.
WASHING machine, any make. AL 3397.
WASHING MACHINE and Ironer in good cond. 12605 Gilmore, N. Hlywd.
WASHING MACHINE, good cond. Wood or coal-burning kitchen stove. TW 9855.
LUGGAGE, several pieces, good quality, matched, 1 or more with hanger. SU 20821.

LOST AND FOUND

Lost and Found has become systematized, and it does simplify things for the clerk not to have to run hither and yon and wonder if maybe somebody stuck it in his bottom drawer until he got around to doing something better with it. Now she just looks through the cards made up on articles turned in and when a card is there at least she knows she is looking for something. You know there is a difference in looking for something one doesn't know whether or not is there and looking for something that is around.

Articles turned in and unclaimed are a man's wrist watch, keys with a "General Foods Sales Co." tag, coin purse with patent belt, glasses, and some eye shades

LOST AND FOUND (Cont.)

that a man left in the housing section.

Among the articles that have been held for a long time, is a gold, heart-shaped locket inscribed "Mother from Bob and Jack." We hate to dispose of this as it has a picture of two cute little boys in it, and we are sure someone would like to have it back.

Uncle Sam says quite a few people leave things besides letters at the Lockheed Branch Post Office. If they are not claimed within 30 days they are sent in to the main Post Office. Maybe you left it at the Lockheed Post Office when you mailed that package.

LOST:

CROSS, black onyx with small gold cross in center. Reward for return. CH 8-9174.
MARINE pin, studded with rhinestone chips. Special memento. Reward. HE 5296.
PARKER fountain pen, initials HEM. Reward. Phone San Fernando 207.

VEHICLES FOR SALE

BICYCLES:

GIRL'S full size, good cond. $30. No. 266.
SILVER King, chromium frame and fenders, new balloon tires. $60. No. 267.

BUICK:

'40 convertible coupe, very good rubber and top. No. 268.
'39 convertible club coupe, good cond. No. 269.

CHEVROLET:

'41 convertible, red leather upholstery, excel. cond. $1200. No. 270.
'40 Cabriolet convertible, deluxe model, good cond. $1150. No. 271.
'37 master deluxe sedan, good tires, mechanically perfect. $450. No. 272.
'36 master deluxe coupe, radio, very clean. $425. No. 273.
'35 coach, recently overhauled. No. 274.
'31 coupe. $175. No. 275.

CHRYSLER:

'42 New Yorker, excellent cond. No. 276.
'38 coupe, radio, heater, A-1 cond. No. 277.
'37 coach, radio, heater, overdrive. $600. No. 278.
'37 coupe, good tires, motor, radio, heater. Sell or trade for sedan. No. 279.

DODGE:

'39 four door sedan, excel. cond. $895. No. 280.

FORD:

'41 club coupe, heater, radio, excel. cond. $1175. No. 281.
'41 coupe, 21,000 miles, Motorola radio, good cond. $1050. No. 282.
'41 super deluxe sedan. $950. No. 283.
'41 super deluxe station wagon, low mileage, good tires. $1795. No. 284.
'40 tudor, pre-war tires, excel. motor, radio, heater. $1095. No. 285.
'39 deluxe coupe, A-1 cond., radio, clock, overdrive. No. 286.
'38 coupe, radio, new paint, good tires. $550. No. 287.
'35 V-8 roadster, good top and tires, rebuilt motor. $350. No. 288.
'29 Model A coupe, rebored motor, new Grade I tire, 2 new retreads. $130. No. 289.

LA SALLE:

'37 sedan, first class cond., radio and heater. $425. No. 290.

MOTOR SCOOTERS:

'40 Powell. No. 291.
'40 Powell Streamliner. No. 292.

MOTORCYCLES:

'38 Harley Davidson, saddle bags and 16" wheels. No. 293.

OLDSMOBILE:

'40 station wagon, new seat covers, radio, heater. $1150. No. 294.
'39 convertible coupe, ivory color, going in service. $850. No. 295.

PACKARD:

'40 two door sedan, motor overhauled, excel. cond. $1245. No. 296.

PLYMOUTH:

'41 club coupe, recently overhauled, good tires and paint. $1195. No. 297.
'41 deluxe four door sedan in good cond., good tires, radio, heater. $1175. No. 298.
'40 deluxe convertible, heater, radio, excel. cond. $1125. No. 299.
'36 four door sedan, 5 very good tires. $300. No. 300.
'35 four door sedan for sale or trade. $295. No. 301.
'35 sedan, radio, good tires, good gas mileage. No. 302.

STUDEBAKER:

'30 Dictator, new top, good rubber, good mileage. $125. No. 303.

Zero Adds Up

A wrecked Jap Zero, worth less than that to anyone in the land of the Rising Sun, has earned its weight in gold in America after being repaired by Lockheed Customer Service.

Resourceful men of this department transformed the twisted wreckage found on a Guadalcanal beach, into an accurate resemblance of its original condition. After first being shown to Lockheed people last October it was taken over by the Naval Aid Auxiliary and has since been touring 125 American cities.

It has been described as "worth its weight in gold" in fund-raising campaigns.

LOCKHEED
Star
PUBLICATION OF THE LOCKHEED AIRCRAFT CORPORATION
BURBANK, CALIFORNIA, U.S.A., OCTOBER 20, 1944
No. 22
ROLL WELD MAGIC
(Story Page 2)

Lockheedian in Orient Reveals Perils of Job

Lifeline of the only Allied fighting front that has yet to enjoy the taste of surging victory, China's Burma Road inches forward today by the toil of Chinese farmers directed by American Army engineers.

One of them is Joseph W. Toland of Alhambra, technician 5th grade, who once worked for Lockheed.

"Ding Hao Highway" is the G.I. name for the famous highway, Toland writes.

Americans Best

As he and other engineers commanded by Col. Robert R. Neyland pass along the road, the Chinese workers rise from the roadside shouting "Mey guo, ding hao," meaning "Americans are the best."

"Ding Hao Highway" is open. But 20 per cent grades, hundreds of hairpin turns and breath-taking heights, with the road balancing itself on the ridge, sometimes above the clouds, cause tremendous problems. Alongside, a budding airport competes for space with rice paddies and corn fields, while tiny, wiry ponies pulling coal-laden carts and herds of cattle make way for supply trucks, frontline-bound.

Build 600 Miles

Toland has traveled the road almost up to the Japanese lines. He's seen the peak of Tien Tz Miao where a hundred coolies busily chewed out pieces of the mountain, making wider the highest and sharpest curve of all. A "tzan tzu" or spade, a bamboo stick with two hanging baskets and a broad Chinese back is all the equipment. With only these, 500,000 men, women and children from 12 to 66 years of age built the first Burma Road.

China: Going Is Tough

Radio Talent To Be Signed

Jack Johnstone, producing and directing Lockheed's "The Man Called X," Blue Network, Saturdays, 7:30-8 p.m. PWT, is organizing a permanent stock company of top-flight players to support Herbert Marshall, the program's star, and Ge-Ge Pearson who portrays his flip young fiancee.

First to have their names inscribed on Johnstone's roster of "regulars" are Steve Geray, former star of the "Follies Bergere" and now one of the films' outstanding character comedians; Jeanette Nolan, for ten years one of radio's most talented personalities; Theodore Von Eltz, a veteran of both stage and screen; and Frank Graham, long recognized as one of the most versatile air-wave actors.

Johnstone plans to add at least ten more players to the stock list as soon as the right ones are available.

FORTY-NINER DAY SLATED FOR SUNDAY TO AID CONSTELLATION

Sunday, Oct. 22, has been designated Forty-Niner Day for certain sections of fabrication and subassembly, it was announced early this week by F. Penn Holter, Factory B works manager. Those employes affected have already been notified by their supervision.

The day follows by two weeks the Sunday devoted by the tooling departments to an all-out effort on behind-schedule Model 49 work. A similar day is to be designated for Factory A and B assembly departments.

"We've been accumulating our energies for a big Forty-Niner Day here at B," Holter said, "and we're expecting a 100 per cent response to our requests for turn-out."

The idea of devoting one Sunday in each division exclusively to Model 49 work came as a result of increased Army demands for Constellation deliveries. The expanding operations of the Pacific war, it was pointed out, have created urgent need for the Constellation's outstanding qualities of speed, range, and capacity. The current Army contract of 260 airplanes calls for deliveries at a rate which accelerates rapidly during the next few months.

"Our goal is high," Holter explained, "and nothing short of our best efforts will enable us to meet it. An added day, a Sunday, will help us immeasurably in catching up on our schedule."

Forty-Niner Day was originally planned as a day of contest, of whisker-growing, of fun, but in view of the seriousness of the need, such ideas were abandoned and the work in the tooling departments on Sunday, Oct. 8, was performed without fanfare or publicity.

"Forty-Niner Day is a joint program," Holter continued. "Mr. Prudden and Mr. Stackhouse are in hearty accord. We all realize the urgency of the need for increased Constellation production—for the war effort —for the peace."

DESLUDGER IS YET IN HIDING

Mystery of the lost 800-pound desludger whose disappearance was described in last week's *Star* was still unsolved at a late hour last night.

Paul Briggs, executive assistant of Reagan Stunkle, customer service department manager, reported having received many tips on its possible location but none of them produced the missing machine. Phone number of Briggs office in Plant B-5 is 6-3319.

STEWARDESS SPOTS EXCITING EVENTS

ONCE she waded through folding money ankle-deep and another time she shocked a famous comedian, but her first air ride with one of Lockheed's ace test pilots was a never-to-be-forgotten experience of Esther Jo Connor, lovely Western Airlines stewardess.

As a 17-year-old Montebello High School student, Esther Jo and her girl friends used to watch pilots at the old East Los Angeles Airport. One of them was Tony Levier, who now flies Lockheed experimental planes.

"Tony kept urging me to take a ride with him, but I had never been up and was timid," she said. "When I learned he had made a sizeable bet that he could persuade me to try it, I felt sorry for him and accepted.

"I regretted it almost before we left the ground in his small plane. His roistering pals were right after us and Tony dodged them with all the aerial stunts in the book. It's a wonder I ever flew again."

Her experience with the actor occurred on a Western Airlines flight from San Diego to the Lockheed Air Terminal.

Miss Connor, who has logged 10,000 hours and a million miles in the air was relaxing in a seat and the noted comic had his arm over the back of the chair as he chatted with her. The girl's blue eyes twinkled as she related the incident yesterday at L.A.T.

"He seemed quite engrossed in the conversation or something," she said, "and his arm dropped to my shoulder. It dropped lower and lower while we talked.

"Suddenly he jumped nearly out of the seat and exclaimed, 'My God! Are all stewardesses equipped like that?'

"His hand had felt the edge of a metal brace I was wearing around my waist as the result of an accident."

Once in a coffee shop just before leaving on a flight to Las Vegas, a man with a ticket to Oakland wanted to change his flight plans when he learned the destination of Esther Jo.

"But that would cost a lot of money," he was told.

To prove he had enough to buy a new ticket, he pulled greenbacks from his shirt till they covered the floor like leaves. He had been lucky at Santa Anita!

Esther Jo Connor

AIR MEDALS GIVEN

Air Medals have been presented to two former Lockheed workers, Flight Officer Harry A. Lindsay with the 8th AAF in England and Lt. Robert W. Hill with the 15th AAF in Italy. Officer Lindsay attended Los Angeles City College and the University of California, while Lt. Hill, former aircraft electrician, is a resident of Glendale and graduate of Glendale Union High School.

Roll Weld Seen As Vital Factor In Manufacture

Accidental invention of the "Gay Nineties," the process of roll-spot-welding as developed by Lockheed half a century later has added strength and speed to the wings of today's warbirds.

Strength, because a joint of metal fused by the heat of an electric current is stronger than the metal itself . . . and speed because spot-welds have replaced rivets to decrease the weight of planes.

Lockheed Invention

What promises to be one of the most important contributions to the sc ence of welding was developed by Lockheed research engineers who have invented a machine called a Spot-Weld Monitor.

According to F. R. Shanley, division engineer of the Engineering Research Department, biggest problem of the trade is the perfection of adequate controls—how to maintain exact standards in the performance of machines set up to produce a weld of given strength.

The Spot-Weld Monitor, Shanley says, seems to be the best answer to the problem.

Using an experimental unit made by Lockheed research engineers as a model, General Electric has been asked to produce Spot-Weld Monitors according to Lockheed specifications.

Guided by George Arrowood, foreman of Factory B-1's Dept. 18-58, and his predecessors, Lockheed has become one of the foremost users of spot-welding in the United States. The cover of today's *Star* is a tribute to the importance of spot and roll welding.

By removing braces from wing interiors and inserting extra gas tanks, P-38 fighting planes gained the cruising range of bombers but not until the strength these braces gave had been replaced by spot-welded doublers.

Production Jumps

Using improved methods of spot-welding, the company jumped its production of drop-tanks from 20 to an average of 278 a day and dropped their cost from $678 to $87 apiece. Other factors were a part of this achievement but spot-welding cannot be minimized.

"Would you be willing to hang from the roof of Los Angeles' 19-story City Hall, suspended by a metal strap you had spot-welded together?"

That's the type of test-question frequently asked of employes in the department by their section supervisor, young, dynamic John Sweeney.

City Hall Roof

When one comes to him with a new spot-weld job of sheer strength, Army specified at, say, 250 pounds, he looks at him and says: "Well, you weigh about 175 pounds, don't you? Would you be willing to trust that weld to hold you suspended from the City Hall roof?"

Cover

ROLL welding holds cover position on the *Star* this week; one of the most important mechanical functions in modern manufacture.

The welder is shown in operation upon a plane cargo door. The photograph was taken by Lockheed.

LOCKHEED LOOKS ACROSS SEAS

HIRES SLUMP; MATTSON BIDS FOR EMPLOYES

"Employment slipped..."

These terse words from M. V. Mattson, employment manager, summarized bluntly the fact that there are "still plenty of jobs at Lockheed." He urged again that referral slips be used and that all employes realize that the need for production personnel is immediate and demanding.

"This last week saw us still in the net gain column for the third successive time," Mattson continued, "but our net over terminations was only 31 as against 179 the week before. We engaged 812 persons and lost 781.

Unlucky Friday

"I think the bogie of 'Friday the thirteenth' had something to do with our slipping," Mattson explained. "Comparing new employment on Fridays 6 and 13, the thirteenth was off 8½ per cent.

"Several persons hired previously to 'go to work on Friday' discovered later that it was the thirteenth and called the employment office to postpone. 'It's a bad day to start a new job any place,' they told us. 'What about coming in Monday?

"Of those we are employing, we gain two women for every man. While we need the women, the demand for men is even greater. This is particularly true on the Constellation line where there is considerable heavy type work to be done. However, terminations now average one and one-half women for every man ... which tends toward a proper balance."

Tuesdays Heavy

Mattson said that Tuesday was always the heaviest day in each week for new hires.

"Apparently, folk think that it's a good idea to get a job early ... but not on Monday; you know ... after Sunday's play or beset by the proverbial Monday 'blues.' So Tuesday is peak and hires fall away from it with surprising regularity. Faster service, then, is available to applicants who choose one of the other days to call.

"But, by all means, tell your friends to come," Mattson stressed, "on Tuesday ... or at any other time. There are good jobs at Lockheed ... and the war is not over.

BARRINGER IS IN NAVY NOW

John B. Barringer, department manager of plant engineering at the Navy-Lockheed Service Center has just left the company to start a two months' indoctrination course at Harvard after being commissioned as a supply corps officer of the U.S. Navy.

One of the designers of the big $3,500,000 modification base at Van Nuys, he joined Lockheed five years ago.

He was born in St. Louis in 1916, was graduated from the University of Arizona and resides in Glendale.

George Beohm . . . and Constellation

LERC Nominees for All Offices Are Selected; Balloting Is Set Oct. 26

Bob O'Hanlon, chairman of the Election committee, last night announced names of nominees for president, vice-president, secretary, treasurer, and members-at-large for the LERC.

The annual election will be held in the private dining rooms of the B-1 Cafeteria Building, Thursday, Oct. 26, following a dinner to be served at 6 p.m.

For the office of president the committee has nominated William Ellis, incumbent, and Jerry Sickler, present vice-president. Ellis was elected to the presidency of the club in April of 1944 and has been chairman of the Salary and Commissary committees. Prior to his term of office he was active in affairs of the recreation club and served as council member. He is a past president of the popular Factory A Penguin Club.

Sickler has been associated with the LERC for the past three years and has served as vice-president for the past three terms, being a member of the Salary and Commissary committees. Formerly he was a member of the Budget and Educational committees.

(Continued on Page 8)

REPRESENTATIVE IS SENT TO AUSTRALIA

Attuned to foreign markets as an adjunct to domestic postwar trade, the Lockheed Aircraft Corporation has just announced appointment of George Beohm, Australian aircraft engineer and former manufacturer, as direct factory representative in that Commonwealth.

Beohm, who has been conferring with Lockheed executives here, has arrived safely in Sydney. For the past three years he has been director of Australian War Supplies Procurement in charge of the Los Angeles office. Prior to that time he was traveling for the Australian government as an aircraft production engineer.

In Flying Corps

Since 1914, when he joined the Australian Flying Corps as an engineer, Beohm has been associated continuously with the aircraft industry ... save for his current war service. He established the Mandated Territories Airways to operate from the New Guinea coast to interior gold fields.

In 1928 he became the co-director of the General Aircraft Company, designing the first Australian-built light plane to carry three passengers, the Genaco. He served, too, as chief engineer for Quantas Empire Airways in Singapore, operating the run from Australia to England, and as ground engineer for Wearne's Air Services, flying a Malay States route.

Will Take Over

Representing Lockheed in Australia and New Zealand at the present time is the firm of Brown and Dureau, Ltd., with whom Lockheed has enjoyed several years of splendid business relations. Arrangements have been made for Beohm gradually to assume the Brown and Dureau spares and service commitments, and expect all negotiations to be completed by the first of the year.

This is the result of the Lockheed postwar policy of shaping a global organization with direct factory representation rather than agency connections. These factory sales and service offices will carry a full line of components for all Lockheed aircraft from small feeder line transports to transocean liners, the forerunner of which is the Constellation.

Supplementing the announcement of his appointment by Lockheed, Beohm said:

"I have had occasion during the three years I spent in the United States to study all the aircraft manufacturers. The American aviation industry has done a phenomenal job. Nowhere else in the world are production marvels being achieved to equal what is being done there.

Ships Win Praise

"Lockheed is doing a splendid job of turning out fighting planes —Lightning P-38's, PV-1 Venturas, and B-17's. Production on all models remains ahead of a stiff schedule.

"Lockheed is thinking, too, of the future," Beohm added. "In fact, it is in the future now— with the finest land-based transport the world has ever seen, the Constellation. It will not be long before this great ship is flying the airways of the world.

(Continued on Page 8)

Forty Loaned to Help with PV's

Expediting wing construction on Lockheed's now famed Venturas for the Navy, 40 men will leave Lockheed Air Terminal at 11 a.m. tomorrow via Navy Air Transport for the Goodyear plant in Phoenix, Ariz. These Lockheed employes will be on duty there for 60 days.

This announcement to the *Star* was made last night by D. T. McGreagor, manager of B-17 and PV sub-contracts for the Lockheed general department. He indicated that a personnel specialist would accompany the loaned employes.

"We want to help Goodyear as much as we can," McGreagor said. "The Navy is calling urgently for Venturas." According to Commander Palmer, Navy representative here, there is no plane so suited for their type of work as the PV's.

"Goodyear has been helping with wings. The Navy needs them rapidly and Lockheed is lending a hand."

New Gadget Made By AAF Lockheedian

One simple hand tool, designed by Pfc. Melvin R. Hoopes, former Lockheed final assembly man, for stripping insulation from wire used in assembling radios, is now saving countless man-hours in the Signal Maintenance Section of an aircraft repair and modification depot ... deep in the heart of England. This word was released officially last night.

VENTURAS AGAIN SLUG JAP CENTERS

With a score of five Jap ships sunk and six damaged, another Navy patrol squadron of Lockheed PV-1's just returned from the Central Pacific for a needed rest and reforming.

Achieving pin-point navigational objectives during night attacks in howling rainstorms, the squadron flew 325 bombing sorties to help wrest control of the Marshall Islands from the enemy.

As reported yesterday by the squadron's commanding officer, Lt. Comdr. Clayton L. Miller of Seattle, night attacks on Mille Island airfield effectively paralyzed the strategic base while American forces moved upon Kwajalein.

First kill was made by Lt. David J. Walkinshaw of Ontario, California, whose Ventura sunk an armed inter-island steamer after three runs at mast height.

Lt. William O. Kuencer of Long Beach, zooming over tree tops of a Jap administrative center in the Marshalls saw a large steamer in the harbor.

Though within range of fighter planes from four enemy bases and 350 miles from his own base, he made three strafing and bombing runs, dropping two 500-pound bombs squarely on the target.

At Ailinglapalap, Lt. Jack M. Swenson of Minneapolis, sank a patrol boat and another vessel was sent to the bottom of Jaluit Atoll lagoon.

Word that the Japs might be expected to conduct an operation from their airfields at Nauru Island brought orders to attack that by-passed area.

The entire squadron of Venturas made the assault and in the face of intense fire from the ground which bracketed every ship, dropped nine tons of bombs on runways and installations.

Fighting PV

Tales of Wild Fighting Related by P-38 Pilots

By JACK PRESCOTT

Streaking head-on toward each other faster than sound were two fighter planes — a Messerschmitt and a P-38. One of them had to give way.

But it wasn't Lt. Phil Tovrea of an Italy-based fighter group who somewhat reluctantly told about it on a visit to Lockheed last week.

Reluctantly because, "Hell," he said, "it's nothing to talk about . . . anyone else would have done the same. He'd have to or else get it, like the Jerry who was after me.

"Our squadron had just shot up an airfield in the Mediterranean theater," said the dark-haired young lieutenant, "when out of nowhere came this flock of ME-109's and it seemed like about 20 of them were all around me.

Out of 'Ammo'

"I hit the deck, but quick, because I was out of ammunition. I was dodging trees and oil derricks when here comes this one Jerry right for me. Why he didn't let me have it with his guns, I'll never know. Maybe he was fresh out of ammo, too. We must have both been doing around 400—that makes an approaching speed of 800.

"I held her right on the deck and he pulled under.

"Whamo! He hit the ground, blew himself to hell and the blast knocked my ship straight up but I kept going. Boy, the landing strip at the home base never looked sweeter than after that mission!"

Details Given

With him as he told the story in the *Lockheed Star* office was Lt. Tovrea's Luke Field training pal, Lt. Bill Caughlin, Calexico native son. Now and then he helped with details of their experiences.

They just had done six months of combat duty together and are home on leave waiting for reassignment. Lt. Tovrea is from Phoenix, Ariz.

"How about that time on the Munich raid?" Bill Caughlin urged.

"Yea," grinned his pal, "but we had altitude and the sun at our backs."

"Well, go ahead and tell him," said Bill. Each tried to make the other "give."

"There were 14 of us in P-38's covering some Flying Forts that had just dropped stuff on Munich. They were tooling along, 'way down below us with the sun at their backs, too.

Air Armada

"All of a sudden we saw what looked to us like about 100 Jerry fighters — mostly Focke-Wulfe 190's and a few ME's—boring in on our bombers from the side, above them and below us. The Forts didn't see them, and thank

(Continued on Page 8)

Gasoline Theft Ends Boy's Job

Casting a character shadow is highly resented by Lockheed juveniles, a small handful of irresponsible youths, few of whom work in the plants, have been caught in what the Plant Protection Department believes is the "meanest trick" . . . stealing gasoline from cars parked in company lots.

The thefts usually occur late at night. The guards nabbed two 17-year-olds. A third got away—after they had cleaned two cars dry in Lot 53. The time was 11:30 p.m. They did a quick job on a Pontiac by removing the gas tank drainage plug, and an equally professional job with a rubber hose on a Rolls-Royce.

This type of theft is typically youthful, Plant Protection Manager E. L. Nichols pointed out, and for this reason, when arrests are not promptly made, suspicion is bound to attach to the innocent as well as the guilty—and this does not take into consideration the serious loss and inconvenience caused the car owner. Arrests led to immediate termination of the only one of the trio belonging to Lockheed. The other taken was turned over to Burbank police.

Won't Mail Out Book Renewals

Don't wait for your supplemental gas ration renewal application to be mailed to you this month, because it won't be.

This warning was issued yesterday by Dale Cosgray, manager of Employe Transportation, who gave as the reason that supplemental ration holders are considered sufficiently experienced with the program after two years to apply for their own applications in ample time to receive the new books. Up to now, renewal notices have been sent out every three months.

Cosgray stresses that every holder of a supplemental book should look at it *now* to make sure of the expiration date, as renewal applications must be completed at the Employe Transportation unit not later than 10 days before the earliest renewal date. *The date is clearly marked on the ration book.* The 10-day margin is allowed to offset any errors which may show up when the board receives the application.

BLANCHARD PROMOTED

Promotion of Lt. Merle Blanchard, former Lockheed employe, to the rank of captain in the 338th Fighter Squadron of the 8th AAF in England, is disclosed by his brother, Leonard, of the Merchant Marine. Captain Blanchard, according to his brother, has three German planes to his credit, an Air Medal and the Distinguished Flying Cross with seven Oak Leaf Clusters.

MOTORBIKE GAS READY

MOTORCYCLE riders should make application now for basic "D" books, it was learned here last night from Dale Cosgray, employe transportation manager.

The forms, he said, must be signed by the registered owner of the motorcycle for which the ration is sought. An agent's signature is not valid. The book contains 40 serially numbered coupons good from Nov. 12.

LIQUOR USE SLAPPED IN MOVE TO MAINTAIN SAFETY IN PLANT

Drinking on, or just before, the job, took a brutal slap last night from E. L. Nichols, plant protection manager. Nichols stressed the importance of absolute sobriety within war production plants.

"At Lockheed," he said, "recent weeks have seen an increase in the number of persons coming to work drunk or part-drunk. In nearly all cases the guards tag such folk at the gates. Some slip through. Spotting such people within the plant and attempting to work leads to termination. Those picked up at the gates by the guards are sent home to regain sobriety.

"While the company does not care to interfere with anyone's private life," Nichols added, "it does feel that a drunk or near-drunk within a factory is a menace to himself and his working companions."

Completes 25th Mission

First Lieut. Lyle L. Crum, former Factory A-1 employe, recently completed his 25th combat mission from an Italian base.

Is it Here?

THESE classified ad columns in the *Star* are provided for employes without charge. If you want to buy, sell, trade, or find or return lost articles, obtain Form 4929 from your department clerk, stationery store, or employe service office. Fill it in and send it to Employe Service Division, Factory B-1. If you wish to check on ads appearing, phone 63041 about all articles.

WANTED

ARCHERY bow, about 45 lbs., and archery equip. SU. 14523.
BENDIX wash. machine. CI. 27859 after 6 p.m.
BIKE, sm. girl's; small kiddie car. SU. 21541.
CAMERA, movie, 8-mm. f.1.9 lens. SY. 42453 after 6 p.m.
CAMERA, Recomar or similar, 9x12 CM. AT. 18935.
DIATHERMY set, home type. Must be reasonable. AL. 5011.
ENLARGER, pref. Argus 35-mm. Goodwin, CR. 12584.
GUITAR, Spanish, plectrum banjo, tenor ukelele. HO. 1491.
HEATER, sm. elec. NO. 26413.
HEATER, med. or sm. elec. Good cond. CHarleston 65651.
HOME, 3-bedrm., in good loc. nr. Magnolia or Toluca Lake. CR. 19460.
HOME, mod. priced or income. Vic. Burbank. CH. 86857.
JACK, 1½-ton hydraulic car. NO. 25256 (between 2-3 p.m.).
PROJECTOR, 35-mm., slide or one to handle 2"x2" Kodaslides. SU. 1062.
SEWING mach., old mod., foot pedal. Any make, pref. not working. AN. 7405.
RING, Masonic. HE. 2660, evenings.
TRAILER, 2-wheel utility. 600-16 tires. CI. 11342.
TYPEWRITER, port. Good cond. 2230¼ Addison Way, Eagle Rock.
WASHING machine, good cond. 4409½ Finley Ave , Los Angeles.
WEIGHTS, bar bell, 100 lb. to 150 lb. 13730 Judd St. Pacoima.

LOST

SPORT coat, gray tweed, lab. Wright's Clothes, Whittier, Calif. CI. 32260.

EXCHANGE

MODEL "E" High Std. auto. pistol, 22 caliber for ???. CH. 69037.
5-RM. unfurn. rental in Whittier for same in NW. L.A. or vic. WH. 61408.
BABY buggy, prewar stl. collapsible for lady's bicycle. SU. 18947.

FOR SALE

ANIMALS
RED pullets, 4 mo. old, cockrells. 7458 Denny Ave., Roscoe.
GOAT, 8 mo. old. Cheap. HI. 2415.

Is it Here?

FOR SALE

ANIMALS (Cont.)
COCKER SPANIEL, pedigree, black. House broken, 8 mo. AN. 19904 after 4 p.m.

CLOTHING
COAT, Norwegian fox fur, med. size. Good cond. 2021 Bonita, Burbank.
COAT, black sealskin, full length. Size 14. WY. 7641, mornings.
COAT, lady's sport, size 14, 100% wool. Never worn. ALbany 9091.
FURS, beaut. pr. red fox. Worn very little. Reas. FI. 7102.
SHOES, 11C, worn once. Camp stove, 45 Colt auto., ctgs. Elec. vibrator. SY. 75112.
SUIT, size 39, navy blue flannel. Army uniform, 39, tailor-made. Prac. new. AN. 18468 after 5 p.m.
SWEATER, white wool, size 38. 2 T-shirts, size 42. Cheap. CR. 63783.

HOME FURNISHINGS
BED, single, iron, springs, mattress; sm. bedrm. desk. SU. 28452 bet. 10 and 2.
BEDRM. set, springs, mattress, dresser, chest, bench, shelves. CH. 86609.
BEDRM. set, twin, blonde wood; dinette 5-pc. set. GR. 1453 after 6 p.m.
BOOKCASE, blonde bird's-eye maple. Adj. shelves. 504 S. Curson, L.A.
CLUB chair, prewar; lamp. Good cond. CH. 86234.
CHAIR, Kroehler, prewar const.; tables; drafting table. 2347 N. Reese Pl., Burbank.
CRIB and mattress, 2. 6549 Teesdale Ave., North Hollywood.
DINETTE set, 5-pc.; 7-pc. Duncan Phyfe din. set. Bunk beds. CI. 31563.
DINING rm. table, chair, lamp; rug, 9x12. Cheap. CL. 64265.
DINING set, 7-pc. walnut Duncan Phyfe. 716 S. Belden Ave., L.A.
DRAPES, 4 prs., like new. Just cleaned. BR. 22056.
KITCHENWARE, aluminum and pyrex. Edna Payne, MO. 12943.
REFRIG., stove, studio divan, inner sprg. matt. and spring. EX. 7419.

MISCELLANEOUS
BABY carriage, rubber tires, steel frame, collapsible. CI. 31742.
BABY carriage, 6 mo. old. Good cond. OLympia 5069.
BABY carriage, prewar Welch, mattress, exc. cond. YO. 6636.
BABY carriage, wicker. Air horns, truck t pe, 150-lb. tank. AL. 1722.
CAMERA, Eastman-Kodak, takes 116 film. NO. 19762.
CART. components, comp. 30-06; oxfords, men's 9D, new. CH. 83213.
CHICKEN coop, 26"x54". HE. 8485.
FAN, G.E., 6" elec. AC-DC current. W. E. Rogers, GR. 8971.
IRON, elec., steam, like new. Golf balls, prewar. SU. 23624.
LATHE, quick change, 9". P. Windheim, 510 Hazel, Glendale.
LUGGAGE, blue Samsonite, 21" trav. case; 1 burn. elec. plate. SU. 23624.
RADIO, Philco car, exc. cond. CHarleston 85770.

Is it Here?

FOR SALE

MISCELLANEOUS (Cont.)
SONOTONE, used 4 mo. E. L. Rapp. 14511 Chatsworth Dr., San Fernando.
TRICYCLE, hvy. const., prewar, stored 3 years, like new. CH. 60712.
TRUNK, wardrobe, large size, like new. HE. 2660, evenings.
TYPEWRITER, Corona Std. Port. 3 yrs. old. CI. 26936.
VIOLIN, 2 bows and case, reas. HO. 3357 between 4 and 6 p.m.
WHEELS, 2 new bike, lam. woods, Weston tires, built up. SU. 27552.

REAL ESTATE
HOME, 2 bedrm., 2-story, dble. garage. 8 mi. from Plt. Immed. poss. SUnland 673.
HOME, 2 bedrm. Fine cond. 10135 Elkwood St., Burbank.
HOUSE, 4 rm., tool house, chick. house, grape arbor. 7458 Denny, Roscoe.
HOUSE, 5 rm. furn., fenced yard. 224 W. Santa Anita, Burbank.

SPORTING GOODS
AMMUNITION, 300 Savage. 150-grain silver-tip bullets. CI. 36309.
BOAT, speed, 14' mahog. 24-h.p. motor. With trailer. Whittier 415258.
SHOES, football, size 10, horsehide, exc. cond. GR. 8971.
SKATES, men's Alfred Johnson black tubular shoe. Size 8. PA. 2866.
TENNIS racket, exc. cond., med. wt., prewar, gen. gut. GR. 8971.

MOTOR VEHICLES
AIRPLANE, sm., single place, new Sczeckley engine. SU. 15258.
BICYCLE, man's prewar Schwinn, new tires, 2 hand brakes. ST. 53862.
CHEVROLET, '39 4-dr. sedan, new paint, recaps, new radio. HO. 6954.
MOTORCYCLE, Army Indian, 2200 mi. W C. Shehorn, CHurchill 92482.
MOTORCYCLE, '40 H.D. 80, just overhauled, extras. 11201 Otsego.
MOTORCYCLE, Harley-Davidson '39-74, exc. mech. cond., clean appear. HI. 5793.
SCOOTER, '44 6 h.p. Custom-built. CHapman 51348.
TRAILER, 18' Schuit '39. Elec. brakes. Good cond. Sleeps 4. 8540 Foothill Blvd. Box 508, Sunland, Calif.

THE LOCKHEED Star
OFFICIAL PUBLICATION OF THE LOCKHEED AIRCRAFT CORPORATION

Issued each Friday for the employes of Lockheed Aircraft Corporation. The *Star* is the official publication of the company. Communications should be addressed to the Editor, *Lockheed Star*, Publicity Department, Lockheed Aircraft Corporation, Burbank, California. Unsolicited manuscripts cannot be returned.

KENNETH CRIST, Editor
Associates:
H. L. Rosson J. H. Prescott

Maj. Richard I. Bong

Major Addresses Lockheed Employes

Carl B. Squier Maj. Richard I. Bong

TWENTY NIPS DRIVEN FROM SKIES BY MAJOR BONG AS TWO PLUNGE INTO SEA AND P-38 AIRMAN REGAINS ACE TITLE

Hirohito's stooges have just completed a fast course at "business college" . . . teacher, Major Richard Ira Bong. And Major Bong again has become America's ace of aces.

To their regret, a pair of Jap fighters forced their way into his sky seminar over the South Pacific last week and left precipitously on a nonstop flight toward the bottom of the sea. Eighteen others fled into their Setting Sun.

That made it a score of 30 kills for the 23-year-old P-38 veteran who told Lockheed workers last June how he used the ships they make to win the approbation of "ace of aces" from Gen. Douglas MacArthur.

Major Bong was then on leave after having blasted 27 Nip planes from the sky to become the leading American fighter pilot of the Pacific theater. That was enough for AAF officers who made him teacher.

As gunnery instructor of the Far Eastern Air Force, it was thought that he would be "more valuable" imparting his know-how to younger pilots and it was understood he would make no combat missions.

Score of Zeros

But last week in the sky "Professor" Bong and his class were rudely set upon by more than a score of Zeros.

"You see," he might have said, "this is the way—" and the Nip intruders were fewer by one . . . "for example," he might have continued as another Jap groaned the wrong way to heaven.

When Major Bong left the Pacific last summer he was credited with 27 planes not including a "probable" over Hollandia Harbor that he felt might be included later in the "sure" column.

Maj.-Gen. Ennis Whitehead of the Fifth Air Force subsequently sent a salvage crew to the Hollandia reef and corrected the official score to 28.

The blond, mild-mannered young pilot with a snub nose has a simple formula he expounds to students seeking to solve Jap extermination.

In the major's own words, spoken during his Lockheed visit, it goes like this:

"Catch 'em with their flying pants down; get in as close as a minimum of safety requirements will permit, and then let 'em have it with everything you've got."

'They Blow Up'

Asked for details of his experiences, Maj. Bong then continued, "The Japs aren't so hot any more. Their best pilots are gone and I don't think they're so crazy to die for their emperor as they'd like to have us believe. The best thing they do is blow up in your face.

"They're scared of a P-38 and it's hard to make them fight. They'll run for it every time if they can. It doesn't matter, though, because we just take after them, run 'em down and blast hell out of 'em. They can't stand P-38 speed and firepower."

Speaking of the "probable," subsequently verified, he said, "The last plane I shot down at Hollandia I scared the Jap pilot to death. I dived on him and he cartwheeled into the ocean with me blasting his way."

Major Bong holds the Distinguished Service Cross, the D.F.C., the Air Medal and at least 10 Oak Leaf Clusters for his work as a pilot of P-38's.

Cigarette Greed Brings Action

Rapid retribution has overtaken the cigarette "bandits" at Plant B-1. The vending machines have been removed from the main LERC cafeteria—not because no cigarettes were available, but because when they did show up they melted like babbitt under the blowtorch of greedy individuals. They were not content with one or two packs, but had to hijack a dozen or twenty, it is said.

The same thing has gone on, according to the Plant Protection Department, with all other machines in the plant area. And Plant B and Lockheed are not alone in the experience: Douglas and many other companies have either removed or sealed the machines.

From now on, everyone in the plant areas will get an even break for, when the canteens and cafeteria get "smokes," they will be sold only over the counter—one pack to a customer and no repeats.

Major and His Ship

Russ Weil Joins Up With Navy for Duty

Lockheed's official "Arkansas Traveler" has gone back to the Navy.

Not for "the duration" will the hundreds of friends and working companions of J. Russell "Russ" Weil chuckle again at his famed Arkansas stories, or pour out their troubles in his interested ear. For Weil left the company this week to reenter the service branch with which he served with distinction in World War I, and in which his 19-year-old son, John, is also serving somewhere in the South Pacific.

Five Years Here

Weil joined Lockheed more than five years ago, coming to his engineering position here from an adventurous career as a bridge builder on the Mississippi. For three years he was plant engineer at B-1 and, when the plant engineering departments at A and B consolidated earlier this year, he became assistant to plant engineer G. S. Rigdon. Weil played a prominent role in the growth of Lockheed units.

His title of "official Arkansas Traveler" is no mere fiction. Some two years ago he was appointed to the post and named "Ambassador of Goodwill" by his life-long friend, Governor Adkins of Arkansas. He has a "signed and sealed" certificate to prove it. This certificate has been proudly displayed in every office he has held in Lockheed and undoubtedly will find a prominent spot in his Navy quarters.

Farewell Party

The women employes of Plant Engineering sadly marked his departure with a farewell party in the Factory B cafeteria. They presented him with many gifts slated for use in his naval career, including "a corn cob pipe, several boxes of seasick pills, and a very special pair of dice." A stag party was also staged in his honor by the men of A and B Plant Engineering departments.

Indicative of the traits in his character which made Weil universally liked at Lockheed is the fact that on the day he left to join the Navy he gave his fourteenth pint of blood to the American Red Cross at the company blood donor station. He reenters naval service as a Chief Petty Officer, Machinist Branch.

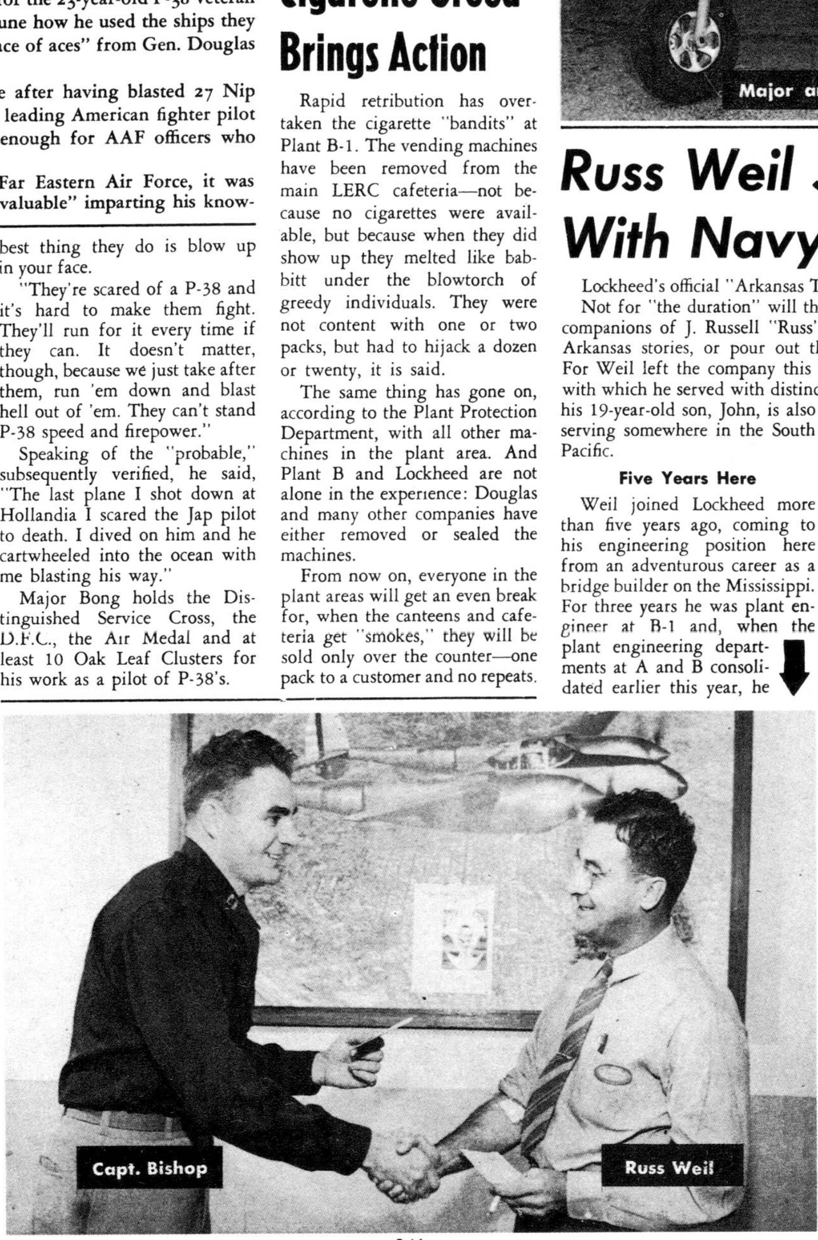

Capt. Bishop Russ Weil

Rangers Offer 5-Point Program For Fall Season

Opening the fall season with a 5-point program of attractions, Mel Graham, program director, invites all Lockheed swing shift employes to join the Swing Shift Rangers in their activities.

Weekly two-hour canters through the Hollywood hills at nominal cost are first in the five incentives offered. In addition the club holds Sunday morning breakfast rides, special social events, and is planning a small rodeo. Fifth attraction to be offered is instruction and help to those who wish to improve their riding technique.

As an incentive to present members, the Burbank Saddlery, Main and Alameda, Burbank, is offering a hand-tooled leather wrist watch band with sterling tip and buckle to the member bringing in the greatest number of new riders during a four-week period, starting Oct. 11, and ending Nov. 1.

The Rangers ride each Tuesday from 10 a.m. to noon at Pico Stables, 420 Riverside Drive.

Newscaster On Program

Of special notice to Lockheed football fans is the appearance of Frank Bull, well-known sports newscaster, as guest speaker at the Factory B day shift Penguin dinner to be held Monday, Oct. 30, 7 p.m., at the Los Angeles Breakfast Club.

Bull, known to all sports fans on the Pacific Coast, will give a resume of thrills and spills in big-time football games of current and past seasons.

Bill Sargent, coach of the powerful Hollywood Rangers, will be on hand with some of his boys to give a few pointers on the "play-for-pay" game.

Concluding the evening's football roundup will be the movie, "Touchdown," showing highlights of the most important games of the past few years with slow-motion shots of "Razzle Dazzle" and tricky scoring plays.

With something new in the way of programs, the Penguins expect to bring out an unusual attendance. Tickets can be had from members or from ticket committees at all plants.

"Dress Rehearsal"

SALES, SERVICE DEPT. PLANS GALA FALL FROLIC

One thousand employes of the Sales and Service Department, with their families and friends, are expected at a "Hard Times" party and dance, Sunday, Oct. 29, at the Los Angeles Breakfast Club, according to an announcement yesterday by the dance coordinator, Seymour Knee.

Les Stevens, former first trumpeter with Ted Fiorito, and his band will set tempo for the three hours of dancing beginning at 9. Stevens and his entire crew are employes of Lockheed.

Executives Help

Carl B. Squier, Lockheed vice president in charge of sales, will head the long list of surprise entertainers on the evening's program, which will be emceed by John E. Canaday. A cowboy band will provide music in the patio.

The dance committee points out that hard-time costumes are necessary for admittance to the party. Surprise prizes will be given to the man and woman wearing the most appropriate garb. A war bond will be given as door prize.

Committee Listed

Committee in charge of the affair includes Lee Morrill, John Feola, Lee Stearns, Ken Lloyd, Jack Munro, Don Blank, Chris Easman, Bob Ritchie, Pearl Fles, Vivian Summerhays and Seymour Knee.

TO CELEBRATE ANNIVERSARY

Celebrating a year's service at the Boulevard USO, Hollywood, Blue Star Service Women of Factory A will hold a Halloween party at that center, Wednesday, Oct. 25.

Halloween dancing will start at 8 p.m. Prizes will be given for games and contests during the evening and fortune tellers will read the future of servicemen guests. A buffet supper will be served by Blue Stars.

Headed by Ella Kennedy, president, special committee chairmen include Thelma Goodman, food; Velma Smith, games; and Esther Schilling, decorations.

Masks will be furnished to all attending and members are requested to come in costume.

During the year the Blue Stars have entertained an average of 400 servicemen each Wednesday night that they have been sponsoring the weekly dances.

PLEA ISSUED TO AID LERC SILVER SAVING

Loss of more than 1000 knives, forks and spoons within 30 days from newly opened Canteen 12, Factory A-1, was reported last night by James Ramsey of the LERC.

"If Lockheed workers would stop to think they are really losing their own property this way they might be more careful," said Ramsey, pointing out that LERC is an employe organization.

"Paper utensils will have to be substituted if this high rate of loss continues," he added.

Most modern of any of the 20 LERC canteens is the new snack bar and fountain of this new unit, near gate three, it has six lanes with three serving sections.

150 dozen doughnuts and coffeecakes and 300 gallons of coffee are served daily. Facilities are available for brewing 180 gallons of coffee at one time and this canteen is the only similar unit having its own dishwashing equipment.

Canteen No. 7, located on the north side of the flying field, was opened yesterday for the convenience of flight engineering, test pilots, and employes of the Fortress assembly line. This is the first canteen to have a complete concrete area.

Latest reports from the engineering department indicate that remodeling changes requested for Canteen No. 5, located near Bldg. 185, will be under way sometime during the coming week.

OPERA CLUB TO MEET TUESDAY

Lockheed Opera Club will hold its first fall meeting at 7:30 p.m., Tuesday, Oct. 24, at 1145 Horn Ave., Hollywood. This is the first house north of Sunset Blvd., and may be reached on the Hollywoodland-Beverly Hills red bus line.

Program for the evening as announced by Frederick Altman, conductor, will include election of officers, auditions, and selection of the first musical presentation for the winter season.

Employes who plan to attend are requested to contact Anne Kalionzes of Dept. 27-29, Factory B-1.

MODEL 80 GROUP TO HOLD DANCE

Employes of the Model 80 development departments will hold a Halloween dance and party, Saturday, Oct. 28, from 8 p.m. to 12, at the Burbank Recreation Center, 1111 W. Olive.

Tom Perkins, chairman, announces that in addition to dancing, there will be ping pong, card games and contests throughout the evening. Refreshments will be served.

All employes working on the Model 80 are invited with their friends and families. Tickets may be purchased from Arden Kitching, engineering group; Lindford Jones, Model 80 planning unit; and from Opal Heckler, Dept. 28-10.

PENGUINETTES WILL ENTERTAIN VETERANS AT BIG COSTUME BALL

Servicemen from nearby hospitals will be guests of the Factory B day shift Penguinettes at a costume ball to be held Tuesday, Oct. 31, at 8 p.m., in the Garden Courts Ballroom on Hollywood Blvd.

Girls will wear fancy dress costumes and the 100 servicemen guests will be provided with masks. Herbert Bloom's orchestra will furnish the music. In rooms adjoining the ballroom, continuous bingo and other card games will be played.

Jimmie Lloyd, Columbia comedian, will emcee the evening's program, which will include "Smokie" Whitfield with his songs and humor and Napua Woodd, dancer from the "Seven Seas," who will be accompanied by Sam Coci from the same night spot. A buffet supper will be served in the lounge room of the hotel.

Special committees are headed by Ethel Thompson, food; Nadine Amandus, tickets; Edith Poritsky, decorations; Ruth Brewer, games and contests; Edna Mattison, program, and Kay Smith, publicity.

Since only a limited number of tickets will be sold, it is suggested that tickets be purchased as early as possible from the ticket committee.

Change Announced For USO Parties

Margo Olson, USO chairman of the Factory B day shift Penguinettes, last night announced a change in plans for parties sponsored by the club at the Boulevard USO, Hollywood.

Weekly dances will continue, but there will be one large party each month, with special entertainment, to replace the weekly Cabaret nights.

First of the special parties will be a masked Halloween Ball to be held Thursday, Oct. 26, at the center. Entertainment and a buffet lunch will be provided for visiting servicemen. Hal Foreman and his orchestra will play for dancing.

Chris Carmen, program chairman, requests that all Penguinettes bring fruit, doughnuts, and other food with decorations suitable for the Halloween season.

Battle Film Scheduled

"The Battle of Russia," showing a Russian campaign to protect their country from the German armies, will be presented by the LERC Educational Committee in Room 4 of the B-1 Cafeteria Building, Tuesday, Oct. 24, for all shifts.

The picture, filmed by more than 400 cameramen, also shows how supplies are sent by the United States and how convoy lanes were maintained.

Short for the evening will be "The March of the Presidents," which gives highlights on the lives of all presidents from Washington's administration.

Free reservations are available at the LERC offices now.

Treat Battle Wounds

Tec 5, Edwin Harmon, 22, former mechanic at Lockheed, is reported to be in Bushnell General Hospital, Brigham City, Utah, receiving special treatment for serious wounds a booby trap explosion caused near Castlefort, above Netturno, Italy, last April 4. He was flown to the Bushnell General Hospital after treatment for five months in an Army hospital north of Naples.

Randolph Nabs Night Shift Golf Title

Trips Poulsen By 1-Stroke Win In Warm Battle

Bob Randolph, swing shifter from Dept. 18-57, A-1, is new champion of the Swing-Graveyard Golf Club after defeating runner-up Kelly Poulsen 78 to 79 at Griffith Park course Wednesday. Poulsen won top honors over 32 night shift contestants that qualified in the club's match play handicap qualifying round at Brookside and Griffith Park courses, Sept. 11.

In Wednesday's championship play Randolph went out in 38 to lead Poulsen by one stroke at the end of the first nine, a lead he managed to hold despite Poulsen's determination to eliminate the one-stroke edge. The runner-up plays out of Dept. 39-42, graveyard shift, A-1. The championship award is a $50 war bond.

Poulsen and Al Peterson have been low-gross favorites since the Sept. 11 tryouts when they led the entire field of 62 entrants with 76 and 75. Poulsen's handicap of 10 gave him the low net of 66. Randolph qualified with a gross 82 with a handicap of 12 for a net 70.

Results of the match for third place between Al Peterson and Pete Brown, both swing shifters at A-1 were not in at presstime. Brown qualified with a gross 83, a 12 handicap for a 71 net.

COMPARE NOTES AS 368 HANDICAP BOWLING SQUADS HIT HIGH SPOTS

With Lockheed's 368 handicap bowling teams now in their fifth, sixth, and seventh week of league bowling, outstanding teams and individuals gradually are working into banner positions in the over-all bowling panorama.

Upset of the week took place in the Friday night North Hollywood loop when the Mixers, last season Lockheed champions who were sharing top honors in the present round with the Jerks, took a four-point shellacking at the hands of the fourth-place Beer Hounds who moved to second position to lower the Mixers to the fourth-place spot they vacated. All this was very pleasing to the Jerks who automatically became top team of the 12-team loop, a position further strengthened by their 3-0 win over the 11th-place Blazers.

Assemblers Tops

In the all-league high team series bracket the Final Assemblers, leaders of the Friday swing shift loop at Olive Recreation, rolled a 2976 to top all comers for all shifts through the first week of October. Second high series was chalked up by the Mixers in the Friday, North Hollywood league with a total of 2924, followed by the Wednesday swing shift Beer Hounds who rolled a 2919 series at Olive Recreation.

The Final Assemblers also copped the all-league high team game honors for the week with 1053 to outpoint the second-place Jerks whose best effort netted 1026. The Wednesday swing shift Roustabouts garnered third spot in the high-game department with a 991 at Olive Recreation.

Win Records Compared

Best win record among the leagues is held by the Wednesday swing shift Chumps, boasting 8 wins in 8 starts, the Inspection No. 1 squad, bowling in the Navy-Lockheed Service Center loop at Van Nuys, who have lost 1 in twelve starts, and the North Hollywood first-placers, the Jerks, who have eighteen wins out of twenty.

Individual Highs

Individual scoring honors show high-series artists scheduled throughout all leagues, all shifts. Bill Sharp, Thursday swing shift member of the Wing Dings, heads the list with 599, followed by D. Brown's 591; G. Riding's 588; E. Fish's 587; Willis Wilhoit's 581; R. LaBeateau's 579; and G. Nelson, seventh best with 578.

Best individual high game for the week was turned in by F. Hancock of the Engineering League at North Hollywood on Fridays, bowling with the A. B. Seers who rolled an enviable 247

Close to Top

Not far behind came Francis Haley of the Thursday swing shift Guttersnipes with a 243, followed by J. Pace of the Dee Tee's with 236, and Carl Ames of the Flight Testers with 235, both bowling in the Tuesday league at Airways. Other high games were R. LaBeateau, Mixers, 231; B. Beechel, 227; G. Nicholls, 214; W. Cuddleback, 214; G. Nelson, 213.

Best high average in all leagues is Fred McComas of the Thursday swing shift Tail Spinners with 186. Tops for their respective leagues with comparable averages are Carl Ames, Flight Tests, Tuesday at Airways, 177; B. Otten, Team No. 7 of the Customer Service League, 175; M. Chapman, Sheep, Friday swing shift at Olive Recreation, 175; B. Robertson, Oh Pees, Wednesday swing shift at Olive, 172; R. LaBeateau, Mixers, 172; H. Erwin and E. Hatch, both of the Night Owls in the Thursday night mixed foursomes at Olive, tie with 172.

Tally Shows Odd Angles

Bowling oddity of the week is the peculiar plight of the Drunkards in the Thursday Mixed Foursome league at Olive. Credited with both the high-team game, 788, and the high-team series, 2175, the team is listed in seventh position of the eight-team bracket.

High individual average for the loop, 172, is a tie between H. Erwin and E. Hatch, both playing with the Night Owls.

NEXT NIGHTER TEE MEET SET

Night shifters' next regular bi-monthly golf tourney will be staged Monday at 8:30 p.m. at both Brookside, Pasadena, and Griffith Park courses, according to word received last night from swing-graveyard golf president, Merle McIntyre.

Membership in the rapidly growing club is open to all employes of the swing and graveyard shifts. An initial fee of 50 cents together with four attested score cards from which the club officers decide handicaps are the only requisites. An additional 50 cents is charged for each tournament to cover cost of awards. Memberships are taken at the LERC offices or at the first tee of either course on the morning tournaments are held.

Winners of the Oct. 9 meet follow:

GRIFFITH PARK	Gross	Hdcp.	Net
K. Kadell	81	12	69
J. Patterson	82	13	69
Al Peterson	76	4	72
K. Poulsen	79	7	72
Al Baggio	83	10	73
Glen Lee	85	12	73
F. Mohr	89	16	73
A. Christensen	93	20	73
BROOKSIDE			
Tom French	82	11	71
Ed Dube	81	7	74
Chas. Kingman	88	13	75
Nick Zelstra	94	19	75

ROOSMAN ELECTED TO HEAD HOBBY CLUB

Bob Roosman, 60-75, as president, heads the list of new officers of Lockheed's LERC Model and Hobby Club elected at a recent meeting. Other officers include Darwin Hyatt, 72-25, vice-president; Tony de Jonkere, 17-04, A-2, secretary and treasurer, and Cliff Nusen, 72-25, program director.

Regular meetings of the club are held first and third Wednesdays of each month in the swimming pool building at Griffith Park.

LERC Activities

DANCE CLUB—Every Thursday, 8 p.m., Allan Rudack Studios, 7213 Beverly Blvd.

BOAT CLUB—Every Wednesday, 5 p.m., B-1 Cafeteria, Private Dining Room.

SERVICE STAR WOMEN—Plant B-1, first and third Wednesdays after work. Conference Room 1, Cafeteria Bldg. B-2, day and graveyard shift, every Wednesday lunch period, 11 a.m. and 3:30 a.m., Conference Room.

CONCERTS—Military band, rehearsal Friday, 9:15 a.m., concerts begin 10:50 a.m., main recreation area, all day shift lunch periods.

DAY PENGUINETTES — Cabaret night hostesses, Boulevard USO, every Thursday evening.

CHESS CLUB—Wednesday, 7 p.m., Rooms 1 and 2, Burbank Recreation Center, 1111 W. Olive.

BLUE STAR WOMEN — Open house, Boulevard USO, 6551 Hollywood Blvd., Wednesday, 7:30 p.m.

BRIDGE CLUB — Thursday, 7:30 p.m., Burbank Recreation Center, 1111 W. Olive.

BOY SCOUTS — Troop No. 13, each Wednesday evening, 7 p.m., in Boy Scout Cabin at John Muir Jr. High School, Burbank. Troop 17, each Wednesday evening, 7 p.m., at Washington Street School, Burbank.

PISTOL AND RIFLE CLUB — Training course, Hoover High School, Glendale, Wednesday, 7 p.m.

DANCES—Swing shift dances after work every Friday at the Burbank Recreation Center, 1111 W. Olive, 1 a.m., Bob Mohr and his band.

TOASTMASTERS' CLUB—(Swing) every Tuesday, 1 p.m., Room 4, Cafeteria Bldg.

GIRLS' SWIMMING—Tuesday, 7 p.m., Hollywood YMCA, 1553 N. Hudson, Hollywood. Swing shift, Tuesday, 10:30 a.m., same place.

MEN'S SWIMMING — Glendale YMCA, each Wednesday, 6 and 8:15 p.m.

SWIMMING—Men and women—Glendale YMCA, every Friday, 8:30 and 9:30 p.m.

BADMINTON—Tuesday and Thursday, 7 p.m., John Burroughs Jr. High gym, Burbank.

VOCAL GROUPS — Hollywood Radio Chorus, Hollywood High School, Room M.A. 71, every Wednesday from 7 to 10 p.m. Victory Singers—Monday and Wednesday, 7 p.m., L. A. High School, Olympic and Rimpau, Room 423.

PLANT TOURS—Contact the LERC office for further particulars.

MUSIC APPRECIATION CLUB—Regular meeting second and fourth Mondays of the month, Cafeteria, B-1, Room 5, 2 p.m. Recordings every Wednesday from 2:45 to 3:45 p.m. Factory B-1 lunch area.

RIDING CLUB—Lockheed Rangers, every Friday, 7 p.m., Pico Stables, 420 Riverside Drive, Burbank. Swing shift, 10 a.m., Wednesday, Pico Stables, 420 Riverside. Call LERC for reservations.

FREE MOVIES—Tuesday, Oct. 24, "Battle of Russia" and the "March of the Presidents" (short), 5:30 and 8 p.m. Swing shift, 1 a.m.

Touch Ball Wars Begin

One and a half hundred Lockheed touch football players donned grid togs this week to open formally the 1944 toucher season. Opening kick-off set the Dept. 28-10, Jet Joes, captained by L. Mierzwa, against the Night Hawks of Dept. 28-26, captained by John Steers. Twelve teams will battle in the North Hollywood Park loop for the chance to meet other day and swing champs in an all-out battle for the 1944 Lockheed championship, scheduled for late December.

Competition Hot

Three former championship teams are entered in the North Hollywood lineup. From B-1 the defending champions are Harry Wildeberger's Office Gang. From A-1, Chuck Townsend has entered the Processors, 1942 champs. Other championship squad is the Template Butchers, piloted by R. Webb, formerly of A-1, now playing out of Dept. 44-52, B-3.

A special meeting of team captains last Thursday, on the eve of the season's opening, resulted in two major changes in the 1944 rules: (1) Players must tag a man below the waist with both hands instead of with one hand as the game was formerly played. (2) Fields will be marked off into three zones with four downs to the zone instead of the former six downs to the field.

Referees for the North Hollywood loop will be Len Meirzwa, Tuesday, Wednesday and Thursday league, and Harold Raines for the Monday and Friday league.

The LERC athletic committee, now scheduling swing shift leagues, name a definite need for more swing shift teams immediately.

Eager Beavers Lead Women's Swing League

Top spot in the Lockheed women's swing shift bowling league at Western Bowl is held by the Eager Beavers with ten wins, two losses, as the loop enters its fifth week. G. Hoffman, lead-off man for the squad holds high individual series with 482 and high average of 152. The team holds high-team series with 1823 and high-team game, 650. J. Bonato, bowling second on the Beaver squad ties with B. Furlong of the Wolfesses for high individual game, boasting 178. Other Beaver squad members are M. Spatz and F. White. In second position are the Hot Tomatoes with 9 wins, 3 losses.

Two new women's day leagues open this week at Sunset and Burbank Bowl alleys, both numbering ten teams. With the addition of these new leagues approximately 200 Lockheed girls are now entered in LERC-sponsored league competition.

Women's Lockheed Lightnings, bowling in the L.A. Women's Major League, Westlake Bowling Alley, Friday at 8:30 p.m., are in second place with 13 wins and 8 losses. They still hold the high-team series for the league thus far with a 2459 series, shot on the opener. On Friday, Oct. 13, the Lightnings met and defeated Gorton's Slender Line, 2 out of 3, rolling a 2410 series, which was high for the evening.

Terminal Sets Traffic Safety Record

PLEA MADE TO FOLLOW RULES FOR VEHICLES

More than 10,000 automobiles and 30,000 pedestrians move within its jurisdiction every day, yet, in four years it hasn't recorded a single accident involving lost time for a Lockheed worker.

That's the astounding record of the Lockheed Air Terminal police department, and to maintain it Chief Fred F. Schrage yesterday issued a warning and a plea for stricter observance of traffic rules.

An increase of violations in recent weeks is blamed on unfamiliarity with regulations on the part of Factory B-1 employes newly transferred to Factory A-1.

Understanding Sought

"All we ask," said the chief, "is cooperation from these people such as we have received in the past and which has helped us build such an enviable record of safety.

"Watch boulevard stop signs —particularly near the traffic circle at the post office crossing. And watch the speed limit."

Particularly vexing, the chief said, is the practice of many Lockheed people who use parking spaces reserved for personnel of the airlines.

Paid Space Cited

"Just because they happen to be empty doesn't mean they can be occupied by anyone. Airlines pay for these spaces and rightfully expect them to be available for their own use.

"Lockheed people have no more right to use parking spaces rented by the airlines than a stranger would have to move into the rented home of a person who might be on a vacation."

Lockheed violators of traffic rules are given warning notices. Continued violations are reported to the Plant Protection Dept. and to the local rationing office.

Lt. J. W. Farris: He Tags Violators

LERC SELECTS CANDIDATES

(Continued from Page 3)

Gene Long, council member, has been nominated for the office of vice-president. He has been associated in LERC affairs for three years, serving on the Entertainment committee. He recently was elected chairman of the Factory B-1 committee.

Al Rankin, present secretary of the club, has been nominated to succeed himself. Also nominated for the office is Charles Dixon. Rankin has shown interest in the LERC for more than four years. He has served on the Executive and Educational committees and as chairman of the B-3 group. Dixon was elected to the Employes' Council in March, 1943, and re-elected in January, 1944.

Third to be nominated for secretary is Ethel Richter. She served for two years as secretary of the VERC prior to the merger and is at present ex-officer member of the LERC.

Walter Martin, incumbent, has been nominated for treasurer. He has served in that capacity since April, 1944. For three years prior to the merger of the recreation clubs Martin acted as treasurer and member of the Executive committee of the VERC. He has no opposition.

Nominees for members-at-large to serve with the officers on the Executive committee follow: Albin "Sarge" Lundahl, Bob Mercer, Al Pimsner, incumbent; Sam Lynch, William Ryker, Don Hayes, incumbent; Frank J. Keefe, Paul Craik, Earl Shriver, incumbent; Friley Peterson, and John Mellquist, incumbent.

Tales of Wild Fighting by P-38 Pilots Told by Airmen on Leave

(Continued from Page 4)

God, the Jerries didn't see us.

"We went down and took 'em by complete surprise. The air was plenty full of busted airplanes for a couple of minutes— broken wings shooting past— Jerries blowing up in your face— some Forts blazing down.

"With our 14 P-38's we got 14 Jerries and dispersed the rest without losing one of our ships."

Phil twisted his hat and looked around the room. This talking for publication wasn't his line.

"That's where he got his Silver Star," volunteered Lt. Caughlin, who accounted for two of the Nazi planes in the same action and won a Distinguished Flying Cross for it.

Record Noted

Phil got four of the 14 in that action and four elsewhere —eight altogether. For shooting down two in a raid near Vienna and escorting a one-engined P-38 back to base, he also won a D.F.C.

"But they should've given the medals to those P-38's—the planes, themselves," both pilots insisted. "It wasn't us that got the Jerries.

"We've flown em. We know. We always got the toughest assignments because our ships could take it and toss it out with extras. Ask the boys at Salerno who saved their day. If they ever fall down on turning out those P-38's here, they're crazy."

They didn't want their pictures taken . . .

But when they heard they were to appear in the *Lockheed Star*, for the men and women who make the "sweetest plane in the sky," everything was okay.

Concluding their Lockheed visit, the two good-looking young pilots went over to Flight Operations to see such P-38 improvements as the dive flaps and aileron boosters, still too new to have been installed on ships they flew in Italy.

Meet Mattern

There they met Jimmy Mattern, Lockheed test pilot who made screaming headlines a few years ago when he flew around the world after being lost in the Siberian wilderness.

Jimmy showed them the new P-38's, and it was hard to tell who thought who was greatest—the famous 'round-the-world flier or the two lads who shot Nazis from the sky and out-nerved a hell-bent Messerschmitt.

Beohm to Australia

(Continued from Page 3)

"The company's policies are advanced in every respect. Only recently it announced the operation of an $800,000 inactive spares plant, employing 2500 men and women working three shifts a day, devoted solely to producing spare parts for all peacetime model Lockheed planes.

"Interested as I am in the future of aviation, I am proud to affiliate myself with a company such as Lockheed."

LOCKHEED SPEED STILL TOPS

Record of 6 hrs., 57 min., 51 sec., set by the Lockheed Constellation for a transcontinental U.S. run, still remains unchallenged in the transport field.

Chest Support Given as 'Buck Club' Advances

Climaxed by the gift this week of $150,000 to the Los Angeles County 1944 War Chest, the two-week-old drive of the Lockheed Buck-of-the-Month Club for new members has proved a notable success, according to a statement issued officially last night by Voltaire Perkins, secretary.

To date the drive has brought in 3000 new members, Perkins said, which, on the basis of a one dollar contribution per month, adds $36,000 a year to the Club's resources for charitable purposes.

Display Permitted

Expressing appreciation for the aid of Union chairmen, LERC representatives, and supervisors in assuring the drive's success, Perkins reminded both new and old Buck-of-the-Month Club members that they are entitled to display a 1944 War Chest Campaign contribution sticker in individual homes and automobiles.

Organized in March of 1942 to funnel all charitable gifts by Lockheed people through one distribution channel, thus evening up everybody's share and incidentally eliminating the multiplicity of solicitations that had bothered employes, the club, to Wednesday of this week, had collected a total of $1,341,652 by the easy, painless method of a voluntary dollar monthly paycheck deduction.

Vital Assistance

Its gifts, during the same period, have amounted to $1,146,652 . . . all to approved organizations working in local, national, and international human welfare fields.

Sightless Lockheed Lad Builds by Touch

PROUD, these days, are swing-shifters of Factory B-1's paint shop . . . proud of William Standage; masker.

He is blind.

For 24 years he has been blind . . . but his eyes are in his fingers. And with his fingers he has "seen," seen giant machinery and the simplest tool. And, too, he has seen a P-38.

Young Bill Standage likes the P-38. He likes its line. And he likes the spirit of victory that seems to be built right into it. So young Bill Standage built a P-38.

He said that he has always wanted to build one.

The scale model is true . . . so true that few with ordinary eyes could have done a better task.

"It wasn't hard to do," he told the *Star*. "About three months ago I came into Dept. 18-14. During lunch periods I'd go to the real P-38 line and feel the fast Lightning. I liked the thrill of it and I could measure its wing-span with my arms. And then my dog, Mitzi, would lead me back to work."

At his bench, during smoking periods and at odd moments, Bill Standage fashioned his model with nothing but his acute sense of touch as his blueprint. He bent scrap wire to form the wings, twin booms, empennage, fuselage and struts. For landing gear wheels he used tubing seals.

Then he wound masking tape around the wire frame and gave it a silver paint job. The photograph, right, shows the product.

His only comment: "I wish it could kill a Jap."

William Standage and Mitzi: He Built Model P-38

ROUTINE JOB TAKES BURCHAM

MILO BURCHAM

MILO Burcham was mourned this week by thousands of men and women—and boys—who knew him only as a flash of silver against the California skies and by the roar of his swift flight . . .

The men and women built the ships he helped to perfect and through the years at Lockheed had thrilled at his wonderfully skillful demonstrations of their handiwork . . .

The boys rode with him—hundreds of them—whenever his flashing ship crossed high above their playgrounds.

Thus they knew him well, these thousands who only watched, and this week when Milo Burcham was laid to rest in Forest Lawn Memorial Park they mourned their hero.

For all who knew him personally, Milo's death in the crash of an airplane he was testing brought a deep sense of grief, and wherever test pilots gathered the Lockheed Chief Pilot was eulogized. He had a host of friends, a legion of admirers, and no enemies.

The end came when Milo took off from the east-west runway at Lockheed Air Terminal and was forced into a low-altitude, down-wind turn, probably by power failure. This flying procedure meant only one thing to other pilots. It meant that the Chief Pilot was thinking of the safety of others, as usual. It was his custom.

"To us who considered him the world's smartest pilot," said one flier, "this *(Continued on Page 2)*

THE LOCKHEED Star
OFFICIAL PUBLICATION OF THE LOCKHEED AIRCRAFT CORPORATION
Volume 1 BURBANK, CALIFORNIA, U.S.A., OCTOBER 27, 1944 No. 23

★ ★ ★ ★ ★ ★ ★

MILO BURCHAM DIES FOR CAUSE OF AIR PROGRESS

(Continued from Page 1)

procedure meant that Milo wanted to avoid even the remotest possibility of a forced landing in areas thick with people, houses, and automobiles.

No Expected Trouble

"Had he taken off as the airliners were doing, any crash might have injured others south of the field. As it was, he was the only victim. Not that he expected trouble. He just didn't want to subject town folk to even hypothetical danger."

Such consideration was typical of the popular pilot whose career began with the sale of a home-made burglar alarm in 1928 to buy a flying lesson and carried him to achievement pinnacles scaled by few.

Milo always insisted on doing the most hazardous tests himself. It was his desire to help young Army Air Force flyers that prompted development of a special course of P-38 instruction he conducted this summer for the Fourth Air Force.

Despite the fact that stunting brought him early newspaper headlines, whenever the safety of others was involved, Burcham was painstaking as a pilot.

"But," said a fellow pilot, "when he was alone over the desert, I've seen him do some of the damndest things a man ever did with an airplane . . . stunts even a bird wouldn't try."

Riding Was Favored

Milo used to drive his old Ford to the stables, a mile from his home where he kept horses for himself, his wife Peggy, and his two sons, Garry, 14, and Vance, 11. From there he would ride "Smokey" 2½ miles to a chicken ranch a block or two from the Pilot House where he would tether the horse and complete the journey on a bicycle. Returning, he'd ride the bike to the ranch, the horse to the stables and the Ford to his home.

One of the few injuries this pilot of the world's fastest airplanes ever had was when "Smokey" slipped on some loose gravel one morning and fell on his master.

To most of the 85 pilots who test Lockheed planes, Burcham displayed the genial personality the public thinks is typical of most fliers. But his intimates knew him as a man of profound depths.

He often took long walks at midnight, pondering some strange problem of flight he had encountered during the day.

Leaned to Science

Burcham was one of the first human beings to peer over the scientific abyss of compressibility . . . to enter that area of high speed in the air where odd behavior of supposedly immutable laws of physics confounded aviation's ablest minds.

That was in the early days of testing P-38's . . . when, from 40,000-foot heights, he screamed earthward faster than any other man ever flew.

With the help of Burcham's observations, Lockheed research engineers have overcome flight barriers created by these strange phenomena of super-sonic speed.

Milo's nine years of pre-Lockheed flying experience included barnstorming, competition in national air races, upside-down flying and other stunts.

But, despite the gasps he drew from admiring crowds, Milo never took chances. Every stunt was carefully rehearsed . . . his plane minutely checked before take-offs.

Though born in Newcastle, Indiana, Burcham considered himself a Californian by adoption. He attended Whittier High School and Whittier College.

'Alarm' Opened Way

The burglar alarm he sold to pay for his first flying lessons was the product of his inventive mind which has created a score of other similar gadgets.

From his well-equipped home workshop Burcham has produced several instruments and devices which engineers have made standard equipment for the Constellation. They were developed on off-hours to answer specific problems he met while conducting engineering test flights of the big transport.

Two of his better-known inventions are a visual oxygen meter that enables a pilot to keep closer check of his oxygen supply in high altitudes and a device, still used, that permits delivery of mail from a plane in flight.

Burcham joined Lockheed in 1937 as a ferry pilot and two years later was sent to England in charge of flight testing at the company's Liverpool division.

Recalled to Burbank, his thoroughness and skill as a pilot brought about his assignment to engineering flight testing where he began testing of P-38 Lightnings.

A visit to the Mayo Clinic to study reactions to high-altitude flying convinced Burcham that decompression of pilots who fly above 30,000 feet was not only desirable, but absolutely necessary. As a result, Lockheed installed decompression equipment for its pilots.

Developed Course

Following his appointment as chief pilot early this year, Burcham developed the unique training course for the Fourth Air Force, flying to bases up and down the Pacific Coast. The same P-38 in which he made the trips was used to demonstrate special flying technique to young pilots of the AAF.

It was a work he loved even better than testing the characteristics of a Lockheed prototype—this teaching others to fly skillfully. His contributions to the science of aviation must be written finally in other chapters at other times, but every pilot knew at that quiet ceremony in Forest Lawn last Tuesday that one of the great fliers of the world had been taken away—too soon.

Cover

THIS week's cover, Lockheed's own Milo Burcham, is presented to Lockheed folk in honor of the memory of a great flier . . . a master test pilot whose loss is mourned by all.

Photograph by Doug White, Lockheed staff photographer.

Telephone Changes Are Held Essential

Corrections for the monthly issue of Lockheed's Telephone directory should be made on Form 4760. The forms can be obtained from stationery stores and should be submitted promptly to Dept. 85-84 when changes occur.

Left to right:
Tony LeVier
Stanley Beltz
Nick Nicholson
Herman Salmon
Bob Harlow
Milo Burcham

FAVORITE PLANES PAY HONOR TO LOST PILOT

Planes he loved, P-38 Lightnings, paid humble honor to Chief Test Pilot Milo Burcham last Tuesday as last rites were said for him in Forest Lawn Memorial Park. The Lockheed ace died in a plane crash on Friday, Oct. 20.

Forming a huge cross and a victor's "V" in clouded skies, the planes moved through the heavens as services in the Church of the Recessional were led by the Rev. Willard O. Trueblood, retired pastor of Friends Church in Whittier.

First squadron of 11 ships in the shape of a cross, came from the Van Nuys air base and was led by Maj. S. A. Long. The second V-shaped squadron from Ontario was led by Maj. M. Millard. Both officers were veterans of the Aleutian Theater of War.

In perfect formation, the two squadrons flown by Army Air Force pilots came over at 3 p.m. and again ten minutes later.

Holding formation the planes then flew over the Lockheed factory in Burbank where they were made and the Lockheed Air Terminal where Burcham used to test them.

Pallbearers were Cyril Chappellet, Lockheed's vice-president; Avery Black, assistant chief test pilot; Joseph Towle, James White, Rudolph Thoren and Anthony W. LeVier, test pilots who were among Burcham's more intimate associates.

The church was thronged with Lockheed officials, pilots who once worked with Burcham and many other of his friends. Surviving are his widow Margaret, two sons, Garry 14 and Vance 11, and his parents, Mr. and Mrs. Charles Burcham.

SWING TELETYPE CUT AT FACTORY B-1

Effective Monday, October 30, the Western Union teletype at Factory B-1 will be discontinued on the swing shift. It will operate during the day shift period only, so departments needing to use it must get their messages in before 4:45 p.m. when the key closes.

Full 24-hour service at Factory A-1, however, will be maintained.

Plants to Hold Realty Options

Including 61 California industrial plants, a 154-page catalog listing properties of the Defense Plant Corporation has been published for distribution to banks, railroads, and chambers of commerce throughout the country.

As announced by the Reconstruction Finance Corporation in the *Wall Street Journal* of Oct. 17, the listed properties include portions of plants operated by Douglas, Lockheed, North American, and other aircraft makers.

Purpose of the catalog, according to Wilbur Wayman, Lockheed's assistant budget director, is to facilitate returning government-owned factories to private ownership as soon as possible. All contracts contain options giving present operators first chance to buy the properties.

30,000 a Day L.A.T.

More than 30,000 persons pass through Lockheed Air Terminal each day. Traffic authorities stress the importance of abiding by terminal regulations.

TED BAKER SETS 11-YEAR PERFECT TIME RECORD

NEVER late or absent since Lockheed hired him 11 years ago in 1933.

That's the record of Ted Baker, P-38 fuselage section supervisor at Plant B-7—a record believed to merit for him the designation of Lockheed's all-time attendance champion.

So far as Factory B attendance officials can determine, Baker's claim is valid.

It wasn't until 1939 that the company began keeping attendance statistics and the Plant B-7 supervisor's record has been perfect since that time.

The facts, affirmed by witnesses, of Baker's record as submitted by Plant B-7 officials indicate he was first hired by Lockheed July 7, 1933, and worked under Wayneat "Pop" Rau in Dept. 9 on the center section.

Because of lost records, Plant B-7 officials explain, Baker was not given official credit for being with the company in 1933 but they submit Miles Sanders, assistant foreman at Plant B-7, as a witness to prove Baker was hired then.

Baker worked on the Electra until 90 ships had been built, then worked on the next two models 12 and 14. When Model 14 became the Hudson bomber in 1938 he stayed with it until the last one came off the line.

In 1942, by then a section supervisor, he was transferred to build the Lodestar where he stayed until his switch last year to his present position at Plant B-7.

Ted Baker

NAVY DAY SEES VENTURA PLEA

FLEET BIRDMEN SEEK AID THROUGH MORE PV PLANES

Navy Day . . . today . . . casts its shadow across the PV production line this morning as Comdr. C. D. Palmer urged more Venturas for immediate military use.

"If we could pile them into Leyte to help the Halsey-MacArthur campaign for total victory then, and only then, could we really celebrate Navy Day," the commander said. Commander Palmer is the senior naval officer at Lockheed.

Talks by the commander and Lt. Comdr. W. R. Stevens at Plant 6 and presentation of a Meritorious Civil Service Award at the Navy-Lockheed Service Center featured Lockheed's Navy Day observance.

Because the Navy enjoyed its first major development under President Theodore Roosevelt, his birthday was selected as the date of Navy Day. Before the buck-toothed fighting man, "Teddy," became President of the United States, he was Assistant Secretary of the Navy.

After this explanation of Navy Day's origin, Comdr. Palmer again urged even greater production of PV's to help shorten the Pacific war.

Speaking both at Plant 6 and Van Nuys, the commander described experiences in the Aleutians where his leadership of a PV-1 squadron brought him an Air Medal, a Distinguished Flying Cross and a commendation from Admiral Chester Nimitz.

Award Presented

At Van Nuys, Lt. Comdr. C. F. Rocheville, Bureau of Aeronautics representative, presented the Meritorious Civil Service Award to Bernard W. Patton, inspector of engineering material, for his suggestion on reworking turret domes which saved costs of $2992.

Pointing out the importance of PV's in Pacific naval operations, Comdr. Palmer expressed the belief that half of the Jap ships destroyed have been sunk by airplanes . . . most of which were attached to the Navy.

"To capture Pacific islands it has always been necessary first to gain air superiority,' he said.

"The PV-1's have been of great assistance in hunting out Jap ships and shore equipment protecting these vital atolls.

"As we know at Lockheed, our PV deliveries have been reduced the last few months. Large deliveries should commence and the fleet is awaiting them anxiously.

"It isn't always the biggest airplane that is of the greatest value . . . a high speed medium bomber like the PV can do a better job than some of our big four-engine ships in hunting out gun emplacements at low altitudes and patrolling the seas in search of all types of shipping.

Need Is Imperative

"Although the PV operates with a smaller crew and burns less gasoline, its greater speed and flexibility enable it to perform some missions far better than the bigger jobs.

"It can land and take off from smaller fields.

"Each of us may think what little more we can do each day doesn't amount to much, but when we add all of these little extras together, it might mean 100 additional airplanes from Lockheed in 1945 . . . and I'm sure that's what we are all trying to do—deliver airplanes to the fighting front fast.

Unfinished Business

"To many, this particular Navy Day's most outstanding significance will be its chastening reminder of the enormity of the job to be done.

"Until Japan is defeated utterly and convincingly, the Navy and all of us at Lockheed have 'unfinished business'."

BLIND LAD IS DONOR

YOUNG William Standage, blind paint shop employe, of Factory B-1, is proud of the model P-38 he built as described in last week's *Lockheed Star*. . . . He is 24 years old and has never been able to see.

He is considered one of the best maskers the department ever had, but he himself wishes he could do still more to help win the war.

Last night he gave a pint of blood to the Blood Donor Bank.

EMPLOYES ARE STILL NEEDED AT LOCKHEED AS TERMINATIONS RISE

Still lots of jobs at Lockheed . . . 3932 of them, to be exact, according to M. V. Mattson, employment manager. "And they all have to be filled," he told the *Star* last night. "These people are necessary to the war, to Lockheed, and to our urgent contracts with the Federal government."

Then Mattson opened the horse's mouth and looked squarely at the teeth.

"Being just plain honest," he said, "since we started this frank campaign for more help we have hired 4998 persons. That sounds excellent . . . and it is.

"But we have had, in the same period, 5243 terminations. That means that we are suffering a net loss and that referral slips still are an essential part of Lockheed's program. Any employe can get a referral slip from his department head. Every employe is asked to do so . . . and use it."

Mattson pointed out that battle-weary servicemen are Lockheed's strongest bulwark for more planes.

"About 400 a day come in for temporary employment," he declared. "They know the need of planes because they have been where Lockheed ships are in ex-

(Continued on Page 8)

RECORD-BREAKING URGE IS CITED AS MODEL MEET GOES ON SCHEDULE

HOPING to break the 87-mile-per-hour speed record held by Rex Bloom, Lockheed Model and Hobby Club members will enter their gas-engine model planes in a contest this Sunday, Oct. 29.

According to president Bob Roosman, the runs will be made over the Commando Course of the Burbank High School, starting at 9 a.m.

Fifteen contestants will fly their U-control models of all classes in a speed and performance contest, first of its kind the Lockheed club has held.

Bloom's black and red model was clocked at 87 miles an hour for the club's record six weeks ago.

Admission to the area is free and Roosman predicts a gallery of approximately 500, judging from the attendance at previous meets.

'CHECK-OUT CHARLEY' SAVES LIVES OF U.S. AIRMEN

TO ENABLE new P-38 pilots to become familiar with instrument and control locations and cockpit procedures, without leaving the classroom, is the purpose of "Check-Out Charley."

An ingenious bit of work by Lieut. W. E. Bullington's instructors in the engineering department of the photo reconnaissance ground school at Will Rogers Field, "Charley" is a cockpit cut from a belly-landed P-38. Set up in the classroom, it contains all instruments and controls, which are connected by an elaborate network of electrical circuits to a one-cylinder emergency generator.

'Engine' Starts

The generator, representing the ship's engine, can be started and operated by the student officer.

The instructors salvaged most of the parts in "Check-Out Charley" from the airplane "graveyard" and it contains parts from B-24's, B-17's, B-25's and even a British Mosquito bomber.

To add another touch of realism, by operating a multitude of switches the red, green and amber recognition lights, the wingtip position lights, the white tail lights and the retractable landing light are lit in a panel mounted on the ceiling of the classroom. By properly setting another series of switches and pressing a button a 100-pound practice bomb suspended from a bracket on the wall is dropped. This represents jettisoning the droppable fuel tanks, which is necessary to prevent fire when a crash landing becomes inevitable.

Changes Pitch

By operating the propeller controls in the cockpit, the student causes a "cutaway" electric prop mounted on a "cutaway" Allison engine on the other side of the room to change pitch.

Improvements Seen

The brainchild of S/Sgt. Lewis Horowitz, S/Sgt. Hugh Connor, Cpl. Henry Schierhold, Pfc. Albert Neuhauser and Pvt. Walter Thoma, the training cockpit has required seven weeks' work thus far and additional installations are contemplated.

Prior to completing this cockpit some accidents were attributed to pilots' lack of familiarity with cockpit procedures and control and instrument locations. Since "Check-Out Charley's" innovation, the number of such accidents has lessened.

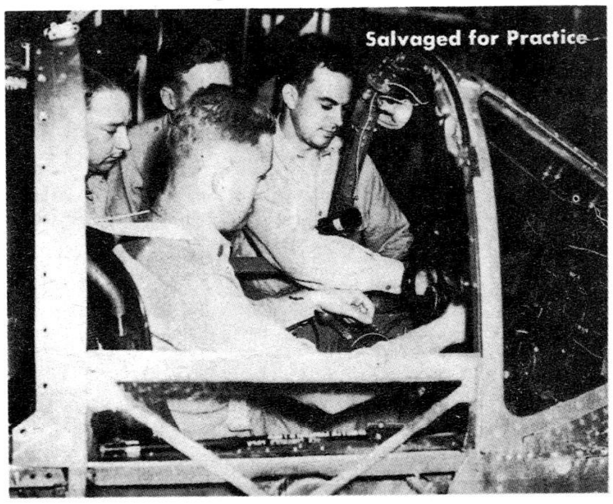

POMONA BACKS WAR CHEST IN CLUB ACTIVITY

Employes of the Lockheed Aircraft Corporation plant in Pomona have, through their Buck-of-the-Month Club, contributed $1000 to the Pomona War Chest in its campaign for $69,500, it was revealed at chest headquarters last night.

The Buck-of-the-Month Club is an organization composed of Lockheed men and women who are voluntarily contributing a small sum regularly for relief of human needs and suffering.

Investigation Made

A committee, consisting of O. V. Trompeter, personnel representative chairman; Milton V. Brunk, president of the Lockheed Employes' Recreation Club, and Ray W. Barnes, union representative, investigates and votes on all requests for contributions.

Through this club, it is possible for employes of the plant to participate in worthy charities and aid deserving welfare organizations, at small individual cost.

Large Sum Given

In the first 28 months of its existence, the Buck-of-the-Month Club, embracing all of the Lockheed plants, has contributed a total of $1,146,652 to worthy charitable, welfare and relief organizations.

The Buck-of-the-Month plan is not copyrighted, and many other industrial concerns throughout the nation have adopted this program with equal success.

Lawrence C. Smith, chairman of the industrial division of the Pomona War Chest drive, as well as vice-chairman of the campaign as a whole, declared: "We of the War Chest appreciate very much this very substantial contribution made to the chest by the members of the Buck-of-the-Month Club.

Employes Commended

"We also would like to commend the employes for formation of such a fine charitable club in their organization. Through this collective contribution program, employes are enabled to make very substantial gifts to all worthy charitable organizations, thereby further aiding in the war with a minimum effort on everyone's part."

Route 6 Bus Service Changes

Discontinuance of interplant bus service on Route 6 serving Burbank Technical Institute and Disney Studios was announced yesterday by H. A. Marriott, manager of the trucking and passenger vehicle department. At the same time he said service on Route 2 would be improved in the near future with an added vehicle.

CERTIFICATE CENTER SHIFTS

Issuance of certificates of availability, formerly made by the recently dissolved placement section of Dept. 90-44 has been transferred to the personnel records section of that division.

B. Steele G. Casebere T. Clinger Lt. Stockton E. Ingram J. Smith

Rangemaster Stockton

GUARD SHOOTING SHOWS PROWESS

If Wild Bill Hickok, Bat Masterson, Sheriff Pat Garrison or any of the other famous gunfighters of the Old West could visit Lockheed today they'd find plenty of congenial company among Lockheed's own gun-throwers, the Guard Division, but they wouldn't find a member of the unit who had ever drawn a gun here in anger.

In the entire history of the Guard Division, no member has ever had to pull a gun, either to protect himself or to defend Lockheed property. . . . Yet every guard keeps his marksmanship skill at razor-edge perfection, as though his life depended on it.

Every Lockheed guard who carries a gun has to earn the right by diligent practice, directed by the Firearms Training unit of the Guard Division under Lt. Jack Stockton. Through cooperation of Burbank's City Council and Police Department, the unit has free use of the Police Pistol Range where shooting is done under ideal conditions. But the training is rugged.

The right to carry a gun, Stockton reports, must be earned by passing stiff target tests and learning to handle firearms *safely* under all conditions . . . and guards must be crack shots with either hand, so that they can still protect themselves if the natural shooting hand is wounded.

"Perhaps you have noticed many of the guards wearing marksmanship medals," remarked Stockton. Believe me, they're not easy to win. Made of bronze, silver and gold, they indicate the ascending ranks of Marksman and Sharpshooter, Expert, and Distinguished Expert.

"A Marksman must score 230 out of a possible 300 points, and 75 out of a possible 100, the first being the total of all points scored in slow fire, timed fire and rapid fire. All must be done with the "natural" shooting hand; and the other is slow fire using his opposite hand. Winning a Sharpshooter medal requires a score of 255 out of 300 and 80 out of 100. The rank of Expert is earned by scoring 270 out of 300 and 85 out of 100; and the Distinguished Expert, must turn in scores of 285 out of 300 and 90 out of 100. All targets are shot on the Standard American Pistol Target at 25 yards."

Only six of the more than 400 members of the entire Guard Division wear the gold medal. They are: Capt. E. Ingram, Capt. T. Clinger, Lt. B. Steele, Lt. J. Stockton, J. J. Smith and G. Casebere. Four others who earned the medal have terminated their service with Lockheed. Twenty-five men wear the Expert silver medal. In all four classes, 245 guards wear shooting medals of various ranks.

This praiseworthy training program was inaugurated in 1941 with Lt. G. Goodrich as instructor, but the U.S. Navy claimed Goodrich after Pearl Harbor. When Lt. Stockton became Rangemaster, Lockheed, Vega and L.A.T. guards were all receiving training. Later, for a time, the Vega guards were trained separately under Rangemaster Clinger, but with consolidation of the guard divisions, Stockton again took charge of the entire group and is given major credit for the present efficiency of the unit.

LINDBERGH IS P-38 'MARVEL'

Col. Charles A. Lindbergh flew a P-38 into Jap-held territory after only five hours of practice, a news report just disclosed here.

According to the release, young fighter pilots of the South Pacific area were amazed at such an unheard-of accomplishment.

The same report said Lindbergh is unofficially credited with shooting down a Japanese plane. His assignment as a civilian expert for the War and Navy Departments has taken him to front bases and on fighter plane flights leading to encounters in which aggressive action has been a matter of necessity.

Much Goes On Little

One coupon from an "A" gas ration book represents four miles on a Lockheed Constellation, greatest of all important planes now in use. No other such transport enjoys so small a consumption of gasoline.

Ambition Realized to Push P-38 Into Enemy's Face in Hun Fight

Fulfilling his ambition to fly the planes he once helped build, Lt. Berkeley Hollister, former Lockheed employe, recently shot down two Nazi planes in an action over Germany.

"We were well into Germany on this particular flight," said Lt. Hollister in a letter received yesterday by his brother, Robert, of Dept. 69-74.

"There were only four of us in P-38s when we saw nearly 40 M.E. 109's ahead and below us.

1st Lt. B. E. Hollister

The four of us made the initial attack and although we received help later, we were able to send the jerries running home.

Overtook Germans

"They turned tail and we followed and overtook them easily. My flight leader shot down three and I was lucky enough to get two. I chased these two and as I got close to the first one I gave him a burst.

"He caught fire and half rolled and I saw the pilot bail out. Then I turned to the other one who was streaking for home. I gave him a couple of bursts and black smoke began pouring out. He went into a steep dive from which I doubt he was ever able to pull out.

'Plenty Scared'

"I received official credit for both planes when my combat film was developed. We were plenty scared, but I guess the Germans were more scared. Now you know why I like a P-38."

Since that letter Lt. Hollister has three more planes to his credit, and has been awarded the Air Medal with three Oak Leaf Clusters to the Air Medal and the Distinguished Flying Cross.

No Charge Is Made For 'Star' Classified

Classified advertisements in the *Lockheed Star* are free to employes. Ask for Form 4929 from a department clerk, at the stationery store, employe transportation, or from employe service. Advertisements are limited to two lines because of space pressure.

Export Airline Shows Huge Gain

Concourse: Rio's Airport

Lodestar: Panair do Brasil

Passengers: Santos Dumont Airport

LODESTARS HELP IN BIG SOUTH AMERICAN RECORD

Lockheed Lodestars, beating through the Brazilian nights on stepped-up schedules, have helped boost the banner of Pan-American's Latin American division.

Express ton miles flown by that unit of the big airline during its last reported 30-day period showed a 155 per cent increase over a comparable 1943 period.

Based on achievements of its entire Latin-American fleet, this report records a 33 per cent gain in passenger miles.

New Night Flights

The part played by Lodestars in this increase consists in the successful operation of new night flights of Panair do Brasil, Brazilian affiliate of Pan-American World Airways System . . . between Campo Grande and Paraguay's capital, Asuncion . . . Rio and Sao Paulo, and others.

Soaring graphs of this burgeoning business in spite of war conditions presage the accuracy of Pan-American's estimates of the potential postwar markets it plans to serve with lightning speed at low rates.

Applications awaiting hearing by the Civil Aeronautics Board are based on a program the company says will offer international mass transportation by air . . . to carry the average man at a cost he can afford throughout the Western hemisphere.

Traffic Is Boosted

A hundredfold increase of its current passenger-mile transport capacity in Latin America with the aid of new equipment is planned.

Air tariffs on the long-distance routes to Rio and Buenos Aires would be as low as 3½ cents a mile. Other substantial reductions are listed.

Typical of proposed fare reductions is the listed new price of $225 for a Los Angeles to Rio de Janeiro passenger ticket which now costs $590. In place of the $670 fare to Buenos Aires, the new rate will be $227.

Cargo capacity of Pan-American's proposed new Clipper fleet would be 17 times greater than that of today's ships, making it possible to handle more than 30,000,000 pounds of air express annually.

More Direct Lines

Proposals before the CAB seek authority to operate more direct services in South America to Rio de Janeiro and Buenos Aires and to connect the company's Latin American network with new gateway ports in the United States.

In addition to Los Angeles, Miami, New Orleans and Brownsville, Tex., passengers and freight would be flown from Charleston, S.C.; Tampa, Fla.; Houston, Tex., and New York.

Newly extended schedules of Panair do Brasil with its fleet of speedy Lodestars are in line with that company's policy of serving all the states and territories in Brazil.

March to West

Ponta Pora, a stop on the new route to Asuncion, is the border capital of the new Brazilian federal state of the same name along the border of Brazil, recently organized as part of President Getulio Vargas' plans for the "March to the West."

In this way, airplanes are creating in South America, a 20th Century version of development in the United States brought on by railroads . . . but it's an infinitely faster change . . . as much faster as the flight of a Lodestar compared to the puffing effort of the Iron Horse.

P-38 TILT SETTLED

Two Marines of the First Division, which the Japanese would rather not hear any more about, got the Lockheed publicity department this week to settle an argument as to whether P-38's have twin fuselages or twin nacelles.

"The facts are," read the reply to their written query, "that the plane has three nacelles and two fuselages.

"Definitions by the National Advisory Committee on Aviation are as follows:

"Fuselage—the body, of approximately streamline form, to which the wings and tail unit of an airplane are attached.

"Nacelle—an enclosed shelter for personnel or for a power plant.

"The booms of the P-38 which are extensions of the engine nacelles in themselves constitute the fuselage and the pilot compartment is not a fuselage but a nacelle.

"This unusual airplane therefore has three nacelles of which two are for power plants and one is for the pilot. And the P-38 actually has two fuselages."

Listen to the Wind

"It isn't the cold that gets you down in the Aleutians," writes one PV flyer. "It's the wind. Sometimes it whips close to 100 knots."

Continental Completes Agreement With Army Transport Command

After two years of operating Army cargo planes on regular schedules over domestic air routes, Continental Airlines last night completed its contract for the work with the Air Transport Command and turned over all Army cargo operations to the domestic transportation division of the command.

As announced by Robert F. Six, president, the contract between Continental Airlines and the Air Transport Command was the last such contract to be terminated. Other similar contracts with commercial airlines flying Army cargo planes were cancelled last month.

Last July Continental celebrated its tenth anniversary of successful operation achieved with the use of Lockheed equipment exclusively.

All of Continental's contract cargo flights were made under the supervision of O. R. Haueter, vice president in charge of operations, Mr. Six said. When Haueter took charge in July, 1942, he faced such problems as setting up a school for training quickly many additional pilots, radio operators, and other skilled personnel; greatly expanding weather-prediction and flight-control facilities; setting up a teletype communication system with Army fields; coordinating airline methods and procedures with the Army.

Whipped Problems

Haueter and his staff, whipping all of these problems and countless others in record time, very quickly had the cargo flights operating with the reliability and regularity of a commercial airline.

During the 2¼ years of operating cargo flights, the airline has flown millions of pounds of rush cargo, including medicines, airplane parts, radio parts and equipment, engine and armament parts. Many of them were desperately needed at the war front. Many flights also carried Army personnel.

Trained Pilot

In addition to flying cargo planes for the Air Transport Command, Continental has also trained approximately 100 Army pilots, checking them out in cargo planes and carrying them as third crew members on cargo flights. Many Continental-trained pilots are now overseas.

Majority of the cargo flights made by Continental were on regular daily schedules over established routes. Continental flight crews at various times also flew special missions to every section of the United States to carry parts and supplies needed to repair grounded aircraft.

Instruction for Employes

RIFLE CLUB OFFERS GOOD TRAINING FOR INDUCTEES

Training completion by 150 Lockheedians was announced yesterday by N. S. Hopkins, president of the Lockheed Rifle and Pistol Club, sponsored by the LERC. In answer to many requests for this type of work, the club received permission from the National Rifle Association, with which it has been affiliated since July, 1942, to organize and conduct a small arms firing school.

The course was outlined by the NRA and has been approved by the War Department. Those who finish six weeks' work are given a written examination, as well as a test in firing. Awards are issued by the NRA according to the score record. Of the Lockheed group, two have scored as experts and all the others are sharpshooters.

The work is given by members of the club who have instructor's ratings and hold qualifying certificates issued by the NRA.

Draftees Favored

While this course is available to all interested employes, those with the least chance of draft deferment are given preference. Instruction is similar to that given by the regular U.S. military service so that, in case of induction, basic rifle school will have been approached.

Commenting on this program of rifle training, Gen. Dwight D. Eisenhower says: "Any young man who has ahead of him prospective service in the armed services will do well to learn all he can about the Army military rifle. If he can become a really capable rifleman, so much the better. Once he has donned the uniform he will find his hours and days so packed with intensive training that he will be pressed for time to learn the many things he should know for his own self-preservation before he is called upon to get the enemy. The one weapon that every man—soldier, sailor, or airman—should be able to use effectively, is the rifle. It is always his weapon of personal safety in an emergency and for many it is the primary weapon of offense and defense. Expertness in its use cannot be overemphasized."

To augment the preinduction training, a follow-up advanced course likewise is offered. Weekly instruction classes are held at the ROTC shooting ranges in the two Glendale high schools. Elementary classes meet each Tuesday from 7 to 10 p.m., and advanced classes each Wednesday at the same time.

In addition to the many men who have taken the training at Lockheed, the club also has issued certificates to 20 women.

Club Women To Hold Election Meet Wednesday

Concluding two years of varied altruistic accomplishments, the Service Star Women of Factory B will meet Wednesday, Nov. 8, in the Studio Lounge of the Hollywood-Roosevelt Hotel to elect officers for the coming year. Only members who have been active in club affairs during the past three months will be eligible to vote.

Esther M. Johnston, chairman of the nomination committee, announces nominees for president as Alice Van Houten, incumbent; Genie Archer, vice-president, and Margaret Olson.

Josephine Murillo, chairman of the B-2 Service Star Women; Evelyn Gibson, and Hazel Austin, sergeant-at-arms, have been named as candidates for vice-president.

Nominated for treasurer are Pat Koerner and Mildred Ashleigh, chairman of the Red Cross Service Unit of the club.

Betty Watkins, chairman of the membership committee, R. Dean White, and Marian Everitt are nominees for secretary.

Nominations for a member-at-large who, with the officers, sets up the executive committee of the club, include Ila Morrow, club historian, and Eleanor Sewall, first president of the Service Star Women.

Cigarettes Controlled

In an attempt to distribute cigarettes among employes of all shifts as fairly as possible, an LERC committee meeting with Lockheed personnel relations officers this week endorsed a new plan of equal distribution to affect all cigarette-vending machines under LERC commissary control.

Vending machines will be located in canteen areas only, and will be equipped with locks. Certain machines will be opened at certain periods throughout the 24 hours for the convenience of employes of the three shifts on days when there are cigarettes for distribution. For day shift the machines will be open a half hour before the beginning of the shift. For swing shift, machines will be opened at 3:15 p.m. and closed at 4 p.m. Graveyard employes will be able to purchase cigarettes from 12 midnight until the beginning of their shift at 12:30 a.m.

"We believe this new plan to be the most practical for an even distribution of cigarettes over the three shifts," explained Earl Shriver, chairman of the LERC committee. "However, success or failure largely depends on the integrity and good sportsmanship of individual purchasers . . . a direct ratio between the number of considerate smokers, content with one pack, and the number of hoarders."

ADVENTURE SHOW IS SCHEDULED

Demand by employes has prompted the LERC educational committee to reschedule the adventure movie filmed by Douglas Erdman, Lockheed flight test inspector, for Tuesday, Nov. 14, in room 4 of the B-1 Cafeteria Building.

Erdman, who filmed the movie in Brazil, Africa and India, will during the evening display some of the curios picked up on his travels.

Next Tuesday, Nov. 7, "Adventures of the News Cameramen" will be shown for employes and their families. This picture is a combination of six films showing the dangers faced by newsmen.

Free reservation tickets may be had for the 5:30 p.m., 8 o'clock, or 1 a.m. shows at the Factory A or B offices.

BLUE STARS TO BRING SANTA TO VETERANS

Well-filled Christmas socks for servicemen in nearby hospitals will be distributed by the Blue Star Women of Factory A during the coming holiday period.

The executive committee, headed by Ella Kennedy, president, asks the cooperation of all members of the club in supplying as many of these gifts as possible.

Regulation socks may be purchased in sizes of 11½ or 12. One of the socks will then be rolled and placed in the toe of the other. As many gifts as desired may be used to fill the sock. It should then be decorated with Christmas tags and seals.

What to Use

Gifts may be selected from the list given below, but it is imperative that nothing edible be used, as some of the recipients of the gifts may be on restricted diets. The following list should be clipped and saved for reference, as it will not appear again in the *Star*.

Black or brown shoe laces, toilet soap, small games, gum, picture postcards, wallet, small puzzles, pocket combs with clip attachment, washcloth, memorandum book, cigarettes, razor blades, stationery, talcum powder, dog tag, toothbrush, shaving cream, handkerchiefs, tooth powder or paste, playing cards, pocket knife, corncob pipe, tobacco, lead pencil and sharpener, small pocket flashlight, or harmonica.

All contributions should be left at the Factory A LERC office at 2425 Avon.

For further information contact Nita Evans, 8-1735.

LERC Activities

MODEL & HOBBY CLUB—Meeting every other Wednesday, 7 p.m., second floor of Swimming Bldg. at Griffith Park. Next meeting, Nov. 1.

CAMERA CLUB—First and third Thursday of the month. Next meeting, Nov. 2, Room 5, Cafeteria B-1, 5 p.m.

DANCE CLUB—Every Thursday, 8 p.m., Allan Rudack Studios, 7213 Beverly Blvd.

FREE MOVIES—Tuesday, Oct. 31, "Adventures of the News Cameramen," 5:30 and 8 p.m. Swing shift, 1 a.m.

BOAT CLUB—Every Wednesday, 5 p.m., B-1 Cafeteria, Private Dining Room.

RIDING CLUB—Lockheed Rangers, every Friday, 7 p.m., Pico Stables, 420 Riverside Drive, Burbank. Swing shift, 10 a.m., Wednesday, Pico Stables, 420 Riverside. Call LERC for reservations.

SERVICE STAR WOMEN—Plant B-1, first and third Wednesdays after work. Conference Room 1, Cafeteria Bldg. B-2, day and graveyard shift, every Wednesday lunch period, 11 a.m. and 3:30 a.m., Conference Room.

MUSIC APPRECIATION CLUB—Regular meeting second and fourth Mondays of the month, Cafeteria, B-1, Room 5, 2 p.m. Recordings every Wednesday from 2:45 to 3:45 p.m., Factory B-1 lunch area.

CONCERTS — Military band, rehearsals Friday, 9:15 a.m., concerts begin 10:50 a.m., main recreation area, all day shift lunch periods.

PLANT TOURS—Contact the LERC office for further particulars.

DAY PENGUINETTES — Cabaret night hostesses, Boulevard USO, every Thursday evening.

VOCAL GROUPS — Hollywood Radio Chorus, Hollywood High School, Room M.A. 71, every Wednesday from 7 to 10 p.m. Victory Singers — Monday and Wednesday, 7 p.m., L.A. High School, Olympic and Rimpau, Room 423.

CHESS CLUB—Wednesdays, 7 p.m., Rooms 1 and 2, Burbank Recreation Center, 1111 W. Olive.

BADMINTON—Tuesday and Thursday, 7 p.m., John Burroughs Jr. High School gym, Burbank.

BLUE STAR WOMEN—Open house, Boulevard USO, 6551 Hollywood Blvd., Wednesday, 7:30 p.m.

SWIMMING — Men and women — Glendale YMCA, every Friday, 8:30 and 9:30 p.m.

GIRLS' SWIMMING — Tuesday, 7 p.m., Hollywood YMCA, 1553 N. Hudson, Hollywood. Swing shift, Tuesday, 10:30 a.m., same place.

MEN'S SWIMMING — Glendale YMCA, each Wednesday, 6 to 8:15 p.m.

Rudy Thoren

Shows Booked By Employes

Following its policy to encourage employe participation and leadership in its sponsored activities, the LERC last night announced a procedure change in selecting motion pictures for lunch period entertainment.

Effective Nov. 4, all movies to be shown in the recreation areas on all shifts will be chosen by employes in cooperation with projectionists, while in the past selections have been made by the LERC or by the film distributors.

All features and shorts for the 13-week period beginning Nov. 4, have been booked, although some change may be made by substitution of later releases from major studios. Short subjects chosen will be releases from OWI and War Department agencies and will include such pictures as "Memphis Belle."

Suggestions for future programs or any ideas which will add to the greater enjoyment of employes during the lunch periods should be directed to Jack Phillips at the Factory A or B LERC offices.

Thoren to Be Guest Speaker

Rudy Thoren, chief flight engineer of Lockheed, will be guest speaker at a luncheon meeting of the swing shift Factory B Penguins to be held Friday noon, Nov. 10, at the Los Angeles Breakfast Club.

Thoren will discuss the Constellation from its blueprint beginning to its record-breaking flight to Washington, D.C., last spring. He will also conduct a forum to answer employe questions regarding the Lockheed giant.

Entertainment for the event will be announced in next week's *Star*.

Toucher Season Gaining Speed

Hawks Win In Runaway

Touch football plunged into the center of the Lockheed sports light this week ➡ as 12 teams of two North Hollywood loops, still keyed from last week's initial scramble for the win columns, buckled down to the serious business of climbing into the lead positions of their respective leagues.

The season's opener, Oct. 16, between the Jet Joes of Dept. 28-10 and the Night Hawks of Dept. 28-26, was an indication of the fast type of ball 1944 toucher fans can expect to see throughout the season and the final battle for the Lockheed all-plant, all-shift championship.

Piloted by John Steers, the Night Hawks blasted their way into a 13-0 win over the cagey 28-10 combination with a series of aerial offensives and spectacular open-field running, featuring R. Bright, Bob Williams, Chuck Middleton and Joe Stein.

First Touchdown

First touchdown of the season was scored when halfback Bright intercepted a pass tossed by the Jet Joes' captain Len Mierzwa in the second quarter. Bright lateraled to Chuck Middleton who ran 40 yards for the first tally.

In the same loop, later the same day, the Template Butchers and P-38 final game ended in a scoreless tie. Opener of the Tuesday league ended after the Office Gang chalked up 35 points, leaving their opponents, the Final Assembly squad scoreless.

Standings Given

Scores and standings for the first week follow:

Interest Picks Up

MONDAY LEAGUE—N. HOLLYWOOD

Team	Dept.	Plant	W	L	Tie
Night Hawks	28-26	B-1	1	0	0
Customer Service Wolves	62-73	B-5	1	0	0
Template Butchers	44-52	B-3	0	0	1
P-38 Final	18-20	B-1	0	0	1
Jet Joes	28-10	B-1	0	1	0
Apprentice Group	90-46	B-5	0	1	0

Team		vs.	Team	
Night Hawks	13		Jet Joes	0
Template Butchers	0		P-38 Final	0
Customer Service Wolves	38		Apprentices	0

TUESDAY LEAGUE—N. HOLLYWOOD

Team	Dept.	Plant	W	L	Tie
Office Gang	18-10	B-1	1	0	0
Processors	27-31	A-1	1	0	0
Tool Engineers	40-34	A-1	0	0	1
P-38 Leading Edge	18-23	B-1	0	0	1
Final Asembly B-17	13-19	A-1	0	1	0
Machine Parts	53-80	B-1	0	1	0

Team		vs.	Team	
Office Gang	35		P-38 Leading Edge	6
Processors	27		Machine Parts	7
Tool Engineers	6		Final Assembly	0

Lockheed Cager-Loop To Open Wednesday

Lockheed's inter-departmental 1944-45 basketball season will open officially at 6 p.m., Wednesday, Nov. 1, at the John Burroughs Junior High School in Burbank with the starting whistle bringing together two promising B-1 squads, Glen Arford's "Dept. 18-20, No. 1," graveyarders, who will tangle with the Machine Parts quintet captained by Lou Thompson, playing out of Dept. 53-80.

Three games will follow the opener at 7, 8, and 9 p.m. At 7 the Rabble Rousers of Dept. 60-86, B-5, will meet the A-1 Oh Bees, engineering department. 18-20 No. 2 will meet the Bummers of 12-19 at eight followed by the nightcap rondo between the department 13-26 squad and 15-08, both of A-1.

The Wednesday night, John Burroughs league, made up of A-1, B-1 and B-5 teams is the first of several leagues to enter this season's bid for top cage honors.

Second league to get under way is now complete and ready for play but temporarily inactive until a convenient gym is located and arranged for by the LERC, sponsors of the cage roundup.

According to the LERC sports office, swing shift leagues are at a standstill due to the fact that not enough teams have been turned in to form leagues. Basketeers not already signed up for league play may do so by sending in team name and roster to either the A or B LERC offices.

Weekly Bowling Roundup Reveals New Highs in All Leagues and All Brackets

Fastest Lockheed league, the 850 scratch loop, bowling at Jackson on Tuesday evenings, is being led in their second week by Carl Burton's Butchers and C. Lyster's Shooting Stars with a three-win, no-loss tie. However, the Butchers lead the two squads in the total pin column by an edge of 128 pins with a 2568. In second spot are the Thunderbowlers and the Ascenders, the former with the total pin high of 2588, also the league's high series. The Butchers tossed the best high game in the first round with 933. Hottest individual scores were those of P. Ulrey of the Produc-tion Service quintet who rolled the high individual series of 611 to tie for the all-league high in that bracket and who also carries the all-league high average of 203.

Still in Front

In the high-team series department the Final Assemblers of the Thursday swing shift league at Olive Recreation still lead Lockheed's 368 handicap squads with a tally of 2976, established three weeks ago. Their score is a safe 52 pins above the second-best Mixers, last year's Lockheed champs whose best efforts in the team series column have been 2924.

The Mixers bowl in the Friday night North Hollywood league. Third-placers, the AAF squad, number-one team of the Tuesday swing shift loop at Sunset, with 2920, are trailed by only one point by the Beer Hounds of the Wednesday swing league at Olive.

Game Race Close

The all-league high-team game, 1053, also held by the Final Assemblers, is being threatened this week by the AAF boys who chalked up a 1052 to displace last week's second-placers, the Jerks of the Friday, North Hollywood league, whose 1026 has become a fourth-place tally, with the Full House quintet of the same league in third place with 1033. Only other team game score besting 1000 turned in this week was a 1007 rolled by the P-38 Pickups in the Tuesday Sunset No. 1 league.

Tallies Boosted

High individual series tallies have been boosted 12 points over last week with Red Duffy of the Outcasts, bowling in the 750 scratch loop at Burbank Bowl and P. Ulrey of the Production Service squad in the 850 scratch club at Jackson both rolling 611 to tie for first-place honors. Best HIG in handicap leagues is 602 recorded by Gordon Melton of the Ramblers in the Burbank Thursday swing league who bested last week's first-placer, Bill Sharp, playing with the Wing Dings in the same loop, by 3 pins. Other high individual series tallies are D. Brown's 591; G. Riding's 588; E. Fish's 587; E. Brashear's 584; W. Wilhoit's 581.

New Highs Revealed

Best individual high game this week is still F. Hancock's 247, rolled for the A.B. Seers in the Engineering Friday league at North Hollywood. Several new names enter the high-game bracket this week with Bud Fink of the Pounders in the 750 scratch league at Burbank scoring 246 to take second spot, and last week's second-placer F. Haley, now tied for third with B. Smith of the Butchers in the Tuesday 850 scratch league at Jackson, both with 243. Six pins behind, in fourth place is Herb Carson of the Flight Test quintet of the Airway alleys' Tuesday league, with 237, followed by J. Pace, 236; R. Follett and C. Ames, 235; R. Labeateau, 231, and B. Beechel, 227.

Jerks Move Up

The best win card turned in this week was the property of the Jerks, leaders of the Friday league at North Hollywood with 25 wins out of a possible 28. Other bests in this department remain the Van Nuys loop's Inspection No. 1 with 11 wins, 1 loss, and the Wednesday swing Chumps with 8 out of 8. At this juncture, the LERC sports office wishes to point out to all league secretaries that this column is made up from score sheets turned in to the LERC office each week before noon on Friday. It is possible that the names and scores here are being bested in other leagues not named, simply because taily sheets of these leagues have not been received from league officers by the Friday noon deadline. Friday night leagues will be included in the following week's roundup.

Ulrey Sets New High

Fred McComas, of the Thursday swing shift Tail Spinners who led the list of all-league high individual averages last week with 186, jumped to 188, according to this week's tally, only to take second spot to P. Ulrey of the 850 scratch Production Service squad whose 203 tops everything so far submitted in this department. Carl Ames, undisputed second-placer last week with 177 dropped to 176 this week to share fifth-place honors with John Cummiskey of the Thunderbirds in the Airways' Tuesday loop. This week's third best is E. Brashear of the Training Transports of the Tuesday Sunset No. 2 league with 183, followed closely by Red Duffy of the 750 scratch league's Outcasts who boasts 182. Others are H. Gullick, 175; B. Otten and M. Chapman, tie with 175; H. Erwin, 173; and B. Robertson, R. LaBeateau, 172.

Men's Doubles Matches Set For Oct. 29

Final playoff for the Lockheed men's doubles tennis championship was promised for the near future yesterday when Art Fiedler, LERC tennis coordinator announced the date of the semifinal match between Craig Cunningham and Percy Haythorn and their opponents, Jim McDaniel and C. S. Fisher as being Sunday, Oct. 29, 3 o'clock, at La Cienega courts.

The match has been delayed several weeks due to Cunningham's illness. The winner of this match will meet the Verne Hughes-Leigh Newcomer duo, already in the finals for the championship.

The semifinal match will be the second time Cunningham and McDaniel will have met in the final brackets of the 1944 Lockheed net tournaments. Previously they met at the same courts as men's singles finalists where McDaniel took three sets out of five to win the championship.

Hughes and Newcomer reached the finals by defeating Richards and Efferts, 6-2, 6-2 in the prelims; Lewis and Miller, 6-2, 6-2; Smith and Pierce, 6-3, 6-1; Phillips and Foster, 6-3, 6-2.

PITCH-PUTT TENETS AIRED

Policies of the new Pitch-Putt club, now numbering nearly a half-hundred players and growing daily, were revealed last night by the club president, Norris McCoy, 38-04 graveyarder.

An entry fee of 50 cents has been established with an additional charge of 25 cents for each of three consecutive weekly rounds, to be held on Wednesdays, beginning at 4:30 p.m., at the nine-hole pitch-and-putt course at Hollywood Way and Victory Blvd., in Burbank. Money collected will go into a prize fund and divided into two flights, A and B. On the fourth Wednesday, members will play a tournament to determine the winner of each flight.

Although two Wednesday rounds have already been played, J. A. Vrooman, secretary, points out that additional golfers are still able to enter the current tournament by paying the entry and round fees and submitting two score cards showing scores of rounds played any time since Oct. 17. Cards should be turned in at either the A or B LERC office.

Lockheed Keglers to Star at Vet Benefit

Lockheed Lightning bowling squad, recent third-placers in the National Telegraphic tourney, and the Lockheed Recreation Club team have been selected to open the all-day Birmingham hospital benefit at Llo-Da-Mar Bowl, Sunday, Nov. 5, it was revealed last night by Mary Jane Hogan, manager of the alleys. The two Burbank squads will be matched against the best from Douglas, El Segundo and North American aircraft plants respectively in exhibition play.

All proceeds taken in throughout the day will be turned over to the rehabilitation center at Birmingham who will use the money to construct bowling alleys for veterans convalescing there.

ARMISTICE, USMC BIRTH REMEMBERED

Two days, this week, are heavy with significance to armed men around the world and to ➡ their kin at home.

Over the face of the globe they are remembering:

An ephemeral armistice, 26 years ago tomorrow.

And they are recalling that, 169 years ago today, the United States Marine Corps was born in a Philadelphia saloon—Tun's Tavern. Now its hardened leathernecks crawl all over the earth—dying sometimes for still that other armistice named "total victory."

Those who die are honored in many ways by proud industries that once employed them.

Air Vengance

But this conflict has disclosed no memorials more fitting than the dedicated war planes Lockheed sends, vengance bent, to distant battle fronts.

Like punishing angels, they rise into the blue sky above Lockheed Air Terminal, carrying emblazoned beneath their guns, the names of Lockheed's own who have given their lives.

On the side of each is engraved an emblem—a gold star inscribed "Resurgam" — "I Shall Rise Again"—and beneath it the name of the former employe to whose memory it may be dedicated.

Relatives Present

Memorial ceremonies, while planes are still on the assembly line, are participated in by relatives working for Lockheed or by fellow workers. Take-offs are without ceremony.

(Continued on Page 5)

For Pfc. Alexander, USMC: Killed in Action

ACCIDENTS ARE CUT IN MANY UNITS

One of the greatest scourges of industry—lost-time accidents—is well on the way to being eliminated in Lockheed plants if a report from chief safety engineer Jack Hatton is any index.

Where once a record of a million accident-free manhours was a phenomenon, such records are now becoming a commonplace in Lockheed plants and departments. For instance:

Hours Roll Up

Plant A-57 at Fresno has accumulated 1,294,973 employe hours since the last lost-time injury which occurred in September, 1943. Superintendent C. U. Wells and Foreman Al Nilmeier attribute this fine safety record to the splendid cooperation of all employes and they have indicated that they hope to top the present Lockheed all-plant record of 1,417,197 employe hours set by the experimental department at Factory B-1.

Plant A-56 at Taft has completed 16 months with a total accumulation of 571,703 accident-free employe hours.

Plant A-55 at Bakersfield has completed 13 months with a total accumulation of 455,259 accident-free employe hours.

Perfect Record

Dept. 38-05, Parts Control—Subassembly, Factory B-1, has not had a single lost-time injury since the present department was created. It has now accumulated 594,532 accident-free employe hours.

Dept. 44-52, Template, Factory B-1, has completed over two years without a lost-time injury and its present total of accident-

(Continued on Page 8)

MAJOR GETS 2 HUNS

Maj. Jules D. Biscayart, 27-year-old fighter pilot and squadron operations officer, has shot down two FW-190's in an air battle west of Magdeberg, Germany, it was learned here today.

The major formerly was a mechanic at Lockheed.

Rudy Vallee Is Bond Drive Star

Lt. Rudy Vallee and his U.S. Coast Guard Band hove to in Burbank this week preliminary to the opening of Lockheed's drive to reach its $4,608,825

Rudy Vallee

quota of the Sixth War Loan. The campaign opens Nov. 20.

The former Yale University undergraduate who crooned his way to fame as a big name band leader entertained all shifts at Factory A-1 on Monday and repeated the program Tuesday at Factory B-1.

Lockheed's quota in the forthcoming campaign can be completed if each employe invests an average of only $75. This is $25 less than the $100 in cash they were asked to contribute for the Fifth War Loan.

Departing from procedure of the last campaign, bonds will be sold on a cash basis and delivered immediately without waiting.

This will be in addition to payroll deduction purchases, which, during November and December will be entirely credited to the Lockheed quota.

To facilitate cash sales special mobile equipment is planned to bring bonds direct to buyers.

Venturas Set Top Safety Record

Greatest safety record in the history of aviation, the Navy said last week, has been made by Ventura PV-1s in the Marshall Islands where performance of a squadron of the Lockheed bombers was 99.96 per cent perfect.

Not one of the medium bombers operating from a Southwest Pacific base was lost during the 61 days of May and June, the report indicates.

Customers' Service Handles All Type Planes for Repairs

Since Pearl Harbor, Lockheed's Customer Sales and Service Division at Burbank has become the hub base hospital for battered fighting planes from the entire Pacific theater of war.

To it, in almost a continuous stream, come America's aerial battleships of every type and size, every make and model—but all with one thing in common, the need for refitting, repairing, or retuning to put them back in fighting trim so they can resume their smashes against the Japanese.

Latest among the long roster of famous fighting planes to put in at the division is the Bolivar, a Liberator bomber that has made 81 missions in the South Pacific, flown 1173 hours, logged 186,000 miles and plastered the Nips with 405,000 pounds of bombs. The famed old warrior, bearing the scars of many sky combats, carried a crew of nine when she landed at Burbank, headed by Lt. Andrew Patrick, pilot, with Lt. James W. Watson in the co-pilot's seat.

None of the crew had flown less than 40 missions in the Bolivar which, as soon as she is put in shape by Lockheed's experts, will again return to duty for further forays against the Nips.

Fixed at Customer's Service

'LIFE BEGINS' FOR MRS. CROW

Life has begun at 64 for Mrs. Roxie Crow. She is a stock clerk in Dept. 38-4 at Factory B-1. She is also the mother of eight children, 28 grandchildren, and more nieces and nephews than you have time to count. Two of her sons, one grandson and eight nephews are in the Army.

This is the woman who has just won one of the largest prizes ever awarded in her unit for a Works Simplification idea, $248. Dept. 38-4 is Stock Control for radio sub-assemblies. Wires for these sub-assemblies have to be wrapped with certainty. The method being employed did not appeal to Mrs. Crow as "most efficient," so she put her farm-wife thinking to work and came up with an idea for a simple rack which enables her to do a better job and, at the same time, cut man-hours approximately in half.

Until Mrs. Crow came with Lockheed nearly a year and a half ago, she had belonged to the pioneering stock of American farm women, so many of whom have entered war plants since Pearl Harbor to build the munitions of war for their sons.

P. K. Berkland Mrs. Crow

Joe Towle Named Chief Test Pilot

LOCKHEED STILL NEEDS HELP TO MEET SCHEDULE

Ringing up its "worst week" in hires in recent months, Lockheed again last night stressed that more than 3000 jobs are available and urged employes to use referral slips to fill essential positions.

"For the week just closed, Lockheed lost 952 persons and engaged only 569," employment manager M. V. Mattson explained. "Our production schedule is not curtailed. We need more help at all factories except Plant 2 and Plant 7. Every other Lockheed unit is stressing the need for aid.

Hinders War Effort

"A net loss of 385 employes within a single week is a serious blow to our war commitments. There is no middle ground. The fight in Europe is still going . . . the war with Japan is far from won."

The Navy office last night emphasized the imperative want of more Ventura planes. Commander C. D. Palmer, resident representative of the Bureau of Aeronautics, pointed out once more that the PV's were the best ship the Navy had to perform their specific missions. Some weeks ago, he said, Lockheed sent skilled employes to Arizona to help with wing construction by Goodyear.

No Substitute

"There is just no substitute," he added. "Help is needed . . . and needed badly."

Men, too, are wanted for the Constellation assembly line. There is considerable heavy work to be done and the manpower shortage is evident.

Joe Towle

ENGINEERING ACE ASSUMES POSITION HELD BY BURCHAM

Joe Towle—J. C. Towle for the record—Lockheed's senior engineering test pilot, was appointed chief pilot for the company this week by Cyril Chappellet, vice-president in charge of administration.

The new chief pilot, who succeeds the late Milo Burcham in the position, will direct the activities of Lockheed's 75 test pilots.

Avery Black continues in his post as assistant chief pilot.

After joining Lockheed in 1939, the 39-year-old flier helped assemble and test Lockheed Hudsons in England, Lodestars for the Union of South Africa and for the Portuguese in East Africa at Mozambique. He is a native of Oregon and graduate of Vancouver.

Altitude Flying

New problems of high altitude flight were a specialty of Towle as an engineering test pilot and he climbed to the substratosphere to find their answers. Working closely with the Army Air Forces Aero-Medical laboratory at Wright Field, O., he added valuable data to its records. Once, Col. Randolph Lovelace, laboratory director, flew piggy-back with him in a P-38, seeking the answer to a particularly vexing question.

After Milo Burcham became chief pilot last March, Towle took over the job of test-flying the Constellation prior to its record-shattering flight to Washington. When the big ship returned with world acclaim for its performance, he continued checking and rechecking. Many minor improvements arose from his suggestions.

Secret Plane

In addition to his testing of the Constellation, Towle has done extensive work on Lockheed's new secret fighter airplane.

Transocean flights of Lindbergh and others lured Towle to his first plane ride at Roosevelt Field, New York, in 1927. He first soloed in Dallas, Texas, the following year. His pre-Lockheed experience includes flying for Fairchild Aerial Surveys, Inc., and seven and a half years with Byrd-Frost, Inc., oil producers.

The new chief test pilot, who has logged many thousands of hours in the air, was married in 1930 at Tyler, Texas, to Evelyn Zarr who was one of his first pupils after he turned instructor. They now reside on a 160-acre ranch in Newhall.

An old biplane its builder couldn't get anyone else to test was one of the first ships Towle ever flew for money.

Made-Up Job

That was in Jacksonville, Texas, in 1928 and the plane was made from odd parts from the wrecks of other old ships. But the plane flew with Towle at the controls and they even carried passengers in it for about a month.

After 25 hours of soloing under instruction of Verne Maguire, since killed in the crash of a plane he was flying for TACA in Central America, Towle test-flew the biplane in Jacksonville. Built by a man named Sam Hall, the plane was so rickety that a more experienced pilot named Jet Hootsell refused to risk his own neck on the test. Hootsell is now an inspector for Lockheed.

Towle got his first license from the Department of Commerce after the required 200 hours of flying time. He worked hard and fast for it because he had been promised a job at a flying school in Dallas, Texas, and he needed that job.

Flew Orion

The first Lockheed plane Towle ever flew was an Orion owned by the Byrd-Frost Oil Company which he joined in 1932.

Crew Chief Sees More War Before Europe Capitulates to Allied Arms

Take it from Staff Sergeant Leon H. Painter, AAF crew chief who learned about P-38's in Burbank, the good U.S. still has goal to go in Europe and, like a football game, that's the hardest part of the fight.

Writing a friend at Lockheed, he expressed surprise at the apparent optimism here about the war.

"Don't let them kid you," he says.

"This is just like a football game. We made the march down the field. Now we have the home team with its backs to its own goal line.

"The next four plays will be tough. And if we don't make it in four plays it's going to be tougher. Now is definitely no time for anyone to lean back. One fumble might change the score."

Sgt. Painter's letter was written to one of his best friends, Furman T. O'Hara of Dept. 39-03, maintenance, Flight Field. It was V-mailed from France just a few days ago in reply to a note from O'Hara deploring wishful thinking of early American victory. O'Hara was trained at Lockheed in October and November of 1942.

Burcham Family Extends Thanks

Deep appreciation of the many expressions of sympathy from friends of the late Chief Test Pilot Milo Burcham, was expressed today in a letter from his family. It was signed by Mrs. Marian Burcham, his widow, Gary and Vance, his sons, and Mr. and Mrs. Charles Burcham, his parents.

The letter follows:

"This is to acknowledge with deep appreciation the many expressions of sympathy, whether flowers, telegrams, cards or letters, or just an unexpressed feeling of regret and a whisper of a prayer for Milo and the ones he left behind."

CONVAIR MAKES LIGHTNING P-38'S

Full-scale production of P-38's is planned in the Nashville Division of Consolidated Vultee Aircraft Corporation now tooling up for the operation under a top priority of the AAF.

At the Tennessee plant last week Lockheed representatives met with Convair officials beside the first P-38 assembled there under the Lockheed assistance program.

LODESTARS SET NEW AIR RECORD

LOCKHEED speed, proclaimed far on wings of streaking warplanes, has added prestige to National Airlines with sleek Lodestars now making air history between New York and Florida.

Whipping along the Atlantic seaboard faster than any other plane on scheduled airline flight, the first ship of a new service sliced an hour from the best previous time of the company's Jacksonville-New York run.

Other Lodestars whittled the schedule still further and brought predictions of flights to be made in "very close to three hours."

President Flies

G. T. Baker, National Airline's president, was at the controls on the inaugural flight when the first ship settled at La Guardia Field 4 hrs., 36 min. after the take-off at Jacksonville's municipal airport.

Very next day, pilot "Skeeter" Royal knocked 21 minutes from this record and, in mid-October, E. J. Kershaw, vice-president in charge of operations, flew the nonstop hop in 3 hrs., 50 min.

At that time, Kershaw said jubilantly, "I believe I am safe in saying that within six months we shall be flying between Jacksonville and New York City in very close to three hours."

Comparable records have been made on the company's new Tampa-Manhattan direct run with a southern terminus on the gulf coast southwest of Jacksonville.

With president Baker again at the controls, another of the company's seven-ship fleet of Lodestars made the first flight of this run in 6 hrs., 20 min.

Airline's President Receives Gold Medal

Urgent demand for service the fast Lodestars give was indicated by more than $22,000 worth of reservations reported by National's New York office the first day they were made available to the public.

Capacity loads of passengers and cargo await each flight and officials of the company have already disclosed plans for further expansion into the Caribbean area and a proposed route to Cairo.

Cow Landing

President Baker, 43, almost landed on the back of a cow in the early days of the company when he was its personnel and the total distance between its payload points was 100 miles. That was in 1934 when it operated a line between Jacksonville and Daytona Beach.

Today, National Airline Lodestars whip through the sky on routes totalling more than 8000 miles a day.

Clubs Plan Joint Meet On Nov. 20

Factory B day shift Penguins and Penguinettes will hold a joint dinner meeting Monday, Nov. 20, at the Los Angeles Breakfast Club, it was announced last night by Jean Maier, president of the Penguinettes.

Entertainment will consist of a variety program, something "entirely new in fun." This meeting will be a change from past meetings as there will be no speakers.

This is the first meeting of the Penguins since appointment of standing committees as announced by John Adams, president. Committees follow: Entertainment, Lloyd Stires, chairman; Larry Wilson and Lem McCarthey. Publicity, Al Mead, chairman; Bruce Kingsbury and Bill Brock.

Constitution and By-Laws, Jack Smith, chairman; Ray Stanton, Ferris Doolittle, and Carl Robinson. Membership, Jack E. Smith, chairman; Erny Blisse and Gregory Ptitsin.

Tickets for the Nov. 20 meeting are now on sale by ticket committee members, or at LERC offices.

New Club Holds First Meeting

Universal Studio talent will headline the list of entertainment for the combined meeting of the Factory A and B swing shift Penguinette clubs to be held Friday noon, Nov. 17, at the L.A. Breakfast Club. The new group will be known as the Lockheed Swing Shift Penguinette Club.

In addition to the stars and entertainers from Universal Studios, special guests for the afternoon will be LERC officials and representatives of Lockheed management.

This will be the first meeting since the merger of the two clubs and advance ticket sales presage a record-breaking attendance. Those who have failed to get their tickets may still buy them from members of the ticket committees at either plant or from the A or B LERC offices.

NLSC ANNOUNCES ALL-PLANT DANCE

One thousand employes of Navy Lockheed Service Center, with families and friends, will attend the second all-plant dance to be held Saturday, Nov. 25, at the Elk's Temple, Los Angeles, it was predicted last night by Bob Ritchie, chairman.

Part-Time Help Needed by LERC

Women are needed to work part time in the LERC cafeterias, it was revealed last night by William Kienzle, personnel manager. Working hours during the day are 10 a.m. to 2:30 p.m. Swing shift hours are 5 to 9:30 p.m.

"Many employes, no doubt, have friends or relatives who would like to work a few hours daily," said Kienzle, "and since experience is not necessary, we feel the cafeteria would give them the opportunity to do their bit."

Employes knowing of anyone interested are asked to call extension 6-3357, Lockheed.

Swingster's Choice

Swing Shifters Select Mohr as Dance Maestro

Appearance of Bob Mohr and his Movielanders at the Burbank Recreation Center after work last Friday marks a new era for swing shift dancers attending the weekly dances sponsored by the LERC.

Selected by the majority of swing shifters as their favorite, Mohr opened an indefinite engagement at the center last week. Only exception anticipated will be Dec. 1, set aside for a special all-plant western jamboree.

Artists Known

The Mohr band has an enviable record in the Southland, including the largest number of appearances in the Pasadena Civic auditorium, and as the featured band at many important spots in Southern California, including the Trianon, Aragon, Casino Gardens, and Casa Manana. Mohr has long been a Monday night attraction at the Palladium.

With and without orchestra, Bob Mohr has been seen on the screen in "The Angels Sing," "Jam Session," "Canterville Ghost," and others.

Vocal spotlight is shared by Janie Johns and Harry Taylor. Janie has been a feature attraction fronting such bands as Ted FioRito, Phil Harris, Anson Weeks, and Dick Jurgens.

Attract Throngs

Opening on New Year's Eve, the LERC swing-shift dances have been a popular recreation for second shifters with a total attendance of more than 25,000 recorded since that date. New dancing hours start at 1 a.m., following work on Friday night, and continuing until 4.

Husbands and Wives To Be Entertained

Husbands and wives of Factory A day shift Penguinettes and Penguins will be special guests at a joint meeting to be held Thursday, Nov. 30, at 7 p.m., at the Los Angeles Breakfast Club.

Art Whiting and his orchestra will play for informal dancing. Entertainment and speakers will be announced next week.

Tickets now are on sale at the LERC offices or from members of the ticket committee.

Plans Are Made By Music Group

Semi-weekly instead of weekly meetings for Lockheed's Radio Chorus were announced last night by Mike Marsman, director. The change was made to provide more individual voice coaching for members.

In addition to regular Wednesday meetings from 7 to 10 p.m., in room M.A. 71 of Hollywood High School, Sunset and Highland, the chorus will meet at the same time and place each Friday.

Voices Needed

Additional voices are still needed for programs planned for the winter season. Plans include a 30-minute broadcast over a local radio station and a Christmas Chorus to sing for veterans in military hospitals in the Los Angeles area.

The Radio Chorus will appear in both the A-1 and B-1 main recreation areas during Thanksgiving week. It is expected that the Christmas program also will be presented in the areas.

Auditions Offered

Employes interested in joining the group may call the LERC offices or Mike Marsman, director, for auditions at the high school Wednesday or Friday evenings between 7 p.m. and 10.

AWARDED CLUSTER

Top turret gunner Orren D. Curl of Glendora, former Lockheed employe, was awarded a second Oak Leaf Cluster to his Air Medal for his participation in the bombing of German war plants.

Donors Sign Up at B-2 and B-7

Honoring employes of the downtown Lockheed plants for their contributions to the Los Angeles Blood Bank, Basil Rathbone, Jimmie Wakeley, Osa Massen, and Mrs. Bradner Lee, chairman of the Los Angeles Red Cross Blood Donor Service, appeared on the stage in the recreation areas at B-2 and B-7 last week.

Rathbone, who served in World War 1, explained the miracles performed by blood plasma during the current conflict. He stressed the constantly growing need for plasma and the necessity for cooperation from every healthy American if the 9000-pint weekly quota for Los Angeles is to be met.

Carnival Plans Made

Penguinettes and servicemen guests will gather for "Carnival Night" Tuesday, Nov. 14, 7 p.m., when the Factory A day shift club will stage their November party at the Hollywood USO.

All decorations and food, under the "Big Top" will be provided by club members. Penguinettes are asked to deliver their food to the refreshment committee, Maureen Carp, Margaret Gunson, Betty Clark, and Gladys Dartford. Food will be served at 9 p.m. from small concessions and carnival booths.

Hosts serving the food will include Jack Newburn, W. W. Aulepp, J. C. Blackington, M. D. Basolo, E. M. Barden, F. Penn Holter, W. Shulver, George Prudden, Roy McKenzie, and Don Fedderly.

The "Great DeVere and his Demonettes," with their tricks of magic, will headline the evening's entertainment. Jane Walton will do acrobatic dancing and contortionist acts. Olive Mae Beach, of the Philharmonic, will sing request numbers. In addition there will be fortune tellers and a handwriting analyst to read the future.

Bill Stanton's orchestra will play for dancing from 7 to 9 p.m. Following the floor show, dancing will continue until 11.

All Penguinette members are asked to arrive promptly at 7 and to bring suitable food and decorations.

TRAVEL FILM TO BE SHOWN

By popular demand of Lockheed employes, Douglas Erdman, globe-trotting Lockheed inspector, will again show his adventure movie in the B-1 LERC cafeteria building, Tuesday, Nov. 14.

Erdman, who traveled 60,000 miles through the West Indies, Brazil, Africa, Arabia, Tibet, India and Australia, brought with him a complete photographic record of his travels. During the time he shot more than 2000 feet of film showing sacred rites, secrets, and living habits of inhabitants of India and the Far East.

The film, which will be shown Lockheed employes and their families on the fourteenth, will show unusual incidents from Brazil, Africa, and India. Day and graveyard shows will be given at 5:30 and 8 p.m. Swing shifters will see the show at 1 a.m., immediately following work on Tuesday night. Free reservation tickets are available at the LERC offices.

'TOPS' NEEDED

Because it may create a false sense of security, a second-class air force is worse than useless—a positive danger, in the opinion of Robert A. Lovett, assistant Secretary of War for Air.

Share Your Ride

"Share your ride" is the safest way to keep in good with the gasoline ration board. It's an advantage to have co-riders.

Rathbone Helps with Volunteers

Hughes-Newcomer Win Doubles Crown

Vern Hughes, Dept. 38-04, B-1, and Leigh Newcomer, Dept. 7-61, B-1, are Lockheed 1944 men's doubles tennis champions today, following a two-set 7-5, 6-2 victory over the runner-up duo, Jim McDaniel and C. S. Fisher. Hughes and Newcomer reached the finals by defeating Don Phillips and F. Foster last month. Cunningham and Haythorn defaulted, giving McDaniel and Fisher an undisputed chance for the championship.

In the first set, played at La Cienega courts last Sunday, both teams started cautiously, followed by an increasing heat with both squads playing a fast, even game, later dubbed "one of the finest sets of tennis played this season" by Art Fiedler, LERC tennis coordinator. In the second set Newcomer and Hughes, playing for the opposition's weak spots, cinched the championship with an easy 6-2 set for the first two games out of the three-game match.

Team of Veterans

Vern Hughes, inactive in Lockheed singles matches this year, is a veteran Lockheed champion, having copped the title in singles for years 1940, '41, and '43. Runner-up in 1942, he lost the title to Vic Seliger. Leigh Newcomer arose to the Lockheed title in singles for the years 1938 and '39.

Jim McDaniel is present Lockheed champion in the 1944 men's singles, and half of the championship mixed doubles team with Gwen McDaniel. He also won the 1944 Griffith Park all-city tournament.

Trophies to Come

Trophies for champions and runners-up will be awarded by the LERC, sponsors of the Lockheed tournament, in a brief ceremony that will mark the close of the 1944 net activities.

P-38 Final Trips NLSC, 22-10 Score

Glen Arford's P-38 Final cage quintet from Dept. 18-20, B-1 looped 22 points last Wednesday at ➡ John Burroughs Junior High to trip the Dept. 80, Navy Lockheed Service Center squad and gain the first inter-departmental basketball victory this season. The game was the opener of the 1944-45 Lockheed inter-departmental cage season. The NLSC boys were held to 10 points.

In the second game on opening night the A-1 Oh Bees from Dept. 72-25, piloted by Dan Birnbaum, defeated Sam Davis' B-5 Rabble Rousers by a closely contested 15 to 7. Dept. 18-20 defaulted in favor of the Dept. 38 squad in the third heat of the day.

Dept. 15-08, A-1, took the nightcap by trouncing Dept. 13-26, also from A-1, 46 to 6. The loop, made up of A-1, B-1, and B-5 teams, plays every Wednesday from 6 to 10 p.m., at the John Burroughs Junior High gym in Burbank.

According to the LERC sports office a number of additional swing shift teams are still needed to round out the swing league schedule. Applicants may send in team name and roster to either A or B LERC office. Scheduling will later be forwarded to team captains by mail. As in all other LERC-sponsored sports, equipment, officials and places of play are all furnished by the LERC free of charge to the players.

Bruner, McClelland Tie In Division Tee Meet

Bill Bruner and Lewis McClelland tied for first-place golf honors last Sunday over a field of 20 contestants in the first of a series of monthly meets planned by the Lockheed Wage and Salary departments.

Seeks Fare Cut

United Airlines is seeking to cut by more than half its prewar passenger fares between California and Hawaii

Lightning Edgers Tromp Forts 14-6 in Stiff Toucher Battle

Week's hottest Lockheed toucher tussle took place at North Hollywood park last Thursday between the P-38 Leading Edge club and the B-17 Final Assemblists. The Edgers won 14-6. However, with neither team scoring in the first stanza, Larry Lappi, P-38 back, tossed an aerial to Art Dillon in the second. He plunged over the goal line after 30 yards of tricky broken-field running to score the first mark. Lappi's conversion made a half-time tally of 7-0.

No Conversion

In the third quarter Final's Bob Clugge grabbed the ball, made a 50-yard dash that ended behind the goal posts for their one and only score, 6 points. Tough P-38 interference foiled their conversion attempt. Also in the third, P-38's Whitey Johnson threw a well-aimed 30-yard pass into the arms of Wolfred Stavenson, who went over for their second goal.

Lappie again made the conversion for the final 14-6.

In the Monday-Friday North Hollywood day loop the Night Hawks secured their first-place position by defeating the Customer Service Wolves, 6-0.

In Second Spot

In second spot are the Template Butchers, whose latest victory was a 12-0 win over the Apprentice group. Len Mierzwa's Jet Joes tripped the third-place P-38 Final squad with a 20-6 win.

Scores and standings in the third week of the North Hollywood leagues follow:

MONDAY-FRIDAY LEAGUE
Weekly Results

Team		vs. Team	
Jet Joes	20	P-38 Final	6
Night Hawks	6	Customer Service Wolves	0
Template Butchers	12	Apprentice Group	0

TUESDAY, WEDNESDAY, THURSDAY LEAGUE—Weekly Results

Team		vs. Team	
Office Gang	7	Processors	0
Tool Engineers	7	Machine Parts	0
P-38 Leading Edge	14	Final Assembly B-17	6

MONDAY-FRIDAY LEAGUE STANDINGS

Team	Name	Captain	Dept.	Plant	W	L	T
2	Night Hawks	John Steers	28-26	B-1	3	0	0
3	Template Butchers	Robert Webb	44-52	B-3	2	0	1
4	P-38 Final	Glen Arford	13-26	B-1	1	1	1
1	Jet Joes	Len Mierzwa	28-10	B-1	1	2	0
6	Customer Service	Eddie Saunders	62-73	B-5	1	2	0
5	Apprentice Group	George Hall	90-46	B-5	0	3	0

TUESDAY, WEDNESDAY, THURSDAY LEAGUE STANDINGS

Team	Name	Captain	Dept.	Plant	W	L	T
1	Office Gang	Harry Wildberger	18-10	B-1	3	0	0
5	Tool Engineers	Henry Jackson	40-34	A-1	2	0	1
4	Processors	Chuck Townsend	27-31	A-1	2	1	0
6	P-38 Leading Edge	Carl Burton	18-23	B-1	1	1	1
2	Final Assembly B-17	Earl Arbuckle	13-19	A-1	0	3	0
3	Machine Parts	Fred A. Lenz	53-80	B-1	0	3	0

Season's Tip Off

LERC's 375 KEG TEAMS BELIEVED U.S. RECORD

New bowling leagues beginning this week raised the total number of LERC-sponsored bowling teams to more than 375, believed to be the greatest number of teams playing under one banner in the entire United States industrial recreation picture.

Notable among the late starters is the new swing shift mixed doubles league that swung into action last Monday, after work, at the Burbank Bowl. Composed of eight teams of men and women, employes of Dept. 57-62, Bldg. 185 at B-1, the mixed fours loop is another indication of the growing interest among Lockheed bowlers of all shifts in mixed four competition.

Help Is Offered

In answer to numbers of requests regarding boy and girlie leagues, the LERC offices voice willingness to set up and coordinate all such leagues as requested by keg fans. There is no charge for services of this kind. All that's needed to get new leagues under way, according to the LERC is "a roster of teams and an interest in the game."

With only 12 league tally sheets turned in from a total of more than 40 leagues by the Friday noon deadline, all league comparisons, usually printed in this space, has been passed up this week as insufficient in scope to be representative of the all-league roundup.

Deadline Stressed

League officers again are reminded that tally sheets must be in at either the A or B LERC office no later than Friday noon each week.

Leagues meeting too late in the week to meet that deadline should submit sheets as soon as completed to be included in the following week roundup.

Girls Swim Meet With Douglas Set

Long-awaited climax of a proposed swimming meet between the feminine aquatic stars of Lockheed and Douglas will take place at the Beverly Hills High School the last week of November.

Claire Hughes, LERC girls' swimming coach and instructor at the weekly Tuesday swims at the Hollywood YMCA, is now forming teams to compete in the various events.

Although Lockheed is now represented by a strong contingent of swimmers from the Tuesday classes, Miss Hughes expresses a need for additional tank talent in all types of swimming and diving to round out a prize-winning team. Girls interested in competing in this event are asked to report for practice at the Hollywood "Y," Tuesday, Nov. 14, at 7 p.m.

World's Largest

Lockheed's LERC is the largest organization of its kind in the world.

All-Stars Set New High Mark

Lockheed's Lightning all-star men's bowling squad, playing the Douglas all-stars as the feature event at last Sunday's benefit exhibition at Llo Da Mar, chalked up one of the best scratch series of the year with 3041, to defeat the Douglas crew by nearly 400 pins.

In the first heat the Lightnings rolled a 964, followed by 1004 and 1073 against Douglas' 902, 860 and 893, totaling 2655. Tom Barbour rolled the best game of the day, 237, and later the best series, 672. Stan Cardinet's series of 612 was second best.

In the other exhibition game of the day the Lockheed Recreation club quintet edged themselves into a 6-point win over the North American squad with 2795 against 2789.

Scores follow:

LOCKHEED LIGHTNINGS

	1st Game	2nd Game	3rd Game	Total
Jim Hogan	178	224	185	587
Bill Barlass	193	180	202	575
Stan Cardinet	176	219	217	612
Tom Barbour	233	202	237	672
D. Beauchaine	184	179	222	585
	964	1004	1073	3041

LOCKHEED RECREATION

	1st Game	2nd Game	3rd Game	Total
Ervin Prue	207	194	177	578
Russ Saunders	183	198	196	577
Bill Ellis	198	174	202	574
Mark Pulis	165	206	177	548
Walt Martin	193	164	161	518
	946	936	913	2795

In addition to the two matches, the bowling show included a match between 20 of the best bowlers in the Los Angeles area that included Lockheed's Jim Hogan. Red Skelton, Harold Lloyd, and other celebrities graced the occasion. Money will be used to construct and maintain bowling alleys at the Birmingham General hospital at Van Nuys.

Drop Tanks Play Odd Roles In War Theatres

Half Sections

Seam Is Welded

Odder than Ripley might imagine are the unplanned uses found for many war implements . . . bathing out of helmets. But probably no invention of the entire conflict has performed more unexpected services than the droppable gasoline tank for fighter planes.

This streamlined container helped hasten victory by lending a bomber's cruising range to the smaller ships . . . and that's what it will be noted for in history books.

Cold Beer Served

To a bunch of Normandy beachhead Yanks, however, it will always mean manna from the skies . . . because an English Spitfire dropped one of the big metal eggs in their midst during a period of tough, hot fighting . . . it was marked "Joy Juice" and contained cold beer.

Lockheed P-38 pilots of the Eighth Army Air Force reconnaissance, speed vital maps and plans across the channel in their 165-gallon drop tanks which they release to command posts of forward battle units.

Sent up for weather information in a routine flight over Trieste, a P-38 pilot encountered two ME-109's at 26,000 feet.

Tank Is Missing

One of them turned away but the other kept coming in on one of those head-on tests to see who gives first. The Nazi plane pulled under and the P-38 pilot felt a grazing collision. He smelled gasoline as he throttled down. Looking over he saw the Messerschmitt spinning to earth and the white silk billow of its pilot's parachute. When he landed one of his drop tanks was missing.

Over in the south Pacific Allan Mogensen, showing the Army how the Work Simplification Plan works, reported seeing black fuzzy-haired natives paddling over sun-spattered water of the ocean in P-38 drop tanks from which they had fashioned catamarans better than they had been taught to make out of tree trunks.

Deductions in Check Due to Federal Laws

Between now and the end of the year, paychecks received by employes participating in the Lockheed retirement plan will carry an extra deduction listed under "miscellaneous" on the check stubs, it was announced here last night.

This deduction, spread over the remaining 1944 paychecks where the total amounts to more than $10, represents the Federal Income Tax on the cost of the life insurance which has been paid by the company as part of the retirement plan. The plan is a combination of an annuity provision and life insurance and, while the government does not require taxing the annuity feature until the time comes for receipt of the benefits by the individual, it has ruled that the cost of the life insurance be taxable income to the individual, income tax upon which must be paid.

All the benefits of the retirement plan, including both annuity and insurance, are paid for by Lockheed but, under the law, the premium on the insurance feature is listed as individual taxable income.

This taxable income—the life insurance premium for 1944—and the tax withheld upon it will be included in the amounts shown on individual earnings statements issued after close of the year.

Newsman Fools 'Erudite' Nip Censors With Word of Yanks

One of the most dramatic incidents of American and Filipino resistance to the Japanese that has come out of the Philippines since Gen. MacArthur's "homecoming" has just been reported by Gordon Williams, war correspondent of the Australian Broadcasting Commission.

When the Nips over-ran the islands and came to Leyte, the printer-editor of Tacloban's newspaper high-tailed it for the hills where he managed, some way, to get out a sheet for the American and Filipino guerillas. But someone betrayed him and he and the press were taken back to Tacloban where the Japanese forced him to produce the Tacloban Shimbun under threat of death to his wife.

However, the intrepid editor was able to give his own slant to the news without the Japs ever being aware of it, thus giving the native population an accurate forecast of the Yank's reconquest of the island, and preparing them for it when it came . . . P-38's and all.

DeHAVEN NOW ACE

P-38 ace Capt. Robert W. DeHaven of Hollywood, has just bagged his fourteenth Zero over Leyte to make him third-ranking flier in the famous Forty-ninth Fighter Group, one of the greatest combat units in the war.

Major Richard I. Bong, No. 1 ace in this group and leading ace in all theaters, recently downed his thirty-third plane in the south Pacific to establish an all-time, all-world record.

Is it Here?

THESE classified ad columns in the *Star* are provided for employes without charge. If you want to buy, sell, trade, or find or return lost articles, obtain Form 4929 from your department clerk, stationery store, or employe service office. Fill it in and send it to Employe Service Division, Factory B-1. If you wish to check on ads appearing, phone 63041 about all articles.

FOR SALE

MISCELLANEOUS

AIR brush, new Thayer & Chandler. 11832 Hamlin, N. Hollywood, after 5:30.
BABY carriage, prewar, good condition. CHarleston 65455 after 5:30 p.m.
BABY buggy, prewar, English coach, like new. 11477 Killion, North Hollywood.
BABY buggy, folding; spring baby scales, jumper swing. HI. 0775.
BABY buggy, leatherette, steel frame, collapsible, rubber tires. CI. 31742.
BROODER, automatic electric heat control. 50-chick capacity. SYlvan 02071.
CAMERA, 16-mm. movie, f2.6 lens. GRanite 4161, room 305.
FIRE extinguisher, small; pruning snips, electric shaver. SU. 23624.
GAS heater, 10-radiant O'Keefe and Merritt. MOrningside 13676.
GUITAR, Spanish, Hawaiian; mandolin, ukulele. 2117 Aaron Street, Los Angeles.
HUB caps, 3 "Ripple Disc" for V-8 Ford. CI. 29588.
LATHE, Dunlap Modeler's, complete with motor, chucks, etc. WH. 5124.
LETTERING set, Minusa dwg. set; 10" slide rule. 11832 Hamlin, N. Hlywd. (eve.)
LIGHT meter, Weston Leicameter. HO. 1507.
LUNCHBOX, metal, good condition. GR. 8971.
OIL heater, duo therm., prewar circulating, with 50' copper tubing. 628 N. Hollywood Way, Burbank.
RADIUS gauges, depth mic. 5" base. Ed Adams. SUnset 26168.
RADIO, '41 G. Motors push button car. Auto. cigarette lighter. CH. 86857.
RADIO, G. E. 3-band console. A-1 condition. SUnset 15692.
COMMUNICATION receiver, R.M.E. 69. Excellent condition. CH. 65062.
DIAMOND ring set, 17 diamonds. AT. 22433.
SAXOPHONE, Buescher "C" with case. Excellent condition. CI. 12623.

Is it Here?

FOR SALE

MISCELLANEOUS (Cont.)

SAXOPHONE, soprano (gold) Conn make. CH. 86406.
SPEED graphic, 4x5, will exchange for other equip. 1804 N. Highland, Hlywd.
TRUNK, good wardrobe; curtain rods. 525 Rosemary Lane, Burbank.
TYPEWRITER, De Luxe Royal portable. R. F. Yung, 1011 Bruce Lane, Burbank.
WAGONS, all-wood, 3 sizes. For boys 2 to 15 yrs. 1059 Western, Glendale.
WATCH, man's 17-jewel pocket Elgin. Never worn. WE. 4504, evenings.

ANIMALS

HORSES, 2 riding, 7 years old, bridles, Army saddle. CH. 64559.
MARE in foal, thoroughbred, sired by Quarter Horse. SUnset 19084.
PULLETS, N.H. M. R. Gilbertson, 7228 Canby, Reseda, Calif.
PUPPIES, Irish Setter, 5 mo., ped. Oakdale Trailer Park, Sunland. L. E. Goodall.

HOME FURNISHINGS

BABY bassinette and stand. Good condition. HEmpstead 6427.
BED, solid panel double walnut. Innersprg. mattress. 13297 Aults, S. Fernando.
BUFFET, maple. Will trade for day bed or ? GL. 8317.
GAS range, white porcelain, 4-burner. W. Arnebeck, 1338 N. Lamer, Burbank.
GAS range, L.R. suite, cocktail table., carpet sweeper. CHarleston 83974.
RUG, prewar American Oriental, 9x12. 100% wool. Like new. STate 44347.

MOTOR VEHICLES

BICYCLE, prewar. A-1 condition. Must sell at once. GL. 8317.
BICYCLE, standard size De Luxe Western Flyer. A-1 condition. SUnland 6729.
BICYCLE, '41 Schwinn, used little. New tires. SU. 28544 between 4-6 p.m.
CITROEN, '39. Good tires, new paint. 14122 Calvert Street, Van Nuys.
MOTORCYCLE, '37 Indian twin, Jr. Scout. 2210 Winona, Burbank.
MOTORCYCLE, Harley-Davidson, includes side car. 11 E. Burbank Blvd., Burbank.
MOTORCYCLE, Army, 4 mos. old. .32 automatic pistol. 1820 Jackson, Burbank.
MOTORCYCLE, '35 Harley-Davidson; '38 Indian. 809 Waterloo, Los Angeles.
MOTORCYCLE, Harley-Davidson, '37-64, '40-61. SY. 44568.
PLYMOUTH '33 4-door sedan. Good tires. Excellent motor. SU. 20334 after 4 p.m.
SCOOTER. CH. 80480.
TRUCK, '31 Ford 1½-ton chassis and cab. Good tires, vacuum brakes. CA. 7601.

Is it Here?

WANTED

ADDING machine, portable typewriter with tabulator. SU. 26168.
ALARM clock. M. Dimsdale, 2844½ Buckingham, Los Angeles.
APARTMENT, furnished, single, in Glendale for young lady. CI. 16739.
BED, folding, small enough to store in closet. 4123 Toluca Lake, Burbank.
CAMERA, 35-mm., in good condition. 1804 North Highland, Hollywood.
'38-'41 coach, club coupe or sedan. Will pay cash. WY. 4427.
'40 Chevrolet or Plymouth club coupe from private party. CR. 14751 after 5 p.m.
CRUSHER, 5-ton open jaw type and set of rolls. NO. 6256.
GOLF clubs and bag, lady's. CI. 35960.
GUITAR, Spanish plectrum banjo, tenor ukulele. HO. 1491, apt. 407, 5 p.m.
HOUSE, equity in 5 or 6-room. Any condition. SUperior 82233.
IRON with heat control. CHapman 52138.
LIGHTMETER, G.E. or Weston master, for serviceman. CI. 33776 after 4:30.
PIANO, small upright. Short keyboard. N. Elsbree, 641 Rosemary Lane, Burbank.
WILL store piano for. use or rent small one from private party. CH. 87209.
REFRIGERATOR, late model. Child's roll-top desk. NO. 0637.
REFRIGERATOR, small electric, small gas stove. NO. 12397.
RIFLE, Winchester, model 70, any calibre. E. L. Jewett, CH. 69037.
ROLLER skates and tricycle, child's. CHurchill 92370.
TRICYCLE, for five-year-old child. SU. 7710.
TRICYCLE, for five-year-old child. SU. 13384.

THE LOCKHEED Star
OFFICIAL PUBLICATION OF THE LOCKHEED AIRCRAFT CORPORATION

Issued each Friday for the employes of Lockheed Aircraft Corporation. The *Star* is the official publication of the company. Communications should be addressed to the Editor, *Lockheed Star*, Publicity Department, Lockheed Aircraft Corporation, Burbank, California. Unsolicited manuscripts cannot be returned.

KENNETH CRIST, Editor
Associates:
H. L. Rosson J. H. Prescott

HALSEY WINS TIGHT RUN

One of the so-far unreported but deadly hazards encountered by Halsey's fleets in the invasion of the Philippines came to light this week in an Australian report on the narrow escape from destruction of its cruiser *H.M.A.S. Shropshire*.

This warship, it is now disclosed, sailed for six hours through the night with an enemy mine fast to her paravane, only 15 feet from the vessel's side. When she altered course at dawn to clear the paravane, the mine floated free but just missed her stern by inches.

Accidents Are Cut in Many Units

(Continued from Page 2)

free employe hours worked is now 848,856.

Dept. 15-23, PV-2 Fuselage Subassembly, Factory A-1, had its last lost-time injury in October, 1943 and it has worked since that time a grand total of 738,320 employe hours without any disabling injuries.

Dept. 15-57, Sheet Metal Subassembly, Factory A-1, has completed more than a year without a single lost-time injury and its accident-free employe hours total stands at 663,095.

Dept. 39-38, Small Tool Repair, Factory A-1, has piled up 405,943 accident-free employe hours and its record has been perfect since June 1943.

"Such records would have been unattainable without the cooperation of every employe," concluded Hatton.

THE LOCKHEED
Star
Volume 2
BURBANK'S QUEEN?
(STORY ON PAGE 2)

DROP TANKS MAKE P-38 TRANSPORT

Add troop transport to the growing list of tough assignments the Army has given to Lockheed's Lightning P-38's. ➡

One in Each Wing

Bomber, rocket fighter, dive bomber, air spy, casualty carrier . . . these are a few of the roles deftly handled by the AAF's battle-toughened glamour girl since her 1939 debut.

Now, special wing tanks to let the ship carry eight or 10 men, plus the pilot, are being made.

With tanks attached, self-contained P-38 pursuit squadrons can carry their ground personnel and equipment right to the scene of Jap action. Minutes after capture of an enemy air base, Lightnings are ready to use it.

Like Drop Tanks

The new carrying devices made by the American Aero Supply Company of Los Angeles are similar in shape and size to the 300-gallon auxiliary drop tanks which carry fuel for long-distance flights. Nose of the tanks is of transparent material to give the occupants light and counteract their feeling of confinement during long hauls. Tanks can carry five occupants each. Lightnings can carry two tanks, one attached to each wing.

Success in the original job for which they were designed automatically suggested other uses for transport tanks, according to P. Philburn, Jr., president of American Aero Supply.

Surprise Enemy

"Fully equipped infantrymen or paratroopers can be hauled at pursuit plane speed to surprise the enemy during lightning offensives," Philburn said. "And recently the tanks have been assigned the task of evacuating critically wounded soldiers from forward areas. Four stretcher cases can be flown to base hospitals for complete medical attention with a swiftness that can mean the difference between life and death."

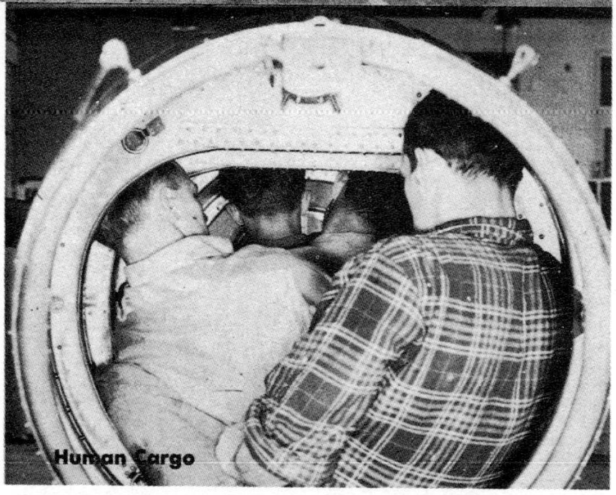

Human Cargo

'LUCKY SEVEN' DRIVE STARTS AT LOCKHEED

Lockheed's $7,000,000 Lucky Seventh War Loan drive opened Wednesday with a "swosh" that still echoes in the tired brain of some 408 Victory committee representatives. After attending classes to "sell" bonds in the most efficient manner, each agent virtually was swamped in the rush of buyers who wanted Lucky Seven deduction cards to be among the first tabulated.

"Although our quota for the Lucky Seventh War Loan drive at Lockheed is by far the largest we have ever attempted," said Victory Committee Chairman Tony Holst, "we've made a wonderful start, and I'm sure we'll succeed this time as we always have before."

Lucky Seven cards will not be distributed again, Holst added. But additional chances on the seven Lucky prizes that will go to 42 Lucky Lockheed winners may be obtained by buying extra bonds through the regular payroll deduction plan. Employes buying bonds for cash are not eligible for prizes at this time, but will be eligible for special awards to be announced at a later date.

CREDIT UNION READY TO AID EMPLOYE TAXPAYER

Filers of short form 1944 income tax returns who will soon be getting bills from Uncle Sam were reminded last night that they can be paid easily with money readily borrowed from the Lockheed Credit Union.

The convenience of making loans on the spot without lost time was stressed in the announcement which pointed out that Credit Union interest rates are lower than those of most commercial houses.

More than 90 per cent of the loan applications recently received were granted, the announcement stated, and the new borrowers were pleased to know they can obtain loans more promptly and economically from their employe-owned and operated Credit Union than elsewhere.

Peterson Elected To LERC Post

Recently sponsored by the LERC, the Accounting Forum revealed last night that William Peterson of Dept. 81-22 had been named president. The group meets every Wednesday in room 1, LERC cafeteria, B-1.

The next meeting will be at 5 p.m., April 25.

FOUR GIRLS SEEK CITY QUEEN BIDS

Four lovely Lockheed entrants in Burbank's combined "Burbank on Parade" and May Queen contest will benefit by last night's announcement by the LERC that all purchases from the club's cafeterias, canteens, and merchandise stores will mean votes for one or the other of the candidates.

The events will be staged on May 4, 5, and 6. Townspeople throughout Burbank will participate.

For every 25-cent sale the purchaser will receive one vote for the candidate of his or her choice.

Girls Named

Lockheed's entrants, appearing on the cover of this issue of the *Star*, are Nell Brown, Dept. 53-70, B-1; Vinola "Boots" Cain, Dept. 28-26, B-1; Patricia Paul, Dept. 81-24, A-1, and Dorothy Burns of Dept. 15-07, A-1. They will vie with 57 other aspirants to the Burbank honor.

Customers of the cafeterias and canteens will receive stubs for their purchases which they will drop in boxes located in the merchandise stores of the Factory A and B-1 cafeterias and labeled with the girls' names.

Votes Count

These will be counted and tabulated to determine the number of votes each entrant is entitled to.

The three days of celebration will commemorate the fifty-seventh birthday of the city.

The May Queen will win not only city honors . . . but a $100 diamond ring and a trip through Warner Bros. Studio and an interview with a talent scout.

All votes or purchase tickets must be turned in by midnight, Monday, Apr. 30.

LIGHTNINGS COVERED YALTA MEET

DEATH of the President recalled to Archie Mobely, Lockheed field representative, the elaborate air cover protection furnished by P-38's for the Yalta conference.

As the principals moved across three continents to their Crimean rendezvous, Lockheed Lightnings of the First Fighter Group gave constant daylight escort.

Including preliminary arrangements, the entire mission took a month. Routes aggregated 16,000 miles. Not a pilot was lost and every rendezvous of ships was made on the dot.

On extremely short notice, Col. Arthur C. Agan, Jr., commanding officer, learned his group had been chosen for the highly secret and involved operation. Taking his three squadron commanders, Colonel Agan flew the routes, planned and arranged for escorting of the late President and Prime Minister Churchill.

Maintaining and arming the P-38's at their several bases, housing and feeding of personnel, planning change of escorts as the passenger transports progressed along the routes to Yalta were some of the problems.

Working in utmost secrecy, alternate routes were planned to allow for adverse weather conditions. Three detachments of ground crewmen were shuttled from base to base. Mechanics and armorers often worked 18 hours a day to keep the proud Lightnings on their toes.

Complete success of the mission particularly on the score of not missing rendezvous even in bad weather brought personal expressions of appreciation from Gen. George C. Marshall, Adm. Ernest King and other dignitaries.

Colonel Agan gave the credit to his squadron commanders, Lt. Cols. Francis J. Pope, Francis H. Harris and Frank G. Jones, as well as his pilots and enlisted crewmen and the P-38's themselves.

Mobely says the American pilots got warm welcomes and high entertainment from Russian pilots in Yalta. From the Americans, Russian children learned gum-chewing, and Russian girls, modern dance steps.

The Lockheed representative reported uniforms of American pilots and their comparative youth were remarkable to the Russians.

This is just one of many notable feats of the First Fighter Group, oldest in the AAF.

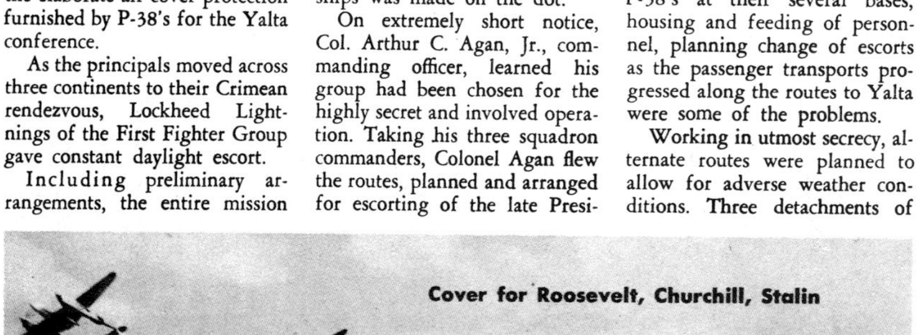

Cover for Roosevelt, Churchill, Stalin

Tissue Here Is Problem

With Plant Protection officials here pointing to theft of Lockheed property as a "grave offense" and promising to take stringent steps, new shortages have been noted in certain specific items.

Among them is lavatory tissue. Under normal conditions, the supply on hand now will last only for four days. It is almost impossible to purchase this item. It has been assumed that store shortage is responsible for shortage within Lockheed plants. Usually, Lockheed maintains a 120-day inventory.

According to Don Buehrig, group supervisor of the purchasing department, the usual need approximates 22,000 rolls a month, but it jumped last month to 30,376. Figures for the last six months are: March, 30,376; Feb., 22,264; Jan., 22,444; Dec., 32,783; Nov., 20,307; Oct., 24,228.

LOCKHEED STILL HAS GIANT JOB

PERSONNEL URGED TO GO THROUGH WAR PROGRAM

After a week of whispered talk among employes about cutbacks, Lockheed executives announced late last night that no immediate policy change toward folk here seems necessary. Lockheed, to all effectual purposes, already has had its "cutback" from Washington. In support of such claims, executive personnel released its production schedule for the remainder of 1945 to all in its organization.

It was pointed out that normal termination rate should care for indicated reduction in personnel. As certain Lockheed plane requirements are reduced, shifts, in so far as possible, will be made to other models. The P-80 schedule will remain at the 100 per cent mark through the remainder of 1945. No cutback is scheduled until next year . . . at the earliest.

Should the war in Europe end today the requirements for Lockheed-made equipment will continue as accent swings deliberately and with "utmost harshness" against the Jap curse.

The truth of the matter is, say executives here, that any accelerated termination rate would thrust this company into a hiring program by June.

List Schedule

Here, then, is the production data released by the company to key personnel:

For May, the P-38 schedule is reduced to 77 per cent of the original order; the B-17, 72; the Constellation remains at 100 per cent. The P-80 stays at 100 per cent. Likewise stays the Ventura.

For June, now, in the same order: 77 per cent of original order; 48 per cent, 100, 100, 100 per cent.

For July: 60 per cent, 50, 100, 100, 100 per cent.

For August: 55 per cent, 46, 100, 100, 100.

For September: 62 per cent, 52, 100, 100, 100.

For October: 37 per cent, 46, 100, 100, 100.

For November: 30 per cent, 50, 100, 100, 100.

By the end of December the P-38 production is presumed to have been completed. The percentages on the other ships follow:

The B-17, 50 per cent of

(Continued on Page 8)

NEWSMEN SEE P-38 CINEMA STAR GLAMOUR

Long a star over the fighting fronts of the world, the P-38 Lightning made its initial bow as a star of the Hollywood variety Tuesday at the Ambassador hotel, as a group of aviation and news writers previewed a new War Department film, "Angel in Overalls," as guests of Lockheed.

The varied tasks of the Lockheed Lightning are strikingly portrayed in scenes selected from official Signal Corps action films made in actual combat in the Pacific theater.

Many Missions

Flying protective cover for a crippled bomber, blasting Jap fighters, ground strafing, dive bombing, and flying dangerous photographic missions over enemy territory, the familiar outlines of the Lightning flashed across the screen again and again.

The name "Angel in Overalls" was won by the P-38's ability to tackle any job, no matter how tough, although as the commentator pointed out, the ship was once described by a novice airplane spotter as two airplanes flying with their arms around each other.

Released Soon

"Angel in Overalls" soon will have factory showings and may be released later to theaters.

This Ship Was Modified

Lodestars to Go In Indies Travel

Plans for spanning the Caribbean with sleek, swift Lodestars touching at West Indies points were announced last night by National Airlines which uses Lockheed equipment exclusively.

The plan involves acquisition of the Caribbean-Atlantic Airlines, Inc., of Puerto Rico, subject to Civil Aeronautics Board approval.

Caribbean-Atlantic Airlines, Inc., operates in Puerto Rico, the Virgin Islands and St. Thomas, linking together the prominent cities of San Juan, Aguadilla, Mayaguez and Ponce and the islands of St. Thomas and St. Croix.

Details of the plan of acquisition have been completed by G. T. Baker, N.A.L. president.

National has applications now pending before the Civil Aeronautics Board for several routes in the Caribbean as extensions to its present domestic system now extending between New York, Miami, Key West, and New Orleans.

DROOP SNOOTS HIT HUNS FOR ONE YEAR

American "droop snoot" bombers . . . modified P-38's, with a bombardier tucked in the nose, have hounded the Germans for more than a year, according to news releases.

Just taken off the "secret list," the ship's job is to lead formations of standard P-38's in fast, high-altitude precision bombing assaults.

Developed by Lockheed engineers stationed in England, the modified Lightnings are used successfully by both the United States 8th and 9th Air Forces.

Employes at Lockheed's overseas overhaul and repair depot built the first model for Army approval. Lieut. Gen. James Doolittle requested the "droop snoot" modification be put on production basis. The aluminum and plexiglass nose compartment was camouflaged to look like a standard P-38.

Carrying the Norden bombsight and all navigation and bombing instruments standard on B-17 Flying Fortresses . . . the 425-mile-an-hour P-38 "droop snoot" is capable of bombing accurately at speeds at least 50 per cent greater than operational speeds of heavy bombers.

On bombing runs the bombardier directs the bombing and does the navigating for the entire formation. Each Lightning "droop snoot" packs 4000 pounds in bombs, half the maximum bomb capacity of heavier bombers.

Impulses from the Lightning's radio installation activate an ingenious bomb release device that allows the bombardier in the lead plane to simultaneously dump the bomb load of every plane in the formation.

VITAL BOOK IS LOST AT PLANT

Lockheed's original vellum copy of Lockheed Report No. 5217, entitled "Method of Improving the Stick Stability at Rearward Center of Gravity in the P-38" is missing, the *Star* was told last night.

Employes are asked to notify the mail girl or call Ext. 8-2957 if they have seen, or know anything about, this report.

'Devilfish' Venturas Slash By-Passed Isles

SPITTING bullets from fiery mouths, dropping bombs from tentacle tips, big green "Devilfish" have been slashing by-passed isles with trails of destruction chasing terror-stricken Japs.

The "Devilfish" were sleek Lockheed Venturas of Navy Patrol Bombing Squadron 150 whose Cmdr. Robert S. Riddell visited Burbank this week with a stirring saga of sweat and tears.

Death of a crew member from a 25-mm. slug and the vengeful destruction of the Jap who fired it was a highlight of his story. Other chapters described a perilous return to base in a wounded PV.

Mascot totem of the squadron was painted on every plane. The turret, humping above the fuselage with its two 50-caliber guns, became the squat, bulbous body of the octopus whence came the planes' names. Long tentacles squirmed fore and aft, wrapping themselves around the fuselage with tips touching the bomb bay.

Covering the Gilberts and Marianas the "Devilfish" flew 1,000,000 miles, spying out enemy activities, knocking out air strips and other installations with no accident casualties.

The squadron's one fatality occurred during a bombing strike on a Jaluit seaplane base. There a sharp-shooting Jap anti-aircraft gunner was the bane of airmen. He was "Gunner Joe" to the Americans. Japs switched him here and there, from one gun to another.

Commander Riddell was bringing his "Devilfish" into a dive when "Gunner Joe" cut loose. A 25-millimeter charge exploded in the plane.

Navigator Kenneth M. Christy of Pittsburgh, Pa., yelled "I'm hit" but Commander Riddell finished the run and dropped the bombs. Lt. Kasimir Kanapicki, copilot, found Christy badly wounded.

Lieutenant Kanapicki administered first aid and morphine to ease the pain. Christy smiled, asked whether the bombs had hit the target, and went unconscious. The copilot left him in charge of another crewman and went back forward to set a course for the nearest friendly base, Majuro. They made the flight in 20 minutes, opening up the "Devilfish" plane for all the speed it could give. But when they landed a surgeon said Christy had been dead 10 minutes.

A few days later a flight of Marine planes swooped over Jaluit with a load of bombs and "Gunner Joe" never bothered our pilots again.

THE CREW: Kenneth Christy T. A. Bennett C. J. Horner Kasimir Kanapicki Riddell W. R. Lyon

Cover

THESE Lockheed beauties on today's cover seek the title of Burbank May Queen for the extensive birthday celebration honoring this city. The story, in detail, is found on page 2, column 5, of this issue.

Left to right, the girls are Patricia Paul, Vinola "Boots" Cain, Nell Brown, and Dorothy Burns. Twenty-five-cent purchases at LERC establishments entitle one to cast a vote for his favorite.

There are 57 other girls in the contest . . . not connected with Lockheed.

Photo by Vic Stein of the LERC.

Radio Station—Griffith Park

AIRPLANE gremlins are getting the hell beat out of them today by Lockheed radio men on a California mountain top. In a brick and reinforced-concrete aerie astride the southern rim of the San Fernando Valley these men are pioneering in the field of aviation communications. Their achievements add luster to Lockheed leadership.

But these achievements are bad news to the little phantom devils spotlighted early in the war by published tales of their pilot-plaguing tricks.

RECENTLY one of the rascals crawled over the shoulder of a helmeted P-38 pilot in the deep blue of the sub-stratosphere. Slyly he pinched the oxygen supply tube. Back in Lockheed's radio testing station a sharp-minded attendant noted a slight

Bill Peale, Coordinator

A Call Is Checked

change in the pilot's voice. Over the ether went a warning. The pilot made ments and returned safely to the earth 32,000 feet below.

Another time a big Army plane was far out over the sea streaking for Ho Part of its power plant began to heat up alarmingly. The pilot's radioed for instructions wasn't heard by his base . . . but it was heard by Lockheed.

Vital part of Lockheed radio operations is the maintenance section supervi A. M. Granich, graduate engineer of New York University. H. W. "Tex" Da sistant, handles test-pilot liaison. Granich and his men design and constru equipment in addition to their maintenance work.

Prior to installation in ships, radio equipment is tested in an insulated room simulated operation conditions. This is done by Dept. 13-07, bench testing, in of Don Robinette, Factory A-1. After installation, equipment is ground-tested field by flight radio technicians. Checks in flight are then made by technicians on all except P-38's and P-80's on which pilots make the tests.

NOT SO long ago the expression "free as the air" was the hottest handy simi "lack of restrictions." It's losing its sting today because radio and radar and tel are staking claims.

Inside Control Room

Beam Equipment

Every radio fan knows broadcasters have to stay on their own beams. If they don't, :nraged listeners soon tell them about it. Before the war, the "hams" had to keep to heir own channels, too. But in the zone of shorter wave lengths the air was still free.

Today, radio strides so fast that far-visioned industries are seeking liens on the still-)pen channels—the wave lengths of high frequency, very high frequency, ultra high frequency, and super high frequency.

That's where Lockheed is pioneering. Last fall the Federal Communications Commission held a pow-wow with representatives of radar, frequency modulation, and television interests, as well as standard broadcasters.

THE subject was postwar allocation of frequencies and Lockheed was the only aircraft maker represented. The need of the industry for adequate consideration in the matter was convincingly put by C. W. Peale, Lockheed's manager of radio operations.

Probably the biggest factor in keeping Lockheed so far ahead of the field is the location of the radio testing station on one of the few suitable, available sites.

For the best functioning of signals in the field of high frequency and above, "line-of-sight" location is needed. Roughly, that means the station should be where a search-ght's beam could find any point it might be necessary to reach with a radio beam.

AND that's exactly where Bill Peale put his station after months of testing possible sites.

A few feet from the corner of the building you can look directly down on the gabled roof of Errol Flynn's home or you can fix your line of sight on any one of many airfields in the Los Angeles area.

Off to the northeast you can see Newhall pass opening directly on the desert where Lockheed's Shooting Stars dart and wheel as their radios are checked with the station.

From this lofty perch you can usually see the entire San Fernando Valley and on a clear day, Catalina and the Isthmus, as well as Palos Verdes, Long Beach, and other distant points.

"It wasn't long after we started construction," said Peale, "before we could easily see how much (Continued on Page 8)

Airport Tower

PICNIC SEASON OPENS

Roll Out the Barrel

Two Outings Set For Week End By Employe Club

Lockheed's 1945 picnic season will begin as a double feature this week, with two groups of the Engineering department holding family picnics on Saturday, April 21.

Dept. 72-25's Electrical and Hydraulics group on the No. 89 project at Plant B-6 will convene at North Hollywood Park, Section No. 6, at 11 a.m. Main feature of the picnic lunch will be a softball game between the Electrical section captained by Bill Crumrine and the Hydraulics section captained by Dick Hayman.

Games Slated

Al Theilman, Frank Lindsey and Ernie Selby, picnic committeemen, announce additional softball games, volleyball, horseshoe games, and races for all members of the family. A regular picnic lunch will be served with refreshments.

Preliminary Design, also a part of Dept. 72-25 at Plant A-1, will hold their family picnic at Griffith Park, Pepper Tree Lane Section No. 1, on the same day, beginning at noon and lasting until 4 p.m.

Ed Fife, in charge of arrangements for the Preliminary Design picnic, stated that a complete lunch including refreshments will be served.

Large Crowd

Softball games, races and other entertainment will be featured. Jack Phillips, LERC's director of outside activities and in charge of picnic arrangements for the club, anticipates more than 100 picnics will be held during the summer months.

Groups of employes who are anticipating section or department picnics are advised to contact Phillips at Plant A-1 LERC office for assistance in arranging their party.

ON THE *Table*

BILL ELLIS Pres. LERC

OUR plant, like the nation, has been a little more serious minded during the past week.

And speaking of seriousness, I could not help but remember the executive committee meeting of March 6. Dr. Adrian Hartog, consul for the Netherlands appeared before the committee to voice the extreme necessity of sharing our extra clothing with the people of war torn lands.

Dr. Hartog's family is in Rotterdam. There, people are dying at the rate of 400 an hour, in bread lines, from starvation or cold. As he talked, emotion overcame him. Through his tears one could see he was wondering about his own family whom he had not seen for many months.

There were tears in the eyes of several executive committee members, too. Unashamed, honest faces, serious in their sympathy.

The employes of Lockheed responded nobly to our clothing drive for those unfortunate people of the Netherlands and the Buck-of-the-Month club also gave $3,000 to the Queen Wilhelmina fund, for blankets. Later, Dr. Hartog appeared before the committee to thank them for their efforts. This time there was not a dry eye in the group as he tried in broken English to convey the deep appreciation of his countrymen.

Again an appeal is being made to all of us. This time the nation as a whole is asked to respond by giving clothing that others might share in our warmth. You have heard the appeals before and will hear more in the future. More eloquent writers and speakers than I will ask for your cooperation. I ask you to heed their call. Prove the generosity of America.

Sometimes a man's best efforts seem to backfire. Easter Sunday a Lockheed employe, frantically in need of a cake, drove out to the A-1 cafeteria and talked an LERC employe into opening up the cafeteria and selling him a particularly attractive cake that was on display. He had a family gathering for Easter dinner and at the last moment remembered seeing the cake on display. Victoriously he proudly set his prize in the center of the gay table. All went well at dinner and it came time to cut the cake. His best efforts failed to do naught but nick the knife. Seems as though the particularly attractive display cake was only a wooden dummy. I wonder if the fact that Easter Sunday was also April 1 had anything to do with it.

CIGARETTE-BUYING CARDS TO BE ISSUED APRIL 25

Cigarette ration cards for Lockheed employes will be distributed Wednesday, April 25, according to word received last night from the LERC Commissary committee, in charge of the new arrangement.

The statement announced that all hourly employes will receive their cards in time card racks Wednesday at the beginning of their shifts. Salaried employes will receive their cards in their pay envelopes the same day.

The ration card will be of regular time card size and bearing the name and clock number of each employe. Only a portion of the full card will be necessary for presentation for smokes and recipients are asked to cut card to proper dimensions as indicated thereon.

Cards not picked up on April 25 will be turned over to the paymaster's department where employes may call for them.

Every employe at Lockheed will receive such a ration card. Validation dates on which holders may claim cigarettes will be announced in the *Lockheed Star* as frequently as the supply is adequate to meet the demands of all card holders.

Employes transferring from one Lockheed plant to another will retain their original card. However, terminating employes will surrender their cards on leaving the company's employ. In that regard, it has been pointed out that it will be necessary to present identification cards along with the ration cards at the time of cigarette purchase.

The ration plan was adopted a fortnight ago by the LERC as the most practical arrangement for cigarette rationing here. At plants A-1 and B-1, cigarettes will be sold at the LERC cigar counters in the cafeterias. Arrangements for distribution in canteen areas at other plants are now under consideration. Further particulars, including the first validation date, will be released in next week's issue of the *Star*.

Ration-Free Shoe Sale

Reworked Marine Corps used issue shoes, being featured by the LERC merchandise stores in the A-1 cafeteria, will continue on sale all next week and are offered to employes ration free, according to Claire Hughes, assistant manager of the stores.

There are no shoes for women, but the stock includes a good range of men's sizes in dark oxfords and hightop work shoes.

In addition to the shoes, the LERC store at A-1 is offering Marine issue shirts and work pants. The store is offering a limited number of heavy wool Marine pants, Army raincoats and sterilized feather pillows.

Girl Scout Troops Sponsored by LERC

Burbank's Girl Scout Troop 8, Brownie Troops 35 and 37 have all gained sponsorship of the LERC according to Gordon Stanton, director of club activities.

All three troops meet at the Washington Street school in Burbank. These latest additions bring the total of sponsored troops to five.

Entertainment Upped at B-3

Artists, hobbyists, entertainers, musicians, even autograph seekers, all employes of Plant B-3, lend their talents to the sparkling array of lunch area programs put on by employes of that plant throughout the month.

With Lewis Brodek as master of ceremonies, the shows meet with the complete approval and interest of all the B-3 employes.

Typical of these programs is the collection of 225 dolls exhibited in the area by Dorothy Darsie, day shift template maker, Dept. 44-52, this week.

These dolls, a number of which were fashioned by Mrs. Darsie, represent authentic folk dolls dressed in the native costume of 23 different countries and include specimens of 12 different American Indian tribal dress.

Dorothy Darsie and Dolls

SWANSON COPS GOLFING HONORS

Doris McAnally Wins Women's Bowling Honors

Doris McAnally won top individual honors at the conclusion of the LERC's first annual women's bowling tournament which ended last week.

Doris won the all-events match with her scratch pin score of 1529 which with her handicap gave her a total score of 1610, equal to 180 average. In the team event, Bunny's Belles, captained by Bonny Shain, rolled down the alleys to an easy win, finishing ➡ with a scratch score of 1672 and a handicap of 246 for a total score of 1918.

Women's doubles was won by Willie Kuhlman and Bonny Shain with a combined total score of 1103.

Singles was copped by Eleanor Clark, who with her 620 total score finished 39 points ahead of the second-place winner, Florence Heberle, who had 581.

Jere Jarrett, committee chairman, stated that the tournament, held at the Sunset Bowling alleys in Hollywood was more convenient from a transportation standpoint.

Ninety Lockheed women making up 11 teams, 14 doubles, 28 singles, entered the contest.

Marcia Westfall Agnes Tarpinian Bonny Shain Willie Kuhlman

Los Lobos Take Lead in Tournament

Setting a tough pace for following competition, Robert Wiehle, captain of the Los Lobos bowling squad from the 755 scratch league at Magnolia, rolled a handicap 2882 to jump to the top of the class-A bracket at last Sunday's opening of the second annual Lockheed all-plant, all-shift bowling tournament at Magnolia in Burbank.

Following in second place with 2742 came the Victory club with the Majors in third place with 2712.

Leaders in the class-B team event on the opening round were the Penguins who tossed over a 2582, twenty pins over second placers, the Blue Chips. Purchasing placed third with 2466.

Class-A doubles was touched off Sunday by Tom Davis' and Don Wilson's handicap total of 1223. McLane and Kimble placed second with 1176. Only one point behind came the third-place duo, Bill Smith and Matt Pohl, 1175.

Nick Boukidis and Chub Howe placed first in the B doubles with 1090. Barrett Uhl took first-place ⬅ singles honors in the A bracket with a 631 scratch that totaled 665 with his 34 handicap, 61 pins over second-placer Russ West and 63 pins over third-placer Bill Durham's 602. Tom Adamson placed first in the B events with a 618 scratch, 10-point spot, for 628.

Slated originally to open last Saturday, the tournament was postponed until Sunday morning out of respect to President Roosevelt. The first of the more than 1400 keglers began rolling at 10:30 a.m., Sunday, with the starting whistle of tournament manager, Stan Cardinet. Three hundred and twelve bowled that day.

Schedule for this Saturday and Sunday shows 24 teams playing at 6:30 and 9 p.m. on both days. Sunday will see 48 doubles events from 10:30 a.m. to 4:30 p.m. and 96 singles contests beginning at 11:30 a.m. and playing through 5:30 p.m.

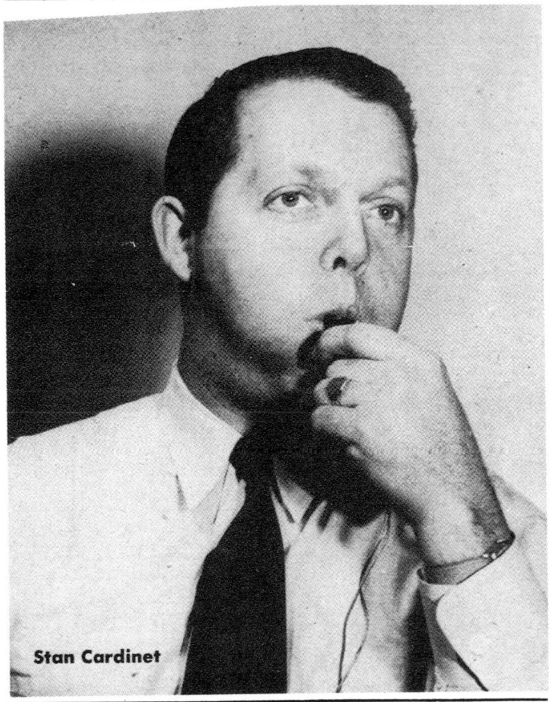

Stan Cardinet

Ticket Reductions Offered When Lockheed Has Day at Ice-Capades

Lockheed day at the Ice-Capades for all three shifts is being planned, according to Hal Davis, recreation division manager.

Arrangements are being made by the LERC to "take over" the Pan-Pacific auditorium where the Ice-Capades are being held on Sunday, May 6, for the swing shift and again on Sunday, May 13, for the day and graveyard shifts.

Tickets will be on sale at the LERC offices at Plants A and B and reservations for Lockheed employes and their families should be made as soon as possible.

Tickets will be offered Lockheed employes at substantially reduced prices.

Need Umpires On Swing Shift

With 58 departmental squads in the softball league battling it out on the diamond in various baseball parks scattered over Burbank, Glendale and North Hollywood, 11 Lockheed employes are handling that unpopular job of umpiring.

Handling the swing shift interdepartmental games by himself is Pat Montgomery.

Activities

BADMINTON—Tuesday and Thursday, 7 p.m., John Burroughs Jr. High School Gym, Burbank.

BLUE STAR WOMEN — Open house, Boulevard USO, 6551 Hollywood Blvd., Wednesday, 7:30 p.m.

BOAT CLUB—Last Wednesday of every month, 5 p.m., B-1 cafeteria, private dining room.

BOY SCOUTS — Troop No. 17, each Tuesday evening, 7 p.m., in Boy Scout cabin, George Washington School at Lincoln and Rowe Sts., Burbank. Troop No. 13 every Wednesday, 7 p.m., John Muir Jr. High School Scout cabin.

BRIDGE CLUB — Thursday, 7:30 p.m., Burbank Recreation Center, 1111 W. Olive.

CHESS CLUB—Wednesdays, 4 to 10 p.m., room 5, B-1 cafeteria.

CONCERTS — Military band, rehearsals Friday, 9:15 a.m., concerts begin at 10:50 a.m., main recreation area, all day shift lunch periods.

DANCE CLUB—Every Thursday, 8 p.m., Alan Rudack Studios, 7213 Beverly Blvd.

FREE MOVIES — Tuesday, April 24, "Camera Thrills of the War," "Angles of Angling," "Eruption of Mt. Vesuvius," "Seasons and Their Causes," and other short subjects, B-1 cafeteria, 5:45 p.m. and 8 p.m. Swing shift, 1:15 p.m.

GIRLS' SWIMMING—Tuesday, 7 p.m., Hollywood YMCA, 1553 N. Hudson, Hollywood. Swing shift, Tuesday, 10:30 a.m., same place.

MUSIC APPRECIATION CLUB—Regular meeting second and fourth Mondays of the month, B-1 cafeteria room 5, 2 p.m. Recordings every Wednesday from 2:45 to 3:45 p.m., Factory B-1 lunch area.

OPERA CLUB—Every Wednesday, 7 to 10 p.m., Hollywood High School, Highland and Sunset.

PENGUINETTE, DAYS — Cabaret night hostess, Boulevard USO, every Thursday evening.

PISTOL AND RIFLE CLUB—Training course, Glendale High School, Glendale, Wednesdays, 7 p.m.

PLANT TOURS—Contact the LERC office for further particulars.

PING PONG—Every Tuesday, 7 p.m., Burbank Recreation Center, 1111 West Olive.

RIDING CLUB—Lockheed Rangers, every Friday 7 p.m., Pico Stables, 420 Riverside Drive. Call LERC for reservations.

SKI CLUB—Contact the LERC office for further particulars, extension 6-1901 or 8-1735.

SERVICE STAR WOMEN — Plant B-1, first Wednesday of the month, after work, conference room 1, Cafeteria Bldg.; third Wednesday evening, 7:30, Hollywood YWCA, 6927 Hawthorne, Hollywood; B-2 day and graveyard shift, every Wednesday lunch period, 11 a.m. and 3:30 a.m., conference room.

SWIMMING — Men and women—Glendale YMCA every Friday, 8:30 and 9:30 p.m.

TOASTMASTERS' CLUB—Swing, every Tuesday 1 p.m., room 4, Cafeteria Bldg.

VOCAL GROUPS — Hollywood Radio Chorus, Hollywood High School, M.A. 71, every Wednesday and Friday from 7 to 10 p.m. Victory Singers—Monday and Wednesday, 7 p.m., L.A. High School, Olympic and Rimpau, room 423.

Three-Way Tie For Low Gross Will Rematch

With three players tied for low gross honors, Howard Swanson walked off with net honors at last Sunday's all-plant golf tournament by shooting a 79 gross with a 12 handicap for a net 67.

The triple tie of 75, shot by Ed Meyberg, Dan Lovejoy and Tom Rassmussen, all at Inglewood was the low gross turned in for both courses and will become a three-way playoff with the winner copping the first prize in that bracket.

Further results in the 300-man event, the second of its kind to be staged by the LERC, follow:

First Flight (70-80)

Name	Gross	Hdcp.	Net
Howard Swanson	79	12	67
Len Morgan	80	12	68
Smeland	85	17	68
G. Pemco	76	7	69
Don Clark	76	7	69
George Batchlor	81	12	69
Jim Sterling	79	10	69
Dan Lovejoy	75	5	70
Bill Paralta	80	10	70
Al Baggio	84	14	70

Second Flight (86-100)

Name	Gross	Hdcp.	Net
Pat Montgomery	93	24	69
Dingham	91	22	69
J. Harvey	92	22	70
Bill Rieger	100	29	71
John Lah	88	17	71
Mike Varanese	90	19	71
Bob Kaiser	91	19	72
Al Potocony	94	12	72
Bill Barlass	89	17	72
H. Hindman	91	19	72

Third Flight (101 and Up)

Name	Gross	Hdcp.	Net
W. Haven	104	29	75
Chet Stalker	103	26	77
Daug Hunt	102	24	78
Les Rauth	102	24	79
Ken Lawrence	108	29	79
C. Ackerman	103	24	79
Bill McCreary	103	22	81
W. Patter	103	22	81
Frank Miller	105	22	83
Mel Cole	105	22	83

Ten winners in the blind bogey bracket of 70-80 at both courses whose net totaled 72 follow:

Name	Gross	Hdcp.	Net
Doug Kruger	87	15	72
Stan Gebovaz	97	25	72
Bill Kirwan	97	25	72
Don Hayes	102	30	72
S. Biegler	87	15	72
Tom Barbour	87	15	72
Bud Lewis	82	10	72
R. A. Holt	112	40	72
Dave Dokemus	102	30	72
Morrow	87	15	72

First and second place winners in the putting contest at Inglewood were Gordon Coster and Pat Montgomery respectively. At Baldwin, J. E. Blaine placed first, Max Elson, second.

Bridge Club Adds Events

LERC's Bridge club is considering rubber bridge in addition to the duplicate bridge presently being played in the club's tournaments.

Glenn Wilkie, Dept. 26-05, Plant A-1, reveals that if sufficient interest is shown, additional instruction in contract bridge will be arranged. The club meets every Thursday at 7:30 p.m., in the Burbank Recreation Center.

MARSMAN TO SING AT B-1

Michiel Marsman, baritone and director of the Hollywood Radio chorus, will appear in a special program at Lockheed B-1 on April 21, and at A-1 on the 28th, in connection with the 7th War Loan Drive. Phyllis Althof, soloist in the chorus will appear with Marsman.

LOCKHEED RADIO WORK SETS PACE

(Continued from Page 5)

greater freedom from fog is enjoyed by the Lockheed Air Terminal.

"Many's the day you can look down into the sun-flooded valley with the terminal's runways clearly visible. Toward the west and southwest in the direction of Mines Field, Clover Field and other airports you can see nothing but thick, impenetrable fog. Our mountains form a barrier to most of the fog blankets that move in from the sea."

The station is hardly more than twice the size of a two-car garage but Lockheed spent more than $100,000 putting it there.

Inside are twenty receiving sets and fourteen transmitters, permitting the station to operate across the entire range of radio frequencies. On them are seemingly a thousand dials, gauges and switches. They're bewildering to a layman but to the eyes of experts who operate them they bring gleams of pride.

Recalls Raid

One of the operators is Harry Dennis just back from the merchant marine. He has a particular appreciation of P-38's. It is tied to a searing recollection of a Jap air raid on Port Moresby in the war's early days.

"I was sitting on a shipload of 100-octane gasoline when they came over," he says, "and the pearly gates seemed pretty close.

"A small handful of our fighters, mostly P-40's, rose to meet more than 100 Nip bombers. But among those fighters were six funny-looking planes with twin tails. They went to work like avenging angels and in a few minutes 76 Jap planes fell in flames. The rest of them high-tailed for home."

Harry sits in front of a typewriter with four loudspeakers facing him. Under the table are four foot-pedals like the bass note keys of an organ. On the end of a rod attached to the typewriter is a tiny microphone. When the going gets rough, Harry cocks his ear to pilots' voices coming from the loud speakers, pounds the typewriter with his fingers, operates the pedals with his feet and talks into the mike. If that sounds easy you belong in a circus.

Others doing similar work are Fred Yule, Lane King, and Ted Rycraft. Their supervisor is R. L. (Bob) Richards, veteran of 16 years in the merchant marine.

Used by Many

Though built primarily for checking radio apparatus of Lockheed planes, the station is made use of at times by nearly every high frequency transmitting apparatus in Southern California, on land or in the air.

For example, "line-of-sight" transmitters in Santa Monica and the San Fernando Valley might not reach each other because of the mountain barriers. But each could reach the Lockheed station and thus deliver the message.

"In communications," says Manager Peale, "you always answer a call, whether it's a man with your company or not.

"Once we heard an Army transport over Colorado trying to get a ground station the pilot could plainly see below. The operator on the ground saw the plane but didn't know it was calling him. We relayed the message to him.

"In the early days, our own pilots were not unnaturally dubious of our new station's value. But after they were helped out of a tough spot or two they became more radio conscious. Now we've become a sort of radio refuge for all pilots in the area. We're on duty 24 hours every day and they feel safe when they come within our range. They know they can always get help through our station.

"We have to know all the answers. Once a PV pilot was worried about his landing gear being stuck. We got a P-38 in the vicinity to look at it. He saw what the trouble was and the PV pilot soon fixed it. They couldn't talk to each other but both could reach us."

Much credit for the fame of Lockheed Radio operations is due to the energy and far vision of young Bill Peale.

Had Wrong Notes

Bill says he was a "ham" operator in high school but majored in chemistry when he started college. He decided that was a bad idea one day when he emerged from chem class with a page full of notes on radio. He joined Lockheed in 1938 and a year later was checking radios on the Hudson assembly lines.

After Peale made a trip to Washington a year ago, the Army and Civil Aeronautics administration called a special meeting of Southern California aircraft manufacturers to discuss airlanes congestion as affected by radio. This led to acceptance in its entirety of the Lockheed Radio Operations manual as standard procedure.

Before the F.C.C. Peale argued the case for aircraft manufacturers so ably that the industry won the right to certain exclusive services of the air.

Lockheed was the first to receive an F.C.C. license for very high frequency transmission and the first to set up a licensed two-way communication between the control tower at the terminal, crash trucks and police cars.

Though admittedly a pioneer in this field of radio, Lockheed's many discoveries and developments have been made available to the industry. Its only interest is to maintain the reputation of its radio operations department as the nemesis of aviation gremlins.

S. T. Sesnon, Jr. — Cyril Chappellet

PLANT WINS FIRST SPOT

For their "outstanding cooperation" Lockheed employes today hold the first citation from the American Red Cross blood-donor service to any Pacific coast industrial organization.

Lockheed's permanent blood-donor station receives the Red Cross mobile unit twice weekly to cover all factory shifts—a record unapproached by any other industrial station.

Many Pints

Since the unit's opening more than a year ago, a total of 23,260 pints of plasma and whole blood have been contributed.

Just recently, at the urgent request of the Navy, facilities were converted overnight to accept whole-blood donations to be flown directly to South Pacific battle fronts. Already the station has applied to Red Cross authorities for a third day of operation to continue plasma donations.

Cyril Chappellet, vice president in charge of administration, under whose authority the unit was established at Lockheed, received the certificate of appreciation this week from William T. Sesnon, Jr., director of the Red Cross blood-donor service.

Holst Present

Present, too, was A. H. Holst, Lockheed Industrial Relations man who directs activities of the blood station.

The citation was signed by Sesnon and Basil O'Connor, national director, American Red Cross; G. Canby Robinson, M.D., national director, blood-donor service; and Guerney E. Newlin, chairman of the Los Angeles chapter, American Red Cross.

COURSES AVAILABLE

New courses available to Lockheed employes include: Industrial Safety Engineering, Hydraulics, Engineering Mathematics IV, Aircraft Descriptive Geometry, Industrial Supervision and Human Relations, Industrial Electronics I, and Applied Ferrous Metallurgy.

Call extension 6-2676 for further information.

Is it Here?

THESE classified advertisements in the *Star* are provided for employes without charge. If you want to buy, sell, trade, or find or return lost articles, obtain Form 4929 from your department clerk, the stationery store, or employe service office. Mail the advertisement to the *Lockheed Star*, Room 244, Bldg. 1-A, Plant B-1.

WANTED

SINGLE apartment L. A. or Hollywood. Write 4915½ Lexington Ave.
FORD model "A" coupe or sedan—good condition. NOrmandy 21916.
TYPEWRITER, Underwood. Prefer portable or Stand. model. CH. 61049 aft. 4.
'37 to '40 Ford sedan, or other. Write 5130 Greenbush Ave., Van Nuys.
UNFURNISHED apt. or bungalow in Glendale or Hollywood. CH. 81658.
FURNISHED apt., 1 bedrm. or large single. NO. 8443 after 4:15 p.m.
REFRIGERATOR for cash. SUnset 22418. 11509 Burbank, N. Hollywood.
CAMERA, super Ikonta A or C special. Cash. WA. 2804.
KENNEDY tool box, 7-drawer-type preferred. YOrk 6633 bet. 5 and 8 p.m.
FORD V-8 body. What have you? 9007 Olive Grove Pl., Sunland.
ELECTRIC refrigerator. Call day or evening. CHarleston 62664.
'39-'41 car, any make. Will pay cash. CI. 16191, anytime.
2-wheel luggage trailer. 712 N. Van Ness, Hollywood.
LAWN swing in good condition. CI. 26402. 356 Vine St., Glendale.
BEACH umbrella, new or used. CI. 18554.
REDWOOD lawn furn., gin rummy set, chaise longue, table, etc. NO. 25024.
ALARM clock in good working condition. 15142 Victory Blvd., Van Nuys.
APT. for single girl in Hollywood district. Might con. sharing. OL. 6864.
MOTORCYCLE—prefer Harley 61 or 74. 1820 Jackson, Burbank.
UNFURN. house to rent. Couple has to have by June 1. OLympia 2473.
PORTABLE phonograph. CHarleston 63203. 3300 W. Clark Ave., Burbank.
2 young men to share room in furnished apartment. CI. 26441 bet. 11 & 3 p.m.
'36 or '38 2-door Plymouth, Ford. Cash. 509 N. Fairview St., Burbank.
SMALL radio in good condition for man overseas. WE. 6735.
'37-'39 Chevrolet coupe or sedan in good condition. NO. 24996.
MODEL A Ford roadster, running condition. CHarleston 86092.
SMALL furnished house for 3 months, near beach. STate 55012.
35-mm. camera for G. I. overseas. 130 "C" S. Cordova St., Burbank.
LAWN swing, good condition, with top. 1721 Maple St., Burbank.
ELECTRIC flat iron in good condition. Urgently needed. SYcamore 47932.
GATELEG table din. room set and '41 auto. 6652 Denny, N. Hollywd, aft. 4.
NEED immediately, size 7 shoes for left-handed bowler. CItrus 32580.
RENT house—apartment. 4 adults. Any location. Reward. SU. 15511.
OUTBOARD motor. Johnson Seahorse or Evinrude. RE. 6242 after 5.

FOR SALE

MISCELLANEOUS

TRAILER with bed, breakfast nook, gas, fan, tires. FItzroy 5397.
5-piece walnut dinette set—6-ft. extension table. WAlnut 9476.
5-piece Philippine mahogany bedroom set. Prewar. RE. 5806.
GATE for driveway, white picket, 8'x4', with post. CH. 68386.
DOUBLE-breasted pin-stripe black suit, size 40; trousers, 35". ST. 73665.
TRUMPET. Nearly new, reasonable. STate 43984.
DRESSMAKING. Specializing in children's dresses, etc. WA. 5676.
CHESTERFIELD set, coffee table, etc. 14749 Runnymede St., Van Nuys.
STUCCO court, 4 units, furnished, garages. 2321 Ridgeview Ave., Eagle Rock.
MAN'S Victory bike, woman's Elgin, prewar. ARizona 37472, evenings.
LADIES' lightweight green suit; blue covert cloth coat. (16). CH. 84265.

Plan No Change In Policy Here

(Continued from Page 3)

original order; the Constellation, 100 per cent, the P-80, 100 per cent, and the Ventura, 100 per cent.

Secret Ship Holds

As portions of Lockheed know, the company is making still other secret models which will remain at 100 per cent production during the remainder of 1945.

These instructions for production were received here from the Air Technical Service Command.

The Lockheed Aircraft Corporation will comply with its expressed desires. It has been indicated that no sharp change is anticipated upon the fall of Germany.

Said Industrial Relations Manager William Aulepp last night: "Tell our people to stay on the job and finish the job. The Japs aren't whipped . . . and neither are the Germans at the moment."

Is it Here?

FOR SALE

MISCELLANEOUS (Cont.)

VACUUM cleaner. "Rexair" conditioner and humidifier. CI. 34693.
DUAL-carburetor manifold for Ford V-8, .22 shells and rifle. CHase 78183.
OUTBOARD alternate-firing Johnson 12, top condition. SY. 61670.
5' 65-lb. Yew wood bow, leather quiver, rid. boots, 9½. 2412 Brigden, Pasadena.
PLATINUM engagement ring, 2 baguette, 16 smaller. 1-kt. center stone. EX. 0184.
DOUBLE bed and springs, dresser, etc. Prewar. CH. 69862.
TWO bicycles and ladies' roller skates, size 4, with white shoes. CH. 60357.
LADIES' pear-shape diamond ring, 60 pts. Plat.-set diamond & sapphires. GL. 0652.
PIANO, bungalow upright; chair, rose. Barkers. SUnland 1721.
BLUE bridesmaid dress, Magnin's, 12-14. HI..6181, apartment 305, mornings.
TUXEDO, 3-piece black broadcloth. Size 39, single-breasted. PArkway 7356.
NEW "Ercoupe" U-control kit. 20% off retail price. CH. 64604.
HOUSE TRAILER, no furnishings. 110 S. Orchard Dr., Burbank.
2 pairs gabardine prewar coveralls—ladies' size 15. CR. 63783.
RACING outboard — 4-cylinder, 55-h.p. Johnson class-E motor. CI. 32542.
V-42 gas cooking stove. Good condition. NOrmandy 25256.
BILT-RITE baby carriage, springs. 6005½ Carlton Way, Hollywood.
TWO-toned gold wedding band, size 5. Apartment 203, HE. 1744.
ELECTRIC Sunbeam Shavemaster. 2306½ Rowe Ave., Burbank.
RADIO, Packard-Bell phono-cord. 7709 Sepulveda Blvd., Van Nuys.
BABY paneled crib and mattress, like new. CHarleston 64457.
AIR wheel tube, 600x16, heavy duty, excellent condition. GR. 8971.
CRAFTSMAN air compressor, overhauled. 544 Harding Ave., San Fernando.
1 lathe, Dunlap metal-turning with accessories. SUnset 12563.
CABINET radio, trunk, suitcases and tools. HI. 5581.
SNARE drum, stand, sticks and brushes. 245 E. Santa Anita, Burbank.
12-ga. Rem. pump and shells or exchange for Woodsman or Stevens. AT. 43174.
LADIES' yellow-gold wrist watch. NO. 13092.
ALTO sax, buffet clarinet, soprano saxes; combination case. FI. 2074.
RADIATOR grills, fenders, V-8 transmission, etc. CI. 35508.
GOLF clubs, steel; sell or trade for left-hand irons. CH. 87573.
BURMESE kittens, make wonderful pets. RUgby 62670.
DRUM set, complete with Hi-Hat, snare, etc. CH. 85414, evenings.
DE LUXE play pen, box springs and mattress. 2100 N. Valley, Burbank.
TELESCOPIC sight, Winchester, for .22-cal. rifle. ARdmore 82084.
HAND garden plow, and hose, 100 feet. CH. 61817.
LADIES' gold, rimless-eyeglass frames. Very cheap. AS. 42365.
PARKER Vacumatic pen and Pea coat. 1125 A. Raleigh, Glendale.
PORTABLE reducing machine, motor perfect. ANgelus 16315 after 5:30.
STUDIO couch, blue, can be used as sgle., double or twin beds. STate 44804.
BED divan. Also double iron bed and springs. CH. 80034.
USED high-oven gas range. Reasonable. WA. 5559.
MEN'S shoe roller skates, size 10, .351 Remington cartridges. AL. 1669.
PAIR rounded fender pants, fit 'most any car. SY. 73380.
HIGH chair, play pen, Crosley car, man's overcoat, 44. CH. 60670.
BROODER, hutches, bucks, dresser, books, ice skates (9). SUnset 15288.
HI-OVEN Detroit gas range, good condition. 1243 N. June St., Hollywood.
DOBERMAN—2½-yr. black male. Army-obedience trained. SUnland 6562.
'39 edition Encyclopaedia Brittanica with bookcase. CH. 61893 after 6.

VEHICLES

1934 Harley Davidson 74. CR. 60547.
MOTORCYCLE, Henderson 4, late model. 1456½ E. Chevy Chase, Glendale.
MAN'S 28" bike, Princeton, prewar. Lady's wool coat, 12-14 yr. WY. 7977.
'36 Harley 74, L-head 'cycle, good tires. FE. 2276.
'35 Pontiac coupe, excellent condition. 1311 C Buena Vista, Burbank.

EXCHANGE

10 acres near L. A. County Park for diamond ring or ? AL. 5972.
PORTABLE typewriter for small piano or radio-phonograph. WH. 3536.
'41 Pontiac sedanette for older model and cash. 2355 Cove Ave., L. A.
2-bedrm. unfurnished duplex in N. H. for house or apartment in L. A. SU. 13071.
PORTABLE Corona No. 4 for later model pica type and cash. CR. 63783.

LOST

BLACK wallet containing gas stamps, etc. 10315 Marcus St., Tujunga.
BILLFOLD in Olympic-Fairfax bus. Reward. 111 N. Wetherly Dr., L. A.
EVERSHARP fountain pen, brown, wide gold band. Reward. CI. 32531.

FOUND

"GLOVE." CH. 60935 between 5 and 6. 1234 N. Parish, Burbank.

FOR RENT

ROOM for 2 men, day workers, near B-1. 2120 N. Brighton St., Burbank.

THE LOCKHEED Star
OFFICIAL PUBLICATION OF THE LOCKHEED AIRCRAFT CORPORATION

Issued each Friday for the employes of Lockheed Aircraft Corporation. The *Star* is the official publication of the company. Communications should be addressed to the Editor, *Lockheed Star* Unit, Lockheed Aircraft Corporation, Burbank, California. Unsolicited manuscripts cannot be returned.

KENNETH CRIST, Editor

Marshall Atwell, Staff Artist — J. H. Prescott, Associate Editor

LOCKHEED'S FUTURE TOLD

Results of Two-Year Survey Place Company in Position of Leadership

Business Outlook Seen as Excellent for Post-war Program; Employes Told of Plans as Peace-time Orders Reach $150,000,000

Lockheed's future, determined through a three-year study by experts, was outlined to management this week. It is a good future; probably the best in the airframe industry.

Through long war years these experts have labored toward just one end: To know what the company would be like when peace came to Burbank.

Succinctly, this is the picture:

The commercial business on the books at the present time totals some $150,000,000. The figure is approached, but neither equaled nor exceeded in the industry on the basis of announcements to date.

To manufacture airplanes in prospect, it has been estimated that 32,000 employes will be required . . . after the Japs have been whipped.

32,000 Employes

As of July 6, Lockheed had 39,347 persons on its payroll. Of this number, 16,566 were direct, productive employes.

To meet postwar schedules some 16,000 direct producers and a like number of indirect employes will be essential, according to estimates handed management. They will build a giant, but still secret, transport, also the now-famed Constellation, the Saturn regional transport, and yet another craft designed, built, and flown . . . to appeal to private plane owners.

Visitors arrive almost daily to see the Constellation in the interests of major airlines. Some come from the far ends of the earth. The pattern has been set for the Constellation to fly in major transoceanic business. Its operation economy has combined with its speed to make it great. Each of the 64-passenger Constellation's engines requires but one quart of fuel for each mile in flight at 15,000 feet at 260 m.p.h. No other ship of comparable size is so economical.

Shifts Emphasis

The fact that the Army has shifted emphasis from the P-38 and B-17 to the C-69 Constellation tends daily to shorten any readjustment period that may arise at the war's close. The ship lends itself to rapid conversion.

Then there's the "big transport job" . . . designed for the Navy. It, too, will convert with speed. Construction of this super-airplane is being pressed.

And now comes the personal ship: Looking to a long-range future, it offers, says management, what may become the greatest opportunity of all for volume production business. Its development possibilities are virtually unlimited.

Lockheed engineers have not waited for the small plane market to develop. For more than two years they have studied its commercial possibilities.

Personal Craft

For purely experimental purposes, Lockheed has built such a plane . . . tested it. The ship, sometimes called the Little Dipper, has proved safe, efficient, and easy to operate. It is all-metal and can be produced at low cost. It can take off and land in a normal-size ballpark . . . with plenty of climb on take-off to clear the backstop.

So convinced is Lockheed of the potential future of the personal airplane field that further experimentation is going forward.

Other such ships will follow.

Lockheed's supervision was informed this week that, when the market is ripe, Lockheed will be ready with a good product, an aggressive distribution program, and an internationally known name.

Authority Cited

Coupled with these facts, high Army and Navy officials this week informed Lockheed that no additional cutbacks in the military program are planned for this company before Japan's defeat.

It also was indicated that the war's close probably would not sound taps for the P-80. Fastest ship in the world's skies, the Lockheed Shooting Star is expected to remain on order to meet replenishment in the nation's permanent air force.

While the war's end may bring a readjustment period that will prevent, through military cutback, transfer of all Lockheed personnel immediately to commercial production, the company program is designed, and ready, to take care of business now pressing . . . from the airlines of the world.

PRESIDENT POINTS WAY TO LOCKHEED'S FUTURE; RAY WINS 'LUCKY SEVEN'

Elemer Coleman Ray, commissary at Plant A-1, won the grand "Lucky Seventh" prize for cash bond purchases.

Lockheed's Lucky Seventh War Loan Drive reached a fitting climax last Saturday with lunch area ceremonies that included three important highlights.

1. Company employes received 18 separate citations from the U.S. Treasury Department for purchasing more than $6,000,000 worth of bonds . . . more than any other war plant group in the Southern California area.

2. An all-expense air trip to Mexico City and 41 other valuable prizes were awarded to winners on the "cash purchase" contest which was carried out during the Lucky Seventh bond drive.

3. President Robert E. Gross told employes that he has good reason to believe peacetime operation at Lockheed will provide jobs for thousands of workers, many more than once thought possible.

Peace Outlook

President Gross, who drew lucky numbers in the prize drawing and accepted one Treasury Department citation on behalf of company employes, said that the company's job in preparing for peace will be as hard as it was in preparing for war.

"But," he added, "with the orders we now have on hand, the future of your company looks extremely encouraging.

"Our first consideration, regardless of all else," President Gross said, "must be in winning the war. I am sure you all know that as well as I do. When that job is done, however, we are not going to let down.

Hard Work

"Although I have seen all too little of you people in the past few months, it isn't because I have wanted it that way. You have been working hard, and I, too, have been working hard.

"For example, Monday morning I am going to take the Model 12 and head east. I am going to take my little black bag with me and I am not going to return until I have it filled with orders for commercial airplanes. We have a substantial backlog of those orders on hand right now. But that isn't enough. We have to keep our company as far ahead of the field in future peace as it is at present, during war.

"We are in this business together. And I sincerely hope that we will continue in it together."

Awards Given

Howard D. Mills, regional director of the Treasury Department's War Finance Division, presented A. H. Holst, chairman of Lockheed's Employe Victory committee and each of the company's bond commandos with individual citations for their part in the drive.

Cleo Riewer represented the commando group at the ceremony. Following is a list of the prize winners:

(Continued on Page 8)

Elemer Coleman Ray

LOCKHEED MEN WIN PRIZES IN MODEL CONTEST

Lockheed prestige soared high among model builders this week in the wake of the Southland's biggest meet in history where Lockheed men and ships took top prizes.

Flying a Vega five-place high-wing model, Bob Palmer of Factory B-1 scored 212 points to win the precision flying class of the first semi-annual U-control tournament at Santa Ana Army Air Base.

Many Spectators

With more than 400 entries and thousands of spectators on the big parade grounds, the meet was described by veteran model enthusiasts as the largest ever held in Southern California. It was sponsored by the convalescent hospital division of the base.

First prize in the Class B scale models went to another Vega ship built by William Given of Engineering Dept. 12 at the Navy-Lockheed Service Center in Van Nuys.

Second Spot

Second place in this class went to Test Pilot John E. Schields with a model of a Great Lakes Trainer. Third and fourth places went to Edward B. Tifft and Palmer of Factory B-1.

Rex Bloom of Dept. 72-25, a former president of the LERC-sponsored model club, piloted the ship of Clarence Beskin, winner of the Class C speed event. With a mark of 117.26 miles an hour, this ship just missed breaking the class world's record of 118 miles per hour.

NEW PENCILS FOR OLD, NOW

Pencil stubs will have to be turned in at Stationery substations to procure further pencil stock, it was announced here last night by R. C. Sargent, manager.

Pencils are becoming scarce, stocks are being replenished by purchasing small lots from whatever source possible, he said.

RECEIVES AWARD

Lloyd Christensen of Dept. 40, Navy-Lockheed Service Center, four of his brothers, and his parents recently received the Congressional Medal of Honor, highest honor in the land, awarded posthumously to Lt. Dale Christensen, killed in New Guinea last August.

Lockheed Mechanic Wins $100 Prize

Ramond J. Stewart, Lockheed experimental mechanic won first prize of $100 in the Snap-On-Tool Corporation's slogan contest, it was learned here last night.

The slogan he submitted was "Tons in the Shops."

Snap-On-Tools, wrenches and hand tools, are used extensively by Lockheed for production, maintenance, and service.

AIR-MINDED FRENCHMEN INSPECT CONSTELLATION

Ten French military and aviation officials visited Lockheed last Tuesday to familiarize themselves with Lockheed commercial and military products. Members of the party who toured the factory area, conferred with engineering executives, and took a flight in the Constellation were: General H. Ziegler, Chief of Mission; Col. C. Razanoff, Assistant Chief of Mission; Lt. Col. C. Teyssier, Maj. A. Esperet, Maj. R. Marshall, Lt. R. Beauvais, Lt. Col. C. Penin, Lt. Col. E. Gibouin, Lt. Col. Albert Ladousse, and Maj. J. Millet.

Hall Hibbard, vice president in charge of engineering; Kelly Johnson, chief research engineer; Joe Towle, chief test pilot, and R. C. Stanton, flight test engineer, briefed the touring party for the Constellation flight.

Roger Lewis, Charles Thomas, and Bob Stoessel conducted the factory tour.

Airlines in U. S. Active

America's extensive airlines system, largest in the world, would be more than 10 times greater than it now is if all of the 554 applications to the CAB for new routes were granted.

Reports the Air Transport Association, these applications embrace 678 new scheduled airline stops over routes totaling 794,296 miles in length.

At the end of 1945's first quarter there were 554 applications for domestic airlines and 100 foreign. Plus 37 for new Alaskan operations makes a grand total of 691 compared to 534 on May 1, 1944.

CHECKS FOR BACK WAGES NOW READY

More than $200,000 in retroactive pay will soon be distributed to Lockheed employes in the form of 11,635 checks, the Industrial Relations department announced last night.

Of this amount, $167,000 in 8335 checks will be distributed next Monday, July 16, to employes in factory labor grades 1, 2, 3 and 4 who may be affected by the National War Labor Board order of March 2, 1945, granting a five-cent-an-hour increase.

Maybe Two Checks

According to the machine accounting section of the payroll division which has been preparing the retroactive payments, certain employs of this labor group are eligible for two checks.

Of those in the labor group employed between March 3, 1943, and July 21, 1944, the smallest check is for 12 cents and the largest $61. Those in this group who were also employed between July 22, 1944, and April 5, 1945, will be eligible for a second check averaging between $20 and $30 each.

Distributed July 30

The remaining 3300 checks worth $104,000 will be distributed July 30 to all employes classified as leadmen between March 3, 1943, and July 21, 1944.

Smallest check in this group, says the machine accounting office, will be for $1.75, and the largest for $127.75.

DIES IN ACTION

Word has been received that Pvt. Dallas McDonald was killed in action on Okinawa. He was former group leader in Dept. 25, Lockheed B-1.

FIRST REHIRED VETERAN HERE

FROM a land where Hudsons once fought surging Jap air power almost single-handed an AAF veteran returned this week to become Lockheed's first ex-employe rehired after a point-system discharge.

He is Wallace E. Hague who helped repair the rugged Lockheed ships and many other warplanes during 27 months in the South Pacific. When 122 points brought his release, he was a master sergeant in the 43rd Service Squadron of the Fifth Air Force.

Now he's at Navy-Lockheed Service Center on loan from the Customer Service Division where he first joined the company in January of 1941. He enlisted before Pearl Harbor's tragedy.

"When I first saw Australia," recalled the blond, 27-year-old Iowa native, "Lockheed Hudsons and a couple of B-34's were part of a thin Royal Australian Air Force buying precious time with blows against a yellow tide.

"At Darwin these ships shared a flying field with American forces and we often helped bind their battle wounds. Again and again they were sent up to slug it out against hopeless odds."

Hague had high praise for Aussie ground crews at advanced bases.

"Sometimes in drenching downpours by day and faltering candlelight at night," he said, "those sleepless men kept their battered Hudsons flying under incredible difficulties."

In addition to 19½ months of combat duty, factors in Hague's point total were the members of his family—a wife and two daughters. He came to California when a youngster and attended Los Angeles high schools. Inglewood is his home.

Wallace Hague

TECHNICAL DEVELOPMENT IN GERMANY STUDIED BY ENGINEER FROM COMPANY

By W. W. BEMAN

Division Engineer, Lockheed Aeronautical Research

It is rather an unusual circumstance that causes an engineer to pause and look at the political machinery that makes civilization run. Yet this unusual circumstance exists in Germany, where for several weeks preceding the Armistice and for a time after, W. Bleakney, head of Lockheed's Flutter and Vibration engineering group, and I visited on a flying trip.

The primary purpose of our mission was to study the technical developments within Germany and to determine what factors could be profitably used.

Dreams, Realities

Many of the things which were under development were fantastic but, most interesting, was the slow realization of the background which made these developments realities.

In Germany, nothing was prohibitively expensive, expense being merely a relative term. The will to do is the determining factor.

No one in this country would have undertaken the expensive

W. W. Beman

development of the super-fantastic V-2 rocket bomb, a tremendous weapon weighing more than 12 tons.

Some Still Doubt

There are people who still scoff at the idea, because it would be prohibitively expensive, that the rocket bomb ever could have been developed to shoot 3000 miles and be effective. Yet, this is a definite technical possibility.

Human understanding and sympathy have been completely suppressed.

To illustrate: A German family had been bombed out of its home in a little town near Berlin.

Members gathered such belongings as they could, and started walking to Aachen.

They traveled some hundred miles to discover Aachen had been obliterated.

Strict censorship was so controlled that is was impossible for one group of people to know what the other group was doing.

Each town, as it was obliterated, felt that it was bearing the whole brunt of the war.

America's important lesson from Germany is to retain the U.S. position in the world, we must do it by research.

American engineers know that technical achievements are in the near future which absolutely confound the greatest imagination—there is no point on the globe which is immune from attack from any other point.

Interplanetary travel at speeds in excess of 3000 mph. is a physical possibility, and once any people has the will to do, this accomplishment may be commonplace.

'MAD MAPPER', EX-TEST PILOT, REACHES U.S.

Former Lockheed engineering test pilot, Lt. Col. Pat B. McCarthy, commanding officer of a Superfortress reconnaissance squadron has returned to the United States for leave and reassignment.

His squadron photographed more than a million square miles of the Japanese homeland in the last eight months.

A veteran of 600 hours of combat flying, Colonel McCarthy has flown photographic mapping missions in nearly every combat theater of World War II. He has completed tours of duty in Labrador, Greenland, the Caribbean, South America, North Africa, the Mediterranean and Red Sea areas, and the China-Burma-India theaters.

The 46-year-old veteran flier's accomplishments as leader of his aerial reconnaissance squadron resulted in his nickname, "Mad Mapper."

He has been flying airplanes since 1924 and has more than 9000 flying hours. For eight years he was a pilot for Delta Air Lines, flying the run from Charleston, South Carolina, to Fort Worth, Texas. At Lockheed he made many test flights on the P-38.

FRATERNITY IS L.A.T. VISITOR

Alpha Eta Rho, national aviation fraternity, of the University of Southern California held its initiation and banquet in the executive dining room of Lockheed Air Terminal recently.

Dinner followed the initiation ceremonies, at which an address was given by regional director of Civil Aeronautics Administration in the Los Angeles area. The group then made a tour of the airport, visited the control tower, weather office, Western Airline servicing shop, and dispatching room.

VISITS PLANT

Headley Crabtree, superintendent of overhaul for British Overseas Airways Corporation, visited Lockheed this week to confer with Reagan Stunkel, general service manager and Charles Thomas, Lockheed sales engineer.

FUNDS LIMITED

Legislation to place specific limit on the use of road funds has been introduced in the Maryland state legislature. It is aimed at circumventing use of commission funds for airport development.

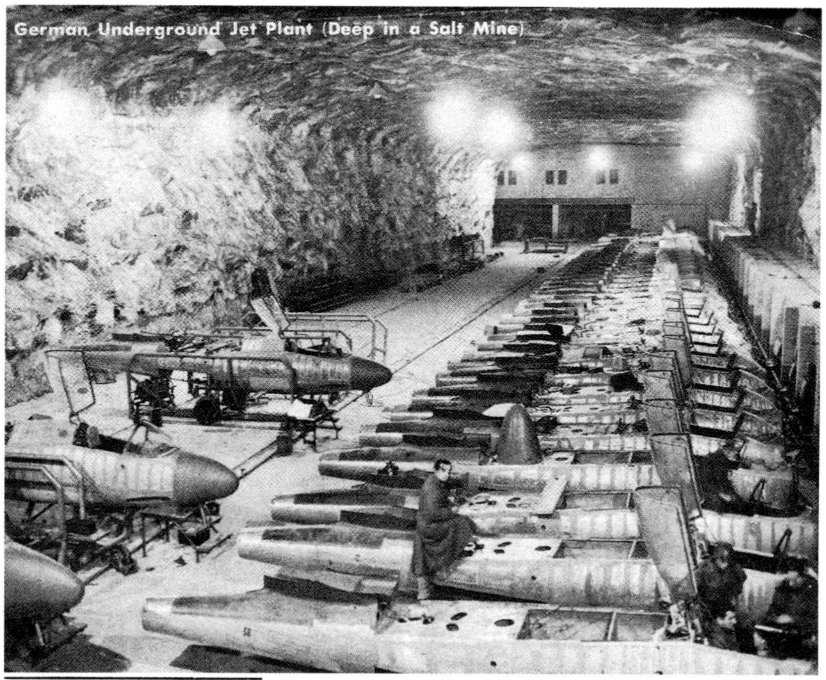

German Underground Jet Plant (Deep in a Salt Mine)

Hibbard Predicts Developments in Aircraft Industry

Jet propulsion, which already has brought revolutionary speed to airplanes, will be adapted to virtually all forms of transportation in the future, Hall L. Hibbard, vice president and chief engineer of Lockheed Aircraft Corporation, said this week.

Turbine engines that absorb all the jet's energy in successive turbine fans, will be adaptable as power units for railroad trains, buses, electric power generators and even automobiles of the future, in the opinion of Hibbard, who addressed 400 businessmen attending a special luncheon meeting of the Los Angeles Chamber of Commerce.

"In aviation, jet propulsion's chief effect will be speed and economy, speed such as we have never known before," Hibbard said. "Our future transport will bring the outposts of the world within a day's flying of Los Angeles.

Accept Impossible

"It takes strong, courageous thinking to visualize this world. We must prepare our minds to accept the impossible—for the impossible is almost upon us."

A jet helicopter that will become "the standard form of family travel" 10 years from now was described by the Lockheed engineer.

"This helicopter can be operated simply and safely," he said. "Cruising speed will be in the neighborhood of 200 miles an hour. Its range will be roughly 500 miles. It will land and take off with no forward motion whatsoever. Should an engine failure occur, the ship can be brought gently to a landing with no power. It will be sold for the price of an automobile."

Warns of 1960 Hitler

Hibbard warned of aircraft scientists who might be ready to supply a 1960 Hitler with tremendously powerful weapons.

"The aircraft industry cannot solve that problem," he said. "Public opinion must provide that solution."

U.S. INTELLIGENCE TEAMS STUDY HUN JET SECRETS

Current *Aviation News* air-war commentary exposes details of German airpower information unearthed by U.S. intelligence teams who are checking details of the world's most powerful reciprocating engine, and information on vast German fighter production schedules.

Thus, full Nazi air progress before Germany's surrender is being slowly pieced together.

Developments on advanced aircraft and engine projects, as well as secret weapons are being studied by American engineers.

Engineers have known for years of German development work expended on their two advanced high-power aircraft engines.

Huge Engine

The latest Bavarian Motor Works engine, the 803, is the world's most powerful reciprocating engine. Consisting of two 14-cylinder in-line units coupled together, it has a reported horsepower of over 3500. The BMW 801 engine is powerplant for the Focke-Wulf 190. It is a 28-cylinder, liquid-cooled type.

The Junkers 24-cylinder liquid-cooled Jumo 222 consists of six blocks of four cylinders arranged around the crankcase. It has a 2500-horsepower take-off.

At the time of Germany's surrender, neither of these engines was in full production, probably because of emphasis of jet-propulsion gas turbines.

German jet secrets revealed indicated that the Heinkel 162 had a monthly production peak of 750 aircraft, assembled in an underground factory. Another factory was reported ready to produce 1250 jet ME-262's by late summer which would have made a total of 2000 jet fighters produced a month.

Turbo-Unit

The HE-162 was powered by a single turbo-jet unit with a thrust power ranging between 2700 and 3000. This is considerably more powerful than the BMW 803 engine used in certain versions of the AR-234 or the Jumo 804 in the ME-262, and other versions of the 234.

The Heinkel jet-fighters have a gross weight of about 6000 pounds. The ME-262 weighs 12,000 pounds.

The Arada 234 twin turbo jet fighter-bombers were first encountered toward the end of 1944. They did not appear to be quite as fast as the jet Messerschmitt 262, which has a top speed of 550 mph., as a fighter.

Maj. Levy Is Transferred

Transfer to San Diego of Maj. Nat E. Levy, commanding officer of the 3098th AAF Base Unit Lockheed Aircraft Factory School was disclosed this week by Charles H. Tigar, manager of the Service Training Department.

The new commanding officer is Major Levy's former adjutant, Capt. Delmer L. Hughes, native of Wisconsin who has been with the regular Army since before the first World War.

Major Levy whose new assignment puts him in charge of the 3095th AAF Base Unit of the Western Flying Training

Capt. Delmer L. Hughes

Command has been commanding officer of the Lockheed unit since Oct. 28, 1943.

Upwards of 20,000 men of the Army Air Forces have studied repair and maintenance of Lockheed-built warplanes since establishment of the base in May of 1942.

The teaching is done by Lockheed men. Army designations of ships studied there are: B-34, A-28, A-29, AT-18, B-17, P-38, C-60 and C-69.

Major Levy was given a farewell luncheon at the Skyroom by civilian and military personnel.

JACQUELINE COCHRAN is the world's Number 1 airwoman. Director of the WASPS, she was the first woman to ferry a bomber, the Hudson, across the Atlantic to England. Holder of five national and international speed records, she is three times winner of the Harmon Trophy as outstanding woman pilot. She is one of the few women in the United States licensed to fly multi-engine craft

Jacqueline Cochran

WOMEN can speak in aviation . . . they have a right to speak. Today they're potent factors in a $20,000,000,000 sky industry. And they know what they want. In the first place, aviation no longer is a man's game. And more; it's no longer a man's means of travel. As a director in Northeast Airlines, I'm interested in what women want.

First, I believe, they want the nice appointments of the skyways. They want comfort. They want relaxation. They want attention . . . you know, just the kindliness of air attention.

"She was such a lovely person . . . the stewardess."

Doesn't that sound just like your wife?

THEN there's another angle: Some 30,000 girls . . . and age-up . . . have applied for Women's Auxiliary Pilot training . . . without a bit of recruiting.

Interested in aviation?

Of course women are!

The truth of the matter is that women are going to set the sky styles.

They'll be sensible about it, too. They won't ask for a lot of gadgets that are impracticable; gadgets that only will add weight and, because of their weight, cut speed. They know that luxury, so called, is no substitute for economy in operation. Most women know the value of money because they have had to deal with it.

64-Passenger Constellation

Air Hostess

Cargo Capacity

The Lockheed Constellation

tyles

By Jacqueline Cochran

Director, Northeast Airlines
as told to
Barbara Sewald

·, the female is ingenious enough to think of many things that are
plane at present and curious enough to find out whether they could
/ithout too much cost or loss of flying efficiency.
y, women want proper pressure inside the cabin and freedom from
nd noise as well as even temperatures. But, so do men.

·hinking of the women's angle one must think more in terms of being
.sh the trip looking fresh, in terms of wholesome drinking water and
ɔits of food, nice powder rooms equipped with lotions and cosmetics,
gloves and knickknacks, methods of keeping up with the flight, and
color schemes.
s said about women travelers on our transports also is true generally
. who fly their own light planes.
ıities of a feminine market in aviation are tremendous. American women
·number men. They control some three-fourths of the nation's wealth
ing power. They have proved to be inveterate travelers by surface

have flown all types of combat aircraft and can do any aerial flying that
o . . . except where unusual muscular strength is required. They know
g. They're interested.

the big companies: In air transportation alone, the percentage of women
about one-quarter of the total.

Rapidly growing air-mindedness of women, revealing their unusual aptitude for nearly every kind of job in aviation, has been brought to light vividly by the service which they have performed during the war with the air branches of the armed forces.

One-third of all WAVES have been on duty with the Navy air arm. WACS and SPARS have played a major role in the vital ground services for the Army Air Forces' Air Transport Command.

Flight nurses already have taken care of 800,000 sick and wounded who have been flown to safety in this war. Many of these people have flown over oceans.

WACS have been serving in more than 150 different capacities related to flying—as grease monkeys, radio operators, dispatchers, draftsmen, inspectors, control tower operators, priority and traffic officers, intelligence officers, and weather experts.

SPARS did notable work in control towers and in charge of Link trainers. WAVES administered tests in low-pressure chambers, acted as air navigation instructors, aerologists' assistants, and instrument mechanics. Women Marines have performed many similar duties. Likewise they have worked as parachute riggers, electricians, hydraulic specialists, propeller specialists, oxygen experts, and in all branches of radio. They have worked with aerial photography.

THESE hundreds of thousands of servicewomen will, on their return to civilian life, be the distaff purchasers of airline transportation privileges.

In a recent airline survey, potential tourists gave preference for postwar world air travel to the British Isles, Continental Europe, Canada, Mexico, and South America. Air Transport Association contemplates tripled travel by air in 1946 as compared with this year . . . an addition of three and three-fourths billion miles!

A quarter-million air travelers will go to Europe each year soon after the end of the war. With London and Paris only 21 to 23 hours away . . . with a proposed fare of less than $400, world air travelers will board a plane at an air terminal in Los Angeles one morning, fly cross-country, see the latest movie at night in a luxurious cabin—a cabin that may even have a clubroom with cocktail bar and tables for bridge—and, at dawn, alight on the continent.

There are six million potential new air travelers as a result of war experiences connected with flying . . . *and women comprise a large percentage of these potential passengers.*

ounge

Stand By to Come Aboard

Swing Shift Dance

LERC TAKES OVER TOOL STORES

Effective July 16, operation of Lockheed Employes' Tool Stores will be directed by the LERC. Leon Fiesinger has been named the new LERC Tool Stores manager. These stores formerly were operated by the Lockheed Aircraft Corporation.

Some weeks ago the LERC executive committee was informed by Lockheed management that the company was going to discontinue its operation of these stores, at which time the executive committee began negotiations to continue this service.

Leon Fiesinger, who was formerly in charge of the Employe Tool store at B-1, a position he held for the past seven years, will now manage the Tool Store department for the LERC at both A-1 and B-1 stores. Fiesinger already has announced plans for enlarging the scope of the LERC Tool Stores by increasing the number of different lines handled. Additional tools, such as garden supplies, electric equipment, and sporting goods will be offered as they become available.

Policy Stable

George Wiseman, coordinator of the LERC, announced last night that there will be little change in the overall policy of the Tool Stores, as they will continue to offer employes first-line equipment at comparable costs to employe. Many items now handled by the stores will be sold at the same prices, as prices for these items are governed by the Fair Trade act and may not be sold for less than the published list price.

Many other items handled by the Tool Stores, which were formerly sold by the company at wholesale, will be increased 10 per cent to cover operating costs.

The stores will be in the same locations.

Outside Salesman

In addition, an outside salesman will be added to the staff who will contact all the outlying Lockheed plants in Southern California and take orders for tools desired by the employes and make delivery on his next visit.

Wiseman points out that these stores being on the grounds of Lockheed will offer the employe a three-way saving of time, gasoline, and money.

Bowl Tickets On Sale Here

Hollywood Bowl general admission tickets at reduced prices are available to Lockheed employes at the A-1 and B-1 LERC offices. The first performance of the 24th season of Symphonies Under the Stars was presented Tuesday night, July 10.

Featuring Leopold Stokowski as music director, the bowl programs from July 10 to Sept. 2 are expected to draw record crowds. Employes are urged to make reservations early.

Regular 90-cent general admission tickets are now on sale for employes at 65 cents, tax included. Good for all feature nights including the nine Russian Ballet performances these reduced tickets are made possible by arrangements between LERC and the Hollywood Bowl Association.

Reservations and season books may be purchased at LERC offices for bowl programs which will feature such stars as Patricia Munsel, Helen Traubel, Jan Kiepura, Jeanette MacDonald, Yehudi Menuhin, and many others.

MOVIE FEATURES FAVORITE STAR

Tuesday's LERC free movie will be "And the Angels Sing," starring Dorothy Lamour, Fred MacMurray, Betty Hutton, and Diana Lynn. This is a close-harmony sister act with no harmony in their love lives and mayhem in their hearts, as Fred MacMurray, the big, bad band leader tries to make love to the whole family at once.

It is the topmost of all the famous fun, music and laugh shows. Also featured in this movie are the songs such as: "It Could Happen to You," "His Rocking Horse Ran Away," and "How Does Your Garden Grow?"

Short subjects will complete the bill to be shown in Room 5, at the B-1 cafeteria.

SHRINE CIRCUS IN LAST DAYS

Only two days remain to see the Shrine Circus, playing to record crowds since Friday, July 6. The Shrine, on its gigantic stage, is offering Polack Brothers' circus, "bigger than ever," with many added features and every act direct from the "big tops" of the country.

There are many wire and trapeze artists and trained animals of all kinds. Likewise, there are Hubert Castle, the only man in the world to do a back somersault through a 22-inch hoop on the tight wire, the Great Antaleks, Mazzimalino Truizzi, sensational juggler, and scores of other professionals.

This show is staged each year to benefit the many Shrine philanthropies and activities, according to Stanton Bruner, general circus chairman and past potentate.

Tickets still may be purchased at either LERC office, extensions 8-1735 or 6-1901.

Plant Dance to Be Held July 14

Announcing plans for an all-plant dance, Jack Philips, LERC assistant recreation director, in charge of arrangements, said yesterday that the dance will be given at the Royal Palm, Saturday, July 14.

Allan Moore and his Rhapsody in Rhythm will furnish the music for the all-department dance in the two ballrooms at the Royal Palms.

This event is the second in a series of all-plant, all-department dances that have proved so popular, according to Philips.

Tickets for this gala event will be limited to 500 employe couples and will be sold by the LERC Recreation offices at both A-1 and B-1. In addition, tickets will be sold at the door. All ticket holders will be eligible for the many door prizes to be awarded during the dance.

Dept. 62-75 to Hold Family Party

Employes of Dept. 62-75 at B-5 will hold a departmental picnic Friday, July 13, at North Hollywood park No. 8 from 5 p.m. to closing. Softball, games, and swimming will be the day's program, said "Scotty" Haynes, picnic committee chairman. The day shift group will be served a complete dinner.

SWING SHIFT DANCES GAIN POPULARITY

Swing shift Friday night dances, long-time favorites of late-working Lockheed people and other night owls, swing into even greater popularity now that the blackout has been lifted. Tonight's Friday 13 program from 1 a.m. to 4 o'clock will again feature the sweet tempos of Les Stevens and his orchestra.

From "jumpin' jive" to "blackout waltzes," music for everyone is programed by the Stevens group for the "lucky 13 swing session." Les Stevens is fast becoming one of California's contenders for national fame.

At Center

Swing shifters will find the Burbank Recreation Center at 1111 West Olive, Burbank, ventilated for comfort and wired for perfect sound. The "coke" bar will be open for the three hours of late dancing and music.

Under LERC sponsorship, the swing dances have attracted "the best in music," according to Jack Philips, assistant recreation director. Swing shifters have swung to swing music of Bob Moore, Jack Riley, Cy Erb, Allan Moore, Art Whitting and other fine aggregations.

Casual Dress

Employes are urged to "come as you are." There are no dress restrictions, said Philips, and ducats may be purchased at the door at the regular price of 85 cents.

Boat Club to Reorganize

LERC's Boat club has high hopes of reorganizing before the midsummer season, according to Red Salisbury, president. Many boat owners now are eligible to apply for increased gasoline rations, he said.

Owners of both inboard and outboard motorboats will be granted increases up to 50 per cent where their craft are used for personal purposes, with larger increases being granted where boats are used to conduct fishing parties, Salisbury was informed by Charles C. Scott, OPA rationing representative.

Increases Told

Inboards, formerly limited to 24 gallons a quarter, will be granted up to 36 gallons for the same period, and outboards, formerly eligible for 10 gallons per quarter, may receive a maximum of 15 gallons for a three-month period.

Boat owners who use their boats for conducting pleasure or hunting parties also will receive larger allotments. Largest increase has been allotted to inboards used in conducting fishing parties, which can receive as much as 1200 gallons for a three-month period as compared with the previous maximum of 125 gallons per quarter.

Salisbury indicated that all Boat club members will be notified by mail in the near future in regard to a meeting to possibly reorganize the club for summer sports.

ON THE Table

BILL ELLIS Pres. LERC

THROUGH the democratic process of an election, this October will bring a contest to determine the LERC officers and executive committee members for the following year. These folk will guide the affairs of the LERC.

The officers and executive committee are elected from within the LERC council, by the council membership. To be eligible for an office, one must have served a minimum of three months on the council.

The point I am calling to your attention is that, in October, you will have a new set of officers and executive committee members. They will be selected by vote from a group you elected to the council in the general LERC council election. Now might be a good time to check the record of your duly elected representative. He is now eligible for an office and, if he has represented you, fulfilling the trust you placed in him, maybe he is good material for the executive committee or an executive office.

Do you as a reader, as a member of the LERC, know who your council representative is? Do you know whether he represents you and your co-workers—or does he represent a group? The point is, does he want to help the employes or himself? You should know what his program is. Ask him!

I know you like fair play; so do I. I earnestly hope all LERC members will interest themselves in fair play and the LERC; not for the good of an individual or a group, but for the good of all.

Last week mention was made of the community work being carried on by Lockheed employes, through their recreation club. The work is something of which you can all be proud. The nation looks to Lockheed for leadership in the science of flight. Local civic and governmental agencies and organizations look to the employes of Lockheed for community leadership. It is just reward for honest endeavor. Let us not betray that trust. Know your own organization and see that the leadership you receive is that for which you voted. Look at the record. Keep the record up-to-date!

Joint Penguinette Meeting Scheduled

LERC's two Penguinette clubs are planning a big joint meeting for July 25, to be held at the Hollywood Roosevelt hotel in the lovely Terrace room, at 7 p.m.

"Lightnings"

SWING SHIFT SOFTBALL TEAM IN FIRST PLACE

By JIM ARBOGAST
LERC Sports Director

Minus the services of Capt. Nick Puglizvich, vacationing in the east, the Lockheed swing shift Lightnings' softball team defeated the tough Douglas Skymasters 5-2 on Tuesday, July 3, and on Thursday, July 5, went into first place in the swing shift Aircraft Softball league by running over the North American Fighters 11-5.

Gilmore, shortstop, setting an example for the rest of the team, drove in all of the five runs for the Lockheed Lightnings. In the fifth inning, second baseman Mutsig singled, rightfielder Coats walked, and centerfielder Wilson, lead-off man, also received a base on balls.

Sharp Single

Gilmore came to bat and hit a sharp single to left field, scoring Mutsig and Coats. In the seventh inning Coats singled and Wilson singled which gave the Lightnings a man on first and a man on second. Gilmore, coming to bat again with men on, fixed his eye on the right field and cracked out a home run over the Skymasters' rightfielder's head, scoring Coats and Wilson ahead of him. The Skymasters accounted for their runs, one in the third and one in the fifth.

Leo Duran, pitcher for the Lightnings, found himself in a hole on several occasions, once with two men on base and no outs and again, with the bases loaded and no outs, but was able to set the Skymasters down without any damage being done. Battery for the Lightnings: Leo Duran, pitching; Sam Polis, catching.

In the feature game of the week, Lightnings vs. North American Fighters, the Lightnings came through to knock Snuffy Smith, Fighter pitcher, out of the box in the third inning when they collected four hits and four runs. Sam Polis doubled, and pitcher Leo Duran also doubled, scoring Sam from second base. Gilmore singled, putting Lightnings on first and third bases.

Field Day

Max Greenberg, third baseman, had a field day at bat collecting three hits out of four trips. He hit a long fly ball to deep right center for a home run accounting for three of the four runs in that inning.

In the fourth inning, Miles, playing first base, got a single, followed by Phillips, right center, who also singled and left fielder, McCambridge, who was the third man in a row to collect a single.

Second baseman Mutsig collected the fourth straight single scoring Miles and Phillips. Sam Polis and Leo Duran each walked with McCambridge scoring on Leo's jaunt. Max Greenberg then collected another single to score Mutsig from third base.

Totals Given

In the seventh inning the Lightnings drew blood again when runs were scored by Gilmore, Freeze and Miles on hits made by Miles, Phillips, McCambridge, and Wilson. The Lightnings collected altogether 14 hits, 11 runs, two errors, and the Fighters collected six hits, five runs, and one error.

Results Told in All-Plant Tilt

First and second round winners in the Lockheed interdepartmental softball championship contest were announced yesterday by Jim Arbogast, LERC sports director, who is handling the tournament.

NORTH HOLLYWOOD
TUESDAY, 5 P.M.

First Round Winner: Team No. 6, Shooting Stars, Ed Saxe, captain.

Second Round Winner: Team (Dept. 27-04 in lead W 3, L O). One week left to play.

GRIFFITH, TUESDAY, 4:30 P.M.

First Round Winner: Team No. 2, Plant 7, Larry Crites, captain.

Second Round Winner: Team No. 3, Inspection P-38's, Royal Jensen, captain.

GLEN OAKS, TUESDAY, WEDNESDAY AND THURSDAY, 5:15 P.M.

First Round Winner: Team No. 3, P-38's League Winner, Leo Dandurand, captain.

Second Round Winner: Team No. 5, Model 49'ers, Walt Johnson, captain.

BURBANK RECREATION
TUESDAY, 5 P.M.

First Round Winner: Team No. 3, Wolves of 29, Albert Voegele, captain.

Second Round Winner: Team No. 1, 3G Jiggers, Ross Earixon, captain.

(Tied for first): Team No. 2, B-17 Final Bombers, Earl Arbuckle, captain; Team No. 6, N.L.S.C., Jack Walker, captain.

BURBANK RECREATION
WEDNESDAY, 5 P.M.

First Round Winner: Team No. 3, Outlaws, Ed Torgeson, captain.

Second Round Winner: (Dept. 24-16, Stores Brusers, Dept. 21-24, tied for first place.) One week left to play.

BURBANK RECREATION
THURSDAY, 5:15 P.M.

First Round Winner: Team No. 1, Office Gang, John Schlueter, captain.

Second Round Winner: (Office Gang in lead). One week left to play.

BURBANK RECREATION
FRIDAY, 5:30 P.M.

First Round Winner: Team No. 3, O.P.'s, R. G. Cople, captain.

Second Round Winner: Team No. 3, O.P.'s, R. G. Cople, captain; Team No. 6, Stores Rebels, Harry Bishop, captain; (tied for first playoff to be held Friday, 5:30 p.m., diamond No. 2, Burbank).

GRIFFITH PARK
MONDAY, 10:30 A.M.

First Round Winner: League winner, Team No. 6, Swingers, Nick Puglisvich, captain.

Second Round Winner: One week left to play.

Playoffs between the first and second round winner in each of the leagues will begin immediately, Arbogast said, and the winner of that contest will be entered in the championship playoff. For the seventh time in a row, he declared, the Office Gang looms as the leading contender for the championship.

Two Groups Plan Picnic July 15

An all-shift picnic for the employes of Depts. 15-13 and 15-59 is set for Sunday, July 15, at Roscoe park, according to Larry Mercier, picnic chairman.

The all-day outing from 10 a.m. to closing will feature softball, games, contests, and prizes. A complete picnic lunch will be served. Other committeemen are Ed Miles and Don Holdon.

Lady Bowlers Win Over N. A.

Lockheed's Lady Lightning bowlers, for the second consecutive time, have won the Lockheed-North American perpetual match trophy by defeating the North American quintet by a score of 2268 to 2118. Florence Dunlap, bowling an anchor position, was high for both clubs, hitting the maples for a total of 540 pins. In this series her first game was 218. Martha Stelling, bowling in third position, collected 503 pins for second high series.

The Lockheed girls are undefeated in match play, having downed Consolidated Convair in a previously scheduled home-and-home series.

Other members bowling for the Lockheed club were: Adel Crumpton, Helen Smith and Jerre Jarrett.

Scorebook results of last week's game show the lady bowlers as follows:

Helen Smith........	123, 156, 180—total, 459
Jerre Jarrett........	134, 156, 141—total, 431
Florence Dunlap	218, 179, 143—total, 540
Martha Stelling..	150, 173, 180—total, 503
Adel Crumpton..	110, 115, 110—total, 335

Lockheed will meet North American again next year and, if they win this third match, they will become permanent possessors of the perpetual trophy.

NONNIE HOEHN GETS SHUTOUT

Nonnie Hoehn, stellar twirler for the Lockheed Lady Lightnings, trounced a determined nine from the Continental Can company with a hot no-run, no-hit, 27-0 game, Monday, July 2, on the Echo Park diamond.

Only three opposing batters reached first, each on errors, in the otherwise air-tight defense of the Lady Lightnings. This game followed closely their shutout performance against the powerful Pasadena Reds, whose roster includes several regulars from the famed Pasadena Ramblers.

Credit was given by Carl Robinson, coach, to Lois Hopper for a pro-catching performance, and to Ruth Tracey for stealing second. Nonnie Hoehn is marked as one of Southland's outstanding feminine pitchers and employes interested in the series should contact the LERC office for specific playing dates and locations.

LADY LIGHTNINGS' SCHEDULE IN THE BURBANK EVENING SOFTBALL LEAGUE (GIRLS' DIVISON)

Lightnings vs. Maison, Burbank Recreation Center, 7 p.m., Friday, July 20.

Lightnings vs. Trinity, Glen Oaks, 7 p.m., Friday, July 27.

Lightnings vs. Magnolia, Glen Oaks, 7 p.m., Thursday, August 2.

Lightnings vs. Moosettes, Glen Oaks, 7 p.m., Thursday, August 9.

Girls' All-Star Bowling Team

Pistol Team Drops Match

Lockheed's "Pistol Packers" dropped a three-position match to the "gun totin'" group from Culver City, evening up two previous wins at the Glendale High range. Bob Lang, spokesman for the LERC club, listed J. Rankin as top man for Culver City with 286 points, and "Hoppy" Hopkins for Lockheed trailing with a score of 275 points.

The informal meet, June 29, at Glendale High, ended a series of matches with the Culver City gunmen. Score was Lockheed, 1054, and Culver City, 1123. Shooting for Lockheed were Jack Teal, Bob Hunter, "Hoppy" Hopkins and George Arwine.

Lang also announced that entries are closed for the pistol class, a six-week course which began July 11 at Hoover High. Applications may be filed with Hopkins for the next pistol class to start at the conclusion of the present course.

Pistol and Rifle club began an inter-club par match on July 6, said Lang. Members shoot against their own individual averages. Greatest individual improvement wins the medal. Employes are invited to participate in the many activities of the club. For information call "Hoppy" Hopkins, extension 8-1922.

Duck Shooters Need Stamps

Lockheed sportsmen are warned that in order to hunt migratory waterfowl, they will have to purchase the new federal "Duck Stamp" on sale at all post offices.

Penalties will be assessed those hunters not carrying the new stamp in their possession while hunting birds, it was announced today by Bud Kuecher, president of LERC's Pistol and Rifle club. Kuecher also stated that rumor has it that the government expects to release ammunition and shotguns for the hunters this fall.

CIVILIANS STUDY HIGH ALTITUDES

Ninety civilian aircraft radar technicians, engineers, test pilots, and crew members ➡ are being given high altitude indoctrination through Lockheed's Aero-Medical section, by request of the Army Technical Service Command, it was announced here last night.

Dr. W. R. MacLaren of Lockheed's medical staff is in charge of the program.

Army contractor personnel who check planes between altitudes of 12,000 to 30,000 feet are taught the use of oxygen equipment and how to recognize two of the physiological dangers encountered in high altitude flying: anoxia and aeroembolism.

Dr. MacLaren conducts two school sessions of two hours each in Lockheed's Research laboratory high altitude pressure chamber at Plant B-1, for the radar technicians.

In addition to pressure chamber work a small classroom is maintained in the Research building to give preliminary instruction in use of helmets and the standard A-14 Demand type oxygen masks.

Three of the ATSC civilian radar technicians are women. Civilian technicians taking the indoctrination program get the same type training given Lockheed's test pilots in their high altitude course.

FOOD TESTED

Frozen food service tested by Naval Air Transport Service, may be used by airlines. The new method of food preparation and handling provides a quick, compact and convenient meal service. It makes use of quick frozen partially precooked meals which are stored in the frozen state until needed, and then cooked in a specially designed oven for a brief period before serving.

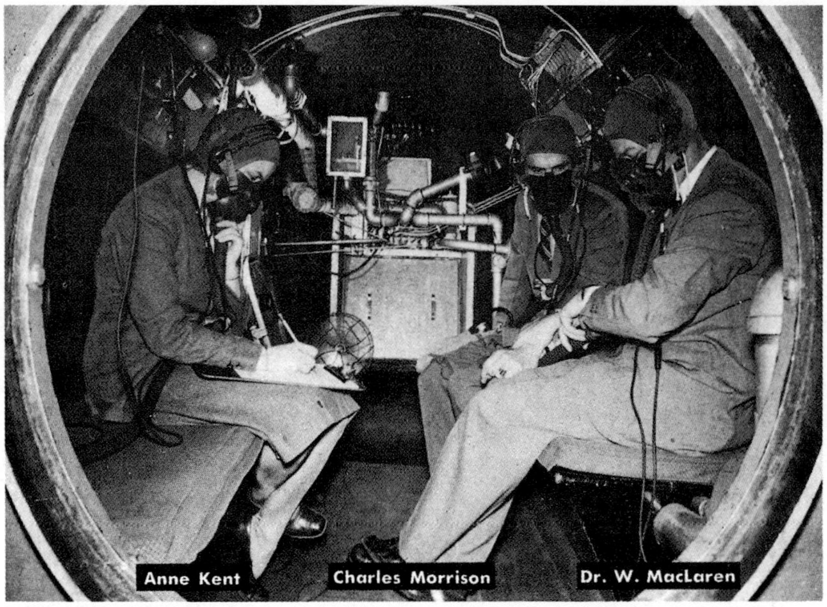

Anne Kent — Charles Morrison — Dr. W. MacLaren

Hourly Employes to See Progress Reports Submitted by Supervision

Beginning with the next company-wide progress report rating day, July 11, each hourly employe will be given a duplicate copy of his report, according to an announcement made last night by R. B. Robertson, personnel manager.

The Employe Progress report, form 3968-2, has been revised accordingly.

The administrative directive indicates that employes must be given their copy of the report, after it has been reviewed by the department head, within one week following each established rating day.

Prompt rating by supervision on the specified rating days, which occur each eight weeks, will be necessary to comply with the new personnel ruling.

The progress report checks on five employe factors: (1) quality of work, freedom from errors, rejections or rework necessary; (2) quantity of work acceptable during an average day; (3) knowledge of operations and methods, technical fitness; (4) dependability, reliability when not supervised, attendance, conduct, attention to safety, and (5) cooperation, teamwork, willingness to follow instructions and to help others.

Five possible grades are: poor, low average, average, above average, and excellent. Supervisory comments may also be made as to whether the job is well done or poorly done.

"Allowing employes to have a look-see at their progress reports will be beneficial in correcting work deficiencies and will allow both supervision and employes to make the most of their jobs," said Robertson.

Lockheed Blackhawk Soldier Back Again

Only Lockheed and only Burbank soldier from the famed Blackhawk division to return to the states was Pfc. Bud M. Fisher.

Private Fisher is looking forward to redeployment to the Pacific for he speaks Japanese like a native. He was employed at Lockheed for two years before he joined the Army.

Propose Free Rides For Wives of Vets

Free transportation for parents or wives on Government-owned ships and aircraft to visit the graves of veterans buried abroad is proposed in a bill before Congress.

LODESTARS ON MARKET UNDER FEDERAL UNIT

Fourteen Lockheed Lodestars have been sold and four leased by the Reconstruction Finance Corporation since May 11, it was learned here yesterday. On that date the ships went on a price tag sale basis. The ships are "Army surplus." Reconstruction Finance Corporation is Surplus Production Board's agent for surplus aircraft disposal.

The planes sold brought a total of $425,000. Total return on four leased Lodestars will be $21,120 annually during the life of leases.

Eighty-eight more Lodestars are still up for sale at Bush Field, Augusta, Georgia. All types are priced at $68,000.

Reconstruction Finance Corporation disposal agencies in California are at Chandler Field, Fresno; Sherman Field, Concord; Ryan Field, Hemet, and Cal-Aero at Ontario.

Air C. of C. Changes Name to 'Industries'

Aeronautical Chamber of Commerce of America, Inc., the national association for aircraft manufacturing industry for more than a quarter-century, has just announced that it has changed its name to Aircraft Industries Association of America, Inc.

LIST LOCKHEED PRIZE WINNERS

(Continued from Page 2)

TRIPS			
1st Prize	Eva L. Kunze	35-39	A-1
2nd Prize	Ray A. Wells	52-42	A-1
3rd Prize	David Lewis	40-34	A-1
4th Prize	Joseph Caldwell	28-25	B-1
5th Prize	J. S. Wilde	28-42	A-1
6th Prize	George S. Godfrey	22-58	B-6
GRAND PRIZE	ELEMER COLEMAN RAY	LERC	A-1
$100 WAR BONDS			
8th Prize	Gertrude Mathews	LERC	B-1
9th Prize	Leonard C. Glahn	22-55	A-1
10th Prize	Naomi Dewey	15-07	A-1
11th Prize	C. G. Voorhies	AAF	B-1
12th Prize	E. Moffatt	27-29	B-1
$50 WAR BONDS			
13th Prize	J. P. Seamons	72-25	A-1
14th Prize	Rufus R. Smith	39-40	A-1
15th Prize	Lillian J. Collins	16-42	B-1
16th Prize	H.F. Strombeck	LERC	A-1
17th Prize	R. W. Garner	88-72	B-1
18th Prize	Earl A. Marcotte	90-44	B-1
19th Prize	John P. Corbett	17-35	A-2
20th Prize	G. B. McDaniel	44-20	B-3
21st Prize	C. S. Morsman	21-24	A-1
22nd Prize	Helen A. Simpkins	12-19	A-1
$25 WAR BONDS			
23rd Prize	A. L. Cunningham	39-46	Whse. 18
24th Prize	R. C. Mortimer	57-51	A-2
25th Prize	L. F. Moore	57-92	B-1
26th Prize	H. F. Strombeck	LERC	A-1
27th Prize	Major Sheldon G. Cooper	AAF	A-1
28th Prize	Mason F. Birlem	51-50	A-1
29th Prize	Vivienne Ballinger	81-02	B-1
30th Prize	Dan A. Trent	88-72	A-1
31st Prize	Franklin L. Naylor	12-20	A-1
32nd Prize	Howard Morgan	39-44	A-2
33rd Prize	Thelma Mahyles	57-59	B-1
34th Prize	Walter Schrack	12-32	B-1
35th Prize	Barney Silver	18-07	B-1
36th Prize	George D. Hammers	39-38	B-1
37th Prize	Rex L. Abbott	83-22	B-3
38th Prize	E. E. Veling	18-28	B-6
39th Prize	Lawrence Petterson	62-73	B-5
40th Prize	Clyde A. Jones	28-26	B-1
41st Prize	E. Smith	39-35	A-1
42nd Prize	Freda Permisohn	90-47	B-1

Is it Here?

THESE classified advertisements in the *Star* are provided for employes without charge. If you want to buy, sell, trade, or find or return lost articles, obtain Form 4929 from your department clerk, the stationery store, or employe service office. Mail the advertisement to the *Lockheed Star,* Room 244, Bldg. 1-A, Plant B-1.

WANTED

PHONOGRAPH, portable or small. RE. 2-1004.

SET matched golf clubs. MO. 1-1674.

BOWLING shoes, size 5½. EX. 2093.

TRICYCLE for 5-year-old. AL. 9445.

RIDERS, Florence & Central to Figueroa, Riverside, B-1, A-1, B-6. PL. 6508.

BOLT action or pump .22 rifle. Trade 12-gauge shells for 16. WA. 2512, Bob.

GUITAR and bass fiddle for girls' orchestra. WY. 8212.

UNFURN. house, N. H. or Brbk., adults, $50 bonus; urgent. CH. 6-7495.

DOLL buggy, collapsible with metal wheels, swing, wagon for 2-year-old. CH. 8-5830.

RIDE to Bldg. 167, B-1, from Brand and Mtn., Glendale, 8 a.m. CI. 1-5646.

TO rent house, furn. or unfurn. Being evicted. 2643 Riverside Terrace, L.A. 26.

KENNEDY kit, 3-drawer. CH. 8-7916 after 5.

BOWLING shoes, lady's, size 6½ or 7. CI. 2-8690.

FORD coupe, '33, '32 or '34, good condition. CI. 2-0137 after 5.

FORD or Mercury, '41 club coupe. CH. 8-4745.

CAMERA, 6-20, for serviceman. SU. 1-3393.

OUTBOARD motor in good condition. HE. 4644.

GREENHOUSE, any size. SY. 4-4121.

RIDERS, Hollywood to A-1, 7 a.m. NO. 1-9762.

PORTABLE sewing machine, good condition. HE. 8580 after 4:15.

FURN. or unfurn. apt. or house for discharged veteran. 1666 W. 12 Pl., L.A.

HOUSE, 2 or 3-bedrm., front and back yard. N. Hllywd or Hllywd. CI. 2-0814.

HOUSE, unfurnished, West Adams district. Extension 6-2273.

TIRE wanted, size 5.25-5.50x17. FI. 5983.

HOUSE, 3-bedrm., adults, 8-yr. girl, max. rent $90. N. Burbank, Glen. FI. 5983.

RIDE to Minneapolis, Chattanooga, Nashville, last week August. Paula Wood, 1740 Winona, Hollywood.

RIDER, 8 a.m., from Sunset & Fairfax. HE. 7485 after 5:30 p.m.

COMPLETE set of indiv. rider manuals. CH. 8-2011 after 5:30 p.m.

RADIO, table or console model, reasonable. NO. 1-0155.

CHILD'S sidewalk bicycle. DR. 9879.

BENJAMIN air rifle or Pellet gun. 5929 Carpenter, North Hollywood.

Is it Here?

FOR SALE

MISCELLANEOUS

TUXEDO suit, 3-pc., single-breasted, size 40. CI. 2-9545.

PORTABLE radio, Packard-Bell, want table model radio. CR. 6-2855.

REDWOOD patio lounges, 2; Spanish guitar, tweed sport suit, worn once. SU. 1-4857.

CHOW puppies, pedigreed, blacks and reds. SUnland 4976.

FREE, house-broken kittens to good homes. CH. 9-3808.

PADDLE board, 11-ft., spruce, new. SEpulveda 7-2623.

MAUSER, big game rifle, 8x60-mm., new, 5 boxes shells, lthr. case. ARiz. 9-2631.

ENAMEL ice box, 25-lb., excellent for mtn. or beach cabin. CA. 1-4011.

FORD fender skirts, light blue, good condition. NO. 2-2126, extension 50.

TRUMPET, gold-plated Conn, perf. cond., attach. & case inc. CHurchill 9-1259.

OREGON property near Eugene, sell or trade. ST. 5-1491 after 4:30 p.m.

SOUND for 8-mm. home movies. SU. 1-5066.

TUB shower doors, prewar, chrome & glass, complete; ironer, fits Thor washing machine. CH. 6-5285.

NEW goatskin motorcycle gloves, medium size; riding boots, size 9. CH. 8-8115.

APRICOTS, tree-ripened, $1.75 per lug. N. Hollywd. near Ventura. SU. 2-3768.

GLASSES, 2 pair, McDonald 1-Gard Vernalite, new. CH. 6-0015 after 5.

FURNISHED house, Mexican type; double lot, secluded; cheap. CH. 8-9991.

NEEDLEPOINT, several pieces, ready to mount. SU. 1-3393.

REGINA vacuum, attach.; men's riding breeches, size 30; bed divan. RE. 4049.

WILSON tennis racket, desk lamp. 624 Salem, Glendale.

DAVENPORT, chair, small dinette set, curtain stretchers. 5933¼ Willoughby, Hollywood.

VEHICLES

BICYCLE, man's Schwinn, prewar, chrome rims, hand brake. CL. 6-6317.

PLYMOUTH sedan, '34, 4-door. CH. 8-6890, 834 N. Myers, Burbank.

HISPANO-Suiza, '33 Studebaker Pres. motor, conv. sedan body. 512 Stanford Rd., Burbank.

YAWL, 23', sleeps 2, head, galley, good condition. HI. 9770, apt. 214 after 6.

FORD V-8 coupe, '35, sell or trade for late model club coupe or sedan. Ext. 6-2428.

STUDEBAKER, '31, good cond., exchange or sell for later G.M. car. 10610 Samoa, Tujunga.

BICYCLE, man's 28", almost new. 1410 Randall, Glendale 1, Calif.

BUICK, '30 light 6, 4-door sedan, new paint. HO. 6954 after 4.

FORD, '31 model A sedan, 5 good tires, O.K. mechanically. SU. 2-8250.

BICYCLE, man's prewar, balloon tires. 1136 Stanley, Glendale.

FORD, '42, or De Soto convertible, trade my '42 Packard Clipper for above. CI. 2-6075.

Is it Here?

FOR SALE

MISCELLANEOUS (Cont.)

SAILBOAT, 12-ft., V bottom, sloop rigged. SU. 1-8313.

POWELL Aviate scooter, '41, less than 5000 miles. CH. 8-2226.

FORD sedan, '30, new paint, excellent tires. NO. 7180.

CHEVROLET coupe, '31; '32 motor, good condition. 3316 Andrita, L. A. 41.

HOUSE trailer, sleeps 2. 3316 Andrita, Los Angeles 41.

DE SOTO Airflow sedan, fair tires, good condition. CH. 8-2129.

MOTOR bike, Briggs motor, 2-way; 70 miles per gallon. CH. 6-5096.

FORD V-8, overdrive and set tires, recaps. 6.00x16. HI. 4947 evenings or Sunday.

CHEV. coupe, good tires, engine rebored, '33 model, radio. 1527 San Fern. Rd.

NASH, '34 4-door sedan, good condition. Good transportation. NO. 4022.

CHEVROLET '32 coupe, 5 good tires, clean. CI. 2-7984.

TO buy Ford or Mercury '41 club coupe. CH. 8-4745.

EXCHANGE

RIFLE shells, 20 boxes .22 long for .22 short. 2643 Riverside Terrace, L. A. 26.

UNFURN. house, 3-rm., low rental for 2 or 3-bedrm. house, unfurn. 3814 Rosemont, Montrose.

MATCHES, 250 books, no dups., for stamp collection. PA. 1846, 5 p.m.

LOST

CHARM bracelet, Olympic-Doheny bus, 8 a.m. 6-30. Reward. SY. 2-6044.

SILVER cigarette case, B-1 cafeteria. Reward. SY. 7-3355.

GOLD-PLATED earring (plain hoop) 2 weeks ago. CI. 1-9846.

FOUNTAIN pen, Sheaffer lifetime, gold name. J. H. Karp. Reward. HE. 7485.

FOR RENT

ROOM, reference necessary. 12755 Hortense, North Hollywood. SU. 1-3937.

THE LOCKHEED Star
OFFICIAL PUBLICATION OF THE LOCKHEED AIRCRAFT CORPORATION

Issued each Friday for the employes of Lockheed Aircraft Corporation. The *Star* is the official publication of the company. Communications should be addressed to the Editor, *Lockheed Star* Unit, Lockheed Aircraft Corporation, Burbank, California.

No unsolicited manuscripts or pictures will be returned and the *Star* cannot be responsible for other than requested articles or photos.

KENNETH CRIST, Editor
J. H. Prescott, Associate Editor
Marshall Atwell, Staff Artist
Barbara Sewald, News

THE LOCKHEED
Star
OFFICIAL PUBLICATION OF THE LOCKHEED AIRCRAFT CORPORATION
Volume 2 BURBANK, CALIFORNIA, U.S.A., AUGUST 3, 1945 No. 31
LOCKHEED
Shooting Star
STORY ON PAGES 4 and 5

PRODUCTION SPEED SETS P-80 BOOST

As advanced as the ship itself are plans now being followed for mass production of Lockheed Shooting Stars.

In the opinion of officials, the new production machine will make the old P-38 assembly line seem as obsolete as Model T Fords did when the Model A appeared.

For the P-38's only, final assembly lines were mechanized. When Shooting Stars get rolling in high gear, subassemblies and details will come from no less than seven belt conveyors.

Simple Means

To help Lockheed men and women build America's top-priority fighter plane faster and easier, many other outstanding production improvements are planned. The comparative simplicity of the Shooting Star, itself, has abetted this aim.

According to L. H. Bradley, assistant to Manager E. H. Roy of the P-80 Manufacturing Planning Department, the entire production machine will be under one roof instead of being separated in five different plants as was the P-38's.

Shooting Stars now roll from a mechanized final line on the former location of Number 3 line of the P-38. The eastern half of what used to be the P-38's Number 2 line will be occupied with the P-80's forward fuselage mechanized assembly line. The aft section assembly line will occupy the middle third of the former location of P-38's Number 3 final line.

Another Boon

One of the biggest innovations is the mechanized wing assembly line just north of the island in the same building. Here entire P-80 wings hang from an elevated track. This installation is now nearing completion.

One of several bench belt conveyor lines will be installed near the foot of the final line. Another will be on the first mezzanine of building 113A. Most of the other lines including the upper and lower flight sections of the forward fuselage, nose, hood door, and keelson will be southeast of the former P-38 final lines.

Tubular Cradles

To eliminate the annoyance of air hose and electric lines being in the way, cradles on the final line are tubular. Air and power lines are piped through these frames from underground lines on reels comparable to the air hose at a service station.

Another big innovation is in the final line whose two halves move at different speeds with the P-80's aft section being added on the last half. Ships on the first half of the line, without aft sections, occupy less space — thus permitting more ships on the entire line.

Cover

WORLD'S fastest plane, the Lockheed P-80 Shooting Star, makes a pleasant pattern as it streaks over desert sagebrush near Muroc in this unusual aerial view by Erik Miller, Lockheed photographer.

Production Line

SAFETY AWARD GIVEN PLANTS IN WAR WORK

Banners of Lockheed's Safety Department waved high last night with receipt of Safety Achievement Certificates from the Department of Labor and congratulatory letters from three Congressmen.

The certificates, signed by Frances Perkins just before her recent retirement from her cabinet post of Labor Secretary, were made out to the following Lockheed plants: A-54, A-55, A-57, A-60, A-2, B-2, and B-7.

Reduced Injury

The certificates were awarded to these plants for their frequency rate of reducing disabling injuries 40 per cent or more in the final half of 1944 as compared to the same period the previous year.

Congratulations on the achievement were written by Congressmen A. J. Elliott, Carl Hinshaw, and B. W. Gearheart to Jack F. Hatton, chief safety engineer.

Accompanying the awards was a letter to Hatton signed by the Secretary of Labor.

Urged to Continue

Urging Lockheed employes to continue their accident prevention efforts, L. M. Bach, vice president in charge of manufacturing, is distributing the certificates.

They are considered among the top war safety awards.

Sgt. England Dies in Philippine Action

Word has been received that Sgt. Dennis England, former Lockheed employe in maintenance on motor vehicles, was killed on Luzon in the Philippines.

His family has received the Silver Star and Purple Heart awarded him for breaking up an enemy counter-attack single handed. Not yet 21, he served with the famed 172nd Infantry.

CONSTELLATION RIDE IS PRIZE FOR TOP AIRMEN

Their first rides in a Constellation pilot's seat made news this week about two men—an RAAF captain from "down under" and a top Lockheed executive whose flying experience began in 1910.

"What a ship!" grinned youthful-looking Group Capt. W. H. Garing as he slipped from behind the wheel of the Constellation soaring high over Lake Arrowhead. "Controls like a sweet dream," raved George Prudden, works manager of Factory A, where the ship was born.

Captain Garing, RAAF staff officer at the Australian Air Mission in Washington, D.C., holds the second highest military award of the British Empire—"Commander of the Most Excellent Order of the British Empire." His lengthy war record includes the flying of 58 different airplane types including most Lockheed ships.

Second Oldest

Prudden, his host for the two-hour test flight, has the second oldest American flying record of any man still actively engaged in the airplane manufacturing industry. Glenn Martin is his senior.

First flight the Lockheed works manager ever made was in a biplane of his own construction. That was back in Minnesota in 1910 when he was a 19-year-old youth.

The captain, whose service in this war has been in both the European and Pacific theaters, has flown Lockheed B-34's, PV-1's, a Vega, Lightnings and Hudsons. His best story concerns Hudsons . . . but not himself.

In Early Days

"Squadron Leader Ian Campbell was the skipper of one Hudson which was jumped by three Zeros," said the captain.

"While slugging it out, some stuff came through the cockpit clipping Campbell's legs so that he couldn't work the rudder pedals. The co-pilot took over. Then he, in turn, was wounded in the wrists.

"With Campbell's good wrists and the co-pilot's sound feet the Hudson was brought back."

In addition to the C.B.E., Captain Garing holds the British D.F.C. and the American D.S.C.

Pilot of the Constellation which carried the delighted captain and his host on the flight over California mountains and desert was Heinz Wegner. The co-pilot was R. G. Field.

BONG TELLS OF FLYING FAST PLANE

By Maj. Richard I. Bong
Lockheed Army Operations Officer

I've only had three hours in the jet Shooting Star and I believe that it takes at least 25 hours in any ship to tell just what it feels like to fly that particular plane . . . but look:

I've flown the P-38 in 500 hours of combat, all time in the Pacific theater, and I know that it's one of the sweetest ships in the skies. The P-80 has lots more speed.

What does it feel like to fly the Shooting Star? Well, it feels like nothing at all. There is absolutely no sensation. You just whip through the sky absolutely free from propeller noise.

Free and Easy

There is no sensation of speed. You know you're traveling fast but flight is free and easy. The P-80 is easy to fly because it's so simple.

A single lever regulates power . . . and that's a good combat feature. You don't have to make a dozen different engine adjustments.

The control surfaces are unusually light, even at high speeds. And, with all this, the plane is comfortable, too.

I like the sleek smooth look of the P-80 on the ground. With its negative gray, polished lacquer coating the plane looks fast, deadly . . . and beautiful.

Different Type

The P-80 Shooting Star is such a different type ship that no true comparison can be made between it and the Lightning P-38.

Combat pilots are sure to like the jet Shooting Star, because, in it, you go back to fundamental reasons for a pilot's love of flying . . . there is a thrill of speed, the thrill of controlling power . . . and the earth and all else become nonentities.

"This Is the Fastest Stuff on Earth"

CONSTELLATION SETS RECORD

NON-STOP NEW YORK TO PARIS PLACES SHIP AS TRANS-OCEANIC QUEEN

In 14 hours and 12 minutes, the Lockheed Constellation C-69 lowered the New York to Paris non-stop flight record by more than 20 per cent, according to an announcement of the flight by the Air Transport Command Tuesday.

The Lockheed Constellation took off from the overcast La Guardia Field in New York at 4:38 p.m. E.W.T., Tuesday, and arrived at Paris at 6:50 a.m., E.W.T. The routine Trans-Atlantic flight spread Air Force observance of its 38th anniversary to the European continent.

The 3600-mile run was made in an average of 253.5 miles an hour. The ship carried the conventional Army interior or litter seats with capacity for 60 persons in addition to a normal crew of six.

Brig. Gen. Lawrence G. Fritz, commander of the North Atlantic Division of the Air Transport Command, was pilot of the Constellation. The plane carried a crew of eleven Army Air Force crew members. Lt. Col. N. E. Timper of the North Atlantic Division of the Air Transport Command was co-pilot.

Cuts Previous Record

The Constellation record flight Tuesday trimmed nearly four hours from the previous New York-Paris record of 18 hours made by a C-54 transport on October 6, 1944, when it carried Gen. George C. Marshall, Army Chief of Staff, and James Byrnes, now Secretary of State, to Europe.

A Lockheed Electra held the official pre-war record for the New York to Paris non-stop flight. It was made in 20 hours and 29 minutes on May 9 and 10, 1937. It was flown by H. T. Merrill and John S. Lambie.

The first non-stop flight from New York to Paris made by Charles A. Lindbergh in his famous "Spirit of St. Louis," was made 18 years ago on May 30, 1927. His flight of 33 hours and 30 minutes was almost 20 hours slower than the new record.

Other Flight Records

Last year the Constellation established a cross country record flight when it was flown on a routine delivery flight from Burbank to Washington in 6 hours and 58 minutes. Howard Hughes and Jack Frye, president of Transcontinental and Western Air, Inc., were pilots on the cruise which utilized only 65 per cent full power.

Tuesday's Trans-Atlantic record is the latest in a long series of inter-city record-breaking performances by the Constellation made in routine hops around the States.

The Constellation's overnight flight from New York to Paris is a forecast of routine Trans-Atlantic service to be available to air travelers in 1946 when the Constellation goes into commercial operation on the world's leading airlines, according to Lockheed officials.

The Lockheed Constellation

General Wires Congratulations

Lt. Gen. Harold L. George, commanding general of the Air Transport Command, last night sent the following telegram to the Commanding General European Division, ATC:

"Please convey to General Fritz and the crew of the C-69 which reached Paris after a flight of 14 hours and 12 minutes from New York, my warmest congratulations on their fine performance.

"It is appropriate that this routine mission was accomplished as a grateful nation salutes the founding of the Army Air Forces 38 years ago today.

"Their flight is a stirring contrast to the hazardous flight made by Charles Lindbergh over the same route 18 years ago and is a fitting demonstration of the progress we have made in the air transport field by applying American engineering and manufacturing skill to war necessity."

HELP FIND THESE BANDITS

Lockheed employes were asked last night to help catch the bandits who stole $111,300 from two bank messengers last Monday within a stone's throw of the Factory B-1 cafeteria.

The holdup, described as one of the biggest here in recent years, occurred between 7:20 and 7:30 a.m. near San Fernando Road and the intersection of Maria and Wilson streets.

Broadcasting a detailed description of the robbers, Plant Protection officials asked to be notified immediately by any employe who might have seen them. Their descriptions follow:

Bandit number one—23 to 25 years old, five feet 11 inches tall, brown hair, light eyes—probably blue—slender build, white man with heavy coat of tan. He was tight-lipped, wore a U. S. Army enlisted man's uniform, a peaked cap (not overseas) and an MP armband. He was nervous.

Bandit number two—23 to 24 years old, white man, five feet eight inches tall, 145-150 pounds in weight, medium build, fair complexion, light-brown hair, small, light-colored moustache. In contrast to his companion, he appeared very calm. He wore a gray felt hat and an action-backed (pleated) tweed sport coat of pebble-dash brown. He appeared to be wearing a round, hourly employe's badge of Lockheed.

Swing, Days to Get Longer Lunch Time

Increase in lunch time from 30 minutes to 42 minutes was announced last night by William Aulepp, director of industrial relations.

The change affects all hourly employes on the day and swing shifts, effective August 13.

This means that the day shift will start at 7 a.m. and quit at 3:42 p.m. Swing will start at 4 and end at 12:42 a.m. Graveyard shift not affected.

Hourly employes who have a 45-minute lunch period now will continue in that status.

NEWS-RADIO MEN HAIL FAST P-80

When calloused reporters and newsreel men utter honest exclamations of amazement, they've really seen or heard something extraordinary.

That's what happened when Lockheed's Shooting Star made its debut this week at Lockheed Air Terminal before an audience of more than 150 newsmen, magazine writers and editors, camera men, and assorted guests.

Fastest Ship

When Chief Engineering Test Pilot Tony LeVier buzzed the Shooting Star along the west-east runway Tuesday morning most of the assembled word-wizards went limp. They looked as though they couldn't believe what they'd just seen and heard—the fastest-moving vehicle known to man.

These assembled phrase-artists could come up with nothing better than such trite baubles as "Oh boy!" or "What a plane!" They were too dumfounded for brilliant expression. Later they were more voluble and at a luncheon in the Factory A-1 cafeteria they fired sharp questions at Lockheed officials.

Maj. Richard Bong, Army Air Force ace of aces, was there as well as Edgar Bergen without Charlie McCarthy.

Comment varied.

Said Nelson "Pete" Pringle, Columbia Broadcasting System commentator recently back from the Pacific War Theater, "When I see the P-80 fly I think of all the skibbies in Japan who'll break their necks trying to see it."

Exciting Ship

Dwight Whitney of *Time* and *Life* magazines—"One of the most exciting things I've ever seen. It turned up the hair on my back."

What impressed Ray Zeman, *Los Angeles Times* assistant city editor, was the unmentionable top miles-per-hour figure on the speedometer. "My main ambition now is a piggy-back ride in one," he said.

Newsmen Talk

Pat Hogan of the *Los Angeles Examiner* was surprised such a small plane could have such a fabulous reputation.

Cleve Herman of the *Herald-Express* said, "It's so simple. Why didn't somebody think of it before? It has possibilities as unlimited as a Roman candle."

Press Views P-80

Francis McCarthy of the United Press, just back from a 41-months stretch in the Pacific War Theater said: "How small it is to be such a ship!"

Said John B. Hughes, radio commentator: "I've heard them in the air but I could never see them. It's the sweetest thing ever!"

100-Yard Dash

Maxwell Stiles, former Lockheed assistant publicity manager now west coast editor for *Aero Digest* had seen the P-80 previously. The former sports editor of the *Los Angeles Examiner* had figured the P-80 could spot the world's fastest runner a mile and half and still win a 100-yard dash. Frank Wyckoff once did it in 9.4 seconds.

Scholer Bangs, west coast editor of *Aviation News* said, "Sometime I hope I can get a ride in it." Larry Black of *Western Flying* and many others were impressed with the ship's mirror-like finish.

"It has about the cleanest design of any ship I've seen," said Gaither Littrell, west coast editor of *Flying*. "Leave it to Lockheed

(Continued on Page 8)

P-80 Shooting Star

By JACK PRESCOTT

Tony Le Vier Visits

Make-Up for a Debutante

Wing Talk

Ladder to the Skies

Out of This World

UTHERN CALIFORNIANS today had the answer to a growing mystery of ghostly roars in the sky. Those astral commotions whose source was suspected but seldom seen sounded like blasts of an un- ly blow-torch. But what caused them? Whence their origins? This the Army told—Lockheed Shooting Stars.

iese fastest airplanes in all the world were the outstanding attraction ie Army Air Forces 38th birthday celebration. In important cities of iation, swarming Americans strained for their first look at the smartest ; in jet propulsion. They marvelled and were amazed.

E the first sketchy announcement of the P-80's existence last March, nthusiasts craned necks skyward for glimpses of the fabulous ship. erning ones thought they could distinguish its prop-less roar. A few) snapped heads in an opposite direction from the sound saw silver glints the horizon. Concerning the half-secret ship fanciful tales sprang up.

)n Wednesday at Mines Field as well as Dayton, Dallas, and Washington, C., the public had the rare pleasure of finding fable no stranger than fact. her planes of the Army Air Forces were there—lithe Lightnings, queenly nstellations and the top performers of other companies.

YING for attention, some flew, others opened their doors baring secrets inquisitive eyes. But the prima donna of them all was Lockheed's Shooting ar.

In the Army's first announcement, the public learned tantalizing facts it few details about the ship. Up to this week it knew that the Shooting ar had outperformed the best of the Nazi's—that it embodied aviation's iost spectacular advance and was a harbinger of momentous developments —precursor, perhaps, of inter-stellar traffic. But few had looked at the ship or its photograph.

This week, thousands saw the actual plane and millions more enjoyed brilliant pictures of the sleek, silky fighter in newspapers, magazines, and newsreels. At the same time, they gulped new details released through press previews on Tuesday at Lockheed Air Terminal and Mitchell Field, New York.

PHOTOGRAPHS showed droppable fuel tanks attached to inner shackles and faired into—of all places—extreme tips of wings. This added to the ane's out-of-this-world appearance—reminded comic-strip fans of a Buck Rogers space ship.

Even Lockheed employes, including hundreds who helped build the ship, avidly read the newly disclosed facts.

The droppable fuel tanks make the Shooting Star capable of equaling the flight distances of long-range fighters. Its ceiling tops 45,000 feet—a mile higher than rated climb of first-line propellered fighters.

THE nose, containing six .50-caliber machine guns and all ammunition boxes can be substituted by a nose with camera equipment, making the Shooting Star the AAF's fastest photo reconnaissance plane.

The wing span is 38 ft., 10½ in.; overall length, 34 ft., 6 in., and height, 11 ft., 4 in. Total weight, empty, is approximately 8000 pounds. Gross take-off weight with maximum fuel load is about 14,000 pounds—two tons lighter than the P-38's top weight. The ship's aerodynamic sleekness is unscarred by exterior attachments. Air scoops and canopy are the only protuberances.

Center line of the sharp, laminar-flow low wing is two inches behind the midpoint of the fuselage. The flat wing tapers at leading and trailing edges.

Control surfaces of both wing and empennage are much smaller than those of conventional planes—totaling less than 45 per cent of the area of the P-38 Lightning control surfaces. With no propeller slipstream or torque to overcome, rudder tabs are eliminated.

The cockpit, topped by a plastic bubble canopy and located forward of the wing in the Shooting Star's long, slender nose, can be pressurized from the General Electric jet engine to give pilot comfort in the substratosphere, propeller clearance being unnecessary.

THE plane's tricycle landing gear is unusually short and light.

The six machine guns merge into the lower part of the lance-like nose, a position that eliminates possibility of gun-flash blinding the pilot. The gun sight is an electrical gyro-lead computing type with a reflex optical system.

The six ammunition boxes containing 300 rounds each are upside down from their position in the Lockheed P-38 Lightning—above the guns that they serve. Standing on the ground mechanics can remove magazines and guns in less than 15 minutes. A gun camera is located in a slight bulge of the right-hand air intake duct.

COMPLETE protection for the pilot comes from use of an armor glass windshield, steel armor plate on the upper forward side of the front bulkhead and back of the pilot's seat and head, and dural plate aft of the front bulkhead.

The Shooting Star's engine was developed by General Electric engineers at the River Works in Lynn, Massachusetts. It actually has but one moving part, an impeller and turbine connected by a shaft, spinning faster than 10,000 revolutions per minute. Air condensed by the impeller frequently is 50 degrees below zero, while the exhaust is a blazing hot, 1500 degrees or more.

The impeller whips air into the combustion chamber from the two intakes molded into the fuselage at the wing roots. Kerosene injected into the combustion chamber burns fiercely in the compressed air.

Velocity of the air and gases are increased by the heat before they strike the turbine buckets. The air gases turn the turbine at great speed and then pass out through the jet exhaust nozzle directly under the P-80 tail assembly.

Unlike conventional-type engines, the G-E jet requires no warm-up. The airplane can move 60 seconds after the engine starts. Efficiency of the engine increases greatly with speed and altitude.

ENGINE output is rated in pounds of thrust. The General Electric super jet develops a maximum thrust several times more powerful than the reciprocating engine used on the P-38 Lightning. Thrust exists when the velocity of the jet exceeds the speed of the airplane. Thrust increases as jet velocity and air mass flow increase.

Only engine control is the throttle. The tachometer that shows the revolutions per minute of the turbine compressor is the principal instrument needed to determine thrust output.

Lockheed-engineered hydraulic aileron boost and balanced empennage controls give the plane a maneuverability limited only by the pilot's ability to withstand the forces of tight turns and pull-outs. It has the fastest roll of any plane in the world.

Control surfaces total only 31.6 square feet, compared to 70.3 square feet on the Lockheed P-38. The P-80 recovers from a spin in one-fourth to one-half turn.

Production manhours for a Shooting Star are approximately half those of a P-38. The plane is constructed in four major assemblies . . . nose section, wing, center fuselage section, and aft fuselage (Continued on Page 8)

LERC Offers Transfusion Service

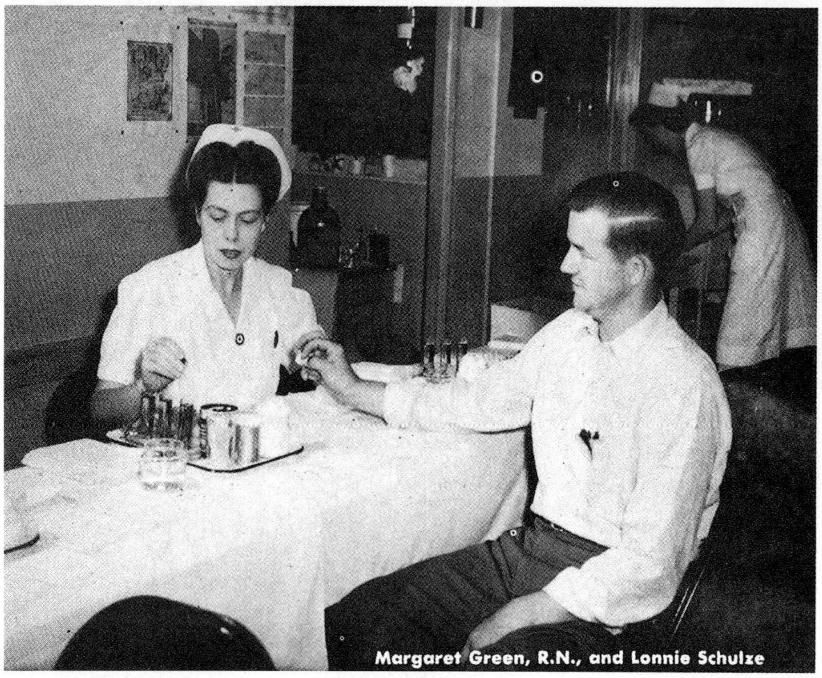

Margaret Green, R.N., and Lonnie Schulze

VOLUNTEERS NEEDED FOR BLOOD DONATIONS

More than 1000 pints of blood have been donated to Lockheed employes and their families through the LERC emergency transfusion service during the past five years, according to Hal Davis, Recreation division manager. The life-saving plasma was given by employes who volunteered to form a blood bank as an aid to fellow employes at time of sickness or accident.

The recent cutback at Lockheed has so depleted the list of donors, said Davis, that new volunteers are needed at once. It is necessary to maintain a fairly large list of donors in order not to place too much of a load on a few people, he said, most of whom are also giving blood regularly to the Red Cross.

Fast Attention

The transfusion service is and has been available for several years to all Lockheed employes and their families who need direct or indirect emergency transfusions. Donations are given at any time of day or night and frequently the transfusion is under way within ten minutes of the first call.

Employes have needed six or seven transfusions, Davis said, and many lives have been saved by this volunteer service. Lockheed people who have benefited from the emergency transfusion services discovered that in addition to securing the correct blood type in a hurry, it has proved a financial saving to the individual.

Committee Named

The LERC Service committee in charge of emergency transfusions is composed of Frank Arrico, chairman; Frank Keefe, John Cooney, and Stuart Simpson. Persons requiring such service should contact either Tony Holst, Ext. 6-2742, or Hal Davis, Ext. 6-1901.

Typical of the service given by the LERC group is the case of Lonnie Schulze, section supervisor in Dept. 18-58. A charter member of the blood bank, Schulze has also benefited from the service.

"I have been repaid fourfold," he said, "for volunteering to aid other employes. My father has been critically ill for the past two months and has received four pints of blood from four employes. Two of the emergency transfusions were given on Sunday, very unexpectedly," he said, "and were credited with saving my father's life."

More Help

The urgent appeal from Davis for volunteers comes at a time when the entire program is in danger of collapsing due to changing personnel at Lockheed.

TOASTMASTERS HOLD TALKFEST AT BREAKFAST

Another new membership drive was instigated by the LERC Toastmasters' club recently, according to Larry Thompson, president. Club members will be divided into two teams with the losing team "wining and dining" the winners at a "ham and eggs brunch" the first meeting in September.

The two teams will be captained by Merle MacIntire and Rex Lorenz, both of Dept. 28-26. The object of the drive is to bring the membership up to a limited thirty members.

A recent innovation is providing an interesting feature at the meetings, said Thompson. Two speakers talk at the same time to train concentration and force of delivery. First half of the program is a table-topic discussion at dinner; the second half consists of prepared speeches by members. Employes interested should call either LERC office, Ext. 6-1901 or 8-1735.

BOWL NIGHT SET FOR AUG. 4

Motion Picture Academy night at the Hollywood Bowl tomorrow, Aug. 4, also will be Lockheed night since the LERC has reserved a block of seats for Lockheed employes and their families.

Academy night will feature Leopold Stokowski and stars Johnny Green, Claudette Colbert, Danny Kaye, Frances Langford, and Frank Sinatra. The many Lockheedians who take advantage of the LERC reserved seat arrangement are promised one of the finest programs of the year, according to the Hollywood Bowl association.

The Bowl program will include selections from "The Horn Blows at Midnight," "Our Town," and "For Whom the Bell Tolls." Highlight of the evening will be a suite of motion picture music featuring excerpts from "The Canterville Ghost," "Lady in the Dark," "Song of Bernadette," "Meet Me in St. Louis," and others. Claudette Colbert will read excerpts from "Bambi," written by Nunnally Johnson especially for Academy night.

Talent Needed, Apply at Club

Instituting a search for professional talent to entertain service personnel at the Hollywood Boulevard USO, the Recreation division of the LERC called for volunteers from Lockheed employes last night.

Dancers, musicians, singers, magicians, and comedians are urgently needed, said Gordon Stanton, assistant recreation director, to provide entertainment every Wednesday and Thursday when the two LERC women's clubs, Blue Star and Service Star, sponsor the USO programs.

The many Lockheed employes who have had professional stage, screen, or radio experience are urged to contact Stanton at Ext. 6-1901.

PENGUINS GIVE GIANT PROGRAM

Gene Coughlin, whose editorials are featured in the *Daily News,* will be guest of honor and principal speaker at the swing shift Penguin and Penguinette meeting on Friday noon, Aug. 10, at the L. A. Breakfast Club.

The swing shift Penguin club, having skipped its July meeting due to the fact that many members were on vacation, has one of the finest of programs to present to its members at the re-opening of summer meetings.

Noted Singers

Mary Hobson Crow, contralto, starring in opera and light opera both in this country and abroad, will sing classical selections. Mary Lou Viregge will entertain with popular songs, accompanying herself on the accordion. Keith Watts, a Lockheed employe in Dept. 38-06, B-1, will give his magic act.

As an extra-special feature, Lyman Gande, piano player-extraordinary and 13 years with Kay Kyser, will be at the Steinway. Anchor-man on the entertainment bill will be popular Pat Hogan who has been received enthusiastically by many Lockheed groups during his 7th War Loan tour here. Hogan, now in the U. S. Navy, will bring along his famous guitar and songs.

Top Amusement

Lockheed employes on the swing shift who are looking for top amusement and a good meal at the L. A. Breakfast Club are urged to get their reservation from one of the Penguin or Penguinette members or contact the LERC offices at B-1 or A-1.

ACTION WANTED ON WRITERS' GROUP

Lockheed employes interested in forming a Writers' club under LERC sponsorship are urged to contact Gordon Stanton, Ext. 6-1901, LERC office, B-1. A small group of employes have petitioned for one, Stanton said.

LERC Movie Features Stars

"Four Jills in a Jeep," starring Kay Francis, Carrol Landis, Martha Raye, and Mitzie Mayfair will be the regular Tuesday free LERC movie on Aug. 7, according to Joe Bell, education committee chairman.

This is a story of movie stars going into the war areas and putting on shows for the armed forces, and is based on Carrol Landis's experience abroad. There are several other guest stars featured in the movie, a musical show with romance and laughter.

PHOTOGRAPHERS HOLD MONTHLY MEETINGS

"Photography in War" was the theme for LERC's Camera club meeting last night at the B-1 cafeteria when Romo Falk, Eastman Kodak research engineer and honorary member of the club, presented his collection of 87 slide films.

The action war shots were projected by a club member, Wally Tyler, while Falk gave a running commentary on the quality and history of each picture. Members of the photographic group, who meet on the first and third Thursdays of each month, praised last night's meeting, calling the war pictures both instructive and entertaining, according to Ed Hollister, club president.

All Invited

Employes interested in photography are invited to the bi-monthly camera sessions, Hollister said. The August 16th meeting promises to be interesting and exciting. Members and prospective members should watch the *Star* for further details.

Members submit mounted photos on the last meeting each month for an intra-club competition. During this meeting, called print night, winners receive war stamps and an opportunity to claim the club's loving cup for one month. At the end of each year the member who has held the cup the greatest number of times is given permanent possession of the cup.

Entries Checked

Subjects for print night are chosen by a salon committee elected by the membership for one year's service. All prints entered are discussed, criticised, and judged by the entire membership.

Winning prints are picked for composition, subject, printing and developing technique, also artistic values. New subjects are chosen each month to keep varied interest. Wally Tyler of Dept. 16-40 holds the cup for this month for his fine prints on the monthly subject, "Landscapes."

Romo Falk

ON THE *Table*

BILL ELLIS **Pres. LERC**

IN previous articles, I have made reference to the LERC Investigating committee. That fact-finding body submitted its report at the July council meeting. The report was a well-written, comprehensive study of Commissary division activity; 7 pages. The committee presented recommendations based upon facts. Personal opinions did not influence its suggestions. That action must be commended.

I thought the recommendations logical. Those requiring detail change will be acted upon as soon as possible. Committeemen compared LERC to two similar organizations in this area. The study revealed, in general, they believed our organization was much better than either of the other two plants visited.

In the committee's opinion, "The LERC has a class 'A' operation for which it need not make apologies to anyone."

The committee reported: "We are willing to leave it in the hands of the council to judge whether or not the investigation has been justified. We have attempted earnestly to do the job fairly and honestly as we saw it, bearing in mind that we were not detectives or efficiency experts but five fellows elected to do a job for which they did not apply. It is our mutual conviction that we would have a better organization if each member of the council could give a similar amount of time and study to the operation of the LERC. Due to the fact that a majority of the complaints concerned the Commissary division, our investigation was confined to that branch of the LERC."

I believe this report has done more toward promoting harmony than any other single council action. The committee should be complimented on its work.

The question I am most frequently asked is: "Who writes your column?" To keep the record straight, I am not attempting to pass as a columnist. These weekly columns are merely facts passed on to you, by me, in my own words. They are intended to inform you on subjects with which your elected representatives are faced. They are honest attempts to justify that purpose.

COURSES GIVEN

In 14,000 of America's 25,686 high schools, aviation courses are being given, according to a report of the Aeronautical Chamber of Commerce.

Johnny Morris

PISTOL CLUB TAKES PART IN NATIONAL RIFLE MEET

LERC's Pistol and Rifle club members are participating in a National Rifle Association-registered match at Glendale Rifle club on Sunday, Aug. 12, at 8:00 a.m. Open to all employes, the match is expected to draw a large Lockheed turnout, both participants and spectators, according to president Bud Kuecher.

Kuecher also announced that the pistol classes held at Hoover High school in Glendale have received excellent attendance. New classes will be open in three weeks. Those interested must sign up now, he said, as the limited list soon will be closed.

Round-Robin

Pistol and rifle par matches are being played off once a week, round-robin, on the R.O.T.C. range at the Hoover High school, Glendale. Casey Jones, Dept. 22-53, and Jack Teal, Dept. 72-25, are all tied up for the top spot in both points and matches. The match is wide open, Kuecher said, as there are four more matches to be played.

A par match is one of the fairest types of shooting with handicaps based on a pre-established average of the individual shooter.

Set-Up Explained

Each contestant shoots against his own average, the greatest personal improvement takes the match. Each improvement moves the average up. The last three scheduled meets should prove to be hotly contested duels.

All members and employes are cordially invited to attend each week, Kuecher said. For schedules or further information contact B-1 LERC office, Ext. 6-1901.

WINTER SPORTS ARE SCHEDULED

Lockheed's touch football league will be formed and ready to begin play by Oct. 1 and LERC's all-star men's and women's bowling teams will be ready for the 1945 season Sept. 1, according to a report by Don Hays, chairman of the LERC athletic committee.

The decision to keep the LERC represented in the bowling and touch football leagues was made at a recent meeting of the athletic committee, Hays said.

The committee headed by Hays, is composed of Al Pimser, Wilkie Byran, Earl Schriver, and Ted Yeats. It guides the destiny of the tremendous LERC sports program.

Other announcements from the athletic group include the scheduling of basketball and badminton for Oct. 1. Schedules and details will be announced later.

Tournament Set By Herald-Express

Third annual Southern California softball tournament sponsored by the *Evening Herald-Express*, will begin play Aug. 12, according to Frank Davis, chairman of the *Herald-Express* tournament committee.

The tournament starting date was set last night by a committee headed by Davis and composed of John Old, sports-writer; Dudley Schumway, city of Los Angeles sports director, and Ken Kellough, North American Aviation Recreation director.

Winners and runners-up in the LERC interdepartmental softball league will be eligible to enter the *Herald-Express* contest, Davis said, and details of the event will be announced in next week's *Star*.

Girls Hold Lead With Forfeit Win

Lockheed's Lady Lightnings, by virtue of a forfeit win over the Trinity girls' team, still hold their second place position in the Burbank City league, according to Jim Arbogast, sports director.

The all-star girls will take part in the Southern California girls' softball championship play in the city league. Seeded favorites in the tourney, the girls will meet top teams from the state.

DAY SHIFT LIGHTNINGS CONTINUE TO WIN IN 2 CITY SOFTBALL LEAGUES

Lockheed's top-flight Lightnings took two softball thrillers last week, one in the Burbank league and one in the L. A. Double-A league, to draw the noose a little tighter on championships in both leagues, and stretch their undefeated winning streak to 19 games.

Star ball flippers, Johnny Morris and Buel Fanning, each took a game in stride, continuing the tight pitching performances that have put the LERC softball group in the lead position in two hot leagues.

Fanning, rapidly proving to be the foremost pitcher in Southern California, KO'd eighteen out of twenty-one Brawley Drug sluggers in a 5-2 game on Monday, July 23, at the Glenoaks diamond. Eleven of the first twelve men to face Fanning were retired to the bench without even touching the fast curve balls delivered by the Lightning pitcher.

Score First

The Lightnings scored first in the second inning when Fanning singled to short left field followed by a hard hit home run by Keith France.

In the sixth inning, Simons started off by doubling, Andy Schubert walked. Robson singled, scoring Simons and Schubert. Robson scored when the next three batters were walked by the Brawley pitcher.

The Brawley team managed to eke out two runs in the last of the seventh inning on a hit by first baseman, Swaboda, and two errors by the Lightning infield when two consecutive bunts were let down by the Brawley batters.

Johnny Morris pitched his usual brand of ball July 25 at Echo Park, setting down thirteen of the Dodge Trophy club by strikeout to collect an 8-0 victory in the L. A. City A-A league.

One Hit

Morris allowed only one hit and had the ball not taken a bad bounce over the second baseman's head, Morris would have rung up another no-hit, no-run ball game to his credit.

The LERC group accounted for ten hits, eight runs and no errors while the Dodge boys collected one hit, no runs and one error.

Highlight of the game in the hitting department came in the sixth when Kenny Hyde singled, Marty Smith walked and Tom McCambridge smacked one over center field for a home run scoring Hyde and Smith.

Record Given

Morris was given air-tight backing by the Lightnings with stellar performances by captain Andy Schubert, Sid Bruner, Connie Gonzales, Max Greenberg and Charlie Simons. The infield clicked with clocklike precision and played flawless ball through the ball game.

BURBANK CITY LEAGUE

Lockheed	Opponent	
4	Peterson Mkt.	3
6	Warner Bros.	0
9	Brawley Drug	0
4	Maxwell	0
3	Armstrong	2
4	Warners	0
12	Peterson	0
5	Brawley	2

Maxwell and Armstrong to be played.

LOS ANGELES CITY AA LEAGUE

Lockheed	Opponent	
1	Enderles	0
5	Dodge Trophy	4
5	Carnation	2
2	18th AAF	0
7	Military Police	0
6	Glasser Bond	1
5	Jr. Chamber of Com.	3
4	Enderles	0
8	Dodge Trophy	0

McDANIELS IN SEMI-FINALS

Jim McDaniels, top ranking Lockheed tennis star and defending champion of 1944, is the first man to advance to the semifinals by virtue of his victory over Charles Sharpe, 7-5, 6-3. McDaniels has departed for the East to participate in the National Colored Championship matches and, upon his return to Lockheed, will meet the winner of the Jack Ryan and R. W. Andrews match.

Vic Seligar, quarter-finalist awaits the winner of Joe Quint, Don Phillips and John Walsh. L. Hastings will meet the winner of the Starr Pierce, R. H. Shatz match.

In the men's class B division, Lou Cruz with two wins over Sid Barnett and James Arbogast, will meet Victor Bantilan, who retired Clay Vaughn and Bob Earl in a semi-finalist match, while Wilbur Lincoln, with victories over Carl Burton and Joe Dorgan, will meet R. E. Spangenberg who defeated Oscar Saenz and E. E. Woodson.

All-Plant Game Will Be Slated

Day shift winner of the LERC interdepartmental softball league semi-final game tonight at 5:30 p.m. at the Olive Avenue center will meet the swing shift victor, Aug. 5, 11:00 a.m. on the Glen Oaks diamond to determine the championship in the all-plant, all-shift contest.

The championship game next Sunday morning will climax a three-month elimination match in which more than 1100 Lockheed employes played top quality softball. The winning team will be awarded medals and the new perpetual trophy. Runners-up will receive medals and an opportunity to enter the *Herald-Express* third annual softball tournament, reported elsewhere in the *Star*.

A large employe turnout is expected for the semi-final game tonight at 5:30 p.m. and the final game, Sunday morning at 11:00 a.m.

Chess Club Moves To Recreation Center

Moving back to its old quarters, the LERC sponsored Chess club will continue regular Wednesday evening meetings at the Burbank Recreation Center, 1111 West Olive.

Eph Koningsberg, president, announced yesterday that the club would meet at 6:30 p.m. each Wednesday.

LOCKHEED SHOOTING STAR MAKES SOUTHLAND DEBUT

(Continued from Page 5)

and tail group. Both nose and aft fuselage are secured by quick-action tension fittings and may be removed for service within a matter of minutes. With the aft fuselage, including the nozzle, removed by detaching three fittings and the tail pipe clamp, the simplified G-E jet engine is accessible for maintenance and may be run up without taking it out of the fuselage. A complete engine change may be finished in less than 20 minutes.

The nose section, aside from armament or photographic equipment, contains compartments for oxygen, radio equipment, and the adjustable landing light.

In the center fuselage section are the cockpit, fuel tanks, and power plant. Space beneath the cockpit holds hydraulic, fuel, and radio equipment.

The aluminum alloy wing of full cantilever design is built in one unit containing retractable sway braces for carrying the droppable fuel tanks or bombs on the wing tip shackles. Ailerons are conventional. The main landing gear, operated hydraulically, folds inboard into the wing.

Smooth As Piano

A glass-smooth "piano" finish that enhances the harmony of the Lockheed fighter's aerodynamic lines adds greatly to the plane's overall speed and performance.

To attain this surface, rivets are cut and surface-ground. A zinc chromate primer is applied. All butt joints are cement filled, and flexible joints are covered with organdy mesh tape.

A surfacer is applied in preparation for the paint, which is baked on in special ovens large enough to hold the entire plane. Light sanding and buffing follow. A specially developed wax is sprayed on and polished.

Eliminates Coolers

Use of the General Electric engine has simplified the P-80's design and production. There is no continuous ignition system to cause radio interference. There is no propeller to hamper forward-firing armament or to provide a clearance or torque problem. The engine has a self-contained lubricating system that eliminates oil coolers, piping and tanks.

Combustion in the engine chamber is complete. There is no trail of flame or smoke emerging from the nozzle. There is no danger of carbon monoxide to the pilot.

Although present engines for the P-80 are designed to operate on kerosene, which reduces altitude fuel problems and fire hazards, modifications in the fuel system would enable them to operate on gasoline of any octane rating with approximately the same efficiency.

Logistics will determine which fuel will be used when the P-80 enters large-scale operations, although kerosene provides best performance.

Pressure in the cockpit is automatically reduced when the combat gun switch is turned on to prevent physical injury to the pilot from explosive decompression should a bullet hit the canopy. Two fluorescent lights are mounted on sides of the cockpit.

WRITERS GAPE AS P-80 BUZZES

(Continued from Page 3)

to create a beauty of such trim lines."

John Canaday, Lockheed public relations director emceed a brief question-and-answer program at the luncheon. Among those introduced were S. E. Gates, district manager and Wayne Allen and R. E. Johnson, engineers of the General Electric Company; Lt. Comdr. W. D. Howell, BuAer representative; Mrs. Rhoda Morris of the Western District Office Air Technical Service Command; L. M. Bach, vice president in charge of manufacturing; Hall L. Hibbard, vice president in charge of engineering; C. L. Johnson, chief research engineer; F. Penn Holter, Factory B works manager; Harvey Christen, superintendent P-80; Rudy L. Thoren, division engineer of flight test; William Ralston, P-80 project engineer; LeVier, Major Bong and Bergen.

Courtlandt S. Gross — Brig. Gen. Muniz

AIRMEN FROM BRAZIL VISIT FACTORY HERE

Air Brig. Gen. Antonio Guedes Muniz and Oswaldo Bittencourt Sampaio of Brazil visited Lockheed Monday and toured the factory area.

General Muniz designed the first Brazilian plane in 1935. He is director of National Motor Factory located near Rio de Janeiro, which was the first Latin-American plant to build airplanes from start to finish. Its first engine was completed in January, 1944.

General Muniz designed two military trainers, the Muniz M-7 and M-9, and the H-1, a light trainer for civilian use.

Member of the Brazilian Air Force, General Muniz said: "The future of Brazil's transportation is bound more and more to the airplane because of Brazil's giant size and its varied terrain."

While at Lockheed, General Muniz conferred with Carl Squier, vice president in charge of sales, Jim Fisher, Lockheed South American representative, Roger Lewis, Ken Smith, and other Lockheed executives.

His last visit was in 1941.

Employes' Libraries Closing Out Books

Closing of employes' libraries has made many books available at reduced prices. Final sales are scheduled for Factory B August 4 through 6, in the library room, building 128, inside gate 11.

Sales at Factory A-1 are listed for August 4 through 8, in the library room at the west end of building 80.

Parcel Post Will Take Heavier Mail

All magazines, periodicals, packages, or bundles of any appreciable bulk or weight, formerly handled by mail delivery girls, will be picked up by a parcel post messenger once daily, according to an announcement from L. W. Wulfekuhler, secretary.

The mail rooms at all plants are to be contacted when such material has to be picked up.

Historic Ship Honors Lockheed Vet's Name

Lockheed's last B-17, No. 8750, which ended production on the most famous bomber of World War II, was christened the Arthur N. Dantzler, honoring a civilian inspector for the Air Technical Service Command who worked at Lockheed. He was killed in a training crash in Florida.

Is it Here?

THESE classified advertisements in the *Star* are provided for employes without charge. If you want to buy, sell, trade, or find or return lost articles, obtain Form 4929 from your department clerk, the stationery store, or employe service office. Mail the advertisement to the *Lockheed Star*, Room 244, Bldg. 1-A, Plant B-1.

WANTED

TRAILER and hitch, 2-wheel. SU. 1-7017.
CAMERA, 16-mm., for serviceman. AN. 1-0767.
UNFURN. 3-bedrm. for liberated internees, rent or lease. CH. 8-8463 after 4.
PISTOL, .22 or .32, or .22 rifle. HI. 8775.
ROLLAWAY, 1 pressed steel. 1926 Bonita, Burbank.
AUSTIN. Art Bloomfield, CH. 8-2986.
CLUB coupe, late model, conv., buy or trade '39 de luxe Ford coupe. CI. 2-1765 after 5.
REFRIGERATOR, late model, good condition. CI. 2-1765 after 5.
HOUSE to rent, adult and 1 child; 1 bedroom necessary. B-7, extension 124.
FORD '41 club coupe. CH. 8-4745.
LAWN mower, vacuum. SY. 7-2996.
ACCORDION, 120-bass. DR. 1780.
MOTORCYCLE, perf. Army Indian "45." Cash. 15164 Normi, San Fernando.
COT. GL. 0065.
REFRIGERATOR, 4 or 5 cubic ft. CI. 3-2580.
CAMERA, Kodak bantam special. NO. 2-1777.
GIRLS, play guitar and bass fiddle for orchestra. WY. 8212.
FORD '36 or '37 or other low-priced car. CH. 6-6166.
ELECTRIC refrigerator. 2137 Dymond, Burbank.
COUPE, '36 or '37. Ext. 6-1551.
PLACE to board two horses and colt in the valley. OL. 5105.
REEL, fresh water, bait casting, level-wind type preferred. CH. 8-4840.
MAPLE-finish writing desk with drawers. Before 3. CH. 8-2915.
CAMERA, 2¼x3¼ flash, any model, cash. RO. 1842.
BEST car that $400 cash will buy, sedan preferred. CH. 6-7835.
STATION wagon, or Chev. club coupe '41 or '42. HI. 9427, eves. or Sundays.
APT., court, furn. or unfurn., to $60. Couple, no pets. CI. 1-4446, eves.
TO rent by 2 refined sisters, dbl. apt. or sm. house L.A. or Glendale. 657 S. Coronado, Rausch.
RIDE for two passengers to Minneapolis on or about Aug. 11. DR. 9971.

Is it Here?

WANTED

RIDE for two to Sioux City, Iowa, on or about Aug. 18. NO. 2-5696.
FLATIRON, small with detachable handle or travel iron, 110 volts. HE. 2536.
RIDERS from Glendale Blvd. and Sunset vicinity to A-1, days. FI. 6729.
PORTABLE typewriter in good condition. RO. 4215.
LOCKHEED couple need furn. apt. Church. Ext. 8-2900.
RIDERS wanted, B-1, A-1, swing, from N. Chevy Chase, Lexington, Monterey Rd., etc. CI. 2-7014.
RIDE, Pico and Main, San. Monica swing, A-1. 240 Bicknell, Santa Monica.

FOR SALE

MISCELLANEOUS

RADIOS, one Philco console, 1 table model. CH. 8-2011, after 5:30 p.m.
COLLAPSIBLE buggy & bathinette, good cond. 1302 5th St., Glendale.
BABY bathinette, prewar buggy, practically new. HI. 6151, Apt. 1930.
PIANO, Braumbach, 5-ft. baby grand, refinished and reconditioned. CH. 8-8373.
ROCK house, 2 bedrms., insulated, fruit, shade trees. 318 Fermore, San Fern.
LEITZ, double condenser, enlarger. Laack f.45 lens, neg. 2¼x2¼. S.M. 4-4504.
BUGGY, steel, chrom. handle, rubber tires, collap. Like new. CH. 8-6704.
GOLF bag, leather, like new, $15. CI. 2-4077.
HOME, N.H. 2-bedrm. 3½ yrs. old. Immediate possession. STate 4-3346.
NEW prewar alarm clock, pr. men's shoes, size 9, 2 ctns. cigs., OL. 7660, 7-9 p.m.
COMB. radio-phono., chair-side model, walnut fiinish. HI. 4635.
BED davenport and chair, library table. 415 Moss, Burbank.
STAMP collection, foreign, some U.S. CH. 8-4495.
BABY buggy, ice box, 50-lb., prewar; 2 goats. 15164 Nurmi, San Fernando.
FIRESTONE, 5-ft., 1-pc. steel bait-casting rod, level-wind reel. SY. 9-6584, aft. 6.
BIRD cage, solid brass, like new. SU. 2-3719.
LOS Feliz home, immediate possession. 3 bedrooms, 2 baths. Owner. NO. 5685.
WALNUT dinette table, 4 chairs, burgundy tapestry upholstered. CI. 8575, 1063 Raymond, Glendale.
STARR spinet piano. CI. 2-9079, Apt. 102.
TWIN beds, metal, brown, sturdy, cheap. 7-6 Imogen, L.A. NO. 1-5552.
MACHINERY handbook, like new, $4. CH. 8-8775.
UNION oak tool box, comp. 1" & 2" micr. & depth micr., telescope gauges, etc. CH. 8-7775.
WEDDING ring, 93-pt. diamond channel setting. Reasonable. GL. 0246.
REMINGTON bolt-action repeater, .22. 403 W. Stocker, Glendale.
BUGGY, baby, Thayer, practically new. OL. 2658, after 6 p.m.
BROADLOOM, 9x15, henna, pebble weave and pad. CI. 2-8384.
PIANO, upright, splendid tone. HI. 8554.
ENGLISH bicycle, generator light, chrome, like new. CH. 8-8115.
ELECTRIC fan. CH. 8-8115.
BASSINET with stand, large size, lined, good cond. 14412½ Califa, N.H. ST. 5-2589.
ELECTRIC mangle, Thor Gladiron. CL. 6-6396.
SWING, child's two place, steel; girl's bicycle. Size 28. CI. 2-5787.
DINETTE table, 4 chairs, walnut finish. CI. 1-5646.

Is it Here?

FOR SALE

MISCELLANEOUS (Cont.)

ICE BOX, 50 lbs., white enamel, good cond. 10206 Haddon St., Pacoima, after 3 p.m.
IRISH setter, AKC reg. female, cheap to good home. SUnland 431.
BABY'S car bed, elec. toaster, Book of Knowledge, 20 vols.; pump action .22 rifle. CH. 8-9033.
ONE dark oak bedroom set, comp. with matt., hardwood drawers. SUnland 380.
BEDROOM set, 5 pc., mattress and springs. CH. 8-3539.
WILTON rugs, 2 with pads, 8x3, 10x6; 3 rugs, 4x6. WH. 6475.
RADIO, 10-tube, all-wave, table model. Perf. cond. 1017 N. San F. Rd., Apt. 43.
ESSICK air cooler, used 50 hrs. Sell $60. CH. 8-1226.
GRAND piano, Fischer; 2 ladies' bikes. NO. 1-2889.
EASTMAN kodak, No. 1 series III, 120 film. Ex. pictures. CI. 1-9657.
OLD Dutch spinning wheel. Chinese mandarin coat, kodaks, elec. mixer. OL. 5264.
ELEC. abrasive motor cutter, 1 hp., for pipe and angle iron. $110. 11425 Eldorado, San Fernando.
EVAPORATOR, cooler type, home air conditioner. $60. 11425 Eldorado, S.F.
GERMAN Police female pup, 8 mos. old, ready for training. $25. 11425 Eldorado, San Fernando.
WARDROBE, 6 ft. CH. 8-2974, after 4 p.m.
ACRES, 2½, 3 mi. from Van Nuys, 60 orange trees, 120 lemon. CH. 8-5149.
HOUSE, 2 bedrm., insulated, dbl. garage, fruit & shade trees. 1926 Fairview, Brbk.
WALNUT-finished modern desk with drawers and shelves. CH. 8-2915, before 3 p.m.
CAR radio, push-button, good condition. CH. 6-0757, after 4 p.m.
BASSINET, de luxe size, set on wheel rack. NO. 2-4514.
SPORT suit, man's all-wool, size 38, worn once. SU. 1-4857.
RAZORS, 2 electric. Schick and Dual Remington. HE. 3752.
DIAMOND, beautiful blue-white, 1¾-k., one diamond each side. AL. 5910.
RADIO, console, $30; cedar chest, good condition. 1510 N. Naomi, after 4 p.m.
TROUT fly rod, like new. SUnland 6384, after 6.
COMMERCIAL acre on paved road in Reseda, trade for house & lot nr. Lockheed, pay balance. EX. 4056.
CAR RADIO, General Motors '34. One unit, $15. Good cond. CI. 2-3402, Marian Kier.
LADY'S dinner ring, zircon set in onyx. Sacrifice. CHapman 5-1324.
OUTBOARD motor, Waterwitch, heavy-duty twin, last model mfg. $110. CI. 1-7032.
BOAT, 30' sloop, hollow mast, stainless-steel rigging, 2 bunks. NO. 7757.
RADIO. '37 Ford Philco, $25, no aerial. CH. 6-9658.

VEHICLES

PONTIAC '38 convertible sedan, radio, new top. CItrus 1-5580.
V-8 motor, '33, good condition. CI. 3-2806. 6-8 p.m.
PACKARD 4-dr. sedan, '38, good cond. Radio. SUnland 6384, after 6 p.m.
MODEL A Ford '31 roadster. Good condition. RE. 5806.
FORD '37 85-hp. 2-dr. sedan, ex. motor, tires. 1919½ W. Victory, Burbank.
FORD coupe, model A, A-1 cond. Inq. Sunday & Monday. 2702 W. Ave. 30. L. A.

Is it Here?

FOR SALE

VEHICLES (Cont.)

TRAILER, 2-wheel, 10x5 body, welded, steel constr., lights, car hitch. CI. 1-5551.
MOTOR bicycle, Whizzer, good cond. 16' factory-built house trailer. 20 W. Mt. View, Altadena.
SCHWINN prewar light bicycle. SU. 1-3381.
MOTORCYCLE, 36-80 Harley Davidson; '29 Peerless, good cond. 1820 Jackson, Burbank.
ARMY Indian motorcycle. 1014 Pass Ave., Burbank.
SACKS motor bike, 2-cycle engine, $140. Good condition. CH. 6-9302.
RYAN St-3KR, just licensed, comp. gone over. CH. 8-7535, 5 to 6 p.m.
MODEL midget racer, super cyclone engine. Almost new. CH. 8-5688.
MARMON sedan, '25, good tires, heavy motor, as is, $100. SY. 9-6584, after 6.

EXCHANGE

TRADE flying time for work on N3N airplane. CH. 8-2129.
FORD '41 de luxe coupe, ex. cond., for clean late-model house trailer. ST. 4-2867
LA SALLE '39 sedan and cash for 2 or bedrm. house, L. A., Alhambra vic. A. 2-7400.
FORD '36 Tudor and cash for '41 light car. AN. 1-0767.
LOT in N. Hollywood, 50x185, down pay. house in valley. 13753 Mercer, Pacoima.
SINGLE apt., all-elec. kit., refrig., garage, V. Nuys, for apt. So. L. A. STate 5-2668.

LOST

SERVICEMAN'S identification bracelet, D. W. Ruliffson. Reward. CH. 3072.
RAY Ban sun glasses, black lthr. case, parking lot 6 on 7-21. Rew. Ext. 6-3278.
COLLIE, toy, vic. S. F. Rd. & Hollywood Way, sable body, white paws, no tail. CHase 7-7367.
FOUNTAIN pen, green marbled, near gate 8, A-1. $5 reward. Boehme, 7425 Tujunga, N. H.
LADY'S Bulova wrist watch, gold, chipped dia., nr. LAT 7-30. Rew. Lowery, ext. 8-1086.

ROOM AND BOARD

CARE for child, plus rm. & board for 1 or both parents, walking dist. B-1. 524 Irving Dr.

THE LOCKHEED Star
OFFICIAL PUBLICATION OF THE LOCKHEED AIRCRAFT CORPORATION

Issued each Friday for the employes of Lockheed Aircraft Corporation. The *Star* is the official publication of the company. Communications should be addressed to the Editor, *Lockheed Star* Unit, Lockheed Aircraft Corporation, Burbank, California.

No unsolicited manuscripts or pictures will be returned and the *Star* cannot be responsible for other than requested articles or photos.

KENNETH CRIST, Editor
J. H. Prescott, Associate Editor
Marshall Atwell, Staff Artist
Barbara Sewald, News

THE LOCKHEED Star
OFFICIAL PUBLICATION OF THE LOCKHEED AIRCRAFT CORPORATION
Volume 2 BURBANK, CALIFORNIA, U.S.A., AUGUST 10, 1945 No. 32

NAVY'S PV-2 HARPOON

STORY: PAGE 3

Breakfast at Lockheed

6400 People Daily Enjoy Breakfast In Cafeterias

More than 6400 Lockheed employes eat breakfast daily at LERC's vast sprawling commissary network to prove that breakfast at Lockheed must be better than "Breakfast at Sardi's." More people eat at Lockheed. That's the opinion expressed last night by Charles Birgy, commissary manager.

LERC's commissary system, consisting of two $1,000,000 cafeterias and 12 in-plant canteens, began serving breakfast some time ago as an accommodation to a few hundred employes. The subsequent growth of the breakfast volume is credited to fast service, low price, and quality food.

Time Given

Breakfasts are served from 6 a.m. to 9:30 a.m., and from 2:30 p.m. to 4 p.m. each day with three lines open to supply fast service.

The piles of raw stock for the huge breakfast service stagger the imagination in this age of ration points. In the adjacent picture, Factory A Chef Ernest Reidel is shown checking only a part of the stock necessary for one day's breakfast at the "A" cafeteria alone.

Consider walking down to the corner market to pick up the ingredients for a cozy breakfast for 6400. You'd need 120 lbs. of butter at 1920 red points and 225 lbs. of bacon or ham currently valued at more than 2000 red points. Then you would want 300 lbs. of coffee, three 100-lb. sacks of sugar, and 30 gallons of cream.

List Continues

Hot cakes, breakfast rolls, and doughnuts made in the LERC bake-shop call for six 100-lb. sacks of flour, three 100-lb. sacks of sugar daily as well as quantities of nuts, raisins, and dried fruits; 4500 eggs and 165 lbs. of shortening plus 60 gallons of milk and 1800 bottles of milk per day.

LERC Activities

ACCOUNTING FORUM — Meets every Wednesday, 5 p.m., B-1 cafeteria building.

BADMINTON—Tuesday and Thursday, 7 p.m., John Burroughs Jr. High School gym, Burbank.

BLUE STAR WOMEN — Open house, Boulevard USO, 6551 Hollywood Blvd., Wednesday, 7:30 p.m.

BOY SCOUTS — Troop No. 17, each Wednesday evening, 7 p.m., in Boy Scout cabin, George Washington School, at Lincoln and Rowe Streets, Burbank. Troop No. 13, every Wednesday, 7 p.m., John Muir Jr. High School Scout cabin. Troop No. 302, every Friday, 7 p.m., 6242 Banner St., Hollywood.

CAMERA CLUB—First and third Thursdays of the month—room 5, B-1 cafeteria.

CHESS CLUB—Every Wednesday, 6:30 p.m., Burbank Recreation Center, 1111 W. Olive, Burbank.

CONCERTS — Military band, rehearsals Friday, 9:15 a.m.; concerts begin at 10:50 a.m., main recreation area, all day shift lunch periods.

DANCE CLUB—Every Thursday, 8 p.m., Alan Rudack Studios, 7213 Beverly Blvd.

SWING SHIFT DANCE—Every Friday night after work—1 to 4 a.m. Always a good band. Burbank Recreation Center, 1111 W. Olive, Burbank.

FREE MOVIES—Tuesday, Aug. 14, "Little Miss Molly," starring Benkie Stuart, Maureen O'Hara, and Tom Burke. B-1 cafeteria, 5:45 p.m. and 8 p.m. Swing shift, 12:45 (after work) in B-1 recreation area.

PENGUINETTE, DAYS — Cabaret night hostess, Boulevard USO, every Thursday evening.

PISTOL AND RIFLE CLUB—Training course, Hoover High School, Glendale, Wednesdays, 7 p.m.

PLANT TOURS—Contact the LERC office for further particulars.

RIDING CLUB—Lockheed Rangers, every Sunday, 8 a.m., and every Wednesday at 7 p.m., Pico Stables, 420 Riverside Drive. Swing shift Rangers, 10 a.m., Wednesday, Pico Stables. Call LERC for reservations.

SKI CLUB—Contact the LERC office for further particulars, extension 6-1901 or 8-1735.

SERVICE STAR WOMEN—Plant B-1, first Wednesday of the month, after work, conference room 1, cafeteria building; third Wednesday evening, 7:30, Hollywood Y.W.C.A., 6927 Hawthorne, Hollywood; B-2, day and graveyard shift, every Wednesday lunch period, 11 a.m. and 3:30 a.m., conference room.

TOASTMASTERS — Every Tuesday, 1 p.m., room 4, cafeteria building.

VOCAL GROUPS — Hollywood Radio Chorus, Hollywood High School, MA. 71, every Wednesday. Victory Singers—Monday and Wednesday, 7 p.m., Los Angeles High School, Olympic and Rimpau, room 423.

Coca-Cola Shortage Imminent

If the coke machine or the canteens are out of "cokes" during this current warm weather spell, don't blame the LERC, blame the cut in the ice quota. So said Jimmy Ramsey, canteen manager for the LERC in the interview yesterday.

Revealing the fact that the local ice companies have cut the quota to Lockheed employes by 25 per cent, Ramsey said that this automatically would mean that the ice delivered per day would not be sufficient to last a complete working day and, for that reason, the canteens would not be able to serve all "cokes" and soft drinks needed during a normal day's period of operation.

One Drink

As matters now stand, the employes on smoking period or during the first lunch period often use up all the available supplies, Ramsey said, and this means that the other employes are without refreshments. Ramsey asked that the day shift employes remember the second and third shift and not drink more than one soft drink during the day.

Because of the run on soft drinks during the warm weather, the milk situation becomes more critical for, when soft drinks are not available, employes are exceeding the normal demand in bottle milk.

Sugar Cut

However, in the case of the soft drinks, difficulty is being met due to another cut in the sugar supply to the soft drink producers, which reflects itself on the amount of soft drinks available to consumers here at Lockheed.

PICTURES READY

Old Timers, please note: The LERC offices at both A-1 and B-1 have copies of the pictures taken at the last Old Timers' affair given at Oakmont Country Club.

P-80 pictures are also on sale now in both merchandise stores.

Forum Celebrates Election Of Officers at B Cafeteria

LAST week, the Accounting Forum celebrated its first six months of continuous activity with the election of new officers at a banquet held in the LERC B-1 cafeteria. The new officers elected to serve for the next six months are:

President, Bob Stevens, Dept. 81-34; secretary, Lou Milligan, Dept. 81-22, and treasurer, Ollie Ingraham, Dept. 81-22. In addition several committee chairmen were elected to new terms.

Guest speakers for the special occasion included three representatives of the Training Department, Perry Arnold, Joseph Schwartz, and Edward M. Lang, all of whom are honorary members and advisors of the Forum.

Ferg Wins Chess Prize

Dick Ferg, Dept. 26-11, walked off with a double victory in LERC's Chess club July match by stealing both the Brilliancy and Chess Ladder prizes . . . proving that chess is any man's game. Ferg's two wins were the first competition victories to his credit.

The Brilliancy prize is awarded to the player who is accredited with the best and most original games during the month's competition. The Chess Ladder prize is given for the most consistent win record. Both prizes rarely are won by one player, making Ferg's double first time win a club record.

Chess club members meet every Wednesday night at the Burbank Recreation Center at 6:30 to 10:30. Employes interested in learning chess or in improving their game are invited. Chess men and boards are furnished and an extensive chess library is available.

MODEL PLANE BUILT BY CLUB

Another high wing model airplane is being built by the members of the LERC Model and Hobby club. It will be flown by U-Control, a method commonly used where the operator controls the plane's up and down movements by two wires. The ship was designed by Rex Bloom of A-1 Engineering. The model is being built so that folks who never have flown before can learn to fly control-line planes.

The active members are willing to help beginners learn the art of control-line flying, if prospective members need help, according to Ted Salamandra, club president. It costs nothing to join this LERC sponsored unit. New members are wanted and may contact either John B. Cesario, B-1, Ext. 6-1650 or Salamandra, A-1, Ext. 8-1441, for further information. Employes are invited to the next meeting Aug. 8, 7:30 p.m. at Griffith Park swimming pool, corner of Los Feliz and Riverside Drive.

Prospective members may see model planes being flown by active members of the club.

NLSC Dance Tops Week

Foremost among the activities planned by the LERC for Lockheed employes will be the Navy Lockheed Service center dance at the Oakmont Country Club on Saturday, Aug. 11.

This affair, wide open to Lockheed folks, will be sponsored by the NLSC day shift and graveyard, all departments. Horace Blanco has charge of the arrangements and tickets may be secured from him or from the LERC offices at B-1. It is also planned to sell tickets at the door. Music will be by Cy Erb and his orchestra.

Special Men's Ties on Sale in Employe Stores

LERC's merchandise stores in "A" and "B" cafeterias have just received a new shipment of men's ties, according to Walter Martin, store manager. The gayly colored, hand-painted foulards have been a popular seller with Lockheed men, he said, and the purchasing staff has found it difficult to keep the stores stocked with the silk ties.

"Foulard ties are almost impossible to find today, and Lockheed employes may appreciate the fine selection offered by the store," Martin said. "From polka-dots to exotic designs, the double width ties of the finest rayon and silk are created in Hollywood's smartest shops for Lockheed employes."

The merchandise stores are now presenting, among many other items, a fine line of leather goods for men. Belts of the best leather available are selling at very reasonable prices, Martin said. He indicated that some excellent hand-tooled items in limited numbers will be available for a short time.

Cosmetics, toilet goods, perfumes and jewelry are among the many lines carried for the convenience of Lockheed women, Martin added, although anyone living near Lockheed is welcome to purchase at the employes' stores. Housewives are invited to drop in from time to time as new lines are constantly being added to the stock.

FACTORY A-1 PICNIC SLATED FOR AUG. 12

Dept. 35-39 at Factory A-1 will have its all-shift family picnic on Sunday, Aug. 12, from 10 a.m. to 6 p.m., at North Hollywood park.

Ties for Sale

ON THE *Table*

BILL ELLIS Pres. LERC

DURING the weeks this column has appeared in the *Star*, I have failed to tell you of one particular department of the LERC . . . about which little is generally known.

The Maintenance Department, headed by George Stokes, is one of the busiest service units here at Lockheed. General maintenance and repairs fall under maintenance jurisdiction. The work-load is heavy and I would like to offer a suggestion whereby we can help . . . and help our canteen personnel, too.

Our canteen areas, located in areas at the mercy of the sun, have grey-painted tables. The covered areas have white tables. Both are a big problem when it comes to keeping them neat and new-looking. This is particularly true when one sits on a table with his feet scuffing another. The next time you see this condition, remind the offender that paint is still costly. You pay for it when you patronize the LERC Commissary. Actually, this is a little point but little points count.

Another point involves cleaning up the areas. If each of us will clean up his own paper dishes and put them in the nearby disposal can, we can take a large work-load from the shoulders of our staff and, at the same time, help keep ready for our fellow employes eating at a different lunch period.

Charles Birgy, manager of the Commissary division, points out another problem: This one relative to cafeterias. Sometimes it seems difficult to find a place to sit. All tables are occupied. Next time you are confronted with this situation, find a table not fully occupied, introduce yourself to the person already there and ask him if he minds your joining him. Such practice will speed you through and, at the same time, you may find a new friend. I know I have made some very interesting friendships through these lunch period meetings. Why not give it a try?

Industrial feeding, a wartime necessity, doubtless will exist after the war. We, here at Lockheed, have a well established, efficient employe operation. I feel certain all will be proud and pleased to contribute to increased efficiency.

SWINGERS BEAT OFFICE GANG 2-1

Score Big Upset in Ball Game

Scoring one of the most startling upsets in interdepartmental softball annals, the ➡ Swingers, captained by Nick Puglizvich, toppled the Office Gang under John Schlueter by a score of 2 to 1 last Sunday.

Odds on favorites, the Office Gang had steamrollered through a tough schedule, meeting and defeating all comers among the more than 60 softball teams in the day shift leagues, while the Swingers competed against 12 teams, winning the swing shift division of the interdepartmental softball league and the chance of playing against the winner of the day leagues.

In the semifinals the Office Gang won the first round game of the 1945 season by defeating the NLSC Fighters by a score of 4 to 0.

Batteries Given

Batteries for the Office Gang were Morris and Cannon, pitchers; Bernie Beckner, catcher. Batteries for the Fighters were Perea pitching; Conway catching.

The Inspection P-38's knocked the Shooting Stars out of the championship play-offs by a score of 5 to 1. The Shooting Stars scored in the first inning when Lincoln walked and Saxe collected the only hit for his team in the ball game when he doubled to center field scoring Lincoln.

The Inspection boys scored three runs in the first inning when Jim Schilling, lead-off man, started the fireworks by hitting a home run.

The P-38's, champions of plant B-6 managed by Leo Dandurand, after trailing by a score of 3 to 1 at the end of the second inning came from behind and pulled the game out of the fire by scoring one run in the third and put on a hitting spree in the fifth inning to tally four runs to win the ball game 6 to 3 over Dept. 21-24. Bob Woodbury started pitching for the P-38 squad but was relieved in the third inning by Joe Stein who held the Dept. 21-24 boys hitless for the remainder of the game.

Only Game

In the only game of the first round played at the Glenoaks Playground on Monday July 30, manager Cople's OP's downed the stubborn NLSC team captained by Jack Walker by a score of 4 to 2. The Navy boys, first to bat in the ball game scored one run in the first inning and Cople's aggregation tied it up at the end of the first 1 and 1. Both teams were scoreless until the last half of the sixth inning when the OP's accounted for three runs on four well placed hits.

Nick Puglizvich's Swingers met and defeated the Mixmasters captained by Larry Nolen from NLSC in a shutout game by a score of 4 to 0. Nick, pitching for the Swingers, allowed the Navy boys only two hits for the seven stanzas striking out six men.

Pitcher Watson of the Navy found himself in trouble at the start of the ball game when he walked Max Greenberg and four consecutive hits by Gilmore, Bagentoes, Phillips and Gardner scored the only four runs of the ball game.

The Swingers earned the right to meet the winner of the Office Gang vs the P-38's on Sunday, August 5th at Glenoaks Playground, 11:00 a.m., for the championship of Lockheed Aircraft.

Cigarettes Will Be Available

CIGARETTE ration No. 4 becomes valid Aug. 16, and like past issues, will be good for two packages of cigarettes. No. 4 will be valid from Aug. 16 to 25 at the "A" and "B" cigar counters in the two cafeterias.

Cigarette booths at Gate 3, A-1, and Gate 7, B-1, will be open only three days for the No. 4 issue. These booths were open five days on rations 1, 2 and 3, however, LERC officials have determined that three days will be sufficient.

Employes are urged to have change ready in order to facilitate the movement through the lines.

Frank Davis Jim Arbogast Capt. Nick Puglizvich

ANNOUNCE WINTER PLANS FOR BOWLING

1945-46 Bowling League schedules have been set to begin Sept. 15, according to an announcement made last night by LERC's athletic department. The statement followed a meeting of the bowling committee, headed by Stan Cardinet.

Scratch leagues are established in the following brackets: 875, 850, 825 and 800 according to Jim Arbogast, athletic director. The usual handicap leagues will be set up, he said, under the LERC athletic program.

All LERC bowling leagues will start Sept. 15, so it is imperative that all team entries be made as soon as possible, Arbogast continued. Entry blanks may be obtained by calling Jim Arbogast, 6-1901, after Monday, Aug. 13.

Lightnings Win Again

During the past week's play, the day shift Lightnings, Lockheed's top softball team, ran its score to 21 straight victories by beating Carnation Milk Company in the Los Angeles league and the Santa Barbara Candy Kids.

The Lightnings topped Carnation 11 to 1 and Santa Barbara 8 to 2. The Santa Barbara game was an exhibition game. The victory over Carnation virtually cinches the title for the Lightnings.

NIGHTERS TAKE TOP NINE 3-2

Lockheed's swing shift Lightnings, captained by Nick Puglizvich, knocked over the North American softball team, currently leading the Southern California Aircraft swing shift league, at Rancho Playground, Tuesday. July 31, by a score of 3 to 2.

Pitcher Leo Duran allowed the North American Fighters only 8 well scattered hits and 2 runs. The outstanding field play of "Antelope" Don Phillips at short center robbed the Fighters of 6 consecutive hits. His agility in covering the 6 balls hit by the Fighters and his one handed catches brought the fans to their feet on several occasions.

This victory moves the Lightnings in undisputed third place and puts them in the play-offs for the swing shift aircraft championship.

LODESTARS PURCHASED FOR TACA AIR ROUTES

Fast-stepping TACA Airways announced yesterday a notable airplane utilization record and the acquisition of eight additional Lodestars for use in Latin America and routes to Mexico City and Miami.

John M. Lockhart, executive vice president, said first of the new ships will probably start service this summer. At the same time he reported Electras and Model 14's had racked up a record 300 per cent better than non-Lockheed ships of the airline.

Replacing tri-motor Fords, two of the newly acquired Lodestars will carry cargo to the Neptune and La Luz mines in Nicaragua, Lockhart said. The others will carry passengers, express and air freight, permitting "faster and more frequent schedules both locally and internationally."

Contracts Cited

New TACA contracts with the Nicaragua mines will run five years. Both mines were accessible only by TACA, which serviced them since they were reopened in 1936, carrying more than 70,000,000 lbs. of air freight to date. Equipment, supplies and personnel, including a spectacular cargo of several 64-ton Bucyrus electric shovels were transported by air.

Thirty pieces of equipment in excess of 5000 pounds each, including sedans and trucks were flown in to the mines in addition to the giant shovels.

The mines were originally discovered by the Indians centuries ago and then rediscovered by the Conquistadores. Both mines were worked sporadically over the years but finally closed down 25 years ago because operations could no longer be conducted on a profitable basis due to their inaccessibility and the consequent transportation problem, that is, until TACA came in with air transportation as the answer to the problem.

Largest Mines

The mines which are primarily gold producers are among the largest of their kind in the world. Each mine employs 3000 people.

Two 4000-foot paved runways are being constructed at each of the mines to accommodate Lockheed Lodestars.

TACA has recently renewed its aviation contract in Honduras for a 10-year period and is in process of doubling its facilities in San Jose and Costa Rica, according to the announcement.

Lockheed Lodestar

Nation Mourns Untimely Loss Of Hero Flier

(Continued from Page 2)

heed folk followed Bong's career with avid and personal interest. They thrilled to his romance with Marjorie Ann Vattendahl, boyhood sweetheart whom he married last February . . . they sympathized with him in his house-hunting attempts here and they spoke with pride of his new assignment with the Army Air Forces group.

Some 500 Hours

Major Bong's log showed 500 hours of blazing combat against the little monkeys of Nippon. Returning from the Pacific theater last year to teach tricks to neophytes at gunnery schools, he remarked: "I guess they don't want to kill me off."

Topping the 26 war decorations held by the young major was the Congressional Medal of Honor, highest award in the hand of a nation. At the funeral in his home town were flowers and condolences from remote parts of the world and all ranks of military and civilian life.

The service was held at 2 p.m., Wednesday, in the Dann Funeral Home of Poplar.

Returned Home

Major Bong's body left Long Beach for Wisconsin, Tuesday night, on a plane ordered by Gen. H. H. Arnold, and piloted by Col. K. C. McGregor, commanding officer of the Sixth Ferrying Group, ATC. On the same plane were Mrs. Bong, her brother, Jerome Vattendahl; a personal friend, Mrs. Clarence Toy, and Maj. Earle Kingsley, official escort.

Besides his widow, Major Bong is survived by his parents, Mr. and Mrs. Carl Bong.

FISHER TELLS AIR POTENTIAL

(Continued from Page 2)

per cent above the level of United States domestic airline service. However, efforts are being made to increase and improve intermediate airfields and ground facilities, and to assemble and make available accurate maps and route information, and to reduce expenses, fees, and permits for international flying," continued Fisher.

Lockheed Electras and Lockheed Lodestars are flown on principal airlines of most of the countries. The low population density is reflected in number of miles flown and in passenger traffic, which is considerably less than United States domestic airlines, but cargo transport exceeds U. S. airlines. It seems that the ideal plane for South American use is a combination cargo-passenger plane with low wing loading for operation out of high-altitude fields with short runways, according to Fisher.

Training to Be Resumed

Tentative plans for resumption of tuition-free vocational training of Lockheed employes in public schools were announced last night.

Preliminary to the start of courses in the fall, questionnaires are being circulated which prospective students are asked to fill out. Suggested courses and schools where they may be given are listed which employes are asked to check for preference.

Questionnaires may be obtained from department heads or the training department office in room 323 of Bldg. 102 at Factory B-1, where they should be returned as early as possible. Phone inquiries will be handled at Ext. 6-2676.

HIGH RANKING VISITORS HERE

Dr. Fernando Lobo, minister-counselor of the Brazilian embassy in Washington, accompanied by Col. John Gillett, Peter Beasleay, and Maj. Leonard Geninsp visited Lockheed this week.

Another distinguished visitor was Albert Dodero, president of Compania Argentina de Navigacion Dodero.

EX-EMPLOYE IS KILLED ABROAD

Word has been received by Mrs. Eugene Atwell of Dept. 72-25, that her husband, private first class in the 161st Infantry, was killed in action near Putlan, on the Island of Luzon, in the Philippines.

Private Atwell was a former Lockheed employe in Dept. 24, Experimental.

HIGH RECORD IS SET FOR SHIPS

Handicapped by tropical heat, dust storms, and the ever-present threat of hostile action, crew chiefs and mechanics of the 13th Air Force "Dirty Dozen" Squadron kept 92 per cent of P-38 Lightning fighters in flying condition at all times, in one of the busiest months of the war.

Is it Here?

THESE classified advertisements in the *Star* are provided for employes without charge. If you want to buy, sell, trade, or find or return lost articles, obtain Form 4929 from your department clerk, the stationery store, or employe service office. Mail the advertisement to the *Lockheed Star,* Room 244, Bldg. 1-A, Plant B-1.

WANTED

ELECTRIC fan, any kind. CH. 8-8115.
FORD, '41 club coupe. CH. 8-4745.
HOUSE, West Adams district, 3-bedroom; unfurnished. Extension 6-2273.
RIDE to Pico and Ocean, Santa Monica, A-1, swing. 246 Bicknell, Santa Monica.
BROWN English riding boots, 9C; 2 pair breeches, size 36-38; sell or trade. GR. 5798 after 6.
RECENT back issue of "Life" for hospital patient. CH. 6-8835.
UNFURNISHED house to rent, mother and son, adults. ST. 5-0448.
TO rent 2-bedroom house or apartment, furnished or unfurnished. GR. 5964.
SIDEWALK bicycle, 2-wheel; exchange or sell child's 2-ladder fire engine, tricycle. OL. 6181.
WASHING machine. NO. 5030.
ELECTRIC heating pad. HI. 3044.
CHEVROLET, '41 or '42 club coupe or station wagon. Priv. party. HI. 4947 Sunday or after 4:15.
TO rent 2-bedrm. house, furn. or unfurn. Urgently needed. References. FA. 1075.
NEWLY married couple urgently need furn. or unfurn. house or apt. OL. 1056.
FURN. apt. vicinity Glendale for Navy man and wife. M. W. Crout, 18-04, B-1.
TRICYCLE for child 3-5 years, good condition. CI. 2-3070.
CASH reward info leading to rental sgle. or dbl. apt. Hllywd., Bev. Hills. Ext. 8-1719, Schlacks.
TWO business women want furn. apt. or small house. CL. 6-7057.
LIGHT deer rifle or .30-.30, and Spencer .30-calibre shells. CH. 8-0274.
GIRLS to play guitar and bass fiddle in girl orchestra. WY. 8212.
SAVAGE rifle, .250-3000, 8c ammunition. FE. 4264.
TO buy or rent desert auto cooler. CH. 6-9293.
AUTOMOBILE, Olds, Buick or Chev., '35 to '38, must be good mechanical condition. GR. 4323 after 6.
TO rent furn. or unfurn. house or apt. Responsible employed couple and child. 9397½ San Fernando Road, Roscoe.
RIDE to Unit 58, near A-2, 8 a.m. shift. 813 Euclid, Los Angeles. AN. 2-4310.
WASHING machine, pay top price. 7409 Farmdale, North Hollywood.
SET Ford wheels, 16", 17" or 19". CH. 5-2477.
TRANSPORTATION for 2 to Oregon about August 12. CL. 6-3512.
YOUTH bed with innerspring mattress. CI. 3-5402.
DUMBBELL set with extra plates, prefer revolving type. HE. 1087.
LATE model car, '39 to '41, good condition, good tires. AN. 1-4440.
OUTBOARD motor to rent, Aug. 13-27, under 3-h.p. preferred. RO. 2428.
SIMMONS Beautyrest mattress and box springs, good conditions. SY. 2-7307.
PROJECTOR, 8-mm., perf. Bell & Howell or equivalent. Cash. CL. 6-8978.

FOR SALE

MISCELLANEOUS

SHOES, woman's white Spectators, 5½AA; man's brown loafers, 8½B; black oxfords, 9B. SU. 1-7601.
SMALL house trailer, sleeps 2, good condition. 3316 Andrita, Los Angeles 41.
MATTRESS, dble. innerspring, box spring, legs attached. CH. 8-1811 after 4:30.
BAUSCH & Lomb binoculars, 6x30, perfect for racing or game. HE. 4644.
COLLIES, few choice available now. 1446 Lakeshore, Los Angeles. FI. 4507.

Is it Here?

FOR SALE

MISCELLANEOUS (Cont.)

PICO-Robertson, 10-rm. duplex, newly painted. Will vacate upper. CR. 5-1386.
FURNISHED home in Burbank. Immediate occupancy. CH. 8-0660, 7 to 8 p.m.
GOLF bags and clubs, $15. Apt. 6, NO. 9251 after 6 p.m.
COLT .38 Detective special, like new. CH. 8-2905.
RIDING boots, lady's, English, size 5, like new, reasonable. CH. 8-3524.
MAHOGANY dresser, dressing table, chair; Hollywood bed, book case, open walnut. SU. 1-3095.
CORNET, Bach Stradivarius, in excellent condition, like new. HI. 4463.
CHICKEN fryers, 8 weeks old; two battery brooders. 10241 La Tuna, Canyon Road, Roscoe. CH. 7-8231.
COCKER, 5 months old, black male; mixed pup. Reasonable. CI. 2-5338.
HOLLYWOOD bed, innerspring mattress, youth's bed, good condition. CI. 1-6411.
STUCCO, 5 yrs. old, 2 bdrms., lg. den, 15 orange trees. 1075 Huntington, S. Fern.
HOUSE, 2-bedroom, with house in rear; double garage. CI. 1-6135.
.22 H. & R. Sportsman revolver. HE. 2807.
USED tennis racket, good condition, reasonable. NO. 1-1366, 10 to 3 p.m.
BABY'S Taylor-Tot, rubber tires, like new. AN. 2-5644.
SLIDE rule, K. & E., with magnifier, in leather case, very good. AT. 1-3445.
COMPLETE industrial management course, La Salle Extension Univ. SU. 2-5978.
GOLF bag, all leather, $15; 2-pc. upholstered liv. rm. set, $45. CI. 2-4912.
REVERSIBLE 100% wool carpet and pad, 14x20 and 7x9, and runner. HE. 1742.
SUNBEAM coffee maker, Pflueger 400-yard deep sea reel. CI. 3-4944, eves.
MAN'S bicycle, photographic enlarger and equipment. CR. 5-3516.
ENGLISH setter shooting puppies, pedigreed, registered. ST. 4-0178 after 4 p.m.
ALL-metal, prewar Coolerator, 50-lb. capacity, $50. SY. 4-7566.
B-FLAT tenor saxophone, "Buffet," good cond., $100. DR. 0020 bet. 5 & 8 p.m.
SIX rooms furniture and elec. appliances. 4613 Cleland, L. A. 42. CI. 3-4645.
DINETTE set, table, 4 chairs, maple finish. CH. 8-2608.
SHOE roller skates, wooden wheels, size 3. 4 dining room chairs, table. CH. 8-9739.
MAN'S watch, Geneva, 17-jewel, waterproof, shockproof, gd. cond. CI. 1-5276.
PIANO. Bush & Gerts, upright, solid mahogany. CI. 2-0558.
SLACKS, brown gabardine, size 42, practically new; good leather belt. AL. 2730.
PINT Stanley stainless steel thermos and steel lunch bucket. CH. 8-8115.
TECHNICAL shop books, 4; slide rule. GL. 0065.
RUGS, 17x11; 3 room-size rugs. CA. 1-4429 before 2 p.m.
BABY scales, 30 lbs. capacity, practically new, all-metal, prewar. PL. 2-8147.
LAWNMOWER, garden tools. UNion 1-3890.
ELECTRIC R.C.A. record player. CI. 1-7847 after 4:30 p.m.
BICYCLE, boy's; hi-oven gas range, good cond. 1816 Val Preda, Brbk., across B-1.
JARS for fruit canning, 1 and 2-qt. canning sizes; alum. ktchnwre. NO. 9834.
RUG, 9x15, like new. 1800 N. Naomi, Burbank.
COFFEE table, oval walnut, perfect condition. SU. 2-9290.
SHAVEMASTER, electric, perfect running order. 1800 N. Naomi, Burbank.
STUDIO couch, prewar, in good condition, also covers. HI. 1672 after 4.
MANGLE, electric. CL. 6-6396.
ELECTRIC console sewing machine, ex. cond., reas. 1124-B Winchester Ave., Glendale, after 5.
HOUSE, lot 50'x140', near transp., by owner, leaving. 9229 Ralston, Roscoe.
GUITAR. in good condition. GR. 5002.
TWO-burner Coleman camp stove, electric fan, cooking utensils. SU. 1-2514.
TAYLOR-Tot, excellent cond. CI. 2-6538.
BLACK dress suit, red velveteen collar, trimmed with Persian lamb, size 16. Magnin. AL. 0951.

Is it Here?

FOR SALE

MISCELLANEOUS (Cont.)

PROFITABLE income prop., good cond., 4 apts., furn. or unfurn. SU. 1-4857.
DAVENPORT and chair, reasonable. CH. 8-3247 or CH. 6-4723 after 5.
BUGGY, good condition, real bargain. RO. 4621. 2832 Somerset Dr.
MAUSER, big game rifle, 8x60-mm., 50 shells, cowhide case, new. ARiz. 9-2631.
AUTO. pistol, .32, some ammunition, sell or trade for .22 rifle. STate 5-2589.
BLEACH walnut 5-pc. bedrm. set, box springs, matt., less than year old. 6556 Bellaire, North Hollywood.
CONN trombone, H-H ballroom type, in excellent condition. CH. 8-3787.
FURNITURE, drapes, garden tools, dog-house. 1838 N. Maple, Burbank.
FREE to good home, 3 half Persian kittens, ex. pets, housebroken. 246 E. Tujunga after 5 p.m.
HAMILTON watch, railroad special, 21-jewel. CI. 7-1610 after 5:30 p.m.
FOUR-piece bedroom set. 1238 Kenwood, Burbank.
COMP. set service mechanic's tools, incl. Craftsman roll-away, reas. FI. 7234.
MAN'S wrist watch with gold-filled exp. bracelet, modern, reas. NO. 2-6163.
METAL cut film developing hangars, 3¼x4¼. GL. 6993.
PROJECTION screen, 30x40, glass bead, perfect condition. CH. 6-8387.
MICROPHONE, Electro voice No. 275, new, with stand. HE. 8775, evenings.
SAILBOAT, registered Star class, with trailer, excellent cond. HE. 8775, eves.

VEHICLES

FORD, '34 coupe, under ceiling. SU. 2-8758 after 6.
OLDSMOBILE, '35 de luxe sedan, ex. mech. condition, good tires. OL. 7184.
WILLYS 77 de luxe sedan, '35. CH. 8-1247.
MODEL A Ford coupe, '28, good condition, excellent tires. GR. 8971.

FOR RENT

MOUNTAIN cabin, Crestline, San Bernardino Mountains. CH. 8-8723.
FRONT bedrm., priv. entrance, 10 min. to B-1, man only. 2015 Parish Pl., after 4.

EXCHANGE

MOTORCYCLE, Harley-Davidson, shaft drive, '42, for an older motor. JE. 5478.
TRICYCLE, 18", sell or trade for 14"; also 10" tricycle, sell or trade for 14". NO. 1-3792.
STAMPS for collections, U. S., foreign; golf set for sale. CR. 5-1776.

LOST

PARKER pen, July 26, Bldg. 80, black-white, chrome. Rew. Larry Strong, SY. 7-6236.
BROWN purse, small, Gov. papers, imp. M. English, 1721 Maple, Burbank.
SHAEFFER lifetime red-brown pencil, gold band. H. Townsend, 53-70, B-1.

THE LOCKHEED Star
OFFICIAL PUBLICATION OF THE LOCKHEED AIRCRAFT CORPORATION

Issued each Friday for the employes of Lockheed Aircraft Corporation. The *Star* is the official publication of the company. Communications should be addressed to the Editor, *Lockheed Star* Unit, Lockheed Aircraft Corporation, Burbank, California.

No unsolicited manuscripts or pictures will be returned and the *Star* cannot be responsible for other than requested articles or photos.

KENNETH CRIST, Editor
J. H. Prescott, Associate Editor
Marshall Atwell, Staff Artist
Barbara Sewald, News

THE LOCKHEED
Star
OFFICIAL PUBLICATION OF THE LOCKHEED AIRCRAFT CORPORATION
PLUMB LINE
ATTACH JACK PAD
STORY, PAGE 3

LOCKHEED FOLKS SEE BIG EVENTS

Globe-trotting field representatives of Lockheed's Customers' Service Division made news this week with goings and comings and letters from the earth's far corners.

The war's end was glad news, but for the most part work went on as usual, according to much of the post V-J Day mail received by Margaret Morris, Lockheed's official letter writer.

★ ★ ★

Tops for nonchalance was reported by William Fossum in his Aug. 21 note dated "Somewhere in India."

Hearing the radio news of surrender, Bill walked out to the flight line of the AAF base where he was stationed and shouted, "Boys, the war is over!"

An Air Force mechanic straightened up from the innards of a P-38 and remarked, "Yeh? Well, how about giving us some dope on how to take out this fuel pump?" And it wasn't just an act, Bill insisted.

★ ★ ★

Less blase, however, were the boys on Okinawa where William Corrao has been helping the Navy take care of PV's. Corrao writes that they shot off all the ack-ack they could lay hands on in addition to giving other weapons a workout. As reported in the press, there were casualties.

"Nevertheless," said Bill, "the war's end only intensified the main topic of conversation about discharge points and the chances of getting home."

★ ★ ★

A similar attitude was reported by Ed Cruz, now on his way home after a long stretch in India. In his last letter he wrote: "Celebrating here doesn't seem important. Most of the boys say, 'Let's get home and do our celebrating when we get there.' "

★ ★ ★

Wally Fryer, homeward-bound from Burma writes that the best thing he could say of the place where he was stationed is the weather, which reminded him of California—warm days and cool, restful nights.

★ ★ ★

George Pentland, recently returned from work with the 13th Air Force, reported seeing the Lockheed PV-1 bearing a scroll with 800 names of the men and women who helped build the ship.

Pentland said the rugged Ventura which he saw at a Philippine base had logged a lot of hours and rolled up a great record for the Navy.

★ ★ ★

Dan Schmittner, in Manila since March, saw the first Jap peace envoys arrive. "Everyone was very quiet," he wrote. "I was too far away to hear what was said but I could see things were very businesslike."

As of Sept. 5 there were 23 field representatives outside of continental United States. Of these there were one each in South America and Alaska, three each in the Mid-Pacific, South Pacific and C.B.I. theaters and one in Panama. Eight were homeward bound.

Make-Believe Land

Down It Comes

'NEVER, NEVER LAND' IS GONE, BUT SECRET IS KEPT FOR NEXT WAR

"Never, Never Land" that once was Lockheed from the air is no more. It vanished with removal of the camouflage which had made this part of the San Fernando Valley look to pilots like grain fields and dusty country roads.

The job was done by the Burkett Fence Co. under contract to the U.S. government. Today workmen are carting away last loads of the dismantled material.

Took Three Months

It has taken three months to remove the overhead netting, burlap and wood bungalows, chicken wire and feather trees, and other overhead foliage which protected this war-vital industry from prying enemy eyes during the past three years.

The means by which camouflage experts made their materials so realistic that new pilots often found it difficult to locate the field must remain secret in the interest of future wartime security, officials said.

Completion of the work is being held up momentarily by the pending appointment of a joint survey committee whose duty it will be to determine damage to Lockheed property and funds needed to restore it. This committee will consist of a representative of the real estate division of the USED, a member from the United States District Engineer's office, and a Lockheed representative. This cost will be in addition to the $236,200 already spent.

Shelters to Go

Yet to be removed are some 315 personnel bomb shelters weighing 140 tons apiece, blackout paint and glass splinter protection, as well as "dead men" concrete anchorage blocks, imbedded timbers, etc.

Part of the chicken wire and heavy timbers were salvaged by the contractors and sold. Monies realized from such sales are to be deducted from the final cost of the removal project, officials said.

Of a crew of approximately fifty workmen engaged in both erecting and dismantling the camouflage only one casualty occurred. This happened when Tracy C. Ming, San Gabriel, plunged to his death from a catwalk at LAT in June of this year.

Worked Together

Both Lockheed and Army personnel were employed in erection of the camouflage originally.

The government has up to six months pending cessation of hostilities to restore the company property to its former state, according to George A. Hart, chief of the management and disposal section of the USED.

LOST ITEMS SEEK LOCKHEED OWNERS

Lockheed employes missing one glove, one earring, umbrellas, purses, combs, or the variety of trinkets that are often lost, may retrieve some of them at the Employe Service lost and found desks at Plant B-6, B-1, A-1, and A-2, according to Dale Cosgray of the Employe Service department.

A large number of lost and found articles remain unclaimed. Any employe who has lost personal property is urged to contact Employe Service.

To Halt Proposals

The Material Branch announced last night that effective Sept. 21, 1945, all operating procedures and systems of the Material Branch will be closed to employe proposals for improvement. This moratorium affects all departments of the Material Branch and will continue through Dec. 31, 1945.

Jack Hatton

Appoint Hatton To State Board

Governor Earl Warren this week appointed Jack F. Hatton, Lockheed's chief safety engineer, a member of the newly created five-man California State Industrial Safety Board.

This safety board will adopt all general safety orders to be enforced by the California State Division of Industrial Safety as well as act as advisors to the State Safety Division.

Publication Wins Award of Citation

The National Council of Industrial Editors announced this week the award of a citation to the *Lockheed Log* as a 1945 leader in its classification because of its "excellence in appearance, editorial qualities and appropriateness to purpose."

The magazine, edited by Roy L. Stevens of Lockheed's Sales Promotion department and under the art direction of Arthur J. Halverson, is Lockheed's external house organ and is distributed throughout the world to airline and business executives.

ARMY CHIEF URGES FUTURE AIR FORCE

Lt. Gen. Harold L. George, chief of the Army Transport command, believes approximately 5000 transport aircraft will be required jointly for civilian and military needs to keep this country adequately prepared for any future war.

PRODUCTION RECORD FOR NLSC NOTED

One completed plane modification for every two workmen employed is the remarkable record of the Navy-Lockheed Service Center, reported last week.

Since the inception of NLSC, with an average of only 1450 employes, 724 aircraft were modified, completed, and delivered to the Navy. This record received special commendation from both the Navy and Lockheed. The figure included those planes delivered up to September 7, 1945, and was released only upon the relaxing of security regulations.

This amazing total included eight different types of craft. During this same period of time, buildings were being constructed, personnel hired and a smooth working organization set up.

Will Restore Levels

Since V-J Day, Navy-Lockheed production has of necessity fallen below par. This has been due to the postwar victory holidays, personnel turnover, and general planning and scheduling readjustments. With personnel problems gradually smoothing out of their own accord, expected production levels will soon be restored, Reagan Stunkel, Lockheed's Sales and Service manager, said.

Officials in charge of the base express pride in the center's wartime achievements and are now putting plans into operation to maintain it at fullest efficiency for peacetime operations.

TELL DANGER OF SOUVENIRS FROM ABROAD

Apprehension of a Lockheed employe polishing a live 50-caliber machine gun cartridge on his work bench brought a sharp warning this week from Plant Protection officials.

The shell, clamped in a vise, might easily have exploded while the employe filed it, officials pointed out, and the bullet could have caused an injury or fatality. The employe said he was polishing it for an ornament without realizing the risk involved.

All Kinds

All sorts of live ammunition, Plant Protection warned, have been sent back from war fronts. Sometimes these articles are abandoned in mail boxes or open lots if they are not actually delivered or brought into the home.

Such articles are dangerous, Plant Protection stressed, and should be cleared through the police department. It was directed that such "souvenirs" should not be brought to Lockheed.

Expand L.A.T. Facilities

The Lockheed Air Terminal coffee shop is expanding its facilities. A new walk-in refrigerator and employes' dining room is being built adjacent to the kitchen. It will occupy a space near the entrance to the Administration building opposite the parking lot.

BUSINESS VIEWS NEW FRONTIERS

ALERT FIRMS PURCHASE RECONVERTED LODESTARS

Trade horizons are being moved from the future into the realm of today by American business, both large and small, if present trends in the purchase of air- → craft are an indication. One of the country's oldest and conservative banking firms is listed alongside newcomers in other fields as purchasers of Lockheed Lodestars with which to carry on their future business.

The Manufacturers' Trust Co. of New York, which has loaned many millions of dollars for purchase of airplanes and their components, acquired its first airplane recently—from Lockheed. In contrast, a young firm in Canada purchased a Lodestar to haul fish. Others were bought by such prominent companies as General Motors Corporation, TACA airlines of Honduras, and *Life* and *Time* magazines.

Hours Mean Dollars

Aircraft purchased were those reconverted from military use, it was announced last night by Lockheed's Domestic Sales department. Many of the purchasers are obtaining their first aircraft for business use, typifying the modern trend where hours saved can mean thousands of dollars.

Interiors of the newly converted Lodestars are many and varied, depending upon intended use. Conversions are being made for executive-type ships, personal transports, standard airliners and cargo carriers.

List Purchasers

Included among recent Lodestar purchasers are: Air Cargo Transport Association of New York, Air France, Armstrong Cork Company, Bendix Radio Division, Baltimore; Byrd-Frost Air Transport Co., Dallas; Canadian Pacific Air Lines, Ltd., Montreal; Jacqueline Cochran, Colombian Petroleum Company, Cucuta, Colombia; Consolidated-Vultee Aircraft Corp., San Diego; Continental Oil Company, Ponca

(*Continued on Page 6*)

L. M. Bach

Bach Directs Victory Fund

Victory Fund officials announced last night the appointment of L. M. Bach, Lockheed vice president in charge of manufacturing, as chairman of the industrial division of the Burbank Victory War Fund campaign, and Armand J. Bas, director of Industrial Relations for Aieron Mfg. Co., as co-chairman.

The Victory campaign of the Burbank Community War Fund opens Monday night when Bach will be host at a dinner given in honor of the presidents and general managers of all Burbank industries at the Sky Room, Lockheed Air Terminal.

Higher Goal

Goal of the campaign is $123,500, an increase of $4000 for the Burbank area over last year's goal. Sixteen war relief agencies, members of the National War Fund, and 15 home-front agencies will benefit from the funds of this year's campaign.

Funds received in the current campaign will carry operation of the agency to January, 1947, at which time the War Fund agency will be liquidated, Burbank Victory Fund officials stated.

Shoots Hole in One On Wilson No. Three

Harold F. Blackmore, formerly with the training department of Plant B-7, scored a hole in one at the Griffith Park Wilson course in a foursome played last Saturday.

The hole in one was made on hole No. 3, a 198-yard, three-par hole, and was made with a brassie.

Blackmore's total score was 83. Other members of the foursome were Carlton Pederson, Joe Garagliano, and Roger Baldwin.

Cover

JOURNEY from a Star shows Lockheed pilot, Nick Nicholson, recording flight data after a substratosphere journey in a P-80 Shooting Star. Photo by Lockheed photographer Larry Larivee.

In Big Demand

Canadians Watch Constellation Make New Northern Speed Record

Proudly displaying her charms before high government and airline officials of Canada, Lockheed's queenly Constellation blasted another speed record this week with a flight of three hours and 33 minutes over the 1064 miles between Winnipeg and Montreal. Figures for the previous record were not immediately obtainable but it was reported the Constellation topped it by a substantial margin.

In the pilot's seat during the flight was Barney Rawson, superintendent of flight operations for Trans-Canada Airways whose current fleet of Lodestars is making air transportation history north of the border.

Arrangements for the demonstration were made by Henri Chappellet, Lockheed's representative in Canada. The big ship was flown north from Burbank by Lockheed test pilots Ray Meskimen and Heinz Wegner.

Other Records

This Canadian record follows closely on the heels of one set by veteran TWA pilots flying their regularly scheduled run between Washington, D.C., and San Francisco in eight hours, 37 minutes, an average speed of 289 mph.

Operating under contract with the Air Transport Command,

(*Continued on Page 7*)

Lt. Col. Langmack

COL. LANGMACK TAKES AAF POST

Assignment of Lt. Col. Charles J. Langmack as Lockheed Army Air Forces plant representative, was announced last night by the Army.

Before coming to Lockheed in 1943, Colonel Langmack was assistant AAF representative at the Boeing plant in Seattle. Previously he was engineering officer at McCord Field, Washington.

Constellation Shines in Service Test, Sets Mark in Round Trip to New York

Continuing the Lockheed Constellation accelerated service test program, Lt. Col. T. W. Rafferty and a special Air Transport Command crew last week piloted a Constellation on a round trip between Burbank and New York, covering the 4960 miles in an elapsed time of 20 hours and 58 minutes.

High-Flying Crew

The eastbound flight was made in 8 hours and 35 minutes while the westbound flight required 9 hours and 51 minutes. Two hours and 18 minutes were spent on the ground at Mitchell Field, New York. The flights were made at less than 50 per cent power. Instrument weather was encountered for four hours on one leg of the trip.

A total of 824 flight hours had been accumulated without overhaul on all of the airplane's four engines prior to the trip, yet Colonel Rafferty reported that all engines functioned perfectly. Although it is customary to remove engines for overhaul at 625 hours, Colonel Rafferty plans to carry these engines up to 1000 hours in a test of their serviceability over extended periods of time.

Flying with Colonel Rafferty on the epochal trip were Major Keith Cantine, pilot; Capt. Don Beeler, copilot; Sgt. Walter Leigh and Sgt. Forrest Smith, flight engineers. They appear, right to left, in that order in the accompanying picture with Colonel Rafferty at the top.

P-80 PLANS GO AHEAD AS MODIFIED

An improved modification of Lockheed's Shooting Star, America's most deadly fighter plane, is now being produced, L. H. Bradley, assistant manager of the P-80 Manufacturing Planning department reported this week.

Added improvements will continue in rapid succession following conferences between the Army and Lockheed officials.

Accelerated production demanded by war urgency having abated somewhat, time allowed now is being well spent in catching up on scheduled modifications, Bradley said. The majority of these are being done with a minimum of changes in the basic structure of the ship, through closest coordination between tooling, material, planning and scheduling. This provides for changes long before the ship bearing the scheduled serial arrives in production.

Special Crews

Highly specialized crews of workmen organized on a functional basis have been set up in production and now are speeding up the program. Thus, an instrument check-out crew can remain with the ship until its work is done instead of having to break the work down into stationized areas.

Southland City Airport Named For Zamperini

They're naming an airport after Lt. Louis Zamperini, former Lockheed spot-welder whose horror experiences of drifting at sea and Jap prison camps thrilled the world last week.

The city of Torrance where he was born and went to high school is planning to name the AAF's Lomita flight strip "Zamperini Airport," according to Grover White, editor of the Torrance *Herald*.

The strip on Pacific Coast highway, Route 101, near the intersection of Hawthorne Boulevard, has been released by the Army, White said, and the city has initiated steps to acquire it as a municipal airport.

Plan Welcome

Meanwhile, plans went forward for a tumultuous welcome to be accorded the native son on his arrival in Torrance, expected any day, White declared. Official word from the War Department that Zamperini is being sent home from the Pacific theater reached the family of the former U.S.C. track star last week. His parents, a brother and two sisters as well as most of Torrance are waiting expectantly.

If he returns by plane, White said, an attempt will be made to have the ship land on the air strip the city hopes to name after the former B-24 bombardier. Arrangements for the welcome program are being made by the Torrance *Herald*.

Night School

Training pays off

by Barbara Sewald

TEACHING agriculture and mechanics in the begir 19th century, Johann Heinrich Pestalozzi, a Swiss, world's first pedagogue to deal with practical : exposed his ideas on training in his book, "How Gertrude Children." Lockheed, realizing the value of practical trair visual aids, work experience, and other educational ch among the first in modern aircraft industry to recognize an organized in-plant training system.

SINCE inception of Lockheed's training program, more s been graduated from professional classes than there are ir sity of California, Columbia, Harvard, Yale and a half of the country's larger universities. More than 152,708 er taken training courses and an additional 556,000 man-hou spent in job-improvement learning.

Functionally, Lockheed's training program has five pl supervised by Carlton Pederson as a part of Industrial Re are grouped as follows: (1) Visual aids, (2) Planning ment, (3) Supervisory training, (4) Area representati Non-supervisory employe training. The visual aids sectio Bill Murray, produces pamphlets, booklets, slide film, ch and illustrations to give trainees visualized materials a breakdowns of complicated procedures.

The planning and development unit works directly wi line supervision. Where additional training is needed, in ing, administration, engineering, or in any Lockheed brar

Supervisory Discussion

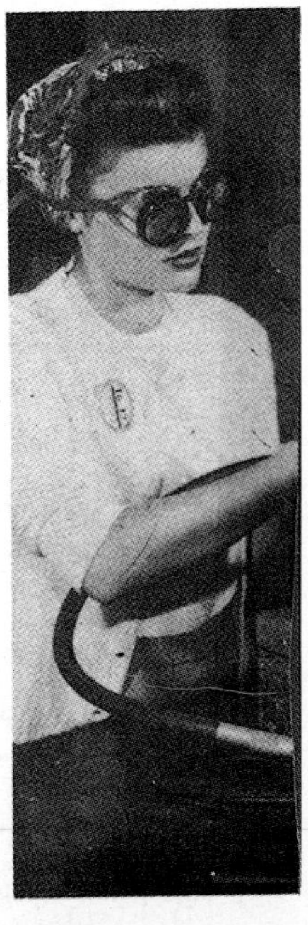

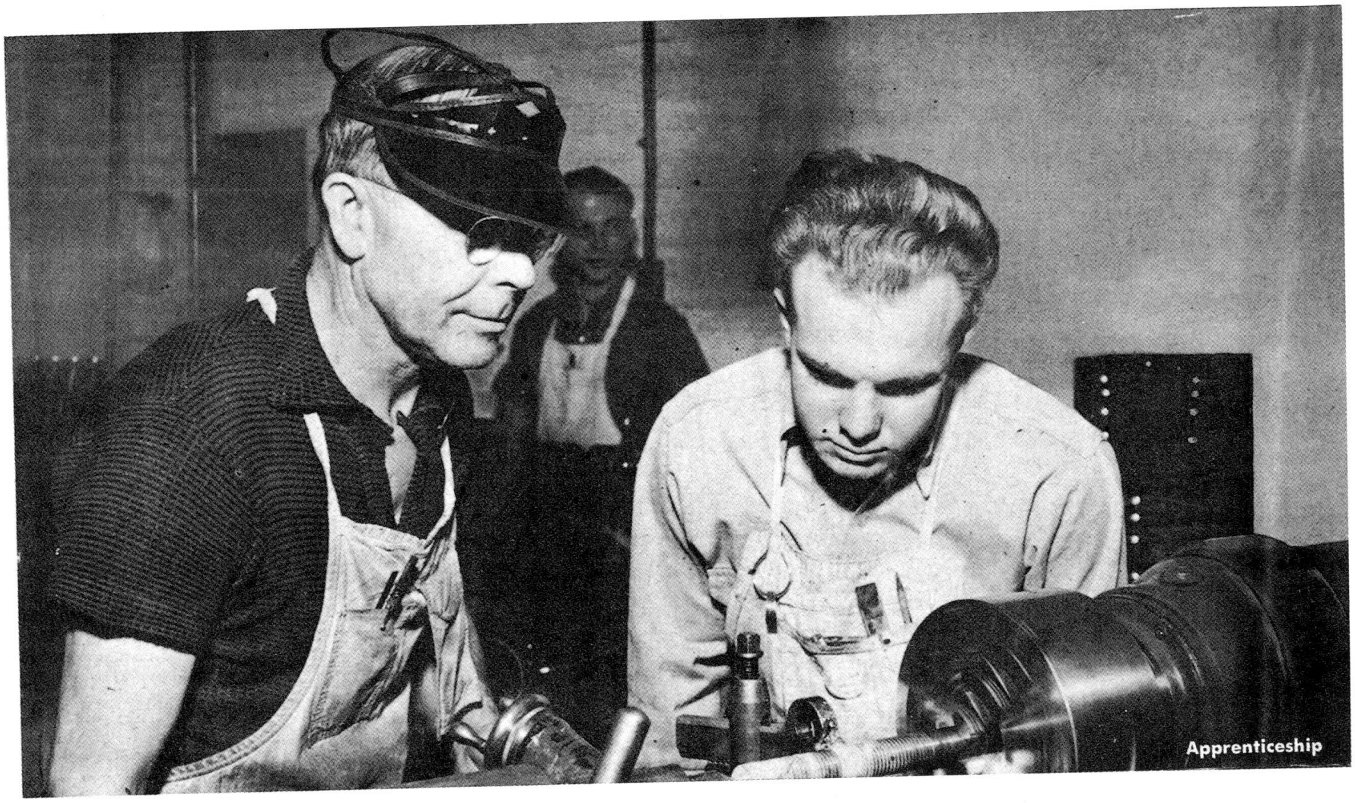
Apprenticeship

of line supervision and the training department meet to develop training program.

Supervisory training, a vital function for smooth industrial operation, is one of the most important phases of the Lockheed training program. Thousands of employes have taken some part of supervisory training. Classes in job instruction have graduated 15,500. Job relations, sponsored by the War Manpower Commission has graduated 2400 students. Work-simplification training has assisted 11,200; labor relations, 5200, and employe rating review, some 5800.

PRODUCTION and cost control instruction has assisted 5600 employes and 4200 studied a course called selection of management personnel. Organization control classes were offered to 1200 employes, while an earlier class in supervisory development gave aid to 15,900.

Three area representatives regularly contact line supervision to determine training needs in the Lockheed organization. They estimate particular corporate needs and coordinate the training program.

Edward Lang is area representative for the Manufacturing office of B-1, for all B plants, and works with Manufacturing Development.

Hatch Farnsworth is area representative for Plant A-2 and the Works Manager's office of Factory A-1.

Joseph Schwarz is area representative for Engineering, Material, Sales and Service, Administration, and the finance branches.

Non-supervisory employe training is arranged for all employes in basic skills, such as welding, or in additional skills, such as an hydraulic specialist. A new production employe is taught how to handle the tools of his trade. At Lockheed, he understands them before he enters actual production as a riveter, driller, welder, or assembler.

BASIC skill training and upgrading instruction has been given to 87,258 employes since the training program began . . . plus an additional training equivalent to 380,000 man-hours. Courses scheduled are similar to those in the present P-80 work center, designed as a transitional training for employes coming in from the discontinued P-38 assembly.

Education coordination with local schools and colleges such as the University of Southern California, University of California at Los Angeles, and California Institute of Technology provided 176,000 man-hours of extension training for Lockheed folk through the program known as ESMWT—Engineering Science and Management War Training.

THESE courses, which ended with the war's close, were developed through cooperation with the training department which requested particular classes to meet specific organization needs. The various schools developed training programs accordingly.

Engineering assistant's training has been given to more than 200 graduate engineers from leading engineering schools. Training courses providing work experience in production and engineering were made available before assignment to Lockheed's technical development department. Lockheed's indentured apprenticeship *(Continued on Page 8)*

Basic Skill

Engineering Knowledge

Ernest Frank

Bob McCrea

New Committeemen Elected by LERC

Bill Ellis, LERC president, invited all Lockheed employes to meet their new officials on the executive committee of the LERC through the columns of the *Star*. Ernest Frank, Dept. 57-44, Plant B-6, was elected treasurer at last month's LERC council meeting. Frank is filling the vacancy created by the resignation of Al Pimsner. Robert McCrea, Dept. 17-57, Plant A-2, was elected a member-at-large on the executive committee to represent A-2 and the outlying plants.

Speakers Meet Every Tuesday

Meeting at 1 o'clock every Tuesday, the Toastmasters are attracting more and more attention from employes wishing to perfect their speaking technique. The group meets in room 4 at the B-1 LERC cafeteria.

A feature of the Toastmasters and one that all of the members strive for is their regular vote for the best speaker of the day from among the group selected to speak at that meeting. Larry Thompson, club president, announces that the Toastmasters will welcome any swing shifters who want to join this active public-speaking group.

Service Groups Ask Assistance

Lockheed's Service Star Women and other LERC-sponsored women's groups are rallying to the call for aid to hospitalized veterans, by opening a drive for materials and articles that are sorely needed. First of the two-point drive is an appeal for men's white handkerchiefs. Lockheed employes are asked to donate as many of these handkerchiefs as they can.

Opal Broderson of the B-1 LERC staff, who is coordinating the drives for the service groups, asks that employes who plan to make donations please wrap the gifts so that they may be kept clean. Large boxes will be placed at the main Lockheed gates and at the cafeterias so that employes may deposit their contributions.

In addition to handkerchiefs, the women report that other materials are needed. These include clean woolens, clean worn or torn sheets and soft linens to be used as malaria 'kerchiefs. This need is great as the 'kerchiefs are used only once and are then thrown away, Mrs. Broderson said.

Clean cotton materials can be made into neck pillows; clean kapok, cotton batting or feathers are used by the service groups to make pillows and cushions. Yarn scraps in any length and color can be used to finish afghan squares.

Rifle Club Forms New Training Class

Bud Kuecher, president of the Pistol and Rifle club, announced today that formation of rifle-training classes is now in progress. New classes will be revised from the old-style pre-induction training and will cover civilian target shooting.

The initial class already in training has become so popular that more classes are being anticipated in the near future.

Interested employes may contact Gordon Stanton, assistant recreation director, Ext. 6-1901, for applications and schedules.

FIRMS PURCHASE ARMY LODESTARS

(Continued from Page 3)

City, Oklahoma; Expreso Aereo Inter-Americano, Habana, Cuba; Fairbanks-Morse Co., Chicago; Foreign Economic Administration, Fleetwings Division of Kaiser Cargo, Inc., Bristol, Pa.; Fruehauf Trailer Company, Detroit, and the General Motors Corporation, Buick Motor Division, Flint, Mich.

Grumman Aircraft Engineering Co. of Long Island, Gulf Oil Corporation, Pittsburgh; Johnson & Johnson, New Brunswick; Lear Avia, Piqua, Ohio; Linas Transcontinentalis de Aereo Transportes SA., Mexico City; Linea Aeropostal Venezola, Caracas, Venezuela; Max Fleischman, Kollsman Aircraft Instruments, Northrup Aircraft Corporation, Page Airways, Rochester, N.Y.; Panair do Brasil, Rio de Janeiro; Pratt & Whitney, East Hartford, Connecticut; Pure Oil Company, Chicago; Reynolds Metal Company, Richmond, Virginia; Sinclair Refining Co., Sky Kraft Paper Corporation, Mobile, Alabama; Square D Company, Detroit; Standard Oil Development, and Superior Oil Co.

Swiftlite Aircraft Corp., Jersey City, N.J.; Texas Co., N.Y.; TWA, TACA airline of Tegucigalpa, Honduras; Warren Petroleum Co., Tulsa, Okla.; Standard Brands, United Nations Relief and Rehabilitation Administration, Washington; Republic Oil Refinery, Pani Airlines, Mexico; Owens-Corning Fiber Glass Company, *Life* and *Time* magazines, Otto Aviation Co., Gannet Company, Rochester, N.Y.; Evening News Publishing Co., Dayton, Ohio; Aero Services, Van Nuys; Ambassador Wm. D. Pauley, and McInnes Products Corporation of Edmonton, Canada.

PRIVATE FLYING CLUB AT NLSC PROVES OUTSTANDING SUCCESS

Increasing interest in private flying has been given impetus by the lifting of wartime restrictions and many Lockheed employes have expressed a desire to form a flying club. One such organization, made up of Lockheed employes, is the Val-Aero Flying Club which has been in successful operation for a number of months.

Val-Aero was formed by Howard Ritchie at Navy-Lockheed Service Center and is incorporated at Van Nuys as a nonprofit organization without capital stock; the purpose of the group is the maintenance and support of educational undertakings, namely, the education and training of its members in the operation of aircraft for pleasure.

Club president is William Walker; Harvey Young, vice president; H. V. Ritchie, secretary-treasurer, and members James Boyce, E. M. Helsabeck, Earnest Corbiel, Donald Johnston, D. O. Wood, James Arthur and Richard Logan, all employed at Navy-Lockheed Service Center.

Members Own Plane

Each of the members of the club advanced ten per cent of the cost of the aircraft which was, in this case, $150.00 per member for their tandem 65-horsepower Aeronica trainer. A trainer, according to Ritchie, founder and secretary of the club, is the ideal airplane for a club, not only because of the comparative ease with which beginners can be instructed in its use but because of the low cost, both initial and upkeep.

After banding together and paying $150.00 each, the members elected club officers and selected a board of directors to handle financial affairs. As to duties, the president is charged with promoting general interest in the organization and appointing committees, the vice president fills in whenever the president is absent and also acts on the board of directors. The secretary-treasurer takes care of dues, flying time and the aircraft logbook, attends to correspondence of the club and sees that the aircraft has its regular C.A.A. 100-hour checks on schedule. In addition to the board of directors, Val-Aero has a regular flying instructor, one of Lockheed's co-pilots, who instructs the beginning flyers and who also serves as air operations officer with the right to ground pilots or plane as he sees fit. This, the club feels, is an important safety check on both personnel and equipment.

Charges Set

Aside from the initial payment for the airplane in which each member owns a tenth interest, the club has worked out a scale of charges which maintains the plane, provides insurance, gasoline, tie-down charges and miscellaneous expenses necessary to maintain a private plane. In this case, the club charges $2.00 an hour for flying time as compared to $8.00 or $11.00 charged by commercial operators. Members, however, are required to sign up for a minimum of four hours flying time each month, payable in advance. Instruction is provided by the instructor at $3.00 per hour.

Costs Explained

The amount charged members for flying time is based on estimated costs per hour. These costs are: 87½c for 3½ gallons of gasoline per hour, 12½c for oil, 40c per hour for estimated engine maintenance and 40c for frame repairs. Added to the amount of 20c per hour for emergency and unexpected contingencies, this makes a total of $2.00 which is flying time charge per hour.

In addition to flying time, each member is charged $5.00 a month for tie-down expenses. This includes hangar space and use of the field, a charge that is made by the airport operators.

Fledglings Fly

That this club is a success is attested by the fact that in July when the club first started, there were only two licensed pilots; six of the members had never flown before. At the present time, only one member of the club has yet to solo. The officers and members of the Val-Aero group will be glad to answer any and all questions regarding their club. Inquiries may be sent direct to them at Navy-Lockheed Service Center or forwarded through the LERC Recreation office at B-1.

C.A.P. Tells Of New Plan

At a special inspection and review held last week for Major Hoyt of the Civil Air Patrol, national headquarters, by the California Fifth Group at the Burbank Recreational Center, Major Hoyt revealed future plans of the C.A.P.

Major Hoyt expressed the gratitude of Gen. H. H. Arnold, Commanding General, Army Air Forces, for the splendid service performed by the C.A.P. during wartime emergency and for the training value to the AAF. It was announced that the Air Power League, composed of the leaders of the aviation industries, has chosen the C.A.P. to be the nucleus for a nationwide organization of air-minded citizens. In particular, the expansion of the Cadet Training Program, which is a part of the C.A.P. activities, will become a more important feature of the organization. For the aid of training courses, the AAF is releasing to C.A.P. considerable surplus materials, and is loaning training airplanes for orientation work.

Lockheed squadrons in the Fifth Group are the A-1, B-1, and B-6 squadrons, which meet every Tuesday and Thursday evenings at the C.A.P. headquarters at 35 E. Magnolia, Burbank. All persons interested in receiving free aviation ground instruction training, and who wish to help the cadet program, are urged to attend a meeting to obtain full particulars for membership.

FORUM HOLDS CREDIT TALKS

Members and friends of the Accounting Forum have been enjoying a series of interesting discussions and lectures of current interest. These forums have been led by men outstanding in the business world, and for the most part, discussions have been on cost control, industrial reports, aspects of cost accounting, the place of the certified public accountant in industry and other such timely topics.

On Wednesday, September 26, Mr. K. R. Naumann will speak on "Federal Credit Unions." All who are interested are invited to attend. Dinner will begin at 5 p.m. at the B-1 LERC cafeteria, after which the meeting will be held.

Lt. John Hedenberg Assigned to ATSC

1st Lt. John W. Hedenberg, 813 W. Burchett St., Glendale, Calif., veteran of 66 combat missions, has been assigned to Headquarters, Air Technical Service Command.

A student of California Institute of Technology, he worked summers at Lockheed Aircraft, before his entry into the service on January 3, 1942.

Aloha Party Set for USO

Hollywood's "Boulevard USO," for the past two and one-half years the scene of operation for Lockheed's USO hostess activities, is about to be closed due to the expiration of the lease on the building at 6551 Hollywood Blvd. The Blue Stars and Penguinettes have given thousands of hours of service to this wartime institution, entertaining servicemen and women in every branch of our armed forces. In recognition of their service, the women of both Lockheed groups are invited to a "swan song" party being given there on Saturday evening, September 29.

The party will be an "aloha" affair, complete with celebrities, a big orchestra, dancing and a special floor show. All the girls who plan to attend are requested to dress in formal or party dresses and are asked to bring two leis.

Completing the week-end activity at the USO on Sunday, there will be an afternoon get-together with a concert, and in the evening, there will be a "goodbye" party with more dancing, more celebrities and a floor show as a climax not only to the evening but to the activities of Hollywood's famous Boulevard USO.

Traffic Preview Brings Optimism

Low-cost Clipper travel for the common man is viewed optimistically by Pan-American Airways after a summer preview of travel on the Horta-Lisbon route. Within two months there were 312 passengers on this route which hardly averages a passenger per trip in the winter. The heavy travel permitted special summer fares well below the cost of first-class steamer passage and within $4 of second-class rates.

UNITED EXPANDS

More than half a million dollars is being spent by United Airlines in modernizing and enlarging its ticket offices to care for anticipated air travel increases in the next five years.

Gals Are Glad To Find Pins At LERC Stores

By KAY ANDRE

Have you been over to LERC merchandise stores lately to check up on what's new and what's due? While wandering by the other day with my one good eye open, I saw quite an abundance of interesting items, among them, bobby pins! Certainly you remember bobby pins! They went out with men, girdles and nylons about three years ago and now they're on the way in again. Also in the pin department I found hair ones, straight ones, and safety ones (aye, what a terrific invention for the hurried and the lazy).

And speaking of pins, how's for some leg make-up? You know, what with summer and tans on the wane, it might be a good idea to latch onto a bottle (leg make-up), just in case you want to go out looking healthy.

And if your legs look healthy, your face will have to follow suit and that calls for make-up and we have it! That includes powder base, sponges, rouge, powder, eyebrows, eyelashes, lipstick . . . everything! Now that you have your face all zooted up, what about your hair? Go wash it! (Of course that involves going back and taking off all your make-up but you can always put it back on and who knows? You might do a better job.)

Well Stocked

What I'm getting around to is the fact that LERC merchandise stores are well stocked with all kinds of hair equipment. Where were we? Oh, yes, you were washing your hair. Well, how's for some combs? We have the practical kind and the dressy kind. I was peering at some smooth little plastic combs that would look razor-edge in one's wig. Go down and look at them!

A reet hair-do always leads to earrings, naturally, and if you're mad about earrings, you'll have somewhat of a field day at that particular counter. And such a variety!

Better Stock Up

Well, now that you're all ready to go, you look down in horror, only to discover that your nails need doing. That's me, again! Merchandise stores have orange sticks, emery boards, nail files, cuticle remover, polish remover and of necessity, polish! Hadn't you better go stock up on these little hard-to-get items while you're thinking about it?

Let's assume by this time that your date (or possibly your poor weary husband) has been downstairs waiting for a half-hour. While he's thumbing through last year's copy of *Vogue*, you're upstairs discovering that you "haven't a thing to wear" . . . at this stage, I leave. I'll chug over to the Sports Bar and see what they have to offer, but until next time, you're on your own! See ya!

Fall Sports Program Announced

Many Leagues Being Formed

Rounding out a full program for sports enthusiasts, the LERC last night announced complete coverage of all types of athletics in its fall schedule, to make full use of the five-day work week. Bowling leads the field with approximately 400 teams entering interdepartmental competition in leagues for both men and women on all shifts. Running a close second, basketball and seven-man touch football leagues now are being organized.

Basic instruction will be given in badminton, and swimming classes will be held twice weekly. Signing up for the men's classes is under way and the women's classes now meet every Tuesday at the YMCA in Hollywood.

Deadline for team entries in the fall touch football league has been scheduled for October 16th. Although response has been good, there are still spots for several more departmental teams in the leagues on all shifts.

At completion of the plant and shift play-offs, winners will meet to decide the Lockheed championship. Department teams must have a minimum of seven men and a squad will consist of 12 men.

Rules Ready

Entry blanks and rules are available at the LERC recreation office at B-1 or they may be secured from any member of the athletic committee.

Entries are still being taken at the LERC sports office for the 1945 basketball leagues. Teams will be set up for regular league, shift and plant championship play-offs at the interdepartmental tournament schedule. Entry blanks obtainable at the LERC office must be turned in by October 22nd. Team captains will then be forwarded a set of rules as compiled by the athletic committee. There are still a few places to be filled in the fall bowling program, especially in the various scratch leagues and in the women's divisions at the various alleys.

Plans are again announced for an all-plant blind bogey golf tournament which should appeal to the many Lockheed golfers. Information regarding time and place may be had at the sports office. Badminton, another popular fall sport, is also being organized with ladder competition planned as well as instructions for beginners.

Touch Football

Basketball

Lightnings in 3-to-2 Victory Over Navy Hospital Squad

Manager Ed Kinzy and his powerful Lockheed Lightnings overpowered the Long Beach Navy Hospital softball squad in the opening game in their quest for the Southern California 1945 softball championship at Recreation Park in Long Beach.

Before a crowd of several hundred enthusiastic rooters, the two teams staged an extra-inning thriller with the final victory of 3 to 2 going to the well-coordinated Lockheed ball club.

The crowd was tense at the last half of the eighth inning with the score tied at 2 to 2 and with Lockheed coming up to bat. Andy Schubert, the first man up to the plate, poled a screaming line drive down the left field foul line for a home run and brought his team another step closer to the coveted championship.

Al Pina starred with his five-hit and twelve-strikeout pitching and, with the hearty support of an airtight infield, led the Lockheed Lightnings to a hard-fought win.

CAMERA CLUB HOLDS OUTING

With gas rationing a thing of the past and an early release anticipated on many hard-to-get photographic materials, the Lockheed Camera Club announced plans this week for the fall season.

Last week the semi-annual salon was held in the LERC B-1 cafeteria with Don Bleitz, owner of the Bleitz Camera Company in Hollywood, judging the many salon prints entered.

September 23rd has been set aside for a field trip to Laguna Beach where the order of the day will be pictures and more pictures. The group is meeting at the Laguna Art Gallery at 10 a.m. At the meeting following this outing, there will be a special competition to select outstanding prints.

CANADIANS SEE RECORD FLIGHT

(Continued from Page 3)

TWA pilots are flying nonstop schedules from coast to coast in approximately nine hours in Constellations. Round-trip flights are made every other day.

"Absolutely tops" is the way TWA pilots such as Captains Waldon Golien and Bronson White express their opinions of the huge transports which are capable of carrying 51 passengers. Plans call for establishment of daily schedules as soon as additional equipment is available.

Routine Flights

No attempts at record breaking are being made on these regular runs, Otis F. Bryan, TWA vice president in charge of war projects, emphasized. "We are merely making routine, scheduled flights and no effort is being made to attain maximum speed," he said.

Harold F. Blackburn, manager of TWA's Intercontinental division, revealed that in a recent test he successfully flew the "Connie" from Washington to Burbank on three engines. "We flew at 16,000 feet and the results were satisfactory from every standpoint," he declared. The Constellation operation is in addition to the redeployment program under which TWA and other airlines are transporting soldiers across the country.

Wide Variety of Tickets on Sale

LERC's mutual branch ticket office now has tickets available for the Pan-Pacific's "Ice Follies of 1946" as well as seats at the "Blackouts," Earl Carroll Revue and many other attractions.

This LERC service saves Lockheed employes time and frequently is able to offer tickets at a reduced price. Employes wishing tickets to any outstanding event should go to the LERC office at A-1 or B-1 and make their reservation.

ON THE *Table*

BILL ELLIS Pres. LERC

ELECTION fever has hit the LERC. The past few days has had at least a dozen different men at the helm, potentially speaking. There are some interesting sidelights on this election business. One is the sudden increase in popularity with some of the LERC staff, of possible new officers.

There exist the usual pre-election jitters that always precede a change in administration. This condition is healthy, in my opinion, for there is the ultimate result of taking inventory of the job and checking on the weak points. That ounce of prevention is worth several pounds of cure if it is taken in time. The candidate line-up has had one addition since last week. Bob Mercer has declared that he is ready and willing to take the job of treasurer. Bob was treasurer a couple of years ago, and apparently is ready to give time to the LERC once again. Time is an important factor in the LERC.

All officers of the club are forced to give a whole lot of time to the club—for free—but they do it willingly when they take on the duties of their office. They do it because they believe in the LERC.

The candidates that have already tossed their hats in the ring are now beginning to wonder about possible "dark horses." That always is enough to create interest. There are other good men with enough of a following to make any office a rough race, right down to the finish line. So, you see, no office is a cinch by any means.

To repeat the line-up as it stands, remember these names. For President, Bob O'Hanlon and Jerry Sickler; Vice President, Al Rankin; Secretary, Marcia Westfall; Treasurer, Bob Mercer.

Talk to your LERC council member about these candidates. Prove your interest in future administration of the LERC as these candidates are willing to do. See that your council member votes in a manner representative of your own interests. After all, you elected him and he is supposed to be guided by your interests, so be sure and tell him exactly how you think.

PLAN SMALLER AAF

Two weeks after V-J Day the Army announced plans to reduce size of the 2,150,000-man Air Forces to a strength of approximately 600,000. This will be the size of its interim air force.

DEEDS OF LOST LIGHTNING PILOT LIVE THROUGH PORTRAIT BY PAL

Lt. Col. Robert B. Westbrook of North Hollywood, a P-38 pilot, and great Jungle Air Force ace who downed 20 Japanese fighters, was lost to ack-ack on November 22 over Macassar Strait in the Celebes. But through a portrait his pal is painting his achievements and personality will live on as compelling inspiration to the men of his command who flew with him.

When youthful Lt. Edwin R. Cunningham, who flew with Westy at the age of 19, was awaiting orders home, after 532 combat hours in a P-38, he devoted his time to an oil portrait of the gallant P-38 Lightning pilot.

The Jungle Air Force is preparing full-color reproductions of the painting for distribution to Westy's comrades, both officers and enlisted men.

ATOM PLANE POWER SEEN AS POSSIBLE

Engineers of the National Advisory Committee for Aeronautics view an atomic engine, utilizing the tremendous energies released through the splitting of atoms as a distant possibility for aircraft propulsion, particularly for supersonic speeds, according to an announcement by the association last week.

NACA scientists point out that until recently the only fuels which could be considered for aircraft engines were those which released energy by chemical reactions in which the atoms themselves are unchanged, but two or more kinds of molecules (fuel and oxident) unite to form two or more different kinds of molecules (exhaust gases).

Atomic reaction involves the breaking up of the atoms themselves and is called a fission type of reaction.

The vast energy potential inherent in atomic reaction is especially significant to aeronautics, not so much because of the power available, but rather because of what it means in terms of range, added pay load, and aerodynamic refinements.

SAW SURRENDER

Lockheed Mail Service employes received a letter this week from a former Lockheed employe, Walter Johnson, aboard the *U.S.S. Missouri* during the Japanese surrender ceremony.

Randall Irwin

Irwin Named As WLB Member

R. Randall Irwin, director of Industrial Relations Service, Aircraft Industries Association, has been named substitute industry member of the National War Labor Board. He will continue to serve part time on the NWLB's National Airframe Panel, of which he has been a member since April, 1944.

Irwin is on leave of absence from Lockheed to serve on the staff of the Aircraft Industries Association. For 10 years he was in charge of Industrial Relations and Personnel for Lockheed.

LOCKHEED-EQUIPPED LINES SET RECORD

July saw three operating records hung up by Lockheed-equipped National Airlines which operates along the Atlantic seaboard. During the month it flew more revenue passenger miles, more revenue miles and more revenue passengers than any other in its ten-year history.

AAF GENERAL LAUDS WORK OF LOCKHEED

Grateful thanks from Maj. Gen. Hugh J. Knerr, commanding general of the Air Technical Service Command, came to Lockheed this week for its part in helping win the war.

Said General Knerr in a letter, "The Army Air Forces' share in the victory was achieved by an inseparable team of combat and production forces.

"In your production of B-17, P-38, P-80, C-60 and C-69 aircraft, you joined with other organizations . . . to supply the AAF with weapons and equipment superior to the enemy's.

"Together we have the satisfaction of knowing that air power—supported, defended, and supplied by ground and sea forces—drove Japan to surrender without an invasion of its home islands.

"You have a stake in our four-point peacetime program to remain a first-rate power: continued research, maintenance of strategic bases, assurance of trained personnel adequate for rapid expansion and a strong industry which can provide planes, guided missiles and other weapons which may decide—or, more important, prevent—future wars."

PASSENGER ROCKET PLANE

First flight by a man-carrying rocket plane was made Sept. 30, 1929, at Frankfort, Germany, by Fritz von Opel, German automobile manufacturer.

FIVE-PHASE PROGRAM AID TO THOUSANDS

(Continued from Page 5)

program, supervised by Svend Pederson, was the first in the aircraft industry and was the first to be approved by the Veterans' Administration for World War II servicemen benefits under the GI Bill of Rights. Seventy-five apprentices have been graduated from the program, divided into three classifications: machinists, tool, die, and jig builders, and airplane service mechanics.

6 Months' Study

Inter-American aviation trainees also study at Lockheed. Five South American students have taken a six months' course of instruction at Lockheed in assembly, production, and customer service operations. These students won scholarships under the International Training Administration, Inc., through cooperation from the Civil Aeronautics Administration.

Lockheed training department's program for the future is among the "tops" in U. S. industry.

Orientation courses for new employes will be streamlined. Plans are made for formalized training for new supervision on an 80-hour training program, using case method of instruction.

University Sponsors

Also on the slate is a Management Institute to be sponsored through leading university graduate schools for Lockheed key personnel. Through instruction in the one-week annual course, management personnel will be able to apply information taught by experts to supervision.

Work experience and vocational training in skills and related subjects will continue. Employe surveys will be utilized.

Junior executive training in all major phases of Lockheed operations is planned so executives from every branch in Lockheed will thoroughly know Lockheed products.

Without textbooks such as "How Gertrude Teaches Her Children," but with maximum use of professional educational facilities in Southern California, Lockheed training has paid off for some 155,000 employes with attainment of higher skills and pleasant employe relations through full job knowledge.

Announce Change For B-1 Canteen

The canteen across the street from the cafeteria at Factory B-1 will discontinue serving hot foods and prepared lunches starting next Monday. The canteen will become a "cold" unit and will continue to serve sandwiches, coffee, pies and soft drinks.

However, a canteen line will be open in the B-1 cafeteria. It will serve the "quickies" such as hamburgers, chili and all the other hot foods now served in the canteen. Line 1 will be used for this purpose.

According to Charlie Birgy, manager of the commissary, this action is being taken in the interest of conservation of personnel and equipment. "It is senseless," said Birgy, "in these times of shortages, to be in competition to oneself directly across the street."

Gas Turbines Used In Jet Propulsion

Ten aircraft and engine manufacturers have announced they are engaged in development of gas turbines for jet propulsion and propeller applications.

Is it Here?

THESE classified advertisements in the *Star* are provided for employes without charge. If you want to buy, sell, trade, or find or return lost articles, obtain Form 4929 from your department clerk, the stationery store, or employe service office. Mail the advertisement to the *Lockheed Star,* Room 244, Bldg. 1-A, Plant B-1.

FOR SALE

MISCELLANEOUS

PUPS, to collies—3. 1125 N. Evergreen, Burbank.
COMB. phono. & radio, table model. HI. 4106, Apt. 117, 2017 N. Argyle Ave., Hollywood.
WALLABY coat, white; football shoes, size 9½, like new. GR. 8674.
SHOTGUN, fox, Savage, 16-gauge, and shells. Like new. 1048 Willard Ave., Glendale.
VACUUM cleaner, $20. 5130 Greenbush Ave., Van Nuys.
DINING room set, mahogany; table, 6 chairs; yellow leather seats; buffet; excellent condition. WY. 3948.
ELEC. record player and changer, walnut case, RCA. SU. 2-7536 after 4.
S. & W., fires .32 Win. cart., & Colt .36 C. & B. cllctrs. arm. 2524 N. Myers, Burbank.
ENLARGING easel, 11x14 inches, like new. HO. 1507.
DOUBLE wedding ring set, yellow gold, reasonable. SU. 1-8939.
8-MM. Mauser sport gun, 4X scope, sling, ammunition. RY. 1-6052.
RIFLE, Mossberg, .22-cal., Lyman sight. CH. 8-2122 before 6 p.m.
BEDROOM furniture, mahogany, 5 pieces; ice box. NO. 2-1245 after 9 a.m.
BUNK beds, box springs, $30; kitchen work table, $8; circulating gas heater, $25. CI. 2-5496.
BICYCLE, man's, good balloon tires, reasonable. WAlnut 7917.
COAT, black, fox collar, size 18; 2 coats, size 16; yellow suit, wool, size 16; 5 pairs of slacks, size 16. GR. 8455.
FUR coat, nut brown caracul, finely matched skins; sacrifice; size 18-20. CH. 8-5904.
NC 200 com. receiver, net price, new. PL. 1-2347.
IRON. CH. 8-9274, call after 4 p.m.
ICE box, Hollywood bed, springs & mattress, blue chintz sofa. 436 Stanford Rd., Burbank (near Glenoaks & Scott Rd.)
CHINESE mink coat, size 34-36, worn only a few times. ATlantic 2-2433.
PAINT spray unit, small but complete. 1041 North Elm Ave., Glendale.
AUTO jacks, 2; new prewar foglite, reasonable. CH. 8-3524.
SHOES, size 11A, man's white buckskin; lady's brown leather pumps, size 7½AA, never been worn. CI. 1-4940.
LAUNDRY, damp or fluff dried, 36-hr. service, done in private home. 1411 N. Broadway, Burbank (near Lockheed B-1, one black W. of San Fernando Rd.)

Is it Here?

FOR SALE

MISCELLANEOUS (Cont.)

CHEST, large black walnut; Haviland china, mirror. Apt. 3, 30 S. Euclid, Pasadena. SY. 2-9755.
HOUSE, 4-rm., 2-bedrm. 4918 Mendota Ave., Los Angeles. CI. 6-7463.
TIRES, 2, 6.00x16 retreads, good condition. CR. 1-9460.
DINING room set, 7 pieces; fire wood, cut and dried. CH. 9-3594.
JUICER, fruit and vegetable, prewar, unused, $7.50. AN. 6222.
BED divan, new cover, since used; good spring construction. NO. 1-6103.
5 ROOMS modern furniture, including range & refrigerator; also Schwinn lightweight bicycle. CH. 8-4112.
COLLIE, male, 3 years old, thoroughbred, no papers. Excellent watch dog. SYlvan 0-2414.
BLACK fur chubby, finger-tip length, excellent condition, reasonable. CI. 3-4942.
TIRE, prewar whitewall, 7.00x16, or trade for 6.50x16 equal. ARiz. 9-3926.
OSCILLOSCOPE. AL. 8737.
TABLECLOTH, crocheted, and buffet runner. CI. 3-4916.
BABY buggy, leatherette, metal construction, with mattress pad, $25. SU. 2-2609.
RABBITS, white, 1 buck, 1 doe with litter, 1 bred. Hutches, crocks, skin stretchers, etc., $20. CH. 8-3974.
DOUBLE bed, four-post, mahogany finish. 411 Elvina Dr., Glendale 6.
WASHING machine, apt. size, new gears and motor, A-1 condition. SU. 1-1182.
THOR mangle, 42-inch, good condition. M. Peterson, 5145 Clinton St., L. A.
STEINWAY, spinet style piano, mahogany. CH. 8-2729.

VEHICLES

2-WHEEL trailer, all-steel, 16" wheels, good tires, fenders and lights. 834½ N. Kingsley Drive, Los Angeles.
STUDEBAKER coupe, 1930, and lightweight bicycle. Phone CH. 6-5240.
TRAILER, 23-ft. National Butaine; 20x20 tarp., venetian blds., good tires. 2709 N. Ontario, Space 6.
STATION wagon, International, 1935. 7810 San Fernando Road.
BUICK coupe, business, 1937-40, good condition throughout, radio. NO. 1-6103.
'37 BUICK 4-door sedan, radio & heater, good condition. T. W. Menehan, 4452 Melbourne Ave., L. A. NO. 1-5267.
'31 CHEV. touring car, all good tires, new clutch, good brakes. CH. 8-4673 after 5.
1940 BUICK special sedan, A-1 condition. OL. 4505.
'33 PLYMOUTH sedan or '34 De Soto Airflow coach. Real bargains. CH. 8-2129.

WANTED

APARTMENT, furn. or unfurn., small, or house for a discharged serviceman and wife. CH. 6-2017.
TWIN beds, Hollywood, complete, and chest of drawers. CH. 8-7876.
FORD V-8 "60" engine, also front axle suitable for trailer. OL. 5567.
RIDE from Sunset and Alvarado to B-1, 8 to 4:45 shift. V. M., Ext. 6-1734, 2126½ Sunset, L. A.

Is it Here?

WANTED

PIANO, small bungalow, studio or upright, in fair condition. FE. 3665 after 5 p.m.
RIDE to Bldg. 185 from 54th & Western. AX. 3-1279.
5-RM. furn. rental, allowing pet. HE. 7630 before 10 a.m.
HOUSE to rent, two-bedroom, unfurnished, or apartment. SU. 2-3010 after 6 p.m.
1934 V-8 coupe, fair condition, cheap. Call after 6 p.m. SU. 1-3948.
2-BEDROOM house or apartment to rent by Oct. 1st, unfurnished. CH. 8-4770.
TOOLS, socket sets, wrench sets, snips, etc., prefer prewar. CH. 6-6484, after 4:30.
LAWN mower, good condition. CI. 2-6402.
FORD, Chevrolet, Plymouth, will pay cash for clean 1934, '35, '36. CI. 3-3269 after 6 p.m.
BLDG. own home, need unfur. 2, 3-bdrm. hse. or apt. to rent for 6 mos. WA. 3668.
RIDE to Pico and Ocean, Santa Monica. 246 Bicknell Ave., Santa Monica, A-1, swing.
TRUNK, also several suitcases. CH. 6-7714.
SINGER sewing machine, treadle. CH. 7-9015 evenings.

EXCHANGE

16-MM. sound projector, sell or trade on '38-'39 light car. CI. 1-1997.
'42 BUICK, super sedanette, for cheaper car, desire '40-'41 Chev. ARiz. 9-3926.
RADIO, table model, for record player attachment. HIllside 6151, Ext. 57.
TYPEWRITER for outdoor furniture, radio, tools, spotlite. CH. 6-4568.
HOLLYWOOD bed, mattress and/or .32-cal. rifle for studio couch. 8000 DeGarmo Ave., Roscoe.

FOR RENT

ROOM for rent, room adj. bath; swing shift. See Sat. or Sun., 1704 N. Buena Vista, Burbank.

THE LOCKHEED Star
OFFICIAL PUBLICATION OF THE LOCKHEED AIRCRAFT CORPORATION

Issued each Friday for the employes of Lockheed Aircraft Corporation. The *Star* is the official publication of the company. Communications should be addressed to the Editor, *Lockheed Star* Unit, Lockheed Aircraft Corporation, Burbank, California.

No unsolicited manuscripts or pictures will be returned and the *Star* cannot be responsible for other than requested articles or photos.

J. H. PRESCOTT, Editor
Barbara Sewald, News Editor
Marshall Atwell, Staff Artist

THE LOCKHEED
Star
OFFICIAL PUBLICATION OF THE LOCKHEED AIRCRAFT
Volume 2 BURBANK, CALIFORNIA, U.S.A., OCTOBER 12,
Story, Page 3

Zamperini Eager To See Lockheed After Welcome

Captain Louis Zamperini tasted fully of a dream last night and found it exceedingly sweet . . . a dream that he had carried through the untold sufferings of 47 days on a storm-tossed life raft and 28 months' tortures in a Jap prison camp.

Friends of one of the nation's great heroes welcomed him home at the Torrance Civic Auditorium with a reception and an ovation that did something to him that all the fiendish torments he had undergone failed to do . . . put a catch in his throat and tears in his eyes.

Zamperini was flown to Long Beach from Letterman hospital in San Francisco last Saturday; less than a month from the time he was liberated from a prison camp and brought to Manila. He was met by his parents, brother Pete, and two sisters, Mrs. Sylvia Flammer and Virginia, who had never relinquished hope that he would return.

Medical Check-Up

The former USC track star is spending ten days with his family at 2028 Grammercy Avenue, Torrance, following which he is to report for a medical check-up at Birmingham hospital in Van Nuys. A 90-day furlough is to be spent in meeting his old friends again and picking up the loose ends, Zamperini said. He has plans for the future but he is not ready to talk about them yet.

One of the first places Captain Zamperini hopes to visit is Lockheed, he said. "I especially want to meet my friends there with whom I worked and see this new P-80 Shooting Star that I've heard so much about. I want to talk over the old days with Cecil Loomis and Odie White who used to work with me in experimental there," Zamperini said.

Awaited P-38's

"My fellow prisoners must have gotten bored with me at times. All I could talk about while in that Jap dungeon was about the P-38 and how I hoped a squadron of them would come over some day when we were outside enjoying our few meager minutes of sunshine. When I received my first mail there were several copies of the Lockheed *Star* and I read every word of all of them. They were my first touch with what had been going on during all those weary months," Zamperini said.

Plans are going forward to name a Torrance airport after the former Lockheed dispatcher. The Army has relinquished control of the site to the surplus property board but the city has not been able yet to complete the purchase deal.

Roger Lewis — Major T. N. Shen — Major Y. S. Yang — K. H. Smith

CHINESE OFFICIALS LAUD CONSTELLATION

Sixteen years ago a plane carrying passengers and mail flew from Shanghai, China, to Hankow in 7 hours. The 539-mile flight marked the beginning of commercial aviation in China. Today, the same line, Chinese National Aviation Corporation, is formulating extensive plans for air service to include all China as an important phase of China's over-all economic development.

This week two representatives from the pioneer Chinese airline, Maj. Gen. T. N. Shen and Maj. Y. S. Yang, visited Lockheed and toured the factory areas. Presently, Major General Shen is with the Chinese Air Force. Ken Smith and Roger Lewis consulted with the Chinese visitors who were especially interested in the Lockheed 4-engine Constellation. Interiors of the Constellation were shown and various technical phases of Constellation operation were discussed.

It was China National Aviation Corporation which pioneered in the unparalleled air service over the "hump." The Chinese name of the airline, translated literally, means "The Middle-Kingdom Space-Machine Family." Pan American Airways, Inc., owns 45 per cent of the airline and the national government of the Republic of China owns the rest. Management of the airline rests with the Chinese; operations with American pilots and executives.

ANNOUNCE NEW NAME

Trans-World Airlines is the name selected by TWA for its intercontinental division which plans to operate Lockheed Constellations on routes crossing the Atlantic.

Surplus Sales Play Minor Role In Future Plans

Recent articles in the daily press stating that 61 California war plants, including Lockheed, have been declared surplus and are offered for sale by the Reconstruction Finance Corporation have been subjects of misunderstanding for some Lockheed employes.

According to Lockheed's budget division, all Defense Plant Corporation properties in use by Lockheed are on a rent-lease basis for commercial work until July, 1946.

Defense Plant Corporation owns only a small portion of Lockheed . . . part of which the company may seek to repurchase at the expiration of its lease with DPC next July.

List Properties

DPC property listing includes: 36.34 acres of Plant A-1 property with buildings 61, 80, 82, 83, 85, and 86, and 887 pieces of machinery; 7346 portable tools, and 188 pieces of automotive equipment.

Its Plant B properties include 34.07 acres with building 185, 2 run-up shelters at B-6, a motor test building at Plant A-2, Burbank, and building 230 at Plant B-3. The DPC's machinery and equipment at B plants include 3711 pieces of warehouse equipment.

Coding of all machinery and equipment in all plants, whether Lockheed owned or not, has just been completed.

WRITING $75,500,000 IN CONTRACTS REMINDS AUTHORS OF PEACE TREATY

The way it seems to L. V. "Larry" Kerber and Roger Smith after writing $75,500,000 worth of Constellation contracts, such a document as the United Nations Charter would be a simple composition.

Kerber, who heads the contract office, and Smith, the legal office, are Lockheed's artisans of legal phraseology. Accuracy is their god. A miss might mean millions.

To be sure, they agree, the United Nations Charter takes in a little more territory. But it also had 50 countries to help write it.

Like the charter's framers, Kerber and Smith had some anxious moments about the success of their creative efforts. Before the final signatures on the record-breaking orders for 103 Constellations were obtained there were many lively debates in smoke-filled rooms.

During the year of meetings with sales and legal representatives, on more than one occasion delegates in a huff have stamped out of the room. But, as with the United Nations conferees, differences were compromised and satisfactory working agreements were finally reached.

What does a contract for several million dollars' worth of airplanes look like?

One of those in the group just negotiated which is typical of the others is a bound, paper-covered volume. Including specifications of the contracted-for ships it comprises some 150 to 200 pages and weighs approximately a pound.

First preliminary discussion involving this particular group of airplanes took place in a midwestern city more than a year ago in September of 1944. At that time representatives of the airline said in effect, "We like the airplane."

At a subsequent meeting in Burbank, negotiations actually began with presentation of Lockheed's standard form contract. This was the basic legal instrument from which the final agreement evolved.

To start with, the airplane had to be defined on the basis of data supplied by the Lockheed engineering branch. Then from the manufacturing and engineering branches came tentative schedules and delivery dates. Probable costs were prepared by the estimating department of the finance branch. Only the employes involved in supplying such information know what a prodigious amount of work is involved.

With representatives of Lockheed's New York and Washington offices cooperating, meetings occurred in various cities and the contract was finally signed a year later.

L. V. Kerber — Roger Smith

NORWEGIAN NEWSMEN GUESTS OF LOCKHEED

As part of their program to secure an over-all picture of American farming, business and industry, a distinguished group of Norwegian journalists visited Lockheed this week as guests of the United States government. They were accompanied by Dan Terrell and Gunnar Martin of the OWI.

Visibly impressed by what they saw and especially voluble in their praises of the Saturn and Constellation, the group met for a press conference with Carl B. Squier, Lockheed vice president, as host.

Among the writers were Olav Brundvand of Bergen's leading newspaper, *Arbeiderblad*. One of the first to start underground press service in his German-occupied country, he was arrested by the gestapo and spent four years in forced labor for the Reich.

Miss Joruun Johnsen, Norway's foremost woman journalist, employed by *Afgenposten* in Oslo, an active member of the home front during the war who as a result spent 14 months in the notorious Grini concentration camp, was with the party.

Other members of the party included such famous personages as M. C. Kirkeboe, editor of the non-political Norwegian *Christian Press;* Oskar Hasselknippe, of *Verdens Gang,* an Oslo paper, and Per Thompson, of the newspaper *Stavanger Aftenblad.*

Hasselknippe made an outstanding record in the Norwegian home-front organization and at the time of his liberation was an officer in command of some 2000 men pledged to the resistance movement. During the occupation he made numerous trips to both Sweden and England for important conferences.

Thompson, a well-known novelist, was imprisoned from October, 1944, until the time of his liberation.

Visitors from Norway

AUTOMOBILES WILL BE BOND PRIZES

AIR TRIP ANYWHERE IN U. S. TOPS OTHER AWARDS IN VICTORY LOAN DRIVE

How would you like to get a brand-new 1946 model console radio this year for Christmas?—Or maybe a new washing machine?—Or a brand-new de luxe model Ford automobile?—Perhaps you would prefer a $1000 Victory Bond?—Or an all-expense air trip for two persons to any city in the United States?

Might even be that you are one of the feminine dreamers that has dared to want a dozen pairs of sheer nylon hose.

You think someone has a hole in their head? Well, then listen to this:

On December 21 — just in time for Christmas—these and comparable awards that add up to 31 grand prizes will be handed to Lockheed employes who hold lucky tickets in the Victory Loan drive which officially starts at Lockheed on October 29.

Victory bonds—identical with War bonds except in name—will be sold by the Lockheed Employe Victory Committee both through payroll deduction and cash sales during the drive.

And with every $25 unit sold goes one chance in the grand prize drawing.

Okay Deductions

On next Wednesday, October 17, you will receive a regular type payroll deduction card with your time card. If you are not buying bonds through this plan at present, this card will authorize deductions in time for you to participate in the drawing. If you are having bonds deducted from your check—and you'd like a few extra chances at the prizes—this card will authorize an increase in your deductions.

Employes are requested to fill out all information requested on the card and especially whether they are paid hourly or monthly.

All bonds purchased between October 22 and December 2 by payroll deduction will auto-

(Continued on Page 7)

Powers Model Enjoys Link Trainer 'Ride'

Lockheed's Link Trainer has had many passengers, but none like lovely blonde Aina Constant, R-K-O movie star who "rode" in it on a recent visit to Lockheed's Pilot House.

Miss Constant, former Powers model and air enthusiast, had her first experience of how it feels to fly blind.

Since 1940 Lockheed test pilots have been learning to fly with instruments as their only guide in a Link Trainer. For instrument rating pilots are required to have six hours of instrument time each six months.

Pilots Learn

In a room off the main corridor of the pilot house Lockheed's Mose Harvey gives three pilots a day orientation problems; simulated takeoffs from Lockheed Air Terminal; instrument procedure to Long Beach, and similar problems, all in a Link Trainer.

When the pilot closes down the hood of the blue and yellow Link Trainer he depends on flight instruments and simulated radio beams to fly a route charted on a map by a "bug" at operator's desk. The "bug" or recorder sits on top of a map, the same type map the pilot is using in the cockpit, and it faithfully records every move the pilot makes by means of a red line on the map.

Bond Prize

LOCKHEED LOOKS GOOD TO TOPFLIGHT NEWSMEN

Hints of Lockheed's research and development into even faster jet fighters, rocket planes and missiles, and jet-propelled transports were given to 25 of the nation's leading newspapermen by President Robert E. Gross and Chief Engineer Hall L. Hibbard at a press conference Tuesday.

"The planes that we began talking about and designing five years ago are the ones now keeping our Lockheed factories busy," Gross said. "We are working today on plans for aircraft that will lead the industry five years from now."

Hibbard said Lockheed's research and development program was being pushed into improvements on the P-80 Shooting Star, world's fastest airplane, into use of gas turbine and jet power for transports, and into the vast new field of inhabited and uninhabited rockets.

Hold Conference

The newspapermen met Gross and Hibbard in the directors' room for a quick conference that preceded a tour of the Constellation and Shooting Star production service areas. They inspected the Constellation now being given finishing touches for early delivery to Transcontinental & Western Air.

News correspondents who attended the conference were Morley Cassidy, Philadelphia *Bulletin*; John F. Chester, Associated Press; Stanton Dellaplane, San Francisco *Chronicle*; C. Edmund Fisher, Pittsburgh *Post-Gazette*; Harold Fleming, Christian Science *Monitor*; Max Forester, New York *Herald-Tribune*; Joseph Garretson, Cincinnati *Enquirer*.

Donald Grant, St. Louis *Post-Dispatch*; William E. Jones, Boston *Globe*; James L. Kilgallen, International News Service; Sandor Klein, United Press; Russell Porter, New York *Times*; Allen Schoenfield, Detroit *News*; Ralph Werner, Milwaukee *Journal*; Anthony Wirry, Chicago *Tribune*; John Zug, Des Moines *Register* and *Tribune*; Raymond F. Zeman, Los Angeles *Times*.

Milton Randolph, Nashville *Banner*; Dick Reynolds, Los Angeles *Daily News*; Bud Hathcock, Los Angeles *Examiner*; and Don Ryan, Los Angeles *Herald-Express*.

SEEK HELP IN DIRECT PRODUCTION

More than 230 spot radio announcements a week plus classified advertising in metropolitan newspapers are asking for some 1800 male employes for various manufacturing departments in Lockheed's largest hiring program since Sept., 1944, according to M. V. Mattson, Lockheed employment manager.

Lockheed needs assemblers, general installers, aircraft and engine mechanics, riveters, sign painters, spray painters, upholsterers, buffers and polishers, wood form block makers, jig builders, plaster pattern makers, die finishers, experienced mechanics, sheet metal workers, tool and die makers, general machinists, machine operators of various types, as engine lathe, grinder, milling machine, and power saw, and forming roll routers, as well as a few other specialized production employes.

Terminations Up

Since V-J Day, voluntary terminations at Lockheed have been on the increase. Much of the personnel loss has been direct labor, which Lockheed expects to replace through the employment program. Since termination of hostilities, 7033 Lockheed employes have terminated, 4968 of which were voluntary terminations. Closing of subplants in northern cities was responsible for a proportion of the 1642 employes terminated during the period since V-J Day on lay-off procedure. New hires total 811.

As Lockheed gradually accomplishes its transition to commercial production, some employes in various branches of the company will of necessity be declared surplus. Today, some 600

(Continued on Page 6)

Lockheed Volunteers Aid Y.W.C.A. Service

Extension of the Y.W.C.A. Counseling Service in which a number of Lockheed women are participating has been made to two new locations, Susan S. Laughlin, women's activities director announced last night.

Not only do many women volunteers from Lockheed help conduct the service, Mrs. Laughlin declared, but many more enjoy the assistance it offers.

New locations are the Southeast Branch, 6111 Huntington Blvd., phone KImball 7133, and Hollywood at 6927 Hawthorne Avenue, GLadstone 5141. Other locations are Central at 941 South Figueroa, TRinity 0461, and Woodlawn at 4260 Woodlawn Avenue, ADams 1-4103.

Cover

POWERS model and pilots . . . lissome loveliness in a Link Trainer. Larry Larrivee, Lockheed photographer, got this candid shot of R-K-O.'s Aina Constant, the first Powers model to visit Lockheed.

Twins Make U. S. and Lockheed See Double

Like the peripatetic peas that they are, the Leto brothers, Al and Frank, bobbed up at Lockheed again this week to renew confusion of fellow employes.

In other words, the Leto brothers are identical twins, who formerly worked in the same department, who were drafted into the armed forces at the same time, served in identical posts, flew the same number of missions, received the same honors, and are returning to work together again in Dept. 44-42 at Plant B-3 in the tooling machine shops.

After eighteen months working as machine parts inspectors and layout men the brothers vainly tried to enlist. Drafted in March, 1943, both served in the 12th Air Force group.

Both boys left the Army at Santa Ana, September 23, as staff sergeants and each wears the air medal with four oak leaf clusters, ETO ribbons with 6 battle stars, the croix de guerre and presidential citations.

The twins were discharged with identical point scores of 87, even though they flew different missions.

Despite the fact that the twins flew many missions, neither boy ever received a serious wound.

When V-E Day came it found them enjoying a well-earned "flak" leave of a week in London. They sailed together from Liverpool on July 22 for this country. And after only three weeks of vacation they were unable to stand inactivity any longer and asked to come back to work.

Both single, the twins live with their widowed mother at 3531 Floral Drive in Los Angeles. They plan to enter UCLA to take the same course in radio and mechanical engineering.

Fay Ellenz Frank Leto Al Leto

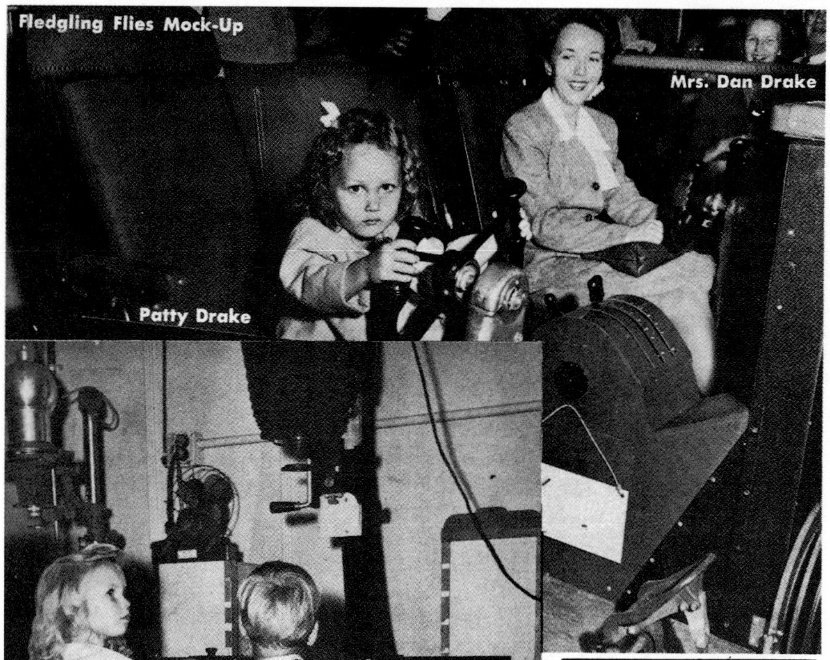
Fledgling Flies Mock-Up
Mrs. Dan Drake
Patty Drake

Youthful Photo Enthusiasts

BIRTHDAY PARTY HELD BY RESEARCH ENGINEERS

Reminiscent of Lockheed factory Family Days, the Engineering Research laboratory at Factory B-1 celebrated the fifth anniversary of its founding with open house last Saturday for all its employes and their families.

More than 500 persons toured the laboratory, each employe acting as guide for his particular party. Machines were not in operation but hundreds of visitors sat in the pilot's seat of cockpit mockups and saw giant weight-testing machines, chemical equipment, expensive metallurgical instruments, hi-altitude testing room, static-testing equipment, and hundreds of other specialized research equipment.

It was the first time the Lockheed employes' families were able to visit the research laboratory because of the highly secret work there during the war years.

Research personnel reported no casualties on Family Day except tired feet and aching necks. The LERC served refreshments to the visitors and many hungry folk had dinner after the tour in the A-1 commissary.

The Lockheed Research laboratory was founded five years ago as an outgrowth of the P-38 engineering experimental section under Al Jacobson. Instrumental in founding the laboratory was Dr. Maurice Nelles and present head of the laboratory, James Gerschler.

NEW DOCK

A trash disposal dock of reinforced concrete with an asphalt ramp leading to it is under construction at the southeast corner of the Constellation hangar, building 304, at B-6.

P-80 Mobile Unit Trains Technicians

Muroc Flight Test Base was visited recently by a mobile P-80 mock-up training unit sponsored by the Air Technical Training Command. This mobile P-80 training unit is scheduled to visit all existing P-80 Army units according to Army announcement.

The unit provides training for technicians and ease of observation on the fuel, control, hydraulic, electrical, and power plant systems of the P-80. This is the first time that a mobile P-80 mock-up has ever been used for training purposes.

New Routes Opened By Dutch Airlines

Extended air routes planned by the Royal Netherlands Indies' Airways call for an initial annual mileage of 6,000,000, it has been announced by N.E.A.L. De Jong, general manager. This includes both inter-insular and inter-continental service.

A projected transpacific operation from Soerabaja covers a route touching Ambon, Hollandia, Motje, Honolulu and San Francisco.

PAN AMERICAN FLYER URGES MUTUAL HELP

"What we achieve in future good will will depend on what we share with our neighbors, in sincere mutual exchange of ideas. Money won't buy co-operation—ideas are the only lasting force."

This opinion on world relationships was expressed today by H. W. Peterson, recently returned from service in South America with the Air Transport Command, who spoke to the Consumers' Advisory Committee at the Pan American World Airways building, Lockheed Air Terminal.

Members of the committee, representing leading women's organizations of Los Angeles, inspected operations facilities for international air travel and partook of a "typical Clipper luncheon" served by airline hostesses.

Hourly Delivery

"We should realize our dependence on our fellow nations. During the war, nearly 90 factories in the United States were depending on hour-to-hour delivery of quartz crystal from Brazil. If a plane had failed or even delayed in the tremendous program of emergency air shipments of quartz, factories would have shut down," Peterson revealed.

In a program arranged by Mrs. Gertrude H. Rounsavelle, member of the Board of Education, the prominent clubwomen were studying air transportation from the viewpoint of the consumer. Mrs. Stella Alkire heads the organization, which is affiliated with the Better Business Bureau, and has as its purpose the interpretation of consumer needs in business.

Time Reduced

"Mass transportation for the average individual will be possible under a program for the utilization of great planes carrying 100 and 200 passengers. The Constellation, C-97 transport, is a powerful plane that will reduce transcontinental travel time to a miraculously short time," Peterson added.

PROPOSE NEW RACES

Air races from London and New York to Sydney, Australia, have been proposed as a feature of a projected Pacific exposition in 1948.

ENGINEERS SEEK STRIKE VOTE IN NLRB PETITION

Announcement was made last night that official notice has been received by Lockheed that the Engineers and Architects association has petitioned the National Labor Relations Board for a strike vote. If the petition is not withdrawn, the vote will be held on or about Oct. 25, officials stated.

The association, which represents about 1900 salaried and hourly employes in various branches of the company, has also taken two other steps in connection with items in dispute with the company.

Officials said the E.A.A. has requested the U. S. Conciliation Service to certify the items currently being negotiated for addition to the agreement of March 22, 1945, between the association and the company, and on which no agreement has been reached, to the National War Labor Board for a decision from the board.

Protest Reductions

The E.A.A. has also protested the pay reduction of salaried employes in their bargaining unit, made in accordance with U. S. Treasury department requirements when the company went to a 40-hour week. They have requested the Conciliation Service to certify this item as a dispute to the National War Labor Board, and have asked for a decision restoring the prior rate of salaries, retroactive to August 20, 1945.

In their petition to the NLRB asking for a strike vote, the E.A.A. stated, "This dispute has arisen as a result of the breakdown of negotiations for a collective bargaining agreement between the parties supplementing the partial and incomplete agreement concluded by them some months ago. Specific issues in dispute include wages, hours of work, seniority, sick leave, holidays, union security, assignability of the agreement, intraplant transfers, anti-discrimination clause and other essential terms and provisions of the contract. Negotiations between the parties which have been in progress for an extended period have come to a complete halt as a consequence of the company's unnecessary delays and its refusal to continue bargaining in good faith."

Always Ready

F. W. Thrane, chairman of the company's negotiating committee, said yesterday, "The company is willing now, and has constantly been willing to resume negotiations and to bargain in good faith with the Engineers and Architects association in order to settle items in dispute."

The E.A.A. petition requesting a strike vote comes as a climax to a long series of negotiations following the certification of the association on December 29, 1944, as the collective bargaining representative for employes in specified engineering job classifications.

According to government rules governing such situations, the association may strike following the vote even if the vote does not favor a strike. If such a strike is called, however, it will violate the no-strike pledge provision in the existing agreement between the company and the association.

This agreement became effective March 22, 1945, following ratification by the association's membership and the company board of directors. This agreement, which is only a partial agreement, was entered into by the company as a result of a request by the E.A.A., although collective bargaining agreements normally are not signed until negotiations have been completed on an entire agreement.

REPAIR GROUP WINS TROPHY

Department 62-73, repair and overhaul, now possesses the Lockheed Factory B safety trophy. This department was awarded the trophy for attaining the largest accumulation of lost-time accident-free man hours of any department in the Factory B organization. This department has not had a lost-time accident since February of 1945.

This achievement is remarkable because of the varied types of work performed by this department—including some of the most hazardous in the industry. An outstanding example has been set proving that any job in the aircraft industry can be carried out safely.

Every employe in the repair and overhaul department is responsible for winning the safety trophy. Should one employe sustain a lost-time injury—it would disqualify the department for the trophy award.

Foreman George Betts, Arnold Haines (chairman of the Plant B-5 general safety committee), members of the general safety committee, and every employe of Dept. 62-73 are to be congratulated on their outstanding accomplishment in winning the safety trophy.

REPORT DESPERATE NEEDS FOR RIDES

Because many people have been transferred from outlying plants and because of shifts and transfers in work places, Lockheed's Employe Service and Transportation department is flooded with requests from employes needing rides. Employes who are driving their cars to work for the first time since lifting of gas rationing regulations and those with room for passengers are asked to contact the Employe Service section.

German Transport Rated as Inferior

German military and civilian air transport industry was generally overrated and far inferior to that of this country in the opinion of J. H. Carmichael, Penn-Central Airlines vice president, first of the airline engineers to report on an inspection trip.

"Practices and equipment which we considered obsolete seven or eight years ago were still standard with them," said Carmichael, one of six airline engineers who made the ten-week inspection trip under Foreign Economic Administration auspices.

HAS MANY GADGETS

The test version of the Constellation, "Old 61," is the most completely instrumented airplane ever to fly.

you ride a Shooting Star

Herman "Fish" Salmon

By HERMAN SALMON

as told to

BUD LILLY

SO YOU want to know how it feels to fly in the world's fastest airplane? An an engineering test pilot assigned to flying Lockheed's P-80 Shooting Star, I can tell you. But first, in order that you may understand fully my sensations in this unorthodox jet fighter, you should know how to fly it yourself.

And if you have even a general idea of the basic mechanics of flying a conventional, stick-controlled airplane, you are eligible for my complete course on how to fly a jet job.

First, of course, you step into the cockpit. You start your engine by pushing the small button there on the instrument panel. Next, set your brakes and move the single-engine control lever to forward position. Your engine is dead cold, so wait 30 seconds and then release your brakes. Proceed with your take-off and flight just as you would in any light sport plane.

You are now a jet pilot. The P-80 Shooting Star is really just about that simple to fly.

I don't say, however, that you will be right at home in its streamlined cockpit on your initial flight. For one thing, the amazing absence of noise—that later becomes such a comfort—undoubtedly will cause you some early concern. The roar of your jet power unit is reduced to a pleasant hum. You are going to find it hard to convince yourself that you have in your control the most powerful aircraft engine in the world. At the same time, your forward motion will seem much too effortless for maintaining flying speed.

You will be confused further if you try to judge your speed without instruments. Unless you are alert to your instruments every minute of your flight, the speed of the Shooting Star will fool you every time. The clatter of a trainer will give you a greater sensation of high speed than you get in the quiet cockpit of the Shooting Star.

Because the Shooting Star is a truly radical departure from conventional aircraft, you will find many other features in it that are mighty strange to you. Both airframe and power unit are totally different from those to which we have become accustomed in years of flying conventional planes.

Still Gets Thrill

Even today, after hundreds of hours in the sleek P-80, I still get a tremendous thrill out of swishing across the skies at the terrific speeds it travels. Not a thrill of speed, but a thrill of controlling what seems to be unlimited power, a thrill of being freed from the binding ties of old mother earth.

HERMAN "FISH" SALMON, Lockheed test pilot for five years, who has logged some 3000 hours' flying time. He has piloted all types of Lockheed ships from the Hudson Bombers he delivered to Canada to Lockheed's P-80 Shooting Star. During barnstorming days he made more than 200 exhibition parachute jumps.

That last statement may sound rather trite. I have heard a great many pilots express the sense of freedom they feel in flying. But never before in my years of piloting fast planes have I approached the exhilaration I find in the swift, almost ghostly, flight of the Shooting Star.

The basic simplicity of the Shooting Star has a lot to do with this new sensation of flight. For many years—since the Wright Brothers first flew at Kittyhawk in 1903, as a matter of fact—airplanes have advanced steadily in speed. The transition from bamboo-and-cloth flying kites to modern all-metal planes, however, has resulted in extremely complicated methods of construction and operation. Flying a high-speed reciprocal-engine plane is a real job. If the average individual wants to master one, he must make a career of aviation.

Simplicity

But in the P-80, we have reverted to simplicity. In my way of thinking, this simplicity is one of the outstanding features of jet propulsion. The P-80 is simple in manufacture, maintenance and operation. The jet engine, although creating more thrust power than any reciprocating engine, has less than a tenth as many moving parts and is much lighter in weight.

Completely lacking are the conventional fighter's propeller, carburetor, generators, ignition system, oil system, radiators, air scoops and the complex controls for these items. The Shooting Star is exceptionally easy to build, service, repair and fly.

More Security

As a pilot I am extremely interested in simplicity of operation. For example, I have only three basic engine instruments—fuel pressure, rpm.'s and engine temperature—to watch while flying the Shooting Star. My sense of security is increased in knowing that I control the acceleration and deceleration of my plane with a single lever. And that I am getting complete operating efficiency through use of this lever. There are no complicated adjustments like manifold pressures and fuel mixtures of the reciprocating engine.

I push my throttle ahead and I go. I pull it back and I don't. It couldn't be much simpler than that.

Cockpit comfort is another thing a pilot looks for—and all too seldom finds—in the plane he flies. The pressurized cockpit in the Shooting Star is unique among today's fighter planes. Pilots fly in complete comfort at high altitudes without cumbersome oxygen masks.

The bubble canopy and location of the cockpit forward of the wing in the semi-monocoque fuselage give excellent pilot visibility in all maneuvers. Standard

(Continued on Page 8)

Lockheed Shooting Star

Glider Clubs To Revive Sport With SCSA Help

Renewed interest in the sport of soaring, virtually discontinued during the war, has stimulated plans of the LERC for a meeting of all interested soaring fans. During the war, many thousands of men were trained in the use of gliders, and in time, the LERC officials believe, the sport may rival that of private plane flying.

Additional impetus has come from new Civil Air Regulations which permit crediting of time in piloting motorless aircraft as flight experience in qualifying for power pilot certificates. Private pilots may have up to one half their time in gliders and commercial pilots one quarter of their log time.

William G. Briegleb, president of the Southern California Soaring association, has agreed to address the proposed meeting sponsored by the LERC and present a plan for the formation of a soaring club.

This club, officials believe, should be under the sponsorship of the SCSA which is in the best position to interpret and enforce the CAA soaring regulations.

Soaring is considered by its exponents to be superior from the standpoint of actual sport to motor-powered flights. In soaring, the actual duration of flight and height reached is determined solely by the skill of the flier.

Similar Plans

Soaring planes now being used by SCSA clubs and by Briegleb's school are of the two-place type which allow for the same instruction as followed by the motor-powered flying clubs. The proposed club would function much like a flying club. Although the initial cost of the glider is less, the flight time costs about the same as in a light plane.

Lockheed employes, both men and women, who are interested in gliders and soaring clubs, are invited to contact the LERC office at B-1, Ext. 6-1901, and leave their names. They will be contacted as soon as sufficient numbers have indicated their interest.

Free as the Wind

SERVICE CLUB SEEKS GIFTS FOR VETERANS

Christmas away from home is bad enough, according to letters from servicemen, but Christmas in a remote hospital is worse.

This is the predicament of thousands of servicemen this year, says Opal Broderson, LERC staff, who is assisting the Lockheed Service Star Women in their drive for gifts to go to servicemen in hospitals here and abroad.

The Lockheed Service Women have pledged themselves to provide gifts for some of the hospitals in this area. To date, the number of gifts contributed has been far from adequate.

Contributions should be turned in at the deposit boxes provided by the LERC or may be brought to either LERC recreation office at A-1 or B-1.

GUEST NIGHT AT DANCE CLUB

"Guest Night" will be featured next Wednesday, October 17, by the LERC Dance club. Special instructions and pointers will be given by Mr. and Mrs. Alan Rudack at their studio, 7213 Beverly Blvd., according to Chris Johnson, club president.

Lockheed employes and friends are invited to learn new dance steps at these Wednesday evening meetings. Special beginning and advanced classes are held for the benefit of those wishing to learn or for those employes who merely want to "brush up." For information, call the LERC Recreation office at B-1, Ext. 6-1901.

Haughton Tells Need Of Production Jobs

(Continued from Page 3)

surplus indirect employes will be terminated. In some instances they may be transferred to direct production. Dan Haughton, assistant to the vice president in charge of manufacturing, says: "Manufacturing positions will be offered to any indirect personnel who qualify for production jobs in the skilled or semi-skilled brackets."

BOY SCOUTS ADD TO MEMBERSHIP

B. H. Keen, Dept. 90-64 at Plant B-1, and Scoutmaster of Troop 13, Boy Scouts of America, announced through the LERC Recreation office at B-1, that Troop 13 now has some vacancies among its patrols and would welcome new members. Boys over the age of 12 are eligible for membership in the Boy Scouts; this troop, which is sponsored by the LERC, meets every Wednesday evening at John Muir Junior High School, Burbank.

ACTION FILM ON LERC BILL

By popular request, LERC is sponsoring as the free movie of the week an all-Army-Navy show. The performance will include the Army's "Special Delivery Japan" and the Navy's "Corregidor to Iwo Jima," "Story of Big Ben," "Now It Can Be Told," and "On to Tokyo." Especially gripping is the story of Big Ben, the unsinkable aircraft carrier, and its fantastic story of a fight for survival through terrific Jap kamikaze attacks.

This special showing will take place at the LERC B-1 cafeteria in rooms 3, 4 and 5. The first performance starts at 5:45 and the second at 8.

Girl Scouts Plan Additional Troops

LERC-sponsored Girl Scouts and Brownie Scouts are looking forward to a busy and successful year under the able leadership of Edna Jacquith, Rosalie Jackman, Mildred Phillips, Roy Beanblossom, Virginia Edgar and Helen Rittgars.

With the fall reorganization, two intermediate and three Brownie troops have been formed, bringing the total number of Washington troops to five. Many plans are being made for Hallowe'en parties, service programs and other fall activities, states Mrs. Hazel Whitmoyer, contact chairman for the Washington Girl Scouts.

At the present time, the Brownie troops are working on tray favors for the soldiers' hospitals throughout the southland.

Swing Shift Rangers Plan Hallowe'en Party

Because of an increase in membership, the Lockheed Swing Shift Rangers have voted to move their meeting place to the Pico Stables on Riverside Drive, Johnny Kuhn, club president, said yesterday.

Don't Fence Us In

Kuhn reported that the Swing Rangers are planning a gala Hallowe'en party for members and their special guests. In addition to regular Wednesday rides and monthly jaunts, they are scheduling hayrides and moonlight rides with the annual fall dance high lighting a busy season.

Time and place of this affair will be announced later. The favorite meeting of the Swing Rangers is their breakfast ride through Griffith Park hills, Kuhn continued. This is a two-hour jaunt that leads to Pepper Tree Lane where the Rangers are served a delicious outdoor breakfast prepared by the Lady Rangers.

Employes, both men and women, who are interested in joining this active group and participating in the fun are invited to contact Gordon Stanton, assistant recreation director, Plant B-1.

Penguinettes to Hold Joint Meet

Lockheed's A and B Penguinette clubs will hold their first fall joint meeting at the Hollywood Roosevelt Hotel on Tuesday, October 30, at 7 p.m.

Called an "Autumn Achievement dinner," the Penguinettes are saluting the women at Lockheed who have been carrying on the hostess and recreation work for servicemen. These include the Blue Star Women, Service Star Women, Lockheed Hollywood Canteen Hostesses, Terminal Lounge Hostesses, Guild Canteen group of Lockheed, and the Junior and Senior Hostesses for Army and Navy camp trips as well as the swing Penguinettes' own service group.

Tickets for this meeting may be obtained at the LERC offices or from the regular ticket committee of both Penguinette clubs. A particularly fine program is being planned as well as the presentation of a "Scroll of Honor" to be signed by all the service groups present.

'BARBER SHOP FOUR' 3 VOICES SHORT

Gordon Stanton this week announced plans for a "barber shop" foursome. Consideration is being given, he said, to the formation of a staff group to help furnish impromptu entertainment on short notice. Anyone interested in getting together to sing some of the old-fashioned songs should contact the LERC office, Ext. 6-1901.

PLANES LAY TELEPHONE WIRE

Planes now can lay telephone wire. In a recent test a twin-engine transport plane laid 16 miles of Army telephone wire in a little more than six minutes over rough-wooded slopes with elevations between 1500 and 5000 feet.

CAFETERIA'S SUPER FOOD HELPS KAY

By KAY ANDRE

As I sit here, typewriter in hand, my alleged mind turns to thoughts, not of love but of food!

Last Saturday night, I trapped my mother and father and an old musty friend into eating at LERC's A cafeteria and the food was terrific (I'm paid to say) . . . I had chicken pot pie with real chicken, no less! That's quite a thing nowadays, you know, to have chicken in chicken pie! I had the same deal not too long ago at a restaurant in town and so help me, it tasted like the three little kittens, complete with mittens. . . .

Trot your whole family out (we can seat up to 1250) and give it a try. And bring the baby, too, 'cause we have high chairs for the occasion . . . and what's more, we have nice soothing music to offer. It's canned, but it's good.

Or have you tried eating breakfast at the cafeterias? If you're a gal, it saves doing the dishes at home, or if you're a man, it saves your wife getting up in the middle of the night to feed you. So you win either way, providing you're a girl, of course. The bacon and eggs are especially good and are getting to be a habit with me. In case you're scratching your head 'way out to here some morning, they also serve ice-cold tomato juice and grapefruit juice . . . merely a suggestion!

For lunch, I usually wrap myself around a vegetable plate and my only complaint is that I can never eat all of it. (I can't decide whether I'm fragile or whether they're overly generous.) . . . The meat at the cafeterias is strictly top-drawer, the reason being that they have butchers who carve all the bodies of cows and things that hang in the refrigerators over at B-1. As a matter of fact, I guess there isn't anything they don't do for themselves. Nice to be independent.

Even if you aren't hungry enough to inhale a whole meal, LERC offers malts, sandwiches, cake, ice cream affairs (you know, sundaes and things) and all kinds of little gadgets. . . .

FLASH—(and not that this has anything to do with the cafeterias) Bill Ellis is now a lady-father. It was a girl (still is as a matter of fact)! She weighed in at six pounds plus and clocked in on the swing shift around nine the night of October 3 . . . congratulations, Jean and Bill!

Cafeterias Need Additional Help

LERC commissary manager, Charles Birgy, sent out a call last night for additional part and full-time help. An urgent need, he said, is felt in the early hours of the morning to serve breakfast to Lockheed day shift employes.

Part-time jobs are also available for the afternoon and evening shifts. Those interested in such work are asked to contact the manager of either the A-1 or B-1 cafeterias.

JEWELRY STORE HAS NEW MANAGEMENT

Operating under new management, the LERC jewelry store and watch repairing department is being handled by Lee's Jewelry Company.

Just Hit It Like This—or

Wear It Like This—or

Dust Like This—It's Wonderful

COMMANDOS SET FOR DRIVE

(Continued from Page 3)

matically entitle the purchaser to chances in the grand drawing.

Then, between October 29 and November 23, you will have an opportunity to buy additional bonds for cash. As in the payroll deduction plan, every $25 unit entitles the purchaser to one more chance in the golden jackpot.

Lockheed's famed Bond Commandos will serve cash customers both on the job and from their permanent booths in front of the main cafeterias at factories A-1 and B-1.

A. H. (Tony) Holst, chairman of the Employe Victory Committee, today announced that Lockheed's quota for the coming drive is $3,750,000.

Most Important

"Our government," Tony said, "feels that the Victory Loan drive is as important as any War Loan drive ever held. Money subscribed will be used to return fighting men and women from overseas, take care of wounded veterans, pay for war goods used by armies of occupation, and to pay government pensions. Also we are all aware that a successful bond sale will be definite insurance against disastrous inflation.

Booklet Written By Lockheedian

To most employes, the California State Unemployment Insurance Act remains somewhat of a mystery. However, Alexis Corfino, of Lockheed Industrial Relations department, has written a booklet which is now on sale at the LERC merchandise stores that gives a comprehensive report on it.

This pamphlet will prove to be very useful as it explains in detail exactly the who, what, when, and where of the insurance act.

Corfino's booklet is on sale at all newsstands as well as at the LERC merchandise stores.

Touch Football Signup to Close

Last call for entrants in the touch football league, Frank Davis, LERC recreation director, said yesterday. Both teams and individual players are needed to fill out the winter football league. October 20 will be the last day for registrations.

Tennis Tilts To Be Resumed

Art Fiedler, LERC's tennis coordinator, announced today that with vacation almost over, the 1945 Lockheed Tennis Championship tournament will get under way again.

In the men's singles, "A" division, which has completed the quarter finals, Jim McDaniels, defending champion, defeated Charles Sharpe, 7-5, 6-3. Lewis Hastings defeated Starr Pierce, 6-4, 6-1. Jack Ryan will meet R. W. Andrews, Jr., in the fourth round and Victor Seliger will meet Don Phillips.

The semifinals of the men's "B" division finds L. M. Cruz winning over V. Bantilon, 7-5, 4-6, 7-5, and R. Spangenberg winning over W. Lincoln, 6-3, 6-1.

Men's Doubles

Playing lineup for the first round of the men's doubles will be: Hughes and Newcomer—bye, Quint and Richards—bye, Wachter and Broberg won over Richards and Effertz by default, Hastings and Pollard—bye, Burchett and Haythorne—bye, Foster and Saenz will meet Winkler and Burkholder, Dewey and Goldberg will meet Earl and Earl, Pierce and Phillips—bye, Bonnie and Walsh will meet Makela and Fiedler, Humphrey and Forrester will meet Carson and Lincoln, Fisher and Wilcox—bye, Shatz and Helzel—bye, Hayman and Johnson will meet Davis and Woodson, Mosley and Horton — bye, McDaniels and Andrews—bye, Seliger and Gay—bye.

Women's Singles

First-round matches in the women's singles give the following lineup: Mary G. Lauck, defending champion in the women's singles event—bye. Margaret Dunlap will meet Clara McGinty, Marjorie Davis—bye, Joan Parker will meet Dove Thomas, Katherine Johnson will meet Chic Roodberg, Alvene Wolff—bye, Josephine Murillo won over Ester Mink by default and Kathleen Turner—bye.

Players listed above are urged to contact LERC office at B-1 for the time and place of their scheduled match.

Default System

Fiedler warns that a rigid default system will be in effect and players who do not show up on time will forfeit their match and consequent position in the tournament. Tennis fans who might be interested in any of the above matches are also invited to attend.

PETECA EXPLAINED BY LERC SPORTS EDITOR

Don Hayes, LERC's athletic committee chairman, is the authority for the following new (to us, at least) game called peteca. At least, he purchased a couple of petecas for the LERC which will be used in the lunch areas.

To date, rules for the game seem a little vague; your sports editor was told that the game was played exactly like badminton, which at first seemed logical because the peteca looks like a badminton birdie with glandular trouble; slightly overgrown, that is.

However, we were told that you don't use a racket but bat the peteca back and forth with your hand. That we tried, and that method, we wish to report, won't work! Unless, that is, you can find yourself four auxiliary sets of arms, which, due to shortages, is rather difficult.

What a Bird!

Even with just a "love pat" the overgrown bird hurtles through the air like a P-80 late for supper. It seems to have two favored places for landing: on the end of your nose or in the pit of your stomach. You can't defend yourself unless you have help. Maybe the reason for this is that the peteca's stern is stuffed full of turkey feathers which must have been taken from a wild turkey. Either that, or a bean bag collided with a turkey in mid-air and came out on top.

After much research, the sports department has come to the conclusion that the peteca can be used to play volley ball with a number of people on each side. This method would reduce the quantity of abrasions on a single player in favor of a larger distribution. You could always single out a player on the opposite side of the net and bean him when he wasn't looking.

Good Flyswatter

There are several other things you can do with a peteca. It makes one of the best desk dusters we have found yet. Its deadly accuracy makes it unexcelled as a long-range flyswatter. With practice, you can pick off a fly from the wall at fifty feet. Extra points could be given for flies in mid-air. Just tossing it back and forth across the desk makes a pleasant exercise during rest periods in the office . . . no points for knocked-over inkwells here, however.

It's nice, though seldom does one find so many uses for a single game.

Ex-Employe Tells Escape from Death

After miraculously escaping death when a 77-mm. Jap shell killed 14 of his buddies and sent him to a Manila hospital for two months, Ralph Meginniss, former supervisor in Dept. 18-06, is enjoying a well-earned 30-day furlough here.

Meginniss saw 8 months of action with the Sixth Division of the U.S. Infantry in the Wawa watershed district and the Cagayan Valley, Luzon, P. I.

Ralph is spending his furlough visiting his brother, C. A. Meginniss, Dept. 34-04, manufacturing engineering.

FASTEST AIR SCHEDULE IS FLOWN BY LODESTARS

Record-breaking silver-streak Lockheed Lodestars are now flying the skies over blue Caribbean waters in the fastest airline schedule in the world.

Caribbean Atlantic Airlines, Inc., proposed subsidiary of National Airlines, recently announced the Caribair Commuter Service operating in Puerto Rico and the Virgin Islands with charter flights to Miami.

A 26-passenger Lockheed Lodestar has been adapted from a 14-passenger ship for commuter service on the airline. The increase in passengers was made possible by removing the original one-passenger seats and replacing them with comfortable upholstered benches on each side of the plane. The benches are equipped with arm rests and safety belts.

Use of the 26-passenger Lockheed Lodestar in Puerto Rico and the Virgin Islands has made possible an 18½ per cent reduction in fares.

Caribbean Atlantic Airline routes over Mayaguez and Ponce, Puerto Rico; San Juan, St. Thomas, and St. Croix in the Virgin Islands are changing hours of travel time into minutes.

The airline recently flew its first charter flight between San Juan, Puerto Rico, and Miami. The flight was made in the record time of 5 hours and 18 minutes. The first flight northbound plane was met in Miami by George T. Baker, president of National Airlines. Baker flew a Lockheed Lodestar in the inauguration flight of the National Airline route from Jacksonville, Florida, to LaGuardia Field, New York, in the record time of 4 hours 36 minutes.

In addition to the 26-passenger Lodestar commuter, National Airlines and its proposed subsidiary, Caribbean Atlantic Airlines, operate a fleet of Lockheed Lodestars which have made many transcontinental speed records for passenger planes.

Salmon Rides Shooting Star

(Continued from Page 5)

cockpit equipment includes attachment for gravity suits to lessen discomfort and danger of blackout in sharp turns and pullouts.

Lockheed engineers have pioneered the field of pilot comfort in the Shooting Star. As a result they have done much toward eliminating pilot fatigue. Personally, I think the jet fighter's cockpit arrangement will exert a profound influence on the development of future pilot stations. I think the days of cramped quarters and inaccessible instruments and controls are just about over.

Fastest Ever

But these are the luxuries of flying, in warplanes at least. Primarily, the pilot is interested in performance. You already know the Shooting Star is the fastest airplane that has ever flown. And, although exact figures are still secret, it is the fastest by a good margin.

Knifelike leading edge of the laminar flow wing and other aerodynamic innovations master the problems of air compressibility encountered when approaching the speed of sound. Wing loading ratio is the lowest of any first-line fighter. Hydraulic aileron boosters and balanced empennage controls make the plane extremely maneuverable. Even with heavy loads of ammunition, photographic equipment, bombs, or auxiliary fuel for long flights, it responds to pilot control quickly with a minimum of effort.

Rate of roll is fastest of any plane in the skies. Rate and angle of climb are superlative. Absolute ceiling is unknown because no pilot has ever been able to take it all the way up. Range is more than ample for any of the distances that pursuit ships are required to fly.

It all adds up to terrific speed with maneuverability limited only by the pilot's ability to take it.

Sleek Plane

Less important than performance but still an attribute in any airplane is appearance. I am sure every pilot takes pleasure in flying a sleek plane, just as every motorist enjoys driving a fine-looking automobile.

The Shooting Star leads the aircraft field for pure beauty of design. Its negative gray, polished lacquer coating was developed by Lockheed research engineers in cooperation with the nation's large paint manufacturers because the jet job's terrific speed necessitated an entirely new approach on surface smoothness. Skin variances of as little as .002 inch appreciably affect the plane's speed. But at the same time, the glass-smooth finish has increased the harmony of the Shooting Star's unbroken aerodynamic lines to give it the appearance of speed even while parked on the ground.

All of these things play their part in your feelings as you fly the P-80.

FRIENDS FETE BILL STYER ON BIRTHDAY

Lockheed's oldest employe in terms of service, police guard Bill → Styer, celebrated his 78th birthday Tuesday at the LERC commissary in a spontaneous party given for him by members of Lockheed's Oldtimers' club.

Not so long ago Hal Davis of the LERC Recreation division asked Styer what he would like to have for his birthday . . . a blonde or brunette. Tuesday, Styer had both. Blonde Doris Finks and brunette Beverly Lewis presented him with a winter trench coat from members of the Oldtimers' club.

Fifty Lockheed employes enjoyed Styer's birthday party, complete with birthday cake and ice cream. Among Lockheed folk present were Cyril Chappellet, Harvey Christen, Police Chief Phelps, "Mop" and Lou Basolo, James Gerschler, Scotty McAdams, Shirley Arnold, Allan Hess, Robert Stansfield, Henry Scullford, Dean Hanson, and Jack Eaton.

Styer was hired by Lockheed aircraft founders, Allan and Malcolm Loughhead in 1928. He has watched the company grow from a machine shop in a shed to one of the world's greatest airplane plants.

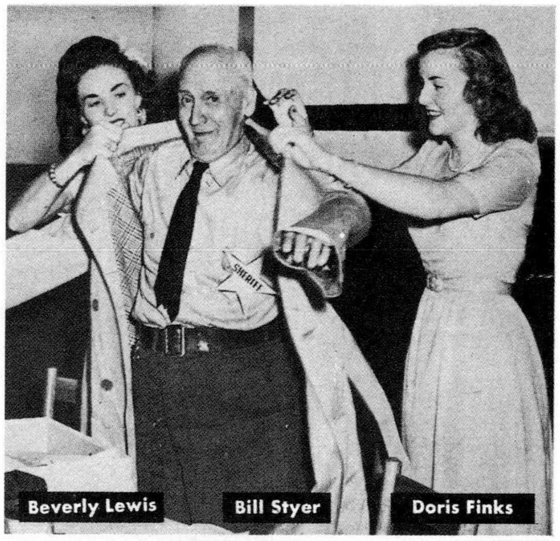
Beverly Lewis — Bill Styer — Doris Finks

LEGISLATORS INSPECT LOCKHEED IN AIRCRAFT INDUSTRY STUDY

Peacetime reconversion, insofar as it affects the aircraft industry, was scrutinized at Lockheed this week by the state legislative committee.

Members of the State Assembly Interim committee on postwar airports and aviation making the visit were seeking background information on the terminal—its facilities, traffic and general problems.

During the week the committee held hearings at the State building in downtown Los Angeles. The purpose of the hearings is to secure data to be presented before the state legislature looking toward establishment of sufficient airports throughout the state to handle peacetime air needs.

Committee members consisted of Ernest W. Debs, Los Angeles, chairman; Sam L. Collins, Fullerton; James G. Crichton, Fresno; Lester McMillan and Frank Waters, Los Angeles.

Is it Here?

THESE classified advertisements in the *Star* are provided for employes without charge. If you want to buy, sell, trade, or find or return lost articles, obtain Form 4929 from your department clerk, the stationery store, or employe service office. Mail the advertisement to the *Lockheed Star*, Room 244, Bldg. 1-A, Plant B-1.

WANTED

FURNISHED single apartment in Hollywood or Glendale. CI. 2-1312.
RIDE from 32nd and Hoover to Plant B-1, days. RI. 3963.
HOUSE to rent, unfurnished, by couple being evicted. CH. 8-9142.
HARD-top coupe body for 1934 Ford V-8, gd. cond. 8-1841, ext. 63 or CH. 9-3555.
'35, '36 or '37 car, good mechanical condition, for cash. HI. 3536 after 4:30.
CANOPY bed, French period preferred. CI. 1-7964, 525 Glenwood Rd., Glndle.
CASH for '37 or '36 Ford, Plymouth or Chevrolet 2-door sedan. SU. 1-7652.
TO rent—2 or 3-bedroom furnished or unfurnished house. MA. 8422.
TO rent—furnished or unfurnished 2-bedroom house or apt. 3 adults. CI. 3-5907.
HIVES of bees and bee equipment. 1503¾ 12th Ave., L. A. RE. 3575.
COCKER spaniel puppy, either sex, for sm. boy. Can only pay nominal sum. CH. 8-8627.
RIDE—Pico and Ocean, Satna Monica, A-1, swing. 246 Bicknell, Santa Monica.
TO rent—2 or 3-bedroom unfurnished house or duplex. FItzroy 8762.
FUR. apt. or house, disabled vet and wife. Ext. 8-1381 or CI. 1-2930 after 6 p.m.
MODEL A Ford, '30 or '31; good tires, engine, brakes, etc. Reasonable. SUnland 3381.
TO rent—1 sgle. or dble. apt. 1525 N. Van Ness, Hllywd. HI. 5111, apt. 118.
1 OR 2 hillside lots in Sunland, Tujunga. Write to 236 Beechwood, Burbank.
OAK or steel 5, 7-dr. tool chest. State cond. & price. PA. 2966 betw. 10 a.m. and 2:30 p.m., also after 6 p.m.
WOMAN, part-time housekeeper. CH. 8-8115.

FOR SALE

MISCELLANEOUS

1941 Powell motor scooter, gd. cond., just overhauled; reasonable. NO. 2-5777.
BABY crib, Kantwet mattress; like new; bargain. BR. 2-1988.
UPRIGHT Baus piano, dark finish, beautiful rich tone, $125. SUnland 6384.
BOOK of poems, just off the press; exquisite gifts. RIchmond 7975.
WHAT am I offered—davenport, chair & end table, good condition. CH. 8-3247.
SET of 4 camera filters—35-mm. f3.5, with holder. CH. 8-2129.
CLARINET, Selmer made, wood B flat, like new; also collapsible baby buggy, good condition, cheap. 4974 Mt. Royal Dr., Eagle Rock.
GATELEG drop-leaf table, hardwood. CH. 6-4603.
FRUIT and vegetable juicer, 2-gallon; Plasti-coat paint. GL. 7732.
LADY'S London tan shoes, size 6½B, worn 3 times; '37 Delco car radio, cheap. UNion 1-3890.
CHEST of drawers, walnut; desk, walnut; bed table, walnut. Gd. cond. ST. 4-1883.
35-MM. Perfex camera, f3.5 lens, case, filters, incl.; A-1 cond., $35. 1802 Rosita Ave., Burbank.
CHICKEN brooder-broiler unit, accommodates 50 chicks to broiler size; factory built Farm-master. CHurchill 9-4334.

Is it Here?

FOR SALE

MISCELLANEOUS (Cont.)

RABBIT hutch, constructed with new lumber, six units, with removable partitions; 2 does. CHurchill 9-4334.
DUAL manifold & conn. for Ford-Mercury. J. Henry water heater. SU. 1-1182.
EASTMAN 8-mm. mag. movie camera, mod. 90, f1.9 lens, case, Weston Cinemaster light meter. CI. 1-3991.
SINGER "Electrified" sewing machine, gd. cond. Jim Bryant, ext. 8-1217 or NO. 2-5203.
LOG-Log duplex decitrig slide rule, new; discount 30%. Call Jim Bryant, ext. 8-1217.
NAVY blue gabardine cardigan suit, size 12; reasonable. SY. 6-8455.
2 SUITS, brown & blue, Rosenbloom, size 16; good buy; almost new. Ext. 6-1244.
COPPER—300 lbs. 14 oz., soft rolled, 15"x24" sheets. AT. 7-1045.
STAINLESS cut film hangers, 1 doz. 3¼x4¼, 1 doz. 9x12 c.m., 3 stainless dev. tanks. ST. 5-4441.
LADY'S ice shoe skates, size 7; children's ice shoe skates, size 1 and 3. 6701 Clybourn, N. Hollywood.
STUDIO couch, dinette table & chairs, coffee table, 3-pc. bedroom set, good cond. 229½ S. Columbus St., Glendale, after 4 p.m.
39 HUDSON 6 sedan. Finish, tires, engine & seat covers like new. CH. 8-2129.
FURNISHED 5-rm., 4½ yrs. Sewer, paved st., fenced, exc. cond. 1609 N. Ontario, Burbank.
BLACK fur chubby, finger-tip length, exc. cond.; also man's black leather jacket. CI. 3-4942.
MAN'S 28" bike, gd. cond.; baby crib & mattress; Taylor-Tot; reasonable. SUnset 2-4536.
4-RM. house, redec., photo dk. rm. in garage. Lot 75x100. $5500. 19 S. Marengo, Alhambra.
DINING room set, small Philippine mhg.; 4 chairs, leather seats and leatherette table pad. OLympia 2642.
COLLAPSIBLE baby buggy, practically new. Perlis, 4041 Los Feliz Blvd. NO. 1-2031.
CHICKENS, layers, meat birds and started chicks. 6546 Odessa, Van Nuys.
HEATER, radiant gas; floor lamp; both excel. cond. ORegon 8-1542. 4512 W. 64th St., Inglewood.
AUX. yawl, flush deck, mahg. const. Built 1941. 26' O.A. x 8'9". Fully equipt., ready for cruising. P.O. box 644, San Pedro.
PISTOL, Colt police, positive, fired once; holster, box of shells. OL. 9356 after 4.
BLK. Forstmann wool coat, beautiful silver fox collar & front trim, 12-14; sacrifice. NO. 9242, apt. 106.
BEAGLE pups, A.K.C. reg. J. B. Rauch, 7923 Hillrose St., Sunland, SUnland 5961 after 7 p.m. or week end.
ELEC. record player, cheap; one baby crib, 38"x58". 7722 Camellia Ave., N. Hollywood.
SUPERCHARGER, Ozone. Installed. CH. 8-9158.
MILK cow, 4 gals. milk, 2 qts. cream; calf, separator, turkeys. SUnset 1-5022.
BLACK fox chubby, 28" long, good condition. Ext. 6-2250, B. Lewis.
28" bike, nearly new, $25. CHapman 5-1703. 1410 Randall St., Glendale.
GULBRANSEN medium upright piano, gd. cond. NO. 2-4447. 1321 Lyman Pl.
BABY buggy with rubber tires, metal frame, prewar; also high chair. AXminster 2-3359.
LOT in Venice. Sm. dn. payment; terms. P.O. box 223, Highland Park Station, L. A.

Is it Here?

FOR SALE

MISCELLANEOUS (Cont.)

KENNEDY tool box & set Starrett tools for machine parts inspection, brand-new a few months ago, will sell cheap as a complete set. E. B. Allen, 621 N. Niagara St., Burbank, after 6 p.m.
16-FT. sloop and trailer, excellent condition. SUnset 1-5449.
BASSINET, like new, large, complete, fully trimmed, $10. 307 E. Garfield, Glendale.
ZENITH console radio, excl. cond. 5825 Satsuma Ave., N. H. SUnset 1-5446.
FURNITURE, complete for 5 rms., prewar, excl. cond.; also baby furniture. CH. 6-9851.
ELECTRIC roaster oven, metal table. CH. 8-6358.

EXCHANGE

VOIGHTLANDER camera, f4.5 lens, 1/400 speed time setting; use 120 film, 8 or 16 exp. Trade for binoculars or drill press. 4415 LaClede Ave., L. A.
¾ BLK. Chesterfield coat for full-length blk. Chesterfield, size 16. HI. 3706.
HOUSE (2-bedrm.), near Lockheed, for 6-rm. house in Alhambra or vic. CH. 6-4608.
VERY nice single apartment in Wilshire-La Brea district for nice double apt. in Wilshire-La Brea district. WH. 7128.
EAGLE Rock, hillside, 5 rms. upstairs, 3-rm. apt. downstairs, for 4 & 5-rm. duplex or 2 houses on one lot. Reasonable rent, Glendale or Burbank. CL. 7-3054.
2-BEDRM. apt., unfurn., nr. B-1, for 2-bedrm. furn., Hollywood or midwest L. A. CH. 8-6358.

FOR RENT

LOVELY large room, adj. bath, with or without breakfast, one or two girls. CH. 6-0757.
PLEASANT room for 1 or 2, swing shift, girls; walking distance. 1451 N. Buena Vista St., Burbank.
ROOM in private home, 4257 Tujunga, N. Hollywood, SU. 24852.

LOST

GREEN handle 2-blade pocket knife. ST. 4-0709.
LADY'S Bulova wrist watch, gold link bracelet, B-1 cafeteria. Reward. Ext. 6-1553.
REWARD, $50 for information on stolen 1939 Buick, brown, license No. 805-591. Oct. 7, eve. from 1144 E. 77th, E.L.A. LUcas 0589.

THE LOCKHEED Star
OFFICIAL PUBLICATION OF THE LOCKHEED AIRCRAFT CORPORATION

Issued each Friday for the employes of Lockheed Aircraft Corporation. The *Star* is the official publication of the company. Communications should be addressed to the Editor, *Lockheed Star* Unit, Lockheed Aircraft Corporation, Burbank, California.

No unsolicited manuscripts or pictures will be returned and the *Star* cannot be responsible for other than requested articles or photos.

J. H. PRESCOTT, Editor
Barbara Sewald, News Editor
La Verne Munt, Associate